A First-Class Temperament

ALSO BY GEOFFREY C. WARD

BEFORE THE TRUMPET:
Young Franklin Roosevelt
1882–1905

Franklin Roosevelt at the helm off Campobello, 1920.

A FIRST-CLASS TEMPERAMENT

THE EMERGENCE OF FRANKLIN ROOSEVELT

Geoffrey C. Ward

BOOK-OF-THE-MONTH CLUB

NEW YORK

Quotations from the letters of Anna Roosevelt Cowles, Eleanor Roosevelt, Sara Delano Roosevelt, Corinne Robinson, and Corinne Alsop in the collection of the Houghton Library, Harvard University, are used by permission of the Houghton Library. Quotations from the letters of Anna Roosevelt Cowles on deposit at the Houghton Library by the Theodore Roosevelt Association are used by permission of the Theodore Roosevelt Association.

Designer: Sidney Feinberg

Printed in the United States of America

For Nathan,
for Garrett,
and for Kelly

CONTENTS

PREFACE

W HEN the White House limousines pulled up outside the house at 1720 I Street in downtown Washington at about five-thirty on the afternoon of March 8, 1933 and a curious crowd began to gather, the old man was still napping upstairs.

His young clerk hurried to wake him.

Justice Oliver Wendell Holmes was ninety-two that day—he had retired from the Supreme Court on which he had served for three decades only a little over a year earlier—and he had celebrated his birthday at a small at-home luncheon attended by his current clerk, Donald Hiss, a former clerk, Thomas G. Corcoran, and an admiring friend, Felix Frankfurter.

It had been a convivial time. Hiss arranged with a fashionable and discreet bootlegger to import several bottles of champagne for the occasion, carefully assuring his employer that the British ambassador had sent them over. The Justice might have barred them, had he known their authentic source. "Young fellow, I don't want you to misunderstand things," he had told Frankfurter with a smile as the bottles were being uncorked. "I do not deal with bootleggers but I *am* open to corruption." But Holmes had enormously enjoyed what he called the "fizzle water," confiding, "This stuff feels good to your face, doesn't it, Sonny?" as he sipped at it through his white mustache, and the champagne and unaccustomed excitement had later persuaded him not to take his usual afternoon drive around the city he had known so well so long. Instead, he stretched out in his bedroom and listened to his clerk read aloud until he fell asleep, still wearing the worn alpaca jacket he favored when he expected no guests.

"Mr. Justice," Hiss murmured, shaking Holmes gently, "I think the President of the United States is outside."

"Don't be an idiot, boy," the old man said, opening his eyes. "He wouldn't call on me."

"I'm pretty sure it is."

Holmes rose from his bed. "Well, we'd better not take any chances. Give me your arm. Get this coat off."

Hiss helped him into his old-fashioned swallowtail coat as, downstairs, Franklin Delano Roosevelt, the new President, was wheeled into the elevator by his eldest son, James. Two Secret Service men squeezed in beside them for the short ride up to the library. Frankfurter and Eleanor Roosevelt came up by the stairs.

It was a novel event, this surprise visit by an American President upon a private citizen in his home, especially at such a critical time. It had been just five days since FDR had taken office in the depths of the nation's worst depression, declaring that "the only thing we have to fear is fear itself," and promising his weary, desperate fellow citizens a "New Deal."

But no President ever had a greater sense of historical occasion than Franklin Roosevelt, and Justice Holmes embodied for him much of American history's sweep; not only had Holmes been the Great Dissenter on the Court since 1902, but he could recall his grandmother telling him how arrogantly the British had acted when they occupied Boston during the Revolution; he had himself known Ralph Waldo Emerson; had been wounded three times in the Civil War, at Ball's Bluff, Antietam, and Fredericksburg.

There was continuity, too, for FDR in the fact that his cousin Theodore had named Holmes to the Supreme Court. The new President himself had first met the Justice in 1913, shortly after he arrived in Washington as a very young, very eager Assistant Secretary of the Navy.

As his unexpected guests entered his study, the Justice rose slowly and stood as straight as he could—"the jacknife won't open," he liked to say about his old man's stoop.

Once everyone had found a seat in the library and Mary Donellan, the Irish waitress and parlormaid, had poured the tea, the conversation was genial and scattered. The President and the Justice talked of boxing—Holmes had watched the rise of "the Boston Strong Boy," John L. Sullivan, with great interest.

Two handsome old swords hung above the fireplace and FDR asked about them. They had belonged to his grandfather, Holmes said; he had used them in the French and Indian War.

"Well, my grandmother goes back as far as the Revolutionary War," FDR said, "but not as far as the Indian wars." (In fact, neither of Roosevelt's grandmothers had been born until after the Revolution ended.)

Holmes was led to another story: "I remember that my governor [his father, Dr. Oliver Wendell Holmes] told me that he was having lunch as a young student, and his father came home from lunch ... with a friend. And the friend said, 'You know, I saw that little West Indian bastard downtown today,' referring, of course, to Alexander Hamilton."

FDR was delighted. He may have mentioned his own mother's warm memory of the Justice's father; when Sara Delano Roosevelt was a little girl visiting her grandparents while suffering from whooping cough, Dr. Holmes had calmed her mother's concern and suggested remedies.

They chatted on for half an hour or so, the parlormaid continuing to pour tea, and when the time came to leave, FDR asked Justice Holmes if he had any final counsel for him.

"Form your ranks and fight," the old soldier told him, and complimented him on the way he had handled himself so far.

After the President and his party had left, the Justice eased himself back into his favorite chair.

"You know," he said to Hiss, "his [Cousin] Ted appointed me to the court."

"Yes, Mr. Justice?"

Holmes considered for a moment before rendering his verdict on this latest President Roosevelt.

"A second-class intellect. But a first-class temperament!"

Holmes was a shrewd judge of men as well as laws. There were always wiser men and women than Franklin Roosevelt in American public life, people who were better informed, more consistent, less devious. But there were none whose power to inspire both love and loathing was so great, none whose political success or apparent self-assurance exceeded his.

This book, like its predecessor *Before the Trumpet: Young Franklin Roosevelt 1882–1905*, is primarily about the development of the distinctive temperament Justice Holmes singled out for praise.

Again, this is not a conventional full-scale biography. It begins with young Roosevelt's honeymoon in 1905, ends just twenty-three years later as he starts his return to public life after infantile paralysis, and deals mainly with character and personality rather than politics or policymaking.

The book is inevitably filled with foreshadowing of FDR's presidential years, but I have tried throughout to examine his early life as coolly as possible, attempting to see him for the evasive young man he was as he first flirted with power, rather than the world leader he would one day become.

"You know," FDR told his admiring friend Henry Morgenthau, Jr., in 1942, "I am a juggler, and I never let my right hand know what my left hand does. . . . I may have one policy for North and [another for] South America. I may be totally inconsistent, and furthermore I am willing to mislead and tell untruths if it will help win the war." He did help win the war, of course, and before that he had restored the confidence of a terrified people—facts which should perhaps be borne in mind when, from time to time, the reader is startled by the apprentice juggler's willingness to "mislead and tell untruths" in the interest purely of his own advancement.

This book will not necessarily please either FDR's admirers or his detractors, and it may also surprise those who have accepted the once conventional wisdom that Roosevelt's life can be divided neatly into two parts: a spoiled, self-absorbed youth cut short by an illness whose searing impact somehow transformed its victim into a thoughtful and compassionate leader. He was indeed spoiled and self-absorbed as a young man, and, for better or worse, I believe that the Roosevelt who could not walk was in most respects very like the one who could. But his terrible ordeal did force him to find qualities within himself theretofore unsuspected, while some of the same characteristics most responsible for turning despair into triumph were among those that most alienated his early detractors—his easy charm, his extravagant ebullience, above all, perhaps, his gift for breezy duplicity.

This is in many ways a group portrait, too, for while FDR sits always at the center—where he invariably liked to be—he is again surrounded by the vivid cast of friends and enemies and family members who helped shape him, among them his extraordinary but complicated wife and no less remarkable and much-maligned mother; Lucy Mercer, the beautiful woman whom he loved, and Missy Le Hand, the adoring woman who loved him; his raffish, doomed friend Livingston Davis; and Louis Howe, the shrewd, ugly little man who devoted his own life to Roosevelt's for complicated reasons of his own.

Their stories, too, are part of his.

So far as possible, the book is based upon primary sources, many of them never before examined. No other biographer is quoted anywhere in it (unless he knew his subject personally), although my debt to the biographers who have gone before me is everywhere apparent.

And it demonstrates clearly, I think, that in the telling of his own life story, FDR was his own least reliable witness, unable or unwilling to tell the truth about his early years for reasons rooted both in his upbringing and in the relentless ambition that upbringing ensured. Few leaders in our history can have labored harder to create a personal past less rooted in reality. There is always both more and less to him than meets the eye.

In part because Franklin Roosevelt was so elusive he appears also to be inexhaustible as a biographer's subject, and it is comforting, as I conclude my study of him, to know that no one will ever have the last word.

—Geoffrey C. Ward

New York City
November 30, 1988

A First-Class Temperament

PROLOGUE

THE END OF ALGONAC

Through the window of Sara Delano Roosevelt's bedroom, a visitor could see that the trees across the Hudson had just begun to turn; the air that stirred the curtains was sweet with the smell of fallen apples from the orchard right behind the house. Mrs. Roosevelt was fond of this room, with its lovely views and still lovelier memories, and early autumn was her favorite season at Hyde Park. But this morning, propped up with pillows on the flowered chaise at the foot of her bed, her back to the window, she was impatient.

It was Saturday, September 6, 1941, and she was waiting for a visit from her son, Franklin. She was eighty-six years old, and had been ailing off and on all summer. Her heart was failing; her memory now came and went. Still, she had refused for as long as possible to concede that she was really ill. In July, she had gone as usual to the Roosevelts' summer home at Campobello on the Bay of Fundy, and no one there had been able to persuade her to eat the right foods or take the rest she needed. In the White House that same month, where FDR was preparing for his first meeting with the British Prime Minister, Winston Churchill, the President had finally become worried enough about his mother to send her a telegram begging her to permit him to dispatch a nurse. FOR MY PEACE OF MIND, he had wired her, I DO WISH YOU WOULD ACCEPT A TRAINED NURSE TO STAY IN THE BACKGROUND BUT HELP IN LITTLE WAYS LIKE DIET.

Put that way, she could not refuse him. FEELING BETTER, she wired back, NURSE ARRIVED MAKES EXCELLENT IMPRESSION. The President was relieved. From the train that was taking him to New London, the first stop on his clandestine journey to the rendezvous with Churchill off Newfoundland, he had written her a note in pencil: "I'm so glad you really are feeling better & that you like the nurse & that you do what she says!" But his mother did not, in fact, always do what the nurse—or anyone else—said. She had refused, for example, to hear of being carried out of her cottage for the long, tiring trip home to Hyde Park at the end of August. Instead, she did her best to stride purposefully down the front steps, head high, saying goodbye to the staff until the next summer, just as she had at the close of nearly every season since 1885. She was forced to stop halfway down, leaning heavily on the banister while she caught her breath. The Reverend Frank R. Wilson, rector of St. James Episcopal Church at Hyde Park, who was summering on the island, had come to see her off and now stood in the yard. She smiled at him as gaily as she could, saying, "You've never seen the 'old lady' in this condition, have you?" then resumed her slow descent and just managed to make it into the back seat of her automobile without help.[1]

The journey home—including a night's stopover at her house in New York—had drained her, and her daughter-in-law, Eleanor, had been so alarmed at her condition that she called FDR in Washington, urging him to come up to Hyde Park as soon as possible. Other members of the family had rallied, too. Sara's younger brother, Fred, bald and portly now, but still tall and imposing, had been in to see her the day before, and her younger sister, Katherine Collier—"Kassie"—had motored up from Tuxedo Park, still so regal at eighty-one that even Sara sometimes felt intimidated by her. She had seemed glad to see them both, though they also thought she seemed very tired, and they had kept their visit short. But as they were about to leave, Robert McGauhey, the British butler who had served her for nearly twenty years, stepped in to say, "A telegram has just come from the President. He will be here tomorrow morning at nine-thirty." Sara brightened

1. Despite her gallantry, there may have been at least one clue that summer that she suspected she might not ever come back to Campobello. One afternoon she had sent for Laura Delano Adams, a favorite grand-niece, who was staying in her family's nearby cottage. When the fifteen-year-old entered, her Aunt Sallie gave her an uncharacteristically extravagant gift, a gold lady's watch covered with diamonds and sapphires, on a heavy gold chain. Laura was dazzled; it was "too feminine for words," she remembered, and she protested a little. Sara insisted that she wanted her to have the watch. It had been very precious to her since her honeymoon sixty years before, she carefully explained, "a gift from your great-uncle James to commemorate the conception of your cousin Franklin." *Source:* Interview with Laura Delano Adams Eastman.

instantly, had suddenly seemed "just like her old self," Fred Delano would remember later.

"I will be downstairs on the porch to meet him," she announced, smiling at the thought.

For all of his fifty-nine years, Franklin had been her first concern. She had always been there to greet him, as eager to see him carried up her front steps as President of the United States as she had been to see him run up them as a boy, happy to be home at last from Groton.

She had not finally been able to make the trip downstairs this morning—she was too weak for that—but her excitement at the prospect of seeing her son had not diminished. She was devoted to every member of her family, but it was always Franklin for whom she longed most deeply, her only child for whom she now had dressed in a silk bed jacket edged with lace, and had had her long white hair wound into a braid with a bright blue ribbon.

Pictures of him surrounded her as she waited: small ones spilled across her bedside table; an early photograph of herself holding him in her arms; portraits of him at school and college; standing with Eleanor and the grandchildren, squinting into the sun; seated at his White House desk. A youthful, life-sized portrait of him hung on the wall; in it, he looked slim and solemn at eighteen.

He wrote to her less often now than he once had, but the chatty, loving, insouciant tone of his letters remained precisely the same as when he was a schoolboy. The small radio on her bedside table sometimes brought him close. She looked forward to every presidential broadcast and always listened intently, murmuring to herself, "Good," or, "How true that is," as her son's familiar voice filled the room, and sometimes, chuckling softly to herself, she would add, "I know some people who won't like *that*."

But even when Franklin was far away, the radio was silent, and there had been no cheerful notes from him for a time, she took comfort in being able to conjure him up vividly in her own mind; a mother could always do that "*inwardly,*" she had once assured him. Earlier that same summer, the rumor had spread among Campobello's summer residents that FDR and Churchill were to meet somewhere nearby, and that the two of them might even come ashore to call upon the President's mother. Sara had not paid much attention. Her son had warned her such a visit was unlikely, and besides, she told a friend,

"No rumors about Franklin excite me *very* much. I already see them in my mind's eye, walking up my little lawn."

As she grew older, she once told another friend, she sometimes liked just to lie back in her bedroom "and remember all the beautiful things that have happened here." Most of those things also centered around her son. He had been born in this house; she had nearly died giving birth to him just down the hall from the room in which she now waited, in the same carved bed in which she still slept each night. She had watched him grow here, reluctantly cutting his long blond curls when he was six, supervising his nurses and his games, seeing to his schooling by a succession of tutors. Always she had sought to inculcate in him the sense that he was important; that he could do anything to which he set his mind, but that, as a Delano and a Roosevelt, he also had an obligation to do good. Three times she had stood proudly beside him on the portico, waving to friends and neighbors as they celebrated his election to the presidency. Those victories had pleased her, but she had not been surprised by them. "I have always thought Franklin perfectly extraordinary," she said once, "and, as I look back, I don't think he has ever disappointed me."

Unpleasant things had happened here as well, painful personal things which had threatened to end forever the air of serenity she had worked so hard to sustain. But, like her son, she did not dwell on them. Her home was her sanctuary, and her son's. That sense of what a home should be had been bred into her by the first of the three men to whom she had devoted her long life, her father, Warren Delano II, who looked down upon her now from an outsized photograph that hung above her bedroom fireplace. His fierce, loving protectiveness toward his family had been so great that "Algonac," the name of his walled estate near Newburgh, had become a code word among his descendants for everything that made one feel safe, tranquil, protected.

Her late husband, James Roosevelt—"dear James" to her, "Mr. James" to almost everyone else, now dead for forty-one years—had felt the same way about Springwood, his own Hyde Park home. "I often wonder why men are so satisfied to live all their lives between brick walls and thinking of nothing but money and the so-called recreations of so-called society," he had written once from its veranda, "when there is so much enjoyment in the country."

So far as possible, she had kept Springwood a self-sufficient haven, just as Mr. James had, a bulwark against a world changing far too fast for her to keep pace. Flowers from her own gardens filled her vases.

Her fields and kitchen plots provided vegetables; her herds and barns and henhouses yielded meat, milk, poultry, eggs. Springwood still had no refrigerator; the ice that clinked in her guests' glasses of iced tea in summer had been chipped from blocks cut from the river the winter before, just as they had been in the time of Mr. James.[2]

The modern world sometimes intruded anyway, and Sara had had to make a considerable adjustment to accommodate some of the men and women Franklin and Eleanor routinely brought home with them: political operatives whose cigars scorched her carpets; mannish social workers; labor organizers from the Lower East Side; profane newspapermen. She had been as gracious as she could to all of them. "I have always believed," she once explained, "that a mother should be friends with her children's friends."[3]

She heard the crunch of tires on the gravel driveway that meant her son had arrived at last. Doors slammed. There were muffled shouts of greeting as the President was lifted into the house and installed in his wheelchair, then wheeled into the small hand-powered elevator and hauled up to the second floor.

He appeared in the doorway, rolling toward her, beaming. "When my son comes and sits there beside me with the smile that is *not* reserved for the voters," she had told an earlier visitor to her bedroom, "I just look at his face and think that it has everything—wisdom and goodness and sweetness."[4]

2. Not long after the President's mother died, the journalist John Gunther asked one of her old servants if the Hyde Park house had changed much over the decades. The man seemed genuinely startled by the question. No, he said: "In the house of such a lady, nothing ever changed." *Source:* John Gunther, *Roosevelt in Retrospect*, page 162.

3. The strain sometimes showed. On a Sunday morning in the early autumn of 1932, Senator Huey P. Long of Louisiana came to Hyde Park to confer with the Democratic nominee for President. Always a flamboyant dresser, he had outdone himself for this occasion, wearing a broadly striped suit, an orchid shirt, and a bright pink necktie—perhaps in a conscious effort to show the patrician Roosevelts that they could not intimidate him. FDR, as apparently cordial and affable as always, invited him to lunch, and the two men discussed campaign strategy, leaving the other guests to talk among themselves. During a momentary silence, Sara's voice could be heard whispering loudly, "Who is that *awful* man sitting on my son's right?"

Once in a while, too, strolling through the grounds, she would stop, fix the nearest newspaperman or Secret Service agent with a glare, then bend over, pick up a discarded cigarette, and carry it inside Springwood, held between her thumb and forefinger. *Source:* T. Harry Williams, *Huey Long*, pages 601–602.

4. She thought it had more than that. In 1903, at her request, he had played Prince Charming in a Sleeping Beauty tableau at a charity event. "When he kisses her head to wake her up," she had confided to her sister, Dora, "he is really beautiful." *Source:* Roosevelt Family Papers, Donated by the Children, FDRL.

That face now resembled hers as much as it did that of the slender young man who peered down from the wall. Her eyes were brown, his were blue, but the smiles with which they greeted one another were the same; so was the stubborn tilt of their chins.[5]

Franklin spent the rest of the day sitting with his mother, telling her of his shipboard meeting with Churchill and talking of old times. They were interrupted only occasionally when a White House aide slipped in with a telephone message too important to delay, or a document that needed the President's immediate attention.

Toward evening, Sara grew drowsy and was put to bed. The President said goodnight, then was taken downstairs for dinner.

At the table everyone agreed that Sara had seemed "quite bright." Perhaps the President's visit had been the tonic she needed. The crisis appeared to have passed. But at about nine-thirty, as she slept, she lapsed into a coma from which her doctors could not rouse her. Her circulatory system had collapsed. FDR was wheeled back into her room and sat with her most of the night; his wife began calling close friends and members of the family to tell them that her mother-in-law was not expected to live.

Sara Delano Roosevelt died shortly after noon on the following day, Sunday, September 7. Her son was at her bedside.

The President's wife was "of course attending to everything," a visiting relative noted in her diary that evening. It was Eleanor who called the undertakers and the rector of St. James; she who tracked down the old lady's checkbooks and began to sort through her clothes.[6]

Her own emotions were tangled. She took time out to dictate a

5. Sara evidently had somewhat ambivalent feelings about their growing resemblance. She once proudly told an artist who was painting her son's portrait that he was sure to have trouble with the jaw; "it is just like mine." But she was not amused in 1939 when the Gridiron Club gave the President the mammoth papier-mâché caricature of him that had served as the center-piece of its annual dinner that year. It portrayed FDR as the Sphinx—an allusion to his long, maddening silence as to whether or not he would run for an unprecedented third term—and its most prominent feature was its jutting jaw. An innocent White House aide asked her if she didn't think it was a pretty good caricature of the President. It was *not*, she said; her jaw was identical to his. Did the aide think this grotesque object looked *anything* like her? *Source:* John Gunther, *Roosevelt in Retrospect*, page 165; Walter Tittle, *Roosevelt as an Artist Saw Him*, page 59.

6. That same night she shouldered a still heavier burden: word came that her younger brother, Hall, his liver destroyed by years of alcoholism, had collapsed at his Hyde Park cottage. She had him sent first to Vassar Hospital in Poughkeepsie, then to Walter Reed in Washington, where she spent as much time with him as she could, doing her best to soothe his agony until he died twenty-two days later, not yet fifty. "The loss of a brother," she wrote later, "is always a sad breaking of a family tie, but in the case of my brother it was . . . like losing a child." *Source:* Eleanor Roosevelt, *This I Remember*, page 228.

public tribute to Sara for her newspaper column, "My Day." It was distinctly unsentimental. Sara had been "a very vital person," Eleanor said, whose "strongest trait was loyalty to her family. . . . There was a streak of jealousy and possessiveness in her where her own were concerned. The word 'grande dame' was truly applicable to her." Privately, she was still less charitable. "I think Franklin will forget all the irritation, and remember only the pleasant things," she wrote to a relative, "which is just as well."

She herself could not forget: "I looked at my mother-in-law's face after she was dead," she confessed to a close friend, "& I understood so many things I had never seen before. It is dreadful to have lived so close to someone for 36 years & to feel no deep affection or sense of loss. It's hard on Franklin, & the material details are appalling & there of course I can be of some use."

It was indeed hard on Franklin, though he did his best to let no one know it. The family gathered for tea in the library late that afternoon. Two of his sons, James and John, had arrived with their wives. Eleanor was there, presiding over the silver tea tray. Betty Roosevelt and Helen Roosevelt Robinson, the widow and the daughter of the President's late half brother, James Roosevelt "Rosy" Roosevelt, had come over from his Red House next door. When FDR joined them, Helen wrote that night, "He looked very tired & worn, but he was wonderful," chatting more quietly than usual with his guests, accepting their condolences with a smile only slightly less broad than customary.

That same afternoon—within minutes of his mother's death, in fact—one of the largest oaks on the place had, without wind or warning, crashed to the ground. FDR was later taken out to see it and sat for a time gazing silently at the broken branches, the upturned roots, the open wound the tree had torn in the earth.[7]

"Those who were closest to him," the playwright and speechwriter Robert Sherwood remembered, "could not presume to guess at the quality of sorrow caused him by his mother's death; one needed only a small realization of the tenacity with which he clung to every surviving link with the lovely world of his childhood—a world fantastically different from the one in which he now lived and fought—to know that his sorrow was very deep indeed. He kept it to himself. He

7. This eerie event—which no sane novelist would dare invent—evidently has a scientific explanation: the soil of Dutchess County is unusually thin over a base of solid rock, so that the roots of even the mightiest trees are poorly anchored. *Source:* Bernard Asbell, *Mother and Daughter: The Letters of Eleanor and Anna Roosevelt,* page 135.

permitted no sign of it to appear on the surface. He wanted no evidence or awareness of it from anyone else."

There was little hint of it at the private funeral held on Tuesday in the large, book-lined library he and Sara had planned together in part to display some of his collections of which they had both been proud. A spray of flowers from her garden lay on top of her mahogany coffin, which rested against the South Wall. Friends and family, servants and tenants sat in a semicircle in front of it while the Reverend Wilson performed the simple Episcopal rites. FDR read out the responses in a firm voice and listened without discernible expression as eight members of the local choir sang his mother's favorite hymn, "Love, Thou wilt not let me go."

He watched, dry-eyed, too, as eight of the men who had worked longest for his mother—among them her chauffeur and butler, and William Plog, the superintendent of the estate, who had served the Roosevelts for forty-five years—bore the coffin to a waiting hearse.

The Secret Service accompanied the President as usual during the three-mile drive north along the Albany Post Road to St. James. Farmers and townspeople stood in small groups beside the road, the men holding their hats in their hands. But when the President's open Ford reached the cemetery itself, Mike Reilly, the commander of the detail, ordered his men back. "You watch out for him," he told one of the President's sons. "I don't think we belong in there, even if Congress says we do."

The President's car was edged as close as possible to the grave site, hemmed in by old stone walls and headstones and tall evergreens. His sons locked his braces, helped him to his feet, and leaned him against the car so that he could stand upright, jaw still set, as the men from the Roosevelt estate lowered his mother's casket into the brick-lined vault beside his father.

Several days later, FDR was at work in the big bright office he had designed for himself in the new Roosevelt Library on the Springwood grounds. He wore a black mourning band on the left sleeve of his jacket,[8] and across from him stood a life-size oil portrait of his mother;

8. The Japanese attacked Pearl Harbor on December 7, 1941, precisely three months after Sara Delano Roosevelt's death. When FDR appeared before a joint session of Congress the following day to ask for a declaration of war, he wore a mourning band. Noticing it in newsreels and newspaper photographs, many Americans assumed he had worn it in honor of the Navy dead; in fact, it was the symbol of his own more private grief. He would wear it for well over the traditional year. *Source:* Jonathan Daniels, *White House Witness,* page 58.

she had commissioned it for him from the artist Douglas Chandor shortly before her last illness.

As he worked, Grace Tully, his White House secretary, quietly sorted through some cartons newly stored in cabinets built for them into the South Wall. She had packed many of them herself in Washington and shipped them north; they held books, mostly, and stamps for his already vast collection.

She was searching for a particular box that one of Sara's closest friends had told a member of the staff about. When she found one that looked unfamiliar she carried it over to the President's desk. He had never seen it before, either. Miss Tully untied the twine that held it closed and, together, she and FDR peered inside. There were a number of tissue-paper bundles, each labelled in the confident hand of the President's mother. One held the gloves she had worn at her wedding. Others revealed snippets of her brown hair and one of her son's, their color precisely matching; his first baby shoes; his lace-trimmed christening dress. Beneath the bundles were stacks of his boyhood letters, carefully sorted and tied up with string, written to her from Groton and Harvard.

Tears filled the President's eyes. He murmured that he would like to be left alone. Miss Tully hurried from the office. No one on his staff had ever seen Franklin Roosevelt weep.

CHAPTER

THE WONDERFUL HUSBAND

THE CAPTAIN of a transatlantic liner was his ship's social arbiter as
well as her commander. In consultation with the purser—and
often only after contacting the home office—he carefully surveyed the
passenger list, selecting from it for his own table in the great dining
saloon that handful of men and women whose prominence was so
obvious that even the most socially ambitious travellers would be willing to accept assignment elsewhere.

This was often delicate work, but not when preparing the seating
for the June 7, 1905, sailing of the White Star liner *Oceanic* from New
York. Franklin and Eleanor Roosevelt were aboard, on their way to
England and the Continent for a delayed honeymoon. Young Mrs.
Roosevelt was the favorite niece of the President of the United States,
the daughter of his late younger brother, Elliott Roosevelt; Theodore
Roosevelt himself had given her away at her wedding. She was only
twenty and unusually tall—nearly as tall as her husband—and surprisingly diffident, with a habit of gazing down at her hands while waiting
for others to speak to her. But there was no question of her social
preeminence. Franklin Roosevelt was not only her husband but the
twenty-three-year-old son of the late James Roosevelt, who had been
a frequent passenger aboard the ships of the White Star line and a good
friend of its late founder, Sir Thomas Ismay.

Eleanor was seated in the place of honor at Captain J.G. Cameron's
right, Franklin assured his mother, in one of the first of the steady,

reassuring stream of letters he and his bride would write home to Sara, "and I next. . . ."

The young Roosevelts had been married for nearly three months before they sailed. They had put off their honeymoon so that Franklin could complete his first year at Columbia Law School and take his examinations. At Sara's urging, they had started their lives together with a week at Hyde Park—"just where my great happiness began," she told them.

We know little of how happy the young Roosevelts were that week. Franklin characteristically left no record of it, while what seems to have remained with Eleanor were a jumble of proofs of her own crippling timorousness. She remembered most vividly that Elspeth McEachern—"Elespie," who had been the Springwood housekeeper since long before Franklin was born—had coldly looked her up and down as she arrived, as if "wondering if I would come up to her expectations as the wife of 'her boy.' "

The morning after their first night together as man and wife, standing in the Springwood parlor near the fire that took the edge off the March wind blowing around the house, Franklin had shown Eleanor one of his most precious first editions. Somehow—"in some inconceivable way," she recalled half a century later, still horrified at the memory—she slightly tore one of the pages. (Perhaps, like a good many of the volumes on her husband's shelves, its pages had never been cut; he was always a collector, not a reader.) In any case, she wrote, "I held it in my hands, frozen with fear. . . . Finally, I made myself tell him what I had done. He looked at me with bewilderment and some amusement. 'If you had not done it,' " he assured her, " 'I probably would [have].'

"What I had dreaded, I don't know," Eleanor wrote, "but I remember my vast relief. That was the beginning of my becoming more mature about my fears of displeasing people."

If so, it was *just* the beginning, and the depth of her fears must have honestly baffled her husband, whose own eagerness to please was accompanied by an inbred sense of his own importance at once strong and unexamined. The orphaned daughter of an erratic, alcoholic father and a distant, self-absorbed mother, and raised by relatives whose interest in her was for the most part merely dutiful, Eleanor had never been able to count on anyone's unshakable affection, was always worried that she would somehow offend those who she hoped would love her, that her failings would drive them to abandon her. Her own lack of self-confidence had been a revelation to Franklin, she once told an interviewer: "He had always been secure in every way, you see, and then he discovered that I was perfectly *in*secure. . . ."

Franklin began to call Eleanor by a pet name, at once fond and faintly patronizing—"Babs," short for "Baby."

After their week together at Hyde Park, Franklin and Eleanor moved into a small furnished apartment Sara found for them on West 45th Street. "Went to F. & E's apartment at Hotel Webster," she wrote the evening after they moved in, "arranged flowers and went to my French lecture. Returned to find my children and brought them home to lunch with me."

The young couple spent just over a month on 45th Street. Eleanor's insecurities were again apparent. She could sew—a childhood nurse had seen to that—but she knew nothing of cleaning or cooking, could not even order a meal properly, or so she remembered. The hotel staff and its kitchens helped, but it was not easy. She was humiliated by her own incompetence, fearful that she was already proving inadequate as wife and daughter-in-law. And when her younger brother, Hall, now a big hearty adolescent, came down from Groton to spend a few days with his sister and her new husband, she was embarrassed by him, too. "He seemed to fill the whole apartment," she recalled, even though he had a room of his own.

Franklin offered her what reassurance he could, while doing his best to keep up with his studies. But it may have been with some relief that the young Roosevelts shifted to Sara's empty, rented brownstone at 200 Madison Avenue when she moved up to Hyde Park at the end of April. Elespie was sent down from Springwood to manage their little household and supervise the cook and waitress. Eleanor was not to worry; Sara would take care of things, and while her children were abroad she would do her best to find them a house to rent for the coming year. The young wife was almost pathetically grateful. "Thank you so much dear for everything you did for us," she wrote to her mother-in-law that spring. "You are just the sweetest, dearest Mama to your children. . . ."

More than anything in the world, that was what Sara wanted to hear. For she, too, was then full of fears. She had long before lost the father she revered, and, more recently, the husband she loved. To the end of her life she would keep near at hand the miniature leatherbound Episcopal Book of Common Prayer she had gripped helplessly the night Mr. James died; a sepia photograph of him in his last days was carefully pasted to the flyleaf, and across from it, written in her hand, the place and date of his death: "10 W. 43; December the Eighth, 1900."

Her great worry now was that she would also somehow lose the son who was all she had left. "How can I be thankful enough to God for you," she once wrote Franklin, "when He has taken from me the love & devotion that have so long been mine?" Nelly Blodgett, Franklin's godmother and Sara's closest friend since girlhood, understood his all-importance: ". . . now, dear Franklin," she told him shortly after his father died, "you are *everything* to your dear mother."

That was not an exaggeration. Sara had faithfully kept a journal ever since her marriage to Mr. James, recording in it much of what she and her husband and their boy had done, together or separately, nearly every day for twenty-four years. Now that Franklin was married and had begun to live apart from her, she rarely bothered to make regular entries unless he or Eleanor (or, later, their children and grandchildren) had come to visit her. In her mind, the daily events of her own life, away from her precious son and his family, were hardly worth recording.

Both Franklin and Eleanor understood her fear, and they tried hard to live up to the pledge Franklin had given her after he told her of his secret engagement. Marriage, he had said then, would "never change what we have been & always will be to each other—only now you have two children to love & to love you. . . ."

Sara did her best to believe that, and Franklin and Eleanor did their best to demonstrate it. They spent nearly every weekend with Sara at Hyde Park that spring, and when they could not come to see her, she often came into town to see them.

But as their departure for Europe drew near, Sara became more tremulous, making plans to have old friends and members of the large Delano clan stay with her while her "dear children" were gone, and worrying over how she could endure the sad anniversary of Mr. James's birth in July without her son to comfort her.

On June 6, Franklin saw that the luggage was put aboard the *Oceanic,* he and Eleanor were to sail the next morning. That evening, Sara presided at a small farewell dinner: Franklin's half brother, Rosy, came, so did Rosy's daughter, Helen, and her new husband and distant cousin, Teddy Robinson, just back from their more lavish honeymoon, a year-long trip around the world. After the guests left, Sara sat up with her children while they each promised to write regularly. She remained cheerful in front of them, but later, alone in her room, she was evidently overcome with emotion too strong to be expressed and could write in her diary only "My dear F and E."

She went with them to the dock early the next morning, and saw them safely to their cabin, but she left the ship long before it sailed, unwilling to trust herself not to break down; ever since her father had been forced to leave his family for a time when she was five, partings had been agony for her, and this one was far more difficult than most. She fled the city for Hyde Park, where her nephew, Warren Robbins, and a young friend came to spend the night with her. "Sweet of them," she wrote that night, "to come when they knew I was lonely."

Aboard ship, Franklin made friends easily, though mostly among older people who were not put off, as men and women his own age still often were, by his sometimes over-eager charm. He reported to his mother that he got along well with all the other passengers at the captain's table: "Mr. Lancaster, an old Liverpool merchant & quite interesting . . . a Mr. Evans, a rich Englishman," and Mr. and Mrs. Monell of Tuxedo Park, who turned out to be neighbors of his aunt, Kassie Collier. "She [Mrs. Monell] is pretty and very nice," he told Sara, "but he is rather a bore, though I fancy pretty well off." There were distant cousins aboard, too, and older relatives of his Harvard friends and classmates.

Franklin moved smoothly among them all, Eleanor doing her best to keep up, perhaps a little startled but not displeased at the impression her husband seemed to make on everyone with whom they came in contact. Even the servants admired him. One morning in their cabin the stewardess drew Eleanor aside to ask if Franklin were English; he *must* be, she said, "he is so handsome and has the real English profile!" Eleanor thought this a great compliment. So would Sara, to whom she confided it. Franklin professed to be embarrassed.

The sea was his element. Everything about ships and shipboard life delighted him. The Russo-Japanese War, in which for the first time in modern history an Eastern power showed that it could more than match a Western one, was still raging, and when Franklin discovered that six Japanese naval officers were aboard, on their way to England to take command of two new warships being built for them in British yards, he left Eleanor's side to talk with them—though "their English is not voluble, and I find myself giving out more information than I receive." He persisted, however, and Eleanor seems to have found it a little wearying. "He is looking well," she told his mother, "and has spent most of his time *trying* to talk to the Japs. He has succeeded a few times."

And he cajoled the captain into escorting him and Eleanor on an exhaustive inspection of the ship, from bridge to engine room. Eleanor gamely pronounced the tour "very interesting," but it had also troubled her, making her "more sorry than ever for the steerage passengers" past whom the captain had hurried them below decks.

When they reached Brown's, the fashionable old London hotel where visiting members of the Roosevelt family traditionally stayed, they were received at the front desk with what seemed to both of them to be more than the usual flurry of deferential courtesy. "We were ushered into the royal suite," Franklin told his mother, "one flight up, front, price $1000 a day—a sitting room 40 ft. by 30, a double bedroom, another ditto, and a bath. Our breath was so taken away that we couldn't even protest and are now saying 'Damn the expense, Wot's the odds'!"[1]

Eleanor later said that she had been "horrified" at this extravagance, embarrassed to find that "in some way we had been identified with Uncle Ted," but Franklin was delighted. No identification could possibly have pleased him more. He photographed the sitting room, filled with carved and polished furniture, its walls covered in silk, a cut-glass vase of complimentary roses on the central table—and so large, Eleanor remembered, "that I could not find anything that I put down." The Roosevelts happily occupied the royal suite for five days before moving on to the Continent.

The trip was to last more than three months and to take the young couple from Britain through France, Italy, Switzerland, Germany, and back to Britain again before they hurried home in mid-September so that Franklin could start his second year of law school. In one sense, it was an uneventful journey, filled with quiet times and fond visits to places already familiar to either Franklin or Eleanor from their childhoods. But now and then along the way, things happened—small things mostly—which highlighted the dissimilari-

---

1. The extraordinary figure Franklin gave as the cost of the royal suite was a characteristic exaggeration; the actual price for five days was £35. To the end of her life he took delight in teasing his mother about the cost of things. Later in the same letter he announced that "we have ordered thousands of dollars worth of clothes, and I am going to send you several cases of champagne, as I know it is needed at Hyde Park." *Source:* Elliott Roosevelt, ed., *FDR: His Personal Letters, 1905–1928,* page 11.

ties between them and hinted at what would one day happen to them and to their marriage.

Of all the sources of Eleanor's insecurities, none was greater than sex. Girls of her class were not encouraged to know much about it. Eleanor's younger cousin, Corinne Robinson Alsop, remembered once having been kissed by a boy in the stable of her family's summer home at Orange, New Jersey. "It frightened me to death," she wrote many years later, "and I discussed with my intimate friends whether I would immediately have a baby." Alice Roosevelt Longworth, Eleanor's more resourceful and slightly older cousin, recalled that by the age of fifteen she herself had managed to glean at least a sketchy sense of the mechanics of reproduction by close study of her own pet rabbits and guinea pigs, supplemented by selective reading of the Old Testament. Eleanor evidently had not, and when Alice tried to tell her something of what her own Bible study had taught her—"probably nothing more than the 'begat' series," Alice recalled—Eleanor "suddenly leapt on me and tried . . . to smother me with a pillow, saying I was being blasphemous. . . . I think she probably went to her wedding not knowing anything about the subject at all."

Alice may have been right. Certainly, Eleanor's own family had been of little help. She herself remembered stumbling upon the word "whore" in the Bible, and asking her Grandmother Hall what it meant. "It is not a word that little girls should use," was the old lady's answer. "There were certain subjects never discussed by ladies of different ages," Eleanor wrote many years later, "and the result was frequently very bewildered young people when they found themselves confronted with some of life's natural situations!"

When she herself was so confronted, Eleanor was evidently not only bewildered but embarrassed and appalled. Many years later, in an awkward premarital talk with her own daughter, Anna, she would warn that sex was "an ordeal to be borne." The conventions of the time had something to do with that attitude; it was how older women of Eleanor's class expected younger women to feel. Her mother-in-law, for example, would have approved: a brashly intrusive grandson once pointedly asked Sara Delano Roosevelt whether she and his grandfather had ever had "any fun." "I knew my obligations as a wife," Sara replied, "and did my duty."

But for Eleanor, something more was wrong. The thing which frightened her most all her life was loss of control—anyone else's, but especially her own. The roots of that fear may have lain in her half-remembered child's impressions of her alcoholic father, as well as her more vivid memories of her mother's drunken brothers and frenzied, temperamental sister, Aunt Edith, known as Pussie. Something, she once told a close friend, had "locked me up" emotionally, had given her "an exaggerated idea of the necessity of keeping all one's desires under complete subjugation."

That struggle was made all the more intense by the strength of those desires. Eleanor Roosevelt craved physical affection as only a person to whom it has been consistently denied can crave it. In some of her love letters to Franklin, written during their courtship, she expressed it openly. "I wish you were here, dear, to kiss me good-night," she had written him more than a year before their marriage, and, again, closer to their wedding day, "I am hungry for you every moment, you are never out of my thoughts. . . ." And she seems to have hoped to find in her mother-in-law a warm source of the sort of physical closeness she had only rarely received from her own distracted mother. "You are always just the sweetest, dearest Mama to your children," she had written as she set sail on her honeymoon, "I shall look forward to our next long evening together, when I shall want to be kissed all the time." And again, "I feel as though we would have such a long arrears of kisses and cuddly times to make up when we get home!" Eleanor Roosevelt harbored powerful passions; the fervor with which she clung to her closest friends throughout her long life would attest to that. But she yearned still more for emotional intimacy.

And that, Franklin Roosevelt could never provide. We know little of what he had experienced of sex before his marriage. He had been slow to develop interest in girls; his pursuit of Alice Sohier, the Boston girl who had spurned him before he began to court his cousin, Eleanor, had been ardent but clumsy. Carousing Harvard boys of his generation sometimes frequented Boston's more discreet bordellos, and he had travelled on his own with classmates during the summer of his sophomore year to London and across the Continent, where opportunities for experimentation were not lacking. He may have learned the rudiments of sex before his marriage, then, but genuine intimacy was beyond him.

Everything in his upbringing argued against it. Before Franklin was five years old, his grandfather, Warren Delano II, had laid down the lines along which he had been carefully brought to manhood. Little

Franklin, the old man wrote then, was "a very nice child, that is, always bright and happy. Not crying, worrying, infractious." His father and mother—but especially his mother—had done all they could to ensure that he always remained "very nice"; that he seemed always "bright and happy."

Unpleasantness of any kind—fear, failure, humiliation, envy, anger—was to be ignored or laughed off. "Life is full of that sort of thing," Sara had told him when he suffered a momentary disappointment at Groton, "and we must be above caring. Only keep up your position and character and let *no one* make you feel small, go ahead your own way, and be kind to everyone if you have the chance. . . ."

He did his best to follow that advice all his life, to live up to his parents' example and expectations. It helped create the apparently serene and cheerful surface with which he learned to face down the sometimes puzzling world beyond Hyde Park. But its cost was a closing off. For, far beneath that surface, unpleasant thoughts inevitably persisted, thoughts that were the opposite of "very nice," and the mere fact of their secret existence had to be carefully guarded. To be asked to share them, even with his wife, was to feel intruded upon, crowded, trapped, exposed. Years of trying to create a life of his own while remaining a dutiful son to his loving but demanding mother had taught him the importance of keeping his own emotional counsel.

"His was an innate kind of reticence," Eleanor once told a friend. "It became part of his nature not to talk to *anyone* of intimate things."

Franklin was kind and solicitous toward his bride—he genuinely loved and cherished her, wanted her to be as happy as he was—but he was inclined to laugh away her fears rather than fully to engage them, as he had been taught to do with his own. And when laughter and blithe exhortations to cheer up did not work, he chose simply to ignore them and go about his business, in the hope that they would somehow go away.

They did not, of course, and neither did his, for there is evidence that he, too, was privately troubled that first summer of his married life. His sleep was tormented by nightmares, Eleanor reported, during which he ground his teeth, tossed about, muttered incoherently. And he began to walk in his sleep. He evidently first did so aboard the *Oceanic*, anxiously fumbling at the door of their cabin in his pajamas, trying to get out, to get away.

It happened at least once more while the young Roosevelts were abroad. One night, when they were staying with friends in a Scottish country house, Franklin suddenly sat up, shrieking in terror. Eleanor tried to quiet him. "Don't you see the revolving beam?" he said, peering up into the empty dark. She had to hold onto him to keep him from bounding out of the room to awaken the household. While she and Franklin were enjoying tea in bed the next morning, she asked him if he remembered what had happened during the night! He said he did, she wrote later, and he "remembered being very much annoyed with me because I insisted on remaining in the path of the beam which at any moment threatened to fall off in its gyrations."

It is impossible, of course, to "explain" anyone else's dream; it is the associations triggered in the dreamer's own mind that matter most. And all we have to work with are Eleanor Roosevelt's memories, written down thirty-one years after the fact. Still, it seems clear that her outwardly tranquil young husband was concealing considerable psychological stress while overseas, fears and anxieties he could find no other way to express than by acting them out in his sleep.[2]

There is one other hint that Franklin may have been undergoing internal tension on his honeymoon. He developed hives which plagued him off and on all summer, and for which no external cause was ever found. "They won't go," he joked to his mother, "so people think I have a flea that can't be killed by any method"; in fact, they sometimes grew so severe that he took to his bed. It worried Eleanor. She thought the hot weather in Venice might somehow be to blame, but cool days and nights in the Alps did not seem to help; she suggested that Franklin stop drinking white wine with dinner, but that did not help either. Nothing did.[3]

2. Franklin was still sleepwalking two years later. In the summer of 1907, Eleanor described one episode to her mother-in-law. She and Franklin and their first child, Anna, were staying in Sara's house at Campobello; Sara was away in Europe: "I have quite forgotten to tell you about Franklin's dream two nights ago, and I know you will be amused for it was so characteristic that I had to laugh when I got over being scared! He sleeps or rather slept until this night episode occurred on the side near the windows and suddenly leaped up, turned over a chair and started to open the shutters! I grabbed his pyjama tails and asked what he wanted and received this surprising answer: 'I must get it, it is very rare, the only one and a most precious book.' After some persuasion he returned to bed, very angry with me and the next morning he knew nothing about it! Now I sleep on the window side as the middle of the room seems a better place to hunt for rare and precious volumes!"

Many years later, when Eleanor reread this letter before it was published as part of her son Elliott's edition of FDR's personal correspondence, she asked that the following note be added: "A.E.R. [Anna Eleanor Roosevelt] recalls that FDR's inclination to have dreams like the one described only existed while he was young, and that in later years none ever occurred." *Source:* Elliott Roosevelt, ed., *FDR: His Personal Letters, 1905–1928,* pages 98–100.

3. It is, of course, impossible to know now whether his hives were caused by an allergy or had an emotional origin. He had suffered from them at least once before, at fourteen, in the summer of 1896. He had then been staying with his parents at Bad Nauheim, the German spa to which his father often went in search of a cure for his bad heart. The fact that he had been

Eleanor's anxieties were more clear-cut than Franklin's. Even before they were married, she had fretted over his constancy, had recited to him lines from a favorite poem and obtained from him a promise always to abide by them:

> Unless you can swear, "For life, for death!"
> Oh, fear to call it loving!

She did not worry initially that he was more likely than anyone else to be inconstant, but rather because she could never quite believe that anyone could love her for herself for long.[4] She was not, finally, lovable in her own mind, and in part because she was not, was always on the lookout for the first signs of the betrayal she was sure would come, that the example of her unsteady father had prepared her always to expect.

That pattern began to be discernible on her honeymoon. At Easton Hall, the grand Lancashire estate of the senior Roosevelts' old friends, Sir Hugh and Lady Cholmley, she took an instant dislike to the three unmarried Cholmley daughters, explaining her "prejudice" against them to Sara as the result of the "artificial" look their fashionable makeup lent them. But, though neither she nor her mother-in-law is likely to have known of it, two summers earlier, Franklin had conducted a minor flirtation with Aline, the youngest and most attractive of the girls. Perhaps Eleanor's infinitely sensitive antennae had picked up in Aline's or Franklin's behavior toward one another some hint of their old relationship, enough to threaten her always fragile self-confidence.

Worse was to come. One evening at Cortina, high in the Dolomites, Franklin announced that he wished to rise early the next morn-

---

in Europe then, too, might seem at first to suggest that there was something in what he ate, drank, or breathed on the Continent that caused an allergic reaction, but it should be remembered that he had been under a good deal of unacknowledged stress that summer as well: within a few weeks he was to be sent off to school to live apart from his mother and father for the first time in his life. *Sources:* Elliott Roosevelt, ed., *FDR: His Personal Letters, 1905–1928,* pages 47, 69, 73; Sara Delano Roosevelt Journal, FDRL.

4. She never succeeded in overcoming this fear. An old friend called her hotel room while she was visiting London very late in her life, at a time when she was among the most admired women on earth. Her secretary, Maureen Corr, took the call and when she told her employer who it was, was instructed to say that she was sorry but Mrs. Roosevelt was too busy to come to the telephone.

"She *wants* something," Eleanor said, after Miss Corr had hung up.

"But Mrs. Roosevelt," the secretary said. "Don't you think people ever love you for yourself?"

"No, dear," she answered. "I don't." *Source:* Interview with Maureen Corr.

ing and climb the 4,000-foot peak called the Falovia. He asked Eleanor to go with him. She demurred; she had done enough climbing the day before. Franklin was sorry but determined to have his climb. Eleanor urged him to go, but silently wished he would stay behind with her; her parched childhood had taught her, she once wrote, "to protect myself from disappointment by not asking for what I wanted."

Franklin went, and he took with him another guest at the hotel, Miss Kitty Gandy, an unmarried New York milliner only a few years older than Eleanor and far more worldly; she smoked Franklin's cigarettes, and she wore one of her own creations, a big hat with a long rakish feather, as they set out.

They were gone all morning. Eleanor did her best to act unconcerned, but as the hours dragged by her worry could not be disguised. Toward noon, the Misses Van Bibber, two elderly friends of Sara's who were also staying at the hotel, invited the now openly nervous young woman to accompany them for a gentle stroll along the lower slopes; they would surely meet Franklin and Miss Gandy on their way down. She did go with them, but somehow the two parties missed one another on the broad mountainside.

When Franklin finally turned up with his flamboyant companion in the hotel dining room after lunch, breathless from his climb and eager to tell Eleanor of the sights he had seen—pink and yellow rocks, slopes of blinding white limestone, tumbling clouds—she greeted him with polite but cold silence. She had lapsed into the isolation which was the only way she knew to deal with her anger—"my Griselda mood," she called it, and sometimes "my haggard days."

Franklin was puzzled by her withdrawal and perhaps irritated by it—he had asked her to come with him, after all. All he'd done was climb a mountain Eleanor hadn't wanted to climb with an older woman whom he thought faintly laughable rather than alluring—but he chose to ride it out, remaining outwardly cheerful and oblivious. Eleanor retreated still further. The result—a long, baffled, aggrieved silence—would be repeated a thousand times during their forty years together.

Eleanor's mood did not improve the next evening. When she said she did not care to attend a dance in the dining room, Franklin went without her. He described the evening to his mother: "The hotel maids, cook, etc. and some of the villagers did a *'Schutplatten'*—the native dance. It beats a cake walk and a court quadrille and a Robinson Virginia reel all to pieces and smacks of all three . . . I danced with the proprietress and talked to the cook and smoked with a porter and had the time of my life."[5]

Eleanor had not had the time of her life at Cortina. She had been "jealous beyond description of Miss Gandy," she later remembered, and "though I never said a word," she did not begin to brighten again until the following morning, when she and Franklin left by carriage to ride over the Stelvio Pass into Germany. It was mid-July, but there was ten feet of snow on either side of the twisting, climbing mountain road, Eleanor wrote, and "the air felt as it does at Hyde Park on a brilliant February day."

Franklin walked alongside the carriage a good part of the way— this was the highest mountain road in Europe, he said, and he did not wish to tire the horses. As they began their descent, the snow gave way to meadows filled with flowers and, perhaps relieved at his wife's change of mood, Franklin stopped to gather for her a bouquet of wild jasmine. It smelled sweeter, Eleanor told Sara, "than anything I have ever had."

Franklin did what he could to allay his wife's myriad fears. He was loving, kind, and attentive, for the most part. The Roosevelts were travelling without servants among older men and women who spent whole afternoons dressing for dinner. Franklin did his best to help, and Eleanor was grateful. "Franklin has been a wonderful maid," she told Sara, "and I've never been so well looked after." He sought patiently to reassure her, too, though her almost ceaseless anxiety must some-times have been trying. She had agonized before embarking on her honeymoon. She did not like to sail; a near-disaster at sea was among her earliest memories, she became queasy at the slightest swell, and she had been afraid that she would disgrace herself. But the Atlantic had been calm, and Franklin's solicitude had helped keep her feeling rea-sonably well. "Eleanor has been a *wonderful* sailor and hasn't *missed* a single meal or *lost* any either," Franklin had told his mother from the *Oceanic*.

5. Lest his mother think he had behaved in a manner unsuitable for a Delano and a Roosevelt, he added that the proprietress and waitresses with whom he had danced "are at least our equals—they consider themselves quite above many of the guests and come of old families of the Tirol, with family trees a thousand years old." *Source:* Elliott Roosevelt, ed., *FDR: His Personal Letters, 1905–1928*, page 36.

His active encouragement could cheer her momentarily, but it could not mask the fact that her fears and inhibitions often made it impossible for her to share his pleasures. His exuberant generosity troubled her, too; after listing all the clothes he bought for her in Paris—"a long stole and big muff of the softest, finest mink I've ever seen," an evening cloak, five evening gowns, an afternoon dress, a tweed coat and skirt and riding habit—she asked her mother-in-law, "Are you horrified at my extravagance? I am, but Franklin hasn't begun to complain as yet." She even worried that her letters home were somehow not what they should be. "You must forgive me dear if my letters are long and dull," she told Sara, "for I can't write like Franklin and I'm really quite ashamed to send you such stupid epistles after his amusing ones."[6]

Franklin had a wonderful time revisiting Osberton-in-Worksop, the sprawling Nottinghamshire estate of Cecil Foljambe, the fourth Baron Hawkesbury. He had first gone there at eleven, travelling out from London alone to see the baron's celebrated collection of mounted birds. "We got to this house at 9," he now told his mother, "and Mr. Foljambe and Lady Gertrude are *just* the same, Mr. F. of course a little older and more feeble, but most delightful and Lady G. hasn't altered one scrap. . . . I remember the house very well and the place, and nothing is altered. This morning I began well by being late for breakfast and at twelve we all went for a walk in the garden. . . . After lunch we went for a long drive with Mr. and Lady F. to Sherwood Forest, the scene of Robin Hood's escapades, passing thro' the Duke of Newcastle's place and two other big fellows!"

Eleanor remembered the same visit as something like a nightmare. The great house that Franklin so admired "terrified" her; there was only one modern bathroom serving all its many rooms, and tin tubs filled with hot water were set up in front of the stone fireplace in their bedroom for bathing, a practice she found disquieting. "Dinner was formal," she wrote later, "and to my horror, there were no introductions. We were guests in the house, and that was considered sufficient." While Franklin chatted effortlessly with his dinner partners, Eleanor struggled hard to find something to talk about with hers.

6. Sara also seems to have sensed her daughter-in-law's need for encouragement: "*Everyone* says lovely things about my Eleanor," she wrote to her children. "Those who have not seen her say they have *heard* she was charming and so I am quite puffed up with pride." *Source:* Sara to Eleanor and Franklin, August 26, 1905; Roosevelt Family Papers Donated by the Children, FDRL.

After dinner, the party moved into the big book-lined library to play bridge—for money, an activity Eleanor's pious Grandmother Hall had taught her to deplore. "My principles would not allow me to do this," she remembered, "so I was carried by my partner. . . ." Since she also played badly, she now felt doubly guilty; she had embarrassed Franklin and she had cost her partner money. "I felt like an animal in a trap," she recalled, not knowing how to act, unable to flee.

In Paris, when Franklin and some visiting Harvard friends took her and Sara's sister, Dora Forbes, to a faintly risqué French farce, in part just to see how Mrs. Forbes would take it, it was Eleanor, not the older woman, who was embarrassed. "I confess my Anglo-Saxon sense of humor was somewhat strained," she remembered, "but [Aunt Dora] had lived many years in Paris and did not give them the satisfaction of turning a hair!" Modern literature, too, sometimes troubled Eleanor: while Franklin lost himself in one of Bret Harte's gold rush tales one afternoon, she tried to read "a French book by Anatole France [though] he occasionally disgusts me so that I have to stop, and yet it is a mild and proper book for the French, devoted so far to the problem of our future life!"

She and Franklin and another young couple lunched together in Paris, at Voisin's. "There we saw *Mrs.* Jay Burden and *Mrs.* Harry Whitney," Eleanor reported to her mother-in-law in genuine shock, "with Mr. Bertie Goelet and Mr. Meredith Hare, so you see it is not fashionable to go out with your husband!" Many years later, the daughter-in-law of one of these ladies was shown this passage. "From what I know of Franklin and Eleanor Roosevelt," she said, "I believe he would already, even on his honeymoon, have rather moved to the other table."

That was unfair to both Roosevelts, but Eleanor knew that she was somehow letting her husband down by her inability to enjoy things as he did, to relish life without rendering judgments on it. "I looked at everything from the point of what I ought to do," she wrote later, "rarely from the standpoint of what I wanted to do . . . I was never carefree. . . ."[7]

7. In her modern study, *Another Chance: Hope and Health for the Alcoholic Family,* Sharon Wegscheider suggests four "Classic Roles" typically played by the offspring of alcoholics. The first two of them are eerily accurate descriptions of Eleanor and Hall Roosevelt.

Like Eleanor, the "Family Hero" is usually the eldest child, the one upon whom the disintegrating family depends when the adults cannot cope. She does well in school, is much loved by teachers, and praised for the selflessness with which she ministers to the needs of others. No

Franklin very often was.

He had climbed his peak at Cortina, had danced with the serving girls, though he knew Eleanor wished him to do otherwise. He was usually solicitous and almost always cheerful, but when it came to a choice between what he wanted to do and what his wife—or anyone else, for that matter—might have preferred, he was rarely deflected from his course. As a beloved only child he had rarely had to compromise with the wishes of others; his parents had provided the only effective brake upon his desires, and his marriage, which was in part for him a declaration of independence from his mother's loving demands, was not now going to keep him from indulging them.

Eleanor had hoped to show him Allenswood, the girl's school outside London where she had spent the three years she later called "the happiest of my life." No place on earth meant as much to her; only her own father had been more important to Eleanor than the school's late headmistress, Mademoiselle Marie Souvestre, who had died of cancer just two days after the Roosevelt marriage. But when the appointed day came, early in their trip, and Franklin discovered he was momentarily short of cash and needed to go to Barings Bank to replen-

---

amount of praise, however, can wipe away the persistent guilt she feels or compensate her for the affection she failed to get from her distracted parent—and for which she often seeks elsewhere and without success for the rest of her life. Consumed by guilt and accustomed almost from infancy to running things, she is fearful when not in control, and therefore cannot seem to *stop* working, often in "the helping professions."

Like Hall, "The Scapegoat" is most often the second child. He wins his parents' attention by acting up when small, cultivates a reputation for being difficult in order to hold that attention (even when his behavior is blamed for the family's ills), and continues it heedlessly into adult life.

Much of Eleanor Roosevelt's complex personality may be usefully seen in the context of having had to cope with her father's alcoholism. According to Judith S. Seixas and Geraldine Youcha's *Children of Alcoholism: A Survivor's Manual,* for example, the children of alcoholics, having been let down by their own parents, often have difficulty ever fully trusting anyone. They idealize self-discipline and feel they must control every aspect of their lives for fear of ever again becoming the helpless victim of the unpredictability of other people. Perhaps because their parents so often seemed to be two diametrically opposed people—loving when sober, dangerous when drunk—they tend unrealistically to divide the world around them into good and bad, black and white, and they are frequently so unsure of the worth of their own opinions that they laugh nervously as they express them in order to head off the laughter of others. (See below, page 638, for an account of how Eleanor was helped to deal with precisely this bad habit.) *Sources:* Sharon Wegscheider, *Another Chance: Hope and Health for the Alcoholic Family;* Judith S. Seixas and Geraldine Youcha, *Children of Alcoholism: A Survivor's Manual;* Janet Geringer Woititz, *Adult Children of Alcoholics.* I also owe thanks to my friend Richard Meryman for the suggestion that I pursue this line. For an account of the relationship between Eleanor and Hall and their unhappy parents, see Geoffrey C. Ward, *Before the Trumpet,* pages 258–303.

ish his supply, he did so, and his bride travelled to her old school on her own. Mademoiselle Samaia, who had been Mademoiselle Souvestre's assistant and now headed Allenswood, received her cordially enough, but Eleanor was sorry she had gone. "It was dreadful without Mlle Souvestre," she told Sara.[8]

In London and Paris, Milan and Florence, the Roosevelts spent hours in second-hand bookshops, bargaining for volumes to add to Franklin's collection. At Paris, he relied upon his own overconfident French to strike his bargains, but Eleanor's Italian was better than his, and when they reached Milan she was pleased when he asked her to translate for him—pleased, that is, until he accused her of always siding with the shopkeepers and resumed negotiating for himself, relying on his own distinctive Italian, "made up," Eleanor later said, from Latin learned at Groton.

The tensions between the Roosevelts were already real, but still muted by the no less authentic love they felt for one another, and by the heady sense of starting out life together that their honeymoon naturally engendered. That feeling may have taken some time to develop, for they were rarely alone. At Liverpool, their first, brief stop after landing at Queenstown, they were welcomed by Eleanor's Aunt Ella Bulloch, the widow of Irvine Bulloch who had served aboard the Confederate warship *Alabama* during the Civil War and, after Appomatox, had settled in self-imposed exile in Scotland with his brother, James, rather than return to a country ruled by Yankees. In Paris, the couple visited Dora Forbes and her husband, Paul, in their apartment on the Avenue de l'Alma. With them they undertook an automobile excursion to Fontainebleau; a tire blew halfway to the château, and Franklin's younger cousin, Warren Robbins, now also touring Europe, photographed him stretching the patched tube over the wooden-spoked rear wheel of the Forbes' big French touring car, while Eleanor and Franklin's aunt and uncle looked on from the shade of a roadside tree.

They also saw a good deal of Franklin's more distant cousin, Hortense Howland, while in Paris. Madame Howland was the French widow of a brother of James Roosevelt's first wife, Rebecca Howland,

---

8. So dreadful, evidently, that she later forgot she had ever revisited Allenswood. Had it been open while she was in London on her honeymoon, she wrote in *This Is My Story*, the first volume of her autobiography, "I should certainly have gone back to the old school, [but it] was closed for the vacation period. . . ." *Source:* Eleanor Roosevelt, *This Is My Story*, page 132.

and Franklin's father had been a trustee of her estate; when a fellow trustee absconded with some of the funds, Mr. James had made them up out of his own pocket—a gallantry for which she remained grateful all her life.[9] She was a minor fixture of Parisian society—appearing briefly in Proust's *Remembrance of Things Past*—and Franklin's good looks frankly dazzled her. Madame Howland's open admiration made him "cross," Eleanor reported, "but I thought her most appreciative as she kept repeating, *'Qu'il est beau, qu'il est charmant!'* " When they were shown to their rooms in the Palace Hotel at St. Moritz, they found them filled with flowers, gathered by the children of Eleanor's aunt, Elizabeth Hall Mortimer, known as "Tissie," who was staying nearby.

But there were plenty of what Eleanor called "nice lazy" times, too; days—or at least long hours—when they could be by themselves and learn more about one another.

In Venice, where they spent ten days, "we saw churches until my husband would look at no more," Eleanor recalled later, "but he was never tired of sitting in the sun at one of the little tables around the Piazza [San Marco] and recalling the history of Venice." She was a tireless sightseer, trained by Mademoiselle Souvestre soberly to assess every monument and artifact she saw; the Scuola di San Rocco, for example, she pronounced "a very fine building decorated by Tintoretto and some minor lights," but the "one or two Titians" it contained she thought not "among his best." Franklin raced ahead of her through the galleries of what he called the "Academica de Belly Arty" (Accademia de Belle Arti), taking in at a gallop "the Paul Veroneses and Titians, etc.—chiefly indecent infants sitting on or falling off of clouds—or scared apostles trying to keep the sun out of their eyes." The Roosevelts shopped together, too, ordering up a set of glasses especially incised with the Roosevelt family crest.[10]

In the evenings, Franklin and Eleanor reclined side by side in a

9. She expressed that gratitude on this occasion by sending home in Eleanor's luggage a pair of diamond earrings for Sara, said to have belonged to Marie Antoinette. *Source:* Eleanor Roosevelt, *This Is My Story*, page 132.

10. Franklin was in such high spirits in Venice that he at least toyed with the idea of extending his honeymoon to include a trip around the world, following closely the itinerary earlier marked out by the Teddy Robinsons; this would have meant delaying his return to law school for a year. He quickly thought better of this scheme, but in the same letter in which he broached it to his mother, he teased that she might like to buy "the furniture and woodwork, also mosaic floors, of one of the old palaces . . ." The price was $60,000. "If you care to have it cable me." Sara did not cable him. *Source:* Elliott Roosevelt, ed., *FDR: His Personal Letters, 1905–1928*, page 30.

gondola and were rowed through the canals, languid journeys made still more pleasurable for Eleanor because of her powerful memories of having glided along the same waterways fifteen years before, next to the father she adored. Elliott Roosevelt had insisted on rowing his own gondola, then, and on singing along with the gondoliers. Franklin did not do that, but he and Eleanor did have themselves pulled to a gathering place of gondolas, where they listened to the old songs and, together, watched the sunset.

At St. Moritz—which Franklin declared "the loveliest place we have seen yet"—he and Eleanor found that their clothes were insufficiently elegant and varied for the main dining room of the Palace Hotel; at mealtimes they were relegated to their own balcony overlooking the lake.[11] "Since dinner," Eleanor reported to Sara from there one evening, "I have been writing this, and [Franklin] has been mending his Kodak and occasionally telling me that I have a wonderful husband, so I suppose he is being successful!"

It was there, too, that they received word from Sara that she had found them a temporary Manhattan house of their own to move into upon their return. Franklin had gently turned down the first one she suggested, a brownstone owned by their old Campobello friends, the Alfred Pells; the rent the Pells were asking was prohibitive, he told her, and it would not be available for the full two years that remained of law school. The new house was also a brownstone, at 125 East 36th Street, owned by a member of the William H. Draper family, also old friends of the Roosevelts, and just three blocks from Sara's own New York home. Franklin cabled his mother immediately: WILL TAKE DRAPER HOUSE, IF IN ORDER, AT $2,400.

She signed the lease the day after his cable arrived: The house was "small," she noted in her journal, "but is to be put in good order. . . . I took it for F., as he cabled me to." Franklin wrote that he and Eleanor wanted to choose the wallpaper themselves when they got back, but in the meantime, the plumbing could be inspected and the refinishers could get started on the woodwork. "Eleanor says that *if* you happen to see in the paper of any sale of servant's cotton sheets, towels, etc. and happen to be in town that day or could write and get us some, she would be very grateful. We are so glad that it is really through you that we get the house. . . ." Eleanor agreed. "Poor Mama,

---

11. Eleanor did not forget this slight. Visiting St. Moritz half a century later, she took considerable pleasure in staying at another fashionable hotel, despite the bewildered protests of the Palace management. *Source:* Interviews with Maureen Corr and Edna Gurewitsch.

I am afraid we've given you lots of work about the house, but I shall be so glad if we get it and it is quite near you," she told Sara, and later, "I am looking forward so much to getting it in order with you to help us. I am afraid my unaided efforts would not be very successful!"

Sure now that they would have a place of their own to live in when they got home, the Roosevelts moved on to Germany, where Franklin wanted to show Eleanor some of the places he had known as a boy. Their journey began badly, at least from Eleanor's point of view. When their train stopped somewhere between St. Moritz and Augsburg, Franklin got down to get himself some beer. While he was gone, Eleanor told Sara,

> four large and burly Germans got into our compartment, and as they at first paid no attention to me, I thought Franklin would find no seat on his return. However, by dint of piling coats and cameras up opposite me I succeeded in keeping it. But to my horror the train began to move and there was no Franklin and I had no ticket and no money! You can imagine my feelings, but luckily we returned to the station and Franklin reappeared. Of course the Germans proceeded to make themselves comfortable and at one time I thought Franklin would burst and a duel would ensue, for one of the Germans, after pulling the blinds across *our* windows, leaned across Franklin and closed the window without so much as saying "by your leave'!"[12]

German boorishness was a constant theme in Roosevelt family letters from abroad. Franklin's mother, especially, had objected to dining with "German swine" at the spas to which she and Mr. James had often gone; now Franklin wrote to her from one of them, St. Blasien, that "by a show of severity I have secured a table on the verandah" of the old hotel, as far as possible from the dining room with its "four long pigsties where the strange assortment of mortals (swine are mortal, *n'est ce pas?*) consume victuals."[13]

12. Over the years, this incident evidently took on heroic proportions in Franklin's memory, at least when his wife was not present to correct it. He had been travelling with his mother and a woman friend of hers, not Eleanor, he told a White House visitor during the war, when a Prussian officer entered their compartment and without a word closed the window. Sara's friend gently protested: she had a headache, she said, and needed the air. The Prussian paid no attention. Franklin opened the window. The Prussian slammed it shut. Franklin opened it again, and when the officer rose to close it a third time, knocked him to the floor. When the train pulled into Berlin, the Prussian had Franklin arrested and only his mother's frantic appeal to the American ambassador got him out of prison.

13. The young Roosevelts also looked with disfavor upon some foreign-born Americans they encountered while abroad. One afternoon at St. Blasien, they eavesdropped on two couples, one English, the other American. "Needless to say," Eleanor told Sara, "the Americans were com-

But if Franklin and Eleanor were scornful of the Germans, they were delighted by the German countryside. They sat together on their balcony at St. Blasien, Eleanor reported, "played piquet, and watched the most wonderful pinky clouds I've ever seen and listened to the band which plays every night. . . ." At the falls of the Rhine near Schaffhausen they walked laughing, hand in hand, along the bottom of the cliff until they were soaked with spray. They climbed up the Feldberg after several days of steady rain to view the Black Forest spread out below them through ragged clouds of rising mist. And from the window of the observation car that took them on to Freiburg, Franklin proudly pointed out to Eleanor the steep, twisting road down which, at fourteen, he and his last tutor, Arthur Dumper, had coasted on their bicycles for eighteen miles; that long, giddy ride was a treasured memory for Franklin, a daring moment of freedom in a boyhood largely empty of adventure.

When the Roosevelts reached Paris on August 11, on their meandering way back to Britain and home, Franklin found a letter waiting for him at the front desk of the Imperial Hotel. It was from the Columbia Law School: he had failed to pass two of his courses, Contracts and Pleading & Practice. He sent his mother a cable immediately, asking that her housekeeper bundle up his law books and send them to him in London; nothing was said about why he needed them. Two nights later, Eleanor wrote Sara her usual chatty letter, in the course of which she noted that Franklin was "sad at having failed in two exams, particularly as he got good marks (b) in all the others . . . if possible he wants to take them again this autumn, as otherwise it will mean very hard work all winter. I am not very confident about his passing. . . ."

Franklin may not have been very confident, either: he again broke out in hives. "Poor Franklin . . . he seems otherwise very well," Eleanor wrote, "isn't it queer?"

On August 14, three days after he had learned the bad news and cabled for his books, it was Franklin's turn to write to Sara. He evi-

---

mon, and the man had evidently been a German at no very distant date. They were impressing the English couple with their wealth, and after explaining that in America there was no such thing as a season for eatables, that strawberries were much better in January than in June, and that of course the price was no consideration, they proceeded to discuss the government of the country, and finally the negro question while Franklin and I pretended to do accounts and . . . nearly expired with suppressed laughter!" *Source:* Elliott Roosevelt, ed., *FDR: His Personal Letters, 1905–1928,* page 52.

dently did not know that Eleanor had already told her of his setback. His letter was, if anything, more jaunty and apparently freewheeling than usual: he and Eleanor wanted the master bedroom in the Draper house painted white, at their own expense, if necessary; he had just bought "some Rembrandt engravings and a cunning little sketch by Claude Lorraine"; with Warren Robbins and several Harvard friends he had gone on "a prolonged toot"; and he and Eleanor had had their fortunes told by Madame Noël, a French clairvoyante who clearly recognized the name Roosevelt: "E. is to inherit a fortune . . . and I am to be President of the U.S. or the Equitable, I couldn't make out which! . . . Forgive haste, writing and uninterestingness, but we are having a scrumptious time. Loads of love, FDR."

Not a word about his failure. Franklin hated always to be the bearer of bad tidings, especially about himself. When he did finally get around to telling Sara what had happened, ten days after he got the news, he coupled it with protestations of bewilderment and hints of injustice, precisely as he had at Groton and Harvard when things had not gone for him as well as he and his parents always assumed they would. He had known all along that he would fail, he now said, but "It certainly shows the uncertainty of marks, for I had expected much lower marks in some of the others and failure in one, and thought I had done as well on the two I failed as in those I passed with B. . . . I am going to work the last two weeks and take the exams on Sept 21 and 22 in the bare hope of getting thru. . . ."

Sara was not unduly discouraged. "You can do a good deal even crossing an ocean," she told him, "if you set apart two or three hours a day for work"; but he would have "to forego the pleasure of a nice loafing time" aboard ship.

She had also sent along a gift, a large check with which Franklin and Eleanor launched still another shopping expedition. It carried with it only one stipulation: Franklin had to use part of it to pay for a series of coaching lessons from a celebrated whip named Howlett. He balked a little at first—more at being told what to do than because he objected to driving itself—but then signed up. Horses were a Roosevelt tradition, and Sara wished Franklin to follow family tradition, in this as in all things. His father had been a skilled whip, after all, and his half brother Rosy had been one of the best in Britain or America; indeed, coaching had been Rosy's chief preoccupation for many years after he married into the Astor family and "retired" from business at the age of twenty-three. Now exactly the same age as Rosy had been then,

Franklin decided to concentrate on learning to drive a pair of horses and a tandem rather than the more showy four-in-hand—he was sure those skills would "be more useful to him," Eleanor said—and when they reached London he ordered up a silver-mounted harness so costly that he had to ask his mother to bring "a small sum of gold" with her to pay the customs duty when she met their ship in New York. "I think $300 will be enough," he said.

Sara was eager to see her children; not since Harvard had Franklin been so long apart from her. "I never knew such angels about writing," she told them, "and I am *so* glad Eleanor says that although you have had such a perfect time you are now anxious to see 'home and mother' again."

But before that reunion could take place, the young Roosevelts travelled to Scotland to visit Eleanor's closest friend, Isabella Selmes, one year younger than she and just married to another of her good friends, Robert Munro Ferguson.

Isabella was an astonishingly beautiful young woman, "one of the loveliest . . . girls I have ever seen," Eleanor remembered. Born in Kentucky and brought up in St. Paul, Minnesota, she had, like Eleanor, lost her father at nine, and had lived during the intervening years in the homes of relatives. Unlike Eleanor, however, she had never been without the love of her mother. Eleanor was fond of both mother and daughter; "there was a glamour about them both," she later wrote, but in Isabella she found a friend and confidante who would prove steadfast throughout her life. They had met in 1903, the year of Isabella's New York debut and the year after Eleanor's. The older girl had helped reassure the younger one, and it was to Isabella alone among her contemporaries that Eleanor had confided the great secret of her engagement to Franklin several weeks before it was announced.[14]

One evening, Eleanor had confessed her private anxiety about

14. "It doesn't seem yesterday that we were snuggled in a bed at Mrs. [Douglas] Robinson's at Orange [New York] discussing your marriage," Isabella would remind Eleanor some years later. "I remember every last detail of it."

Evidently, the secret had inadvertently been broached still earlier within the Theodore Roosevelt family, though neither Franklin nor Eleanor may have been aware of it. In the summer of 1904, Eleanor had spent several weeks with her uncle and aunt, the Douglas Robinsons, at Isleboro, Maine. Writing the next year to her own secret fiancé, Bob Ferguson, Isabella had warned him to be circumspect, reminding him that "Even our well regulated Eleanor, when at Isleboro, left a 'My own dearest Nell' letter lying on her dressing table. It was after that that 'Aunty Corinne' wondered at some of honest Eleanor's 'little white lies' about Franklin." ("Nell" was then Eleanor's pet name for Franklin; it had also been a pet name within the family for her late father.) *Source:* Eleanor Roosevelt Papers, FDRL; Ferguson Family Correspondence, Arizona Historical Society.

marriage itself and about "next winter's terrors"—the intimidating social gauntlet a big Roosevelt wedding would force her to run. Isabella had helped calm her fears, and the next day Eleanor expressed her gratitude: "This is only a line to thank you for your kindness and patience of last night. You were very, very sweet to me and I only hope that someday I may have the chance to help you, dear, as much as you helped me . . . I'm feeling quite sane again, so you need worry no more about me!"

For all of Isabella's beauty and vivacity—unlike Eleanor, she was besieged by eager suitors from the moment she made her debut—she was also unusually empathetic, seeming to understand the fears and frailties of her friends almost by instinct. When the Roosevelt engagement was finally announced, for example, she had urged Eleanor to try to "Be as happy as you are good and sweet and true"—wise counsel which Eleanor was sadly never able to follow.

Eleanor and Isabella would remain close, though circumstances often kept them physically apart and they had to be content to keep in touch through correspondence, producing over the next four decades a body of intimate letters which Isabella herself once called "a volume of friendship."

Eleanor was enormously fond of Isabella's new husband, Bob Ferguson, too. He was a tall, diffident Scot, the youngest son of an old family who had been sent to America to make his fortune. He was a former Rough Rider and an intimate of the Oyster Bay Roosevelts—he had been a hunting and ranching companion of Theodore Roosevelt in 1891, and it was to him that an exultant TR had shouted: "Look at all these damned Spanish dead!" on the bloody slope of Kettle Hill. He admired the man he always called "the Colonel" with a fervor that approached worship, and was especially proud that all of TR's children called him "Mr. Fergie." He now worked alongside Eleanor's uncle, Douglas Robinson, as a trustee of the vast Astor estate.

Eleanor had first come to know him during her childhood—he had been a friend of her father's as well as of Theodore—and when she returned from school in England to make her debut, he had won her undying gratitude by sensing her shyness and making certain that several of his far younger friends were attentive to her. He had been confined to his bed with a racking cough on the Roosevelts' wedding day, but Eleanor was so fond of him that they had stopped their carriage on the way from the wedding to Grand Central, where they were to take the train to Hyde Park and their first night together, to see him—a kindness that Ferguson never forgot.

He was thirty-six years old in the summer of 1906—he had once been one of a number of young men who paid court to Theodore's older sister, Anna, and his sudden decision to marry Isabella, eighteen years his junior, had astonished everyone, including Franklin and Eleanor. "I don't think anything nicer than this has happened since our own wedding," Eleanor had written Sara when she got word of it at St. Moritz, "but we were overcome and I can hardly believe it now!"

The Fergusons were honeymooning, too. Bob was still not well—was taking the waters near Novar, one of his family's ancestral homes, and may already have been suffering from the tuberculosis that eventually killed him—but, Eleanor noted, Isabella had had a wonderful warming effect on him. "They all adore her here and she looks prettier than ever," she told Sara, "though she says she is freezing to death. It is impossible to imagine how sweet she and Bob are together, for I would not know him for the same man. He has become demonstrative, if you can believe it, and they play together like two children!" The Fergusons and Roosevelts had "great fun," Isabella told her mother, "comparing housekeeping notes" on the Manhattan "bandboxes"— brownstones—both couples had rented by cable, sight unseen.

The Roosevelts enjoyed themselves at Novar and at Raith, a second Ferguson house near Edinburgh. It rained a good deal, and Franklin had begun to study for his make-up examinations in the mornings, but he managed to find opportunities to play golf at St. Andrews, to survey the tenant farms, and to take long slow walks with Eleanor through the heather. Sir Robert and Lady Helen Ferguson, Robert's oldest brother and sister-in-law, were enthusiastic supporters of the Liberal Party, and British politics was a constant topic of conversation at their table. The Fabian Socialists Sidney and Beatrice Webb came for lunch one day. Eleanor identified them to Sara as writers of "books on sociology." "Franklin discussed the methods of learning at Harvard with the husband," she wrote, "while I discussed the servant problem with the wife!" After dinner that evening, Robert's younger sister, Edith, showed Franklin and Eleanor a portfolio of her own political cartoons. Franklin was delighted by them; Eleanor found them "very amusing," too, she said, "though I miss the point as I don't know half the people."

Twice during their stay with the Fergusons, Franklin again had to come to Eleanor's rescue. At tea alone with Lady Helen one afternoon, she was asked, "Do tell me, my dear, how do you explain the difference between your national and state governments? It seems to us so confusing." Eleanor, the niece of the President of the United States, could provide no answer. "I had never realized that there were any differences to explain," she wrote; the curriculum at Allenswood had not included much information about her homeland. "I knew that we had state governments, because Uncle Ted had been Governor of New York State. My heart sank, and I wished that the ground would swallow me up."

At that moment, Franklin strolled in, back from a long walk with Sir Ronald. While Lady Helen poured him a cup of tea, he did what he could to explain the American system. "He was adequate," Eleanor remembered, "and I registered a vow that once safely back in the United States I would find out something about my own government."

Later in their stay, Eleanor was asked to open the local flower show. "Any young English girl would have been able to do it easily," Eleanor wrote later—by which she meant any English girl of her own class—"but I was quite certain that I could never utter a word aloud in a public place." She could snip the ribbon, thank the crowd, and declare the show open, she told Franklin that morning, but that was all; he would have to do the real speechmaking. Perhaps privately exasperated at having again to compensate for her timidity, he did not consult her on what to say, sitting in their room by himself and scribbling out his remarks in pencil, with many erasures and emendations. The result was Franklin Roosevelt's first known speech as an adult, delivered before a small gathering of crofters. It started off well enough—Franklin was already good at creating a bond with his audience, however tenuous—but before he had finished his remarks the respectful attentiveness of his listeners must have been placed under considerable strain:

> I must thank you again for your very great kindness and hospitality and tell you how much we appreciate this opportunity of meeting you here. Indeed, neither of us can think of you as foreigners or strangers for several of Mrs. Roosevelt's ancestors were Scotchmen & my own great great grandfather was in exile to America after the Scotch Rebellion. And I was fortunate, too, in having a Highland nurse so that I passed my early years with kilts on the outside and oatmeal and scones in the interior. For especially good conduct a piece of shortbread was my reward, and I can assure you that my *desire* to be good [was] irreproachable.
>
> Mr. Ferguson has asked me to tell you something of our American gardens, but judging from amateur observations on two short walks here on Thursday I must confess that the average of your gardens seems somewhat higher than of ours. I have been especially struck by the general

neatness of your flower gardens, as well as by the taste in the selection and arrangement of the flowers. I imagine that with us the relative value of the land is lower than it is here, and that this may account for our tendency to spread our gardens out too much. But in our village gardens, especially in New England, the resemblance to yours is more marked. Perhaps with us the tendency is more to combine the flowers and fine vegetables and that vegetables form a rather larger proportion of our diets. Our average garden contains not only potatoes and cucumbers and peas, beans, onions and carrots, but also the small beet, the egg-plant, the yellow sweet potato, the lima bean, and the Indian sweet corn. And even most of the small gardens have two or three glass frames, an inexpensive way of raising in a climate like this, or like that of our northeast coast, many vegetables which the poor soil and bad weather would otherwise destroy. Perhaps one reason, aside from the cheapness compared to meat, why vegetables play such an important part in America is that our womenfolk excel in cooking them. Instead of water, we cook them nearly always in milk, and this, of course, makes them more nutritious, besides bringing out the flavor.

Eleanor thought this speech "very good," or so she told her mother-in-law—though later she admitted that for years afterwards the family liked to tease Franklin about its imaginative version of American cooking—and she carefully clipped out a local newspaper story about the opening and sent it home to Sara, who proudly glued it into her scrapbook. Franklin was more realistic about his performance: "I had an awful time of it and wasn't even introduced. I had to wander up to the front of the platform and the foolishness of my smile was only equalled by the extreme idiocy of the remarks that followed. You can imagine what a speech on gardening, and the raising of vegetables in general by your son must have been like, and I will say nothing more except that my appetite for those damned weeds has since that time departed!"

However irritated Franklin may have been at having had to stand in for his wife, no hint of it was conveyed to Sara. Eleanor had opened the show "very well," he reported, "and spoke clearly and well"— though, in fact, she had hardly spoken at all. Triumphs were to be shared; disappointments were kept to himself.

The Scottish reporter who covered the Roosevelts' first public appearance noted that Franklin's remarks had been interrupted several times by laughter and applause, but the crowd had shown the greatest enthusiasm when Eleanor was introduced. The local official who began the ceremony had seen no need to say anything more than that "Mrs. Roosevelt had a connection with the President of that great country, the United States (Loud applause)—a gentleman whom the world was applauding (Applause). . . ."

That applause echoed everywhere Franklin and Eleanor went during the final days of their honeymoon. Even the Fergusons' tenants were eager to talk of Uncle Ted's latest triumph, Eleanor was surprised to find. "They all seemed to know about it and take an interest. It is nice news, isn't it?" On September 5, 1905, the same day Franklin and Sir Ronald were playing golf at St. Andrews, the Portsmouth Treaty was formally signed, ending the Russo-Japanese War. Theodore Roosevelt had been instrumental in arranging the talks at the U.S. naval base at Kittery, Maine, just across the Piscataqua River from Portsmouth, New Hampshire, that had at last led to peace. The political risks had been considerable; many of his advisers had warned him against involving himself in trying to settle a complicated foreign conflict that was of little interest to most Americans. But, as he told a friendly reporter while the outcome was still in doubt, "I thought it my plain duty to make the effort," and that effort had now paid off. A Republican congressman had been waiting in the downstairs hall at Sagamore Hill to see TR when the news came that peace was at hand. The beaming President had pounded down the stairs, his visitor remembered. "It's a mighty good thing for Russia," he said, "and a mighty good thing for Japan. And," he added, thumping his own chest with pleasure, "a mighty good thing for *me*, too!"

It was indeed a mighty good thing for him. Newspapers on both sides of the Atlantic declared him a peacemaker. Summing up feelings on the Continent, the Berlin correspondent for the *New York World* wrote that President Roosevelt had emerged from the negotiations as "the most important figure in international statesmanship." The Nobel Committee would later award him its Peace Prize.

No one was more impressed than Franklin. "Everyone is talking about Cousin Theodore," he wrote Sara from London in the last of his honeymoon letters, "saying that he is the most prominent figure of present day history." Franklin eagerly agreed with that assessment; he admired Theodore Roosevelt more than any man on earth.[15]

15. Franklin's mother's admiration for him ran a close second to her son's. After a 1904 visit to the Roosevelt White House, she had reported to Franklin: "He is, as he always was, the most simple, natural person one c'd find and so warm hearted with his really great capacity for work

On September 12, the day before the young Roosevelts sailed for home, he left Eleanor at Garlant's Hotel to finish packing their trunks and hurried into the street, a tall, slender figure in a straw boater, peering at the crowds through pince-nez he had bought nine years earlier in open emulation of his Cousin Theodore.

He had one more important stop to make. At Henry Graves & Company, Ltd., Printsellers & Publishers, located at Number 6 Pall Mall, he wrote out a check for £25 and waited while the clerk wrapped his purchase—a silver-point drawing by the British artist C. J. Becker of his vigorous, triumphant hero.

& thought. As I think of him I wonder how *small men* can criticize & belittle him. . . ." *Source:* Roosevelt Family Papers Donated by the Children, FDRL.

CHAPTER

2

MR. FRANKLIN

On the morning of September 27, 1905, Sara Delano Roosevelt set out from Springwood for Poughkeepsie in her carriage. With her were her son and daughter-in-law, back just eight days from their honeymoon. Sara and Eleanor wore wide hats to shield them from the sun that filtered through the branches above the Albany Post Road. Franklin wore a bowler. Robert Simms, the family coachman, kept the horses trotting smoothly. The Roosevelts were on their way to the Dutchess County Fair.

Franklin and Eleanor had had a difficult voyage home from Europe. The sea was rough; Eleanor was often ill; Franklin had been preoccupied with his law books. And when the *Kronprinz Wilhelm* nosed into her New York berth at 10:00 A.M. on September 19 and they looked down and saw Sara waiting on the dock to greet them, they had been glad to see her.

She had been glad to see them, too, and to greet Duffy, the Scottie pup they had bought in Scotland, the first of several that would tumble through the Roosevelts' lives.

While Franklin saw to the luggage, Sara had taken Eleanor home with her to 200 Madison Avenue; the young couple's new house was still not quite ready for them. They all dined together that evening. Afterwards, alone in her room, Sara had noted in her diary, "We are all so happy."

Franklin had taken his make-up examinations at Columbia two

days later and passed them easily; his second year of law school would begin the following Monday.

But this afternoon at the Poughkeepsie fair grounds, he faced another test: he was to drive his father's old sulky in the trotting meet, behind Bobby, the handsome, Kentucky-bred horse that had been a gift to Mr. James from Sara in the last year of his life. Both Franklin and his mother seemed to see in Bobby a living link with Mr. James, a symbol of the happy time when all three were still together. "I don't think Franklin ever loved any other horse," Eleanor once said.

Sara now rode him nearly every day she was at Hyde Park, roaming the estate to check that her men were seeing properly to their chores, just as her husband had.

Franklin rode the old horse on weekends. The men who worked for the family and the people of Hyde Park village already called him "Mr. Franklin," just as they had called his father "Mr. James," and as he rode around the place or into the village on Bobby in his English riding clothes and polished boots, they remarked on how much he already seemed like the old man.

It had been a quarter of a century almost to the day since Sara's husband had brought his young bride north along this road to her new home at Springwood. He had raised and raced fine trotters for many years, and even after he abandoned the sport—because, he said, the tracks had been taken over by a new and vulgar element, more interested in making money than improving bloodlines—he had always kept a stableful of fine horses for his own use, and had continued to drive his own carriage until just a few days before his death. A Springwood visitor who had gone out driving with the elder Roosevelts during Mr. James's last days recalled that he seemed so frail Sara had gently suggested he might hand the reins to the coachman; he had been uncharacteristically angry. "No, Sally," he had snapped, "I am not dead yet." One of his last projects had been to build an imposing new building to house his horses, topped with a tower and a bright copper weathervane emblazoned with his initials.[1]

The Dutchess County Fair had always been a highlight of his year, a chance to match his trotters against those of his neighbors, and Sara had often watched proudly as he drove one or another of them to victory around the mile track known as Ruppert's Park. She had not

1. The same weathervane still turns on its tower, high above the rose garden in which FDR is buried. In his mother's mind as well as Franklin's own, Springwood always belonged first of all to Mr. James.

been back to the Fair since his death; perhaps the memory of having seen him so happy there so many times was still too painful for her. But this year was different. Franklin felt ready to vie for his father's old honors.

Mr. James had made certain that both his sons were brought up to love and understand horses; everyone in the family agreed that that knowledge was one of the most important marks of a gentleman. "No man who knows nothing about horses," Sara's brother-in-law, Price Collier, had written in his book *Riding & Driving*, "no matter how charitable he may be. . . . No matter how ecclesiastically regular [or] . . . conspicuously tender-hearted he may be to children . . . and the poor, has any business on or behind a horse." (Sara had admired that sentiment so much that she snipped it out of a review of Collier's book and pasted it into her personal scrapbook.)

Horses and coaching had become almost an obsession with Rosy, and Franklin, too, had been an enthusiastic horseman since the age of two, when he was taken around Springwood on the front of his father's saddle. One of the earliest of Franklin's boyhood drawings to have survived shows a man with a top hat, perhaps Mr. James himself, at the reins of a sulky. On his seventh birthday, he had been given his own pony to feed and care for; at eleven he rode twenty miles alongside his father to visit his Delano grandparents at Algonac. After Mr. James's death, Sara had made sure Franklin continued to drive and ride, renting him a horse and carriage to use while at Harvard and, after he began law classes at Columbia, paying for his membership in the New York Riding Club on East 58th Street so that he might rent a mount and explore Central Park in his spare time.[2] And she had made certain that even in Paris on his honeymoon he took the time to polish his driving skills.

At the fairgrounds, Sara and Eleanor took their places in the stands.

---

2. That he was never quite so keen about riding as his mother wished him to be is suggested by the fact that he failed to pay his dues to this club as soon as Sara stopped doing so for him. In December 1908, his old friend and Harvard classmate, Tom Beal, now a Boston banker, wrote him a somewhat embarrassed note:

> You have not paid any attention to [the club's] letters and the result is that they are now all feeling very sore at you. Yesterday, a meeting was held and it was voted to post your name in the club house and then if your dues were not paid, to strike your name from their list. They are very unwilling to do this, for it will be the first time they have been forced to take such action.

Franklin paid up—he had owed $100—but resigned from the club soon thereafter. *Source:* Franklin D. Roosevelt Papers, FDRL.

Old friends and acquaintances of Mr. James greeted his widow, and she introduced them to her daughter-in-law.

Franklin went off to the stables to see that all was ready for the race. The Roosevelt grooms had outdone themselves. The silver trappings on the harness, incised with the three feathers of the Roosevelt crest, were polished until the stable boy could see his face in them; the horse's mane and tail were carefully brushed and curried; its hooves varnished, its ankles wrapped in white puttees that set off its high-stepping gait.

The meet began. There were three one-mile heats and, each time, as the big, old horse thudded past the stand, Franklin stared straight ahead, jaw set with concentration, the reins held in his gloved left hand, as he had been taught by Mr. James and Rosy, the long flexible whip gripped in his right. He wore a high collar and tie—reinsmen, at least, still *dressed* like gentlemen—and his bowler was jammed down on his head to keep it from blowing off in the rushing wind.

Franklin and Bobby won two blue ribbons that afternoon, one for trotting, the other in the saddle horse competition.[3] Eleanor was "very proud," she told him in a note written after he had caught the train back to the city later in the afternoon. "You don't know how nice you looked dear! I feel a little like 'Evangeline' and the 'lovely shape.' " She felt "quite lost and sad" without him, she added, ". . . so I don't think we will try this experiment again, do you think? Incidentally, I hope you miss me dreadfully, too!"

Sara was just as pleased with Franklin's performance; how proud her husband would have been to see his son take first place. Like his father, like his half brother, Franklin was making a name for himself as a horseman.[4]

In later years, Sara was often asked what her ambitions for her son had been when he was young. Her answer was invariably the same: "I hoped that he would grow up to be a fine, upright man, respected in his home and in his own community. I hoped that he would grow up to be like his father." That was the goal to which she had dedicated herself since Franklin's birth with what had always seemed to her

3. Twenty-eight years later, in 1933, another Springwood horse, ridden by Franklin's daughter, Anna, won first prize at the same County Fair. The horse's name was "New Deal." *Source:* Poughkeepsie *Sunday Courier,* September 3, 1933.

4. She was not pleased that same afternoon when Simms, her coachman, failed to win the tandem race. He had been "rather *muddled* with drink when he got home from the fair," she noted, and some months later—after several stern talks with him had failed to persuade him to take the temperance pledge—she dismissed him. *Source:* Sara Delano Roosevelt Journal, FDRL.

complete success. In a letter to Endicott Peabody, his old schoolmaster, written shortly after Mr. James's death in 1900, Franklin had echoed his mother's wish: "It is indeed a terrible loss which Mama and I have sustained, but I can only be thankful that my dear Father was spared long enough for me never to forget him, and to know what he would have wanted me to do."

All the evidence available in the autumn of 1905 suggested that Sara was still succeeding. Franklin had been graduated from Harvard and was attending law school, just as his father had; he was taking an increasingly active interest in the running of Springwood; and, best of all from Sara's point of view, he had made a suitable marriage without seeming eager to separate himself from his mother. The newlyweds had happily managed on their own during their summer abroad, but they now easily fell back into the state of loving dependency upon Sara that had characterized their first weeks together as man and wife. With her, they again constituted an almost inseparable trio, attending together dinner parties, plays, public events.

The young Roosevelts did move into their own small rented house on 36th Street—Franklin called it his "14-foot mansion"—in mid-October. But Sara helped Eleanor pick the wallpaper and hired the cook, waitress, and housekeeper.[5] Nearly every evening when she was in the city she dined with her children, either at her house or theirs; when she came to their home, Franklin always walked her the three blocks back to hers.

And Franklin and Eleanor spent almost every weekend with Sara in Hyde Park, experiencing what Sara herself once called "life as it should be lived."

From there, on October 11—Eleanor's twenty-first birthday—Sara wrote to her daughter-in-law:

My darling Eleanor,
    I am thinking much of you & wishing you every happiness for the coming year & many years to follow, & I pray that my precious Franklin may make you very happy & thank him for giving me such a dear, loving

5. Franklin's own account of this period includes no mention of her own supervisory role: "The house was extremely simple, but very cosy," he said many years later, speaking in the third person. "Franklin had his treasured books and prints around him, and Eleanor, who was instinctively a home-maker, had done wonders with the little place." (For an explanation of why this and many other memories offered in Sara's book about her son's early years as if they came from her were actually his, see note, pages 515–516.) *Source:* Sara Delano Roosevelt (as told to Isabel Leighton and Gabrielle Forbush), *My Boy Franklin,* page 66.

daughter. I thank *you* also darling for being what you are to me already. This is straight from my heart.

I felt you were not at all well yesterday & hope today is a better day. You looked so white & tired. . . .

With dear love & 21 kisses & one more to "grow on,"

Your devoted
Mama

Eleanor looked white and tired because she was pregnant. Her illness aboard the *Kronprinz Wilhelm* had been more than seasickness. Sara had suspected it first while Eleanor was at Hyde Park, and called a local doctor, who confirmed it. The baby was due in late April or early May.

Franklin was pleased, though possibly a little startled that things were happening so fast; he had told Alice Sohier, the first young woman to whom he had proposed marriage four years earlier, that he had sometimes been lonely as an only child, and that, as a consequence, he wanted eventually to have at least six children of his own. Here again, his Cousin Theodore seems to have provided additional inspiration; during the brief, boyhood visits to Sagamore Hill that were among Franklin's fondest memories there had been six boisterous young Roosevelts with whom to play.

Sara was pleased, too, and hoped that the baby would be a boy and be named after Mr. James.

Eleanor's emotions were more complicated. One of her great, secret worries had now lessened; until the doctor told her she was pregnant, she wrote later, "I had been seriously troubled for fear that I would never have any children and my husband would therefore be much disappointed." That fear, at least, would now be laid to rest. But new ones replaced it. Pregnancy had simply happened to her. There had been no conscious decision by her or by Franklin to have a child, and anything beyond her control held special terrors for her. She was now frightened that she would be unable to bear up under the pain of childbirth. "I never said anything," she remembered, "though I was afraid I might not conduct myself with proper self-control." To confess that fear, she was convinced, would shock Franklin and his mother, make them think less of her.

Sara sensed her anxiety anyway, and did her best to ease it, though the examples of successful childbearing she offered—Chinese peasant women she had been told about during her childhood, who sat on hard benches and gave birth without a murmur—were not reassuring. More useful was a chance remark made by one of Eleanor's own friends, also pregnant that winter. "When I am a little afraid of the future," her friend said, "I look around and see all the people there are in the world and I think that, after all, they had to be born, and so nothing so very extraordinary is happening to me."

"When things happen to you that are inevitable," Eleanor concluded, "there is a kind of courage that comes from sheer desperation. If it is inevitable and has to be met, you can meet it."

Her pregnancy made Eleanor rely still more heavily upon her mother-in-law. With Franklin away all day attending classes at Columbia, Sara tried hard to build up her daughter-in-law's strength, to prepare her for motherhood. The two women went driving almost every afternoon; they shopped together for a layette, and in the mornings strolled along the road at Hyde Park or up and down Fifth Avenue, gazing into store windows. As the day of her delivery drew near, Eleanor's stoical calm won her mother-in-law's highest praise. "She is wonderful," Sara confided to her journal, "always bright and well."

The Roosevelts had a family Christmas together at Springwood. Rosy was there; so were Bob and Isabella Ferguson, also back from their honeymoon. Franklin surprised Eleanor with a hand-made calendar illustrated with his own photographs of their honeymoon—the white peaks above the Stelvio Pass, Franklin changing the tire on the road to Fontainebleau, Eleanor, slender and lovely in their Venice gondola, holding her husband's straw hat. She was delighted by it.[6]

For two days in February, Sara and Franklin did leave Eleanor briefly in the care of her cousin, Mrs. Henry Parish, while they hurried down to Washington for Alice Roosevelt's wedding to Nicholas Longworth, a freshman congressman from Ohio.[7]

6. Sara's feelings upon seeing it may privately have been less warm than she let on. On Christmas morning four years earlier, Franklin had presented her with an almost identical calendar depicting *her* first trip to Europe with him the first summer after the death of Mr. James. (This 1902 calendar was only recently rediscovered tucked away in a Springwood library cabinet, and was kindly shown to me by its discoverers, Diane Boyce and Susan Brown, both then of the National Park Service.)

7. "Franklin was there but Eleanor was not," Alice remembered later. "She couldn't go because that was indecent. A pregnant woman at a wedding, going around *showing* herself! That just wouldn't do!"

In fact, Eleanor may have been privately relieved at not having to attend. The White House always made her "rather nervous" then, she remembered. "Alice was so much more sophisticated than *I* was. . . ." *Source:* Michael Teague, *Mrs. L.,* page 128; Interview with Eleanor Roosevelt, Robert Graff Collection, FDRL.

The wedding in the East Room of the White House on Saturday morning, February 17, was the social event of the year, and not even his wife's pregnancy could keep Franklin from attending. Some three hundred carriages waited in line for the gates to open at eleven-fifteen that morning. Franklin and his mother occupied the very first one, with Cousin Bamie and her husband, Admiral W. Sheffield Cowles.

Alice had agreed to be a bridesmaid at Franklin's wedding, but only because she was Eleanor's first cousin. Franklin had not been asked to be an usher at hers. He was still a relatively unimportant Roosevelt; at least one newspaper listed him among the guests as "Frederick Delano Roosevelt," and those that bothered to explain his presence identified him simply as the husband of the President's niece. He stood next to Sara, who was dressed in black lace and wearing a black hat with plumes, and watched with all the other guests as a band struck up the march from *Tannhäuser* and the President and his daughter walked to the improvised altar. Two rows of young men, led by Theodore Jr., formed the aisle; each of them was closer to Longworth and the President than was Franklin.

Sara retained warm memories of the White House ceremony: "Alice looked remarkably pretty and her manner was very charming. Theodore, our President, was as always cordial and interesting, and Edith [his wife] very sweet and nice."

Franklin left no written record of his impressions but they must have been distinctly mixed. After the vows had been exchanged and the guests had crowded around the bride and groom to offer their congratulations, a wedding breakfast was served in the state dining room, a daunting array of dishes—lobster and cold meat, croquettes and sandwiches, cake and ice cream, wine and coffee—which one newspaper described without irony as "dainty." While the guests filled their plates and raised their glasses, the President and his new son-in-law withdrew into the private dining room, followed by a laughing, jostling band of young men. TR himself swung shut the doors behind them.

Porcellian was in secret session. It was the most exclusive of all the Harvard clubs, the one to which TR, and the Reverend Endicott Peabody of Groton, and Franklin's own father had all belonged, and in which he had thought himself entitled to membership as an undergraduate four years earlier. Its rejection of him had been a deep humiliation; fifteen years later he would still count it "the greatest disappointment of my life." Now it was to exclude him again.

Nicholas Longworth was fifteen years older than his bride, already bald and with a deserved reputation as a womanizer. But he was able and amusing, and—very important to his new father-in-law—he, too, belonged to Porcellian. In private, the bridegroom and the President enjoyed calling one another "Brother Longworth" and "Brother Roosevelt." ("My father wanted me to meet all kinds of people," Alice remembered later, "but not to marry them.")

This meeting of the Porc, far from its Cambridge clubhouse, followed club tradition. There was always a "Brothers' Room" at Porcellian weddings, a private place to which the members retired for a round of toasts and club songs. Lewis, the club's elderly black steward, was imported to preside over the punchbowl.

Through the solid door that now separated him and the other guests from the inner circle, Franklin could hear the high, animated voice of the President as he toasted his son-in-law and the shouts and laughter of his listeners, but he could not make out the words; nor could he catch all the lyrics of the special Porcellian songs that followed.

After the rites had ended, the President and his son-in-law emerged, laughing, to rejoin the bride and make their way into the Oval Room for a formal photograph. Franklin again stood by with his mother as the trio gingerly took their places on a photographer's pedestal imperfectly disguised beneath a slippery Oriental throw rug. But when the cameraman asked that someone tall reach up to adjust Alice's veil, Franklin eagerly stepped forward to oblige; he had at last found a small part to play.[8]

In New York, on May 2, Sara and Eleanor walked and rode together as usual. They lunched at Sara's home and dined that evening at Franklin's. After dinner, Sara noted in her journal, while they were all playing cards, "E. had some discomfort." Blanche Spring, a short, sturdy English nurse, had already been engaged, and the next morning she called Sara at nine to say that labor had begun. Dr. Albert Ely was

8. "I wish I had a picture of *that*," Alice said many years later.
   During FDR's presidency, there were rumors that he had once hoped to marry Alice, and that she had been in love with him. Alice herself always emphatically denied that she had ever had the slightest romantic interest in her distant cousin: "Nothing could be further from the truth," she said. "I don't think it crossed either of our minds." One of Alice's nephews, who knew both of them well, explained that "Alice was a delightful person but even as a girl she was a buzz-saw. Franklin was far too smart to ever get himself caught in that." *Source:* Michael Teague, *Mrs. L.,* pages 128 and 157; Interview with W. Sheffield Cowles, Jr.

summoned, and the three of them attended Eleanor all morning while Franklin paced downstairs. A girl was born at 1:15 P.M. She would be named Anna Eleanor, after her mother; Isabella Ferguson was made her godmother. Sara pronounced the baby "beautiful," though big— ten pounds, one ounce—and Franklin was delighted. Helen Roosevelt Robinson dropped in the next day; "a *very* pretty baby," she noted, "and Franklin was beaming."

Eleanor remembered much later that the baby had been "just a helpless bundle" at first, "but by its mere helplessness [had wound] itself inextricably around my heart." But Eleanor felt helpless, too. She knew little of motherhood: her own mother had been distant and distracted; most of those who had cared for her after her mother's death had been merely conscientious; and her own childhood fantasies— centered always around living with her absent father—had not in- cluded caring for children. "I never had any interest in dolls or little children," she wrote, "and I knew absolutely nothing about handling or feeding a baby. . . ."

Again, she looked to Sara for help. Nurse Spring had cared for many babies and was kept on for a time to look after both Anna and her mother. She "took care of me and of the baby single handed," Eleanor remembered; "she adored babies, and she tried to teach me something about their care."

So did Sara. Eleanor was a reluctant, anxious pupil. In later years, she would blame her unhappiness as a young mother on the fact that she had had servants: "If I had to do it over again, I know now that what we should have done was to have no servants in those first few years; I should have acquired knowledge and self-confidence so that other people could not fool me, either as to the housework or as to the children. However, my bringing-up had been such that this never occurred to me, and neither did it occur to any of the older people who were closest to me. Had I done this, my subsequent troubles would have been avoided and my children would have had far happier child- hoods."

Certainly, the ever present nurses did come between her and her baby. But most of the young mothers Eleanor knew did well enough with nurses; so had her mother-in-law, who had always felt that "every mother ought to learn to care for her own baby, whether she can afford to delegate the task to some one else or not," and who had never hesitated to dismiss any nurse or governess who dared try to come between her and her son.

Eleanor's real trouble lay within. Her own accounts of her children and their doings, both in the letters she wrote during their infancy and in her much later autobiographical writings, are singularly joyless. For her, young children seem to have been for the most part merely sources of further anxiety—fragile, undisciplined, uncontrollable—precisely what her younger brothers had been to her when she was herself a little girl and charged with their welfare by her unhappy mother, her drunken father, and her own exaggerated sense of responsibility. When her youngest brother, Elliott, died of diphtheria when she was eight, it was she who sought as her dead mother's surrogate to console her father; ever afterwards, she would seek dutifully to be a mother to Hall, to make him feel "as if he belonged to somebody," she said, even if in truth he could never belong to her. Since the age of eight (with the singular exception of the three terms she spent overseas at Allenswood), she had always felt obligated to worry over her brother. Caring for her own children would now seem to her in some sense merely an addition to that constant burden.

Miss Spring left in June, adding to Eleanor's uneasiness. "Poor little Eleanor," Sara noted in her journal, "is upset by it, though she is brave." "I felt quite helpless & miserable," Eleanor wrote Franklin from Hyde Park, "at the thought of all the things that may happen to the baby."

The new nurse hired by Sara did not help; she was only slightly older than Eleanor and, while she was experienced with infants, she too was fearful, constantly watching her charge for telltale signs of illness. Anna did fall ill while staying at Hyde Park at the end of her first summer; a high fever caused a convulsion. Franklin and Eleanor rushed her to New York, to their pediatrician, Dr. L. Emmett Holt. Sara was alarmed. "It seems sad to let them go," she noted that evening, "but poor Eleanor is anxious to have the baby near New York doctors and it is best so, so I can do nothing and yet feel the responsibility keenly and Baby is so lovely and so fond of being with me."

Anna recovered quickly, and Eleanor hired a new and more reassuring nurse, "a friendly old Irish woman who had brought up babies for many years." But her own feeling of desperation did not lift. One evening when the nurse was out and the Roosevelts were getting ready for dinner guests, Anna would not stop crying. "Our guests began to arrive," Eleanor recalled. "I called the doctor. He asked me if I 'thought she might have a little wind, and was I sure I had gotten up all the bubbles after her last bottle?' I did not dare tell him I had completely forgotten to put her over my shoulder. . . . He suggested that I turn her on her tummy and rub her back, so, with my guests arriving downstairs, I told Franklin he would have to start dinner without me." Eleanor did as she was told and the baby fell asleep. "I went down to dinner but I was so wrought up by this time that I felt I had to go and look at her several times during the evening, and finally succeeded in waking her up before the nurse came home. I was obliged to leave my guests again. . . ."

Dr. Holt, the pediatrician whom Eleanor consulted, was, as she herself later wrote, "the great baby doctor of that period." His small, clearly written book, *The Care and Feeding of Children: A Catechism for the Use of Mothers and Children's Nurses,* went through fifteen editions between 1894 and 1934. Anxious, and baffled by her infant, but infinitely conscientious, Eleanor found in Holt's rigorous teaching a reassuring set of rules by which to raise her babies, to regain some semblance of command over a life that she felt was spinning further and further out of control.

Holt's book, written in question-and-answer form, stressed discipline and regularity above everything else: by the age of three or four months, it said, all properly raised infants ate, slept, and moved their bowels at fixed times during the day and night. Those that did not easily fall into the correct pattern were to be left crying in their cribs until they conformed, which, Holt assured his readers, rarely took more than three hours. Crying was beneficial in any case—"It is the baby's exercise"—and a woolen band worn at all times around the infant's abdomen ensured that it would not rupture itself while shrieking.

He was no less relentless about other aspects of children's lives. Before the age of seven, "A stale lady-finger or piece of sponge cake is about as far in the matter of cakes as it is wise to go"; lemonade was forbidden until ten, as were corn, jam, "all pies, tarts and pastry of every description," and any vegetable that had not first been boiled and mashed very fine (". . . it is almost impossible to boil vegetables too much").

Bad habits were to be broken early, too; simply tying a baby's arms to its sides at night might discourage it from sucking its thumb, but "in more obstinate cases it may be necessary to confine the elbow by small pasteboard splints to prevent the child from bending the arm so as to get the hand to the mouth."

Dr. Holt was stern with mothers who sought physical closeness with their children, a practice he considered old-fashioned, unsanitary, unscientific:

> At what age may playing with babies be begun?
> Babies under six months old should never be played with; and the less of it at any time the better for the infant.

> What harm is done by playing with very young babies?
> They are made nervous and irritable, sleep badly, and suffer from indigestion and in many other respects.

> When may young children be played with?
> If at all, in the morning, or after the mid-day nap. . . .

> Are there any valid objections to kissing infants?
> There are many serious objections. Tuberculosis, diptheria, syphilis, and many other grave diseases may be communicated in this way . . . Infants should be kissed, if at all, upon the cheek or forehead, but the less of even this the better.

Eleanor did as she was told, grateful that she had found a set of regulations to live by—and in the process she lost whatever chance she might have had to build the warm physical bond she had never known with her own mother, whom she described as having been "kindly but indifferent," or with her reclusive Grandmother Hall, who had brought her up, Eleanor once said, "on the principle that 'no' was easier to say than 'yes.' " "She felt a tremendous sense of duty to us," Anna Roosevelt once said of her mother, ". . . but she did not understand or satisfy the need of a child for primary closeness to a parent."[9]

One of Dr. Holt's most sternly held beliefs was that every infant should have an "airing" once a day for up to five hours; this, the doctor promised, would "renew and purify the blood and [was] as necessary for health and growth as proper food." This meant that even when the weather was too bad to take the baby outside, it was to be dressed in a "bonnet and light coat," laid in its carriage, and "all windows . . . then thrown wide open."

Eleanor took this counsel with special seriousness, and, perhaps with Holt's personal encouragement, had a sort of basket built of wood with chickenwire on the top and sides, and hung it out her back bedroom window on the second floor. Anna was placed in it each

9. Many years later, Eleanor was asked what had been the single worst mistake she had made in her life. She replied without hesitation: "Too much belief in discipline when my children were young." *Source:* Eleanor Roosevelt, *The Wisdom of Eleanor Roosevelt,* page 110.

morning for her nap. The baby often cried—it was especially cold there, on the shady side of the house—but Eleanor tried to pay no attention. "There are no real objections . . . to an infant's sleeping out of doors," said Dr. Holt. Finally, an indignant neighbor bustled over and threatened that if the baby were not brought inside instantly, she would report the Roosevelts to the Society for the Prevention of Cruelty to Children. "This was rather a shock for me," Eleanor remembered, "for I thought I was being a most modern mother. I knew you should not pick up a baby when it cried, that fresh air was very necessary. . . ."

Sara, too, was a great believer in the benefits of fresh air: "I do nothing but preach fresh air to Nurse," she reported once to Eleanor when she was taking care of one of the children, "who takes it in a chastened spirit."[10] And she agreed wholeheartedly with Dr. Holt's emphasis on cleanliness in the nursery, but his severity about scheduling and his strictures against going to a crying child appalled her: "I told [the nurse] she *must* get up and turn [Anna] over and soothe her," she noted in her journal one evening. A quiet struggle then began between Eleanor and her mother-in-law over whether or not the children were being spoiled by their grandmother; it would grow steadily in intensity over the years, and never be resolved.

At Anna's birth, Franklin's boyhood friend Edmund P. Rogers offered his congratulations, then added, "Old Father Franklin will have to be very sedate and [staid] now!" But Franklin was not. His "attitude on nurses and other household affairs was strictly hands-off," one of his children later wrote. Eleanor was to take care of such things and, if she was not up to it, his mother was. But he delighted in the baby and paid little attention to Dr. Holt's warnings; he relished playing with her precisely as his father had relished playing with him. He rolled with her on the floor, and carried her on his shoulders, Eleanor reported, with her short fat legs sticking out on either side of his head. His joy in his daughter was tangible and effortless, and Anna returned it. "It's no wonder that I wanted to be a boy instead of a girl,"

---

10. She thought the outdoor basket was overdoing things, however, and in later years enjoyed teasing her daughter-in-law about the "cage" in which her granddaughter had been aired. "The story was told . . . by Granny," Anna recalled, "[who] delighted in her preamble to the effect that Eleanor was foolishly following a newfangled idea of bringing up children. . . ." *Source:* John R. Boettiger, *A Love in Shadow,* page 48.

she recalled, "and that Father was my childhood hero—not politically or as a world leader—just as a man and *my* father."

The easy, instant bond between father and daughter seemed honestly to bewilder Eleanor. "I watched her being dressed," Eleanor wrote Franklin when the baby was eight months old, "& she kept her eyes fixed on the door & said 'pa pa pa' all the time!"

Everyone remarked on Anna's beauty; she had very blond hair, bright blue eyes, a cheerful, adventurous disposition. Only Eleanor's father had ever told her that *she* was beautiful as a child, and she had not believed him. Anna seemed far more Franklin's child than hers.

Now, her husband's love and attention were still further divided. Eleanor grew increasingly dissatisfied with what she came to see as his inattention, still more silently resentful of his absences. "The baby is not behaving very well," she wrote him from Hyde Park, where he had left her while he attended a Harvard class dinner in Cambridge, "and I am feeling helpless. I hope you had a comfortable night & that the dinner was a grand success."

Eleanor had idealized Franklin when he was courting her, precisely as she had idealized her father when she was a small girl and would idealize the other objects of her affection throughout her life. Disillusionment was inevitable. Her standards were impossibly high. "I was so serious," she wrote later, "and a certain kind of orthodox goodness was my ideal and ambition, and I fully expected that my young husband would have these same ideas, ideals and ambitions . . . what a tragedy it was if in any way my husband offended against these ideals of mine. . . ."

There was the matter of church, for example. On bright Sunday mornings Franklin preferred playing golf with his friends to attending services, leaving Eleanor to occupy the family pew with Sara; in the winter, he sometimes went skating or sailed his ice boat across the frozen river. "We are going to church in a few minutes," she wrote him while visiting Oldgate, her Aunt Bye's home in Farmington, Connecticut, in June of 1907, "& I am wondering what you are about to do. Not church I am sure."

For years, she wrote much later, whenever she took the children to church unaccompanied by her husband, she felt "a kind of virtuous grievance . . ."

Sara often shared in that grievance; one of the strongest bonds between mother- and daughter-in-law in those early years was their common distaste for Franklin's more frivolous side. "F. skated," Sara noted one winter morning when Eleanor was very pregnant. "I went to church." Afterward, "E. walked up to meet me." Franklin did not. Two days later, Sara noted, she and Eleanor walked together while "F. skated and shot clay pigeons at the Rogers'."

In an idle moment some time early in their marriage, Franklin began to write a novel. He never got beyond a two-page prologue before setting it aside. Its hero was to be George Richards, a young self-made Chicago millionaire, a manufacturer known as "the Soap King of the West." He was unlike his creator in everything except what Franklin called the "good, solid New England ancestry" that kept him from indulging in vulgar display.

But in Mrs. Richards, he may have drawn a portrait of the sort of wife he himself had hoped for, the kind of wife his mother had been to his father:

> Mrs. Richards . . . seemed just as capable of managing economically and without friction an establishment that boasted of 3 servants as she had been when she did all the cooking and the housework in 3 rooms. Browning Clubs and other uplifting agencies among the fashionable ladies of the Chicago of that day meant nothing to her. Her husband, her children and her house were to her the beginning and the end. Yet it must not be thought that Mrs. Richards was austere or a home drudge; she was loved and admired by her neighbors.[11]

If that was Franklin's idea of what his wife should be, Eleanor did her dogged best to live up to it. Husband, baby, and home did now form the parameters of her world, just as nearly everyone around her had always told her they should. Memories of her father further reinforced that impulse. "The word 'Home' meant everything to him!" her Aunt Ella had reminded Eleanor shortly after her wedding. "A little home especially appealed to him and he loved everything domestic. All little orderly homey ways—all the refinements of a woman's taste in arrangement—dainty ways, flowers and all that was beautiful. He

11. Franklin got little further with a second novel at about the same time, scratching out just four pages in a guest room at Steen Valetje, the vast Barrytown country house his Uncle Warren Delano III had inherited from his childless uncle, Franklin Hughes Delano. This one concerned a young man named Egbert, the son of John Valentine, a celebrated bibliophile who lives in a Gramercy Park mansion and obtains, shortly before his death, a copy of the rarest book in the world. "Egbert was different from his father in just one respect," it begins. "The old gentleman had loved a rare volume better than himself, better than all the rest of the world. Egbert inherited the love, but had found in a certain fair lady a love distinct and even greater." *Source:* FDRL.

would have loved to see you developing into a famous little house-wife."

She had long since abandoned any thought of resuming the sort of settlement work she had found so satisfying before her marriage; Sara—seconded perhaps by Dr. Holt—had warned her that working among the poor would expose her to illnesses she might carry home to her own nursery. Instead, she now followed meekly in her mother-in-law's wake, attending a series of history classes Sara had organized in New York, and at Hyde Park sometimes attending the sewing classes Sara had instituted so that local girls could support themselves as ladies' maids—at year's end, the teachers received a shiny ten-dollar gold piece tied in a lavender ribbon; the pupil who showed the most promise got a silver thimble. Eleanor also accompanied Sara to meetings of the After-Care Association that sought to provide comfort and support for patients recently released from the Hudson River State Mental Hospital just down the Albany Post Road from Springwood. (Interest in this hospital and its patients was also a family tradition; the hospital stood on the site of Mount Hope, the house in which Mr. James had been born, and he had served for a time as its unpaid manager.)[12]

If Eleanor could not be Franklin's enthusiastic lover, was not permitted to be his intimate, was unable fully to share even in his pleasure in their child, she could at least be useful to him, could become his helpmate. "The feeling that I was useful," she once wrote, "was perhaps the greatest joy I experienced." If, as she believed, it was impossible for others truly to love her, they might at least be made to need her.

Eleanor now began to undertake for Franklin the same admonitory tasks Sara had once performed. She reminded him to pay his bills on time and not to be late to class; she saw that his clothes were cleaned and mended and that he sent proper thank-you notes at holiday time; she even made sure that he remembered his mother's birthday and that he wrote to her when she thought he had put it off too long. "I was

12. A local home for those with hearing and speech disorders was still another of Sara's charities. She reported to Eleanor on one of its meetings in 1907: "I went in a motor, taking Mrs. Ashton to Miss Brimigie's for tea for our poor old deaf mutes. It was pleasant to see how happy they all were, admiring the view and walking about. Nearly all had little pads and pencils, so we had charming conversations, such as 'It is cool today,' 'What a beautiful place,' 'I notice you have grown fat.' To this last I answered, 'I must stop eating so much,' smiles and deprecatory gestures." *Source:* Roosevelt Family Papers Donated by the Children, FDRL.

one of those who served his purposes," she wrote after Franklin died; she was then referring to her years as First Lady, but she had begun doing that in the very early years of their marriage.[13]

Eleanor served still another of Franklin's purposes by remaining close to his mother; her proximity provided Sara with at least some of the loving companionship, the daily attention, that she had always expected of him. (While his mother, in turn, could offer Eleanor some of the affection for which she yearned, and along with it, the practical counsel about raising children and running a household that no one else had ever bothered to provide her with.)

"He lived his own life exactly as he wanted it," Eleanor would say of her husband much later. By helping to care for one another, the two women in Franklin's life helped free him to pursue that independent course.

But life for him was not always carefree. Later that winter, the young Roosevelts, with Hall, Anna, and her nurse, spent Christmas and New Year's with Sara at Springwood. The Teddy Robinsons were staying next door at Rosy's. Several of Franklin's Harvard friends joined them there; so did his young cousin, Corinne Robinson. On December 28, there was a dinner and dance for fifty at Crumwold, the Romanesque mansion of Colonel Archibald Rogers, just up the Albany Post Road.

Sara enjoyed watching the handsomely dressed guests dance across the marble floor of the immense foyer beneath the antlers of the deer and elk and moose of which the colonel was so proud. Franklin enjoyed the evening, too. He was a lithe, enthusiastic dancer and he had come to parties here all his life; had attended his first one as an infant in his mother's arms, in fact. "Baby wanted to dance," Sara had noted then. "I could hardly hold him."

Eleanor watched with Sara as Franklin whirled past with partner after partner; she did not feel like dancing, she said, and Sara worried that for several days her daughter-in-law had seemed uncomfortable, "not at all well."

---

13. She served others' purposes as well. "If you happen in your wanderings to see anything nice and not too expensive," Hall wrote her two weeks before Christmas in 1907, "which I could give to Grandma, Auntie Maude, Auntie Edith, and Auntie Pussie," would she please just pick them up? "Also a few toys for Uncle Eddie's brood and Auntie Maude's. . . ." Though she was not feeling well that season, she made all her brother's purchases without complaint. *Source:* Eleanor Roosevelt Papers, FDRL.

Three nights later, on New Year's Eve, there was a second dance at Crumwold. Eleanor went home to Springwood with Sara shortly after it began, urging her husband to stay on and enjoy himself. He did—he had "a lovely time," Corinne Robinson recalled—and did not get back to Springwood until nearly four in the morning.

The next day, having herself slept till ten-thirty at the Red House next door, Corinne dropped by to say hello on her way back to Crumwold for lunch. Franklin met her in the entrance hall, she remembered; he was pale, "dejected and very cross." He had had very little sleep, he told her. His mother had awakened him and ordered him to come down to breakfast at the usual hour—eight o'clock—as punishment for having stayed out so late, especially when his wife was unwell. Franklin was then twenty-four years old, married, and a father.

Franklin took Corinne upstairs to see Eleanor, who was still in bed, then offered to escort her to Crumwold. They stopped along the way to see the flowers that filled the newly built greenhouse at the edge of Sara's rose garden, and while they were quietly talking there, Corinne remembered, the steam pipes rattled suddenly, and Franklin, "his nerves being on edge, uttered a wild shriek and jumped with fright. I laughed and said, 'Don't be frightened. It's *not* Mama.' "

The indisposition that had sent Eleanor home early from the dance was hemorrhoids, the legacy of having borne such a big, heavy baby, and so painful and debilitating that surgery was finally required. The operation was performed later that January in her own bedroom in the New York house, while for four hours Sara and Franklin sat nervously downstairs. "Pretty serious," Sara noted. In fact, the surgery almost proved fatal. Eleanor had weakened herself over the preceding months, feigning good health for fear of embarrassment, and for the rest of her life she would remember drifting back to consciousness to hear Dr. Ely saying, "Is she gone? Can you feel her pulse?"

Ill health and suffering were always signs of weakness for Eleanor, additional evidence of her own inadequacy, further cause for silent anger at herself. Although she was in great pain after the operation, she would admit it to no one, refusing instead to respond in any way to those who came to visit her, and demanding that both of her bedroom windows remain open to the January winds, day and night. "My disposition was at fault," she wrote later, "rather than my physical condition." Franklin, Sara, and Miss Spring all wore overcoats during their brief visits, and on the evening of the 30th, they gathered around her bed to celebrate Franklin's twenty-fifth birthday, the candles on the cake Sara's cook had baked and decorated bravely flickering in the cold air.

Franklin continued to go to classes. His decision to attend the Columbia School of Law had represented an uncharacteristic break with family tradition, and it was his mother who had first urged him to make that break. He had originally planned to attend Harvard Law School, as had his father and his half brother, but Sara had found her long separation from him while he was living in Cambridge hard to bear. "I want you to think seriously of coming to the Columbia Law School which now stands very high," she had written him in his second year of college. "I know Brother Rosy feels that after your college course is over you ought to be in your own city and get to be known among the best men, also be nearer Hyde Park. I feel so very strongly . . . so I merely wish you to think seriously of it, and to realize how much it will be for you and for me, for you to be near your own home, and not too much out of reach." Franklin may not then have agreed—he said nothing at all about it in his next cheerful letter—but by the time he actually had to decide where to go, in the spring of 1904, he had an added incentive to abandon Cambridge for Manhattan: Eleanor was there, living with her cousins, Henry and Susan Parish. By moving to the city he had been able to see her as often as the complex ground rules of their clandestine engagement permitted.

Like Harvard, Columbia was an old institution. King's College, from which it slowly evolved, had been chartered in 1754, and its earliest home had stood on what is now Park Place, not far north of the comfortable residences of Franklin's Roosevelt ancestors. In 1880, when Theodore Roosevelt attended classes there, the Columbia School of Law still occupied a single, battered old house at 8 Great Jones Street. Like Franklin, Theodore Roosevelt had been a young, married Harvard graduate then, eager to get on with his adult life; like Franklin, too, he did not attend classes for very long.

TR had walked the fifty-four blocks to and from law school every day to keep in shape. But in the fall of 1904, when Franklin travelled to his first Columbia class, he had to take the new IRT subway, for the university itself had shifted far northward in the mid-1890s, to a still unfinished campus beyond 114th Street on a rocky West Side escarpment, 150 feet above the Hudson. The new buildings had displaced the old Bloomingdale Insane Asylum—a white-bearded asylum groundskeeper who had been asked to stay on could not be dissuaded from calling the heedless Columbia students who walked across his newly seeded lawns "inmates"—and some of the surrounding countryside was still occupied by squatters' shacks and farm animals. (The older residents continued to call the neighborhood by its original name, "Goatville." "Morningside Heights," the new one coined by the park planner Frederick Law Olmsted, had taken a while to catch on.)

The massive, domed University Library, designed by Charles F. McKim, of the firm of McKim, Mead & White, dominated the new campus. The School of Law occupied the four floors of its north wing. Its faculty was not especially distinguished in Franklin's time (it would not improve until after 1910, in fact, when Harlan F. Stone became dean),[14] but the work was rigorous and the atmosphere serious and scholarly, unlike the Harvard Franklin had known. "We were up at the school at Nine O'Clock in the morning," one former student remembered, "and very often we didn't get into bed until Five. If we got to bed at Three, we felt we were getting a sound night's sleep."

And there were other differences. "I am anxious to hear about your first day," Eleanor had written Franklin as he began his studies in the School of Law, "and whether you found any old acquaintances or had only Jew Gentlemen to work with." Anti-Semitism, especially that directed at Jews newly arrived from Eastern Europe, was then open and almost universal; the Roosevelts were no more immune to it than were most other members of their class.

The student body at Columbia was beginning to reflect the abrupt social transformation of the city it now sought to serve. When Theodore Roosevelt attended the School of Law a quarter of a century earlier, one man, Professor Theodore Dwight, had constituted the entire faculty, and TR's fellow students had all been members of the same Protestant upper class from which he came. Since then, however, New York had been flooded with immigrants. "On they go," wrote H. G. Wells after visiting the immigrant reception center at Ellis Island in 1905, "from this pen to that, pen by pen, towards a little wicket—the Gate of America. Through this wicket drips the immigrant stream—all day long, every two or three seconds an immigrant, with a valise or bundle . . . into a new world."

14. In 1942, FDR raised Justice Stone to Chief Justice of the U.S. Supreme Court. That same year he wrote to a friend that he thought the appointment an especially good one because while attending the Columbia School of Law he had "sat at the feet" of Harlan Stone and had "never regretted it." In fact, Stone did not arrive until Franklin had left the school. *Source:* PPF 4450, FDRL.

They altered that world as they entered it, sometimes at the rate of five thousand a day; nearly two out of three New Yorkers had now been born abroad, and the Lower East Side—where Eleanor had worked at the Rivington Street Settlement before and during her engagement—was perhaps the most densely packed place on earth, with more than 300,000 persons per square mile.

Columbia's move uptown and its transformation from a small, cloistered collection of schools and pre-professional programs into what Seth Low, its former president, hoped would be "the great metropolitan university" were, in part, a reaction to those changes.

There were seventy-four members of Franklin's class at the School of Law; perhaps twenty of them were Jewish. Percentages like these then bred a certain defensiveness among some Columbia graduate students. One member of the law school class of 1900, for example, made a point in his memoir of remembering that most of his fellow students had been "a very *nice* crowd of men . . . Harvard, Yale . . . Princeton."[15]

Another former law student, a Jewish immigrant's son from Hester Street on the Lower East Side who had worked hard to get into the School of Law, remembered that he "hated" Franklin Roosevelt while they were both at Columbia. Young Roosevelt had seemed to him then the living symbol of all those to whom everything for which he had himself been forced to struggle had been granted for the asking.

That resentful fellow student cannot have seen very much of the object of his hatred, for Franklin spent as little time as possible at Columbia. His attendance record was spotty; during his first year he had been absent seventy-three times; the second year he missed about half that many classes. He made few friends during his time on Morningside Heights and only rarely joined his fellow students after class for nickel schooners of beer at the ramshackle College Tavern that was still the sole structure on Broadway between 120th and 122nd Streets. His circle remained largely restricted to relatives and to young men he had known at Groton and Harvard. Nor did he study more than

15. At a New York dinner during those years, Nicholas Murray Butler, Low's successor as Columbia's president, and Woodrow Wilson, then president of Princeton, offered mock tributes to one another's institutions. In the course of his remarks, Butler expressed elaborate sympathy for Wilson who, he said, must be perpetually exhausted from having to oversee what amounted to a nonstop country club; Wilson responded by saying that Butler must be still more weary, for, as Scripture made clear, "He that keepeth Israel can neither slumber nor sleep." *Source:* Interview with H. Alexander Smith, Columbia Oral History Project, Columbia University.

he had to in the library, preferring to do his reading in the relative comfort of his home.

"I hope you will move a comfortable chair and table under one of the lights," his mother once wrote him from Hyde Park, "so as to see the print of those charming and comprehensible law books!" Franklin did not always find them comprehensible, but he never failed a course again after his first year, relying on his rare ability to read and remember complicated material just long enough to make use of it. Neither Mr. James nor Rosy had ever seen the law as more than a good grounding for a gentleman to have, the most useful possible training for a young man who would need to know how best to manage the family properties. Franklin saw no need to alter their assessment. He was interested in the law only insofar as he could make practical use of it. Mostly it bored him, and nothing his professors could do seemed to arouse his interest.

The two men who had failed him during his first year of law school were polar opposites. Henry S. Redfield, who taught Pleading and Practice I, was a singularly dull lecturer, reciting from his tattered notes in a faint monotone while worrying his gray, square-cut beard. On the flyleaf of his textbook for Redfield's class, *Selected Cases on Code Pleading and Practice in New York* (written by the professor himself), Franklin pencilled a bit of doggerel about him:

REDFIELD ON BLEATING
BAH! BAH! BAH!
We are little bored sheep
That have lost their way
    Bah! Bah! Bah!
Gentlemen lawyers off on a spree
Wrong from here to eternity
God ha' mercy on such as Redfield
    Bah! Bah! Bah!

Redfield's students routinely cut his classes, falling back on last-minute cramming to get through.

Charles Thaddeus Terry, who taught Contracts, on the other hand, did not lecture at all; he was a big, sardonic, tough-minded man with a red beard, who intimidated even the most self-confident students with his supercharged Socratic questioning. "Any failure to grasp or state the elements of a problem," one graduate recalled, "any omission in the logical process, any looseness in the thought or in the language expressing it, was ruthlessly exposed with dramatic swiftness." Terry forced his students to think for themselves; he called on the future Judge Harold Medina every single morning for four months one year because he was sure Medina could be counted upon to give him an argument, and when a more timorous student once suggested that his side of the debate must be correct because a recent Supreme Court decision had said so, Terry just grinned. "And you *believed* them, did you?"

The method or quality of the teaching Franklin received, then, had little effect upon his enthusiasm for the subject. He was always impatient with abstractions and uninterested in the law on its own terms, and he had trouble keeping his mind on his studies; while listening to Professor Jackson E. Reynolds's lecture on Bailments and Carriers one afternoon toward the end of his second year, he penciled himself an exasperated note: *"For pity's sake, get that I.C.C. Act down pat."*

Many years later, Professor Reynolds rendered his own brutal judgment of Franklin's law school record and reputation: "Franklin Roosevelt was not much of a student [at Columbia] and nothing of a lawyer afterwards. . . . He didn't appear to have any aptitude for law, and made no effort to overcome that handicap by hard work. He was not a worker and he flunked. He passed my courses [Agency and Bailments and Carriers]—I imagine because they had some interest for him . . . he was interested in public utilities . . . that kind of public ramification, I suppose, interested him. . . ."[16]

16. This may not have been an entirely objective opinion. Reynolds rendered it in 1949, after serving for many years as president of the First National Bank of New York. He was a life-long Republican, and a good friend of Herbert Hoover, who had been the manager of the varsity football team on which Reynolds was right halfback at Leland Stanford Junior University.

In October of 1934, FDR was asked to address the annual meeting of the American Bankers Association. Feelings between the banking world and the administration were then strained, and, according to the economist and speechwriter Raymond Moley, it was hoped that "the occasion of the speech would be a hatchet-burying ceremony." Sharing that hope, the President asked that his old instructor introduce him. But when Reynolds's proposed remarks were shown to the President they included a mild joke about having been Roosevelt's teacher at Columbia. Moley was present when FDR read the offending passage: "He had a baleful look," Moley noted. "It was obvious that public reference to his law studies wasn't calculated to improve his good humor. Apparently he didn't regard them as among the most significant achievements of his career."

The Secretary of the Treasury, Henry Morgenthau, Jr., was assigned the delicate task of persuading Reynolds to delete this and one other offending passage. Reynolds was outraged at first, threatening not to appear at the banquet at all, but finally agreed to the deletions. The President's speech was hailed as a conciliatory gesture toward business, Moley wrote later, "But the atmospheric conditions in which [it] was perfunctorily delivered approached the frigid. The President was scarcely pleasant, either to his audience or to Reynolds." *Sources:* Interview with Jackson E. Reynolds, Columbia Oral History Project, Columbia University; Raymond Moley, *After Seven Years,* pages 296–298.

On June 19, 1906, a few days before Anna was christened, Franklin took the eight-hour examination for admission to the New York Bar. It was unusually hot in New York, and his sinuses—which always bothered him when he was under stress—made concentration difficult. Nonetheless, Eleanor told him she was sure "you are going to pass all right."

He did, though he had to wait with the rest of the hopeful would-be attorneys in the city until the following February to find it out. Franklin was then twenty-five years old, empowered to practice law and soon to be a father for a second time. He saw no need to undertake another rigorous year of law school; an LLB degree held no special appeal for him. He told Columbia he would not return to classes in the spring.[17]

What he needed was a job. His name and connections now helped him get one. In this, too, he was following his father's approved path; after law school, Mr. James had used his family's contacts to secure himself an apprenticeship in a Wall Street firm before launching his business career.

Edmund L. Baylies was a partner in the prosperous Wall Street firm of Carter, Ledyard & Milburn, whose major clients included the Astor Trust, the massive legacy of money and New York real estate upon which Rosy depended for his support. He was the firm's expert on admiralty law, the specialty for which Franklin might have been expected to show the most enthusiasm in law school because of his love of the sea. (In fact, he had never taken a course in it.) Both he and Franklin belonged to the New York Yacht Club. The eager young man may have seemed the right sort for the firm. Rosy almost surely put in a good word for his younger half brother; perhaps it also occurred to Baylies that it might at some time prove advantageous to have a Roosevelt, the husband of the President's niece, in an office that

17. On June 10, 1940, FDR travelled to Charlottesville, Virginia, where his son, Franklin Jr. was a member of the graduating class of the University of Virginia Law School. Professor Leslie Buckler was assigned to board the *Magellan*, the President's private railroad car, and keep him company until preparations could be made for him to be taken off the train. The two men chatted amiably enough, and the subjects of law and education inevitably came up. The President said that he was delighted, of course, that his son had earned a degree, but *he* had never seen the need for one; he had simply taken the bar exam and gone to work.

Professor Buckler was a little too quick to agree to suit Roosevelt; he, too, was a lawyer without a degree, he said; he had been allowed to take the Maryland Bar exam upon returning from France in 1918.

FDR was not pleased with the parallel. Yes, yes, he said, "But *you* are not President of the United States." *Source:* Conversation with Louis Auchincloss, then one of Buckler's students.

was then busily engaged as counsel for several of the giant trusts Theodore Roosevelt was determined to dissolve.

According to Jackson Reynolds, the former professor who was so critical of Franklin's performance as a law student and who was close to two of the firm's senior partners, the young job seeker received still more direct help in obtaining a position. Sara herself asked for an interview with one of the two senior partners, Lewis Cass Ledyard, commodore of the Yacht Club and an old business ally of Mr. James, and asked him to find a place for her boy.

In any case, in June, Franklin received the letter from Mr. Baylies he had been hoping for:

> I have talked over with Mr. Ledyard the question of your coming to our office, and I find that we can arrange to have a place for you at such time as you may wish to come here in the autumn, not later than October 1st, preferably a week or so earlier.
>
> In case you come to us the arrangement with you will be the same as we usually make in such cases, that is to say, you will come to us the first year without salary, and after you have been with us for a year we would expect, if you remain, to pay you a salary which, however, at the outset would necessarily be rather small.

Twenty-two years later, in the autumn of 1929, Governor Franklin Roosevelt of New York was invited to address the Columbia Law School alumni dinner. Columbia's President, Nicholas Murray Butler, sat next to him, chatting affably. At some point during the evening, Butler was heard joking with the governor, "You will never be able to call yourself an intellectual until you come back to Columbia and pass your law exam." Roosevelt laughed and threw back his head. "That just shows how unimportant the law really is," he said.

Franklin, Eleanor, Hall, and Anna spent the summer of 1906 alone at Campobello. Sara sailed for Europe in July to visit friends and members of the family, and did not return until late September. With her went a list of the new clothes Franklin wanted her to order made up for him in London by the same gentleman's tailors who had outfitted his father; he would not go to Wall Street underdressed:

1 Dinner Coat, Waistcoat and Trousers.
1 Winter suit—Dark grey.

2 Pair Brown Linen or Khaki very thin Riding Trousers with
belt straps and no extensions and 1 pair gaiters to match.
2 Evening Waistcoats, single breasted. All this from Tautz.
. . . .
1 Pair black [laced] boots like the last.
1 Pair black Riding boots, a little bigger on the instep and ½
inch more at the top.
This from Peal.[18]

Eleanor was again pregnant that summer—she was already not "a
graceful person," she warned her mother-in-law, who had offered to
buy her lingerie in Paris—and she spent most of her time in the cottage
with Anna, her latest nurse, and Miss Spring, now back again to help
prepare for the new baby. Whenever fog or rain settled in, Franklin
stayed with her, playing with Anna. Eleanor seemed to enjoy the
infant whenever Franklin was with her. "The Baby is too sweet," he
reported to Sara, "and makes us shriek with laughter when she puts
her whole hand into my cup of tea." Eleanor and Franklin watched
with fascination as the baby began to crawl after Duffy, then managed
her first tottering steps, finally progressed to pushing her own carriage
for short distances across the lawn.[19]

And at least once, when the baby's nurse was suddenly called away,
Eleanor fed and bathed and put Anna to bed all on her own, astonished, she said, at how "easy" it was. But when Anna became cross and
impatient, she was less pleased, more anxious. "My lady Anna is the
mischief itself," she wrote, "and I shall be glad when Nurse returns
to manage her, as Nurse Spring and I, not being used to her, have had
some quite hard struggles with little tempers and wildest animal spirits
which break out at inopportune moments!" The morning after the
nurse returned, Eleanor wrote that "Anna is very happy to have
[Nurse] back, but I am glad to say I think she missed me a little last
night."

18. Moses Smith, for many years the Roosevelts' tenant farmer, was once asked how young
Mr. Franklin had dressed. His clothes had been elegant and well tailored, Smith remembered,
but unlike those worn by some of the family's more sporty friends, they had never been "exorbitant." *Source:* Interview with Moses Smith, National Park Service.

19. This was altogether too rapid progress for Sara. "I cannot understand her wheeling her
perambulator on the grass," she wrote from Europe, "it seems a great strain on the tiny person.
Be careful, one often hears of children beginning too soon to walk and to use up their strength
and it leads to trouble with the limbs and even with appendicitis." *Source:* Roosevelt Family
Papers Donated by the Children, FDRL.

While the baby slept, Franklin sometimes took Eleanor for gentle walks along the beach or picnics on nearby islands. She seemed relatively content at Campobello. "E. is well and doesn't seem unhappy," Franklin told his mother with apparent relief. "I am ditto as to health and can vouch for the state of my feelings."

Franklin took gossipy pleasure in the doings of the other summer residents whom he and his mother had known, but not necessarily admired, since he was a small boy. Sarah Hoppin, a distant and divorced cousin, somber and pious, fond of gray gloves and dark veils even on the sunniest days, especially irritated him, and he liked pretending to his mother that she was behaving scandalously. "Our attempts to see Sarah Hoppin have failed (here the Doxology should be sung)," he told his mother, "tho' we caught Mr. [Travis] Cochran coming away from her house at 10 yesterday morning. It looked badly—especially as she was still in bed (here should be sung Hymn 142—Oh come all ye faithful) (In case we don't see Sarah all summer Hymn 684 should be sung—Peace, perfect Peace)."

Eleanor, too, seems to have taken a critical view of some of the Roosevelts' neighbors. "We went to tea at the Sturgisses, a very quiet evening," Franklin reported. "Eleanor was overcome by the general untidiness and 'sloppy weather' effect of the Sturgiss mansion, and by the bad manners and 'revolting appearance' of Marius Prince (the quotations are hers!)."

Franklin always enjoyed himself on the island, and even with his marriage and the birth of his first child, the pattern of his life there, established during his boyhood, remained largely unchanged. Franklin went out each day and did things while Eleanor waited for him to come home and tell her about them, just as he had reported to his parents during his elderly father's long decline. Eleanor never expressed her resentment at having to stay behind, but it cannot have been easy for her, for example, when her laughing husband rolled up his trousers and went wading with his pretty young cousin Laura Delano, and with Frances Dana De Rahm, one of the loveliest girls he had known during his days at Harvard, now married to a classmate.[20]

20. Younger women—especially much younger women—frequently developed crushes on Franklin. Frances Porter, a summer resident of Campobello, recorded her own feelings for him in her diary for 1902. She had been fourteen then, and he was twenty:

August 2. Went to the "Hop." FDR was there and he is a perfect peach.
August 4. Saw FDR playing golf.
August 5. Had a conversation with FDR on the pier and took a picture of him.
August 7. We had a Salimagundi Party. FDR . . . was the star of the crowd.

Eleanor did take secret golf lessons in the hopes that she might sometimes play alongside Franklin—just as his mother had when he was a boy—only to abandon them when he took a look at her tortured swing and told her she might as well give up trying. And she tried hard to conquer her uneasiness about the sea; she fished for flounder alongside Franklin, and undertook at least one longer voyage, to St. Andrews, New Brunswick. The trip went well, Franklin reported to his mother, and "though slightly rough in Passamaquoddy Bay for a few minutes E. did not show the least paleness of cheek or tendency to edge towards the rail!"

Harvard friends came up to visit Franklin, just as they had in the past, and, now joined by Hall—who had become at least for a time the admiring younger brother he never had—they undertook long sailing and canoe trips. "I had to stock the boat up with food for the first few days," Eleanor recalled, "and after their return they always told me what delicious things they had had to eat on the boat. Apparently their idea of perfection was a combination of sausages, syrup, and pancakes for every meal, varied occasionally by lobsters or scrambled eggs. My husband was the cook as well as the captain, and was very proud of his prowess."

On one trip to Oak Island, off Nova Scotia, where Franklin hoped to find a pirate's buried treasure,[21] his party did discover a cormorant's

---

August 11. Mary Prince, Rosalie Channing and I followed FDR around in the golf tournament. He was killing. I found FDR's ball for him.

August 12. Did an errand to Mrs. R's and talked to FDR. He's great.

August 20. FDR took a crowd on a moonlight walk. Mary, Rosalie and I watched them start.

September 1. This AM we girls caddied for the boys. I tried to get FDR but Mary got ahead of me.

September 4. Mary, Rosalie and I drove down the North Road. On the way back, FDR threw a golf ball and nearly hit us!

September 5. Met FDR and Julia Tevis driving. He blushed.

September 6. FDR asked me to the "Shindy" tonight with all the crowd. We went and there was a band and it was fine, but he and Julia Tevis spent the whole evening on the piazza and spoiled it all!

Source: Margaret L. Suckley Papers, FDRL.

21. As President, FDR often used the story of the Oak Island treasure and his failure to find it to prevent visitors from bringing up topics he did not wish to discuss. On his first meeting with Franklin in 1933, his newly appointed Secretary of Agriculture, Henry A. Wallace, listened in wonder as the President-elect spun the tale out for an hour and a half, while Senator Key Pittman of Nevada drummed his fingers, waiting for a chance to talk about his own pet subject, silver. Pittman never got his chance.

Rexford Tugwell, one of Roosevelt's early advisers, agreed, remembering "a long story about a keg of rum from Haiti which he used for the same purpose." *Source:* Interview with Henry A. Wallace, Rexford G. Tugwell Papers.

nest at the top of a tall tree on a rocky island. Hall was sent up to bring it down, along with the four baby birds it held, so that Franklin could send them to the American Museum of Natural History in New York. Hall made the climb all right, but the nest and its contents reeked so, Eleanor wrote later, that when they got back to Campobello, "he had to take off all his clothes and leave them on the beach and scrub himself before he could enter the house."[22]

In late July, Henry and Susan Parish made their careful way northward to Campobello for a visit. The Parishes were among the dutiful relatives who had cared for Eleanor and Hall after their parents died. Cousin Henry was thin and retiring—"the kindest person I have ever known," Eleanor once wrote. His wife was something else again: tall and imperious, given to huge hats and steady complaints. Still, Eleanor felt grateful to her for having once taken her in.

The elderly couple arrived at Eastport, Maine, by the afternoon train in the midst of a dense fog. Franklin and Eleanor had sailed across the bay blindly to pick them up, Franklin's instinctive navigational skill keeping them right on course, the *Half Moon*'s auxiliary motor providing the power, and they had managed to get their slow-moving relations down the steep, slime-covered steps that led from the dock to the water without mishap. But it was dark by the time everyone got aboard for the return trip and a kerosene lantern was hung from the main boom to help Franklin see the compass.

The schooner slid slowly through the fog, Franklin gripping the wheel and peering into the darkness while keeping up a steady stream of cheerful talk to ease the Parishes' anxieties; neither of them much liked to sail. Eleanor recalled what happened next: ". . . the man on the bowsprit called out, 'Hard aport,' and there, above us, loomed the Lubec docks, with just enough room to shear off. Much annoyed and completely mystified, my husband reset his course for Campobello, realizing we had come through a narrow passageway and just by luck had not found ourselves in the tide running through the 'Narrows.' About three minutes later, 'Hard over' came from the bowsprit, and we just missed a tiny island with one tree on it, which was entirely off our course."

22. Hall was sixteen that summer and developed a crush on a fourteen-year-old girl staying at a nearby cottage. One evening, according to FDR, Hall returned dreamily to the Roosevelt cottage at nine o'clock, and said to Franklin, then twenty-five, and Eleanor, twenty-two, "Tell me something—was it customary to hold hands on the porch when you and Eleanor were young?" *Source:* Elliott Roosevelt, ed., *FDR: His Personal Letters, 1928–1945,* Vol. 2, page 768.

Franklin, embarrassed to appear so inept in front of the Parishes, finally realized that the iron in the swinging lantern was attracting the compass. The lantern was moved, and with the help of a box of matches he managed to make Campobello without further incident.

Cousin Susie had been terrified, however, and during her weeklong stay refused again to set foot on board a boat, emerging from the cottage only to play a few ponderous sets of tennis and grumble about the rainy weather. Her chronic unhappiness was aggravated by her addiction to a patent medicine laced with opium, Eleanor once admitted to Isabella, but it was the useless life she led that was the real cause: "She cares for no one sufficiently to forget herself.... She was a spoiled child & a spoiled woman & never was forced to sink her own feelings in anyone else's good." Only by so sinking one's own feelings, in forgetting oneself in thoughts of others, could one's existence be justified, Eleanor believed. In any case, neither she nor Franklin was unhappy to see Cousin Susie go.

In August, Franklin took Hall and Livingston Davis, one of his closest Harvard friends, on a long sail to Bar Harbor, where the Davis family had their summer home. It was a stormy trip over "a very troubled sea," Franklin told his mother; "Hall and Livy thought discretion the better part of valor and remained rolled in blankets on deck, while I steered for about ten hours." But once ashore, the sun shone: "I dined with the Davis family . . . went to the swimming pool, saw thousands of people I knew, had my hair cut . . . played tennis . . . and went again to dine at the Davis'."

While Franklin was away, a letter arrived from Sara in Paris. Two of Franklin's booksellers' bills from his honeymoon two summers earlier had yet to be paid; the shopkeepers had been dunning her sister, Dora Forbes, who hadn't known quite what to do. Sara paid the bills instantly, but she was greatly embarrassed by her son's irresponsibility. "I will say nothing," she wrote, "as it will do no good, [but] it *is* a surprise as I am not accustomed to this way of doing business, my dear Franklin, and if you love me you will be more careful in the future."

Eleanor responded at once: "I can't tell you how sorry I am that you and Aunt Dora have been so bothered by F's bills . . . F. will have your letters as soon as he returns and I hope he will feel as ashamed as I do; and as sorry that your trip should be marred by such occurrences."

Franklin was not ashamed. He had settled *one* of the bills, or so he claimed; the check must somehow have gone astray; and he had told the other dealer he would have to wait for some time before he was paid. "I simply haven't had the money till now," he wrote to his mother. "Hereafter, I shall pay cash!" In his very next letter to Sara he suggested that she might like to help him and a friend buy a nearby island.

Franklin went to his new fifth-floor office at 54 Wall Street for the first time on September 23, 1907. "I shall think of you on the 23rd beginning work," his mother had written from Europe. "I know you will in many ways be glad to start. Try to arrange for systematic air and exercise and keep away from broker's offices, this advice free gratis for nothing." And she was suitably awed when her son met her on the dock on the 28th: "F. has begun *law* in Carter, Ledyard & Milburn's office," she wrote that evening.

Franklin was not awed. He had written her in Europe that he was about to become "a full-time office boy," and his attitude was made still more clear in the mock advertisement he wrote out and sent to her when he had his first personal stationery printed up:

Franklin D. Roosevelt
Counsellor at Law
54 Wall Street
New York
I beg to call your attention
to my unexcelled facilities
for carrying on every
description of legal business.
Unpaid bills a specialty.
Briefs on the liquor question
furnished free to ladies.
Race suicides cheerfully
prosecuted. Small dogs
chloroformed without charge.
Babies raised under advice
of expert grandmother,
etc., etc., etc.[23]

23. Nearly everything in the advertisement refers to something that had happened while Sara was away.

The "unpaid bills" in which he said he specialized were those his mother had paid for him in Paris. The leisurely pace at which he sometimes paid his creditors was a frequent source of embarrassment to Sara (though she was herself not over-eager to settle her own accounts; she did not pay Tiffany's for the $4,000 pearl collar that was her wedding present to Eleanor, for example, for nearly four months).

"The liquor question" was discussed between them often and, like so many of their loving

The firm was deeply embroiled in major cases: Commodore Ledyard included among his clients the American Tobacco Company; John G. Milburn represented Standard Oil of New Jersey. Both giant combinations were under attack from the government under the provisions of the Sherman Anti-Trust Act when Franklin joined the firm, and when, in 1911, the U.S. Supreme Court finally held that each of them had to be dissolved, Ledyard and Milburn orchestrated shrewd plans of dissolution that would do as little personal damage to management as possible.

As the most junior of the firm's five clerks, Franklin came nowhere near such important cases. Each of the senior partners had his own comfortable office, with a cannel coal fire. Franklin and his fellow clerks shivered at rolltop desks in a big, cold room which they shared with a dusty stuffed seal, once a courtroom exhibit in an international dispute with Britain over Bering Sea sealing rights in which one of the firm's founders had represented the United States.

Franklin spent much of his first year running errands, and found even that initially bewildering. "Somebody, the day after [I started work] . . . said, 'Go up and answer the calendar call in the Supreme Court tomorrow morning,'" he remembered much later. "'We have such and such a case on.'

"I had never been in a court of law in my life.

"Then the next day somebody gave me a deed of transfer of some land. He said, 'Take it up to the County Clerk's office.' I had never been in a county clerk's office. And there I was, theoretically a full-fledged lawyer."

He learned fast, liking least the hours he spent in the law library searching out references and helping to prepare briefs for the partners.

---

conflicts, never resolved: throughout his adult life, Franklin enjoyed a stiff drink; neither his mother nor his wife ever stopped disapproving of the custom.

The next line has to do with the trials of Eleanor's second pregnancy. "Race suicide" was what Cousin Theodore was sure would befall the American people if birth control spread too widely among them. "It is self-evident," he wrote, "that unless the average woman, capable of having children, has four, the race will not go forward", and, again, "The woman who shrinks from motherhood is as low as a man of the professional pacifist, or poltroon type, who shirks his duty as a soldier." (Sentiments like these, his daughter Alice later said, "humiliated, shamed and embarrassed me," and while her father was in the White House she founded with three other young woman a secret organization called the Race Suicide Club—or so she later claimed. "Thank God [it] was not unmasked" by the press, she added. "Coming on top of my other eccentricities, it might have proved the final straw.")

The small dog Franklin had in mind for chloroforming was his mother's yippy black spitz, "Touton," which he and Eleanor had fed and cared for all summer. *Sources:* Sara Delano Roosevelt checkbooks, Roosevelt Family Papers, Business and Personal, FDRL; Albert Bushnell Hart, ed., *Theodore Roosevelt Encyclopedia,* pages 45,498; Michael Teague, *Mrs. L.,* page 82.

American Express was a major client; its wagons seemed perpetually to be backing into pedestrians, turning too sharply into traffic, rolling through store windows; baggage got mislaid; crates of eggs arrived cracked; an actor's wardrobe trunk failed to arrive in time for a performance. Franklin devoted days to discovering precedents for assessing responsibility when a thief impersonated an expressman or a chauffeur failed to watch where he was going, and he also did his best to master the rapidly changing rules of the American road:

> Upon approaching a person walking in the roadway of a public highway, or a horse or horses, or other draft animals, being ridden, led or driven thereon, a person operating a motor vehicle shall give reasonable warning of its approach, and use every reasonable means to insure the safety of such person or animal, and, in the case of horses or other draft animals, to prevent frightening the same. . . .

He found such work drudgery, but he was fascinated by the new worlds his practice took him to outside the office. At the end of his first year he was promoted to managing clerk, paid a salary for the first time—ten dollars a week, handed to him in cash inside a yellow envelope—and placed in charge of the firm's business in the Municipal Court on Rivington Street.

Nothing at Springwood or in Europe, at Groton or Harvard or Columbia, had prepared him for the grimy courthouse corridors, or readied him to mix with the kinds of people he met there: loungers and small-time lawyers, dubious or desperate plaintiffs, self-important judges, witnesses both credible and incredible.

Most of the suits Franklin defended there involved American Express, but he also appeared on behalf of the Breakwater Home for Seamen against a man who claimed its watchman had shot and wounded him "while he was approaching [the] premises for the purpose of lodging;" and he defended Greenwood Cemetery in Brooklyn against the estate of an old Irishwoman.

Eleanor Roosevelt was once asked whether her husband had ever enjoyed the law. "I don't think he liked really legal work," she answered, "but he enjoyed the contacts that it brought him with people. . . . it was a very good education because he learned a good deal that he never had an opportunity to know anything about before, the ambulance chasing lawyers that he would be against and then the conditions of people's lives that he could never have known anything about. He always said afterwards that that kind of court practice had been one of the most valuable things he ever did . . . he liked [that] kind of law . . . because it did take him into contact with people."

For the first time in his life, Franklin found himself competing— and sometimes winning—in a world where breeding counted less than cunning, and good manners could be overcome by aggressiveness and the ability to maneuver.

Even his contests with the shabby storefront lawyers he and the other men at Carter, Ledyard & Milburn routinely dismissed as ambulance chasers proved educational; he learned that there was more to them than simple greed. One of his courtroom opponents left a record of his dealings with Franklin; he was the same young man from the Lower East Side who had been so envious of Roosevelt at Columbia. At some point before 1910, he found himself facing Franklin in Municipal Court in a petty property loss suit against American Express. The lawyer had then still been so poor, he remembered, that "I had gotten into the habit of taking off my collar when I left the court, [and] wrapping it up in a piece of tissue paper, so that I could use it a good many times.

"Many of these cases were brought because it was sometimes possible to prey upon a corporation," he admitted. "Roosevelt suspected me of connivance. Perhaps he was right. He never showed it in court, though outside I caught him looking at me for just a fraction of a second with contempt.

"In any event . . . I had to win this case. I had no money to buy food for my family." Franklin had had the law and the facts on his side, the attorney remembered, but he represented a big corporation, while his own client was a poor widow and the emotional appeal he made on her behalf had clearly swung the jury. Franklin saw that it would be best to settle out of court.

"He decided to come to my office to talk it over," the lawyer continued.

> He looked up my address. I had no office. He came to Hester Street. I was away. My wife was not there, my . . . mother was. She knew all about this particular case. I had told Roosevelt . . . that I would settle with him for $300. He had beaten me down to $150. The actual loss was about $18. I had taken the case on a 50-50 split and I had to have at least $15 as my share. . . .
>
> My mother saw the chance to compromise, to really get hold of some money for me. She broke into tears and pleaded with him to give me at least $50 on the case. He had the whole story out of her in five minutes. When I returned, I found a note from him:

I am sorry not to find you in, but I would be glad to settle this case for $35. I cannot get myself to believe that it is worth a cent more, probably less. Enclosed is a small personal check which I am sure you will not return until you are well out of [your] temporary difficulties.

> Most sincerely,
> Franklin D. Roosevelt.[24]

Franklin's first tentative forays into the New York slums may have fascinated him, may even have made him sympathetic to the plight of some individual men and women, but there is little evidence that they initially fostered in him any general sense that anything needed to be done to improve things, a fact which sorely tried his wife. One morning during his time at Carter, Ledyard & Milburn, he and Eleanor had an angry quarrel over a check for fifty dollars he had promised to write to the Robert B. Minturn Hospital for Scarlet Fever and Diptheria on East 16th Street, an institution that served mostly the desperately ill children of Jewish and Italian immigrants. Franklin had evidently forgotten or neglected to send the contribution; the hospital asked Eleanor about it, and she confronted him. He tried to laugh it off—he would get around to writing the check; she insisted he do so right away. Franklin finally stalked off to the office, then sent a messenger home to Eleanor with a bouquet of lilies and a gallant but teasing note:

> Dear Lady,
> Your beauteous bounty requires more than a merely verbal display of homage and praise, hence this.
> The honored draft for fifty plunks has gone the way of all, to R. Minturn, and you can pat your little back about fifty times and with eyes raised Heavenward exclaim in accents of deep content, "Yea! I have saved the lives of a score of blessed little men of the 'Chosen Race'! Surely, "this is no joking matter." . . .

> Your slave,
> FDR

He appeared in police court on behalf of several Harvard friends arrested for being drunk and disorderly in Times Square, and some

---

24. This story, complete with a suitable moral—the lawyer wept, paid the money back in six months, and vowed never again to take a split-fee case—first appeared in one of the earliest and most admiring Roosevelt biographies, Earle Looker's *This Man Roosevelt* (pp. 49–52). By 1932, its source—who evidently told Looker he wished to remain anonymous—had become "a lawyer of good repute," according to the author, "possessing a fine mind that [had] struggled up to its right level from obscurity, poverty and even filth."

For the record, an examination of Franklin's check stubs from the period at the FDRL did not yield evidence of the check he is said to have written out during his brief visit to Hester Street, but he may have had accounts on other banks of which no records have survived.

family business came his way, too, most of it desultory. Rosy and his cousin Douglas Robinson engaged him to sue a laundry owner for default on his mortgage payments on a building they owned. He represented several of Eleanor's wrecked Hall relatives in the petty suits in which they seemed unable to avoid involving themselves. Her alcoholic Uncle Vallie fell behind in his payments to a sanitarium in which he had stayed all too briefly; Franklin arranged a revised schedule of payments and made sure the checks were sent out on time. "I wish I were in a position to send my steam yacht for the summer or give you a new auto," Vallie wrote Franklin, "but I am poor. I will however be glad to call on you at your office . . . & take you out to luncheon & you can have whatever you like. I have been told by so many that you are doing so well . . . downtown & I am so glad. There is nothing in this world so encouraging as feeling that one is advancing."

Aunt Tissie Mortimer thanked him for helping secure her a lease: "Honestly, I don't know what I'd do without you and [Eleanor] to always depend on." Aunt Pussie, whose eccentricities had now driven her very close to madness, needed Franklin's help to protect what little money she had left; he did help, though her gratitude to him seemed somewhat limited. "I'm not worrying about life or *anything,*" she explained to him, "for I've found what I've been seeking for years— One Path of Truth."

He did well enough for the firm in petty cases. He was given the job of keeping the docket in his bold, slanting hand; he was personable with the important clients he ushered in and out of the partners' offices; but he did not greatly impress the senior partners and, most particularly, he did not impress Mr. Ledyard. The commodore was a formidable figure; big and broad, with a ruddy complexion and a crisply waxed white mustache, he somewhat resembled his good friend and predecessor as head of the Yacht Club, J. Pierpont Morgan, the elder. One of Franklin's fellow clerks remembered him as "very powerful, high-tempered and able. . . ." Ledyard found the young Roosevelt basically frivolous, lacking in the industry and seriousness a future partner required.[25]

"Everybody called him Franklin and regarded him as a harmless

25. Hall Roosevelt seems to have seen this coming. Writing from Groton in October of 1907 to thank Franklin for "the good time you gave me last summer," he added, "How is business? A good fat loaf, I guess, as Eleanor says it seems to agree with you, and getting up early and working hard would never agree with you except on the theory that variety is the spice of life!" *Source:* Eleanor Roosevelt Papers, FDRL.

bust," an old acquaintance remembered many years later. "He had a sanguine temperament, almost adolescent in its buoyancy." Part of the problem may have been that the object of much of the firm's most important work was the making of money—the Stock Exchange itself was one of Ledyard's clients—and money in itself never interested Franklin much. The Roosevelts had always had enough of it to support their comfortable lives; so had the Delanos. Franklin would always have a hard time keeping his mind on the earnest pursuit of more, for himself or on behalf of others.[26]

A member of the firm recalled that Franklin had tended to "dance on the tops of the hills," leaving his less nimble colleagues to hard labor on the slopes below. He found those who took that labor too seriously faintly ludicrous. One day, Franklin amused his fellow clerks with a few lines of surreptitious verse about the most industrious of their number, John G. Milburn, Jr., known in the office as George, to differentiate him from his father, the senior partner:

> Everybody loafs but Milburn
> He's at work all day.
> Gets down town at sunrise
> Gee! He earns his pay!
>
> "Come quick and lunch at Walter's,"
> Says Crawford on the phone.
> "Not much—can't leave the office,"
> Says George in injured tone.

Franklin himself preferred long, chatty lunches, a fellow clerk remembered—soup, roast beef, dessert, and coffee at the Exchange Buffet or *arroz con pollo* at any one of several Spanish restaurants along Water and Pearl Streets—and he was then notorious in the office for his enthusiasm for elegant clothes. "Some suit, eh!" he said when he turned up one morning in crisp chalk-striped flannel fresh from Brooks Brothers, and when he later had to go out on business in a rainstorm and returned soaked and wrinkled, his colleagues cheered.

---

26. That pursuit had bored his Cousin Theodore, too, and had helped make him abandon any idea of a career in the law before he had even finished his first year in law school: ". . . it happened that I had been left enough money by my father not to make it necessary for me to think solely of earning bread for myself and my family," TR would write in his autobiography. "I had enough to get bread. What I had to do, if I wanted butter and jam, was to provide the butter and jam, but to count their cost as compared with other things. In other words, I made up my mind that, while I must earn money, I could afford to make the earning of money the secondary instead of the primary object of my career." *Source:* Theodore Roosevelt, *Theodore Roosevelt: An Autobiography*, page 55.

One splendid spring afternoon, Franklin and another clerk, Grenville Clark, were dispatched across the Hudson to New Jersey to serve some papers. They did not hurry back, stopping instead to watch several innings of baseball at the Polo Grounds, during which Franklin enjoyed a beer or two. When he and Clark returned to Wall Street very late in the afternoon, the commodore demanded an explanation. Franklin, even more cheerful and eager to please than usual, offered a long and implausible one. Ledyard cut him off. "Roosevelt," he shouted, "you're drunk!"

Some years later, the commodore would tell a friend—with a good deal of exaggeration—that "in the time that [Roosevelt] was in the office, he never did a piece of work anybody . . . could use. He was utterly useless." Ledyard himself had finally gone to Sara, he said, and "told her that it was no use," her son would never be a good lawyer; he didn't have the concentration, wasn't willing to do the work.[27]

Franklin appeared in his only known criminal case in the spring of 1910. Judge James T. Malone of the Court of General Sessions assigned him to defend one Herman Bassman, a middle-aged compositor, against a charge of second-degree assault. The complainant was Jeremiah G. McCarthy, a sixty-seven-year-old proof reader, who said that Bassman had stabbed him in the wrist with no provocation.

Both men lived in a crowded tenement at 1848 Second Avenue, near 86th Street, in the predominantly German neighborhood known as Yorkville. The struggle took place in the foyer around midnight on the evening of April 4. When Franklin interviewed his client in the City Prison he found that both men worked in the printshop of the *New York Financial Chronicle*, and that there had been bad blood between them for some time. Bassman swore he was innocent.

Franklin located several witnesses to the struggle and set out his findings in a sheaf of cryptic pencilled notes, along with still more brief reminders to himself of the proper procedure to follow in a jury trial:

Grounds of Challenge
Acquaintance

27. Franklin's own memory of his performance at Carter, Ledyard & Milburn was characteristically positive: "In short order he found himself well on the road to acquiring a fine general practice and went at his job with the zest that has characterized every act of his life." (For an explanation of why this and many other memories offered in Sara's account of her son's early years as if they came from her were actually his, see note, pages 515–516.) *Source:* Sara Delano Roosevelt (as told to Isabel Leighton and Gabrielle Forbush), *My Boy Franklin*, page 66.

Affinity
Age—21 to 70
Drink.

As the trial opened on May 3—Anna's third birthday—the prosecutor opened his case by taking McCarthy step-by-step through his lurid tale of having been suddenly and inexplicably attacked by his knife-wielding former friend and, when Franklin cross-examined him, he stuck to it hard. Mrs. Josephine Burger, who had for seven months been McCarthy's "housekeeper," living with him in his flat, backed everything he said; she vowed she had seen the whole thing.

Franklin called his client to the stand to offer his version of the same events. He had been in his room on the second floor with *his* companion, Mrs. Waters, he said, and about midnight had opened the door on his way to the toilet. McCarthy was standing at the bottom of the stairs, reeling slightly, and when he spotted Bassman he began to shout, "There's the Bastard! The Pimp!"

Bassman admitted that he had stormed down the stairs in his shirtsleeves and vest, carrying not a knife but the pipe he had been smoking. Franklin's notes summarized the struggle that followed:

McC. grabbed def't and def't grabbed McC.
Def't told him to quit.
No blows. Shoved McC. up against the wall. Shook himself
    free & went upstairs.

Somehow, McCarthy had scratched his wrist during the scuffle. A few minutes later, as Bassman was relighting his pipe back in his room, a police officer arrived to arrest him.

What had been the cause of their initial quarrel? McCarthy, who kept a "poker joint" in Hartford, Connecticut, owed him money and refused to admit it, Bassman said, and had once tried to strike *him* with an iron pipe.

Franklin called other witnesses to confirm his client's story and to cast doubt on McCarthy's. Four other tenants had watched Bassman climb the stairs after the shoving match in the foyer; none had seen a knife. Nor had the wound McCarthy suffered been serious: the night of the incident the officer at the station house desk asked if he needed medical attention for his bleeding wrist. McCarthy was indignant. "What? For *that?*" he'd said. He seemed to stagger a bit, too, as if he'd been drinking.

The case was never even deliberated by the jury; the judge directed a verdict of not guilty.

Attorney and client shook hands. Friends and members of the family crowded around, plainly dressed working people from an immigrant neighborhood, offering their congratulations to the tall, slender young man with the famous name, wearing his carefully tailored English suit, smiling and blinking behind his pince-nez, reaching out to shake their hands.

The Roosevelts' second child was born on December 23, 1907. Characteristically, Eleanor had everything ready well in advance; she had filled all the family's Christmas stockings—"even [those for] Baby Anna and Miss Spring!" Sara marvelled—and had written a long note for Franklin, telling him just what the nurse was to do with Anna while she was herself unable to supervise things, and where he was to find the address tags for the big, shiny cans in which fresh milk arrived from Sara's Springwood herd by train nearly every morning. She also listed the names and telephone numbers of those she especially wanted him to call once the new baby had arrived—Grandmother Hall, Cousin Susie Parish, Isabella Ferguson, Helen Robinson, her Aunts Bye and Corinne Robinson.

Sara's name and number did not need to be listed. Franklin called her first, and asked her to hurry over at two-forty-five in the morning. When she got there, Franklin threw open the front door, shouting, "A son all right, Mummy!" The baby was even larger than his sister had been, "very fat and handsome." "Eleanor and baby doing well," Sara wrote the next day. "I hope he will be *James*."[28] He was, though he would not be so christened until the following September.

He did not at first do well, "cried every night all night," Eleanor remembered. He refused to eat according to Dr. Holt's exacting schedule, and when he did eat, often developed indigestion afterwards. Miss Spring was invited back to help out, but the winter of 1907–08, Eleanor wrote later, was "one of the times in my life which I would rather not live over again." Things got worse that spring when James

28. Many years later, Eleanor remembered how she had felt when she learned that the baby was a boy: "James . . . will never know with what joy and relief I welcomed him into the world, for again I had been worried for fear I would never have a son, knowing that both my mother-in-law and my husband wanted a boy to name after my husband's father. Many a time since I have wished that two girls had started our family, so that Anna might have had a sister, and in the end I reached a point where boys were almost commonplace, but my heart sang when James was safely in the world." *Source:* Eleanor Roosevelt, *This Is My Story,* page 150.

developed pneumonia. Miss Spring nursed him through it. On a brief visit to New York, Isabella Ferguson reported to her husband that "E. seems so relieved and happy over the baby. Has only 1 nurse now, and says he is doing finely, but is most awfully weak, poor little soul, and pathetic."

Dr. Holt insisted that the recovering baby should not spend the summer at Campobello; he needed to be nearer at hand in case of a further emergency. The Roosevelts looked around for an alternative and thought they had found it in a small cottage built on stilts on the boardwalk at Seabright, New Jersey. It was not the sort of place to which they were accustomed; the neighbors on either side, Eleanor remembered, were "so close that I could hear them ordering their food for the day every morning."

Sara was disappointed that her children would not be coming to Campobello, but she was also understanding: "I think the cottage on the ocean sounds perfect, as the *air* is what you go for, and really if it is healthy the furniture makes absolutely no difference." She decided to spend her own summer at Hyde Park so that she could visit Seabright from time to time.

Franklin and Eleanor, her brother Hall, the two babies, their nurse, and Miss Spring all moved to the Jersey shore in early June. Franklin commuted to and from his Wall Street office every day, driving his own new Ford.[29]

It was a crowded, uncomfortable summer. Eleanor was again pregnant and ceaselessly anxious about James. Anna expressed her resentment of the newcomer about whom everyone else was being so solicitous by pushing him and his carriage off the porch; only the soft sand onto which he fell saved him.

"I played no games," Eleanor wrote, remembering those weeks. "I could not swim, I was feeling miserable again, all day long I spent with the children or walking up and down [the] boardwalk." She tried to learn to drive Franklin's Ford. He thought that "a capital idea," until he returned from work one evening to find that while turning into the driveway she had damaged the gatepost, ripped off

---

29. For some reason he was never able to discover, this car ran reliably only in high gear. "He used to wait until the ferryboat was quite clear of people," he told an interviewer, "then start for it in a rush, hoping to be able to get the car to stop before it rolled off at the other end. As soon as the ferry had pulled into the slip and had unloaded its passengers, Franklin would start up again, and in no time at all be up the hill and on his way to the seashore." *Source:* Sara Delano Roosevelt (as told to Isabel Leighton and Gabrielle Forbush), *My Boy Franklin*, pages 66–67.

a section of the porch, and badly dented his new car. She was mortified. "I suppose the average person would have taken this calmly," she wrote later, "but I felt so terrible at having injured something which was not my own . . . and at having spoiled everybody's pleasure that I never again touched a car for many years."

A sudden three-day storm lashed the Jersey coast in July, driving the sea over the boardwalk and into the cottage itself. Duck boards were laid across the floor, but the cook quit and Eleanor had to find a new one.

Although he had been with Carter, Ledyard & Milburn for less than a year that summer, Franklin managed to arrange a full month's vacation for himself. He spent none of it with his family.

In June, his Uncle Warren Delano III invited him along on a weeklong horseback inspection of some potentially rich coal lands in the Cumberland mountains around Harlan, Kentucky. Franklin eagerly accepted.

Sara sent him a soft gray hat to wear on the trip, adding, "If you do not like it, you must buy one, as it is most important to guard against sunstroke on long rides and also to have a brim to protect your eyes as well as head and back of neck. I hope you and Uncle Warren will have a lovely time, it will be rough, but a very interesting experience for you." She may in fact have hoped that it would prove more than merely interesting. She must have known that Franklin was growing weary of the law; the trip might now awaken in him some interest in a business career. It may even have been Sara's idea. Certainly she would have liked nothing better than for Franklin to take an interest in the industry from which both his father and his grandfather had profited handsomely; maybe, if her son showed enough enthusiasm, Warren would someday be willing to take him into the business.

The trip was a real adventure. They got as far as Pennington Gap, Virginia, by rail, running through "a succession of wonderful valleys and hills," Franklin reported to Eleanor at Seabright; "in some places we were over 2,000 feet up, and the train ran thro gorges that for sheer beauty beat anything that we saw in the Black Forest." At sunrise the next morning they took a second train to a coal station called Hagan, where Uncle Warren had arranged to have horses waiting for them.

"We formed a cavalcade of five," Franklin said, "Mr. Whiteley, Mr. Wolfe [both managers of local iron mines], Uncle Warren, Mr. Sewell, W.D.'s local attorney, and your hubby. My horse is small but wiry and sure footed. Uncle Warren rode a mule, as the horse intended for him had a sore back."

The party reached the top of Cumberland Mountain in mid-morning, Franklin reported to Eleanor, "and had one of the most magnificent views I have ever seen," the blue ridges of the Cumberlands cascading away in every direction. They picked their way along the ridge for a hour or so, "got lost, came over the top and started down into the valley over what [the others] thought was a trail. I thought otherwise—for half an hour we slipped, slid and fell down the slope, the horses slipping, sliding and almost falling on top of us, and ended up in a stream at the bottom. Uncle Warren said it was about the roughest ride he has ever had here."

They stopped for a lunch of chocolate bars and spring water, then headed up and over Black Mountain "on a so-called wagon road— positively the worst road I have ever seen or imagined," and finally pulled up at the house of Henry Smith, a wealthy farmer who lived just outside Harlan where they stayed overnight. After breakfast the next morning, they "sat around for an hour, discussing legal and political affairs," then rode into Harlan, their headquarters for the week.

Franklin was impressed by the countryside through which he rode each day: "The sides of the valley going up 2,000 feet, heavily wooded with great poplars, chestnuts and a dozen or two other deciduous trees and every mile or so a fertile bottom with fine crops and a stream of splendid water." He also enjoyed being treated more or less as an equal by his older companions; "last night I sat up till eleven discussing law with Mr. Sewell," he told Eleanor. And he was interested, as always, in the individuals he met along the way. In Harlan they took rooms at the Imperial Hotel, a rambling unpainted structure, run by an enterprising young county judge named Lewis. "He and his wife do all the work and he waits on table," Franklin reported. "He is 29 only and they have been married 15 years and have two children."

But Uncle Warren's business held no real attraction for him. He visited working mines—there is a snapshot of him, hands on hips and wearing a suit and tie, looking on while two miners, bent nearly double, push past him a car filled with coal—and he helped scout likely sites for new shafts every day he was in Kentucky, but there is not one word about them in his letters to Seabright.

In late August he went away again, this time with Hall, on a moose-hunting expedition to Newfoundland. He was gone almost three weeks, canoeing up the Humber River with Indian guides, camping along the shore, growing a mustache (which he wisely shaved off before returning to the office), finally getting his moose with Mr. James's old rifle. Hall got one, too. On his way home on September 12, Franklin wired Eleanor: FINE TRIP ONE HEAD EACH. . . .

Her pleasure in his success may have been tempered a bit by circumstance. While he was gone she had had to cope with still more problems: "The laundry stove wouldn't work. . . . The colored man wouldn't hear of seeing to the grass and flower beds (!), washing the stoop once a week and doing the shoes for less than $4 a week." Finally, she had organized the family's complicated move back to the city.

The Roosevelts never repeated their Seabright experiment: ". . . both my husband and I," Eleanor wrote later, "were accustomed to the country with plenty of space around us, with not many human beings nearby, and trees and lawns to look at, and we decided that never again were we going to spend a summer in that particular type of place, so we left it with few regrets."

James, whose health had steadily improved despite the difficulties of the summer, was christened at Hyde Park on September 27, 1908, in a ceremony organized by Sara and filled with echoes of the Springwood past. "Baby was squeezed into Franklin's long christening dress," Sara wrote. Her brother Warren, and sister Annie Hitch, were present. Helen Robinson was James's godmother; his godfather was Franklin's roommate at both Groton and Harvard, Lathrop Brown. Following the rites at St. James, the party rode back to Springwood in carriages. Sara served tea to her guests and, like the widow of an English lord celebrating the arrival of a new heir, distributed gifts to all the servants and the farmers on the place "in honor of the name."

Afterwards, Franklin, Eleanor, Sara, and the guests all played croquet, the men in their summer flannels, the women in long dresses, moving through the lengthening shadows on the lawn until, Helen Robinson remembered, "it got too dark to see."

CHAPTER

3

ALMOST THERE

I n 1942, Helen Robinson sent FDR all five volumes of the journals her grandmother, Rebecca Howland Roosevelt, had kept during her twenty-three tranquil years of marriage to Mr. James. The President had copies of them typed up for his new library at Springwood, then returned the books to her; he had found them "fascinating," he said, but "I must confess that neither you nor I would have found [the life along the river they described] very exciting."

That lack of excitement was already evident to him in 1908. Living his father's life no longer satisfied him. Neither did the law. Eleanor had suspected it would not. "He will not find himself altogether happy with the law he is studying at Columbia," she had told her Auntie Bye while Franklin was still attending classes, "unless he is able to get a broad human contact through it."

Naturally gregarious but barred throughout his boyhood from contact with anyone outside the small circle of close friends and family members of whom his mother approved, then educated among boys and young men most of whom had been brought up in circumstances only slightly less circumscribed than his, Franklin was hungry to know other worlds, to move among new kinds of people. His time at Carter, Ledyard & Milburn had provided him only tantalizing glimpses of those worlds, but it had persuaded him that he could function well enough among men and women whose backgrounds were different from his own.

He was eventually assigned to admiralty cases, working under Edmund Baylies, the partner who had hired him. This was a little more interesting than his earlier work, and in later years he liked to suggest it had involved him in romantic and complex litigation having to do with drama on the high seas. But he probably came closer to the truth when he referred to "those ferryboat cases I used to handle" in a letter to his former boss, written shortly after he left the firm. His growing restlessness was a source of some concern to Sara, and when she saw that Judge Henry E. Howland, an eminent distant cousin, was quoted in the newspaper on the subject of the personal rewards of a law career, she clipped the article and read it aloud to her son, then pasted it in her scrapbook in case there were further debate: "Being a lawyer," the judge said, "if a man enters into the spirit of the work properly, is exciting, interesting, diverting and amusing, whether a man is successful or unsuccessful, or is somewhere between. . . . As someone has said, the glory is in the combat, not in the victory."

Franklin was sometimes diverted by the combat, but he already had far larger victories in mind. One especially slow afternoon at the office, he and several of his fellow clerks sat at their desks and talked about their hopes for the future.

When his turn came, Franklin allowed as how he didn't plan to practice law forever. No, he thought he'd enter politics and eventually become President of the United States. He planned first to get himself elected to the New York State Assembly, then win appointment as Assistant Secretary of the Navy, and finally become governor of New York. "Anyone who is governor of New York," he explained, "has a good chance to be President, with any luck."

Years later, one of those who had listened to his musing recalled that no one in the room that day had laughed, a fact he then solemnly attributed to Roosevelt's "engaging frankness . . . the sincerity and reasonableness of what he had to say."

Yet had any other twenty-five year old in that room expressed the same ambition—no matter how frank, sincere, or reasonable he seemed—his friends would have been at least privately amused. Just three New York governors or former governors had gone on to the presidency by then—Martin Van Buren, Grover Cleveland, and Theodore Roosevelt—and it was only the fact that Franklin and TR shared a last name that made the young man's heady vision of the future seem remotely plausible. It was his cousin's swift climb to power that Franklin hoped to follow, rung by rung.

"I think Franklin always intended to go into politics," Eleanor once told an interviewer. "I think Uncle Ted was responsible for that." Certainly, a political career had been in the back of his mind at least since his sophomore year at Harvard, when he told Alice Sohier and others of his plan to become President.[1]

Politics had fascinated Franklin's father, too, but always from a safe, decorous distance: he contributed to campaigns, helped pick local candidates, served one two-year term as town supervisor of Hyde Park, and lobbied quietly in Washington on behalf of the railroads he managed and a canal through Nicaragua that never got built. "I have always refused to accept any nomination for Public Office," he wrote toward the end of his life, "[and] repeatedly refused nomination for Congress, State Senate and Assembly."

Rosy had edged the family one step closer to active participation in public life. Twice, President Cleveland had sought to persuade Mr. James to enter government service; each time he had declined, obtaining instead diplomatic posts abroad for his eldest son. Rosy was as engaging as he was rich, but both posts had been more decorative than demanding.

A New York newspaper writer, assigned in 1896 to write admiring portraits of the leaders of the American community in London during Rosy's time there as *chargé d'affaires,* did what he could to make him seem able and important as well as ingratiating, but the effort it took was obvious:

> A capital sportsman and an all-round good fellow . . . [he] has shown English society that we [Americans] possess men who can take a hand in the encouragement of honest sport, and at the same time fulfill those public functions which men in Mr. Roosevelt's position are so frequently called upon to occupy. . . .
>
> Mr. Roosevelt is a member of the Four-in-Hand Club in New York, and takes a great interest in English sport, having hunting boxes in the

1. Mary Marvin, the wife of Franklin's first law partner, Langdon P. Marvin, remembered having met about 1920 a member of Franklin's Harvard class to whom he had also confided his hope of winning the presidency. "I can remember so well sitting out with him at a party," she quoted him as having said, "and he was perfectly definite about so many things for the future and [Roosevelt] said, 'I know I want to try for the Presidency of the United States.' " *Source:* Interview with Mary Marvin, Columbia Oral History Project, Columbia University. Also see Geoffrey C. Ward, *Before the Trumpet,* page 253.

most famous counties. He is known by all his friends as a great lover of horses, and his capital pair of imported American trotters show that he is an excellent judge of how a good horse should be. As becomes an up-to-date sportsman, Mr. Roosevelt is a cyclist, but it is difficult indeed to think of any sport in which he is not capable of taking an active share. . . .

The position of Chargé d'Affaires is . . . by no means an easy one. The duties require tact of the highest kind. Presentations at Court, admissions to the Royal Enclosure at Ascot, and other great social arrangements have to be regulated by this official, and the nature of these *entrées* makes it an extremely difficult thing to refuse them. It has, however, to be done, as the demand greatly exceeds the supply, hundreds asking for what only four or five can obtain.

In appearance, Mr. Roosevelt is . . . very prepossessing and combines all the qualities that prove attractive in society . . . . . . to Mr. Roosevelt we can point with confidence as one in whom the honor of our country is in safe keeping—whether it be in the world of fashion, the world of sport, or the more serious world of business.

Appointive office appealed to Rosy all his life; he doggedly contributed large sums to those Democratic presidential candidates who met his conservative standards in the frank hope that one of them would win and restore him to the glamour and ease of another foreign capital. But the idea of personally engaging in electoral politics—clamorous, sweaty competition for the votes of men whom he believed his social inferiors—was quite another matter.

It had been Theodore Roosevelt who first demonstrated that a member of the family might remain unmistakably a gentleman while immersed in politics—might "go into politics," in Sara's words, "but not *be* a politician." It had not been easy. His father, Theodore Roosevelt, Sr., like his friend Mr. James, had always spurned politics, and when in the interest of Civil Service reform he permitted President Rutherford B. Hayes to place his name in nomination for collector of customs at New York in 1877, the bitter losing struggle with the Regular Republican machine that followed broke his health and hastened his early death—or so his worshipful son always believed. On his deathbed, his father had written that while he did not regret having become embroiled in a battle for principle, "I feel sorry for the country. We cannot stand so corrupt a government for any length of time."

TR took up his father's struggle. He would enter the lists himself, full-tilt, and run for the New York State Assembly at twenty-three—

he was still a law student at Columbia. When he told friends of his plans, he remembered, they had laughed at him; "politics were 'low,' " they said, "not controlled by 'gentlemen' . . . I would find them run by saloon-keepers, horse-car conductors, and the like . . . rough and brutal and unpleasant to deal with."

He was not discouraged. "If this were so," he told them, "it meant merely that people I knew did not belong to the governing class—and that I intended to be one of the governing class. . . ."

Some of his own relatives were upset at first. "We thought he was, to put it frankly, pretty fresh," his cousin Emlen Roosevelt wrote later. "We felt that his own father would not have liked it, and would have been fearful of the outcome. The Roosevelt circle, as a whole, had a profound distrust of public life." Eleanor's Grandmother Hall, she remembered, always "looked upon Uncle Ted as a strange and curious phenomenon. He was . . . in politics, and she considered politics as something just beneath contempt . . . something you never talked about."[2]

But TR's immediate family rallied to him, and so had Mr. James. Theodore Roosevelt made his first speech in the assembly chamber at Albany on January 24, 1882, just six days before Franklin was born, and when his mother visited Hyde Park to see the new baby later that year, Mr. James enthusiastically read aloud to her and Sara a newspaper account of a testimonial dinner held in New York to honor Theodore's relentless assaults on Tammany Hall.

As he grew to manhood, and with the enthusiastic approval of his parents, Franklin had followed every stage of TR's career with eager admiration, even adopting Roosevelt pince-nez and Roosevelt adjectives ("bully" and "dee-lighted"), and cheerfully enduring the teasing of Harvard classmates who, in part perhaps because of these affectations and his fondness for good times, liked to call him "Kermit," after the third and hardest-drinking of the President's four sons.

Franklin was immensely proud of his kinship with TR—to the end of his life he thought Theodore Roosevelt "the greatest man I ever knew"—but that kinship had an unsettling side as well. Cousin Theodore became a sort of benchmark against which the younger Roosevelt

2. Some members of the family never forgave Theodore Roosevelt for sullying his hands with politics. Several years after TR's death, an elderly uncle came upon workmen laboring to rebuild the brownstone in which he had been born, as a historical monument. "I don't see why you are making such a fuss," he told them, "I used to hate to see him coming down the street." *Source:* Edmund Morris, *The Rise of Theodore Roosevelt,* page 144.

seems to have measured himself and, at least privately, must often have found himself wanting. It is impossible to know just how conscious his attempts at emulating TR were, but he must have been at least privately aware that in no field had he proved the equal of the young Theodore: even his big, boyhood collection of birds and birds' eggs was less encyclopedic than Theodore's had been; his academic record at Harvard, where TR had earned a Phi Beta Kappa key, was undistinguished; he saw his social career there as inferior, too, because he had not been invited to join Porcellian; his marriage to Eleanor had brought him only to the periphery of the inner circle at Oyster Bay.

Instead of unduly discouraging Franklin, these relative failures seem to have served him as a spur, further impetus to succeed, to show himself a worthy inheritor of his cousin's greatness.

Theodore Roosevelt was not only his young cousin's boyhood hero; he was also the great exemplar for the Reverend Endicott Peabody of Groton, a frequent, vigorous visitor to the school who could be counted on to exhort the boys (who eventually included all of his own sons) to involve themselves in the running of their country. "If a man has courage, goodness and brains," he told Franklin and his fellow graduates in 1900, "no limit can be placed to the greatness of the work he may accomplish—he is the man needed today in politics."

All his life, the rector worked to ensure that his boys would carry those ideals into the reform of government. During Franklin's time at Groton, the Reverend Sherrard Billings, the school's best-loved teacher and one of Peabody's two closest associates, delivered a sermon called "A School-Boy's Salvation." Sara kept a copy of it, with those passages marked which seemed to her to epitomize the message she and Mr. James hoped their son would carry away from Groton:

> If people are rich, their money often brings, together with many advantages, a deplorable softness of life that is enough to emasculate any boy—something it is hard for other influences to counteract. If, on the other hand, people are poor, there is often seen ignoble discontent that makes riches important out of all proportion. We have one advantage in America, to be sure. A boy, with a fortune or without it, looks forward to doing something, but the ambition imbibed from the average home is to be a power in some worldly way, to "get on," and the Bible never says "get on," and God never said it. . . .
>
> To be daring, to be of use to your fellows, to have a directly beneficient life—these aims, I believe, appeal to the boys of this generation as forcibly as to those of any generation in the past. They are immeasurably

more attractive to them than any sordid ambition, any overcautious desire to provide for themselves and to make sure of comforts enough for their old age. . . .

Despite the earnestness of Peabody, Billings, and their colleagues, sentiments like these had washed pleasantly over most of Franklin's fellow students at Groton. In the end, all but a handful of Peabody's boys settled amicably enough into pursuit of fortunes still larger than those that had sent them to the school in the first place.[3]

Franklin did not. He loved the easy, comfortable life he and his parents had led at Springwood—few men have been more deeply rooted in a place and its distinctive way of life than was Franklin Roosevelt—yet he also yearned for adventure, sought new challenges, wanted to excel, to be in charge.

His ardent identification with Theodore Roosevelt accounted for part of that. So did the reinforcement he received for it from family, friends, and teachers. After his father's death, his mother and his Uncle Fred Delano both often suggested that he look to TR for guidance as to how to live his life, and the Reverend Billings himself told Franklin in 1905 that it had been "a dream of mine for some years that you would be a man widely useful to your country," and he saw in Franklin's marriage to Eleanor a powerful impetus toward that end.[4]

But other young men all over the nation admired TR, even dreamed of emulating him. Franklin would actually do what they only dreamed.

The special quality of life at Springwood helped make the difference. For the first fourteen years of his life, Franklin was the center of that tranquil universe. Every element of life there—his parents and

---

3. Groton did produce its share of public figures besides Franklin, including Dean Acheson, W. Averell Harriman, Sumner Welles, and Francis Biddle. But no more than its share.

4. Billings's feelings for Franklin approached the worshipful. The following fervid note was written one Christmas Day from Boston's Union Club, probably while Franklin was still unmarried and attending either his final year at Harvard or his first at the Columbia School of Law:

Dear Franklin,

I have just been at the Cathedral where Bishop Sherril preached an excellent sermon on *how God does His work through human personality.* For illustration he said there was a "man sent from God" named *Abraham Lincoln* and one named *Pasteur,* and others. I kept thinking of you. And I pray with all my heart that men will say of you that he was a man sent from God to help the world in its dire need. I have faith to believe that years hence as they look back men will say just that.

Forgive me for writing so intimately

Yours affectionately,
Sherrard Billings.

Source: Roosevelt Family Papers Donated by the Children, FDRL.

fond relatives, his tutors and governesses and servants, the people of
the village who hailed him as "Master Franklin" and lifted their caps
to him and his father as they rode along the Albany Road—had served
to reinforce his sense of his own central importance.

His second fourteen years had seen that order disrupted by contact
with the world beyond Hyde Park. "He went to Groton and Harvard," Mike Reilly, the blunt chief of the White House Secret Service
detail, once said of FDR, "he was raised alone and he had just about
everything he wanted throughout his youth, so it would be just a little
too much to expect him to be 'one of the boys.' He never was 'one of
the boys,' although he frequently made a good try. It was such a good
try that it never quite came off."

Reilly was speaking of FDR's difficulty in finding common ground
with men, like himself, who had been brought up outside the world
of old money and special privilege. But he had things only partially
right, for Franklin had never been one of the boys at Groton or at
Harvard, either. His fellow students had found him too ingratiating,
too sinuous. He had been denied what he believed to be his rightful
position at the center of things—by the rector who had not made him
senior prefect, by the members of Porcellian who had refused him
membership, by his Harvard classmates who had not elected him their
class marshal, by the senior partners at Carter, Ledyard & Milburn who
still treated him as a glorified clerk.

He had been *the* boy throughout his most formative years, and it
seems likely that his fascination with politics, with winning the approval of the voters and attaining the highest possible office, was at least
in part an effort to replicate what would always seem to him the natural
order of things.

Not surprisingly, Franklin was not the only member of the former
President's extended family who hoped to follow TR's political path
as far as it would take him. Eleanor's Aunt Ella Bulloch wrote to her
of how odd it seemed that so many members of the family were now
"in the limelight," with "Uncle Ted in the extraordinary position of
being the arbiter of the Republican destinies. He has certainly infected
you all with large ambitions as citizens and I am sure will be proud of
you all."

Teddy Robinson, the son of TR's sister Corinne and now married
to Franklin's niece and contemporary, Helen Roosevelt, was about to
announce his candidacy for the New York State Assembly. Joseph

Alsop, Jr., recently married to Corinne Robinson's daughter, Corinne, was involving himself in Connecticut politics. Theodore Roosevelt, Jr., the President's own eldest son, was, at twenty, still too young to run for office but already full of plans to do so; the newspapers liked to call him "the Crown Prince," and one or more of his younger brothers, Kermit, Archie, and Quentin, could reasonably be expected to follow suit when their turns came.

All of these potential rivals were as close or closer to the ex-President than Franklin was, and all of them were Republicans.

It seems curious at first that so ardent an admirer of Theodore Roosevelt as Franklin should have chosen to enter politics as a member of the Democratic opposition.[5] He had been an enthusiastic Republican as a Harvard freshman; had marched through a rainstorm in support of the McKinley-Roosevelt ticket, joined the Republican Club, and faithfully attended the lectures it sponsored by members of the new administration.

There was a good deal of Republican sympathy in his own home, as well. Eleanor had been brought up to believe that "Republicanism and respectability went hand in hand." So had Sara, who would initially have been happy to have her son return to the Grand Old Party to which her own father had been uncompromisingly loyal. Mr. James's preference for the Democrats had always been something of a problem for her. "I know so very well every feeling of your dear father," she once wrote Franklin, "and I know that being a democrat never prevented his taking the right side in a contest and he . . . felt very strongly . . . the necessity of always opposing Tammany and vice."

5. In retrospect it evidently sometimes seemed curious even to FDR, and he invented a story to make it seem less so. As President, he often told friends and family members that TR himself had initially sought to enter politics as a Democrat, and had only joined the GOP when the local Democratic bosses turned him away. There is no evidence whatsoever to support this tale, but it may have served to make Franklin more comfortable with his own decision to become a Democrat.

In fact, party loyalty was never more than a tactical matter for either of the Roosevelts; each saw his party primarily as a vehicle for personal power. Initially, at least, TR had remained faithful to his father's party in large part because it seemed most congenial to a young man of his rarified breeding. As early as 1882, he privately confessed to a friend that "Really, though elected as an Independent Republican, I hardly know what to call myself. As regards civil service, reform, tariff reform, local self-government, etc., I am quite in sympathy with Democratic principles; it is Democratic practice that I object to. Besides as I am neither of Celtic descent nor yet a liquor seller, I would be ostracized among our New York Democrats. I cannot join myself with the party that, at least in my city and State, contains the vast majority of the vicious and illiterate population." *Sources:* Interview with Margaret L. Suckley; TR to Joseph Henry Adams, November 20, 1882, quoted in Albert Bushnell Hart, *Theodore Roosevelt Encyclopedia*, page 538.

Mr. James's own loyalty to the Democrats had, in fact, always been tenuous; he had been a Whig as long as he could, and only when that grand old party disintegrated in the 1850s had he reluctantly drifted over to the Democrats. Nor did he always stay there; he was a conservative and selective Democrat, often backing the Republicans when he thought their candidates more responsible and gentlemanly than those of his own party. His friend Grover Cleveland was his political hero; civil service reform, small government, and the obliteration of Tammany Hall were his issues. He thought William Jennings Bryan a shameless demagogue, campaigning under a false flag, and he had eagerly voted for "our cousin" TR for governor of New York in 1898 and again for Vice President just a few weeks before he died in 1900.

Yet as early as his sophomore year at Harvard, Franklin had evidently decided to become a Democrat. His reasoning was crisp and pragmatic. The Republican Party was filled with young members of the family whose claims to the President's mantle were more plausible than his. Only as a Democrat could a Roosevelt from outside Sagamore Hill hope to rise very high—and Franklin Roosevelt would never willingly settle for less.[6]

The problem was how to find himself a handhold in the Dutchess County party. It evidently never crossed his mind to enter politics in the city in which he lived and worked most of the year, as Cousin Theodore had. Like his father, Franklin always saw himself as a country gentleman; in 1915 he told a friend who had mistakenly listed his address as Manhattan that "I never have been and hope I never will be a resident of New York City," and in 1944 he still enjoyed listing his occupation as "tree grower." City life was always an unavoidable and slightly distasteful necessity for him, and the political issues that then interested him—clean government, an end to boss rule, economy, the same issues that had been his father's—were not likely to make him welcome at Tammany Hall.[7]

Casting about for some way to get started in the country, the best

6. Franklin eagerly explained his reasoning to Alice Sohier during one of their evenings together that year. Her father was a life-long Republican; so would she be, and, at least in retrospect, she thought Franklin's straightforward explanation "the most calculating, unprincipled thing she'd ever heard." *Source:* Interview with Emily Shaw, Alice Sohier's granddaughter.

7. As a state senator in 1911, he told a newspaperwoman that "I might almost say that the political salvation of the country lies with the country men and boys. . . . The lives of you city people are artificial. . . . From just such [country men] who think and argue over national and political matters comes the material that makes our best lawmakers and who in time will see to it that only the men that will serve the people wholeheartedly and unreservedly will be elected to office." *Source: The New York Globe,* February 26, 1911.

he could come up with on his own was a run for his father's old post of Hyde Park town supervisor, and some time in early 1910, he quietly made his interest in it known to influential local Democrats.[8]

Meanwhile, Franklin had become a homeowner, courtesy of his mother. At Christmas in 1905, she had handed him and Eleanor a sheet of Springwood stationery. On it was a cheerful sketch of a brownstone with smoke curling from its chimney, and beneath it a brief note: "A Christmas present to Franklin and Eleanor from Mama Number & Street not yet quite decided—19 or 20 feet wide."

She wanted to build them a house. It had taken nearly three years to buy the land, draw up the blueprints, oversee the building, and furnish and decorate the rooms. During that time, she made two major changes in the plan. She had initially hoped to build in her old neighborhood in the East Thirties, but when Altman's department store went up at Madison and 35th, she decided that "the encroachment of trade" required her to move her family much further north. Also, her initial sketch had shown a narrow brownstone with a single front door, but in the end, she had ordered built two adjoining houses with twin doors at 47 and 49 East 65th Street. Franklin, Eleanor, and the children were to live at 49; Sara herself would move in next door a few days before Christmas 1908.

In that day, it was common enough for widows to live with their

8. In later years, Franklin's initial eagerness to run even for that job became a running joke between him and his Hyde Park supporters. Shortly after FDR defeated New York Governor Thomas A. Dewey and was elected to a fourth term as President in 1944, Arthur Smith, the local postmaster sent him a poem, "dreamed up," he said, "while celebrating your re-election."

> Here we sit, celebrating with wine,
> Because you left Dewey far behind.
> Some may say he was on your heels,
> But that's only the loser's disgruntled squeals.
> For you came through as we knew you would.
> There was never a question but that you could.
> Even though a couple more states went a-drift
> We are planning for your 5th.
> Which will be better than a 4th, by far,
> Congratulations, FDR.
> Oh, if you no longer President would be,
> Come back to Hyde Park, and between you and me,
> With the help of your neighbors, and half a break.
> This town from the Elephant we will take.
> With Elmer Van Wagner [the incumbent Supervisor] as your adviser
> We'll give you that job as Supervisor. . . .

The poem "made a tremendous hit with the President," according to William Hassett, FDR's secretary. "All poetry should strike a prophetic note," he added, "and it seems to me that Elmer Van Wagner's job will be endangered sooner or later." *Source:* PPF 6823, FDRL.

children. "Some of [my] friends were surprised" that Franklin and Eleanor had not shared their home with her during the first years of their marriage, Sara later told an interviewer. She had prized her own independence too highly for that, she said; besides, as she told Eleanor, Mr. James had often said that while "it was one thing to have children dependent upon you, [it] was intolerable to be materially dependent on them."

The adjoining houses had seemed a sensible compromise. Sara may, in fact, have got the idea from the Parish household, where Eleanor had stayed before her marriage; Cousin Susie's mother, Mrs. Mary Ludlow, lived next door, and on the Roosevelts' wedding day the folding doors between the two drawing rooms had been opened to accommodate the guests.

Franklin eagerly worked over the plans; he was fascinated all his life with architecture and construction. Eleanor rarely expressed an opinion; she was made uneasy by conflict or argument of any kind, still did not wish to have to defend her own views against those of her husband or her mother-in-law.[9]

Franklin and Eleanor moved in during the autumn of 1908. A few weeks later, Franklin wandered into their bedroom to find Eleanor sitting at her dressing table unable to control her sobbing. He was astonished. What on earth was wrong?

"I said I did not like to live in a house which was not in any way mine, one that I had done nothing about and which did not represent the way I wanted to live. Being an eminently reasonable person, he thought I was quite mad and told me so gently and said I would feel different in a little while and left me alone until I should become calmer."

Emotional outbursts by women always unnerved Franklin; life with his carefully controlled mother had left him utterly unprepared for them. "Nothing could bother him more," his daughter remembered, "than to have one of the females [closest to him] burst into tears. . . . If it's a personal thing [he felt]—go somewhere else and settle it."

9. In the first volume of her autobiography, Eleanor wrote that she had "left everything [about the new house] to my mother-in-law and my husband." But she did evidently take at least a small part in the discussions, for on August 22, 1907, she wrote Sara from Campobello that "Franklin and I have been working over the plans for lighting, bells, and telephones which [Charles A. Platt, the architect] sent us two days ago. All the arrangements seem very good except in one or two bedrooms where I think he has made a mistake as one would want lights over dressing tables it seems to me and not in the four corners of the room." *Sources:* Eleanor Roosevelt, *This Is My Story*, page 152; Elliott Roosevelt, ed., *FDR: His Personal Letters, 1905–1928*, page 122.

Eleanor did eventually calm down—she had been "acting like a little fool," she later wrote—but she was beginning to see that she had sacrificed too much in order to be accepted by her husband and his mother, that she was simply "absorbing the personalities of those about me and letting their tastes and interests dominate me."

She much later came to understand that her vision of what her marriage to Franklin should be had been hopelessly romantic. But that belated realism did little to ease the pain of discovering what a bad bargain she had made. She had buried herself—her wishes, desires, talents, personality—and in exchange had hoped to find a confidant in her husband, and in her mother-in-law, the affectionate, forgiving mother she had never had. Both, she now began to feel, had let her down. Franklin and his mother often differed, but their first loyalty was still to one another.

At Hyde Park one morning early in their marriage, Eleanor asked if she might ride Bobby, Mr. James's old horse. The tall animal was saddled for her by the stable boy, and she started off. The ride, along the shady path that led northward along the bluff to the Rogers' estate, began well enough; off to her left the slow-moving river and the blue hills beyond were lovely. But then, apparently responding to some signal she had not meant to give, her mount suddenly began a plunging gallop, leaping over obstacles, crashing along the path. Nothing she could do would make him stop; she clung helplessly to his neck, ducking her head to avoid the tree branches rushing overhead. No one could see her, no one could hear her calls for help. The big horse ran on and on, then stopped as suddenly and unaccountably as he had begun, and started gently trotting home to his stable. Franklin, she learned later, had trained Bobby to begin to gallop at a certain point along the path, and to slow again at another; it was a secret he and Sara shared, and neither mother nor son had bothered to tell Eleanor about it. She would not ride again for many years.

In January 1909, Theodore Roosevelt invited Franklin and Eleanor to come down to Washington for one more visit before he relinquished the White House to his chosen successor, William Howard Taft.[10]

10. TR was uncharacteristically leaving the White House without a fight at fifty, largely because of a spectacular political blunder of his own making. After serving out most of William McKinley's term, he had won a smashing popular victory in his own right in 1904, and in the

(The President was careful to play no favorites among the young members of his family who hoped someday to pursue political careers; Joe Alsop and Teddy Robinson were also invited for separate visits; so was his own son, Ted.)

Franklin was eager to go. Eleanor, who had been unable to attend her Cousin Alice's White House wedding with Franklin because of her pregnancy, was seven months pregnant again, but this time she resolved to go with him anyway, though Sara was sure she should not. They stayed three days.[11] It had been "a very interesting visit," Sara noted, "but Eleanor got terribly tired. I am thankful she is back."

Shortly after she got back, Eleanor began to keep a diary. In it, her bitterness was increasingly evident. Her days were now still more tightly intertwined with Sara's. She made faithful entries each evening for a little over a month and a half. During those seven weeks, she never failed to have either lunch or dinner with her mother-in-law, except when Sara was out of town, and sometimes they shared both meals. They drove and shopped and strolled and paid calls together, too.

The children seemed to bring her little pleasure: "Brother [James] fell out of his chair this Morning. Anna did not come to breakfast because she said, 'No, I won't!' " "Anna and I had a tussle about being tucked up and going to sleep." "Took chicks in to tea [with Mama] and behaved very badly about Brother."

Franklin was now away from her more and more often, leaving the house and boarding the Third Avenue El at 7:30 A.M. to be in court on time, dawdling on his way home from the office on Saturday afternoons to pore over naval prints at Gottschalk's Old Print Shop on Fourth Avenue, making evening engagements on his own. Eleanor did

---

heady atmosphere of that election night had gratuitously declared, "On the fourth of March next I shall have served three and a half years, and this three and a half years constitutes my first term. The wise custom which limits the President to two terms regards the substance and not the form. Under no circumstances will I be a candidate for or accept another nomination."

His wife Edith and daughter Alice were watching as he made his announcement. Both flinched visibly. TR spent much of the rest of his career torturously explaining that he had meant only that we would not run again in 1908; "I was not thinking of 1912," he later wrote, "nor of 1920, nor of 1940," but his words would jubilantly be used against him by his opponents when he sought to win the presidency back four years later.

It was a lesson Franklin Roosevelt would not forget. *Source:* Theodore Roosevelt, *Theodore Roosevelt: An Autobiography,* pages 402–403.

11. Long enough for Sara to send her son a telegram asking what date his Harvard friend Livingston Davis was coming to Hyde Park for a visit. It arrived in what must have been the first envelope ever addressed to "Franklin Roosevelt c/o The White House." *Source:* Roosevelt Family Papers Donated by the Children, FDRL.

not openly object to what she called his "sprees"—she was determined to try not to badger her husband as she felt her mother had her father—but the air of patient martyrdom with which she greeted him when he got back made her feelings clear, and she kept a meticulous record of where he told her he was going and the hour at which he returned: "Franklin went to a poker party at August Belmont's"; "F. dinner and theatre with Teddy R[obinson]. F. played poker with Teddy, etc. in PM. Knickerbocker Club Annual Meeting returned home 4 AM"; "*He* [Franklin] *went off* at 10:30 to Boston. . . . F.D.R. came home [Sunday] morning. He did not go to church"; "F. went to the Harvard Club dinner and got home 3:30 A.M. I dined with Mama"; "F. back to Harvard Club [after dinner at home], staying with Charlie Bradley [a Harvard classmate] after his work is done and getting home at 12 PM"; "FDR has club dinner got home about One"; "F. Stays at the Bar Association till 9:30."[12]

She sometimes found him inattentive even at home; when his mother gave a dinner party for his attractive young cousin, Jean Lyman, and Eleanor did not feel up to attending, Franklin slipped next door afterwards "to smoke." Another evening, Livingston Davis and his new wife, Alice Gardiner Davis, came for dinner. Afterwards they all played bridge until Eleanor went to bed at midnight: "F. and Mrs. D. sat up after that!"

The baby was due early in March. On the 16th, Sara and Eleanor walked more than a mile and half, hoping to bring on labor. Eleanor made the final entry in her diary on the 17th: "St. Patrick's Day. Mother's Birthday. Our 4th Wedding Anniversary!"

The Roosevelts' third child was born the following morning, an especially handsome boy weighing eleven pounds, whom they named Franklin Jr. Franklin asked Hall, at Groton, to register the new baby as a prospective student. "Tell F. that I have reserved a space for the kid under the name of FDR," Hall wrote back, "and so if he changes his name he may not get in."

When Eleanor, the three children, and a phalanx of nurses and servants made their way to Campobello that summer, they moved into a second house of their own. Mrs. Hartman Kuhn, the Roosevelts'

---

12. "If he would go out—which he did—with the men to play poker," his daughter recalled, "and came home with a breath [smelling of liquor] on him, she died. She just couldn't stand it." *Source:* Interview with Anna Roosevelt Halsted by Bernard A. Asbell, Anna Roosevelt Halsted Papers, FDRL.

island neighbor since the 1880s, had recently died. She had been fond of all the Roosevelts, but especially of Eleanor, who had often come over to read poetry to her in the afternoons, and perhaps she sensed the younger woman's growing need for a place of her own, out from under her mother-in-law's fond but often critical gaze. In any case, in her will she had suggested that if Franklin and Eleanor wished to have her big, brick red "cottage" (it had thirty-four rooms), Sara should be able to buy it for them, fully furnished and "with everything in it," including "linen, china, [and] plated ware," Eleanor recalled, for $5,000.

It was the first home Eleanor ever considered her own and she revelled in the fleeting sense of independence it inspired. "I have moved every room in the house around," she warned Franklin, "and I hope you will like the change." When Franklin wrote that he wanted to bring up with him a caribou skin to put in front of the living-room fireplace, she told him exactly where to find it in the New York house: "All fur rugs are done up in . . . paper in [the] trunk room on 5th floor. Your blankets, rubber things, etc., are in the same place. Try to only make a little hole in finding the rug. The key is in my drawer."

Eleanor enjoyed the relative informality of island life. "There was no telephone . . . no electricity," she remembered. "There was a little coal stove on which you did all your cooking, and the lamps sometimes smoked, and [you] had to learn to take care of them, and you went to bed by candlelight. But it had great charm." And it was hers. Even the cold fogs that curled in off the Bay of Fundy suited her. Settled comfortably in front of the fireplace with a good book, she was able to cut herself away from the demands of those around her, to lose herself in literature.[13]

But she missed Franklin back on Wall Street, and resented what she considered his erratic letter writing. "I was horribly disappointed yesterday," she told him in August, "with your hasty little scrap of a letter after not getting anything for two days." And she found filling in for him with the children arduous. She tried taking them sailing on

13. This was evidently a self-taught technique. In a diary fragment written at Tivoli, shortly after she returned from Mlle Souvestre's school at seventeen in 1902, she described how she planned to withstand the noisy turbulence of her Grandmother Hall's household: "There's a tinman doing the roof over the new porch. Pussie is having a tailor. There is a carpenter finishing the same and a painter on a rickety scaffolding putting the final coat of paint over the whole thing. There is a continuous bang, bang, bang! and Vallie has gone to the woods to get away and I have settled myself in a chair in the midst to prove [that] by the aid of an interesting book I can become oblivious to everything. . . ." *Source:* Eleanor Roosevelt Papers, FDRL.

the *Half Moon* as he would have: "I think they will sail rather seldom together as James goes round and round the cockpit and won't sit still and Anna kicks him whenever she can." Things weren't much better on land: "Brother is bawling because he is alone with Anna and I have told Nelly [his nurse] he must learn to stay alone," she reported to Franklin, and again, the next day, "Brother howls all the time that he is left alone, and I fear the neighbors will soon object to my discipline." Nearly everything about the children still seemed beyond her control: "Anna is upset today, so I am told, though I haven't seen her long enough to judge for myself. Mama and Nelly think so however, so she has gone to bed and had a dose of castor oil!"

Franklin wrote to say that overwork would keep him from coming up as soon as he had hoped. Eleanor was disappointed—"George Milburn is no use at all, & I think it is a shame you have to do so much of his work—" and perhaps unsure that his excuses were entirely truthful: "I can hardly wait for next Saturday and I hope you are looking forward to it more than to any of the past weekends."

The new baby's health was a more serious source of worry. "Baby Franklin is exquisite but always looks delicate," Sara noted in August, "tho' nothing seems really wrong. I hope the darling will grow stronger. . . . He is *so* pretty and sweet." A new nurse was called in; she agreed that the baby looked "delicate," and noted that he had begun to breathe rapidly.

When the summer ended it was decided to leave the baby at Springwood with Sara. Perhaps Dr. Holt suggested that the crisp country air would somehow help. Franklin and Eleanor took turns coming up by train several times a week.

"The baby seems to have a very bad cold tonight and we have sent for Dr. Gribbon," Eleanor wrote Franklin from Hyde Park in early October." The new nurse arrived at 2 and she won't do. . . . She wishes to be called *Miss* and she won't eat off kitchen china. . . . I wonder what you did last night and are doing tonight, do be sure to write. . . ."

An especially loving nurse named Marie Lund was finally hired, but the baby did not improve. By early October, he was eating irregularly, steadily losing weight. On the 22nd, a local doctor thought he detected a heart murmur; the baby's breathing began to quicken even further.

On Friday, October 29, "Baby cried often in the morning," Sara noted, but by noon he was "sleeping sweetly in his pram" and she thought it would be safe to drive up the road to lunch at a friend's home. "At 2, Annie the housemaid telephoned me to come as Baby was ill. I *flew* home . . . Dr. Gribbon was here, holding precious Baby. He just got here in time as the little heart had almost stopped. . . . I telephoned Eleanor. She and Franklin came at 8:30 bringing Miss Spring [and the two younger children]."

The next morning, Franklin and Eleanor bundled up the baby and carried him to New York, Dr. Gribbon in constant attendance aboard the train. The nurse was left behind with Anna and James. "Poor Marie Lund is left here and is heart broken," Sara wrote. "No one can help her. She is alone in her room."

A Manhattan specialist confirmed that Franklin Jr. had endocarditis—inflammation of the thin membrane that lines the heart.

"Some hope is held out," Sara noted that evening. "Darling Eleanor is brave, and Franklin helps and supports her hopeful spirit." Sara tried to support it, too. The baby "must and will get well," she told Eleanor. She entertained the children by sending them to see the chickens on the tenant's farm and assured Eleanor that they were fine, "laughing and playing." She had been "reading up 'endocarditis' in Flint's book," she added. "He says the outlook is hopeful. Of course, sometimes it leaves delicacies or produces bad after-effects, but no doubt with a baby the after-effects are more likely to be outgrown. I keep seeing that lovely little *patient* expression & I realize what it all means to *you*, dear. It certainly seems incomprehensible. . . ."

Sara's confidence could not alter the facts; neither could Franklin's.

On the 31st, he telephoned his mother. "I went to town," she remembered, "though just as I left F. said 'don't come down.' I simply had to go. When I got there, E. said, 'Oh, I am so glad you came.' Drs. Carr and Irving, nurses Spring and Battin there. I cd. hear every cry all night from my room where I lay, useless."

Nov. 1st. At a little before 5 I went in. Dr. Carr said "He is holding his own." At a little before 7 A.M., Franklin telephoned me to my room, "Better come, Mama, Baby is sinking." I went in. The little angel ceased breathing at 7:25. Miss Spring was asleep in her room, but Dr. Carr and Miss Battin did what they could. Franklin and Eleanor are most wonderful, but poor Eleanor's mother's heart is well nigh broken. She so hoped and cannot believe her baby is gone from her. He was 7 months and 9 days old, a beautiful flower he always seemed, and yet the delicacy was there and he could not overcome it.

Nov. 2nd. I sat often beside my little grandson. It is hard to give him up and my heart aches for Eleanor.

Nov. 3rd. . . . We brought the little lamb home to our Churchyard. Rosy was there. He and Plog had the little grave ready. . . . Again last night I sat 5 hours beside the little angel and wondered why he had to go. . . .

Nov. 5. . . . Eleanor is perfectly marvelous the way she bears it.

Eleanor was haggard but stoical, accepting the condolences of friends and relatives with calm dignity. But privately she blamed herself. It seemed "cruel," she said, "to leave him out there alone in the cold."

The death of her baby was further vivid proof to her that she was unfit for motherhood. Eleanor had been unable to breast-feed him; one of the doctors had even suggested that the baby might have lived had he not been bottle-fed.

Worse still, she had not been at her baby's side when he was fatally stricken; she had entrusted him instead to her mother-in-law, and that fact, though perhaps never mentioned between them, must also have contributed to the bitterness she later felt toward Sara.

"I reproached myself very bitterly for having done so little about the care of this baby," Eleanor wrote later. "I felt he had been left too much to the nurse and I knew too little about him, and that in some way I must be to blame. I even felt that I had not cared enough about him."[14]

Franklin was saddened, too, but quickly recovered, something for which his anguished wife found it hard not to blame him; it made her "bitter" against him for a time, she said much later, and she may in fact never have entirely forgiven him. "I think that a baby as young as that never means as much to a man," she once told an interviewer who asked her about her husband's reaction to the baby's death, "and I think he felt badly, but Franklin was always—always had so much to do that he—he accepted practically anything that happened and just went on from there. . . . I never saw him let down. . . . It was like closing a door."

The death of his son may have had a greater impact on Franklin than Eleanor would later allow herself to remember, for some time early in 1910 he joined the board of the New York Milk Committee. Infant mortality in the crowded city was appalling—more than one

14. Her feeling that she must somehow be at fault may also have been in part an unconscious echo of the helpless guilt she had experienced at eight when her youngest brother Elliott fell fatally ill and she had been unable to do anything either to improve his condition or to console the sorrowing father she adored.

thousand babies under a year old died in Manhattan alone the summer Franklin Jr. fell ill, nearly half of them bottle-fed as he had been—and much of the trouble was traced to milk that was either adulterated or unpasteurized, or that had been drunk from bottles prepared by mothers who did not understand the importance of sterilization. The committee had been established ten years earlier "to improve the milk supply of New York City and to educate the public to the proper use of milk for infant feeding," and from its headquarters on East 22nd Street it now ran a chain of storefront milk stations in the poorest parts of the city. Known as the "houses with the blue front" because of the distinctive paint used to edge their white-curtained windows, they offered pure milk and free medical advice to mothers otherwise unable to afford either; signs in English, Italian, and Hebrew welcomed newcomers.

Franklin's public identification with this cause may have been the direct outgrowth of a tragedy that had affected him personally, but it also marked the first faint stirring of a social conscience that had lain largely dormant since his days as a member of the Groton Missionary Society. He had come at least a little distance from the young man who had so recently made fun of his wife's solicitude for the ailing children of East Side immigrants.

Within a month of her baby's burial, Eleanor was pregnant again.

It was a grim winter, a difficult year. Eleanor was unwell and grieving, did not respond either to her husband's attempts to cheer her up or her mother-in-law's daily visits. They all tried hard to be brave at Christmas. Eleanor even decorated a tree—"so lovely of her when she misses Baby so," Sara noted—but nothing seemed to help.

Franklin began to spend still more time away from home. Perhaps trying to explain his increasing absence to herself, his mother decided that he was "as usual interested in law work."[15]

In fact. however, it was not law but politics that now held him. The year 1910 promised to be a good one for young, reform-minded New York Democrats. The Republicans were deeply split between progres-

15. Years later, the youngest son of Eleanor's great friend Isabella Ferguson asked his mother why she thought Franklin had gone into politics. Isabella answered that while she could not say for certain, she had always thought part of the answer lay in his desire "to escape the complications of his private life." Certainly that desire must have provided added impetus. *Source:* Interview with John S. Greenway.

sives and conservatives; in the 1909 assembly elections, several progressive Democrats had triumphed in traditionally Republican upstate counties. Encouraged by their success, one of the state's most magnetic reformers, former Mayor Thomas Mott Osborne of Auburn, announced the formation of the Democratic League of the State of New York, pledged to provide the voters with progressive candidates opposed to Tammany Hall. Among the upstate Democratic leaders who rallied to him were two of the most powerful party officials in Dutchess County, Mayor John K. Sague of Poughkeepsie, and Judge John E. Mack, the county's district attorney.

Some time early that year, Mack dropped by to see Franklin at Carter, Ledyard & Milburn, ostensibly delivering some papers for Sara to sign as a favor for the Roosevelt family lawyer, John Hackett. (Mack had begun his career in Hackett's office.) His power rested on the safely Democratic Irish and Italian wards of Poughkeepsie. Some years earlier, he had won the permanent affection of a good many of his constituents by letting public drunks go free, provided they signed a petition requesting him to lock them up for six months should they get into trouble again. But he was also shrewd enough to have worked hard to appeal to Protestant and Republican farmers as well, earning the gratitude of some of them by making chicken stealing burglary in the third degree rather than mere petty larceny.

The Democrats faced a serious problem in the fall election, Mack told Franklin. Democratic Assemblyman Lewis Stuyvesant Chanler of Barrytown seemed unhappy with his post. An Astor and therefore Franklin's distant cousin by marriage, Chanler had been elected lieutenant governor of New York in 1906. Because he had carried the state for the Democrats while his running mate, the publisher William Randolph Hearst, had not, he had briefly been a dark horse candidate for President in 1908, then had won the gubernatorial nomination only to lose the election to Charles Evans Hughes. After all that excitement, he was said to have grown bored with a mere assembly seat.

If Chanler did, in fact, decide not to run for reelection in November, might Franklin possibly be interested in running? If so, victory was reasonably sure; the assembly district, centered in Poughkeepsie, was heavily Democratic, and Mayor Sague would provide all the help he could.

No one now knows for certain whose idea this offer was, but its author may well have been Thomas Mott Osborne himself. He had first met Franklin in the spring of 1904, aboard the *Prinzessin Victoria*

Luisa on which the young Harvard senior and his mother had cruised the Caribbean. They quickly discovered that they were both members of Alpha Delta Phi, Harvard's "Fly Club," and the older man had been immediately attracted to the handsome, gregarious young Democrat with the right sentiments and the famous Republican name.

Whatever the source of the invitation, Franklin could hardly credit his luck. Nothing would please him more, he told the judge; just tell him what to do, where to go, whom to seek out. Mack suggested that he spend some time on weekends in Poughkeepsie, getting to know the local Democrats.[16]

But before Franklin could throw himself wholeheartedly into politicking, there were family hurdles to overcome.

Eleanor, pregnant and still mourning the loss of her second son, raised no real objection. "I listened to all Franklin's plans with a great deal of interest," she recalled. "It never occurred to me that I had any part to play. I felt I must acquiesce in whatever he might decide to do and be willing to go to Albany . . . I was having a baby, and for a time at least that was my only mission in life."

Sara, however, to whom politics, especially *Democratic* politics, still seemed distasteful and undignified, presented a genuine obstacle; without her personal—and financial—support, he could not afford to run. She was not pleased at first; the sort of broad human contact which a political life demanded was precisely what she and Mr. James had sought to shield Franklin from all his life.

But, as so often happened when her son made up his mind, Sara eventually gave in. She could see that politics was what Franklin really wanted; he was clearly restive as a lawyer; and there was no hint as yet in any case that he planned to make a full-time career of public life. In the end, she was less opposed to his plans than were some other members of the family, or so she remembered. "I was one of the few sympathizers Franklin had among his own people," she told a friend.

16. In November 1932, FDR received a letter from an attorney named Edwin De T. Bechtel, who had joined the firm as a clerk the year after Franklin did and had stayed on to become a partner. He, too, had been in the room when Franklin and Judge Mack had first discussed a run for the Assembly.

Roosevelt was now governor of New York, precisely as he had predicted, and was less than a week away from being elected President. "It thrills me," Bechtel wrote, "to realize that your decision in 1910 as you sat at your old roll-top desk at 54 Wall Street and the political principles which you chose then and have always followed should have led to such a very marvelous goal."

Enclosed with the letter were photostats of two pages from a ledger Franklin had kept as managing clerk, sent along "as a reminder of old times." *Source:* Legal Papers, Roosevelt Family Papers, Business and Personal, FDRL.

forty-one and considered the young Roosevelt "a boy," but he knew enough about the realities of power on the great estates to show the expected deference.

"How do you do, Mr. Roosevelt," Leonard answered, taking Franklin's hand.

"No, call me Franklin," Roosevelt said, "and I'm going to call you Tom."

For the first time in his life, Franklin was asking a resident of the village which existed primarily to serve the likes of his family to address him as an equal.

He explained that he was eager to get into politics and that the Dutchess County chairman, Edward E. Perkins, had told him that Leonard was the man to see in Hyde Park if he wanted to get ahead.

The middle-aged house painter told the young patrician that a good way to start would be to come to the committee convention at the Hyde Park town hall the following Wednesday night and introduce himself.

"I'll be there, Tom," Franklin said. "I'll come up from New York."[17]

Leonard was initially impressed. Chairman Perkins never really was; he was an unsentimental banker, a steadfast upstate ally of Tammany Hall, willing officially to back the Poughkeepsie leader's candidate—provided he could be counted on to pay his own campaign bills—but distrustful of Roosevelts in general and of Franklin in particular, finding him overconfident, foppish, probably unreliable. Franklin did little to alter that opinion. Perkins called him at Springwood one summer morning and asked him to come into town as soon as he could to meet some important Democrats. Eager to make a good impression, Franklin, who had been out riding, did not take the time to change, arriving at Perkins's bank office in boots and jodhpurs. The chairman looked him up and down with little enthusiasm. "You'll have to take off those yellow shoes," he said finally, "and put on some regular pants."

Franklin spent as many weekends as he could that summer meeting people in Dutchess County—hiring a man with a trap to meet him at

---

17. Thirty-four years later, on Election Day 1944 at the Hyde Park town hall, it was Tom Leonard who helped FDR into the voting booth for the last time. The President had trouble closing the curtain and was overheard by at least one reporter to mutter to his old ally, "Tom, the Goddamned thing won't work." Reported in *Time*, this produced an avalanche of mail, most of it from clergymen, objecting to the President's blasphemous language. FDR thought it best to claim he'd been misquoted. *Source:* Presidential Press Conference, November 21, 1944.

the Hyde Park depot every Friday evening after work—and he managed just two brief stays at Campobello. Eleanor begged him to come up more often, to stay longer. Pregnant and still dressed in mourning, she felt more isolated than usual; Hall, too, was away, visiting Yellowstone and Yosemite National Parks with schoolmates. "I miss you dreadfully," she told Franklin in July, "and feel very lonely but please don't think it is because I am alone. Having other people wouldn't do any good, for I just want you." And again a few weeks later: "If you don't get off Friday, I shall weep! I want you so much and I miss you so far more than I can say. . . ."

But even when he was on the island she found him distracted by his own plans. Years later, writing of herself in the third person, she said she remembered well a young wife, "who wept many tears because after an absence of some weeks, her husband on his return talked to her more about his business than about his love for her with the result that she thought the romance and glamor of marriage were gone forever."

At about this time, Eleanor began each night to tie three-year-old Anna's hands above her head to the top of her crib with silk cord. Many years later, Anna asked her mother why that had been done. "Her answer was simply that I masturbated and this was the prescribed cure. . . . [She spoke] in a tone which precluded any further questions. The indication was clearly that I had had a bad habit which had to be cured and about which one didn't talk."[18]

Franklin was twenty-eight years old in 1910, still slim and exuberant and to all outward appearances little different from the Harvard sophomore he had been a decade earlier—"White skin and fair hair," Eleanor recalled, "deep-set blue eyes and clear-cut features. No lines as yet in his face. . . ."—and as eager as ever to be at the center of things. A friend remembered him leading a troupe of picnickers to a favorite spot and leaping across a stream too broad for anyone else to follow, "like some amazing stag."

He undertook two long sailing and fishing trips, leaving Eleanor

18. Dr. Holt probably provided the justification for this practice; he did not spell out in his manual precisely how this "most injurious of all . . . bad habits . . . should be broken up just as early as possible," but he did warn that "Medical advice should at once be sought," and it seems likely that Eleanor consulted him and was told just what she must do. Later, the silken cords were replaced by "bells," Anna remembered; "aluminum-type contraptions which covered my hands and had air holes in them. These were 'heaven' to me because I made up marvelous stories: the holes were windows in castles; people lived behind those windows and had wonderful adventures." *Sources:* L. Emmett Holt, *The Care and Feeding of Children,* pages 193–194; Anna Roosevelt Halsted's memorandum to herself, quoted in Bernard Asbell, ed., *Mother and Daughter: The Letters of Eleanor and Anna Roosevelt,* page 20.

alone again with his mother, and spent a good deal of time organizing the annual Campobello field day. A "grand horse race" was announced, and when the appointed hour came and there seemed to be no entrants, he quietly unhitched a pair of horses from an unguarded carriage and challenged another summer resident to a bareback contest. Franklin galloped home the laughing, easy winner.

At the end of August, Eleanor and Miss Spring returned to New York, Eleanor recalled many years later, to "sit" and await a new baby. "The other two children returned to Hyde Park with my Mother-in-law. She was in and out of New York and so was my husband, who was making his campaign for State Senator."[19]

On September 23, 1910, the Roosevelt's fourth child was born. Eleanor insisted that the boy be named Elliott, in memory of her beloved father. From the first, the new baby suffered from what Eleanor herself called "a rather unhappy disposition." Having blamed herself for the death of one child, she now lacerated herself for her new baby's troubles. "I think . . . I was partly to blame," she wrote much later, "for certainly no one could have behaved more foolishly than I did practically up to the time of Elliott's arrival, and I should have known better."

"I was so glad to hear about the new nephew," Hall wrote to Eleanor. "Anna and James will have a new object in life. . . . Franklin won't be able to be so extravagant with his political campaign, now that there is a new addition to support."

That campaign had very nearly not begun at all. Some time that summer, Franklin had taken Lewis Chanler to lunch in New York. His motives for the invitation are not clear. Some remembered being told that he had meant to encourage the assemblyman to think of running for the U.S. Senate; perhaps he simply wanted to gather campaign tips from the man whom he expected to give up on his behalf the assembly seat he was so eager to fill. Chanler had always been his "ideal of a public man," Franklin said, but his admiration now underwent a grave strain, for his hero had changed his mind. Running for the Senate was far too chancy, he said; he had no intention of abandoning the Assembly for Franklin or for anyone else. Life might be a little tame there,

---

19. Again, her memory of the misery she felt altered the facts. While Sara and the children did go to Springwood, Franklin spent most of September with Eleanor in New York, attending to his law practice during the week and confining his visits to Poughkeepsie politicians to the weekends.

but it was far livelier than it would be without any office at all. Franklin left the table pale and angry.

He went to Mack and Perkins, and threatened to run as an Independent rather than abandon the field; he had already gone too far willingly to turn back. They suggested he might now think of running for the State Senate instead of the Assembly. Mack warned him his chances were no better than one in five; no Democrat had been elected from the 26th District since 1856—except for Mr. James's friend and neighbor, Thomas Jefferson Newbold, who had slipped through in a freakish three-cornered race in 1884. If Franklin was willing to try, Mack thought he could have the nomination without any trouble. "At that time it was made by a committee of three, of which I was one," the judge recalled. "I was sure of another and quite sure of the third."

"I'll take it," Franklin said.[20]

The committee duly nominated him. Their choice needed to be ratified formally at the annual session of the Dutchess County Committee in Poughkeepsie on October 6. Mack volunteered to make the nominating speech and, many years later, he remembered the gist of what he had said: "In the European countries, from their early youth, men were trained for diplomatic or other posts. . . . That was not true in this country, but the young man whom I am now asking you to endorse has had training in civic matters from his youth. . . . In addition to that, he has travelled all over most of the world, especially in Europe, and that he spoke at least two languages beside our own. . . . French and Italian, and that he was now ready to carry on the heritage of his birth and be our candidate. . . ."

There was an awkwardly long silence before a member of the committee, John J. Meara, seconded the nomination, but no one actually objected. Franklin was the nominee.

His acceptance speech was long on vigor, short on specifics.

"I thank you heartily for the honor you have done me. . . . But even

---

20. There is a familiar tale that a delegation of local politicians called upon him in 1910 to offer the Senate nomination, only to have him say, "I'd like to talk to my mother about it first." "Frank," one of the professionals is supposed to have answered, "there are men in Poughkeepsie waiting for an answer. They won't like to hear you had to ask your mother," whereupon Franklin gulped and said, "I'll do it." It's a good story but almost certainly apocryphal: there is no contemporary evidence that any such delegation ever waited upon him, and it seems inconceivable that even a youthful Franklin Roosevelt would ever have even inadvertently implied that he was not his own master. *Sources:* Variations of this tale appear in many books, including Allen Churchill, *The Roosevelts,* page 209; Henry Noble MacCracken, *Blithe Dutchess!,* page 79; Ted Morgan, *FDR: A Biography,* page 112.

more do I thank you for giving me an opportunity to advance the cause of good government under the banner of the Democratic Party.

"As you know," he continued, "I accept this nomination with absolute independence. I am pledged to no man; I am influenced by no special interests, and so I shall remain. In the coming campaign, I need not tell you that I do not intend to sit still. We are going to have a very strenuous month. . . ."

There was polite applause. "Well, the *name* sounds pretty good," one committeeman muttered to another.

No one thought Franklin would win. "The Democrats have made their nominations and put their ticket in the field . . . ," said the Republican Poughkeepsie *Eagle*.

> They have made a new and valuable discovery, Franklyn D. Roosevelt, younger son of the late James Roosevelt. This is one of the exceptional branches of the Roosevelt family that is Democratic in politics. Young Mr. Roosevelt is a graduate of Harvard and this is his first jump into politics. Presumably his contribution to the campaign funds goes well above four figures—hence the value of his discovery, which we doubt not was made by that astute politician, Mr. Perkins. [Incumbent Republican Senator John F.] Schlosser, we imagine, will not be greatly disturbed by Mr. Roosevelt's candidacy.

Sara put the best face she could on his news: "Franklin recd. *nomination* for State Senate. . . . Franklin will be here [at Hyde Park] now a great deal."[21]

Franklin would sleep at Springwood often during the coming weeks, to Sara's delight, but his days were spent on the campaign trail—long, strenuous days, just as he had promised the men who had nominated him.

The battle began at an open-air rally in Bank Square at the center of Fishkill Landing, the home of Senator Schlosser, the idea being to cause the largest possible stir in the heart of the incumbent's territory. Young Ferdinand Hoyt, the local Democratic candidate for the Assembly who was, like Franklin, a fledgling New York lawyer, was to join him on the platform. The two youthful candidates nervously went over one another's speeches at dinner at Hoyt's home that evening, then faced their first large crowd. Morgan Hoyt, the assembly nomi-

---

21. She may have been slow to warm to the notion of a political career for her son, but once he was committed to the race she had no doubt of the outcome; within two weeks of his nomination she was referring to the surrounding countryside as "his district." *Source:* Sara Delano Roosevelt Journal, FDRL.

nee's older brother and chairman of the Fishkill Democratic Committee, introduced Franklin.[22]

The speeches went well enough, the elder Hoyt remembered, and when they got together again after the meeting, "the boys fairly hugged one another, with exchanges of 'You were great, Frank,' and 'You were swell, Ferd.' "

The two candidates made an important tactical decision that same evening. They would follow a precedent established by Lewis Chanler in earlier elections and campaign throughout the district by automobile.

Franklin hired an open two-cylinder Maxwell touring car, painted bright red, from Harry Hawkey, an itinerant Poughkeepsie piano tuner with a grandiose mustache and a gazeteer's knowledge of the district's back roads gleaned from years of calling on customers. Hawkey had his automobile tricked out with flags and bunting and served as Franklin's chauffeur and aide for the duration of the campaign at twenty dollars a day. Ferdinand Hoyt rode with him; so did Richard E. Connell, the editor of the Poughkeepsie News-Press, who was the nominee for Congress. Connell, who had been running unsuccessfully for so long in this heavily Republican region that he had begun deliberately to befriend schoolchildren in the hopes that when they grew up they might remember and vote for him, was an old-fashioned stump speaker; he ended his standard speech waving a flag and shouting that he stood for "The same old flag that waved at Lexington, the same old flag Sherman carried on his march to the sea. . . ." Franklin greatly enjoyed his company and his spread-eagle style, but he borrowed from him for his own use only a single phrase, the familiar opening, "My friends . . ."

For five exhausting weeks, Franklin, Connell, and Hoyt spent all day nearly every day on the roads of Dutchess, Putnam, and Columbia counties, racing along at 22 miles an hour, flags snapping in the autumn air. When a carriage or a hay wagon appeared ahead of them, they pulled over and shut off the engine—frightened horses might alienate their owners on Election Day.

One morning, rounding a blind corner near Silver Lake, the Max-

22. Hoyt went on to introduce FDR seven more times during his political career—once again for senator, twice for governor, and four times for President—each time in the place where his first campaign began. At the opening of his fourth campaign for the presidency in 1944, the President began by saying that "Morg Hoyt has been introducing me on this same spot for the last 100 years." Source: Morgan H. Hoyt, "Roosevelt Enters Politics," The Franklin D. Roosevelt Collector.

well ran over a puppy. Franklin ordered Hawkey to stop, hunted up the owner, apologized profusely, and paid him five dollars. The farmer, who had lost three puppies on the same corner without ever having a driver stop before, expressed his astonished gratitude and—according to FDR many years later—persuaded fifteen of his fellow Republicans to vote for the conscientious Democrat.

Young Jefferson Newbold, Franklin's next-door neighbor, went along for the ride the first few days; he had heard colorful tales of his father's brief political career and he was languidly amused by the crowds of farmers and townspeople whose favor Franklin seemed so eager to win. It was all quite exciting at first, but then he grew bored by the sameness of the speeches—there were sometimes ten a day—and weary of the rigors of road travel. The Maxwell had neither roof nor windshield, so that on dry days, dust enveloped the passengers whenever the car rolled to a stop, and when it rained—and it rained often that autumn—the passengers slid on rubber rainshirts over their dusters and hunkered down until Hawkey could find shelter in a barn or beneath an especially big tree.

Franklin hardly noticed; he was having a grand time meeting new sorts of people. One was Thomas M. Lynch, the admiring son of a Poughkeepsie florist whom he took to addressing as "my wild Irish rose." Lynch bought two bottles of champagne and put them in his cellar, pledging not to open them until his new friend was nominated for President.[23]

Nothing seemed to lessen Franklin's enthusiasm for campaigning, not even the foul ball that accidentally arched into the car and bloodied Connell's nose one afternoon as the Maxwell passed through the village of Wiccopee. In fact, Franklin's impetuousness nearly knocked him out of the race. On October 10, running to climb aboard a moving Poughkeepsie streetcar, he slipped and fell, badly bruising an elbow and cutting his knee; had he not been wearing a brown felt hat that helped cushion the blow to his head, he might have been far more seriously injured.[24] A doctor had to be called, and Eleanor and Sara took turns soaking his wounds in disinfectant.

23. Twenty-two years later, after FDR accepted that nomination, Lynch broke out the bottles in his friend's Chicago hotel room. "We had a little ceremony," Eleanor recalled, "and each person [who had worked so hard for him] had about a thimbleful." *Source:* Interview with Eleanor Roosevelt, Robert Graff Papers, FDRL.

24. Thereafter, he would always campaign with a hat, partly out of superstition, partly because he liked to have something with which to wave.

He was back campaigning the next morning, though he limped and his arm was badly swollen, and it was Eleanor's twenty-sixth birthday. He managed to call her from the road the next evening. She wrote him two days later:

Dearest Honey,

I was so glad to hear your voice last night & I do hope you really feel better. Your lovely lilies are still fresh & you know I love them better than anything. I also love the cups which came on approval & which will go so well with the plates you got me last spring I think.

Ever so many thanks, dear, & I only wish you could have been here. . . .

Devotedly,
Eleanor

Franklin spoke from the porches of general stores, atop hay wagons in the fields, in dairy barns and at milk stations, sometimes standing on the back seat of the Maxwell itself; he talked "any place," one of his companions remembered, "where a group of farmers could be brought together. I think I worked harder with him than I ever have in my life."

He was not yet a polished or especially persuasive orator; his speeches were filled with high-flown allusions, transparent flattery of his audience, and tributes to his own integrity. His notes for a rally at Pleasant Valley, a small town not far from Poughkeepsie, have survived, scribbled out in pencil on hotel stationery:

Humboldt the great traveller once said: "You can tell the character of the people in a house by looking at the outside." This is even more true of a community—and I think I can truthfully say that of all the villages of Dutchess County, and I have been in pretty nearly every one, there are very few that appear as favorably as Pleasant Valley. This Library Building, the splendid trees, and the generally neat and prosperous appearance of the community as a whole all point out that the people inside are made of the right stuff.

You look here as if you stand for progress.

And it is just this standing for something that I want to say a word about.

. . . .

Doughnut [personal shorthand for one of Franklin's favorite political metaphors: unlike a doughnut, he liked to say, government did not work if it had even the smallest flaw at its center].

. . . .

There is just the same difference between the man who stands for something positive and he who stands for something merely negative.

Carlisle calls them constructive man and the stationary man.

And he goes on to prove that the stationary man is more than that—he is a destructive man, and then he goes on and utters his cry:

"Rise, you people of England, rise up and *make* something."

. . . .

This country has progressed since its beginnings more than any other probably in the history of the world. And it is due to one thing more than any other, it is a country where more men than in other countries have made things.

. . . .

Not confined to material side of life—

Take the example set by our Social Service. . . .

The rest of the speech is lost, but pinned to its first page was a newspaper clipping quoting lines attributed to Abraham Lincoln that evidently provided Franklin with his peroration: "I am not bound to win, but I am bound to be true. I am not bound to succeed, but I am bound to live up to what light I have. I must stand with anybody that stands right, and PART with him when he goes wrong."

Some of his listeners thought he overdid things. A friend remembered that after the candidate ended one crossroads rally with a promise that "when I see you again I will be your State Senator," an old bearded farmer in a straw hat muttered to himself in a voice that carried through the gathering, "Like hell you will!" Franklin joined in the laughter before gunning off to the next stop.

He was at his best shaking hands and working a crowd. "A topnotch salesman," Tom Leonard, the house painter, remembered, "because he wouldn't immediately enter into the topic of politics when he met a party . . . he would approach them as a friend and would lead up to that . . . with that smile of his. . . ."[25]

No knot of lounging farmers, no main-street saloon, no front porch crowd was too small for Franklin to overlook. He startled and pleased a gang of Italian railroad workers repairing track near Brewster by leaping from his car and seizing their hands, chatting away in what

25. A quarter of a century later, comparing FDR with his predecessor as President, Senator Huey P. Long of Louisiana said more or less the same thing: "[Herbert] Hoover is a hoot owl. Roosevelt is a scrootch owl. A hoot owl bangs into the roost and knocks the hen clean off and catches her while she's falling. But a scrootch owl slips into the roost and scrootches up to the hen and talks softly to her. And the hen just falls in love with him, and the next thing you know, there's no hen." *Source:* Frederick Lewis Allen, *Since Yesterday,* page 151.

they only gradually realized was his distinctive version of their language.

Sometimes his eagerness got the best of him. Campaigning in the Harlem Valley on the eastern edge of the district late one afternoon, he stopped in front of a small-town hotel, bustled inside, and invited everyone in the bar to have a drink. After all had ordered, and the bartender had begun to fill mugs with beer, Franklin asked him, "What town is this?"

"Sharon, Connecticut," he answered, continuing to pour. Franklin paid up anyway, and told the story on himself for years.[26]

He saw to nearly everything himself, applying to the smallest details of his campaign the same intense attention he had previously reserved for his collections of stamps and books and stuffed birds. He ordered up 2,500 celluloid campaign buttons and 500 placards to be hung in store windows, and he carefully wrote out personal checks to cover advertisements in twenty-four local newspapers, from the Amenia *Times* and Hillsdale *Harbinger* to the Cold Spring *Recorder* and Wappinger *Chronicle*.

In the cold evenings, Franklin and Connell sought to keep warm by jointly bellowing endless choruses of an old song as they banged along the dark, rutted road to still another rally:

> Are we almost there?—Are we almost there?
> Said the dying girl as she neared her home.
> Be them the tall poplars what rears
> Their lofty heights against Heaven's big dome—
> Are we—al—most there—

Women could not then vote, of course, but Hawkey noted that large numbers of them attended Franklin's evening rallies, held in grange halls or small-town theatres; ". . . they came to see as well as hear (as I heard several ladies say) the handsomest candidate that ever asked for votes in their district. He might have stepped out of a magazine cover picturing a typical college man of the day, descended from the best honest-to-goodness American stock."

The Republicans at first sought to defeat the Democrats as they had in the past, by ignoring them. This time it did not work. As the

---

26. As did most of FDR's stories, this one varied with the telling; sometimes he had just finished speaking from the top of a haystack when he discovered where he was; sometimes he was told his location by some of the schoolchildren Connell courted so assiduously.

campaign ground on, Franklin and his colleagues drew larger and larger crowds. Connell's oratory and Franklin's good looks, charm, and energy were only partially responsible.

Cousin Theodore had a lot to do with their good fortune. He had returned from Africa in June pledged to political silence. "There is nothing I can say," he told reporters who then asked him for his views. "There is one thing I want, and that is absolute privacy. I want to close up like a native oyster."

But Theodore Roosevelt could no more remain silent than an oyster could talk. He was alarmed at what he took to be the increasing conservatism of President Taft and by the growing power of the political bosses, Republican and Democratic, in his own state. Insurgent Republicans all over the country implored him to return to public life and defend the progressive policies for which he had once fought so hard. Perhaps most important, he was only fifty-two years old, with nothing much to look forward to, certainly nothing capable of engaging his enormous energy so completely as had the presidency.

In July, he attended the thirtieth reunion of his Harvard class at Cambridge and marched in the academic procession alongside Governor Charles Evans Hughes of New York. Hughes—soon to be elevated to the U.S. Supreme Court—was then locked in a struggle with the New York legislature, where old-line Democrats and Republicans had joined forces to block his bill that would have required direct primaries in elections for state offices, and as the two men walked together across the Yard, the outgoing governor called upon the ex-President publicly to express his hope that the bill would pass. He did so that same evening, and when the bill was defeated anyway, TR allowed friends to nominate him to be the temporary chairman of the New York Republican Convention, to be held at Saratoga late that September.

To defy him, his ancient enemy, Boss William S. Barnes, Jr., put up a candidate of his own for this essentially meaningless post. TR won the power struggle at Saratoga on September 27—four days after Elliott's birth, a little over a week before Franklin's own nomination for the State Senate—and then, declaring that the New York Republicans now faced a choice between becoming "the party of progress or the party of the Bourbon and the reactionary," he swung the gubernatorial nomination for his old friend, Henry L. Stimson, and won passage of a platform in which the direct primary was the central issue. Barnes and the old guard responded by offering only tepid support for their own ticket.

Franklin had followed these developments closely and, initially at least, with some alarm. Cousin Theodore had been glad to bless Franklin's entry into politics back in June; after all, he was then himself safely above the battle. But by midsummer, it had seemed likely that TR would soon stump the state on behalf of Stimson. If he were to campaign in Dutchess County for the Republican slate and say anything even remotely disparaging about his youthful Democratic kinsman, it might end Franklin's political career before it got started. Franklin was worried. He had not dared approach the ex-President again directly, but in mid-August, Bamie Cowles arrived at Campobello with her small son, Sheffield. Franklin discussed the problem with her. Would she ask her brother what his plans were? She wrote him right away. Franklin was "a fine fellow," TR replied, though he still wished he were not a Democrat. In any case, he said, "Franklin ought to go into politics without the least regard as to where I speak or don't speak."[27]

Now, as the campaign continued, the fact that the former President was in the thick of things worked to Franklin's advantage. The Republicans were split and dispirited. Franklin was free to lash out at bosses in both parties, to appear to soar above partisanship, to be seen as fighting alongside his great cousin against privilege, graft, and corruption wherever they were to be found.

Senator Schlosser had voted against the Hughes reforms and was only lukewarm about the Stimson candidacy. Did Franklin support Hughes's policies, a man asked at one stop. "You bet I do," the candidate answered. "I think he's one of the best governors the State has ever had," and he would have been able to pass his reform program if it had not been for the disloyalty of the reactionaries in his own party, men such as Schlosser. "That's what I am glad to hear," shouted his questioner. "I'm going to vote for you."

Franklin gleefully exploited his last name. He professed to be "dee-lighted" by everything—the weather, the reception he received, his prospects on Election Day—precisely as TR almost always was, and at least once after he was introduced he smiled and said, "I'm not Teddy." The crowd laughed. "A little shaver said to me the other day that he knew I wasn't Teddy—I asked him why, and he replied: 'Because you don't show your teeth.'"

TR had provided Franklin with the combative example he needed to get into politics, had helped arm him with many of the political

27. In fact, Theodore Roosevelt did speak in Dutchess County during the campaign, at the County Fair at which Franklin had won two blue ribbons for his horsemanship five years earlier. He charitably made no mention either of Franklin or his Republican opponent.

principles he took with him into the field, had even given his tacit approval to his joining the opposition. Now, he indirectly helped make his untried cousin's unlikely victory possible.

Even Theodore Roosevelt finally was made to serve Franklin Roosevelt's purposes.

"Last week," a grinning Franklin told a Poughkeepsie crowd on the last day of October,

> Mr. Connell and I went on an automobile speaking tour through Dutchess County. . . . It was a success in every way. . . . The effect on the Republicans was, to say the least, amusing. One Republican leader in southern Dutchess was so upset at our success that he sent out the report that our car had been upset in the Pawling mountains and we had all been killed. . . . [I]t acted as a boomerang. The crowds were bigger than ever and people from all the countryside turned out to hear the corpses. But the trip did more. It woke up the Honorable Hamilton Fish [Connell's opponent, the incumbent Republican congressman, and father of the congressman of the same name who would so strenuously oppose FDR before World War II]. He so far forgot himself as to launch forth in an attack on the trip and on me.

The Republicans had bestirred themselves too late. Fish charged that Franklin was a carpetbagger, who pretended to be a Dutchess County farmer but was actually a resident of New York City, and that his automobile tour of the district amounted to an undignified "vaudeville tour for the benefit of the farmers."

The Poughkeepsie *Eagle* now attacked him with new vehemence as false to his famous cousin's ideals: "Franklyn Roosevelt represents just the opposite of what Theodore Roosevelt stands for. The News-Press reports him as managing clerk of the firm of Carter, Ledyard & Milburn of 54 Wall Street, New York City. It is well for the electors of this Senatorial District to bear in mind that this firm are the lawyers for some of the great trusts. . . ." Franklin, who had refrained from personal attacks on his older opponent for fear of seeming too aggressive, now replied in kind. "I had a particularly disagreeable opponent," FDR remembered many years later, "and he called me names . . . and I answered him in kind. And the names that I called him were worse than the names he called me. So we had a joyous campaign." Schlosser, he now said, was the pliable creation of the Dutchess County Republican boss, Lou Payn, a chief lieutenant of Boss Barnes and known to friends and enemies alike as "the Sage of Chatham."[28]

"Whether it is that [Schlosser] has represented the Sage of Chatham by long distance 'phone, or whether it is that he has represented nobody at all except himself I don't know," Franklin said, adopting the familiar, inclusive style of which he would later become the master, but "I do know that he hasn't represented me and I do know that he hasn't represented you." By contrast, Franklin pledged to tour the district twice each year to learn what was on the voters' minds.

He did not often directly address the charge that he was not a bona fide resident of Dutchess County, perhaps because there was a good deal of substance to it.[29] But his supporters indignantly answered that he was so deeply rooted in the district he hoped to serve that fully two thirds of the farmers who came to hear him had known and admired his father, and he himself paid lengthy, loving tribute to his native region at almost every stop:

> In the course of the last two weeks I have been travelling from town to town, from farm house to farm house, in these magnificent counties along our great river, and my heart has grown glad and I have thanked God that it fell to my lot to be born and to have lived as one of the people of this Hudson Valley. For with every new face that I have met it has been impressed upon me that here we have a population that is truly American

28. Even for his time and place, Payn's corruption was ripe. As governor of New York in 1900, TR had taken considerable deadpan pleasure in removing him from his post as state superintendent of insurance because, he said, Payne, "being a frugal man, out of his seven thousand dollars a year salary" had somehow managed to save "enough to enable him to borrow nearly half a million dollars from a trust company, the directors of which are also the directors of an insurance company under his supervision." This was only a momentary setback; accused of voting tombstones in a later case, Payne responded that he invariably cast the votes of the dead as they would themselves have wanted them cast: "we always respect a man's convictions." *Sources:* Kenneth S. Davis, *FDR: The Beckoning of Destiny,* page 241; Nathan Miller, *FDR: An Intimate History,* page 68n.

29. On Election Day, a letter from Franklin did appear in the Hudson *Republican* answering the accusation. It was at least misleading: "I desire it clearly understood that I was born and brought up at Hyde Park . . . that my name has always been and will always be there. I own real estate and personal property in Dutchess, pay taxes on it in Hyde Park and in no other place. I have regularly voted there, and in no other place. It is true that for three years I have practiced law during the winter months, but have severed my connection with the office in which I worked. . . ." All of Franklin's real estate was, in fact, located in New York City and on Campobello Island. His mother owned Springwood; Franklin would not purchase his own first parcel of land at Hyde Park until the following year. Nor had he resigned from Carter, Ledyard & Milburn, and would not do so until January 9, 1911. *Sources:* F. Kennon Moody, *FDR and His Neighbors: A Study of the Relationship Between Franklin D. Roosevelt and the Residents of Dutchess County,* page 318; photostat copies of pages from Carter, Ledyard & Milburn ledger, FDRL.

in the best sense of the word; a people alive, a people desirous of progress and of real representation and honest, efficient government. . . .

At Poughkeepsie, answering the charge that he was waging an unseemly campaign, he borrowed a page from Connell's gaudy book: "I want to ask Mr. Fish a few questions. Does he sneer at our trip . . . because we [carry] and [are] not ashamed to carry on our automobile the American flag? Or was it because we did a thing he never did—went about among the whole section and gave the people a chance to see their candidates, to meet them face to face, and to find out what they stood for . . . ?"

And again and again he assured his listeners that he was not merely running for the novelty of it, as other rich young candidates sometimes had. "If you elect me to represent you I will be a real representative. I will devote my energy and my time to your service alone. I will represent every one of you. I'll be your representative every day of the 365, every hour of the 24. That is my promise. I ask you to give me the chance to fill it. . . ."

Sara and Eleanor went at least twice to hear him speak, at Poughkeepsie on November 6, and at Tivoli, near Oak Terrace, the home of the Halls, on the 7th, the final day of the campaign. With them came doting aunts and uncles from both sides of his family.

Franklin still "spoke slowly," Eleanor remembered, "and every now and then there would be a long pause, and I would be worried for fear he would never go on. . . . He looked thin then, tall, high-strung, and at times, nervous."

Franklin himself remembered these two appearances as disastrous attempts to match the fervor with which Connell wound up each meeting. He "waxed truly eloquent," he much later told an aide, "was rhetorical and oratorical both—mixed his metaphors and otherwise so amused his relatives they begged of him not do it again." Perhaps the presence of so many assembled Roosevelts and Delanos and Halls had temporarily unnerved him.[30]

30. Many years later, talking to an aide, FDR blamed his poor showing in front of the family on his having forgotten a lesson learned earlier. He had been eighteen or so, spending the summer at Campobello, he said, when the guests at one of the two Campobello hotels objected to a new golf course, laid out and paid for by the summer residents. "As secretary-treasurer, FDR was called upon to explain the plans governing the use of the course to a meeting of the summer colony. He was, of course, without experience as a public speaker. Afterward he was delighted when none other than Mr. Justice Horace Gray of the Supreme Court of the United States congratulated him on the clarity and simplicity of his presentation. . . . The Justice also counseled

He made his final appearance of the campaign on election eve at the little red-brick Hyde Park town hall where Mr. James had often read out the returns to the townspeople on election days. While Sara smiled her approval, he ended by saying, "You have known what my father stood for before me, you have known how close he was to the life of this town, and I do not need to tell you that it is my desire to follow always in his footsteps."

Franklin received the election results at Springwood the next evening. It was all good news. The Democrats swept twenty-six governorships, the state, the district,[31] and Franklin had run ahead of the whole New York ticket.

Sara got into the spirit of the evening, proudly jotting down the returns in her firm, confident hand on a sheet of her stationery, with its heading "Hyde Park on the Hudson":

Franklin carries Poughkeepsie by 927
Hyde Park & two election districts by 139
Carries Hudson by 499
Fishkill 128
Second assembly district of Dutchess 900
1069 Majority[32]

Franklin celebrated by handing out fourteen dollars' worth of good cigars.

---

him to stick to that style of public speaking." The Poughkeepsie failure marked the only time he ignored that advice, or so FDR said. *Source:* William D. Hassett, *Off the Record with FDR, 1942–1945,* page 159.

31. Richard Connell won his seat in Congress at last that evening, only to die of a heart attack ten months after taking the oath of office. Franklin served as the chairman of a committee that built an especially apt memorial to him at Poughkeepsie—the Richard E. Connell Memorial Playground. *Source:* Franklin D. Roosevelt Papers, Papers as State Senator, FDRL.

32. Franklin's actual victory margin was still better; he won by one thousand one hundred forty votes. Sara's sense of priorities was not permanently altered, however; in her journal entry for that day, she gave the latest weights of her grandchildren before noting her son's political triumph.

CHAPTER

4

❧

THE AWFULLY MEAN CUSS

FRANKLIN was no stranger to Albany. His father's duties as vice president of the Delaware & Hudson Line had been fairly light but had nonetheless frequently taken him upriver, to the railroad's head office in the state capital, and as a small boy Franklin had sometimes come along aboard Mr. James's private car. Franklin's father and mother also had a number of Albany friends high in the administration of Governor Grover Cleveland, and all three Roosevelts had been special guests at the inaugural of Theodore Roosevelt as governor in 1899.

When in Albany, Franklin and the senior Roosevelts had most often stayed on Capitol Hill with their friend Mrs. John Van Schaick Lansing Pruyn, at Number 13 Elk Street, on the fashionable block named "Quality Row" for the wealthy old Albany families that lived along it. Huybertie, Mrs. Pruyn's pretty daughter, and one of the few children outside the family with whom Sara permitted Franklin to play, much later recalled that her own family and their neighbors on Elk Street had always "seemed apart to me from other less fortunate people," that the street itself, with its turreted houses and big walled gardens, had seemed a refuge "from the busy hum of men." Ten servants made the Pruyns comfortable, including a coachman in a fur hat who in winter took Huybertie and her friends to skate on the Erie Canal or to dances at the Fort Orange Club in one of several family sleighs. "Everything was on runners," she remembered, "from the station sleighs . . . and delivery sleighs to the finest type of Canadian or Russian turnout. The whole city presented a gay and charming picture. . . ."

That picture had changed by 1910. The city Franklin saw when he emerged from the Renaissance vastness of the new Union Depot on the morning of Sunday, December 31, 1910, was very different: streetcars now clanked along the snowy streets where he had once glided in the Pruyn family sleigh; an imposing new Flemish Gothic headquarters for the old D&H was going up across Union Square, part of the "Beautiful Albany" program intended to rescue the once proud waterfront from the bad times that had befallen it as the river traffic dwindled; the elder Pruyns had died, Huybertie herself had married and moved away, and saloons and rooming houses were beginning to threaten the calm gentility of Capitol Hill.

Despite what he might have heard, a wealthy friend who had spent time in the capital had assured Franklin, there were still "an unusually large number of nice people in Albany, and knowing them will undoubtedly make Eleanor's time there pass more pleasantly. I shall be only too glad to let a few of them know that you are going to be in Albany this winter." In the meantime, he suggested, Franklin should join the Fort Orange and Country clubs right away.

"Jimmy Wadsworth [a young millionaire Republican assemblyman from Geneseo] had an attractive home there," the friend added; the assumption was that Franklin would want one just like it. He first tried to rent a house on Quality Row itself, then settled for a large, comfortable one at 248 Upper State Street, in a quiet cobbled neighborhood several blocks west of the Pruyns' old home. He had had to choose it largely on his own; Eleanor was still too distracted and anxious after the birth of Elliott to play much of a role. (In later years she could not even remember looking at the house before they moved in.)

Their new home seemed "palatial after New York," Franklin noted in the journal he began keeping on New Year's Day, 1911, and he was especially pleased to discover a fist gripping a club carved into the coat of arms above the study fireplace; it seemed nicely reminiscent of his cousin's Big Stick and over the coming months he would enjoy pointing it out to visiting reporters. A full staff of servants was hired to make life as agreeable as possible.

Life in Albany for most legislators was nowhere near so agreeable; few could afford to bring their families to the capital. More characteristic was the experience of Alfred E. Smith when he had arrived six years before. A freshman assemblyman then—he had worked his way up to Speaker by the time Franklin arrived—who had never been more than a few miles from his Lower East Side constituency and had to rely on his $1,500 legislator's salary to support himself, his wife, and five children all year, he had doubled up with another newcomer in a room on the seventh floor of a decaying wooden hotel called Keeler's. An icy wind blew steadily off the frozen river through its riddled walls, and just before dark, Smith noticed that there was no fire escape. As a veteran of a Manhattan hook and ladder company, he knew what could happen if a fire broke out. He and his friend took turns keeping watch all night, then moved the next morning into furnished rooms elsewhere for the rest of the session.

Franklin paid $4,800 a year to rent his Albany house, a figure that did not include the wages he paid the servants but was already more than two and a half times the annual salary paid to his fellow senators. The contrast was not lost on his legislative colleagues.

Al Smith never tired of telling of his first visit to the new Roosevelt home. One evening early in the session, his friend and fellow Tammany man Senator Robert F. Wagner told him he had an appointment to see Franklin; Smith thought he'd go along.

They stood together on the stoop and rang the bell. A butler in formal dress answered the door.

"Senator Wagner and Assemblyman Smith to see Senator Roosevelt," Wagner said.

The butler was polite but clearly unused to unexpected visits by strangers. "I know the Senator is expecting Senator Wagner, but . . ."

He frowned at Smith.

"That's all right," answered the Democratic leader of the Assembly, smiling and gently pushing his way inside behind Wagner, "I'll come along, too."

Francis R. Stoddard, a young contemporary from a wealthy family who would himself soon enter New York State politics, but more conventionally—as a Republican assemblyman rather than a Democratic senator—remembered watching Franklin's early career "because he was a gentleman in politics, and I was interested in how he would get along with people who were decidedly different. . . . If he had been a Republican, he might have met people who were more or less his type, that is, the old American type. . . ."

If Franklin were to succeed in politics, he would have to learn how to function among new American types, to pick his way among new American issues.

The new house which so pleased Franklin initially appalled Eleanor. She found it chaotic and threatening at first, further evidence that her life was not hers to control, and she set about grimly putting things to rights. "I have always had a passion for being completely settled as quickly as possible, wherever I lived," she later explained. "I want all my photographs hung, all my ornaments out, and everything in order within the first twenty-four hours. I think it was my early training which made me painfully tidy. I want everything around me in its place. Dirt or disorder makes me positively uncomfortable!"

The children continued to distress her, too. Elliott remained chronically fretful. She had hired a new English nurse for the older children and a wet nurse for the baby because she could not feed him herself and did not wish to risk the health of another child through bottle feeding. The wet nurse bothered Eleanor's conscience. She "spoke no language known to us," she remembered. "I think she was a Slovak. My sense of duty made me feel a great responsibility about her baby, so I visited the home where the baby was boarded, a very poor but clean tenement, and went through agonies for fear her child would not do so well when I took her up to Albany. She soon became so homesick and worried about her baby I had to let her go, but by that time little Elliott seemed to be pretty strong and well. For several years I kept in touch with her, and had a bank account for her baby."

Just before the move to Albany, the doctor told Eleanor that James had now developed a heart murmur and must not over-exert himself. "He was a fairly tall though thin little boy, and quite a load to carry," she remembered, but, terrified that she might lose another child, she saw that he was carried up and down stairs all winter. (For that reason, Franklin noted that it was a special comfort that the Albany house had "only three stories instead of six.")

The pace of political life soon left Eleanor little time for the introspective brooding that she had been unable to halt since the birth of her first child. "Here in Albany began . . . a dual existence for me," she remembered, "which was to last all the rest of my life. Public service, whether my husband was in or out of office, was to be part of our daily life from now on." She did not yet really enjoy politics, but it "was a wife's duty to be interested in whatever interested her husband, whether it was politics, books, or a particular dish for luncheon. This was the attitude with which I approached the first winter in Albany."

On January 2, Franklin attended the inauguration of the new Democratic governor, John Alden Dix, in the assembly chamber, and was secretly embarrassed when the invocation was nearly drowned out by the jubilant rattle of the Hyde Park fife and drum corps drifting up from Union Station; a large delegation of triumphant Democrats from his district had arrived.[1]

Hurrying down the Capitol steps after the ceremonies and loping toward his new home, Franklin found the street filled with a large happy crowd of constituents. ("Four hundred strong!" Franklin later said; his mother thought there had been two hundred and fifty.) He pushed through them, shaking hands and shouting greetings, then stationed himself in the doorway of the dining room and ushered everyone inside for a buffet lunch. Eleanor and Sara "made a hit with the whole delegation," Franklin noted, moving among the guests, passing trays of sandwiches and boxes of victory cigars. (Sara marvelled later at how "splendidly" her daughter had managed this event, which would have been unimaginable to both of them just a few months earlier.)

Franklin and Eleanor slipped away briefly in mid-afternoon to pay a formal call on the new governor and his wife, then hurried back so that he and Ferdinand Hoyt could lead the beery, laughing crowd to the railroad station for the trip back to Poughkeepsie.

When he got home again, Franklin noted later, the governor was on the telephone asking "us to go up to the Executive Mansion for a little informal dancing. Accordingly E.R. and I hurriedly dressed, drove up and had a very delightful evening. It was almost a family party, only the military aides, two or three Albany girls and ourselves being there."

The next evening, the freshman senator, his wife and mother dined with the governor and Franklin's reformist patron, Thomas Mott Osborne, at the home of William Gorham Rice, Cleveland's former secretary and a close friend of Mr. James.

A new state senator, one Albany newspaperman wrote, was customarily "of an importance somewhere between that of the janitor and

---

1. Years before, on those rare election nights when local Democrats managed to eke out a victory, some of the same musicians who now hailed Franklin's triumph had serenaded his father at Springwood.

a Committee Clerk." Yet even before he made his maiden speech, Franklin Roosevelt already found himself something of a celebrity in Albany.

Sara left for Hyde Park two days later, then wrote a letter to her children, filled with pride and pleasure:

> Dearest Eleanor & Franklin,
>
> It seems like a very strange dream to be here & to think of you dear things all settled in that big Albany house & my boy sitting in the State Senate, a really fine & dignified position, if only lived up to as it should be & I know it *will* be by my dear one. Every man who has the highest conception of the country's good & of the great trust reposing in its government must & will help others to the same high standard of honesty & truth & the welfare of the people. I was *so* interested today & were I to be with you I should be very often in that gallery!

She was not in fact often with them during Franklin's time in Albany. Politics quickly accomplished what Franklin's marriage had not: it placed at least a little distance between her and her son. It was a field in which her wide acquaintanceship counted for less than it might have in law or business. Most of her husband's old friends from the Cleveland era were back numbers now; Albany was an unattractive and uninteresting city compared to New York and Boston; she would not find many of the men with whom Franklin associated especially congenial.[2]

Still, she watched every aspect of his career with fascination. As always, she expected great things of her son.

Franklin had proved himself an attractive, energetic candidate on the back roads of Dutchess and Columbia counties, but no one knew what sort of leader he would be once he left the campaign trail.

Again, Theodore Roosevelt provided him with his model. TR had begun in politics by making his way each evening to the Twenty-First District Republican Association, a dingy club above a saloon on East 59th Street. He always wore a frock coat and top hat. Some of the regulars "sneered" at first, he himself recalled, but "I made them

---

2. Though if they were her son's allies she struggled to find qualities in them to admire, at least in public: many years later, for example, when Al Smith was running for President, one of her friends is said to have asked her in shocked tones whether it wasn't true that Smith had placed spittoons throughout the Governor's Mansion. It was, Sara said without a pause, and the wonderful thing was that the governor never missed. *Source:* James Roosevelt and Sidney Shalett, *Affectionately, FDR*, page 55.

understand that I should come dressed as I chose." And as a freshman member of the Assembly in 1882 he had continued to be both over-dressed and overbearing. An assemblyman named John Walsh never forgot his first sight of him, bustling into the chamber, then pausing dramatically before striding to his seat:

> Suddenly our eyes and those of everybody on the floor, became glued on a young man who was coming in through the door. His hair was parted in the center, and he had sideburns. He wore a single eye-glass, with a gold chain over his ear. He had on a cutaway coat with one button at the top, and the ends of its tails almost reached the tops of his shoes. He carried a gold-headed cane in one hand, a silk top hat in the other, and he walked in the bent-over fashion that was the style of the young men of the day. His trousers were as tight as a tailor could make them, and had a bell-shaped bottom to cover his shoes.
>
> "Who's the dude?" I asked another member, while the same question was being put in a dozen different parts of the hall.
>
> "That's Theodore Roosevelt of New York," he answered.

Only one man still on the floor when the new Senate session opened on January 4, 1911, had been present in the legislature when TR made his vivid debut twenty-eight years before. He was Thomas A. Grady, a red-faced Tammany veteran with a gray walrus mustache who had been deposed as Democratic leader by his fellow Democrats because of his alcoholism just the day before, and now sat slumped behind a heap of roses left on his desk by sympathetic admirers.[3]

When the clerk reached the name "Roosevelt" in the roll call and a soft voice answered "here," Grady gingerly parted the flowers to get a look at the newcomer taking his seat at desk 26 in the last row. Grady's memories of TR were baleful at best, and the advent of an-other Roosevelt did not improve his mood on this traumatic morning. A *New York Times* reporter recalled what Grady saw:

> . . . a young man with the finely chiseled face of a Roman patrician, only with a ruddier glow of health. . . . Nature has left much unfinished

3. Before drink and a set of inferior false teeth undermined his oratory, Grady was one of the most admired speakers in Albany, celebrated for the ardor he brought to Tammany's cause. A former Senate page recalled him at the zenith of his powers:

> He could slay you with a sentence. . . . One day he had made a mistake as to which side he was to argue on, and he argued well for about twenty minutes. He was tugged at the back of his coat, and he slapped the hand of the coat-tugger away. . . . Finally there was a whispered conversation. . . . "Mr. President," [he said] "I have given you every reason I can think of which can be argued in favor of this measure. I will now give you the reasons against it." He argued better on the contrary side and beat the bill.

Source: Interview with Reuben A. Lazarus, Oral History Collection, Columbia University.

in modeling the face of the Roosevelt of greater fame. On the face of this Roosevelt, younger in years and in public service, she has lavished all her refining processes until much of the elementary strength has been lost in the sculpturing.

Senator Roosevelt is less than thirty. He is tall and lithe. With his handsome face and his form of supple strength he could make a fortune on the stage and set the matinee girl's heart throbbing with subtle and happy emotion. But no one would suspect behind that highly polished exterior the quiet force and determination that now are sending cold shivers down the spine of Tammany's striped mascot.

Grady and the other Tammany men were not actually frightened of him, but they were wary; a good many shared the concern of Timothy "Big Tim" Sullivan, the huge boss of the Bowery, who is supposed to have said when he first spotted Franklin's name among the Democratic winners in November: "Well, if we've caught a Roosevelt, we'd better take him down and drop him off the dock. The Roosevelts run true to form. . . ."

They would soon learn how true to form this Roosevelt ran. The term of the incumbent U.S. senator, Republican Chauncey M. Depew, would expire on March 4. Senators were then still elected by a majority of both houses of the legislature. There were 200 legislators in all, 114 of them Democrats. The Republicans were sure to renominate Depew. The Democrats were to caucus on January 16 to choose their challenger; fifty-eight votes constituted a majority, whose decisions were binding on all the men attending.

Franklin had already shaken hands with all the would-be candidates at informal meetings in the cavernous lobby and dimly lit corridors of the old Ten Eyck Hotel, where a good many legislators and lobbyists rented rooms. He had liked best Edward M. Shepard, the conservative but reform-minded Brooklyn attorney for the Pennsylvania Railroad around whom the old-time Cleveland Democrats who had known his father rallied. Shepard was "without question the most competent to fill the position," Franklin noted in his journal, "but the Tammany crowd seems unable to forgive his occasional independence. . . ."

The most likely Tammany candidate was rumored to be a former lieutenant governor and assembly speaker, William F. Sheehan, known in his younger days as "Blue-Eyed Billy," and anathema to old Cleveland men and young progressives alike. He was personally charming but privately corrupt, a millionaire who had made his first fortune while boss of the Buffalo machine that fought the reforms of

Grover Cleveland, first when Cleveland was mayor of the city, then while he was governor. (Cleveland's loathing for Sheehan was so great that in 1882 he had threatened to abandon the governor's race if "that man Sheehan" appeared anywhere on the ticket.) More recently, Sheehan had moved to Manhattan, where he served as the director of a dozen public utility companies and had entered into a law partnership with Judge Alton B. Parker, the Democratic presidential candidate whom TR had swamped in 1904. Progressive Democrats deplored the nexus he seemed to embody between big business and the party bosses. Cleveland conservatives could forgive neither Sheehan's tawdry past nor his attempts to undermine their hero.[4]

Unconcerned about his critics, Sheehan had smoothed the way for his Senate candidacy by contributing heavily to the campaigns of several newly victorious legislators who would now be granted an opportunity to express their gratitude.[5]

"Sheehan looks like [Tammany's] candidate at this stage of the game," Franklin wrote. "May the result prove that I am wrong! There is no question in my mind that the Democratic Party is on trial, and having been given the control of the government chiefly through up-state votes, cannot afford to surrender its control to the organization in New York City."

The results proved him right. Charles F. Murphy was the head of Tammany Hall. The 1910 Democratic sweep had given him more personal power than any Democrat had wielded since the time of the notorious William Marcy Tweed in the late 1860s, but Murphy was a new kind of boss, the antithesis of his noisy, ham-fisted predecessors. A big, taciturn man in spectacles, he had learned his politics by doling out favors while leaning against a lamppost in front of his saloon,

4. Franklin's opposition to Sheehan and the fact that he was Mr. James's son alone were enough to endear him to some old Cleveland allies. Franck Taylor, a Kentuckian who had known Franklin's father, wrote to express his admiration: "though I know nothing of you personally, I fancied you bore the Grover Cleveland stamp. A somewhat varied experience of 25 years . . . has taught me that the men—and the descendants of the men—of the Cleveland cohorts, are the real Americans whom I was brought up to respect and admire. Politics *may* be a game . . . played with marked cards, and I dislike to feel vindictive, but I have never been able to forgive the men, who so bitterly assailed our old Chief in days gone by." *Source:* Franklin D. Roosevelt Papers, Papers as State Senator, FDRL.

5. Franklin had evidently been on the list of candidates whom he hoped would accept his help. Back in October he had written to the would-be state senator, offering to have the Democratic *New York World* sent each day until Election Day at his own expense to all "Republican and doubtful voters . . . in your county or in any of the counties in your senatorial district." No one knows whether Franklin accepted the offer. *Source:* Franklin D. Roosevelt Papers, Papers as State Senator, FDRL.

Charlie's Place, on Second Avenue, but prided himself on his gentlemanly discretion—his first nickname was "Silent Charlie"; later, friends and enemies alike thought it best to defer to him as "Mr. Murphy."[6] Now he conducted his business over lunch each weekday at Delmonico's, seated at a table which rested on four carved tiger's paws in a private dining room the press loved to call "The Scarlet Room of Mystery." His weekends were spent at Good Ground, his Long Island estate, where he bred bulldogs and played golf on a private course.

His genteel air was deceptive. "The Quiet Boss" could be as hard as any of his noisy predecessors. Sheehan was his choice to fill Depew's Senate seat. He had quietly worked out an arrangement with the boss of the hopelessly outnumbered Republicans, William S. Barnes, Jr., of Buffalo, who had promised not to fight the Democrats' nominee harder than appearances required.

Murphy controlled a hefty majority in the Democratic caucus, and he expected all good Democrats to go along. Those who didn't would be sorry.

Like Theodore Roosevelt nearly three decades earlier, Franklin was spoiling for a fight. Like him, too, he seemed bent on making a reputation right away as an uncompromising reformer. That was the sort of behavior expected of a Roosevelt; the sort he expected of himself.

TR had infuriated the regulars of both parties at the outset of his first assembly term by ignoring the tradition that freshmen legislators should defer to their elders, noisily forcing an investigation instead that embarrassed such influential men as Cyrus W. Field, Jay Gould, and Russell Sage.

Franklin had been prepared to bolt the session's very first caucus, "even at the expense of harmony and possibly of my whole future," had it not replaced Senator Grady (whose "habits and . . . character" he told his diary he deplored) with Senator Wagner as president pro tem of the Senate.

Now he seemed almost eager to consider it again.

When word reached him a few days before the second caucus that Sheehan was Murphy's final choice, Franklin went for a long walk to

6. Once, at a Tammany Fourth of July picnic, Murphy was seen not to have joined the braves in singing the Star Spangled Banner. A reporter asked an aide for an explanation. "Perhaps," said the aide, "he didn't want to commit himself." *Source:* Alfred Connable and Edward Silberfarb, *Tigers of Tammany Hall: Nine Men Who Ran New York,* page 237.

think things through. He met William Church Osborn, an influential Putnam County reformer, on the snowy sidewalk and told him that he could not find it within himself to vote for Tammany's man, no matter what the caucus decided. He was not alone; several assemblymen, led by Edmund R. Terry of Kings County, felt the same way, and had already announced their intention of boycotting the caucus.

Franklin resolved to join them.

He was not the instigator of the insurgency that followed, nor even its prime organizer. As the regular Democrats gathered in the Capitol for the caucus at nine o'clock Monday evening, January 16, Franklin was just one of twenty-one insurgents who crowded anxiously into a room at the Ten Eyck and worked up a manifesto to explain their absence. They had stayed away, they said, because of their belief that "the votes of those who represent the people should not be smothered in the caucus; and that the people should know just how their representatives voted, untrammeled by any caucus action; and that any majority . . . should be credited to the representatives in the Legislature and not someone outside the body."

Some favored one candidate, some another; some were genuine independents; others belonged to rival machines and were acting under orders from their bosses, or just didn't like Murphy. But all were agreed on one thing: Under no circumstances would they support Billy Sheehan.

This was the opening salvo in a war that would be waged without a break for two and a half months.

Day after day, the rebels met in the library of Franklin's house on State Street. Again, this was less a sign of his prominence, perhaps, than an acknowledgment that he may have been the only member of the group who had an Albany house of his own in which to meet. Assemblyman Terry called it the insurgents' "harbor of refuge," and Franklin "the shepherd of the flock."

Louis Howe, a veteran Albany stringer for the *New York Herald,* wrote that the insurgents seemed "terribly in earnest . . . [and], led by a 'new senator' without experience in the game, who looks like a boy, they have proved an ability to meet cunning with determination rarely shown by older men. Never in the history of Albany have 21 men threatened such total ruin of machine plans. It is the most humanly interesting political fight of many years." It was also very good copy for Howe and his colleagues.

Franklin was never actually the leader of the insurgency—its decisions were made democratically—but in part at least because of the newspapers' fascination with his name, which made "a big racket, like an alarm clock," according to the *New York Times,* he became its spokesman.

Day after day, the men got together in the library at 10:00 a.m., marched together to the legislature to vote and eat lunch, returned to smoke in the late afternoon, went out again for supper, and came back for the long evening. "There is very little business done at our councils of war," Franklin told a reporter. "We just sit around and swap stories like soldiers at the bivouac fire."

Anna Roosevelt's earliest memories of her father dated from these days. She was then five, she wrote, and "It seemed to me that on too many occasions Father would come home from work and shut himself up . . . with a lot of other men. I was forbidden to interrupt. But curiosity got the better of me and one day I sneaked into the room, *with* Father and his political cohorts. I had sense enough not to utter a sound. . . . But pretty soon I noticed that the air began to smell and was filled, right up to the ceiling, with smoke. It wasn't long before I began to cough, rub my smarting eyes and wish I could get away. Of course, I was discovered." All her life she would associate cigar smoke with politics.

The thick blue smoke seeping up the stairs and into the nursery above finally forced Eleanor to have the smallest children moved to the third floor. But, despite the inconvenience, she found herself more and more deeply interested in the fight her husband was waging and in the men that struggle brought into her house. Assemblyman Terry himself often slipped into the living room to read his own earnest poetry to her while she knitted, and around midnight he helped her pass the beer, cheese, and crackers that, she remembered, were her "gentle hint that the time had come for everyone to eat, drink and go home."

Increasingly absorbed in her husband's struggle, she was learning to enjoy at the same time her relative independence from the mother-in-law upon whom she had once leaned so heavily. "For the first time," she wrote, "I was going to live my own life . . . I wrote my mother-in-law almost every day . . . but I had to stand on my own feet now, and I think I knew that it was good for me. . . . I was beginning to realize that something within me craved to be an individual. What kind of individual was still in the lap of the gods!"

She sometimes sat in the Senate gallery in the afternoons, watching Franklin cast his fruitless vote, before hurrying home to have tea with the children and their nurse.[7] And once she tried having Anna, now five, lunch with her and Franklin, "but after spending a solid hour over the meal on our first attempt, returned her to her nursery. . . . I still lived under the compulsion of my early training," she remembered, "duty was . . . the motivating force of my life, often excluding what might have been joy or pleasure."

Tammany struck back hard at the insurgents. At an early interview in the Ten Eyck, Sheehan had warned Franklin that it would. No one else had been present, but as soon as he got home Franklin wrote down the gist of Sheehan's threat. "He said in substance: 'Having a majority of the Democratic Caucus which according to all precedence should elect me, this action against me is assassination. I will give up my law practice and devote my time to the vindication of my character, and I will go into the counties where these men live and show up their characters—the character in which they have accomplished this thing.' "

In the event, Sheehan's noisy forays into enemy territory were less effective than the more subtle pressure Tammany could exert on the rebels behind the scenes. Patronage was quietly withheld. (Franklin had been made chairman of the Forest, Fish and Game Committee, but his appointee as clerk, his friend Morgan Hoyt of Fishkill, was fired.) Hometown banks threatened to foreclose on rebels' mortgages. One insurgent, who owned a small newspaper, was threatened with withdrawal of state notices.

Eleanor remembered that "my blood boiled" at these stories. "I realized that you might be a slave and not a public servant if your bread and butter could be taken from you. . . ." Franklin's, of course, could not be taken from him, and he somewhat grandly promised to use his personal fortune to help his strapped colleagues stay true to the cause. "Some of us have means," he told a reporter, "and we intend to stand by the men who are voting for principle. . . . They shall not suffer because they are faithful to the people." The Buffalo *Enquirer* was especially impressed by this pledge: "How poor and mean by comparison are the egotistical donations of a Carnegie or the Pharisaical 'philanthropy' of a Rockefeller! A man of wealth like Senator Roosevelt,

---

7. At least one of Franklin's opponents was evidently struck by her quiet charm. Senator Tom Grady, the Tammany veteran whom her husband had helped unseat as Senate president, would write her on St. Patrick's Day: "Be with the insurgents and if needs be with your husband every day in the year but this—today be 'wid us.' " *Source:* Joseph P. Lash, *Eleanor and Franklin*, page 173.

who interposes his financial power to . . . protect public men from all the evils of corrupt coercion, recalls an elder day of patriotism, when rich men were the defense and not the menace of the State."[8]

Tammany attacked Franklin in other ways, too, first spreading rumors that he was anti-Catholic: Sheehan was a Catholic, Shepard a Protestant. "There's nothing the matter with Sheehan," Al Smith told one visitor to his office. "He's all right, except he's an Irishman. That's all they've got against him." The Reverend Patrick Ludden, Catholic bishop of Syracuse, charged that Franklin and his colleagues represented a rebirth of the "old spirit of Knownothingism" that had barred Catholics—and especially Irish Catholics—from getting ahead.

Franklin was stung by the charge. At least three members of his embattled band were themselves Catholics; several were committed to support a Catholic, John D. Kernan, for the Senate, if Sheehan's name were withdrawn. "This is absolutely untrue!" Franklin responded. "We do not ask and we do not care from what stock a man may have sprung or what his religious beliefs may be. All we ask is that he be a fit man for United States Senator."

But he counterattacked clumsily, alleging that Sheehan was the creature of the notorious Wall Street operator, Thomas Fortune Ryan.[9] (The evidence he marshalled to back up this charge was not calculated to reassure Catholic voters about his lack of religious bias; both men, he confided to a newspaperman, had been spotted attending the same ten o'clock mass at St. Patrick's Cathedral—though when pressed by reporters he had to admit that they had not actually *sat* together.)

8. No one knows how much of his wealth really was so interposed. The newspaper owner, for example, was allowed to go under. Any substantial sums would have had to come from Franklin's mother, and neither her nor her son's checkbooks for the period reveal any payments to his threatened colleagues.

9. Ryan was an immensely rich Tammany ally, whose personal fortune—estimated at more than $200 million—was originally built in street railway franchises, the same business in which Sheehan had enriched himself. His interests eventually grew to include the American Tobacco Company, the Equitable Life Assurance Society, and investments in gold, diamonds, copper, and rubber in the Belgian Congo. A partner once pronounced him "the most adroit, suave and noiseless man" in American finance, and his reputation was so tainted and his behind-the-scenes influence peddling thought so ubiquitous that at the 1912 Democratic National Convention, William Jennings Bryan would force through a resolution calling upon the party to repudiate any candidate "who is the representative of or under obligation to J. Pierpont Morgan, Thomas Fortune Ryan, or August Belmont." *Sources:* Stewart H. Holbrook, *The Age of the Moguls;* Matthew Josephson, *The Money Lords;* Walter Lord, *The Good Years: From 1900 to the First World War; Dictionary of American Biography.*

Despite his disavowals, young Franklin did almost surely share in the anti-Catholic, anti-Irish prejudices of his time and class. His father had called the Irish "Paddys" and preferred not to have them working in his house; for conservative Democrats like Mr. James, Irish loyalty to their party had always been something of an embarrassment. During Franklin's boyhood, Irishmen were routinely ridiculed in newspaper and magazines, including nearly every copy of *Punch* that Franklin's parents sent him at Groton. Eleanor Roosevelt, too, had been brought up to believe the Irish corrupt, drunken, and benighted.[10]

Franklin would learn tolerance as he went along, dictated by the realities of power; he would finally prove shrewd enough never to allow his private prejudice to deny him access to any individual who might be useful to him. Later, both he and his wife regularly employed Irish Catholics as close aides.

But there was always, even in Franklin's dealings with Irish party leaders, an air of jaunty patronization. He enjoyed telling Irish stories in a broad and unpersuasive brogue, and began at least one presidential speech with a wolfish grin and the words "Fellow Dimmycrats." The point of the joke was the absurdity of a Roosevelt talking like that, the incongruity of his making such an appeal.[11]

Over the years, FDR and the Irish leaders used one another for the benefit of both—each would have been far less powerful without the other—but their mutual affection never ran very deep.

James Aloysius Farley, so flamboyantly Irish that he signed his letters in green ink, would serve Franklin Roosevelt loyally and well for a dozen years as campaign manager, party chairman, and postmaster general. The popular perception, encouraged by both men and reinforced by countless smiling photographs, was that he and FDR were warm personal friends as well as political allies. Part of Farley's

10. Even describing her fondness for Senator Grady in the first volume of her autobiography, published in 1937, Eleanor wrote that "he was a very charming Irishman, in spite of the fact that he liked his Irish liquor somewhat too well." Her feelings on the subject never entirely changed. "Franklin was always surrounded by Catholics," she told a friend toward the end of her life, ". . . They were determined to *see* that he was always surrounded." *Sources:* Eleanor Roosevelt, *This Is My Story*, page 172; Irine Reiterman Sandifer, *Mrs. Roosevelt As We Knew Her*, page 86.

11. Raymond Moley, a member of the Roosevelt brains trust and an acute observer of politics, especially New York politics, once described the "mixed reasons" the state's "better people" always had for opposing Tammany: "The reasons which they do not express are that Tammany suggests alien ancestry, religious affiliations antagonistic to those of most native Americans, and generally the 'lower' and poorer element. The reasons expressed are the corruption, the misgovernment and the autocracy of the machine. These latter evils are not to be minimized. The former, however, are important and pervasive." *Source:* Raymond Moley, *27 Masters of Politics in a Personal Perspective*, page 34.

job in the early days of their partnership was to persuade his fellow Irish party professionals that in spite of what they might have heard about Roosevelt's youthful anti-Catholicism, they could work with him, just as he did. Farley published the first of two autobiographies in 1938; in it, he reiterated that old refrain, writing of FDR, that "there isn't a snobbish bone in his body."

A decade later, the President having died and after a bitter break with him over Farley's own presidential ambitions in 1940, he published a second book in which he allowed his old resentments to show. The "relationship between Roosevelt and me had been basically political and seldom social," he now said. "Strange as it may seem, the President never took me into the bosom of the family, although everyone agreed I was more responsible than any other single man for his being in the White House. Never was I invited to spend the night in the historic mansion. Only twice did I ever make a cruise on the presidential yacht. Both . . . were political. Never was I invited to join informal White House gatherings. . . . Mrs. Eleanor Roosevelt once said, 'Franklin finds it hard to relax with people who aren't his social equals.' I took this remark to explain my being out of the infield."[12]

Murphy's men also charged that young Roosevelt was not really a Democrat, that he had somehow been sent into their midst to undermine them by TR himself.

"Are you an admirer of your uncle-in-law?" a *New York Times* reporter asked him toward the end of January.

12. Some of FDR's biographers have questioned whether Mrs. Roosevelt could or would ever have said such a thing about her husband, and she herself vehemently denied it to her son, James. Still, whether or not she said it, there was some truth in it. FDR was genial and buoyant with almost everyone, of course, but virtually all of those whose company he sought when not on the job were men and women of his class, many of them distant members of his own large and tangled family.

Then, too, among Franklin's social peers, it was thought bad form to discuss business on social occasions. Politics was merely FDR's business. It was Farley's life; he had little to say about anything else. (Ed Flynn, the Bronx boss, on the other hand, was an Irish operative broad-gauged enough to talk amusingly about other things. "Politics has never been my vocation" he once said, "but it's been an avocation . . . I've had a lot of fun with politics but I've always been in the position where, if anything happened, it wouldn't make a damned bit of difference to me." The President delighted in his company.)

In 1976, sixty-five years after Franklin entered the state Senate, Daniel O'Connell, the veteran boss of Albany County who had worked closely with FDR during his governorship and presidency, and who was then in his ninetieth year, still echoed the sentiments of the young Roosevelt's Irish colleagues of 1911. "I got along all right with Roosevelt," he told Jon Margolis, a reporter for the Chicago *Tribune*. "He was all right, but he was a bigot. He didn't like Tammany. He didn't like poor people. He was a patronizing son of a bitch, he was." *Sources:* James Roosevelt and Sidney Shalett, *Affectionately, FDR*, page 27n.; Transcript of interview with Edward J. Flynn, Columbia Oral History Project, Columbia University; Jon Margolis, " 'The Boss' Who Out-Daleys Daley," Chicago *Tribune*, April 2, 1976.

"Why, who can help but admire him?" Franklin responded, and predicted that Cousin Theodore would make a political comeback: "It is only a question of time before people generally will appreciate what he has done in arousing the public conscience and in driving corruption out of politics."

But as to Sheehan's charge that he was his kinsman's agent, "That's absurd. Why, I haven't seen my distinguished cousin since the first of the year. We've had absolutely no communication on this subject."[13]

This may not have been as sweeping a denial as Franklin's embattled Democratic allies might have hoped for. The first of the year had been just a few weeks earlier, after all. Nor was it strictly accurate; he had received a cheering note of encouragement from TR only a week before the newspaper interview: "Just a line to say that we are all really proud of the way you have handled yourself. Good luck to you!"

On January 30, Franklin's twenty-ninth birthday, Murphy summoned him to a private meeting. Was there any chance he and his allies would change their minds and vote for Sheehan?

There was not, Franklin said. There was nothing personal in their opposition to Sheehan; it was just that their constituents did not want him, and he was "altogether too closely connected with the traction trust in New York City."

According to Franklin, Murphy responded that he was "entirely convinced your opposition is a perfectly honest one. If at any time you change your minds, let me know."

Meanwhile, Sheehan's candidacy was dead. Murphy's support for him had been purely pragmatic. So was his decision now to abandon him; if Sheehan had too many enemies for victory, someone else would have to be found with fewer. But first, Sheehan himself had to be convinced of the hopelessness of his cause so that he could gracefully withdraw. Would Franklin help Murphy do that?

13. From the first, Franklin seems to have known almost by instinct how to intrigue the press while telling reporters no more than he wanted them to know. "Senator Roosevelt . . . was in one of his mysterious moods," a reporter for the *New York World* noted on January 7, after a rumor spread that he and Boss Murphy were to hold a private meeting.

Reporter: "Were you consulted in the arrangement of this conference?"
Franklin: "That would be telling."
Reporter: "Well, why not tell?"
Franklin: "Because I don't want to."

Franklin had been in office precisely one week, but that sort of exchange with the press, combining breezy access with tight control over what was and was not printed as a result, would be repeated countless times through the 998 press conferences he held during his presidency.

He would. Franklin invited Sheehan and his wife to lunch on February 2. It was a stiff occasion, Eleanor remembered: Franklin chatted away in his most determinedly amiable manner, before he and Sheehan retired to the study for a talk that lasted nearly three hours, leaving her and Mrs. Sheehan to talk "about the weather and anything else inconsequential that we could think of, while both of us knew quite well that behind the door . . . a really important fight was going on."

When the Sheehans had left at last, Eleanor asked Franklin, "Did you come to any agreement?"

"Certainly not."

A little later a reporter from the *New York American* called. "Mr. Sheehan is delightful, personally," Franklin told him, "but that is one thing, the senatorship fight is another."

The first alternative to Sheehan proposed by Murphy was his own son-in-law, Dan Cohalan. The insurgents said no.

The deadlock continued.

Among those who had most enthusiastically congratulated Franklin on his election in November was an old friend, Langdon Parker Marvin. Eight years Franklin's senior, Marvin had also attended Groton and Harvard and had served alongside him at Carter, Ledyard & Milburn before becoming a junior partner in the Wall Street firm of Jerome & Rand. "I was much interested in your candidacy," he wrote,

> and, despite my affiliation with the party of your illustrious kinsman, much pleased at your election. You will be quite the boy wonder and certainly the pride of Albany. May this first big step lead on to the heights attained by the aforesaid illustrious kinsman, and the White House again resound with Roosevelt revelry. . . .
>
> PS.   (a)—I want to be Chief Justice.
> (b)—Send me an invitation to the coming-out party in the White House of fair Alice's successor.
> (c)—Lunch with me some time & tell me how you did it.

They had lunched a few weeks later. Franklin met Marvin at the corner of William and Wall and they adjourned to a nearby restaurant. Marvin was weary of his subordinate status at Jerome & Rand; Franklin needed a New York office of his own, he said, "a *pied-a-terre* . . . to do law work when not in Albany." A new partnership seemed the answer. "He said very definitely that he wanted an office *with me,*"

Marvin recalled many years later. "We discussed the question of whether or not we could get any clients, but he was always an optimist, and finally we decided to go ahead and get an office together and see what we could do!"

Another former clerk at Carter, Ledyard & Milburn, Henry S. Hooker, signed on as well. The new firm was to be named Marvin, Hooker & Roosevelt. In early January 1911, all three men resigned their posts. Marvin rented space for them at 52 Wall Street, just next door to the established firm that had given them all their start, and solicited advice from his new partners as to just how they would like the firm's announcement card and letterhead to look.

Then, suddenly, Franklin began to stall. Already deeply embroiled in the Sheehan fight, he apparently became afraid that some of his partners' clients might damage his reputation, and, perhaps more important, he was disturbed as well that he was not going to have the top billing among the partners to which he believed his ambition, his new political prominence, and his celebrated name entitled him.

In late January, Marvin wrote him a frankly exasperated letter:

> Dear Franklin:
> Unless you have some real reason for not joining Harry Hooker & me in our announcement cards I think you had better let us put them out as already planned. You suggested first, you will remember, that you & I send out cards, but later assented to Hooker's joining in. I cannot see how any reflection can fall on you from this. Hooker's client, Battershall (Rev. W.W.'s nephew) is not coming with us—he was connected with Allen Ryan (not Thomas F.)[14]—but since he is not coming, that cannot touch you. And though Hooker has done & probably will do business for Allen Ryan, there is to be no partnership [between Ryan and Hooker], so no reflection—if there could be any—on you. Of course Hooker is not Ryan's only lawyer—merely a youngster to whom R[yan] occasionally gives business. So I am sure you need not be timid on this score.—As for me, I assure you that my clients cannot disgrace you—I only wish I had more to take a chance on. If you have any feeling that your political prominence will suffer through being placed third on the list, you must remember that you are still young in the law and that it will be a source of strength to you to have it known that you have older associates.
> It is a source of strength to all of us to have it known that there are three on the job—people will give business to a combination when they might hesitate to give it to a lone practitioner. If you send out an individ-

14. Allen A. Ryan, Thomas Fortune Ryan's son, also had Tammany ties, and some years later would be forced to resign from the New York Stock Exchange by its Business Conduct Committee after the collapse of a dubious stock deal he had engineered.

ual card, it will be somewhat awkward to explain how any business of yours will be done in New York with you in Albany.

Your name is also, of course, of help to Hooker & me—especially with your present prominence in politics—but that, I am sure, you will not grudge. We shall be assisting you not only with our names, but also in running the office for you.

I hope, therefore, you will leave the card matter as it has already been planned.

As for letterhead, Harry and I suggest that we follow somewhat the form of the Jerome & Rand one at the beginning of this letter. . . .
Langdon P. Marvin
Harry S. Hooker
Franklin D. Roosevelt
Counsellors at Law

52 Wall Street
New York_____, 191__

. . . .

Albert de Roode
William S. Mitchell [these last two were junior partners; de Roode was a Harvard classmate who had served with Franklin on the *Crimson*]

There are a number of initial expenses that we shall have to incur—paper, some books, etc.—also I have had a man today to see about putting green linoleum on the whole office, but find it would cost about $100. Have you any rugs, chairs, book-cases, etc., you could loan—and have you your own desk? The partitioning is going up & will look finely. You & I have a bully room. . . .

To cover initial expenses, salaries (stenographer & office-boy) & rent, it seems best to establish a common fund, in the names of us three, each putting in $500 at the present time. Can you send me a checque for this? Of course an account will be kept and later adjusted. We thought it would be wise to make the deposit in the N.Y. Life Ins. & Trust Co., our landlord.

I am sorry to bother you with all this, but we have to get under way & unless you have some contrary views you can merely leave the whole thing to me. You must, however, get up a list of names to send cards to. If our cards go out together, I'll check up the Harvard Club & Bar Association (only those likely to be interested) and you can limit yourself to the legislature, class and personal friends.

If you would rather go over all this with me personally, wire me tomorrow morning . . . where you expect to spend Sunday.

We are all proud of the young Senator—& congratulate you on the stand you have taken & the fight you are making & leading. You have certainly plunged right into the vortex. Best regards to Mrs. Senator. . . .

Life in the vortex left Franklin little time for law. Despite the hard work of Franklin's partners, the firm never did very well—and, according to Franklin's mother, her son's identification with the struggle against Sheehan actually lost the firm one of its first clients.

"*We want more business*—and *big business,*" Marvin exhorted Franklin in 1912. "Keep this in mind & watch for Legislative Committee work, etc. We can investigate anything the State needs looking into." But Franklin never landed the big clients of whom Marvin and Hooker had evidently dreamed.

"He did a few law jobs from time to time," Marvin recalled many years later, "but not very many . . . I don't remember any cases he handled. . . . He didn't specialize in any kind of law—he wasn't there much. He would come in occasionally when he was in New York—he would write letters. . . . I had always thought he would be a great business getter, but he was too busy with other things to bother much. . . ."

As the weeks dragged on, the hostility of the Democratic majority toward Franklin and his allies intensified. Most of the Tammany men bitterly resented having to stay in Albany all week; unlike Franklin, most of them needed to return home regularly to supplement their incomes. (So did many of the insurgents, for that matter.)

Nor did he make himself more popular by attacking the education and upbringing of his opponents. In their shortsightedness, he told one writer, the Tammany men reminded him of the "hopelessly stupid" children of "hillbillies" whom an Eastern schoolmaster was sent south to teach. When he discovered that his students did not even know the name of the capital of the United States, Franklin said, he ordered them to ask their parents when they got home that night. The next morning not a hand went up when he asked again about the capital.

"The school teacher lost his temper. 'Here, you,' said he to the tallest boy in the school. 'Stand up. Now, did you ask your father . . . the name of the Capital . . . ?'

"The boy nodded a stupid affirmative.

" 'Well,' said the schoolmaster. 'What did he say?'

" 'Pap low'd . . . as how he didn't know and he didn't care a damn.' "

That, Franklin concluded, was the sort of men that followed Boss Murphy.

By mounting such personal attacks he risked transforming his reputation for bold independence into notoriety as a willful and intransigent snob.

Even Sara may have seen the danger. She had been asked by Franklin not to bother Cousin Theodore about political matters; his dealings with his cousin now that he, too, was in public life were delicate and easily misinterpreted, and he preferred to handle them himself. But his mother always set her own priorities, and she was clearly worried about how her boy was getting on at Albany. A little talk with TR might help straighten things out.

One afternoon in February she hurried into the opulent lobby of the Waldorf-Astoria, asked the man at the desk for writing paper, then settled herself at a table and wrote an uncharacteristically breathless note to her son.

> Thursday 3PM
> Dearest Franklin,
>
> I *had* to see Coz. Theodore today about the Plant, Flower & Fruit Guild meeting and he was *so* nice about you & said he knew how proud I must be, etc. He said, "Franklin is doing just right, there is only one thing I hope he will keep to, *not to tie to one special man* but to the good cause. Not to say Shepard and no other." Then he quoted from a novel and said, "I would be glad to play with the angels, but the angels are not playing about just now." He thinks you are splendid and *as usual* was dear & nice. . . .
>
> Devotedly,
> Mama[15]

Uncle Fred Delano urged similar caution. While he was proud of his nephew and wished him "God speed" in the struggle against Sheehan, he also issued a warning: "Don't let your reform friends induce you to undertake too many things which may look right but which are untried—most reformers make the mistake of thinking that the toughs and the boodlers are invariably on the wrong side and that anything they oppose is therefore the desirable thing."

Frederic A. Delano had learned his principled pragmatism the hard way, and of all the members of his family outside his own home who

---

15. Franklin might have been further instructed by a letter TR himself once wrote to Senator Depew:

> How I wish I wasn't a reformer, oh, Senator! But I suppose I must live up to my part, like the Negro minstrel who blacked himself all over!

Source: Richard Hofstadter, *The American Political Tradition,* page 206.

offered him counsel over the years, Franklin may have listened most closely to him. A tall, calm man—Sara always admired what she called his "wonderful nature"—he was the youngest of Warren Delano's sons. He revered his father's memory and shared his devotion to the family (even becoming its unofficial chronicler in a series of pamphlets written late in life), but he had veered sharply from the old man's unshakable conservatism. After leaving Harvard in 1885, he had worked as a surveyor and mine superintendent, then joined the Burlington Railroad, where he stayed for twenty-one years, eventually rising to the position of general manager. While with that railroad he had often served as what he himself called "a strikebreaker," doing everything from "firing an engine to actually running an engine or acting in the capacity of yardmaster," sometimes with a pistol on his hip. That experience, he later wrote, "was a very unpleasant but valuable one, in that it enabled me to consider pretty clearly the rights of the employee as well as those of the employer. I learned to see that the employee had a good deal of the right on his side, although there were extreme leaders on the labor side who were as much at fault as the most hard-boiled employers."

He often disagreed with company policy toward its workers, he wrote much later, but "My attitude was that I had enlisted in the service of the Burlington and did whatever I was told to do." During the railroad strikes of the mid-1890s, he was superintendent of terminals. "The method adopted by all business in those days," he remembered, "was that of cutting down expenses to a minimum by reducing wages, throwing men out of work, etc. . . . I had to carry out these orders, and was naturally impressed with the cruelty of it, and on the other hand, with the generosity of the very poor to their friends. When I used to ask about this or that man who had been dropped from the payrolls and was without work, I would be told by those still at work that they were contributing to the support of their friends."

His sympathy for workers and skepticism toward the motives of big businessmen may have further intensified after 1905, the year of Franklin's marriage, when he was himself driven from his job by one-eyed Jim Hill, the implacable railroad builder, who had seized control of the Burlington through means Uncle Fred thought questionable and merged it into his mighty Great Northern network.

Thereafter, he began to devote more and more time to public service. In 1906, he was instrumental in winning approval of the Chicago Plan, which sought to preserve the beauty of that city's lakefront. (A talk with his uncle about this scheme, FDR once said, had first persuaded him of the importance of planning as "the way of the future.")

The welfare of his widowed sister and her only son was always important to him. He wrote to the fatherless young man often, urging him to study hard, to be loyal to his alma mater, above all to maintain the standards of conduct set by his late father and by his Cousin Theodore. His was always a voice for change wedded to caution. Reformers, he warned Franklin in the midst of the Sheehan fight, "are . . . impatient in trying to undertake too much and too many things, instead of making *slow but steady* progress. I would rather be called conservative and reactionary than impractical and visionary; and I think you can accomplish more real reform in that way. . . . I shall watch your career with the greatest interest and sympathy. Here's success to you, and strength to your good right arm!"[16]

16. Later, he would serve in a bewildering number of unpaid but important public positions including membership on the Federal Industrial Commission and the Federal Reserve Board under Woodrow Wilson and, under Calvin Coolidge, the chairmanship of the National Capital Park Commission, which helped develop a comprehensive city plan for Washington, D.C.

A memorandum he wrote privately in 1933 outlined the essentials of what became the National Recovery Administration; the President sent it along to his Secretary of Commerce, saying he thought it "right but perhaps a little ahead of its time." The following year FDR made him head of the National Resources Planning Board; he served until the agency was disbanded in 1943, and received a good many official communications from the White House addressed to "Dear Uncle Fred."

In 1935, an old acquaintance wrote him to protest what he called "the wild and extravagant experiments" of his nephew's New Deal. "I used to very much enjoy business," he said, "but now it is getting to be a chore every morning to go to work for we are being hampered so . . . that it hardly seems worthwhile trying to keep a business going. . . . I know you are a life-long Democrat and I should think it would be even harder for you to see how the party has strayed than for those of us who are in the opposition."

Uncle Fred mailed a copy of his heated reply to FDR:

Now as to politics, I have been a Democrat—or as we called it when I first voted for Cleveland in 1884, a "Mugwump." I did that greatly against my parents' wishes but on what I believed to be highly conscientious motives. Since then I have usually voted the Democratic ticket, and if I was a Liberal in 1884, I am even more of a Liberal today. During my business career I have been so horrified at the methods of wealthy men in banks and corporations that the necessity of reforms was obvious. I agreed with Theodore Roosevelt when he called them "malefactors of great wealth," and while I have tried to do my full public duty even . . . when Republicans were in power, I have been impressed that after 12 years of Republican methods, a change is absolutely necessary.

If I were to tell you in a very few words why I am a Democrat, I would say (1) that I have always believed in a liberal rather than a conservative point of view; (2) that while a man of large wealth or superior ability is able to shift for himself, there are a lot of people down in the ranks who need a friend. . . .

Going back over my experience, I have known many people of means, and I have been astonished by the fact that great wealth has a terrible deadening effect. They not only grow more and more dumb, but singularly unable to see the other fellow's point of view; furthermore, that appears to me to be more so in our country than in Great Britain. There, the landed

By mid January, Franklin had abandoned the candidacy of Edward Shepard; as Lewis Chanler and others had explained to him, Tammany's charge of anti-Catholicism could only be met by his coming up with an acceptable Catholic nominee. When Mayor Sague of Poughkeepsie wrote Franklin protesting that "it will be a fatal mistake to turn [Shepard] down," he filed the letter after scrawling "No Ans[wer]" across the top.

The next two months were spent in a sometimes frantic search for someone—anyone—who would provide a mutually acceptable alternative to Sheehan and Shepard. That pursuit proved as chastening and educational for Franklin in its way as had been his rejection by the young men whom he had supposed were his friends in Porcellian, for in the corridors of Albany nothing was quite as it seemed.

Franklin sought, through Theodore Roosevelt's secretary, William Loeb, Jr., to discover from Boss Barnes himself whether they might together be able secretly to settle on an Independent Democrat whom both they and the Republicans could support for the Senate instead of either Sheehan or Depew. He was certain, he said, that they could come up with a nominee who was "conservative in regard to business interests and yet a man whose position can never be questioned by the radical element of society."

"Mr. Barnes said that he could not do it," Loeb recalled, "because his arrangement with Mr. Murphy was that he was not to interfere in Mr. Murphy's plans about the senatorship."

He then tried to work quietly toward the same end through Francis Lyde Stetson, the former law partner of Grover Cleveland, whose clients included both J. P. Morgan and Thomas Ryan. That didn't work either.

---

gentry have long appreciated that with wealth and high position, there comes a duty to society, and every student of government or politics is aware that Great Britain is far ahead of us in all social or remedial legislation; and under their set-up they don't "bleat" about it but take their medicine.

I do not pretend to be the official defender of the present Administration; that is not my privilege, but I would be a skunk if I were not loyal to this President. . . . Of course he has failed in some of his efforts; of course he has had his disappointments . . . but in the main he must be happy that he has succeeded, that we have turned the corner, that many great pieces of social legislation have been put upon the Statute books, that the man in the street has the right to feel that he not only has a friend in the White House, but a friend who will try to help him and come nearer doing so than some other well-wishers. . . .

Sources: Frank Freidel, Franklin D. Roosevelt: Launching the New Deal, page 418; Otis L. Graham and Meghan Robinson Wander, eds., Franklin D. Roosevelt: His Life and Times, page 330; Frederic A. Delano Papers, FDRL.

In mid-March, Lang Marvin invited Franklin to address the annual Harvard Club dinner. Franklin agreed—President A. Lawrence Lowell of Harvard and Major Henry Lee Higginson, the Boston philanthropist and Civil War soldier, were to be among the other speakers—then begged his new partner for help: ". . . for Heaven's sake write me out something to say—I have no thoughts yet." Marvin, busy trying to drum up the law business for which Franklin had so little time, responded with some asperity: "If you can only elect a Senator by Friday, you will have plenty to talk about, and if you do not you still ought to be able to chin through 5 or 10 minutes of talk. . . ."

He had had to improvise; there was still no new senator. A hostile Albany newspaper now wrote of Franklin, "there seems nothing left for the poor man but to keep on insurging."

Franklin and the others boycotted a second Democratic caucus on March 27, evidently on the bad advice of Stetson and his friends, and thereby denied the nomination to a genuinely admirable candidate, Samuel Untermeyer, a progressive businessman who had battled a variety of trusts and championed the rights of consumers in the insurance industry. Tammany happily seized upon this error to charge that for all their high-minded posturing, young Roosevelt and his allies were nothing but the tools of one Wall Street faction engaged in a cynical war for profits. (Both sides of the Senate struggle had learned the appeal of progressive rhetoric.)

When the end finally came, it came quickly.

On the night of March 29, a fire swept through the west end of the Capitol, killing a watchman, destroying the state library, and gutting both legislative chambers. The weary legislators now had to meet in cramped quarters in the old City Hall across the street. Their impatience intensified.

The next day, Murphy proposed to Franklin the name of still another nominee, State Supreme Court Justice Vincent Dowling. With it came a threat to publish an indignant letter from the rejected Samuel Untermeyer himself, lending support to Murphy's charge that the insurgency was a fraud orchestrated from Wall Street, unless Franklin and his friends agreed to support this latest candidate at the caucus to be held the next day.

Dowling was a much-admired jurist, and the insurgents, now almost as anxious as the regulars to end the deadlock, went along.

Then the signals changed again. Dowling declined the nomination the next morning, and Murphy smoothly substituted the name of another judge—Justice James Aloysius O'Gorman, a former Tammany Sachem and past president of the Friendly Sons of St. Patrick who had displayed a degree of independence from the machine while on the bench but was thought by Murphy far more likely even than Sheehan to prove pliable when it mattered most.[17]

The insurgents were gathered in Franklin's library when this alarming news arrived. Two men immediately left the room to vote for O'Gorman. The insurgency was coming apart. Franklin tried to persuade the rest to hold the line, but once Smith and Wagner had reassured him that there were to be no reprisals against those who had held things up so long, even he decided to vote for Murphy's man.

On the afternoon of March 31, Franklin and the ten most dogged rebels walked together along State Street, past the big ice-shrouded Capitol Building, blackened by smoke and patrolled by militiamen with fixed bayonets, and filed into City Hall. As they shouldered their way into the crowded chamber, the jubilant regulars jeered and sang chorus after chorus of the Tammany anthem.

When the time finally came, Franklin stood and did his best to explain his vote, struggling to be heard above the steady hissing:

> Two months ago a number of Democrats felt that it was our duty to dissent from certain of our party associates in the matter of selecting a United States Senator. The party had been restored to power after seventeen years of Republican misrule. We have followed the dictates of our consciences and have done our duty as we saw it. I believe that as a result the Democratic Party has taken an upward step. We are Democrats—not irregulars, but regulars. I take pleasure in casting my vote for the Honorable James A. O'Gorman.

That pleasure must have been severely limited. The insurgency had been broken. Murphy had won the Senate seat for a man at least as malleable as Sheehan would have been. Even sympathetic newspapers saw O'Gorman's victory as a defeat for the insurgency.[18]

Franklin, as he had been taught to do from infancy, did his exuberant best to seem oblivious of his defeat. Just two days later, as guest speaker before the YMCA of Greater New York—his topic was "Poli-

17. O'Gorman's nomination pleased Murphy for another, more personal reason: it created a vacancy on the bench that his son-in-law, Dan Cohalan, could happily fill.

18. So did most of the insurgents. Of the twenty-four men who had stuck by Franklin in the long struggle, just fourteen won renomination by their party; only four of those survivors—including Franklin—were reelected in 1912. The party itself did poorly overall that year, too, and a good many defeated regulars and their supporters blamed Franklin and his allies for raising issues like bossism which the Republicans had been able to exploit.

tics and the Young Man"—he as good as claimed victory. "I have just returned from a big fight," he declared, "a fight that went 64 rounds, and there was fighting every second of those 64 rounds. This . . . fight was a free-for-all . . . and many of the other side got good and battered. As for the condition of the insurgents, I exhibit my physical condition as a sample. The insurgents received few scratches, and have suffered little. . . . Everybody is happy now. The battle ended in harmony, and we have chosen a man for the people who will be dictated to by no one."

Less than two weeks later, however, at the Legislative Correspondents' Association annual dinner, Franklin had to smile through still more humiliation while a newspaperman dressed as a Tammany brave sang a song called "Our New Senator—Jim O'G.":

> Said Franklin D.: "There's got to be
>   Some new insurgency,
> We've got some boys to make a noise
>   And leader I will be;
> For weeks and weeks we fought the fight
>   Against Old Tammany,
> But I can't figure out as yet,
> Just what was handed me."
>   Chorus
>   Tammany, Tammany,
> Franklin D., like Uncle "The.",
> Can't compete with Tammany;
>   Tammany, Tammany,
> Skies are clearin', keep on cheerin',
> Tammany . . .

As late as 1920, according to Judge Joseph M. Proskauer, one of Al Smith's closest advisers, there was still among New York party professionals "a tendency to laugh at Roosevelt a little for [the Sheehan] performance. . . . According to the gospel [FDR] won a great victory. [But the] victory was that instead of getting Sheehan, who was a pretty good upstate lawyer, they withdrew him and nominated [O'Gorman whom they] would much rather have had nominated in the first place. . . ."

A large part of the electorate believed the gospel, however, including —to Franklin's intense relief—his own normally Republican constituents, who had delighted in his twisting of Tammany's tail.

Over the years, Franklin and his allies would spread his version of the story far and wide, and as time passed, he himself seems to have come to believe that he really had won a famous victory.

In a personal sense, of course, he had, and for him that was always what mattered most: within six months of his first election to office, the Sheehan fight had made him a national symbol of reform. An editorial in the Cleveland *Plain Dealer* must have especially pleased him: The writer confessed that he had originally assumed that this young Roosevelt, being rich, had entered politics just "for 'fun,' " but his battle against Sheehan had persuaded him that he had been wrong. If none of Theodore Roosevelt's own sons proved worthy of their father, he continued, "may it not be possible that this rising star may continue the Roosevelt dynasty? Franklin D. Roosevelt is, to be sure, a Democrat, but this is a difference of small import. In other respects, he seems to be thoroughly Rooseveltian."

And, in embarrassing Boss Murphy and his Republican counterpart, Franklin had also added to the groundswell of public enthusiasm for an amendment to the U.S. Constitution providing for the direct election of U.S. senators. In May, he led the five-hour floor fight on behalf of a resolution requiring the New York congressional delegation to vote in favor of such an amendment, and—given his unpopularity among his colleagues, perhaps as much in spite of his advocacy as because of it—it was finally adopted by twenty-eight votes to fifteen. (The Seventeenth Amendment became effective two years later.)

In any case, Franklin eventually allowed the warm memory of his first fame to distort the cold facts of his earliest political defeat. "Do you remember the old Sheehan fight of 1911?" he asked a long-time friend in 1928, when he was running for governor of New York and had long since papered over his old differences with Tammany Hall. *"When the final Murphy surrender came* [author's italics], the flag of truce was brought to me by Assemblyman Alfred E. Smith . . . and State Senator Bob Wagner. What a change has taken place all along the line!"

The scars of the Sheehan battle did not heal during Franklin's time in the state Senate. He was never much liked by his Democratic colleagues.

Part of the problem was that Theodore Roosevelt continued to set the standard for Franklin—not the pragmatic, private TR, who had himself been forced to learn the limitations of politics through hard experience, but the public crusader for good, the noisy, chesty wielder of the Big Stick.[19]

Murphy and his cohorts, Franklin charged at Buffalo months after the Sheehan struggle had ended, "must, like the noxious weed, be plucked out, root and branch. . . . For those of you who are fond of hunting, it is no longer necessary to go to the Canadian Rockies or the Jungles of Africa for sport; there is bigger game and better hunting right here in New York State. . . . The hunt is on, and the beasts of prey have begun to fall. . . ."

The impact of such assaults on their targets was similar to that the young Theodore had produced as well. Patrick E. McCabe, the clerk of the Senate, for example, denounced Franklin's Buffalo address as "bristling with the conceits of a silly prig. . . . Disloyalty and part treachery is the political cult of a few snobs in our party who . . . are political accidents. . . . [Party leaders] are largely responsible for this embarrassing situation because they have humored and coddled too much the little fellows, fops and cads who come as near being political leaders as a green pea does to a circus tent. Some leaders may stand for the impudence and arrogance of these political prudes, but I won't."

Franklin was never so flamboyant as his cousin had been when young, but he did sometimes deliver speeches in dinner clothes, literally peered down his nose at his colleagues through pince-nez—Al Smith liked to call them Roosevelt's "pinchers"—and spoke in a distinctive accent that combined the curiously Anglophile tones of old New York with a distinctive, langorous hauteur cultivated at Groton and polished on Harvard's Gold Coast.[20]

19. Relatives and friends reinforced Franklin in the role. Rob Roy Alexander, a Harvard classmate and now a Cleveland banker, for example, wrote that he hoped "your Big Stick grows to be as mighty as that other Big Stick we hear so much about." Another classmate, Ned Bell, wrote from Teheran, where he held a minor diplomatic post, praising him for leading "that noble band of 'Boy Scouts' to victory at the Battle of Albany." (Like many other college friends, he addressed Franklin as "Kermit," after TR's third son.) "My dear Kermit, permit me to offer you my sincere congratulations. Apparently no homestead in the darkest depths of the Rockies or Alleghanies . . . is complete without your portrait in oils or chromo. . . ." Source: Franklin D. Roosevelt Papers; General Correspondence; Harvard Class of 1904, FDRL; Roosevelt Family Papers Donated by the Children, FDRL.

20. His early attempts at proving himself a regular fellow sometimes backfired, too: he caused a sensation one evening when, in a clumsy effort to smooth over his old differences, he ventured into a boisterous Tammany ball wearing not only dinner clothes but gleaming gold cuff links, an affectation then thought foreign and effeminate by all but the toniest New Yorkers. Source: Interview with John J. Fitzgerald, Frank Freidel Papers, FDRL.

Some reporters wrote that he reminded them of an earnest young clergyman, and it was just that air of piety that seemed to arouse the most indignation among his opponents. When a Democratic budget bill was called up one June evening, Franklin astonished senators of both parties by demanding to know why it included $881.54 to improve a bridge at Wappinger's Falls in his district.

Chairman James J. Frawley, chairman of the Senate Finance Committee, explained that it was meant to benefit the senator's constituents.

Franklin said he did not care. He knew of no such need and thought the money ought to be returned to the state treasury.

Tim Sullivan muttered, "Frank, you ought to have your head examined."

A Republican, delighted to see Democratic overspending pointed up by one of their own, suggested that Franklin's protest would one day "stand as a monument, greater than any that has ever been or will be erected to perpetuate the achievements of his illustrious relative." Another welcomed him to join the Republicans, "the party of *real* economy and retrenchment."

The Democrat leadership set the bill aside for a day to see if Franklin thought better of his objection. He did not.

A few days later, he took on Frawley once more, charging this time that the senator's failure to report out a fire-fighting bill would make him personally responsible for the loss of the state forests that were sure to burn that summer. As Frawley, a florid, paunchy Tammany man, rose to his feet and began to sputter his reply, Senate President Wagner interrupted: "Senator Roosevelt has gained his point. What he wants is a headline in the newspapers. Let us proceed to our business."

The charge that Franklin was more interested than most of his colleagues in getting into the papers was made often, partly out of envy. From his first day in Albany, he seemed to understand—just as his cousin had—the importance of appealing directly to the public through the press. His famous name initially stirred the newspapermen's interest in him, but his own innate sense of drama kept it tightly focused.

He had less luck at first with photographers. The day after the Sheehan fight began, a cameraman caught him in earnest conversation with another young politician. The photographer was not certain which man was which, and when the picture was published, the other man—wearing an elegant silk hat—was identified as "Senator Roosevelt, who says he will never vote for Sheehan."

The next time his face appeared in a newspaper, his features were printed so dark, according to the *New York Evening Telegram,* that "the complexion rivaled that of Jack Johnson in its ebon hue." When it was shown to Franklin, he joked that while it might provide grounds for libel, he did not plan to sue "because that picture ought to make me solid with the negro vote in my district."

Another portrait was still more unfortunate: his normally smooth face somehow furrowed with "deep lines of age and care," the eyes "pointed to port and starboard," and his mouth "wandered uncertainly across the face like a Boston business street."

"This is the limit," he moaned when he saw it. "I could stand the others but when this reaches the family . . . they will say, 'Heavens, how Frank has suffered under the strain of battle,' and they will send up six doctors and an insanity expert on the next train to lead me to some quiet retreat."

On June 22, Franklin and Senator Frawley clashed again. That evening, the Tammany leaders called a surprise Democratic caucus to adopt a binding position on a controversial highway bill. Before the voting could begin, Franklin rose to announce that he would not abide by its result.

Frawley had had enough. "I move that the senator from the Twenty-Sixth be excluded from the caucus."

While the regulars cheered, the chair appointed Frawley a committee of one to escort Franklin from the room. "He walked over, took the Dutchess County man by the arm," the *New York Evening Globe* reported, "and gently led him to the door. Of course, it was all done good naturedly, but nevertheless there was meaning beneath the smiles. . . ."

In the corridor outside, Franklin made a lame attempt to mimick even his cousin's shrill combativeness. During his time in Albany, TR had knocked down one of his fellow legislators with his fists, and threatened to unman another. Now, when Frawley, who had once been a successful amateur boxer, joked to reporters that he would face Franklin any time, anywhere, "in a pulpit or a rat pit," Franklin boasted right back that Frawley should beware; he weighed "one hundred and seventy pounds, stripped," he said, and had been "quite a boxer" at Groton. (It was a good thing the fight never came off; Franklin had fought precisely one bout at school, against a boy named

Fuller Potter, both smaller and younger than he, and had lost, retiring early with a bloody nose.)

Nothing—not even the daily derision of his fellow senators—was seen to discourage or disturb Franklin. That apparent imperturbability was part of what so irritated his opponents. But the effort evidently took its toll. In late June, as Eleanor and the children were packing for their summer at Campobello and just a few days after he was escorted from the caucus, he collapsed with a fever of 104 degrees. He was exhausted; his tonsils were raw and swollen, his sinuses throbbed, as they often did when he was undergoing extreme stress. After a few days he seemed to be on the mend and it was thought best for Eleanor to take the children northward and wait on the island for him to come up for a rest as soon as the session ended. His mother was left in charge.

He did not continue to improve. Doctors, summoned by Sara, fussed over him, flushed out his sinuses, prodded his tonsils, fed him cocaine. "I feel a good deal like a rag," he wrote Eleanor from Springwood after three more days back in bed, "and have lost nearly ten pounds . . . I can't tell you how I miss you and Mama does not in the least make up."

Finally, Eleanor hurried down to Hyde Park in the heat to nurse him. It took him three full weeks to regain his feet, but by the closing days of the session, still pale and drawn but again outwardly serene, he was back in the Senate leading the fight for a direct primary bill.

On July 18, sitting at his back-row desk on the floor, he wrote notes to both his wife and his mother. He told Eleanor he had just "raised a riot" by calling for immediate action on the bill, which its Republican and Tammany foes had hoped quietly to bury; and to Sara he said he "had dropped a bomb . . . [that] provoked a 3-hour discussion and I was called some choice names. . . . It is now 6 PM & we shall probably sit here till midnight." Then, recalling his mother's perpetual anxiety about his health, he added, "I am going to send out for a glass of milk soon."

The bill did not pass—Franklin denounced its opponents to his wife as "asinine"—but a few days later the legislature finally recessed, and he was able to come up to Campobello for nearly six weeks of sun and sailing and rest.

At some point during that otherwise tranquil time at Campobello, perhaps while Franklin and Hall were undertaking their customary voyage down the Maine coast aboard the *Half Moon*, Eleanor and her mother-in-law clashed over what seemed on the surface a simple issue.

Eleanor thought that since she and Franklin were clearly going to spend all but a few days of the coming fall and winter in Albany, they should keep their New York townhouse closed and board out the servants they wished to retain. During their infrequent visits to Manhattan, they could stay with Sara.

Her mother-in-law, who may still have hoped that Franklin would weary of politics and return to the law, considered this a foolish economy, and, perhaps more important, did not like the implication that her family would so rarely be with her in the coming months.

In the past, Eleanor might have been expected quickly to retreat. It had taken her nearly six years to oppose openly the wishes of the mother-in-law whose affection, approval, and advice she had once so desperately sought, but this time she held her ground. When Sara saw that Eleanor would not change her mind, she seemed to back off, and when her mother-in-law left the island for Hyde Park in early September the younger woman thought everything had been settled.

It had not been, at least so far as Sara was concerned, and when Franklin stopped at 65th Street on his way back to Albany and the start of the second legislative session in September, she took him aside for a little talk. "I have just finished talking to Mama," he wrote Eleanor afterwards. "She began about the New York house. I told her we had made all arrangements to have the servants boarded out. She was quite upset and although I said it didn't matter, I *think* she has written you to have the servants stay! I don't know quite what to say about it; it would certainly be nice to have them here in November and December, but on the other hand we have practically decided not to. Do just as you think, dearest, and you know I'll back you up!"

Eleanor—who thought she and Franklin had *actually,* not "practically," decided, and who must surely have been uncertain that he would truly back her up in any serious confrontation with his mother—was furious, but at Sara, not at her wavering husband:

> Really, Honey, it becomes ludicrous! She made an offer, then withdrew it and now wants to renew it! I think she had better decide another time before speaking and as I wrote you it would be foolish to get new servants and put them in her house, as Lydia is going. I expect to let Emily go also as I overheard a conversation which made me decide that she talked too much even though she might seem nice to me! ... After Cousin Susie [Parish] is in town I'm sure she will love having us stay there if we want to anytime and I would rather do it than go to Mama's now!

In the long, often trying struggle between the two women in his life, Franklin would always do his skittish best not to take sides more often than was absolutely necessary. "I think as far as Father was concerned," his daughter once said, "his feeling was that he didn't want to take on responsibility he didn't have to . . . and as long as the females in the family . . . wanted to do it, why, let them do it." Franklin loved and felt loyal to both his wife and his mother, and he could never bring himself finally to choose between them. Neither of them ever found him a reliable ally. Each took out her anger over that fact upon the other.

Sara had been defeated for the moment—Franklin and Eleanor did close their townhouse that fall, and they stayed with the Parishes during at least one of their infrequent visits to the city—but she would not be supplanted easily as the central woman in her son's life. Not long after Eleanor and the children returned from Campobello, Sara privately recorded her pleasure that "*Our* three children are well and very sweet" (author's italics), and when Franklin vaguely said he "needed an auto," she instantly bought him a Hudson and gave it to him—on Eleanor's birthday in October.

By then, Franklin, Eleanor, and the children were back in Albany, living in a still larger rented house at Number 4 Elk Street. One of its chief attractions may have been that it had been built by Martin Van Buren, a Democrat and the first governor of New York to reach the presidency. Franklin devoutly hoped to be the next.

The Roosevelts did a good deal of entertaining, and Eleanor took it upon herself to provide a welcome to the anxious wives of newly arrived newspapermen and newly elected legislators. One of these was Helen Robinson, whose husband, Teddy, had just been elected Republican assemblyman from Herkimer. Most of the Roosevelts' friends were fairly sedate; the Robinsons preferred what Eleanor recalled as "a gayer and younger group" with whom she, at least, did not feel at ease, and "I think I must have spoiled a good deal of the fun for Franklin . . . though I do not remember that I ever made much objection to his being with them as long as I was allowed to stay at home."

But if Franklin was sometimes frivolous and fun-loving when away from the Capitol, he more than made up for it on the floor, as Frances Perkins noted. Miss Perkins was a small and plainly dressed Mount Holyoke graduate, a suffragist and social worker who was often in

Albany that autumn, lobbying on behalf of labor. Over the coming years, she would coolly observe Franklin at every stage of his career, assessing his strengths and weaknesses and speculating as to their sources, gleaning knowledge of his mercurial personality that would one day make it possible for her to survive and prosper as Secretary of Labor throughout FDR's presidency. Few of his contemporaries ever understood him as well. Franklin the freshman state senator, Miss Perkins remembered, was "tall and slender, very active and alert, moving around the floor, going in and out of committee rooms, rarely talking with the members, who more or less avoided him, not particularly charming (that came later), artificially serious of face, rarely smiling, with an unfortunate habit—so natural that he was unaware of it—of throwing his head up. This, combined with his pince-nez and great height, gave him the appearance of looking down his nose at most people."[21]

Big Tim Sullivan, who rarely said an unkind word about a fellow Democrat, was once heard to mutter after a talk with Franklin, "Awful arrogant fellow, that Roosevelt."

"I can see 'that Roosevelt' now," Miss Perkins wrote many years later, "standing back of the brass rail with two or three Democratic senators arguing with him to be 'reasonable' . . . about something; his small mouth pursed up and slightly open, his nostrils distended, his head in the air, and his cool, remote voice saying, 'No, no, I won't hear of it!' "

In a rare moment of retrospective self-criticism, FDR himself agreed that his political debut had not been as gracious as it might have been. "You know," he told Miss Perkins, "I was an awfully mean cuss when I first went into politics."

As a boy, Franklin had sometimes been permitted to take part in the strenuous "point-to-point" hikes Cousin Theodore liked to organize on summer weekends, the Roosevelt children and their guests

21. She had first seen him in 1910, at a Gramercy Park tea dance. "Roosevelt had just entered politics with a Dutchess County campaign," she recalled, "which was not taken too seriously either by Roosevelt himself, his supporters, or his friends. The Republicans and farmers had voted for him largely because of his name. It was the era of Theodore Roosevelt and we were all still under his spell. . . . There was nothing particularly interesting about the tall, thin young man with the high collar and pince-nez and I should not have later remembered this meeting except for the fact that in an interval between dances someone in the group I joined mentioned Theodore Roosevelt, speaking with some scorn of his 'progressive' ideas. The tall young man . . . made a spirited defense of Theodore Roosevelt. . . ." *Source:* Frances Perkins, *The Roosevelt I Knew,* page 9.

scurrying after the Colonel as he strode briskly toward some agreed-upon destination through the woods around Oyster Bay. The game had a single inviolable rule: obstacles were to be overcome, not circumvented; one pushed through brambles, waded streams, crawled under fences or scrambled over them, and never, never went *around* anything. Sometimes older people took part. His sister Corinne recalled one race during which TR came upon "an especially unpleasant-looking bathing house with a very steep roof." She prayed he would somehow contrive to lead the pack around it. Not a chance. "I can still see the sturdy body of the President of the United States," she wrote long after, "hurling himself at the obstruction and with singular agility chinning himself to the top and sliding down the other side."[22]

Point-to-point was a good metaphor for Theodore Roosevelt's style of leadership—or at least for the style he liked to advocate. Adversaries were to be met and overcome, head-on.

Franklin admired his cousin extravagantly, and when his own children were big enough he would organize strenuous paper chases of his own along Campobello's shoreline. But his basic personality was quite different from TR's. The creative uses of indirection, for example, were built into him from infancy. Raised alone by loving but anxious parents, he had learned early that the best technique for getting one's way was often to do one thing while chattering pleasantly about something else.

This is an oversimplification, of course. FDR could be bold. TR was sometimes indirect. But this and other intrinsic differences between them finally made Franklin's almost worshipful imitation of his cousin impossible to sustain. He was simply not credible trying to seem like someone he was not. His own distinctive personality emerged slowly but steadily, and he came eventually to shed the superficial

---

22. TR's games could be intimidating as well as exciting, especially for visiting children, like Franklin and Eleanor, who were not accustomed to adventurous play. At an August 8, 1939, White House press conference, President and Mrs. Roosevelt competed with one another trying to convey the special terrors of afternoons spent racing up and down the dunes near Sagamore Hill:

FDR: . . . we children were awfully terrified because it was awfully steep and the sand went down with you, and you were darned lucky if you did not end, halfway down, by going down, head-over-heels.
Mrs. R.: Uncle Ted lined you up and you had to go at a run.
FDR: And go down the steep dune.
Mrs. R: And coming back you had to go up again and you slipped down two steps for every one you went up. . . .
FDR: The other way around, one for every two, otherwise you wouldn't get up!
Mrs. R: Yes, and you always had to climb.
FDR: It was a very difficult process, with real danger to life and limb.

aspects of TR's personality that had never really suited him. The mature FDR was neither shrill nor bellicose nor hyperkinetic.

But in 1911, "Franklin stood out for being a little disagreeable," Frances Perkins remembered. "If I'd been a man serving in the Senate with [Tim Sullivan and others like him] I'm sure I would have had a glass of beer with them and gotten them to tell me what times were like on the Old Bowery. Franklin Roosevelt had none of that. And they didn't like him. . . ."

He seemed in fact just the sort of over-serious young man Senate veterans enjoyed playing tricks upon. It was a tradition, for example, that the senator occupying the farthest seat to the right of the Speaker's rostrum should each morning provide a red carnation for the buttonhole of each of his colleagues in the back row. Franklin religiously followed custom, carrying a crimson bouquet as he entered the chamber every day, and always wearing one bright blossom himself.

One Wednesday morning, a large number of women suffragists came to the capital to show their support for a bill awarding the vote to women. When Franklin and an equally handsome Republican Senate colleague, J. Mayhew Wainwright of Westchester, each wearing his carnation, sauntered out of the Senate chamber and tried to strike up a conversation with some of the younger suffragists gathered in the corridor, the women turned away from them.[23]

This was not the usual reaction of young women when Franklin Roosevelt approached them, and he and Wainwright were utterly mystified. It happened several times. Finally, one older suffragist, perhaps from sheer force of habit, began to argue for her cause, then broke off, apparently exasperated. "Of course," she said, "it is of no use to talk to either of you, as you choose to show your dislike of our work so plainly."

Franklin asked her what she meant and learned that one of his opponents had quietly spread the word among the women that he and Wainwright wore their carnations as badges of membership in a secret anti-suffrage club whose motto was "Woman's place is at the fireside, not the polls." Nothing either of the young senators could think to do that afternoon would convince the indignant visitors that they had been the victims of a joke.

Part of the reason Franklin had such trouble persuading the women

23. The two senators with whom Franklin then felt most comfortable were Republicans: Wainwright and Josiah Newcomb; both were wealthy and from Westchester County, and were the sort of men Franklin's mother most admired. *Source:* Transcript of interview with Frances Perkins, Columbia Oral History Project, Columbia University.

that he was not their enemy may have been that he was so hesitant about proclaiming himself their ally. His air of moral superiority was combined with what then seemed to many reformers and regulars alike an unusual sinuousness when it came to complicated or controversial issues.

He was not himself opposed to votes for women, for example—though both his wife and his mother were—but he saw no reason to alienate voters who were opposed. "I think it is a very great question whether the people of the state as a whole want it or not," he told advocates of both positions in 1911, and so he urged a statewide referendum to decide the question. Woman suffrage advocates were disappointed. What sort of progressive was this Roosevelt? How could he not see that the same logic that demanded the direct primary required votes for women? How else could boss rule be overthrown and democracy be made direct?

Not until the spring of the following year would Franklin decide it was safe for him openly to advocate woman suffrage.[24]

Congressman Richard Connell, with whom Franklin had campaigned in 1910, remained an enthusiastic, avuncular ally. After the Sheehan fight was over, he had written to congratulate his youthful friend on the "priceless example" he had set for "the young men of our state and country who contemplate participation in public life. You might have been . . . a cog in a revolving wheel which runs the merrier for the hearts being crushed beneath it. Instead . . . you walked right into the foreground where belong the men of the day . . . the men upon whose courage and character our republic may well rest in confidence."

But there were hearts Franklin was willing to crush to get ahead, and one of them turned out to be Connell's.

24. When Franklin did finally support votes for women, Eleanor was startled. "I had never given the question really serious thought," she remembered, "for I took it for granted that men were superior creatures and still knew more about politics than women . . . I cannot claim to have been a feminist in those early days."

She had not changed her mind since 1908, when her Aunt Pussie had argued with her about votes for women. "You seem surprised that Auntie P. is a suffragette. . . . ," Hall wrote her then, "the most surprising thing to me is that she's trying to convert *you* of all people." Two years later, the two women had clashed over the subject again, and Eleanor was so vehement then that Hall had worried about his sister's uncharacteristic loss of "self-control."

Much later it amused Franklin (and annoyed Eleanor) for him to claim that he had been persuaded to support woman suffrage only after the beautiful suffragist Inez Mulholland lobbied him while perched prettily on his desk. That was "a very good story," Eleanor was careful to explain in the first volume of her autobiography, ". . . but as a matter of fact, he came out for it two months before that memorable visit." *Sources:* Nathan Miller, *FDR: An Intimate History,* page 86; Eleanor Roosevelt, *This Is My Story,* page 180; Eleanor Roosevelt Papers, FDRL.

Two bills occupied the legislature in the late summer of 1911. One was a new charter for New York City, backed both by Tammany and by William J. Gaynor, the reform mayor, whose hand over appointments it would greatly strengthen. The other was a reapportionment bill which, in the interest of extending Tammany's hold into the city's suburbs, would have sacrificed Connell's upstate district to the Republicans. "It seems pretty rough on poor old Connell," Franklin told Eleanor early in the session. "Everybody is up in arms about it here, and I am doing my best to get it changed, but I don't personally think there is any chance."

Franklin first aligned himself with the reformers who opposed the new charter on the grounds that it would gravely weaken civil service and greatly strengthen the city machine. The cause would provide "a fine opening," he told a reporter, "for an energetic trouble-maker" and he was looking forward to another good fight, and one in which he held the balance of power. With just three Democratic allies in the Senate, and the help of the Republicans, he could block passage of the charter.

Gaynor sent an emissary to Albany to work with Franklin, hoping to smooth out those features of the bill which were most troublesome to him. At the same time, Tammany quietly offered Franklin a deal that blended threats with promises. If Franklin could find it within himself to come out in favor of the revised charter, Connell's district would be left unmolested and, at the next election, the old congressman would be shouldered aside and Franklin could have the congressional nomination. If he refused to go along, on the other hand, the machine would do all that it could to defeat him. "Get smart," one Tammany man told him. "If you want to go someplace we can fix it. But if you haven't got the sense, we'll fix it so you won't go anywhere."

Robert S. Binkerd, a New York attorney and lobbyist for the Citizen's Union, took Franklin to dinner at the Ten Eyck one evening, still certain that Franklin was four-square for reform. But as they ate and he reiterated his group's opposition to the new charter, he noticed that Franklin seemed restive, distracted. Finally, perhaps weary of Binkerd's preachments, Franklin interrupted him. He was not even a citizen of New York City, he protested. Why should he jeopardize his political future on behalf of the people of that distant city?

Binkerd remembered being outraged. ". . . [Y]our legal residence may be Hyde Park," he told the younger man, "but you and your family have been in New York City for a hundred years, and the idea that you haven't any obligation to the people of New York is nuts."

The news that Franklin was wavering spread fast in good government circles and his old friends were upset. IF YOU VOTE FOR [THE CHARTER] I SHALL FEEL LIKE RETIRING PERMANENTLY FROM POLITICS, Thomas Mott Osborne, Franklin's first political patron and still the state's preeminent Tammany foe, wired him. FOR GOD'S SAKE DON'T COMPROMISE.

Franklin wavered again.

Now the Gaynor men appealed to him to hold fast. CONFIDENTIAL. AFTER ALL OF THE FALSIFICATION AND ABUSE I BEG YOU TO STAND BY ME IN THIS CHARTER MATTER, the mayor himself wired Franklin. IT IS HONEST AND FREE FROM WRONG OF ANY KIND.[25]

He finally voted against Gaynor and the charter.

Franklin's inept maneuvering had done him no good. The charter was eventually passed; Connell's district was divided and Franklin never was nominated for Congress. Worse still, he had begun to develop a reputation even among some of his old allies for shiftiness and hypocrisy which his implausible protests that his positions on the charter and reapportionment had never had anything to do with one another did nothing to refute.

"He was a very uncertain factor," one prominent member of a good government group who had called upon him during the charter fight recalled. "No one could ever tell how he was going to vote. . . ."

On Saturday, March 25, 1911, just four days before the Albany Capitol fire tipped the balance against Franklin and the other insurgents in the Sheehan fight, another far more fateful blaze had broken out in the crowded interior of the Triangle Shirtwaist Company that occupied the three top floors of a ten-story New York City loft building just off Washington Square. The flames, sparked by a discarded cigarette, spread fast among the paper patterns and bolts of cloth. The doors to the stairwell would not open. There were no fire escapes. Scores of women found themselves trapped inside. One hundred were burned alive; another forty-six jumped or fell to their deaths, screaming, some of them with their hair in flames.

No one was found legally at fault in the trial that followed.

25. It cannot have been easy for the embattled mayor to have to beg a favor from this young upstate politician who seemed to hold the fate of his city's charter in his inexperienced hands; in private, Gaynor and his aides called Franklin "Mr. Damn Fool" and "Mr. Know-It-All." Source: Louis H. Pink, *Gaynor, the Tammany Mayor Who Swallowed the Tiger,* page 173.

The owners of the building were allowed to collect some $65,000 in insurance on their damaged property. Twenty-three families of the dead sued and received a total of $1,725—$75 per life lost.

The Triangle Fire produced new demands for reform—for laws to regulate working hours and conditions; end child labor; establish building codes; provide worker's compensation. In June, the State Senate and Assembly created the New York Factory Commission. Robert Wagner was chairman; Al Smith was vice chairman; Frances Perkins was chief investigator. Over the next three years the commission produced a flood of thirty-two reform bills that would one day serve as models for the nation.

Franklin would vote for them, but with little apparent enthusiasm. He knew precious little of the lives led by those less fortunate than he, even in Dutchess County, and he had inherited his father's distaste for city life. Nor was he notably sympathetic to labor. (Asked his opinion as to the right to strike just a week before the Triangle Fire, he had confused strikes with boycotts. "There is no question in my mind," he wrote, "that we cannot permit legislation which will legalize the practice of boycotting.")

Nothing was more important to Miss Perkins or her allies than the fifty-four-hour bill for women and children which stalled in the spring of 1912. Tammany itself was split. Manufacturers close to Murphy had persuaded him to oppose it; Smith, Wagner, and their followers were for it.

Every vote counted.

Franklin was reluctant to commit himself. Miss Perkins took it upon herself to try and enlist him personally, believing that an appeal from a genteel, well-brought-up advocate of labor's position might somehow turn the trick. He would not even grant her an interview, tossing his head back and dismissing her with "No, no. More important things. More important things. Can't do it now. Can't do it now. Much more important things."

Miss Perkins found this behavior bewildering; it would have been simpler to tell her she had his support, even if she didn't.

On the day of the roll call, two votes were needed to pass the bill. They were cast at the last possible moment by Big Tim Sullivan and his younger cousin, Christy, whom Miss Perkins managed to call back to the chamber from the night boat that was about to take them to New York. (Big Tim told her he was defying Murphy and voting for the bill because "I seen my sister go out to work when she was fourteen and I know we ought to help these gals by giving 'em a law which will prevent 'em from being broken down while they're still young.")

Franklin did not even bother to attend the session, though he did eventually see that his vote was recorded as having been for the bill.

Miss Perkins recalled her disappointment that "Franklin Roosevelt did not associate himself actively with this [legislation], which was a measure of the progressive politicians of 1912. I took it hard that a young man of such spirit did not do so well in this, which I thought a test, as did Tim Sullivan . . . [who was] undoubtedly corrupt. . . ."[26]

This inconvenient fact evidently bothered Franklin, too, in later years, and so, as he so often did, he simply altered the past to suit the present.

Campaigning for governor in New York City in 1928, he spoke warmly of "One of the first measures that we started in 1911 . . . the

26. Sullivan was indeed corrupt, in charge of gambling and prostitution below 14th Street. (The New York "Sullivan Law," the nation's first to bar the carrying of concealed weapons, was sponsored by him so that police officers in his pay could plant pistols on members of his rivals' gangs, then hustle them off to jail.)

But he had a sentimental side as well. Every year on his mother's birthday, he distributed tickets entitling each of the 2,000-odd children in his Bowery Ward to a free pair of shoes. And in the state Senate he could often be counted upon to favor legislation that would benefit the poor. When an upstate senator opposed to the fifty-four-hour bill claimed that the factories in his home town were so pleasant women preferred working in them to staying home, Sullivan demolished his argument. "Mr. President, I wish to endorse everything my honored friend, the senator from Troy, has just said. I've seen the shirt factories of Troy, and I want to tell you that it's a fine sight, too, to see them women and girls working in those bright, airy places the Senator has so eloquently described. But I also want to tell you that it's a far finer sight at noontime to see the fine, big, upstanding men fetching around the women's dinner pails."

Sullivan thrived on the gritty, intensely personal politics of the teeming wards where his word was law. He served one term in Congress but found it too anonymous, too far removed from the voters. "There's nothing in this Congress business," he once told a reporter. "They know 'em in Washington. The people down there use 'em as hitchin' posts. Every time they see a Congressman on the street they tie their horse to him."

Big Tim's private life was tormented. He had contracted syphilis, deserted his family, and fathered at least two illegitimate children, and only a few months after he cast his decisive vote for Miss Perkins's bill was confined to a mental institution, a victim of paresis. In 1913, he escaped, wandered along a nearby railroad track, and was killed by a passing freight. Twenty-five thousand people attended his funeral.

Many years later, in the White House, FDR recalled to Frances Perkins that Sullivan had often said that "the America of the future would be made out of the people who came over in steerage and who knew in their hearts and lives the difference between being despised and being accepted and liked." Then the President provided an epitaph that would have astonished his youthful self: "Poor old Tim Sullivan never understood about modern politics, but he was right about the human heart." *Sources:* Alfred Connable and Edward Silberfarb, *Tigers of Tammany Hall*; Kenneth S. Davis, *FDR: The Beckoning of Destiny 1882–1928*, page 268; George Martin, *Madame Secretary*, page 92; Frances Perkins, *The Roosevelt I Knew*, page 13; M. R. Weber, *Tammany Hall*, pages 501–510.

fifty-four-hour law for women and children in industry. In those days a fifty-four-hour law was considered the most radical thing that had ever been talked about."

Five years after that, about to be nominated as President, he approved a *Saturday Evening Post* article written by his closest aide, in which he was portrayed not only as having been present at the final vote on the bill but as the central figure in a suspenseful drama. It had been "young Senator Roosevelt," according to the article, ". . . deeply interested in the passage of a 54-hour bill," who had ordered that Tim Sullivan be summoned from the night boat—'But he won't come,' they objected. 'Yes he will—tell him he has to and I said so.' " Meanwhile, Franklin had held the floor with a filibuster on the habits and plumage of Dutchess County birds until "a sleepy Tim Sullivan appeared on the Senate floor."

Not one word of this tale was true.[27]

Still, the young senator did slowly realize that if he were to hope to play a larger role in the Democratic Party he could not afford to alienate labor or let Tammany Hall out-reform him; by reelection time in 1912, he was a consistent advocate of workmen's compensation, winning the endorsement of the State Federation of Labor, and the following year at a legislative hearing he publicly endorsed all thirty-two of the bills proposed by the Factory Commission.

Franklin was learning. The *source* of an idea, he was coming to see, was less important than whether the idea worked or not. Good could be done—and his own career could be pressed forward—by working

---

27. Frances Perkins was never persuaded that he had ever even really *voted* for the bill. "I always thought he hadn't voted for it," she remembered many years later.

But at a presidential press conference on August 26, 1938, he again referred to his alleged leadership of the fight. In a breezy discussion of name-calling in what he called the Tory press, he suggested to the reporters jammed into his tiny office at Springwood that it might be "fun for some of you to dig out the file of papers of 1911 and 1912, great fun—this is off the record—and see the names that Bob Wagner and I were called in those years. Communists? Of course. Hell, we were working for a 54-hour law for women and children in industry and the *Herald-Tribune* was turning somersaults every day, saying it was communistic for women and children to work 54 hours a week."

Marvin McIntyre [the President's secretary]: You did not brag about being a Communist?

FDR: We were that kind of Communists and we bragged about it. We admitted it. And after that [Triangle] fire, the *Herald-Tribune* did the same thing. . . . Oh, they said it was terrible for the girls to be burned up, but when it came to factory legislation for inspection, they opposed it. It is an old story . . . [but] like the elephant, I have a long memory."

alongside people whom his father or his half brother could not have imagined as allies.[28]

Yet the goals toward which he worked remained murky. He was loud against "bosses" and "the machine," as his father and mother would have wanted him to be, and he was no less noisy in favor of "good government" and "modern ideas"; but definitions of these terms were hard to come by, and the real, day-to-day needs of many of his constituents were still alien to him.

In later years, for example, Franklin spoke often of his natural kinship with the farmers of his district, yet during his first Senate term he was little more attentive to the concerns of the dairymen and fruit growers of his three counties than he had been sensitive to those of Tammany's big-city constituents. And when, during his reelection campaign in 1912, a program was being developed to benefit them on his behalf, it was such a novel notion to him and to others that, he confessed to a friend, "You will be amused to hear that I am blossoming out as the particular friend of the farmer. . . ."

The small-bore moral issues that most exercised his churchgoing constituents did not interest him at all. He didn't care whether baseball was played on Sundays or not—his own father had been against it, yet it did seem a little unfair, he told one agitated correspondent, for rich men like himself to be able to play golf while the less prosperous were forbidden "a quiet game of baseball in the afternoon when it does not disturb anyone"—but he voted to ban it when his mail ran heavily that way. And he was perfectly capable of the sort of public piousness that some of his correspondents expected; voting against a bill that would have eased the state ban on racetrack gambling, he explained his position to a group of approving clergymen in terms that would have especially pleased his father: "While I am personally devoted to horses

---

28. Boss Murphy was learning, too. Some years later, Miss Perkins visited him on behalf of new factory legislation. He listened attentively, then asked, "You are the young lady, aren't you, who managed to get the fifty-hour bill passed?"

She was.

"Well, young lady, I opposed that bill."

"Yes, I so gathered, Mr. Murphy."

"It is my observation that the bill made us many votes. I will tell the boys to give all the help they can to this new bill. Goodbye."

Then, just as she murmured her thanks and was about to leave his office, he asked, "Are you one of these women suffragists?"

"Yes, I am," she answered, worried that she might have alienated him again.

"Well, I am not, but if anyone ever gives them the vote, I hope you will remember that. You would make a good Democrat."

Source: Frances Perkins, *The Roosevelt I Knew*, pages 24–25.

and to races I have always felt that a sport cannot be a healthy one if its existence depends on gambling."

He also echoed his father when it came to public school education. As a member of the Hyde Park school board, Mr. James had been a strong advocate of vocational classes—sewing for girls, for example, and carpentry for boys, rather than more academic subjects that would only take time away from preparation for the life of service to the great estates that he thought the local schools should provide. Franklin agreed, at least during his time in the Senate. "I have been objecting for some years," he told a constituent, "to some of the unnecessary frills which are taught in the Hyde Park school and which take the place necessarily of more practical and valuable work."

He was most consistent and effective when it came to conservation. And it was in this area, more than any other, that young Franklin Roosevelt sounded most like his older, steadier self.

It was an interest to which he had been born, and in which he had been bred. Rides through the family forests alongside his father were among his earliest memories, Mr. James pointing out the special qualities of each variety of tree, making sure that his men preserved the finest old stands intact. And it had been the great cause of his cousin, Theodore.[29]

As chairman of the once somnolent Forest, Fish and Game Committee, Franklin brought the issue center stage, first by sponsoring an Albany appearance by Gifford Pinchot, creator of the U.S. Forest Service under TR, who showed a series of lantern slides to demonstrate the permanent damage done in China by the sort of heedless timber cutting now threatening to denude the Adirondacks, then by demanding a bill to require state regulation of timber harvesting, state inspection of deforested private lands along watersheds, and compulsory reforestation, paid for by the landowners themselves. Private interests were indignant; state interference with their right to do whatever they wished with their lands, they said, was plainly unconstitutional. Franklin complained that "scores of people representing the

---

29. Eleanor Roosevelt believed her husband's life-long interest in forestry had also been encouraged by his boyhood visits to the Black Forest with his ailing father. Franklin had showed it all to her on their honeymoon, she remembered: "These forests were so beautifully kept. When the trees matured they were cut in certain areas, and as they were cut, new trees were planted. He pointed out to me how every twig was gathered up in winter for firewood by the peasants and how beautifully cared-for and cultivated the forests were." *Source:* Eleanor Roosevelt, *Franklin D. Roosevelt and Hyde Park: Personal Recollections of Eleanor Roosevelt,* page 30.

lumber interests" testified against the bill; a great many more worked against it behind the scenes.

A new forestry bill was finally passed at the session's end in April, but most of its tough provisions had been excised beforehand. Another conservation-related bill backed by Franklin, which would have permitted the state to flood its own forest lands in the interest of providing public power, died in the Assembly. (He would return to the struggle for public power as governor of New York, seventeen years later.)

Speaking before the progressive People's Forum at Troy on March 3, 1912, in the thick of his struggle for a tough timber bill, Franklin came as close as he ever came during his early years in politics to setting forth a philosophical basis for his political actions.

"If we go back through history," he began, ". . . we are struck by the fact that . . . the Aryan races have been struggling to obtain individual freedom." That struggle had largely been successful. "It is a sweeping statement to make but taken as a whole today, in Europe and America, the liberty of the individual has been accomplished."

Now, Franklin continued, Americans were engaged in a new "struggle for the liberty of the community," which had a "higher and nobler meaning. . . . We have found that if every man does as he sees fit, even with a due regard to law and order," he often fails to "march on with civilization in a way satisfactory to the well-being of the great majority of us." Competition, he added, "has been shown to be useful up to a certain point and no further. Cooperation must begin where competition leaves off and cooperation is as good a word for the new theory as any other."

It was lack of "cooperation" that had stripped the mountains of China of their forests and now threatened New York State; that made cities and farms mutually antagonistic; that kept labor and capital from progressing together—"There is no such thing as a struggle between labor and capital."

"If we call the method [by which progress will one day be brought about] regulation, people hold up their hands in horror and say 'unamerican,' or 'dangerous.' But if we call the same identical process co-operation, these same old fogeys will cry out 'well done.' "

But then, perhaps concerned that he not himself alarm any fogeys who might be present, he added: "How must the liberty of the community be attained? It will not be attained at once—whether the Democrats or the Republicans or the Socialists say so. . . . It must be worked out by keeping ever in view the cause of the condition, and it must be worked out by keeping ever in view the other great essential point— law and order."

Franklin's address included within it awkward echoes of Theodore Roosevelt and his old schoolmaster, Endicott Peabody. And his efforts to find reassuring ways to say what some then considered radical things seem strained.[30]

But it did demonstrate that he was beginning to carve out fresh positions for himself in an America already different from the one his father had known just a dozen years earlier.

30. The mature FDR was not given to philosophical musing about his actions, but after his election to the presidency in 1932, he did evidently write (though he never published) a short essay entitled "How I am going to Conduct my Responsibilities." In it he was still clearly searching for the most reassuring possible language with which to offer new ideas. The basic fact of American life, he now said, was "*inter*dependence—our mutual dependence one upon the other—of individuals, of businesses, of industries, of towns, of villages, of cities, of states, of nations."

CHAPTER

5

THE SPLENDID TRIUMPH

WHEN THE 1912 Senate session recessed in April, Eleanor was called upon to close up the Albany house and move the household back to New York all on her own. Franklin and Hall were off on an even longer cruise than usual—all the way to Panama, to see the nearly completed Canal that Theodore Roosevelt had begun. Hall, who was about to be graduated with honors from Harvard, was soon to enter engineering school. "I am taking the trip chiefly on Hall's account," Franklin told TR in asking for an introduction to George Washington Goethals, the chief engineer, "and feel that it will help his future engineering career if he could see the Isthmus intelligently." The ploy worked: thanks to Cousin Theodore, Franklin, Hall, and Franklin's friend and Republican Senate colleague, J. Mayhew Wainright, were received by Goethals and his subordinates as important personages.

Eleanor had been asked along, but she had not wanted to leave the children, and did not relish a long sea voyage. "I do wish you were here," Franklin wrote her from his cabin aboard the United Fruit Company's SS *Carillo,* "it is hard enough to be away from the chicks, but with you away from me I feel too very much alone and lost. I hereby solemnly declare that I REFUSE to go away the next time without you . . . I can't tell you how I long to see you again. . . . Give a great deal of love and kisses to sister [Anna] & Brud [James] and Snookums [Elliott]—I am just so crazy to see my four precious ones again that I am almost tempted to turn around . . . and sail straight back. Take good care of yourself, dearest, and *please* don't overdo it in moving. . . ."

This was in a sense a return trip for Franklin, who eight years before had cruised the Caribbean with his mother, and he was careful also to keep her informed of his progress. The sea was calm all the way, "like the overworked mill pond," he told her from the ship, and the weather a little too warm: "We all go about in our shirts, no coats except at meals, but trousers, of course. The few women are also still entirely covered, but we anticipate what greater heat will bring forth.

"It seems so natural to be down in these seas again," he added, "and I only wish you were with us, and I almost expect to see you every time I go on deck."[1]

The *Carillo* docked for a day at Kingston, Jamaica, where Franklin and his companions hurried ashore to buy white tropical clothes, then engaged an automobile for a fast tour of the local attractions. Their first stop was the old church in Spanish Town, where Franklin looked into the register and rediscovered the signatures of "Mrs. James Roosevelt and F. D. Roosevelt, Feb. 25, 1904," and noted a memorial slab in the floor dedicated to the memory of a Briton who, its inscription read, "came with the forces who conquered the Island and having performed various services both civil and military—with great applause he departed this life on the —— day of —— 1692." This legend, Franklin wrote, showed "the importance of correct pronunciation."

They went on that afternoon to explore the former residence of the royal governors, then wound along the Rio Cobre, past "great creepers and clinging crooked trunks of trees," to visit a natural bridge before heading back to their ship through fields of sugar cane. When the party's spirits momentarily flagged in the heat, Franklin stopped the car, he noted in a letter meant for Eleanor, and "a drink of cocoanut water, procured by a naked nigger boy from the top of the tallest tree, did much to make us forget the dust." Telling his mother about the same incident, he was a little less crude, saying that "we sent a darky boy up a tree. . . ."[2]

1. "It gave me great pleasure that you 'wished I had been there,' " Sara answered. "To tell you the truth I was wild to go and could easily have done so, but I did not like suggesting it, as I felt it was pleasanter for you and Hall to go 'unhampered.' " *Source:* Sara Delano Roosevelt Papers, Roosevelt Family Papers Donated by the Children, FDRL.

2. As a young man, Franklin used the word "nigger" privately without embarrassment, just as his father had when young. His handwritten caption for one of the snapshots he made at St. Thomas on his 1904 Caribbean cruise reads: "Niggers coaling the P.V.L. [*Princessin Victoria*

In the Canal Zone itself they called upon Goethals, who told Franklin, "We like to have Americans come down, because they all say it makes them better Americans." Certainly it had an inspirational effect on Franklin, but his enthusiasm was intensified by the fact that the Canal carried with it a host of family associations. Colon, at the Caribbean end, had once been named Aspinwall, after its founder and Franklin's great-uncle by marriage, William H. Aspinwall; Mr. James had spent years seeking funds with which to build a similar canal through Nicaragua; Franklin had himself debated earnestly on behalf of his father's waterway while a schoolboy at Groton, his argument fortified by documents sent to him from home. Above all, the Canal provided him with the most vivid possible example of the impact of his Cousin Theodore upon the world.

Six passenger trains chugged across the Isthmus every day, hauling nearly twenty thousand awed tourists in 1912 alone. At Goethals's order, Franklin and his companions were given a personal observation car in which to ride through the steep-walled, nine-mile Culebra Cut behind their own special engine "over tracks and switches among the blasts and drills and steam shovels and dump trains," Franklin proudly reported home, "the whole trip personally conducted by Commissioner [Admiral Harry Harwood] Rousseau, who, I take it, is probably more the right-hand man of Goethals than anybody else."

"I can't begin to describe it," he told Sara, "and have become so enthusiastic that if I didn't stop I would write all night. The two things that impress me most are the Culebra Cut, because of the colossal hole made in the ground, and the locks because of the engineering problems and size. Imagine an intricate concrete structure nearly a mile long and three or four hundred feet wide, with double gates of steel weighing 700 tons apiece!"

While Franklin was away, the *Titanic* sank off Iceland. With her son far off at sea, Sara was unable, she said, "to get my thoughts away from the awful disaster, it seems too terrible to be true. The confidence in the 'unsinkableness' of the great ship, the shortage of

---

Luise]" and the margin of a 1911 speech contains a crisp pencilled reminder to himself: "story of nigger."

The editors of his personal letters altered both "nigger" and "darky" to "colored" when the Panama letters were first published in 1948; I have restored the original wording. *Sources:* Geoffrey C. Ward, *Before the Trumpet: Young Franklin Roosevelt 1882–1905*, page 47; Arthur M. Schlesinger, Jr., *The Age of Roosevelt: The Politics of Upheaval*, page 430; Elliott Roosevelt, ed., *FDR: His Personal Letters, 1905–1928*, page 184; Franklin D. Roosevelt Papers, Harvard College Papers, FDRL.

life boats . . . no search lights, all these faults are doubtless common to all the great liners. Such warnings are, I suppose, necessary from time to time and for a time great care will be taken. . . ." Many well-known passengers had been lost, she added, "but oh! the tragedies in the steerage as well."[3]

Franklin arrived home safely, landing at New Orleans on April 30 to find Eleanor alone there, waiting for him. While Hall hurried back to Cambridge, Franklin and Eleanor took the train to New Mexico, where Bob and Isabella Ferguson were living in the hope that the warm sun and dry air would halt Bob's tuberculosis. (Sara had gently complained to Franklin that Eleanor would not "hear of my going to New Orleans!"—did not even want her to travel with her as far west as Philadelphia, in fact—but she had put the best face on it she could, adding: "I think you and she will have enough to talk about to keep it up till you get to Silver City!")

The Fergusons were still living in tents in a remote place called Cat Cañon. The closest railroad depot was Silver City, as Sara suggested, but Franklin and Eleanor discovered that the train only reached that outpost three times a week, and so decided to get off at Deming, rent an automobile, and drive to Silver City where they were to be met.

It was June in the desert, hot and glaring and utterly unlike anything either of the Roosevelts had ever seen before, and at first they found it fascinating. Eleanor never forgot the colors of the distant mountains, the sense of limitless space, punctuated only here and there by jagged mesas. But as the hours went by, they began to grow anxious. Sand from the unpaved road crept into the tires and chafed the inner tubes; again and again Franklin had to pull over to patch one or another of them. They passed only one other human being all day, a

3. Those were not the tragedies that most concerned Rosy. Colonel John Jacob Astor IV, his brother-in-law and director of the Astor empire, had been aboard, and for a time Franklin's half brother spent his days at the Carter, Ledyard & Milburn offices working with Commodore Ledyard to help untangle that empire's bewildering affairs upon which his own sizable income largely depended.

When Rosy and the commodore had completed their work on the will, the bulk of Jack Astor's huge fortune—some $87 million—was found to have been left to young Vincent, nine years Franklin's junior and a life-long friend and admirer. (The colonel's charities had added up to less than $50,000, most of it given to St. Paul's, his old school and Groton's great rival.)

The complex legal work involved in settling such a vast estate inevitably contributed to the prosperity of Franklin's old law firm. "Apparently the noble firm of C. L. and M. have fallen on their feet as usual," Franklin would write to John Lytle, another former clerk, the following autumn, "for most of their millionaire clients have passed away within the last year or two and the pickings must be fat, indeed! All the same, confidentially, I never regret the determination to leave them and try some other line of attack. Do you?" Sources: Virginia Cowles, *The Astors*, pages 123–146; Franklin D. Roosevelt Papers, Papers as State Senator, FDRL.

distant and oblivious horseman. The narrow, empty road seemed to stretch on forever. Dusk began to fall, the hot wind blowing across the desert turned cold, and Franklin, still wearing his thin Panama suit, started to shiver. It seemed likely that they would have to spend the night in the open.

Then, far ahead of them on the desert road, they saw first a cloud of dust and then the car that was stirring it up. Martha Selmes, Isabella's mother, sent to pick them up at Silver City and worried when they did not arrive, had driven out to find them.

The life the Fergusons had carved out for themselves at Cat Cañon was a revelation to Eleanor, and perhaps to Franklin as well. As the sixth child of a Scottish landowner, Robert had inherited comparatively little money and had originally been sent to America to find a way to make his own living. Since his illness, he had relied on a modest pension from the Astor Trust, supplemented by regular payments from a compassionate older brother. Isabella's father had died when she was a child, and she and her mother had often had to make their home with relatives before her marriage. But the Fergusons had been a prominent and popular couple in New York drawing rooms before tuberculosis drove them west, and the adjustments they had made with such apparent cheerfulness astonished Eleanor.

Isabella had described their surroundings to Eleanor in a series of breathless letters. "If only you were alongside this warm but pleasant [day]," she had written shortly after arriving in New Mexico. ". . . Surely Anna & James & Elliott would like feeding chickens and building rock houses and going on most cautious barefoot strolls on the path between tents. . . . The practical odds & ends of everyday living as we do keep one's hands so full. Indeed, you'd find it hard to believe till you'd seen it for yourself."

Now, she and Franklin could see it for themselves: the tidy, open-sided tents; baths in a tin tub filled with hot water at dawn by a Mexican boy; the vegetable patch Isabella herself tended. The two children, Martha, now just six, and Robert, four, were thriving, Eleanor noted, on a diet that included "pork and beans and all kinds of canned food which would have been considered absolute death to children of their age in eastern surroundings."[4] The family's milk was left each evening on a neighbor's fence post, halfway to town.

---

4. Before too long, the Ferguson children would learn to ride and shoot and begin to supplement the family income by trapping and skinning rabbits, skunks, coyotes, and wild cats and selling the pelts to a St. Louis furrier. *Source:* Interview with Martha Ferguson Breasted.

In the evenings, sitting quietly with Bob and Isabella and her mother in front of the big tent they called "the living room," they watched the fading light play over the landscape, just as Isabella had described it—"pink and blue far hills & sandy near ones with scrubby dwarf evergreens that break the desert sweep . . . the air . . . marvelous and still."

And at night they slept beneath a vast black sky filled with brilliant stars, the silence broken only occasionally by the cries of distant coyotes and by the sound of Bob's deep, anguished coughing coming from the tent in which his illness forced him to sleep alone.

Eleanor greatly admired the single-minded devotion with which Isabella cared for her husband. Much younger than he and very beautiful, she seems never to have regretted her decision to marry him. When his disease was first diagnosed in 1908, his doctors told him he had just six months to live; Isabella refused to believe it and, thanks in large part to her attentions, he had now lived four years (and would survive for another ten).

Caring for him was not easy. Medical experts agreed that the best advice for sufferers was "Never stand when you can sit. Never sit when you can lie." Now gaunt, weak, and hollow-eyed, he had once been an active, energetic outdoorsman—a rancher and hunting companion of Theodore Roosevelt, a Rough Rider, and an explorer who had undertaken a 500-mile trek through the Canadian wilderness—and he seems to have suffered almost as much from inactivity as he did from his illness, striking out verbally sometimes at those who cared most for him out of hopelessness and frustration.

There was the constant fear, too, that he might somehow infect the children or Isabella herself. Tuberculosis was still America's most feared disease; only infantile paralysis was coming to seem as sinister. No one was sure how TB spread; no one knew of any cure. The patient's silverware was kept separate; so was the linen. Bob's children were not to touch their father, and he was never to touch them—or his wife.[5]

5. The uncharacteristically desperate tone of one of Isabella's letters to Eleanor, written in 1918 from the mountain homestead she and Bob had built by then, hints at how burdensome the simplest household logistics could be, how isolated she and her children sometimes felt. Bob was just then "having a long, tedious pull-up from such a sinking point," she said. (The course of the disease was notoriously unsteady, a succession of false hopes, raised and dashed.) An earlier letter from Eleanor had hinted that the Roosevelts were not going to Campobello this summer. "Bob, Mother and I," Isabella wrote, "are wondering so *hopefully* if you & Franklin would consider sending Anna & James out here to us for the summer or a portion of it. . . . It would spell *heaven* for us & . . . You must understand it would mean stopping on the other side of the

Isabella seems to have accepted it all with remarkable cheer, taking pleasure in her surroundings, making the best of each day as it came, getting to know the neighbors scattered across the rugged landscape. "When I think now," Eleanor wrote years later, "of the endless care that went into the upbringing of two children in the same house with a man who was slowly dying of tuberculosis, I marvel at the fact that Isabella was able to create the impression that life was joyous, that the burdens were not heavy, and that anyone who was not living that kind of life was missing something."

When the time came for Eleanor to shoulder a burden almost as heavy, Isabella's example would help strengthen her resolve.

Franklin and Bob talked politics. Both Fergusons admired Franklin's recent battle against Tammany—they had followed it eagerly in the armloads of Eastern newspapers they received by mail—but from Cat Cañon, Albany politics looked a little pallid. "It's quite true," Isabella once wrote Eleanor, "that one is not a proved politician [in New Mexico] till he's been shot at a certain number of times in the public plaza!" Bob's greatest enthusiasm was reserved for the likelihood that TR was about to return to the presidential lists, if not as a Republican, then as the nominee of a new Progressive Party. His affection for the man he always called "the Colonel" was, if anything, greater than his visitor's—lunch and dinner in the canyon were announced by a dented bugle blown at San Juan Hill.

Franklin was excited by the prospect of his cousin's return to public life, too; but he was already dedicated to the presidential candidacy of Woodrow Wilson, the reform-minded former professor and president of Princeton who had been elected governor of New Jersey on the same day he had won his own Senate seat.

He had first met the governor late the previous autumn, when Wilson already seemed the front runner for the 1912 nomination, and Franklin had hurried to Trenton to talk with him to see what he might

---

house from Bob—possibly putting the boys in a tent house—& Bob has everything separate—China, glass, spoons, forks, etc. & no one ever goes into his bathroom—& if they should come I'll have everything of his washed in separate vessels—(a matter that the Drs have not thought necessary)—but we'd play on the safe side. . . . I'd never be able to tell you what such a chance to have ours together would mean!!—or how I long to come to know my god-daughter. . . ."

The Roosevelt's gently demurred, perhaps because they still thought the risks of infection too great. Isabella did get to know Anna on her brief visits back east, but the Roosevelt and Ferguson children would remain only what Franklin once called "delightful myths to each other" for many years. *Sources:* Eleanor Roosevelt Papers, FDRL; Ferguson Family Correspondence, Arizona Historical Society; Interview with Martha Ferguson Breasted.

do to help his candidacy in New York State. The governor had wanted to know what Franklin thought his New York prospects were. Not good, Franklin had told him; while there was widespread public support for him among the rank and file and perhaps a third of the ninety most likely delegates to the national convention leaned toward him, Boss Murphy controlled the majority and, because of the unit rule, all were bound to vote as he dictated.

Nonetheless, Franklin said, he believed that conditions might soon change. Boss rule was doomed, not only in New York City but all across the state, he told Wilson; the future lay with the independents like himself. He eagerly volunteered to see what he could do to build support for the governor.

Although it seems unlikely that he would have admitted it to Bob Ferguson, Franklin's early enthusiasm for Wilson was at least as pragmatic as it was principled. He genuinely admired Wilson's winning fight against the same sort of machine he faced in Tammany—the New Jersey governor had successfully blocked election to the Senate of a machine nominee more noxious than Sheehan, then gone on to win passage of a flood of progressive legislation in just four months—and he may also have been especially attracted by Wilson's air of Protestant rectitude, so reminiscent of his own father and of Endicott Peabody.

But he also saw in the governor a potential winner with whom it would be prudent to cooperate early. The Democrats had lost four presidential races in a row. Wilson, a transplanted Virginian who had managed to win power in a traditionally Republican state, seemed to promise at least the possibility of victory for a national party that had, from Franklin's point of view, for far too long been under the domination of William Jennings Bryan and his Western and Southern allies.

After Franklin's two rugged years in Albany, it was clear to him that if he were to rise further in New York politics, he would have to do so without the help of the machine. By allying himself with Wilson he stood at least a chance of circumventing it—and perhaps even of winning for himself a spot in a new Democratic administration at Washington.

By the time Franklin reached New Mexico, he had already been hard at work for seven months alongside his old ally, Thomas Mott Osborne, trying to organize upstate support for Wilson in the face of Tammany's hostility. The battle had not gone well: so tight was Boss Murphy's grip that when the state Democratic Convention met in

Manhattan in April and Franklin invited a host of upstate delegates to a Wilson dinner, only twenty dared even reply and only three accepted.

Still, the showdown would not come until the Democratic National Convention at Baltimore in late June. Although Franklin was not a delegate or even an alternate—Murphy had made sure of that—he planned to attend as leader of a band of one hundred fifty members of a hastily organized "New York State Wilson Conference," and see what might be done from the gallery.

While Bob and Franklin talked of the coming campaign, their wives took long walks together. Isabella described her problems finding good help in a West that was still distinctly wild—"Last week, I thought I had a really good boy, but I found he was wanted for the murder of his own brother, so I had to let him go to jail." She introduced Eleanor to several other TB exiles in Silver City, and drove her twenty-five miles to Burro Mountain near Tyrone, where the Fergusons would soon build a handsome ranch house and begin to homestead. Eleanor, who still could not drive, felt hopelessly inadequate, she remembered, and when they stopped to cook themselves a meal, "it took me hours to peel a few potatoes, which should have been done in a few minutes."[6]

Eleanor's admiration for Isabella never wavered. "I know no one, least of all myself," she would one day write her, "who could have done with their life what you've done with yours." And Isabella responded in kind, keeping a photograph of Eleanor and her children always on her living room table—"the center of our family circle"—and telling her own mother that should anything ever happen to her, the children were to be sent to stay with the Roosevelts for at least half of every year. (Later, when she heard a wealthy friend's husband complain about the burdens his wife bore overseeing a houseful of servants, she told him, "I know one Eleanor Roosevelt who has four

6. The Fergusons knew a number of wealthy easterners whose adjustments to Western life had not been so smooth as theirs. According to Isabella, one millionaire got down from his private car at Silver City, accompanied by a private physician, sauntered into the shoemaker's shop, looked around, and "slapping him on the back said, 'I say, if you'll move out of your house today and let me move in tomorrow, I'll give you $15,000.'" The shoemaker told him to go to hell.

Others adapted in their own way. A Dr. Ricketts of New York, his wife and sister, were "a most delightful surprise in parts so remote," Isabella told Eleanor. "For diversion he runs koyotes down across the plains by motor." The Ricketts lived just across the Mexican border in Cananea, and when a running battle between rival rebel bands was about to begin there, the doctor "had carpets and chairs taken to the cellar so [that he and the ladies] could be comfortable during the shooting." Source: Eleanor Roosevelt Papers, FDRL

children & moves them all six times a year—& does everything else besides.")

Franklin may have felt a bit left out in New Mexico; he was not the focus of things. Bob Ferguson was far older than he, had actually fought alongside his cousin, Theodore, and had befriended Eleanor long before Franklin began to court her. Isabella, too, was much more his wife's friend than his, and his over-eager efforts to make her warm to him sometimes put her off. Isabella liked Franklin but never entirely trusted him; even in those early days, she much later told her son, she had found him "pretty elusive."

On the day the Roosevelts left to take the train back home, Bob was feeling well enough to ride along as Isabella drove. He suggested they take in an especially handsome mountain view. Afterwards, returning to the desert floor by an unfamiliar road, they came to a crossroads, two arrow-straight desert tracks leading toward horizons that seemed identical to Eleanor and the Fergusons. Bob admitted that he was not really sure which one led to Deming.

Franklin did not hesitate. "You go straight ahead," he said. "I remember the contour of those mesas the day we drove over." He was right, and it was this demonstration of what Eleanor called "Franklin's remarkable memory" that he liked best to recall about this trip in later years.

It was a crowded spring for the Roosevelts. In early June, Hall—not yet twenty-one—was to marry a Miss Margaret Richardson, still younger, of Marion, Massachusetts, to whom he had been secretly engaged for more than a year. He had not told either Eleanor or Franklin about it until the end of the previous summer—and then only at the insistence of his fiancée's mother.

His reluctance to confide in his sister and brother-in-law was perhaps understandable. Several years earlier, at Campobello, he had flirted mildly with a number of girls, including Carolyn Sturgis, the daughter of Dr. Russell Sturgis, a Boston physician and island neighbor, whose old New England family had been linked long before with the Delanos through the China trade. Franklin and Eleanor had both kidded Hall unmercifully about his "harem" that summer, and Franklin had later told exaggerated stories about it to friends and family. Hall was furious: "By the way," he told Eleanor, "you might advise F. to be careful what he says about me, especially when it isn't true, as other people believe him when they see his face but . . . have never been initiated. I heard what he said as host a while ago at a dinner party and I wish he would behave himself."[7]

Sara had made things still worse. She decided Hall's courtship of a girl from a fine family so closely tied to hers should be encouraged, and during a visit to Boston in 1910 had evidently told members of the Sturgis clan that Hall's interest in Carolyn was serious. Hall complained to Eleanor about that, too. "I am now under obligation to the family and all bound in such a manner as I had always carefully avoided. I prefer to do my own choosing and to carry out all such diplomatic relations without expert assistance." When he had finally made it clear to Carolyn that he wished only to be her friend, he told his sister, he "incurred the hatred of the whole [Sturgis] tribe," and so, when he did develop a serious interest in another girl, he kept it to himself.

Eleanor worried that both Hall and Margaret—an attractive debutante who loved outdoor sports and dancing, with whom, Eleanor confessed, she seemed to have little in common—were too young to marry, but since she herself had been thought very young when she married Franklin, she found it difficult to argue with their plans.

Besides, Hall was uninterested in what the rest of the family thought. "As for telling anyone of our engagement, don't worry," he told his sister. "I have never had the slightest intention and you can decide all questions of precedence . . . if anyone expects to be told first, let's tell 'em all at the same time . . . and see them fight it out as to who got there first."

Hall was about to come into his inheritance from his late parents, and, as Eleanor wrote later, he "had . . . very naturally a great desire to have a home of his own for he had always lived either with my grandmother or with me . . . he had curiosity about life much as I had had, and a desire to possess something which was really his own."

For Eleanor, Hall's marriage provided both relief and regret. Ever since her mother's death she had felt responsible for her brother. She had "thought about him a great deal, loved him deeply, and longed to mean a great deal in his life" she wrote. "I think at this wedding I felt as though my own son and not my brother was being married. . . ."

7. Hall himself had contributed memorably to his own legend as an eager suitor within the family that summer by setting out from the Campobello cottage with a young woman to scale "The Old Friar," the steep, jagged landmark that guarded Friar's Head. Whether he had deliberately planned it or not, the tide crept in while he and the girl were still climbing, so that he had several hours alone with her on the summit while Eleanor and Sara anxiously peered at them through binoculars to ensure that nothing untoward occurred before the tide went out again. *Source:* "Conversations Between the Four Roosevelt Brothers. . . ."

Not long after the wedding, Franklin hurried to Baltimore for the Democratic National Convention. In the weeks since he and Bob Ferguson had talked presidential politics in New Mexico, the stakes had risen. On June 22, the Republican old guard in Chicago had ignored Theodore Roosevelt's successes in the primaries, crushed his progressive rebellion, and renominated his former friend and chosen successor, William Howard Taft, for President. ("I don't want to fight," Taft had said when TR first entered the primaries against him, "but even a rat in a corner will fight.")

The ex-President had bolted the GOP and vowed to soldier on as the nominee of a third, Progressive Party. With the opposition sundered, a Democratic victory seemed not only possible for the first time in twenty years, but likely.

Eleanor went to Baltimore with Franklin, but did not enjoy herself. They had rented a small house with two other couples, sight unseen. It turned out to be a dreary place: the beds were lumpy, Eleanor recalled, there was no silverware, the maid was poorly trained, and the Roosevelts' bedroom overlooked an alley from which "the most unearthly sounds emanated."

Franklin hardly noticed. This was his first national convention, and he revelled in it. He spent hours working the lobbies and corridors, shaking hands and talking up his candidate. Reporters and delegates alike from distant states were curious to meet this un-Republican Roosevelt.

One of them, Josephus Daniels—national committeeman, editor of the Raleigh (North Carolina) *News and Observer*, old friend of Bryan, close counselor to Wilson—was especially struck by him. "He was in a gay humor," he remembered, "and I thought he was as handsome a figure of an attractive young man as I have ever seen. At that convention Franklin and I became friends—a case of love at first sight."

Franklin did himself more good by circulating among the party leaders than he did Wilson. His was an almost entirely peripheral role that week in Baltimore. He and Eleanor had good seats in the gallery, but she spent most of her time there alone while he organized his small claque of cheering New Yorkers, and gossiped with reporters in the press box. When a floor demonstration for Wilson's chief rival, House Speaker Champ Clark of Missouri, began, and the Baltimore regulars allowed several outsiders to slip inside and swell its ranks, Franklin led a shouting band of one hundred upstate Wilsonites in their wake, shouting, "We Want Wilson!" as loudly as they could. Murphy's delegates glared as he swung by.

Eleanor found the convention exciting, she remembered, but also hot and confusing. After the tenth ballot, Murphy threw Tammany's support to Clark and he pulled ahead of all his rivals, but by only a single vote; he needed two thirds to win.

On the fourteenth ballot, William Jennings Bryan, who had come to Baltimore in futile search of a fourth presidential nomination, sweat running down the sides of his bald head but his voice still thunderous, threw his support to Wilson, vowing that he could never vote for Clark or any other man who had accepted support from Tammany or its shadowy Wall Street allies, among them the son of Mr. James's old friend August Belmont.

Mrs. Belmont, sitting near Eleanor, rose to her feet in indignation and stalked from the hall, threatening to work against the Democratic Party for its ingratitude toward her generous husband.

Eleanor was still more startled when, during a floor demonstration for Clark, the Speaker's pretty daughter permitted herself to be carried around the hall on the shoulders of his cheering supporters: "Such things simply did not happen to ladies, in my code!"

Finally, Franklin seemed so busy and so preoccupied, Eleanor wrote, that "I decided my husband would hardly miss my company, as I rarely laid eyes on him," and she left town to take the children up to Campobello.

Indeed, Franklin barely noticed as the balloting ground on. Finally, on Monday, July 1, the weary delegates nominated Woodrow Wilson on the forty-sixth ballot.

WILSON NOMINATED THIS AFTERNOON, Franklin wired Eleanor at Campobello. ALL MY PLANS VAGUE SPLENDID TRIUMPH.[8]

Franklin's plans were clear enough on one thing; Whatever happened in the presidential race, he now wanted first to be renominated for his state Senate seat, and then to be reelected.

A few months earlier those goals had seemed beyond his reach, and he had spoken to several friends as recently as January about dropping out of politics until the atmosphere for reform improved. The Democratic machine's opposition to him had been immovable; traditionally

8. Franklin Roosevelt was delighted; Theodore Roosevelt was not. On the way to the convention, Franklin told a reporter, he had run into TR's son, Kermit, who had said, "Pop was praying for Clark." *Source:* Ernest K. Lindley, *Franklin D. Roosevelt: A Career in Progressive Democracy,* page 105.

Republican voters in his district appeared to be edging back toward their ancient allegiance; Lewis Stuyvesant Chanler's reelection to the Assembly by just seven votes in the most safely Democratic neighborhood the previous November was the proof.

Now that the Republicans were split, and two candidates would be sent into the field to divide the opposition, Franklin's reelection seemed attainable. But first he had to be renominated. Ed Perkins, the Democratic Dutchess County chairman who had always viewed Franklin with suspicion, was still less enthusiastic about him after his well-publicized battle with Tammany.

Fresh from the Baltimore convention, Franklin had joined Osborne in forming still another reform organization, the Empire State Democracy, and at its first meeting he had called upon all Democratic progressives to desert Murphy and rally to Wilson. Again, Murphy had quietly outmaneuvered him. The Tammany chief let it be known that he would back the party's nominee for President, and even pledged that the upcoming state convention would be allowed to pick an unbossed candidate for governor. The Empire State Democracy was made to seem shrill, amateurish.

"I am just back from a long day in which I have covered 150 miles in the machine," Franklin wrote Eleanor at Campobello in July. "I have seen all the 'henchmen' in Claverack, Hillsdale, Copake, Ancram, Pine Plains, Bangall, Stanfordville, Clinton and Salt Point! I ran straight up to Columbia County, then turned East, came down the Harlem Valley and thence home. The day was perfect, the machine went well"—a nice contrast with the day before, which he had spent trying to rally support in Poughkeepsie. "It appears that Tammany and 'the Interests' are really making an effort to prevent my renomination," he continued. "This is done by several agents who are trying to stir up the old Sheehan business and are taking advantage of the starting of the Empire State Democracy to howl about 'Discord' etc. Of course the trouble is that Perkins has no spine, but he knows now if he listens to [Tammany headquarters on] 14th Street, he will have a perfectly delightful little fight on his hands that will not stop easily or quickly."

Despite Perkins and Tammany, Franklin was renominated unanimously on August 24. His acceptance speech was notably conciliatory. "I realize," he said, "that in places the Democrats are not in accord . . . and to have success, I believe in unity."

Sara's reaction was mixed. "In *one* way I wanted you all in New York," she told her son from Paris, where she was visiting her sister, Dora, "but to be sensible & unselfish, I am glad & I hope you will be elected because I *know* how honest & fearless you are & that nothing will change you when you know what is honest & right. . . . I hope the 'bull moose' party will endorse you of course it *ought* to, to be true to its principles." It was now clear that Franklin's interest in politics was not waning as she had once hoped it would; on the other hand, she did not think it had corrupted him, either.

Sara's hope that Franklin would somehow win the backing of the Bull Moose party was symptomatic of the struggle between political and family allegiances that began in 1912, and that would continue to smolder among Franklin and Eleanor's family and friends through the presidential years.

However outwardly genial they seemed, the Oyster Bay Roosevelts and their closest allies would always see Franklin's refusal to support TR in 1912 as a kind of betrayal. The Colonel considered that race as something like a holy war. "We stand at Armageddon and we battle for the Lord," TR had said when the Republicans rejected him in June, and nothing that had happened since had dampened his fervor or that of the other members of his family. Teddy and Helen Robinson were working hard for the ex-President, Sara told Franklin from Paris, and then warned, "*Don't* pin any faith to Teddy. I know a few things from 'away back' which I can't repeat but *he* is not a friend to you & I am glad you need never look to him for help in *anything*, tho' I am devoted to Helen, and think she is all right when not influenced by her little husband. This is *entre nous*, strictly."

The Fergusons, too, threw themselves into the Bull Moose campaign. A great congress of Rough Riders was held at their homestead when the Colonel stopped at Albuquerque, and Isabella took the children to see a mock gun battle put on in his honor—seventy-five years later, her daughter Martha still vividly remembered the terrifying noise of it. TR had seemed tired but "more loveable than ever," Isabella reported to Eleanor, and "of you he said so much that warmed my heart.

"It does seem too bad that 'Uncle Theodore' should have to carry such an undue load," Isabella continued, "but, after all, in the end his achievements may become all the more sure and clear—He might perhaps not have wished to run against Woodrow Wilson & it would have been easier to step aside & let the break come in the

Democratic as in the Republican ranks, but when he puts his hand to an undertaking he never pulls back—or quits until it is finished— he's doing a wonderful world's work—a great world's work—and he will succeed. . . ." A very large part of the growing national "resentment against machine methods and & their results," she continued, "is due directly to his leadership—and teaching. His wisdom & patience being as fully appreciated as his fighting crusader qualities."

Franklin, too, was thrilled by his cousin's struggle against the Republican regulars. "It is indeed a marvelous thing," he had written back in June, "that [TR], acting with the support of untrained militia, has succeeded in overcoming the well-organized opposition of the trained soldiers of the Republican Party." But his own future now depended upon a Wilson victory.[9]

One afternoon in early September, Franklin and Eleanor returned to the New York house, its furniture still shrouded for the season, planning to spend just one evening having dinner out with Bob Ferguson's brother, Ronald, before moving up to Springwood (where they had left the children) for the autumn campaign. But by dinner time Franklin was violently ill with a high fever and severe stomach pain, unable to dine or even to stand up for very long. Eleanor took Ronald out to dinner.

Franklin was not better when she got back, did not improve the next day. A doctor was called who pronounced himself mystified. Franklin's condition remained the same for ten days, Eleanor running up and down stairs with trays, bedding, patent medicines that proved worthless. She, too, began to feel ill.

Finally, an anxious Sara returned from Europe, saw that Eleanor

9. Even Sara, devoted as she was to her son's cause, was evidently not at all sure she favored Wilson over Cousin Theodore. She would demonstrate her continuing ambivalence by attending the climactic Manhattan rallies of both candidates, and on election night it was to Bull Moose headquarters, not Wilson's, that she went, escorted by Franklin's law partner, Harry Hooker.

The Springwood household was not the most deeply divided in the extended Roosevelt family that autumn. Nick Longworth, Alice Roosevelt's ambitious husband, was the congressman from President Taft's Cincinnati district. She, of course, was passionately in favor of her father. He was torn, as she told a friend, between his father-in-law "and his Ohio obligations toward Mr. Taft. Father recommends he remain with Mr. Taft to protect his future in his home state."

Alice's husband and father finally met at Sagamore Hill that summer, and on its piazza, side by side in rockers, agreed that Longworth would stay above the struggle, so far as he could, and—far more difficult for either of them to guarantee—that Alice would maintain a discreet silence until Election Day.

was "so hot I was frightened," and took charge, summoning a doctor who diagnosed typhoid fever and told both Roosevelts to stay in bed. (Eleanor blamed the stateroom water on the steamer that had brought them south from Campobello for infecting them; both she and Franklin had heedlessly used it to brush their teeth.)

Eleanor recovered rapidly.[10] Franklin languished.

It seemed a disaster. He was sure he could not win without mounting the sort of strenuous backroad campaign that had gained him his seat two years before. Perkins and the regulars would do nothing to help his candidacy and some of them might quietly do what they could to torpedo it.

Worse still, he had had the bad luck to fall ill in New York, not Hyde Park; the old charge that he was really a Manhattan swell and not a Dutchess County man was sure to be revived. (He actually had himself driven up to Springwood so that he might at least recuperate there, exhausted himself in the process, and was ordered back to the city by his doctors.)

Day after day, he lay alone in his Manhattan bedroom, feverish and haggard—he looked like Robert Louis Stevenson in his final days in Samoa, Eleanor remembered—unable to do much more than fret. He did not even cheer up for long when his mother wrapped him in blankets and drove with him to the river to watch several battleships steam by. His political career seemed to have come to an abrupt end.

In October, farmers harvesting their crops along the roads of the twenty-sixth senatorial district began to notice what may have seemed at first a familiar sight. The same big, red, two-cylinder Maxwell slammed its way past them that they had seen at election time two years before. Harry Hawkey, the Democratic piano tuner, was again at the wheel, wearing a duster, goggles, and his flaring gray mustache. But there were no flags flying this time, no bunting was draped along the sides, and someone else was sitting in the back—someone utterly unlike the tall, handsome young Senate candidate with the famous name who had pulled over then to shake their hands.

10. No sooner was she back on her feet than she received a desperate wire from Hall. Margaret had given birth to a boy who was ill. She hurried to Boston, she remembered, "but after weeks of anxiety the baby died without our ever being entirely sure what was wrong with it." Eleanor stayed as long as she could, caring for the grieving mother and nursing her brother, who had collapsed with appendicitis the same week his son died. *Source:* Eleanor Roosevelt, *This Is My Story,* page 193.

This man was small and ugly, his face deeply pocked, his head sunk between his shoulders, a cigarette dangling from his lower lip. He stared straight ahead, leaning forward every so often to urge Hawkey to drive faster.

His name was Louis McHenry Howe, and without his help it is hard to see how Franklin Roosevelt could ever have become President.

Howe's own early life had been nearly as unlike Franklin's as was his appearance. Born at Indianapolis, Indiana, in 1871, he had been surrounded since early boyhood with failed dreams and missed opportunities. His father, Captain Edward Porter Howe, was a short, fat, bearded Civil War veteran whose big plans had finally come to nothing. He had married a wealthy widow, Eliza Blake Ray, the daughter of the president of the Bank of Indiana, bought a handsome house, got a good job with the Franklin Insurance Company, and, with his wife's fortune—plus money borrowed from banks, his company, even his church—began to buy up real estate and to build a downtown business block named after himself.

The Panic of 1873 wiped him out. He lost everything, had to flee with his wife and five-year-old son to Saratoga Springs, New York, where he was given rooms in Dr. Strong's Remedial Institute, a boardinghouse and sanitorium run by his brother-in-law.

In a matter of months, Ed Howe had gone from up-and-coming young businessman to poor relation. He would eventually scrape together enough money to buy a modest house of his own in Saratoga, but he never really recovered from that humiliation, either financially or emotionally.

His wife kept up a brave front, but the tensions her husband's failure surely caused may have helped exacerbate the chronic asthma that already wracked her frail five-year-old son. Louis was always small for his age, a pale little boy with a bulbous nose, jutting ears, and enormous brown eyes. He was fond of books—Thomas Carlyle's *Heroes and Hero-Worship* was an early favorite—and writing dreamy, overwrought poetry, and he was thought too weak at first by his anxious parents even to play with other children.

Saratoga Springs was a curious place, combining a fashionable resort for the wealthy horse fanciers who flocked there each summer with a conventional upstate small town and a center for the treatment of well-to-do sufferers from various ailments. Like Franklin, who spent several summers with his parents at European spas, Louis spent much of his childhood surrounded by the sick and dying.

Ed Howe and his family never really fitted in: they were not ill; they had too little money to take what they themselves may have believed to be their rightful place among the wealthy; and, as newcomers with airs, they were not especially welcome among the permanent residents. Ed's politics did not help, either: he was a vociferous Democrat in a largely Republican town. He worked as a free-lance reporter for a while, then bought a failing weekly, the Saratoga *Sun*, and turned it into a partisan newspaper whose costly printing innovations—three colors and bold headlines—were not enough to guarantee a profit. He did a little better running the printshop connected with the paper and, during the four years of Grover Cleveland's first term as President, was rewarded for his steady partisanship with appointment as Saratoga postmaster. But by the time Louis was seventeen or so, his father was struggling again, moving inexorably toward the nervous breakdown that would make his last years still more bleak.

Louis was tutored at home at first—bronchitis and a possible heart condition had been added to his asthma by the time he entered adolescence, and shortly after that internal damage done by coughing caused him to be fitted with the truss he would wear daily for the rest of his life. He was then sent to the Temple Grove Seminary for young ladies just across the street, where he and the principal's son were the only boys. Plans to send him on to Yale fell through; he never attended any college.

Instead, he went to work for his increasingly distracted father; at the age of twenty-one he became co-editor and part owner of the *Sun*, spending much of his time out trying to drum up business for the printshop—for a time, thanks to him, the firm did fairly well printing advertisements that were wound around the handles of buggy whips. He also picked up extra money as a reporter, both for his own paper and, during the racing season, as a local stringer for the *New York Herald*, chronicling the doings of the rich.

Somehow he found time to join in the activities of other young people. He threw himself into golf and tennis, for example, with more energy than skill—his size and frailty usually defeated him. He was better at bicycling, but this only added to his troubles. Spinning along a country road one afternoon, he caught his toe in the spokes and was hurled, face-first, into the gravel; the scars, with their deeply imbedded dirt, remained with him all his life. He became a good card player at the Saratoga casinos, laid siege to a succession of visiting young ladies with little success, found his greatest satisfaction in amateur theatricals, writing and directing and starring in his own plays. Only on stage, where he could fulfill his own or someone else's imaginings, did he feel fully satisfied.

The real world then seemed to offer him little hope. He had been raised to savor the tastes and refinement bred by wealth and social distinction, but without any clear sense of how he might attain them for himself. His father had been unable to amass either wealth or power; the effort to do so had shattered him. Louis, who loved his father, and who saw himself as even more unattractive than he really was—"one of the four ugliest men in New York," he already liked to say, for fear that others might say something like it first—could not imagine how he could do better on his own.

The first two decades of his adult life mirrored with eerie accuracy the downward course of his father's life. Like Ed Howe, Louis pursued and eventually married a young woman whose social position and wealth were far greater than his own; like his father, too, he would deeply disappoint her.

In the summer of 1896 he began to court a well-connected young visitor to his uncle's sanitorium, Grace Hartley of Fall River, Massachusetts, who had been brought to Saratoga by her widowed mother in the hope of heading off the attentions of a persistent young Irish Catholic suitor. The Hartleys were influential and prosperous[11]— Grace herself had recently come into a considerable inheritance—and Mrs. Hartley was determined to shield her daughter from fortune hunters. In this, she saw Louis Howe as an ally at first; he was attentive and diverting, but clearly not the sort of young man she needed to worry about—even Grace said later she had not been "a bit impressed with him" at first.

Mrs. Hartley underestimated both the little man's devotion and his staying power. He escorted Grace for long shady walks down Broadway and took her dancing at the Grand Union Hotel, where Victor Herbert sometimes conducted the orchestra. He wrote to her that winter, saw her again in the summer of 1897, visited Fall River in 1898, saw her secretly at the home of a sympathetic Boston girlfriend that summer and, again secretly, at a friend's home in Saratoga. Finally he told her that he was planning to go overseas to cover the Spanish-American War and that he wished to marry her before he went. She

11. They were related to another important Fall River family, the Andrew Bordens, whose daughter, Lizzie, had severely embarrassed them all four years earlier.

believed him, and in November of 1898 they stole into Vermont to be married by a justice of the peace.

The next day, Grace returned quietly to her mother's home and Louis went back to Saratoga, his marriage still a secret. He never went to the war—it ended before he could get himself organized—but he did continue to visit the Hartley home, to the growing annoyance of Grace's mother, who couldn't understand why he had not long since given up his suit.

Finally, as Grace told the story, she and Louis were found out but sworn to secrecy; a formal wedding was held in Fall River in the spring of 1899, and they moved into a comfortable Saratoga home, bought and furnished for them by Mrs. Hartley. A daughter named Mary was born a year later.

After that, nothing went right. The newspaper faltered. Louis mortgaged his new home to save it. Mrs. Hartley was enraged. When Grace again became pregnant, she returned to Fall River to be with her mother. The new baby was a boy, whom they named Edward Hartley. Louis hurried to his wife's bedside. The Howes reunited in Fall River, returned to Saratoga, then split again.

The *Sun* and its printshop fell into the hands of collectors in 1899. The Howes moved into his parents' home for a time, where, now a thirty-year-old married man with two children, he was still treated as if he were a small boy and fined a quarter if he came late to table. (Howe would always be especially understanding of Franklin's diffi- culties with his own mother.)

Grace could not stand it and fled again to Fall River. That pattern would be repeated throughout the Howes' turbulent marriage; they were rarely together for more than a few months, sometimes a few weeks, in any year. Instead of living together, they wrote one another long, anguished letters; he apologized again and again for having brought his wife so low and painted increasingly implausible pictures of how things would be once they turned the corner that seemed steadily to recede. Grace berated him for his failures, blamed him for disappointing her, for being inattentive to her and to his children. Both Louis and Grace believed she had married beneath herself.

Louis eked out a meager living—$10 a week—working as a part- time reporter for his old paper's new owner, and when he was dis- missed even from that job, humbly sought new assignments from the man who had fired him in spite of Grace's fierce scorn: "wild horses wouldn't have forced *me* into it—go out on the road and run up trade for a man who had just discharged me! Not much!"

He tried to make money at cards, at the track, writing travel pieces for magazines. He also dug hard on behalf of the *Herald*, supplying facts for staff writers to turn into stories, and wrote a society column during the season. (This last was not so easy as it sounds. "Getting a respectable showing of Society" in a slow year, he remembered, was "like marching 6 supers 'round & 'round the stage to represent an army.") And he occasionally covered a real story; his best known beat was Theodore Roosevelt's rattling buckboard ride down from Lake Tear-of-the-Clouds and into the presidency the night William McKinley died.

In 1906 he agreed to serve as an Albany stringer for the *Herald* during the legislative session. By the time Franklin arrived at Albany five years later, Howe was a capital fixture, nicknamed "the water rat" by one of his colleagues for the enthusiasm with which he burrowed through old records in search of facts, and thought especially shrewd at assessing the public mood and predicting political races.

Power fascinated him. He was immensely ambitious but unable to conceive of winning power for himself; his odd looks and repeated defeats had persuaded him of that. But he wanted to be as close to it as he could, and to get there he needed to find some candidate who would provide him with that access. In 1906, he thought he had found his man in Thomas Mott Osborne, the big, handsome former mayor of Auburn, who seemed likely to rise at least as far as the governorship. When that happened, Louis Howe hoped to rise with him. "I feel the turning point has come in our fortunes, dear," he wrote Grace, when he first went on Osborne's payroll at $40 a week, "and I don't want to make any mistakes."

Osborne was then seeking to block the gubernatorial candidacy of Tammany's candidate, William Randolph Hearst. Howe had been hired by Osborne to travel upstate cities and towns gathering information and getting to know local leaders who might be persuaded to buck Boss Murphy, then send him lengthy confidential reports on prospects for reform.

The 1906 effort failed—and Hearst was badly beaten by Charles Evans Hughes in the November election—but Osborne had found Howe useful, and from time to time put him on his payroll to serve as adviser and secret operative, exploiting his credentials as a supposedly objective reporter to gather intelligence within the ranks of the regulars and, sometimes, even to slant his stories to make the opposition look bad. Howe also hammered out hundreds of letters over Osborne's signature to local politicians, small-town editors—anyone thought likely to champion his candidate's cause. "Isn't it funny Osborne wants me to be practically his private secretary," Louis wrote Grace. "That is the kind of job you have always been poking me up to getting."

Despite Howe's energy and diligence, it was not a close or easy relationship. Osborne admired Howe's ability but he was never personally fond of him. He disdained the little man's eccentric attire—Louis smoked incessantly, scattering clouds of ashes wherever he lighted; he wore both belt and suspenders at all times; and he hid his thin neck within a stiff, soiled, oversized collar which made him seem still smaller than he was—and he distrusted Howe's eagerness to bend the truth or even to suggest temporary alliances with the enemy if he thought that by doing so, Osborne's cause—and his own—could be advanced.

Howe genuinely shared his patron's strong anti-Tammany sentiments. They had been his late father's views as well. (Ed Howe died, still luckless and in debt, in 1908.) But his progressivism was always leavened by a deep cynicism, engendered perhaps by having spent so many years as a failure, the object of his wife's derision, relegated by his own appearance and abrasive personality to the fringes of power wielded by men who, while more attractive and personable than he, were nowhere near as intelligent—or so he believed. "You can't adopt politics as a profession and remain honest," he much later told a student audience in an uncharacteristic moment of public candor. "If you are going to make your living out of politics, you can't do it honestly."

Above all, perhaps, Osborne was wearied by Howe's persistent wheedling for raises, his nagging pleas for a permanent job. In the spring of 1909 he fired Howe, then reluctantly hired him back when told a doctor had given Louis only two months to live. The crisis passed, but Howe's hold on his job was clearly slipping.

The following year, Louis helped Osborne organize the Democratic League, the reform organization that had backed a number of young upstate reformers, including Franklin, for the legislature. By then, still more had gone wrong. Howe's mother died. A third child was born, a second son, only to die within a week. (Another son, named Hartley, would be born in November 1911.) Grace grew ill. Louis himself endured a recurrence of his old heart trouble and fretted that his shaky position with Osborne would soon end.

And Osborne himself began to seem a less dependable sponsor than he once had. He was eloquent, bold, immensely attractive, apparently a model father to the four strapping sons for whom he cared after the early death of his wife. But he was also vain, bombastic, and unforgiving. His 1910 bid for the governorship had failed, broken largely on the stony shoals of his own excessive rhetoric (he had refused even to parley with Tammany, whose ranks, he said, were filled with "dogs" and "curs").

And so, when Louis Howe watched young Franklin Roosevelt stride to his new Senate seat in January of 1911, he may have already been looking for some new political comer with whom to identify himself, someone who shared his own progressive views but was less inflexible and more congenial.

No newspaperman proved more friendly to Franklin and the anti-Sheehan insurgency during the 1911 standoff than Howe. He wrote a fulsome tribute to the still untested senator long before he had any evidence with which to back it up, offered him experienced counsel during the Sheehan fight, and, when Franklin began to work with Osborne on Woodrow Wilson's behalf in 1912, did most of the hard daily work on behalf of both the New York State Wilson Conference and the equally short-lived Empire State Democracy. He understood completely Franklin's ultimate ambition: even before the Baltimore convention he was addressing him as "Beloved and Revered Future President."

But Wilson's victory failed to pay off for him, at least at first. He had given up his *Herald* job after the governor was nominated, assuming he would now work full time for Osborne's organization. But after the Democratic nominee made his peace with Tammany, Osborne withdrew his financial backing. With it went Howe's job.

Louis wrote Franklin an angry letter. He had been assured, he said, that his "insurgent friends were going to fight it out to the finish. . . . I went into this game against my inclination, but T.M.O[sborne] said it was his 'last fight' [so] I jumped into the game. When I left T.M.O. at the train for Baltimore he told me that if Wilson was nominated he was going on with the fight and I promised him then that I would give up my place . . . and . . . stick by him instead."

Howe was now desperate. "If you can connect me with a job during the campaign," he continued, "for heaven's sake help me out, for this mess is bad business for me." He left for his summer cottage at Horseneck Beach, Massachusetts, to puzzle out what he might try next. He seemed to have failed again, to be once more on his own, without prospects.

Then, one morning in September, Eleanor Roosevelt wired him from New York. Howe had no telephone. He picked up her telegram at Lulu Hammond's General Store. Franklin had fallen ill with typhoid fever, it said, and he had asked her to see if Howe might be persuaded to come down to New York and talk with him about taking over his stalled campaign.

Louis took the next train.

Neither Eleanor nor Sara was notably glad to see him. His personal habits put them off. They objected to the cigarette smoke with which he filled the sickroom, ostentatiously throwing open the windows as soon as he had left—"Remember, I was still a Puritan!" Eleanor wrote much later—and they feared that his long, laughing, closed-door talks with Franklin about strategy would exhaust the patient. Sara noted only "Mr. Howe here a good deal" in her diary.

Accustomed to the disdain of others, Louis pretended not to notice. "I am hated by everybody. I have always been hated by everybody," he once said, "and I *want* to be hated by everybody." The only thing that mattered to him was the approval of the pale, anxious young candidate who had asked for his help.

For the few weeks that remained before Election Day, Howe was to all intents and purposes Franklin's surrogate. He moved his small family to a boardinghouse in Poughkeepsie, rented a room in a downtown hotel called the Morgan House, hired Harry Hawkey and his red Maxwell, and took off after votes.

His energy was as great as Franklin's had been two years earlier, but more shrewdly focused on winning specific, doubtful constituencies. He devised what he called "a great farmer stunt," for example—a bill to protect farmers from commission merchants, the middlemen who pocketed the difference between the low prices they paid to farmers and the high ones they charged consumers—then addressed multigraphed "personal" letters over Franklin's signature to hundreds of farmers, informing them of his new campaign on their behalf and enclosing a stamped, self-addressed envelope in which to send him their comments. Similar letters promised shad fishermen that license fees would be lowered, and apple growers that Franklin would introduce a bill to standardize the size of their barrels.[12]

12. The partial text of one of Howe's carefully targeted posters:
TO FRUIT GROWERS!
    I am convinced after careful consideration that the current law making a 17⅛ inch barrel the legal standard for fruit is injust and oppressive to fruit growers. I pledge myself

Howe also took out full-page newspaper advertisements—unprece-dented in upstate races—in which he pledged Franklin's support for woman suffrage, trumpeted his new-found devotion to labor, and took out after the Republican bosses. Copy was sent to the ailing candidate for his last-minute approval: "Here is your first ad. . . . As I have pledged you in it I thought you might like to know casually what kind of a mess I was getting you into. Please wire o.k., if it's all right. . . . Your slave and servant, Howe."

It was always all right.[13]

Franklin turned over his checkbook to Louis and was soon notified that it was overdrawn; in his haste, Howe had added rather than subtracted as he went along. The candidate himself managed to raise campaign funds from his wealthy friends, dictating appeals to his mother sitting at his bedside, then mailing the checks on to Howe for deposit.[14]

---

to introduce and fight for the passage of an amendment to the law making a standard fruit barrel of 16½ inches. This barrel to be the legal standard for fruit and to be marked "Standard Fruit Barrel . . ."

Franklin D. Roosevelt
Candidate for State Senator.

When Franklin Roosevelt says he will fight for a thing he won't quit until he wins— you know that.

Source: James MacGregor Burns, *The Lion and the Fox,* page 45.

13. It was not all right with Sara. She had been taught that one of a gentleman's first duties was to keep his name out of the newspapers. Paying perfectly good money to put it there seemed to her unsuitable, perverse, further evidence of Louis Howe's bad influence on her son. *Source:* Rita Halle Kleeman, *Gracious Lady,* page 257.

14. Jefferson Newbold, Franklin's admiring young Hyde Park neighbor, was one of those who loaned him cash for the campaign. The morning after Election Day he claimed to be "completely broken . . . praying that your Mother is as wealthy as reported so that I can get some money back!"

Newbold was interested in politics but the opportunities it offered for new experiences that so delighted Franklin merely alarmed him. He told Franklin of a visit to Manhattan Democratic Headquarters, where his family's fortune had won him a place on the Finance Committee. He had been visiting the committee chairman, Henry Morgenthau, Sr., he said, when "a timid knock was heard on the door, it opened, and a blame ugly face made its appearance. . . . Things happened so quickly that I suddenly found that Woodrow the Great was being introduced to me! After a few pointless remarks about the weather, etc., we ambled out to the elevator, arrived safely at the street . . . entered awaiting limousines, Woody going with Mrs. [Borden] Harriman who was waiting coyly for him in her own buzz-wagon, and then we proceeded to a 'Tariff Exhibit.' Once there we were parted, after a real fight, in which I lost my hat & temper, & broke most of my fingernails, to say nothing of the third commandment. I attained the platform, was hauled and pushed up some steps, almost through Mrs. H., whose figure I found myself trying to preserve in the most unseemly manner, (it is the first time I have ever had my arms around another man's wife, but I couldn't help it!). Finally, we reached some chairs, and I sank down exhausted. . . . Then the show began. Have you ever been to a massed meeting in New York City? It reminds me of a tin of American sardines, everybody was packed close together, and they all smelt! A guy, who had not been introduced to me, got on his pedal extremities & at his first utterances

Howe also drove all over the district, sometimes with Grace at his side, to encourage party workers and seek out waverers for whom Franklin might wangle jobs at Albany should they come over to his side: one demanded a position that paid "2500 or more," Louis reported; another would be content to work as a coat-room attendant.

"I'm having more fun than a goat," Howe told his new employer. Campaigning delighted him: the promises kept and broken; the maneuvering; the heady sense that his decisions could alter the future. He enjoyed himself even when things didn't go precisely as he'd planned.

In the last week of the campaign, Franklin's Republican opponent, Jacob Southard, for example, dredged up the old charge that he was anti-Catholic.[15] But when Frank Cleary, a prominent Hyde Park Democrat, threatened to urge his fellow Catholics to oppose Franklin, Howe found him a job in the State Engineer's Office, then told him that he had to thank Franklin and John Sague, former mayor of Poughkeepsie and Franklin's old sponsor, now running for the late Dick Connell's seat in Congress. "This pleased Sague very much," Howe reported, "and everyone is happy and singing the doxology."[16]

---

the mob yelled. The more he said, the more noise was made, and I decided then and there that I would never run for President. I couldn't stand the racket."

Another wealthy young man named Penfield had accompanied Newbold to the rally. He now murmured that "he needed a drink or he would die." The two pushed their way to the back of the platform and got out through a window. "Then," Newbold continued, "I . . . discovered that I had ten minutes to catch the 12:50 train. I told my sorrows to Penfield, he rose to the occasion, and got me to the station in his sixty Mercedes with one minute to spare! It was some experience for a young one, believe me, New York politics are interesting, but too speedy. Old Dutchess for me, for when you really come down to it, there's no place like Home!" *Source:* Franklin D. Roosevelt Papers, Papers as State Senator, FDRL.

15. Franklin dictated an aggrieved response, which he hoped to persuade a sympathetic Republican sign and to send to the Poughkeepsie *Eagle:*

May I as a Republican express [my protest] through your columns against the manner and tone of your recent editorials on one of our Dutchess County neighbors, Mr. Franklin Roosevelt of Hyde Park. Many other Republicans have told me that while they may not agree with Mr. Roosevelt's expressed views, they resent what appears on your part a definite attack both on his good faith and his personality. . . . What he says is always simple and to the point and he is the last person in the world to be called condescending. He is less like a snob than any man I know. . . .

He never sent the letter; "I still think it is probably best to leave the thing in its grave," he told Howe.

16. From his sickbed, Franklin had quietly supported Sague for the nomination against another of his early patrons, Lewis Stuyvesant Chanler, suggesting that Chanler was both too languid and too parsimonious to make a successful run. ("Someone told Chanler the nomination would cost him twenty-five cents in postage," Howe had told Franklin, "and he threw up both hands and cried never, never, never.")

Chanler, whose own political star's fading had coincided with the rise of Franklin's, and who had thought young Roosevelt's first term in the state Senate a shrill embarrassment, was now

Cleary turned against his benefactor, however, and, with three days to go before Election Day, again began to urge his fellow Catholics to desert the Democratic candidate. This so exercised Tom Newbold, next door, that he hired two Burns detectives to watch the polling booths on Election Day.

They were not needed. Franklin won by a larger margin than he had two years earlier, outrunning even Woodrow Wilson. Had his Cousin Theodore not also been running, the result might have been different; the combined votes of Franklin's two opponents outnumbered his.

But clearly, the ugly little man had proved himself indispensable. For the next twenty-three years Franklin Roosevelt and Louis Howe would rarely spend more than a few days apart.

Franklin returned to Albany in January of 1913, still so pallid and so weak that Eleanor worried about him and he sought to reassure her: "I'm very well & taking care of myself—wearing rubbers, brushing my teeth, etc., etc." His new committee appointments pleased him. "I drew Chairman of Agriculture," he told his wife, "ranking member of Conservation (the old Forest, Fish & Game) & also member of Codes, Railroads & *Military Affairs!* This isn't bad & I am particularly glad that the other members of Agriculture give me control of the committee as against our N.Y. City friends."

But he was not pleased at the prospect of plunging into a new legislative struggle with the old guard, a struggle in which he was sure to be still more isolated than he had been the year before. "We are going to have a very interesting tho' somewhat difficult session," he told William Church Osborn, "and I fear it will take a good deal of tact and tenacity to come out of it with a whole skin."

Then, shortly after he arrived, he was summoned to Trenton to see President-elect Wilson. Either then or later he made known his inter-

---

infuriated, and saw in the younger man's failure to back him evidence of vindictiveness. Chanler had refused to resign from the Assembly in 1910, so that Franklin might run safely for his seat; Franklin, he believed, was now wreaking his revenge.

According to the family, Chanler never got over what he saw as this base betrayal, and when Franklin ran for governor in 1928 he could not bring himself to vote for him. Nor could he vote for a Republican. So, reluctantly, he cast his ballot for the Socialist candidate. At that time, the Redhook votes were still counted in the library of Rokeby, Chanler's ancestral house that had been built by William B. Astor. There was a good deal of consternation when a lone Socialist ballot appeared, and finally Chanler himself felt duty-bound to confess what he had done. *Source:* Interview with Bronson Chanler.

est in a Washington job.[17] He was considered for several—including Assistant Secretary of the Treasury and Collector of the Port of New York, both of which he politely declined—before he got the offer he had been waiting for.

Josephus Daniels was to be the new Secretary of the Navy. On the morning of Inauguration Day, March 4, 1913, he wandered into the crowded, cavernous lobby of the Willard Hotel. Franklin hurried across to congratulate him on his appointment. The courtly middle-aged editor shook hands with the tall young senator he had liked so much at the Baltimore convention.

"How would you like to come to Washington as Assistant Secretary of the Navy?" Daniels asked.

Franklin did not hesitate. "How would I like it? I'd like it bully well. It would please me better than anything else in the world. . . ."

The symbolism of his appointment was lost on no one. Daniels noted it in his diary: "His distinguished cousin TR went from that place to the Presidency. May history repeat itself," and in announcing the news, the Secretary's old paper captioned a youthful portrait of Daniels's new assistant: "He's Following in Teddy's Footsteps." TR himself wrote Franklin a short congratulatory note: "It is interesting that you are in another place which I myself once held. I am sure you will enjoy yourself to the full as Ass't Secty of the Navy and that you will do capital work."

Returning briefly to Albany to wind up his Senate affairs, Franklin paid a courtesy call on the Senate president pro tem, Robert Wagner, with whom he had tried to maintain cordial relations despite their political differences. Franklin said he was going to Washington to take the Navy job, then wondered aloud whether he was doing the wise thing.

Wagner, normally an impassive man, had some difficulty disguising his joy. Franklin's departure would make his own job a good deal easier. "Go, Frank, go!" he told him as he walked with him to the door and shook his hand. "I'm sure you'll be a big success down there."[18]

17. He may have already been reasonably sure of a federal appointment even before he went back to Albany. For the first time that winter he rented rooms in the Ten Eyck for himself and Eleanor alone, planning to remain in town just two or three days at a time, as if he knew he would not be staying long and wanted to keep the children from having to undertake two moves in the same season.

18. At least one Navy man remembered hearing that Franklin's appointment had actually been engineered by Boss Murphy himself, so eager was he to see him moved out of Albany. *Source:* Frank Freidel interview with Admiral Frederic Harris, Freidel Papers, FRL.

CHAPTER

6

THE ENDLESS ADDICTION

FRANKLIN was sworn in as Assistant Secretary of the Navy on March 17, 1913, his eighth wedding anniversary. "I didn't know until I sat down at this desk," he wrote Eleanor from his new office on a sheet of handsomely embossed official stationery, "that this is the 17th of happy memory. . . . My only regret is that you could not have been here with me;—but I am thinking of you a great deal & sending 'wireless' messages!"

He also remembered to write his mother:

Dearest Mama—
I am baptized, confirmed, sworn in, vaccinated—and somewhat at sea!

For over an hour I have been signing papers which had to be accepted on faith—but I hope luck will keep me out of jail.

All well, but I will have to work like a turbine to master this job—but it will be done even if it takes all summer.

Your affec. son,
Franklin Delano Roosevelt

"You can't imagine the happiness you gave me . . . ," Sara answered. "I just *knew* it was a *very* big job, & everything so new that it will take time to fit *into* it. Try not to write your signature too small, as it gets a cramped look & is not distinct. So many public men have such awful signatures. . . ."

Endicott Peabody wrote, too, pleased that his strenuous efforts to have Groton boys enter public service seemed to be paying off at last.

201

"Your friends at Groton," he wrote, "—and they are numerous—are delighted over your appointment to High Office. It is a great triumph of Honesty & Loyalty over the lower powers which are trying to best the Country. . . . With you and Jake Brown [Lathrop Brown, Franklin's roommate at both Groton and Harvard, just elected to Congress as a Democrat from Long Island] among our rulers we are feeling very influential!"

Franklin was just thirty-one years old in March 1913, seven years younger than Theodore Roosevelt had been when he first occupied the same desk, twenty years younger than his new chief, half the age of many of the admirals with whom he would soon have to deal. And he looked still younger—so young, in fact, that when he made a mildly cynical joke at a pre-inaugural dinner, a naval officer's wife who had no idea who her youthful dinner partner was had remarked loudly, "Naughty, naughty. Little boys just out of college should not say such things."

But all his life he had loved the sea and the Navy; only his father's wish to keep him close to home had kept him from attending Annapolis rather than Harvard. His mother and his grandfather Delano had taught him to be proud of his seafaring heritage; he himself collected naval prints, books, and memorabilia, and spent weeks each summer at the helm of his own yacht. His Cousin Bamie was right when she told Bob Ferguson that Franklin's new job was the "one thing about which he has always been keen."

It was the parallel with TR that pleased him most of all, of course, and a few days after he began work, when Daniels left him in charge while on an inspection tour, he could not resist telling a reporter, "There's a Roosevelt on the job today. . . . You remember what happened the last time a Roosevelt occupied a similar position?" Eleanor, who at that point still rarely criticized her husband, told him she thought this "a horrid little remark." (What had happened then was that TR, sitting at the same desk at which Franklin now sat, had waited until his unwitting superior, Secretary J. D. Long, was away from the office having his painful corns attended to, then ordered Commodore George Dewey's Asiatic Squadron to steam toward Hong Kong with orders that "IN THE EVENT OF DECLARATION OF WAR SPAIN" he was to mount "OFFENSIVE OPERATIONS THE PHILIPPINE ISLANDS.") Franklin had no such obvious insubordination in mind as yet, but even the possibility of such power was giddy.

The daily work of his office was traditionally routine. In theory, he was to oversee procurement, supply, and civilian personnel, help prepare the budget, and to manage the 65,000 men who worked in the shore installations. In practice, he would seek to spread his influence wherever his indulgent chief did not specifically forbid him to go. "I get my fingers into about everything," he once exulted to Daniels, "and there's no law against it."

Charles H. McCarthy, an able private secretary who had served Franklin's predecessors, was already in place to help him sort through everyday naval affairs, but he eagerly imported Louis Howe, whose loyalty was always to him alone, to handle more delicate matters: "Dear Ludwig . . . Here is the dope. Secretary—$2,000—expect you April 1, with a new uniform." Howe characteristically answered that he would take the job, "though it will break me." In fact, he had never been offered anything like such a sum, and he hurried down to Washington, bringing his family with him. (Later, he would be promoted to Special Assistant, at an additional $1,000 a year.)

Franklin spent the spring alone in rented rooms, first at the New Willard and then at the Powhatan Hotel, then moved into the house at 1733 N Street which his Cousin Bamie had offered to rent to him and "dearest, dearest Eleanor," six blocks down Connecticut Avenue from his office in the vast old State, War and Navy Building that stood just across the street from the White House. Eleanor and the children would spend the hot months at Campobello, as usual, and not join him in Washington until the autumn.[1]

Eleanor's summer with the children was not so smooth as some had been.

To begin with, there was new trouble with her mother-in-law. Maude Livingston Hall, the youngest of Eleanor's aunts, had recently divorced Larry Waterbury, a handsome polo player addicted to gam-

1. Sara did not entirely approve of this long separation, and in July, when Franklin developed some sort of stomach ailment, she raced down to Washington to be with him, administering liberal amounts of calomel.

"Tummy isn't according to Hoyle yet," he told her after she had returned to Springwood, but he was better: "I loved having you, and you saved my life," he told her, "but I'm too sorry we couldn't have done some nice things together." He did add that the doctor had told him that two grains of calomel at a time was rather "a large dose!"

Sara was mortified. The following December, writing from London, she was still apologizing to Eleanor for her excessive zeal: "the best doctors over here refuse to give calomel, as it is an accumulative poison. . . . Think how I feel about the dose Franklin received from my hand. It may still be poisoning him." Franklin assured her he felt fine. *Sources:* Elliott Roosevelt, ed., *FDR: His Personal Letters, 1905–1928,* Vol. 00, page 205; Sara Delano Roosevelt Papers, Roosevelt Family Papers, FDRL.

bling, who had left her with two small children and no money. That, from Sara's point of view, was bad enough. But afterwards, to pay her debts, Maude had dared run a dress shop for a time, and had even considered acting as hostess for a restaurateur interested in attracting an especially high-toned clientele. Eleanor, upon whom all the Halls continued to rely (they were "floating islands," Isabella once wrote, while Eleanor was the Rock of Gibraltar), invited Maude and the children to stay with her on the island. Eleanor was fond of her beautiful, red-haired aunt, but startled when Maude asked if she might bring along a gentleman friend, a Mr. David Gray. She finally agreed, making it clear that Mr. Gray was to stay in the nearby village of Welshpool, and that she would herself act as chaperone for the far older couple.[2]

Eleanor knew that her mother-in-law would be appalled even at this arrangement, and asked Franklin to break the news of Gray's coming visit to his mother while she was visiting him briefly in Washington. He did, then warned Eleanor, "she made no comment."

Gray was an amiable, sensitive man, the son of a Buffalo editor, fond of horses and writing short stories about the outdoor life; his comedy, *Gallops*, had opened and closed quickly on Broadway. He enjoyed poetry, too, and read it aloud well, to Eleanor's great pleasure—but he also seemed to her to lack something, to be a little vague, ineffectual. Still, she told Franklin, if Maude decided to marry him—and clearly that was what he wanted—"he will take good care of her."

Sara, while remaining outwardly amiable toward all concerned, was inwardly furious: at Maude for her shameless behavior in inviting Gray to her quiet island, at him for coming, at Eleanor and Franklin for tolerating them both. At the mention of Gray's name, Eleanor noted, Sara "fairly snorted"—"does she snort any more?" an amused Franklin asked a week later from the relative safety of Washington— and Eleanor was certain she was "in for a grand scene with Mama and

---

2. Appearances were important. It amused Eleanor that when Harry Hooker, Franklin's law partner, visited her at Campobello once while he was away, Sara accompanied him and Eleanor wherever they went so that no one might misunderstand.

It had not amused her, however, earlier when, visiting Boston, Franklin had run into Alice Longworth, she had invited him to her hotel room for a drink, and he had gone. "Actually, it wasn't really in my room," Alice remembered. "We just sat on a trunk in an alcove nearby and drummed our heels on it as we drank green mints and felt like leprechauns on a roof. Somehow, Eleanor got to hear of it and was very annoyed and said to Franklin, 'No one would know that you were her cousin. You were seen going to a woman's room. I think it would be a good idea if you and Alice didn't see each other for some time." *Source:* Joseph P. Lash, *Eleanor and Franklin*, page 181; Michael Teague, *Mrs. L.*, page 157.

tears, one of these days." (Whether or not the grand scene ever took place, the couple was married that October in a hurried civil ceremony at the Poughkeepsie town hall, arranged and witnessed only by Eleanor and the Roosevelt family attorney, John M. Hackett. Sara did not attend. In 1940, Franklin would appoint David Gray Minister to Ireland.)[3]

Worse for Eleanor than family tension was Franklin's absence. During this summer—and most of the summers that followed while he was Assistant Secretary—he was able to spend only a few days at a time on the island. She lived for his letters when they were apart, filled with jaunty but terse accounts of happenings in Washington, in which the real subject was, as always, himself. Within ten days of taking office, with Daniels out of town and Eleanor still in New York, he had told her of "a most interesting day . . . I was suddenly called upon by the President to make all arrangements for sending surgeons, attendants, supplies, etc. out to the flood district in Ohio—I had a hectic time getting the machinery going, but the force leaves tonight, & I had some interesting work in co-operation with the Secretary of War & General [Leonard] Wood."

One Friday in July, he told her that "the Secretary and I worked like niggers all day on all the things he should have decided before & as I expected most of them were turned over to me! The trouble is that the Sec'y has expressed half-baked opinions in these matters & I don't agree—I know that he would decide right if he'd only give the time to learn—However he has given me carte blanche & says he will abide by my decision. Yesterday . . . he said very nice things to me."[4]

---

3. Maude Gray died in 1952, the last important link with Eleanor's childhood. Her husband lived on, however, until 1968, and during Mrs. Roosevelt's last years was often a guest at Val-Kill, her house near Springwood. Still elegant in his Edwardian tweeds, he was also increasingly eccentric. While still in Ireland—he did not resign his post until 1947, two years after the President's death—he had fallen under the influence of an Irish medium and frequently sent Eleanor thick packets of indecipherable spirit writing which purported to be messages from FDR on the Other Side, dealing with various matters of state as well as what Gray termed "the nigger question."

He also became alarmingly outspoken with advancing years; when Nikita Khruschev visited Mrs. Roosevelt at Hyde Park, Gray introduced himself to the Soviet premier as "her wicked uncle," and just after the leader of a later Russian delegation had finished assuring her of the love and respect all the Soviet peoples felt for her, he was heard to mutter, "And when you get ready to drop that atom bomb on us, I hope you will think of dear Mrs. Roosevelt." *Sources:* Eleanor Roosevelt Papers, FDRL; Joseph P. Lash, *Eleanor: The Years Alone,* paper 313–314.

4. Eleanor tempered her pleasure at Daniels's kind words with a gentle caution: "I think it is quite big of him to be willing to let you decide. Most people want to put their opinions through at all costs whether they are half-baked or not! It shows great confidence."

He was disappointed with a public appearance at Chancellorsville, Pennsylvania:

> The day . . . was not thrilling—very much a one-horse affair & the whole celebration apparently run without good management, I was driven around town interminably—a dirty coal mining town & didn't get an opportunity to really see the only interesting part, the mines & miners themselves! I spoke in a picnic grove, & went from there to the 3:05 B&O train—stood on the back platform nearly all the way to Washington as the scenery was wonderful all through S. Western Pa. & then to Cumberland & down the Potomac to Harper's Ferry. We passed thro' Mt. Savage [the site of a Delano mine] where Uncle Warren started work.

Franklin could be self-deprecating, but almost always about an event in which, despite his alleged inadequacies, he nonetheless held center stage. "Funny isn't the word to describe the scene last night at the 62nd Anniversary of the Conferring of the Rebekah Degree [International Order of Freemasons]," he told Eleanor,

> when, with the Lady Grand Master on my arm, I brought up the rear of a two by two procession which marched five times round an enormous hall. At least a thousand persons engaged in the solemn proceedings & when I had tried three excruciatingly humorous stories on them without getting a smile I launched into an extemporaneous and highly pathetic discourse on loyalty, patriotism and the debt of gratitude the human race owes to its females of the species. There were few dry eyes in the house when I finished & I am going to take up heavy tragedy when I leave this job. I'm glad, oh, so glad, you weren't there—it was hard enough as it was to keep my face anywhere near straight.

In August, it looked for a time as if American forces might be impelled to intervene in Mexico, and Franklin would be able to make good on a promise he had made in a speech delivered just two weeks after taking office; if actual fighting began south of the border, he had said then, he would be compelled to resign his new post, "follow in the steps of T.R. and form a regiment of rough riders."

In 1911, a rebel army led by the diminutive reformer Francisco Madero had driven the eighty-one-year-old Porfirio Díaz into exile, after more than three decades of harsh dictatorial rule that had benefited mostly Díaz, his wealthy allies, and American and British oil and copper speculators. A gentle moderate, Madero moved too slowly toward land reform to please the radical revolutionaries who had fought alongside him, too rapidly to suit the conservatives who were allied with the resident Americans and had the backing of the U.S. ambassador. In February 1913, the commander of Maderos's army, Victoriano Huerta, overthrew his president, then had him assassinated. President Taft's ambassador, Henry Lane Wilson, still on the job, was pleased; so were many of the fifty thousand Americans living in Mexico at the time. The newly elected President of the United States was not, however, and as soon as he took office he refused to recognize a regime he considered murderous, headed by a man he thought "unspeakable."

This marked a real break with past American foreign policy which, since the time of Thomas Jefferson, had generally recognized established governments no matter how they had become established. "My ideal is an orderly and righteous government in Mexico," the President eventually declared, "but my passion is for the submerged eighty-five per cent of the people of that republic who are now struggling toward liberty." That struggle took the form of four bloody and confusing rebellions led by rival leaders, in which Americans sometimes found themselves caught up. Oil drilling stopped. Mines closed down. A handful of Americans were killed in the crossfire. William Jennings Bryan, the new Secretary of State, urged all of his fellow countrymen to leave Mexico.

Wilson's critics charged that his Mexican policy of what he called "watchful waiting" was misguided sentimentalism, sure to prolong anarchy. There were loud calls for him to change his mind, even to send troops to defend American interests, and Theodore Roosevelt began contacting his old Rough Riders, eager to saddle up and lead them into combat again.

One Saturday afternoon that August, Franklin and the President (separately) attended a Washington Senators baseball game, prompting Franklin to write Eleanor a letter written more or less in the dialect style of Peter Finley Dunne's "Mr. Dooley:"

> Dearest Babs—
> It was a foine ball game Saturday, & me & the President graced the ancient & hon'rable game with our dazzling prisince, amid the plaudits of the worshipping proletariat—Yistirday Oi held divine service with the misses Millie & Frances [the Cowles' black maids] at our palatial abode, fearing [sermons by Professor] Droppers of Williams College & by Professor Bullock iv Harrr-vard University—The Discoosion ranged from hoigher ayconomics to the raising iv cats.
>   Today the dulcet air is more dulcet & me & the President are working

in our shirtslaives, & thr-rowing kisses to aich other out iv the window.
Our little brown brithrin the Mecks arr shtill foighting bloody dooels at
twinty miles range dhropping [dirty] epithits into each other's camps at
the did of night. What they call the internashnal sitooation is unchanged,
though the awful heat in the capitol city will probably drive this gr-rate
& powerful nation into the neighboring State of Intervention before
autumn, and thin its name would be changed to the State of Invasion.
Anyway, as me friend Dooley would say, it would be an imminently
righteous acquisition iv Territory in a Holy Cause

Your perspiring F.

The nation did not invade. The territory was not acquired. (In fact,
that November President Wilson would pledge that "the United
States will never again seek one additional foot of territory by conquest.") And Franklin missed his chance at the easy military glory that
might have propelled him still faster along his cousin's path, perhaps
even under TR's own command.[5]

One day that summer, Eleanor left the island to shop at Eastport,
Maine. While she was gone, the older children helped collect the
rotting seaweed and driftwood that were periodically burned on the
beach below the house to improve the smell at low tide. The blaze was
lit and burned quickly. Elliott, now three, and thought to be suffering
from some congenital weakness of the legs, was wearing stiff steel
braces fastened with bands of leather. Somehow he toddled or fell
backward into the smoldering ashes while the nurse was looking elsewhere, and was badly burned on his legs, where the ashes were trapped
beneath the straps, and on one of his hands with which he had tried
to slap the pain away. Eleanor's letter to Franklin describing what had
happened is curious, longer than most of her summer letters, but
failing even to mention the accident until the very end. "He only cried
a little . . . ," she assured her husband. "Nurse says that they are only
skin burns. . . . He ate more supper than usual & has gone placidly to
sleep so it can't hurt much."

Misled by her brief dismissal of the accident, Franklin answered in
the same spirit: "I'm too sorry about Elliott's burn. Hope it is healed."

---

5. Some measure of his interest in getting to Mexico may be seen in a letter he wrote to his
mother at about this time. Warren Delano Robbins, the son of Sara's sister Kassie and her first
husband, was Third Secretary in the Paris Embassy and had written Franklin for help in winning
a transfer. Mexico was suggested and inquiries were made about his joining the staff there. When
Kassie Collier heard of it she was *horrified*: Mexico was dangerous, no place for her boy. Sara
urged Franklin to intervene. He wrote back that he had done so, "though I don't want it thought
that I can get him any place he wants. . . . Personally, if I were in the Dip[lomatic] Service I
would beg for Mexico, as it is the only place just now where there is real action." *Source:* Elliott
Roosevelt, ed., *FDR: His Personal Letters, 1905–1928,* pages 206–207.

Eleanor's response was instant and indignant: "You are casual about Elliott's burn but he had a very bad hand & it won't be healed for some time . . . he is a very brave young man."

Part of her anger may have been a means of allaying her own guilt at having been away when Elliott was injured. But part of it, too, was surely her frustration at finding herself still more often alone with the children on the island than she had been in the past.

Franklin's notes from Washington, short and telegraphic as they usually were, often included brief messages for the children—"Kiss the chicks & tell Elliott I will get right to work on the aeroplane when I get back", "I love Elliott's photos—The 'Boy Hero'!!"; "I'm *too* sad about the bunny's demise—and only hope the funeral & making of the tombstone will console the chicks . . . was it the lopsided one?"

And, now and again, there were hints as well of the old love between him and Eleanor. "All well & *crazy* to see you"; "I long to be with you again & you can't imagine how I miss you all the time." After returning to Washington after one brief visit in 1916, he would write that "I am anxiously awaiting you Saturday & only wish we could have another walk in the woods like last Sunday."

But his short stays on the island actually included little time for his wife. His mother hovered. The children clamored for his attention. He often brought guests with him, whom Eleanor had to look after; on his first visit to Campobello that summer, he ordered the battleship *North Dakota* to anchor offshore for the Eastport Fourth of July celebrations, and she found herself organizing dinners, teas, and bridge games for all the senior officers, not only while Franklin was with her but for several days after he had returned to Washington. When he told her he would try to come back to the island in August, she replied that she was fearful of another big visitation.

"No, no more battleships coming," he wrote back. "I may come up in a destroyer, but that means only 3 officers!"

"I shall welcome you on a destroyer or with a whole fleet," she said, "if you will just come a little sooner on their account, but of course the destroyer will be easier to entertain!"

She tried her best to sound cheerful, but Franklin knew that she was still unhappy, neither truly absorbed in their beautiful but clamorous children nor fully occupied elsewhere, and surrounded by his friends and family and his mother's, only rarely her own. And he also knew that he himself had neither the time nor the ability to make her happy for long. After her Aunt Maude left the island, Franklin wrote her that he hoped she would come back the following year because "I know what a delight it is to Eleanor to have you and I am afraid I am sometimes a little selfish and have had her too much with me in the past years, and have made life a trifle dull for her really brilliant mind and spirit."

Franklin and Eleanor managed a few more days together at summer's end, and on the lurching train that took him south to Syracuse where he was to make still another speech, he scribbled Eleanor an unusually emotional note: "I do so wish the holiday had been longer and less interrupted while it lasted. I felt Tuesday as if I was really getting back to earth again—& I know it is hard for both of us to lead this kind of life—but it is a little like a drug habit—almost impossible to stop definitely."

It was an addiction he never really tried to end.

Auntie Bye's Washington house was a handsome four-story brick structure with a small walled garden. For Franklin, it constituted still another historic link with TR, who had lived in it during the brief interregnum between McKinley's death and his widow's departure from the White House; during his presidency he had walked there so often in the evenings to talk things over with his shrewd older sister that it was known to the press as the Little White House.

Eleanor had visited there often too, as a girl, finding in its cheerful, old-fashioned clutter and in her fond and understanding aunt sources of calm and security absent from the homes of the other relatives in which she stayed. "We're really very comfortably settled now in this dear, bright house," Eleanor told Isabella shortly after the family had moved in, "& I feel very much at home, chiefly because Auntie Bye has lived here. . . ."[6]

Sara, who arrived for an extended visit some time after Eleanor and the family moved in, found it snug, too, once she had made her own mark. "Moved chairs and tables," she noted in her diary, "and began to feel at home."[7]

6. The Cowles home was still gas-lit. One of Elliott Roosevelt's earliest memories was of his mother admonishing him, "You must never, *never*, play with the gas." *Source:* Elliott Roosevelt and James Brough, *An Untold Story: The Roosevelts of Hyde Park*, page 17.

7. Sara's first visit to her son's Washington home had been delayed by a sudden trip to Europe. Price Collier, the gentleman-writer who had married her sister Kassie after the death of her first husband, had died instantly of a heart attack while hunting on the ancient estate of his friend, Count Wedell, on the Danish island of Fünen. Sara had hurried across the Atlantic to be at her grieving sister's side and to offer solace on the sad voyage home. Kassie had been staying in Paris with her children when the bad news came, and in a letter to Franklin and Eleanor, Sara described the scene in the Danish castle, as Kassie described it to her: "Count

"Will you tell me if there are any people I ought to call on at once," Eleanor asked her aunt even before she moved down, "for I don't know a soul in Washington & am afraid of all kinds of stupid mistakes." Bamie instructed Eleanor in the intricacies of afternoon calls in the capital. Each day she set out in a carriage with a cardcase and made between twenty and thirty stops—Monday on the wives of Supreme Court justices; Tuesday, congressional wives; Thursday, Cabinet members; Friday, diplomats. Whenever the mistress of the house was home, Eleanor stammered through the same stiff introduction: "I am Mrs. Franklin D. Roosevelt. My husband has just come as Assistant Secretary of the Navy." She earnestly tried to limit each conversation to six minutes so that no household would go uncarded.

Sometimes James came along in a blue suit and long black stockings to act as her footman, knocking timidly on some stranger's door, placing his mother's card in the hand of the butler, then scurrying back down the steps and into her carriage. A girlhood friend who came to visit remembered that "the only way to talk to her was to ride along and snatch bits of conversations between . . . stops."

"I'm trying to keep up with my calls," she told her Auntie Bye six weeks after she moved in, "but it is quite strenuous. I've done all the Cabinet, Pres. & V. Pres., justices, Speaker, NY Senators, & some others, also some Congressmen. All Embassies, Counsellors, Naval Attachés, & there are only a few less important Ministers & the Military Attachés left. Besides, I've paid dozens of calls on people who've called on me."

On Wednesdays, she received at home, never able to predict who or how many her visitors might be. She reported on one "rather frantic" Wednesday afternoon to Isabella, "with strange little Navy ladies & foreigners & the Miss Pattens, all mixed up together." (The Miss Pattens were Washington fixtures, three wealthy spinster sisters named Mary, Josephine, and Nelly, each so fond of gossip that someone suggested that the best way to spread a scandal was "Don't telegraph. Don't telephone. Tell-a-Patten.")

There was little time for shyness. There were luncheons, teas,

---

Wedell took them to his chapel in one wing of the schloss, where they found Price sleeping the sleep of death looking well and young, with candles burning around him." There was a Protestant service in the family chapel, led by the count's own clergymen who had painstakingly translated both prayers and hymns into phonetic English, and then a long coach ride to the nearest train station, the coffin draped in an American flag, for the final journey to the crematorium at Copenhagen. *Source:* Sara Delano Roosevelt Papers, Roosevelt Family Papers Donated by the Children, FDRL.

dinners, big formal ceremonies. "We stood and shook hands with some 500 . . . people this afternoon at the Daniels'," Eleanor reported to Isabella one evening, "until Franklin began introducing me as *Mr.* Roosevelt!"

There were new duties for Eleanor outside Washington, as well, and she found them both exhausting and tedious, at least at first. In November, she and Franklin's younger cousin, Laura, accompanied him on an official inspection tour of naval installations along the Gulf Coast. In New Orleans, Eleanor complained, they found themselves in the company of "prominent political (not social) citizens"—a distinction then still important to her. At the official banquet in Biloxi, she told Bob Ferguson, "I found we were expected to head the procession to the dining room, it being there the custom apparently for husbands and wives to go in together & sit together! Laura confided in me later she longed for a husband as her partner hadn't even buttoned his shoes. The meal also was odd: oysters, soup, chicken salad, turkey, etc., being the order! & then the speeches were the best of all & I felt quite ashamed that F. could give so little real colour to his & that his grammar was even passable!"

But she was adjusting fast; when invited along with a number of the Cabinet wives to watch naval target practice from aboard the *Rhode Island,* she alone among them, and despite her customary seasickness, put on dungarees and scaled the skeleton mast to get a better view. "There seems to be so much to see and know and to learn and understand in this big country . . . ," she told her Aunt Maude after one early foray beyond the capital, "and so few of us ever even realize that we ought to try when we've lived in the environment that you and I grew up in."

Eleanor may sometimes have found her ceremonial tasks wearying. Franklin delighted in his. Nothing pleased him more than to stride aboard a naval vessel to the deafening sounds of the seventeen guns to which his post entitled him—four more than rear admirals with forty years seniority received.[8] He took to wearing a dark blue naval cape on ceremonial occasions, and when he discovered that the Assistant Secretary of the Navy had no distinctive flag—only the President of

---

8. When the *North Dakota* had steamed into the Bay of Fundy that first Fourth of July, he made a point of boarding her in white flannels while the big guns boomed. He would have dispensed with the salute, he claimed later, but he knew the children and the neighbors would be disappointed. Not all the children were pleased, however; at the first sound, Anna covered her ears and hid her face in her mother's skirt.

the United States and the Secretary then had them—he designed his own, and made sure it was flown whenever he arrived at a Navy yard or boarded a naval ship.

He never tired of the sight of American warships under full steam. "The big gray fellows were magnificent as they went past," he wrote Eleanor after reviewing the fleet off Hampton Roads, "with all hands at the rail, and I only wish a hundred thousand people could have seen them."

And he enjoyed as well the glittering social life to which his new post and family connections now entitled him.

There had not been a Democratic administration in Washington since Grover Cleveland had quietly departed fifteen years earlier, and the elite among the city's more or less permanent residents—the "cave dwellers," they liked to call themselves—were mostly Republicans who regarded the Democratic newcomers, in Alice Longworth's words, as "odd beings." The personal austerity with which Woodrow Wilson and his wife approached public life added to their sense of alienation: the new President held no inaugural ball and refused to accept proferred memberships in either the Metropolitan or the Chevy Chase clubs.[9]

Franklin happily belonged to both by the time Eleanor and the children arrived; in fact, she said many years later, it was her belief that the eagerness of the capital's two most exclusive clubs to have him as a member had helped somewhat to compensate in his own mind for the Porcellian's rejection.

The Franklin Roosevelts were thought of less as Democrats than as Roosevelts by the cave dwellers, some of whose opinions of the newcomers they themselves seemed to share, at least at first.[10] At a luncheon given by Mrs. Daniels for the President's daughters, Eleanor

9. Older residents were especially upset by Mrs. Wilson's public concern for the plight of the capital's black poor. "If Mrs. Woodrow Wilson intends to spend as much of her time slumming in the alleys of Washington as she has been doing of late," wrote a reporter for *The Clubfellow and Washington Mirror* in 1913, "then it will not be very difficult for her to gratify her oft-repeated remark that she will not spend over $1,000 for dresses. Just what Mrs. Wilson is to gain by driving through these alleys quite baffles Washington." Eleanor Roosevelt would one day be criticized in the same tone for the same concerns. *Source:* Jonathan Daniels, *The End of Innocence,* page 86.

10. This identification with TR had its awkward side, as well. Henry D. Breckinridge, the new Assistant Secretary of War, invited Franklin to join the Washington Fencer's Club, to which "your distinguished kinsman gave great impetus." Franklin, who did not know how to fence, answered that while it would be "bully" to be a member, he simply did not have the time. *Source:* Franklin D. Roosevelt, Papers as Assistant Secretary of the Navy, FDRL.

told Sara, she found herself seated next to "Miss Eleanor Wilson, who is nice but, dear me, breeding is somewhat lacking in this political flower of the land."

Franklin and Eleanor were frequent guests at the homes of many of Theodore Roosevelt's old friends. They dined often with the frail, witty old British ambassador, Sir Cecil Spring-Rice, who had once fondly said of TR, "You must always remember that the President is about six," and from whom Franklin found it impossible to conceal his admiration for England in its growing quarrel with Germany. They saw the French ambassador, Jules Jusserand, too, so devoted to TR that he had once waded Rock Creek wearing only his gloves rather than abandon one of the President's vigorous point-to-point hikes. Henry Cabot Lodge of Massachusetts, a Rooseveltian champion of a powerful Navy and soon to become Woodrow Wilson's most implacable enemy in the Senate, sought them out.

And they sometimes called upon Henry Adams at his home on Lafayette Square, just across from the White House. Frail and sour in his mid-seventies, a widower since his wife's suicide in 1885, he flaunted a wry pessimism which Eleanor often found trying "When I ask [him] how he feels about things," she told Isabella, "he says, 'I'm only glad I'm not responsible for them!' " Once, when Franklin expressed impatience at the pace with which the administration seemed to be moving, Adams hushed him. "Young man," he said, "I have lived in this house many years and seen the occupants of that White House across the square come and go and nothing that you minor officials or the occupants of that house can do will affect the history of the world for long!" Franklin smiled politely and did not believe a word of it.

Franklin and Eleanor also frequently saw the Longworths. Nick was still in residence when they first arrived in Washington, although he had lost his seat in the House by a mere seventy-eight votes in the November election, and Alice was still Washington's foremost hostess in exile. (They would soon leave for a two-year sojourn in Cincinnati, living at Rookwood, the big brick Longworth family house that Alice once recalled as "*enchanting*, it was so awful.") Although Nick's cheerful philandering had already made their relationship more an alliance than a marriage—Sara believed Longworth "a cad"—evenings at their home were informal, boozy, often hilarious. Franklin enjoyed them. Eleanor did not. "I went to dine when Franklin was away the other night," she told Isabella, "& one of the lady guests had a cocktail, 2 glasses of whiskey & soda & liquers & 15 cigarets before I left at 10:15! It was a funny party, but I'm glad I'm not so fashionable."

Alice recalled reciprocal dinners at the Roosevelts' with still less pleasure: "They would have rather fine and solemn little Sunday evenings where one was usually regaled with crown roast, very indifferent wine, and a good deal of knitting. I remember going there once with my stepmother, who maintains that she could always tell when I was bored because I appeared to swell up. My eyes recede and my face becomes fat. My stepmother said she thought I was going to lose my eyes that evening. Both Eleanor and Franklin could be very boring together. But not when he was without her. Then he asserted himself."

The Roosevelts' closest shared friends were a small circle of slightly older officials and their wives who dined together informally at least twice a month. Franklin K. Lane, the plump, amiable Secretary of the Interior, and his wife, both from California, were the oldest members of the group. The rest were more or less the Roosevelts' contemporaries: the third Assistant Secretary of State, William Phillips, and his wife Caroline, an Astor and an old friend of Eleanor's; Adolph Miller, an economist and soon to become a member of the Federal Reserve Board, and his wife Mary;[11] and Charles Hamlin, Assistant Secretary of the Treasury, whose amusing wife, "Bertie" Pruyn, had been Franklin's boyhood friend in Albany.[12]

All of them greatly liked the Roosevelts and most left their impressions of the Franklin Roosevelt they knew then. Franklin had seemed to overshadow his wife, they all agreed.

Lane admired his abundant self-confidence. "Young Roosevelt

11. Lane had introduced Franklin to Adolph Miller while walking in Lafayette Park after lunch one day in 1913. They shook hands at the foot of the equestrian statue of Andrew Jackson and when Miller heard the newcomer's name he asked if he were related to TR.
"Yes, distantly," Franklin answered. "What is it about him that you admire most?"
"His dynamic virility," Miller said.
Franklin nodded, and Miller thought that then and later, the younger man was always measuring himself against his cousin's great example. *Source:* Interview with Adolph Miller, Columbia Oral History Project, Columbia University.

12. Franklin was very fond of Bertie, only tolerant of her much older husband, who had been his instructor in government when he was a Harvard undergraduate. "A really splendid person," he told Eleanor, "though not exciting." Then, he added, "incidentally & *pour vous,* I *think* I helped him get him the place [at Treasury]." (It seems unlikely that he needed Franklin's help in 1913—Hamlin had held the same post in the second Cleveland administration, while young Roosevelt was still in his first year at Groton.) Much later, as President, FDR did appoint Hamlin special counsel to the Board of Governors of the Federal Reserve System. *Source:* Franklin D. Roosevelt Papers, Papers as Assistant Secretary of the Navy, FDRL; Elliott Roosevelt, ed., *FDR: His Personal Letters: Early Years,* page 480n.

knows nothing about finance," he told a friend, "but he doesn't *know* he doesn't know."

Phillips remembered him as "brilliant, lovable, and somewhat happy-go-lucky . . . always amusing, always the life of the party." But there had been no signs of greatness: "he was not a heavyweight . . . not particularly steady in his views."

Franklin's years as Assistant Secretary of the Navy represented the only time in his political life he ever acted as anyone's subordinate. Nothing in his early training had prepared him for the role of follower. Yet he would spend nearly eight years at it, almost as much time as any President (except himself) occupied the White House.

It was never easy, either for him or for his chief.

It would be hard to conjure up two men whose backgrounds and training for their shared task were more different than Franklin Roosevelt and Josephus Daniels. Even their looks were in vivid contrast. Roosevelt, nineteen years younger than Daniels, was tall, slender, exuberant, taking the office steps each morning three at a time and, after 1917, doing so after an hour of strenuous outdoor exercise with Cabinet officers and their subordinates under the stern eye of the veteran Yale football coach, Walter Camp. "Mr. Roosevelt," Camp reported, "is a beautifully built man with the long muscles of the athlete. . . . His spirit is resilient, and his effect upon others is . . . salutary in that he imparts some of his own vitality." Daniels himself wrote that Franklin was "as handsome a figure of an attractive young man as I had ever seen."

The Secretary was short, paunchy, and utterly uninterested in exercise;[13] a carriage driven by a black coachman and drawn by a stately matched pair of horses named Nip and Tuck took him to work each morning and brought him back again at day's end. Even his features seemed soft and round: his small, blue eyes were kindly, his mouth invariably turned up at the corners in a courtly smile. He wore old-fashioned black frock coats in winter, wrinkled white suits in summer, and string ties in every season.

If, as the Secretary liked to say, his initial meeting with Franklin at the 1912 convention had been "love at first sight," it had been a one-sided infatuation. Franklin had been at his most publicly winning that afternoon—a witness to their handshake recalled that Daniels had

13. Many years later, he would take private comfort from the fact that while "Walter [Camp] and his pupils have passed [away] . . . I was strong and vigorous when I celebrated my 83rd birthday." *Source:* Joseph L. Morrison, *Josephus Daniels: The Small-d Democrat,* page 96.

turned and introduced Roosevelt to William G. McAdoo, the vice-chairman of the Democratic Party, and Congressman Cordell Hull of Tennessee, and that the young state senator "appeared to be in high spirits at being in the company of these men"—but privately Franklin remembered having thought the North Carolinian "the funniest looking hillbilly I had ever seen."

Daniels spoke and thought and acted as deliberately as he moved, and he had lived a distinctly landlocked life. He was born in the tiny North Carolina hill town of Wilson, in the midst of the Civil War, and had been raised by his widowed mother, the local postmistress, who supported her three sons on a percentage of the stamps she cancelled. (When he was a boy, Daniels remembered, a dime had "looked as big as a cart wheel.") Mrs. Daniels had been burned out three times during the war, and the memory of her bitterness over that and the accidental death of her husband at the hands of Confederate troops who had mistaken the ship he was sailing on for a Union vessel, helped make her son, he said, an instinctive "hater of war."

He remembered his home town as "a democracy with a small 'd' . . . a community free of caste or social chasms," and when he briefly studied law at the University of North Carolina Law School at Chapel Hill, he had indignantly refused to join a fraternity because he thought such organizations betrayed "the democratic spirit." He belonged to just two organizations, he liked to say in later years, the Methodist Church and the Democratic Party: "You could go into either and get out of either of your own free will. If either demanded allegiance or principles not deemed sound, you just quit affiliating without explanation or asking the consent of anybody. Every other organization had in it the probability of caste."

For most of his life he was a newspaperman. He had gone to work as a printer's devil at fourteen, worked his way up to editor of the Wilson *Advance* before his nineteenth birthday, and by 1885, when Franklin Roosevelt was three, already owned his own paper and had been made state printer in gratitude for his editorial loyalty to the Democratic Party. At thirty-one in 1893—precisely Franklin's age when Daniels hired him—he briefly served in Washington as chief clerk of the Interior Department under Cleveland, but when the Democrats were driven from Washington again, he returned home, took over the Raleigh *News and Observer*, and made it one of the most influential newspapers in the South.

Daniels was an uncompromising white supremacist, instrumental in making North Carolina a one-party Democratic state again after

Reconstruction by disfranchising black voters. His racial views would remain adamant—although he did come to deplore the Ku Klux Klan for its lawlessness, and much later confessed that his early editorials had been "cruel in [their] flagellation . . . too cruel"—and he was personally offended the first time he dined with the Roosevelts in Washington and found that they had imported white servants from New York to cook and wait table; in his part of the country such tasks were for blacks alone.

But on other issues his had been a progressive Southern voice; he was opposed to child labor and sweat shops, in favor of the regulation of utilities and the right of unions to bargain, savage in his denunciations of the Tobacco Trust and the railroads. He was also deeply suspicious of the rich and well-born—though this prejudice had not prevented him from marrying the granddaughter of a governor of his state, an ardent *Mayflower* descendant and Daughter of both the American Revolution and the Confederacy, with a handsome old family house in Raleigh, shaded by ancient oaks—and he was the close friend and stalwart ally of the man whom Mr. James, Rosy, and their conservative Democratic friends had all considered an apostate, William Jennings Bryan. Daniels had acted as the great orator's publicity director in every presidential race since 1896, patiently waiting for the day when his friend would finally make it to the White House, and he had performed the same job for Woodrow Wilson in 1912.

Bryan never did make it, of course, and now after seventeen years of common struggle, he and Daniels found themselves Cabinet colleagues; Daniels at the Navy, Bryan as Secretary of State. Daniels shared fully in Bryan's anti-imperialism following the Spanish-American War, his pacifism, his fundamentalist piety, even his celebrated abhorrence of alcohol.[14] He especially admired Bryans's pledge that there would be no war while *he* was Secretary of State, applauded his old friend's campaign to persuade thirty nations to sign arbitration treaties with the United States, and was the proud possessor of one of the plowshare-shaped paperweights that Bryan had ordered made from old guns.

Daniels's link with the Navy he now headed was tenuous but important to him. His father had been a ship's carpenter whose only

14. It had been a condition of Bryan's taking his new job that he not be required to serve anything more potent than grape juice or water to his official guests. One Russian diplomat in Washington, asked to try to remember the last time he had willingly drunk water, is supposed to have thought for a long time, then answered that he believed it might have been during his time as an attaché at Rome in 1879. *Source:* Mark Sullivan, *Our Times: The United States 1900–1925*, Vol. 5, page 150n.

legacy to his son had been his box of tools. His brother-in-law, Worth Bagley, had been a naval ensign stationed off Cuba in the weeks before the Spanish-American War began, and was widely mourned as "the first to fall" in that conflict when he was killed in an exchange of fire with Spanish ships. These apparently disconnected facts left Daniels with two emotions, according to his son—an affection for the Navy, "only surpassed by his devotion to the Democratic Party and the Methodist Church," alongside a visceral suspicion of anything that smacked of spit-and-polish militarism. Military ceremony, he once said, was all "more or less flummery," and his fond wife's first emotion at hearing of his appointment was "hilarity" at the notion of him in a top hat receiving the salutes of naval officers in full uniform.

Those officers and their civilian admirers shared her skepticism but not her fondness for him. His appointment frankly appalled them, and he did little in his first months on the job to ease their minds. He persisted in calling warships "boats," addressed groups of sailors as "young gentlemen" rather than the more nautical "my lads" because he refused to recognize social distinctions at sea, and sometimes even stopped to shake hands with the seamen lined up for inspection. He also ordered that sailors be trained to say "left" and "right" rather than "starboard" and "larboard"; sent desk-bound admirals to sea at intervals they considered far too short; opened the Naval Academy to enlisted men, encouraged civilian instructors to join its faculty, and sought to transform warships into floating "universities" so that sailors would be better prepared to return to civilian life. And he declared an end to the serving of wine in the officers' mess, not only because he believed in temperance but because he thought it undemocratic for officers to have access to alcohol at sea when enlisted men did not.

Daniels was a favorite target for cartoonists—in one drawing, he was shown dressed as Little Lord Fauntleroy, struggling to master a book titled *How to Tell Ships from Automobiles*—but he never seemed to mind much, and his wife papered one entire wall of their home with the signed originals. With his drawling ways, his teetotaling, and his disdain for fashion, he seemed to epitomize everything that the Roosevelts' Washington friends thought wrong with the new administration in whose service Franklin now found himself.[15]

To the new Secretary's old friends, Franklin must have seemed a

15. In an early letter to Isabella, Eleanor worried that Franklin might find the expectations of such a man too exacting: ". . . as his Chief, Mr. Daniels, is a tremendous worker, I think F. will be kept at it pretty hard." *Source:* Ferguson Family Correspondence, Arizona Historical Society.

distinctly odd choice as his closest aide, for young Roosevelt seemed to embody, on the glossy surface at least, a good many of the things against which the editor had battled all his life. "Democracy with a small 'd' " had had precious little to do with Franklin's prominence. He owed his swift rise very largely to his wealth and celebrated last name, a name which had never previously appealed greatly to Daniels. When it had been suggested in 1908 that TR be made president of Harvard, for example, the *News and Observer* had run an especially blunt editorial: "By all means [Theodore] Roosevelt should be elected president, John D. Rockefeller bursar and Elihu Root professor of political economy if Harvard is to teach absolutism, greed and usurpation."

Further, Franklin was a Groton boy and a Harvard man,[16] devoted to just the sort of exclusive clubs Daniels deplored. Franklin's father had helped run the southern railroads that the Secretary believed had bled his state, and young Roosevelt himself had once worked for Carter, Ledyard & Milburn, the law firm that represented the Tobacco Trust whose power and influence Daniels had fought since the early 1890s.

His motives for choosing Franklin seem to have been very largely political. He felt he needed a northeasterner to offset his own Southern background, and Roosevelt's was a name likely to help disarm naval officers otherwise suspicious of the new Secretary.[17] Then, too, he was realistic enough about his own shortcomings to know that a vigorous young assistant with at least an enthusiastic amateur's knowledge of the Navy would make his work easier. And he was genuinely charmed by Franklin's exuberance and energy—one acquaintance said the young man was then "as eager to please as an airedale pup"—and even before their meeting at Baltimore, Daniels had admired his fight against Billy Sheehan, whom he had despised since Cleveland's time. His new assistant would be "a fine co-worker," he confided to his diary after obtaining Woodrow Wilson's approval of his choice, though he

16. Groton was "a caste school," Daniels said, and Harvard a place where "conservative and Republican ideas prevailed." *Source:* Interview with Josephus Daniels, Frank Freidel Papers, FDRL.

17. Franklin's Cousin Bamie, as shrewd about political life as she was about people, understood that merit had played a secondary role in winning him his new position. "Is it not fine about Franklin's app't," she told Bob Ferguson. "I have not yet heard by what happy combination he got the one thing about which he has always been keen. The Navy has been his hobby. He has a fine Naval library & such nice old naval prints." *Source:* Ferguson Family Correspondence, Arizona Historical Society.

still did not know Roosevelt very well: on Franklin's first day at the office, Daniels noted that "Mr. Frederick D. Roosevelt . . . arrived today."

The contrast with his chief made Franklin look very good indeed to the admirals. So did his own infectious love of ships and the sea. Even before he was sworn in as Assistant Secretary, he had asked to be allowed to inspect the Brooklyn Navy Yard and arranged to have a boat pick him up for the ceremonies at the New York Yacht Club, in full view of his friends and fellow members. Wilson Brown, a junior officer that spring, but later a vice admiral and naval aide to FDR in the White House, commanded the barge sent down the East River to fetch him:

> The [commandant's] barge was one of the smartest in the whole Navy. Its mahogany hull shone like a mirror, its brass work could decorate a Tiffany window, and a hand-picked crew showed their pride in the boat by some of the fanciest woven mats, hand lines, and boat cloths the eye of seaman ever beheld.
>
> The story was young at that time about the prairie congressman who, upon visiting his first ship, stared down an open hatch in genuine astonishment. "By gum," he exclaimed, "It's hollow, ain't it!" Would the new assistant secretary be as ignorant as this? Probably not, I decided, for he was a Roosevelt and a Harvard graduate. We were almost the same age. . . . Like nearly everyone else in the Navy I had become a staunch admirer of Theodore Roosevelt, not only for his leadership, but his showmanship, flamboyant though it was.
>
> All I knew of Theodore's young cousin, Franklin, was that he'd stepped into politics not long after leaving Harvard. I'd met few Harvard men and shared some of the prejudices against them. In the mind of a Navy man, there was the usual curiosity about a political civilian executive. . . . All of us were fearful that the entire Wilson Administration . . . would be hostile to the armed services. The new Secretary of State, William Jennings Bryan, had lectured throughout the country on the virtues of pacifism and the need for total disarmament. Our new Secretary of the Navy, Josephus Daniels, was believed to be a fervent disciple of Mr. Bryan. . . . Would . . . this young Roosevelt . . . follow in those pacifist footsteps? . . . [Then] the coxswain put over his helm. The barge eased alongside the New York Yacht Club wharf and tied up.
>
> I can see to this day the new assistant secretary-to-be as he strode down the gangplank to the club float with the ease and assurance of an athlete. Tall . . . smiling, Mr. Roosevelt radiated energy and friendliness. We shook hands, and he introduced me to some friends with him. . . .

Most sailors are accustomed to the gushing enthusiasm of visitors aboard ship. . . . We take it for granted, and we take for granted, too, an enthusiasm which leads them either to muster a misplaced vocabulary in an attempt to show themselves at home or to maintain a guarded silence in the hope of avoiding mistakes. . . .

Once aboard the barge, [Roosevelt] showed immediately that he was at home on the water. Instead of sitting sedately in the stern sheets as might have been expected, he swarmed over the barge from stem to stern during the passage to the Navy Yard. With exclamations of delight and informed appreciation he went over every inch of the boat from coxswain's box to engine room. When she hit the wake of a passing craft and he was doused with spray, he just ducked and laughed and pointed out to his companions how well she rode a wave. Within a few minutes he'd won the hearts of every man of us on board, just as in the years to come he won the hearts of the crew of every ship he set foot on. . . . He demonstrated . . . the invaluable quality of contagious enthusiasm. . . .

Franklin might be a bit young for the job, the veteran officers felt, but he was genuinely knowledgeable about naval matters and was, at least at first, respectful toward career men—whose number he had once hoped to join himself.[18] He knew Europe first-hand, having crossed the Atlantic some twenty times. (Daniels had never even visited Canada.) Above all, he was a Roosevelt in an anti-Roosevelt government, an admirer of the works of Admiral Alfred Thayer Mahan on the importance of seapower, an advocate of a "big Navy" and an active role for it to play overseas.

Franklin did his best publicly to distance himself from his chief's more controversial actions. He was thankful to be out of town, for example, inspecting naval installations on the West Coast, when the Secretary's ban on shipboard wine went into effect, and so was spared the wrath of the officers. "I know how greatly you regret not being here at the time to share in some of the glory," Howe wrote him from Washington. "As it is of course, I can tell the newspapermen nothing except that you are away and naturally know nothing about it."[19]

Privately, he was eager that his new Washington circle understand

18. He was not invariably deferential, however. Already in June 1913, he had his clerk send an acerbic note to the admiral in charge of the Bureau of Supply and Accounts: "The Assistant Secretary desires that the first paragraph of the attached letter to Congressman O'Brien be rewritten in such a way that he will be able to understand what is meant." *Source.* Alfred B. Rollins, *Roosevelt and Howe,* page 116.

19. Franklin's boyish boastfulness would eventually extend even to the liquor ban. During World War II he solemnly assured his aide, Bill Hassett, that it had been he, not Daniels, who had issued it. "The Chief took the blame," he said, "but he didn't formulate the order at all. I did." He didn't. *Source.* Jonathan Daniels, *The End of Innocence,* page 129.

that he, too, found the Secretary's ways quaint and unpolished. He loved to tell of the time he and Daniels dined aboard a warship off Hampton Roads. An aide entered, saluted the Secretary, and said, "I wish to report, sir, that all is secure."

Naval protocol called for Daniels to reply simply, "Very well."

But, according to Franklin, he had said instead, "Well, I declare! That's fine! I'm mighty glad to hear it."

"At first, [my husband] was quite contemptuous of Mr. Daniels," Eleanor remembered, so openly so at dinner one evening that even Franklin's admiring older friend, Secretary Lane, felt called upon to admonish him. "You should be ashamed of yourself," he told him. "Mr. Daniels is your superior and you should show him loyalty or you should resign your office."

Franklin did not resign. But he did chafe.

Over the years there would be serious, substantive differences between the Secretary and his restless assistant. They differed over the proper size of the American Navy and the state of its readiness; about the likelihood of U.S. entry into World War I; about the desirability of that entry; about the way to wage the naval war once America was engaged. Daniels really was slow, sometimes, and rarely saw the need to make a decision before the ground had been carefully prepared for it.

Yet something else was at work as well. It was not that the older man failed to give the younger one his head. Few assistant secretaries in Washington history can have been given freer rein than was Franklin Roosevelt; he exaggerated only slightly when he much later told an aide that Daniels had said he wanted him to be Acting Secretary "even if I have only stepped out to the washroom."

The problem lay rather within Franklin's own expectations of himself and his rightful place in the world. The simple fact was that he thought no man should be his chief, that things were in their proper order only when he was at the head of the list. He had been raised to believe that, and nothing that had happened to him since he first ventured beyond the walls of Springwood had persuaded him that life should be ordered otherwise.[20]

20. Some saw trouble coming early. As a courtesy, Daniels had consulted Elihu Root about Franklin's appointment back in March of 1913. Root, who had been TR's Secretary of State, had broken with him in 1912, and was then Republican senator from New York, had responded very carefully. "You know the Roosevelts don't you?" he asked. "Whenever a Roosevelt rides, he wishes to ride in front."

A Syracuse newspaper, recalling Franklin's turbulent time in Albany, headed its story of his appointment, WATCH OUT JOSEPHUS. Daniels, for his part, remained serene. "A chief who fears

However complex his innermost feelings were about his chief, Franklin took care to maintain in his presence an appearance of cordial, almost filial affection; he had had a good deal of training at home and at Groton and elsewhere in keeping to himself all but his warmest feelings about older people.

For Christmas in 1913, for example, Franklin gave Daniels a framed photograph of a watercolor of the nineteenth-century battleship *North Carolina,* a gesture which greatly touched the older man; it was "my most prized . . . present," he noted in his diary, "the work of a famous artist." When the clamorous evangelist Billy Sunday came to town, the Secretary was so enthusiastic about his preaching that he lent him the Navy Band to play hymns before and after his exhortations and asked him to lead prayer meetings at his home. Franklin gravely attended several of these, and also dutifully escorted Eleanor to at least one of Sunday's revivals. (Eleanor was relieved to find the former baseball player's preaching more dignified than she'd feared, she told Sara, though she still felt as if she were at a show rather than a religious service. Her husband admired Sunday's ability to move a crowd.) Franklin was also publicly supportive of the Secretary's strong views on drink and gambling, although a bottle of Scotch and a deck of cards were always available in his own adjacent office, once the Secretary had left for home.

The younger man may have often been scornful of his chief, but he was at the same time shrewd enough to see that for all of Daniels's weaknesses, authentic or exaggerated by his own restiveness and ambition, there were lessons to be learned from him as well.

The Secretary viewed the world very differently from the way Franklin had been brought up to see it. An only slightly too enthusiastic admirer later wrote that Daniels had been

> one of the few living men who had the exact combination of qualities needed to grapple with the Navy as it was in 1913. He had no personal friends in the Navy, and he had the Puritan's conscience and stubbornness. He entered the department with a profound suspicion that whatever an Admiral told him was wrong and that every corporation with a capitalization of more than $100,000 was inherently evil. In nine cases out of ten his formula was correct: the Navy was packed at the top with dead wood,

that an assistant will outrank him," he wrote in his diary, "is not fit to be chief." *Sources:* Frank Freidel, *Franklin D. Roosevelt: The Apprenticeship,* page 156; Franklin D. Roosevelt Papers, Papers as Assistant Secretary of the Navy, Scrapbook 1, FDRL; Josephus Daniels, *The Wilson Era: Years of Peace 1910–1917,* page 127.

and with politics all the way through, and the steel, coal and other big industries were accustomed to dealing with it on their own terms. With all that, he had sound judgment of men coupled with an innate affection for the rebel.

Years of political experience had taught the older man the ways and means with which to deal effectively with Congress; he spent much of his time as Secretary on the Hill, doing the sort of amiable, indispensable lobbying on the Navy's behalf that the impatient, impulsive younger man would then have found impossible. One-eyed "Pitchfork Ben" Tillman of South Carolina, chairman of the Senate Naval Affairs Committee, for example, was a crude, chronically disheveled racist, whom Daniels had no difficulty in pronouncing "my best friend in Washington."

As his predecessor had left the big, chandeliered Secretary of the Navy's Office for the last time, he slammed his hand on the huge desk and said to Daniels, "Keep the power *here!*"

He needn't have worried. For all his rumpled, patient manner, Daniels could be very tough. One admiral remembered that whenever he differed with the Secretary, he felt "as if I had tried to scratch a diamond with an iron file."

Franklin watched from the sidelines as, twice during his first months on the job, his chief beat back attempts by the admirals to usurp his power. On May 9, 1913, Japan lodged a forceful protest with Washington over new and blatantly discriminatory California laws aimed at barring Japanese aliens from owning land. The Joint Board of the Army and Navy—an exclusively advisory board of military planners—met to formulate an American response. General Leonard Wood, who had commanded American troops in Cuba and was one of TR's most enthusiastic allies, argued that war with Japan was only days away, and that the Navy should immediately move five cruisers from their station in the Yangtze River to Manila so that the Philippines would be protected.

The next morning, Rear Admiral Bradley A. Fiske, aide for operations, conveyed the board's recommendations to Daniels, asserting that the Secretary of War, Lindley M. Garrison, had already approved them.

Daniels was furious: only the Commander in Chief could give the Secretary of the Navy orders. He was sure that Japan did not want war, and in any case, if war did come, the Philippines were indefensible; the force available was too small and too far away. The President backed Daniels, and when Fiske and his allies protested the decision to the White House, Wilson barred the Joint Board from convening again without his permission.

Not long afterwards, Fiske displayed before the Secretary a handsome new table of organization for the Navy Department, aimed, he said, at streamlining things. All department business would be conducted through his Office of Operations—fifteen uniformed officers who answered only to him—he explained, while he and he alone reported to the Secretary. Surely, the Secretary could see the logic of it, and, he continued in a deeply sympathetic tone, it would ease the Secretary's great burdens—which, Fiske had actually warned Mrs. Daniels, might weaken her husband's health.

The new set-up was "admirably drawn," Daniels told him when he had finished. "Beautiful and as perfect a diagram as I ever saw."

Fiske beamed.

But, Daniels said, "you have put the Secretary of the Navy on the top of the Washington Monument without a telephone." If implemented, this attempt to "Prussianize the American Navy" would leave the Secretary with "little power except to draw his breath and draw his salary."

Fiske's plan was out of the question.

The admiral then sought to persuade Congress that the department should be reorganized along the lines of his original proposal.

Daniels returned to the White House. The President again backed his Secretary, and when Daniels himself subsequently reorganized things so that a new Chief of Operations became responsible, under the Secretary, for the operations of the fleet and the preparation of war plans, Wilson suggested that since no admiral could be found who favored his plan for this powerful post, he should appoint a captain. He did just that. Captain (later Admiral) William S. Benson, then commander of the Philadelphia Navy Yard, was appointed, an elderly Georgian with a white mustache who shared Daniels's moderation, his deliberate Southern manner, and his suspicion of wily foreigners. Fiske was never even considered.

Although Franklin had privately supported the Joint Board's bellicose plan for the Pacific Fleet and had evidently also told Fiske he had his support for Chief of Operations, he could not help having been impressed by the skill with which his chief worked his will upon the brass.[21]

And he admired, too, Daniels's efforts to slash costs and frustrate profiteers, not because he then shared the former country editor's instinctive suspicion of big business, but because economy would allow more construction and the political benefits that went with it.

Franklin especially admired, and swiftly emulated, the unfailingly polite but utterly unyielding way in which Daniels dealt with overly greedy naval contractors. In the spring of 1913, the younger man was present when representatives of Midvale, Carnegie, and Bethlehem Steel all presented identical bids for making armorplate.

Daniels took it calmly enough. "Gentlemen," he said. "This, I am afraid, is collusive bidding for you, all three, to arrive at exactly the same figure. I am afraid I have got to throw the bids out and ask for new bids."

The lobbyists each solemnly assured the Secretary that they had come to the same figure by sheer coincidence.

"Well," the Secretary said, "the bids are rejected and we will open new bids at twelve o'clock tomorrow. Sharpen your pencils, think it over during the night, and don't have another coincidence."

"I loved his words," FDR recalled, remembering the businessmen's expressions as they left, and his own and Daniels's pleasure at their distress.

But they came back at noon the next day with precisely the same figure.

That was not accepted, either. Instead, Franklin was dispatched to New York to solicit a bid from a visiting British steelmaker. It was substantially lower, and, according to the Secretary's son, "by another coincidence, all [then] agreed to meet the price."[22]

---

21. Franklin came to share Daniels's amusement at Admiral Fiske's loquacity. He was "extremely able," FDR recalled to a 1943 press conference, but would not stop talking—"had no 'terminal facilities.' "

Once, travelling back to Washington together aboard the interurban after a long day with the admiral at Annapolis, he and Daniels passed a billboard for a well-known manufacturer of automobile parts. "Read that," the Secretary said. "That's the truest . . . sign that has ever been put up in this country."

The sign read, "FISK TIRES." *Source:* Press Conference 879 (February 12, 1943).

22. It should be noted that Daniels's own account of this confrontation makes no mention either of Franklin's contribution or of the British threat. The Secretary concluded that the government should build its own armorplate plant, and managed to win passage of a bill authorizing construction at Charleston, West Virginia. It was begun in 1917, but built too slowly to affect

By 1917, Franklin would routinely act the same way. That year, Joseph P. Kennedy, the assistant manager of the Fore River shipyard at Quincy, Massachusetts, was sent to Washington by his boss, Charles M. Schwab, the powerful chairman of Bethlehem Steel, to see the Assistant Secretary. Schwab's men had finished building two battle-ships for the government of Argentina before World War I began, but Schwab refused to deliver them until he was paid.

Franklin received Kennedy with his usual elaborate cordiality. They had been dealing warily with one another for at least two years. Kennedy then thought Roosevelt a spoiled rich man's son of a type with which he was altogether too familiar from his own years at Harvard; Franklin's opinion of Kennedy in those days is nowhere recorded.

Kennedy delivered his message: no money, no ships.

Franklin assured his visitor the money would be forthcoming; the State Department would collect it on Schwab's behalf. No one wanted an international incident over such a trivial transaction.

Kennedy said that was not good enough.

The Assistant Secretary said that was "absurd."

Kennedy persisted.

Franklin walked him to the door, his arm around the smaller man's shoulder. It was always a pleasure to see Joe. He hoped he'd look him up again when he was next in town. But if Schwab would not give up the ships, the Navy would have to come and get them. Kennedy tried once more.

"Hope to see you again, very soon," Franklin said, and turned back to his desk.

Kennedy assured his boss that it was all bluff. Schwab agreed.

A few days later, four tugboats nosed into the Fore River yard, each filled with armed Marines. They landed, briskly pushed the workers aside, commandeered the new ships, and towed them out to the Argentinian crew waiting offshore.

Joe Kennedy stood by, helpless. Much later he remembered that Franklin had been "the hardest trader I'd ever run against. . . . I was so disappointed I broke down and cried."

---

wartime production. *Source:* Josephus Daniels, *The Wilson Era: Years of Peace 1910–1917,* pages 351–363.

Dwarfed by his big desk in the cramped anteroom just outside Franklin's far larger office at the Navy Department, Louis Howe was a startling sight. He invariably wore a stained but recognizably navy blue tie and slicked down his few remaining wisps of gray hair as faint concessions to his boss's desire to run a shipshape department, but his suits were as rumpled and ash-strewn as ever, and his expression when visitors arrived to see Franklin was often anything but hospitable.

Visiting admirals, accustomed to crisp uniforms and gold braid, found his presence disconcerting at best. Once, Franklin liked to recall, he suggested to an officer that he might send Howe to inspect a ship rather than come himself. "If you do, do you know what will happen?" the officer is supposed to have answered. "As soon as he comes aboard they will take him up on the foc'sle, strip him and scrub him down with sand and canvas."

Out of bitter experience, Howe laughed harder at jokes like that than anyone else, even when they came from the man to whom he was so doggedly loyal. (When, much later, a newspaperman first used the phrase by which he was thereafter most often described, he took to answering his telephone, "Medieval Gnome, here.") But he remained at his station in the outer office, controlling access to his boss.

George Marvin, a former master of Franklin's at Groton, then an assistant editor of *World's Work,* was one of the few old friends whose comings and goings Howe was powerless to limit. In a brief memorandum written many years later, Marvin's scorn for his friend's secretary is still palpable. Howe was "physically a very little and very ugly man of no prepossessions," he wrote, whom Franklin "had picked . . . up at Albany. . . . It always made Howe extremely sore when a few others, like myself, passed through his office, without any reference to him, on our way to see the Assistant Secretary. Howe was a vindictive, as well as an extremely astute individual, and he never forgot his earlier inferiority complexes. Many visitors to the . . . office . . . complained of Howe's bad manners and self-importance."

They complained of other things as well. His first loyalty to his boss sometimes seemed out of place at the Navy. Daniels himself once complained that Howe "would have sidetracked both President Wilson and me to get Franklin to the White House," and the Secretary's son, Jonathan, a teenager during the war years and a frequent visitor to the Navy Department, remembered him as seeming "like something that had come from under the dark, damp side of a stone, very dry and dusty all the same."

Complaints of this kind never seemed to bother Franklin.

His appeal for Howe can be summarized in a very few words. Franklin was a likely winner who would provide the little man with some semblance of the power he craved. Louis, Eleanor told an interviewer many years later, after she had forged her own strong friendship with Howe, "had an enormous interest in . . . having power, and if he could not have it . . . himself, he wanted it through someone he was influencing. I think he loved power."

But why did Franklin saddle himself with an intimate adviser whom so many people could not abide? The answer to this as to so many questions about him lay in his own ambition.

Many of Howe's most obvious liabilities—his eccentric looks, his untidiness, his obvious and unapologetic cynicism, the quirky personality that the charitable found merely gruff but others thought repellent—were assets from Franklin's point of view. For they ensured, as no verbal assurances ever could have, that Howe would always be beholden to him, would never dare try to overtake or excel him. Only by absolute loyalty to Franklin's advancement could Howe hope to advance, and both he and Franklin knew it.

And because of it, Howe's word could be trusted when almost no one else's could be.

Franklin did not normally take criticism well, distrusting the critics' motives rather than considering seriously what they had to say. Howe provided no possible grounds for distrust. Therefore, if he told Franklin—as he often did, and with vehemence, then and later—that he was making a mistake, he had to be listened to. Only Louis Howe could have spoken to Franklin Roosevelt as he was once overheard doing over the telephone: "You damned fool! You can't do that! You simply can't do it, I tell you! . . . If you do it, you're a fool—just a damned idiotic fool!" Howe was "the best adviser Roosevelt ever had," recalled an admiral who dealt often with both the Assistant Secretary and his assistant during the Navy years, "because he had the guts to say 'no.' "

And Louis's strengths, less obvious to outsiders than his liabilities, neatly filled chinks in Franklin's ability to lead and maneuver. Josephus Daniels understood: "Howe would look after a lot of things that Roosevelt didn't have time to do. [He] had no personality, no charm, but he knew politics and forgot himself. He would have laid on the floor and let Franklin walk over him."[23] Howe was a tireless laborer on behalf of their common cause, a workaholic long before that ugly but descriptive word was coined. (His family would one day come to blame Franklin and Eleanor for stealing him from them, but had the Roosevelts not existed it seems clear he would have found other objectives to occupy his restless, driven mind, away from his tense home.)

Franklin was not fond of paperwork. He had great energy and his ability to absorb bits of disconnected information was astonishing, but his concentration span was short; he had never much liked swotting up—at Groton, at Harvard, at Carter, Ledyard & Milburn, even in the state Senate, he liked to do as little studying as possible—as contrasted with Al Smith, for example, who helped himself master the legislative art by virtually memorizing the annual blizzard of bills and amendments.

Paperwork was a Howe specialty. He read fast, wrote fast, dictated fast, scattering cigarette ashes over everything as he went, and his newspaperman's training had taught him how to deal with the press, how to distill from vast amounts of material those essential facts which his boss needed to function at his best, and how to make even the most apparently wearisome labor seem somehow entertaining enough to hold his interest.

A series of long, detailed letters, written to accompany fat packets of mail forwarded from Washington to Campobello, where the Assistant Secretary took a week's vacation at the end of his first June on the job, show something of Howe's method. He enjoyed gossip and intrigue at least as much as his boss did, and he knew how interested Franklin always was in his own press, and so he peppered his lengthy summaries of office business with tidbits that he knew would keep Franklin reading. "I understand the President is going off on the *Mayflower* [the Presidential yacht] with his doctor and nobody else for three or four days. . . . I don't know just what this means, but I take it the heat has got him finally," appears precisely halfway through a four-page letter filled with complicated information regarding every-

---

23. Howe's willingness to remain in his chief's shadow was second nature to him, and he insisted always that Franklin's other aides follow his example. "Remember this," he instructed one newly hired member of the Roosevelt campaign staff in 1932. "You're nobody. Your name means nothing. Your face means nothing. So I don't want to catch you or anyone else crowding hiself into the picture to get some personal publicity. But the thing you've got to worry about night and day, and work for night and day, is this man Roosevelt and the cause he represents." *Source:* Stanley Hyman interview with C. Edgar Brown, FDRL.

thing from New York politics to a contract for "blue cloth hats," all of them demanding, at least briefly, the Assistant Secretary's undivided attention.

Another of those early letters, with nineteen numbered points, includes, as item 12: "To take the bad taste out of your mouth from the batch of papers under item 11, I am sending you a press notice of yourself from Mansfield, Ohio, which is rather cleverly written. This, I trust, will put you in good humor for Number 13." Still another big envelope arrived with a note promising "all kinds of horrid, stupid things and a scandal or two on the way."

Impatient, overconfident, the youthful Franklin too often preferred action to reflection, was inclined to move fast and by instinct. Howe, on the other hand, was if anything too cautious; he never wanted to risk their shared future on anything far short of a sure thing. His aide's inborn hesitancy irritated Franklin sometimes, but in quieter moments he, too, realized he needed the "toe weights" that Louis often said he was only too happy to provide.[24]

Howe's distrust of piety, the weary skepticism with which he approached most people—especially politicians—must also have been bracing for Franklin. His wife and mother were never satisfied unless he were jousting with what Groton's rector had called "the lower powers." Neither were the other family members and friends whose opinions he'd been raised to value.

He worked hard to make them and his constituents all feel that he was invariably righteous and uncompromising, never stopped seeking the approval of those closest to him. Yet it was clearly impossible for him to function effectively if he treated those with whom he had to work as anything like "lower powers." The sentiments of people like his godmother, Nelly Blodgett—who had greeted his reelection as state senator as proof that "the means you will use to gain your ends will *always* be honorable and generous"—were well meaning but hopelessly out of touch.

If Franklin had not known that before he entered politics, he certainly knew it now, yet that guilty knowledge was still a secret within his household—a secret that would never be comfortably shared—and it must have been refreshing to have in Louis an in-house comrade who acknowledged it, too.

24. He kept at this to the end. According to FDR's first Vice President, John Nance Garner, Howe's final words to him, delivered in a whisper on his deathbed in 1936, were, "Hold Franklin down!" *Source:* John Gunther, *Roosevelt in Retrospect*, page 85n.

Howe displeased Eleanor and the children by turning up at 8:15 A.M. sharp each morning to walk with him to the Navy Department, wheezing to keep up with his tall boss as he laid out the day's crowded schedule. He acted as Franklin's critic and goad sometimes, but he also often signed his letters "your slave," a joke in which there was more truth than laughter. For he was willing, even eager, to perform chores that might have angered a less devoted, more self-confident assistant. He kept track of the tiniest details of Franklin's life—WHERE DO YOU WANT YOUR STRAW HAT FORWARDED? he once wired the Assistant Secretary, who was aboard a train heading west, REPLY FROM NEXT STATION—and he pored over gallery catalogues looking for naval prints and rare books for Franklin's collections, then placed the bids and picked up the merchandise.

Howe's carefully cultivated raffishness appealed to Franklin, too. He knew things and was willing to share them—about the racetrack, about low lifes, about the private doings of politicians—that the young Roosevelt had never had the opportunity to learn on his own. For all his energy and outer gloss, Franklin was still a remarkably unsophisticated young politician. Frances Perkins once wrote that Franklin's Harvard education "in itself [constituted] a political handicap."[25] Continuous exposure to Louis Howe would help him get over it.

In a sense, Howe would be the last and most important of the succession of tutors who devoted their lives for a time to answering Franklin's queries, showing him how to do things on his own.

Unlike them, however, Louis was enlisted for the duration.[26]

There was no line dividing Franklin's ambition from Howe's, and, together, they now tackled the burden of Navy business. Like Franklin, Louis got into everything from shipbuilding to the design of uniforms, bond drives to the brands of toothpaste sold aboard

25. For all his public fealty to his university, FDR later seemed to agree at least in part with this assessment. In 1940, the President grew very fond of the young Texas congressman, Lyndon B. Johnson, and expressed his special enthusiasm for him to his Secretary of the Interior, Harold Ickes. Johnson, he said, was "the kind of uninhibited young [professional]" he himself would have been "if he hadn't gone to Harvard." *Source:* Thomas G. Corcoran's and Eliot Janeway's independent accounts of conversations with Ickes, as quoted in Robert A. Caro, *The Path to Power: The Years of Lyndon Johnson,* page 668.

26. "I really can't think of anyone who had a total friendship with Franklin Roosevelt," Frances Perkins remembered. "He revealed a good deal of himself to Louis Howe out of sheer necessity, but I don't think that there was ever the friendship between equals between them. I hate to say it, but I think Louis was always more in the category of a high-grade intellectual servant." *Source:* Transcript of interview with Frances Perkins, Columbia Oral History Project, Columbia University.

ships. (Secretary Daniels remembered that from the first Howe seemed to know "all the tides and eddies of the Department," and a Navy veteran would marvel in 1916 "how a man not connected with the Naval Service can have obtained in three years the detailed knowledge . . . that is possessed by Mr. Howe.")

Howe was a superb investigator, digging out the facts and figures with which his boss impressed congressmen and dazzled unwary officials. He often acted as troubleshooter, too, visiting the yards incognito to interview the men and putting even uncooperative admirals through brusque interrogations. (It pleased him to learn that he was known by some officers as "Roosevelt's gumshoe.") He continued to work hard at sparking Franklin's interest in the minutiae the job sometimes demanded, handing on troublesome communications pinned to brief notes showing he sympathized: "This makes me tired, but I suppose it's all right"; "I honestly have forgotten what all this means"; "What in the world shall we do about this?"

He also made a determined effort to acquaint Franklin with the issues troubling labor, ushering delegations of workingmen in and out of the office, sometimes more often than his boss liked. Howe was no more instinctively friendly to labor's cause than was Franklin—he, too, was an upstate New Yorker with little experience of industrial life— but he foresaw the enormous power labor voters would one day wield, the importance of winning and holding the friendship of their leaders, and he made certain his boss saw it, too. "I want you all to feel that you can come to me at any time in my office," Franklin was soon telling union spokesmen, "and we can talk matters over. Let's get together, for I need you to teach me your business and show me what is going on."

They did get together. The Assistant Secretary's office became a clearinghouse for labor complaints. Franklin listened and learned. "The laboring men all liked him," Josephus Daniels remembered. "If there was any Groton complex (which there was in his social life), he did not show it in the Department. Our policy was always fair compensation." Later, Franklin liked to boast—with only slight exaggeration—that during his years on the job, the Navy never had "a single strike or even a serious disagreement."[27]

27. Howe acquainted his young boss with the need to do something for black voters, as well, as FDR recalled in a conversation with his own Secretary of the Navy, Frank Knox, in early October 1940. Roosevelt and Knox were trying to find symbolic ways to placate civil rights

Eleanor once suggested to an interviewer that Franklin's overseeing of the Navy Yards—and Louis Howe's frequent interventions on
labor's behalf—had been very largely responsible for having made her
husband "more than just a very nice young man who went out in
society and did a fair job but [was] perfectly conventional about it."

Franklin may sometimes have had to be pushed by Howe to interest himself in departmental details, but he always had time for matters
that had nothing whatsoever to do with defense but everything to do
with maintaining and expanding his power back home.

By the autumn of 1913, the New York Democratic Party was in
even worse disarray than usual. Tammany's hand-picked governor,
William "Plain Bill" Sulzer, an erratic orator who had pledged to be
his own man during his election campaign and then made the mistake
of believing his own rhetoric, had run afoul of his patrons. When he
threatened to expose their corruption, he was impeached for his independence, convicted, and removed from office. Louis had been careful
to keep Franklin from publicly siding with either camp during the
prolonged struggle in Albany, preparing what he called "nice pussy-
footing answers" for his boss to sign when the embattled Sulzer begged
him for help.

Sulzer was driven from Albany and replaced by a dependable
regular, Martin H. Glynn, but the noisy battle had contributed further
to Tammany's reputation for ruthlessness. At the November elections,

---

leaders who were pressing for full integration of the armed forces. The President thought it might
be helpful if "we had a colored *band* on some of these [Navy] ships, because they're *darned good
at it.* . . . Look, to increase the *opportunity,* that's what we're after."
Then, he argued for the appointment of black spokesmen:

In the Navy Department in the old days I had a boy who volunteered by the name of
Pryor [Frederick D. Pryor, secretarial clerk to General Edwin "Pa" Watson, the President's
military aide at the time FDR was speaking]. . . . He used to be my colored messenger. A
young kid, and Louis Howe was terribly fond of him. And when we got back here in
thirty-three, Louis Howe said to me, 'The one man I want for my office is Pryor.' Well,
Pryor, *now,* is one of the best fellows we've got in the office and he handles all my . . . cases
from the Department of Justice. . . . He summarizes the whole thing. . . . A great boy.
. . . He was just a clerk in the Navy Department and I used *him.* [Black] People went to him
with any kind of question. Can we do *this?* Can we do *that?* Can we get another opening
there? And he was of very, very great service. I think you can do that in the Army and the
Navy . . . get somebody colored [who will act as] the clearinghouse.

Shortly after this conversation, the Secretary of War, Henry L. Stimson, added to his staff, as
a civilian aide, the first black federal judge, William H. Hastie. *Sources:* "The FDR Tapes,"
American Heritage (February–March 1982), page 24; Frank Freidel, *Franklin D. Roosevelt: The
Apprenticeship,* page 203.

Murphy had lost his grip on the New York mayoralty to a fusionist reformer, John Purroy Mitchel, but Democrats of every kind had gone down to defeat.

Franklin was already growing restive at the Navy Department. He enjoyed his new job in many ways. He took enormous pleasure in presiding over the nautical ceremonies of which he had dreamed as a child, revelled in his new proximity to national power, found the exalted company he now routinely kept in harmony with his sense of himself, liked nearly everything about life in Washington, in fact, except the summer heat.

But he found much of the work tedious. Believing himself fit for command and grand strategy, he had to deal instead with the day-to-day details of departmental housekeeping.

Perhaps more important, he fretted that the turbulent course of political events in New York State, where he believed the next step on his steady ascent would have to be taken, might leave him behind. The first statewide direct primary ever held in New York State was scheduled for September of 1914. Franklin had led the fight for just such a primary while at Albany. The way was now open for someone to take the case against Murphy to the voters. Unless a candidate could be found to do that effectively, he was sure, the Republicans would sweep the state.

To Franklin, it seemed intolerable that a rival reformer might be afforded the opportunity to mount that challenge.

He asked the President privately to anoint him as his agent, empowered to build an anti-Tammany organization throughout New York. Wilson withheld approval, wishing neither openly to betray the reformers who had backed Wilson for the 1912 nomination nor to alienate the regulars in Congress, whose votes were still needed to enact the host of progressive bills that constituted the President's New Freedom.

Franklin determined to see what he could do without help from the White House. To stand a chance of defeating Murphy's machine, he first needed secretly to build an organization of his own. "This is a delicate game we are playing," Franklin wrote from the Navy Department to Louis M. Antisdale, editor of the Rochester *Herald* and one of his most trusted political allies, "and what success we have achieved so far has been due largely to our ability to keep our mouths shut and keep out of the newspapers."

It was indeed a delicate game. Franklin was by no means the most important New York Democrat in Washington. Senator O'Gorman saw no special reason to be helpful to him; no member of the 1911 Democratic legislative caucus had cast his ballot for the senator more reluctantly than had young Roosevelt, and he thought Franklin distinctly unreliable. William McAdoo, now Secretary of the Treasury and soon to be the President's son-in-law, was more friendly, often willing to help Franklin on specific matters, but harboring presidential ambitions of his own. And several other old reform allies of Franklin's were dreaming dreams almost as large as his.

In spite of the odds, and with Howe's shrewd and tireless help, Franklin attempted to corner federal patronage in as much of New York State as he could manage.

Treasury positions were McAdoo's domain. Neither Howe nor Franklin was able to make much headway prying jobs out of the State or Justice departments, either. But thousands of civilian Navy positions were under their control, and at the Post Office Department, Howe carefully cultivated Daniel C. Roper, the Assistant Postmaster General, a young South Carolinian honestly bewildered by the unique intricacies of New York politics and at first genuinely grateful for the little man's offer of help and his straight-faced expressions of interest in improving the quality of postal service throughout the state. Soon, in open defiance of the civil service laws, Roper was routinely submitting to Howe the names of the three top scorers on the competitive examinations for each vacant office. Armed with this information, he and Franklin were often able to shunt aside machine nominees and to win appointments for men thought more likely to be friendly to their interests.[28]

No town was too small, no federal job too insignificant, no potential bloc of votes too unimportant for Franklin to ignore. When he learned that the Davy Crockett Hook and Ladder Company of Poughkeepsie was planning a Washington excursion, he invited them all to the Navy Department and asked "Whether they would not like to be shown over the Navy Yard where the big guns are manufactured." He interested himself even in picking rural letter carriers.

Sometimes, Howe arranged to swap favors with officials in other departments on his behalf; thus; for example, he managed a safe shore assignment at Boston for a friend of the Postmaster General at the request of that official's private secretary, who begged that his letter be

28. In 1933, FDR would name Roper his Secretary of Commerce.

kept out of the files, promising to "reciprocate when opportunity offers." (Howe kept the letter, as insurance against the Secretary's ever going back on the pledge.)[29]

"I conceive our part of the game just at present is to wash our hands entirely of matters below the Bronx," Franklin told one supporter. He learned not to attack Tammany on its own ground. An early attempt, made jointly with McAdoo, to have his friend Mayor John K. Sague of Poughkeepsie appointed Collector of New York had been scuttled at the last moment by the President's small, shadowy aide, Colonel Edward M. House, to avoid the Tammany cries of betrayal that would surely have followed. But he and Howe did their best to ensure that the power of Murphy's machine did not spread beyond its natural borders. "I think Senator O'Gorman is dreaming of assuming the leadership of up-state," Franklin warned a friend, "but so long as our endorsement is necessary to get the post-office appointments . . . just so long will these appointments come to us first."

He could not always satisfy those who sought favors from him. "I supposed you had more common sense," he wrote one disappointed politician, "than to believe in the silly newspaper stories that I am the official patronage dispenser for the State of New York. . . ."

He never did become the official dispenser, but it was not for want of trying. He was not the first ambitious young federal appointee to try to build an organization back home through patronage, nor would he be the last. But the scale of the operation he and Howe conducted was extraordinary; there are forty-three large boxes of patronage correspondence among Franklin's papers in the Franklin D. Roosevelt Library at Hyde Park, and these do not include all the letters Howe drafted—a good many have turned up elsewhere, of which file copies were either destroyed or never made. Nor do these files reflect the bulk of the patronage business he and Howe undertook, most of which was done on the telephone or across the Assistant Secretary's desk. "Come

29. The pleasure Howe and Franklin took in the deft maneuvering the patronage struggle required was almost palpable. Clayton Wheeler, one of the original anti-Sheehan insurgents in the state Senate, now in the Assembly, suggested a man named Truman Lewis for postmaster at Sidney. When Lewis sent in his résumé, he was found to be seventy-two years old, well past the legal appointment age. Rather than risk personally offending this good friend of a friend, Franklin asked Wheeler, "How would it be for us to write a little note commending him to the Postmaster General and getting a reply regretting that his age makes his appointment absolutely impossible and forwarding him the letter. There would be no trouble about doing this." *Source:* Franklin D. Roosevelt Papers, Papers as Assistant Secretary of the Navy, FDRL.

see me," Franklin told one upstate supporter. "There are a number of things that I do not want to put on paper."[30]

He had few illusions about the permanence of the loose antimachine alliance he and Howe were nailing together. "I realize perfectly that ⅔ of [our new friends) would slide back at the prospect of any loaves and fishes from the other side," he told Antisdale. He had to be able to produce jobs and favors for his friends consistently, to demonstrate the benefits that upstate politicians could derive by allying themselves with him, and to persuade them, too, that defying him could be costly.[31]

To do all that, Franklin sometimes needed to be able to imply a closeness to the President that was never really present.

Others were working at cross-purposes with him, most notably Colonel House, who was quietly trying to make some sort of accommodation between the reformers and Governor Glynn to keep the party together and New York votes for his chief's domestic program intact on Capitol Hill. Franklin argued that such an effort was doomed to failure; that Murphy could be counted upon to dominate any coalition into which he was willing to enter. Still, if anyone's claim to the President's support had any legitimacy it should have been House's.

This inconvenient fact bothered neither Franklin nor Howe. In December, Louis floated a story in the *New York Sun* suggesting that unless Governor Glynn made an open break with his Tammany patrons, the President hoped Franklin Roosevelt would enter the race against him. Franklin's denials of his own interest in the governorship that followed at regular intervals thereafter were both too frequent and too eagerly indignant to be credible.[32]

30. Years later, even FDR seems to have been a little embarrassed by the scale of his patronage effort—and by some of the youthful wheeling and dealing it revealed. Speaking at a Washington dinner for the trustees of his still unbuilt library in 1939, he said his papers having to do with patronage "form an interesting historical record of appointments of that particular type of public service, showing the progress that we have made in twenty-five years."

31. In this last, especially, Howe backed him to the hilt. "[Louis] paid no attention to how *he* was treated," Eleanor remembered, "but if someone did something [to the Boss] which he thought was a double-cross, he was the most relentless enemy I have ever known. No one ever got away with doing something to Franklin, and I used to say years afterwards, 'Why did you do that to so-and-so?' And he would say: 'Don't you remember twenty years ago [what he did]?' And I would say: 'Good Heavens. I had forgotten all about it.' And he would say, '*I* never forgot it.'" *Source:* Interview in Robert D. Graff Papers, FDRL.

32. One of those who did not believe them was Governor Glynn, even though Franklin carefully sent one to him: "By the way, if you happen to run across the inspiring idiot who started the report that I might be or under any circumstances could be, a candidate for Governor, you

In March 1914, Franklin made a clumsy attempt to force Wilson's hand. The *New York World*, he told the President, had asked him to write "an article on the New York situation." He had "steadfastly refused," of course, because "I do not think it is right for me to speak if it is to be construed as voicing the opinion of the Administration." But the newspaper was being very persistent. Might he come see the President "for five minutes" to discuss what he might usefully say?

Wilson was too busy to see him, but in a short note the President urged strongly that Franklin refuse to write anything, since "the plot is not yet clear" as to what was likely to happen in New York.

Franklin's political maneuvering was interrupted briefly in early April, 1914 when Daniels sent him west to inspect naval installations on the Pacific coast. While he was there, the Mexican situation erupted once again.

The USS *Dolphin*, the same vessel on which Franklin had often enjoyed sailing back and forth from Campobello, had been anchored off Tampico, stationed there to shield American lives and property. A boat went ashore to pick up supplies and three members of its crew were arrested by a hot-headed Mexican colonel in Huerta's army. The local commander apologized and released the men, but Admiral Henry T. Mayo, acting without authority from Daniels, demanded far more: the colonel had to be punished, there must be a formal apology made by high-ranking Mexican officers in uniform aboard the *Dolphin*, and the American flag had to be hoisted on Mexican soil and given a twenty-one-gun salute—all within twenty-four hours. ("I'm afraid Mayo is not a good 'watchful waiter,'" Howe wrote Franklin.)

To Daniels's surprise, President Wilson—whose dislike of Huerta had intensified steadily since their initial confrontation—backed the admiral, and when Huerta refused to order the flag salute, dispatched warships to Mexico.

Nothing could have pleased Franklin more. At last, action seemed near, and he was to be in the thick of it. Travelling up and down the coast, he promised that the Pacific installations would be strengthened, and implied to reporters that he had been sent to oversee naval mobilization, to ensure that "Every warship on the Pacific Coast is [ready]

---

will do me a real favor by taking him into a quiet corner and firmly convincing him that he is absolutely mistaken." *Source:* Franklin D. Roosevelt Papers, Papers as Assistant Secretary of the Navy, FDRL.

for sailing in fighting trim on a moment's notice." (In fact, Daniels had merely asked him to "make such suggestions as you think wise.")

War, Franklin confided to one newspaperman, was now very close: "We're not looking for trouble, but we're ready for anything"; punishment was necessary for those whose "studied insults [were] aimed directly at the nation."

On April 20, a German vessel laden with war materiel for Huerta arrived at Vera Cruz. After consultation with the White House, Daniels ordered the Navy to seize the customhouse and ensure that no German arms came ashore. Nineteen Americans were killed in the street battle that followed.

Franklin was in his element. He doubled the work force with which a radio installation was being built at San Diego, arranged for fleet and Marine movements from Washington to southern California, and wired Daniels to send him the department's plan for action on the west coast of Mexico.

He had been scheduled to return to Washington, but now he clearly hoped to stay on and direct those operations himself. History again seemed to be repeating itself; the opportunity had finally come to earn for himself the sort of warrior's reputation TR had made just sixteen years earlier.

Daniels decided it was time to rein Franklin in. He called him home in the gentlest possible way, having Howe send a carefully worded wire:

> SECRETARY SAYS THAT AS MOST OF THE VESSELS ON THE WEST COAST WILL BE DOWN IN MEXICO AND IN VIEW OF THE GREAT HELP YOU CAN BE TO HIM IN WASHINGTON, HE THINKS THE WISE COURSE IS FOR YOU TO RETURN AS ORIGINALLY PLANNED.

Franklin followed orders, but boarded his train with great reluctance. While he was travelling back across the continent, Wilson agreed to submit the dispute to the ABC powers of Latin America, Argentina, Brazil, and Chile. Franklin may not have known that the President had opted for a peaceful solution, but he was certainly aware that the arbitration offer had been made. Nonetheless, he issued bellicose statements at almost every stop.

What would happen next? he was asked at Minneapolis. "War!" he said, "And we're ready! . . . I do not want war, but I do not see how we can avoid it. Sooner or later, it seems, the United States must go down there and clean up the Mexican political mess. I believe that the best time is right now."

"The war spirit is sweeping the west like a prairie fire!" he told a Chicago newspaperman. ". . . Many persons and newspapers are openly advocating annexation as the only solution. . . . The sentiment appears to be growing."

In fact, it was shrinking, and with it another chance at military fame for Franklin Roosevelt. Back at the office he received a firm but gentle dressing down from his chief, after which he refused all further comment on the Mexican crisis. "Of course things at the moment look quiet and not as warlike as last week," he wrote a friend in early May, "but I am not convinced the worst is over."

Sadly for Franklin, it was.[33]

After the Mexican conflict failed again to materialize, Franklin's frustration with his job seems to have intensified. The practical limitations of his position had now been made clear to him. He became more determined than ever to find a way to regain a political foothold in New York State.

He had been Assistant Secretary of the Navy for eighteen months; his cousin had held the post for just thirteen, then gone on to Cuba.

Franklin was behind schedule.

Yet his efforts to build his own organization seemed to backfire. When Franklin successfully blocked the Irish candidate for postmaster of Poughkeepsie favored by Ed Perkins in June, for example, his early enemy was so angered that he resigned his post as finance secretary of the state party, loudly repeating the old charge that Franklin was not so much anti-Tammany as anti-Catholic. The Poughkeepsie *Times-Union* headed its story of the new appointment NO IRISH NEED APPLY, and warned the President not to listen to "the young and rash Roosevelt . . . [who is] animated by racial and religious prejudice . . . rather than by actual hostility to Tammany."

Even some of Franklin's oldest allies were alienated by the divisive anger his efforts to build his own candidacy appeared to inspire. Leaving his own post as state party chairman that spring, William Church

---

33. More than two years later, he was still hopeful of a border war. "The Mexican situation is going through one of its periodically peaceful revivals," he told Eleanor, "but the pendulum will swing back to intervention in a week or a month or a year. I don't care much which as it is sure to come and at least the Army and Navy are gaining by every hour's delay." *Source:* Elliott Roosevelt, ed., *FDR: His Personal Letters, 1905–1928,* page 304.

Osborn, for example, bemoaned the sad state of his party and blamed much of it on "self-appointed little busybodies who have the President's ear and . . . may have convinced him that many perfectly good Democrats are only Tammany heelers." Franklin responded with biting sarcasm, "congratulating" his old mentor on quitting a job for which he had always been ill-suited. Eleanor found this a dubious tactic: "Isn't it just a bit patronizing? If I were [Osborn] I would rise up and smite you for an impertinent youth."

His impertinence does not seem to have been shaken. But his confidence may have been, for nothing now seemed to go his way. He toyed with the notion of seeking the Progressive Party's nomination for governor, but backed away swiftly when the rumor reached him—false, as it turned out—that TR himself might want it. "If Colonel Roosevelt is a candidate . . . ," he told a reporter, "I will not run against him. You know blood is thicker than water."

Meanwhile, Franklin's hollow victory over Perkins, and rumors that forty more postmasterships were about to be awarded to his anti-Murphy allies, brought Tammany's anger to a head in late July. Congressman John J. Fitzgerald of Brooklyn, chairman of the powerful Ways and Means Committee and spokesman for some twenty regular Democrats in Congress, publicly warned that he would find it hard to continue to support an administration which permitted a sub-Cabinet official to imply that he was speaking for the President when he charged that Tammany men like himself spoke for "crooks, grafters and buccaneers."

Woodrow Wilson, who saw no need to imperil passage of the blizzard of reform bills that comprised his New Freedom in order to further the ambitions of his glossy young Assistant Secretary of the Navy, issued a statement declaring that *he* did not consider Tammany congressmen "crooks, grafters and buccaneers."

Clearly, not even Franklin Roosevelt dared now suggest that he was the White House candidate for the governorship. That office was beyond his grasp—"thank God," he told Eleanor bravely—and his final public statement on the subject was as nautically jaunty as he could make it: "When I said I was not a candidate . . . I did not say it in diplomatic language, but seafaring language, which means it."

By then, events elsewhere again seemed likely to hold his attention. On July 14, he told Eleanor, he had arrived at the office to find "an interesting situation in Haiti and Santo Domingo, with a hurry call for marines from the State Department. I saw the President about it, also Mr. Bryan and Bill Phillips, and by 5 p.m. had 700 marines and two ships in motion towards Guantanamo."[34]

Later in the month, he steamed north to Campobello for a short visit. There, the news reached him on the 28th that Austria-Hungary had declared war on Serbia. A full-scale European conflict seemed only hours away. The next morning, he travelled down from Campobello to represent the Navy at the ceremonies inaugurating the Cape Cod Canal from the deck of the first of six destroyers that steamed past "a great many thousand people [who] lined the bank, with countless automobiles and much noise of welcome." A fierce current pushed the little fleet past the tent where the speeches were to be made, the destroyer could not anchor, and Franklin and the other dignitaries finally had to go ashore by motor launch. Afterward, he travelled all night by boat, automobile, and train to Washington, feeling, he said, "a good deal like P. Revere."

He was sure that "the greatest war in human history" was beginning, that the United States would almost certainly be drawn into it, and that the Navy must be readied instantly for any eventuality. But when he got to the office, he found only gloom:

> To my astonishment on reaching the Dept. nobody seemed the least bit excited about the European crisis—Mr. Daniels feeling chiefly very sad that his faith in human nature and civilization, and similar idealistic nonsense was receiving such a rude shock. So I started in alone to get things ready and prepare plans for what ought to be done by the Navy end of things. . . .
>
> These dear good people like W.J.B. and J.D. have as much conception of what a general European war means as Elliott has of higher mathematics . . . I nearly boil over when I see the cheery "mañana" way of doing things. . . .

34. This incident apparently inspired one of FDR's favorite stories. According to him, an agitated William Jennings Bryan raced into his office one afternoon, shouting, "I've got to have a battleship! White people are being killed in Haiti, and I must send a battleship there within twenty-four hours!"

The Assistant Secretary said that would be impossible. "Our battleships are in Narragansett Bay and I could not get one to Haiti in less than four days steaming at full speed. But I have a gunboat at Guantanamo and I could get her to Haiti in eight hours if you want me to."

"That is all I wanted to know," Bryan said, and turned to leave, then stopped in the doorway.

"Roosevelt," he said, "after this, when I talk about battleships don't think I mean anything technical."

Sources: Slightly varying versions of this story appear in many places, including Frank Freidel, *Franklin D. Roosevelt: The Apprenticeship*, pages 237–238, and Ernest K. Lindley, *Franklin D. Roosevelt: A Career in Progressive Democracy*, pages 115–116.

The department was able to spare him the next day, however, for a previously scheduled public appearance at Reading, Pennsylvania. There, an incumbent Democratic congressman in a tight race for renomination had managed to wangle from Daniels an anchor from the *Maine* for presentation to the citizens of his city. His opponent pronounced the anchor a fake, implying that the Navy Department was somehow manufacturing *Maine* relics in the interests of its friends. Franklin travelled to Reading on July 31 officially to present the anchor. Who better to attest to the authenticity of a Spanish-American War relic than a Roosevelt? He did it with spirit (though the incumbent still lost the primary): "The Reading unveiling . . . was a great success," Franklin told Eleanor, "—fine parade—lots of bands—ending with an impassioned oration by hubby to 5,000 people in the park!"

On the train back to Washington he received the news that Germany had invaded France.

"A complete smash up is inevitable," he told Eleanor, "and there are a great many problems for us to consider. Mr. D. totally fails to grasp the situation and I am to see the President Monday a.m. to go over our own situation." Whether that situation was the coming war or his own momentarily thwarted political ambitions we do not know. Wilson had no time for the young Assistant Secretary, on Monday or any time that week; his wife of twenty-nine years was dying of cancer.[35]

Franklin continued to find playing a secondary role both uncomfortable and unnatural. It seems to have been difficult for him to admit even to himself, let alone to his wife and mother, that he was not really in charge—that Daniels and the President were.

Three days later, Franklin still saw himself at the center of things. "Alive and well and keen about everything. I am *running* the real work, though Josephus is here! He is bewildered by it all, very sweet but very sad!"

Eleanor was sympathetic. "I am not surprised at what you say about J.D. or W.J.B. for one could expect little else. To understand the present gigantic conflict one must have at least a glimmering of understanding of foreign nations and their histories . . . I can see you managing everything while J.D. wrings his hands in horror. There

35. She died on August 6. "It is too horrible about Mrs. Wilson," Franklin wrote Eleanor. "The President has been truly wonderful, but I dread a breakdown. The funeral is Monday at the White House, I don't yet know whether Assistant Secretaries will be expected to go or not." They were not expected to go. *Source:* Elliott Roosevelt, ed., *FDR: His Personal Letters, 1905–1928.* pages 245–246.

must be so much detail to attend to all the time and so many problems which must, of course, be yours and not J.D.'s."

Franklin was named to two emergency interdepartmental committees—one to aid Americans stranded abroad, the other to maintain neutrality. The latter included creation of a coastal patrol to ensure that belligerent warships did not stray too close. "Most of the reports of foreign cruisers [seen] off the coast," Franklin told Eleanor, "have really been of *my* destroyers." His secretary, Charles H. McCarthy, told Howe, "the Boss has been the Whole Cheese in this European business. . . ."

That frenzied summer proved nearly as eventful for Eleanor, now pregnant for the fifth time, and for other members of the family as it did for Franklin.

One morning in June, the telephone had rung in Bamie Cowles's home in Farmington. It was Rosy, calling from Poughkeepsie. She was surprised, thinking him at his country home in Scotland for the summer.

He had something important to tell her, he said, something he could not discuss over the telephone; she must come see him right away. He was on his way to New York.

Bamie, who was now severely crippled, said that would be difficult.

Rosy insisted. He had come home to undergo surgery, he said, and might not survive. Before the doctors operated, he had to "settle his affairs."

Bamie hurried to the city. Rosy was indeed about to be operated upon—for gall stones—and, as she told the story later, "the affair he had to settle" turned out to be his long, secret liaison with a British shopgirl, Betty Riley. Bamie's discovery of that relationship some years before in London had forced her to reassess her own hope of marrying Rosy, but despite the shock she had remained his friend ever since. She liked him above all for his effortless charm; "he was the sort of man," one of Eleanor's closest friends once said, "that made you feel sort of pleased that you were a woman." Bamie's own son would remember him as "everything a gentleman should be—and no more."[36]

36. Rosy also gave Bamie investment advice when asked, rarely urging her to buy because of what he saw as the perpetual threat from labor. "I don't know," he'd say, "I just feel as if their employees might strike." And once, when she did invest in railway stocks he had recommended and they did poorly, he insisted on buying them back at the price she'd paid for them, a gesture she thought "very gallant." *Source:* Interview with W. Sheffield Cowles, Jr.

But she was also a little scornful of his hypochondria and his dependence upon her whenever he got into trouble. When a genuine crisis finally did come, she liked to say, she was sure that she and Betty would somehow find themselves together, standing watch on either side of his bed.

That is precisely what now happened. Worried that he might die and thereby leave Betty without funds, he had brought her back to America with him, planning to marry her once Bamie had given her the family's blessing. Bamie did so, and Rosy went under the knife. Afterwards, Isabella wrote, just "as [Bamie] prophesied, she and the lady each held a hand" until Rosy decided he would survive, after all.

Eleanor evidently visited him in the hospital and at least shook Betty's hand. Sara would not do so, still appalled at the scandal their long liaison had caused—so reminiscent, for her, of the relationship between Rosy's son, Taddy, and a New York prostitute whose discovery, she believed, had hastened her husband's death—and disgusted that now that he was on the mend, Rosy again saw no hurry to get married.[37] (It was actually Betty who was most uneasy about marriage. A mere clergyman's daughter, she felt herself far beneath Rosy's family and worried that the Roosevelts would never welcome her. But bachelorhood suited Rosy, too; for one thing, a member of the family recalled, whenever a group of his sporting friends got together for a convivial week along a likely trout or salmon stream in Scotland or Scandinavia, with the stipulation that no one bring his wife, Rosy alone could still come accompanied.)

"She [Sara] never mentioned Rosy's affairs to me!" Eleanor reported to Franklin from Campobello. "Except to remark that life was full of problems and of course those who had no principles were never much troubled."

The couple sailed for Plymouth, England, on board the *Kronprinzessin Cecilie* so that Rosy could continue his recuperation at one of the comfortable European spas Mr. James had favored. Then, on August 4, word reached the ship that Great Britain had declared war

---

37. During Hall Roosevelt's sad last years when, hopelessly alcoholic and wholly unpredictable, he lived in a little house near Springwood, provided for him by his solicitous sister, he, too, had a mistress who faithfully tended to him, a white Russian émigrée named Mrs. Zena Raset. Hall was often asked by Sara to come to Sunday dinner at the big house; although no one ever knew what state he would be in or what he might do, Hall was family. "Mrs. Raset was never invited," a close friend of the Roosevelts remembered. "It was the old, old idea. It's the woma who pays." *Source:* Transcript of interview with Marion Dickerman, Columbia Oral History Project, Columbia University.

on Germany; World War I was under way. The *Kronpinzessin Cecilie* was carrying some $13 million in gold and silver; rather than have the money fall into British hands, the owners ordered her captain to reverse his course in mid-Atlantic and race for the safety of some American harbor, every porthole covered at night to elude British pursuers. From shipboard, Rosy wired Sara that he and Betty planned to be married once they reached American soil.

Since he was at last apparently determined to make an honest woman of his mistress, Sara felt she could now receive the couple. She wired back that if he waited to marry until he reached New York, she would attend the ceremony, permit him to use her house, and invite the newlyweds up to Campobello.

Rosy did not wait. The German ship slipped into Bar Harbor, Maine, under the protection of a thick fog, and he and Betty were married immediately. He toyed with the notion of sailing back to England aboard the *Olympia* for the duration of the war—the couple had many more friends there than they had in the United States—but evidently decided another wartime voyage was too risky, and accepted Sara's invitation to visit Campobello instead.[38]

"She says she feels it her duty to make things as decent as possible," Eleanor explained to Franklin. "She told me yesterday she would talk it over with Helen [Roosevelt Robinson, Rosy's daughter] as Helen understood her point of view but I made her feel like a stranger by my curious attitude and I assured her I had no attitude & no opinion and she became enraged and said that she couldn't understand!"

To Isabella, Eleanor was more frank. She had heard a very great deal about the importance of living up to Roosevelt and Delano standards from her mother-in-law, and Sara's discomfiture over what she called "Rosy's matrimonial adventure" frankly amused her. "The situation was so funny at times for such a respectable and conventional family to be mixed up in," she wrote, "that I occasionally pinch myself to make sure it's true. . . ."

Sara herself rallied nicely, presenting her customary serene surface to the outside world. "Rosy & his wife have been here over a week," she told Isabella. "She is very nice and of course absolutely unselfish

---

38. By sheer coincidence, it would fall to Franklin to oversee the delicate negotiations with England that permitted the interned *Kronprinzessin Cecilie* eventually to be brought safely from Bar Harbor to Boston.

& devoted to him & he seems devoted to her. This is a rare case of 'surpassing love of woman' in my opinion. . . ."[39]

Isabella and her children were nearby that summer, caught on the East Coast when her daughter Martha developed severe colic and Isabella was told it would be best for the eight year old to recuperate for several weeks before taking the long train trip back to New Mexico. Isabella moved into a cottage rented by relatives at North East Harbor on the coast of Maine. By mid-August, Martha seemed well enough for Isabella to make a three-day visit to Eleanor at Campobello. She had never been there before, and reported on the Roosevelts to Bob. "This is the most delightful small family I ever saw," she wrote. "Each one a slice of Eleanor. . . . The baby is due any day—in fact I dreamt it was going to greet me today . . . and all is in serene order. F. arriving today, having made up his mind to run for the U.S. Senate. E. supposes he undertakes it backed by Progressives as well as Democrats. The children are perfect delights, wicked as you please and loving and generally charming. Elliott melts Eleanor at every turn! as I have never seen anyone else do. She's a pulp in his hands."

Franklin's last-minute decision to run for the Senate, announced the day before he came to Campobello, had been so sudden that he had consulted neither his wife nor Howe (who was also on vacation, at Horseneck Beach) beforehand. MY SENSES HAVE NOT YET LEFT ME, he somewhat sheepishly wired Louis afterwards.

The move had been suggested to him by Louis Antisdale, now leading an upstate faction which wanted him to join an independent ticket headed by John A. Hennessy, a flamboyant, Irish-born newspaperman who claimed to have a "little black book" filled with damaging information about Murphy and his machine. Franklin had based his impulsive decision to make the race on a string of dubious presuppositions: that President Wilson would publicly smile upon his candidacy (his evidence for this was evidently a vague promise from Secretary McAdoo, who urged him to run and whose own closeness to the President Franklin apparently overestimated); that he could win both the Democratic and the Bull Moose nominations; that Boss Murphy

39. Once she and Rosy were married, Betty Riley Roosevelt was treated as a full-fledged member of the family. She outlived her husband, remaining in the Red House next door to Springwood, and, during the presidential years, often spent the evening playing cards in the library of the big house with her stepmother and rough contemporary, Sara. A fragile, reticent, unassuming old lady in black, she attended Franklin's funeral in 1945, and did not herself die until 1948.

would field a second-rate candidate against him; that unless he ran, all the gains the upstate reformers had won in their struggle against Tammany would wither away.[40]

All of these assumptions would prove false, but politics was at least momentarily shelved once Franklin reached the island.

Isabella left for North East Harbor just an hour or so before Franklin arrived, and the baby—who would be the second Franklin Delano Roosevelt, Jr.—came earlier than expected. Franklin wired Daniels, FUTURE ADMIRAL ARRIVED LAST NIGHT, then described events in greater detail to Isabella a few days later:

> All is well, though Eleanor had a harder time than before. Now, however, she swears she has never felt better in her life! Never again will I trust her mathematics! It was pure luck that I decided to come Sunday. Dr. Ely was due today [from New York] & of course is now not coming. I sent the Half Moon for Dr. Bennett at 11:30 PM Sunday, and after he got here we all settled down & Eleanor had a quiet night & slept soundly. She was up & about the house up to noon on Monday & the baby arrived that evening at 6:45. He weighed 10¾ pounds & is splendid in every way.
>
> I am thankful to say Dr. Bennett proved excellent & even Miss Spring was thoroughly satisfied.[41] The children are all wild with excitement, but Elliott refuses to surrender the title of Baby and firmly suggests that "It must be called Other Baby." I have suggested the name of Isaac after my grandfather & great great grandfather, but this is not met with enthusiasm, especially as the baby's nose is slightly Hebraic & the family have visions of Ikey Rosenfelt, though I insist it is very good New Amsterdam Dutch.[42]

40. For once, Howe's cautious pessimism deserted him. He shared Franklin's hope that the machine nominee would be William Randolph Hearst, agreeing with his boss that it would be both "magnificent sport and magnificent service" to run against the publisher. And he had persuaded himself that Tammany would be reluctant to field a strong candidate against a man who appeared to have Woodrow Wilson's ear: "They haven't a thing to say against you," he told Franklin, "and no one is anxious to bell the cat—particularly when they have an idea that the President occasionally pats him on the back and calls him 'pretty pussy,' and gives him a saucer of warm patronage milk." *Sources:* Franklin D. Roosevelt Papers, Papers as Assistant Secretary of the Navy, FDRL; Louis M. Howe Papers, FDRL.

41. Dr. E. H. Bennet—whose name was consistently misspelled with two "t's" both by his most celebrated patients and by their biographers—had his office in Eastport and usually confined his Campobello practice to year-round island residents; the wealthy summer people either went elsewhere for treatment or, as the Roosevelts always had before, imported their own physicians from Boston or New York.

After delivering Eleanor's son, Bennet expressed astonishment to Miss Spring: "She is just like one of us!" *Source:* Joseph P. Lash, *Eleanor and Franklin,* page 194.

42. The younger Roosevelts evidently had their ancestors on their minds during those years. Hall and Margaret had gone to the Yukon in the summer of 1914, where Hall was to work as a mining engineer. Margaret became pregnant, and Hall asked his sister to send a nurse to her

That kind of jocular anti-Semitism was nearly universal in the wealthy American circles in which the Roosevelts moved, and none of them was immune to it.[43] But it never reached in Franklin the curious degree of viciousness exhibited, for example, by Rosy. The fear of encountering Jews—and other lesser breeds—often spoiled Rosy's otherwise remarkably comfortable travels. A ceremony at the Cathedral of St. John the Divine in Manhattan, for example, was rendered distasteful for him because no special seating had been provided for the trustees (of whom he was one) and he had been forced to mix with "nigger clergy standing everywhere." A month of motorboating on Lake Placid proved tolerable only because the cottage he rented was on an island—"thank goodness, otherwise we should catch a nose disease. The whole village reeks of Jews." Bermuda, where Rosy maintained a handsome winter home, was also often alarmingly crowded with "Mostly an awful class of Jews, most objectionable when sober, and worse when drunk." Even Aix-les-Bains seemed to him to be filled with "An awful lot of Jews, mostly of the detestable American variety. I am ashamed to hail from the U.S.A."

Franklin was always fond of his half brother, but a little startled by his virulence. At the end of World War I, Rosy would ask Franklin to do him a favor. "I have been made chairman for the town of Hyde Park of the United War Work Campaign," he wrote. "(Y.M.C.A., Y.W.C.A., Natl Cath. War Council, Jewish Welfare Board, Salvation Army, War Camp Community Service.) . . . Do you think you could speak for me on the afternoon of Election Day, outside on the Ball Ground, and tell . . . of the necessity of backing them up . . . everyone

---

in the wilderness. Eleanor had felt "a bit hopeless" at first, she later admitted, but managed somehow to find a Scandinavian woman who "consented readily to go in by dogsled." When the baby was born in the spring, he was named "Claes van Rosenvelt Roosevelt," after the 17th century founder of the American family. Good sense eventually prevailed, however, and Franklin acted as Hall's attorney in having the baby's name officially changed to "Henry Parish Roosevelt" after the rich, retiring cousin who had been so kind to Hall and Eleanor after they were orphaned. *Sources:* Eleanor Roosevelt, *This Is My Story*, page 217; Franklin D. Roosevelt Papers, Papers as Assistant Secretary of the Navy, FDRL.

43. Although they did differ among themselves. Eleanor still seemed to see no contradiction between her fondness for the children with whom she had once worked at the Rivington Street Settlement and the scorn she then felt for their elders. In 1920, she would refuse to read *Woodrow Wilson-An Interpretation* by Maurice Low because, she wrote, its author was "such a loathsome little Jew. . . ." Mr. James had had a scattering of very wealthy Jewish friends, including August Belmont, and he told Sara several times that, while "he did not have one drop of Jewish blood as far as he knew . . . if he were a Jew, he would be very proud of it." Much later, when Sara heard that the Nazis had marched into Austria, her first thought was for "those poor Jews." *Sources:* Roosevelt Family Papers Donated by the Children; Kleeman Notes, Rita Halle Kleeman Papers, both at FDRL.

would come if you were to speak. I don't think I should have anyone but you. . . . Politics of course strictly barred. . . ."

Franklin, who was coming home to vote in any case, was happy to oblige, but could not resist kidding Rosy a little about his private obsession. VERY GLAD TO SPEAK ELECTION DAY AFTERNOON, he wired back. WILL MAKE SPECIAL APPEAL FOR JEWISH WELFARE BOARD.

Franklin's own eagerness and ability to seek help and support from Jews, Catholics, and others outside the Roosevelt circle continued to startle both his mother and his wife. Eleanor was surprised, for example, one day in Washington when her husband brought home for lunch a young man he had only recently met named Felix Frankfurter, "an interesting little man," she told Sara, "but very jew," and she hated an evening with Bernard M. Baruch: "The Jew party [was] appalling. I never wish to hear money, jewels, or labels mentioned again."

Her husband had seemed to be having a wonderful time, just as he did later when the Roosevelts dined with Cardinal James Gibbons of Baltimore. "What a keen, interesting old face he has," Eleanor wrote, "85 & as quick & interested as a young man. He admired F's looks enormously & was interested in him because as we went in F. told him about his cousin [the] former archbishop of whom I'd never even heard! We were quite a distinguished party & the good Catholics all curtsied & bowed low & kissed his rings!"[44]

Henry Morgenthau, Jr., was Franklin Roosevelt's closest Jewish acquaintance. Morgenthau was the wealthy son of a still wealthier German-Jewish father who had been an important backer of Woodrow Wilson in 1912. After attending but not graduating from Phillips Exeter and Cornell, Henry Jr. had fled to Dutchess County to get out from under his father's overbearing influence and had become a gentleman farmer, growing apples and raising dairy cattle on a large rolling estate near East Fishkill. His wife, Elinor Fatman, was a graduate of Vassar; her mother had been a Lehman.

44. Franklin was in fact very distantly related both to James Roosevelt Bayley, an Episcopal convert to Catholicism who had been James Gibbons's predecessor as archbishop of Baltimore, and to Bayley's aunt, Elizabeth Ann Bayley Seton, known as "Mother Seton" and canonized thirty years after FDR's death as America's first Catholic saint. According to FDR's son James, his father especially enjoyed teasing his mother about "My great aunt, Mother Seton." Sara "always rewarded him with the reaction he was striving for—an explosively reproachful exclamation of 'Oh. Franklin!'"

Perhaps it was on the occasion of the dinner Eleanor described in her letter that Cardinal Gibbons told FDR a story he enjoyed repeating in later years. Not long after the cardinal had returned from a visit to Rome, someone asked him if he believed in the infallibility of the Pope. He did indeed, he answered; "I may say, however, that I saw the Holy Father many times and each time he called me Jibbons." *Source:* Nathan Miller, *The Roosevelt Chronicles*, pages 133–137.

Franklin first sought him out in 1915 for some of the same reasons local politicians had contacted him five years before: Morgenthau was young, vigorous, inclined toward the Democrats—and rich. He invited him to lunch one weekend at Springwood, hoping to persuade him to run for county sheriff. Morgenthau declined to run, but Franklin pronounced him "an awfully nice fellow and one who will be a tremendous asset to us in the county. . . . Certainly, we ought to do everything possible to keep him interested."

FDR once gave Mrs. Morgenthau a photograph of himself and her husband together in the back seat of a car inscribed "For Elinor, from one of two of a kind." Certainly, Franklin and Morgenthau shared many things: they were both gentleman farmers who enjoyed comparing notes on everything from selective timbering to the growing of squash; they were both progressive Democrats opposed to Tammany; their wives grew fond of one another, too, despite Eleanor's initial envy of Elinor's formal education. (Even Sara admired her, writing Eleanor after the couple came to tea with her for the first time, "Young Morgenthau was easy and yet modest and serious and intelligent. The wife is very Jewish but appeared very well.")[45]

Morgenthau was a shy, formal man, balding and myopic, tireless but retiring, who owed his public prominence almost entirely to FDR. He seems from the first to have been devoted to Franklin, to have seen in him, perhaps, qualities he only wished he possessed himself—magnetism, exuberance, gaiety, self-confidence. In 1928, after Franklin had appointed him chairman of the New York State Agricultural Advisory Commission, the first of the series of important jobs he would hold under FDR as governor and President, his wife wrote Franklin a note that mirrored perfectly Morgenthau's attitude toward his fond patron. "Henry always goes about his work with a real feeling of consecration," she wrote, "but the fact that he is working under you and for you, fills him with . . . enthusiasm. . . . The part which pleases me most is that while you are moving on in your work . . . it gives Henry a chance to grow. . . ."

He could grow, then, but only in Franklin's shade.

So could other Jews, upon whose skill and talent he would draw eagerly all through his career. Judge Samuel Rosenman was a speech-

---

45. One of FDR's grandsons remembers hearing the President tell mildly anti-Semitic stories in the White House. Morgenthau laughed as hard as anyone in the room. The protagonists were always Lower East Side Jews with heavy accents, men of quite another class from Franklin Roosevelt and his Duchess County neighbor. *Source:* Interview with Curtis Roosevelt.

writer and close aide from 1928 onwards; Sidney Hillman and Rose Schneiderman advised him on labor matters; David Niles served in the White House; Ben Cohen drafted key New Deal legislation, and (with his Irish partner, Thomas Corcoran) rallied liberal opinion on Capitol Hill.

Jews constituted about 3 percent of the United States population during FDR's presidency, yet they represented approximately 15 percent of his top appointments, a disproportion bigots routinely denounced as evidence of a "Jew Deal," and which provided the Nazis with one pretext for their charge that the President was himself a Jew.

Jewish voters eagerly responded to his attentions, especially admiring his widely published response to a pointed inquiry about his own ancestry: "In the dim distant past [my ancestors] may have been Jews or Catholics or Protestants. What I am more interested in is whether they were good citizens and believers in God. I hope they were both." And they clung to FDR with special fervor during the Holocaust years; in 1940 and again in 1944, they would give him nine out of ten of their votes.

That loyalty was understandable. Even during World War II, public opinion polls repeatedly showed that anywhere from 15 to 24 percent of Americans still considered Jews "a menace to America."[46] FDR seemed to be their best, perhaps their last, hope. Still, he always felt he had to tread carefully, and those Jews who worked most closely with him often found it wisest to bury their Jewishness, to avoid being seen by him—or by others in his administration—as overly concerned with specifically Jewish issues, even when those issues involved the survival of their co-religionists in Europe.[47]

46. The ubiquity of anti-Semitism, even in World War II Washington, is made vividly clear in Jonathan Daniels' edited diary, *White House Witness*. Among those clearly infected: ex-Governor James Michael Curley of Massachusetts, United Mine Workers' chief John L. Lewis, numerous high-ranking officers in the Army and Navy, various State Department officials, and, within the White House, the President's secretary, Bill Hassett, his press secretary, Steve Early, and Daniels himself.

47. Samuel Rosenman seems to have been especially anxious to distance himself from those Jews who felt the President was insufficiently committed to their cause. On October 16, 1943, for example, a delegation of several hundred Orthodox rabbis sought to present FDR with a petition calling on him to create a rescue agency to deliver the European Jews from the Nazis, and to pressure the British into opening Palestine to the survivors. His aide, Bill Hassett, recorded the President's irritation at their proposed visit—and Rosenman's maneuvering as well: "The President told us in his bedroom this morning he would not see their delegation; told [his secretary, Marvin] McIntyre to receive it. McIntyre said he would see four only—out of five hundred. Judge Rosenman . . . said the group behind this petition not representative of the most thoughtful elements in Jewry. Judge Rosenman said he had tried—admittedly without success—to keep the horde from storming Washington. Said the leading Jews of his acquaintance opposed

FDR's willingness to work closely with Jews, even to have them routinely staying with him in the White House and at Springwood, seems to have puzzled even his most admiring Hudson River neighbors. One of them did his earnest best to explain it to his son: "It just shows you how smart FDR is, to have all those smart Jews working for him."

Franklin may have felt that way, too.[48]

Franklin was sorry to have missed Isabella's first visit to Campobello, he told her toward the end of August; he had hoped to show her a lot of the lovely sites that "make this place compel." He was looking forward to a very strenuous Senate campaign, he said, "as Tammany will doubtless put up a respectable rubber stamp against me. I am going to keep trying to clean out that old gang if it takes twenty years."

He planned to "have a destroyer come up September 1 & go down [to Washington] about the 4th. . . ." If Isabella were still going to be home at her uncle's Maine cottage, he thought he might stop by for dinner. She wrote back to say that she would be happy to see him.

Franklin's visit made a considerable stir at York Harbor, a remarkably sedate vacation spot where, as Isabella told Bob, "liveried footmen announce the people and usher them thro' the blueberry patches" to picnics on the stony beach.

Isabella's daughter Martha never forgot her "Uncle Franklin's" arrival. When word came that his destroyer had anchored offshore, she and her mother, and her brother Bob, hurried down to the water and watched as a launch was lowered and drew slowly toward the beach. Isabella pointed Uncle Franklin out to her, standing in the boat, smiling "and so handsome," wearing a dark blue naval cape.

When the launch reached shallow water, two uniformed sailors slipped overboard and carried Franklin through the waves so that his shoes would not get wet on his way to dinner.

---

this march on the Capitol. . . ." *Sources:* William D. Hassett, *Off the Record with FDR*, page 209; David S. Wyman, *The Abandonment of the Jews*, pages 151–152.

48. Something of his underlying view of the real position of Jews and Catholics in the United States may have been revealed in a conversation he held in the White House in 1942 with Leo T. Crowley, an economist and a Catholic, who had recently become Custodian of Alien Property. Over lunch, FDR said, "Leo, you know this is a Protestant country, and the Catholics and Jews are here under sufferance. It is up to you [Crowley and Henry Morgenthau] to go along with anything that I want. . . ." *Source:* Henry Morgenthau, Jr., Papers, Presidential Diary, Vol. 5, January 27, 1942, FDRL.

The Senate campaign got off to a slow start. The candidate did not bother to come down to New York to attend the kick-off rally at Carnegie Hall, preferring, as Howe said, to stay at Campobello and "play with [his] destroyer," though he did ask for a copy of the Republican platform so that "he could shoot holes in it." Nor was he good about answering Louis's barrage of worried letters and telegrams: "Is it your idea to wait until your youngest can act as your stenographer before writing to me?"

Howe did everything he could think of to fill in. He had "any number of pictures of your handsome self printed and sent upstate for distribution," he told his boss, and he tried to apply the same techniques that had done well for Franklin in the three counties he had won in 1912 to the entire state: "I am playing the game the same way. . . . Letting Tammany look after its strongholds and letting Hennessy look after the cities while I go gunning up in the rural districts which Tammany never thought worth looking after." But he had least one new trick. He drafted a standard letter to the editors of 316 Democratic and Independent newspapers, he told Franklin, "asking them for advertising rates and saying how valuable you found newspaper advertising in your state senatorial campaign. It only costs 2 cents each to do this and some of them will surely fall for it and others will print your letter because it booms newspaper advertising. I have used some of your nicest stationery and have had each letter written separately [by a member of the Navy Department staff, on his or her own time] because I want to impress the rural mind." A thick batch of them arrived at Campobello for the candidate to sign and mail just before he sailed south.

Despite Howe's ingenuity and the energy Franklin eventually brought to the race, everything after that went wrong. The Progressives showed no interest in an alliance. The Tammany "rubber stamp" Franklin had hoped for turned out to be James W. Gerard, an upright and independent-minded wealthy Democrat who was currently U.S. Ambassador to Berlin. Franklin sought through intermediaries—including the Secretary of State—to persuade the President to ask Gerard to decline the nomination and stay put overseas, but Wilson would not take sides. Gerard kept at his post, refusing to come home and campaign on the lofty ground that to do so in such perilous times would be unpatriotic; if the voters demonstrated that they wanted him in the Senate, he would, of course serve. That, too, would be his duty.

Thus, Franklin could neither claim to be the administration's candidate, nor aggressively attack a Tammany nominee whose high principles ostensibly prevented him from campaigning. And Progressive voters who might at least have rallied to Franklin's name were barred, of course, from the Democratic primary.

He did what he could, crisscrossing the state four times in seventeen frenetic days. While Eleanor and the children pinned up a Roosevelt poster on the cottage wall at Campobello, and James passed out campaign buttons to bewildered Canadian passers-by, Gerard continued to remain above the distant battle; Franklin complained bitterly that he was finding it hard to campaign against "moles." He was further hampered by the fact that John Hennessy's rich brogue and shrill attacks on Tammany only served to remind upstate Protestants of why most of them had always remained Republican.[49]

Eleanor wrote Isabella on primary day: "When we haven't been thinking about the war, we've been thinking of F's campaign & now the primaries are over & I'm anxiously waiting to hear the result. He doesn't stand a chance of winning, but I hope he'll run well [enough] to encourage them for future battles against Mr. Murphy."

He didn't. Franklin was swamped three to one, losing all but twenty-two of the state's sixty-six counties.

"I wonder if you are disappointed," his mother wrote. "I hope you are not. You made a brave fight and now you can return to the good and necessary work of the Navy Department, which you must have missed all these weeks."

Characteristically, Franklin assured her he was not disappointed,[50] and professed to find a victory even in this debacle, publicly claiming that "I . . . was beaten only because of the solid lineup of New York City." (Gerard, in turn, would be badly beaten in November by the Republican nominee, James Wadsworth, an old friend and golfing partner whom Franklin now termed representative of "all that is most reactionary in the most reactionary wing of the reactionary Republican Party!")[51]

49. Even Howe uncharacteristically overlooked an important detail: several thousand copies of a handbill advertising Franklin's new pro-labor record, meant to be handed out at factory gates, had to be withdrawn when someone noticed that they bore no union label.

50. His chief, who understood politics and politicians far better than Sara did, saw through Franklin's bravado. Young Roosevelt had been "hurt" by the voters' rejection of him, Daniels noted in his diary.

51. In late October, Colonel Edward House, Woodrow Wilson's closest confidant, wrote to McAdoo: "Gerard's friends are very anxious for Franklin Roosevelt to come out strongly for him.

Yet both Franklin and Murphy learned a valuable lesson from the 1914 elections: an upstate progressive could not win the state without help from the big-city machine; Tammany could not win without a progressive candidate. Some sort of alliance, however uneasy, was the only guarantor of Democratic power.

That same year, Franklin took on another machine, more genteel and subtle than Tammany but no less tightly united when threatened by an outsider.

Franklin was a loyal son of Harvard, just as his father, his half brother, and his Uncle Fred had all urged him to be. He tried never to miss the Harvard-Yale Game—Eleanor always bravely pretended to care about its outcome, too—and faithfully attended Harvard dinners in Boston and New York and Washington, no matter how busy he was, carefully saving all the elaborate menus listing "Roast Plover with Jelly à la Houchee-Couchee," "Punch, Punch, and Ever So Much More Punch," and "Smello Bado Perfecto Caruso" cigars.[52]

But few defeats had ever bothered Franklin more than the fact that in his last year at Harvard he had been denied the most prestigious

---

I think he is making a mistake in not doing it. Could you not talk to him directly or have Sec. Daniels do so?" Either McAdoo or Daniels showed the letter to Franklin, who returned it with "NUTS F.D.R." scrawled across the top.

Franklin did express his formal regret at Gerard's defeat, but, according to James Farley, never forgave the ambassador for having opposed him. In 1935, U.S. Ambassador Breckinridge Long let it be known that he wished to be withdrawn from Italy. "I took the opportunity to press for the appointment of [Gerard] wartime ambassador to Germany and a faithful servant of the Democratic Party," Farley remembered. "Roosevelt was evasive, saying he did not want to make any commitment for a long period after the 1936 election. I had proposed Gerard for Paris; Roosevelt promised favorable action, but William C. Bullitt was named. I suggested Gerard for Rome; Roosevelt was sympathetic but William Phillips was nominated. Gerard told me to cease my efforts, holding that Roosevelt would never forget the defeat he suffered at Gerard's hands in . . . 1914. Nonetheless, I persisted and succeeded in having Gerard named as the President's representative at the coronation of King George VI in [1937]."

Gerard's own disjointed autobiography makes no mention of his early contest with FDR, but does allege that while he had supported Roosevelt before 1932 and "had contributed money whenever he needed it for his payroll, giving it to Louis Howe, Roosevelt's grand vizier," the President had never delivered on pledges to make him Ambassador to Italy or Great Britain.

In March 1943, evidently at Eleanor's suggestion, Gerard wrote out a six-page summary of his services to the party and the promises he believed had been made to him and then broken. Eleanor sent it to FDR with a pencilled note: "F.D.R. Read the end. He is very bitter. E.R." *Sources:* House letter in collection of Franklin and Eleanor Roosevelt Institute, FDRL; James A. Farley, *Jim Farley's Story*, page 56; James W. Gerard, *My First Eighty-Three Years in America*, pages 32–324; PSF Gerard, FDRL.

52. His enthusiasm for his alma mater, however, did not approach that of the father of his college roommate Lathrop Brown, who, whenever he passed through New Haven on the train with his three sons, ordered them all to get down and spit on the platform. *Source:* Letter to the author from Herbert Barry III, Lathrop Brown's grand-nephew.

honor his class could bestow—the chance to be one of just three class marshals. Six men had been nominated, himself included; he had come in a close fourth in the vote, a victim, he believed, of a secret agreement among certain, mostly Boston-based clubmen to vote as a bloc for the three men who came in ahead of him. His own election two days later as permanent chairman of his class committee had done little to ease his resentment.

The class Decennial was to take place in Boston in June 1914, and Franklin seems to have seen in the planning for that event an opportunity to win back some of the prestige he believed had been unfairly taken from him ten years before. In December 1913, he began quietly lobbying to have the planning committee for the anniversary expanded to include some friends who, like him, lived west of Boston.

He found a number of allies with resentments as keen as his. Roy Smith Wallace, for example, a Philadelphia attorney, who had been elected class secretary in 1904, had recently been asked to resign his post by one of his fellow officers simply because he did not live in Boston. He had considered it, Wallace told Franklin in a letter he marked as "exceedingly confidential," but had not done so because of "the fact, which you recognize as well as I, that I was elected by a group of men who were not the dominant men of our class but who were rather the outsiders, a good many of whom have taken occasion to say to me that they were glad I was Class Secretary because I knew them and they knew me and they took great satisfaction in knowing one of the class officers personally and having a first name acquaintance with him and in feeling that in a way they were represented in the counsels of the class." (By "outsiders," he said, he meant "the non Boston group.")

Franklin suggested that all the officers of the class resign simultaneously, and that a new vote be taken by *all* members of the class, not just those who were able to make it to Boston for the June festivities. After all, he told Wallace, all of them—himself included—had really been elected by the outsiders, who actually constituted a "great majority of the class, [if] a majority which up to that time had rarely, if ever, made itself felt," and the officers should be made really to represent those who elected them or expect to be replaced. He thought the June celebration itself might be the time to put this idea forth.

Wallace backed off a little: there was indeed a "hot feeling of resentment against the Boston leadership," but he thought the resignation and new election should follow the Decennial, not precede it, in order to avoid complicating the celebration with "factional spirit."

Franklin said he agreed, then went ahead on his own to offer places on the Decennial planning committee to several classmates sympathetic to his cause, all in the interest, he said, "of wider representation and heartier participation."

Three Boston members of the committee, including Arthur A. Ballantine, whom Franklin had edged out for editor of the *Crimson*, and Tom Beal, with whom he had often cruised along the New England coast, responded with some heat.[53] They, too, claimed to be interested in widening representation, and for that reason, they said, had already asked several non-Bostonians to play their traditional part—as fund raisers.

But they were utterly opposed to allowing anyone else actually to take part in making the arrangements. If that were even contemplated, they would themselves feel obligated to resign. In order to ensure that all went smoothly, they planned now to appoint "an executive committee composed of the Boston men who will have full power and carry out all details."

At the Decennial itself, feelings were somewhat strained. Franklin and his allies circulated among their classmates, urging resistance to any effort to force non-Bostonians from office.

When the men of '04 filed into the dining room at the Hotel Dorset for the final dinner, Franklin must have been pleased to see that a caricature of himself in a top hat, dwarfing admirals and pulling a fleet of warships on strings, decorated the back of the sheet of song lyrics

53. Franklin evidently never got over the fact that his old friend Tommy Beal had opposed him. Nineteen years later, when Beal, president of the Boston Clearing House during the banking crisis, wrote him a note of congratulation on his inauguration as President in 1933, praising him for his stated resolve to balance the budget and expressing his "readiness to acknowledge [that] I was wrong when I voted against you," he got back an angry note from FDR: "I feel I want to be perfectly frank with you. During the campaign I was told by several people of things you were supposed to have said and it is only fair for me to tell you that because of what I felt to be a very old and real friendship these alleged remarks hurt. I am sure you know me well enough to be sure that I would have no feeling you should vote for me because of friendship. On the other hand, I felt that because of this friendship, such remarks should have been made directly to me."

Beal sent him back a long, equally frank apology in which he wrote that he did not know what "you heard that I said . . . I have never forgotten the good times which we had together in the old days. . . . I did say that I could not vote for you" out of honest political differences, and that "you were obstinate and ambitious . . . [but] in my opinion the very characteristics which I have criticized have shown themselves as most helpful to us all in the emergency. . . ."

The President remained unmoved. The "honest differences" had never bothered him, of course, he said, but "I must admit . . . that I am a little amused by your use of the word 'ambitious' because you had not been in touch with me in any way during these years . . . but much the best way is to let bygones be bygones. . . ." *Source:* PPF 183, FDRL.

that rested next to every classmate's place card.[54] But Arthur Ballantine was the toastmaster and made an unfortunate joke about the controversy to which Franklin, as one of four speakers, felt obligated to respond. "I felt that I was placed in a somewhat difficult position on the evening of the dinner," he later told a friend, "but I tried to carry out my responsibilities in the interest of the whole class, and, while I suppose some men are not particularly happy over the failure of their little plan to go through, I think the great majority of the class will back us up."

For the second time that year, he had badly misjudged the extent of his support. Perhaps the great majority of the class did not really believe Boston's hold on Harvard affairs would ever slacken. Possibly Franklin had fewer friends among the outsiders than he thought he had; after all, he had never during his undergraduate days been notably sympathetic to those students who did not live on the Gold Coast. Maybe his classmates simply had more important things to do. In any case, the backing upon which he had counted largely failed to materialize.

At the annual class committee meeting, held in the Boston Harvard Club on December 19, Franklin faced his antagonists alone. To give the appearance of fairness, the Boston men made him temporary chairman of the meeting—"politely shoved" him into the job, he wrote in an angry letter to a friendly classmate he finally decided not to send—then, one by one, they voted down nearly every one of his suggestions.

He had come to the meeting armed with the proxies of two of his fellow "westerners," Laird Bell of Chicago and Roy Wallace of Philadelphia; they were disallowed. Only men actually present in Boston could vote.

He proposed that actions involving general class policy be passed

54. The invitation to the Decennial also made a labored reference to Franklin's job—and to Daniels's order barring alcohol aboard naval vessels:

> ... It is said that the personnel of the liquid division of the Class of 1904 absolutely refuse to have anything to do with a Decennial Reunion conducted exclusively on a grape juice system of irrigation. . . . Later: Assistant Secretary of the Navy Roosevelt . . . told your correspondent that the scope of the order was exaggerated. No interference is projected with the Decennial other than that 1904 men boarding the battleship on which Mr. Roosevelt intends to convey the Class of 1904 to New London in the event that the Committee is too poor or too stingy to take it there out of the general fund, will have to bring their own booze carefully concealed in their hip pockets. He added that there were no sailors in the class anyway, except certain gentlemen who, upon occasions had been at least "half seas over"— and then some.

Source: Franklin D. Roosevelt Papers, Harvard College Class of 1904: General Correspondence, FDRL.

on by the whole committee, with distant members being polled by mail when time permitted; he was overruled, he told a friend, and a quorum was "placed at the ridiculously small number of five." Clearly, Boston was not about to relinquish its grip.

New officers were then elected: Arthur A. Ballantine, chairman; Payson Dana, secretary; and James Jackson, treasurer. All three were Boston men.

"Temporary Chairman Roosevelt wished his vote recorded as opposing the election of all of the officers of this Committee from Boston," the temporary secretary noted in his minutes, "and suggested that one or more vice-chairmen should be elected from some place outside of Boston. . . . It was the opinion of all the other members present, however . . . that as practically all class matters can be most conveniently and promptly attended to in Boston, it was advisable to have Boston men as officers. . . ."

Franklin had lost again, had in fact been forced out of his ten-year chairmanship, and gained nothing but animosity in exchange.

Outwardly oblivious, as always, he continued regularly to attend Harvard events as if nothing awkward had happened, greeting old friends and enemies alike with the same broad grin. In 1917, he was elected to the Harvard board of overseers by the alumni; distrust and dislike of him was still largely confined to the members of his class who knew him personally.

Two years later, at the fifteenth reunion of his class, held at New London, he arranged to receive his classmates on the deck of a destroyer, the USS *Palmer*, a showy occasion which even some old friends found grating. One was Walter Sachs. "At lunch on the second day, Franklin made his grand entrance. . . ." he remembered. "He had that characteristic way of throwing his head back and saying 'How are you Jack?', and 'How are you, Walter?', and 'How are you, Arthur?'

"I know I had the feeling, 'Hell, Frank, You can't put on all that stuff with us, we knew you from the old days!' "[55]

55. In 1919, Sachs and Franklin were two of "seven men from outside Boston" elected to a new class committee to serve through their twenty-fifth reunion in 1929. Although *eight* Bostonians were elected the same day, thereby ensuring that in a close vote their control over class affairs would remain intact, the class secretary only half in jest described the election of non-Bostonians as "our Bolshevik revolution." *Source:* Franklin D. Roosevelt Papers, Harvard College Class of 1904: General Correspondence, FDRL.

CHAPTER

7

❧

THE PLACE

POLITICIANS often find themselves making claims for themselves
that in the harsh light of the next day must astonish even them.
Franklin Roosevelt managed this better than most, but even he may
have been at least a little surprised at himself for remarks he made
when, just a few weeks after he signed on as Assistant Secretary, his
chief sent him down to Raleigh, there to address the student body of
the Agricultural and Mechanical College.

The struggling young school—a scattering of buildings out near
the Fair Grounds—was a point of special pride with Daniels, who
served on its board of trustees, boosted its every activity in his newspaper and, when he was at home, taught a group of students its Sunday
School lessons. Those students were poor for the most part, North
Carolina farmers' sons hoping to learn how to eke a better living from
the region's tired soil than their fathers had. Daniels saw in them the
hope of his state's future, and he wished both to show them off to his
new Assistant Secretary, and, perhaps, to let his neighbors know that
he now had a Roosevelt working for him.

Eleanor came south, too, tall but retiring, in a big hat that largely
hid her face, but Franklin was the center of things, wearing a bowler
hat and a handsomely tailored double-breasted suit, escorted across the
dusty campus by the college president. His short speech was entitled
"Stay East Young Man," and its familiar message was that the frontier

was dead, that new conditions required Americans to restore their own soil rather than seek out new land to exploit.

But it was the opening words with which he sought to identify himself with his listeners that were most memorable. "I am a hayseed myself," he told these hardscrabble farmers' sons, smiling as he tossed his head, "and proud of it!"

Certainly, Franklin Roosevelt loved the land, had been brought up to love and respect it since, as a very small boy, he had accompanied his father on his daily rounds at Springwood, but the farming to which he was accustomed was utterly unlike anything most of his North Carolina listeners had ever seen.

Neither he nor his parents had ever much liked the term "estate." Springwood was always "the Place" to the Roosevelts. But it had been established as a gentleman's country home, whose tenant farmers' first duty was to produce crops and poultry and dairy products for the table of that gentleman and his family; since the death of Mr. James in 1900, it had been run by his widow as closely as possible along the lines he had laid down in 1867, when he moved to Springwood with his first wife, Rebecca Howland.

It had been Franklin's hope that as he grew to manhood, he would inherit some control over the Place. On his honeymoon abroad he had held "many long and interesting talks . . . on farming and cattle raising" with old friends of Sara's with whom he and Eleanor stayed, and, he had told his mother, his "plans for Hyde Park now include not only a new house but a new farm, cattle, trees, etc. . . ."

In fact, however, both of them always knew that in the end, only her plans for Springwood mattered. Sara was in charge, she alone could approve changes; that would be true to the day she died. Her late husband had left the Place in her hands. "I see him in every room," she told her sister, Dora. "I hear his voice at every turn." After a visit to Springwood, Bamie Roosevelt, who had introduced Sara to Mr. James and to whom he had once proposed marriage, wrote to thank her hostess. "You are sweet to judge me so kindly in my dear home," Sara answered, "but *you* know how much lovelier it would be if James were here & I always realize how he is needed here & yet I have tried to keep something of the same atmosphere."

Whenever conflict arose between her and her son, she held the upper hand, for she alone controlled the bulk of the family fortune. "For years," Franklin's son, James, would recall, "she squeezed all of us—Father included—in that golden loop."

She liked her son to oversee things when she herself could not; he had at least twice left Campobello one summer early in his marriage to travel down to Hyde Park to urge a crew to greater efforts in making a gravel path through the woods, and he had later been assigned the delicate task of getting Rosy to pay half its cost. (Rosy did finally pay up, calling the path "the 'Boulevard,' " and claiming it had made him "stony broke"; still, he added, "it's a fine road all the same, and all credit to you for putting it through. Don't be surprised if you see a sign 'for sale' or 'to let' on Road gate!!!")

And Sara shared Franklin's interest in forestry. In the spring of 1911, she wrote that she had been

> worrying for a long time about our woods, & after a conversation with Mr. [Archibald] Rogers [the owner of Crumwold, the much grander and far more formal estate just up the road], who has studied the subject for years past with government experts, etc. & has worked hard himself, I have decided to go to work seriously this autumn & try to clear all the dead wood out, a very large undertaking, & then to cut in the right way & *sell*. This will improve the woods, & we can begin to have young nurseries of trees. The first thing I want to do . . . is to clear near the Railway, where the old dead wood of ages lies.

Franklin then began, with her approval, an oversized farm journal in which he recorded precisely what had been planted where, which fields had been fertilized when, the numbers of trees planted and cut. And he hired a forestry expert to go over the Place with him; William Plog, the estate superintendent, came along too, jotting recommendations as to which varieties of trees would fare best on the cleared portions of the long, uneven slope that ran between the old house and the rail line that edged the river.

But he did want some land of his own with which to do whatever he wished, and so, in 1911, he bought 194 acres adjoining the eastern edge of his mother's property, the first segment of a smaller, semi-detached empire that he would slowly amass over the years.

On most of his land—and much of his mother's—he would for the next three decades conduct experiments in forestry, demonstrating to himself, if not to the entire satisfaction of his neighbors and "fellow farmers" of Dutchess County who he always hoped would follow his lead, that exhausted, overgrown land could be made profitable again through the planting of seedlings and the harvesting of lumber and Christmas trees. He planted 8,000 seedlings in his first year; had some

65,000 more in place by 1928; and would plant more than 300,000 during his lifetime.

But the farm itself—its fields and herds and flocks and beehives—remained under his mother's exclusive care. "She supervised very closely," her superintendent remembered, "went over there pretty nearly every day." As a young man, Franklin sometimes chafed under this arrangement, arguing that with modern methods he could put the old farm on a paying basis, as it once had been in his father's day. Sara would not hear of it.

The fact was that neither Sara, nor the son who was so much like her, was ever eager to share power.[1]

Some of the supposed conflict between them over Springwood may have been play-acting. Franklin enjoyed teasing his mother; she liked teasing him back, and enjoyed, as well, acting out her role as grande dame. At breakfast he would sometimes urge his guests to have extra helpings of eggs, explaining that they must be especially good because they were the most expensive in the world, costing his mother fifty cents apiece. The eggs were produced precisely as they had been in his own boyhood, Sara would reply; and they would continue to be produced that way.[2]

Sara was no more yielding about the big Springwood dairy herd, begun by Mr. James and allowed to multiply out of all proportion to need over the intervening years. It produced *safe* milk for her family and friends, she said; it always had, and, "so long as I am alive, Franklin, it is a matter of no consequence to me whether the cows make money or not."

The Springwood farm may have been inefficiently run, but its yield was rich, a wholesome flow of old-fashioned food: huge strawberries ("the best in the world," Franklin said), golden honey, crisp green asparagus, fresh corn and eggs, "cream," a frequent visitor recalled, "you could cut with a knife." Springwood milk and chickens and

1. This could sometimes cause confusion at the Springwood table. Eleanor once brought two Vassar girls to lunch with her mother-in-law during the White House years. One of the students, up on current events, asked the First Lady what her husband was going to do about the budget.

"Budget? Budget?" said Sara. "What does the child mean? Oh, but Franklin knows nothing about the budget. *I* always make the budgets." *Source:* Transcript of interview with Roland Redmond, Eleanor Roosevelt Oral History Project, FDRL.

2. She meant it, too. When, some time during the 1930s, Democratic Congressman Francis Ryan Duffy of Wisconsin wrote to the President offering him a very good price on a constituent's chickens, FDR had to dictate a note to his secretary: "Tell Ryan Duffy I have no chickens of my own and that my Mother has special chickens she does not want to mix with others." *Source:* PPF 1-G, FDRL.

barrels of apples and potatoes were shipped to the younger Roosevelts wherever they happened to be—New York, Albany, Washington, Campobello. "I've written to ask Plog if we could have 1 fowl & 1 chicken twice a week from the Place," Eleanor wrote Sara from Washington in 1913 ". . . for the chickens here are not good. . . . I thought you wouldn't mind."[3]

The farm continued to supplement the family's diet for decades; when James Roosevelt was a student at Harvard in the late twenties, he was still receiving shipments of Springwood eggs and cream three times a week, precisely as his father had at the turn of the century. (Eleanor thought this "a terrible waste," by then, James remembered, "but I enjoyed it, and Father never did anything to stop it.")

Franklin's initial resentment of his mother's resistance to change seems to have waned as his own public life outside Springwood grew more turbulent, and the Place became for him more and more what it had always been for her, the reassuring symbol of calm and security.[4] His eldest son believes that, in the end, one of the things about his grandmother which his father came to admire most was that "she could be counted on to keep Springwood just as it had always been, which was how he really wanted it, how we all really wanted it." "Father never tried very hard to make the Place modern or efficient," he added, pointing out that after Sara's death in 1941, when Springwood was FDR's at last, to do with as he wished, he changed almost nothing.[5]

3. According to Eleanor, constant access to the sort of the abundance to which he had become accustomed at Springwood became one of Franklin's life-long, unstated assumptions. "He took flowers for granted," she told an interviewer as an example of what she meant: Springwood's gardens had always provided them in warm weather; the Springwood greenhouse made sure fresh blossoms were regularly shipped south to brighten the New York house in winter. "If he walked into a room and there were no flowers, he would say . . . 'There's something wrong,' but he wouldn't be able to tell you why.' [Flowers were] just part of his life." *Source:* Interview with Eleanor Roosevelt, Robert D. Graff Papers, FDRL.

4. He had been his mother's strong ally in several controversies that threatened to alter the Roosevelts' traditional, tranquil way of life. In 1913, for example, he had urged Governor Sulzer to veto a bill that would have allowed an interurban car to clank past Springwood every day along the Albany Post Road. "This matter," he told the governor, "affects not only residents along its whole length from New York to Albany, but hundreds of thousands of travelers all over the country who know its historic and scenic features."

Two years later, he hired a New York attorney to appear on his mother's behalf at a hearing to protest a planned bus route along 65th Street, explaining that his mother "believes the residential character of the street should be maintained." The interurban was beaten back; the buses were not. Franklin Roosevelt's writ never ran in New York City. *Source:* Franklin D. Roosevelt, Papers as Assistant Secretary of the Navy, FDRL.

5. Rexford G. Tugwell, a member of FDR's original brains trust, economist, agricultural expert, and perceptive observer of his chief, wrote of the Place's impact upon the President's perception of his fellow countrymen:

During the 1930s, however, he did take it upon himself to rename the Place. Springwood, the name his father had chosen for it, he decided, was meaningless, "like Bellevue, or Oak Hill, or the Willows. . . ." It should be called "Krum Elbow," he said, claiming that to have been its original name.[6]

Howland Spencer, a very distant and very wealthy cousin who deplored the New Deal and its author with special vehemence and lived just across the Hudson, loudly objected: *his* estate, plainly visible from Springwood, had always been called Crum Elbow, he said. The President was a usurper.

"There is no reason in the world," FDR shot back, "why anybody owning land on either side of the river abutting on the 'Crum Elbow,' or 'Turn in the River,' should not call their Place 'Crum Elbow' if they want to, but the fact remains that the land owned by my Mother and myself was called 'Crum Elbow' by the original occupants two hundred years ago."

Spencer was not mollified.

FDR asked the Board of Geographical Names, U.S. Department of the Interior, to make a formal decision regarding who had the more legitimate claim to the old name. Perhaps not surprisingly, a decision was duly rendered in favor of the President of the United States—Crum Elbow Point was designated as "A point on the *east* bank of the Hudson River about 4½ miles above Poughkeepsie, Dutchess County, New York."

Howland Spencer had been outgunned.[7]

[Roosevelt was] it cannot be too much emphasized, a child of the country. . . . Cities . . . were clustered out there on the periphery of existence, curious agglomerations to be visited on occasion; but they were not by any means the center of things to him as they were to so many of his contemporaries. He would never really regard them as other than a perhaps necessary nuisance. Moreover, he could not quite believe that people raised in them could have the whole worth of others with country backgrounds. His idea of an ideal enterprise would be a farm, one suspiciously like Springwood.

Source: Rexford G. Tugwell, *The Democratic Roosevelt*, page 24.

6. The historical basis for this was the fact that in the 1790s a house had still stood on the Roosevelt land called alternately "Krum Elbow" and "Crooke's Delight." The President understandably chose the first of the two names. *Source:* George Y. Wilkins, *A Report on the Birthplace and Home of Franklin D. Roosevelt* (unpublished), National Park Service.

7. Outgunned, but not daunted, Spencer resorted to his last weapon: he deeded his property to the Harlem messiah, Father Divine, who brought to it boatloads of his followers on weekends. To Spencer's fury, the Roosevelts made no public objection to their new neighbors. (Father Divine had earlier attempted to purchase the Frederick W. Vanderbilt estate in Hyde Park itself; its owner, Mrs. James L. Van Alen, refused to sell to him, and FDR was later instrumental in having the mansion taken over by the National Park Service.) *Source:* F. Kennon Moody, *FDR*

The whole controversy frankly appalled Franklin's mother. To reject the name by which she had always known her own home seemed to her a betrayal of Mr. James's benevolent ghost, and once, when she overheard a guest using "Crum Elbow" in conversation, she was quick to correct him. He apologized, and explained that he had heard the President himself use it.

"Franklin doesn't know *everything,*" she said.[8]

The Springwood house itself was also a source of some contention between mother and son for a time. Franklin wanted almost from the moment of his marriage to build onto it, perhaps hoping to match the more palatial country places of some of his Harvard and Hudson River friends, possibly to create a more suitable setting for the rising young statesman he was already determined to become.

Although she did wire the old house for electricity in 1908, Sara otherwise held the line, shoring up a porch here, having a hole in the roof patched there, rather than entertain the notion of major alterations. Springwood was too full of sacred memories for her to want to change it.

But by 1914 the young Roosevelts had four children, and when they descended upon her with their retinue of nurses and maids they managed to fill even her beloved old house's many rooms with so much cheerful tumult that Sara, too, saw the need to expand.

Even before his mother chose an architect, Franklin had begun to doodle sketches of the house as he would like to see it transformed. Sara showed the drawings to Francis Hoppin, an old Campobello friend, the former husband of a distant cousin, and a fashionable architect who

---

and His Neighbors: A Study of the Relationship Between Franklin D. Roosevelt and the Residents of Dutchess County, pages 164–165.

8. Sara never abandoned her conviction that she was all that stood between the Place and revolution. During her son's presidency, she liked to have his black maid Lizzie McDuffie recite poems for her. "She asked me to give 'The Deserted Plantation' by Paul Lawrence Dubar, eight times," Mrs. McDuffie remembered. "Often she would shake her head and say, 'that's the way Hyde Park will be when we are all gone.'"

Sara was also utterly mystified by the need for Social Security. One day, Mrs. McDuffie recalled, "she called me out on the front porch and made me sit down and discuss the theory of pensions with her. 'Don't you think I take good care of my help on this place? . . . Shouldn't they be able to save some money for their old age, but not expect pensions?'"

Mrs. McDuffie was evidently not persuasive, for Sara managed to overlook Social Security payments for several years before her son discovered it and quietly made up the difference himself. *Source:* Chapters of an incomplete autobiography by Lizzie McDuffie, FDRL.

was "doing a little work for Mr. Vanderbilt," Sara told her son, "and he is *enthusiastic* and says 'Franklin has got the idea, exactly.'"

Hoppin had his commission. He "is full of taste," she told Franklin, "and will do anything for me with pleasure and enthusiasm and is in our neighborhood just now."

The renovations, too, were to be a project shared only with her son. "Do not speak of it to Eleanor, it is too uncertain and I want to surprise her if I do it." Franklin made his mother an intricately detailed scale model of the house as it would look when finished. (Sara thought the model "a real work of art," but somehow failed to hold onto it as she did to nearly every other artifact of her son's early life.) Elliott C. Brown, a Harvard friend of Franklin's, was hired as contractor.

The old buff-colored clapboards were ripped off; the verandas on which Mr. James had so enjoyed reading were dismantled. The south tower, in whose attic room Franklin had often played as a boy, was lowered, and a second tower built to match it to the north. The front roof was raised to hold a third-floor nursery. Three-story wings— built, at Franklin's urging, out of native stone brought to the site from the old walls that twisted through the Springwood forests—were added onto either side of the central section, which was stuccoed gray to match them. A broad porch with a sweeping balustrade formed a new and far more stately entrance.

Franklin delighted in the project, urging on the carpenters, going over the plans for every room with Elliott Brown.

Sara encouraged him in that, too. "She had the great idea," Eleanor once said, "that a home should be run for a man," and certainly much of the public portion of the house seems to have been planned as a showcase for her son and his collections. The tall panelled wall in the front hall was covered with the naval prints and cartoons he now collected as assiduously as he still sought out stamps. To the left, there was a life-sized bronze statue of a seated Franklin, commissioned in 1911 by his godmother, Nelly Blodgett, as a gift for his mother from their mutual friend, the fashionable sculptor Paul Troubetskoy, whose brother Pierre's oil portrait of Sara hung just down the hall.[9]

Behind the statue was a specially built glass-fronted case that held his boyhood collection of native birds, shot by him, then stuffed by professional taxidermists in New York and Poughkeepsie.

9. The statue ended at the thighs, because, the sculptor is supposed to have told Franklin's mother, "I can't see Franklin with legs." *Source:* Olin Dows, *Franklin Roosevelt at Hyde Park,* page 81.

Franklin and Eleanor, honeymooning in Switzerland, 1905.

This previously unpublished honeymoon snapshot of a haggard Franklin, suffering from hives, was taken in Venice by his bride, who later posed for him in the gondola at right, holding her husband's hat.

Franklin comes in a winner behind his father's old horse "Bobby," at the Dutchess County Fair in Poughkeepsie, 1905, and takes Anna for a walk at Campobello two years later, while Eleanor (left) and Anna's nurse, Blanche Spring (center), look on.

Franklin (above, hands in pockets) has a close-up look at manual labor at one of the coal mines owned by his uncle Warren Delano in Harlan County, Kentucky in the summer of 1908. Restless as a novice lawyer, two years later he began to spend weekends at Springwood (right) in hopes of persuading local Democrats to nominate him for some office.

Franklin campaigning for the state senate in 1910 (Eleanor is just behind him in the large hat). Roosevelt was already "a top-notch salesman," a witness remembered, "because he wouldn't immediately enter in the topic of politics, . . . he would approach them as a friend . . . with that smile of his."

Group portrait made by Eleanor during the Roosevelts' visit to the Fergusons near Silver City, New Mexico, in May, 1912. Left to right: Mrs. Tilden Selmes, Isabella's mother; Isabella Selmes Ferguson; Robert Ferguson; and Franklin.

Livingston Davis and Franklin at Hyde Park during the winter of 1913.

FRANKLIN D. ROOSEVELT.
Lawyer, Clubman and Statesman.

Roosevelt's qualifications for his post as Assistant Secretary of the Navy, as seen by H. R. Mianz of the Washington *Herald*, March 22, 1913.

The Roosevelts of Washington, 1916. Left to right: Elliott, Eleanor, Franklin, Franklin, Jr., James, Sara, John, Anna.

The Assistant Secretary of the Navy on the Western front, 1918. To his left is Admiral Charles P. Plunkett, commander of the naval battery in which Franklin hoped to serve as a lieutenant commander.

Franklin samples some of the "sublime Scotch" that kept him and his party warm while fishing in the rain in Scotland on August 30, 1918.

The most attention was lavished on the library that occupied the entire south end of the first floor, a huge room with "plenty of room for books, books, books," Sara said, ". . . simple woodwork, with perfect finish. . . ." Franklin's leather-bound sets soon lined the long walls, and specially built cabinets on either side of the west fireplace held his stamp albums. Glass-covered shelves were built into the cabinetry, under which were displayed his coins, medals, and other knicknacks. The Roosevelt coat of arms was deeply carved above the huge Italian marble fireplaces at either end of the room. A portrait of Franklin's great-great-grandfather, Isaac Roosevelt, attributed to Gilbert Stuart, hung at the eastern end of the room; an anonymous portrait of his great-grandfather, the first James Roosevelt, stared back from the opposite wall.

Franklin loved the library so much that in his instructions for his own funeral, written in 1937, he would ask to have his casket placed in front of the fireplace before burial, so that he could spend one last night in it before he was buried in his mother's garden.[10]

His mother felt the same way; it was already *"so* home-like," she thought, though she was a little startled at the house's size for a time (it now encompassed thirty-five rooms, eight of them intended for the servants, plus nine baths), and took to calling it "our new hotel."

Her grandchildren loved it, too. For them, it came to represent the safe center of an increasingly tumultuous world, much as it had for their father. "Hyde Park," Anna once told an interviewer, "was very definitely my most favorite Place in life . . . Hyde Park was home, and the only Place I ever thought was completely home. . . ."

Her brothers felt the same way.

The children's memories of the Place were bound up in part with the active presence of their father. "Franklin comes tomorrow for 4 days," Eleanor told Isabella from Springwood one summer during his first Washington years, "the first & only holiday as far as I can see that he expects to have. The children are wild with joy & have planned enough things to keep him busy for a week."

"My happiest memories of Father, my most carefree escapades of childhood," James wrote, "all seem centered [at Springwood]." The children came closest to holding Franklin's attention at Hyde Park; he

10. In the end, this was not done; his family did not find his funeral instructions until after his burial. For an explanation, see Geoffrey C. Ward, *Before the Trumpet: Young Franklin Roosevelt 1882–1905,* page 3.

swept them up in the activities he had always loved, seemed content to act toward them precisely as his own father had acted toward him before illness slowed him down. "He inundated us with fun and action," James remembered, "and with love, too—but in his special way, which was both detached and overpowering."

In the mornings, in the early days, Franklin took Anna riding through the woods with him, just as his father had once taken him. She treasured the memory of those rides, huddled in front of her father on the saddle of her grandfather's old horse Bobby, as he "point[ed] out varieties of birds as they darted by. His favorite rides were to wood plantations he had put in. Some were close to wood roads and some were in the most unexpected spots in peaceful, deserted glens deep in the woods."

In summer, Franklin swam with the children, either in his father's old ice pond or up the road, where the Rogers' pond featured its own elaborate bathing pavilion built of branches with the bark left on in the already old-fashioned rustic style, and he made and sailed model boats with them on the Hudson from the boathouse at Rosedale, the estate on which his father had been raised, just down the shore.

In winter, he took them ice-boating on the frozen river, the only sound besides their laughter the rushing wind and the creaking of the ice. When coasting on the hill behind the house, James recalled, Franklin was "like a kid himself. He would chase us back up the steep road at a pace so fast our lungs would ache with the . . . cold air," then plunge with them down the hillside again. Those who fell off were not to cry.

Sara often watched them coast, standing at the edge of the snowy bluff, bundled in furs, Elliott recalled. Eleanor sat alone inside by the fire.

At Christmas, too, Franklin was the exuberant center of things. He supervised the cutting of the tall tree that always stood in the center of the library, and he placed each of the scores of candles that decorated it in its holder, climbing a ladder to reach the highest branches while the children offered noisy counsel from below. (To the end of his life, the Roosevelt tree blazed with candles, a bucket of water nearby in which stood a cane with a big sponge tied to it for dousing sparks.)[11]

11. There was another holiday custom at Springwood that echoed the era of Mr. James. On Christmas Eve, all the men and women who worked on the Place trooped up to the house with their families, everyone dressed in his or best, to see the big tree and the decorations and to receive from Sara's hand their bonus checks. As Anna and the boys grew older, they were encouraged

Franklin carved the turkey himself, too, proudly producing slices so thin, he liked to say, "you can almost read through them," a skill he had mastered at Groton, where every young gentleman was taught to perform this holiday rite. And after the feasting and the opening of the presents, piled in gaudy heaps on library chairs around the tree, one for each child, he read aloud Dickens's *A Christmas Carol,* another Groton ritual, performed there by the rector himself. It was evidently an irresistible performance. James remembered sitting still and listening, wide-eyed, to his father's "clear, confident voice . . . soaring into the higher registers for . . . Tiny Tim, then shifting into a snarly imitation of mean old Scrooge."[12]

Eleanor apparently liked the new Springwood, too, at least at first. "You would not know the home here," she told Isabella when it was finished. "We all have big rooms & I think it's very home-like & for the chicks it is now ideal."

But later she would change her mind. "For over forty years," she wrote at the end of her life, "I was only a visitor there."

That feeling was, to some extent, inevitable. She *was* a visitor for forty years, after all.

Springwood was Sara's house. She had lived there for sixty-one years before she died, for twenty-two years before Eleanor first entered it as a young woman. It was always her home, the center of her world, crowded with mementoes of her own long life and those of her Delano forebears.

Sara continued to the end of her life to see to every detail of daily life there; she planned the menus with the cook and housekeeper; saw that the maids overlooked no dust; cut and arranged the flowers from gardens meticulously tended under her sharp eye; kept count of all the linens, just as she had when Franklin was seven and had gravely

---

to save out of their allowances enough money to buy a little gift for one of the employees' children. Since their allowances were small, Elliott remembered, "our giving tended to be restrained, possibly a dime-store ring for a girl like Florence Depew, daughter of . . . Granny's chauffeur . . . I lost my heart to her." *Source:* Elliott Roosevelt and James Brough, *An Untold Story: The Roosevelts of Hyde Park,* page 102.

12. In 1936, a recording of this annual ritual was evidently made at the White House, complete with an interruption by a small grandchild who wanted a glass of water. Two portions of it were poorly recorded and the President may have re-recorded them the following year. According to Fred W. Shipman, the first director of the Franklin D. Roosevelt Library at Hyde Park, FDR "wanted the matter kept secret and the records stored away, not to be played until after his death." Over the intervening years they seem to have disappeared. *Source:* PPF 450, FDRL.

followed her from room to room, writing down with a stubby pencil her careful running tally of towels and tablecloths and bed covers.[13]

Still, Eleanor's deep bitterness was at least partially understandable. Sara made few concessions, even to her family. Things ran on her schedule; her guests obeyed her rules. A Chinese gong on the stairs was tapped once, precisely half an hour before lunch and dinner, and again just five minutes before food reached the table.

It was unwise to be late. "[My mother-in-law] never would allow outsiders to criticize any member of her family," Eleanor remembered, "but she herself was quite free to criticize anything . . . she felt was wrong. In fact, she felt it her duty." Sara would have agreed with that assessment. "I was talking with Fred Weekes [a distant cousin] yesterday," she once wrote Eleanor, "about Kassie and [her daughter] Sallie, and I said I thought my sister . . . and I were very different. She always thinks anything her daughters do is the *right* thing. With me, my love for my own makes me more critical than I would be of strangers."

The grandchildren were inspected before they took their places at the table. "My dear, you have a decided stable odor," Anna remembered her grandmother saying to her once, after she had come in from a hard morning's ride. "A bath, of course, will cure it. And don't forget, you must wear a dress for lunch!"[14]

Sara always sat at the head of the dining room table, facing her son.

---

13. Despite her best efforts, things did not always run smoothly. In February of some unknown year she was forced to write the following letter to the family lawyer, John T. Hackett, from her New York home:

> I have just had a disagreeable experience. A Scotch laundress named Julie Wallace was taken suddenly ill, & we got her moved to a Maternity hospital just in time for her baby to be born there. She has been in my service for about a year and a half & I never suspected anything wrong. The father of the child is John Simpson, a stableman on Rosy's place, about 30 years old & unmarried. If I go to Hyde Park to try to get him to marry her, he will probably get away. I think he ought to provide for her to the child—She told the doctor that she would not marry John, that he was having an affair with another woman!
>
> She says she told John the child was coming and he paid no attention & did not offer to marry her—What can one do? He certainly ought not to go "Scot free"—she has no means of support, & the man ought to pay for her board & the baby has to be with its mother for some months to come, even if she could board it out by next autumn & take a place again. Let me know if you can see the man & require him to support the woman.
>
> > Very Sincerely yours,
> > Sara D. Roosevelt

Hackett's response no longer exists. *Source:* Franklin and Eleanor Roosevelt Institute, FDRL.

14. Sara never stopped trying to teach her descendants manners. In 1935, she had built on the Springwood lawn a little white playhouse that became known as "the Swan House," after the long-necked brass knocker on the front door. It was her hope that her small great-grandchildren would serve one another formal tea there in the afternoons. *Source:* Rita Halle Kleeman Papers, FDRL.

"I sat anywhere," Eleanor remembered.

Franklin's favorite boyhood foods were often served: hot corn-bread, kedgeree, minute pudding—a soft, smooth mush sweetened with hot molasses, "certainly more like baby's cereal than anything else," Eleanor recalled. His behavior was sometimes monitored, too. Once, at dinner, her youngest grandson, John, used the word "damn." Sara frowned but said nothing. A few moments later, FDR himself used it. "Our little Johnny learns his language from the stable," she told the family, "and Franklin apparently learns it from Johnny."

Eleanor was scrutinized, too, and often found wanting. A member of the family remembers Sara saying to her daughter-in-law, in front of dinner guests, "If you'd just run your comb through your hair, dear, you'd look *so* much nicer."

Her answer, as always in those days, was, "Yes, Mama." Once grateful for such advice, she had now begun to find it humiliating.

In the library after dinner, Franklin and his mother each had a special chair—matching, high-backed Governor's chairs after 1932—on opposite sides of the fire.

Again, Eleanor sat wherever there was room.

From infancy, Eleanor had felt at home nowhere; had been unsure where she belonged or how to behave in order to make herself welcome. Now to be required, year after year, to spend weeks—sometimes months—at a time, often without her husband, in this place where everyone else in her family seemed so eager to be, and yet to feel always apart from it, alien, orphaned again, became an agony. "It was my husband's home," she told an interviewer, "and my children had a sense that it was their home. . . . But for me, it was not . . . home." Her complicated struggle with the mother-in-law whom she continued both to resent and rely upon centered, often, on Springwood and the children.

Eleanor was now less anxious about her offspring than she once had been. They had survived too many childish colds and other ailments for her to fear their imminent deaths with every fever. (They had endured so many that one visitor to their Washington home noted the Roosevelt children seemed to lack the most basic instruction in how to blow their noses.)

In fact, Eleanor's sympathy with illness was severely limited; it was a sign of weakness, she believed, even for children to give in to it. Once, James was severely afflicted with poison ivy while Eleanor was away. When she returned, Anna took her to her brother's bedroom, explaining how uncomfortable he was, how little sleep he'd had. "I'll never forget my surprise," Anna remembered, "when Mother calmly said, 'You silly boy, you ought to know better than to get near poison ivy.' "

"Up to a certain point," Eleanor wrote later, "it is good for us to know that there are people in the world who will give us love and unquestioned loyalty . . . I doubt, however, if it is good for us to feel assured of this without the accompanying obligation of having to justify this devotion by our behavior." For Eleanor, who had received so little of it as a child, maternal love often seems to have been conditional, meted out as a reward for good conduct.

For sympathy, the children turned to their grandmother.

She was solicitude itself when any of them was hurt or ill.[15] At six, James fell off his pony, Daisy, at Hyde Park. "He slid off over her tail & her hoof must have touched his chest & chin as both are scratched," Eleanor reported to Franklin. "He did not seem really hurt at all but cried hard & Mama brought him in & had him lying down before I knew anything was wrong. . . . I would have made him get on again if only for assurance. . . ."

Above all, Sara's love for all her grandchildren was unqualified, her fascination with them apparently unending. Anna remembered that her busy parents' morning greetings were perfunctory pecks on the cheek over the breakfast table, but "when I was sent . . . to say Good Morning to Granny as she finished her breakfast in bed, her kiss and hug were indeed warm—almost suffocating. . . ."

Everything about her grandchildren seemed to interest Sara—how they dressed, what they ate and read and weighed—and they repaid her loving interest with overwhelming affection for her. "When I said goodnight after hymns to the children," she wrote in her journal at the end of one visit to Washington, "Anna and James *both* said 'I *wish* you were not going away, *do* come back soon,' and were very sweet and loving. I hate to leave my grandbabies."

Toward the end of her own long life, Eleanor wrote bitterly that Sara's devotion to her grandchildren had grown not so much out of

15. Solicitous, but strong-minded and old-fashioned. Her remedy for poison ivy was a coat of varnish. To induce vomiting, the patient was encouraged to swallow a raw oyster, tied to a string; the string was then slowly pulled back up. This last was invariably effective, but at least one patient who endured it was unable even to look at raw shellfish for decades afterwards. *Source:* Interview with Laura Delano Adams Eastman.

love as out of her desire to "hold on to Franklin and his children; she wanted them to grow up as she wished. As it turned out, Franklin's children were more my mother-in-law's children than they were mine."[16]

While it may seem odd that Sara should have considered Franklin and Eleanor's offspring "our" children, as she herself sometimes wrote that she did, it also seems likely that had she not so considered them they would have led still more troubled lives than they actually did.

Sara had provided for her son what Anna once privately admitted her own mother had failed to provide for her—"consistent, warm, spontaneous love."

She tried her best to do the same for her grandchildren, and Anna, at least, remembered her as having been "the most solidly important" adult in her childhood; she was "far more than a grandparent," she added. "She was inextricably interwoven with the Place."

Eleanor remembered her mother-in-law once asking her, "Why don't you tell the children what's right and what's wrong?"

"Because," she answered. "I don't know myself."

Sara had no doubt that *she* knew, but she could not always be with her grandchildren.

For the children of the wealthy, nurses and governesses traditionally helped clarify such questions, sometimes with considerable severity. But the Roosevelt children recalled the women employed to care for them in their earliest years as a succession of horrors, each grimmer than the last. The worst of them, almost surely psychotic, was named "Old Battle Axe" by her frightened, abused charges. All the children suffered at her hands. She knocked Anna to the floor, knelt on her, and slapped her face for failing to be sufficiently ladylike, and on another occasion sent her to school with a wad of cotton in her mouth. When the teacher asked her to remove it she said she could not; her nurse had told her it must still be there when she got home because she had told a lie. She locked both Elliott and Franklin Jr. in dark closets for hours at a time, once breaking off the key in her inexplicable fury. James was made to spoon down an entire jar of hot mustard because he had dared watch her slather her meat with it when she told him to avert his eyes, and she later draped him in his sister's dress, hung a sign that said I AM A LIAR around his neck, and forced him to parade up and down in

16. Anna later agreed. "I was raised," she once said, "more by Grandmother than by my parents." *Source:* James Roosevelt and Sidney Shallett, *Affectionately, FDR,* page 51.

front of the Roosevelt house on East 65th Street, because she thought he had not told her the truth about brushing his teeth.

Perhaps Eleanor's eerie obliviousness to what this woman was doing to her children resulted in part from the fact that she may herself have been the victim of a furtively abusive adult companion when she was a girl living in her Grandmother Hall's gloomy house.[17] In any case, nothing the governess did seems unduly to have disturbed Eleanor; nothing, that is, until she discovered an empty whiskey bottle in the nurse's dresser.

To the daughter and niece of alcoholics, secret drinking was unforgivable. The woman was gone the next day.

Much later, Eleanor would blame Sara for having hired her children's first nannies; she had herself still been too meek, she said, ever to oppose her mother-in-law, and the act of dismissing this worst of them had been a liberating experience. "From the time I got rid of that person," she remembered much later, "and took over the selection of the type of nurses I wanted, I began to have more confidence in my ability to handle the children."

It is hard to credit that someone like Sara, who had been so concerned that everyone with whom her own son came into contact be precisely the right sort, should have guessed so wrong so many times when it came to her grandchildren. (Her own chief worry about the women she hired to help with Franklin, she once explained, was that they would spoil him through too much adoration.)[18] Her own standards for children's behavior were lofty, to be sure. James once told her he was about to wash his dirty hands: "A gentleman's hands may be *soiled*, James," she told him, "but they are never *dirty.*" And she insisted to Anna that no lady ever crossed her limbs when seated.

Perhaps, her reasoning had run, if the children's own mother was indecisive about what was right and what was wrong, it was all the more important that their nurses and governesses not be.

17. For speculation about this episode, see Geoffrey C. Ward, *Before the Trumpet: Young Franklin Roosevelt, 1882–1905,* pages 291–292.

18. Nor, had she been in daily charge, is it likely that Sara would have overlooked the sadistic behavior of "Old Battle Axe." As it was, she kept a sharp eye on her grandchildren's nurses whenever she was with them. Once, when Franklin Jr. was an infant, she wrote in her journal, "I noticed that . . . sometimes when he was supposed to be sleeping in the open . . . [the windows] were closed again in an hour." She spoke firmly to the nurse and was pleased afterwards to see that "yesterday they were open from ten to two . . . so I hope by watching that he may have more air. . . ." *Source:* Sara Delano Roosevelt Journal, FDRL.

But it is also possible that Eleanor herself played a larger part in the selection of the women who cared for her children than she later liked to remember. For her offspring did honestly bewilder her, precisely as she had bewildered her own mother, and if a would-be nurse seemed suitably well mannered; if she considered rules and deportment important; above all, perhaps, if she seemed likely to keep the children quiet, under control and out of danger, then mother-in-law and daughter-in-law alike may have found her suitable.

The noise the children made, their quarrelling and messiness, still grated upon Eleanor. When she took them to visit her sedate, elderly cousins, Susie and Henry Parish, who had once taken her and Hall in when they were children and whom she had always tried then to please by her own perfect manners and by attempting to keep her erratic brother under control, she was especially embarrassed by the children's behavior—they "have been the wildest things you ever saw & about ready to jump out of their skins," she complained to Franklin. She blamed that behavior on their having yet another nurse assigned to them, "a new person [whose] authority they still question. . . ."

In fact, as Anna wrote, all the Roosevelt children quickly learned that "the Nanny or nurse . . . did not have to command . . . respect because they came and went, always replaced by someone else." The result was a good deal of anarchy, which alarmed Eleanor but which she was apparently powerless to halt. When in New York, James and Anna filled paper bags with water and gleefully dropped them on passers-by on East 65th Street. A little later, Elliott would test the accuracy of his new air rifle by shooting holes in the stained-glass window across the street.

The obstreperousness that so irritated his wife was to Franklin evidence of the kind of childish high spirits of which he had been allowed so little as a boy. "Oh, let them scrap," he told one nurse, when James and Elliott tussled. "It's good exercise for them!" And before Eleanor and the children arrived for a stay at Springwood, he suggested that she "Let the chicks run wild at Hyde Park. It won't hurt them."

Like his own father, Franklin refused to accept responsibility for day-to-day discipline; that was his wife's task, or the nanny's. Once, during the early Albany years, Eleanor had forced him to spank James by actually placing a hairbrush in his hand and saying, "Franklin, you *must* spank this boy."[19]

Eleanor recalled more characteristic occasions. At Hyde Park one day, she sent her youngest son to his room. After a time she looked in to find him gone. "I went straight to the study," she remembered, "where I found him crying his heart out in his father's arms with his head buried in his father's shirtfront. My husband sat tipped back in his desk chair looking entirely miserable and quite guilty because he knew he was not upholding discipline."

For Franklin, who disliked unpleasantness of any kind and preferred always bringing good news to bad, such a gentle talking to was reprimand enough; the merest hint of parental disapproval, after all, had been all that had been required to correct his own behavior when he was a boy.

Once, James stole ten dollars from his father's wallet and used the money to buy Anna a Christmas watch. On Christmas morning, he was much admired for his generosity by everyone else, including his astonished sister, but his father, who had missed the money, later took him into his study and quietly asked if he had indeed taken it.

James tearfully admitted that he had.

Franklin paused for what seemed to his son a very long time. People went to jail for that sort of thing, he said finally, even if it had been done in a generous spirit. It could be forgiven once, but "If it does happen again, I shall have no choice—and I shall not hesitate, though I would regret it—but to call the police, and let them handle the matter as they see fit."

Meanwhile, the secret would remain theirs alone.

James repaid the debt, and long after his father's death, asked his mother if FDR had ever told her of the incident. He had not.

Franklin could be an exacting parent, especially if one of his children threatened his own good times; his daughter remembered having been reduced to tears when, as a very small girl sailing with him off Campobello, she had been too slow in carrying out his barked commands.

And he was very often absent, causing a good deal of anxiety which

19. James remembered one other paternal spanking, delivered one Sunday morning during the Washington years after he had refused to accompany his parents to church and forced his father, in cut-away coat and striped trousers, to crawl under a bed and drag him out. So far as James knew, these were the sole occasions on which his father delivered a spanking to any of the children. *Source:* James Roosevelt and Sidney Shalett, *Affectionately, FDR*, page 82.

Eleanor had to do her best to allay. At Campobello in 1913, she told Franklin, "Elliott feels a calamity approaching" because of his father's departure. The following summer: "Elliott sends his love and wants you to return at once as 'he has no one to take care of him.' " Again, in 1915: "It seems very lonely and strange without you ... Elliott after he got home [from seeing Franklin off to Washington] last night gave way completely & I found him alone in the day nursery waiting for his supper & crying hard. When pressed for a reason he said 'I don't want *my* father to go 'way.' I consoled him by suggesting that he make you lots of boats & horses before you get back & he told me this a.m. he was 'working hard.' "

As a child, James Roosevelt remembered wondering "why [Father] ever had to leave this paradise [Springwood], and why we had to troop after him." In later years, he would still wonder "why we had so little of Father" in those early years.

Sara worried over his absences, too. When, some time in the autumn of 1914, he failed at the last moment to bring James with him and join his wife and daughter for a weekend at Hyde Park as he had promised her he would, she was furious:

Dearest son

It is a *great* disappointment not to see you, Langdon [Marvin, Franklin's law partner and James's godfather] is very sad over it, so is Rosy, so are we all. . . . I miss my dear James. I am glad he has the natural feelings of a nice boy and misses us all. I am sure he must feel queer to be without his mother today and yesterday, as no doubt you are too busy to be devoted to him. . . .

It is such a comfort to have Eleanor and a few peaceful days with her beloved children will do her no harm! She accomplishes so much in her quiet way, and is always so sweet and cheerful, never nervous or cross and I just count on these few days. Try to get some fresh air, and also some time with dear little James. He will never forget what you do for him now.

Ever your devoted
Mother

When Franklin did find time for his children, he clearly enjoyed himself and them. Eleanor did not seem to do so; the closest James ever felt to her as a small boy, he remembered, was when she read aloud to him because Dr. Holt had said, "I had to have my 'quiet times.' . . . It is sad she seldom had other occasions to unbend."

All three of the senior Roosevelts had great powers of concentration, Anna remembered, and none liked to be interrupted. But it was her mother who resented it most: "When Mother was concentrating—talking to someone, reading or working at her desk—she had a . . . chilling way of putting me in my place. This way persisted throughout her life so I remember very well the sound of the low but cold voice which said, 'What do you want, dear?' It was not a question, just an unmistakable announcement that she was busy and preoccupied."[20]

Nowhere was the difference between the children's parents more sharply drawn than it was at bedtime. Anna remembered the gravity with which Eleanor approached their evening prayers: "Mother came to the nursery for this ritual. We knelt at her knee for prayers, and at our bedsides if we were alone with the nurse. If nurse complained of our behavior, Mother's disapproval was quite evident, usually expressed by dampening down the warmth of her goodnight hug and kiss."

If the chicks were awake when Franklin returned home, on the other hand, he bounded up the stairs to say goodnight to them, wrestling or staging a pillow fight if there was time, in any case staying long enough to stroke the back of each sleepy child and murmur "snug as a bug in a rug?"

By 1915, the children, who had learned to endure their father's absences, were having to adjust to their mother's as well, as she began to accompany her husband on inspection trips around the country.

Eleanor greatly enjoyed her travels, although she sometimes found them exhausting; she loved seeing new things, spending time with her husband and away from her charges. But, as always with her, joy bred guilt. "I hated to leave my children," Eleanor remembered, "but once out, my fears were quiescent until we were about two days from home, and then they were revived in full force, and the last night I usually imagined all the terrible things that might happen to the children before we saw them again. They might fall out of a window, or into the fire, or be run over! Those last nights were certainly bad ones, and I was relieved to get home and find everything running smoothly."[21]

20. "It has always seemed to me," Anna once wrote, "that the greatest contradiction in my parents was, on the one hand, their supreme ability to 'relate' to either groups of people or individuals who had problems, and on the other hand, their apparent lack of ability to 'relate' with the same consistent warmth and interest to an individual who was their child." *Source:* John R. Boettiger, *A Love in Shadow,* page 73.

21. In her autobiography, Eleanor added that "there really was no cause" for such anxiety, since her capable mother-in-law always "had an eye to the children." But the first Franklin Jr.

Meanwhile, Sara was in charge. Her pleasure in having the children to care for was palpable. She interrupted a letter to her son early one morning because, she told him, she had looked up from her writing desk in the crowded little first-floor room she called her "snuggery" to see Anna and James in the doorway, looking "like bright young robins, ready for breakfast." Her reports to Franklin and Eleanor on the children were always admiring, reassuring: "Baby [Franklin Jr.] is too sweet, so happy and such a lovely disposition. Anna and James have just gone to bed and said 'be sure to give our love to them, grandmama' "; "Baby is splendid, had his one big movement in the morning as before. . . . Just weighed Babs—He has regained his 7½ ounces (lost last week) since *Saturday* and looks the picture of health"; ". . . the children did their 'surprise' for me and I was enchanted, and much surprised that they could act so well. James is a born actor and Anna was also very good"; "James looks so well and so grown. He is so happy that he just laughs with joy."

She was indulgent with her grandchildren. "We . . . quickly learned that the best way to circumvent 'Pa and Mummy' when we wanted something they wouldn't give us," James remembered, "was to appeal to Granny." And, according to Eleanor, James and Anna especially "always treated [Sara] with an affectionate *camaraderie* which won from her almost anything they desired."

James remembered planting a garden one spring at Hyde Park: "Granny's idea of teaching me self-sufficiency was to provide the land, the seeds (free) and lots of advice, then purchase my crop at prices 50 per cent above the market. Father contended with some asperity that it was 'unrealistic' to pay me 150 per cent of parity. All he got was a hurt response that surely 'dear James' should be encouraged in his commendable display of initiative."

That was how she usually dealt with Franklin and Eleanor's protests that she was spoiling her grandchildren. "When we objected," Eleanor wrote, "she looked at us quite blandly and said she hadn't realized we disapproved. She never heard anything she did not want to hear. . . ."22

---

had also been under Sara's care when he was fatally stricken in 1909, an event for which Eleanor continued to blame herself directly—and perhaps, subconsciously, her mother-in-law as well. *Source:* Eleanor Roosevelt, *This Is My Story,* page 213.

22. Sara was not always so deaf. She once overheard her own servants at Springwood complaining that she was "chicken-hearted" when it came to disciplining her grandchildren; that she spoiled them; and that, as a result, they were "bad children." She reported this angrily to

On the other hand, there were certain things about which she felt strongly. She believed, for example, that one could not be too careful about choosing children's companions. Once, when she and Eleanor and the children were at Campobello, James struck up a friendship with a small boy who owned a pony on the island. Eleanor encouraged it, although she did not know his family. Sara chastised her, and Eleanor appealed to Franklin in far-off Washington for support: "Do you think it dreadful of me to let the children pick up acquaintances?" (He did not think it dreadful, he told her, but "very delightful for the chicks to have a friend with a pony!")

The nurse who lasted longest and whom the children liked most was "Connie," Elspeth Connochie, a Scotswoman who helped get Elliott through the long series of ailments that plagued him during his earliest years and who combined genuine affection for her charges with a determination to teach them the discipline their parents had been unable to impose.[23]

Sara liked her, too, but did think her alarmingly lax when it came to allowing the children too prolonged access to their friends. Once, when Franklin and Eleanor were away, Connie allowed James to stay for two nights with a friend who lived at Tuxedo Park. "It is a surprise James's staying away 2 nights as I was told one," Sara wrote her children, "... if I had been asked before permission was given I should have said certainly no visiting! Aunt Kassie also would have said no, but she says Connochie had accepted for 2 nights and said to her 'Mrs. Wheeler says you know her very well.' Aunt K. says she has seen her 2 or 3 times. I suppose it was pleasant to Connochie to allow James

---

Eleanor, then added: "But one sh[d] keep as clear of the opinion of that class as possible I am sure, for they blow hot & cold, the best of them, & if any of them speak to me of how *nice* the children are, I shall not even answer. One thing that makes for good behavior at table is that we all know everything goes upstairs & outside." *Source:* Joseph P. Lash, *Eleanor and Franklin*, page 197.

23. James Roosevelt and most of FDR's biographers accept Eleanor's recollection that she alone chose the nurses and governesses that followed in the wake of "Old Battle Axe." But as late as March 1918, Eleanor was writing her mother-in-law from Washington to ask her "to hunt me up a Scotch nurse ... ," and it is hard to believe that Sara did not have at least a hand in the hiring of Connochie, who so resembled her son's beloved nurse, Helen McRorie, known as "Mamie."

Nor can it be entirely an accident that when the time came to employ a French-speaking Mademoiselle, the Roosevelts settled upon a young and diminutive Swiss girl named Seline Thiel, so like Franklin's own favorite governess, the Swiss Jeanne Sandoz.

Sara kept an eye even on Mlle Thiel. "Our day will be very full," Eleanor told Isabella from Washington one winter, "as the chicks have learned a new French play for our Christmas gift, which is to be given after lunch before the Christmas tree! Mlle is quite an actress, which I think makes Mama feel she is on the verge of not being a proper person to be with the young!" *Sources:* Roosevelt Family Papers Donated by the Children, FDRL.

the pleasure, while she is in authority, and I shall say nothing of course. . . . of course Connochie wants to have the children look back with pleasure on her time in charge, that is natural."

Natural or not, a few days later Sara made sure it did not happen again: "Connochie & I had a talk last evening. . . . I asked her not to invite any boy to *stay* here as I felt it was always a mistake for children to *visit* & she C^d ask any of them for tea & lunch. . . ."

Springwood and the other Hudson River homes of Sara's friends were customarily closed up during the winter months, and in the serene days of Franklin's youth their absent occupants could be reasonably sure that they would return from their New York houses in the spring to find them unmolested. But times were changing, and in the winter of 1915–16, several river estates were burglarized.

When a thief broke into Colonel Rogers' Crumwold, just two doors north of Springwood, he got away with $15,000 worth of silver, including, Rogers told Franklin, "most of my best yachting cups." The outraged colonel persuaded the prominent men of Dutchess, Putnam, and Columbia counties to put up a $5,000 reward, used his considerable influence as a Standard Oil official to import detectives from the New York City Police Department, and finally called upon Franklin for help from the federal government.

Rogers was certain, he told the young man he had known since Franklin and his own sons had studied their lessons together in a schoolroom in Crumwold's big round tower, that the culprit was a man named Ralph Rose, a deserter from the armed forces and fugitive from justice who, some years earlier, had robbed the little West Park post office. Rose was part of what Rogers called "the river gang . . . *newcomers* [who] have been here about two years"; his father was "a bad egg," too—though his brother Robert, a carpenter who had worked for Franklin's mother at Springwood, "seems all right."

The colonel was frustrated, he wrote, by the lack of official concern over these robberies. He seemed unable to impress upon the authorities that important people were being victimized: "Mrs. Winthrop Sergeant, Tom Hunt, Louis Church, Vincent Astor, Captain Zabriskie & half a dozen others. . . . We are making some progress," he continued, "but it is very discouraging to run up against a lot of rotten district attorneys who will not give search warrants or act promptly. I have a sworn statement from a thief in Sing Sing about the location of a lot of 'Swag' concealed in a barn cellar belonging to the proprietor of a road house not far from Catskill, [but] I am sure that when we finally search the place it will all be gone."

In any case, would Franklin see what sort of records the federal authorities might have on Rose? "It is time to nail him, and I want as many things against him as possible, so as to put him away for as long as possible."

Franklin responded instantly: "I felt terribly about the loss of your cups," he told the colonel. "It seemed like the hardest kind of luck, and I am sure you would have much rather had them take instead other things of even greater value, but with less associations attached to them." He had already "set the Army, Navy and Marine Corps searching their records," he assured Rogers, had written the Postmaster General of the United States about the West Park robbery, and was himself "getting hotter and hotter about [the burglaries] every day."

Franklin's search turned up a description of Rose, a list of his aliases and the past crimes for which he was still wanted. But even armed with this, Rogers' agents failed to find him or any other burglar, and when Franklin accompanied Eleanor and the children as far as Hyde Park on their way north to Campobello that June, the River families were still nervous.

One warm night, ten-year-old James Roosevelt, sleeping in his father's boyhood room at the head of the Springwood stairs, awoke to see the dark, seated shape of his father outlined against the window, a shotgun across his lap.

"What is it, Pa?" he asked.

"There may be a burglar in the vicinity," Franklin answered in a voice his son remembered as "strangely formal," and, "I intend to remain here all night if necessary, to apprehend him. You are to pay no attention to me. Go back to sleep."

James was understandably unable to do that, and remained rigid and wide-eyed in the dark. Toward dawn, father and son heard the unmistakable crunch of footsteps in the gravel driveway, coming toward the house.

"Father stood up—suddenly he was at least eight feet tall—and pointed his gun through . . . the window," James remembered. "In tones that seemed to me capable of frightening even Jack the Ripper, he thundered: 'Halt! Who's there?' "

"Don't shoot, Mr. Roosevelt," said a frightened voice from below. "It's me!"

It was the Roosevelts' groom.[24]

The real burglar was finally shot down one night in August, as he fled along a wooded road within the walls of Rhinecliff, Vincent Astor's estate north of Rhinebeck. Visiting his mother for the weekend, Franklin drove up with a neighbor, Tracy Dows, to see the spot where it happened.

The dead man's name was Fred Cramer, not Rose, and while he had not lived long enough to confess his crimes, the burglaries along the river ended and the sheriff asserted there had never been a gang at all.

The Place seemed safe again.

24. James Roosevelt understood from his father that the groom he had surprised was never seen again: "For years Father wondered if he might not have been working with a burglary gang." This seems, however, to have been FDR's way of making his own performance a little less anticlimactic in retrospect, for in fact the groom, whose name was Robert, had also been sitting up for the burglars (along with Franklin, an especially hired night watchman named Clements, and Duffy, the Roosevelts' now-venerable Scotch terrier). *Source:* James Roosevelt and Sidney Shalett, *Affectionately, FDR,* pages 56–57; Elliott Roosevelt, ed., *FDR: His Personal Letters, 1905–1928,* pages 315–316.

CHAPTER

8

TOO DAMNED SLOW FOR WORDS

I N MARCH 1915, Franklin and Eleanor left their children in Washington with Sara and travelled to San Francisco. Franklin had been appointed one of the federal commissioners to the Panama-Pacific Exposition. The Roosevelts' best Washington friends were all going—William and Caroline Phillips (Phillips, too, was a commissioner), the Lanes, and the Millers—and old Harvard friends of Franklin's, Livingston Davis, Owen Winston, and their wives were to meet them on the coast. It was "to be a splendid party," Franklin told Livy Davis, "perfectly bully."

If, in Franklin's view, the Wilson administration was still unable to grasp the enormity of the war now raging in Europe—the initial German offensive had smashed its way through Belgium and into France only to stall just short of Paris; trenches stretched from Switzerland to the English Channel; no end to the fighting was in sight—the planners of the Exposition at San Francisco were ruefully aware of its impact. The fair had initially been meant to mark both the resurrection of the city after the 1906 earthquake and the official opening of the Panama Canal, the great achievement engineered by Theodore Roosevelt that had so excited Franklin three years earlier, and which had then been almost universally hailed as the most heroic effort of the age.

But when the first vessel—a cement barge named the *Cristobal*—made the initial ocean-to-ocean trip the previous August, news of its passage had been relegated to the inside pages, suddenly overshadowed by the coming of the war.

Franklin had been given the task of orchestrating the official opening celebration on the Secretary's behalf, and until fighting broke out overseas, his plans had been suitably grand: more than fifty warships of many nations were to assemble at Hampton Roads, then steam through the Canal and arrive off San Francisco to herald the Exposition's opening.[1] President Wilson himself was to be aboard the leading vessel, the old battleship *Oregon,* which in 1898 had raced 12,000 miles around the Horn of South America in just sixty-seven days to take part in the Battle of Santiago Bay.

None of this happened. The naval parade was cancelled early, Daniels concurring with the admirals that so large a proportion of the fleet should not be sent to the Pacific at a time when, if war came, it was most likely to come from the Atlantic. And at the very last moment, the President decided not to attend the opening at all, unwilling to leave Washington even briefly in such critical times.

The war had affected Exposition plans on shore as well. The round-the-world airplane race was cancelled; so was the international yacht race; so were plans for a celebration of "One Hundred Years of Peace Among English-Speaking Peoples." All the belligerents cancelled plans for pavilions, except France—and its exhibition of art by Monet, Rodin, and other modern masters was often marred by the presence of jeering demonstrators from San Francisco's German community.

The Roosevelts' cross-country trip aboard a special train was as jovial as Franklin had hoped it would be, made awkward only by the fact that the President's personal representative, Vice President Thomas Riley Marshall, and his wife, Lois, were to join it at Chicago. The Vice President was as unlike the Roosevelts as he could be. He had been a progressive Democratic governor of his native Indiana, but had been picked as the New Jersey governor's running mate almost exclusively because of geography. (Marshall had no illusions about the office he held; he liked to introduce himself as "President Wilson's Vice," and compared the Vice President to a cataleptic: "He cannot speak; he cannot move; he suffers no pain; yet he is perfectly conscious

---

1. It did not help Daniels' reputation for nautical knowledge that an invitation had gone out over his signature inviting the navy of Switzerland to take part. *Source:* Josephus Daniels, *The Wilson Era: Years of Peace 1910–1917,* page 213.

of everything that is going on around him.") He was neither notably polished nor well connected; a graduate of Wabash College, a self-made lawyer, and an enthusiastic Mason with a ragged gray mustache; a little man, dwarfed by his large wife and rarely seen without a big cigar. (He is best remembered for a remark made while presiding over the Senate during an especially tedious debate over the nation's requirements: "What this country needs is a really good five-cent cigar.") Nor was he wealthy—he felt the need to supplement his $12,000 Vice President's salary by lecturing, travelling alone and usually unrecognized, from town to town by train—and he believed that "unless the tendency of certain men to accumulate vast fortunes is not curbed, America may face socialism or paternalism." Eleanor dismissed him to her Aunt Maude as a "good deal of a socialist with a desire for the millennium and, it seems to me, no very well worked out ideas for how we are to get there."

As the train roared along the Great Salt Lake in the shadow of the Wasatch Mountains, the party hurried out onto the observation platform to exclaim at the view. Marshall emerged late, removed his cigar just long enough to say, "I never did like scenery," and strolled back inside.[2]

The Roosevelts found Vice President Marshall ludicrous, as did most of their Washington friends; he and his wife were entirely the wrong sort to represent the administration, and Franklin was especially contemptuous of the Hoosier's ignorance of naval ceremony.

A quarter of a century later, in the summer of 1941, FDR took time out to dictate a two-page memorandum recalling the Vice President's performance in California:

> I had arranged for a review of the Pacific Fleet on the afternoon of the third day, all of us to go on board the Flagship . . . the fleet to pass us in review through the Golden Gate.
>
> Then came the fun. I went on board first with full honors and my flag was hoisted. Then came Lane, Phillips and Miller and their families, followed by the Vice President and Mrs. Marshall and their party. I had previously designed a flag for the Vice President—white with the Presi-

2. The Vice President lacked utterly the sort of rich man's gallantry that inspired Secretary Lane to jump down at the first California stop and buy out the depot florist's shop, so that when Eleanor and the other wives opened the doors of their compartments that morning they were greeted with huge baskets filled with blossoms and a card that read, "The Land of Flowers Welcomes You." "This was the kind of thing which Frank Lane was always doing," Eleanor remembered, "and was one of the reasons why people loved him and found him such a charming companion." *Source:* Eleanor Roosevelt, *This Is My Story,* page 220.

dential arms in the middle, but without stars, on the theory that the Vice President can hold no command rank.

We were lined up thirty feet from the gangway. . . . The Vice President's barge came alongside, the band and the side boys [enlisted men lining the deck] were all set, and in a minute the Vice President's silk hat and frock coat appeared at the top of the gangway. He had a cigar in his mouth, yellow gloves in his left hand and a cane in his right. . . .

The Vice President stopped at the head of the gangway very correctly and stood there while the four ruffles were given on the drum. But when the Star Spangled Banner was started, confusion followed. The poor man had an awful time shifting his cane to his left hand with the gloves. He reached for his hat, got it half way off, remembered the cigar, put his hat on again, got the cigar out of his mouth, fumbled it in with the gloves and the cane, and got his hat off again just before the National Anthem finished. Then came the reverse process—back went his hat, back went the cigar, and back went the cane into his right hand.

At that awful moment the first gun of the salute was fired almost over his head. He jumped two feet in the air and stayed there during the whole of the nineteen guns.

Utterly confused by that time, he stepped down on to the deck below the line of four side boys on each side, shifted his cane once more and reached out for the hand of the first side boy. The latter, utterly confused, also broke into a broad grin, reached in turn and shook the Vice President warmly by the hand.

By this time . . . I had started forward and we rescued the Vice President before he had completed shaking hands with all eight side boys.

"It was a bit pathetic," FDR said, and then, perhaps not wishing to be on the record as having been too harsh, he added, "but on the whole the Vice President carried out his mission splendidly and was evidently very popular wherever he went."

At the time, however, Franklin and Eleanor had both simply felt embarrassed to be seen in his crude company. That summer, as a token for their help in getting through such ceremonies, Mrs. Marshall sent the Roosevelts a gift. "There appeared a box yesterday from Gorhams," Franklin told Eleanor, "with Mrs. Marshall's card enclosed— and twenty-four (24!)—silver corn handlers or whatever the name is—finger-savers, anti-burners, comme-il-fauts, etc. I am overcome, not with remorse but with delight of getting some reward for our great kindness to her. . . ."

Despite the reduced scale of things at the fair, there was plenty to see and a frenetic schedule to follow, with formal luncheons and dinners and an international ball one evening at which, according to the newspapers, Eleanor towered above the Vice President in a white satin gown with a long train and "magnificent jewels of diamonds and pearls."

Franklin and Phillips spent several days striding from pavilion to pavilion in top hats and tailcoats, carrying canes and taking turns snipping ribbons and offering enthusiastic dedicatory remarks.[3]

"F. doesn't have time to breathe," Eleanor marvelled to Sara, "but he seems to thrive on it." She and Franklin and their friends did snatch the time to ride the cars through the five-acre model of the Panama Canal that was the showpiece of the Zone of Joy, listening through "telephonic communication with a phonograph" to a guided tour of the Canal's wonders, and they wandered together along the Avenue of Progress beneath the floodlit 453-foot Tower of Jewels, its fifty thousand suspended glass prisms shifting constantly in the Pacific breeze.

Franklin and Eleanor had a good time in California, but now and again the strains between them showed. Eleanor grew bored with the hoary yachting stories Franklin and his classmates never tired of retell-

---

3. At the Palace of Fine Arts, he was especially struck by a life-sized bronze study of a kneeling nude, done more or less in the style of Rodin by the young sculptor Ralph Stackpole. Years later, building himself a retreat at Hyde Park, the President remembered the statue, and asked friends in California if they could help track down the artist—whose name he'd forgotten—and see if he might have a copy to place on the grounds of his new cottage.

The result was an embarrassment: the original plaster cast had been lost, and Stackpole had greatly changed his style over the intervening years in any case. Instead of trying to recreate the statue Franklin had admired, he carved an entirely new version in stone. William Hassett described it: ". . . a huge hulk of a female in domestic travertine, big breasts, mammoth in all of her proportions—no curves, no grace, no delicacy. The woman was in a kneeling position, to be sure; but her head was square, neck set on the shoulders on an angle, sides straight, no beauty at all, hands hanging down like great hams, to which were attached square fingers—modernist in every aspect."

FDR was horrified, and Stackpole's explanation did not help: "Big mass movements in thinking and labor naturally reflect in art. The slender and graceful belong less to us now. I've tried to make heavy and strong forms. She is more bent and the burden heavier. Too, I thought of the great building of your administration, especially of Boulder Dam."

In his *FDR: A Biography*, Ted Morgan makes a good deal of Roosevelt's fondness for this statue, suggesting that it represented for him "an idealized woman ready to do a man's bidding, which he, with a strong-willed mother and a strong-willed wife, had never known," and adding that he had the modernist version placed outside his bedroom window. But he didn't; FDR followed his secretary's suggestion and had it installed about as far from his bedroom as he could—on the north side of his new library behind a screen of evergreens.

Eventually, he did obtain a model of the original statue, eight inches tall, and kept it among the many knickknacks that lined the mantel of the hilltop cottage he built for himself near Springwood. *Sources:* William D. Hassett, *Off the Record with FDR: 1942-1945*, pages 31–32; Inventory of contents of Top Cottage, Margaret L. Suckley Papers, FDRL.

ing; "They could hardly be talking a minute," she remembered, "without breaking into some reminiscence."[4]

Franklin showed irritation when his wife slipped into his mother's too-familiar role of earnest exhorter.

William Phillips remembered sharing breakfast with the Roosevelts in San Francisco.

Eleanor asked Franklin if an expected letter had come.

"Yes."

"Well, have you answered it?"

"No, but I will."

"Don't you think, Franklin, that you should answer it promptly?"

"Oh, I'll answer it promptly. I'll attend to it."

"Don't you think . . . that it would be best if you answered it now?"

"All right, I'll answer it now!"

He left the table to do so.

This is the earliest instance recorded by an outsider in which Eleanor publicly pressed her husband to do something he was reluctant or not quite ready to do. Hundreds more just like it would be enacted over the coming decades.

Although Franklin had been in charge of the preparations for the California trip—and figured prominently in them—both he and Howe were let down by how little press coverage he personally received. Louis teased him about it from Washington: "Mr. Daniels thinks he has quite a good joke on you. He called my attention to the fact that no published account in the East of the various fetes and functions for the Vice President has mentioned that you were there, or thereabouts. You had better tell Phillips to fire whoever is acting as press agent for your blooming commission and try to get at least a line in amongst the patent medicine advertisers."

Franklin got his line while visiting Los Angeles, where word reached him that a new American F-4 submarine had failed to return

---

4. Recalling Franklin's delight in one of these stories, centering around Tom Beal's having slipped while climbing into the *Half Moon* with an armload of provisions so that he was covered with "eggs, berries, butter, cream, and so on," Eleanor in 1937 came as close as she ever did in print to detailing the streak of cruelty that sometimes ran through her husband's humor: "My husband has a really good sense of humor and can enjoy a joke on himself as well as those on other people, but I used to be very much amused in those early days at the evident relish with which some of the young men laughed at someone else's expense and how much more forced was the laughter when they themselves were the victims!" *Source:* Eleanor Roosevelt, *This Is My Story*, page 224.

to the surface after a dive off Pearl Harbor; all hands on board were lost. He hurried to the harbor and went aboard another submarine.

"Come on, boys," he shouted to the sailors who lined the wharf. "Don't you want to go along? Plenty of room. Glad to have you." Several filed aboard and followed him below.

The sea was choppy, the sky lowering, but Franklin ordered the commander to dive while spectators along the shore cheered.

When the submarine returned to the surface and all were safely back on shore, one of the passengers told a reporter that the Assistant Secretary had "taken off his coat and dug right into everything."

"It was fine," Franklin told the press, "and for the first time since we left Washington we felt perfectly at home."[5]

That was precisely how his Cousin Theodore would have acted. Nothing had dimmed Franklin's admiration for TR, least of all the ex-President's increasingly vocal impatience with the administration in which his young cousin served, and the two branches of the Roosevelt family still treated one another with gingerly solicitude, overlooking political differences, at least in public, each side determined to avoid an open break with the other.

Before undertaking his arduous trip up the Amazon in October 1913, TR had been given a farewell dinner in Manhattan by 2,350 Progressive admirers. Franklin did not attend, remaining at his Washington desk, but Eleanor made the trip north. "A most wonderful ovation," she reported to Isabella, ". . . the people came in crowds & put in chairs all around the tables so that waiters couldn't serve & so they just gave up & retired. Uncle Ted made a splendid speech chiefly for the recall of judicial decisions. Absolutely clear & logical yet very amusing. . . . I wish F. could have heard him but I was glad he did not hear Mr. Gifford Pinchot [the toastmaster], who made what I felt was

5. The favorable stories his bold dive fostered would be at least partly offset later, when news that the Controller of the Treasury had initially refused to approve payment for his expenses on the California trip was somehow leaked to the New York papers.

Franklin was furious. He thought the Controller's questioning of his expense account "exceedingly rude and uncalled-for. . . . One might think from this opinion that I had been guilty of trying to charge up a private train across the continent." He did not submit vouchers or receipts as Assistant Secretary of the Navy, he explained, and there was therefore "absolutely no reason" why he should have done so when travelling on behalf of the National Exposition Commission, and he had *required* a Pullman drawing room, he said, because of "official conferences with the Vice President." *Source:* Franklin D. Roosevelt Papers, Papers as Assistant Secretary of the Navy, FDRL.

an ill-advised and dangerous [anti-Wilson] speech and I like him so much that I felt quite grieved."

Her uncle wrote her a cheerful note just before embarking the next morning:

Darling E.,

Just a line to say how deeply touched I was to see you at the dinner. Give my love to F.; I hear from all sides how well he is doing. . . .

TR's jungle trip came close to killing him. Already blind in the left eye from a White House boxing mishap, he injured his leg which became badly infected, lost thirty-five pounds, and developed a debilitating and recurrent tropical fever. "The Brazilian wilderness," a friend wrote, "stole away ten years of his life."[6]

Nonetheless, he had plunged into the 1914 mid-term elections with as much of his old energy as he could muster, and when he stumped upstate New York on behalf of the Progressive nominee for governor, Sara invited him to stay with her at Springwood, as he occasionally had in simpler times. He gently turned her down. "I have a letter from T.R.," she told Franklin, "saying that he hesitates about staying here, fearing it is an 'error from Franklin's standpoint' as he is attacking the administration, and that he is only thinking 'of Franklin's interest.' Of course, it is very kind of him, but why should he go on a tour deliberately to attack the Administration, is what I cannot see the wisdom of. I think no one gains by pulling others down. It is not a noble or high-minded viewpoint."[7]

The spring of 1915 represented the low point of Theodore Roosevelt's career. Defeated at the polls in 1912 and again in the congressional elections of 1914, his Progressive Party was in tatters. He was genuinely alarmed at the growing menace of Germany, but so far unable to find a way to express that alarm without seeming merely disgruntled. "The Kaleidoscope has been shaken," he told a friend that spring. "All the combinations are new and I am out of sympathy with what seems to me to be the predominant political thought in this

6. "At your age, why did you do such a thing?" a friend asked him when he got back. "I had just one more chance to be a boy," he answered, "and I took it." *Source:* Joseph L. Gardner, *Departing Glory*, page 295.

7. TR's letter to Sara had been especially tactful. He wanted "dear Sally" to be assured that "If it were not for the campaign, there is no place where I would rather go. And, of course, if the matter has been made public, it might be better to go anyhow."

country." To another admirer, who wished to write a history of the Progressives, he suggested an obituary, instead, "for I am more like a corpse."

To make matters worse, TR found himself on trial at Syracuse, the defendant in a potentially costly lawsuit he was by no means sure of winning. The year before, trying to broaden the appeal of his New York Progressives, he had urged his followers to support some anti-Tammany Democrats. "The interests of Mr. [William J.] Barnes, Jr. [Republican boss of Albany and state chairman of the GOP], and Mr. Murphy are fundamentally identical," he said, "and when the issue between popular rights and corrupt and machine ruled government is clearly drawn, the two bosses will always be found on the same side, openly or covertly, giving one another such support as can safely be rendered. . . ."

Barnes sued him for libel the next day, asking $50,000 in damages. TR's lawyers had been able to obtain a change of venue to Syracuse—Barnes's grip on Albany was thought to extend even to prospective jurors—but the ex-President's failure to persuade old allies to come forward and testify as to what they knew of collusion between the party bosses deeply disappointed him. Few were willing to risk alienating such powerful party figures.[8]

Franklin was a rare exception. He responded eagerly to his cousin's invitation to testify as to what he remembered of the behind-the-scenes alliance between the Republican and Democratic machines during the Sheehan fight. It must have been a triumphant moment for him: he was being asked to help Theodore Roosevelt; his hero actually needed him.

On the morning of May 4, a newspaper photographer caught a smiling Franklin striding to the Syracuse courthouse alongside TR and his attorney. In the courtroom, the ex-President looked on as the self-assured young Roosevelt proudly identified himself as his "fifth cousin by blood and a nephew by law," then added with a grin, "I've known him for some time."

Shortly before the end of the Sheehan struggle, Franklin testified, he had himself gone to see Boss Barnes at the Fort Orange Club in Albany to ask him one final time if, in the interest of good government

8. Even Louis Howe had balked at testifying on TR's behalf. While assuring the ex-President's lawyer that he had always considered Barnes's grip on Albany "a far more sinister and evil thing . . . than Tammany at its worst," he claimed to have too poor a memory for "dates and instances" to be a good witness. *Source:* Louis M. Howe Files, FDRL.

and an end to the long deadlock, the Republicans couldn't be persuaded to join forces with the embattled insurgents and agree to support an independent Democrat for Senator Depew's seat. All Barnes would say was, "No, we can't do it now," refusing either to confirm or deny that he was acting in tacit collusion with Murphy. His refusal to act, Franklin said, spoke for itself.

Barnes's attorneys could not shake his story. Nor could they persuade the jury that this apparently earnest young Roosevelt was simply a Democrat with a partisan ax to grind.[9]

TR beamed.

"Franklin Roosevelt was up here yesterday," he wrote to his wife the next evening, "and made the best witness we have had yet, bar [former assemblyman and Bull Moose stalwart, Frederick] Davenport."

The jury took just under forty-three hours deliberating, but the ex-President was exonerated on May 22. When Franklin wrote to congratulate him, he responded, "You have a right to congratulate me on the verdict because you were part of it. I shall never forget the capital way in which you gave your testimony and the impression upon the jury."[10]

On the afternoon of May 7, while the trial was still in progress, a messenger slipped into the courtroom and handed TR a telegram. A German submarine had sunk the British liner *Lusitania* off the Irish coast. Almost 1,200 people had drowned; 128 of them were Americans. The ex-President declared the sinking "piracy on a vaster scale of murder than the old-time pirates ever practiced. . . . It seems inconceivable that we can refrain from taking action in this matter, for we owe it not only to humanity but to our own national self-respect." The next day he apologized to his attorneys for having possibly damaged his

9. Franklin was a very different sort of witness from TR, who testified on his own behalf with such vigor that Barnes's attorneys had had to ask the judge to order him to "confine himself to words, and not . . . answer with his whole body." *Source:* Joseph L. Gardner, *Departing Glory,* page 330.

10. Some months later, at Oyster Bay, the subject of the libel trial came up and a friend asked TR how much in damages he had been awarded.
The colonel grinned.
"Would you mind saying that again?"
The friend did so.
"My dear fellow! *I* was the de-*fen*-dant!"
Source: Henry F. Pringle, *Theodore Roosevelt: A Biography,* page 577.

own case—there were two German-born citizens on the jury—but there were more important things than losing a libel suit. "I've got to be right in this matter," he told a friend.

Franklin certainly thought he was right.

He had believed for a year that the United States belonged in the war; that if it did not intervene to help the Allies, Germany would one day attack an isolated and unprepared America. Now he was sure of it. And he found terribly disappointing Wilson's declaration three days later that there was such a thing as "a man being too proud to fight. There is such a thing as a nation being so right that it does not need to convince others by force that it is right." Both the older and the younger Roosevelt must have agreed with the *New York Herald* headline the next morning: WHAT A PITY THEODORE ROOSEVELT IS NOT PRESIDENT!

Back in 1913, Isabella Ferguson had written Eleanor that she and Bob both hoped "Franklin may take the bull by the horns and demand and work for an adequate navy in the face of all disapproval, as Admiral Fisher did." Admiral of the Fleet Lord John Arbuthnot "Jacky" Fisher, First Sea Lord from 1904 to 1910 (and again from 1914 to 1915), had, largely through the application of his personal credo—"ruthless, relentless, remorseless"—kept the strength of the Royal Navy comfortably ahead of that of its German rival, often over the objections of politicians stung by his arrogance and lack of tact and weary of his warnings about the growing threat of war. (Even Fisher's friend and disciple, Winston Churchill, could not credit his 1914 prophecy that the Germans would one day wage unrestricted submarine warfare on commercial vessels. Such a thing was "frankly unthinkable," he told Fisher; ". . . I do not believe this would ever be done by a civilized power.")

Franklin admired Fisher as he admired his cousin, but direct confrontation was not his way; he rarely wanted to have anything to do with the bull's horns. Nor was he ever in command. Still, over the next two years, and despite the fact that he was a prominent member of the Democratic administration, Franklin would draw closer to Theodore Roosevelt's bellicose views, not further from them, would work alongside him, sometimes in secret, to ready the nation for the struggle each was uncertain President Wilson would ever willingly lead.

It was a delicate, difficult role that Franklin chose to play, demanding not only his characteristic enthusiasm and energy but also his highly developed skills at maneuver and deception.

Theodore Roosevelt had broken openly with Wilson's foreign policy back in the spring of 1914, resigning his post as associate editor of *Outlook* magazine because he felt "in honor bound to stand in strong opposition to the administration," which, in international relations, he wrote, has "meant the abandonment of the interest and honor of America." He had at first been uncharacteristically vague as to which side of the war raging in Europe he favored. "I am not taking sides . . . ," he said, when Germany first invaded Belgium. "When giants are engaged in a death wrestle, as they reel to and fro they are certain to trample on whoever gets in the way of the huge, straining combatants, *unless it is dangerous to do so.*" Only a powerful, independent defense could ensure that such accidents did not occur, he believed, and Wilson's "little arbitration treaties which promise impossibilities," negotiated by Bryan—"a professional yodeler, a human trombone"—had proved worse than useless.

Franklin never had a moment's doubt as to which side he favored. On August 19, 1914, Woodrow Wilson had called upon all Americans to remain "impartial in thought as well as action" in the interest of strict neutrality. For Franklin, that would prove an impossible request: everything in his upbringing had taught him to admire the British and despise the Germans. Even his household staff reinforced those inbred sympathies. "My new [British] governess has three brothers at the front, one wounded," Eleanor told Isabella, "so we feel rather close."

On the day Wilson declared American neutrality, Franklin wrote Bob Ferguson that he sympathized with the invalid Scottish Rough Rider's frustration at being unable to fight for Britain: "Even I long to go over into the thick of it & do something to help right the wrong. England's course has been magnificent—Oh, if that German fleet would only come out and fight!"[11]

---

11. In 1939, when FDR proclaimed that the United States would "remain a neutral nation" in the renewed struggle between Britain and Nazi Germany, he would carefully add, "but I cannot ask that every American remain neutral in thought as well."

Wilson himself was never privately neutral. The same week he called for impartiality, he told his brother-in-law, Stockton Axson, that a German triumph would be a disaster, leading to universal militarism. "The United States itself, will have to become a military nation, for Germany will push her conquests into South America, if not actually into the United States." And five months later, when Brand Whitlock, the U.S. Ambassador to Belgium, told the President he was four-square for the Allies, Wilson responded with considerable vehemence: "So am I. No decent man, knowing the situation and Germany, could be anything else. But that is only my own personal opinion and there are many others in this country who do not hold that opinion. In the West and Middle West frequently there is no opinion at all. I am not justified in forcing my opinion upon the people of the United States and bringing them into a war which they do

That summer, as Franklin had chafed at the administration's inactivity and mounted his own futile campaign for the Senate, TR stumped the country for the Progressives, and called for greatly increased American armaments. His was the loudest voice to support that cause, but two others were perhaps as effective on Capitol Hill—Senator Henry Cabot Lodge of Massachusetts, ranking member of the Senate Naval Affairs Committee, and his son-in-law from the same state, Representative Augustus P. "Gussie" Gardner, chairman of the House Military Affairs Committee.

Josephus Daniels had a grudging respect for Theodore Roosevelt, believed Lodge to be a fair man, and was himself normally both patient and forgiving, but he despised Gussie Gardner, whose prominence he believed owed very little to his own abilities and a great deal to his wealthy upbringing, his schooling at Groton and Harvard, above all to his marriage to Constance Lodge, whose father's wealthy friends could be counted on to fuel his congressional campaigns. Daniels' voluminous memoirs, published almost thirty years after he left the Navy Department, are remarkably free of rancor, but an exception was made in Gardner's case: the Massachusetts congressman had been, he said, "the most vicious assailant of the Naval establishment in Congress . . . a blatant and bitter critic." (As further evidence of his contempt for Gardner, in his diary he quoted approvingly Wilson's suggestion that the congressman should "go to hell," near-blasphemy in Daniels' pious lexicon.)

Franklin and Eleanor, on the other hand, felt "really at home" with Mrs. Henry Cabot Lodge, Eleanor wrote, and the white-bearded senator was personally cordial to them both. And Gardner and the Assistant Secretary who was twenty years his junior but otherwise identical in background and breeding genuinely liked one another—the congressman admiring young Roosevelt's brisk speed and efficiency, Franklin seeing in the older man a powerful potential ally in his behind-the-scenes struggle for a bigger Navy.

When Gardner mounted a shrill, all-out assault on the administration's military posture, alleging incompetence and inefficiency, and demanding an investigation by a special National Security Commis-

---

not understand." *Source:* Robert H. Ferrell, *Woodrow Wilson and World War I 1917–1921,* page 9; for a discussion of the Roosevelt family's feelings toward the Germans among whom they summered so often, see Geoffrey C. Ward, *Before the Trumpet: Young Franklin Roosevelt, 1882–1905,* pages 149–150n.

sion, Franklin supplied him with ammunition with which to back his charges. Just two days after Gardner launched his attack, Franklin issued on his own authority a shrewdly worded statement intended simultaneously to suggest support for the President while hinting that departmental affairs were indeed worth looking into: because the Navy was short 18,000 men, it said, thirteen of its second-line battleships were out of commission. "The enclosed is the truth," he told Eleanor, sending her a copy of his statement, "and even if it gets me into trouble I am perfectly ready to stand by it. The country needs the truth about the Army and Navy instead of a lot of the soft mush about everlasting peace which so many statesmen are handing out to a gullible public."

The press picked up the story, delighting in this evidence of dissension within the administration, and, probably at the insistence of his chief, Franklin hastily issued a half-hearted "clarification" in which he denied having "recommended" additional men, since such recommendations were not "within my province."

Wilson scoffed at Gardner's charges and refused even to consider either the greatly increased Army or the compulsory military training which TR, Lodge, and Gardner all favored in public, and which Franklin favored in private. "We shall not alter our attitude toward the question of national defense because some amongst us are nervous and excited," the President told Congress; the time had not come to "turn America into an armed camp." When Daniels appeared before the House Naval Affairs Committee a few days later, he offered a moderate, Wilsonian shipbuilding program and called for no additional men.

Franklin, appearing before the same committee a few days later, managed again through the selective use of statistics and skillful use of innuendo to undermine his chief without ever seeming openly to contradict him. Although he was careful to assert that he was not discussing policy, the inescapable conclusion to be drawn from his five hours of testimony was that the Navy was indeed undermanned, inefficient, and far from ready for action should action be called for—just as Daniels's critics charged.

He also displayed for the first time in public his extraordinary ability to overwhelm his questioners with facts and figures, absorbed through intensive last-minute briefings and retained just long enough to disarm potential antagonists. The Assistant Secretary, said the *New York Sun,* had "exhibited a grasp of naval affairs that seemed to astonish members of the committee who had been studying the question for years."

Franklin was no less delighted with his own performance: it had been "really great fun," he told Eleanor, "as the members who tried to quiz me and put me in a hole did not know much about their subject and I was able not only to parry but to come back at them with thrusts that went home. Also I was able to get in my own views without particular embarrassment to the Secretary."

"War is in all our thoughts & the horror of it grows," Eleanor told Isabella. "We are most distinctly 'not ready,' & F. tried to make his testimony before Congress very plain & I think brought out his facts clearly without saying anything about the administration policy which would, of course, be [disloyal?]."

Over the next few months, Gardner continued to attack Wilson and his Secretary of the Navy, and the Assistant Secretary continued to dine at his home and to provide him with information behind the scenes—provided the congressman agreed not to reveal his source. Years later, someone asked Daniels how he could have endured his assistant's friendship with so fierce an enemy. "I did not require," he answered, "that his friends be my friends."

Meanwhile, on January 24, 1915, the British battle cruiser fleet met and mastered a German squadron, just as Franklin had hoped it would. The next day, the Germans declared the waters surrounding Britain a war zone, and warned that their U-boats would sink any Allied ship that ventured through it: merchant ships of neutral nations would enter British waters at their own risk. Wilson warned that Germany would be held to "strict accountability" for any harm to American lives or property resulting from violation of "acknowledged [neutral] rights on the high seas." In offering that warning, he failed to make clear whether he planned to hold the Germans accountable for damage done to neutral *ships,* or to neutral passengers and goods carried on Allied ships.

Wilson still hoped and believed that America could remain above the battle. No member of his Cabinet was more fervently supportive of that hope than Josephus Daniels, and the President returned that loyalty in full measure. The unfounded story spread that in the interest of strict neutrality, Daniels had banned from all naval bases the singing of the popular British marching song "It's a Long Way to Tipperary." (Frank Cobb, the editor of the *New York World,* asked, "Why should a Navy that has Josephus Daniels for its Secretary *wish* to sing?")

At luncheon at the White House someone made light of the controversy. Wilson flushed. "I have never seen the President angry before.

I never want to see him angry again," a guest recalled. "His fist came down on the table."

"Daniels did not give the order that 'Tipperary' should not be sung in the navy," the President shouted. "He is surrounded by a network of conspiracy and of lies. His enemies are determined to ruin him. I can't be sure who they are yet, but when we do get them—God help them."

Franklin was never one of Daniels' enemies, exactly—his fondness for his chief was genuine, though tainted always with condescension and sometimes with over-eagerness to assume the older man's duties—but he was never a dependable ally, either.

In mid-May, Daniels and Franklin each addressed the same Manhattan banquet. Their hosts were the members of the Navy League, a Big Navy organization made up largely of retired admirals, the shipbuilders and munitions makers. Franklin spoke first; he clearly felt himself among friends, and went out of his way to flatter his audience. "Most of our citizens don't know what national defense means," he told his hosts, as they smoked their cigars and sipped their brandy. "Our extraordinary good fortune in our early wars has blinded us to the facts. Let us learn to trust to the judgment of the real experts, the naval officers. Let us insist that Congress shall carry out their recommendations." The Big Navy men banged the table in loud approval.

Unlike Franklin, Daniels was in enemy territory; the applause as the Secretary rose was perfunctory, and no more enthusiastic when he sat down again. He, too, favored a strong Navy, he said, but went out of his way to praise "the forward-looking Sixty-Third Congress" for concentrating upon enacting Wilson's progressive domestic program and—perhaps deliberately using one of Franklin's favorite analogies—he attacked those "depressing pessimists, who are resolved to see nothing but the hole in the donut. . . ."

The two men were publicly as cordial as ever after dinner, but one reporter present noted the substantive difference between them. The Assistant Secretary, he wrote, "seems not so self-satisfied as his chief" with regard to the Navy Department's performance.[12]

Franklin was worried that he had gone too far this time, and wrote Eleanor a relieved note from Washington a few days later: "The Sec'y is back. . . . I have only seen him for a moment and he seems cheerful

---

12. Daniels eventually refused to have anything to do with the Navy League, boycotting even its annual dinners. Franklin, on the other hand, always attended and remained on cordial terms with its president, Colonel Robert M. Thompson, throughout his own tenure at the Navy Department.

and still glad to see me!" Two days later, he dined at Daniels' home and reported that the Secretary and his wife were both "cordial (!) but no reference was made to the New York episodes."

In fact, neither Daniels' allies nor his adversaries ever fully trusted his young assistant, who then had the habit, his friend William Phillips remembered, of saying "Yes, of course," to nearly everyone, seeming to agree with each visitor, but actually speaking only "from the social compulsion to maintain a pleasant exterior." Admiral Bradley Fiske recalled leaving a letter to Daniels with Franklin, urging a greatly accelerated readiness program. He received no response from the Secretary, he remembered, but he had expected none. The Assistant Secretary, however, pronounced his letter "bully," Fiske said, and promised "that he would do what he could to secure action. Needless to say, Mr. Roosevelt never did anything at all in the matter."[13]

Franklin was playing a difficult double game, trying to remain in the good graces of the President of his party, at whose pleasure he served, without losing the affection of the kinsman he had admired since boyhood. It was increasingly clear that Wilson and Theodore Roosevelt had come to hate one another: Wilson was "the worst President by all odds since [James] Buchanan," TR said, "at heart neither a gentleman nor a real man," "a true logothete, a real sophist," "always utterly and coldly selfish," "a silly doctrinaire at all times and an utterly selfish and cold-blooded politician always." Wilson felt no more warmly toward his clamorous predecessor, but refused to reply in kind. "The way to treat an adversary like Roosevelt," he told a friend, "is to gaze at the stars over his head."

Franklin would discover during his years as Assistant Secretary that the eagerness to please which he had honed as the only son of an elderly father and a fond but critical mother, and which formed so central a part of his early charm, did not work so well when those he sought to please despised one another, as Wilson and TR did. In trying

---

13. Franklin and his chief eventually came to be of one mind about Admiral Fiske, whose self-important memoranda, usually delivered at day's end with a request for immediate action, had been a trial for both of them.

"Old man Fiske," FDR recalled in 1943, "about . . . when the Secretary was thinking of going home, almost every day would bring [Daniels] a . . . twenty-page typewritten article on armor, or some new form of machine gun . . . which no layman could possibly understand, and tell the Secretary he had to read that because he wanted action on it in the morning."

One morning, Fiske came to Franklin, asking for the Secretary's opinion on three of his latest proposals. A search of Daniels' desk failed to find any of them.

Franklin called Mrs. Daniels.

"Hmm," she said, "I think I can find them. . . . I am going up to his closet. I think they are in the right hand rear tail of his spare cutaway coat." Source: Press Conference 879 (February 12, 1943).

to win the approval of both masters, Franklin would succeed only in incurring the suspicion of each, and many years later, in a rare moment of retrospective self-criticism, he confessed to a close presidential aide that his performance at the Navy Department had in some ways been an embarrassment to him.

Sometimes the strain showed even then. One afternoon, a Navy Department aide remembered, as "Assistant Secretary Roosevelt and I were going over the mail . . . Louis Howe burst into the office, a strange gleam in his eye, to lay a calling card down on FDR's desk. It read 'Colonel Roosevelt.' Franklin . . . sprang to his feet as though Howe had exploded a bomb. 'What!' he exclaimed in alarm. . . . [It] was obvious he thought his belligerent cousin had come to the Navy Department to breathe fire at Wilsonism and demand some impetuous action. Then the door opened and in strode—not Teddy—but Harry Roosevelt . . . another cousin, with a grin on his face stretching from ear to ear." Henry Roosevelt was a captain in the U.S. Marines but a colonel in the Haitian gendarmerie, and had had the misleading cards printed up as a gag. Franklin did his best to seem amused.

On June 8, 1915, William Jennings Bryan resigned as Secretary of State, unable any longer to support an administration which in his view had abandoned genuine neutrality, firmly protesting German submarine attacks while failing to act with equal vigor against the British counterblockade of German ports that also threatened American shipping. The *Lusitania*, he pointed out, had carried munitions, which seemed to him like "putting women and children in front of an army."

Franklin was delighted to see Bryan go. "What d'y' think of W. Jay B.?" he asked Eleanor. "It is all too long to write about, but I can only say I'm disgusted clear through. J.D. will *not* resign!"[14]

And then, eager to align himself with the President's new and

14. Franklin's scorn for Bryan was based in part on genuine disagreement over policy, but some of his pleasure at the Nebraskan's departure was also the product of class. After attending a formal dinner given by Bryan's successor, the former State Department counselor, Robert W. Lansing, Franklin told Eleanor, "It was a delight to see a Secretary of State who is a gentleman and knows how to to treat Ambassadors and Ministers from other civilized nations." (Daniels, for his part, thought Lansing "meticulous, metallic and mousy.")

In 1934, faced with renewed controversy over neutrality and munitions making, FDR wrote Daniels a letter in which he said, "Would that W.J.B. had stayed on Secretary of State—the country would have been better off." Some writers have suggested this constituted a genuine change of heart about Bryan's stewardship; it seems to me more likely that he was telling his old chief what he wanted to hear. *Source:* Jonathan Daniels, *The End of Innocence*, page 177.

tougher stance, he wrote Woodrow Wilson: "I want to tell you simply that you have been in my thoughts during these days and that I realize to the full all that you have had to go through. . . . I feel most strongly that the Nation approves and sustains your course and that it is *American* in the highest sense."

A few days later, Daniels, still grieving over the departure of his old friend from an administration he believed now drifting inexorably toward war, took his assistant to lunch. As they walked toward the Hotel Shoreham, Daniels poured out his worries, and Franklin later pencilled a scornful memorandum summarizing them: "As we were walking over, Mr. Daniels talked of the difficulty of our position: that Germany might not agree to give up her submarine warfare—that if she did not & refused to do so ever so politely, what could we do? He seemed worried & bewildered, questioning without even daring to suggest to himself any answers."

"Do you think the people would stand for raising an army?" Franklin asked.

"No," Daniels replied, "it would create terrible divisions of opinion. You know, it was just that that made Bryan resign—this fear of the next step if Germany does not give in. It is a mistake to look too far ahead, to cross the bridges before we get to them; it is sufficient to take each step as it comes up."

"This reminds me," Franklin added, "that [the Secretary of War, Lindley] Garrison told me yesterday that Daniels has said to him 'I hope I shall never live to see the day when the schools of this country are used to give any form of military training—If that happens it will be proof positive that the American form of government is a failure.' "

Franklin thought this "line of talk . . . entirely typical" and entirely wrong. The President was being deprived of informed military counsel precisely because men like Daniels and Bryan found discussion of future steps "disagreeable." Daniels was right that there was no point in merely breaking off diplomatic relations—"The German submarine warfare would be conducted in the same way in violation of law & humanity"—but military and economic steps short of war could be used to demonstrate American determination. We could not go on "negotiating by notes & more notes . . . of this there is a limit—witness the War of 1812."

In this opinion, too, he echoed Theodore Roosevelt. At Sagamore Hill, some weeks after the *Lusitania* was sunk, TR and Alice were reading the newspapers in the library. She noted aloud that Wilson had sent another protest note to Germany.

"Did you notice what its serial number was?" TR asked. "I fear I have lost track myself; but I am inclined to think it is No. 11,765, Series B."

At six o'clock in the morning on July 1, 1915, the telephone rang in Louis Howe's apartment. It was Franklin: Eleanor was away at Campobello, and he had a terrific pain in his right side. His sleepy aide was unsympathetic, at first. "Oh, take a pill," he said. "It's nothing but that cherry pie and glass of milk you had for lunch [yesterday]. I told you not to eat it."

The pill did not help. Franklin called back. He could barely stand up, the pain was so intense. Howe summoned a doctor and hurried over. It was acute appendicitis, and Franklin was rushed to the Washington Naval Hospital for surgery. Eleanor took several days to reach Washington from Campobello; his mother, in New York when she got the news, was at his bedside the next evening, bringing with her a silk kimono as a gift. It was "a real beauty," Franklin told her when he felt better, ". . . and at last I have something respectable and not bulky to wear to take on visits to the country houses of my rich friends!"

He would spend most of the next two months recuperating, first at his Washington home, and then on his beloved Canadian island. Daniels, who now had to perform both his own job and his assistant's, and would have to rearrange his own summer plans, nonetheless ordered the Secretary's yacht *Dolphin* to take his stricken assistant north, accompanied by his Groton friend, George Marvin, as soon as he could comfortably travel. The Secretary returned fatherly solicitude for his subordinate's frequent disloyalty:

> The doctor has just telephoned me that your temperature is normal. . . . You can therefore make your arrangements to go to Maine as soon as the doctor will let you travel, feeling perfectly free, and it will be a pleasure for me to remain on deck. You need the salt air and bracing climate after your stay in the hospital. For the present, you need to rest and sleep, with your mother near you. Your friends will look for your early getting out and ready to play. . . . [My] love and happiness that you are getting on so finely.

Franklin lolled about the Campobello cottage for five weeks, fashioning sailboats for his children until even he wearied of it; laughing, despite his stitches, over *Ruggles of Red Gap,* sent to cheer him by the Fergusons; and exclaiming over his nine-year-old daughter's newly acquired skills in the kitchen. "This A.M. Anna had her first cooking lesson and shelled all the peas for lunch and made the bread and butter pudding and you can imagine her pride," Eleanor told Isabella in late July. "Cousin Susie says I should not take time from culture and higher mind to teach her such things, but I wish *I'd* learned young!"

While Franklin was out of action, Woodrow Wilson dramatically changed course. On July 23, he asked the Army and Navy departments to draw up plans for "an adequate defense" to be presented to Congress in December; Daniels asked Franklin to begin thinking about how work in the Navy Yards could be accelerated. Preparedness had suddenly become the President's cause—though Theodore Roosevelt dismissed his version of it as *"half-*preparedness." For the next twenty-one months, the argument within the administration would turn on the *pace* of readying for war, not its essential wisdom.

Franklin returned to the department in mid-August, eager to serve as Acting Secretary while his chief took time off, and promising Louis Howe, "That means things will hum." They did. On August 19, a German submarine sank without warning the British passenger liner *Arabic* off the Irish coast; two Americans were among the forty-four dead and, since the ship had been heading for New York and carried no contraband, Wilson considered this a deliberately unfriendly act toward neutral America. "I have seen Lansing today," Franklin wrote Eleanor, ". . . and I think the President really will act as soon as we can get the facts. But it seems very hard to wait until Germany tells us her version and I personally doubt if I should be quite so polite."

Eleanor thought the *Arabic* sinking "an outrage," too, and so did Sara. "I feel a little as TR feels, in fact, a good deal," she told her son, ". . . there is one thing that [Wilson] must remember—the time for dealing with the German criminals is over." But the German ambassador vowed that this latest sinking had been an error, contrary to orders, not to be repeated. The crisis momentarily eased.

Franklin took a plan for a Council of National Defense to oversee industrial mobilization directly to the President, only to be put off. "It seems that I can accomplish little just now as the President does not want to 'rattle the sword,' " he told Eleanor, "while Germany seems anxious to meet us more than half way, but he was interested and will I think really take it up soon."[15]

On September 2, Franklin announced on his own initiative the creation of a Naval Reserve of fifty thousand men and squadrons of private power boats. In this, he had in mind a naval version of General Leonard Wood's civilian camp for the training of Army officers at Plattsburgh, New York, to which were steadily flocking young gentlemen of his class, including Hall Roosevelt, and three of TR's own sons. (The journalist Richard Harding Davis, just back from covering the European war, took training at Plattsburgh, and recalled that his squad had included "two fox-hunting squires from Maryland, a master of fox hounds, a gentleman jockey from Boston, and two steeple-chase riders who divided between them all the cups the country offers.")

"Today I sprang an announcement," Franklin told Eleanor, "... and trust J.D. will like it! It is of the utmost importance and I have failed for a year to get him to take any action, though he has never objected to it. Now I have gone ahead and pulled the trigger myself. I suppose the bullet may bounce back on me, but it is not revolutionary nor alarmist and is just common sense."

There was no ricochet. Daniels did not oppose the Naval Reserve—in fact, he would eventually name its first seagoing trial the "John Paul Jones Cruise," angering his assistant who felt a proprietary interest and had wanted to name it himself. But Daniels did urge that the reserve be run along strict democratic lines, not as a seagoing club for Franklin's fellow yachtsmen.[16]

15. Congress eventually did create such a council, backed by a number of administration officials, of whom Franklin was only one. Nonetheless, he told a Preparedness advocate who had also urged such a body, "without intending to throw bouquets at myself, I think I am the only person in the administration who realizes the perfectly wonderful opportunities, nationally and politically to accomplish something of lasting construction." *Source:* Frank Freidel, *Franklin D. Roosevelt: The Apprenticeship,* page 255.

16. The Secretary's concern was justified. Franklin's classmate Livingston Davis, himself an enthusiastic amateur sailor, served as a scout for potential reserve officers on Franklin's behalf. Here he recommends a new acquaintance, Guy Lowell: "Harvard 1892 ... Very rich, salt-water baby, raced yachts ... [at] Kiel, Spain, and Marblehead ... has large acquaintance all over the globe has offered his services. ..."

Franklin himself concentrated his own recruiting on the most prestigious schools, assuring the chairman of the Yale *News,* for example, that he hoped "very much there will be a large number of Yale men on the cruise. ... We want to get as representative a body of men as possible." Following the first cruise, in the summer of 1916, a Harvard reserve officer wrote to thank Franklin for the good time he'd had at sea in precisely the same tone in which he would have expressed his gratitude to his host for a rewarding weekend in the country: "The cruise was not alone educational but social life was most agreeable and I formed many acquaintances

Rumors of German perfidy were everywhere. Sara breathlessly reported to Franklin that she had heard from a friend that "the big grey buildings of the German Brothers across the river from Hyde Park ... [are] full of ammunition," and that summer, when a small fire broke out at Springwood after the crew working on its remodelling had left the site for the evening—doing less than $200 damage—the *New York Times* concluded that it had been the work of German saboteurs. "No damage done," Sara told Franklin, "but it makes me sad that *anyone* c'd do such a thing."

Her friends—the wealthy, mostly Republican older men and women among whom Franklin had been raised—increasingly deplored what they saw as Wilson's timidity. "I went to tea with Mrs. [Levi] Morton [widow of the former Republican Vice President]," she reported to her son, "and she says 'people pin their faith to Franklin and feel absolutely safe where *he* is concerned, as they know he is straight and can be depended on.' I said I felt that was the best that could be said of a clever man."

In February 1916, Franklin developed still another illness, a throat infection this time, and was sent away by his physician to spend two weeks resting and breathing fresh sea air at Atlantic City under the care of his mother. It was "purgatory," he assured Eleanor; Atlantic City was "the place of departed spirits," and he was back within a week, his throat still raw.

While he was gone, Lindley Garrison resigned his post as Secretary of War because the President continued to refuse to advocate universal military training.

Like Franklin, Eleanor was torn between the President she admired and the kinsman she revered. "These have been very exciting times down here," she told Isabella, "and I am sorry to say F. has been laid up for three weeks with the nastiest kind of throat. . . . One hears so much discussion of the P. and Congress and Mr. Garrison that one hardly knows what to think. I do think Mr. Garrison has always been

---

with men of prominence . . . which I hope to retain for many years." (In 1937, FDR himself would admit, "it was just a nice yachting cruise.")

Wealthy yachtsmen knew they had a kindred spirit at the Navy Department and demanded a good deal of his attention throughout his tenure. In August of 1917, Louis Howe would report to Franklin that he was unable to respond to a request from two other prominent amateur seafarers—the department store magnate Rodman Wanamaker and Stanley Mortimer, the husband of Eleanor's Aunt Tissie—to have "semi-automatic guns" installed on their yachts. The Bureau of Ordinance reported that only two such guns had yet been delivered by the Driggs Company, and they were intended for regular naval vessels. *Sources:* Joseph William Coady, *Franklin D. Roosevelt's Early Washington Years (1913–1920)*, pages 69 and 71; FDR Press Conference, July 27, 1937; Franklin D. Roosevelt, Papers as Assistant Secretary of the Navy, FDRL.

a bit hot-tempered and autocratic but his position was very trying. Mr. Wintie Chanler blew in from Boston last night and he seemed to feel that everything the President has done is hopeless and he and Mr. Henry Adams had decided there was nothing for the P. to do but resign. Alice, I gather feels the same way, so that must be Nick [Longworth's] feeling and, I suppose, Uncle Ted's."

Franklin did not want Wilson to resign, but he continued to complain privately at the pace of Preparedness and when, perhaps at Howe's instigation, newspapers suggested that he might be in line for Garrison's job, he was not displeased. (Franklin was evidently never really in the running; Wilson named to the post the diminutive, cautious reform mayor of Cleveland, Newton D. Baker.)

Franklin's rough contemporary and counterpart at the War Department, Assistant Secretary Henry C. Breckinridge of Kentucky, had resigned alongside his chief, issuing as he left office a personal protest at Wilson's policies. Franklin and Breckinridge had watched one another carefully since their simultaneous arrival at the capital, and at fleet exercises early in their time together in Washington, they had tested one another. "We climbed, and vaulted, and lifted, and ran, and in every instance there was a tie," Franklin told Eleanor. "I am three years older, but there we were, in a perfectly even contest every time."

Their militant views matched, too: each was an ardent admirer of Theodore Roosevelt; each believed America belonged in the war. But Franklin does not seem to have considered resigning. Confrontation was not his way.[17]

John Aspinwall Roosevelt, Franklin and Eleanor's sixth and final child (and the fifth to survive), was born in Washington on March 13, 1916.

The baby's arrival was not allowed unduly to interrupt his parents' crowded schedules. He was born that evening between the time Franklin went out to dinner and when he came home again.

The first Wednesday afternoon after the baby's arrival, two sena-

17. According to Daniels, Breckinridge's dramatic exit did not have the impact the volatile young man had hoped for.

"Have you heard the sad news about Henry Breckinridge?" Kentucky Senator Ollie James asked Daniels the day after he left the War Department.

"No."

"He is suffering from a cold. He hung his head out of the window all night expecting to hear the newsboys shout, 'Henry Breckinridge has resigned. . . . The Government is in peril!' " *Source:* Jonathan Daniels, *The End of Innocence*, page 184.

tors' wives arrived downstairs for tea. The Roosevelt butler explained that Mrs. Roosevelt might not be able to see them, but he would check with her maid. He hurried upstairs while the ladies waited, still wearing their coats and a little put out. It was Wednesday, receiving day, after all.

The butler returned. Would the ladies please follow him upstairs? They did so, still baffled, and found Eleanor propped up in bed, her newborn son in her arms. Only his arrival, she earnestly explained to her visitors, had kept her from being downstairs to serve them tea.

She seems to have been less anxious about the birth of this baby than any of the others. Childbirth now held fewer terrors for her than it once had; Sara was not even summoned for the lying-in.[18]

But there may have been another reason for her increased calm, as well. It had always been Franklin's hope that he would one day have six children, the same number that had crowded the home of his cousin, Theodore. This stringent requirement had been one of the things that had persuaded the beautiful Alice Sohier to reject his proposal of marriage in 1902, before he began to court his plainer cousin.

While there is no certain evidence that any such bargain was struck before she and Franklin were married, Eleanor had now herself given birth to six babies (five of whom had survived), and the Roosevelts would not have any more.

The sleeping arrangements in the new Springwood, completed that year, implied at least that they would help ensure this by occupying separate bedrooms. There were three bedrooms above the big new library, two large and one small. Sara occupied one of the large ones; her son had the other. Eleanor slept in the third.[19]

18. Still, displaced not only by nurses and Sara but also by her own inborn insecurity, her continuing sense that they, not she, must know best, Eleanor had not found for herself a fulfilling domestic role; she still seemed to belong nowhere, to have no clear emotional role to play within her family. Less than three weeks after John was born, Franklin took Anna and James to Hyde Park for a visit. "Wee babs [John] is getting so cunning and now has a bath in his rubber tub," Eleanor wrote to Anna, "& Miss Spring says *she* knows [author's italics] you'll love to see him."

Eleanor didn't know how Anna would feel; only Miss Spring did. Perhaps she wasn't sure how she felt herself. *Source:* Bernard Asbell, ed., *Mother and Daughter: The Letters of Eleanor and Anna Roosevelt,* page 15.

19. At the very end of her life, Eleanor would carefully explain that it had only been her husband's infantile paralysis in 1921 that had separated her from him at night. Until then, she wrote, "he and I had shared a bedroom in the new wing, directly over the big library–living room; after his illness, I took the small neighboring room, and his mother made the sitting room of our suite into a bedroom for herself."

I suspect this is not strictly true, but rather was her effort to provide the most palatable possible answer to the questions of postwar Springwood visitors, many of whom were genuinely puzzled by her oddly spartan sleeping arrangements. The story of Franklin's romance with Lucy Mercer

Such abstinence by couples who did not wish more children was common in 1916, when birth control was still forbidden by the Episcopal Church and made illegal by state statute.[20] But beyond that, it may have come as a relief to Eleanor, who had always seen sex as an ordeal, devoid of pleasure.

The decade during which, Eleanor herself once wrote, "I was always just getting over a baby or about to have one" was over, and according to Anna, her mother said "that was the end of any marital relationship, period."

Franklin was just thirty-four years old and still so youthful-looking that a testy Wisconsin congressman ordered him to stub out his cigarette while he waited to testify before a House subcommittee, later apologizing that he'd mistaken the Assistant Secretary for a junior clerk.

But his impact on women was now considerable. The air of fragility that had once made his Oyster Bay cousins call him "Miss Nancy" and "the feather-duster" behind his back was largely gone. Bamie called him "my debonair young cousin," and her elderly husband, Admiral W. Sheffield Cowles, teased him that "the girls will spoil you soon enough, Franklin, and I leave you to them." An especially fervid Sunday feature writer described him as he stood in his office one winter afternoon, leaning easily on the mantelpiece in front of a blazing fire, a bronze bust of John Paul Jones looking on over his shoulder; the reporter thought he presented an altogether "engaging picture of American manhood":

---

was not yet widely known; nor did most people outside the Roosevelts' circle understand how rarely she stayed in her mother-in-law's house after Val-Kill, her own Hyde Park cottage, was completed in 1925.

More important perhaps, her assertion goes in the face of two letters written to Franklin by his mother more than two years before his illness: in the first, written on June 14, 1918, she writes of buying a new desk for "her" (Eleanor's) room; in the second, written about a year later, Sara refers to the two big rooms as "yours and mine" (see below, footnote, page 460). *Sources:* Eleanor Roosevelt, "I Remember Hyde Park," *McCall's* (February 1963); Roosevelt Family Papers Donated by the Children, FDRL.

20. "Contraception was just never mentioned," Alice Longworth remembered. "I had a most wonderful German doctor, Dr. Sophie Nordhoff-Jung, and she knew a good deal on the subject, but most of my contemporaries were far too shy even to ask their doctors about such matters. I think most American doctors of the time would have been absolutely horrified, fearing lawsuits. . . . But not dear Dr. Sophie. I still have a letter written to me shortly after I was married by my sister-in-law, Nan Wallingford, who was then the mother of three. In it she begged me to send her 'one of those cunning, labor-saving devices' so that she might save her 'tottering reason.'" *Source:* Michael Teague, *Mrs. L.,* page 57.

Through the wide windows rays of dazzling light, reflected from the snow-clad expanse of the White House grounds across the street, caught the clean lines of his face and figure and threw them into sharp relief. They, the air of alertness they conveyed, the natural pose, were the sort of thing one sees in the work of American illustrators more often than in real life. The face was particularly interesting. Breeding showed there. Clearly cut features, a small, sensitive mouth, tiny lines running from nostrils to the outer lines of the lips, a broad forehead, close-cropped brown hair, frank, blue, eyes, but above all, the proud, straight upstanding set of the head placed the man.

A Washington hostess remembered him from his time at the Navy Department as the most "desirable" man she had ever met, and a San Francisco society woman who met Franklin and Bill Phillips during their visit to the Panama-Pacific Exposition recalled that "they were the most magnetic young men I ever saw. I had no *idea* that the Democratic Party ever recruited that type of person."

In June, Eleanor and the children left as usual to spend the summer at Campobello. During the summers, out from under Eleanor's constraints, Franklin could relax, could revert to being what she once called "a typical Metropolitan Club young man," bibulous, carefree, sometimes surrounded by pretty girls.

This was not the impression Franklin liked to convey to his wife and mother. "I long so to be with you," he told Eleanor, ". . . this bachelor life isn't what it's cracked up to be." To hear him tell it, Franklin's life as a summer bachelor was chaste and uneventful, filled mostly with toil performed bravely despite the humid heat that made sleep difficult. "I took two cold baths and changed my pyjamas three times and finally found two bats in the room!" he reported to Eleanor during his first summer in Washington. "So I moved into the middle room with a sheet and managed to get about four hours. . . ."[21]

---

21. Eleanor rarely expressed much sympathy with her husband's complaints about the heat. Sara was more solicitous and offered counsel as to how best to deal with it:

> The heat must be pretty bad, but after all it hurts no one if one chooses to take proper care of oneself as to liver & kidneys. Your grandfather [Warren Delano II] lived in a climate [Canton, China] where he had nine months of heat, much of it damp & sticky & intense heat night & day without a let-up from the age of *21 to 33*. He started in doing what all his friends did & found he was not well, so he adopted his own wise rules & kept well. This has always made me feel that what we could do for ourselves is what counts & I feel sure you must realize it after your serious illness in New York when your liver was in a pretty bad condition. [Evidently a reference to the jaundice her son suffered on the eve of the announcement of his engagement in the fall of 1904.]

Source: Roosevelt Family Papers Donated by the Children, FDRL.

There were social engagements, usually written up in the same world-weary, misleading tone he had used when describing to his mother the parties and dances he attended as a Groton schoolboy. Everything was pretty boring, he seemed to say; no one need worry that he was having *too* much fun:

> Dearest Babs—
>
> Yesterday I had a very busy time as the Secretary went to Annapolis & left me about a thousand loose ends to tie up. I stayed here until just in time to dress for dinner & went out to Chevy Chase with [Rear Admiral and Mrs. Victor Blue]—a nice dinner of ten—Comte . . . de la Rocca (or something similar), and Mrs. Emory, a Norwegian . . . & a Miss Somebody, friend of Belle Hager's—also an unknown female. Everybody danced afterwards, except self who lost his nerve, & Mrs. Blue & the Miss Somebody who had a sore on her leg—so I had a peaceful evening & really enjoyed watching the antics of the 3 or 4 hundred other bipeds on the floor. . . . Am feeling very fit & going to bed early. Kiss the chicks. . . .
>
> Your devoted
F.

In fact, Franklin almost always had a good time, whatever he was doing, and there were events he did not bother to report to Campobello. In late June, for example, he told his wife that he was coming north to attend the Hyde Park wedding of Elihu Root's niece, Ruth Wales, to his Harvard classmate, Harry DuPont, but he did not bother to explain that he planned to stop on the way at the New York Harvard Club for the festivities marking Harvard's triumph in the annual Harvard-Yale Boat Race. Nigel Law, a young British diplomat eight years younger than he, came along and much later remembered the fun they'd had that night:

> It was naturally a gay evening. Someone suggested that we should go over to the Yale Club and give them a friendly cheer. A party of us with linked arms, every other man carrying a bottle of champagne, set off. Arrived there, we found that all members had gone to bed except two who from the balcony had heard our approach. (I think we had a rudimentary brass band with us.) The two Yale men, with most hospitable courtesy, asked us all in for a drink. . . .
>
> We then all went away, Franklin and I to spend the night or what was left of it, at a hotel. The following morning we were called at 5 a.m. and set out for the Hudson River, where we embarked on the *U.S. Torpedo Boat. Destroyer No. 59.* Franklin, as Assistant Secretary of the Navy, then

took charge and we proceeded up the Hudson at such speed that our wash nearly sank some barges moored to the bank.

The only breaks in Franklin's daily routine, his letters implied, were golf at dawn on the Chevy Chase course, poker at the Metropolitan Club, and solitary midnight drives out into the countryside in the family's new Fiat to escape the heat.

These drives were curtailed in mid-August, to Franklin's fury, when his chauffeur, Henry Golden, smashed up the automobile, breaking his leg in the process. Franklin was "mad clear through," he told Eleanor, and asked Louis to look into what had happened. "I think our nice Golden has been a weak, miserable wretch," Franklin reported; he had cheated his employer on repairs, gasoline, and tires, and "I think he was joy-riding last Sunday night and that others were in the car and were hurt too. I am now looking up other patients in other hospitals. If so, of course, I get no insurance and the car is pretty badly smashed, as it turned completely over. . . ."

Louis pieced together what had happened. Golden, whose chronically ailing wife had been a subject of special concern to Eleanor, had become interested in other women:

> One . . . in particular took a great liking to him at first, and he went joy riding . . . with the usual high-balls needed to prove oneself "a good fellow," then the skirt got her grip on him and he started to slide faster. . . . As he got in deeper and the girl demanded more he began to drink more. . . . Then the smash came and as soon as that happened, the girl shook him. . . . His anxiety as to whether his wife knew about the girl is a good sign. No man is beyond redemption as long as he don't want his wife to find out.

After paying Golden's medical bills, Franklin fired him.

"Isn't it horrid to be disappointed in someone," Eleanor wrote her husband when she heard about Golden, ". . . it makes one so suspicious!"

Perhaps she may have felt in the revelation of the chauffeur's infidelities echoes of her own fears about Franklin's faithfulness, fears which had beset her on her honeymoon and had never entirely lifted. If so, the fact that she had to spend nearly four months away from him that summer, instead of the usual two, can only have made matters worse.

Infantile paralysis raged along the East Coast in the summer of

1916. Twenty-seven thousand Americans were affected. Nothing like it had ever been seen before. Medical authorities were baffled, both as to its causes and its special virulence; the consensus seemed to be that the long damp spring had something to do with it. The epidemic hit New York the hardest—there were 19,000 cases in the city, 2,448 of them fatal—but it was already spreading outward from the cities by July. When desperate New York parents tried to spirit their children out of town, they were turned back unless they had a certificate of good health signed by a physician; at small-town depots, hand-lettered signs greeted those who did manage to escape: NEW YORKERS KEEP OUT. WE SYMPATHIZE BUT WE HAVE CHILDREN.

Before Franklin managed a few precious days on the island late that month, his mother, still in Hyde Park, told him that her friend and neighbor Mrs. Tracy Dows was "not allowing [her children] *off the place* at all, on account of the infantile paralysis epidemic which might come into the country. The doctors advise this course. There are 4 cases in Poughkeepsie, brought from Brooklyn. When you go to Campobello, you ought not to kiss the children till you have washed and disinfected (nose and mouth especially) as it can be carried from people one meets traveling."

Franklin spent part of his short stay on the island swatting the scores of buzzing flies that congregated in one sunny window of the cottage—one theory held that flies carried the infectious germ—and when he got back to Washington, they were still on his mind: "The infantile paralysis in N.Y. and vicinity is appalling. *Please* kill all the flies I left. I think it really important." Eleanor and the children did their best to comply.

The epidemic on the mainland worsened. Sara wrote her son from Campobello that "this awful disease . . . is spreading. I trust our island will be 'immune.' " Campobello did prove immune, but in August, the disease intruded upon Springwood itself: Mildred Butler, the three-year-old daughter of Sara's coachman, was stricken. (She would fully recover.)

In late August, Franklin wrote to Eleanor:

> The Sec'y was accused in Congress of intention to use [the official Secretarial yacht] *Dolphin* to campaign in Maine—hence he is scared blue and *Dolphin* won't be allowed within 1,000 miles of Maine till after September 11. I think *then* the Sec'y will use her for a week or so & I might get her about the 20th. I am really upset at the thought of bringing

you all down by rail. There is much I.P. in Boston, Springfield, Worcester, etc. & even in Rockland & other *Maine* points. Also the various villages are keeping motorists with children out & it would be difficult to get to [Hyde Park] by motor, even if mine were in shape. It will take at least a month of repairs.

Franklin did not arrive on the island to pick up his family until the end of September. The voyage south to Hyde Park took three days, made memorable for the commander of the *Dolphin*, William D. Leahy, by the turbulent Roosevelt children—"brats" he called them privately thirty-two years later—who roamed the deck and banged in and out of the pilot house without an admonitory word from their parents, and interrupted by a short stop in New York Harbor so that the family doctor could be rowed out to look over the baby, whose heart had seemed irregular to his anxious mother. (It was not.)

Franklin gave Sara strict instructions as to how the family was to avoid infection between the landing just below her house and the safe haven of Springwood itself: "By [the time we arrive] I hope all will be fumigated, but anyway whether it is or not I think the children ought not to go in any of our autos or carriages or sit behind Butler. Therefore, could not Rosy or his man come down to the River to bring up Eleanor, Caton [the childrens' latest English nurse], FDR, Jr. and [John Roosevelt]. The rest of us can walk!"

Seven thousand people died of polio that summer, almost all of them children.

The Roosevelts returned to Washington unscathed.

Had there been no epidemic, Franklin would still have seen little of his family in the summer of 1916. It was a presidential year, and as a Roosevelt who both believed in Preparedness and was at least publicly loyal to Wilson, he was especially useful to the embattled administration. He spent much of his time campaigning, "more out of Washington than in," Eleanor told Isabella, touring northeastern states with large naval installations.

It was an uphill struggle. The country was still overwhelmingly Republican. Wilson had owed his narrow 1912 victory to the fact that the opposition had been fatally split between the regular Republicans, led by Taft, and the Progressives and their champion, Theodore Roosevelt. In December 1915, he had called for a greatly expanded defense program—including $500 million to build a Navy "second to none"—but Congress had been slow to enact it and many voters, especially in the Midwest, where pro-German sentiment was strong, were alarmed by the President's new stridency. Wilson's recent remarriage, too, had been thought unseemly by some because his courtship of Edith Galt, the widow of a Washington jeweler, had begun less than seven months after his first wife's death.

And no one knew what Theodore Roosevelt was going to do. TR himself did not know. "*I most earnestly* hope the Republicans will *not* nominate me," he had told Bamie early in the year, "for my belief is that the country is not in a heroic mood; and unless it *is* heroic and willing to put honor and duty ahead of safety, I would be beaten if nominated." Nor did he wish to make a second Wilson victory possible by another futile run as a Progressive. But he did want desperately to be President again, and thought he might be able to make it if he could somehow simultaneously win both the Republican and Progressive nominations in June.

In this, he underestimated the residual hatred the old guard felt for him. Only the Progressives nominated him in the end, and he turned them down, urging instead that they support the the Republican nominee, Justice Charles Evans Hughes of the Supreme Court, a former governor of New York, so handsome in his silvery whiskers and so prim in manner that TR had once dismissed him as "the bearded lady." He and the Colonel had once been friends and political allies, but after Hughes abandoned progressive politics for the bench in 1910, and later refused to testify on TR's behalf in the Barnes trial, relations between the two men had been severely strained. TR now determined to overlook all that and to campaign hard for him, even though the Republican platform called for strict neutrality: "At his worst [Hughes] will do better than Wilson," he told friends, "and there is always the chance that he will do very well indeed."

"Theodore," a tearful Corinne Robinson told her brother, "the people wanted you." TR smiled ruefully: "Do not say that; if they had wanted me *hard* enough, they could have had me." He was more blunt with Bamie: "Well, the country wasn't in a heroic mood! We are passing through a thick streak of yellow in our national life."

Meanwhile, in an effort further to undermine the Colonel and to woo his old followers, Wilson had done his best to implement the most important planks in the 1912 Progressive platform, backing domestic legislation that he had once opposed as "unwise and unjustifiable" because it tended to favor "a single class of the community"—low-cost loans for farmers, a ban on interstate traffic in goods manufactured by workers under sixteen, an eight-hour day for railroad workers, a tariff commission to systematize national trade policy.

He had also appalled conservatives and pleased progressives in both parties by naming to the Supreme Court Louis D. Brandeis, a stalwart liberal and the first Jew ever to be appointed to that bench. The battle over Brandeis's nomination had been bitter and prolonged, suffused with the crudest kind of anti-Semitism. What the young Roosevelts thought of the Brandeis appointment at the time is not known; Franklin much later paid tribute to the justice's liberalism, but both he and Eleanor were in 1916 close to Franklin K. Lane, who had himself lobbied quietly for the seat.[22]

Although Franklin had nothing to do with Wilson's new domestic program, he believed it both solidly in the Theodore Roosevelt tradition and good presidential politics. Still, he sometimes found himself hard-pressed to defend it within the family. One summer evening in New York he took time out from campaigning to accompany his mother to dinner at the East 69th Street home of his uncle, Warren Delano III, his mother's white-bearded eldest brother, who had inherited his late father's implacable Republicanism as well as a handsome share of his fortune, and who had at least qualified access to the far larger inheritance of his wife, Jennie Walters, as well.[23]

Sara's sister, Dora Forbes, was present too, visiting from Paris. Franklin managed to steer the conversation away from Wilson's domestic program until after dinner, he reported to Eleanor, but then his host erupted against the Democratic administration and the dangerous radicalism he believed it actively encouraged. "Uncle Warren gave the

22. Two years later, after the financier Bernard Baruch had been appointed chairman of the powerful War Industries Board, and the Roosevelts' good friend Cecil Spring-Rice, the British ambassador, had been replaced by Lord Reading, also a Jew, Eleanor reported approvingly to Bob Ferguson a remark of Henry Adams: "Jews are trumps just now!" *Source:* Ferguson Family Correspondence, Arizona State Historical Society, Tucson.

23. She had initially been disinherited by her eccentric, widowed father, William Thompson Walters, for having dared leave his household to marry. The old man had left his huge fortune to his son, Henry, but he, in turn, had generously divided it with his sister when his brother-in-law went broke in the coke business.

Jennie Walters Delano was a vast, bosomy woman, who rarely let anyone forget for long that her father's fortune, not her husband's industry, was the source of the family's very considerable comfort. Her size was a source of special amusement to Franklin. In August 1916, he got word that her son-in-law, Frederick B. Adams, planned to bring her upriver to Hyde Park in his yacht. "Some undertaking," Franklin wrote Eleanor. "I hear Fred is to enlarge his boat." *Sources:* Interview with Laura Franklin Delano Adams Eastman; Elliott Roosevelt, ed., *FDR: His Personal Letters, 1905–1928,* pages 324–325. For the story of the curious Delano-Walters courtship, see Geoffrey C. Ward, *Before the Trumpet: Young Franklin Roosevelt, 1882–1905,* pages 100–102.

usual line of talk 'agin' the government,' " Franklin reported to Eleanor, "and I delivered eulogy per contra. Think it did Aunt Doe good at least!"

There was a new militance to Wilson's public appearances that summer. On Flag Day, June 14, Preparedness parades were held in half a dozen Eastern cities. Wilson led the Washington procession himself, marching at its head, a flag over his shoulder. Franklin marched, too. "The Navy Department made an excellent showing," he told Eleanor, "[and when] I passed the President's reviewing stand I was sent for to join them in the stand and spent the next four hours there!" (This may have been evidence more of Wilson's political canniness than his personal enthusiasm for the Assistant Secretary. Theodore Roosevelt was almost daily questioning the sincerity of his devotion to a strong defense, and the newspapers the next day would feature photographs of the President standing four-square for Preparedness, a grinning *Democratic* Roosevelt at his side.)

Wilson planned to have his party's convention also stress his new-found toughness. But the address by the convention chairman, Senator Ollie M. James of Kentucky, struck a different, more responsive note, exalting the President as a peacemaker for wringing "from the most militant spirit that ever brooded above a battlefield an acknowledgement of American rights and an agreement to American demands . . . without orphaning a single American child, without widowing a single American mother, without firing a single shot, without the shedding of a single drop of blood. . . ."

The delegates cheered for twenty minutes, and Wilson emerged as his party's nominee with a new slogan: "He kept us out of War." The President himself was a little uncomfortable with it—"I can't keep the country out of war," he confessed to a member of his Cabinet. "Any little German lieutenant can put us into war at any time by some calculated outrage"—but he was shrewd enough to see its potential power at the polls.

Hughes proved a pallid, reticent candidate, who tried to remain faithful to his party's pledge of strict neutrality, but was quickly eclipsed by TR and his other interventionist supporters; by midsummer he was promising greater "firmness" than Wilson had displayed when dealing with the Germans.

Daniels was a special Republican target: billboards in Eastern cities warned that "A Vote for Wilson Is a Vote for Daniels," and the new Mrs. Wilson and the shadowy Colonel House both sought behind the scenes to jettison him. Wilson would not hear of it: Daniels was loyal, able, and represented his last link with the Bryan wing of the party. "I know of no one," the President told him, "I trust more entirely or affectionately."

The Secretary characteristically rode out the storm in silence:

> I made it a rule from the first never to reply to critics, but to content myself with clear statements of policies. There were no serious criticisms until I denied lush profiteering to the armor-plate, smokeless powder and other trusts which had been robbing Uncle Sam; until I thwarted the well-oiled lobby determined to exploit the Navy oil reserves; until I put an end to drinking on Navy ships and shore stations; introduced a measure (too small) of democracy and promotion by merit . . . and refused to abdicate and let officers enamoured of Prussianism run the Navy.

When Hughes himself sneered at Daniels for his efforts at educating sailors as well as training them for life at sea—"we must pay less attention to punctuation and more to targets"—Franklin was given the job of firing back. "Does Mr. Hughes not know what the Navy knew, that the Navy in march 1913 was a hollow shell, and that complete reorganization was imperative?" he asked. " . . . I can show him millions of dollars, item by item, saved through common-sense business organization, I can show him an organization that would not break down in case of war. I can show him long-range shooting with big guns that has surprised and delighted every officer in the fleet. . . . The navy is growing; it must grow more. It is using the appropriations widely and honestly. All it needs now is boosting, not knocking."

A few days later, he added that "Misquotations and misrepresentations—yea, *lies*—have been used by the President's opponents. I say 'lies' because this is a good 'Roosevelt' word to use."

He even indirectly defended his chief before the Navy League—at a dinner which Daniels himself declined to attend: "Every minute taken up in perfectly futile and useless arguments about mistakes in the past slows up construction. . . . Worse than that, it blinds and befogs the public as to the real situation and the imperative necessity for prompt action. How would you expect the public to be convinced that a dangerous fire was in progress, requiring every citizen's aid for its extinguishment, if they saw the members of the volunteer fire department stop in their headlong rush toward the conflagration and indulge in a slanging match as to who was responsible for the rotten hose or lack of water at a fire a week ago?"[24]

Franklin's election-year enthusiasm for the Navy Department whose policies he had so recently deplored in private led him in one springtime speech incautiously to attack the record of Theodore Roosevelt himself—who, perhaps not coincidentally, was out of the country, sailing with his wife in the Caribbean at the time. When TR had sent the Great White Fleet on its world cruise in 1907, Franklin charged, its sixteen battleships had been fitted out at the expense of the rest of the Navy; it had been necessary to "strip many other vessels of their officers," he said, "and, to borrow, here, there, and the other place." When the older Roosevelt got back, he responded to his young cousin's criticism with a reprimand made all the more devastating for its uncharacteristic gentleness. "My memory was not in accord with the statement as you made it," he told Franklin, and he had taken the trouble to check that memory with a well-informed veteran officer who agreed with him. Franklin was embarrassed, apologized abjectly, swore he had "tried right along to give only correct facts," and promised to "take the first opportunity to say something about the correct figures. . . ."

The odds still seemed to favor Hughes, but Franklin did his cheerful best to keep up Democratic morale. After visiting Maine (where state elections were held on September 11, nearly two months before the rest of the country voted), he told reporters that he had surveyed "a large number of men . . . factory hands, mechanics, and storekeepers [who] were regular Republicans who had never voted for a Democrat. These men did not wish to announce publicly that they would vote for Wilson, but told me that this was their present intention. . . ." These newly minted Wilsonians did not turn up at the polls on Election Day; Maine went Republican as usual, as would all the states in which Franklin campaigned.[25]

24. That hose would reappear in FDR's rhetoric twenty-four years later, when the President used it to explain the idea of lending arms to embattled Britain.

25. FDR would hone this technique of the phantom poll that invariably backed his own view while in the White House. His actual contacts with ordinary Americans were always severely limited, first by the dictates of his class and, later, by his relative immobility.

This never stopped him from claiming all sorts of close friendships with visitors—a Chinese laundryman, a baseball player, a dirt farmer, a garage mechanic—who "dropped in" for convenient chats, but whose visits somehow escaped the notice of his staff.

As the campaign ground to its conclusion, Theodore Roosevelt outdid even himself in the violence of his denunciatory language. Wilson had spent part of the summer in a rented cottage called Shadow Lawn on the Jersey shore, providing TR with the theme for an especially savage assault four days before Election Day:

> There should be shadows enough at Shadow Lawn, the shadows of men, women, and children who have risen from the ooze of the ocean bottom and from graves in foreign lands; the shadows of the helpless whom Mr. Wilson did not dare protect lest he might have to face danger; the shadows of babies gasping pitifully as they sank under the waves. ... Those are the shadows proper for Shadow Lawn; the shadows of deeds that were never done; the shadows of lofty words that were followed by no action; the shadows of the tortured dead.

Even Wilson had come to believe that he could not win, and on election night the early returns seemed to bear him out. Hughes easily carried the Eastern states, and Franklin left New York Democratic Headquarters at the Biltmore at midnight and hurried to catch the last train back to Washington with his friend Secretary Lane, certain that Wilson had lost and joking a little wanly that he and the State Department counselor Frank Polk, a fellow Grotonian and Harvard man, would form a new law firm and be back practicing in Wall Street by spring. (Hughes thought he had won, too, and went to bed early so that he would be well rested when he met the press the next morning as President-elect. "The President cannot be disturbed," his son is supposed to have told an early morning caller.)

But the next day, back at his Navy Department desk, Franklin scrawled an exultant note to "Dearest Babs": "The most extraordinary day of my life. After last night, Wilson may be elected after all. It looks hopeful at noon." It continued to look hopeful, as the Western and

---

Merriman Smith, the veteran UPI reporter, once called him on it.

The garage mechanic, FDR told one wartime press conference, had complained to him that his wife was unhappy over the high price of strawberries in February. Why waste money on such extravagances, the President said he had told his visitor; such extravagance only made it harder to hold the line on prices.

Six months later, FDR told the same reporters that a mechanic had come in to convey his wife's complaint about the high price of asparagus out of season. Why didn't they eat something else? he said he'd answered. Why contribute to inflation by wasting their ... wages on unnecessary luxury items?

Smith raised his hand and asked if that was the same mechanic who had come in a few months earlier complaining about the price of strawberries.

The press conference exploded in laughter. FDR laughed, too: "My God, Merriman. It's true. It *is* true. It was the same man!" *Source:* A. Merriman Smith, *Thank You, Mr. President,* pages 73–74.

Midwestern votes rolled in, slowly erasing Hughes's lead. California finally tipped the balance, and Franklin told Eleanor that he had framed a victory telegram that he would have liked to send to his irascible Republican uncle:

W. DELANO

BARRYTOWN

THE REPUBLICAN PARTY HAS PROVED TO ITS OWN SATISFACTION I HOPE THAT THE AMERICAN PEOPLE CANNOT ALWAYS BE BOUGHT.

FDR[26]

In the same letter, he returned to a familiar theme: "I have any amount of work to do and J.D. is too damned slow for words—his failure to decide the few big things holds me up all down the line."

"Toward the end of January, 1917," FDR wrote in an unpublished memorandum dictated in the White House, "I decided that it was time to inspect the occupation of Haiti and Santo Domingo by the United States Marines." In fact, the decision had been his chief's, not his, to make, and it had taken him some time to persuade Daniels that he should be permitted to undertake what would amount to a paid Caribbean holiday.

His mother had objected to the trip, worried about political unrest on the island and concerned that the glaring tropical sun would worsen his nearsightedness. Eleanor tried to reassure her: "I think F. is tired and needs the change. Also, it is good for all men, young men especially, I imagine, to occasionally do something with a spice of risk in it. Otherwise they lose the love of it." Sara, unpersuaded but acquiescent, insisted that Franklin promise to wear dark glasses and a pith helmet.

The Marines were now in charge of both halves of the Caribbean island of Hispaniola, and the Navy Department, of course, was in charge of the Marines. There had been at least seven bloody revolutions in Haiti since 1902. A tiny, educated Haitian elite profited from the misery of their two million fellow countrymen, in collusion with

---

26. He was so jubilant over Wilson's triumph that he even dared make a barbed joke about Theodore Roosevelt to a reporter. "It is rumored," he said, "that a certain distinguished cousin of mine is now engaged in revising an edition of his most famous historical work, *The Winning of the West.*"

the Frenchmen who controlled its finances and the Germans who had taken over the railroads and retail trade, and had helped arm the hundreds of *cacos*, jungle-dwelling mercenaries, whose machetes were for hire by any would-be President willing to pay their daily rates. Finally, in July of 1915, after President Guillaume Sam had ordered the massacre of 167 prisoners loyal to the regime he had only recently overthrown, a Port-au-Prince mob retaliated, chasing the President into the French Legation, dragging him out from behind a bedroom dresser, hacking him into six pieces and parading them separately around the city.

President Wilson, worried that European powers might intervene if such chaos was allowed to continue too long, ordered Daniels to send in the Marines. Franklin had been at Campobello when that order came, still recuperating from appendicitis, much to his chagrin. "It is certainly a curious coincidence that as soon as I go away we seem to land marines somewhere," he told his chief.

The Marines restored order, subdued the *cacos*, and compelled the Haitians to accept a treaty which permitted the American President to appoint officials to supervise island finances, public works, public health, and the police, and to agree to a Constitution which made their half of Hispaniola virtually an American protectorate. (A cable from the commander in the field to Daniels suggests the character of the intervention: NEXT THURSDAY . . . UNLESS OTHERWISE DIRECTED, I WILL PERMIT [THE HAITIAN] CONGRESS TO ELECT A PRESIDENT.)

Daniels was uneasy, both with the occupation of Haiti and with the 1916 seizure of the Dominican Republic, and he was not amused when Franklin's jocular friend, Secretary of the Interior Lane, took to greeting him at Cabinet meetings with "Hail, the King of Haiti!" He felt that the American occupation of Hispaniola, whatever its initial motivation, smacked of just the sort of imperialism he had always opposed. The whole Caribbean adventure, he told Franklin, "was a bitter pill."

It was nothing of the kind for his assistant, itching to see action, enamored of the same kind of overseas adventuring that so appealed to his Cousin Theodore, persuaded that the United States needed to play an active role in the Caribbean to keep out the European powers.

Franklin was eager to get started on what he termed his venture into the "Darkest Africa of the West Indies." Major General George Barnett, the Marine commandant, accompanied him; so did John A. McIlhenny, a frequent golf partner and chairman of the Civil Service Commission, and George Marvin, his old friend and former schoolmaster, now assistant editor of the *World's Work* and already lapsing into the alcoholism that would ruin his career.[27]

Franklin had hoped that the reform mayor of New York, John Purroy Mitchel, would also join the party; he thought Mitchel would enjoy it, he said, "especially as we shall have the opportunity to call on their Excellencies, the Presidents of Cuba, Haiti and Santo Domingo. I am told only one of them is coal black." But Mitchel's schedule had not permitted him to take time off.

Livingston Davis found the time. Livy's fondness for Franklin bordered on adoration. Taller and beefier than his famous friend, with a carefully trimmed black mustache, he was equally handsome and high-spirited, and he shared Franklin's enthusiasm for golf, for yachting, and for the sort of convivial evenings favored by Harvard clubmen. Davis had married well after college, and had settled into a lucrative if unexciting life as a Boston broker, but he was always ready to drop whatever he was doing if an invitation arrived from the illustrious classmate whose success he surely admired and may secretly have wished to share.

Livy thought the itinerary Franklin had drawn up—travelling by destroyer, first to Havana, then to Haiti, crossing the island from Port-au-Prince to Cap Haitien on horseback, then on by boat to Santo Domingo—was "superb." Then he added, "I have heard tales of a very risqué theatre in Havana which if true should be too good to miss. Tell George Marvin [who was to arrive in Cuba first] to investigate, and procure tickets . . . I will be host for the crowd."

That was the sort of contribution Livy liked to make to his friend's well-being; he was "your jolly boy," he once told Franklin, ever eager to help provide a good time.

From the first, the members of the Roosevelt party enjoyed themselves. On their first night in Havana, according to Livy's diary, they consumed "several rounds of delicious daquiries," dined on the hotel roof, "after which we were entertained by a special performance of Spanish dancers, then proceeded to the theatre to witness Tortola

---

27. Marvin became one of many old friends to whom the Roosevelts remained loyal despite his weaknesses. His drinking drove him from job to job for years; loans from Eleanor and Franklin kept him alive and they several times pulled strings to find him positions they thought he might be able to fill. At the end of her life, Eleanor kept two old letters in her Val-Kill desk: one, from her long-time secretary Malvina Thompson, renewed what she called her "yearly pledge of my devotion to you," to which her employer had added, "a pledge always kept." There was a note from Marvin, too, promising to reform, on which Eleanor had written, "a pledge broken within a month." *Source:* Joseph P. Lash, *Eleanor: The Years Alone,* pages 237–238.

Valencia in some wonderful dancing." At intermission, they stepped out to the Gallego Club for more drinks, and later continued on to a café for several more early morning rounds. (They evidently never got to the "very risqué theatre" to which Davis had so looked forward, perhaps because they had been joined at the last moment by another friend of Franklin's, Lucien Kinsolving, the Episcopal bishop of Southern Brazil.)

The next morning, hung-over but "silk hatted, frock coated, etc.," Franklin managed to complete a formal call upon President Mario Garcia Menocal and was gratified that the Cuban chief executive seemed "distinctly the gentleman–business man," committed to "orderly progress . . . & not . . . radicalism." (Menocal had in fact won office through appalling fraud, and just a few days after Franklin's visit, a popular uprising in Havana came close to overthrowing him. Wilson blamed German agents for the revolt and sent in troops to quell it; they would remain in place for five years.)

Franklin then hurried on to lunch at the country club, followed by an afternoon drive into the countryside with Livy, during which, he wrote, they "hoped . . . to see Madame Abreu [?], a recent but torrid conquest of Marvin's, who has a magnificent country [house], keeps monkeys, apes, & other retainers. . . ." But they got lost, turned their touring car back toward Havana, and first killed a goat, then blew a tire, making them late for the train that was to take them on to Santiago. The train was held for the important guests, however, and once aboard, Franklin remembered, "we had not been going long before we were all invited into the private car of Benny Van Horn, the President of the Cuba railroads. He is a son of my father's great friend, Sir William Van Horn, President of the Canadian Pacific. . . . Benny provided all the liquid nourishment necessary—and more."

A destroyer, the USS *Wainwright*, took them on to the harbor of Port-au-Prince, where at dawn the next morning the Atlantic Fleet was spread out for Franklin's inspection—seventy-two ships, drawn up in two parallel lines that stretched for three miles. Franklin and the destroyer's commander stood together on the bridge as the *Wainwright* steamed down the corridor between the warships, each vessel that carried guns firing the Assistant Secretary's salute as she passed.

Franklin and his companions, all in top hats and cutaways despite the growing heat, went ashore for formal ceremonies of welcome. Franklin loved telling of his reception:

When we landed at the end of the long pier, we were met by a number of gentlemen in frock coats and silk hats. I assumed erroneously, that they were the Mayor of Port au Prince and representatives of [the President]. . . . As they stepped forward with a scroll, I bowed and delivered the speech I had intended as my official address . . . I had translated [it] with a good deal of difficulty into French and delivered it thus.

We all entered automobiles and to the shore end of the wharf we drove, where we were met by another delegation. This time it was the Mayor, and as I had but one speech, I redelivered it. . . .

Then to the Palace of the President, where we were ushered upstairs into a red plush and gold drawing room where we met the President and his Cabinet, and I made the same speech for the third time.

After the palace ceremonies—which were marred, for Livy and Franklin at least, by the warmth and sweetness of the champagne served—they reviewed the Haitian gendarmerie, run by the Marine Major who had helped pacify the island and now policed it, Smedley Darlington Butler. He was just the sort of man to delight a Roosevelt. Thin and wire-tough, with a raptor's nose and a glare so fierce that his men called him "Old Gimlet Eye," he had begun his career under fire in Cuba at sixteen, been wounded and awarded the Congressional Medal of Honor for bravery at Tientsin during the Boxer Rebellion, and had later splashed ashore with the Marines in Honduras, Santo Domingo, Mexico, Nicaragua.

He had little affection for the people who came under his control. (Years after he had moved on, Nicaraguan mothers still kept their children quiet by saying, "Hush! Major Butler will get you.") Poor Haitian civilians were "niggers" and "coons" to Butler and his fellow officers; those who resisted American rule were "gooks." But the general reserved his greatest scorn for members of the small, educated elite. "Those who wore shoes," Butler said, "I considered a joke." When he shared a room with his handpicked president, a tall, grave black man with a sweeping gray mustache named Sudre Dartiguenave, the Marine occupied the bed and the head of the Haitian government slept on the floor.

Franklin may privately have been no less contemptuous of his hosts than were his companions; many of his favorite stories about his visit to Haiti centered on color. At a luncheon of fifty-two different dishes in honor of Dartiguenave and his Cabinet aboard the American flagship, the USS *Pennsylvania,* Franklin noticed that John McIlhenny, "who came from New Orleans, was not eating much. After the Haitian officials had been piped over the side, I asked what the trouble was. He said: 'Did you see the Secretary of Agriculture who sat opposite me? He was 6'6" and must have weighed 250 lbs. He ate with both hands—everything in sight—two helpings of every dish. I was fascinated—too fascinated to eat. I couldn't help saying to myself that man would have brought $1,500 at auction in New Orleans in 1860 for stud purposes.' "

The next evening, the Haitian president gave a formal dance for his guests from Washington at which Franklin was amused by the sight of white Marines waltzing with "Haitian ladies . . . beautifully dressed in Paris clothes . . . [with] yellow powder instead of flesh-colored powder on their countenances."

But whatever Franklin's private feelings were, his upbringing dictated that he be unfailingly courteous to the Haitians he met: it was a gentleman's duty always to be civil, even to his inferiors. At one point during the official ceremonies, Franklin, General Butler, and the Haitian president were to ride together in the back seat of a new presidential Buick. Dartiguenave bent to get in. Butler reached for his collar to haul him back so that the Assistant Secretary could take precedence. "Very gracefully," Marvin noted, "F.D. stepped aside with '*Apres vous, Excellence,*' raising his hat and giving the gigantic Dartiguenave his proper place on the right side of the rear seat."

Franklin also favorably impressed his hosts because he spoke to them in French, which few American occupiers ever bothered to learn. Marvin, who had visited Haiti twice before, "helped F.D. with some of these talks and supplied him with information which prevented any possible *faux pas* with extremely sensitive colored 'Democrats,' as well as with anecdotes which implied a familiarity with Haitian customs and Haitian history." (Franklin would later become the acknowledged master of this political technique, relying upon his alert staff to provide him with enough intimate details about his audiences and their surroundings to seem virtually omniscient wherever he happened to be.)

The highlight of the trip was to be a four-day horseback ride north through the island's lush interior which, until the Marines arrived, had sheltered the *cacos*. General Butler accompanied him, determined to have him see only what he wished him to see, and brought along fifty Marines and one hundred fifty Haitian gendarmes for protection. The days were hot and strenuous, Franklin remembered, the nights cool and comfortable, "though we heard rifle shots from the hills, and an occasional bullet going by overhead." (He alone seems to have recalled the distant shooting and the nearby bullets; no mention is made of them in long, anecdotal accounts of the trip written by two of his companions.)

Riding at the head of the long, single-file column on his own London-made saddle sent down from Hyde Park, and wearing a Marine uniform, Franklin had a marvelous time. He loved the wild, green countryside where curls of blue smoke rising into the still bluer sky were the only signs of human habitation, admired the laughing washerwomen at work along the streams, shot doves on the wing. He learned to mix a cloying Haitian cocktail that included eggs, brown sugar, and dark rum, and when, on his thirty-fifth birthday, an old village woman brewed coffee for him using a dirty sock for a filter—or so he liked to remember—he pronounced it the best he had ever tasted.

"It was a tough ride," George Marvin remembered, "tropic heat, rough trails. . . . We forded rivers, climbed elevations, slept *al fresco*. . . . [Franklin] was always gay and animated. . . . and he never got tired." Those who did not bear up as cheerfully as he did were mercilessly baited.

"On this trip," Franklin wrote, "good old Livy Davis became the butt of the party." Davis complained about his horse all the first day, saying that its "gait was very jiggly and tiring," and demanded that his orderly bring him a different one the next morning. "The orderly changed saddles but brought back the same horse," according to Franklin, "and . . . Davis was full of praise for the new steed." Near the village of Hinche, the whole party stripped to swim in a creek. "We were having a wonderful swim in a state of nature when, on looking up, we found that the entire female population was lining the banks. They had never seen a white man in this condition before and seemed to take it quite calmly. We came out, dried, dressed—all except Davis, who insisted on sending for his bathing suit before coming out."

Later, Livy kicked over a kerosene lamp, spilling fuel through McIlhenny's bedding, and then was badly bitten by the red ants over whose mound he had heedlessly laid his own blankets.

His host roared at all of it. Livy did not mind the ribbing if it meant he could be close to Franklin. "Of course, this trip has been the biggest event of my life," he told his friend when it was over, "and it is utterly impossible for me to express my gratitude to you for taking me along."

On the last day, at Franklin's request, General Butler led him up a steep green hillside to see Fort Rivière, an old French masonry fortress which had been the scene of the Marines' final victory over the *cacos*. Butler had personally led the assault on Fort Rivière. With just one company to back them up, he, a sergeant named Ross L. Iams, and a private had together scrambled up the slope, bullets pecking into the ground all around them, and reached the foot of the wall, only to find that the sally port through which they had hoped to rush had been bricked up. The only way in was a four-foot-wide storm drain, and the *cacos* at its far end were firing steadily through that. Butler and Iams plastered themselves against the wall. "I had never experienced a keener desire to be some place else," Butler remembered. "My misery and an unconscious, helpless pleading must have been written all over my face. Iams took one look at me and then said, 'Oh, hell, I'm going through.' "

Iams shouldered his way into the drain, with Butler and the private right behind him. The fort's startled defenders somehow missed all three, and before they could reload, the Marines were among them. Fifty-one *cacos* were shot dead, twenty-nine inside the fortress, the rest as they jumped from the parapet and tried to flee into the jungle. Precisely one Marine was injured, hit in the face by a stone. "We were fighting a people who did not know what sights were for," an officer testified later, "and in a tight spot they threw away their rifles and reached for rocks." No prisoners were taken.

When Secretary Daniels heard of this action he was horrified and ordered the Marines to mount no more offensives against the *cacos* "to prevent further loss of life."

Franklin, on the other hand, was so impressed at having been shown the scene of Butler's courage under fire that when he got back to Washington he recommended a second Medal of Honor for him.[28] Nothing Butler did thereafter won anything but praise from the Assistant Secretary, and Franklin's enthusiasm for the Marines seemed so unquestioning that two over-eager junior officers dug up the white

28. Franklin's own account of this action, written long afterwards, provides a vivid example of his chronic inability to leave history alone. The drain was only *two* feet high, not four, he claimed; Iams had hung his hat on the muzzle of his pistol, then pushed it before him through the drain until "he felt two machetés descend on it," then leapt into the courtyard, where, "with a right and a left . . . [he] got both Cacos, stood up and dropped two or three others. . . . Then ensued a killing, the news of which put down all insurrections we hope for all time to come." There were not seventy but *three hundred* Haitians within the fortress, FDR continued, "and Butler and his 18 companions killed over 200 of them. . . ." *Source:* Franklin D. Roosevelt, *Trip to Haiti and Santo Domingo, 1917,* unpublished memorandum, no date but clearly written during the presidential years. Franklin D. Roosevelt, Papers as Assistant Secretary of the Navy, FDRL.

skulls of two *cacos* and offered them to him as souvenirs. He did not finally take them home with him, but he did order crated up an eighteenth-century French cannon found at Fort Rivière, and eagerly rattled through a heap of confiscated bladed weapons to claim for his collection an engraved sixteenth-century Spanish cutlass which he later persuaded himself must once have belonged to a member of the party of discoverers led by Don Diego Columbus.

While waiting for lunch along the road one day, Franklin and his friends were entertained with songs and dances performed by a gang of perhaps one hundred captive laborers, a fraction of the six thousand Haitians impressed against their will by the Marines under an old colonial French law which permitted tax defaulters to work out their service on the roads. Pay was minimal and sometimes nonexistent. Workers were not allowed to visit their families. Marines with rifles guarded them, and men who tried to flee were shot.

Butler was proud that his roads cost less than $250 a mile, and once joked to Franklin that "it would not do to ask too many questions about how we accomplished this work." Franklin agreed. "Well Done," he cabled, when Butler later informed him that a road had been completed to Cap Haitien. And when a revolt against the brutality of Butler's gendarmerie flared in 1918, Franklin supported the Marine suppression of it that took another year of fighting and fifteen hundred Haitian lives.

In 1922, Roosevelt wrote a brisk defense of the Wilson administration's Haitian policy. Before the United States intervened, "the inhabitants of Hayti, taken as a mass, were little more than primitive savages," he said, and their nominally Christian faith "had been greatly changed by the recrudescence of the primitive religions of Africa, which, it is well established, included in many cases the well-known forms of human sacrifices." Haiti had no more been "a Republic in our accepted sense of the term, than were the principalities of India, before the advent of the British." It was true that the Marines had been forced to kill "several hundred" of the "tens of thousands . . . [of bandits] who infested the countryside," but they had also protected the people from those bandits, built roads and hospitals, ensured honest collection of taxes, cleaned up disease-ridden ports, "and, in general, established peace throughout the island for the first time in a century and a quarter."

"If the readers of this could see," Franklin wrote, "as I saw, what the Marines accomplished in Hayti they would go in a body to Washington and beg that the United States carry on its work."[29]

Franklin's own enthusiasm for Haiti took the form of plans for personal investment. (So did that of his friend McIlhenny, who soon left his Washington job to become "financial advisor" to the Haitian government with an eye to profiting personally from the occupation.) Franklin thought Fort Rivière, the hilltop scene of the killing of the *cacos*, might be turned into a first-class resort, and was especially struck by the potential of the lush little island of La Gonave in Port-au-Prince Bay. Eleanor remembered that when he got back from Haiti, he announced that he was going to buy the island, start a cattle ranch, and move the family there during the winters. ("Franklin could never travel anywhere in the world without wanting to buy land there. . . . He just loved land," she said, ". . . so I was a little calm about the fact that we were moving to [La Gonave] and after about three or four months we didn't move.")[30]

Franklin did not see as much as he had hoped to see in the Caribbean. The party moved on from Cap Haitien to the Dominican Republic by ship. On February 3, he and his party were dining in the flower-filled courtyard of an old Spanish colonial house at Santiago de los Caballeros, the guests of Marine Colonel T. P. Kane and his wife. "Toward the end of dinner," Franklin remembered, "my orderly brought me a code message just received over the field radio set. I went out to decode it."[31] It was from the Secretary of the Navy and read:

29. Bitter at having been passed over for Commandant of the Marine Corps, General Smedley Butler himself came to have a different view. In 1935, he reviewed his own career for the November issue of *Common Sense*:

I spent thirty-three years and four months as a member of our country's most agile military force—the Marine Corps. . . . And during that period I spent most of my time . . . [as] a racketeer for capitalism. . . . I helped make Mexico . . . safe for American oil interests in 1914. I helped make Haiti and Cuba a decent place for the National City Bank boys to collect revenues in. . . . I helped purify Nicaraguans for the international banking house of Brown Brothers in 1909–1912. I brought light to the Dominican Republic for American sugar interests in 1916. I helped make Honduras "right" for American fruit companies in 1903. In China in 1927 I helped see to it that Standard Oil went its way unmolested.

He also confessed that often in Haiti, his Marines "went wild . . . and hunted the cacos like pigs."

30. Franklin also later explored the notion of starting a chain of variety stores across Haiti, writing to a dubious McIlhenny in 1922 that "I cannot agree that just because the Haytian native population does not use knives, forks, cups, etc., that they will never use them. As a matter of fact, I feel convinced that during the next generation the Haytian population will adopt the standards more generally in vogue." *Source:* Franklin D. Roosevelt, Papers as Assistant Secretary of the Navy, FDRL.

31. He had to go elsewhere to decode it because he had to consult a pocket dictionary. The cipher in which it was sent was of his own devising, based on the dictionary's page numbers and

BECAUSE OF POLITICAL SITUATION PLEASE RETURN WASHINGTON AT
ONCE. AM SENDING SHIP TO MEET YOU AND PARTY AT PUERTO PLATA
TOMORROW MORNING.[32]

Wilson had handed the German ambassador his passports. American entry into the war at last seemed near. Franklin and his party ended their holiday, he remembered, and started for home aboard the collier USS *Neptune.*

> As we headed north through Caicos Island passage on our way to [the naval installation at] Hampton Roads [Virginia] no lights were showing, the guns were manned and there was complete air silence. . . . We landed . . . on the morning of February 8th. The colonel in command seemed utterly surprised, insisted there was no war, that no special preparations were going on and that he had no orders from Washington to stand by.
>
> Late that afternoon we were back in Washington. I dashed to the Navy Department and found the same thing—no diplomatic relations with Germany broken off, no excitement, no preparations, no orders to the fleet at Guantanamo to return to their home yards on the East Coast.
>
> But that is another story.

---

order of words. He, Howe, and Secretary Daniels always carried copies of the same little crimson-covered book, and to further ensure the authenticity of their most secret messages, he and Howe ended each of their telegrams to one another with "Algonac," the name of the Delano home at Newburgh and a Roosevelt code word for "all is well."

This was the second code Franklin is known to have devised; the first, kept exclusively to himself, was for the most closely guarded secrets in his Harvard journal; in it, he recorded his infatuation with Alice Sohier and his growing love for Eleanor. *Source:* Two little dictionaries and a brief explanation by FDR of how they were once used may be found in Franklin D. Roosevelt, Papers as Assistant Secretary of the Navy, FDRL. For an account of Franklin's earlier private code, see Geoffrey C. Ward, *Before the Trumpet: Young Franklin Roosevelt, 1882–1905,* pages 253–255, 307–308, 313.

32. According to FDR, he was unable to disguise his excitement when he returned to the table. Mrs. Kane asked what had happened. He said he wasn't sure, but that the Secretary had said the recall was "based on political conditions."

> Mrs. Kane looked at me in horror, and said, "What can 'political conditions' mean? It must be that Charles Evans Hughes has led a revolution against President Wilson."
> I replied, "My dear lady, you have been in the tropics too long!"

Source: Franklin D. Roosevelt, unpublished *Trip to Haiti and Santo Domingo, 1917,* Papers as Assistant Secretary of the Navy, FDRL.

CHAPTER

9

HONNEUR OBLIGE

INAUGURATION Day, March 5, 1917, was clear, cold, and windy in Washington, Franklin noted in the diary he had again begun to keep (and would again soon abandon). But the ceremonies in front of the Capitol were oddly listless, nothing like Theodore Roosevelt's exuberant swearing in that had so excited Franklin and Eleanor a dozen years before. The crowds along Pennsylvania Avenue were sparse and curiously silent. Woodrow Wilson and his new wife rode to the Capitol in a carriage shielded by a hollow square of cavalry and mounted policemen. Armed soldiers were conspicuous on nearby roofs. Washington had not seen such tight security since Abraham Lincoln had ridden along the same route on the eve of the Civil War.

The President's address was grim, too: The country was now committed to "armed neutrality" in defense of its rights at sea, he reminded his listeners, and "We may even be drawn on, by circumstances . . . to a more . . . immediate association with the great struggle itself." But he still remained hopeful that if America remained true to its principles, the "shadows that now lie dark upon our path will soon be dispelled and we shall walk with the light all about us. . . ."

Franklin was not impressed with the President's performance: "Too far away to hear address—Little enthusiasm in crowd." Later, he sat behind Wilson in the reviewing stand for the inaugural parade, and while he thought the Navy units marched especially well, he deplored the fact that the President was shielded from the wind: "Awful mistake to review troops from glass cage."

Franklin's unhappiness was not entirely due to his distance from the focus of attention. His frustration at the President's reluctance to declare war and his impatience with Daniels had reached some sort of peak, and he had decided to take still bolder action behind the scenes, even if it cost him his job. He had already written a note to his New York tenant, Thomas W. Lamont, a partner in the firm of J. P. Morgan, warning that his own plans were now uncertain and that the Roosevelts might need to move back into their house the next winter. Lamont answered that he and Mrs. Lamont were disappointed; they had hoped that after the election, "Mr. Daniels might desire to retire to private life, so that we could have the satisfaction of seeing you Secretary of the Navy!"

Franklin shared that hope. At six that evening, he slipped through the crowd gathered across from the White House to watch the inaugural fireworks display, and told the guard at the gate he had an appointment with Colonel House.

House was a tiny, retiring Texan with exquisite manners and a silken voice that rarely rose much above a whisper. No one other than the First Lady herself was then closer to the President. He had long been persuaded that the United States should intervene on the side of the Allies, and had already sought without success quietly to remove Daniels from office because he believed the President's closeness to him was politically damaging. In both those endeavors, Franklin was a natural ally, and as they talked the younger man volunteered what he reported to his diary as "some guarded views about condition of Navy."

Evidently sensing that Franklin was holding back, the colonel invited him to come see him and talk some more, out from under the constraints imposed by the White House. Both he and Franklin were to be in New York five days later; House's home was just a step away from the Roosevelts' twin townhouses on East 65th Street. The two men would confer again on Sunday morning.

"Does it not seem more or less a joke that we made that wild dash north just one month ago?" Franklin had written Livy Davis shortly before Inauguration Day. The Assistant Secretary had raced back to

Washington from Haiti in early February, eager to enter the war at last, only to find the administration still reluctant to act.

Wilson's reelection and the German decision to stop sinking merchantmen without warning that preceded it had encouraged the President to undertake one final great effort to end the war by negotiation, and he had asked each side to state the terms under which it would cease fighting. It was his hope that he might negotiate peace between them himself. Neither party responded favorably. Nonetheless, in January, the President had told Congress that the war must end in "a peace without victory," followed by "not a balance of power but a community of power."

TR had denounced such talk as unworthy of an American President: "It is spurned by all men of lofty soul, by all men fit to call themselves fellow-citizens of Washington and Lincoln or of the war-torn fighters who followed Grant and Lee." Justice could only follow victory.

It was too late for Wilson in any case. The Germans had already resolved to risk war with the United States to defeat the Allies. As of February 1, they pledged to sink any vessel of whatever nation detected en route to any Allied port. On February 3, the day Franklin was called back from Haiti, a U-boat sank the *Housatonic*, and Wilson had severed relations with Germany. But he refused to go further toward war. "He is a very cold and selfish man," TR wrote privately, "a very timid man when it comes to physical danger.... As for shame he has none, and if anyone kicks him, he brushes his clothes, and utters some lofty sentence."

Shortly after he got back to the capital and with Daniels momentarily out of town, Franklin had asked for an appointment with the President. As Acting Secretary, he requested permission at least to bring the fleet north from Guantanamo Bay so that it could be fitted out in case of hostilities. The President refused to grant it. "I want history to show," Franklin remembered his saying, "not only that we have tried every diplomatic means to keep out of the war; to show that war has been forced upon us deliberately by Germany; but also that we have come into the court of history with clean hands."

Franklin wanted action now. Wilson did not wish to move until he had the people with him, and was especially wary of advisers like the young Assistant Secretary whom he believed too close to the military men he so distrusted. "It is the *Junkerthurm* trying to creep in under cover of the patriotic feeling of the moment," he told Daniels. "They will not get in."

Wilson's reelection had not ended the clamor among Preparedness champions for Daniels' resignation and, with Howe's off-the-record encouragement, several newspapers were suggesting Franklin as the best possible replacement: The Chicago *Post*, for example, urged the appointment of the Secretary's "virile-minded, hardfisted civilian assistant. . . . [whose name] uncuriously enough is Roosevelt." Colonel Thompson, the head of the Navy League, asked Franklin himself whether he would object to a letter-writing campaign aimed at removing Daniels and making him Secretary. If the Assistant Secretary replied, he kept no record of it in his files, but within the next few weeks, letters from union leaders in Navy Yards all over the country arrived at the White House, urging that Franklin be given the post should Daniels leave the Cabinet.

Daniels still had no intention of leaving, however, and Franklin had to be careful how he handled such requests. When an old Harvard friend also encouraged Franklin to consider replacing his chief, the younger man issued a high-minded demurral: "Personally I have no use for a man who, serving in a subordinate position is continually contriving ways to step into his boss's shoes and I detest nothing so much as that kind of disloyalty. I have worked very gladly under Mr. Daniels and I wish the public could realize how much he has done for the Navy. I would feel very badly indeed if friends of mine should unwittingly give the impression that I was for a minute thinking of taking his place at the head of the Navy."

But if that was Franklin's genuine feeling at the time, Louis Howe evidently chose to ignore it: George Creel, formerly of the *New York World* and appointed head of the new Committee on Public Information in April, remembered putting out tracers to find the source of all the "old canards" about Daniels now reappearing in the newspapers and finding "their source in none other than Howe; whereupon I went over and let him have it right between the eyes. Of course he insisted he was only explaining and defending 'Uncle Joe,' but I told him if I heard any more of his phony explanations and defenses I would carry the matter to Woodrow Wilson who had a very precise idea of what constituted loyalty.'"

Congress had adjourned on Inauguration Day without passing a presidential request that would have permitted Wilson to arm mer-

chant ships; a small bloc of anti-war senators led by Robert M. LaFol-
lette of Wisconsin—"a little group of willful men, representing no
opinion but their own," Wilson called them—had filibustered it to
death.[1]

On Friday, March 9, Franklin noted, the White House issued a
"statement that W. has the power to arm & *inference* that he will use
it. J.D. says he will by Monday. Why doesn't President say so without
equivocation?" He spent Saturday in Boston, first inspecting the
Charlestown Navy Yard—ahead of schedule in making war plans and
enlisting private boats for the Naval Reserve, he noted, but "due to
local initiative & *not* Department help"—and then lunching with his
class at the Harvard Club, where he "spoke quite freely about Navy."

As promised on Inauguration Day, Franklin spent a second hour
with Colonel House on Sunday morning in New York and later noted
the highlights of their conversation in his diary: "Outlined principal
weaknesses of Navy—J.D.'s procrastination—[Captain William] Benson's dislike of England—failure to make plans with France & England
& study their methods—necessity if war comes of going into it with
all force—money, Troops, etc. He was sympathetic & agreed to main
points."

Already intriguing with Wilson's closest adviser, Franklin hurried
that evening to the Metropolitan Club to take part in a secret conclave
with some of the President's most deadly enemies. At 8:00 p.m. he
dined in a private room in company distinctly odd for a member of a
Democratic administration to be keeping: Cornelius Bliss, former finance chairman of the Republican Party; General Leonard Wood;
J. P. Morgan, Jr.; Elihu Root; George von Lengerke Meyer, Josephus
Daniels' militant predecessor as Secretary of the Navy; Walter Edge,
Republican governor of New Jersey; John Purroy Mitchel, the fusionist mayor of New York and an enthusiastic graduate of the officer's
training camp at Plattsburgh; and Cousin Theodore.

Even in this group of eager interventionists, Franklin aligned himself with the most militant. He summarized the table talk in his diary:
"Discussion of 1. how to make administration steer clear course to
uphold rights 2. how to get active increase army & navy. Decided to
use Governor's Conference to demand this. Root inclined to praise

---

1. Another member of this band was James Aloysius O'Gorman, the New Yorker named to
the Senate when Franklin and his fellow Albany insurgents blocked William Sheehan back in
1911.

administration's present course—TR wanted more vigorous demand about future course—less indorsement of past. I backed TR's theory."

Back in Washington, he found nothing had changed. "Told J.D. things not satisfactory Boston & worse NY. He said nothing. . . . Asked Sec'y in presence Benson that matters pertaining to naval district defense be put under me. To be discussed tomorrow. Something *must* be done soon to organize & expedite work." That evening, news came that the Germans had torpedoed the *Algonquin*.

The next day, Daniels, Admiral Benson, and Franklin together went over their new instructions for arming merchantmen. Daniels thought it "a rather solemn time, for I felt I might be signing . . . the death warrant of young Americans"; Franklin was annoyed that Daniels had rejected the Secretary of State's suggestion that armed vessels be permitted to fire without warning on any submarine not flying its colors.

The Secretary still hoped that total war could somehow be averted, but nothing he or Wilson or anyone could do could slow the events that now seemed to tumble one upon the other, out of anyone's control. On March 15, Czar Nicholas II of Russia abdicated in favor of Aleksandr Kerensky's constitutional monarchy. The conflict seemed more clear-cut to Wilson now that there was no longer a despotic power on the Allied side. On March 18, the *City of Memphis, Illinois,* and *Vigilancia* were all torpedoed.

Two days later, the President polled the ten members of his Cabinet as to what he should do next. One by one, nine of them urged him to go before Congress and call for a declaration of war. The Secretary of the Navy was the last to speak.

"Well, Daniels?" Wilson prompted.

With tears in his eyes, the weary pacifist struggled for a moment for words that would not come, composed himself, and acquiesced in war; even for him, there now seemed no alternative. "If any man in official life ever faced the agony of a Gethsemane," he wrote later, "I was the man during the first four months of 1917. From the beginning of the war in Europe, I had resisted every influence that was at work to carry the United States into the war."

The American ambassador in London urged that a high-ranking naval officer be dispatched right away to England, there to set up liaison with the Admiralty and ascertain immediate British needs in the common struggle to come. Daniels and Wilson agreed, and asked Admiral Henry B. Wilson to accept the job. Wilson preferred sea duty.

Daniels' second choice was Rear Admiral William S. Sims, the president of the War College. Sims was a brilliant, impatient officer, tall and handsome, with a perfectly barbered silvery beard, who had first risen to prominence in 1901 when, as a young officer, he ignored channels and wrote directly to President Theodore Roosevelt to warn him that American gunnery was dangerously inaccurate. Instead of punishing him for his brashness, TR looked into the situation, found the young man was right, put him in charge of improving target shooting, and made him his naval aide. In 1908, Sims had again found conservative bureau chiefs and older officers unwilling to listen to his warnings, this time about serious defects in the design of American battleships. Unable to move his superiors to action, he anonymously supplied inside information to a writer, who then published an exposé in *McClure's* Magazine. A congressional investigation again substantiated most of his charges, but many of the older officers never forgave him for bringing naval weaknesses out into the open.

In choosing Sims for the delicate London mission, Daniels was willing to overlook the admiral's continuing closeness to TR and his repeated attacks on Daniels' own policies, because he believed him able, energetic, and well connected with the British admirals. Franklin admired Sims extravagantly, wished always to be in his good graces, and two years later, when the press lauded the admiral for his part in winning the Allied victory, would falsely claim that it had been he, not Daniels, who had been responsible for his appointment. His story, first told to newspaper reporters in April of 1919, was that the cable requesting an American officer be sent to London had been buried on the Secretary's desk when the President came to call; that he, Franklin, had wandered in, pulled it from beneath the pile, showed it to Wilson, and suggested Sims' name. Not a word of it was true.

On the evening of April 2, Wilson appeared before a joint session of Congress. Franklin sat with Daniels on the floor of the House chamber and barely managed to secure Eleanor a seat in the gallery. It had not been easy to get in. A soft spring rain had fallen all day and the big crowds around the Capitol had pushed into its corridors, holding flags and arguing with little knots of last-ditch pacifists. Senator Henry Cabot Lodge exchanged first angry words and then blows with one peace advocate—a Princeton athlete who was pulled away by the police.

The President was grave and his voice low and strained as he recalled his efforts to avoid taking part in the conflict. The Germans had left America no option, he said; they were "guilty of throwing to the winds all scruples of humanity. . . . There is one choice we cannot make, we are incapable of making: we will not choose the path of submission and suffer the most sacred rights of our Nation and our people to be ignored or violated." America would not fight for conquest, but for "peace and justice. . . . The world must be made safe for democracy." He called upon Congress to accept for America "the status of belligerent which has . . . been thrust upon it," and asked for a national draft of half a million men, and "the immediate full equipment of the navy in all respects."

"It is a fearful thing," the President concluded, his voice rising for the first time,

> to lead this most peaceful people, into the most terrible and disastrous of all wars, civilization itself seeming to be in the balance. But the right is more precious than peace, and we shall fight for the things which we have always carried nearest our hearts. . . . To such a task we can dedicate our lives and our fortunes, everything that we are and everything that we have, with the pride of those who know that the day has come when America is privileged to spend her blood and her might for the principles that gave her birth and happiness and the peace which she has treasured. God helping her, she can do no other.

Each senator and congressman had been handed a miniature American flag on the way into the chamber. Now they stood and cheered and waved them. The silence of those scattered few still opposed to war was hardly noticed in the frantic blur of red, white, and blue.

Franklin had been preoccupied during the speech by banging sounds that seemed to come from directly overhead. On the way out, he learned that a Secret Serviceman had thought he saw someone lurking above the chamber during the address, and had given a silent alarm; the sound Franklin had heard had been the agents scurrying across the tin roof.

Eleanor "listened breathlessly" to the President, she remembered, "and returned home still half-dazed by the sense of impending change."

Four nights later, the two youngest Roosevelt children, Franklin Jr., not yet three, and John, barely a year old, were just dozing off in their beds in the fourth-floor nursery.

Suddenly, the door banged open. Their mother stood in the doorway. A shorter, stockier silhouette appeared behind her. The light went on.

"Boys," she said. "This is Uncle Theodore."

The Colonel strode across the room, his big teeth showing, and threw back the boys' covers.

"I don't care what *anybody* says," he roared. "You don't belong in bed yet." He grabbed a wide-eyed boy under each arm, turned, and pounded down all four flights of stairs, shouting, "*These* two piggies are going to market!"

Franklin Jr. had been too young and terrified to remember more than that bumpy descent in later years; James, seven years older and also awakened from sleep just down the hall, could recall watching the great man stride back and forth in front of the blazing fire, shouting about something and waving his arms. His mother listened and quietly poured coffee, James remembered. His father, too, was uncharacteristically silent.

Theodore Roosevelt's excitement was understandable. America was at war at last. His place was at the front. He was staying with the Longworths while in Washington, but he had stopped by to ask Franklin to help persuade the administration to let him raise his own division and lead it in France.

Franklin agreed to try. The next morning, he slipped out of his office and across the hall to the office of Newton D. Baker, the Secretary of War, to convey his cousin's wish to see the President. He said nothing about TR's visit to his own chief, though Daniels suspected that his assistant was behind a subsequent telephone call from Senator Claude Swanson of the Naval Affairs Committee, urging him to intercede with the President on TR's behalf.

Baker visited the Longworth home and heard the Colonel out, and the next day, TR went to the White House to seek the President's approval. It was an awkward meeting.

"Mr. President," Roosevelt remembered telling Wilson, "what I have said and thought, and what others have said and thought is all dust in a windy street, if now we can make your [war] message good. Of course, it amounts to nothing, if we cannot make it good. But if we can translate it into fact, then it will rank as a great state paper, with the great state papers of Washington and Lincoln. Now, all that I ask is that I be allowed to do all that [is in] me to help make good this speech of yours—to help get this nation to act, so as to justify and live up to the speech, and the declaration of war that followed."

Wilson was correct but patronizing and noncommittal, reminding his visitor that modern war was no "Charge of the Light Brigade." The war was to be fought by a conscript army. TR said he would publicly support the new draft, but while the new army was being trained, there would be a role for volunteers, too: "I could arouse the belief [in Europe] that America is coming. I could show the Allies what was on the way."[2]

Wilson rendered no final judgment but promised to consult the War Department. ("I had a plain talk with the President," TR told a reporter later, "and if it were anyone but Mr. Wilson, I'd say it was all fixed up.")

"Well, and how did the Colonel impress you?" Joseph Tumulty asked the President.

He had liked him, Wilson said. "He is a great big boy. . . . There is a sweetness about him that is very compelling. You can't resist the man."

But Wilson could and did resist him. His War Department recommended against volunteer units in general, and Theodore Roosevelt in particular. The Colonel was too old at fifty-eight, in poor health, half-blind, and had been out of touch with military developments for twenty years. Brigadier General John J. Pershing, fresh from a largely futile search for Pancho Villa below the Mexican border and about to command the American Expeditionary Force (AEF) in France, wanted no part of a subordinate so accustomed to running things on his own. And Wilson himself did not wish to reward his old adversary with command.

His final, formal rejection of TR's offer in late May seemed calculated to wound: "It would be very agreeable to me to pay Mr. Roosevelt this compliment, and the Allies the compliment, of sending an ex-President, but this is not the time for compliments or for any action not calculated to contribute to the immediate success of the war.

2. Georges Clemenceau, not yet premier of France, echoed this argument. "He is an idealist imbued with simple vital idealism," he said of TR in an open letter to Wilson; Roosevelt's was the "one name which summons up the beauty of American intervention." The battle-weary soldiers of France needed a miracle to restore their spirits: "Send them Roosevelt!" He was right at least about the symbolic power of TR's name; when the first American troops finally reached France that summer, and paraded down the Champs-Elysée, Parisians shouted, *"Vive les Teddies!"* Source: Joseph L. Gardner, *Departing Glory,* pages 371–373.

The business now in hand is undramatic, practical and of scientific definiteness and precision."

"I need not assure you," he added in a telegram to the Colonel himself, "that my conclusions were based entirely upon imperative considerations of public policy and not upon personal or private choice."

TR was deeply angry: "I think the decision was a bitter blow from which he never quite recovered," Eleanor remembered. Franklin was angry, too. "We ought to have sent TR over with 100,000 men," he told Daniels in August when the Russian front collapsed and the Germans seemed about to seize Petrograd. "This would not have happened."

All four of Theodore Roosevelt's sons volunteered for duty as enlisted men, but Pershing promised their father that so long as they were physically qualified, they could all serve as officers under him in the AEF. "We boys," TR's youngest son, Quentin, later told a friend, "thought it was up to us to practice what Father preached." Their eagerness to fight delighted their father. "I should be ashamed of my sons if they shirked war," he once wrote, "just as I should be ashamed of my daughters if they shirked motherhood."

During his visit to Washington, TR had been insistent that Franklin not shirk war, either. "You *must* resign," he had told him. "You must get into uniform at once!" It was an exhortation he would repeat frequently, to his young cousin's acute embarrassment. "Uncle Ted was *always* urging Franklin to resign," Eleanor recalled.

Franklin did try to resign, only to have Daniels tell him that the President himself was against it. "Neither you nor I nor Franklin Roosevelt has the right to select the place of service . . . ," Wilson told him. "Tell the young man . . . to stay where he is."[3]

Franklin's motivation for volunteering was mixed. He really did want to go overseas to help "right the wrong," as he had told Bob Ferguson as soon as the war began, but he also had his private agenda: "Around the Department," Daniels remembered, "it was said that, inasmuch as his cousin Theodore left the position of Assistant Secretary to become a Rough Rider, later Governor of New York and then President, and both had served in the Legislature of New York, Frank-

---

3. For once Leonard Wood agreed with the President: young Roosevelt's departure from the Navy Department, he said, would be "a public calamity." *Source:* Kenneth S. Davis, *FDR: The Beckoning of Destiny, 1882–1928,* page 461.

lin actually thought fighting in the war was the necessary step toward reaching the White House."

The motivations of those who urged him to stay a civilian may have been mixed, as well: his energy and ability were undeniable assets to the war effort, but it might also have been politically embarrassing to have a Democratic Roosevelt, known for his militancy, leave his post while the furor over the President's rejection of the "Roosevelt Division" was still fresh in the public mind.

In any case, Franklin did stay where he was. For the first time in his career he had chosen a path that diverged from that blazed by Theodore Roosevelt, but he brought to the new task of waging the naval war he had wanted for so long a full measure of Rooseveltian vigor and impatience. From the moment war was declared he acted with a brashness surprising even for him. That very day a reporter asked him if the fleet had been mobilized. He didn't know, he said uncharacteristically, "but you have a right to know. Come along and we'll find out."

He shoved through Daniels' door without knocking, the reporter struggling to keep up. "Here's a newspaperman," Franklin said to the startled Secretary. "He wants to know, and all the rest want to know, whether the fleet has been ordered mobilized."

Daniels maintained his composure: "Tell the young man that an announcement will be made in due course."

"You see . . . ," Franklin told his visitor, shaking his head as he closed the Secretary's door behind him. "It was the best I could do."

Three days later, he startled his chief again, with a request that he be permitted to name one of Daniels' harshest critics among the retired admirals, Herbert Winslow, as his own assistant, thus undercutting both Daniels and Admiral Benson, whom Franklin thought slow and anti-British. (According to Admiral Sims, Benson had cornered him in his office just before sending him off to Britain and wagged a finger under his nose. "Don't let the British pull the wool over your eyes," he said. "It's not our business, pulling their chestnuts out of the fire. We would as soon fight the British as the Germans.")

Daniels turned Franklin down: "No division of power as to operations," he noted in his diary.

Meanwhile, dispatches from Admiral Sims in London revealed that the Allies, far from being on the road to victory, as Wilson and his Cabinet had believed, were in serious danger of defeat. Allied merchant ships were being sunk by German submarines faster than they could be replaced: 900,000 tons had gone to the bottom in March; identical losses were expected by the end of April. Britain had just three weeks worth of grain on hand; once that was gone, the islands could be starved into submission.

"It looks as though the Germans . . . [are] winning the war," Sims said to Admiral Sir John Jellicoe, the First Sea Lord and his old friend.

"They will win," Jellicoe said, "unless we can stop these losses—and stop them soon."

"Is there no solution to the problem?"

"Absolutely none that we can see now."

Sims was further astonished to learn that the British were as yet only rarely using destroyers to escort merchant vessels; diverting destroyers to convoy duty, the Admiralty told him, would expose the Grand Fleet to German attack. There were simply not enough ships.

Sims called for American destroyers. "We cannot send too soon or too many," he said.

Franklin shared Sims' sense of urgency, and it was greatly intensified later in the month when first a British Mission, headed by former Prime Minister Arthur Balfour, and then a French one, whose major figure was Marshal Joseph Joffre, the hero of the Battle of the Marne, travelled to Washington to determine just what sort of aid they could expect from Woodrow Wilson. Franklin met with both delegations, and informally urged each to press for all that they needed in the way of ships, men, and *materiel*. [4]

At a Navy League dinner for the British Mission in early May, Franklin expressed some of the frustration he—and they—continued to feel. The Allies had listened to a lot of vague promises, "fair words and more fair words," he told the dinner guests, but no troops had yet arrived in Europe. "It is time [Congress and the people] insist on action *at once*. Action that will give something—definite ships, definite men—on a definite day."

Eleanor agreed. "Franklin listened to all the polite platitudes and false hopes," she told Sara, "and was called upon to speak last. . . . It was solemn and splendid and I was glad he did it and I think a good

4. He also pledged to other British officials that thirty U.S. destroyers would soon be dispatched to Britain, although neither Daniels nor Wilson had yet authorized him to do so. Roosevelt saw earlier than his superiors that the best way to beat the U-boats would be to concentrate Allied power at the junction of the sea lanes off Southwest Ireland—"the Western Approaches." (The ships were eventually sent.)

many people were but I shouldn't wonder if the Secretary was annoyed."

Balfour and Joffre, however, were understandably delighted by this militant young Roosevelt, and when Sara found that the French marshal was staying at the Fifth Avenue mansion of Henry Clay Frick, she asked if she might present to him three of Franklin's children—Anna, James, and Elliott—all of whom she was then nursing through the whooping cough. The marshal made room in his schedule, and Sara shepherded her pale, feverish grandchildren inside the mansion and up the sweeping marble staircase "to a little bedroom, and Joffre kissed all three children . . . who were so sweet and appreciative. Then the perfectly charming, brave Joffre spoke to me of my son in a most lovely way, I felt quite queer and rather like shedding a tear but managed to behave decently and thank and tell him the children would never forget seeing him, etc. . . ." (She did not neglect, either, to ask for an autographed photograph of the old soldier, which she had framed and set in a place of honor on the mantelpiece of the Springwood library.)[5]

Franklin kept up the pressure, seemed everywhere at once. He dictated letters and memoranda with such speed and accuracy that his stenographers worked in relays, one furiously scribbling while another, in an outer room, typed up the letters he had taken. "He was a perfect dictator," recalled his head stenographer Renah H. Camalier, "clear enunciation, perfect English, and everything that goes with it. He was as near a perfectionist as I've known." Everything he dictated was signed and sent out the same day, and one of his primary complaints about his chief was the too stately pace of Daniels's correspondence. "I happened into the Secretary's office this afternoon," he wrote in a memorandum to himself on July 27, 1917, "and found him signing a big batch of Bureau of Navigation mail. The letters were dated July 5th."

"The old machine is creaking horribly," he told his old political

5. Sara met Balfour, too, and was almost as impressed. She first attended a Saturday night screening of "wonderful war pictures showing *all* of the Battle of the Marne and those wonderful tanks, which look like pre-historic monsters," she wrote her son, followed by a "charming little speech" from Balfour which, "without any apparent effort and in a *low* clear voice, could be heard perfectly over Carnegie Hall." The next morning she attended a special service at the Cathedral of St. John the Divine, where the trustees escorted the members of the British Mission to their pews. Rosy was a trustee and so she got a chance to speak briefly with Balfour. He "evidently liked it *all*," she reported, "he is both musical and religious, and wins all hearts, mine included." *Source:* Roosevelt Family Papers Donated by the Children, FDRL.

ally William Church Osborn; the war at sea could be lost "unless scissors are applied to the red tape." He wielded his own scissors with glee. Under his ardent urging, Navy purchasers had already bought up so many supplies before war was declared that the President called him in and told him, "Mr. Secretary, I'm very sorry, but you have cornered the market. . . . You'll have to divide up with the Army"—or so he liked to remember.

When the slow rate at which cantonments were being built threatened to force a halt to recruitment, Franklin obtained an officer's commission for his friend Elliott C. Brown, the contractor who had rebuilt Springwood, and gave him a free hand. The pace of building nearly doubled and costs were cut drastically while the bureaucrats struggled to keep up. After he had completed one medical building, Brown received an official procurement form asking for details about the "proposed" structure; he filled it out in voluminous detail and clipped to it a photograph of the finished structure before sending it back. "Things are underway in great shape," Brown assured Franklin from a New York City campsite. "You will have some beautiful requisitions to sign someday, but I'm getting everything bought before sending them in! So it makes no difference what anyone does with them." Franklin promised to "sign the requisitions with my eyes closed."

"Who is the man . . . who is pushing things along?" asked the *Wall Street Journal* in an editorial calling for Daniels' replacement that Howe may have helped inspire. "That's easy: Franklin D. Roosevelt."[6]

Franklin bombarded his chief with stiff memoranda:

6. Such newspaper stories only confirmed Franklin's own sense of his central role in the war effort. During World War II, with concern over German agents again acute, Franklin or someone on his staff found a revolver in the drawer of a table in the Roosevelt's New York home. FDR dictated a memorandum for his files explaining its presence:

In the spring of 1917, just before or after we declared war, the Secret Service found in the safe of the German Consul in New York, a document headed: "To be eliminated." The first name on the list was that of Frank Polk [Undersecretary of State; mine was the second, followed by eight or ten others.

As a result, the Secret Service asked us both to carry revolvers as we both habitually walked to and from our offices. I was given the revolver and the shoulder holster. I wore them under my arm for three or four days. Although a fair shot with a revolver, I realized that it would take me about 30 seconds before I could reach inside my overcoat, haul out, cock, aim and fire. By that time I would normally be dead, with the assassin half a mile away!

I put the revolver in the top table drawer where it remained for 25 years.

We have only Franklin's word for this story, and it is a little hard to understand why the Germans should have chosen to eliminate two sub-Cabinet officials in advance of their superiors. *Source:* PSF Anecdotes, FDRL.

Dear Mr. Daniels—

Do please get through two vital things *today*.

1.) Get that Interior Building or give it to War Dept. & let us take latter's space here

2.) Authorize calling out Naval Militia *& Reserve*. It is essential to get them if we are to go ahead.

FDR

Someone else in the office saw this note, marvelled at Daniels's forbearance, and scrawled across its top in pencil, "Do you *always* follow his advice?"

Daniels did not. Nor did he enjoy his assistant's unwillingness to abandon his pet enthusiasms: Both men urged the rapid construction of the "splinter fleet" of 110-foot wooden submarine chasers that proved useful off Europe, but Franklin was also persuaded that the Navy needed a fleet of fifty-foot patrol boats with which to prowl the American coast. Without them, he was sure, German submarines would slip into American harbors and inlets—even attack Campobello. "I meant to tell you," he would write Eleanor that summer, "that if by any perfectly wild chance a German submarine should come into the bay and start to shell Eastport or [Welshpool], I want you to grab the children and beat it into the woods. Don't stay to see what is going on. I am not joking about this, for though it is 500 to 1 against the possibility, still there is just that one chance that the Boche will do the fool and unexpected thing."

Daniels was unpersuaded. He called these little vessels Franklin's "hobby" and thought them a dubious proposition. "Good in smooth water," he noted in his diary, "but useless in a storm. "I fear buying a lot of junk." So did the experts. The Secretary turned him down. The General Navy Board backed the Secretary. Franklin let contracts for fifty-foot boats, anyway, without authorization, and at one point evidently allowed Howe to promise a captain who served on the General Navy Board a promotion if he would reconsider his decision.[7]

Later, Franklin's critics would charge that he had been heavily influenced in this effort by Arthur Patch "Pat" Homer, the Ameri-

7. Franklin never abandoned his belief in the importance of small-boat patrols. W. Sheffield Cowles, Sr., the elderly retired admiral whom Bamie Roosevelt had married, volunteered to head the Connecticut River patrol, prowling that placid waterway on the lookout for submarines. "I am delighted that you are having such interesting work," he wrote to "Uncle Will" in the fall of 1917. ". . . I have a theory that the only reason we have not had a lot more internal attacks, explosions, etc. is because of local patrols of this kind." *Source:* Franklin D. Roosevelt, Papers as Assistant Secretary of the Navy, FDRL.

can representative of Sterling Motors, a British firm eager to provide engines for the diminutive fleet. Homer was a big, red-faced promoter, celebrated both for his geniality and for the expensive liquor he dispensed liberally from his suite at the Hay-Adams. He flattered Franklin, sent him lobsters, offered him the presidency of a new boat-building firm once the war was over, and, much later, claimed to have conspired with him and Colonel House to supplant Daniels at the Navy Department.

Emory S. Land was then a young officer who accompanied Franklin to motorboat shows at which, he once said, he acted as the Assistant Secretary's "aide, water-carrier and sword-swallower" while doing his best to provide businesslike advice on the construction of small boats and submarines. His boss's greatest weakness in those days, he said many years later, was that "there was always some friend of his who had his ear . . . some damned crook bastard who was pulling his leg."

"FDR was a sucker for anyone who was a classmate or a member of the Newport crowd," John M. Hancock, who had been in charge of Navy purchasing, remembered. "Riches and social position gave a man great validity." Land agreed. "There was someone selling paint," he remembered, "a classmate perhaps: Valentine Paint Company. FDR was always talking up Valentine Paint."

Homer was the most unsavory of Franklin's cronies, Hancock recalled, "a double-crossing son of a bitch," whose impact on both Roosevelt and Howe mystified him. Homer was not a classmate, not of Franklin's social class. But he had enormous charm, and he was an unabashed operator, a doer, "a thoroughly live person," in Franklin's words, sharing Franklin's impatience and scorn for channels. Twice, Franklin had dispatched him to England, first to bring home a seaplane engine, then to bring back an entire seaplane—"What I want is the definite result of getting a seaplane over to this side," he told a naval officer in London, "and I do not care whether it is done officially, unofficially, or otherwise." Homer got it done. He was entertaining, too, overflowing with gags, schemes, big plans: "An extraordinary salesman," with a "colorful imagination," Eleanor recalled, ". . . the kind of salesman that always appealed to Franklin. . . ."

The younger Navy officials with whom Franklin worked admired his zeal and the speed with which he responded to their requests, but some came to distrust the way he and Howe seemed so often to award contracts to firms that could benefit them politically later on. One admiral later claimed he had known no naval officer during the war who thought Franklin "an honest man. Everyone considered him a slippery bird." Others thought him simply too eager to please, too prone to say yes to his latest visitor. To circumvent this, Hancock and his colleagues worked out a reasonably foolproof system: before they went to him with a contract to sign, they wrote a telegram announcing its award. The minute Franklin affixed his bold blue signature—and before the advocates of a rival contractor could get to him—the contract was made public. The first time they worked this on him, Hancock recalled with grudging admiration, Franklin still managed to make political capital out of it, calling an interested politician to say that "While we would have liked to help you out," he was sure the man would understand that things were now on a "war footing" and had to be done differently.

Another enthusiasm of Franklin's, better directed toward victory than the fleet of small boats he so stubbornly refused to abandon, was his determination to build an anti-submarine mine barrage across the two stretches of sea every German submarine leaving or returning to its home base had to cross, the English Channel and the North Sea between Norway and Scotland. It was not entirely his idea, though he later liked to imply that it had been. "Why don't the British shut up the hornets in their nests?" Woodrow Wilson himself had wondered aloud to Daniels long before America entered the war. "We are hunting hornets all over the farm and letting the nests alone."

But had it not been for Franklin's relentless persistence, it is unlikely that it would ever have been tried. Daniels and Admiral Benson were dubious about it; in his diary, the Secretary called it a "stupendous undertaking . . . of doubtful practicality." Admiral Sims was skeptical, too, agreeing with the British Admiralty which, he said, had looked into the matter and found it "quite infeasible." The North Sea was too stormy; the cost of manufacturing the 400,000 mines that would be needed was prohibitive; and the painstaking sowing of them only a few feet apart under the constant threat of German attack would prove too dangerous.

Franklin refused to believe it and went so far as to argue the case for the mine barrage with Balfour during his May visit. Later that same month, a Massachusetts inventor named Ralph C. Browne stopped by Franklin's office, bringing with him a miniature model of something he called the "Browne Submerged Gun," an anti-submarine weapon which was set off when a long, electrified copper antenna, suspended below a buoy, was brushed by a metal object. Franklin saw instantly that the antenna might be adapted to set off rows of mines simultaneously and ordered tests made off New London as soon as possible. They were spectacularly successful in June; far fewer mines would now be needed to do the job.[8]

Despite the tests, Sims continued to echo British doubts. After all, he wrote from London, "the people over here are fighting for their very existence"; they had therefore "examined . . . every scheme," could not help but resent suggestions made by inexperienced Americans, and had had "very bitter experience with every new mine that they have designed and developed. . . ." Sims' condescending tone, and what Wilson had come to see as his slavish admiration for British expertise, angered the President. "Every time we have suggested anything to the Admiralty," he told a group of naval officers in confidence that summer, "the reply has come back that virtually amounted to this, that it had never been done that way, and I felt like saying, 'Well, nothing was ever done so systematically as *nothing* is being done now. . . .'"

Franklin redoubled his efforts, and when Daniels and Benson still seemed to share Sims' doubts, conferred several times with the President, whose impatience he encouraged. On October 3, on his own initiative, Franklin authorized manufacture of 100,000 of the new firing devices. Two weeks later Wilson and the Cabinet endorsed his plan, and Daniels dispatched an admiral to London, charged with winning the Admiralty's approval. The British acquiesced.

Having won his battle, Franklin did his best later that month to make certain Wilson remembered who had been most responsible for seeing that the President's plans were carried out. He wrote a "Confidential" memorandum entitled "Proposed Measures to close English Channel and North Sea against submarines by mine barrage." It was ostensibly meant only for his chief, but he simultaneously sent a copy of it to Wilson. ("I know you will not mind . . . ," he blandly assured Daniels, "as I have discussed it with him several times.") Its tone was peremptory; its meaning unmistakable:

8. In 1928, telling a reporter of Browne's visit to his office, Franklin said he had been "a typical inventor just like one of the thousands of crank inventors who pestered the Navy Department . . . with a beard and a regular inventor's bag . . . [he] looked like a crank." Browne wrote to protest—he had been clean-shaven, for one thing, and had come to the Navy Department highly recommended by qualified Navy engineers. Franklin apologized.

This is, of course, nothing more or less than a resurrection of my proposition, which with all earnestness possible, I called to the attention of the President, the Secretary of the Navy, the Chief of Operations, the General Board, (etc., etc.) . . . during the months of May and June past. . . . I reiterated the need for haste. I know how unseemly it is to seem to say "I told you so," but it is a literal fact that, while the British Admiralty may be blamed in part, our own Navy Department is at least largely responsible for failing to consider this proposition seriously through all these months—May, June, July, August, September and October, which have gone over the dam beyond recall. . . . We have done altogether too much amiable "consideration" of this matter. . . . I dislike exaggeration, but it is really true that the elimination of submarines from all the waters between the United States and Europe must of necessity be a vital factor in winning the war.

"I . . . have given the Sec'y a very stinging memorandum," he wrote to Eleanor the same day, "and sent a copy to the President. *Some day they will make interesting reading.*"

In late February 1918, a special convoy of twenty-four lake cargo ships finally set out for Scotland, loaded with 22 million pounds of TNT, 50,000 feet of wire cable, and the casings for 100,000 mines. In June, they began to be sown in the North Sea at 300-foot intervals in three tiers, the first at 45 feet, the second at 165 feet, the third at 240. Seventy thousand of them were in place when the war ended.

It was an extraordinary technical achievement; even Sims later said it had been "one of the wonders of the war." And the mines did account for at least three and possibly six enemy submarines. But because it had not been completed when hostilities ended, its efficacy was never really tested. This did not dissuade Franklin from believing to the end of his life that the impact of the "mere fact of the existence of the barrage" on German naval morale had played a decisive part in the Allied victory.

In early April 1917, Franklin received a letter from the popular American novelist Winston Churchill, a friend both of Wilson and of the Navy (he had attended Annapolis), volunteering his pen for the duration. Whether Franklin had in mind emulating Admiral Sims' clandestine 1908 collaboration with the writer for *McClure's*, he now tried something very like it. Accepting Churchill's offer, Franklin

pointedly suggested he take on more than "mere 'write-ups,' or recruiting posters of Navy life."

The novelist took the cue and in the course of writing a series of
newspaper and magazine articles on the modern Navy, heard a good
deal from naval officers about Daniels' alleged failings, enough so that
he told Franklin the department was "suffering from hookworm—
certainly not through any fault of yours."

Franklin was very pleased. If Churchill felt that way, he said, he
should tell his friend in the White House of his concern; Wilson would
be sure to listen to him. To aid Churchill in his work, Franklin wrote
for him on May 10 an anonymous ten-page memorandum, detailing
his chief's alleged dilatoriness on several fronts. No real plan had been
drawn up immediately upon the severing of relations with Germany
on February 3, he wrote, nor had the fleet been brought north for
refitting until the end of March—though "the matter was discussed
and discussed and discussed. . . ." No effort had been made to ascertain
Britain's needs, though "for at least a week beforehand it was definitely
known that war would take place." There had been delays in building
an adequate coast patrol and raider squadrons. Although the Secretary
had been told "hundreds of times" that naval training facilities were
inadequate, his indecision about expanding them had resulted in miserable living conditions, and "contagious diseases of every form, from
spinal meningitis to measles, [have] taken a large toll of the men."
While it was "absolutely true that the Secretary has saved the Government much money by dickering with steel plants, shipbuilding companies, etc. etc., [it was] also an absolute fact that the savings . . . [have]
been eaten up many times by the fact that when war actually came on
April 7, the Government had to jump in and purchase millions of
dollars worth of supplies at higher figures in order to make up for the
deficiencies."

The most pressing current need was to work out with the Allies
a coordinated plan to combat the submarine menace—"not in six
months, but in two weeks"—"the Secretary's whole time is spent with
people who divert his attention from one subject to another, with the
result that he . . . is scattering his energies among a mass of absolutely
uncoordinated details."

Franklin's summation was especially scathing:

. . . the business of the Department is not going forward as a whole,
but is going forward half-heartedly along unwarranted lines. The Chief

of Operations, Admiral Benson, proceeds cautiously and slowly from day
to day with little questions of despatching gunboats around the West
Indies, with pleasant chats with American and foreign officers, who also
come to talk about a hundred different subjects, and every matter of real
moment is delayed from 24 hours to 24 weeks. . . .

The whole question resolves itself down to this: In the Secretary's
office the least that can be said is that there is constant delay and lack of
decision—so much, in fact, that the actual naval operations in this country
by the United States have been seriously threatened. The delay of two
months, which has already occurred, has, in all probability, meant the loss
of many thousands of tons of merchant shipping. The same delay . . . if
it is carried to its logical conclusion . . . may mean . . . the actual winning
of the war by the enemies of the United States. Furthermore, there are
certain officers in close touch with the Secretary, such as Admiral Benson,
who think and act exactly along the same lines as the Secretary does. They
do not grasp the broad situation, they fail to come to decisions and spend
their time magnifying ridiculous details. Further down the line among the
various Bureaus and in the general business organization of the Department and the navy yards there exists an exceedingly bad *esprit de corps*.
The morale is slack and the result is shown in every transaction the Navy
Department makes at the present time.

Churchill's final report to the President was far more temperate and
balanced than Franklin's secret memorandum had been—the writer
was careful to consult other knowledgeable authorities before writing
it—but it evidently persuaded Wilson gently to urge Daniels to bring
younger, more active men into the procurement process. The Secretary was glad to comply. "I had heard [Churchill] was going to criticize
me rather severely," he noted in his diary.

Franklin professed to be pleased, too, at least when reporting to his
family. Churchill's talks with Wilson had been "pretty satisfactory,"
he told Eleanor; he was "encouraged to think that [the President] has
begun to catch on, but then it will take lots more of the Churchill type
of attack."

The children's whooping cough kept Eleanor from taking them to
Campobello until late July, more than a month later than usual. She
had been reluctant to leave Washington even then. Franklin had a cold,
seemed tired and irritable, overworked at the department, frustrated by
his chief's deliberateness and his own inability to take charge.

But Eleanor sensed that something else was wrong as well. Franklin seemed unusually anxious to see her on her way north. They had

quarrelled before she finally left on July 14, and two days later Franklin wrote a somewhat sheepish letter to Campobello, as close as he easily came to an apology and meant to reassure his wife:

Dearest Babs,

I had a vile day after you left, stayed at home, coughed, dozed, tried to read and work and failed even to play Miss Millikin [a game of solitaire then popular in Washington society]! But today I am practically all right and have been here at the office as usual, except for lunch with [Commander de Blaupré, the French naval attaché, and his wife] and am going to dine with Warren and Irene [Robbins] alone. I really can't stand that house all alone without you, and you were a goosy girl to think or even pretend to think that I don't want you here all the summer, because you know I do! But honestly you ought to have six weeks straight at Campo, just as I ought to, only you can and I can't. I know what a whole summer here does to people's nerves and at the end of this summer I will be like a bear with a sore head until I get a change or some cold weather—in fact as you know I am unreasonable and touchy now—but I shall try to improve. . . .

Kiss the chicks for me all round, and many many for you.

Your devoted
F

He wrote again the next day, just as solicitously:

Dearest Babs,

It seems years since you left and I miss you horribly and hate the thought of the empty house. Last night I thought I heard a burglar and sat at the head of the stairs with the gun for half an hour, but it turned out to be the cat. . . .

Write me all about the *Half Moon* and the house and place. The chief thing I worry about is fire, and you must see that the extinguishers are filled, that the fireplaces in the rooms are pointed up, and that no large fire is left when you go to bed.

I wonder how the chicks like Campo this year?

Evidently you told Mama I had a cold. I have had a telegram and a letter!

Love and kisses to you all. . . .

Despite the warmth of these letters, Eleanor was right. Franklin had indeed been anxious for her to leave town.

He had fallen in love with another woman—Lucy Page Mercer, Eleanor's own social secretary.

Lucy was tall—nearly as tall as Eleanor—and had the same blue eyes and long, light brown hair, but she was far more graceful, far more beautiful, and at twenty-six, almost half a dozen years younger. Alice Longworth remembered Lucy as "beautiful, charming and absolutely delightful," with a "really lovely" face and "always beautifully dressed." Anna recalled liking to be greeted by her warm smile whenever she returned from school to find Miss Mercer working in her mother's sitting room. A friend remembered seeing her seated on the Roosevelts' rug, Eleanor's mail spread around her, briskly separating letters, bills, and invitations into neat piles; "she was a charmer." Another friend wrote of her extraordinarily fresh complexion, "*fort animé,* . . . brilliant . . . transparent." Still another remembered her low, throaty voice—in such contrast with Eleanor's high, unsteady one— and a smile "the most beautiful and winning I have ever seen."

Much later, Alice Longworth made a point of telling one interviewer that Lucy was also "very well-bred." In fact, her family heritage was every bit as distinguished as the Roosevelts', although she was a Catholic and the circumstances under which she was brought up were far more pinched. Her mother, Minnie Tunis Mercer, was a Henderson from North Carolina, who had been married twice, first to an Englishman named Percy Norcop, who helped her go through most of her fortune before she divorced him as an adulterer in 1886; then, two years later, to Carroll Mercer, whose daughter, Violetta, she bore just seven months after the wedding. Lucy, the second daughter, was born in 1891.

Carroll Mercer was descended from the Catholic founders of Maryland, who had settled on Chesapeake Bay in the 1630s. He was handsome and charming, well known as a hard-riding "sportsman" in New York and Washington as well as Baltimore, but left by his impecunious father without the funds that would have made such a life permanently possible. The military provided him with a small income and something more or less congenial to do. He became first a Marine officer—despite a year's suspension for having twice been drunk on duty—and then an Army officer, serving as Commissary at the Battle of San Juan Hill and rising to the rank of major before retiring in 1901. Thereafter, he would list his profession simply as "gentleman."

At the turn of the century, the Mercers had been sought-after members of the younger crowd of cave dwellers. Minnie, who moved from engagement to engagement in a large brougham complete with liveried coachman and footman, was considered by one society reporter "easily the most beautiful woman in Washington society . . . to be invited to one of her dinners was in itself a social distinction that qualified one for admission to any home." Her beauty and flamboyance put off some of the more staid members of the society in which she shone—she was seen smoking cigarettes in public, for one thing, and she had been sensationally divorced—but men found her irresistible.

Her husband belonged to all the leading clubs, including the Metropolitan and Riding clubs, and he helped found Chevy Chase. But he also continued to drink steadily, and his alcoholism was eventually complicated by diabetes and Bright's disease.

Lucy's parents quarrelled constantly, while allowing most of what was left of Minnie's fortune simply to dissolve. "They just *spent* it," a relative remembered, still disbelieving half a century later. In 1903, when Lucy was twelve, they separated. Minnie moved to New York with her daughters, and found work in the newest of the very few professions thought suitable for ladies of her class who found themselves embarrassingly short of funds: she became what was then called an "inside decorator," bringing her refined tastes to bear on the parlors and ballrooms and foyers of the newly rich.

Lucy inherited her mother's beauty, but little of her fondness for dramatics. Minnie saw to it that she and Violetta were sheltered as far as possible from the showier side of her New York life, and managed to send them to spend at least one year abroad, being educated in an Austrian convent where even the sisters found Lucy's lack of worldliness unusual: a nun confiscated her lacy nightgowns as soon as she unpacked them, muttering that they were far too sophisticated for a girl of seventeen, the sort of thing a *prostitute* might wear. Lucy did not know what a prostitute was.

In 1912, Minnie moved back to Washington, to an apartment this time, not a house, and took a job in "an art establishment," suggesting the proper sort of paintings to add refinement to the homes of freshman congressmen. Her estranged husband came back, too, but lived apart from her and worked for a time as manager of the Riding Club of which he had once been a prominent member. It seems likely that only Catholicism kept the Mercers from divorce; Minnie is thought never to have seen nor spoken to her husband again, though her daughters visited him from time to time when he was ill.

Minnie was able to support herself through her gallery work, but she could not provide adequately for her girls. Violetta became a trained nurse and eventually married the wealthy physician for whom she worked; Lucy, just twenty when her mother returned to the capital, found only occasional work as a decorator. The refinements which she had been encouraged to attain—perfect manners, good taste, social ease—were not intended to translate easily into a professional career; nor were young ladies like Lucy expected to consider such a thing. Hard times were to be considered transitory, standards and appearances were to be maintained, while they bravely became governesses or social secretaries to more prosperous matrons and waited for the good marriage that would rescue them from their predicament.

In the winter of 1914, Eleanor Roosevelt—then pregnant with the second Franklin, Jr. and still a little intimidated by the sheer volume of invitations to be sent out and received, rejected or accepted—had hired Lucy Mercer to help her three mornings a week. Eleanor often consulted her Auntie Bye about her new duties as an official's wife, and it seems likely that it was she who suggested that the timorous young woman she called "my darlingest niece" employ Miss Mercer to help her unravel the mysteries of Washington society. The Mercers had lived during Lucy's girlhood on N Street in Washington, just a few yards from Bamie's home; it would have been like her to have befriended the lovely little girl and, later, to have been aware of her need for the right sort of job; it would have been like her, too, to have told Eleanor of the girl's troubled girlhood, and of her separation from the charming but turbulent father so reminiscent of Eleanor's father and her own beloved brother, Elliott Roosevelt—whose disintegration she had been powerless to stop. Certainly, had Eleanor been told of it, that would have endeared Lucy to her. She knew first-hand the impact an unsteady parent could have on a sensitive young girl and she was, all her life, drawn most strongly to those whom she felt needed her help. Without the encouragement of someone whom she trusted as implicitly as her beloved aunt, it is hard to see how a wife so prone to jealousy and distrust as Eleanor was could have welcomed into her own home someone as young, lovely, and charming as Lucy Mercer.

At first, Lucy seems to have been treated by both Roosevelts precisely as a governess would have been treated. When, for example, Franklin returned to the house unexpectedly during the first spring she worked for the family, and found things in disarray, he had his chauffeur telephone "Miss Mercer, who later came and cleaned up." But Lucy quickly proved an efficient secretary, who understood from the inside the Washington society that then still intimidated her employer, and she brought to her duties a dignity and warmth that especially appealed to Sara; Miss Mercer was "so sweet and attractive and adores you, Eleanor," she once told her daughter-in-law. When, from time to time, an extra woman was needed at the last moment to fill out a dinner party, Lucy began to be asked to attend. She had become a part of the Roosevelt household.

She remained one for three years.

Precisely when she and Franklin became lovers is not known (although that they did seems undeniable, and that they had done so by the time she left Eleanor's employ more than likely).

His attraction for her was easily understood. He was handsome, debonair, amusing, and, as Lucy must soon have known, not always happy at home. Like the absent father whom she loved but rarely saw, Franklin was also much older than she. She was unqualified in her adoration of him; more than a quarter of a century later, she would still long for "his beloved presence . . . his ringing laugh . . . all the ridiculous things he used to say," a glimpse of "his extraordinarily beautiful head."

That quality of uncritical love, in turn, must have formed a large part of her appeal for Franklin. Lucy was dignified, beautiful, intelligent, and, unlike Eleanor, she loved listening to his plans, never disbelieved his stories, saw no need to direct his activities or keep his standards up.

He was happy in Lucy's company; she was happy in his. And as the months went by, the growing attraction between Franklin and her secretary must have become evident to Eleanor herself, frightened always that her fears of her husband's infidelity would be confirmed. Those fears may have accounted in part for her resentment at being separated from Franklin for so long by the polio epidemic of the previous year.

That his romance was always threatened with discovery may actually have added to its appeal for Franklin; he delighted all his life in harboring secrets from those who thought themselves closest to him. But the *reality* of discovery—the wounds it would leave, the anger that would surely follow, the accusations of betrayal, the loss of the approval of his wife and his mother that meant so much to him—was a different matter, and he did all he could to stave it off.

One weekend in June, Franklin took Eleanor and a party of friends on an excursion up the Potomac on the Navy yacht *Sylph*. Harry Roosevelt was aboard; so were John A. McIlhenny and his wife.

Lucy came, too. Her ostensible escort was Nigel Law, her handsome near-contemporary from the British Embassy. Law was nearly as admiring of Franklin as was Livy Davis. ("I found [Roosevelt] the most attractive man whom it was my fortune to meet during my four years in America," Law recalled much later, ". . . a man I loved and admired.") Like Livy, too, he seems to have enjoyed performing tasks for Franklin's amusement. The party went ashore at George Washington's birthplace at Wakefield, Virginia, where, he remembered, "I was stung by poison ivy for the first and last time because I climbed a wild cherry tree in bathing trunks to pick the fruit for Franklin. Probably . . . Washington had overlooked that particular tree." Law evidently also acted as Franklin's cover on such expeditions, pretending, for the sake of appearances, that he and not his married older friend was Lucy's companion.

He proved so plausible a suitor for Lucy that when he left Washington for London that autumn, *Town Topics* hinted at a romance between them, but he may not have fooled Eleanor that Saturday. In any case, a week later, Lucy no longer had a job.

Eleanor was going away for the summer, of course. There was little Lucy could do for her until the autumn, and perhaps, with America finally at war, Eleanor was able to explain her decision in purely patriotic terms; she and Franklin would be far too busy with the war effort to lead the sort of social whirl they had known in peacetime. That explanation would have been in keeping with other decisions she was making that spring: she had recently joined the Patriotic Economy League, for example, a group of prominent Washington women who signed pledge cards vowing to dress simply, save food, and curtail unnecessary entertaining for the duration.

But if she hoped that by gently letting go her social secretary she would keep Franklin and Lucy from seeing one another, she was to be disappointed. For on June 24, barely a week after her trip down the Potomac with the Roosevelts, Lucy Mercer enlisted in the Navy as a Yeoman (F) and was assigned to secretarial duties at the Navy Department. With Lucy and Franklin working together every day in the same building, Eleanor's reluctance to leave town in July had understandably increased.

So had Franklin's guilty irritation at her reluctance to leave. An article published in the *New York Times* on July 17, shortly after she had finally left and had received his half-apology, provided him with the excuse for a burst of angry sarcasm at his wife. Under the headline HOW TO SAVE IN BIG HOMES, Eleanor was quoted earnestly explaining to a reporter just how her household saved food.

Mrs. Roosevelt on her pledge card said that there were seven in the family, and that ten servants were employed. Each servant has signed a pledge card and there are daily conferences. Mrs. Roosevelt does the buying, the cooks see that there is no food wasted, the laundress is sparing in her use of soap, each servant has a watchful eye for evidence of short-comings on the part of the others; and all are encouraged to make helpful suggestions in the use of "left-overs". . . .

"Making the servants help me do my saving has not only been possible but highly profitable," said Mrs. Roosevelt . . . "Since I have started following the home-card instructions prices have risen, but my bills are no larger."

Franklin was merciless:

All I can say is that your latest newspaper campaign is a corker and I am proud to be the husband of the Originator, Discoverer and Inventor of the New Household Economy for Millionaires! Please have a photo taken showing the family, the ten cooperating servants, the scraps saved from the table and the hand book. . . .

Honestly, you have leaped into public fame, all Washington is talking of the Roosevelt Plan, and I begin to get telegrams of congratulations and requests for further details from Pittsburgh, New Orleans, San Francisco. . . .

Eleanor was mortified. "I do think it was horrid of that woman to use my name in that way," she wrote, "and I feel dreadfully about it because so much is not true and yet some of it I did say. I will never be caught again that's sure, and I'd like to crawl away for shame."

With his family away at last, Franklin was now free, like so many of the capital's "summer bachelors," to do pretty much whatever he pleased. There were new opportunities for country drives, quiet suppers, picnics in the parks; and for more long, leisurely overnight trips up and down the Potomac and the James, dining on deck by the light of Japanese lanterns, stopping to swim or to explore the shady grounds of the old mansions that stood here and there along the riverbank and were so reminiscent of those along the Hudson back home.

Livy Davis, down from Boston, came along on some of these excursions. Nigel Law and Lucy continued to come, too. It was inevitable that Eleanor would learn that Lucy had been along; too many other people who Eleanor knew were aware of it for the secret to be kept. Therefore, Franklin now found it best to mention her presence in his letters to Campobello, but casually, in decorous tandem with

Law or as part of a large congenial group of friends, and always in connection with harmless subjects that had nothing to do with his real feelings.[9] The chatty, insouciant tone of his summertime letters was still precisely that of those he had written as a Harvard undergraduate to throw his mother off the trail of the young women in whom he was then interested.

> The trip on the *Sylph* was a joy and a real rest, though I got in a most satisfactory visit to the fleet. . . . Such a funny party, but it worked out *wonderfully!* The Charlie Munns, the Cary Graysons, Lucy Mercer and Nigel Law, and they all got on splendidly. We swam about four times and Sunday afternoon went up the James to Richmond. We stopped at Lower and Upper Brandon, Westover[10] and Shirley and went all over them, getting drenched to the skin by several severe thunderstorms. Those old houses are really wonderful but *not* comfy!
>
> I found much food for thought in the fleet—things not right and due to old lady officers and lack of decision in Department.

Later that summer, Franklin reported to Eleanor that after golf one Sunday, he had driven to a friend's country place near Harper's Ferry.

9. FDR continued to do the same thing literally to the last day of his life. On the evening of April 11, 1945, he chatted with his daughter over the telephone about how her ailing son was doing and plans for a Warm Springs barbecue the next day. Anna knew that he had again been seeing Lucy Mercer, now the widow of Winthrop Rutherfurd; in fact, she herself had sometimes acted as hostess at small White House dinners attended by her father's old friend when her mother was out of town. "There was a funny little thing there," she said years later, remembering that final telephone conversation with her father. "Lucy Mercer was also at Warm Springs. . . . [She was in fact within earshot as father and daughter spoke.] He never once mentioned Lucy Mercer. . . . In other words, his private life was his private life. . . ." *Source:* Transcript of interview with Anna Roosevelt Halsted, Columbia Oral History Project, Columbia University; a letter from Lucy Mercer Rutherfurd to Anna proves that she was present during the telephone conversation, Bernard Asbell, ed., *Mother & Daughter,* page 188. For a discussion of the origins of FDR's well-honed technique for keeping his own counsel while seeming to reveal all, see Geoffrey C. Ward, *Before the Trumpet: Young Franklin Roosevelt, 1882–1905,* pages 251–255.

10. Westover was the handsome home of the Byrd family, among the first of the First Families of Virginia. Nigel Law recalled the unannounced visit by Roosevelt and his guests:

> Franklin and I and some of the party landed at the bottom of the garden and rang the bell. A darkie servant came out and he was told to say that the Under Secretary of the U.S. Navy would be glad to be allowed to visit the house and garden. The servant looked doubtful and soon came back with a curt "No." For a moment we were nonplussed for we particularly wanted to visit this famous old place. Then Franklin had an idea. He said, "Maybe they don't like Yankees in these parts. You send in your card." So as a joke I told the man to take my card, on which I was described as 3rd Secretary of his Britannic Majesty's Embassy. To my surprise he came running back to say, "The Master wants you all to come right in." Franklin was much tickled by this Southern rebuff to federal authority, and kept laughing over it all afternoon.

Source: Jonathan Daniels, *The End of Innocence,* page 236.

"Lucy Mercer went and the Graysons and we got there at 5:30, walked over the farm—a very rich one, run by two sisters—had supper with them and several neighbors, left at nine and got home at midnight! The day was magnificent. . . ."

When he thought he could rely on the discretion of close friends, he did not report his times with Lucy to his wife. He sometimes met her in the evenings at Corcoran House, the elegant mansion of Edith Morton Eustis, whom he had known and admired since his boyhood, which stood conveniently on R Street between his office and his home. Edith was one of the five handsome daughters of the late Vice President Levi Morton, a friend and Dutchess County neighbor of Franklin's parents.[11] Her husband was William Corcoran Eustis, a sportsman and sometime diplomat from the South, who owned still more stately homes in Virginia and South Carolina. Edith was fond of both Franklin and Lucy, and dependably close-mouthed.

Alice Roosevelt Longworth had Franklin and Lucy both to dinner, too, when she knew that her retiring cousin was away—"He *deserved* a good time," she once explained. "He was married to Eleanor." Franklin mentioned these dinners in his letters to Campobello, but said nothing of other guests.

Alice had first noticed the lovers laughing together as they drove past her in Franklin's open car, and called him at his office to tease him about it.

"I saw you twenty miles out in the country," she said. "You didn't see me. Your hands were on the wheel, but your eyes were on that perfectly lovely lady."

"*Isn't* she perfectly lovely," he replied.[12]

But Alice's discretion was not foolproof, and at least once she seems to have wanted to tell her cousin what her husband was doing. One afternoon in Washington, Eleanor encountered Alice in the rotunda of the Capitol, she innocently reported to Franklin, and "She inquired if you had told me, and I said no and that I did not believe in knowing

11. The Morton girls were praised in their day by the Washington *Capital,* not only for their beauty and social prominence, but for the fact that they had been "taught to wait upon themselves and take care of their clothes. Whenever they came in from a walk or drive they put away their own gloves and wraps and hats, not in the careless way of children, but *carefully.*" Source: Jonathan Daniels, *Washington Quadrille,* page 166.

12. Cousin Bamie's son, W. Sheffield Cowles, Jr., recalled years later that he, too, had seen Franklin and Lucy driving around Washington together—"often, I used to think, *too* often." Source: Interview with W. Sheffield Cowles, Jr.

things which your husband did not wish you to know, so I think I will be spared any further mysterious secrets!"[13]

If Eleanor had hoped by this letter to prompt Franklin to reveal anything, she was disappointed; his response to it was as jaunty and opaque as ever. Nothing was said of Eleanor's meeting with Alice, or what she might have wanted to confide.

"I don't think you read my letters," Eleanor once chided her husband, "for you never answer a question and nothing I ask for appears!"

All his life, Franklin answered only the questions he felt like answering, yielded only what he wished to yield.

That same crowded summer, he had been up to something else of which neither his wife nor his mother approved. On Independence Day, he was one of four speakers who addressed the annual Tammany Hall celebration in New York. A newspaper photographer posed the tall Assistant Secretary and Boss Murphy together after the speechmaking. Murphy still proudly wears his broad, embroidered Tammany sash. Franklin has taken his off, and holds it, rolled up as tightly as possible, in his fists. Neither man smiles very widely.

"Rosy was in town yesterday," Sara wrote her son a few days later, "& says 'they all feel quite upset at the T. Club [appearance] as T. is working against [John P.] Mitchel [the reform candidate for mayor] &

---

13. According to Alice, she and Franklin shared still another secret in wartime Washington. Bernard Baruch, then head of the War Industries Board, was believed to be conducting an affair with May Ladenburg, the beautiful daughter of a senior partner in the German-American banking house of Ladenburg, Thalmann & Company whose loyalties were thought suspect. Because Alice was a friend of hers, she was asked to suggest the best places in Miss Ladenburg's studio to plant microphones. She was happy to oblige: "All I was being asked to do," she said later, "was to look over transoms and peep through keyholes. Could anything be more delightful than that?" A microphone was duly hidden beneath the mattress of a suspended bed in which she entertained her lover.

Franklin was called in to provide a guest staying in the Ladenburg home with a sheaf of false but official-looking documents about the disposition of the fleet, with instructions to leave them around the house in the hope that his hostess might be overheard discussing them with Baruch.

Alice and several Secret Servicemen then gathered in an adjoining stable to listen to the tryst. Nothing momentous was recorded, she remembered, although "We did hear her ask Bernie how many locomotives were being sent to Rumania or something like that. In between the sounds of kissing so to speak. . . . Of course we were doing a *most* disgraceful thing in the name of looking after the affairs of our country, but it was sheer rapture!"

It especially pleased Alice that when she and Franklin laughed about the incident in the White House years later, Eleanor said, "You know Alice, I have always disapproved of what you and Franklin were doing!" They had been most unfair to May Ladenburg. Source: Michael Teague, *Mrs. L.*, pages 162–163.

Franklin's speaking strengthens Tammany.' Uncle Warren says one of the papers has pictures of you and *Murphy* side by side—All this rather upsets me, I confess."[14]

Franklin offered what reassurance he could: "Don't let the July 4th Speech worry you—Anybody in the state of NY will tell you where I stand, and you must remember that the meeting was a purely patriotic one & that it was addressed by a Democratic Senator from Colorado, a Republican Congressman from California, a New York Progressive, and an upstate Democrat, myself."

But in fact his presence was inevitably taken by Tammany as he had intended it to be taken—as evidence that he no longer wished to be considered its implacable enemy; that in the interests of party unity (and his own future) he knew he needed to make the best peace he could with the big-city Democrats who had taken such pleasure in defeating him for the Senate nomination three years earlier.[15]

When Franklin developed yet another cold in August, he did his best to keep his mother from coming down to take care of him. The cold was almost gone, he wrote, and, "If I get another or a tummy ache, I will wire you to come." Otherwise, his busy schedule would not permit him to pay enough attention to her to make the trip worthwhile, he told her; he left the house at 7:15 a.m. for exercises with Walter Camp, lunched at his desk, and came home only in time for a late dinner.

In fact, however, his cold was not gone; combined with a recurrence of his old throat trouble, it put him in the hospital for four days—and Eleanor, not her mother-in-law, hurried down this time to nurse him.[16]

14. She was never able to stay upset with her son for long, and her letter's chastening tone is quickly abandoned: "I am glad to have your new photos. They are *almost* very good. I suppose I am difficult to satisfy . . . with dear loving messages. . . ." *Source:* Roosevelt Family Papers Donated by the Children, FDRL.

15. He had already demonstrated his good faith while clearing all appointments at the Brooklyn Navy Yard with Tammany Congressman John J. Fitzgerald, chairman of the Ways and Means Committee. Fitzgerald, who also visited Franklin's office at the Navy Department often to convey constituents' requests for favors, remembered him many years later as having been "very, very cooperative."

16. His fever shot up dangerously shortly after Eleanor arrived, and she had to decide whether or not to cable the news to Louis Howe, then aboard a naval vessel bound for an inspection of the Guantanamo naval base in Cuba. Grace Howe advised against it. "You'd better not let him know [Mr. Roosevelt] is worse," she told Eleanor, "that is unless you want him to jump right off that ship and swim ashore and rush right back. . . ." Eleanor held off until the fever subsided. *Source:* Lela Stiles, *The Man Behind Roosevelt,* page 53.

Sara stayed on the island, sleeping in her children's cottage to keep an eye on things despite the presence of a nanny and governess. "I hope you are daily gaining," she told her "Dearest son." "You certainly were unlucky to get that horrid illness, but I think fortunate to have the most lovely person to rush to you as she did and stay." Perhaps Sara sensed that there had been friction between her children, even that her son seemed alarmingly restless, for she went on to remind him of the rare qualities of her daughter-in-law: "Irene [a wealthy friend] spoke to Aunt Kassie of Eleanor with *such* admiration and affection, she is clever enough to see how different E. is from some of *her* friends!"

Franklin and Eleanor evidently had words again during her visit, and before Eleanor returned to Campobello, she made him promise to come to the island the following week. "I hated to leave you yesterday," she wrote him. "Please go to the doctor twice a week, eat well and sleep well, and remember I *count* on seeing you the 26th. My threat was no idle one."

The nature of that threat is not known, but it seems most likely that she meant to bring the children back to Washington if Franklin did not appear. Franklin made it to the island in time and stayed long enough to forestall her premature return.[17]

When Eleanor and the children did finally come back to Washington in the fall, it was to a new home. They had outgrown the house on N Street. The fault for the move, Franklin had told his Cousin Bamie, "lies only & entirely with FDR, Jr. and JAR!" whose arrival had made her home into "a sardine box." The new, rented house at 2131 R Street was larger, with a garden big enough for the boys to play catch in, and two blocks closer to the office and the White House.

Eleanor's life was different, too. She was thirty-four that autumn, and a dozen years of marriage had failed to bring her the happiness she had hoped for. She still found Washington social life both tedious and intimidating. Motherhood held few joys. Her marriage had not provided her with the ideal, intimate partnership for which she longed. Most important, perhaps, from her point of view, neither her children nor her husband needed her constant attentions, and unless she were needed she always found it difficult either to feel loved or to provide

17. Franklin also tried to write his wife more frequently: "You have been a marvelous correspondent," she told him that autumn, "& it has been such a pleasure to see your handwriting daily." *Source*: Roosevelt Family Papers Donated by the Children, FDRL.

love to others. Anna, James, and Elliott now attended day schools. Nannies and governesses saw to the smaller children's wants. Franklin, ever anxious for her approval, nonetheless led his own increasingly busy life, into which she was allowed to penetrate only so far, and the summer's strains, still imperfectly understood by her but no less threatening, had worsened the relationship between them. Her own closest friend, Isabella Ferguson, lived too far away to see often.

Until the autumn of 1917, she still had little life of her own, then; was still focusing all of her Roosevelt energy and intelligence and organizational skill on domestic tasks altogether too small to bear their weight. Eleanor Roosevelt could never take on new tasks, learn new things, meet new people for herself alone—that, she would have thought selfish, evidence of a failure to sink her own needs in the needs of others—but she could find it within herself to do those things in the interests of people she thought more needy than she. Soldiers and sailors did need her, she convinced herself, and she rushed to fill that need.

"All my executive ability, which had been more or less dormant up to this time, was [now] called into play," Eleanor later recalled. "The house must run more smoothly than ever, we must entertain and I must be able to give less attention to it than ever before. The children must lead normal lives; Anna must go to the Eastman School every day, and James and Elliott must go to the Cathedral school, which was out in the opposite direction. . . . My mother-in-law used to laugh at me and say I could provide my chauffeur with more orders to be carried out during the day than anyone else she had ever listened to. . . ."

She had begun her war work in a small way, just as other, more conventional Washington matrons began, by organizing her own household to save food; embarrassed as she had been by the newspaper interview about her home economies, she did not "crawl away in shame," as she had said she would.

That summer at Campobello she had also knitted ceaselessly for the Comforts Committee of the Navy League—the soft, steady clicking of her needles would accompany her everywhere she went for the rest of her life, keeping her hands busy even when she had momentarily lighted.

This activity, too, produced its own tensions. When she nervously left Washington for Campobello in July, she had left Lucy Mercer, no longer her employee but an active knitter herself, in charge of her

"Wool Saturdays," distributing yarn and gathering up completed scarves and socks and sweaters from the other members of her circle. Eleanor had insisted—perhaps as a not so subtle reminder that for all the good manners and knowledge of Capitol society Miss Mercer possessed, the younger woman was not to think herself an equal—that Lucy's work was to be performed as part of a purely business arrangement, and enclosed a check in payment for all the trouble she had taken. Lucy, no less sensitive, returned the check with a somewhat formal letter:

> My dear Mrs. Roosevelt—
>
> It is shocking to think your letter has been on my desk a week—and unanswered.
>
> Of course you are the mistress of the situation and I must abide by your wishes! I am only too sorry to have been unbusiness-like, for I know that is annoying.
>
> I regret, too, that I must return the cheque for subtraction and give you more trouble as the two last wooley parties were not held—according to the Assistant Secretary's instructions[18]—and on the 21st of July I was not there! I have not written you about it all as I knew you would hear at first hand. I went for a little while last Saturday to answer questions and list what came in—and to tell the dear ladies the distribution would in all probability be resumed. Poor dears, they are so distressed!
>
> Affectionately,
> Lucy Page Mercer

Eleanor sent the check back again, she told Franklin, "saying I knew she had done far more work than I could pay for. She is evidently quite cross with me!"

18. Even knitting had become part of the struggle between Daniels and his old enemies that summer. Colonel Thompson of the Navy League charged that the department had colluded with radical labor leaders to thwart an investigation of West Coast sabotage. Daniels answered that the charges were utterly false and suggested Thompson resign from "what had come to be an unpatriotic organization." The colonel replied that he would resign his post only if the Secretary resigned *bis.*

Daniels then angrily barred all Navy League representatives from naval facilities—even the knitted goods turned out by the women of the League's Comforts Committee were not to be distributed among the men—and Mrs. Daniels and a formidable society leader, Mrs. Edward Stotesbury, were asked to form a new committee under the neutral auspices of the Red Cross.

Franklin, who did not wish unnecessarily to anger his chief, especially when Daniels knew of his past closeness to Thompson, insisted that Eleanor now withdraw from the League committee. She protested a little—"I think Mr. D. has made a mistake to refuse all garments from them. People will be discouraged. . . ."—but acquiesced.

"*You* are entirely disconnected," Franklin told her, "and Lucy Mercer and Mrs. [Charles A.] Munn are closing up the loose ends." *Source:* Jonathan Daniels, *Washington Quadrille,* pages 122–123.

Back in Washington, Eleanor ventured further; she helped Mrs. Daniels organize the Navy Red Cross, and began going to the Red Cross canteen at Union Station through which trainload after trainload of soldiers now passed every day. She made and wrapped baskets full of sandwiches and brewed buckets of coffee in a tin-roofed shed in the rail yards, handed out postcards to the boys, then gathered them up, censoring their messages and seeing that they were mailed; and, often alongside Mary Patten, the eldest and most indiscreet of the gossipy Patten sisters, she also ran the little notions store that provided cigars, cigarettes, chewing tobacco, and candy bars at cost—never failing to make the correct change or keep perfect records.

"General [Leonard] Wood has been here," she wrote Isabella, "& F. has been fearfully depressed by what he tells. Hopeless incompetence seems to surround us in high places & yet the *men* who go are fine. I know that, for I see trainload after trainload go to ports . . . & it's a liberal education in the American soldier! My heart aches much of the time. . . ."

No task was too onerous for Eleanor to undertake, and she was quietly scornful of those women of her class who found canteen work unsuitable. "I remember one lady who came down escorted by her husband to put in one afternoon," she wrote later. "I doubt if she had ever done any manual labor before in her life, and she was no longer young. The mere suggestion that she might have to scrub the floor filled her with horror, and we never again saw her on a shift."

Her cousin Alice, who loathed any activity undertaken out of a sense of duty and had always refused to pay the rigorous social calls Eleanor had been too conscientious to avoid, now resisted canteen work as well. She turned up at Union Station once or twice but did not return, telling her admirers she had developed a mysterious ailment called "canteen elbow" that made it impossible to pour coffee or ladle soup. Twice, Eleanor told Isabella, Alice had asked her

to see if *I* want her to work anywhere. . . . It is a pity so much energy should go to waste. . . . She's a born hostess & what an extraordinary mind, but as far as real friendship & what it means . . . she hasn't a conception of any depths in any feeling. . . . Life seems to be the long pursuit of pleasure & excitement & rather little happiness either given or taken . . . the blue bird is always to be searched for in some new & novel way. I sometimes think lives of many burdens are not really to be pitied for at least they live deeply and from their sorrows spring up flowers but an empty life is really so dreadful!

Certainly, Eleanor's was full. "Instead of making calls," she remembered, "I found myself spending three days a week in a canteen down at the railroad yards, one afternoon a week distributing [yarn] . . . two days a week visiting the naval hospital, and contributing whatever time I had left to the Navy Red Cross and the Navy Relief Society." She sometimes rose at 5:00 a.m. to get to the canteen—"do not you think Mother should not go so early?" James complained to his grandmother.

Eleanor was "the willing work horse," Franklin's Aunt Kassie said, and nothing seemed to drive her from the traces; one busy morning, slicing loaves of bread on a bread-cutting machine, she cut her finger almost to the bone. "There was no time to stop," she remembered, "so I wrapped something tightly around it and proceeded during the day to wrap more and more handkerchiefs around it, until it finally stopped bleeding." By the time she could have the doctor visit her that evening, it was too late for stitches; the scar stayed with her all her life.

On October 5, 1917—about two weeks after Eleanor returned to Washington and plunged into her new life—Lucy Mercer, who had been promoted from Yeoman 3rd to Yeoman 2nd class, was relieved of her duties at the Navy Department "by Special Order of the Secretary of the Navy." No reason was given for Daniels' action.

It has been suggested that "hardship" was the cause. Lucy's father, Carroll Mercer, had died in September. Neither Lucy, nor her mother, nor her sister attended the funeral; the pallbearers were all old, harddrinking friends from Mercer's carefree days as a clubman.[19] But it is hard to see how her leaving the Navy would have done anything but worsen her financial plight. Her father's small legacy was still in the hands of an elderly but still vigorous aunt; she no longer had her Navy salary or her part-time position with Eleanor; and she somehow had to come up each month with her $39 share of the rent on the apartment she still shared with her mother.

Perhaps another explanation makes more sense. Daniels must have seen Franklin and Lucy together often at the department, may have suspected something of their relationship, might have had those suspicions confirmed through rumors that reached his wife. (Bertie Hamlin

19. "At the church," *Town Topics* reported, "they may have reflected on what the primrose path had brought to their associate, but the same afternoon as they talked things over at the Metropolitan Club, they did not look very grave." *Source:* Jonathan Daniels, *Washington Quadrille*, page 124.

remembered that Mary Patten, Eleanor's loquacious canteen partner, and Mrs. Thomas R. Marshall, who may have discerned the Roosevelts' condescension toward her husband, the Vice President, two years earlier and was a close friend of Mrs. Daniels, had both eagerly spread stories about Franklin and Lucy that fall. Alice Longworth, too, may have begun to talk to her large circle of friends.)

The Secretary was as rigorous about the sanctity of marriage as he was forgiving about Franklin's frequent disloyalty to him. When his own brother-in-law, who supervised the *News-Observer* in his absence and had twice lent him the funds with which to rebuild his business after disastrous fires, let it be known that he was contemplating divorce so that he could marry another man's wife, Daniels wrote back: "If you are resolved in this course, no action should be taken and no lawyer consulted until you have made your home in some other place than Raleigh, North Carolina." (The brother-in-law fled to Texas.)[20]

Perhaps Daniels now felt that for the good of the service—and the reputation of the smitten young assistant of whom he was still fond despite everything—it was best that Miss Mercer move on.

In any case, she did so. Still, Franklin and Lucy arranged to see each other from time to time, and to write one another letters.

That October, both Eleanor's brother, Hall, and Quentin Roosevelt, the Colonel's youngest son, managed to make it into the infant

20. Daniels's puritanism was unshakable. When he visited Paris for the first time in 1919, and he and Mrs. Daniels were taken to see *Henry VIII* at the Paris Opera, he was so appalled, he wrote, by the scanty costumes worn by the dancers, and by the "risqué remarks" made by the actors, that he would have walked out if he had not been concerned that his French hosts would be insulted.

Congressman Lathrop Brown, Franklin's Harvard roommate, once wrote to ask that a constituent's son be reinstated in the Navy despite an embarrassing indiscretion. Louis Howe replied that in instances like this, Franklin was powerless:

Now about your young friend . . . who appears to be one of nature's noblemen and to have nothing against him except that he has broken most of the Ten Commandments. I am willing to admit that if we bar from the Navy every gent who has become mixed up with a beautiful female we would have to put most of our ships out of commission and I am afraid we might lose an admiral or two, but in this case the young man was unfortunately caught with the goods. You have run against one of the Secretary's strongest antipathies. And while I know Mr. Roosevelt will speak to Mr. Daniels about the case again, I honestly do not think he has a chance on earth. Do you want one of those "we are doing everything on earth to get this done because of the affection for the Congressman" letters or not? Will send you a masterpiece that will convince your friends that Mr. Roosevelt is sitting on Mr. Daniels' doorstep every night waiting for a chance to make one more plea when he comes home to supper, if that will ease the strain any.

Sources: Josephus Daniels, *Editor in Politics*, pages 83–84; Lela Stiles, *The Man Behind Roosevelt*, pages 44–45.

Air Force, though each suffered from such weak eyesight that he had to memorize the eye charts in secret before taking the test.

Eleanor called upon her Grandmother Hall to break the news of her grandson's enlistment in person. The old lady was appalled. Hall was a young gentleman, she said; why could he not simply pay a substitute to go to war in his place? That, after all, had been what both of Eleanor's grandfathers had done during the Civil War. Eleanor, who usually treated with infinite patience the perpetually depressed grandmother who had cared for her, was outraged. "Gentlemen," she told her, owed the same debt to their country as did all other citizens; paying someone else to do one's duty was unthinkable.[21]

Times were changing, had already changed.

On the evening of October 14, 1917, a rare event occurred at Springwood, an argument in which Franklin and Eleanor were ranged together on one side and Sara stood alone. The subject was the future of Springwood itself.

A discussion of Algonac seems to have set it off. Sara's beloved childhood home had caught fire the previous winter. The fire had begun in the attic on a bitterly cold March night and spread slowly enough downward so that although the house was finally gutted, many of the family's most precious mementoes on the lower floors had been carried to safety by friends and neighbors who came running when they saw the glow of the flames. Sara's widowed sister, Annie Hitch, who now lived at Algonac year-round, had watched it all helplessly from a chair on the lawn, wrapped in furs.

Kassie Collier happened to be visiting Sara in New York when word came of the disaster, and she and her sister had sat weeping in her library with their arms around one another at the thought of their father's great house in ruins, the house that to them and to many of their descendants had always represented everything that was safe, secure, and unchanging.

Although Warren Delano II had been dead for nearly twenty years, there was no thought among the Delano children of abandoning the site. A telegram from Uncle Fred arrived the morning after the fire vowing that the house would be rebuilt right away. Annie shifted into the gatekeeper's cottage while the crews went to work, and she was

21. Many years later, Eleanor was still a little startled by her own vehemence: "This was my first really outspoken declaration against the surroundings in which I had spent my childhood, and marked the fact that either my husband or an increasing ability to think for myself, was changing my point of view."

able to move back into Algonac in late August, just three weeks or so before the three Roosevelts gathered in the Springwood library.[22]

Sara was greatly relieved. The fire had been a great blow to her, and it pleased her now to think that the Delanos would continue to occupy the site her father had chosen for them. Like the still older Delano house at Fairhaven, Algonac was a symbol of the family, to be preserved forever.

So should Springwood be, Sara thought, and she evidently asked her children to promise that after she was gone the Place would always remain in the Roosevelt family.

Franklin, who loved the Place as much as she did, did not feel that he could give that pledge. Springwood was costly to run; there was no guarantee the children would be able to afford to keep it up, much as *they* loved it. The world was at war.

Eleanor gently agreed.

Sara was horrified. She had struggled for seventeen years to preserve the way of life set out for her and for her son by Mr. James.

The argument was not resolved that evening. Neither side would yield. Sara took Franklin and Eleanor to the depot, where they caught the late train to New York. Their parting was unusually strained.

A little over an hour after her children left, and while they were still rattling toward the city, Sara sat down at the desk in her snuggery, and there, surrounded by framed pictures of the ancestors whose example she urged her son to keep constantly in mind, she wrote "Dearest Franklin & Dearest Eleanor" an uncharacteristically anguished letter.

> ... I think of you almost in New York and I am sorry to feel that Franklin is tired and that my views are not his, but perhaps dear Franklin you may on second thoughts or *third* thoughts see that I am not so far wrong. The foolish old saying "noblesse oblige" is good and "honneur oblige" possibly expresses it better for most of us. One can be democratic as one likes, but if we love our own, and if we love our neighbor, we owe a great example, and my constant feeling is that through neglect and laziness I am not doing my part toward those around me. After I got home I sat in the library for nearly an hour reading and as I put down my book and left the delightful room and the two fine portraits, I thought: after all,

22. Mrs. Hitch had been unnerved but not undone by the fire, and when a local reporter blamed it on the recent wiring of Algonac for electricity, she wrote immediately to correct him; the old chimney had been at fault, she said. She felt it important to correct the wrong impression he had given "out of justice to the contractors and in the interest of those who might be prejudiced. . . . against the use of electricity." Even in adversity, she knew her duty as a Delano always to offer "a great example" to her neighbors. *Source:* Roosevelt Family Papers, FDRL.

would it not be better just to spend all one has at once in this time of suffering and need, and not to think of the future; for with the *trend* to "shirtsleeves," and the ideas of what men should do in always being all things to all men and striving to give up the old-fashioned traditions of family life, simple home pleasures and refinements, and the tradition some of us love best, of what use is it to *keep up* things, to hold on to dignity and all I stood up for this evening. Do not say that I *misunderstood*, I understand perfectly, but I cannot believe my precious Franklin really feels as he expressed himself. Well, I hope that while I live I may keep my "old-fashioned" theories and that *at least* in my own family I may continue to feel that *home* is the best and happiest place and that *my* son and daughter and their children will live in peace and happiness and keep from the tarnish which seems to affect so many. Mrs. Newbold's theory that children "are always just like their parents," is pretty true, as *example* is what really counts.

When I *talk* I find I usually arouse opposition, which seems odd, but is perhaps my own fault, and tends to lower my opinion of myself, which is doubtless salutary. I doubt if you will have time, dear Franklin, to read this, and if you do it may not please you. My love to our fine little James, and to you two dear ones.

Devotedly,
Mama

CHAPTER

10

A BREATHLESS, HUNTED FEELING

Ｌ IVINGSTON DAVIS came to Washington in the autumn of 1917, about the same time Lucy Mercer left the Navy Department. He had left his job at a Boston brokerage firm that summer without having anything much else in mind, and his wife Alice had written to Eleanor that she was worried about him: "He is waiting for a job to fall into his hand & cannot be persuaded that they don't come that way. He feels that to go to Washington & ask for a job is asking a favor—not offering a service. . . . I think Livingston has dim hopes that by waiting he might be of some use to Franklin but at least he could be at something else in the meantime."

Eleanor invited Alice and Livy to Washington for a weekend. "I felt sure," she told Franklin, "you & he could talk things over & find something." They did. Franklin appointed Livy his special assistant, and placed him nominally in charge of problems having to do with civilian employees, the Naval Reserve, and the state militias. Davis was to be his "right bower," or Jack of Trumps, Franklin told a Boston newspaper, and Sara, who greatly admired both Livy's looks and manners, was sure that "he is very efficient & will prove of real help."

But his worshipful friend's contribution to the war effort did not in the end prove great—Davis was best remembered for having supervised the "Eyes for the Navy" campaign, under which several thousand yachtsmen and bird-watchers volunteered their binoculars, telescopes, and opera glasses for the duration.

It is safe to say that Livy was not overburdened with duties. When he visited New York on Navy business, for example, he included a round of nightclubs: "Good dinner at Ritz. Went to Winter Garden where was usual bully show. Great! Then to Palais Royal where was bully show . . . assisted in selling [war] bonds, together with chorus. Had bully time, reaching Harvard Club at 2:15." And he recorded what he liked best about an official visit to the Norfolk Navy Yard: he "Got to fire 14″ 50. cal. three times," was permitted to bring home some real gunpowder in his pocket, and, "on way back saw 300 lb. depth charge released off raft. Killed thousands of fish!"[1]

Livy's real job, as he himself remembered it, was "to [ease] in every way possible the burdens thrust upon [Roosevelt's] shoulders"—and to provide his friend with good times. He seemed to go everywhere with his boss, applauding with shipyard workers as the Assistant Secretary exhorted them to help make *this* Kaiser "Wilhelm the Last"; taking off with him from the Navy flying field to scatter Liberty Loan pamphlets over the capital; laughing with Franklin when the formidable Hollywood comedienne, Marie Dressler, fell on top of him at a Liberty Bond rally; and, after the crowd dispersed, helping him wangle an autograph from another movie star, Mary Pickford.

In his elegant maroon leather *Excelsior Diary* for 1918 (identical with Franklin's for the same year), Livy recorded the "bully times" they had together—a more or less constant round of lunches, dinners, parties, and public relations stunts. They lunched nearly every day, often with Franklin's junior law partner, Harry Hooker; frequently knocked off early to swim at the Chevy Chase Club—"On the porch in bathing suits drinking mint juleps. Elysium!!"—or to get in a round or two of golf before attending a cocktail party, and often went to dinner after that, then on to play poker or attend the theatre. "Lunch w. FDR, then with him and Adm. Benson to watch French ace fly—

---

1. Franklin's time was not entirely filled with arduous work, either. He found time to design a bookplate for his personal naval collection and have it printed up by the Bureau of Printing and Engraving, for example, and to amass excerpts that amused him from letters sent to the War Risk Board by semi-literate dependents of veterans seeking financial assistance:

HE WAS INDUCTED INTO THE SURFACE
I AM HIS WIFE AND ONLY AIR
I AM WRITING IN THE YMCA WITH THE PIANO PLAYING IN MY UNIFORM
I WAS DISCHARGED FROM THE ARMY WITH A GOITER WHICH I WAS SENT HOME
PLEASE SEND ME A WIFE'S FORM
MY MOTHER IS DEAD ON BOTH SIDES

Source: Franklin D. Roosevelt Papers, Papers as Assistant Secretary of the Navy, FDRL.

Perfectly Thrilling, then on to dinner and a play at the Winter Garden, 'Doing Our Bit,' very gay. Went behind scenes and met [the star, former heavyweight champion] Jim Corbett." There were long drives through Virginia, too—"FDR and I left in his auto at 11:30 for a little 'giro' to find his radiator cap lost the previous night."[2]

Livy's private life was also hectic. Married to Alice, and with an adopted son who was one of Franklin's many godsons, Davis was ardently pursuing a woman identified in his diary only as "E. Davie," and seems, at least in the pages of that journal, to have been in a state of almost perpetual tumescence. "Dallied around on [the Chevy Chase Club] tennis courts with a couple of beauts when [Alice] arrived"; "Took Postmaster General's two cutey daughters to dinner-dance. Danced till 2:30"; Mrs. George Barnett, the wife of the Marine commandant "appeared bewitching in her daughter's bathing suit"; "Sat between Mrs. Birmingham and Mrs. de Silva [at dinner]. Both peaches . . . ran home alone with Mrs. S. in full moon"; "Sat next to Mrs. Spear. Danced till 3, champagne flowing like water." Livy found "charming" even the "female dentist" who scraped his teeth.

One Sunday in March, Livy and Harry Hooker "picked up Cathleen Nesbitt—actress—& took her up to FDR. Did not go in."

Harry Hooker did. Franklin's badly smitten law partner had followed the beautiful young British actress, then touring in the play *General Post*, down from New York. Eleanor does not seem to have been home; at least Miss Nesbitt had no memory of her having been there. Many years later, the actress did remember the five Roosevelt children "tearing around under our feet" at lunch, and then the unexpected arrival of a secretary to say that some sort of female delegation from Illinois had arrived.

"They say you promised to see them," the secretary told Franklin. "I'm afraid you did."

"Holy smokes," she recalled his answering. "Did I? Why did you allow me? Tell them . . . tell them . . . I'm detained at the White House on important . . . business . . . ssh! I hear them in the hall." He dove behind the sofa, surrounded by his giggling children. The secretary showed the ladies out after letting them peer into the living room, apparently empty except for Harry Hooker and Cathleen Nesbitt.

2. Livy's daily proximity to Franklin was a source of some concern to Louis Howe, who was excluded from fully sharing in his chief's social life and was distrustful of any other person who sought to get too close, but especially one who so eagerly encouraged his irresponsible side. *Source:* Interview with R. H. Camalier, Frank Freidel Papers.

"You can come out now," Hooker said after they had gone, and Franklin and the children all emerged, flushed and triumphant.

"What a handsome man Roosevelt was," Miss Nesbitt remembered many years later. "I fell in love with him at first sight."[3]

As Franklin divided his time more and more often between amusing himself with Livy and his war work at the office, and with her fears about his feelings for Lucy Mercer still fresh, Eleanor found herself increasingly isolated and unsettled. During the winter of 1918, she again began to write almost daily letters to the mother-in-law from whom she had only recently begun to free herself, letters filled with renewed need for maternal reassurance. "Much love, always, dear Mummy," she closed one note in January. "I miss you and so do the children. As the years go on, I realize how lucky we are to have you & I wish we could always be together. Very few mothers I know mean as much to their daughters as you do to me."

"I wish you were *always* here!" she told Sara again a month later. "There are always so many things I want to talk over and ask you about and letters are not very satisfactory are they?" And when, on March 17, 1918—St. Patrick's Day and Franklin and Eleanor's wedding anniversary—Sara sent "my dear children" a congratulatory telegram, Eleanor's response was especially fulsome:

> Thirteen years seems to sound a long time and yet it does not seem long. I often think of what an interesting, happy life Franklin has given me and how much you have done to make our life what it is. As I have grown older I have realized better all you do for us, and all you mean to me and the children especially and you will never know how grateful I am nor how much I love you dear.

On May 15, 1918, Franklin and Josephus Daniels waited with the President, the Postmaster General, and other dignitaries on the lawn of the White House for the ceremonial arrival of the very first airmail delivery from New York. Democratic politicians had begun to talk of Franklin for the New York governorship, and when the subject of Al Smith's possible candidacy for that office came up, he made a point of reminding the President that while Smith was undeniably able, he was

3. Cathleen Nesbitt, who had hoped to marry Rupert Brooke, the handsome English soldier-poet who died aboard a French hospital ship in the Aegean Sea in 1915, eluded Harry Hooker and a host of other equally eager suitors on both sides of the Atlantic and married a British barrister fond of amateur theatrics, Cecil Ramage. She died in 1986 at the age of ninety-eight.

also a Catholic and would therefore not run well upstate. Wilson said that such considerations should be ignored in wartime: "People are every day reading the casualty lists of American boys of every creed."

Franklin gravely nodded his agreement. The conversation was interrupted by the noisy arrival of the biplane, skidding to a stop across the lawn. When the mail pouch was opened, Mr. and Mrs. Daniels had three letters. Franklin asked his chief for one of the stamps for his collection. "Of course, he got it," Mrs. Daniels remembered much later. "Nobody could refuse Franklin anything."

A few weeks later, Daniels noted in his diary that Wilson had said Franklin " 'ought not to decline to run for Gov. of NY if it is tendered to him.' I talked to FDR, who was pleased at the President's view."

Franklin was surely pleased by the President's support. Ever since he had made his wary peace with Tammany the summer before, there had been talk of his running; in a tough Democratic year, his famous name and record as a rural progressive seemed likely to appeal to the farm vote traditionally denied to big-city Democrats.

But Franklin no longer wished the nomination. If he were to leave the administration to run for office with the nation still at war, he and Howe now reasoned, Republicans could effectively charge either that personal ambition had overcome his patriotism or that his work at the Navy Department really wasn't as important to the war effort as he had implied it was. And the war showed few signs of ending: major German drives toward Paris had twice been beaten back that spring, in part by American troops, but German morale remained high.

"F. is certainly *not* going to run for Governor," Eleanor assured Isabella. "It has been suggested, but he could not leave the Dep't. during the war for anything but a destroyer! His one hope now is that he may get abroad as he feels there is much he could do over there."

Franklin was determined to go to Europe. For fifteen months, in fact, he had been laying siege to his chief's office, begging to be permitted to go to the war zone "to form an intelligent opinion on which to base appropriate action." His pleas were bolstered by repeated calls from Admiral Sims in London for *someone*—either Daniels or Roosevelt, it didn't matter to him—to come and see things for themselves; such an official visit would provide the department with a fresh perspective, he said, and would have "a good effect on the spirit of our people. . . ."

Franklin saw a rather larger role for himself. "It is obvious . . . ," he wrote Daniels, "that while of course Admiral Sims has been magnificent in the way he has handled the work, it would be a great help to him to have me go over there for a short time to help him co-ordinate the business end. . . ." Daniels had turned him down, writing "No" in his journal.

Now, with American forces facing the likelihood of a renewed German offensive, Franklin's desire to go abroad had intensified still further. All four of TR's sons were in the service; two had been decorated for valor. If he was not to take an active part in the fighting he must at least be able to say he had seen it first-hand. Other civilian officials were planning to go—"[Herbert] Hoover [U.S. Food Administrator] is going some time in July," he told Eleanor. "So is [Edward R.] Stettinius [in charge of Army purchasing] & [Edward] Hurley [chairman of the shipping board] goes in August, possibly—all very vague but beginning to crystallize."

Franklin did not wish to be left behind, but Daniels had not been inclined to cooperate. There was still time for good-humored exchanges between him and his assistant:

Secnav
1. I beg to report
(a) That I have just signed a requisition (with four copies attached) calling for purchase of eight carpet tacks.

ASTANAV

Why this wanton extravagance. I am sure that two would suffice.

J.D.

But the older man was increasingly distrustful. The previous September, he had had a visit from Grenville S. MacFarland, editor of the Boston *American,* who had brought disturbing news. Daniels noted it carefully in his diary that evening: "*Carthage delenda est.* R[oosevelt] If not loyal sh'd not hesitate. [He] told [Republican Senator John] Weeks [of Massachusetts] Navy Department was not conducted properly & you sh'd be certain."

Two days later, the Secretary repeated the story, and used the same Latin quotation. It translates as "Carthage must be destroyed," and had been the slogan of Cato the Censor, the bellicose Roman statesman and orator who repeated it whenever he spoke before the Senate; his oratory had helped bring on the Third Punic War that finally ruined Rome's great rival before it grew too strong to resist conquest. The allusion can be read two ways: Daniels may have thought Franklin, like Cato, was a warmonger, heedless of the bloody cost of his enthusiasm;

or he may have felt that he had himself put off too long the unpleasant task of crushing the subordinate who might one day destroy him.

In either case, Daniels' patience was fraying, and he began to keep more careful notes on his disputes with Franklin, perhaps building his case for a final confrontation, should their relationship continue to deteriorate:

> *October 29.* . . . Roosevelt after reading report of General Board for a barrage across No. Sea, said "I told you so last May."

> *Nov. 6.* . . . FDR wanted to name destroyers Indian names. No. Hold for heroes. We may lose many before this war ends.

Daniels charitably attributed some of his troubles with Franklin to pressure from TR. On January 24, 1918, the Colonel had visited Washington—"to set up a rump government," the Secretary thought, "and failed." He also saw Franklin and Eleanor, and the very next morning, according to Daniels, "[Democratic Congressman William B.] Olivier [of Alabama] talked to FDR. He [FDR] said speed was not being made, so TR had been in town two days."

Daniels also noted a disturbing story about a contract Franklin had unwisely awarded:

> *June 15.* Confer with [Secretary of War] Newton F. Baker and Solicitor General [John W.] Davis. A clerk in C&R (Bureau of Construction and Repair] had written he had secured contract for certain parties at highest prices by using much bull on Asst Sec'y.

> *July 26.* Clerk in C&R grilled to find out who was concerned in giving out info. about bids. [Eugene] Sullivan was arrested in Boston. He gave stipulations so his concern [the Quaker City Raincoat Company] could bid. Said he had to use a good deal of bull on FDR to get him to give contract to his favorite—who was not lowest bidder.

By the time Daniels wrote that entry, Franklin had made it to Europe. His personal desire for a voyage overseas had not moved the Secretary, but political considerations finally did. The House Naval Affairs Committee was to make its own tour of naval installations that summer. By sending Franklin on ahead, Daniels hoped, shortcomings in the management of the naval war might be found and remedied before hostile congressmen could ferret them out.

And so, on Monday, July 1, Franklin at last got the permission he had been waiting for. "The O.K. has been given," he wrote Eleanor, "and I am to go very soon—Don't tell a *soul*—not even Mama . . ." Then he stepped next door to tell Livy that he was to come along, too, as his aide. Davis recorded his own delight in his diary: "About 4:30 was changing combination of [the office] safe when FDR came in and told me to pack up my old kit bag. Hand slipped and drove screwdriver into bone of index finger of left hand. Too excited to get combination straight and after much fussing abandoned all attempts."

Livy raced to tell his mistress. She was initially upset—"gave me Hell," he noted—but the next afternoon he "Picked up E.D. at 4:30 & went out to Clearwater Brook. Had supreme time & came home completely purged."

Franklin boarded the USS *Dyer* at New York on July 9, having written the President a note saying he now hoped the question of his candidacy for governor would never reach the state convention; it would be a mistake, he felt certain, for him to "give up war work, for what is frankly very much of a local political job in these times."[4]

Neither Sara nor Eleanor was permitted to see him off since he was sailing under secret orders. At Springwood, surrounded by the grand-children who would spend the summer with her, his mother grieved at his going to the front; he remained, as Eleanor wrote, "the center of her existence."

Nineteen years later, running for reelection as President in August of 1936, FDR made an appearance in the great outdoor pavilion at Chautauqua, New York, where William Jennings Bryan had often preached pacifism before America entered World War I. Domestic issues were uppermost in the minds of most voters in that Depression year, but the President felt it necessary at least once during the campaign to pledge his determination to isolate the American people from any new war in Europe.

"I have seen war," FDR said with great solemnity, his voice rising

4. Before leaving, Franklin publicly endorsed an old insurgent ally for the governorship, William Church Osborn. But at the same time, or so he later claimed, he was privately telling an emissary from Boss Murphy that Al Smith should be the nominee. When the Tammany man confessed that Murphy was worried about Smith's religion, Franklin said, he adopted Wilson's high-minded stance, telling him that "in war-time, the church to which he belonged would not be raised as an issue in any community."

Rejected by Tammany, Osborn unexpectedly resolved to challenge Smith in the September primary and contacted Howe seeking Franklin's further support. By then, the Assistant Secretary was safely abroad—where Howe urged him to stay, maintaining "a masterly absence" until after the primary, the first week in September. He did as he was told.

Osborn lost and Franklin immediately endorsed Smith. He believed 1918 would be a Republican year, and fully expected his old antagonist to lose, leaving the way open for a run of his own, two years later. Instead, Smith won. *Sources:* Frank Freidel, *Franklin D. Roosevelt: The Apprenticeship*, pages 341–342, note; Alfred B. Rollins, Jr., *Roosevelt and Howe*, page 113; Ray Stannard Baker, *Woodrow Wilson: Life and Letters.* Vol. 8, *Armistice.* pages 264–265.

in its fervor. "I have seen war on land and sea. I have seen blood running from the wounded. I have seen men coughing out their gassed lungs. I have seen the dead in the mud. I have seen cities destroyed. I have seen two hundred limping, exhausted men come out of line— the survivors of a regiment of one thousand that went forward forty-eight hours before. I have seen children starving. I have seen the agony of mothers and wives. I hate war."

But if hatred was the emotion the sights and sounds of war kindled in Franklin, they did so very slowly. During his eight weeks overseas in 1918 he seems to have had a uniformly grand time. Nowhere in Livy's jaunty diary of what he and Franklin saw and did, or in Franklin's own carefully selective day-by-day account of what he was up to, sent home to be read aloud to the family, is there so much as a hint of anything but enthusiasm.

Franklin would at last see for himself the battlefields about which he had been so excited and on which other Roosevelts were distinguishing themselves. He would get to meet and talk with a whole series of his heroes. And he would be away from Washington, where even a man who revelled in secrecy and was as accustomed as he to keeping his own counsel must have found exhausting the strain of keeping his wife from knowing of his continuing relationship with Lucy Mercer. As he travelled back and forth between Britain and the Continent, he would find letters from both women waiting for him.

Captain Edward McCauley, Jr., his chief of staff, and his orderly, Marine Sergeant W.W. Stratton, accompanied Franklin aboard the brand-new destroyer, the USS *Dyer*. The rest of his party—Livy, Elliott Brown, Captain Victor S. Jackson, and his stenographer, R. H. Camalier, were to find their way to London aboard another vessel.

Franklin took over the captain's cabin, setting up a framed photograph of his children on the dresser and wearing what he called "my destroyer costume—my own invention,—khaki riding trousers, golf stockings, flannel shirt & leather coat—very comfy & warm, [and] does not soil or catch in things!" The *Dyer* was to help escort a troop convoy through the war zone.

Franklin exulted at being at sea:

> ... the good old Ocean is so absolutely normal—just as it has always been—sometimes tumbling about and throwing spray like this morning— sometimes gently lolling about with occasional points of light like to-night—but always something known—something like an old friend of

moods and power. . . . But now though the Ocean looks unchanged, the doubled number on lookout shows that even here the hand of the Hun False God is reaching out to defy nature; that ten miles ahead of this floating City of Souls a torpedo may be waiting to start on its quick run; that we can never get our good Old Ocean back again until that God and the people who have set him up are utterly cut down and purged.

The torpedoes never materialized, though there were two night-time alarms during the stormy, zigzag crossing—each time, Franklin eagerly raced to the bridge, barefoot and wearing his silk pajamas, to scan the dark sea—and on another occasion the captain took a floating keg for a periscope and fired three shots at it before realizing his mistake. The only real dangers Franklin faced were a near-miss with a second Allied convoy in the fog and the accidental detonation of a 4-inch gun aboard the *Dyer* itself during a drill.[5] "I am more than glad that I came this way," he wrote home on July 13, " . . . I have loved every minute of it."

The next day was Sunday, July 14, Bastille Day. That morning, as Franklin "read much, slept much and ate much" aboard the *Dyer*, Lieutenant Quentin Roosevelt, just twenty years old, took off from Orly field outside Paris at the controls of his Nieuport 28. With him flew seven other planes from the 95th "Kicking Mule" Aero Squadron of the 1st Pursuit Group. Their mission was a sortie behind the German lines in the Marne Salient.

Quentin was the youngest and perhaps the best loved of Theodore Roosevelt's four sons, ardent, high-spirited, and eager, despite severe nearsightedness, to equal or surpass the achievements of his older brothers. He had begun training at Plattsburgh at just seventeen while still a Harvard sophomore and was already engaged, to Flora Payne Whitney, the lovely young daughter of Harry and Gertrude Vanderbilt Whitney. His parents thought the elder Whitneys showy, but they liked Flora, whom Quentin called "Fouf," and TR had tried to arrange for her to travel to France so that before his son went into combat the

5. The dearth of torpedoes disappointed Franklin, but his creative way with history later helped him get over the letdown. The *Dyer's* engines did go dead for about an hour off Fayal in the Azores, making her "an easy mark for submarines," he reported to Eleanor, and while the destroyer floated there a submarine was in fact spotted several miles away. Over the ensuing months, that sighting grew steadily closer until, while running for Vice President in 1920, Franklin would tell a reporter that the enemy vessel had come up first on one side of the ship and then the other. *Source:* Frank Freidel, *Franklin D. Roosevelt: The Apprenticeship*, pages 346–347.

young couple might marry and have "their white hour together." Regulations had defeated him: women without specific tasks to perform were barred from travelling to Europe.

On July 5, just nine days before this morning's takeoff, Quentin had survived his first dog fight. "You get so excited," he wrote home afterwards, "that you forget everything except getting the other fellow, and trying to dodge the tracers, when they start streaking past you." On the 10th he shot down his first enemy plane, just north of Château-Thierry, then toasted his success at dinner with his brother Ted's wife, Eleanor, who was stationed with the Red Cross in Paris. His squadron mates called him "the Go and Get 'Em Man" because of his eagerness for combat. "Whatever now befalls Quentin," his proud father told his mother when he got the news, "he has now had his crowded hour, and his day of honor and triumph." In a letter to Ted, Jr., he was still more exultant: "The last of the lion's brood has been blooded!"

Now, as Quentin's squadron flew above the battlefield near the little red-roofed village of Chamery, seven German planes appeared. "They came out of nowhere," one American airman remembered. "Christ, but the air was full of Fokkers." The squadrons roared toward one another. Precisely what happened next is unclear: "to tell you the truth," the same pilot recalled, "each pilot was busy looking out for his own hide."

Somehow, Quentin split off from his comrades. Two German planes flew at him at once, firing as they came. His engine sputtered, and his plane rolled over, then plunged downward, spiralling until it smashed into a rutted field below. There had been no smoke or flame; perhaps, his fellow pilots hoped, he had survived, to be taken prisoner.

On the morning of the 16th, a reporter ran up the steps at Theodore Roosevelt's Oyster Bay home with a puzzling telegram his office had just received: WATCH SAGAMORE HILL FOR——. TR came outside to read it, then closed the door so that his wife would not be alarmed, and told the reporter he feared it meant "something has happened to one of the boys."

No further news came until early the next morning when the newspaperman, tearful now, returned with word that Quentin had been shot down. He had in fact been dead before he hit the ground, two machine-gun bullets through his head. German aviators had seen to it that he was buried with full military honors because he was the son of Colonel Roosevelt, whom they believed to be a great American, and they had marked his grave with a simple cross and the wheels of his airplane.[6]

The Colonel paced the piazza with the reporter. "But Mrs. Roosevelt!" he said at last. "How am I going to break it to her?"

He straightened his shoulders and went inside. After half an hour, he returned with a prepared statement: "Quentin's mother and I are very glad that he got to the front and had a chance to render some service to his country, and show the stuff that was in him before his fate befell him."

TR later expressed both his pride and his private anguish in a letter to his old comrade-in-arms, Bob Ferguson:

> Well, Bob, when you and I had the chance we did our duty, altho it was on such an infinitely smaller scale; indeed, if I had not myself gone to war in my day I don't think I could have borne to send my sons to face death now. It is bitter that the young should die; [but] there are things worse than death, for nothing under Heaven would I have had my sons act otherwise than as they acted. They have done pretty well, haven't they? Quentin killed, dying as a war hawk should . . . over the enemy's lines; Archie crippled, and given the French war cross for gallantry; Ted gassed once . . . wounded seriously, and cited for "conspicuous gallantry"; Kermit with the British military cross, and now under Pershing. Dick [Derby, one of TR's sons-in-law] knocked over by a shell. . . .

In a letter to Isabella, Eleanor sounded very like her uncle. "The family has been wonderful about Quentin," she said. "He was instantly killed by 2 bullets holes in the head . . . so he did not suffer & it is a glorious way to die." To Franklin, she revealed more: her heart ached for Uncle Ted and Aunt Edith, she said; "Think if it were our John, he would still be a baby to us."

6. The Germans were not uniformly gallant: one soldier carved souvenir cigarette boxes from parts of Quentin's plane, and another photographed his sprawled body, then had the picture printed up as a postcard for sale back home. Several copies of this ghastly photograph eventually found their way back to the Roosevelt family.

After the war, Edith Roosevelt visited the site, ordered a stone monument built, and made arrangements for a local family to tend the grave. Following World War II, however, the body was exhumed and reburied in the American military cemetery at Sainte-Laurent-sur-Mère, next to that of Quentin's brother, Brigadier General Theodore Roosevelt, Jr., who had died of a heart attack a week after D-Day.

The original monument was brought back from France to the lawn at Oyster Bay, where it continues to baffle visitors who think Quentin buried beneath it. *Source:* Interview with Dr. John A. Gable, Executive Director, Theodore Roosevelt Association.

Franklin landed at Portsmouth on July 21 and was delighted to be met on the quay by a large group of officers that included Admiral Sims[7] and Rear Admiral Sir Allan Frederick Everett, Naval Secretary to the First Lord of the Admiralty. ("I am told it is a very great honor to have had Everett sent down to meet me," he told Eleanor. "Personally, I think it is because they wanted to report as to whether I am house-broken or not.")

Rolls-Royces took Franklin and his party to London and the Ritz Hotel, where he had "a magnificent suite as the guest of the British Admiralty." It was a heady time for an American official to be in the British capital. The streets with which Franklin was so familiar from his many boyhood visits were now filled with Americans in uniform, and newspapers reporting on the Western Front, where another German thrust had been blunted, were full of praise for American troops: "The counter attack in the Rheims salient has heartened everybody enormously," Franklin reported; "our men have undoubtedly done well. One of my Marine regiments has lost 1200 and another 800 men."[8]

Franklin's orders from the Secretary were "to look into our Naval administration" and help coordinate its efforts with those of other American agencies. But he was also authorized "for such other purposes as may be deemed expedient by you on your arrival." Within hours he was volunteering to take on a delicate diplomatic assignment that he hoped would be good both for the war effort and for his own career.

Sir Eric Geddes, First Lord of the Admiralty, evidently planted the idea in his mind. Geddes "had awfully nice eyes and a smile," Franklin

7. Admiral Sims' delight in seeing Franklin was qualified. He was in charge of 45 stations, 250 ships, 570 aircraft, and over 8,000 men, and visiting dignitaries took precious time. "Times have been pretty strenuous up here . . . ," he told a fellow officer a few days before Franklin landed. "This will be further complicated by the arrival of Assistant Secretary Roosevelt, who is coming to make a 'look-see.' "

"Junkets were our bane," remembered Robert Dunn, one of Sims' aides and an old Harvard acquaintance of Franklin's: "Congressmen, inventors, labor leaders—and Franklin Roosevelt. "How's the job? And Josephus?" I asked him over Scotch. His eyes fell to the glass. 'Gosh, you don't know, Bobby,' he said gravely, after a pause. 'What I have to bear under that man.' " *Sources:* Sims Papers, Library of Congress, courtesy of Michael Simpson; Robert Dunn, *World Alive,* page 276.

8. Franklin's proprietary identification with the Marine Corps, begun when he wore a Marine uniform while riding across Haiti in 1917, never entirely ended. Discussing interservice cooperation during World War II, FDR often spoke of the Marines as "we." *Source:* Eric Larabee, *Commander in Chief,* page 256.

wrote, "but is more like a successful American business man than any British Cabinet Officer one is accustomed to picture." He flattered his young visitor, accompanied him on an inspection tour of British and American bases—"Geddes inspects a yard very much as I do—He walked them off their feet & took a special interest in the wood saws"— let slip selected British secrets, made a show of seeking out Franklin's opinion on matters already decided, and joined with him in issuing joint radio messages which Franklin cabled to Daniels "in the interests of the *entente cordiale.*" ("I hope he gave them to the press," he wrote home.)

The British were alarmed at conditions in the Mediterranean, where the enemy was now sinking more Allied shipping than it was in the Atlantic. The Italians insisted simultaneously upon total control of Allied naval activity in that region and near-total passivity. Little was being done to halt German and Austrian U-boats from slipping down the Adriatic to prey on Allied vessels. The British wanted action, Geddes explained, and believed the only way to get it was to create a unified naval command, with a Briton in overall command.

Franklin, as impatient as the British for aggressive action and personally eager always to find a larger role to play than his superiors had envisioned for him, volunteered to go to Rome and press for the British plan. He needed little urging to bring the matter up with other British officials as he made his official rounds in London. Not surprisingly, they were uniformly enthusiastic, promising to get approval for his mission from the French, while Franklin was shrewd enough to deflect Geddes' hint that he accompany him to Rome. "I am convinced this would be just the wrong move," he told Eleanor, "as the whole situation is . . . deadlocked . . . and my business is to find a way out or a compromise. I cannot do this if the Italians think the British are bringing me along as 'Exhibit A' to prove that America takes wholly the British line. . . ."

To Daniels, whose inbred suspicion of the British Franklin always had to keep in mind, he explained things slightly differently: "The trouble seems to be chiefly with the Italians themselves and a certain amount of jealousy of the French in regard to the Atlantic and of the British in regard to their rather condescending attitude about things in general. . . . The Italians may not love us . . . [but] at least they know that we have no ultimate designs in the Mediterranean."

On July 29, Franklin was received at Buckingham Palace by King

George V, an event upon which he reported in proud detail to his mother, whose fascination with royalty he fully shared:

> The King has a nice smile and a very open, quick and cordial way of greeting one. He is not as short as I had expected, and I think his face is stronger than photographs make it appear. This is perhaps because his way of speaking is incisive, and later on, when he was talking about German atrocities in Belgium, his jaw almost snapped. . . .
>
> I . . . remarked something about having been to school in Germany and having seen their preparation for the first stages of the war machine. The King said he went to school in Germany, too, for a year; then, with a twinkle in his eye—"You know I have a number of relations in Germany, but I can tell you frankly that in all my life I have never seen a German gentleman. . . ."
>
> He was a delightfully easy person to talk to, and we got going so well that part of the time we were both talking at the same time. I understand that this type of interview is supposed to last only fifteen minutes, but it was nearly three-quarters of an hour before the King made a move. . . ."[9]

That evening he attended a dinner for the war ministers at Gray's Inn, where, to his horror and without warning, he was called upon to speak after Lord Curzon, General Jan Smuts, and other senior Allied statesmen had all offered their views. He did his best, but it was not enough to impress at least one of the guests to whom he was introduced, the Minister of Munitions, Winston Churchill, who evidently did not bother to disguise his disdain for the tall, breathless young visitor from Washington. "I have always disliked [Churchill] since the time I went to England in 1918," FDR told Joseph P. Kennedy, his Ambassador to the Court of St. James's, at the White House in 1939. "He acted like a stinker at a dinner I attended, lording it over all of

---

9. Franklin did not report his entire conversation with the king to his wife and mother. Twenty-three years later he remembered a story the British sovereign had told him:

> When he was visiting a hospital in Scotland containing several hundred sailors wounded in the Battle of Jutland, he stopped for a moment at the cot of a burly Britisher who had a large tattooed portrait of the King on his bare chest.
>
> The King congratulated him on patriotism, and the sailor proudly pointed out a tattooed portrait of the Queen between his shoulder blades, a . . . portrait of the Prince of Wales on his right arm, and one of Princess Mary on his left arm.
>
> The King congratulated him again on his patriotism and loyalty, whereupon the British sailor said:
>
> "That ain't the half of it, your Majesty. You should see me behind. I 'ave two other portraits—I am sittin' on the Kaiser and Von Hindenberg."

Stories like that were not to be read aloud at Springwood. *Source:* PSF "Anecdotes," FDRL.

us. . . ." In a subsequent conversation with Kennedy he added that Churchill had been "one of the few men in public life who was rude to me."[10]

Franklin did better the next day with the Prime Minister, David Lloyd George, or so he reported to Eleanor: Lloyd George had been "very greatly pleased" with his assurances that so long as the war continued, American labor would have no sympathy for British strikers, "& intimated that he had decided on a firmer hand [with strikers] in the future." In the evening, Franklin attended a dinner at the House of Commons and afterwards had a "long talk with Mr. [Arthur] Balfour . . . [then Foreign Minister] while we walked up and down the terrace in the dark." Balfour assured him that "everyone understands" that it was the American Marines who had "stopped the rush at Chateau Thierry" and that the British Cabinet had warmly endorsed his trip to Rome.

Franklin clearly felt himself at the heart of things in London—"in spite of all people say," he wrote, "one feels much closer to the actual fighting here"—but there was also time to go to the theatre, visit old family friends, and enjoy a "great old talk" at the St. James Club with Livy and another Harvard classmate, Ned Bell.

Franklin and Livy also found opportunities for a good deal of shopping, using an Admiralty car with a uniformed chauffeur to do the driving and guard their packages. "My old friends, the silk pyjamas, have gone up from 30 to 60 shillings," Franklin wrote home, "& I only got 3 pairs instead of the 6 pairs I wanted!!"

"I do wish you would write me," Franklin had urged Eleanor in a shipboard letter, "if you can think of any small thing Mama or the children would like me to get. I would ask you to do the same thing in regard to yourself, but I fear you would suggest table-cloths or feather-dusters. If you *could* by way of a change think of yourself, I

10. Churchill entirely forgot this encounter, and as the Atlantic Conference opened in 1941, innocently said how glad he was at last to meet for the first time the man with whom he had been communicating so cordially by telephone and cable. More than a little annoyed, the President said they *had* met previously. Churchill said he did not think so, then, taking note of FDR's evident displeasure at having been forgotten, hastily agreed. Much later, the wartime Prime Minister would make elaborate amends in his memoirs, recalling how allegedly impressed he had been in 1918 by FDR's "magnificent presence in all his youth and strength."
Franklin's initial dislike of Churchill was in the Roosevelt tradition. TR had not liked him, either: "Churchill was here in about '99, after the war in Cuba," Alice Longworth remembered. "My father was then Governor of New York. . . . [Churchill] didn't get up when older men came in or when women came in. And he puffed on a cigar, and was generally obnoxious." *Sources:* Joseph P. Lash, *Roosevelt and Churchill,* page 394; Carol Felsenthal, *Alice Roosevelt Longworth,* page 247.

would perhaps find it in London or Paris." James, then ten, replied that he would like "the kaiser's helmet and, if possible, the kaiser himself," but Eleanor's response was characteristically practical: Sara wished a black bag from Paris, Anna needed "6 new nightgowns & 6 prs of drawers," the boys required "knit stockings with turn-over tops." She wanted nothing for herself except two pairs of gloves.

The two friends also drove out to Waldorf Astor's magnificent country estate, Cliveden, in Buckinghamshire. Nancy Astor, Franklin told his wife and mother, "is just the same, enthusiastic, amusing and talkative soul as always. . . . Of course this place is wonderful and I am so glad to see it. They live in the big house with only woman servants—everything comfortable, food about like ours, only a scarcity of sugar and butter."[11]

He toured the hospital for eleven hundred wounded men that had been established within the building that housed the Astors' tennis courts: "It is not more than a quarter full just now, but of course will be again when another batch comes over. . . . The men get very good care, and the walking cases have the run of the Cliveden gardens and grounds. Mrs. Astor is wonderful with them . . . they all adore her. Down on the bank, overlooking the Thames, the Astors have turned an Italian Garden into a really perfect little cemetery. . . ."

With Franklin overseas, Eleanor carefully divided her summer between her children and her war work. She had at least toyed with the notion of going abroad herself that spring; the Red Cross had asked if she would be willing to organize a canteen in England, as Mrs. Theodore Roosevelt, Jr., had already done in Paris. "I really won't go abroad," she had reassured Sara, "but it is a fearful temptation because I feel I have the strength and probably the capacity for some kind of work and one can't help wanting to do the real thing instead of playing

11. Much later, when Cliveden had become a symbol of British appeasement, Franklin would remember this visit differently. The Astors and their other guests—including "a number of the British cabinet"—he told a 1942 press conference, had "spent all Saturday evening indoctrinating me on all of the terrible hardships that people in England had gone through. They hadn't had this to eat or that to drink . . . for a long, long time. They hadn't had any butter, and they hadn't any bacon, and so forth. They had to really tighten their belts enormously. And I was being indoctrinated because I was the first 'near' cabinet member to go to the other side in the war.

And the next morning I was late for breakfast, and sat down, and suddenly realized that all the food was on the sideboard, like most British breakfasts. And I went over to it, and the first hot dish I took the cover off was just piled high with bacon. And the hostess said, 'What! Only one bacon?' I said, 'Yes. . . . You know at home, I have gone without bacon for a year and a half, in order that you good people might have it.' " *Source:* Press Conference 831 (June 9, 1942).

at it over here." And she was frankly envious of Franklin for being able to go: "I hate not being with you and seeing it all," she told him after his visit with the king. "Isn't that horrid of me!"[12]

But if she could not go overseas, she would not abandon her new life outside her home. "The war was my emancipation and education," she told a friend many years later " . . . I loved it. I simply ate it up." She went to Hyde Park to settle the children in with Sara before Franklin left. "Hot though the Hudson River was, I felt the children were old enough to stand it," she wrote; there would be no time for Campobello.

Then she returned to Washington to work for a full month at the Red Cross canteen. "I . . . spent all day and most of the night at the canteen," she remembered. "I had nothing else to do . . . and in the heat to which I was quite unaccustomed, I was anxious to keep busy. No place could have been hotter than the little corrugated-tin shack with the tin roof and the fire burning. . . . It was not an unusual thing for me to work from nine in the morning until two or three the next morning, and be back again by ten. The nights were hot and it was possible to sleep only if you were exhausted."

Franklin worried that she would do too much and damage her health. "I've come to the conclusion that you only feel heat when idle," she assured him, and she was very rarely idle. "We've become the fashionable sight," she told Sara on July 27, "and yesterday Mrs. Woodrow Wilson came to look on and brought Lady Reading [the wife of the British ambassador] and Mrs. [Newton D.] Baker and Miss Margaret Wilson [the President's daughter] worked with us! It rather tries my soul, but is good for my bump of deference!"

She had promised Franklin and his mother that she would spend the entire month of August with the children at Springwood, and it was surely no accident that faced with that claustrophobic prospect— and with Franklin safely overseas and unable to tease her—she took still another step toward independence: she learned to drive, steering the Roosevelt Stutz through the streets of Washington from her home to Union Station every morning while Huckins, the patient family chauffeur, offered rapid-fire suggestions from the running board. Despite a couple of close calls with streetcars, she told her husband, "Huckins says I'm doing finely."

12. Among the many duties she assumed that summer was the old one of making sure that Franklin did not ignore his ever anxious mother. Please, she begged him, "when you don't write Mama, send messages to her [in other letters], otherwise I have to invent and that is painful!"

Now, she would be able to come and go from Springwood on her own, would no longer have to ask her mother-in-law's permission just to go to town. She used the car often that August to take the children swimming at the homes of friends along the river and to pay dutiful visits to her big, bleak childhood home at Tivoli where Grandmother Hall still lived. Her grandmother had come to seem to her a pitiable figure. "Her willingness to be subservient to her children isolated her," Eleanor wrote; she was unable to see her children's faults and "her gratitude for their affection was . . . almost pathetic and showed how little else she had in life." Such dependence had been bad for her grandmother, Eleanor thought, and still worse for her children—her alcoholic uncles, Eddie and Vallie, and her beautiful but erratic Aunt Pussie, whose chronic unsteadiness, Eleanor believed, could be traced to their mother's inexhaustible patience with their weaknesses; it would "have been far better . . . had she insisted on bringing more discipline into their lives simply by having a life of her own."

Eleanor had begun to do just that; she even sought to conquer her deep childhood fear of water and learn to swim that summer, struggling to keep afloat as she dangled from a long pole held by her mother-in-law's butler.

On July 31, Franklin and his party set out from Dover for Dunkirk, aboard a British destroyer with the Assistant Secretary's flag fluttering from the mainmast—"the first time this sort of thing has ever happened on a British ship." He was at last on his way to the Western Front where, thanks again in part to American troops, the Allies had just driven the Germans north of the Marne River.

Two "magnificent limousines, each with two Poilus on the front seat and rifles in a rack in front of them," met Franklin and his party at Dunkirk and roared toward Paris at high speed, through Calais and Boulogne and Beauvais along roads pocked with bomb craters and so dusty that Franklin stopped to "change from my seagoing suit to khaki trousers, leather puttees and a gray coat."

In Paris, the French government put them up at the Hotel Crillon in "wonderful rooms on the troisième, southwest corner." Franklin had instructions from his mother to look in upon various members of the family living in and around the city. His first telephone call, made as soon as he got into his room, was to his Aunt Dora Forbes, Sara's older sister, who had refused to leave her Paris flat even when the

Germans shelled the city and seemed on the verge of seizing it.[13] Franklin had breakfast with her before beginning his first round of official visits and later took her for a day-long drive to Versailles and back, just as he had on his honeymoon thirteen years earlier.

Franklin also paid his respects to the Oyster Bay Roosevelts present in Paris: "I went out at tea time to see Ted and Eleanor and found them in a nice little house just beyond the Arc de Triomphe," he noted. "Archie was there also, looking horribly badly." Both of TR's sons were recuperating from serious wounds: Ted Jr. had been hit in the leg; Archie's arm had been broken, his knee shattered by shrapnel. "They both have really splendid records," Franklin wrote, records he still yearned somehow to equal.

Meanwhile, he had to content himself with official business. He was received by the Minister of Marine, the Minister for Foreign Affairs, Marshal Joffre, and the President of France, Raymond Poincaré—to whom he found he had to introduce himself, since no one had bothered to tell him "who I was." The high point of his visit was an interview with the premier, Georges Clemenceau:

> I knew at once that I was in the presence of the greatest civilian in France. He did not wait for me to advance to meet him at his desk, and there was no formality such as one generally meets. He almost ran forward to meet me and shook hands as if he meant it; grabbed me by the arm and walked me over to his desk and sat me down about two inches

13. She would do the same thing a quarter of a century later, in September 1939, when the Nazis seemed about to strike. While other Americans anxiously fled for home, she stood her ground, issuing a formal statement through a spokesman to newspapermen who asked what the President's aunt planned to do:

Madame is determined to remain in her Avenue George V home as long as it is tenable. . . . After all, she has lived in Paris for almost forty years. All the friends of her whole life are here. You cannot expect a woman of her age to move out and start her whole life anew. Madame is in excellent health and in excellent spirits. Although she finds living in wartime Paris different from before, she is not uncomfortable, for the present, [and] is not making any emergency plans.

Not even Sara, who had travelled to Paris for the purpose the previous spring, had been able to persuade her older sister to change her mind. Back in the United States, the President's mother grew increasingly concerned as the weeks and months went by, and finally called her son at the White House. The news from Europe was *too* alarming, she told him; he must send a battleship at once to pick up Aunt Dora and bring her safely home. FDR gently explained that not even the President of the United States could issue such an order.

Sara was furious: What was the *point* of being President?

Dora Forbes did finally make it back to America the following spring—her fiftieth crossing of the Atlantic—just before the Germans marched into Paris. She died at Algonac on July 20, 1940, with her brother Fred and sisters Sara and Kassie at her bedside. She was ninety-three.

away. He is only 77 years old, and people say he is getting younger every day. . . . He launched into a hair-raising description of the horrors left by the Boche in his retreat—civilian population—smashing of furniture— slashing of paintings—burning of houses—and he said—"these things I have seen myself. . . ."

Then still standing, he said—"Do not think that the Germans have stopped fighting or that they are not fighting well. We are driving them back and will keep them going back because we are fighting better and every Frenchman and every American is fighting better because he knows he is fighting for the Right. . . ." He spoke of an episode he had seen while following just behind the advance—a Poilu and a Boche still standing partly buried in a shell hole, clinched in each other's arms, their rifles abandoned, and the Poilu and the Boche were in the act of trying to bite each other to death when a shell had killed them both—and as he told me this he grabbed me by both shoulders and shook me with a grip of steel to illustrate his words, thrusting his teeth toward my neck.

That evening, Franklin reported to his family, he and his party dined quietly at their hotel. He did not detail what happened afterward. The House Naval Affairs Committee had arrived and was also staying at the Crillon. After dinner, Franklin accompanied them on a lively tour of Parisian nightclubs, beginning at the Folies-Bergère, but soon moving on from there in the wake of a knowing midget hired as a guide. When they got back to the hotel around four o'clock in the morning, they found the entrance barred by an iron gate. Republican Congressman Sidney Mudd of Maryland, a massive man and drunker than his companions, leaned heavily on the bell, setting off a loud insistent gong that roused the staff and woke many guests. (One of them was Herbert Hoover, staying on the floor above Franklin and his party; the next morning, he demanded to know who the noisy revelers had been.)[14]

The following evening, Franklin, Livy, and the rest plunged back into Paris nightlife, dining this time at the Café de Paris. Franklin described this dinner to his wife and mother, solemnly assuring them that since no alcohol could be served to any man in uniform, their fellow diners had been "extremely happy, no rowdiness and wonderfully little intoxication." But these strictures evidently did not apply

14. The congressmen had been just as boisterous in London, Admiral Sims' aide Robert Dunn remembered: "The bunch tried to crash Sims' office, demanded drinks and women, went to see 'their' ships at Scapa Flow, and stole the foot mat from Admiral Beatty's barge. Due for an audience with King George, some were reeling along the Strand—the war to them." *Source:* Robert Dunn, *World Alive,* page 276.

to Franklin or his staff, for when they left for the front at last at 6:00 a.m. the next day, Sunday, August 4, Livy was badly hung over and so were most of the other members of his party.

A French naval officer named Pamard and the American naval attaché at Paris, Captain R. H. Jackson, rode with Franklin in the first of three big gray touring cars assigned to him, each with a tiny pair of American and French flags snapping from its radiator cap.

Captain Jackson had already annoyed Franklin by trying to shepherd him through his formal appointments in Paris at a brisker pace than he liked. Now he made things worse. Ordered to ensure Franklin's safety, he was determined that the Assistant Secretary visit only areas securely in Allied hands. This was to be Franklin's one opportunity to see the fighting for himself, and he was no less determined to get as close to it as he could.

As the little convoy moved eastward toward Château-Thierry, winding its way among wounded soldiers and the overladen carts of refugees returning to their newly liberated villages to see if their homes were still standing after four years of war, the two men clashed angrily. Franklin was not interested, he said, in "late rising, easy trips and plenty of bombed houses, thirty miles or so behind the front." When Jackson continued to argue, he relieved him of any further responsibility for his travels; from then on, he told Eleanor, "for four days I ran the trip."

Franklin pushed his party from one battlefield to the next, curious, keen, tireless. "I managed to get my boots and leggings off and fell in," he wrote by flashlight one evening after finding a place to sleep in an empty, battered house, " . . . 1:00 AM and a thoroughly successful day."

"Such tireless energy as Roosevelt's, I have never known," Captain Edward McCauley remembered later, "except perhaps for his kinsman, Theodore Roosevelt. I thought I was fairly husky, but I couldn't keep up with him. In a letter to my wife I complained bitterly that it didn't seem to matter to him what he ate, where or when he slept or if he ever got a bath."

Franklin insisted on walking part way into Belleau Wood:

> In order to enter the wood itself we had to thread our way past water-filled shell holes and thence up the steep slope over outcropping rocks, over-turned boulders, down trees, hastily improvised shelter pits, rusty bayonets, broken guns, emergency ration tins, hand grenades, dis-

carded overcoats, rain-stained love letters, crawling lines of ants and many little mounds, some wholly unmarked, some with a rifle stuck, bayonet-down, in the earth, some with a helmet, and some, too, with a whittled cross with a tag of wood or wrapping paper hung over it and in a pencil scrawl an American name.

And he took elaborate pains to enhance the reputation of the men he continued to call "my" Marines: he made a point of noting a dinner conversation with a French general who, he said, "told me with his own lips" that he had personally ordered Belleau Wood renamed "Bois de la Brigade de Marine," rather than "Bois des Américains," as un-named "jealous individuals" in the Army were now claiming, and he issued orders that the Fifth Marines be permitted to wear their corps button on their collar points so that their khaki uniforms could instantly be distinguished from those worn by Army troops.[15]

He reviewed troops, called upon senior officers unannounced, dashed inside village churches to survey the damage "done deliberately and maliciously by the Huns," contrasted the "stolid, stupid look" of German prisoners with the "awake and intelligent" ones of their French captors, and longed for a chance to strike a blow at the enemy himself. At the battered village of Mareuil-en-Dole, not far from Rheims—abandoned by the enemy just twenty-four hours earlier, and where dead horses and "a little pile" of unburied German corpses offended "our sensitive naval noses"—he finally got his wish. The Sixth United States Gun Battery was shelling the German lines only seven miles away, and "Just as we descended from the motors," he wrote, "a loud explosion went off very close by."

Much later he told a friend what had happened next:

> We were walking along, that is picking our way through what we were told was a quiet sector in no danger from the big German guns . . . now and then stopping to use the glasses so as to see more plainly what was all intensely interesting, when an explosion . . . seemed to plant a shot right in our midst. . . . Commander Brown jumped clear of the earth by

15. This struggle for celebrity between the Marines and Army had begun right after Belleau Wood, when an inexperienced AEF censor referred to all the men who initially went into action there as Marines, thus making them, rather than the regular army men who fought well at the same time, the war's first American heroes. The controversy had surprisingly long-running repercussions: During World War II, General Douglas MacArthur, who had served with the army's Rainbow Division on the western front, refused unit citations to Marines on Bataan in part upon the dubious ground that they had received quite enough attention during the last war. *Source:* Robert H. Ferrell, *Woodrow Wilson and World War I 1917–1921*, page 69.

a couple of feet. Captain McCauley made a sound like nothing earthly. I danced. . . . From the bushes on our right came wild howls of laughter, shrieks and screams of glee which upon investigation proved to be a gun crew of our own army. . . . They had seen the group of American Naval officers coming up and just wanted to see how the Navy would stand fire.

After Franklin and his companions got over their fright, the gun crew invited them into the thicket where, as he told Eleanor, "We visited the other guns of the battery of 155's [and] fired one of the guns. . . ."[16]

"The members of my staff have begun to realize what campaigning, or rather sight-seeing, with the Assistant Secretary means," Franklin wrote home, "and Captain Jackson is still visibly annoyed because I upset his comfortable plans for an inspection of regions fought over a month ago."[17]

Approaching Verdun, he stopped his caravan again to survey the scene of fighting which had yielded 900,000 casualties:

For a few moments it didn't look like a battlefield, for there was little or nothing to see but a series of depressions and ridges, bare and brown and dead. Seen even from a short distance there were no gashes on these hills, no trenches, no tree trunks, no heaps of ruins—nothing but brown earth for miles upon miles. When you look at the ground immediately about you, you realize that this earth has been churned by shells, and churned again. You see no complete shell holes, for one runs into another,

16. The memory of this proximity to combat remained vivid all Franklin's life. Visiting France in 1931 and without asking directions of anyone, he had himself driven to the spot with his son, Elliott: "We found the roads, the slope, the bushes, the wall and the broken roof [of a barn] exactly as I had described them after 13 years. There was a new section of wall, and, too, the new tile just where the hole had been."

On December 11, 1944, he dictated a memorandum about this event in which his own role had characteristically enlarged. Not only had "We . . . [author's italics] fired one of the guns," as he had written home in 1918, but Franklin now had twice personally "pulled the lanyards, and a spotting plane reported that one shell fell just short of, and the other directly on, the junction and seemed to create much confusion. I will never know how many, if any, Huns I killed."

If such a report had actually been made from the air in 1918, it is impossible to believe he would not have boasted of it in his original letter home. Source: PSF 151, FDRL.

17. Franklin's anger at his overprotective attaché did not diminish: he had him removed from his Paris post as soon as he could, and, a year later, when the captain was made U.S. naval commander in the Azores, attempted to have him ousted from that job, too, telling Daniels the appointment had made him "rather upset" because of Jackson's lack of "tact and good manners." Sources: Frank Freidel, Franklin D. Roosevelt: The Apprenticeship, page 358n; Frank Freidel interview with Edward McCauley, Jr., Freidel Papers, FDRL.

and trench systems, and forts, and roads have been swallowed up in a brown chaos.

Within the battered citadel itself, where he and his party were entertained at "a splendid dinner" that included filet of beef and truffles, he was shown the original signboard with the defiant message— "*Ils ne passeront pas*"—that had inspired its French defenders during the long German siege, and he insisted upon exploring its fetid underground passages himself, "although . . . I could not help feeling that it is the same air being breathed over and over again."

Later, near Fort Douaumont, and still closer to the fighting, he was issued a steel helmet and gas mask and stood out in the open so long at a sharp turn in the road called "L'Angle de Mort," snapping pictures of all that remained of the village of Fleury, that German observers had time to call in artillery. A colonel hurried his important visitors out of harm's way, "and sure enough, the long whining whistle of a shell was followed by the dull boom and puff of smoke of the explosion at Dead Man's Corner we had just left."

Franklin grew so excited that he left on the running board of his car his suitcase filled with important papers; a French soldier later found it by the roadside and returned it to him at his Paris hotel.

On August 8, Franklin travelled to Rome by private railroad car.[18] Again he enjoyed the attentions of senior officials: Baron Sonnino, the Foreign Minister, "did a very unusual thing in not only receiving me but in talking to me for half an hour. [An American diplomat] said he had never known him to be so chatty and cordial, as he has rather the reputation of a bear." He held a forty-five minute press conference— "an unusual occurrence for Italy," he told Eleanor, "and they loved it, apparently, and it did good. . . ."[19]

18. "We are quite surprised about your going to Rome," Sara wrote proudly to her son, "and how splendid to go to ITALY!"

Livy Davis was not asked to go along, but found plenty to do in Paris while he waited for his friend to return. That evening, according to his diary, he dined with Eliott Brown and another aide: "Mrs. Leslie Melville, a wild-cat adventuress sat at next table w. a fox terrier, which Brown persisted in whistling to. Came out of dining room late to find them talking to her. I joined group & she started thru door. I followed others didn't so she & I strolled up Champs Elysees & back to hotel." The next day he accompanied another woman to her hotel and managed to besiege at least two more before sailing home with Franklin in September. *Source:* Roosevelt Family Papers, FDRL; Livingston Davis Diary, FDRL.

19. The reporters might have loved it more, had all the freewheeling things he said actually been translated. But unbeknownst to him, an official of the American Committee on Public Information present at the press conference had arranged to tug on the translator's coat whenever

And in a meeting with the Italian chief of staff and Minister of Marine he did not hesitate to encourage greater naval aggression in the region. Austria was near collapse, he argued; concerted action by the combined Allied fleets could destroy its fleet and open the Dalmatian coast to attack. He found the younger Italian officers eager for battle, but their older superiors adamantly against it. At one point he wondered aloud at the wisdom of keeping the entire Italian Battleship Fleet within the harbor at Taranto for a full year, not allowing them to steam into the open sea even for fleet drill or target practice.

"Ah," said the chief of staff, "but my dear Mr. Minister, you must not forget that the Austrian fleet has not had any [practice] either."

"This is a naval classic," Franklin told Eleanor, "which is hard to beat, but which perhaps should not be publicly repeated for a generation or two."

He thought he had done better with the Prime Minister, Vittorio Orlando. "Things have worked out all right," he reported to Daniels before boarding the train back to Paris; he had persuaded Italy to agree to "a commander-in-chief for the naval forces in the Mediterranean." But he had not so persuaded him; Orlando had agreed only to a chairman of a joint naval staff and had only gone *that* far when promised that Italy would continue to have the final say over operations in the Adriatic.

His chief was not pleased. The French complained that Franklin's impetuous attempt at negotiating among the Allies had undercut them. Daniels assured the Secretary of State that he had never authorized his assistant to "say who should command" in the region. Woodrow Wilson himself sent a terse note to the Navy Department, asking that henceforth he be told of any further civilian missions to Europe, as "too many men go over there assuming to speak for the government."

Franklin's first venture into diplomacy had been an embarrassment rather than the triumph he had hoped for.[20]

Only momentarily daunted, he took his party southwest to inspect all the anti-submarine bases along the Atlantic coast from Bordeaux to

---

he felt Franklin's remarks insufficiently discreet. At least twice, the Assistant Secretary's words were ignored. *Source:* Frank Freidel, *Franklin D. Roosevelt: The Apprenticeship*, page 362n.

20. By the end of the month, even Franklin realized his mission to Rome had been a failure: "Frankly I have not reached the milk in the cocoanut," he confessed to Geddes. "My visit to Italy not only made me feel that it will be impossible to get the Italian battleship force placed under Allied command, but the whole political situation down there is such that we should not attempt to force this issue." *Source:* Franklin D. Roosevelt, Papers as Assistant Secretary of the Navy, FDRL.

Brest. "[A] frightfully busy week," he wrote Eleanor, "—on the road each day from 6 AM to midnight—& we have done all manner of interesting things . . . all by auto—flying stations, ports, patrols, army stores, receptions, swims at French watering places, etc. etc."

Livy was more succinct: "FD having joy ride."[21]

They bought lace at Quimpèr, had "a delicious swim" at dawn on a deserted beach—Livy regretted that it had been "too early for chickens"—and "all had a fly" in a dirigible tethered to the U.S. naval station at Paimboeuf. At Paulliac on the 14th, Livy noted, "5,000 men [were] drawn up for us . . . several thousand were eating & [we] had lunch on a raised dais while a band of singers entertained. FD made them a very good speech. . . ."

In it, he told the enlisted men "they must always realize that hundreds of thousands of other men . . . at home would give anything in the world to change places with them.

"It is hard for me to go back to a dull office job at Washington," he added, "after having visited the lines where our boys are making history."

More than ever, Franklin wanted to make that kind of history, too, and as they drove from port to port, he and Livy talked seriously of resigning their posts for active duty.

The previous year, back in Washington, Franklin had urged that a naval battery of 14-inch, fifty-caliber guns—originally intended for use aboard battle cruisers and with an effective range of twenty-five miles—be mounted on railroad cars for use against the Germans on the

21. Franklin's party moved faster than the French villagers were used to, and in one village the pilot car knocked down an elderly priest trying to cross the road. Franklin ordered his driver to stop and ran up to see if the old man was all right. He was only slightly injured and when Franklin asked him what the Navy might do for him in the way of compensation, FDR reported during World War II, he said he could not accept anything from "the American Navy, which was doing so much for the cause of saving France."

Then could he do something for the church?

The priest's eyes filled with tears. All his life he had hoped to collect enough money to have the stained glass windows releaded.

How much would it cost?

One thousand francs, more than his poor flock could possibly raise.

Franklin wrote out a Navy requisition for $200 right there on the bonnet of his car and gave it to the grateful priest.

"Several months later," FDR said, "an officer reported to the Assistant Secretary that he had been in the church and the work of re-leading . . . was nearly completed and that in one of the bays of the church a perpetual candle had been lighted by the old priest in honor of the American Navy. . . . I have no doubt that now, in 1942, it is still burning—unless the Germans have put it out." *Source:* PSF 151, FDRL.

Western Front. That battery was at last being readied near Sainte-Nazaire, and on the 17th, Franklin drove up to inspect it.

The battery commander, Rear Admiral Charles P. Plunkett, hurried to welcome him, a wiry veteran with a gray mustache, wearing an Army officer's hat and uniform with two stars on his shoulder, indicating the rank of either rear admiral or major general depending upon the branch of service to which he belonged.

"Captain McCauley," Franklin said, turning and winking broadly to his aide, "who is this Major-General?"

"Mr. Secretary, that is Admiral Plunkett. . . ."

"Admiral," Franklin continued, looking Plunkett up and down, "you are out of uniform." The Assistant Secretary was dressed in tie and tweed jacket and puttees, wearing a soft hat and leaning on a cane.

"Much perturbed," the admiral tried to explain. Regulation whites were too conspicuous and easily soiled for work on land, he said; and navy blue was far too heavy for this hot work. Repeated letters to the Navy Department requesting permission to make the change had gone unanswered.

Franklin threw back his head and laughed: he had only been joking, he said; permission was hereby granted. The two men inspected the first train of thirteen cars, each with "U.S.N." painted on its side, ready at last to move toward the war after six weeks of argument with French authorities, who had feared that the 90-ton guns would destroy the railroad bridges over which they had to pass.

Franklin yearned to go with them: by signing on he could simultaneously fulfill two long-standing dreams—to take part in front-line combat and to be a naval officer. He asked the admiral if he might join the battery. According to him, Plunkett wanted to know first "if I could swear well enough in French to swear a French train onto a siding and let his big guns through. Thereupon, with certain inventive genius, I handed him a line of French swear words, real and imaginary, which impressed him greatly, and he said that he would take me on . . . with the rank of Lieutenant Commander."

"Somehow I don't believe I shall long be in Washington," Franklin wrote Eleanor from Brest three days later. "The more I think of it, the more I feel that being only 36 my place is not at a Washington desk, even a Navy desk. I know you will understand. . . . Kiss the chicks—I wish I could see them each day and tell them of the wonderful things their country is doing here. A great deal of love from your devoted F."[22]

Back in Paris again, Franklin held a press conference to report on the rapid progress the Allies were making in combating submarines. The members of the press "were all in full dress suits, with white ties," he reported to Eleanor, " . . . nearly all of them were the *rédacteurs*— the editors—of the papers. They were having the privilege of being received by '*Monsieur le Ministre.*' Apparently, it caused the most awful furor." Determined to make the story "just as big as I possibly could," Franklin was in his element: he dispensed with his translator, sat on the edge of a table, and told the newspapermen that he would address them in the overconfident language first made famous by his cousin Theodore, "Roosevelt French." The reporters were dazzled, and made much of his assurances that the war effort was "over the hump."[23]

The Assistant Secretary had hoped for a formal invitation for his party to visit British headquarters at the front, Captain McCauley remembered, but "the invitation was not as cordial as it might have been, and the trip was called off" in favor of a quick, courtesy visit to General Douglas Haig by Franklin alone. He and Livy and two officers then sped north along the coast to Belgium, where they watched an inconclusive battle between destroyers and submarines just off the beach, inspected a home for five hundred war orphans, lunched with King Albert I at his château near his headquarters at La Panne, and

---

22. Later in the trip, he pencilled a note to Josephus Daniels:
PRIVATE FOR THE SECRETARY—*London, September 4.*
    For your information only I have long thought of my proper duty in this war and now after organization work is nearly completed I am certain I should be in active service in some capacity. Army has asked me to consider work in France but in view of long associations I naturally prefer Navy if possible and therefore will ask you about October first for a commission in Navy or Marines that will insure service at front. I do not need to tell you how hard it will be for me to end our work together, but know you will understand.
                                                                    Roosevelt.

A quarter of a century later, FDR sought to remind Josephus Daniels of this letter. Daniels did not remember it, however, since Franklin had never actually sent it. *Sources:* Frank Freidel, *Franklin D. Roosevelt: The Apprenticeship*, page 367n; Jonathan Daniels, *The End of Innocence*, page 270.

23. According to Franklin, they were also impressed by his assertion that members of the American Cabinet met with the press once and sometimes twice a day and tried to persuade the far more remote members of the French Cabinet to follow the American example. The next morning, he said, he had breakfast with Clemenceau, who "came at me, just like a tiger, with his claws out," threatening to resign rather than receive the press. "So I darn near overthrew the Government and lost the war." *Source:* Frank Freidel, *Franklin D. Roosevelt: The Apprenticeship*, pages 367–368.

took a drive with him to a nearby village where one wall of the old town hall had been torn off by a shell the previous day. The old town records lay exposed to the weather, hundreds of brittle pages tied with tape. Franklin asked to see some and an aide hurried inside and brought an armful out to the car. Most were sixteenth-century reports from the village fishing fleet. Franklin told the king he wanted to come back after the war and examine the records more carefully to see if he could find proof of a pet theory of his—that French and Flemish fishermen had been blown all the way west to Nova Scotia and New England long before those coasts were settled.

That night, returning to Paris by motor along unfamiliar, twisting roads and without lights, Franklin shook with fever. Livy took his temperature: it was 102 degrees.

He chose to ignore it, continuing to charge around Paris, even finding time to shop for books in the little shops along the Seine across from Notre Dame, until it was time to leave for Britain once again.

At the end of August, Franklin and Livy were in Scotland, where they inspected the North Sea mine barrage and the battleship squadron at the Firth of Forth, fished for salmon, and drank like undergraduates. At Strathpeffer, a former spa whose hotels had been commandeered as hospitals for wounded sailors, they "had a few rounds of Scotch," Livy noted, followed by "a wonderful dinner," after which their host "brought out some real chartreuse. Had private parlor, so sang and told stories till 1 A.M. Wonderful time going to bed, FDR finding a fox in his bed, Jack dressed up and Brown coasted downstairs."

The next morning Franklin insisted everyone turn out for fishing. Livy described the day:

> Brown, FDR, Jack and I with Wallace drove out to Black Water belonging to Sir Arthur Mackensie in pouring rain in a dos-a-dos. [Ghillies] late in coming so all had some Scotch and had a fine sing-song. All in regular clothes, low shoes, etc., but no one got a strike. Weather was so dour all had to keep it out with copious draughts of sublime Scotch so all sang all the way home. While clothes were drying, Wallace concocted a brew of hot Scotch, honey, and oatmeal served in beakers. All had at least two, and on descending found all guests and servants assembled so all hands to parlor formed circle and sang *Auld Lang Syne*.

All this conviviality—plus an ill-timed puncture—made the party nearly four hours late for an inspection at Inverness. The men had been waiting in the rain since ten, and when Franklin finally drove up at 1:45 p.m., Davis noted, their commander, Admiral Joseph Strauss, was "spitting mad." After what must have been a somewhat tense official luncheon, Franklin and his party drove on fortified with still "more Scotch and all got out at Perth for delicious and extremely jolly dinner. Had sing-song in train till bed time at 10:30. One of the jolliest days of my life!"

Franklin pushed on alone the next day to visit old family friends, while Livy and the rest of the party went back to London. They joined forces again on September 6 for one last round of good times before heading home. Davis again noted some details:

> Worked at hotel, then went to Coliseum to see Russian dancers in "The Good Humored Ladies." Thence . . . at 6 FD, Lt. Heyden and I went to American Officers Club in Lord Beaconsfield's house on Curzon Street. Several delicious rounds of c.t.'s [cocktails] and saw many friends. Returned to hotel where had a very rough dinner . . . Lt. Com. Jack Garde, and John Roys brought in Prince Axel [nephew of the king] of Denmark and his staff. . . . Came in. Everybody got drunk. All finally faded away except FD, Brown, Jackson and I. Stayed up until 4:30 pitching coins, playing golf, etc.
>
> Sept. 7—Up at 7 to pack. All feeling very rocky. . . .

Langdon Marvin, Franklin's law partner who happened also to be in London as part of a Red Cross unit, helped him pack his bags before dawn. Franklin was weak and pallid, but he did confide that he was going to hurry right home, resign his post, and at last "get assigned to the big guns at the front."

Shortly after the USS *Leviathan* set sail from Brest for New York on September 12, Franklin collapsed in his cabin, suffering from double pneumonia. Livy and McCauley fell ill, too; so did Prince Axel, and most of his suite. Spanish influenza, the pandemic that would take 20 million lives worldwide that year, raged through the ship. Several officers and men died during the five-day voyage, and were buried at sea.

Franklin spent the journey in his bunk, shivering and semi-coherent.[24]

24. Franklin gravely attributed his illness to having stood bareheaded in the rain at Brest during the prolonged funeral of Allied seamen lost to German torpedoes, and Eleanor echoed his belief in her autobiography. He did attend such a funeral—thirty-seven men had died, and even Livy thought the ceremonies "very impressive." But it seems at least as likely that Franklin initially fell ill after swimming off the French coast; he had had a fever off and on for two weeks before boarding the *Leviathan. Source:* Livingston Davis Diary, FDRL.

Eleanor, still at Hyde Park, knew nothing at first of his illness but she was worried nonetheless, for she had not heard from him for days, did not know when he was to come home or where he might be. Finally, she wrote Louis Howe to see if he knew anything: "if you have any definite news of my husband who seems rather shrouded in mystery, please let me know." Six years after he had taken over her ailing husband's campaign for the state Senate, Louis was still "My dear Mr. Howe" to her, and she was "Mrs. Roosevelt" to him.[25]

Howe knew no more than she did about Mr. Roosevelt's plans or precise whereabouts, he said, but promised to write the minute he heard anything; in the meantime, he would see if he could arrange to have the Roosevelt family pew a little closer to the altar of St. Thomas Church for the coming winter, as she had requested.

While she fretted, word came of another Roosevelt family tragedy. Eleanor's uncle, Douglas Robinson, who had given her father a job and treated him with extraordinary generosity and patience while he fought his long, losing battle against alcoholism, had suddenly died. She went to Herkimer for the funeral and to do what she could to comfort her grieving Aunt Corinne. Uncle Theodore was there too, of course, and after the services he took her aside to speak to her about Franklin. She was still his favorite niece and he had no wish to wound her, but the death of his son had made still more stern his views on a young man's obligations. It was Franklin's plain duty to get into this war, he told her: she *must* use her influence as his wife to persuade him to enlist. Eleanor flushed with anger—she felt it was her husband's choice, not hers; besides, Franklin had tried to join the Navy and been told to stay where he was by the President himself—but she did not openly disagree.

A wire from Franklin, sent before he embarked on the *Leviathan,*

25. Her hostility toward him was sometimes hard for her to conceal: "I had a little conversation with Mr. Howe this a.m.," she told her husband not long after he sailed for Europe, "about (Frederick D.) Pryor seeing to forwarding mail when he was not on his holiday!

Oh dear but Mr. Howe is in the air! Mr. [?] is in hospital for a month. He has no good stenographer. The mail is piling up. Pryor can't have a holiday till you come home. He [Howe] alone kept you from being nominated for governor. Now he doesn't know what to do as you came out for Osborn & he is staying in the race & Al Smith wanted your endorsement & he (Mr. H.) could get no answer as to what the White House wished you to do, etc. My guess is, he's making himself the little nuisance, however, I soothed him by suggesting that as you were out for Osborn you'd have to stick till he withdrew which would doubtless be soon & perhaps he could find a better stenographer so he ended by telling me to tell you that all was well & he would write soon!

Source: Roosevelt Family Papers Donated by the Children, FDRL.

finally arrived at Springwood: UNDER NEW DRAFT LAW PLEASE REGISTER ME AT HYDE PARK PERIOD ALL WELL.

Louis Howe, who shared Eleanor's apprehension at Franklin's eagerness for combat, tried to reassure her about his plans: "I wonder if he knows that it has been practically decided to accept no volunteers whatever under the new draft, and also that married men with children are not going to be called. I fear that he will have a somewhat strenuous time getting the President to waive regulations, particularly as I feel the President has sufficient judgment to know that things would go very badly here if he should leave."

The same day she heard—from someone else—that Franklin had fallen ill aboard ship. She tried not to worry, hoping the return voyage would provide him the rest he needed. Her mother-in-law was badly frightened at the news that he was ill, however, and both women were waiting with a doctor when the *Leviathan* finally docked at New York on September 19.

Franklin was still so weak that he had to be carried off the ship to an ambulance, and borne up the front stairs of his mother's East 65th Street house by four orderlies.[26]

Mail from anxious friends and relatives arrived, full of concern for Franklin's health and praise for his exertions overseas and his decision to enlist. Theodore Roosevelt wrote to say that he was "*very* proud" of Franklin, and promised that when he felt a little better Eleanor would tell him "of our talk about your plans." Bob Ferguson congratulated him on going "into the big gun business—I think it's fine—a good example to many & sure to produce results for us all."

The children, kept from their father at Hyde Park for fear of infection, wrote affectionate, teasing notes. "Be sure not to spill anything on Father when you feed him!" James told his mother. Anna, now twelve, wrote for permission to keep the big, frisky German Shepherd puppy Sara had won for her in a raffle at the Rhinebeck Red Cross Fair—Franklin agreed and she named the dog "Chief"—and she sent him a gift:

26. Thomas W. Lamont still occupied Franklin's own adjoining house.

"When the boat docked and we went on board," Eleanor would later recall in her autobiography, "I remember visiting several of the men who were still in bed. My husband did not seem to me so seriously ill as the doctors implied. . . ." Franklin's condition was in fact grave, and I suspect the scorn implicit in this passage reflects less Eleanor's authentic feelings at the time than the bitterness that began only a few days after Franklin's return and which understandably colored her every memory of those weeks. *Source:* Eleanor Roosevelt, *This Is My Story,* page 268.

Dear Father

I am sending you these little pictures of Indians and boy scouts, you can make a very nice little picture if you put them together. Ask Mother to put them together for you, and stand them up against something. I hope you feel better and will be all right again very soon. Goodbye Father, I wish I could kiss you. Mother will kiss you for me.

Love from
Anna

Louis Howe had been in almost hourly touch with Mr. Roosevelt's doctors by telephone, he told Eleanor, and had not wished to disturb his employer.[27] She thanked him for being so considerate as *"not* to telephone, which has been the bane of our existence." But now that the patient was better, Howe said, "Do assure Mr. Roosevelt that things are really going smoothly, and you might tell him that I showed the seemingly impossible by being ready for his arrival without a single unanswered letter or unattended to piece of work. . . . Politically speaking, he is taken ill, which is the usual Roosevelt luck, at the perfectly ideal time for taking the stump [on Al Smith's behalf]!"

The political future was on the children's minds, too, as Sara—back at Springwood now so that Elliott's birthday would not go unnoticed—explained to her son:

My garden club meeting was pleasant, & Franklin, Jr. & Johnnie handed cakes & sandwiches & behaved like perfect gentlemen. The evening before F. Jr. said "Granny, I intend to run for the Presidency, & I am beginning my campaign at your tea." I said: "how will you do that?"

"Oh, I shall get to know people, & when my name comes up, they will vote for me"—So I answered, "That's a good idea & if you wait on people quietly & do not drop the sandwiches & cakes, & are helpful, people *may* say: 'Oh, he must be one of those nice little boys who helped us. I think I will give my vote to him.' " He took it quite seriously & went to sleep. . . .

But for Franklin and Eleanor themselves, the future seemed suddenly uncertain. Their marriage was coming apart. While unpacking her husband's effects in a guest bedroom of her mother-in-law's house,

27. A letter to Franklin from Bill Phillips confirmed this: "Your faithful Howe keeps me informed day by day, so I feel that I know intimately every event connected with your illness. His gloom, which *was* prodigious, has completely disappeared. (I use his face as my daily barometer of your condition. . . .)" *Source:* Franklin D. Roosevelt, Papers as Secretary of the Navy, FDRL.

Eleanor had come upon a bundle of love letters to Franklin from Lucy Mercer.

With this discovery, she confided later to a friend, "the bottom dropped out of my own particular world, and I faced myself, my surroundings, my world, honestly for the first time."

Every deep fear her childhood had inculcated in her was confirmed. Nothing lasted. Those she loved most and to whom she gave herself most fully—first her father, now her husband—would always desert her. She was in truth what her tactless Aunt Pussie had once told her she was: too plain, too dull, too unhappy, to sustain the love of any man.

Ethel Roosevelt, TR's younger daughter, remembered Eleanor weeping on her shoulder one evening during her engagement to Franklin. "I shall never be able to hold him," she had sobbed then. "He is so attractive."

Now she knew she had been right.[28]

Nor was Franklin the only person who had betrayed her. Lucy had been her secretary, the trusted confidante who had answered her mail and often dined at her table. She feared that Franklin's friends, too, were aware of what had happened—Livy Davis, Nigel Law, perhaps others as well. Members of her own family and his also knew; Alice Longworth and other eager Washington gossips had seen to that. Her humiliation was all the more damaging for being public.

We know nothing first-hand of what went on between Franklin and Eleanor that autumn. Nor do we know when Sara discovered what had happened.[29] But the story Eleanor told her closest friends in later years was that she confronted her husband with the letters from his lover and told him she was willing to step aside and grant him a

28. "If she really loved somebody," Eleanor's niece, Eleanor Wotkyns, once said of her aunt and namesake, "she just gave her whole love to them, and it was then tender. She would be hurt if it wasn't returned in that same way, and maybe this is what happened with herself and Franklin. I mean, he would be much better able to put various relationships in perspective, and that seems more normal. I remember Tommy [Eleanor's long-time secretary, Malvina Thompson] used to say of ER that she felt she was adolescent in a way. . . . She had loved her father just blindly. She knew that he drank too much and he was perhaps not a very balanced person, but if she loved him, she just really loved him. And the same with Hall. So she couldn't see any balance, perhaps, in the most vital relationships of her life. . . ." *Source:* Interview with Eleanor Wotkyns, National Park Service Val-Kill transcripts, FDRL.

29. Sara's diaries for the years 1917, 1918, and 1919, which might have provided clues, no longer exist, although those for 1916 and 1920 do. It seems at least possible that some member of the family—perhaps Sara herself—discreetly destroyed these volumes before the rest were given over to the FDRL.

divorce if, after considering its impact upon the children, that was what he wanted.[30]

Together, according to family legend, they told Sara of the fragility of their marriage. "It was all very well," she said, "for you, Eleanor, to speak of being 'willing to give Franklin his freedom.'" And if her son really wished to leave his wife and five children for another woman and bring scandal upon his family, she could not stop him; but he must understand she would "not give him another dollar," and he could no longer expect to inherit his beloved Springwood.[31]

Louis Howe, too, is said to have proffered advice, reminding Franklin that divorce would end his political career.

With the crisis still unresolved, Eleanor took the children to Washington to begin school. Franklin was moved up to Hyde Park where he stayed two weeks, recuperating and presumably continuing to discuss the future with his mother, while, as Eleanor wrote, she commuted "back and forth until the whole family was settled together again."

Franklin and Eleanor finally returned to Washington on October 18. Livy met them at the station. Franklin "seemed fairly well," he thought, though he was still surprisingly pale and drawn despite his familiar grin.[32]

It was a haggard autumn. Franklin just managed to make it back to the office when first three of the family servants, then all five children, and finally he himself fell ill with influenza. "There was little

---

30. "Eleanor was smart to put it the way she did," a member of the Oyster Bay branch of the Roosevelt family recalled. "If she'd put it as a choice between the two women, she wouldn't have stood a chance." *Source:* Interview with W. Sheffield Cowles, Jr.

31. "I don't think one can have any idea of how horrendous even the *idea* of divorce was in those days," Alice Roosevelt Longworth recalled many years later. "I remember telling my family in 1912 that I wanted one and, although they didn't quite lock me up, they exercised considerable pressure to get me to reconsider. Told me to think it over very carefully indeed. . . . Not done they said, emphatically." *Source:* Michael Teague, *Mrs. L.,* page 158.

32. Livy's shipboard influenza had also turned into double pneumonia, and he had written earlier to Franklin from The Homestead at Hot Springs, Virginia, where he had gone to recuperate:

Oho! My boy! My boy!

How's ums boozums wuz? Mine at long last is on the road to recovery, for this morning I stood on the greensward for almost an hour & beat out golf balls to a nigger, but the exertion tuckered me so that I had to beat it back to the hotel and flop into bed. . . . Well, old Top, my best wish is that you may not be as weak as I feel.

Thine,
Liv.

difference between day and night for me," Eleanor recalled. A doctor came twice a day to look over all the patients, but it was she who nursed what she called this "galaxy of invalids," rushing from one bedside to the next, while keeping an especially anxious eye on John, who developed bronchial pneumonia as well as influenza and was kept in a crib in her room.

"These emergencies of domestic and family life were extremely good training," Eleanor wrote, but those crowded weeks were far more than that for her; they provided her once again with an essential role to play, more demands to be met, helped forestall the brooding that might otherwise have crushed her. When Elliott developed double pneumonia, she finally hired a trained nurse for him, but instead of resting she then devoted yet more time to her Red Cross duties, waiting until the children were asleep, then driving out each day with gifts and "a word of cheer to the poor girls lying in the long rows of beds" in hospital wards set aside for stricken government clerks.

"In all our contacts," Eleanor once wrote, "it is probably the sense of being really needed which gives the greatest satisfaction and creates the most lasting bond."

Three thousand five hundred people died of influenza in Washington alone that year; people moved about the empty streets in gauze masks. Everyone in the Roosevelt home recovered, and Franklin went back to work, doing his best to act as if all was well at home.

But Livy Davis was not fooled: something was very wrong with his old friend. He and Franklin continued to play golf but, for the first time since they had first played together at Harvard, Livy won nearly every game. "Never saw FD play so poorly," he noted in his diary on December 3, and after their round that morning, he and Franklin had sat together, having what Livy called "a Bully talk."

Perhaps it was then that Franklin told his old friend of his wife's discovery of his romance, of the recriminations that followed, and of his decision to give up Lucy Mercer and try to rebuild his marriage to Eleanor.

Many years later, after both the Roosevelts had died, Eleanor's cousin Corinne Alsop assessed for an interviewer the impact on Franklin of his romance with Lucy Mercer. It "seemed to release something in him," she remembered. Until then he had seemed to her "to look at human relationships coolly, calmly and without depth. He viewed his family dispassionately, and enjoyed them, but he had in my opinion a loveless quality, as if he were incapable of emotion."

Franklin had married "very young and immature, and had a life sheltered by 'Mama,' " she continued. La Rochefoucauld had said, "*Il y a des bons marriages, mais il n'y en a point de délicieux.*" "On the whole," the Roosevelt marriage had been a good one, but "in my opinion it lacked the *déliceux.*"

She maintained that there had been no real scandal. When the crisis came, Mrs. Alsop believed, "Everybody behaved well and exactly as one would expect each of the protagonists . . . to behave. Lucy Mercer, a Catholic, could not make up her mind to destroy the family, and she would not marry a divorced man. Eleanor was tolerant, understanding, troubled but very kind, and was willing to give Franklin his freedom. Mama was regal, autocratic and adamant. She refused to give Franklin one penny if he got a divorce. The obstacles were insuperable, Franklin accepted the situation, and Lucy and Franklin parted. . . ."[33]

Her cousin exaggerated Eleanor's kind tolerance: the wound inflicted by Franklin's betrayal remained raw to the end of her life. "I have the memory of an elephant," Eleanor told friends years later. "I can forgive, but I cannot forget," and her rancor can only have been

---

33. "I know that marriage would have taken place," one of Lucy's cousins told Jonathan Daniels many years later, "but, as Lucy said to us, 'Eleanor was not willing to step aside.' " As Joseph P. Lash was the first to point out, that was not what happened, but it is perfectly possible that that is what Franklin *told* her had happened, to soften the blow as they parted.

The writer Murray Kempton once speculated as to what might have followed had the decision gone the other way, had Franklin resolved to give up Eleanor and his career for Lucy Mercer. He got the sequence of events out of order, but his imaginings are worth recounting, anyway:

> Somehow, though, cruel as it is to think of an America deprived of Eleanor Roosevelt, there is a fugitive fantasy that together he and Lucy Mercer had sacrificed her immortal soul and his own high destiny. There these two will endure in the imagination, growing old together, say near Newburgh, he languidly farming and dimly drawing wills and litigating country quarrels and she stealing now and then into the dreary little church to grieve a while for the spiritual loss that had bought their happiness. The Depression is hard on him; but, when he dies, he has managed to recoup by selling his remaining acres for a postwar housing development. His obituary is exactly the size the *Times* metes out for former assistant secretaries of the Navy who had been nominated for vice president of the United States in a bad year for their party.
> She lives a long while afterward, is restored to the Church, and works in the Library and always thinks of him tenderly. They would, we may be certain, have brought it all off far better than the Windsors, and hardly anyone would have known they had.

Sources: Jonathan Daniels, *Washington Quadrille*, page 145; Joseph P. Lash, *Eleanor and Franklin*, page 226; *New York Review of Books*, April 15, 1982.

compounded by the slowness with which Franklin had come to his decision; years later, she still believed it had been Howe's warnings, not the children's welfare or any residual love for her, that had finally tipped the scales against his leaving her for a new life with Lucy.[34]

"This past year had rather gotten the best of me," Eleanor would soon write to Isabella. "It has been so full of all kinds of things that I still have a breathless, hunted feeling. . . ."

Among the papers found at Eleanor's New York bedside after her death in 1962 was a tattered, faded newspaper clipping of a poem, "Psyche," by Virginia Moore:

> The soul that has believed
> And is deceived
> Thinks nothing for a while
> All thoughts are vile.
>
> And then because the sun
> Is mute persuasion,
> And hope in Spring and Fall
> Most natural,
> The soul grows calm and mild
> A little child,
> Finding the pull of breath
> Better than death . . .
> The soul that had believed
> And was deceived
> Ends by believing more
> Than ever before.

Across the top of the clipping she had written "1918."

The Roosevelts now tried almost too hard to please one another: Eleanor did her best to be the gay, enthusiastic partygoer her husband wished she were—"Last night's party was really wonderful and I enjoyed it," she told Sara bravely, " . . . I actually danced once"; and Franklin attended church faithfully for a time—"a great sacrifice to please me," Eleanor told Sara—even became vestryman of his father's

---

34. "Eleanor could be hard," her close friend Marion Dickerman remembered. " . . . I know she *tried* to forgive but hers was a not a forgiving nature, really."

In later years, Eleanor would encourage other people close to her (including her own daughter) who were trapped in unhappy marriages and in love with other people to end them. *Sources:* Kenneth S. Davis, *Invincible Summer*, page 93; Bernard Asbell, ed., *Mother & Daughter: The Letters of Eleanor and Anna Roosevelt.*

Hyde Park church, St. James, and did his best to make her feel included in his work, laboring alongside her in the evenings to edit his reports from Europe into a publishable article.[35]

He also played a more active role within the family: helping Anna with algebra, taking Elliott for horseback rides, paying James a quarter a round to caddy for him at Chevy Chase.

Meanwhile, world events had outrun Franklin Roosevelt. Back in October, while still too ill to return to work, he (or Louis Howe) had planted a newspaper story saying that he planned to leave the department for active duty. As soon as he could muster the strength he had told Daniels of his intentions and at eleven o'clock on the evening of October 31, he called upon the President to announce his plans. But Wilson again discouraged his leaving government: he was "too late," Franklin remembered his saying, the President "had received the first suggestion from Prince Max of Baden . . . the war would be over very soon."

Franklin held onto a slim hope that the negotiations would some-how falter: on November 9, he wrote his old friend Lathrop Brown—now in the Tank Corps—that "the consensus of opinion seems to be that the Boche is in a bad way and will take anything, but I am personally not so dead sure as some others. If the terms are turned down and the war continues, I think I shall get into the Navy without question."

But two days later, at 5:00 a.m. on November 11, the conflict that had taken the lives of 10 million young men ended in Marshal Foch's railroad car in the Forest of Compiègne.

For Eleanor, "The feeling of relief and thankfulness was beyond description." But for Franklin, relief and gratitude were mixed with disappointment: he had missed the Great War.[36]

"We've lived in suspense from day to day," Eleanor told Isabella two days after the Armistice, "never knowing what would happen

35. This work was never finished; the letters did not appear in print until Elliott published them in his collection of his father's letters in 1948.

36. In 1921, Groton School planned a permanent monument, listing the names of all gradu-ates who had served in the armed forces. Franklin insisted that his name belonged with the rest: "Though I did not wear a uniform, I believe that my name should go in the first division of those who were 'in the service,' especially as I saw service on the other side, was missed by torpedoes and shell, and had actual command over 'materiel' navy matters in Europe while I was there." Source: Frank Freidel, *Franklin D. Roosevelt: The Apprenticeship*, page 337.

next & no one making any definite plans . . . F. had a horrid time but is really quite well again, though he'll have to be careful this winter. Of course now that the war is over he can't go out & join the Naval guns at the front as he had his heart set on doing. He is anxious to be sent back to see to Navy things over there, but so far the Secretary can't be brought to see that some civilian with authority must go over. In time, however, F. may convince him. . . ."

Bitter that he had not been in combat, and that he had even been denied the role of civilian wartime administrator in Europe he had sought so long, Franklin now first asked Daniels for—then *demanded*—permission to return to Europe, this time to oversee naval demobilization.

The Democrats had lost control of Congress that autumn, despite a strong partisan appeal from the President, and as soon as they took their new seats, the Republicans were sure to investigate the Navy Department's conduct of business abroad, where millions of dollars had been hastily spent, sometimes without even the semblance of a contract. Daniels was inclined to let Admiral Sims supervise the dismantling of the installations for which he had been responsible. But Franklin wished to do it himself, and suggested to Daniels that he owed it to his own reputation to send him abroad since he wished "your administration of the Navy to continue without scandals or criticism." When that gentle hint of possible trouble to come did not move his chief, he took a tougher line: if he were not allowed to sail for Europe, he told Daniels in early December, he would have no choice but publicly to disclaim responsibility for department policy.

The Secretary still resisted. Franklin continued to press, asking now that Eleanor be allowed to accompany him even though official policy still barred women without official duties from accompanying their husbands to what had so recently been the war zone. Her ostensible reason for wanting to go was straightforward enough: Franklin was still weak from the autumn's illnesses; she wanted to keep an eye on her husband, to keep him from falling ill again under the strain of his official duties. "I [hate] to go," she told Isabella, "but I [am] afraid to let F. go without me as I know the climate & many discomforts might be hard for him after pneumonia. . . ." But there was more to it than that. She had been envious of his earlier trip even before she learned of his continuing romance; now, she did not want to sit home alone again, wondering what he was up to.

On Christmas Eve, Daniels finally gave in, signing travel orders allowing both Roosevelts to sail to Europe. Sara Delano Roosevelt may have had something to do with his change of heart. In town to spend Christmas with her children, she called upon the Secretary at his office that afternoon. He simply noted "Mrs. James Roosevelt——" in his diary that evening, but it seems likely that she shared her fears for her son's delicate health with the sympathetic Secretary, who continued, despite everything, to treat Franklin like one of his own sons. Neither she nor Daniels would ever have explicitly mentioned the recent rift between the young Roosevelts, but each knew the other was all too aware of Franklin's weaknesses and, in time, Sara may have helped Daniels delicately to see that Eleanor's steady presence would be a good influence on Franklin, would help ensure a successful mission and be of benefit to all concerned.[37]

In any case, after a hectic holiday, during which Eleanor managed to entertain around the Christmas tree not only her own big family but "12 sailors from Mrs. [Franklin P.] Lane's Convalescent Home and 12 sailors from the Naval Hospital," and with the children safely in Sara's care, she and Franklin took the train to New York. The next day, aboard the USS *Aztec*, Franklin reviewed the returning Victory Fleet during a snowstorm. A remarkable photograph taken on the bridge that afternoon shows the toll that dispiriting fall and winter had taken on both Roosevelts: beneath a wide black hat, Eleanor is grim and almost skeletal; Franklin, also thin and drawn, stands at attention at the rail, his bowler hat held over his heart, hair plastered to his head by melting snow.

"FDR standing bareheaded nearly froze to death," Livy Davis noted in his diary. He was again to accompany Franklin to Europe and joined the Roosevelts on New Year's Day as they boarded the USS *George Washington*, Franklin's former aide Captain Edward McCau-

---

37. Four years earlier, in the summer of 1914, Daniels and his wife had visited Springwood. Sara had reported then having been "incensed" to hear from the rector of St. James that a relative had said to him, "Isn't it dreadful Franklin is compelled to associate with that terrible man, Daniels?"

"What do you mean?" the rector said. "Secretary Daniels is a man of the highest character and Franklin admires him very much."

"But you do not know about him and his habits," the lady answered. "I have just returned from Washington and was told by truthful people that the Secretary has affairs with all the Navy ladies."

The Daniels's and the Roosevelts alike had laughed then at the absurdity of scandal touching anyone in their comfortable circle. *Source:* Josephus Daniels, *Editor in Politics*, pages 83–84.

ley, Jr., now commanding.[38] Also included in the Assistant Secretary's party were Commander John M. Hancock of the Naval Supply Corps, who was to do the extensive detail work, and Thomas Spellacy, a genial Connecticut politician whom Franklin had brought along as legal counsel—"nice," Eleanor told Sara, "but of such a different kind that there is little common meeting ground for anything beyond acquaintanceship."

"A heavy sea," Livy noted the day after they sailed, "whole dining room wrecked by heavy roll, also my breakfast landing on top of waiter's head." Despite the constant pitching and rolling, the Roosevelts enjoyed the voyage. They had a luxurious suite—two rooms and a bath. Franklin exercised every day with Walter Camp. Eleanor enjoyed reading *The Education of Henry Adams*—"but sad to have had so much and yet find it so little"—and conversed enthusiastically in French with members of the Mexican and Chinese delegations going to the peace talks just getting started in Paris. After giving a luncheon for the delegates, Livy noted, Franklin "made a characteristic felicitous speech wh. was ably replied to by a Chink educated at Yale."

On Sunday evening, January 5, there was a band concert in the crew's theatre, followed by a gala dinner and speeches by Franklin, and by Charles J. Schwab, the steel magnate who now headed the Emergency Fleet Corporation, and whose vigorous, straight-from-the-shoulder speechmaking "captivated the entire personnel of the ship," according to Eleanor. Then the Roosevelts and their party settled down to watch Charlie Chaplin in *Shoulder Arms*—"Funniest movie I ever saw," Livy thought.

That same evening in Oyster Bay, Theodore Roosevelt sat reading in his children's empty nursery.

He was only sixty, but badly overweight, and just home from six weeks in a New York hospital. He had checked in on the day the war ended, suffering from inflammatory rheumatism that rendered his left arm useless, and weary with grief over Quentin's death and the frustration of having had to sit out the war. "Ugh!," he told Bob Ferguson, "It isn't pleasant for the old man to be reduced to doing nothing but talky-talky."

38. Just before sailing, Franklin gratefully took delivery of four cases of "Old Reserve" whiskey at just $1.90 a bottle, courtesy of his old friend John I. McIlhenny, now president of the U.S. Civil Service. It seemed clear that Congress was going to pass the Prohibition Amendment and send it on to the states, "but 47 East 65th Street," Franklin wrote to McIlhenny, "is for the time being at least on the 'wet' list!" *Source:* Franklin D. Roosevelt, Papers as Assistant Secretary of the Navy, FDRL.

Old friends who visited him in the hospital had found him physically weak but still pugnacious. When the admiring Kansas editor, William Allen White, came to call, he was first turned away: the former President was too heavily medicated to see visitors. He left a note saying that General Leonard Wood was planning to announce his candidacy for President in 1920, and that if the Colonel was interested in running himself, he should make his desires known to the party. Upon reading the message, TR sent three different couriers to track White down and bring him back to his bedside. "Well, probably I shall have to get in this in June," he told the editor and showed him a pencilled draft of the Progressive platform on which he already planned to campaign.[39]

"I seem pretty low now," he told another visitor, "but I shall get better. I cannot go without having done something to that old gray skunk in the White House." He was delighted that Wilson's call for a Democratic Congress had backfired so spectacularly. The election results had been a "stinging rebuke" to the President, he told Ted Jr.; Wilson "has no authority whatever to speak for the American people. . . ." "We did an unparalleled thing," he wrote to his friend Rudyard Kipling, "and took away the Congress from him, on the issue that we stood for, forcing the Germans to make an unconditional surrender. I took a certain sardonic amusement in the fact that whereas, four years ago, to put it mildly, my attitude was not very popular, I was now the one man whom they insisted upon following and whose statements were taken as the platform."

He had already denounced the Fourteen Points upon which Wilson hoped to base a lasting peace as "fourteen scraps of paper"; now he offered only carefully qualified support for the proposed League of Nations: "Would it not be well to begin with the League which we actually have in existence, the League of the Allies who have fought through this great war?" he asked in the Kansas City *Star*. "Let us at the peace table see that real justice is done as among these allies and that . . . the sternest reparation is demanded from our foes. Then let

39. He had gently turned away supporters who had urged him to run for governor the previous autumn, but he had never given up hope of returning to the White House. "I have only one fight left in me," he had told his sister, Corinne Robinson, then, "and I think I should reserve my strength in case I am needed in 1920."

Even some old enemies supported his candidacy. A Midwestern Progressive leader told the Republican boss William Barnes, Jr., whom TR had defeated with Franklin's help in the 1915 libel trial, that he thought the ex-President would be nominated in 1920 'by acclamation."

"Acclamation, hell!" Barnes answered. "We're going to nominate him by assault!" *Sources:* Sylvia Jukes Morris, *Edith Kermit Roosevelt*, page 424; Herman Hagedorn, *The Roosevelt Family of Sagamore Hill*, page 406.

us extend the privileges of the League as rapidly as their conduct warrants it to other nations."

It was his hope to help monitor that conduct as President once again.

He had come home again to Oyster Bay on Christmas Day, his pain reduced but complaining of shortness of breath and still too weak from anemia and fever to do more than take short walks around the lawns. A nurse moved in to keep an eye on him; the family doctor stopped by twice a day.

Now, while he turned the pages, his wife played solitaire. A fire crackled in the fireplace. He closed his book and gazed into the flames, Edith Roosevelt remembered, and "spoke of the happiness of being home, and made little plans."

"I wonder if you will ever know how I love Sagamore Hill," he said.

James Amos, his old White House valet, helped him to bed about midnight, then sat quietly in a nearby chair as he fell asleep. The next morning around 4:00 a.m., Amos woke with a start. The Colonel was breathing strangely. The valet rushed to awaken Mrs. Roosevelt and the nurse. Both women hurried into his room. "Theodore darling!" Edith called, leaning over him. He did not answer. He seemed "just asleep," she said, "only he could not hear."

He had died of a pulmonary embolism, a blood clot in the lung.

"The old lion is dead," Archie cabled to his brothers overseas.

"Death had to take him sleeping," Vice President Marshall said, "for if Roosevelt had been awake, there would have been a fight."

Woodrow Wilson was already in Europe for the peace talks about to begin at Paris. A messenger brought him the news as he sat in his railroad compartment at Modena, in northern Italy. Two reporters, strolling along the platform, stopped to watch his face as he read the telegram: it registered first surprise, they said, then pity, then "transcendent triumph." He scrawled a hasty note to Edith Roosevelt; he first said he had been "grieved" to hear of her husband's death, but before he sent his message he amended it to read "shocked."

That afternoon, Edith Roosevelt and TR's sister, Corinne Robinson, whose affection for her brother had eclipsed even her love for her late husband, took a long, cold walk together around the grounds at Oyster Bay. As they turned and started back they heard the unfamiliar whine of aeroplanes and looked up into the reddened sky above the house: pilots from the Long Island airfield where Quentin had trained were dropping laurel wreaths over Sagamore Hill.

The funeral was held at Oyster Bay on Wednesday. As the pall-bearers carried Theodore Roosevelt's coffin through the snow-covered trees to a hilltop grave at Oyster Bay, and the family followed along behind it, a New York police captain stepped up to Corinne: "Do you remember the *fun* of him, Mrs. Robinson? It was not only that he was a great man, but, oh, there was such fun in being led by him."

The news reached the Franklin Roosevelts aboard the *George Washington* by wireless on the 6th. Both were stunned. "My cousin's death was in every way a great shock," Franklin told Daniels, "for we heard just before leaving that he was better—and he was after all not old. But I cannot help thinking that he himself would have had had it this way and that he has been spared a lingering illness of perhaps years." " . . . I think much of Aunt Edith," Eleanor wrote Sara, "for it will leave her very much alone. Another big figure gone . . . and I fear the last years were for him full of disappointment."

"I never saw anything like Paris," Eleanor reported to her mother-in-law. "It is full beyond belief and one sees many celebrities and all one's friends! People wander the streets unable to find a bed and the prices are worse than New York for everything."

Livy and the Roosevelts stayed at the Ritz, the other members of their party at the less splendid Continental. But the lobbies of both hotels and the streets surrounding them were filled with an astonishing variety of foreigners. Delegates from everywhere on earth had congregated to ensure their own place in the settlement being discussed at Versailles: Armenians, Ukranians, Bessarabians, Koreans, Polish shepherds wearing caps of black fur, and desert Arabs in flowing white robes elbowed their way past French war widows dressed in black.

Wilson had been in Europe for two weeks. He had arrived with a retinue of more than twenty academic advisers eager to help him redraw the boundaries of Europe but not a single member of the United States Senate that would have to ratify whatever treaty he signed.[40]

The reception the President had received everywhere he went was almost frightening in its intensity; schoolchildren at Plymouth, wear-

40. Alice Longworth, whose grief over her father's death would soon turn into unrelenting hatred for the man who had in her view wrongfully supplanted him in the White House, had written already of Wilson's "amazing trip to Europe, preparations for which exceed in grandeur those for the Field of the Cloth of Gold or the Queen of Sheba's visit to King Solomon. The apes and the peacocks alone are lacking, and there are those people unkind enough to say that even they will go along in one form or another." *Source:* Jonathan Daniels, *Washington Quadrille,* page 175.

ing American flags, cushioned his path with rose petals; banners hung across Parisian boulevards hailed him as "Wilson the Just"; farmers lit votive candles in front of his photograph in cottages all across the Continent.

But there were disturbing rumors already floating among the delegates, Eleanor reported. There was "much discussion about the President's not having yet been to the front which is worrying the French very much. They feel he should see the devastated regions before the conferences, and of course our own boys are very anxious to have him see where they have fought and existed, for one couldn't call it living. Also he has been to no hospitals and Mrs. Wilson only to two so far. . . ."

The Roosevelts had nothing directly to do with the peace talks. Franklin's task, in Commander Hancock's words, was to "lubricate the discussions" with the French, bringing to negotiations over the sale of naval property his distinctive combination of affability and toughness. He did well, setting up boards to settle the claims of private citizens and disposing of all manner of naval supplies to the French government, despite its chronic reluctance to commit itself before sufficient time had passed to force down prices.

His most impressive feat—"The most successful thing I pulled off in Paris," he called it—came in talks with André Tardieu, the French Minister of Liaison with the Allies, over disposition of a naval radio station near Bordeaux. "The French had backed and filled for over six weeks," he reported to Daniels, "and I finally put it up to Tardieu, and told him that if they did not wish to keep the Lafayette Station themselves, I would take it down and ship it home. . . . They agreed to take it the next day." The price, Eleanor confided to Sara, was "22,000,000 frcs. This is a big success but don't mention it!"[41]

While Franklin tended to business, Eleanor saw to Aunt Dora, strolled along the Champs-Elysées to gaze at the captured German

---

41. This tale, like to so many others, quickly grew in the retelling. Nigel Law much later recalled how Franklin described the negotiations to him as soon as he got back from Europe:

He was having an argument with the French over the price at which he would sell them a radio aerial. . . . The French were obstinate and offered a ridiculous sum counting on the fact that the cost of dismantling and removing it would be prohibitive. But just when a deadlock had been reached . . . a messenger handed a telegram to FDR which read, 'Dismantle and ship aerial to America.' The French opposition at once collapsed. . . . FDR had of course arranged for the telegram before he went to the meeting. He told me this story with much gusto.

Source: Jonathan Daniels, Washington Quadrille, page 161.

guns, accompanied Mrs. Wilson to military hospitals—in one of which she found both her uncle, David Gray, and Theodore Roosevelt, Jr., laid up after corrective surgery on his shattered knee—and ordered up two costly gowns at Worth's ("F. bore it like a lamb").

Early in the morning on January 18, the Roosevelts set out by motor for Boulogne, where they were to catch the boat for England. Wedged in the back seat between Franklin and Livy, Eleanor was in great pain. She was said to be along to safeguard her husband's health, but it was Eleanor, not Franklin, who now fell ill. She had developed pleurisy in her right lung; every jolt along the shell-pocked road was agony. Nonetheless, Franklin noted, "she insists on doing everything, getting out of the car at all points of interest."

" . . . [Belleau] Wood with its few bare sticks to mark what once been [trees] gave one an even more ghastly feeling than the shelled & ruined towns," Eleanor told Isabella. "The sea of mud on every side also must be seen & what the men lived through who fought there is inconceivable."

They stopped near Ham to have a look at the half-exposed skeletons of a German gun crew, still dressed in shreds of gray wool, then spread out their lunch on the base of a missing monument in the Cathedral Square at St. Quentin—"the figure itself [had been] carried off to Hunland," Franklin reported. Eleanor, too ill to eat the beef-paste sandwiches provided by the Army commissary, but not wishing to admit how badly she felt or to hurt anyone's feelings, wandered away from the party and discreetly buried her sandwich in the rubble of the shelled cathedral.

Near Cambrai, their motor suffered a puncture, giving Franklin, Eleanor, and Livy an opportunity to explore the elaborate system of trenches and view the St. Quentin canal, where British troops had smashed through the Hindenburg Line against overwhelming odds. " . . . [I]t seemed a very wonderful feat," Eleanor told Isabella, "for the cut is some 60 feet up, very steep and just mud from top to bottom & they had to slide down & cross & climb up in the face of machine gun fire!"

It had been "a very wonderful day," Franklin wrote, "and one we shall never forget." That evening they reached Amiens, where they were to spend the night. A British officer assigned to escort them to their hotel and take them sightseeing the next morning explained that women were not as yet permitted to tour the war zone; Eleanor would have to stay behind. "When I told him that we had already visited the entire battle area," Franklin proudly reported to his mother, "he almost fainted and had visions of court martial."

The next day they moved on to London.

Admiral Sims had not looked forward to Franklin's visit—"The Assistant Secretary could not form any intelligent opinion upon all of the various things we have to settle over here without giving his whole time to it for six or seven months," he told a friend. "There are over thirty stations he would have to visit and look into. . . . The consequence is that he is practically confined to looking wise and approving what is recommended by local commanders and headquarters."

And Franklin's brashness when he finally arrived did not help. Sims greeted him cordially enough, and assembled the staff. Franklin told them all how happy he was to be in Britain again, how proud he was of the job the Navy had done. Then he added that he had come over to make sure that when the Republican Congress got around to investigating the administration's conduct of the war, the Navy, at least, would come out clean.

Sims bristled: the Assistant Secretary need not have come if that was the reason for his visit, he replied; he was prepared to take full responsibility for every decision he had made.

It was an awkward beginning to Franklin's mission to Britain, but in fact comparatively little was left for him to do. Sims had already begun the demobilization process and Commander Hancock was available to settle the particulars. "F. works morning and afternoon," Eleanor reported to Sara, "but gets home for lunch and tea about 5:30 and he's really not overworked."

Franklin was fine, but Eleanor remained ill, haunted by a rasping, uncontrollable cough. A doctor came to their suite in the Ritz to examine her, prescribed bed rest and, alarmed by her thinness, urged her to be examined for tuberculosis when she got home. She stubbornly insisted she was well enough to see old friends and family members; to shop for clothes for Anna, attend the theatre, and dine on sandwiches and champagne at the Admiralty while watching silent footage of the surrender of the German Fleet. Franklin insisted on taking her temperature one evening, found it well over 100, and "to my rage," she said, forbade her to attend a dinner.

On January 31, Franklin left with Livy for the Continent to visit Belgium and inspect Marine bases in occupied Germany, where women were again expressly forbidden to go. "I hate to miss the trip . . . ," Eleanor noted in her journal, "and to have him going off without me." She moved in with Franklin's cousin, Muriel Robbins Martineau, for a few days before travelling on to Paris, with Commander Hancock as her escort, to be reunited with her husband.

Franklin's cross-Channel voyage from Dover to Ostend aboard the American destroyer the USS *Farnell* was halted well offshore because of a thick fog bank that hid the surrounding waters. Unswept mines were thought to be in the vicinity, and the skipper, William F. Halsey, was not willing to risk taking his ship through them until he could see where he was going. Franklin and Livy paced the deck for two hours. They were scheduled to lunch with King Albert at Brussels and Franklin believed it "absolutely necessary" that they be there. Finally, he commandeered a motorboat and sped toward shore, taking his chances with the floating mines rather than miss his royal luncheon.

They made it in time—"one of the most delightful things in my life," Franklin said—and toured forts and inspected Canadian troops at Liège. Then Franklin moved on into the occupied Rhineland, where even Livy was not permitted to go, and where he looked forward to a special treat: the sight of the Stars and Stripes streaming above the great fortress of Ehrenbreitstein that he had seen often during his boyhood summer visits to Germany. But when his motor came around a curve in the river, the flagstaff above the citadel was bare. Furious, Franklin stormed into the commanding officer's headquarters, demanding to know "Why the Hell the American flag is not flying. . . ."

The answer—out of respect for German sensibilities—did not satisfy the Assistant Secretary of the Navy. Upon his return to Paris he would accost General Pershing himself on the subject: failing to raise the flag was "a very grave error," he later said he told the commander of the AEF. "The German people ought to know for all time that Ehrenbreitstein flew the American flag during the occupation."

"You are right," Pershing said, "it will be hoisted within the hour." According to Franklin, it did not come down again until the last American had left German soil.

Franklin did not permit the incident at Ehrenbreitstein to spoil his triumphal mood: after inspecting a Marine brigade on the bank of the Rhine, he told the men that they were especially privileged to be serving in Germany. Then, patting his pocket where he said his steamship tickets were kept, he declared how happy he'd be to trade them for a Marine uniform. According to legend, one private shouted back, "*I'll* swap you!"

Back in Paris, Eleanor was unhappy and increasingly anxious without Franklin. "Somehow I feel lost and lonely in a strange town alone and I do get so blue," she confided to her diary. "I suppose it must be the result of pleurisy." Ceaseless activity helped drive off depression: she shopped, looked up friends, took Aunt Dora with her on a tour of the Val de Grâce Hospital which specialized in plastic surgery. "I don't see how she stands it," she told Sara, "and yet one must grow accustomed for she seemed to like hearing about all the horrible operations and I could hardly bear to look at the men with the horrible face wounds."

Her anxiety grew steadily. She expected Franklin on the afternoon of February 8. A dinner was scheduled with Commander Hancock at eight, but when Franklin had not arrived by eleven, Hancock thought it best to go back to his hotel and return the next day. Eleanor waited alone in her room at the Ritz, fearful that something had happened.

Franklin did not turn up until well after midnight, and when he did, his arms and those of two companions were filled with "all kinds of 'loot' from battlefields and Germany," so many souvenirs that a pair of orderlies had to be assigned the job of packing them for the trip home: this time, James would have plenty of German helmets to choose among.[42]

Eleanor was less interested than Franklin might have liked in the stories he tried to tell her about his "interesting and delightful trip" as he ate the cold supper she'd kept for him.

And when he came weaving home in the early hours of the *next* morning, having attended a hilarious and impromptu reunion of the Fly Club with Livy and several other Harvard men who happened to be in town, she was still angrier.

For Eleanor, Paris still seemed a dangerous, seductive city, not the sort of place in which her husband should be on the loose. Its women were too worldly, too brazenly made up—"exaggerated, some pretty but all chic [and] you wonder if any are ladies. . . . ," she told Sara.

42. Franklin had also bought "several trunksful" of old books for his collection at very low prices in German towns along the Rhine. *Source:* Ernest K. Lindley, *Franklin D. Roosevelt,* page 182.

"I've decided there is very little real beauty in France!" She had seen the city's impact on one member of the family: Munro Robinson, Aunt Corinne's son, had been very brave at the front, but was now drinking heavily and "behaving dreadfully" in Parisian society, she wrote; and she was glad Franklin had arranged for Auntie Bye's only son, Sheffield, to join his staff and sail home with the Roosevelts: the French capital was "no place for the boys, especially the younger ones, and the scandals going on would make many a woman at home unhappy."[43]

Livy met the Roosevelts for breakfast in the hotel dining room the next morning, and "Found FD and E very cool [to one another] as he had been to Fly Club dinner night before." Eleanor still distrusted Franklin; he still chafed under her distrust.

She was annoyed with Livy, too, and in Franklin's absence he had provided her with an incident with which she could now make that annoyance plain. Livy had not been happy at being forbidden to accompany his friend to Germany and when, after the long drive back to Paris, he arrived at the Ritz and found that the room and bath he had asked for right next to the Roosevelts would not be available for twelve hours (during which he was welcome to occupy another room on the same floor), he had made a loud, temperish scene at the front desk, "as much upset as though he had been a refugee in one of the devastated areas." " . . . I thought the poor manager's head would be torn off!" Eleanor told Sara. "I have decided that trips of this kind either make very firm friendships or mar them. . . . Livy is lazy, selfish and self-seeking to an extraordinary degree with the outward appearance of being quite different. Franklin is too loyal ever to change in his feelings, but I am deciding more firmly every day that the estimate I've been making of him for over a year is not far from right."

She had begun making that estimate the previous winter, when Livy started monopolizing Franklin's spare time. Since then, nothing had happened to change her growing conviction that his influence on her suggestible husband was malign. Now, she made those feelings plain to Franklin.

In any case, rather than return to America with the Roosevelts, Davis decided to stay on in Europe and work under Herbert Hoover

43. Sara echoed her feelings: "One hears a great deal here from returning officers and privates," she wrote her children. "One tale is that the common soldier behaves better than the officers, asking 'Where is Napoleon's Tomb,' 'Where is the Louvre gallery,' etc. The officers say: 'Where is Maxim's?' " *Source:* Roosevelt Family Papers, FDRL.

as an administrator, helping to feed the desperate people of Czechoslovakia.

President Wilson was sailing home aboard the *George Washington*, planning to stay in Washington just long enough to sign bills passed since his absence before hurrying back to Paris for further negotiations. Franklin and Eleanor were to go home with him. They had played no role in the peace talks, of course—a friendly newspaperman would give them their first look at an advance copy of the draft Covenant aboard the boat train—but they were both keenly interested in all that was happening.

On February 15, they left Paris for Brest in a drizzling rain. Bretons cheered from the rooftops, and Franklin must have enjoyed it when, from time to time, the troops who lined the tracks craned their necks to peer into their compartment in hopes of seeing the Wilsons and mistook his thin face for that of the President.

Aboard ship, Franklin was eager to hear about the Treaty from Wilson himself, but at first it did not seem likely that he would get the chance: the President kept mostly to himself, walking through a formal inspection at Franklin's side with little enthusiasm, and ignoring even the boxing matches specifically staged for his entertainment on Washington's Birthday, saying, according to Eleanor, he "neither cared for boxing nor had the time to waste." "He seemed to have very little interest in making himself popular with groups of people whom he touched," she added.

Eleanor herself sat through the bouts, feigning enthusiasm though they sickened her, continuing to fulfill her duty as a politician's wife. But with Livy no longer taking up Franklin's spare time, she also had begun to introduce him to stimulating fellow passengers whom she thought he might otherwise overlook. "She used always to be telling [him], 'I met so-and-so,'" Sheffield Cowles remembered. "He's an interesting fellow. You should talk with him. *He's* interested in more than sailing.'" It was a role she would play for the rest of their lives together.

That same day, to Franklin's relief, the Roosevelts were invited to be among the President's guests at lunch. Two things stayed with them afterwards: Wilson said he had read no newspapers since the war began; his secretary, Joseph P. Tumulty, clipped all the important stories for him. "This is too much to leave to any man," Eleanor noted in her diary. And he had spoken with genuine emotion of the League: "The United States must go in or it will break the heart of the world for she is the only nation that all feel is disinterested and all trust."[44]

The next day was Sunday, and after services that morning Franklin and Charles Schwab were both scheduled to address the men. Franklin, who had been outshone by Schwab on the trip to Europe, was determined to do better this time. He wrote out several drafts of his remarks in his cabin and read them aloud to Eleanor and Sheffield Cowles before he was satisfied. "Even *then* he wasn't very good," Cowles remembered,[45] and Schwab brought the men to their feet by presenting them with the money to buy a new film projector for their mess.

That evening, Wilson was persuaded to leave his stateroom and attend another show in which sailors dressed as chorus girls in pink tulle cavorted across the deck. One, bolder than the rest, ran down into

44. As Assistant Secretary, Franklin had seen to President Wilson's accommodations aboard the *George Washington* and had arranged to have set up in his stateroom a replica of a desk once used by the ship's namesake that had been on display in Wanamaker's department store. Later, he somehow managed to purchase this desk—at which Wilson had worked over his draft of the Covenant while travelling to and from Europe—and set it up in his own office in his new library at Hyde Park in 1940.

Some time during World War II, Wilson's widow, who had hoped to have the historic desk for her husband's old home on S Street, attended a dinner at the White House.

"How do you like the wineglasses, Mrs. Wilson?" the President asked.

She said she thought them very handsome

"I got them off the *George Washington* for five cents apiece."

Mrs. Wilson innocently said that reminded her of a story. After the President had returned for the last time from Paris, she said, Secretary Daniels asked Wilson if he would like the desk he had used aboard the ship. Wilson said he could not accept it; it belonged to the government.

Daniels reminded him that it did not; the desk had been a personal gift to the President from Rodman Wanamaker.

Wilson said in that case he would like very much to have it.

Daniels called back a few days later, deeply embarrassed, to say that the desk could not be found. He was terribly sorry. Mrs. Wilson added, "We never found out what happened to it."

FDR said *"I can tell you. I have it, and what's more, you're not going to get it away from me."*

Mr. President, she said, "you're nothing but a common thief."

Perhaps chastened by this confrontation, the President later dictated a memorandum to his secretary, claiming that he had carefully informed the Wilsons that the desk was up for sale and had only bought it for himself when they expressed no interest in it.

Later, Mrs. Wilson told friends, "I should have sued him for that desk."

(The desk on display at Hyde Park at the time of this writing is a copy; James Roosevelt, the President's eldest son, has possession of the original.) *Sources:* Gene Smith, *When the Cheering Stopped,* page 275; Alden Hatch, *Edith Bolling Wilson: First Lady Extraordinary,* pages 271–272; James Roosevelt (and Sidney Shallett), *Affectionately, FDR,* page 79n; PSF 178, FDL.

45. He was still *"terrified"* of speaking then, especially in French but in English, too," Cowles remembered, and credited the vice-presidential campaign of 1920 with having finally made his cousin Franklin a vivid, off-the-cuff orator. *Source:* Interview with W. Sheffield Cowles, Jr.

the audience, leaned his rouged face close to the President's long pale one, and chucked him under the chin. Franklin never forgot the expression on Wilson's face as he recoiled.[46]

One afternoon on that voyage home, Franklin and Sheffield Cowles stood together on the bridge of the *George Washington*, bundled against the cold wind, watching the big, gray destroyers gliding through the gray-green sea on either side of the President's ship, and talking of Theodore Roosevelt and what his loss would mean to the family and the country. Franklin was uncharacteristically depressed and ruminative.

The "greatest disappointment in his life," Franklin told his young cousin, had been his rejection by the Porcellian, TR's club—and his own father's. "That made a great impression on me," Cowles remembered. "I thought he was *quite* successful. After all, as Assistant Secretary of the Navy he rated a nineteen-gun salute."

That success had never been enough for Franklin, but the once bright future now seemed dark to him. The war was over, and he had missed the fighting, he told his young cousin. He should have listened to Cousin Ted and left for the front the minute the war began, instead of staying behind in Washington. If he had, he could have commanded one of those magnificent destroyers. Now, without a combat record of which to boast, with his old rival Al Smith in the governor's chair

46. The *George Washington*'s original destination had been New York, according to a story Franklin loved to tell, but after she was under way, Wilson told Captain Edward McCauley he wished to land at Boston. The newspaperman Arthur Krock recorded Franklin's memories of what happened next:

> To Eddie McCauley's consternation he discovered he had no chart aboard for a Boston landfall, and would have to feel his way, with such assistance as I, who had long sailed the ocean off New England, could give him. I explained that this could be very slight, considering the difference between navigating a sailboat and an ocean liner. One night, in the course of Eddie's quandary, which was concealed from the President, I was awakened in my berth by a shuddering noise. Thinking the *George Washington* must be aground, I rushed to the bridge in my pajamas and bathrobe to discover that the ship's engines had been reversed and cut off—that was the noise—and that she lay between two jagged rocks, with little way between, facing a shoreline with a row of summer cottages.
> I recognized the settlement as Nahant, where I had frequently made port. And in a general way I was able to tell Eddie where he would find Boston harbor. . . . He then gave the order for backing the ship out of its perilous location, and proceeded safely to Boston. President Wilson, who had not been awakened . . . was never told of what happened.

Krock told this story to Captain McCauley, then retired, and asked him how much truth there was in it.

"None," the captain said. There had been a thick fog off the New England coast but Franklin had nothing whatsoever to do with guiding the *George Washington* through it. *Source:* Arthur Krock, *Memoirs: Sixty Years on the Firing Line,* page 156.

at Albany, the political future looked grim, and—perhaps unknown to Cowles and certainly unmentioned by Franklin himself as he stared out to sea—his marriage was still in tatters.

Because of the greatness that would come to Franklin Roosevelt later in his life—and because of his own cheerfully grandiose sense of himself at every age—more has often been made of his career at the Navy Department than should have been. He was more cheerleader and expediter than maker of decisions, often in the public eye, but largely because his busy chief had neither the time nor the inclination to be there. In the 604 densely printed pages of Josephus Daniels' published diaries, his Assistant Secretary's name appears just 113 times, and then as often as not only when he was making trouble.

During the early struggle to maintain civilian control over the admirals, arguably the greatest single achievement of Daniels' tenure, Franklin had largely been an onlooker. None of Franklin's most intense enthusiasms—the building of fleets of fifty-foot patrol boats and 110-foot submarine chasers, the creation of the Naval Reserve, the North Sea mine barrage—materially affected the outcome of the naval war. And Franklin's two swashbuckling wartime trips to Europe may have been good public relations but they were unimportant in the overall scheme of things.

His actual role in the winning of the war had been relatively small, then, but he had displayed a great natural gift for gettings things done, for learning fast and making decisions swiftly, for getting along with all sorts of people, and for getting the Roosevelt name into the newspapers.

He could not have known it then, peering through the fog, but despite the death of Cousin Theodore, that name would continue to stand him in good stead.

CHAPTER

11

~~~

THE SIMON-PURE POLITICIAN

ON TUESDAY afternoon, July 6, 1920, Sara Delano Roosevelt motored south along the Hudson to Algonac. Eleanor and the children had left Hyde Park on Sunday, on their way to Campobello for the summer, and Franklin was far away in San Francisco, a New York delegate to the Democratic National Convention that had just nominated Governor James M. Cox of Ohio for President. She was pleased that he had gone to the convention, as she was whenever her son got what he wanted: ". . . I can imagine that the time at San Francisco will be most interesting and I hope 'elevating,' " she wrote in reply to the telegram he sent assuring her of his safe arrival, ". . . but I fancy the last epithet is not very likely in a crowd of every sort of politician."[1]

Sara had tried to come to terms with the increasingly public lives her children now led. "I can't tell you how happy I am that you are both doing all these interesting things and seeing these interesting people," she had written to Franklin and Eleanor when they were in Paris the year before, "and it seems to me public life is so peculiarly what you are fitted for, even tho' you are so extremely nice when leading the simple life at Hyde Park!"

But that simple life often seemed lonely to Sara when her family

---

1. Sara never entirely reconciled herself to political conventions, even when they were certain to nominate her son. "I shall 'listen in' to the [Chicago] Convention," she told FDR just before he was to be nominated for an unprecedented third term in 1940. "I hope it will be dignified & not *too* awful." *Source:* Roosevelt Family Papers Donated by the Children, FDRL.

was away, and so she had come down to visit her sister, Annie Hitch. Second only to Springwood, the old Delano house, now rebuilt after its disastrous fire—though without the great tower in which she had once slept—and still surrounded by deeply shaded lawns and landscaped gardens, was Sara's favorite place to be. She was working among the flower beds she had tended as a girl, enjoying the breeze off the Hudson and the familiar, sweeping view of Newburgh Bay, when a servant called to her from the house. She was wanted on the telephone.

She made her way inside and was handed the receiver. It was her Hyde Park neighbor, Mrs. Thomas Newbold, and she had wonderful news. The Democrats had nominated Franklin for Vice President of the United States.

Sara was pleased but not totally surprised. More than a week earlier, Langdon Marvin, Franklin's law partner, had written her that his nomination for Vice President would "strengthen the ticket very much," and earlier that day several telephone callers, including Mrs. Newbold's husband and her older brother, Warren Delano, had called to say that Franklin's nomination now seemed likely.

Her first thought, as always, was of the family. "I telegraphed to Eleanor and to Rosy as soon as I heard the news," she wrote to her son, "and also to Nelly [Blodgett, her closest girlhood friend and Franklin's godmother]."[2]

2. Rosy and Betty were fishing for salmon in New Brunswick when they got word of Franklin's nomination. Rosy's delight in his half brother's good fortune was only slightly tinged with jealousy, as his letter to Eleanor makes clear:

July 7, 1920
Upsalquich, New Brunswick
Dear Eleanor,
Hurrah for the Democrats! "Ma's" telegram has just come by canoe. Won't "Ma" have to buy a whole new set of new hats to contain her head! Now for the family photos in all the papers. From left to right, John aged four, Franklin aged six, Elliott, James, Anna, etc., Mrs. Roosevelt, the Vice President, and in the back row the Vice President's mother, and perhaps his elder Brother, on the wall at the back of the picture portraits of the Roosevelt ancestors as hung on the walls of his baronial residence on the Hudson!!!!

His letter to Franklin, sent the same day, omitted the reference to his own comparative obscurity:
Dear Franklin,
. . . To say that we were thrilled does not express it!! Betty suggested two days ago that Cox and Roosevelt would sound well, and I told her nothing so good as that could happen! . . .
It is a good clean ticket. Thank goodness they had the sense to put Wilson, McAdoo and Palmer in the soup. . . . I think you have a good chance of winning out.
Anyway, it won't hurt you a bit for the future, if you don't win. An older man might be shelved by it, but such an honor to a young man will always help. I really suppose you

"All my love and interest goes to you," she continued, "and as always, is centered in you. . . . My regards and best wishes to our future President. Your devoted Mother."

Franklin was not really surprised by his nomination either, though he liked to say he had been. He had sought a more prominent political position for months, in fact, and with a single-mindedness so reckless that it led him dangerously close to political ruin. And he had learned in the course of his sometimes desperate maneuvering that his fortunes could not be severed from those of the two men whom he had served so impatiently for more than seven years, Woodrow Wilson and Josephus Daniels.

The Roosevelts had returned to America from Europe in late February 1919 with no clear idea of what the immediate future held. "We've had an interesting trip," Eleanor then wrote her Auntie Bye, "& F. thinks he succeeded very well with his demobilization of all possible stations in Europe. . . . He says he now expects to go into business this summer for a time so we may be in New York next year & there may be a little more time which we can call our own."

Secretary Daniels left for Europe in mid-March to attend an Allied naval conference and was gone until mid-May, leaving Franklin in charge. Fearful the Acting Secretary might do something impetuous during the two months he planned to be away, he left detailed instructions on nearly every subject likely to come up during his absence. The bureau chiefs, for example, could be expected to ask Franklin to approve their recommendations and forward them on to the new Republican chairman of the Naval Affairs Committee. He was to refuse to do so: "It would be very well . . . for you to have a drawer and put them all in it so that we can make a study of them, and we will discuss them when I get back."[3]

---

would rather have gone over to the Senate, as more interesting than presiding over it. I love to think of you calling Lodge and the other gray beards to order!!

I fancy that Tom Lynch and John Mack promptly got drunk, when the result came, and I don't blame them, either.

I suppose you will have to resign (after the yacht races) and stump the country. I wish I knew a little more about Cox, and whether he is in good health!!!

We do congratulate you most heartily, and are very much puffed up with pride. . . .

Source: James Roosevelt Roosevelt Papers, FDRL.

3. Daniels' anxiety was justified. Even Herbert Lehman, who was a civilian aide in the Navy Department in World War I and would one day be Franklin's Lieutenant-Governor and an admirer of his chief so ardent that the journalist Arthur Krock dismissed him as "a sort of pet

". . . [T]hings have been so quiet here as to be almost terrifying," Franklin reassured his chief after Daniels had sailed. "Literally nothing has happened outside of the routine work, which, however, has been voluminous." To Livy Davis, he was a good deal more expansive: "You ought to see the change in the carrying on of the Department work. I see civilians at the old building from 9 A.M. to 10:30, then I see the Press, and then dash down to the new building in a high-powered car, and from that time on—11 A.M.—see no outsiders, Congressmen, Senators, or anybody else. The Department mail is signed at regular hours, and absolutely cleaned up every day, with the result that nothing is taken home, mislaid, lost, et cetera, et cetera!"

And when a reporter from a newspaper known to be hostile to his absent chief asked for an interview, Franklin was happy to oblige. "The Assistant Secretary cannot leave Washington for a day," the writer assured his readers after talking with Roosevelt. "If he does the machinery of the great department stops automatically. . . . Recreation has no place in his daily routine. . . . The strain is telling on him; he has a heavy cold . . . but he stays at his desk. . . . The short-sightedness of his superior [in not appointing two additional assistants, as Franklin had earlier requested] makes such sacrifice necessary."

Among the thousands of pieces of paper to which Franklin affixed his bold blue signature that busy spring were several orders he would later greatly regret ever having signed. All of them touched upon the subject of homosexuality.

Josephus Daniels was against sin in every form—it was he who had persuaded the city authorities at New Orleans to close down the Storyville district in 1917, because he believed his sailors were being corrupted by the bordellos that flourished there.[4] And, in common with most Americans of his time, he believed homosexuality, like prostitution, was a vice, to be rooted out wherever it was found.

Newport, Rhode Island, was both the site of a naval station and one

---

dog," admitted that Roosevelt's casualness about paperwork could be dangerous: It was "much easier to get FDR's signature. [Daniels] was much more critical, a much more careful man. He'd sometimes say, 'Well, leave the papers here with me. I'll study them.'

"When I went up to FDR he'd say, 'Are these all right?'

"If I said, 'Yes,' he'd put his signature on them."

Source: Transcripts of interviews with Arthur Krock and Herbert Lehman, Columbia Oral History Project, Columbia University.

4. Storyville's closing had historic consequences for American music: New Orleans jazz musicians, including Louis Armstrong, were forced to take their fiery gospel northward.

of the bases from which the Atlantic Fleet operated, and the Navy Department had been receiving reports of rampant vice in and around the handsome old town ever since the war began. Brothels proliferated. Drugs and illicit liquor were sold openly. The mayor and the police seemed unwilling to do much about any of it—and may in fact have been quietly sharing in the profits.

In any case, in June of 1917, Daniels remembered, "[w]omen prominent in the social life of Newport, joined with owners of summer homes and with many mothers who came on from their homes to see how their boys were being looked after," and appealed directly to the Navy to act. After consultation with local citizens, Daniels sent a list of just "some of the known and verified places of ill resort" to the local authorities and asked for immediate action.

The press sensed a good story, and John R. Rathom, the flamboyant, 250-pound Republican editor of the Providence *Journal*, enthusiastically endorsed Daniels' findings. "The situation in Newport is about as bad as can be," he told the Secretary. "These places have been recognized by the police for years; they have been allowed to operate without any hindrance whatever, and orgies of the most disgraceful character have been carried on for the benefit of sailors, and frequently witnessed by police officers themselves as spectators." Rathom ran a series of front-page articles alleging among other things that "houses of prostitution of the lowest type have been maintained under the patronage of city officials, with police officers actually detailed to keep visitors in orderly line, awaiting their turn. . . ."

The publicity split Newport into two camps: those demanding reform, and those who resented all the lurid attention being paid to their city and insisted, in Daniels' words, "that there was no unusual immorality extant." Hoping to quiet things down, the Board of Health declared an official Clean-Up Week, rounded up nineteen known prostitutes, had them examined, found six were diseased, and ordered them out of town. This, the mayor assured the naval commandant, had been "a great, big step" toward improving conditions.

Daniels said he "couldn't agree that a finding that thirty-three percent of the 125 known and admitted prostitutes in the city . . . were diseased was even a little step toward reforming the general immoral condition of the town."

A highly publicized sweep of the brothels followed, but, as Rathom wrote Daniels, "Dozens of the women returned to Newport without ever having left the island at all, and several of them were met with automobiles as they left Bristol Ferry and told . . . they could come back."[5]

Finally, the Secretary acted on his own, ordering naval police stationed in front of every known brothel with orders to bar the door to any man in uniform.

Things got better for a time, but in early 1919 the complaints started again. New bordellos had opened for business; liquor and drugs were again plentiful. Newport, one local clergyman told his congregation, had once more become "a Hell Hole of grog shops." And there were new and, for the Secretary, still more disturbing rumors of widespread homosexuality among the sailors themselves. A little band of homosexual seamen, calling themselves "the Ladies of Newport," boldly attended YMCA socials every Saturday night in search of fresh recruits. Even the forty-six-year-old Episcopal chaplain of the Naval Hospital, Samuel Neal Kent, was said to be involved, taking lonely-looking young men home with him to his parish house.

The Secretary was disgusted: ". . . I [had] exhausted every one of the regular channels in an effort to clean up conditions," he said later, ". . . and it was not until failure after failure had followed the first efforts to effect any permanent reform that I became convinced that in cooperation with the Department of Justice, the Navy itself must take steps to secure [a] wholesome environment for youths sent to Newport for training."[6]

Before leaving for Europe, the Secretary left orders with the Newport commandant to name a court of inquiry and "clean the place up."

Captain Edward H. Campbell, the station commander, was assigned the task of setting up the court. Unsure how best to proceed, he asked Lieutenant Erastus Mead Hudson of the Medical Corps, a recent Harvard graduate and a physician in civilian life, to look into

5. Such cooperation between Rathom and Daniels ended abruptly during the 1918 elections, when the editor's telegrams were evidently leaked by Daniels or someone in his office to the Democratic candidate for Congress as ammunition with which to unseat the Republic incumbent. "It was my first intimation," Rathom later said, "that the Secretary of the Navy was using personal knowledge in order to boom his own political party." *Source:* Lawrence R. Murphy, *Perverts by Official Order,* page 198.

6. The Navy had always considered homosexuality a punishable offense. Louis Howe was paid $40 to write an article for Franklin to sign in *Scientific American* entitled "The Problem of Our Navy," whose point was "Men must live straight if they would shoot straight," and he once prepared a report for the Secretary on "Homo-sexualism" in Philadelphia: "From ninth street to Juniper Street," Howe warned, "the corners contain from one to five male perverts, or 'fairies,' waiting for the street cars coming with their loads of sailors from the Navy Yard." *Source:* Louis Howe Papers, FDRL.

the seriousness of the problem. During the course of his investigation, Hudson spoke with a former detective named Ervin Arnold, serving as a machinist's mate, who claimed that his nine years as a detective had taught him how to "detect a sexual pervert by watching him on the street as to his walk, manner and bearing"; he argued that homosexuality at Newport was so rampant that the only way to make any inroads against it would be to recruit a squad of likely-looking enlisted men and send them out into the surrounding neighborhoods to be solicited.

On March 15, Captain Campbell named Lieutenant Hudson to a four-man court of inquiry and Arnold was ordered to begin collecting evidence. He recruited thirteen newly enlisted sailors, moved into a special office provided for him at Red Cross headquarters, and set about entrapping homosexuals. "You people will be on the field of operation," Arnold told his men. "You will have to use your judgment whether or not a full act is completed. If that being the fact, it might lead into something greater. You have got to form that judgment at the time you are on that field with that party."

How much Franklin knew of the methods Hudson and Arnold were using at Newport will probably never be known—Roosevelt always contended that he knew no details until September—but on March 22, 1919, shortly after his chief left for Europe, he asked the Attorney General, A. Mitchell Palmer, for help in purging Newport. "The Navy Department," he wrote, "has become convinced that such conditions of vice and depravity exist . . . as to require a most searching and rigid investigation with a view to finally prosecuting and clearing out those people responsible for it." Not only were Newport civilians still trafficking in drugs, liquor, and prostitution, but they were also "fostering dens where perverted practices are carried on. . . . This department, eager for the protection of its young men from such contaminating influences, desires to have the horrible practices stopped. . . ."

Meanwhile, the men of Hudson's unit were busy, bringing about the arrests of eighteen sailors in a single week in April. Fourteen of them were eventually court-martialed, two deserted, and two received dishonorable discharges, while the sailors whom they had allegedly propositioned and upon whom they had performed fellatio were officially praised by the court of inquiry for "their interest and zeal in their work in assisting the Judge Advocate and in the best interests of the naval service."

That same month, R. Livingston Beekmann, the governor of Rhode Island and "a very old friend" of Franklin's, sent the Reverend Charles P. Hall, the field director of the Newport Red Cross, to see Roosevelt.

Things at Newport were worse than the department knew, Hall said.

"What do you mean by that?" Franklin remembered asking him.

"Everything. Drugs, prostitution, perversion." The current court of inquiry couldn't halt all this because those who worked for it had already become too well known. Sending in a team of civilian investigators wouldn't work, either; they'd be spotted as soon as they got down from the train. The only hope was a secret Navy unit. Hall urged Franklin to see Lieutenant Hudson.

On May 1, Hudson and Arnold, the former detective, were brought to Washington for a talk with the Assistant Secretary. They would later allege that it had been a lengthy discussion. Franklin said it lasted less than five minutes, that over the next few days he spent no more than thirty-five minutes on the Newport investigations, and that "at no time were the details of how the methods of investigation had been or were to be conducted mentioned by me or to me."

However long they talked, whatever they talked about, four days later, the Assistant Secretary sent a confidential memorandum to the director of Naval Intelligence, Rear Admiral Albert P. Niblack. In connection with the work of suppressing "moral perversion and drugs" at Newport, Franklin said, he wished Hudson and Arnold placed in Niblack's office; "It is requested that this be the only written communication in regard to this affair, as it is thought wise to keep this matter wholly secret."

The admiral was unenthusiastic; civilian vice was not a proper subject for Naval Intelligence to investigate. Besides, he had no budget from which to pay for such an extensive undercover probe and a private detective, hired to conduct an independent investigation, warned that while Lieutenant Hudson was undeniably "sincere," he was also "inclined to have rather exaggerated and imaginative ideas concerning the manner and form of conducting investigations."

Impatient with Niblack, disappointed that the Justice Department had been slow to involve itself, and still without the restraining influence of his absent chief, Franklin detached Hudson to new duty, and handed him a letter addressed "To whom it may concern" which stated that the lieutenant was "engaged on important work in which

I am interested and any assistance you can render him will be appreciated."

In June, Franklin attached Hudson to his own office, designating him "Commanding Officer of a group of enlisted . . . men who have been assigned . . . certain confidential special duties as agents of the Assistant Secretary of the Navy. This group or unit, will bear the name: 'Section A—Office of the Assistant Secretary,' or simply: 'Section A—OASN.' " All orders and correspondence pertaining to the secret activities of Section A were to be routed through Franklin's own stenographer; all orders—including one attaching Hudson to his office for "duty of such a nature that he does not have written orders"—were to be signed by the Assistant Secretary himself. All bills were to be paid out of the Secretary's own Contingent Navy Fund.

Hudson sought guarantees from Franklin that the investigative methods the men of Section A were employing were legal and legitimate—though, again, how specifically he spelled out his concerns about those methods is unclear. To allay his fears, Franklin twice sent him to see Justice Department officials; both assured him that whether or not the ends justified the means morally, his agents were committing no indictable offense. A Newport attorney was also assigned to work with Hudson as a special legal adviser.

Reassured, Hudson now recruited a total of forty-one enlisted men for Section A, ten of them between sixteen and nineteen years old, and sent them into the field. In July, they brought about the arrests of sixteen civilians—including a librarian, a waiter, a butler in a wealthy citizen's home, several summer visitors, and Father Kent himself, who was handcuffed and locked up, charged with being "a lewd and wanton person."

Samuel Kent was widely respected in Newport, a familiar presence in the parlors of its wealthiest homes, much admired for what seemed to be lifelong devotion to the welfare of boys and young men. A fellow minister put up $400 bail, and when two young sailors testified in uniform at Father Kent's trial on August 23 that they had been told to become sexually involved "to the limit" in order to obtain evidence against him, he was acquitted, and a search began to see who in the Navy had authorized such practices.

On September 3, two prominent Newport citizens, the Reverend Stanley C. Hughes and Hamilton Fish Webster, called upon the Assistant Secretary—Daniels was again away, in Hawaii this time—to protest the methods that had been used to seize Kent. Franklin insisted that the chaplain had been guilty as charged and implied that the judge who exonerated him had either been incompetent or bought. But he also said he was astonished at the thought that men of the U.S. Navy had been used to entrap anybody. "If anyone has given orders to commit immoral acts," he assured his indignant visitors, "someone will swing for it."

The clergymen were not satisfied. Franklin urged them to take their complaints to Captain Richard Leigh, acting chief of the Bureau of Navigation. After hearing them out, Leigh told Franklin he believed the sailors attached to Section A might indeed have overstepped the bounds of propriety, and that Lieutenant Hudson should be ordered to cease his work until an internal investigation could be made. Orders to that effect were issued by Leigh and confirmed by Franklin on September 4.

Daniels returned to Washington on September 21 to find waiting in his outer office James DeWolf Perry, the Episcopal bishop of Rhode Island, come to register his personal protest at what had been done to tarnish the reputation of Chaplain Kent. Daniels asked Admiral Niblack to look into the matter. He did so, read through the files, had Hudson and Arnold interviewed, and evidently heard enough sensational details to convince him that Kent had in fact been guilty— Niblack was especially incensed that homosexuals had selected the YMCA as the favored site for their seductions. A second trial, he told the Secretary, should result in the proper verdict and vindicate the zeal of Section A. Daniels agreed: according to Hudson, the lieutenant was then told that both Daniels and Franklin were "very much pleased" at the work of his unit and concurred in an investigator's suggestion that they be "commended." All the evidence was turned over to the Justice Department, and Kent was tracked to a Michigan sanitorium where he had gone after suffering a nervous breakdown. There, he was arrested and charged with having violated a federal wartime statute that made it unlawful "to receive any person for the purpose of lewdness" within "reasonable distance" of a military installation.

A federal trial was set for the U.S. district court at Providence in January.

On April 12, about three weeks after Franklin first alerted the Attorney General to the need for a federal investigation of vice at Newport, he signed an order restoring to active duty ten Navy men who had served sentences in the naval prison at Portsmouth. This, too, seemed more or less routine department business at the time.

Josephus Daniels hated sin, but he did not hate the sinner, and believed in the cleansing power of repentance. The Navy had a duty, he said, to do all that it could to rehabilitate those unfortunate young men who had transgressed its laws, and when he visited the naval prison at Portsmouth, New Hampshire, shortly before the war and found that its inmates were outnumbered by their Marine guards, and that the men incarcerated behind its walls, most of them guilty only of overstaying their leaves, routinely received dishonorable discharges upon completion of their terms, he resolved to transform this harsh and "archaic" system.

To do so, he turned to Thomas Mott Osborne, one of Woodrow Wilson's original supporters in New York State and an old political patron of both Franklin and Louis Howe. In the years since the three had fought Tammany side by side in Albany, Osborne had built a reputation as the nation's most successful—and most publicized—penal reformer. Appointed chairman of the New York State Commission on Prison Reform in 1913, Osborne spent a week in Auburn State Prison masquerading as convict "Tom Brown," then wrote a best-selling book about it, *Within Prison Walls*. As warden of Sing Sing from 1914 to 1916, he had championed a system of self-discipline for prisoners that emphasized rehabilitation rather than punishment.

He seemed just the sort of man Daniels was looking for.

But there was another side to Osborne. His effectiveness was sometimes undercut by breathtaking arrogance; he was given to talking of big, shadowy plots against him; and, as a public figure, he suffered from still another, far more serious flaw, dangerous and secret, of which Franklin and Howe, normally up to date on political gossip, were evidently unaware. Not long after they left Albany for Washington in 1913, Osborne began disappearing from his home at night to haunt workingmen's bars and hobo jungles, elaborately costumed and made up, according to his own terse diary, variously as a minister, doctor, "Dude, Old Gent, Mexican, Italian, Colored Gent." He was often accompanied on these nocturnal masquerades—for which he never offered any coherent explanation—by a handsome, muscular young man whom he had found in a reform school and employed ostensibly as a handyman. Widespread whispering about his midnight rambles had helped torpedo his political career in New York State and lent credence to later rumors that his friendships with good-looking young convicts were more complicated than they first seemed.

Osborne made many enemies at Sing Sing: conservatives attacked him for coddling prisoners; Tammany politicians, already bearing ancient grudges against him, were further angered by his elimination of graft from the prison system; still others charged that he had forced homosexual advances on the men under his charge. It is impossible to know now how much truth, if any, there was in the more violent assaults on his character. Certainly they did not intimidate him: When accused of various crimes, including sodomy, in 1916, he fought back in court and was exonerated.

That there might be some validity to any of these charges was apparently unthinkable for Franklin. Osborne had been among the first people to encourage his political career; he was still magnetic and imposing at sixty, still a vigorous foe of the big-city bosses and a warm friend of the Astors and Chanlers and other old acquaintances along the Hudson; above all, he was a gentleman, a Harvard graduate, a fellow member of the Fly.

And so when, in January of 1917, Daniels asked Osborne to investigate the naval prison system, Franklin was especially enthusiastic. Osborne went about his work with his usual panache. Enlisting in the Navy as seaman Tom Brown, he got himself arrested and sentenced to a week cutting ice aboard a rotting prison ship to see for himself how the men were treated before taking command at Portsmouth in August, wearing the white uniform of a lieutenant commander in the Naval Reserve. Portsmouth "has been a scrap heap," he told Daniels. "You wish me to make it one of humanity's repair shops." He did away with prison walls, had all but a handful of guards reassigned, set up classrooms, tennis courts, and a baseball diamond, and personally coached the new drama club. He paid as little attention as possible to Navy procedures—once, when his immediate superior, the admiral commanding the Portsmouth Navy Yard, sent for him, he replied, "I'm too busy. Come over and see me"—and he routinely took his problems over the heads of the admirals directly to Daniels or his old friend, Roosevelt.

More important, he encouraged his "graduates" to return to duty when their time with him was up. America was at war, he argued: "Is the ex-convict morally unfit to fight the Savage Hun?" Four thousand of the six thousand sailors who passed through Portsmouth Prison under his command were sent back to the fleet.

To the old-line officers, all of this was blasphemy, further evidence of the amateurism and sentimentality fostered by Josephus Daniels. *The Army and Navy Register* suggested that if Osborne and his adherents had their way, the services would soon become "a refuge for criminals." Discipline would falter; men undergoing hardships at sea, their commanders said, were already longing for the far pleasanter surroundings at Portsmouth, with its baseball games and amateur theatricals.[7]

No officer was more incensed by Osborne—or the man who appointed him—than Admiral William S. Sims, now home from Britain and back at his old post as president of the Naval War College at Newport. Sims remained bitter at what he perceived to have been wartime slights at the hands of Daniels, to whose stubbornly countrified presence as head of the Navy Department he had never been reconciled. The Secretary had scuttled his friend Admiral Bradley Fiske's plan for reorganizing the department, had been slow to ready the Navy for war before it came, in Sims' view, and tardy in sending destroyers to Britain once it began; he had overruled Sims' opposition to the North Sea barrage, appointed a commander of the naval forces in France whom Sims disliked, had even refused to allow him to accept honorary membership of the British Admiralty, a gesture never before made by Britain to a naval officer of any other nation.[8]

While still overseas, Sims had written a fellow officer that he looked forward to the day when he could reveal "a number of rather disagreeable facts" to whatever congressional committee looked into the conduct of the war once it had ended. Since returning home he had been appalled anew by the activities of Section A at Newport and the Osborne regime at Portsmouth Prison. And a new insult had been added to his old injuries: when a New York publisher asked him to write a book about his wartime experiences in the spring of 1919,

7. Many years later, Admiral Richard L. Conolly recalled what it had been like to command a ship whose crew included twenty-three "Portsmouth graduates:" "Nobody could own a watch. They'd steal you blind." Of those aboard, "only two or three were any good at all," he said. "Maybe only one that was rehabilitated. [The program] had been highly unsuccessful. And they blamed Franklin D. for that." *Source:* Transcript of interview with Richard L. Conolly, Columbia Oral History Project, Columbia University.

8. In a letter to Daniels, Wilson explained his rationale for refusing Sims' request: "I appreciate fully the spirit in which this honour is offered Sims, and I wish he could accept it; but I am afraid it would be a mistake for him to do so. The English persist in thinking the United States is an English people, but of course they are not and I am afraid that our people would resent and misunderstand what they would interpret as a digestion of Sims into the British official organization...." *Source:* Josephus Daniels, *The Wilson Era—Years of War and After,* page 494.

President Wilson expressed concern to Daniels that the outspoken admiral might be indiscreet. Sims was summoned to Washington, where Franklin was given the delicate task of exacting a pledge that he would abide by Article 1534 of the Navy Regulations, which barred public criticism of the Navy Department by active officers. Sims agreed, though he privately thought the article a relic of the Spanish Inquisition. "From this," he told his close friend Admiral William F. Fullam, "you will see that although I may call a spade a 'spade,' still I am under practically a gentleman's agreement not to mention unfavorable spades. . . . You may be sure that, at the proper time, I will tell the truth as I understand it."[9]

That time, Sims was sure, would soon be at hand.

"Amid a world of people who are having fearful domestic trials," Eleanor wrote to Isabella in the spring of 1919, "I seem to be sailing along peacefully." The reason for this new tranquility was simple, she explained. "I have acquired . . . a complete darky household."

She acquired it soon after her return from Europe. Two servants who had been with the family for years had decided to leave her employ without warning while she was away—"one cannot count on *any* of them," she had complained to Sara from Paris when one of the Springwood maids also left her job—and the others had proved quarrelsome after she got back. Many years later she explained how she arrived at her solution:

> I decided that life in Washington would be simpler if I took colored servants who could be obtained there, which would obviate my having to go to New York to find new white ones. In a day or two I had a new cook, kitchenmaid, butler and housemaid. Perhaps it is my early association with Aunt Gracie [Bulloch], and her tales of the old and much-loved colored people on the plantation, perhaps it is just the Southern blood of my ancestors, but ever since I had been in Washington I had enjoyed my contact with such colored people as came to work for me. I have never regretted the change. . . .
>
> Mrs. Selmes [Isabella's mother], years ago, told me that, properly trained, the colored people were the most faithful and efficient servants in the world. . . . The colored race has the gift of kindliness and a fund of humor. Many difficulties of life are met with easy laughter and a kindly

9. He went ahead and wrote his carefully nonpartisan chronicle. Called *The Victory at Sea*, it was serialized that summer in the *World's Work* and would win Sims and his collaborator the Pulitzer Prize when published in book form in 1920.

tolerance toward other people's failings. Though their eyes may mirror the tragedies of their race, they certainly have much to teach in the enjoyment of the simple things of life and the dignity with which they meet their problems.

At the time, Eleanor was not sure she had made the right decision. "Darky servants came," she noted nervously in her journal on March 15, "others left!" ". . . [H]eaven knows how it will all turn out!" she wrote Sara. Still, she soon found her new staff less likely to sulk or talk back than their white predecessors had been, "pleasanter to deal with and there is never any question about it not being their work to do this or that." And in her new cook, Nora Gibson, she found a tireless worker who would remain with the Roosevelts for years, patient even when last-minute invitations required her to bake four hams at a time or produce gallons of grapefruit punch at a moment's notice.

Sara disapproved of the change. Whenever possible, she and Mr. James had employed British or Scandinavian servants; blacks, she feared, were unreliable.[10]

With her household now running comparatively smoothly, Eleanor was able to devote still more time to worthy projects outside her home. War work had officially ended, of course, but Eleanor's pace did not slow. "I have been in Washington off & on all summer," she told Isabella, "& while most of the gay side, in the shape of French and English officers, has disappeared, it is a very interesting place to be. Now everyone is concerned over strikes & labor questions & I realize that we are entering a new era where the ideas & habits & customs are to be revolutionized if we are not to have another kind of Revolution!"

Eleanor herself had entered a new era. That March, the Red Cross sent her to inspect St. Elizabeth's Hospital where the Navy was still housing battle-shocked sailors.

"I cannot do this," she remembered thinking to herself. She was terrified of insanity, of getting too near anyone who had lost what she called "the power of self control." But she insisted on going, anyway. *"You must do the thing you think you cannot do,"* she would write one day of this decision, adding her own italics. Fear cripples if it is not conquered.

10. Eleanor continued to employ black servants through the White House years. Her housekeeper, Henrietta Nesbitt, recalled that "the first criticism" she heard of her employer "was when Mrs. Roosevelt brought in all colored help, instead of the mixed staff the [Herbert] Hoovers had in the kitchen. Mrs. Roosevelt and I agreed that a staff solid in any one color works in better understanding and maintains a smoother running establishment." When members of the White House staff, including FDR's black valet, Irvin McDuffie, and his wife, Lizzy, the President's maid, visited Springwood, they were fed separately from Sara's servants.

She never forgot the awful sound of the door locking behind her. "Locked in with the insane!" she wrote. "I wanted to bang at the door, to get out. But I was ashamed of myself. I would not have shown my terror for the world."

The ward was long, dark, and narrow, lined on each side with cots on which the men sat or lay staring, some mumbling to themselves, others in chains.

"At the end of the ward," she remembered, "standing where the sun coming through the window touched his golden hair, stood a handsome young man. He did not see us. He saw nothing but some private vision of his own. He kept muttering."

"What is he saying?" she asked a doctor.

"He keeps repeating the orders at Dunkirk to go to the shelters."

"Will he get over it?"

"I don't know."

Haunted by the terror that never entirely vanished, she nonetheless made herself visit the ward once a week, distributing flowers and cigarettes and stopping to talk with the troubled men.

When she discovered that there were not enough attendants in the naval hospital to provide the men with proper care, she made it her business to stop in and see her friend Franklin K. Lane, the Secretary of the Interior, under whose jurisdiction St. Elizabeth's was run. When she urged him to inspect the hospital for himself, she remembered, "He confided to me that the last thing he wanted to see was a hospital for the insane." She persisted, and Lane finally saw to it that the appropriation for the hospital was raised. Meanwhile, she had arranged for the Red Cross to build the men a recreation room, obtained $500 from the Colonial Dames to set up a program for occupational therapy, and organized a shop in which the patients could raise their own funds by selling hand-made wares.

Nor was Secretary Lane the only official from whom she sought improvements. She also lobbied Secretary Daniels and her own husband hard, she told Isabella, "trying to get restrooms established for the girls at the [Navy] Department and with a woman doctor in charge!"

Despite the zeal with which Eleanor continued to devote herself to social work in Washington, the wound left by Franklin's romance with Lucy Mercer showed little sign of healing. The self-confidence she had built up so painfully was still paper-thin; beneath it hid despair and cold anger.

She and Franklin worked hard to please one another. She kept up a crowded social schedule, though the late hours it demanded inevitably made her "a dead dog" the next day, and Franklin tried to remember to get home on time for lunch and dinner. When he forgot, Eleanor scolded him over the telephone and sometimes drove down to the department herself to fetch him. "Dined alone," she noted in her diary on April 10 after bringing her protesting husband home before he had finished his work. "Franklin nervous and overwrought and I very stupid and trying, result a dreadful fracas."

When they found time to be alone together now it often seemed forced, artificial, self-conscious. "I wish we did not lead such a hectic life," she told him once, "a little prolonged quiet might bring us together & yet it might just do the opposite! I really don't know what I want or think about anything anymore!"

She did know that she wished to spend as little time as she could with her mother-in-law. The two women had been allies in the struggle to maintain the Roosevelt marriage, but the price Sara exacted for her qualified support had come to seem too high. Now that Eleanor knew she could never be fully certain of Franklin, and had begun to build her own increasingly independent life outside the precincts of the family Sara considered sacred, she found the older woman's bland self-esteem increasingly intolerable. The "serene assurance" of Sara and her sisters, Eleanor wrote, their "absolute judgments on people and affairs . . . make me want to squirm and turn bolshevik."

The strain between herself and her mother-in-law was now palpable. One evening in May, Eleanor found herself dining alone with Sara at Hyde Park. "I might just as well not have eaten," she noted in her diary, "for I promptly parted with it all."

In July, she took the children from Springwood to the Delano homestead at Fairhaven. Sara stayed behind, and "I feel as though someone had taken a ton of bricks off me," Eleanor told Franklin, "and I suppose she feels the same."[11]

One evening that winter, the Roosevelts were expecting dinner guests. Eleanor went upstairs to say goodnight to the children and hear their prayers. As she leaned over Elliott, she collapsed in tears on his pillow. The nine year old was alarmed. "I had not heard her cry before in this uncontrolled, hopeless way," he remembered.

His father appeared in the doorway, asking what was wrong.

"I just can't stand to greet all those people," his mother sobbed. "I

11. If she did, she was careful not to let anyone know it. "A letter from Mama this morning," Franklin wrote Eleanor. "It will amuse you as she says everything is going smoothly."

know they think I am dull and unattractive. I just want to hide up here."

Later in the year, the Roosevelts attended a dinner at the Chevy Chase Club, followed by dancing. As always, young women surrounded Franklin; as always, he enjoyed their attention. After a time, Eleanor decided she wanted to go home. He preferred to stay on, to keep dancing. Eleanor told him she would go home alone, that he should stay and have a good time. She did not ordinarily allow him to stay at parties later than she did now, but she permitted it on this occasion, perhaps because his cousins Warren and Irene Robbins, also attending, were the Roosevelt's house guests and could be relied upon to bring him safely home.

At her front door, Eleanor discovered that she had forgotten her keys. The children's nurse must have been asleep upstairs. So were the children. There may have been other servants as well.

She did not ring the bell.

Instead, she sat down on the doormat in the vestibule and waited, brooding. She was still sitting there, grim and sleepless, when Franklin and the Robbinses arrived not long before dawn, "all flushed with wine and good cheer," according to Alice Longworth.

Franklin was astonished.

Why on earth hadn't she rung the bell or gone next door and asked to use the telephone, he asked, unlocking the door.

She had not done that, she said, because "I've always understood one should try and be considerate of other people."

Then why hadn't she hailed a taxi and driven back to the club for his key?

"I knew you were all having such a *glorious time,*" she said, "and I didn't want to *spoil the fun.*"[12]

On Friday, October 3, Eleanor was at Hyde Park. There she noted in her journal that evening: "Mama and I have had a bad time. I should be ashamed of myself and I'm not. She is too good and generous and her judgment is better than mine but I can *learn* more easily." It seems

---

12. At this point in retelling this story, Alice liked to add, "So noble, so noble." Mrs. Robbins, the eyewitness from whom she heard it, was more blunt: *she* would not have blamed Franklin then, she said, "if he had slapped her hard."

In the Oyster Bay branch of the family, Joseph Alsop remembered, the sort of patient martyrdom Eleanor displayed was known as the "I am not angry, only a little sick at heart" ploy, so named from "the first sentence of a long-ago letter, circulated after the event, from the virtuous victim to the rich perpetrator of an unconventionally vigorous loving approach." *Sources:* Joseph P. Lash, *Eleanor and Franklin*, page 243; Joseph Alsop, *FDR: A Centenary Remembrance*, page 67.

likely that Sara had implied that Eleanor was devoting altogether too much time to her own causes, spending altogether too little with the children and with Franklin. And her daughter-in-law seems to have responded with a rare outburst of anger in which, perhaps for the first time, she dared openly to put her own desires above those of her family. A few days later she offered her mother-in-law an apology, at once abject and still filled with fury:

> I know, Mummy dear, I made you feel unhappy the other day and I am so sorry I lost my temper and said such fool things for of course as you know I love Franklin and the children very dearly and I am deeply devoted to you. I have, however, allowed myself to be annoyed by little things which of course one should never do and I had no right to hurt you as I know I did and am truly sorry and hope you will forgive me.[13]

Franklin came up the next day, only to leave again for New York to speak at an American Legion dinner. Livy Davis was going to the city with him. The evening was sure to end in one of their sprees.

At St. James Church the next morning, she found herself unable to take Holy Communion. Her anger and bitterness were still too great, too unyielding more than a year after she had found confirmation of Franklin's betrayal, for her to pretend, even to herself, that she felt the requisite "love and charity" toward those around her.

She would return to the Communion rail, was slowly building a new kind of partnership with her husband, but those emotions would never entirely lift.

Back in Washington, she took to driving out alone to a little grove of pines in the cemetery in Rock Creek Park, where stood a life-size bronze figure of a brooding, hooded woman. Her late friend Henry Adams had commissioned it from Augustus Saint-Gaudens as a memorial to his wife Clover, whose suicide in 1885 Washington gossips attributed to her having heard rumors that her husband had fallen in love with another woman and had made her pregnant.[14]

---

13. "In all the years I only lost my temper with my mother-in-law once," Eleanor wrote later, "and that was over the training of the children. I made up my mind then I would never lose it again. She forgot all about it the next day, but I have remembered it all my life." *Source:* Joseph P. Lash, *Love, Eleanor,* page 86.

14. In his provocative study of Clover Adams, Otto Friedrich cites the scholarship of Ernest Samuels to prove that geography made it impossible for Adams actually to have been the father of the daughter born to Elizabeth Cameron, wife of Senator James Donald Cameron, after Mrs. Adams's death; he and Mrs. Cameron were in different parts of the country when the child was conceived. But he believes there may well have been a romance and acknowledges that the rumors of one were real and widespread. *Source:* Otto Friedrich, *Clover,* pages 330–331.

Eleanor Roosevelt found special solace in this inscrutable statue for the rest of her life. She evidently felt a sense of kinship with the long-dead woman who had believed herself betrayed, but she may also have permitted herself some pride that she had not succumbed to the kind of despair that had driven Clover Adams to kill herself, that threatened always to engulf her, and that only ceaseless activity seemed to forestall.[15]

The big Boston crowds that had greeted Woodrow Wilson and his party on their return from Europe aboard the *George Washington* in late February 1919 were so enthusiastic that even Calvin Coolidge, the Republican governor of Massachusetts, was moved to uncharacteristic effusion. "We have welcomed the President with a reception more marked even than that which was accorded to General George Washington," he told a mass meeting at Mechanic's Hall, "more united than could have been given at any time during his life to President Abraham Lincoln. We welcome him as the representative of a great people, as a great statesman, as one to whom we have entrusted our destinies, and one whom we are sure we will support in the future in the working out of that destiny, as Massachusetts has supported him in the past."

Wilson smiled as the crowd cheered. Sitting near him on the platform, Franklin and Eleanor clapped with special enthusiasm. It had seemed to them then that despite Republican majorities in both houses of Congress and the deep personal enmity of the new chairman of the Senate Foreign Relations Committee, Senator Henry Cabot Lodge of Massachusetts, Americans were overwhelmingly in favor of the President and the League of Nations Treaty toward which he was working at Versailles. "The people seemed to have grasped his ideals," Eleanor remembered, "and to want to back them."

The President returned to Paris to finish his work on the Treaty in early March, his optimism undimmed by the round-robin Lodge had organized and had thirty-seven senators sign—enough to block ratification—declaring that they could not accept the Covenant in its original form. When Colonel House suggested that some degree of accommodation with their concerns might eventually be required,

15. "In the old days when we lived here [in Washington]," she told a close friend whom she took to the cemetery in 1933, "I was much younger and not so very wise. Sometimes I'd be very unhappy and sorry for myself. When I was feeling that way, if I could manage, I'd come here alone, and sit and look at that woman. And I'd always come away somehow feeling better. And stronger. I've been here many, many times." *Source:* Joseph P. Lash, *Eleanor and Franklin,* page 358.

Wilson dismissed the thought. "I have found," he said, "that you get nothing in the world that is worthwhile without fighting for it."

Almost three months later, when Franklin travelled to Chicago to speak before the Democratic National Committee on May 29, he was still filled with that confident spirit. His address, the most important he had yet delivered, was a fighting call for what he called "sane liberalism."

The Republicans, he charged, were now blindly committed to "the policies of conservatism and reaction, the principles of little American-ism and jingo bluff. . . ." The only objective of their bankrupt foreign policy was automatic opposition to the wishes of the President of the United States. "I asked a prominent member of that party who hap-pens to be an intimate personal friend of mine," he said, "what is the purpose or policy of Senator Lodge as Chairman of the Committee on Foreign Relations. He said 'That changes from day to day. When Mr. Lodge reads his morning paper at the breakfast table and sees what the President has said or done, his policy for the next 24 hours becomes the diametrical opposite.' "

The Democrats, Franklin said, presented a vivid contrast:

> Beginning with the Congressional elections of 1910, followed by the triumphal selection of a progressive Democrat to lead the ticket . . . in 1912, the party has become established on definite principles. During its first four years, it has carried through more great measures for the good of the whole population than any other party in any similar period. During the past two years, it has been responsible for guiding the Nation through the most stupendous war in history. . . .
>
> So we are approaching the campaign of 1920—approaching it with the broad principles settled in advance; conservatism, special privilege, partisanship, destruction on the one hand—liberalism, common sense idealism, constructiveness, progress, on the other.

The speech impressed the party leaders present and caused a brief, flattering stir in the newspapers. New Yorkers began to talk of Frank-lin for governor, if Al Smith decided to run for the Senate, or, if Smith preferred to stay in the Governor's Mansion, for the Senate, against his old Albany friend, James Wadsworth.

Some enthusiasts even began to boom Franklin for President. One of these, Judge Henry M. Heymann, went so far as to send out public-ity material headed "Roosevelt for President" to the newspapers. These packets unfortunately arrived unsigned and postmarked

"Washington," and when editors wondered if Roosevelt might actually be sending out anonymous advertisements on his own behalf, he wired his admirer to stop. "Thanks for your action in nipping my Presidential boom in the bud," he wrote the judge later. "Being early on the job is sometimes wise and sometimes not. I sometimes think we consider too much the good luck of the early bird, and not the bad luck of the early worm."

Still, he was pleased by the attention and delighted with the political options that seemed to be everywhere opening to him.

At about eleven-fifteen on the warm evening of June 2, 1919, Franklin and Eleanor were coming home from a Washington dinner party. As Franklin parked their Stutz in a rented garage several blocks from the house on R Street, they heard a thunderous explosion.

Franklin joked that a souvenir shell he had brought home from France must have fallen off the mantel. But when he and Eleanor reached the street and heard sirens and screaming from the direction of their own house, they broke into a run. Four of the children were away in Hyde Park, but James had stayed behind to study for his Groton entrance examinations.

As they raced along the sidewalk, Franklin far in the lead, Eleanor, hobbled by her long dress, struggling to keep up, they first saw policemen milling around in front of their house, and then the appalling damage done to the front of the brick home of the new Attorney General, A. Mitchell Palmer, right across the street. Its front wall seemed about to collapse. All the windows were blown in, the front door shattered and torn from its hinges. The street and sidewalks were blanketed with leaves and branches blown down from the trees and the air was still thick with the acrid smell of cordite.

An anarchist had been blown up by his own bomb, evidently just as he placed it before Palmer's front door. A human leg lay in the path to a neighbor's house, another was in the street. Part of a head had come to rest on a nearby roof.

All the windows in the front of their own house had been smashed, too, and there was blood mixed with bits of flesh on the front steps.

From inside, they could hear Nora the cook shrieking that the world had come to an end.

There was no sign of James.

Franklin took the stairs to the second floor two at a time, threw open the door of the boy's bedroom, and rushed inside. James was standing in his pajamas, barefoot amid the smashed glass, watching the police hold back the growing crowd. "I'll never forget how uncommonly unnerved Father was when he . . . found me standing at the window . . . ," James recalled. "He grabbed me in an embrace that almost cracked my ribs. About this time, Mother, her skirt hoisted above her ankles, arrived, and cold water was thrown on my emotional scene with Father. 'What are you doing out of bed at this hour, James?' she inquired, as if bombings and dismembered anarchists were everyday occurrences. 'Get yourself straight to bed!' Then, she proceeded to soothe the hysterical cook."

With James safely back in bed, Franklin hurried across the street to see what he could do to help. The Palmers had just gone to bed in the back of the house when the bomb went off, and so no one had been hurt. Franklin offered to take the family in for the night, but Mrs. Palmer, badly frightened, wished to be taken to some safer haven, so he got his car and drove her and her daughter to the home of friends. The Attorney General thanked him for his help, reverting in the excitement to the Quaker speech of his boyhood—"Thank thee, Franklin."

Alice and Nick Longworth soon arrived. "As we walked across [R Street] it was difficult to avoid stepping on bloody hunks of human being," she remembered. "The man had been torn apart, fairly blown to butcher's meat. It was curiously without horror . . . a large number of pieces had been assembled on a piece of newspaper, and seemed no more than so much carrion."[16]

While the police went about their grisly business, Franklin helped gather up page after page of anarchist literature that had been impaled on bushes and trees by the force of the blast. The pamphlet was entitled "Plain Words" and signed "The Anarchist Fighters."

"Now we are roped off," Eleanor reported to Sara the next morning, "and the police haven't yet allowed the gore to be wiped up on our steps and James glories in every bone found! I only hope the victim was not a poor passerby instead of the anarchist!"

"Father still was feeling unusually tender and solicitous toward

16. In the end, neither a fragment of the anarchist's collar that revealed a Chinese laundrymark nor tattered patches of his green-and-black striped suit led anywhere: he was never identified.

me," James remembered—tender and solicitous, that is, until he hurried to the breakfast table with an interesting object he'd found on the lawn and asked what it was. "I've never seen such a reaction from Father!" he remembered. "He paled, grabbed it from me with his napkin—it was a piece of the anarchist's collar bone—and took it out to the police. He never did finish his breakfast."[17]

The morning newspaper reported that the bomb that blasted Palmer's home was just one of eight that had gone off at the same hour in widely scattered cities. The bombs did little serious damage—only the man who tried to blow up the Attorney General was killed—but they signalled the start of the unprecedented assault on civil liberties that came to be known as the Red Scare. Palmer was its zealous instigator. "The blaze of Revolution was sweeping over every American institution of law and order," he wrote later, and ". . . eating its way into the homes of the American workman, its sharp tongues of revolutionary heat . . . licking at the altars of the churches, leaping into the belfry of the school bell, crawling into the sacred corners of American homes, seeking to replace marriage vows with libertine laws, burning up the foundations of society."

For many Americans, society's foundations did seem alarmingly vulnerable. Prices were high. Production fell. Thousands of returning veterans clamored for jobs. Four million Americans would go out on strike in 1919—one out of every five industrial workers. The President was still far away in Paris, and the Treaty to which he was devoting virtually all of his time came to seem less and less important.

The war years had witnessed widespread mistreatment of unpopular minorities of all kinds—German Americans, socialists, anarchists, Communists, pacifists, members of the Non-Partisan League and the Industrial Workers of the World. Now, more frightened people came to share Palmer's conviction that the Bolsheviks were somehow behind the unrest. Even Franklin, whose innate self-confidence made him less fearful of foreign radicals than most other young men of his class,

17. In April of 1929, a package addressed to Governor Franklin Roosevelt and containing a home-made bomb began to smoke and putter at the New York Post Office. It was dismantled safely (and later turned out to have been a hoax, prepared by the porter who said he discovered it in hopes of a reward). FDR professed not to be concerned: "I am very sleepy," he told reporters from Hyde Park when he got the news. "I am going to bed and expect to sleep well." But he could not resist adding that a similar bomb had been sent to him and dismantled while he was Assistant Secretary of the Navy, a story for which there was not a shred of evidence. *Source:* Frank Freidel, *Franklin D. Roosevelt: The Triumph,* page 66.

sometimes succumbed. Addressing a women's luncheon not long after his return from Europe, he solemnly warned that membership in the League would be America's best defense against the official Bolshevik policy of free love.[18]

The liberalism for which Franklin had been such an exuberant spokesman in May was already falling from fashion. The country to which Woodrow Wilson was about to return at last from Paris had changed.

The President came home to Washington with his Treaty on July 8. Alice Longworth and a friend parked near Union Station as the President's train pulled in and she was pleased to see that only a small crowd had turned out to greet him, made up mostly of people "of the sort to whom any man who happens to be President is a spectacle." "We were against the League," she remembered much later, "because we hated Wilson, who was a Family Horror. He couldn't do any good in our eyes because he had beaten Father. . . ." Then she drove to the White House. The crowd there was satisfyingly thin, too, and as the Wilsons passed through the gates she embarrassed her companion by crying out a curse: "A murrain on him, a murrain on him, a murrain on him!"

On July 10, the President drove to Capitol Hill to lay the document before the Senate. The Treaty, he said, had come about "by no plan of our conceiving but by the hand of God who has led us into this way. . . . We cannot turn back. We can only go forward, with lifted eyes and freshened spirit, to follow the vision. It was of this time that we

18. The basis for this charge—which Franklin evidently believed at the time—was the lurid, clumsily forged "Decree of the Socialization of Women," then being circulated widely as an official Soviet document. "All women," it said, "according to this Decree are exempted from private ownership and are proclaimed the property of the whole nation," and all "Men citizens have the right to use one woman not oftener than three times a week for three hours."

More characteristic was his response when the commandant of the Boston Navy Yard dismissed two machinists because of their politics in December 1919: "Now my dear Admiral, neither you nor I can fire a man because he happens to be a Socialist. It so happens that the Socialist party has a place on the ballot in almost every state. . . ." At about the time Franklin wrote this letter, the New York Assembly expelled five duly elected Socialist members as "Little Lenins, little Trotskys in our midst."

Sara deplored the Bolshevik Revolution with special vehemence all her life, and when her son officially recognized the Soviet Union in 1933, threatened never to return to the White House. She was back within two weeks, of course, and her feelings about recognizing the revolution were kept firmly within the family. *Sources:* Geoffrey Perrett, *America in the Twenties*, page 58; Frank Freidel, *Franklin D. Roosevelt: The Ordeal*, pages 30–31.

dreamed at our birth. America in truth shall show the way. The light streams upon the path ahead, and nowhere else."

Senator Lodge, convinced that public opinion favoring the Treaty was still running too strong for him to risk a vote on its ratification, set about delaying that vote, first insisting upon a word-by-word reading of the document that took nearly two weeks, then staging six more weeks of hearings at which representatives of aggrieved ethnic minorities were encouraged to offer their objections: Italians, outraged that Yugoslavia had been awarded Fiume; Irish, who felt betrayed because the Treaty said nothing of self-determination for them; Germans, angered by the crushing reparations the Allies now demanded from their defeated fatherland.

Meanwhile, anti-League speakers began moving across the country charging that membership would mean submitting variously to domination by the Pope, by "dark" peoples, by the British Crown. Their expenses were paid by two enormously wealthy men whose loathing for Wilson nearly equalled Lodge's own: Henry Clay Frick of United States Steel and the banker Andrew Mellon.

There were twenty-five bloody race riots in American cities that summer—including Washington, where Franklin was spending the summer alone. On July 19, a rumor spread through the Capitol that a white woman had been attacked by blacks. The chief of police ordered searched all black citizens found on the streets after dark. Hundreds of uniformed soldiers, sailors, and Marines stormed through poor neighborhoods, shooting into apartments, beating up men and women caught outside their homes. Blacks armed themselves and began shooting back. At least fifteen people were killed, ten of them white. For four days, the police were powerless to stop it.

The rest of the Roosevelt family was at Fairhaven, where Eleanor, the memory of the Palmer bombing fresh in her mind, became increasingly agitated. "I am worried to death," she wrote her husband, "even if something is wrong, why don't you let me know. I'd always rather know than worry. I couldn't sleep at all well last night, thinking of all the things which might be wrong!"

"The riots seem to be about over today," Franklin reassured her on July 23, "only one man killed last night. Luckily, the trouble hasn't spread to R Street and though I have troubled to keep out of harm's way I have heard occasional shots during the evening and night. It has been a nasty business and I only wish *quicker* action had been taken to stop it."[19]

Despite domestic turmoil and the efforts of the League's opponents outside Washington, there were still only fourteen Senate "Irreconcilables," opposed to participation in the League in any form. The rest of the Republicans in the Senate might have been persuaded to vote for a modified Treaty—and Wilson might even have been willing to accept enough modifications to win them over—had the author of those modifications not been Henry Cabot Lodge.

The Massachusetts senator was counting upon that fact. When an anti-League colleague, James Watson of Indiana, suggested to him that their cause looked hopeless since 80 percent of the people seemed to favor the President's League, Lodge only smiled. "Ah, my dear James," he said. "I do not propose to defeat [the Treaty] by direct frontal attack . . . you do not take into consideration the hatred that Woodrow Wilson has for me personally. Never under any set of circumstances in this world could he be induced to accept a treaty with Lodge reservations appended to it."

Watson thought that a slim reed on which to hang so great a cause.

"A slender thread!" cried Lodge. "Why it is as strong as any cable with its strands wired and twisted together."

Wilson "could have had his League at any time," Alice Longworth wrote later. "All he had to do was take the reservations. . . . We were not irreconcilable but we were against the League *in that form.*"

When told in August that he would have to accept at least some of Lodge's modifications, Wilson answered, "Never! Never! I'll appeal to the country." He would ignore the Senate and barnstorm across the nation, rallying the people to the cause he had come to believe literally holy.

Wilson was not well. He had already suffered what seems in retrospect to have been an initial stroke in Paris in April, and was haggard and gray; his face twitched convulsively; his hands trembled. Members

19. The newly formed National Association for the Advancement of Colored People urged Josephus Daniels to restrain his sailors and Marines. The Secretary took no action, apparently believing the blacks had brought the trouble on themselves. Franklin seems to have agreed. "With your experience in handling Africans in Arkansas," he told a Harvard classmate now living in the South, "I think you had better come up here and take charge of the Police Force." *Sources:* Herbert Shapiro, *White Violence and Black Response*, page 154; Frank Freidel, *Franklin D. Roosevelt: The Ordeal*, page 30.

of his Cabinet urged him to abandon the idea. His wife and his physician, Admiral Cary T. Grayson, told him he would be risking his life if he made the tour.

Wilson overruled them all. When a newspaperman privately suggested to the President that he clearly was not well enough to undertake such a trip, he answered: "I don't care if I die the next minute after the treaty is ratified."

On September 3, Wilson and his wife, Admiral Grayson, and Joseph Tumulty, the President's secretary, boarded the blue-painted presidential car *Mayflower* at Union Station and began steaming west. During the next twenty-two days the President would travel 8,200 miles through fourteen states, delivering more than forty formal speeches and countless trackside talks. Changes in altitude now made him dizzy; he found it increasingly hard to breathe and suffered unrelenting headaches.

At Pueblo, Colorado, on September 25, he spoke of the debt he felt he owed all the young men he had reluctantly sent to war: "There seems to me to stand between us and the rejection of this treaty, the serried ranks of those boys in khaki, not only those boys who came home, but those dear ghosts who still deploy upon the fields of France."

He stopped speaking, his eyes filled with tears, his shoulders shaking. He took a deep, shuddering breath, then continued, his voice low and hoarse: "I believe that men will see the truth, eye to eye and face to face. There is one thing that the American people always rise to and extend their hand to, and that is the truth of justice and of liberty and of peace. We have accepted that truth and we are going to be led by it and it is going to lead us and through us, the world, out into pastures of quietness and peace such as the world never dreamed before."

That evening, in his darkened compartment aboard the *Mayflower*, he suffered a second stroke.

The tour was cancelled. At the insistence of the President and his wife, Admiral Grayson announced only that the President was suffering from "nervous exhaustion." The train bore him slowly back to Washington, where he was seen shuffling into the White House on his own, the left side of his face frozen and drooping. He would not leave that house again for more than a few minutes at a time until the inauguration of his successor, seventeen months later.

At about the time Wilson returned to Washington, it was announced that King Albert of Belgium was soon to arrive in New York for what was sure to be a hero's welcome. Despite the routine nature of most of what he did at the Navy Department, Franklin's sense of himself remained resolutely exalted; he had dined twice with the king in Europe, and now was eager to be seen at his side. William Phillips wandered into Franklin's office one morning to find his young friend fumbling through a drawer full of letters. Phillips asked him what he was after. He was looking for envelopes "addressed to me as 'Your Majesty,' or 'Lord Roosevelt,' or some other crazy title, indicating royal rank," Franklin explained. "I'm going through them to pick out the ones I think would amuse the King. . . . Don't you think it will amuse him?"

But on October 1, Franklin learned that no one had thought to include the Assistant Secretary of the Navy in the official welcoming party. Franklin stormed into Daniels' office, and the Secretary later summarized the conversation that followed: "Roosevelt. [Secretary of State] Lansing to meet King of B. He [Franklin] 'went up in the air.' R. said it was 'stupid.' Phillips said the P. had selected the men to go and he c'd not add. I advised FDR to drop it & save embarrassment."[20]

The next day, the President collapsed in his bathroom, his left side totally paralyzed. On the 17th, a prostatic obstruction blocked the President's bladder; he survived that without surgery somehow, but it was more than two weeks before he could even be lifted out of the bed in which Abraham Lincoln had once slept, and placed gently in a chair. His sight had deteriorated; his speech was difficult to understand, his signature shaky and unrecognizable. Mrs. Wilson and Dr. Grayson barred his room to callers. Executive government stalled; important positions went unfilled; requests for action went unanswered. Vice President Marshall was kept as much in the dark as anyone else. The Cabinet could not decide whether it would be in bad taste to meet without the President, and Senate Republicans suggested Wilson be

20. Some of Franklin's embarrassment at having been left out may have been caused by his having somewhat exaggerated his own closeness to the king in letters to his mother, to whom the young monarch was a special hero. She, too, evidently envisioned herself in royal company, as she wrote her son: "I dreamed last night that King Albert came to stay, & I was overcome by the shabbiness of my house and wakened, thinking of the wonderful preparation the titled people of England have always made for Royalty—However, I imagine he will pay no *private* visits. If I knew *ahead* that he was coming, I could easily make the entire end [of the house] over the library very nice but I should have to have time to arrange it as a suite—Yours & mine, and *we* would take the old rooms."

For his part, while Josephus Daniels admired the king's bravery and bearing, he could not help but be amused by his royal fondness for medals; while in Washington, he wrote, Albert "decorated almost everyone that rendered him a service, giving a medal to the chauffeur who drove his car." *Source:* Josephus Daniels, *The Wilson Era—Years of War and After,* page 495.

declared incapacitated. "I am not interested in the President of the United States," Mrs. Wilson told a delegation of concerned Democrats. "I am interested in my husband and his health."

Admiral Grayson's bulletins continued to be bland and uninformative. Competing rumors spread that the President was sulking or syphilitic or wholly mad.

Franklin knew nothing of what was happening upstairs in the White House—on October 18, while Wilson lay unconscious and close to death from the obstruction in his bladder, he, Livy Davis, and the aviator Richard E. Byrd set off for a nineteen-day moose hunt in Nova Scotia—but Admiral Grayson reported the President's condition frankly to Josephus Daniels.

"If you would tell the people exactly what is the matter with the President," Daniels told Grayson, "a wave of sympathy would pour into the White House, whereas now there is nothing but uncertainty and criticism."

"I wish I could do so," the weary physician said. "But I am forbidden. The President and Mrs. Wilson have made me promise to that effect."

On the afternoon of October 30, the Belgian king and queen were ushered into the President's bedroom, the first callers in more than three weeks. They found Wilson still in bed, wearing a dressing gown and a startlingly white beard, grown because his doctors had feared shaving him would unnecessarily tire their frail patient. He managed a short chat with his royal visitors, who were besieged by reporters as they left the White House. They had brought him a set of fine china, they said, and left him sitting up against the pillows, peering through a magnifying glass at one of the plates, trying to see the little painted scenes.

"When . . . we heard he had grown a beard," Alice Longworth recalled, ". . . we wondered whether he kept it outside or hidden under the sheets." "Think of this week," she wrote to her Auntie Bye, "the Peace Treaty debate, the illness of that sissie in the White House, labor in a desperate snarl, the visit of the Belgians—yet Father in everyone's mind, his name on their lips, and his memory in their hearts."

A week after the Belgians' visit, the Democratic minority leader, Senator Gilbert Hitchcock of Nebraska, was let in to see the President for a moment. It was now clear that he could not muster even a majority of the Senate in favor of the League without restrictions, let alone the two thirds needed to ratify. He must negotiate further with Lodge; otherwise, American entry into the League would not be possible.

"It *is* possible! It *is* possible!" the President whispered.

"Mr. President, it might be wise to compromise—"

"Let Lodge compromise!"

"Well, of course, he must compromise also. But we might well hold out the olive branch."

"Let Lodge hold out the olive branch!"

The bearded old man sank back on his pillow.

On November 18, with the final Senate vote now very close, Hitchcock came again to ask the President to change his mind. Mrs. Wilson herself leaned down to ask, "For my sake, won't you accept these reservations and get this awful thing settled?"

The President grasped her hand. "Little girl, don't *you* desert me; that I cannot stand. Can't you see I have no moral right to accept any change in a paper I have already signed? It is not *I* who will not accept it; it is the nation's honor that is at stake. Better a thousand times to go down fighting than to dip your colors to dishonorable compromise."

In that spirit he dictated a note to his supporters in the Senate: "I hope that all true friends of the Treaty will refuse to support the Lodge reservations."

The next day, November 19, Wilson's followers dutifully voted down the amended Treaty. Then, Lodge's backers defeated the version Wilson had brought home with him from Paris.

"Senate defeated the treaty," Daniels wrote in his diary after dinner at the Roosevelts' that evening. "Lodge has one passion. Hatred of Wilson."

Across town, Alice Longworth celebrated Wilson's defeat with the Irreconcilables; Mrs. Warren Harding, the wife of the Republican senator from Ohio, cheerfully scrambled the eggs.

"Alice says she is quite happy about politics & Mr. Lodge is the greatest man in the country," Eleanor wrote Isabella. "I can't say I entirely share her feelings, tho' I wish the President had been more willing to accept reservations. Still, I do wish he could have had the League. I want it behind us & a free hand for all the many domestic problems. . . ."

The atmosphere in Washington, a journalist remembered, was now "one of bleak and chill austerity, suffused and envenomed by hatred of a chief magistrate that seemed to poison and blight every ordinary human relationship and finally brought to a virtual stoppage every routine function of the Government. . . . The White House was isolated. . . . Its great iron gates . . . closed and chained and locked."

Outside those gates, the invalid President's enemies mobilized their forces. Few were more eager to attack than Admiral Sims, and Daniels himself now gave him what seemed like the perfect opening. At the Secretary's request, all commanding officers—including Sims—had formally submitted their recommendations for awards to be conferred upon men who had served under them during the war. But in December, Daniels made public his own list of "Medals of Honor, Distinguished Service Medals, and Navy Crosses Awarded," which differed greatly from those Sims and his fellow officers had sent in.

In an angry letter to the Secretary dated December 17, Sims protested the Secretary's action: Daniels, he said, had arbitrarily overruled the judgment of the immediate superiors of the men in question, had based his own awards on the erroneous assumption that service at sea was more important than service ashore, and, against all naval tradition, had honored officers who had suffered defeats or lost their ships.

As a dramatic symbol of his protest, Sims declared that he would not accept the Distinguished Service Medal meant to be conferred upon him—and made sure the *Army and Navy Journal* was made aware that he had done so. Two fellow officers followed suit. Daniels' action, Sims told a friend, had afforded him "a unique opportunity . . . to express an opinion in a very dignified way and thereby to . . . turn down Mr. Daniels and his exploitation of the Navy for political purposes."

Nineteen twenty was an election year, and the Senate Naval Affairs Committee, now headed by Senator Frederick Hale, a Republican eager to discredit the Democrats for the way they had waged the war, immediately appointed a subcommittee to look into the question. Hearings were scheduled to begin on January 16.

Sims was the most admired officer in the Navy, president of the War College, author of a widely read popular account of the naval war, hailed on both sides of the Atlantic as the chief architect of the Anglo-American naval alliance.

Franklin had always admired him—he had been raised to revere naval heroes in any case, had enthusiastically backed his demands for more men and ships in the early days of the war, and privately thought Daniels' refusal to permit officers to accept foreign honors had been wrong-headed. He had eagerly hurried to New York to meet the admiral when Sims returned in triumph the previous spring and escorted him to Washington, where he had made a point of telling the press—falsely—that the admiral's appointment had been his idea and no one else's, and he had successfully urged Harvard to grant Sims an honorary degree (a ceremony repeated at Yale, Tufts, and Juniata that June).[21]

And he privately continued to court his favor. Sims' close ally, Admiral Fullam, stopped in to see the Assistant Secretary that November and later reported on his conversation to his friend: "I have just had a chat with Franklin Roosevelt. *Confidentially*, you should have heard him speak of Daniels and his regime as well as the Benson-Blue infliction!!"

Sims did not himself think much of young Roosevelt, whose brash, ebullient presence in Britain he had found wearying in the busy summer of 1918, and whose references to domestic politics while visiting London the following year he had found positively offensive. But he also knew that Franklin had a long record of private criticism of his chief, and may have hoped that by making a friendly gesture toward him now he could persuade him to move still further away from Daniels, even perhaps to testify against him in the hearings to come.

In any case, not long after Franklin returned from his New Brunswick hunting trip, he underwent surgery for tonsillitis—he was still susceptible to every sort of childhood disease, a legacy of his closeted boyhood—and while he lay in bed, a handwritten letter from the admiral's wife arrived, ostensibly for Eleanor but containing a dark warning for her husband.

> My dear Mrs. Roosevelt,
>   I heard something recently which I feel it is only fair to pass on to you and Mr. Roosevelt.
>   A high-ranking officer in Washington told a lady there that the order to use enlisted men as decoys in the sad business which has stirred Newport so deeply came from the Assistant Secretary of the Navy and that the Secretary of the Navy was in no way responsible for it.

21. He had proposed five names for honorary degrees, all of them men whose favor he had worked to win: His friends Franklin K. Lane and William Phillips, Major General Enoch Crowder, Judge Advocate General of the Army, Sims, and Samuel Gompers, president of the American Federation of Labor. Harvard honored only Sims. *Source:* Franklin D. Roosevelt, Papers as Assistant Secretary of the Navy, Box 101: "Harvard Matters," FDRL.

I thought it was only right that you should be in possession of this information.

I hope that all the members of your family are well. . . .

Very sincerely,
Anne H. Sims

Clearly, Sims and his friends had more than medals in mind. The second trial of Samuel Kent, the chaplain whom the sailors of Section A had snared, was set for January 4, just twelve days before Sims was to begin his testimony, and Franklin's own role in the scandal was likely to come under sharp scrutiny.

Roosevelt replied carefully to Mrs. Sims' letter on Christmas Eve, doing all that he could to shift whatever blame might eventually be assessed.

My dear Mrs. Sims:

Your letter to Eleanor came when I was in the hospital having my tonsils out. As soon as I got back to the Department, I asked Admiral Niblack just what he had said about the Newport case, and he tells me that he never intimated, and could not have intimated, that the order to use enlisted men as decoys came from me. He says he did state what was the truth, that as a result of the court martial cases, I gave orders in the usual form to Dr. Hudson to conduct an investigation, and did this on the recommendation of the Bureau of Navigation. As I think I told you when you were down here, the order to Dr. Hudson was exactly similar to orders we have given hundreds of times before. In other words, he was told to investigate, as any other officer would be told to investigate. The means he was to use were neither ordered nor discussed—I suppose on the natural assumption that as an officer of the navy he would conduct the investigation in proper form. After Mr. Daniels got back from the Pacific Coast, the question came up again of dropping the investigation, and Mr. Daniels himself, under Admiral Niblack's recommendation, directed that the investigation proceed. I understand that the Navy cases are now proceeding and that the Department of Justice cases will be tried the first week in January.

As to the method of Dr. Hudson in conducting the investigation, there is absolutely no question that if he issued orders which were improper, he should be held to strict account by a Board of Investigation or court-martial.

I don't need to tell you that I feel just as deeply about this as you do.

Give my love to the Admiral. I hope to be able to run up to

Newport next month or early in February. Strictly between ourselves, I should like to shake the Admiral warmly by the hand.

Franklin still hoped to avoid publicly taking sides in the controversy to come as long as he possibly could—his warm feelings for the admiral were still to be kept "strictly between ourselves"—but the wind seemed now to be blowing steadily away from Josephus Daniels and Woodrow Wilson, and Roosevelt was warily preparing to sail with it.

Earlier that day, Fullam had stopped to chat with Franklin, who went out of his way to assure Sims' close friend that he was in full sympathy with the admiral's views. "I was amazed and *delighted,*" Fullam reported to Sims, "at his open condemnation of Daniels, Blue and Benson."

That same evening at Newport, Admiral Sims began writing a long letter to the Secretary of the Navy. He entitled it "Certain Naval Lessons of the Great War," but its intent was not educational. He hoped to use it as a weapon with which to drive the hated Daniels from office.

Eleanor had sent the Fergusons a framed family photograph for Christmas, and on January 6, 1920, Isabella wrote from New Mexico to thank her:

> You & yours have been the real delight of my Xmas. I've carried the photograph from table to table, from room to room & it seems but yesterday that I stood alongside in the white taffeta & saw you step over the border & now dear I simply can't say the pride that wells up with the tears when I try to tell you the admiration there is for the way you have carried yourself & the grand success you've made. . . . I have only one regret about the photograph. It looks alarmingly like the ones of families that end up in the White House & that I am not sure I would wish for anyone I loved. . . .

Franklin would ordinarily have been buoyed by such a letter, but he was nowhere near so ebullient as usual that week.

Walking her dog along R Street on the morning of Saturday, January 10, Franklin's boyhood friend Bertie Hamlin encountered him just leaving his house. "He has had his tonsils out and has been ill, too," she noted in her diary that evening; "he looks poorly for him. He had two of his boys and a dog with him and we walked along together. Several of the children have had or are having chicken-pox—James is to have his appendix out—Eleanor was getting out 2,000 invitations for Navy teas. He said he did not expect to run for the Senate—that even if he wanted it or could get it—he thought it stupid."

Franklin's uncharacteristically foul mood may have had a number of causes other than those Mrs. Hamlin noted. The family's finances were in poor shape after seven years of entertaining on a Navy salary and he would soon be forced to ask his mother for still another loan.[22]

With the President incapacitated and his administration largely immobilized, 1920 did not look good for the Democrats, and Franklin did not want the nomination for any office if it did not promise victory. "I am perfectly frank in saying that I would not run this Autumn for Dog-catcher," he told a friend that winter, "if the Democrats nominate a party hack or a reactionary or a Bryan at San Francisco."

Admiral Sims' appearance before the Senate subcommittee was now less than nine days away; just the day before, Chaplain Kent had been exonerated for the second time, this time in federal court, and the presiding judge had lashed out at a system of entrapment that had required American sailors to subject their persons to "indignity." The Providence *Journal,* whose editor, John Rathom, had cooperated with Daniels in cleaning up Newport two years earlier, had now begun to call for a full-scale investigation to find out which naval officials had sanctioned the activities of "Section A—Office of Assistant Secretary," just who had made young Americans enlisted in the U.S. Navy "perverts by official order."

"What do the people in your part of the country think of Mr. [Herbert] Hoover?" Eleanor asked Isabella in a letter written the day after Mrs. Hamlin noted Franklin's atypical pessimism. "He's the only man I know who has first hand knowledge of European questions & great responsibility & understands business, not only from the capitalistic point of view, but also from the worker's standpoint."

Eleanor's enthusiasm for Hoover was genuine, and shared by millions of Americans of both parties. He had emerged from his years as chairman of the Belgian Relief Commission, Food Administrator, and director of European relief programs with an unmatched reputation

22. "You are not only an angel which I always knew," he would tell Sara after he received a handsome thirty-eighth-birthday check at the end of the month, "but the kind which comes at the critical moment in life! For the question was not one of paying Dr. Mitchell for removing James' insides, the Dr. can wait, I know he is or must be rich, but of paying the gas man and the butcher lest the infants starve to death, and your cheque which is much too much of a Birthday present will do that. It is so dear of you."

for efficiency, idealism, and nonpartisanship.[23] "I am not a party man," he said, and, "I must vote for the party that stands for the League." Ralph Pulitzer of the *New York World* endorsed him for President that month. Walter Lippmann wrote that Hoover represented "all that is at once effective and idealistic in the picture of America." The *New Republic* was for him, pronouncing him a "Providential gift to the American people for the office of pilot during the treacherous navigation of the next few years." So were the *Saturday Evening Post* and *Ladies Home Journal,* William Allen White, Jane Addams, Louis D. Brandeis, and a two-to-one majority of the Harvard faculty.

But Eleanor's interest in the Great Engineer on January 11 may well have been intensified by an excited conversation with her husband the night before. For the gloom that encompassed Franklin early on the 10th had lifted considerably later in the day when Louis B. Wehle, a Kentucky attorney and member of the War Industries Board who had known and admired Franklin since their days together on the Harvard *Crimson,* came to call.

Democratic presidential prospects looked grim, the two friends agreed. But Wehle now thought he had come up with a ticket that stood a real chance of victory: Hoover for President, Franklin for Vice President. Hoover was from California; Roosevelt from New York; both were big, doubtful states, without which it would be hard for the Democrats to win. Hoover was thought to be especially popular among American women who would be voting for the first time in 1920. Franklin would add the luster of the Roosevelt name.

Wehle had already tried out the idea on influential Democrats and had found them enthusiastic. "Frank," he remembered telling his host, "you have everything to gain and nothing to lose. . . . Whether you win or lose, you would suffer the stigma of mediocrity that seems to attach to the Vice Presidency or to one who tries for it. But you are young and you could live it down for several reasons: first, you bear the name Roosevelt; second, you have a first-rate record of public service. . . . and third, in your campaign tours you would make a great number of key acquaintances in every state."

"You can go to it so far as I am concerned," Franklin said. "Good

23. Not everyone was impressed: Josephus Daniels remembered listening to Hoover describe how he was feeding the desperate people of Belgium "as coldly as if he were giving statistics of production." *Source:* Richard Norton Smith, *An Uncommon Man: The Triumph of Herbert Hoover,* page 88.

luck! And it will certainly be interesting to hear what the Colonel says about it."

The colonel was Edward M. House, once Wilson's closest adviser and still a party elder. Wehle sought him out the next day in his New York apartment. House was enthusiastic; in fact, he had been quietly boosting Hoover for President since January. "It is a wonderful idea," he told his visitor, "and the only chance the Democrats have in November."

But was Hoover a Democrat?

Franklin's old friend tried to find out from Hoover himself. As he outlined his proposal, Wehle recalled, Hoover listened with "his head bent toward his desk blotter, making marks with a pencil. . . . I could not catch his eye for a clue to his thoughts." Finally, still without looking up, he said, "I don't believe that I want to get into a situation where I have to deal with a lot of political bosses."

Wehle slapped the desk top, he remembered, and Hoover started. As he looked up, "I caught his eye and held it." "Let me tell you if you expect ever to get into American political life," Wehle told him, "you'll have to take it as you find it. You can't make it over first from the outside."

According to Wehle, Hoover did not argue further, and "Before I left, . . . assured me that he would phone House and try to make an engagement with him for that evening."[24]

Franklin's hopes for a Hoover-Roosevelt ticket were still high. "I had some nice talks with Herbert Hoover before he went West for Christmas," he wrote a friend. "He is certainly a wonder, and I wish we could make him President of the United States. There could not be a better one."

An unsigned article filled with fulsome praise for Thomas Mott Osborne's rehabilitative work at the Portsmouth Prison had appeared in the January 4 issue of the *Army and Navy Journal*. "[T]he younger Navy officers," it alleged, "particularly the commanders of the destroyers, have taken the view that every chance should be given to those guilty of infractions to expiate in a Navy atmosphere their derelictions and have an opportunity of coming back into the service. They

24. He did see House, then or later, and told him that while Democratic interest in him was flattering, he was a progressive Republican and hoped to instill in the GOP something of the old spirit with which Theodore Roosevelt had briefly imbued it.

have held that every way should be open to the enlisted man to come back to the ship a better man for having learned his lesson."

At least one young former destroyer commander believed that to be a lie. Captain J. K. Taussig, who had commanded the first division of destroyers to reach Queensland in 1917, had already asked to be transferred to the Naval War College from his post as Director of Enlisted Personnel in the Bureau of Navigations because he felt that his warnings about the propriety of permitting offenders—especially those convicted of sodomy—to return to duty had been ignored by Daniels and Roosevelt. Now, unable to contain himself—and perhaps unaware that the article he deplored had been written by the Assistant Secretary of the Navy himself—he wrote an angry rebuttal which concluded: "The good men of the ships must, of necessity, owing to the intimate way of living on board and the requirements of working in the same confined places, associate to a more or less extent with these moral perverts, and thereby be exposed to contamination. . . . In the redemption of an individual we should not permit the degradation of the Navy."

Franklin responded no less angrily. He had never intended to argue that men convicted of *moral* offenses should go back to sea, he said—"There can be no two opinions on that score"—but only two men convicted of sodomy had returned to active service in the two years since Osborne had taken command, or so he claimed, and both of them had done so under unique circumstances. "Anyone who, like Captain Taussig, attempts to give the wrong impression, deliberately or otherwise, can only harm the service itself," he continued, and he only hoped that the captain had "merely through lack of knowledge made a false statement."

Stung by this semi-official reprimand and with the encouragement of his mentor Admiral Sims, Taussig formally demanded from the Secretary of the Navy a court of inquiry and at the same time took his case to John Rathom, already launched upon his series of sensational articles about the Newport vice investigation and eager for fresh ammunition with which to assault the Navy Department.

The Assistant Secretary's letter, Taussig charged, "questions my veracity, impugns my motives, and tends to publicly discredit me." Nearly a hundred morals offenders had been returned to service, he said, not just two; in April of the preceding year, Franklin Roosevelt himself had signed an order returning ten of them at once. Privately, Taussig charged that those men whom Franklin had so favored were uniformly men of his own class, young gentlemen from the best schools who had gone astray; less well bred offenders were driven from the service.[25]

The controversy forced Daniels to appoint a board to look into conditions at the prison. It had three members—Rear Admiral A. S. Halstead, commander of the Portsmouth Navy Yard, Rear Admiral Herbert O. Dunn, commander of the First Naval District, and Franklin himself, as senior member. Dunn was an amiable ally of Franklin's—his cordiality perhaps enhanced that same month when the Assistant Secretary helped his wife's nephew obtain an appointment to Annapolis—and evidently agreed with him that "we can work out [the] Portsmouth Prison trouble if we of the service can only get together on these things and not air our dirty linen in public."

The committee visited the prison briefly, and looked into various

---

25. Much later, when another "gentleman" similarly strayed, FDR would act in precisely the same manner. On September 17, 1940, aboard a special train carrying mourners back to Washington from the Alabama funeral of Speaker of the House William Bankhead, the Under Secretary of State, Sumner Welles, reeling from far too many whiskeys, propositioned several black porters whom he had summoned to his special compartment. All of them turned him down and one lodged a formal complaint with the Southern Railway Company.

Welles was the great-nephew of Charles Sumner; a Groton boy who had been a page at Franklin's wedding; a Harvard classmate of Eleanor's brother, Hall; a seasoned diplomat whose career Franklin had helped to launch; a married man who, under normal circumstances, carried himself with such dignified hauteur that a British diplomat once complained, "It's a pity that he swallowed a ramrod in his youth." His alcoholism and his private sexual habits were common knowledge among his social and professional peers, however, who ignored them as perhaps unfortunate but certainly not something to be discussed with inferiors.

William Bullitt, also a friend of the President, former Ambassador to the Soviet Union and to France and the legatee of an old Philadelphia family, was not an inferior, and he loathed Welles, whose job he may have hoped one day to have. In any case, he thought, the incident with the porters would provide him the perfect vehicle with which to rid the State Department of his enemy. He spread the story as widely as he could in Washington, hoping the rumors would force the President to seek an investigation. They did, and J. Edgar Hoover confirmed the sordid details.

Months then went by, while Bullitt pressed for further action. Finally, he confronted the President about it in the spring of 1941. The story was true, FDR admitted, but he had assigned a bodyguard to ensure that the offence would not be repeated.

What of the danger of blackmail? Bullitt asked. FDR said he was aware of that but not sure how to handle it; Welles was a useful old friend and he wanted to keep him where he was.

In that case, Bullitt said, he would himself have to resign. The President was "thinking of asking Americans to die in a crusade for all that was decent in human life. He could not have among the leaders of a crusade a criminal like Welles."

FDR rang for his aide, General Watson "Pa, he said, "I don't feel well. Please cancel my appointments for the rest of the day."

Eventually, more than two years after the incident aboard the funeral train, the President did ask for Welles' resignation: the official reason given was that Mrs. Welles had not been well.

Roosevelt never forgave Bullitt. Adolph Berle called upon FDR shortly after Welles had left the government. "He said Bullitt had just been there," Berle remembered. "That on Bullitt's entry he had appointed himself St. Peter. Two men came up: Sumner Welles, and after chiding him for getting drunk, he let him in. The second Bullitt. After paying due tribute to what Bullitt had done, St. Peter accused him of having destroyed a fellow human being and dispatched him to Hell." *Source:* Will Brownell and Richard N. Billings, *So Close to Greatness: A Biography of William C. Bullitt,* page 297.

charges—one man had disappeared with $9,449 in cash and jewelry belonging to his fellow inmates; another had made off with some Liberty Bonds. Its findings strongly upheld Osborne's leadership. "There isn't very much" to the charges against the prison management, Roosevelt told the press.[26]

Taussig was not mollified, and Franklin, alarmed to find himself again at the center of a potentially damaging controversy, but confident always of his ability to disarm potential enemies through personal charm, asked the captain to come see him at the Navy Department. Surely they could work something out. The two men talked for two hours, but the officer refused to back down. Finally, with Taussig impatient to catch his train back to Newport, Franklin called in one of his secretaries and dictated a statement that was supposed to represent the views of both men. Taussig never saw it typed up, however, and when it appeared in the *Army and Navy Journal* he disowned it entirely.

Franklin then wrote him a letter blandly offering the still angrier captain just two choices: his request for a court of inquiry should

26. Shortly thereafter, Osborne was allowed to resign his command and return to civilian life. Daniels wrote him that his "policy of helpfulness and hope [would be] continued" so long as he was Secretary of the Navy, "for you have taught the navy and the country that prisons are to mend men, not to break them."

Osborne continued to arouse controversy. An additional, unstated reason for his resignation may have been a pending $25,000 alienation-of-affections suit filed against him by a woman who charged that he had persuaded her fiancé, a young former convict who had become Osborne's closest aide and sometime "bodyguard," not to marry her. Osborne was eventually acquitted for lack of evidence.

He never held another important post. Gifford Pinchot, the progressive governor of Pennsylvania, almost appointed him warden of the Eastern Penitentiary at Philadelphia in 1923, but backed off when rumors of old scandals at Sing Sing and Portsmouth reached him. Osborne denounced Pinchot for cowardice and returned to his home at Auburn.

Late in the evening on October 20, 1926, a reporter on the city desk of the Auburn, New York, *Citizen* received a telephone call: An unknown man had been found dead on William Street. It had been a slow news day; maybe this would make a story. The reporter hurried to the scene. The man lay in a pool of light, a policeman leaning over him. No one recognized the corpse; there was nothing in his wallet to indicate who he was. The newspaperman bent closer. The dead man was wearing false whiskers; false teeth were fitted over his real ones; small coils of wire distended his nostrils; a milky glass eye stared up at the night sky. Slowly, the reporter penetrated this last disguise: Thomas Mott Osborne was dead at sixty-seven.

Not even his bizarre death made Franklin back away from his support of Osborne. In 1933, *Osborne of Sing Sing*, a worshipful account of his public career by Frank Tannenbaum, was published with a laudatory intoduction by FDR.

I could locate only one other book on Osborne, a baffled but hugely admiring study by Rudolph W. Chamberlain called *There Is No Truce*, published in 1935. Its author was clearly mystified and pained by Osborne's double life but also unable or unwilling honestly to examine it; the best he could do was to assure his readers that Osborne "exhibited not the slightest trace of transvestism. . . . Not once did he put on a female disguise. To him that would have been an unnatural act."

Osborne and his curious career deserve a modern, more objective study.

"either be withdrawn by you, or [it will be] pro forma refused by the Secretary on the ground that the matter was one of misunderstanding and has been satisfactorily ended. Will you let me know which you think is the best thing to do?"

Taussig refused to accept either option. "The truth of the matter . . . ," he said, "which fact was more impressed on me during our conversation, is that you do not understand my attitude in this matter, and that it was impracticable, under the conditions, for you to make a statement that would have been satisfactory to me."

Daniels eventually refused to grant Taussig's request for a court of inquiry. There would never have been a controversy, he told the captain, had the officer not violated the spirit of Article 1535, which barred Navy personnel from writing for the newspapers.

Captain Taussig had no choice but to subside, but he remained unsatisfied, angry and eager for revenge. Many years later, he was asked to sum up his impressions of the Franklin Roosevelt he had known at the Navy Department: "tremendous personal charm," he said, ". . . rather less than perfect in matters of personal integrity."

When Franklin sat down to breakfast on the morning of January 14 and unfolded his copy of the *Washington Post,* he found buried inside it a distinctly unsettling story: Admiral Sims had sent to Secretary Daniels what the newspaper called "a frank and fearless exposé of the hopeless . . . maladministration, mistakes and blunders into which the American Navy has fallen as a result of Mr. Daniels' policies."

"Certain Lessons of the Great War," the letter to Daniels which Sims had begun writing on Christmas Eve, had been carefully leaked to the *Post* in advance of the awards hearings. The charges it contained were sensational and sweeping—because of the dilatory incompetence and anti-British bias of Secretary Daniels, the admiral said, half a million lives had been lost, 2.5 million tons of shipping had gone to the bottom, $15 billion had been wasted. Suspiciously similar charges had been made on the floor of the Senate by Boies Penrose, the Republican boss of Pennsylvania, and had been generally dismissed as overzealous partisanship. But now, coming from Admiral Sims, the same indictment seemed to carry enormous weight. As the *Post* said, "If this officer, who is generally regarded here and abroad as one of the most competent naval authorities in the world finds it necessary to expose Mr. Daniels' management of naval affairs and frankly and fearlessly undertakes the task, it is not probable that Senators will show lack of interest."

Franklin had had nothing to fear from the medals controversy, but if the admiral's new indictment did nudge the full Senate Naval Affairs Committee into launching a second, wider-ranging investigation of the Navy Department, as suddenly seemed likely, his own actions would inevitably come into question, and he could no longer hope to remain above the struggle between Daniels and Sims.

Over the preceding months, Franklin had quietly given both parties to that struggle reason to believe he sided with them. Years later, Franklin himself would tell a campaign biographer that Sims and Daniels had each asked him to testify on their behalf, and that he had replied to both that while he was, of course, willing to appear, each should know that he would feel compelled to be utterly objective, to speak of "the good as well as the bad." "Both sides of the controversy were pleased—and disturbed" by Roosevelt's frankness, his biographer claimed, adding: "They should have known that he was not willing to be merely partisan."

At the time, however, frankness was not what he displayed. Franklin may have privately thought Sims' renewed attack "scandalous," as he wrote Livy Davis; "It does seem a pity does it not, that really fine, interesting men seem so often to lose their heads completely. The net result of all this will be, of course, to hurt the Navy. . . . The hurting of a Secretary or an Assistant Secretary, who are but birds of passage is very incidental and very unimportant, but the Navy has gone on nearly 150 years, and we hope will always go on; therefore its reputation is of importance."

But his real concern was his own career. He was genuinely fond of his chief but dismissive of him, too, and certainly unwilling to see his own future spoiled by too close identification with him.[27] He could not yet tell how the Sims investigations would come out, but he felt sure that it was in his interest to separate himself somehow from

27. Events on the evening of the day Sims's letter was leaked to the newspaper offered a vivid example of the differences of class and culture that still separated the Assistant Secretary from his chief.

The Eighteenth Amendment went into effect at midnight, January 15. The stroke of twelve found Josephus Daniels standing in a pew at the First Congregational Church of Washington, singing the doxology at a special ecumenical service called by jubilant prohibitionists to celebrate "the Passover from the old era to the new." Joining their voices with his were William Jennings Bryan, Bishop James Cameron, Jr., of the Methodist Church South, and Congressman Andrew J. Volstead of Minnesota, author of the prohibition enforcement bill that defined intoxicating liquor as any beverage containing more than one half of 1 percent alcohol.

Across town, Franklin, too, was on his feet, but he had a champagne glass in his hand and was toasting the late John Barleycorn at the Metropolitan Club, where a special dinner of the Harvard Class of 1904 had been called "to celebrate prohibition."

Daniels, to make the Secretary's enemies continue to consider him an ally rather than an adversary.

And so, on February 1, 1920, Franklin cut himself loose from the freshly beleaguered man whose restless subordinate he had now been for nearly seven years—and he did so without warning and with a callous abandon astonishing even for him.

Standing before fifteen hundred people at the Brooklyn Academy of Music, he declared that in 1917, in the interest of Preparedness, "I committed enough illegal acts to put me in jail for 999 years," acts about which neither the Secretary of the Navy nor the President of the United States had known anything.[28]

Two months *before* war was declared, he added, "I saw that the Navy was still unprepared and I spent $40,000 for guns [to arm merchant vessels] before Congress gave me or anyone permission to spend any money." This, he said, had been "opposed by the President."

What was more, he claimed, it was he, not Daniels, who had chosen Admiral Sims for his important post in London.

Daniels, whose first word of Franklin's remarks came from the next morning's newspapers, was astounded at this attack from the young man with whom he had been so patient for so long. What was more, those facts which were not simply false in Franklin's claims were wildly exaggerated. He checked his recollections with Admiral Ralph Earle, Chief of Naval Ordinance: All of Franklin's supposedly illegal orders for materiel had been cleared with the Secretary in advance, Earle assured him.

Daniels, not his assistant, had armed the merchant ships; Franklin had been enjoying himself in the Haitian jungle at the time. Daniels had also picked Sims.

Coming on the heels of the admiral's assault, Franklin's betrayal was doubly wounding. Even Livy Davis was appalled: "What in the world is the matter with you for telling the public that you . . . committed enough illegal acts to keep you in jail for 900 years?"

Franklin, for his part, behaved as if nothing untoward had happened—"FDR came in as usual," Daniels noted in honest wonderment the next day. The Secretary demanded an immediate retraction. Franklin evidently first said he had been misquoted, then contacted

---

28. The same line had gone over well three weeks earlier before the Newbyrgh New York Chamber of Commerce, without garnering much publicity. *Source:* Scrapbook, Franklin D. Roosevelt, Papers as Assistant Secretary of the Navy, FDRL.

Marvin McIntyre, head of press relations, and ordered up a mild "clarification." Daniels asked to see it before it was handed to the newspapers and was startled again: "He [Franklin] wished news bureau to send out explanation that did not explain and I told McIntyre nothing went out without my approval."

Daniels could barely bring himself to speak to his assistant.[29]

On February 4, just three days after Franklin's betrayal of his chief, a telegram arrived for Eleanor from New York. It was from Forbes Morgan, the long-suffering husband of her mercurial Aunt Pussie; she and her two daughters had burned to death in the converted stable in which they lived on Ninth Street in Greenwich Village. (Her son William Jr. had been away at boarding school.)

Eleanor boarded a train and hurried north. Aunt Pussie had helped raise Eleanor, but she had also cruelly and repeatedly reminded her of her plain features, her shyness, her utter lack of the coquettishness that she and the other women of the Hall family cultivated. "For the practical things of life Pussie had no gift," Eleanor remembered, "but she still had all her charm and much of her beauty, and her spell fell on everyone who came in contact with her." Both childish and child-like, she had veered between exuberance and despair, dabbled in religion but could not seem to remain faithful to her husband, and, largely incapable of taking care of herself, had relied on relatives to get her through her frequent emotional crises. As a young girl Eleanor herself had spent hours trying to soothe her, and as an adult she later remembered calling at her home to find that still another maid had just been fired, leaving Pussie's nine-year-old daughter Eileen to do the best she could to care for her mother and her household.

Now Eileen, her sister, and their mother all lay dead. Eleanor arrived in the midst of a blizzard, and when she found snow blocking cross-town travel, trudged back and forth across Central Park several times seeing to the bleak details. "It was one of those horrors I can hardly think of," she wrote much later, ". . . To this day I cannot bear any funeral parlor." Then she led "a sad little group" of relatives

29. In November 1944, Norman Littell, a Justice Department employee, was engaged in a noisy dispute with his chief, Attorney General Francis Biddle. In an effort to quiet him, FDR sent his daughter, Anna, as an emissary. "The President told me to tell you that, when he was Assistant Secretary of the Navy," she said, "he had resolved that, if ever there was a disagreement on policy with his chief, he would resign before it became a real disagreement. At the slightest shadow of a suggestion of such a disagreement . . . he would tender his resignation." When Littell failed to take the hint, Roosevelt fired him. *Source:* Norman M. Littell, *My Roosevelt Years.*

upriver to Tivoli and saw that the three coffins were laid in the family vault.[30]

At about the time Eleanor rushed to New York, her friend Mrs. Frank Polk in Washington got a telephone call from her old friend, Lucy Mercer. Some time after leaving the Navy Department, Lucy had become the governess for the children of Winthrop Rutherfurd, a wealthy widower and sportsman nearly twice her age with big houses at Allamuchy, New Jersey, and Aiken, South Carolina. In his youth, Rutherfurd had been a glittering figure in American society, a fox-hunting partner of Rosy's and Eleanor's fathers', and the handsome admirer of Consuelo Vanderbilt, whose suit was rejected by her mother only in favor of the Duke of Marlborough's.

Rutherfurd's first wife had died in 1917. She had been Alice Morton, the daughter of former Vice President Levi Morton and a Hudson River neighbor of Sara's, and she had left him a widower at fifty-five, with six children to care for. Edith Eustis, who had quietly entertained Lucy and Franklin in her house together back in the summer of 1916, was the late Mrs. Rutherfurd's sister; perhaps she helped arrange the young woman's new position; perhaps Franklin had discreetly helped, too. In any case, Lucy had proved a firm friend to Rutherfurd, and that winter stood by him as he watched his teen-aged son Lewis slowly die of an undisclosed ailment. Sometime during that long death watch she had agreed to marry the grieving father.

Now, Lucy was calling Mrs. Polk to ask a favor. She was about to be married, she said, and felt she owed it to Franklin to tell him so before he read about it in the newspapers, but she also did not feel, as an engaged woman, that she could write to him directly. Would Mrs. Polk tell him? She agreed to try.

An invitation to tea at the Roosevelts seemed to provide just the opportunity she needed. But with Eleanor pouring tea and amiable talk going on all around her, Mrs. Polk could think of no plausible excuse to take Franklin aside to deliver her message. Finally, as she and her husband put on their coats and started toward the door, she announced Lucy's marriage plans, addressing her remarks to Eleanor but in a voice loud enough so that Franklin could not help overhearing. He "started," a member of the family wrote, "like a horse in fear of a hornet," but said nothing.

We have no way of knowing what, if anything, the Roosevelts said

30. Eleanor's Grandmother Hall was already interred there; she had died August 14, 1919.

to one another about Mrs. Polk's news after their guests left, but on February 14, Eleanor added a postscript to her weekly letter to Sara: "Did you know Lucy Mercer married Mr. Wintie Rutherfurd two days ago?"

The Wilson administration continued dangerously to drift.

On February 2, the Secretary of the Treasury had submitted his resignation.

The Roosevelts' friend Interior Secretary Lane followed suit on the 5th, feeling that his integrity had been questioned by the President, who refused either to see him or to answer his memoranda suggesting that Navy oil fields be leased to private drillers.

On the 7th, Wilson wrote to Robert Lansing, his Secretary of State, demanding to know whether it was true, "as I have been told, that during my illness you have frequently called the heads of the executive departments of the government into conference." When Lansing said it was indeed true—"in view of the fact that we were denied communication with you, [we thought it] wise for us to confer informally together"—Wilson demanded his immediate resignation.

Even the President's most devoted admirers were stunned: Wilson's letter to Lansing suggested that for fully four months he had not even been aware that the Cabinet was meeting. "The President's letter can only be considered that of a sick, peevish man," Eleanor wrote to Sara, "as I think everyone is more really seriously worried than at any time." Questions about the President's sanity were raised in Congress; the Los Angeles *Times* called the dismissal of Lansing WILSON'S LAST MAD ACT.

At the Navy Department, Franklin continued to act as if he had never publicly undercut his chief, even inviting the Secretary and his wife to dinner on the 17th. Mrs. Daniels accepted, although Daniels had not wished to go. On the 16th, Daniels noted in his diary, both Mrs. George Dewey and Admiral Samuel McGowan told him "they were glad we are going to the FDR's." But the next day he was himself still not sure he should attend: "Dinner FDR to go or not to go?"

In the end, the Daniels did go to dinner, but the Secretary was still angry and four days later, on February 21, he called at the White House, wishing to discuss with the President at least the possibility of having to replace his disloyal subordinate. Conditions there made him think better of it at the last moment, as he cryptically noted in his diary that evening.

"I hate L," said E. Wanted T to tell L that Major S must be sent back or would not receive. T. refused. Must put it on other grounds.

FDR persona non grata with W. Better let speech pass.

Some translation is necessary. While waiting to be ushered into the President's bedroom, Daniels discussed with "T"—Joseph Tumulty—the sudden dismissal of "L"—Secretary Lansing—still a topic of furious newspaper speculation. The unauthorized calling of Cabinet meetings had provided the President with the excuse he wanted, the President's secretary explained, but it had not been the real cause. Lansing's loyalty to the unaltered Treaty had long been suspect, but perhaps more important was the hatred that "E"—Edith Wilson—felt for Lansing on a purely personal basis.

That hatred had its origins in a Washington dinner party held more than a year earlier at which an official of the British Embassy, Major Charles Craufurd-Stewart, was said to have repeated a current joke about the second Mrs. Wilson:

"What did Mrs. Galt do when the President proposed to her?"

"Fell out of bed."

Somehow, Edith Wilson had heard of it. So had the President. Craufurd-Stuart had been asked to leave the country.

Then, on September 25, 1919, the day the President collapsed at Pueblo, the former British Foreign Minister, Viscount Grey of Fallodon, had arrived in America with confidential word that a treaty with some reservations might still be acceptable to England. He had been waiting for an appointment ever since. Grey was nearly blind, had to wear blue spectacles and be led by an aide wherever he went, but it was neither his handicap nor Wilson's that had kept the two men from meeting. It was because, as Franklin's friend Bertie Hamlin wrote, "to everyone's astonishment," Lord Grey had seen fit to bring the tactless Major Craufurd-Stuart back to Washington with him as a member of his personal staff.

Wilson made it clear that he would never meet with Grey so long as the man who had denigrated his wife remained in America. The envoy refused to send the major home; Craufurd-Stuart swore he had never gossiped about Mrs. Wilson, and Grey took him at his word. The result was a long stand-off, deeply embarrassing for State Department and Foreign Office alike.

Lansing did his best to work out some sort of compromise and it was in doing so that he had evidently earned Mrs. Wilson's wrath. Not long before the President wrote his bizarre letter to his Secretary of State—Tumulty now told Daniels—Mrs. Wilson had insisted that *he* pass the word to Lansing that Craufurd-Stuart must be withdrawn because of his insults to her. Tumulty had gently demurred, suggesting that grounds other than dubious dinner-table gossip must be found for such a serious breach of diplomatic courtesy. (Tumulty, too, would quickly fall from Mrs. Wilson's favor.)

On December 22, and at Lansing's urging, Grey had reluctantly severed the controversial Major from his staff—though he still remained in Washington attached to the embassy—in the hopes that this concession would persuade the President to receive him. It did not.[31]

Three days later, on Christmas Day, Lord Grey and his closest aide Sir William Tyrell had gone to dinner at the Franklin Roosevelts on R Street. Grey's long friendship with her Uncle Theodore was the basis for Eleanor's invitation, and among the other guests beneath the Roosevelt tree were Sara and TR's daughter, Alice Longworth. It was a cheerful occasion; the only untoward moment came halfway through dinner when it was discovered that James had German measles and had to be taken up to bed.

But Woodrow Wilson, already distrustful of Franklin, soon learned that Lord Grey had been a guest in his home. Neither he nor his wife would ever forgive or forget that fact, and when Grey, back in England and once again a private citizen, wrote a letter to the London *Times* suggesting that Britain would be willing to accept all but one of the Lodge reservations, their anger at the British diplomat and all his American friends only intensified.[32]

Now, as Daniels was shown into the President's bedroom, intending to take up the question of dismissing his assistant, he found the President already choleric toward Franklin—"FDR persona non grata." Wilson may have heard of Franklin's Brooklyn speech—it is impossible to know what he was told during his illness and what was kept from him—but he was certainly aware that Franklin had dared entertain Lord Grey.

31. Perhaps because by then the President had heard still another dinner party rumor: that Grey himself had been overheard expressing his hope to Senator Lodge that the Treaty might one day be adopted with his reservations. *Source:* Jonathan Daniels, *The End of Innocence,* page 299.

32. Long after both Woodrow Wilson and FDR were dead, Mrs. Wilson was pressed by an interviewer for her impressions of the Franklin Roosevelt she had known during World War I. "He was socially wonderful—truly he could charm the birds off the trees," she said. "I thought him more charming than able. . . ." *Source:* Alden Hatch, *Edith Bolling Wilson: First Lady Extarordinary,* page 243.

Daniels backed off. With three Cabinet members gone from the government since the first of the month and the President's mental state now a matter of public debate, perhaps he felt that the sudden departure of a fourth prominent official, particularly when the department in which he served was already under Republican attack, might be more than the beleaguered administration—or the sick President—could handle. In any case, he decided, "Better let speech pass."

Once again, the forbearance of Josephus Daniels had saved Franklin Roosevelt's career.

One of Franklin's greatest strengths as a politician—and a source of unending distress to many of his puzzled admirers—was his apparently sunny ability to accommodate his views to sudden, dramatic shifts in circumstance that would have bewildered a less sinuous and subtle man. By mid-February, informal word had reached him that Herbert Hoover would not declare himself a Democrat. Eleanor still clung to her belief in Hoover: she and Franklin had dined with him the night before, she told Sara on March 7. "Mr. Hoover talked a great deal. He has an extraordinary knowledge and grasp of present-day problems."

But on March 30, Hoover officially declared himself a progressive Republican. There would be no Hoover-Roosevelt ticket.[33]

33. In 1932, FDR told his biographer Ernest K. Lindley that he and Franklin K. Lane had dined with Hoover in the winter of 1919 and, together, urged him to run for President. All he needed to do, they said, was let slip that he was a Jeffersonian Democrat. He was so popular, they assured him, that just that announcement alone would win him an impressive number of delegates to the Democratic Convention—and form the basis for a certain victory in 1924. (They may have been right: in April, weeks after he announced his Republicanism, Hoover still handily defeated William G. McAdoo, the front runner in the *Democratic* primary in Michigan.)

In any case, Roosevelt and Lane thought they had persuaded him, and when Franklin went to dinner at the home of the widow of his friend Republican Congressman Augustus Gardner some time later, and Mrs. Gardner—the daughter of Henry Cabot Lodge—said Hoover was about to announce that he was a Republican, he loudly denied it. Mrs. Gardner just as vehemently said she knew it was true, and that it was her father and Senator Boies Penrose of Pennsylvania who had talked him into joining the GOP.

After telling this tale to Lindley, Franklin asked that it be deleted from his book because, with Hoover in the White House, it "would not go so well!"

Much later, in a letter to another Roosevelt biographer, Frank Freidel, Hoover himself went to some pains to deny the story. "So far as I recollect Lane never mentioned the Presidency to me. . . . Mrs. Gardner's supposed statement is also apocryphal. Both Penrose and Lodge bitterly attacked me over my whole period of public life. . . . So you will see it is unlikely that they sold me the Republican Party."

Franklin and Lane may well have at least discussed the presidency with Hoover that winter; many others did so—including Homer Cummings, the chairman of the Democratic National Committee—so many that it is perfectly possible the former President did not "recollect" it. And the news of Hoover's announcement that he was a Republican must have been upsetting to Franklin and may actually have first reached him at the Gardner's table where he often dined.

But that Lodge and Penrose persuaded Hoover to join the GOP is impossible to credit, still

By then, too, Franklin's fear of the impact of Admiral Sims's attacks had begun to lessen. The admiral turned out to have overreached himself: his most serious charges struck even many senior officers who had privately been contemptuous of Daniels as shrill and unprovable. The Navy, they felt, should not have been attacked so openly by one of its own: Admiral Hugh Rodman, who had commanded American vessels in the North Sea and argued hard and often with the Secretary, spoke for many when he assured Daniels that "As a matter of principle . . . I wish to combat [Sims'] statements and help preserve the deservedly good name which the Navy earned during the war." A Rollin Kirby cartoon in which Sims was depicted shooting a revolver at the Navy's war record with the caption, "Something the Enemy Never Did," was widely distributed. The widow of Admiral George Dewey sent Daniels a message: "Go after them. Give them Hell. That is the message George Dewey would give if he were here. . . ."

And, like so many other Navy men who were fooled by Daniel's slow-moving manner—like Franklin himself, for that matter—Sims had greatly underestimated the Secretary's tactical skills. The stiff-necked admiral, testifying grandiloquently in his crisp uniform, may have had an arguable case in strictly military terms, but Daniels, rumpled and genial, knew precisely how to make it politically indefensible in a country traditionally suspicious of military show.

To the charge that only commanders knew who was most deserving of honors, Daniels pointed out that Sims had wanted the Distinguished Service Medal for a naval aide "who had only trod the deck in a sumptuous office in London, and recommended only a Medal of Honor to men, who, under fire and in the perils of torpedo attack, bore themselves with courage. . . ." Nor had Sims named more than a handful of enlisted men for honors.

Daniels could not agree, either, that in the new age of "under-sea assassins," brave commanders whose ships were sunk, should be exempted from honors simply because that had been the traditional practice in the age of sail.

---

another product, I believe, of Franklin's creative memory. For him, the two senators had become symbols of all that was partisan and reactionary among the Republicans, and I suspect that the invention of this detail, which made Hoover seem at once indecisive and hopelessly conservative, was too appealing for him to resist.

Hoover himself once explained his reasons for finally rejecting Democratic blandishments that spring: "I knew no Democrat could win in 1920 and did not see myself as a sacrifice." *Sources:* Elliott Roosevelt, ed., *FDR: His Personal Letters, 1928–1945*, pages 193–194; Frank Freidel, *Franklin D. Roosevelt: The Ordeal*, pages 58–59; David Burner, *Herbert Hoover: A Public Life*, pages 150–157.

And the Secretary made no apology for having given precedence to men who had fought at sea over those who performed mere "desk duty, far from danger." "The position of Admiral Sims in placing shore duty above sea duty, in the danger zones," he added, with his familiar tight smile, "is no doubt influenced by his own record" as naval attaché at Paris and St. Petersburg during the Spanish-American War.

It was quickly clear that Daniels was going to survive—"[T]hings are quiet," Franklin told his mother on February 11, "the Sims episode being . . . of less public interest as time goes on"—and he shifted course accordingly, passing up few opportunities to pledge his allegiance to Daniels and to the Navy for which, he now wanted the public to understand, they both stood. He denounced what he called "three-to-two" history—there were three Republicans on the subcommittee and only two Democrats—and boasted that despite ninety-seven investigations since the war ended, the Congress had been unable to uncover a single "embalmed beef and paper-shoe" scandal of the kind that had corrupted the Republican-run Spanish-American War.[34]

"We are so well fortified, not with perfect wisdom but in things accomplished . . . ," Daniels told reporters before he entered the hearing room a second time to answer Sims' charges in early May, "that the more people learn about the work of the Navy in the war, the more satisfied they will be that we did a good job. We are proud of our record."

Again, Daniels made his accuser, not the Navy Department, the topic of debate, deftly painting a devastating portrait from whose effects the admiral's reputation never entirely recovered. Sims was a prima donna, according to Daniels, a petty egotist altogether too fond of the "glitter" of naval life, slavishly devoted to the British, inex-

34. As late as March 30, however, Franklin and Louis Howe were still evidently hedging at least some of their bets. In 1919, Franklin had signed a contract with Harper & Brothers to write a book, *The Work of the Navy Ashore*, which, its prospective editor hoped, would be an account of "the tremendous thing that has been done in the Navy Department in the last six years." Howe was paid $500 to write the early, purely historical chapters but, despite Eleanor's urging, Franklin had never actually got around to writing anything. In January 1920 the editor wrote a tactful note asking how the manuscript was coming. Franklin stalled for almost two months: the awkward fact was that he did not know which side of the Sims controversy then still building in Washington he wished to be on. "My part of the work is practically completed," Howe finally wrote the publisher on March 30 with unusual frankness, "but Mr. Roosevelt has hesitated, particularly during the investigation, in having what would be a rather frank resumé of Navy ways of doing business appear." The situation should have been clarified by June, he thought, and the Assistant Secretary would begin writing then.

In the end, the book was never written. *Source:* Franklin D. Roosevelt, Papers as Assistant Secretary of the Navy, FDRL.

perienced in the real business of the Navy—"the struggle at sea"—and willing to do or say almost anything to soothe his wounded vanity, including villifying the victorious American Navy.

As an old newspaperman, the Secretary also knew how best to orchestrate the appearances of those admirals who testified on his behalf, distributing their opening statements among the sixty Washington press bureaus early in the day so that they—and not the possibly damaging interrogations that followed—would yield the afternoon headlines. Toward the end of the hearings, an Associated Press reporter congratulated the Secretary on "getting out of so many pretty tight holes." Daniels smiled and placed his hands on the younger man's shoulders. "Yes," he said, "and I can't tell you how much I appreciate all *you* have done for me."

The Sims hearings ran from March 9 to May 28 and during much of that time Franklin lived in daily dread of being called to testify. No possible political good could come of being publicly confronted with his own previous undercutting of the Secretary to whom he had now pledged such fealty. He sought to head off that threat by publicly promising to make Chairman Hale regret it if he were summoned to appear. Franklin's ploy worked—or Hale may have simply felt that Daniels' effective performance had already done damage enough to his party's cause. In any case, Roosevelt—who admitted to Livy Davis he'd been "somewhat lucky"—was asked only for written recommendations.

In these, too, he managed to ally himself more closely with his chief than ever before. "Frankly," he told the committee, "the most serious problem with the Navy now, as it has been in the past, is Congress." As for Admiral Sims, the War College under his leadership had become "a holier-than-thou aggregation of officers at Newport," he charged, entirely out of touch with "the actual life of the Navy"; he, for one, was grateful that certain "gold-laced gentlemen" had been thwarted in their effort to have the Navy controlled by a European-style general staff unanswerable to their civilian superiors.

This attack, coming from a man who had only recently been so flattering, was especially galling to Sims and his friends.[35] "Roosevelt's case has been surprising to me," Admiral Fullam wrote Sims. "I

---

35. Rear Admiral Benton C. Decker, a Sims ally and Commandant of the Seventh Naval District, was moved to denounce Franklin in a letter to the *Army and Navy Journal*, pointing out while that admirals might be "gold-laced gentlemen" to the Assistant Secretary when seeking "to ingratiate himself with the workingmen . . . they are not scorned as 'gold-laced gentlemen' when he meets them in the rich clubs of New York and Washington." *Source:* Frank Freidel, *Franklin D. Roosevelt: The Ordeal*, page 49.

thought a *little* better of him [than Daniels]. But his remarks about the War College and 'gold-laced gentlemen' sickened me. This and the vice ring business left him in a bad plight."

Sims responded in kind. "I have long known the kind of man that Mr. Roosevelt is," he wrote. *"He is a simon-pure politician."*[36]

Franklin had been spared having publicly to account for his divided loyalties in front of the Senate Naval Affairs Committee, but he still faced an ordeal of his own.

The acquittal of Chaplain Kent in January had inspired the bishop of Rhode Island and a dozen Newport clergymen to appeal directly to the President for a full-scale investigation of the activities of Section A. A "score of youths," they charged, "enlisted in and wearing the uniform of the United States Navy [had been] instructed in the details of a nameless vice and sent through the community to practice the same . . . to entrap certain designated individuals. . . ." The churchmen demanded that the President "eliminate from the Navy all officials, however highly placed, who are responsible for the employment of such execrable methods."

Franklin continued to deny everything. As for charges that naval officials had used "highly objectionable methods in collecting evidence," Roosevelt told the editor of the Boston *Herald.* "If that is true, I will not only apologize to you, but take great pleasure in resigning my present office."

On January 17, Daniels appointed a court of inquiry to look into the Newport scandal, headed by Admiral Dunn—the same friendly

---

36. The apparent ease with which Roosevelt altered his views led some even among those who otherwise supported him to question his sincerity. Raymond Moley, a one-time aide, suggested that such critics missed the point:

> I have been asked many times by those who know of my long association with Roosevelt: "Is he"—or was he—"sincere?"
>
> When time permitted, I always answered that sincerity, as a quality known to the generality of people, is not fairly applicable to a politician. Or to put it another way, in a category of virtues appropriate to a politician, sincerity occupies a less exalted place than it does among the qualities of a novelist, a teacher, or a scientist. And that is in no way damning the politician, for he may exalt virtues such as kindness, understanding and public service far beyond those who sniff at his lack of sincerity. . . .
>
> The politician creates illusions. His words must be selected not because they are the most forceful or descriptive in conveying exact facts and situations, but because they will produce in the minds of hearers or readers the reaction desired by the speaker or writer. What, therefore, does sincerity, as we talk this virtue to our children, have to do with the calculations of a politician?
>
> Ultimately, the considerations of a politician are not based upon truth or fact; they are based upon what the public will conceive to be truth or fact.

Source: Raymond Moley, *27 Masters of Politics in a Personal Perspective*, pages 42–43.

officer who had served alongside Franklin during the gentle probe of conditions at Portsmouth.

John Rathom, the editor of the Providence *Journal,* had kept up a drumfire of articles and editorials about the scandal, strongly suggesting that the real culprit was the Assistant Secretary of the Navy. To these, Franklin now made furious objection; since the newspaper's editor knew that a court of inquiry had been established to sift facts from fiction, he said, public accusations against individuals were "disingenuous and dishonorable . . . morally dishonest."

Rathom retaliated by reprinting his most sensational story, headlined VICIOUS PRACTICES IN U.S. NAVY DENOUNCED BY CLERGY OF NEWPORT, and mailing copies of it to editors all over the country. Franklin himself sent a copy to the chairman of the Senate Naval Affairs Committee, urging that he seek to suppress such stories on the grounds that they would damage naval recruitment: "Any mother reading the headlines . . . would very properly hesitate before allowing her son to enlist in the Naval Service. In fact, it is believed that any average citizen reading this article must be led to believe that the Navy as a whole is a pretty rotten institution, and that it is not a proper place, either on its ships or in its training camps, for young Americans to be."

But instead of investigating Rathom, Senator Hale eagerly appointed still another subcommittee to look into the charges the editor was making.

On May 20, the day before Daniels wound up his testimony in the second Sims hearing, Franklin went before the Dunn court.

He proved a glib, defiant witness.

He knew nothing whatsoever, he said, of the activities of the men under Hudson and Arnold before Section A was created in June of 1919.

> Q. Do you mean to tell this court that if there was a Court of Inquiry at Newport that the Assistant Secretary of the Navy wouldn't know about it?
>
> A. Not necessarily, and certainly not about its details. . . .
>
> Q. Mr. Secretary, did you know that in nine instances, between the 18th of March and the 14th of April, that certain naval [operatives] had permitted sexual perverts in the naval service to suck their penis for the purpose of obtaining evidence . . . ?
>
> A. The answer is no. I knew absolutely nothing about the court or its methods or its personnel. . . . In view of the fact that the Acting Secretary is called upon each day to pass on anywhere

from 20 to 100 court-martials, courts of inquiry, and boards of investigation cases, to go into details would require ten lives instead of one day. . . .

Nor had he ever been told of the specific methods used by Hudson's men once they were attached to his office.

Q. Who would be responsible for the acts of men in an organization so constituted?
A. The officer in command.
Q. Did you give [the men] any instructions or orders as to how the details should be carried out.
A. Naturally not.
Q. Would that not have been your duty, since these men were attached to your office?
A. Absolutely not.

Lieutenant Hudson had been in command, not he, Franklin said. Several times during the summer, Hudson had reported to him that "the investigation was proceeding very satisfactorily," but only "in general terms. . . ."

Q. And on none of these occasions you asked him what methods he was using?
A. Absolutely not.
Q. Why not?
A. Because I was interested merely in getting results. I was not concerned any more in finding out about their methods than I am concerned in finding out how the commanding officer of a fleet takes the fleet from New York to Newport. What I want to know is that he gets the fleet over to Newport.

Ervin Arnold had testified that during his visit to the Assistant Secretary on May 1 he had personally handed the operative's report on Samuel Kent, explicit in its details as to just how the evidence against him had been gathered, to Roosevelt, who had at least looked through it in a "rough way" while he was in his office. ("I happened to be an Episcopalian," Franklin testified, "and was rather glad, personally, that the Reverend Mr. Kent had been acquitted. . . .") But under cross-examination by a Newport attorney representing Kent's fellow clergymen, Franklin continued to maintain his utter ignorance of what the secret squad attached to his office had been doing.

Hadn't he even *read* the letter he'd signed, establishing Section A? "Whoever brought it into my office stated the general purpose and tenor of the letter," Roosevelt answered, "and I glanced over it in all probability not reading it word for word, and probably only reading a couple of lines of each paragraph."

Q. You were aware of the fact that one of the subjects of investigation was unnatural crime?

A. One. Sodomy was one of four or five other vices which were to be investigated.

Q. As a lawyer, how did you suppose that evidence of such a crime could be obtained?

A. As a lawyer, I had no idea. That is not within the average lawyer's education.

Q. Did you give that matter any thought whatsoever?

A. Not any more than how were they going to close the whorehouses or [stop] the sale of drugs?

Q. Did you realize as a lawyer . . . that investigations in such matters often lead to improper actions on the part of the investigators?

A. I never had such an idea. Never entered my head. No, sir.

Q. Were you aware that unnatural crimes are not commonly committed in the open?

A. Neither is prostitution nor the selling of drugs committed in the open.

Q. How did you think evidence of these things could be obtained?

A. I didn't think. If I had I would have supposed they had someone under the bed or looking over the transom.

With such denials, Franklin hoped he had put the matter to rest and could return to the two subjects that continued to consume him: his own political future and that of his party.

One day that spring, Dr. Grayson permitted President Wilson to go for a little drive. He looked gaunt and waxen, a blanket across his lap. Mrs. Wilson rode beside him. He did not stay out long, and as the chauffeur drove him back through the White House gate, a little knot of men and women stood clapping on the sidewalk. The President lifted his good hand in a wave and did his best to smile. Tears stood in his eyes. "You see," he said to his wife, as he was being lifted from the car, "they still love me!"

Mrs. Wilson turned away so that he could not see her weep. The crowd, made up of friends and family of Secret Service agents, had been arranged by the chief of the detail, Colonel Edmund Starling.

Wilson had lost touch with reality. Unable to walk unaided, to write a coherent letter, even to engage in a conversation for more than a few moments before losing the thread of what was being discussed, he now let it be known that he wished to run for an unprecedented third term as President of the United States.

None of the Democrats most likely to be nominated at San Francisco in June were up to the job, he told visitors. William G. McAdoo of California—"dear Mac," the President's own son-in-law and former Secretary of the Treasury—was lacking in the requisite "powers of reflection." It would be "futile" to run A. Mitchell Palmer: the public had wearied of his repeated warnings of a revolution that never seemed to start, and he was detested by liberals and labor leaders. The nomination of Governor James M. Cox of Ohio, Wilson added, "would be a joke."

The Republicans met at Chicago in mid-June. Senator Lodge presided as chairman. The overriding issue of the campaign to come, he told the delegates, was simple: "Mr. Wilson and his dynasty, his heirs and assigns, or anybody that is his, anybody who with bent knee has served his purposes, must be driven from all control, from all influence upon the Government of the United States. They must be driven from office and power."

There were two leading candidates for the Republican presidential nomination: Governor Frank O. Lowden of Illinois, an attorney and self-made millionaire, and General Leonard Wood, Indian fighter, Rough Rider, and confidant of Theodore Roosevelt, whose zealous advocacy of Preparedness before the war had so irritated Wilson that he had been denied an active command once it began.

Corinne Roosevelt Robinson—TR's worshipful sister and Eleanor's "Auntie Corinne"—delivered the seconding speech for Wood, the first address ever delivered by a woman before the national convention of either major party: ". . . We do not want any more visionaries," she told the delegates. "We do not want a fleeting glance of fleecy, dissipating cloud. We want realizable ideas, and we want to realize them. . . ."[37]

Warren Harding had scant enough vision to suit any Republican,

---

37. Some years later at a summer gathering of the Oyster Bay Roosevelts at which Eleanor but not Franklin was present and after a good many drinks, Teddy Robinson asked his Democratic cousin to dance, then without telling her he was doing so, put a recording of this address on the turntable and whirled her around and around the room while her aunt excoriated her party and her Republican relatives roared.

"It was everything Eleanor hated," an eyewitness remembered. "Teddy had had too much to drink. The political joke wasn't funny. Everything was too hilarious." *Source:* Interview with W. Sheffield Cowles, Jr.

but he was just one of several dark horses as the balloting began. Lowden and Wood quickly deadlocked, the convention adjourned for the night, and on the thirteenth floor of the Blackstone Hotel in the early morning hours of June 12, party leaders settled upon the Ohio senator. He was nominated that afternoon. For Vice President, the Republicans picked the taciturn governor of Massachusetts, Calvin Coolidge, who had caught the national imagination the previous autumn by calling out the National Guard to crush a strike by Boston policemen, declaring, "There is no right to strike against the public safety by anybody, anywhere, anytime."

As genially bland as he was handsome, Harding was a small-town newspaperman with a determinedly narrow view of the presidency. Promising "Not heroism but healing, not nostrums but normalcy," he planned to wage a dignified and old-fashioned front-porch campaign like the one conducted twenty years earlier by his political hero and fellow Ohioan, William McKinley, and even arranged to have McKinley's original flagpole brought over from Canton and set up until Election Day in his own yard at Marion.

On June 18—six days after Harding and Coolidge were nominated; just ten days before the Democratic Convention opened—Wilson allowed himself to be photographed at his desk and gave an interview to the *New York World* in which he said that he would not endorse any candidate, and was confident the convention delegates would not "permit themselves to be led astray. . . ."

For Woodrow Wilson, the path the Democrats should follow was clearly marked: they must renominate him for President; otherwise, the League would die.

One afternoon that June, John L. McCrea, aide to Hugh Rodman, the newly appointed commander of the Pacific Fleet, happened to pass the Assistant Secretary of the Navy in the main corridor on the second floor of the Navy Department.

Roosevelt stopped him. He knew the admiral was about to sail for San Francisco, he said. Exactly when was he to leave?

That very afternoon, the aide answered.

"I was hoping to see Admiral Rodman before he left."

The admiral was at the bank. The aide offered to go and tell him he was wanted.

That wouldn't be necessary, Franklin said, if the aide could give him a message: He planned to reach San Francisco a couple of days before the convention opened on July 28, and had been having trouble getting a hotel room. Since the fleet was going to be there, in any case, "I am wondering if Admiral Rodman couldn't arrange to quarter me and an aide on his flagship. . . . No hurry about an immediate answer. Just ask the Admiral if he will be good enough to drop me a note. . . ."

Rodman, a rugged, plain-spoken man "never sparing in reproach or criticism," according to an officer who served under him in the North Atlantic, had quarrelled with the Assistant Secretary over the wisdom of building fifty-foot boats early in the war and had cursed out Louis Howe when he clumsily suggested that a favorable vote for his boss's little fleet might win him the appointment to sea duty he craved. He was not especially fond of Franklin. "I don't like it one damn bit," he told his aide when he heard of Roosevelt's request, "but . . . I suppose we'll have to do it. The . . . Assistant Secretary demanding accommodations—Can you beat it?"

He was still more displeased a few days later to learn that Secretary Daniels also wished to stay aboard the *New Mexico*. He liked the Secretary no better than his assistant, and had defended him in the Sims hearings only because he believed in so doing he was also defending the Navy. Rodman sent word that there was only one suitable stateroom aboard the flagship, and that Mr. Roosevelt had already reserved it for himself. A telegram from the Secretary settled the matter: I SHALL STAY ON NEW MEXICO MAKE OTHER ARRANGEMENTS FOR THE ASSISTANT SECRETARY SIGNED DANIELS.[38]

Since Franklin was a member of the New York delegation for which hotel rooms had long been booked, the story that he was having trouble getting accommodations was almost surely false. More likely,

38. The Secretary might not have attended the convention at all had he not felt an obligation to help save his friend the President from himself. His primary motive for heading west was to ensure that the new Secretary of State, Bainbridge Colby, and other misguided Wilson enthusiasts were not successful in renominating the President who, his anxious physician had said, could not survive a third campaign.

He boarded the *New Mexico* in Texas and sailed through the Panama Canal and up the coast to San Francisco, slept aboard throughout convention week and dined often with Rodman and his staff. One day at lunch he said he needed a haircut and asked the admiral if he knew of a good barber shop in town.

"We have an excellent barber shop on board, sir," the admiral said. "His shop is close to your cabin, Mr. Secretary. We'll be glad to make an appointment for you."

Daniels thoughtfully fingered the shaggy nape of his neck "Thanks Rodman," he said, "but I think I shall have my hair cut ashore. There are so very many men in the Navy who would like to cut my throat I don't think I should chance it. . . ." *Source:* Unpublished memoir by John L. McCrea, FDRL.

he thought a cabin aboard a warship would provide an especially impressive backdrop for his activities at the convention. In any case, he quickly arranged a cabin for himself aboard the battleship *New York*, and on the eve of the convention gave an on-deck dinner for the entire New York delegation.

Franklin clearly intended to emerge from the convention as more than merely a New York delegate, and to help ensure that result had brought with him a small delegation of his own that included his Navy Department secretary Renah Camalier; Grenville T. Emmet, with whom he and Langdon Marvin had just formed a new law firm; and his three oldest and most trusted political allies: Lathrop Brown; Judge John E. Mack of Poughkeepsie, who had first come to him with the notion of running for office; and Tom Lynch, the Poughkeepsie florist who was his golfing partner, and who, a full decade earlier, had put away two bottles of fine champagne against the day Franklin became President.

Looking back on the 1920 Democratic National Convention almost a quarter of a century later, H. L. Mencken remembered it as "the most charming in American annals. . . . It made history for its voluptuous loveliness. . . . Whenever I meet an old-timer who took part in it we fall into maudlin reminiscences . . . and tears drop off the ends of our noses. It came within an inch of being perfect."

The weather was wonderful; accommodations were plush; the people friendly. But above all, Mencken remembered the "incomparable Bourbon" poured freely for delegates and newspapermen alike, courtesy of the mayor, James "Sunny Jim" Rolph, Jr., a Republican whose boosterism easily outstripped his partisanship. Prohibition had officially begun five months earlier, Mencken recalled, and arriving delegates, already accustomed to "hair oil, Jamaica ginger and sweet spirits of nitre," feared that San Francisco would offer nothing better than "paint remover and sheep dip."

> What a surprise awaited them! What a deliverance was at hand! The moment they got to their hotels they were waited upon by small committees of refined and well-dressed ladies, and asked to state their desires. The majority at the start were so suspicious that they kicked the ladies out; they feared entrapment by what were then still called revenuers. But the bolder fellows took a chance—and a few hours later the glad word was everywhere. No matter what a delegate ordered, he got Bourbon—but it was Bourbon of the very first chop, Bourbon aged in contented barrels

of the finest white oak, Bourbon of really ultra and super quality. It came in quart bottles on the very heels of the committee of ladies—and there was no bill attached.

The auditorium in which the convention opened on Monday, July 28, was also a revelation; a relic of the Panama-Pacific Exposition Franklin had helped inaugurate six years earlier, it had been completely refurbished and was "so spacious, so clean, so luxurious in its comforts and so beautiful in its decorations," Mencken wrote, "that the assembled politicoes felt like sailors turned loose in the most gorgeous bordellos of Paris."[39]

Downstairs, in the spacious basement, smiling young women in white served up "West Coast delicacies at cut-rate prices," and even the men's rooms were showplaces—"lined with mirrors . . . staffed with shoe-shiners, suit-pressers and hat-cleaners, and outfitted with automatic weighing-machines, cigar-lighters, devices releasing a squirt of Jockey Club perfume for a cent, and recent files of all the principal newspapers of the United States."

In the huge convention hall itself, the freshly painted walls were tastefully hung with pastel fabrics. A single, spectacular note of color was provided by a vast American flag—billed as the largest ever made—that draped the pipes of an enormous organ. The doors were kept standing open to let in the balmy ocean air and from their chairs the delegates could watch the warships of the Pacific Fleet riding at anchor in the Bay, courtesy of Josephus Daniels and Franklin Roosevelt.

Instead of the traditional ward heelers armed with clubs for keeping order in the aisles, women in white "moved prettily through the delegates, armed only with little white wands," Mencken remembered,

39. Mencken had attended the Republican Convention in Chicago that spring "and was thus keen to the contrast. The hall in Chicago was an old armory that had been used lately for prize fights, dog shows and a third-rate circus, and it still smelled of pugs, kennels and elephants."

Along with the other delegates, Franklin had a lively time between sessions. One evening, the Vallejo Chamber of Commerce gave a banquet in honor of Daniels and Roosevelt. (Vallejo was the home of the Mare Island Navy Yard.) "The night of the banquet it was suggested that the guests go to various rooms in the Stewart Hotel for refreshments—this despite Prohibition," John L. McCrea remembered. "About seven . . . that evening, when the guests had [had their drinks and] were gathering in the banquet room I was standing in the vicinity of the elevator bank on the main floor. Suddenly, an elevator plummeted by and hit with a *crack* in the elevator well. . . . [then] bounded up about six feet and there came to rest. One of the persons I saw crawling out of the elevator was the Assistant Secretary of the Navy."

Years later, when McCrea was FDR's naval aide, he asked the President if he remembered this incident. He did: "How could I forget it?" *Source:* Unpublished memoir by John L. McCrea, FDRL.

"and every wand was tied with a blue ribbon, signifying law and order. When one of these babies glided into a jam of delegates with her wand upraised they melted as if she had been a man-eating tiger, but with this difference: that instead of making off with screams of terror they yielded as if to soft music, their eyes rolling ecstatically and their hearts going pitterpat."

Franklin made his first mark on the proceedings—and the authority of the lovely wand bearers faced its first challenge—even before the opening ceremonies were over. Spotlights played upon the giant flag as it was slowly raised to reveal a huge oil portrait of Woodrow Wilson and the band began to play. The delegates cheered and rose to their feet in sentimental tribute to the broken man who had restored their party to the White House eight years earlier. Soon the aisles were choked with marching delegates and the standards of all the states swayed above the crowd—all the states, that is, except New York, where Boss Murphy's men were under orders to remain in their seats and Judge Jeremiah T. Mahoney held the standard firmly in both hands.

Franklin and at least one other delegate, Mayor George R. Lunn of Schenectady, were determined to march, too. They went together to William W. Farley, chairman of the state committee, and, shouting to be heard above the din, got reluctant permission for individual delegates to join the demonstration. Then, as the *New York Tribune* reported, "imbued with zeal and clothed with authority as they thought, [the two] swooped down upon the standard" and seized hold. Judge Mahoney and several of those closest to him held on. There was a brief scuffle before Franklin wrenched the standard high above the crowd and stepped off into the aisle to the cheers of hundreds of delegates.[40]

40. The story of the struggle for the standard quickly grew in the telling. "When I wanted to take the standard I was told that New York would remain seated," Franklin soon told a reporter. "I didn't like that and I grabbed the standard. About half a dozen men grabbed me and we had a jolly fight, but I got the standard and it was paraded."

A week after the convention, a Roosevelt enthusiast would swear that Franklin had been all alone in wresting the standard from Mahoney, and in the course of doing it had felled two Tammany men with "a right and a left with his fists"; it had taken "a clean uppercut" finally to win him the flag.

Judge Mack remembered that there were just three men holding onto the standard, not six, when Roosevelt (and Mayor Lunn) approached, and Judge Mahoney himself recalled that there were only two, and that "FDR couldn't budge it until Mr. Murphy sort of bowed to let it go and we let it go. The whole thing probably took less than four seconds. . . . There wasn't even an angry gesture."

Somehow, Tom Lynch got hold of the battered standard and in 1932 presented it to FDR,

"You & Tammany don't seem to agree very well," Eleanor wrote as soon she had read the next day's newspaper account of the struggle on the floor. "Mama is very proud of your removing the state standard from them. I have a feeling you enjoyed it, but won't they be very much against you in the State Convention?"

In fact, the struggle for the standard was, as William Farley said, simply a misunderstanding, more symbol than substance. It now served the long-term interests of both Franklin and Murphy that the New York delegation seem united, and they were careful to be seen on the floor in apparently amiable conversation with one another.

At Franklin's convention-eve reception for the New York delegation on the quarterdeck of the USS *New York*, Al Smith introduced Roosevelt to his family for the first time. Much later, the governor's daughter Emily remembered "being impressed only as any other young girl would have been at meeting an Assistant Secretary of the Navy, and one so handsome, so debonair, and with a family name so universally known."

Even Emily Smith, who worshipped her father, would not have called Al Smith handsome. He was forty-seven then, nine years older and four inches shorter than Franklin; his once lean figure was developing a paunch, his sandy hair was thinning, his formidable nose had been reddened by unaccustomed exposure to the California sun, and his gold-capped teeth were clamped as usual upon a moist cigar. But through his own efforts he had managed to make his own family name universally known among Democrats, winning the governorship in 1918, a year of otherwise almost unmitigated disaster for his party, and then proving himself an able chief executive, championing civil liberties and calling for a progressive program that included a minimum wage law; an eight-hour day for women; state ownership of hydroelectric power; and state doctors and nurses to minister to the rural poor, all over the violent objections of a Republican legislature dominated by Theodore Roosevelt's old nemesis, Boss William Barnes.

Now, his name was to be entered into nomination as New York's favorite son, and some time during their chat aboard the *New York*,

who proudly hung it on the wall of his old study at Springwood where it remains. *Sources:* Palmer Interview with John E. Mack, FDRL; Frank Freidel, *Franklin D. Roosevelt: The Ordeal*, page 63; newspaper interview with Horace Hawkins, Scrapbook, Franklin D. Roosevelt Papers, 1920–1928, FDRL; Transcript of interview with Judge Jeremiah T. Mahoney, Columbia Oral History Project, Columbia University.

after some amiable but necessarily gingerly reminiscing about their days together in Albany nine years before, Smith evidently took Roosevelt aside to ask if he would be willing to second his nomination. Franklin jumped at the chance.

Smith was Boss Murphy's candidate, and Franklin had not initially favored him for the gubernatorial nomination in 1918—he had in fact first wanted the nomination himself, then wanly supported an old anti-Tammany ally, William Church Osborn, finally delayed returning from his inspection tour of Europe until after the New York primary that September so that he could avoid taking sides.[41] And while relations between him and Smith had always been correct, they had never been genuinely cordial.

For all his noisy geniality aboard the *New York*, Smith's memories of Franklin in Albany were not really warm: young Roosevelt's pious intransigence had made life for the whole Assembly unnecessarily burdensome, and like his friend Robert Wagner, Smith had been delighted to see him pack his bags for Washington in 1913. He had dismissed Roosevelt as a "morning glory," the term Albany veterans applied to newcomers who were showy at the dawn of their careers but faded fast. Franklin's inept campaign for the Senate nomination in 1914 only confirmed Smith's conviction that Roosevelt was an impractical "damn fool," a showy snob whose word could not be trusted, who talked too much and did too little, and was unwilling to work hard enough for the success he so nakedly craved.

Smith knew that Roosevelt's new-found willingness to work with Tammany—signalled by his close cooperation with New York congressmen during the war, and his July Fourth appearance alongside Boss Murphy in 1917—was purely tactical, but he thought he could make good use of it, nonetheless. Roosevelt's last name still had broad appeal beyond New York City and precisely because he had once so noisily opposed the regulars, a public demonstration of his support would lend Smith's candidacy a special kind of credence.

And there was a second compelling reason for picking Franklin to speak on his behalf. Smith was a sentimental man, and had asked a boyhood hero to be the first to place his name in nomination. William Bourke Cockran was a veteran silver-haired Tammany orator whose fervid style of speechmaking Sir Winston Churchill once credited with

---

41. This did not prevent him from much later claiming that he had always been for Smith and had even been personally responsible for reconciling suspicious upstate leaders to his candidacy. *Source:* Frank Freidel, *Franklin D. Roosevelt: The Apprenticeship*, pages 342–343.

having helped to shape his own. He was also a Roman Catholic, as was Smith, and neither major party had ever nominated a Catholic for President—neither had even seriously considered the possibility, for that matter. As the most prominent Protestant Democrat in the state, Roosevelt's willingness to appear on Smith's behalf would help broaden the governor's appeal.

Franklin had few illusions about any of this: he was "window-dressing," he knew. But it was in his interest to go along. For all his hopes of the vice-presidential nomination, his most likely option that fall still seemed to be a run for the Senate, and he needed the backing of Murphy and the regulars if he had any hope of victory in what looked to be yet another bad Democratic year. They were devoted to the governor, Frances Perkins remembered; he had risen from their ranks, understood their problems, could be counted upon to keep his word: "Smith *knew* he was the beloved of the organization . . . one of the boys that made good. He knew they couldn't be pried loose from him."

But they would always be leery of Roosevelt. Despite his eagerness to ingratiate himself, he remained an outsider without the "full, honest support of the people who pulled wires in his own political party. He had to play them. He wasn't their bird."

Playing them now required that he display hearty if not heartfelt enthusiasm for the presidential candidacy of Al Smith.

"I've always thought that two items were driving elements of Roosevelt," Frances Perkins once told an interviewer. "One was a desire to outshine Al Smith. The other was to outshine [Cousin] Ted. I know it. These two items were so deeply buried in his subconscious that he could hardly have been aware of them, but they were always driving elements, driving him to do things. They were partly what made him so active when there was a great deal of indolence in his nature."

Over the coming years, Franklin Roosevelt and Al Smith would each repeatedly find he needed the other. Both men came bitterly to resent that fact. It is not surprising that they were such uneasy and mutually suspicious allies. Nothing in their backgrounds suggested they could be friends.

The tenement flat above a barber shop at 174 South Street on the Lower East Side where Alfred Emanuel Smith was born in 1873 was about as far as one could get from Springwood. Smith's father was a freight handler with a broad mustache and a fondness for Democratic politics: the last time he ever left his apartment it was to vote the Tammany ticket. Al's mother, Catherine Mulvehill Smith, was an immigrant tailor's daughter so pious that she put into a drawer her husband's certificate of membership in the New York Volunteer Fire Department because she feared the unclothed Neptune that was its central figure might impair her children's morals. Her devotion to her son, her determination that he should excel, was extraordinary even for that time and place, and his gratitude was expressed each evening when he knelt in front of her to receive her blessing before going to bed, a practice he continued whenever he visited her to the end of her life.[42]

The Smiths were by no means the poorest residents of their neighborhood, as Al's younger sister, Mary, was once careful to explain: just down the block lived children who had no shoes. But certainly their surroundings and circumstances would have seemed threadbare to the Roosevelts. Some of Franklin's earliest memories were of ships, the great liners that took him and his parents to and from Europe each summer, the yachts and sailboats in which he sailed up and down the Hudson or around Campobello. Al Smith's first memories centered on ships, too, the great array of sailing ships tied up at the wharves just across the cobbled street whose bowsprits arched almost to his second-floor window. "The rigging of the sailing vessels afforded a very good gymnasium," Smith remembered. He and his friends clambered from one ship to the next, played tag among the packing boxes on the wharves and stickball against the walls of warehouses in the shadow of the Brooklyn Bridge, and on warm days they swam naked in the East River.

Franklin was brought up in splendid but lonely isolation on the Hudson; his infrequent playmates were close relatives, the children of country gentlemen like his father, or the offspring of family employees encouraged to do as they were told by the young master. Smith learned

42. Sara Delano Roosevelt was invariably polite to Al Smith, though she often privately found his presence trying; he was emphatically not the sort of man with whom she had ever wished her son to associate himself, even for purely practical purposes. But she did admire his closeness to his mother.

Although Mrs. Smith lived to look on proudly twice as her son was inaugurated as governor, she died in 1924, and so never saw him become his party's presidential nominee, a source of special sadness to her son. Welcoming Roosevelt to Albany as his successor as governor in 1929, Smith bowed to Sara from the rostrum. "I congratulate the mother," he said. "It is a great day for her. I remember my mother. My mother was on the platform for two inaugurations. I know how she enjoyed it and how she felt about it."

Sara's eyes filled with tears. *Source:* Frank Freidel, *Franklin D. Roosevelt: The Triumph,* page 21.

to hold his own in the crowded, clamorous streets filled with Irish, German, Italian, Jewish, and Chinese children.

Both Franklin and Smith attended churches named for Saint James. Franklin's was Episcopal, of course. Smith's had once been Episcopal, too, but had been acquired by the Roman Catholic Church in 1827, from old-line Protestants like the Roosevelts, who had then already begun fleeing north to escape the rising tide of immigrants crowding into lower Manhattan. His mother hoped for a time that he would become a priest and saw to it that he became an altar boy at seven, that he attended the parish school and pumped the organ for Mass. Smith was a practicing Catholic all his life. As governor, Miss Perkins remembered, he "could often be heard at his early morning shaving concerts, intoning in his deep baritone the responses of the Mass and even the priest's part." His Catholicism was an integral part of him—indeed it was the central fact about him in the minds of millions of American voters—but he himself took it pretty much for granted: he knew nothing of theology, understood little Latin, had never thought very much about the separation of church and state.

At fourteen, Franklin was a new boy at Groton, his chief concern that he escape the hazing of the older boys. Al's father died when he was fourteen, forcing him to leave the eighth grade and become the financial mainstay of his grieving family, selling newspapers while holding down a second job as a "truck-chaser," racing up and down the waterfront to tell teamsters where to go next for three dollars a week. He graduated from that to working in a pump house, and to a job as "assistant book-keeper," which required him to rise before dawn and trundle barrels of iced fish for twelve hours a day, six days a week, at the Fulton Fish Market. (In later years, he liked to say he had been educated at that institution and had an "FFM" to prove it.)

He did not allow his new and sobering responsibilities to dampen his high spirits. In a neighborhood where boys often relied on their fists to get their way, Al always preferred to employ words. "He could talk faster and louder than any boy in the ward," an old friend remembered, "and as he grew up his voice increased in volume and his dexterity with words also. . . . A boy or man can't fight and laugh at the same time, and Al Smith could make anybody laugh." He had won school-boy prizes for oratory, loved to perform monologues—"Cohen on the Telephone" and "The Face on the Barroom Floor" were special favor-ites—and particularly prized the fervid speechmaking of Bourke Cockran, pasting especially ripe examples of the Tammany congressman's prose into a little scrapbook and committing them to memory.[43]

"He was talking all the time, at parties, reciting or dancing. He was quite a boy at jigs, and *he* thought he could sing, too," an old friend remembered. She and some girlfriends once planned a picnic without him, and told him so. "Oh, you'll ask me," he said. "You won't be able to get along without the talent."

At nineteen, Al was hired to stand outside a newspaper office and bellow out round-by-round reports of Jim Corbett's victory over John L. Sullivan as they clattered in over the wires because his huge voice could easily reach the outermost edge of the big, noisy crowd. Soon afterwards, he began spending his evenings at the local Tammany headquarters—Tom Foley's saloon on the corner of Oliver and Water streets. Foley was a huge man, a one-time blacksmith and full-time Tammany ward boss who distributed pennies among the neighborhood children and political favors among their parents, and was always on the lookout for glib, ambitious young men to strengthen the organization. Smith began making election speeches, and at twenty-one was rewarded with a patronage post as an investigator for the courts that paid him $800 a year to chase all over the city serving summonses on reluctant jurors.

Smith enjoyed the prestige his first white-collar job brought him, but he did not yet think politics would be his career. He wanted to be an actor, and had often starred in amateur productions staged in the cellar of St. James, where he specialized in comedy and heroic roles but disliked playing the villain; the hissing of the audience made him uncomfortable. Al Smith always wanted to be loved.

His favorite part was as Congressman Bardwell Slote in a hoary comedy called *The Mighty Dollar*. Slote was a standard-issue comedy character, a plain-spoken American full of scorn for pomp and pretense whose candor was rewarded at the final curtain. As Slote, Smith got to rasp out his suspicion of aristocrats who claimed their ancestors had come over on the *Cauliflower*, and his disdain for "what they call society! I'd like to have a contract to supply society with all the powder and paint it uses. It would beat a government contract by a large

43. Smith almost wept in San Francisco when the old orator agreed to place his name in nomination. "I am about to achieve the joy of my life," Cockran assured him. "For as long as I can remember at national conventions I have been fanning the wind either against somebody or against something. At last I have an opportunity to be *for* somebody." *Source:* Richard O'Connor, *The First Hurrah*, page 125.

majority." The stock Briton who begins the play as Slote's enemy and becomes his friend assures him as he is about to go off with the girl he loves and the fortune his honesty has won him, that "if I can aid you to climb the political ladder you may rely upon my support, even to the presidential chair."

"And that's where I am going to land," Slote says, "by a large majority."

"One of the most remarkable conditions of a new country," the Englishman responds as the curtain falls and the audience begins to applaud, is "that the road is open to him, and a man may be my employee today, and my president in the future."

As Smith took his bows in the church basement, he and his audience, made up mostly of newcomers and their children, shared that article of American faith. But he was already spending his evenings as an extra in melodramas just to be near the Broadway stars he soon hoped to join, and actually won himself speaking parts in two Broadway melodramas, *Blossoms* and *The Confederate Spy*, and so might never have sought to test it for himself had he not fallen in love with an Irish girl from the Bronx named Catherine Dunn—known to him always as "Katie."

Her father was an Irish contractor who had literally moved up in the world—Katie had in fact been born in Smith's own Fourth Ward, and Al later liked to refer to his trips north to 170th Street to see her as journeys into "the wilderness"—and he was adamant that a would-be actor was not a proper match for his daughter. Al paid steady, stubborn court to Katie Dunn for five years, haunting her father's parlor to join her in duets of "Sweet Violets" and "After the Ball," before he finally agreed to give up what he called the "wig-paste profession" for the safer and more sedate world of politics.

Mr. Dunn finally gave his blessing and Al Smith and Katie Dunn were married in 1900. Franklin and Eleanor Roosevelt would tour Europe on their honeymoon five years later; the newlywed Smiths spent theirs at Bath Beach in Brooklyn. Like the Roosevelts, they would eventually have five children.[44]

For many members of Franklin Roosevelt's family—and especially for his mother—his decision to enter politics had been a step down. For Al Smith, the same choice represented a big step up. The most coveted

---

44. Challenged by a fellow Catholic to explain why he didn't have still more, Smith replied, "Don't blame me. Remember, for twelve years I have been a member of the Legislature and had to spend my winters in Albany." *Source:* Richard O'Connor, *The First Hurrah*, page 90.

positions in business and the professions were still by and large barred to Roman Catholics with no college education, and for an aggressive, articulate city youth like Smith, politics represented the fastest available route to the prominence and power he sought and which the unshakable encouragement of his mother had taught him was his due.

In 1903, Smith was elected to the New York State Assembly by a margin of almost five to one. He arrived in Albany, a skinny blue-eyed thirty year old, in March of 1904, and almost as soon as he had unpacked his bag, mailed his mother a postcard:

> Dear Mother: This is a picture of the Governor's residence. I'm going to work hard and stick to the ideals you taught me and some day—maybe, I'll occupy this house.

That move must then have seemed very far away. He brought with him a top hat and dinner jacket, courtesy of a group of friends who had not wished to have it said that their representative had gone to the state capital underdressed, but he found few opportunities to wear them. The old Protestant Albany families that would welcome Franklin and Eleanor Roosevelt so warmly when they arrived seven years later did not invite the Catholic newcomer from the Bowery into their parlors—not even after he was elected Majority Leader in 1911 and Speaker in 1912. He would later preside over weekly dinners of his own, and legislators from both sides of the aisle would compete for the honor of joining him for corned beef and cabbage washed down with schooners of beer, but he never forgot the snub. The stories he liked to tell about the relative opulence of Franklin Roosevelt's first home as a freshman state senator were frankly laced with envy, and when, upon being elected governor, he promptly received an invitation to dine from one prominent leader of capital society, he took considerable pleasure in turning it down. "I have been in Albany fifteen years now," he told an aide. "I have met all the members of that family socially a number of times. This is the first time they have invited me to their home. Governor Al Smith may be different from Assemblyman Al Smith to them—but not to me."

The new freshman's gravest initial disappointments were political, not social. "Don't speak until you have something to say," Tom Foley had told him. "Men who talk just for the pleasure of it don't get very far." Silence was never Al Smith's natural state, but he needed little urging to keep quiet: "I can tell a haddock from a hake by the look in its eye," he complained to an old friend, but he was utterly baffled by the steady flow of legislation across his desk—"in two hundred years I could not tell these things from a bale of hay."

The job seemed beyond him. But during his second session, he had as his Albany roommate state Senator Robert F. Wagner, a German immigrant from a Manhattan neighborhood similar to Smith's, who had managed to put himself through law school at night. Together, they sat up night after night poring over pending legislation, while Wagner helped Smith see how to cut through the thickets of legal language. Al Smith would eventually exhibit a mastery of the details of lawmaking unmatched by any other New York politician in his lifetime; he was not only self-made but self-taught.

And he learned fast. He was first known as "the Assemblyman from the Bowery," consciously playing up his brassy big-city ways and loyally serving the interests of the Quiet Boss, Charles Murphy, who came up from New York to see him and set policy every week. But he also soon won a reputation even among the opposition for industry and bluff integrity. "If it comes to the point where I've got to break my word to the fellows I'm working with here each day," he said. "I'm willing to quit this legislative game."

He was a realist, scornful of reformers as a rule, and usually uninterested in any legislation for which the votes could not be mustered, but also fair-minded and sensitive to shifts in public opinion. He opposed the direct primary system, championed by Franklin and other enemies of the machine, for example. "This sort of thing is only the squawk of the fellows on the outs," he rasped, "the squawk which, like Niagara, runs on forever." But when pressure for it proved irresistible, he was perfectly frank about having changed his mind—"Within four hours I've become an advocate of direct primaries," he told his colleagues. "Maybe I did it because I had to. But never mind, I did so."

The Triangle Fire and Smith's vice-chairmanship of the Factory Commission formed in its aftermath (Robert Wagner was the chairman) took him all over the state for the first time—he had never been in a woods before he went to Albany, had never even seen a farm until he took the train upriver to the capital—and it brought him into daily contact with an extraordinary generation of activist social workers whom he would call upon for help throughout his years in government—among them Frances Perkins, Henry Moskowitz, and Moskowitz's future wife, Belle Lindner. Miss Perkins made sure that Smith and Wagner saw with their own eyes the inadequate fire escapes, the unshielded machines that maimed and scalped workers, the six year olds snipping beans in an upstate cannery at dawn.[45]

Boss Murphy and Al Smith now began to see both the good politics and the simple justice of reform. The result was a flurry of unprecedented legislation aimed at protecting the individual against the hazards of an industrial society, much of it shouted through the legislature at record speed by the carnival barker's voice of the Speaker. "At times bills on the calendar are rushed through at the rate of eight a minute," the *New York Times* reported, and Smith could be withering in debate. When conservative clergymen descended upon the capital to request that canneries be exempted from the fifty-four-hour bill, he took the floor: "I have read carefully the Commandment, 'Remember the Sabbath Day, to keep it holy,'" he said, "but I am unable to find in it any language that says, 'except in the canneries.'" Canneries were included in the bill.

Smith was the dominant force at the Constitutional Convention of 1915, too, more than holding his own among the eminent Republican lawyers who constituted the majority of the delegates. "Of all the men . . . ," Elihu Root admitted afterwards, "Alfred E. Smith was the best informed on the business of the State," and even Sara's old friend Ogden Reid, publisher of the devoutly Republican *New York Tribune*, thought Smith "a true leader, a genuine compeller of men, a man of wit and force and an instinctive grasp on legislative practice. . . ."

So far as it was possible for a successful politician, Smith refused to pose as something he was not. "I never read a book for entertainment in my entire life," he once claimed, and he tried never to appear more learned than he really was. At the height of the Red Scare in 1919, an overly erudite aide, Judge Joseph K. Proskauer, composed for Governor Smith a message with which he was to veto three bills that would have sharply curtailed civil liberties, larding it with quotations from past champions of free speech—Thomas Jefferson, Benjamin Franklin, Alexis de Toqueville. Smith asked for a rewrite: "Tell Pros-

---

45. Smith was not surprised—though Franklin may have been—when the investigators revealed that "the vilest and most uncivilized conditions of labor in the state" had been uncovered in a factory at Auburn, owned by the anti-Tammany prison reformer Thomas Mott Osborne, Roosevelt's ally. *Source:* Richard O'Connor, *The First Hurrah*, page 71.

kauer," he said. "I know who Jefferson is, and I may be supposed to know who Ben Franklin is; but if I quote Tocqueville everybody will say 'Al Smith never wrote that. He never heard of the man.' "[46]

"You know," Franklin once said to Frances Perkins in the friendly but patronizing tone he often used when discussing the governor with men or women who were Smith's allies as well as his, "Murphy always made it a point to keep Al Smith honest. He never let Al get smeared or tangled up with any of the dirty deals. He took great pains that they should never involve Al in any of these things because he thought he was a capable fellow and could go far."

Smith's detractors exaggerated his liking for flashy suits, implied that his opposition to Prohibition was evidence of alcoholism, hinted that he led a disreputable private life and must be on the take.[47]

"Nothing embarrasses me," Smith said. He was no prude: he liked a bawdy story and a stiff drink, but he was also a devoted family man. Frances Perkins sometimes walked home to the Governor's Mansion with him in the evenings. There, they inevitably found his wife waiting for him in the pink parlor, surrounded by "rather beefy furniture" left over from Grover Cleveland's time, but looking "pretty as a pin and prettily dressed."

"Well, Katie," the governor said, "got something to eat? Let's have some beer."

Trays of sandwiches and cold beer appeared. Smith put his arm around his wife. "What about a little music, Katie?"

She sat down at the piano and began to play one of the old songs

46. Smith was never quite so simple and straightforward as he seemed. Frances Perkins once looked into his origins and found that while he always claimed to be Irish—and was so considered by the overwhelmingly Irish organization that backed his rise—he was in fact a blend of Italian, German, English, and Irish strains. *Source:* Matthew and Hannah Josephson, *Al Smith: Hero of the Cities,* pages 12–19.

47. Smith's probity was never plausibly challenged during his lifetime. In 1928, however, Thomas L. Chadbourne, a prominent New York attorney and investor in Manhattan private subway and elevated railway companies, alleged in his autobiography that he had given Smith more than $400,000 in cash and stock options over the years in an effort to have the subway fare raised above a nickel. The fare was never raised, Chadbourne wrote bitterly, because of Smith's cowardice, dishonesty, and "Irish Tammany sense of gratitude." "Smith was determined not to be frank with me," he added. "I suppose he thought that if he were he would lose his meal ticket because that is just what I had been to him for years."

The autobiography was not published until 1985 and when it was, the chapter covering Chadbourne's relationship with Smith was deleted, on the advice of Chadbourne's old firm, Chadbourne, Park, Whiteside & Wolff. The *New York Times* revealed the missing material in a front-page story on May 22, 1985.

they'd sung together during their courtship. Al leaned on the piano and sang along.

When the time finally came in San Francisco to nominate Smith, Bourke Cockran's remarks were characteristically ardent: "We offer him to you as President of the United States. We will accept no compromise in the convention. If you take him we will give you the state of New York and if you reject him, we will take him back and run him for Governor!"

But, according to Mencken, Cockran's fervor had little to do with the extraordinary demonstration that followed. After one unwise chorus of "Tammany"—which, Mencken said, "suggested only Romish villainies to the delegates from the Bible country"—the band leader swung into "The Sidewalks of New York."

> . . . [A] murmur of appreciation ran through the hall, and by the time the band got to the second stanza someone in a gallery began to sing. The effect of that singing, as the old-time reporters used to say, was electrical. In ten seconds a hundred other voices had joined in, and in a minute the whole audience was bellowing the familiar words. The band . . . switched to "Little Annie Rooney," and then to "The Bowery," and then to "A Bicycle Built for Two," and then to "Maggie Murphy's Home," and so on down the ancient line of waltz-songs. . . . The scene was unprecedented in national conventions and has never been repeated since, though many another band leader has tried to put it on: what he lacked was always the aid of Jim Rolph's Bourbon. The first delegate who grabbed a lady politico and began to prance up the aisle was full of it, and so, for all I know, was the lady politico. They were joined quickly by others, and in ten minutes Al was forgotten, the convention was in recess, and a ball was in progress. . . . By the end of the first half hour the only persons who were not dancing were a few antisocial Hardshell Baptists from Mississippi and a one-legged war veteran from Ohio. For a while the chairman [Senator Joseph Robinson of Arkansas] made formal attempts to restore order, but after that he let it run, and run it did until the last hoofer was exhausted.

Franklin waltzed with his fellow New Yorkers, but with one eye on the stage, and when he saw the signal to come up and begin his seconding speech he was so eager to get there that he vaulted several rows of chairs rather than be slowed down by the dancing delegates. Tall and smiling, standing at a convention podium for the first time in his career, he was effusive in his praise for the governor, who was for him at best a wary, temporary ally:

The past half hour has shown that the Great Democracy of the state of New York is an integral part of the Democracy of the nation [*Applause*], and that is another reason why we from New York sent to this Convention the name of our beloved Governor. I love him as a friend; I look up to him as a man; I am with him as a Democrat, and we all know his record throughout the nation. . . . Yes, the Democracy of New York is united . . . and so, knowing that he has been a Governor in the open, we know, too, that this Convention is a Convention in the open. The nominee of *this* Convention will not be chosen at 2 A.M. in a hotel room! [*Applause*]. . . . In the Navy, we shoot fast and straight. Governor Smith, in that respect, is a Navy man [*Applause*]. . . .

The impression Franklin made on the delegates, Grenville Emmet reported to Langdon Marvin, "could not have been better." Frances Perkins thought he had made himself "one of the stars of the show." Once, she had been put off by his hauteur. Now, she was struck by his energy. Franklin seemed "better looking than he used to be, somehow. . . . more amiable . . . [he] mixed more with people . . . more slaps on the back with odds and ends of people." She much later discussed the change she'd seen with Franklin himself, and he attributed it in part to his having often lunched in Washington with members of the New York State Democratic Committee who wanted favorable treatment from the administration. He had found then, he said, that "They aren't mean, bitter creatures. They won't insist upon patronage, provided they think they're getting attention . . . a little attention, a little prestige, a little notice" were often all they needed.

"What you saw in San Francisco," Miss Perkins remembered, "was his being nice to all these people he'd taken out to lunch." He had "learned to be very nice to people. . . . I'm sure he didn't start out being attracted to people as people. I'm not sure he was, [even] at this time." But he had learned how to feign the genial enthusiasm required to build the bridges he needed to advance his career.

On the first seven ballots, Franklin voted with his delegation for Al Smith. The two-thirds rule virtually ensured a long, wearying series of ballots and it was feared that the supporters of McAdoo and Palmer might produce a deadlock at San Francisco.

If that happened, James Cox, the third-term governor of Ohio, was waiting in the wings. Colorless but shrewd, Cox was favored by Murphy and by other big-city bosses, because he was a moderate Wet untainted by any link with the unpopular administration and uncommitted on the controversial League. Like Harding, Cox was an Ohio newspaper publisher whose determinedly lackluster views seemed designed to alienate no one.

When Smith at last withdrew his name and Murphy ordered his men to switch to Cox on the eighth ballot, seventy New Yorkers dutifully followed suit. Franklin, Mayor Lunn, and eighteen others voted for McAdoo.

As the days and the ballots went by, each vote tallied in pencil by Franklin, Cox's total steadily rose while first Palmer's fell, and then McAdoo's. The governor's prewar record proved progressive enough to placate McAdoo's disappointed adherents, while Palmer's backers came to admire Cox's aggressive advocacy of Americanism once the war began—including his authorship of a statute that forbade the teaching of German in any public, private, or parochial elementary school for fear of undermining the loyalty of schoolchildren.

Finally, shortly after midnight on the morning of Monday, July 6, Cox won the nomination on the forty-fourth ballot, and the exhausted delegates adjourned till noon, when they planned to pick their vice-presidential nominee.

In the hectic bargaining that finally put his man over the top, Murphy had hinted that he would not oppose Franklin for any office he might want, senator or Vice President, provided Roosevelt and his allies refrained from challenging his last-minute efforts to swing the delegation to the Ohio governor. To make that promise a reality, Franklin's friends, including Judge Mack, Lathrop Brown, and Tom Lynch, fanned out through hotel lobbies and dining rooms, and stumped up and down the aisles, listing for any delegate who would listen the strengths young Roosevelt would bring to the ticket: He was an easterner and would therefore provide geographical balance; he could help ensure that the Democrats carried New York, without which the ticket was almost surely doomed; as a government official, he would please those Democrats still loyal to Wilson; above all, the famous name he bore would appeal to those progressive Republicans who had hoped this year to vote again for Theodore Roosevelt and had been sickened by the nomination of Warren Harding.

Meanwhile, Edmund H. Moore, the Ohioan who had managed Cox's fight on and off the floor, called his candidate to ask him whom he favored. It was dawn in Dayton, and the governor, still in his newspaper office and short on sleep, was understandably terse. "Naturally, I've been thinking about this a good deal," he said, "and my choice is young Roosevelt. His name is good, he's right geographically, and he's anti-Tammany. But, since we need a united front, go to see Charlie Murphy and say we won't nominate Roosevelt if he objects. He can suggest other names."

Moore did as he was told. "This is the first decent treatment I've ever received from a Presidential candidate," said Murphy, who had been kept at arm's length by the Wilson White House. "Thank you. This young Roosevelt is no good, but if you want him, go ahead and we'll vote for him."[48]

Judge Timothy T. Ansberry, another Cox intimate from Ohio who had also favored Franklin for the nomination, was given the job of putting his name before the convention.

At the last moment it occurred to him that his candidate might be too young: the Constitution required him to be at least thirty-five.

He found Roosevelt near the speaker's platform.

"How old are you?" he asked.

"Thirty-eight. Why do you want to know?"

"I'm going to nominate you."

"Do you think I ought to be around when you do?" Franklin asked.

"No," Ansberry said, "I'd leave the hall."

The judge made his way to the podium as Franklin hurried out a side entrance. "The young man whose name I am going to suggest," Ansberry said, "is but three years over the age of thirty-five prescribed by the Constitution . . . but he has crowded into that short period of time a very large experience as a public official. . . . His is a name to be conjured with in American politics . . . Franklin D. *Roosevelt!*"

Other delegates rose to second his nomination, including Al Smith, whose praise for the wealthy upstate Protestant who had seconded his own nomination for President a few days earlier was friendly but less than fulsome. Roosevelt was "a leader in local legislative reform," Smith said, "who, during the present administration, has held a position of great power and importance. . . ."

48. Murphy's motives for agreeing to Franklin's nomination have never been entirely clear. He may well have been grateful to Cox for his courtesy, as he said he was, but that wouldn't seem to have been enough to overcome his visceral dislike of the young man who had brashly challenged his leadership in 1911 and been a thorn in his side ever since. Perhaps, like the Republican bosses who urged young Theodore Roosevelt for the same office in 1900, he hoped the nomination would simply make him go away. If so, like them, he would be disappointed.

Other candidates withdrew. Just before the rules were suspended and Franklin was nominated by acclamation, Josephus Daniels made his way to the podium to attest to his continuing affection for his assistant:

> I wish to say that to me, and to five hundred thousand men in the American Navy, and to five million men in the Army, it is a matter of peculiar gratification that this Convention unanimously has chosen as a candidate for Vice President that clear-headed and able executive and patriotic citizen of New York, the Assistant Secretary of the Navy, Franklin D. Roosevelt. And I wish to add that his service during the great war . . . was chiefly executive only because, when the war began, and he wished to go to the front, I urged him that his highest duty was to help carry the millions of men across and to bring them back. . . .[49]

Admiral Rodman had been ashore all day. When he returned to his flagship after dark that evening, the agitated staff duty officer met him at the gangway. "Admiral," he said, "your cabin is occupied by *politicians*. Secretary Daniels brought a boat-load of them out here, including the Assistant Secretary of the Navy who was nominated today for the Vice Presidency. The Secretary invited them for dinner, and they are now in the midst of it. I doubt there is room for you."

"The nerve of the guy," Rodman muttered, straightening his shoulders and making his way toward his crowded quarters.

49. "Franklin's nomination . . . really didn't require much shoving . . . ," Grenville Emmet wrote to Langdon Marvin from San Francisco. "He had played a fine part all through the convention and when Cox was nominated . . . sublime availability geographically as well as from every standpoint was so apparent . . . he went through in quick time." *Source:* Frank Freidel, *Franklin D. Roosevelt: The Ordeal,* page 51.

CHAPTER

12

THE BRILLIANT CAMPAIGN

FRANKLIN came home to Hyde Park from San Francisco aboard the Knickerbocker Express on the afternoon of July 13. Townspeople had hung the little brick depot with bunting and strung naval flags and pennants from tree to tree across the Albany Post Road.

"Look at the navy flags," Franklin said as he got down and began shaking hands with old friends. "This is a real navy reception!"

A parade of flag-draped automobiles took him to Springwood. He stopped his car at the big stone gateposts his father had put up just after the Civil War, so that a happy crowd of several hundred townspeople waving miniature flags could escort him on foot up the tree-lined drive, accompanied by the rattle and blare of the successor to the same Democratic band that had hailed Grover Cleveland's election victories here in the time of Mr. James.

Eleanor, travelling alone all day and all night from Campobello, failed to reach Springwood in time for Franklin's homecoming. "This certainly is a world of surprise, isn't it?" she'd told Sara when word reached her of her husband's nomination. " . . . [H]e must be thriving on honors and excitement. Anyway, it is nice to know he's well." But his mother, wearing a high-necked summer dress and holding a black fan, stood waiting for him on the broad portico he and she had planned together. He smiled and waved when he saw her, then ran lightly up the steps and into her arms and they embraced while a newsreel cameraman took pictures. Perhaps embarrassed to be seen displaying such public affection but too overcome to remain aloof, Sara hurried her son inside to tell him how proud she was. "I kept wishing for your Father," she told Franklin a few days later, "but I believe he knew and was with us. . . ."

Scores of congratulatory telegrams and letters from friends and family members, classmates, and political acquaintances in both parties greeted Franklin on his return to the East Coast.

"The fact that I do not belong to your political tribe does not deter me from offering my personal congratulations to an old friend," wrote Herbert Hoover. "I am glad to see you in the game in such a prominent place, and, although I will not be charged with traitorship by wishing you success, I nevertheless consider it a contribution to the good of the country that you have been nominated, and it will bring the merit of a great public servant to the front. If elected, you will do the job properly."

The President of Franklin's own party had been less enthusiastic. The news of Cox's nomination had been greeted in the White House by a stream of presidential curses so violent that they had alarmed Wilson's valet. Tradition called for the incumbent to send expansive telegrams of support to his party's nominees, expressing satisfaction at the delegates' collective wisdom and confidence in the victory to come. Instead, he sent a single formal line to each man. To Cox, whose candidacy he had thought ludicrous and whose position on the League was still unclear, he said only: PLEASE ACCEPT MY HEARTY CONGRATULATIONS AND CORDIAL BEST WISHES.

Franklin's nomination may have pleased him even less: his congratulations to the vice-presidential nominee were merely WARM, his wishes only GOOD.

In the interest of greater Democratic unity, Franklin and Governor Cox called upon Wilson at the White House on Sunday, July 18. "Young Roosevelt acted as a sort of master of ceremonies," a Republican newspaperman reported to Henry Cabot Lodge, "ushering Cox into Tumulty's room where the correspondents had assembled; the candidate for vice president was bright and boyish and a little silly in his exuberance—the thing has gone to his head."[1]

1. Lodge agreed. Franklin had "talked well in the early years of the administration," he said. "He is a pleasant fellow whom I personally liked, but now that the administration is coming to a close we can see that when it came to the point, he did exactly what Daniels wished him to do. He is a well-meaning, nice young fellow, but light. . . . His head [is] evidently turned and

Roosevelt and Cox had to wait fifteen minutes while the paralyzed President was wheeled out to the portico. "He is a very sick man," the governor whispered to Franklin as they came in sight of the motionless figure in the rolling chair, and Mrs. Wilson remembered all her life the expression of shocked sympathy on Roosevelt's face as he drew closer to the leader whom he had not seen for ten months. Wilson sat stiffly, his frozen left side and useless arm hidden beneath a shawl on this warm summer afternoon, his long jaw slack, eyes on the ground. Not until Cox stood above him did he look up and try to speak. "Thank you for coming," he said. "I'm very glad you came."

Franklin remembered that there were tears in Cox's eyes. "Mr. President," the governor said. "I have always admired the fight you made for the League."

"Mr. Cox," Wilson said, "that fight can still be won."

"Mr. President, we are going to be a million per cent with you, and your Administration," the governor promised, "and that means the League of Nations."

"I am very grateful," Wilson managed to say. "I am very grateful."

"I wish that every American could have been a silent witness to the meeeting between these two great men," Franklin told reporters. "Their splendid accord and their high purpose are an inspiration."

Cox sat down at Tumulty's desk and drafted a statement making the League the paramount issue of his campaign. Wilson's promise to the world, he said, "I shall, if elected, endeavor with all my strength to keep."[2]

On July 25, Franklin took the wheel of the destroyer *Hatfield* and steered her smoothly through the tricky Lubec narrows and into Passamaquoddy Bay, assuring her nervous captain that he had taken destroyers through the same waters four times before with no damage, then brought her safely to anchor off Welshpool. He had in fact been

---

the effect upon a not very strong man is obvious." Source: Kenneth S. Davis, *FDR: The Beckoning of Destiny*, page 616n.

2. If the candidates had hoped by this gesture to persuade the President to issue enthusiastic statements on their behalf, they were to be disappointed. Shortly after their visit, Wilson confided to Josephus Daniels that he was still "resentful, deeply resentful" toward Roosevelt; he refused repeated entreaties to speak out for the ticket, and when he did finally issue a statement on October 27—reading his remarks in a weak voice to a group of pro-League Republicans standing awkwardly around his wheelchair—he urged voters to "test the candidacy of every candidate for whatever office by this question: Shall we or shall we not redeem the great moral obligations of the United States?" Neither Cox nor Roosevelt was mentioned by name. *Source:* Gene Smith, *When the Cheering Stopped*, page 168.

sailing to and from Campobello aboard warships for over seven years without incident, taking pleasure in the impression his dramatic comings and goings made upon the people of Campobello and Eastport. But now, because he was a candidate for national office, his voyage attracted a new, more critical kind of attention.

What right had Roosevelt to use a "fighting ship belonging to the American Navy and to the AMERICAN PEOPLE . . . for commuting purposes?" Hearst's *New York Journal* demanded. "What right has a man to burn up coal enough to heat the homes of fifty families all winter to carry his 165 pounds . . . to a summer resting place? Is a first-class ticket . . . not good enough?"[3]

From now on, nearly everything Franklin did would be subject to similar scrutiny; every member of his family would have to learn to accommodate the intense curiosity of outsiders.

For Eleanor, it was agony. "My grandmother," she remembered, "had taught me that a woman's place was not in the public eye, and that had clung to me all through the Washington years. It never occurred to me to do more than answer through my secretary any questions that the reporters asked about social events. I gave as little information as possible, feeling that was the only right attitude toward newspaper people where a woman and her home were concerned."

Beyond her own Washington circle, Eleanor was still largely unknown, and as soon as Franklin was nominated, Louis Howe wired to ask for a recent photograph of her for the newspapers. Always embarrassed by her looks and distrustful of all cameras, she had answered: ARE NO PICTURES OF ME. The result was that a photograph of someone else, cropped from a picture that showed the Roosevelts and others attending a Washington Senators game together, was widely circulated as a portrait of her. And when a Washington newspaper published comparative profiles of the candidates' wives, it said, "Mrs. Roosevelt is essentially a home woman [who] seems especially to dislike the official limelight," and quoted an anonymous and patronizing "friend" who volunteered that "She is too much a Roosevelt to be anybody's prize beauty, but she's pure gold!"

Eleanor herself gave just one tentative interview, to a reporter from the Poughkeepsie *Eagle News*:

3. Had the newspapermen been still more alert they might also have asked what had entitled him to halt the warship at Boston while sailors brought aboard a 21-foot sloop, the *Vireo*, and lashed her to the deck so that he could present her to his children.

"Yes I am interested in politics, intensely so, but in that I think I am no different from the majority of women, only that, of course, I have followed my husband's career with an interest that is intense because it is personal. But I have never," and she emphasized her words, "campaigned for him. I haven't been active in politics in any way, and so you see there isn't much of a story to be found in me.

"My politics? Oh, yes, I am a Democrat, but," and here she paused, "I was brought up a staunch Republican,—and turned Democrat. I believe that the best interests of the country are in the hands of the Democratic party, for I believe they are the most progressive. The Republicans are,—well, they are more conservative and we can't be too conservative and accomplish things."

She would, of course, accompany her husband on his campaign tour, she continued, "if Mr. Roosevelt wants me to," but she much preferred to remain at Campobello with the children.

Shortly after Franklin landed on the island, a newsreel cameraman arrived with orders to get informal footage of the candidate and his family. He set up his equipment on the lawn of the Roosevelt cottage and asked Eleanor to pose. The minute or two of film made that day bear vivid witness to her self-consciousness. Frozen in flickering close-up, she tentatively picks a flower at the cameraman's prompting. Asked to smile, she seems fearful and close to physical pain, squinting into the sun, her prominent, uneven teeth cruelly exposed. Then she leads her tumbling brood down the cottage stairs and toward the camera. The governess who has dressed and combed her charges so that her mother can be seen in public with them stands half-hidden in the shrubbery. Anna's big German Shepherd, Chief, leads the way, barking silently and wagging his tail so furiously that John, the youngest child, clings to Eleanor's hand in fright. The older boys are in knickers, scowling and seemingly resentful, outshone—as is Eleanor herself—by Anna, now fourteen and nearly as tall as her mother, with golden hair that streams to her shoulders.[4]

4. Sara, too, had to learn to deal with the newspapers her upbringing had taught her always to avoid. Shortly after her son's nomination, the *New York Evening Post* sent a young reporter up to see her at Springwood. She gently refused to say anything about herself or her son, other than that he was devoted to his home at Hyde Park. The newspaperman was impressed, anyway: "There is a stark and undeniable atmosphere of noncompromise about this house and its lady ... there is no necessity ever to speak of what is one's belief [in such surroundings; it is so certain and so sure."

Sara would be careful throughout her son's career to maintain a polite but suitably distant relationship with the newspapers. But once, in 1932, it occurred to Louis Howe that if she could

By contrast, the candidate himself is a natural performer before the camera, smiling and self-confident whether sitting in a wicker chair on the lawn in his striped summer jacket, puffing a pipe, or standing on the porch pumping the hand of the feathered chief of the local Passamaquoddy tribe. As he sits in a dory offshore, pretending to read the pile of mail in his lap, the wind catches one page and sends it flying above his head; without seeming even to lift his eyes he reaches up and plucks it from the air.

Among the hundreds of letters he actually read and answered that week was one from an old Groton friend, Ellery Sedgwick, now the editor of the *Atlantic Monthly*. The former president of Harvard, Charles W. Eliot—Sedgwick said—might be persuaded to come out in print for Cox, but was worried by the fact that the governor had been married twice. Could Franklin reassure him on that score?

He did his best:

> You undoubtedly know that there has been divorce trouble in the Harding family also. Mrs. Harding was divorced by her first husband, and almost immediately afterwards married Mr. Harding.[5] I hate, of course,

---

be persuaded to provide enough motherly anecdotes for a series of magazine articles about her son's boyhood, it might help win the woman's vote. Two young women working in the Democratic headquarters were assigned the task of interviewing her, Gabrielle Forbush and the actress Isabel Leighton.

The two campaign workers garnered enough stories for the first two of three articles, to be serialized in *Good Housekeeping*. Sara had never seen *Good Housekeeping* before, or so she said, and when shown a copy said only that "It seems to have a great many advertisements."

The magazine's editor was delighted and chose to rush the first installment into print even before the final one was written, trumpeting its publication on the sides of delivery trucks in foot-high letters: MY BOY FRANKLIN BY SARA DELANO ROOSEVELT.

Sara was appalled: "My name is going all over town on *trucks,*" she said, and she was further horrified to read that her collaborators had included in their article the fact that she had been given too much chloroform at her son's birth, the sort of intimate detail she would never have wished known outside the family. When the two young women came to interview her again, she was polite as always, but explained that "she was sorry, she couldn't remember anymore."

Desperate, and with a deadline approaching fast, the two interviewers telephoned FDR at the Governor's Mansion in Albany. "Mama is like that!," he said, laughing, and invited Miss Leighton up to sit with him while he spun out enough stories about himself as a young man to fill out the series (and the final third of the saccharine little book that was eventually made from them, *My Boy Franklin*), all admiring and all told as if his mother had volunteered them herself.

Toward the end of her life, when an overly solicitous member of the President's staff said he'd be happy to shield her from the press, Sara replied, "Young man, I talked to newspapermen before you were born." *Sources:* Transcript of William Stickle's 1967 interview with Gabrielle Forbush, FDRL; Doris Faber, *The Mothers of American Presidents,* page 78.

5. In fact, nearly five years passed between Florence Kling's divorce from Henry DeWolfe in September 1886 and her marriage to twenty-five-year-old Warren Harding on July 9, 1891.

More germane perhaps was the question of Harding's two mistresses. The first, married to the proprietor of a Marion dry goods store, was sent on a round-the-world tour with her husband

to have this sort of thing enter into the campaign at all, but if the Cox divorce is made a factor by the opposition, you may be sure that the Harding divorce will be brought out also. . . . [Dr. Eliot] need not be in the least worried about the family record of Governor Cox. I . . . would not want my name used in any way, . . . [but his] first wife was a really impossible sort of person. . . .

On August 6, Franklin was in Washington to take formal leave of the Navy Department. Two thousand employees turned out to say good-bye. Daniels awarded Franklin a silver loving cup, Mrs. Daniels sent him a big bouquet of red, white, and blue flowers, the president of the Metal Trades Council at the Washington Navy Yard presented him with a teakwood gavel fashioned from the old rail of the presidential yacht *Mayflower* in gratitude for his cordiality toward labor. Roosevelt stood on a flag-draped table to thank the crowd. "No matter what happens on November second," he said, "my heart will always be with the Navy. If things go all right on that date, I feel quite certain that the capital is going to hear a whole lot more of the Navy than it has ever heard before." Then a Navy band saw him off at Union Depot.

He left behind a farewell letter to Daniels in longhand:

MY DEAR CHIEF,

This is not goodbye—that will always be impossible after these years of close association—and no words I write will make you know better than you know now how much our association has meant. All my life I shall look back,—not only on the *work* of the place—but mostly on the wonderful way in which you and I have gone through these nearly eight years *together.* You have taught me so wisely and kept my feet on the ground when I was about to sky-rocket—and in it all there has never been a real dispute or antagonism or distrust.

Hence, in part at least, I will share in the reward which you *will* get true credit for in history. I am very proud—but more than that I am very *happy* to have been of help.

We will I know keep up this association in the years to come—and please let me keep on coming to you to get your fine inspiration of real idealism and right living and good Americanism.

during the campaign and paid $20,000 plus a monthly sum thereafter throughout Harding's presidency under an arrangement negotiated by Albert Lasker, his campaign's publicity director. His second, far younger mistress, Nan Britton, reaped no such benefits but after the President's death published a book about their affair to recoup her losses and provide for his illegitimate daughter. *Source:* Francis Russell, *The Shadow of Blooming Grove,* pages 81–83, 401–403.

So *au revoir* for a little while. You have always the
Affectionate regards of
FRANKLIN D. ROOSEVELT[6]

The Secretary wrote Franklin an affectionate reply for which Eleanor and Sara both thanked him: "My thought and feeling has been that of an older brother," it said in part, and "I shall share in the happiness that [comes] to you in your beautiful home life and we will indeed be brothers in all things that make for the good of our country."

That evening he added a few more personal lines to his journal: "[Roosevelt] left in the afternoon but before leaving wrote me a letter most friendly or almost loving which made me glad I had never acted upon my impulse when he seemed to take sides with my critics."

Daniels, whose fondness for his assistant seems to have grown rather than diminished with time, did gently point out to an interviewer toward the end of his long life that he thought some Roosevelt biographers had been a bit unfair in portraying him as "a sort of slow fellow." Newton D. Baker, he remembered, had taken him aside during the 1932 presidential race and said, "Joe, I've been reading these campaign biographies of Roosevelt. Did *you* ever do anything [at the Navy Department]? I wouldn't stand for that."

"I never knew a campaign biographer who didn't claim everything for his candidate," Daniels told Baker, and pointed out that unlike Franklin, *he* had never been running for President; if he had been, and a campaign biographer had gone to work, "FDR would probably be only barely mentioned."[7]

---

6. Many years later, Eleanor shrewdly summarized relations between Daniels and her husband:

> At first, [Franklin] was quite contemptuous of Mr. Daniels. Mr. Daniels was a provincial country editor and wore funny clothes and knew nothing about the Navy. Franklin knew a great deal about the Navy, but nothing whatsoever about Congress . . . the Navy all loved him and probably would have fooled him; because the Navy and all the services are a close group. There is more politics within them than you can realize if you have [never] lived close to it, and they usually manage their civilian heads and their civilian heads never know it. Mr. Daniels was managed to a certain extent, but he had a shrewd country editor type of mind and he carefully found out what was going on. . . . Franklin at first knew all these things and saw all these things from the point of view of the Navy . . . the Navy is always ready to get everything it can. Every service wants that. They played up to Franklin very much and they would even bring him certain requisitions and papers to hold until the Secretary went away, so that Franklin would be sure to sign them. I think the Secretary always knew. He was a very wise man. . . .

Source: Transcript of interview with Louis Eisner, FDRL.

7. Franklin kept his promise that he would continue to call upon Daniels, appointing him at seventy his Ambassador to Mexico in 1933.

Franklin, Eleanor, Anna, and James travelled to Dayton for Governor Cox's formal notification ceremony on August 8. Cox was cocky but short, with pince-nez and a receding chin, and as the candidates marched together through the streets to the Fair Grounds, waving their straw hats, Franklin towered above him. But despite appearances, Cox was very much in charge.

Franklin had at least officially been a subordinate at the Navy Department for almost eight years, and nearly every day during that time he had chafed at having to take orders from another. He knew the vice presidency had historically been an empty office, but thought he might be able to change it: If he and Cox were elected, he assured one newspaperman, "the old idea about the Vice Presidency is going to be knocked into a cocked hat. . . . There is plenty of opportunity in that position for the use of brains and energy, and . . . four years from now, [it] is going to be a highly respected and live-wire office."

Franklin urged Cox to announce that *his* Vice President would be allowed to sit in on Cabinet meetings. Not a chance, the governor said; if he did so, the Senate over which he would have to preside would think Franklin a White House "snoop."

Roosevelt hid his disappointment, and the two men promised a fighting campaign. Together, Franklin said, "We will drag the enemy off the front porch."

Franklin's own notification ceremony took place at Springwood at noon the next day. Some five thousand people sat and stood beneath the old oaks, including Daniels, William McAdoo, and Al Smith.

Sara sat next to her son, gazing intently up at him as he spoke. Eleanor and the two oldest children sat off to his right in the bright summer sun.

"Two great problems will confront the next administration," he said, "our relations with the world and the pressing need of organized progress at home." The world was already too interdependent for America ever to return to isolation; "it was impossible to be in this world and not of it." On the domestic front, there "is no reason why

---

Daniels outlived his far younger assistant by almost three years, and when he accompanied Roosevelt's body home to Springwood in the spring of 1945 was "the most sincere mourner" aboard the funeral train, according to the veteran newspaperman Frank Kluckhorn. He "invited me into his compartment and then burst into tears in talking about 'Franklin' and what a 'fine boy' he had been. The tears streamed down his face. . . ." *Source:* Joseph L. Morrison, *Josephus Daniels: The Small-d Democrat,* page 245.

the effectiveness of the National Government should not at least approximate that of well-conducted private business. . . ."

> Some people have been saying of late: "We are tired of progress, we want to go back to where we were before; to go about our business; to restore 'normal' conditions." They are wrong. This is not the wish of America. We can never go back. The "good old days" are gone past forever; we have no regrets. For our eyes are trained ahead—forward to better new days. In this faith I am strengthened by the firm belief that the women of this nation, now about to receive the National Franchise, will throw their weight into the scale of progress and will be unbound by partisan prejudices and a too-narrow outlook. . . . We cannot anchor our ship of state in this world tempest, nor can we return to the placid harbor of long years ago. We must go forward or flounder. . . .

An airplane flew low over the crowd, and the earnest candidate paused before continuing:

> America's opportunity is at hand. We can lead the world by a great example. . . . The Democratic program offers a larger life for our country, a richer destiny for our people. It is a plan of hope. . . . Our opposition is to the things which once existed, in order that they may never return. We oppose money in politics, we oppose the private control of national finances, we oppose the treatment of human beings as commodities, we oppose the saloon-bossed city, we oppose starvation wages, we oppose rule by groups or cliques. In the same way we oppose a mere period of coma in our national life. . . .

Sara offered lemonade and cake to everyone on the lawn, and had expected to serve a full-scale lunch inside to as many as two hundred especially invited friends and dignitaries. Instead, some five hundred hungry Democrats trooped into her house, where, as Eleanor wrote, "for so many years only family and friends were received." Somehow, she managed to feed them all and, she later told a friend, "after she thought everyone had left, she found lunching in her dining-room and pleased as Punch, a little tailor from Poughkeepsie with his fat, good-natured wife. She greeted them with the same graciousness that she might have bestowed on any of the invited guests."[8]

---

8. Moses Smith, the Roosevelts' long-time tenant, was among the local people who were received inside Springwood for the first time that day. "I were invited," Smith remembered proudly many years later, ". . . to attend the notification . . . which ceremony was held at the big house in the library, and we passed in a single file by the dignitaries and [I am] very mindful of Mr. Roosevelt presenting me to Senator Joseph T. Robinson of Arkansas, the Chairman of this Nominating Notification Committee. He introduced me in this manner: 'Moses, I want you

After everyone had gone home at last, she and her gardener went over the grounds to see what could be done to restore the ruined lawns.

Among the family members attending the celebration was Sara's silver-bearded older brother, Warren Delano III, who lived at Steen Valetje, his splendid mansion at Barrytown, less than half an hour's drive up the river. He was fond of his nephew and sent his "heartiest congratulations" to him upon the widespread approval his nomination had won even among Republicans. "It is a most unusual 'ovation,'" he said, "and something for you, your children and all your devoted friends to prize most highly and for all time!" But he had privately been disappointed when Franklin failed to enter the coal business to which he had gone to some trouble to introduce him in 1907, and was frankly appalled by his politics. His own adherence to the Republican principles of the father whose memory he revered made him profoundly uneasy at any Democratic ceremony, even one honoring a member of the family, and he slipped away as soon as he decently could.

Like his father before him, Warren was an adventurous businessman: he managed to lose three large fortunes during his career. Like him, too, he took seriously his duties as what his younger brother, Fred, called "the natural head of the family." He presided over Thanksgivings in the family homestead at Fairhaven, doled out funds from his parents' wills as their executor, expected his siblings to consult him about decisions both major and minor, and blanketed the walls of his home and New York office with photographs of friends and family members.

Among his many hobbies was the breeding of fine horses—his belief that the draft horse would never be supplanted by the automobile was unshakable and he was said to have imported the first Norwegian duns into the United States—and in September of 1920 he was in charge of all the equine events at the Dutchess County Fair.

At home on the afternoon of the 9th, he decided to drive Belle, an elegant and untried young horse, to the Barrytown depot to pick up a trunk for one of the many house guests planning to spend the week of the Fair with him. She was a high-strung animal, and he hoped to be there and back before a passing train could startle her.

---

to meet Joe Robinson,' which I always considered as one of his very friendly gestures toward his neighbors." *Source:* George Palmer interview with Moses Smith, National Park Service.

She trotted to the depot without incident but it took longer than he had planned to see that the trunk was secured to the buggy, and as the men worked, an approaching express suddenly sounded its whistle south of the station. The horse began to plunge. Warren grabbed the reins, swung up onto the driver's seat, and managed to get her under control again just as the engineer gave a second loud blast on the whistle, much closer than before. This time, the terrified horse lunged forward, careening around the side of the station and onto the tracks directly in front of the onrushing train.

The impact tore the horse to pieces. The locomotive carried the buggy 150 feet before it could come to a stop. Warren was found still sitting on its seat, the only sign of the accident a small abrasion on his forehead. He had died instantly of a broken neck. Passers-by carried him into the little brick depot and laid him on a bench. Mrs. Elizabeth Chapman, a neighbor and old friend of the family who happened to be nearby, planted herself in front of the window to block the view of gawkers until men from Steen Valetje could be summoned to carry him home.

Word of the accident spread along the river. At dusk that evening, Sara saw her neighbors Colonel and Mrs. Archibald Rogers hurrying toward her across the lawn. The grim set of their faces gave them away. "My beloved brother Warren was taken from us suddenly," she wrote in her diary with an uncharacteristically shaky hand that evening, "thrown from his wagon at the station—God help us!"

Franklin, off campaigning in Maine when he got the news, was unable to attend the funeral. For some members of the Delano family, this may have eased a growing awkwardness. Sara would of course always be welcome among them. To the Delanos, family always mattered more than anything else. But her late husband's affiliation with the Democratic Party, which her father had believed the home only of drunkards, Southern traitors, and unruly and ungrateful immigrants, had always been a matter of some strain within the family, and her son's sudden prominence as a national Democratic candidate was now a source of considerable embarrassment. His early career as a Democrat in the state Senate had been tolerated—he had, after all, made it his first order of business to oppose Tammany—and they had admired his work at the Navy Department, but this new nomination, clear evidence of his willingness to abandon his battles with the big-city machine, was profoundly disturbing.

The Delanos—with the exception of Uncle Fred—were immovably Republican but their servants were not.[9] On the morning of Franklin's triumphal return to Hyde Park from San Francisco in August, Peter Mahon, who had been first groom, then coachman, and finally chauffeur at Algonac, had tricked out Mrs. Hitch's automobile with flags and bunting, sure that she would wish to drive down and greet her nephew in it. When his employer emerged from the house, she told him firmly to remove all the decorations before she got in: she would be there to welcome Franklin, of course, but she would not help advertise his campaign. To do so would imply a disloyalty to her father's party no Delano would wish to leave in the public mind.

To ensure that none of their neighbors misunderstood the family's position, George R. Bishop, an old friend of Warren's, wrote a letter to the Poughkeepsie *Eagle News*. In it, he recounted a conversation with Warren that took place not long before his fatal accident; Mr. Delano had said he planned to vote against his nephew and lamented the day that "my sister [Sara] broke away from the family traditions and stood on the other side."

No one regretted that breaking away more than Sara's widowed elder sister, Kassie Collier, who lived with her daughter Katherine at Tuxedo Park. His great-aunt was so regal, James Roosevelt remembered, that even Sara sometimes seemed intimidated by her. Eleanor yearned to look like her, and a young relative, leaving her bedroom when her great-aunt was ninety, found herself kissing the old lady's extended hand "because it seemed the thing to do." The sturdy conservatism that was her father's legacy had been intensified first by her late husband, Price Collier, and then confirmed by the immobile views of her friends and neighbors within the tall, barbed-wire fence that then enclosed America's wealthiest and most exclusive community.

Tuxedo had been created by the sportsman and tobacco magnate Pierre Lorillard IV in the mid-1880s as a comfortable summer sanctuary for those wealthy New Yorkers who wished to flee the vulgarity of the new generation of millionaires then elbowing its way toward the top of society in their city. At Lorillard's direction, Italian and Slavic immigrants—eighteen hundred of them, housed in a huddle of makeshift shacks placed well outside the fence—carved it out of the rocky Ramapo Hills in less than a year. The self-contained community included stables, stores, a police force, a trout hatchery, a splendid club-

9.This had greatly annoyed Sara's father, who had once threatened to fire any man on his place even suspected of having voted for Grover Cleveland.

house overlooking a lake (no one could then live in Tuxedo unless he or she were a member of the Tuxedo Park Association), and imposing mansions, called "cottages" by their owners, of which the smallest had five bedrooms and the largest included fourteen rooms for the servants alone.[10]

Emily Post, who grew up at Tuxedo, recalled that it "was the most formal place in the world. Nobody ever waved or hello-ed or hi-ed. . . . You bowed when you shook hands . . . and first names were considered very bad form. . . . There were only five men . . . who called me Emily—and never in formal Society."

The gulf between residents of the village and the community of servants and their families—many of whom still occupied the supposedly temporary shelters constructed to house the men who built the place—was rarely crossed. Herbert C. Pell, Lorillard's nephew and a frequent guest at the Price Collier dinner table as a boy, remembered his cousin, Mrs. William Kent, explaining why the son of the Tuxedo Association manager who collected rents and lived in the Park could never be invited to dinner despite his exquisite manners: she really could not have a man at dinner one day, she said, who might have been dancing with her housemaid the night before.

"The purpose of a man's life [at Tuxedo] was to get money . . .," Pell recalled. "At a dinner, the richest man sat at the hostess' right, the next richest at her left and so on. After dinner, the ladies left and we would drag our chairs up and listen to the richest man talk about money and how to make it . . . and . . . the iniquities of Theodore Roosevelt. That class hated TR and raved against him far more than they ever did against Franklin. By the time Franklin came along there was no less hostility, but there was less surprise."

The Depression would threaten Tuxedo's survival. Trust funds dissolved; investments failed; some cottages were boarded up, others sold fast at low prices to people who stood little chance of ever becoming members of the Association. Kassie did her complacent best to ignore what was happening all around her, and, despite politics, Sara continued to visit her and her niece at Tuxedo to the end of her life. Sometimes after a few days in her sister's company she would attempt delicately to mediate between Franklin and the critics among her

10. When William Waldorf Astor, one of Tuxedo's original settlers, abandoned America for England in 1890, he told a reporter that Tuxedo was the only "fit place for a gentleman to live" in the whole country. *Source:* Frank Kintrea, "Tuxedo Park," *American Heritage,* (August–September 1978), page 71.

friends and family members who struggled to moderate the violence of their denunciations of her son only out of respect for her.[11]

Grace Tully, FDR's secretary, recalled one exchange between mother and son.

"Franklin, darling," Sara asked, "why is everyone opposed to so much of your program? A number of people have told me that they don't think it will work."

"Mummy," the President answered, "I think I know who you have been talking with, and if I'm right, they are people who don't understand the first thing about government, never having served in it, nor have they the slightest conception of the great problems facing the nation. Their only worry is that they might find themselves having to get along with two automobiles instead of three, but they don't give a hoot for the man who not only can't afford a car but is unable to feed and clothe his family. These are the people I'm concerned about and if I succeed in raising their standard of living, I won't lose any sleep over some of our friends who are opposed to my Administration."

Warren Delano's eldest son, Lyman, inherited Steen Valetje. His love of luxury was considerable: the sole task of one of his men, a servant remembered, was to rise early each morning and rake the long curving driveway that circled around the vast clipped lawn "so that Mr. Delano's tires would crunch only on fresh gravel." And his Republicanism was, if anything, more unyielding than that of his father or his grandfather. Shortly after he moved in, he noticed a portrait of Thomas Jefferson included among those of other founding fathers on the ceiling of the library, and ordered it painted over; the founder of the Democratic Party would not be honored in any home in which Lyman Delano lived.

Relations between him and the New Deal President whose every policy he deplored were distinctly cool, but when one of his daughters

11. Kassie Collier continued to maintain correct if not cordial relations with Sara's son and daughter-in-law so long as FDR was alive, and she did attend his funeral—she owed that much to her late sister—but afterwards she refused categorically to grant interviews to any biographer seeking what she called "the aggrandizement of the Roosevelt family."

Her daughter, Katherine D. P. Collier St. George, ran for Congress as a Republican in 1947, basing her successful campaign in part on vociferous denunciations of her late cousin, Franklin. When she spoke to a women's meeting at Tuxedo, she was careful to observe the old social distinctions that she and her mother believed central to the village's existence: "Ladies of the Park," she began, smiling toward a small cluster of elegantly dressed women up front and then, nodding toward the rest of the crowd, "and women of the village." *Sources:* Rita Halle Kleeman Papers, FDRL; Frank Kintrea, "Tuxedo Park," *American Heritage* (August–September 1978), page 76.

was to be married in 1937, FDR was asked to attend. He was Aunt Sallie's son, after all, and had to be included.

Bronson Chanler, the seventeen-year-old grandson of Lewis Stuyvesant Chanler, the wealthy reformer whose seat in the New York legislature Franklin had hoped to inherit in 1910, attended the reception at Steen Valetje with his father. There were tents on the rolling, shady lawn that afternoon, he remembered, and clusters of men in formal clothes and women in summer gowns were scattered across the vast shady lawn, sipping punch and champagne.

There was no sign at first that FDR was present, other than that his open car was parked next to the north side of the huge house. Bronson's father, Lewis Stuyvesant Chanler, Jr. went to look for him; he wanted his son to have the experience of shaking the President's hand. The Chanlers found him virtually alone, his back to the festivities, sitting in a wicker chair on the terrace and gazing out at the slow-moving Hudson. Perhaps only at a Delano wedding would the presence of the President of the United States have been virtually ignored, but among Delanos, of course, he was merely a Roosevelt.

FDR greeted the elder Chanler a little too effusively as "Stuyvie"—a nickname to which Bronson's father had a special aversion—then asked the boy to sit down and chat with him. Many years later, Bronson no longer remembered just what they talked about but he had then been attending St. Paul's, and thought they might have joked about that school's ancient rivalry with Groton.

In any case, after a few minutes it was clear that FDR felt he had stayed long enough and signalled to the Secret Servicemen waiting a little distance away. Once Roosevelt was settled in the back seat, the four uniformed state policemen who made up his escort simultaneously kicked their motorcycles into action.

The sudden noise startled the guests still standing beneath the trees, and as they watched the President's car move slowly past them and he began to smile and wave his hat, some who had consumed more punch than others began to boo. The sound grew louder, carrying clearly across the broad lawn.

FDR kept grinning until he disappeared between the old stone gates, but the booing was "very noticeable," Chanler remembered, "he couldn't have missed it. Even to a schoolboy, it seemed appallingly rude."

Franklin K. Lane, who had helped hone the graceful remarks Franklin delivered at his official notification at Springwood, had not been able to be present for the ceremony itself; he was already confined to bed with the illness that would soon kill him. But he wrote the young friend he understood so well a warm but shrewdly admonitory letter:

> Dear Old Man,—
>
> This is hard work—to say that I can't be with you on this great day in your life. You know that only the mandate of the medical autocrats could keep me away. . . . I know that you will not allow youself to become cheap, undignified or demagogical. Remember that East and West alike, we want gentlemen to represent us, and we ask no man to be a panderer or a hypocrite to get our votes. Frankness and language and simplicity and a fine fervor for the right are virtues that some must preserve, and where can we look for them if not from the Roosevelts and the Delanos?
>
> It is a great day for you and for all of us. Be wise! Don't be brilliant. Get plenty of sleep. Do not give yourself to the handshakers. For now your word carries far, and it must be a word worthy of all you stand for.
>
> I honestly, earnestly, ask God's blessing on you.
>
> As always
> Franklin K. Lane
>
> Our love to your dear Mother,—proud, happy Mother,
> —and to Eleanor.

"During three months in the year 1920," FDR said many years later, "I got to know the country as only a candidate for office or a traveling salesman can get to know it. . . ." That education began at Chicago on the evening of August 10, when he boarded the *Westboro*, a private car coupled to the end of a regularly scheduled passenger train, and headed west on a speaking tour that would take him 8,200 miles through twenty states in eighteen days. Franklin delivered an average of seven formal addresses on each of those days, not counting an unknown number of exuberant off-the-cuff remarks delivered from the back platform; in just two days, racing across the state of Washington, he would speak twenty-six times, beginning at dawn and winding up well after midnight.

Three friends from the Navy Department campaigned with him.

Franklin's advance man was Stephen T. Early, a former Associated Press reporter and editor of the American Expeditionary Force newspaper *Stars and Stripes,* who had covered the Navy Department before the war. Steve Early's reports on Democratic prospects, scrawled on hotel stationery late at night, provided the congenitally optimistic candidate with healthy doses of cold-eyed realism.

Marvin McIntyre, the skeletal, soft-spoken former Kentucky news-paperman who had been in charge of Franklin's public relations at the department, served in the same capacity aboard the *Westboro,* seeing that local newspapermen were comfortable during their time aboard, ushering local dignitaries in and out of Franklin's compartment more or less on schedule.

Renah Camalier, Franklin's big, rotund Navy Department stenog-rapher—known to his employer as "Camy," and to the newspapermen aboard as "Old Roly Poly"—strained to hear Franklin's increasingly hoarse voice over the clacking of the wheels, then tapped away at a borrowed typewriter, producing speeches and press releases as needed in time for the next stop.

Tom Lynch was aboard, too, dispensing checks. The campaign was chronically short of funds—Franklin had himself put up $5,000, and his mother would add another $3,000 before the race was over—and the candidate wanted someone he trusted completely to pay the bills and keep track of what little money was left.

The West was thought still to be a stronghold of Progressivism, and a friendly journalist had outlined the stance he thought Franklin should take while campaigning there. Roosevelt, he told the candidate, should make the voters feel that "you are the political and spiritual heir of Theodore Roosevelt, that [TR] was an essential and fundamental democrat, the exponent of liberalism and progress, that the Democratic party inspired by Wilson now stands for everything the great Roose-velt represented."

Franklin needed little urging. He had seen himself as his cousin's political and spiritual legatee since boyhood, and now liked to wink and introduce himself to his audience as "a progressive Democrat, with accent on the word 'progressive.' " "I do not profess to know what Theodore Roosevelt would say were he alive today," he told one Western crowd, "but I cannot but help think that the man who in-vented the word 'pussy-footer' could not have resisted the temptation to apply it to Mr. Harding."[12]

In later years, Franklin did not much like to be reminded of the

---

12. Franklin claimed to have received 2,500 letters and wires of congratulations upon his nomination, and that when those from friends and family were subtracted from the total, fully one third of the rest were from progressive Republicans who felt betrayed by their own party. *Source:* Interview with the Baltimore *Sun,* July 18, 1920, Roosevelt Family Papers Donated by the Children, Campaign of 1920 Clippings, FDRL.

advantages his late cousin's name had given him. "They chose me [to run for Vice President] because my name had become known during the war," he assured the biographer Emil Ludwig. "It was also intended that as an official I should be the connecting link between Wilson and Cox, who had not been a member of the federal administration, especially the war part of it."

But newspaper headlines from the summer of 1920 attest to the importance of his family connection to politicians and voters alike: FRANKLIN ROOSEVELT'S CAREER PARALLELS COUSIN TEDDY'S . . . LIKEN CAREER OF ROOSEVELT TO COUSIN'S . . . COUSIN OF TR IS PICKED FOR SECOND PLACE . . . THE DEMOCRATS HOPE NAME OF ROOSEVELT WILL DRAW VOTES . . . ALL THE WORLD LOVES A ROOSEVELT.[13]

"The Boss should take here," Steve Early reported from Minnesota. "They like his name and his kind. This was a TR state & I hope it will be an FDR state next." A Montana party official called upon Franklin to deliver "rough, peppy Americanism" speeches, "snappy . . . with typical Roosevelt conduct." Reporters in the Rockies wanted to know whether he planned to take time out from his tour to hunt bears. A fair number of the Western voters who turned out see Franklin evidently did so because they thought him TR's son. "I voted for your father!" they shouted. "You're just like the Old Man!"

This kind of confusion—and Franklin's growing skill at stirring his audiences—soon worried the opposition. "Admirers of Theodore Roosevelt and the Roosevelt family," the Chicago *Tribune,* assured its readers, "cannot be fooled by a name. It sounds well but is an empty sound. . . . The name is inspiring, the candidate is not. . . . If he is Theodore Roosevelt, Elihu Root is Gene Debs, and Bryan is a brewer."

The Oyster Bay Roosevelts were divided as to how to respond to Franklin's candidacy. Few members planned to vote for him, but it was hard to know how public to make one's opposition to the candidacy of a member of the family, however distant, who was married to a niece whom Theodore Roosevelt had greatly loved. Only exhaustion and a hectic schedule, Corinne Robinson assured Franklin in mid-August,

13. The connection was not universally made, however. At a track-side ceremony in Colorado Springs, on the way east from San Francisco, Franklin had valiantly struggled not to laugh when the bibulous Republican mayor unexpectedly announced that despite his party affiliation, he planned to vote for the League, for Governor Cox, and for his fine young running mate, "Franklin Rosenfelt." *Source:* Charles McCarthy to Louis Howe, 1924, Louis Howe Papers, FDRL.

had prevented her from immediately "sending you my love and interest in this new adventure. I wish we were working for the same
political party & that I could be behind you, for you & Eleanor are very
dear to me. . . . I am so proud of all you have done to achieve your
honor. My dear love to you both, and politics or no politics, I am
always and affectionately your 'Auntie Corinne.' "

Theodore Roosevelt, Jr., was a good deal less cordial. "Ted was
always the instigator of anti-Franklin feeling," a relative remembered;
he "always felt that Franklin was getting everything he was entitled
to."[14] Still hobbling from his war wounds, the late President's oldest
son had been elected to the New York State Assembly from Nassau
County in 1919 with a record majority, then sought his party's nomination for governor that same summer only to fall short of the convention votes he needed. This defeat—and Franklin's simultaneous
triumph in San Francisco—deepened his conviction that his Democratic cousin, whom he and his brothers and sister had once dismissed
as a "feather-duster" and who had failed to obey TR's exhortations to
leave civilian life and face enemy fire in uniform, was a usurper who
had no right to wear the Roosevelt mantle and to whom things had
always come too easily. And when the Republican National Committee asked him to undertake a cross-country speaking tour of his own
to undo whatever damage Franklin might be doing, he gladly agreed,
leaving his wife, Eleanor, to campaign for his reelection to the Assembly in his stead. At Sheridan, Wyoming, talking to a group of his
father's old Rough Riders, he declared Franklin "a maverick. He does
not have the brand of our family."

Stung by this attack from a prominent member of the family which
he had once been eager to join, Franklin fired back, recalling that in
1912, "when another Roosevelt was working with his coat off to save
the Republican Party from that same old gang that now has it by the
throat," Harding had called Theodore Roosevelt "first a Benedict
Arnold and then an Aaron Burr. This is one thing at least *some* members of the Roosevelt family will not forget."[15]

14. TR, Jr. was "mad for publicity," the same kinsman remembered. During the 1920s he
accompanied young Roosevelt to a heavyweight title fight at Madison Square Garden, which was
spoiled for the President's son when a promise to introduce him from the ring somehow fell
through although he had paid a public relations man to arrange it. He was "quite an exhibitionist,
really," and "always arranged to be the last to come into dinner as if he were living in the White
House. That's a little bit mean, but it's true." *Source:* Interview with W. Sheffield Cowles, Jr.

15. As late as 1932, Eleanor felt called upon to write to thank her Aunt Corinne for "not
making speeches . . . I think it's swell of you not to do it when all the rest of the family seem

"Personally," Eleanor wrote her husband's secretary from Campobello, "I had wanted Franklin out of government service for a few years at least. So, in spite of the honor, I really feel rather unselfish when I wish for his success." She had hoped that after nearly eight years in Washington, and the shattering impact of his relationship with Lucy Mercer, she and her husband had might have some relatively uninterrupted time together to try to rebuild their damaged marriage. Instead, he was now racketing across the landscape, far away and out of touch.

"Oh dear! I wish I could see you or at least hear from you," she wrote Franklin as he set out for the West. "I hate politics!" She and the children followed the campaign as best they could: James wrote his father to report that he had won a prize at the annual Campobello Field Day, then added, "I think all your speeches are very good, and I love to read them in the paper besides the comments. The *World* praises them and the *Tribune* condemns them. I think the *World* is right."

Franklin scratched out a hurried note from St. Paul, Minnesota, on Sunday, August 15:

> Dearest Babs,
> . . . This is the last day of rest till September. I have had a wonderful experience so far but it is tiring. The Chicago meeting on Wednesday was a wonder. Thursday in Wisconsin *very* strenuous. Friday only 2 speeches, one in Minnesota and one here, but both in big auditoriums. Yesterday four speeches in four towns of South Dakota and a motor trip of 80 miles. There is no wire from you and I fear you did not get mine. All my love. I do hope all goes well. Keep some sort of diary *please* or I know I will miss some of the things that happen
>
> > Your devoted
> > F

He wired from Bismarck, North Dakota, the next day: SPLENDID RECEPTIONS MINNESOTA SOUTH AND NORTH DAKOTA SO SORRY MISS FRANKLINS BIRTHDAY GIVE HIM MY SPECIAL LOVE ALL WELL.

Eleanor had often felt lonely and unhappy at Campobello, but now a new note began to creep into her letters; she was frankly envious of

---

to feel so very much more active than usual. I do see, though, how annoying it must be to have people saying and thinking Franklin is a near relation of Uncle Ted's & I do hope they realize that we personally never sail under false colors intentionally." *Source:* Corinne Roosevelt Robinson Papers, Harvard University.

all the excitement which she was not permitted to share. Reminding Franklin that he had not written to his Aunt Dora, she allowed some of her resentment to show: "I hate to add these personal things when you're under such strain and wish I could do them, but I can't, and they're the kind of things which do mean so much to other people who don't happen to have all the interesting things you have to fill their minds."

She was angry when he agreed at the last moment to speak at a Brooklyn rally on Labor Day instead of coming up to the island for five full days of rest as he had promised. "Of course it is hard to refuse," she told Sara, "but I do think he should have cut Monday out and come here directly, however, there is no use in saying anything."

Steve Early was pleased by the reception Roosevelt received at almost every Western stop. The crowds liked the candidate, he assured Louis Howe: "Without exception, [Roosevelt's appearances] were excellent for the Boss. He is speaking easier, going good, and will be a finished product of oratory before we see New York again."

Newspapers paid a lot of attention to Roosevelt's easy grin and ingratiating manner: ROOSEVELT SMILE WINS ITS WAY THROUGH KENTUCKY; FLYING 86 MILES TO FILL SPEAKING DATE . . . ONLY SERVES TO BRIGHTEN ROOSEVELT SMILE. The engineer aboard one of the trains that pulled the *Westboro* from stop to stop concurred. "Do you know," he told a reporter, "that lad's got a 'million vote smile' and mine's going to be one of them."

A reporter for the *New York Post* assessed his impact:

> [Roosevelt] gets the last ounce of appeal-power out of each sentence. The physical impression leaves nothing to be asked—the figure of an idealized college football player, almost the poster type in public life . . . making clean, direct and few gestures; always with a smile ready to share. . . . He speaks with a strong clear voice, with a tenor note in it which rings—sings, one is tempted to say—in key with . . . [an] intangible, utterly charming and surely vote-winning quality.

But for all the excitement his presence caused in the crowds that turned out to see him, Franklin's message was not getting through. The crowds were simply not interested in the League: "The rank and file of the people want to know what they are going to get," Early reported. "The war is over for them. . . . They are thinking closer to home, [of] their bread baskets and not their war allies. The big issues to them are those which will bring them something personally, and individually and not nationally."

Still more damaging to the Democrats' cause was "The bitterness toward Wilson . . . evident everywhere. . . .," Early wrote. "He hasn't a friend. . . . There is good sentiment in favor of *a* league of nations," but precious little for the version Republican orators were carefully coached always to call "Mr. Wilson's League."

In his anxiety to transform his personal popularity into votes on Election Day, Franklin sometimes went too far. His penchant for being "brilliant" rather than "wise," in Franklin K. Lane's knowing formulation—his eagerness to win over the crowd, *any* crowd—first became apparent on August 18 when, standing on a staircase at a farmers' picnic at Deer Lodge, Montana, and jabbing his points home in the style of his late cousin, he launched into an overconfident defense of the League. The opposition had charged that Britain would control the League Assembly because its six dominions would inevitably vote as instructed by the Crown. "The United States has a lot more than six votes which will stick with us through thick and thin. . . ." Franklin assured his audience. "Does anyone suppose that the votes of Cuba, Haiti, Santo Domingo, Panama, Nicaragua and the other Central American States would be cast differently from the vote of the United States? We are in a very real sense the big brother of these little republics. . . ."

And then he added: "You know I have had something to do with running a couple of little Republics. The facts are that I wrote Haiti's Constitution myself and, if I do say so, I think it a pretty good Constitution."

The line went over well with the farmers, and so he cheerfully repeated it later that day at Butte and Helena, as well.

He had not written the Haitian Constitution, of course. Nor had he ever run a republic. And the opposition was already making an issue of the brutality with which the Marines had conquered and now held Haiti. Their nominee gleefully took Franklin at his word: Roosevelt's remarks had been "the first official admission of the rape of Hayti and Santo Domingo, . . . the most shocking assertion that ever emanated from a responsible member of the government of the United States," Harding said. "I will not empower an Assistant Secretary of the Navy to draft a constitution for helpless neighbors in the West Indies and jam it down their throats at the point of bayonets borne by U.S. Marines."

Franklin's response was to deny ever having said anything of the sort and to denounce the local stringer for the Associated Press for having deliberately twisted his words. It didn't work: thirty-one citizens of Butte who had been present promptly signed a document swearing that they had heard it, too. "To have misquotations follow a candidate from one city to another in this fashion," wrote an unsympathetic Spokane editor, "must be annoying, to say the least," and the *New York Telegraph* suggested that the incident had revealed the youthful Democratic nominee as "a spoiled child, to be spanked."

Eleanor loyally noted that "the Republican papers, having nothing very bad against you, have simply been trying to treat you like an amiable young boy. Belittlement is the worst they can do."

It was bad enough. Roosevelt did not mention Haiti again during the campaign, but since the black voters who cared most about the issue were already in the Republican camp, his mistake probably cost few actual votes.[16]

To ensure no further misunderstandings—and perhaps because Franklin seemed likely to make more news than did most vice-presidential candidates—the Associated Press dispatched a top reporter to cover the candidate full time. His name was Stanley Prenosil, and Franklin made sure that he was treated well aboard the *Westboro*, carefully instructing his New York headquarters to delay at least one press release until the reporter could file an exclusive.

Two days after he made his Haitian blunder, Franklin's train steamed across Washington toward Centralia, where just a few months earlier an unprovoked armed attack on an IWW headquarters by American legionnaires had left four veterans dead. One Wobbly, Frank Little, had managed to escape, only to be hunted down and jailed, then seized by a mob, possibly castrated and, begging for death, strung up and hauled down from a railroad bridge three times as the lights of parked cars illuminated his body so that men sitting in them could riddle it with rifle bullets. No one was prosecuted for his murder.

Franklin told the citizens of Centralia how pleased he was to be with them.

16. Franklin never wavered in his denials: In 1928, the *Nation* ran a series of articles on American relations with Haiti and referred in one of them to the "Roosevelt Constitution." It was all "old stuff and nonsense," FDR told the editor, Oswald Garrison Villard:

1. I never admitted in a public speech that the constitution of Haiti was the best ever.
2. I never said I had written that constitution.
3. It is a deliberate falsehood to call it the Roosevelt Constitution.

Source: Frank Freidel, *Franklin D. Roosevelt: The Ordeal,* page 82.

I particularly wanted to make this pilgrimage. . . . I regard it as a pilgrimage to the very graves of the martyred members of the American Legion who here gave their lives to the sacred cause of Americanism. Their sacrifice challenged the attention of the Nation to the insidious danger to American institutions in our very midst. Their death was not in vain for it aroused the patriotic people of our great nation to the task of ridding this land of the alien anarchist, the criminal syndicalist and all similar anti-Americans. Here in the presence of your honored dead, I pledge to the Nation our determination to carry on this patriotic work— to make certain that the land, throughout its breadth and width, shall be made unsafe for those who seek by violence to destroy the Constitution and the Institutions of America.[17]

Franklin spent a few days campaigning in Republican Maine where the governor's race, to be settled in a separate election on September 19, was again being billed as a harbinger of likely national results in November. Josephus Daniels and William McAdoo campaigned there, too, hoping at least to keep the opposition victory margin below twenty thousand.[18]

Then he returned to New York, still exhilarated by the crowds he'd seen out west but appalled at the sloth and indecision that gripped Democratic Headquarters.

Charles H. McCarthy, Franklin's former secretary at the Navy Department, whom he had asked to run the office and keep an eye on the fight to hold New York State, agreed with him. McCarthy was a natural worrier—thin, tense, losing his hair—but nothing did seem to be going right. There was little money to be had anywhere—the Republicans would eventually outspend the Democrats nearly six to one—and almost none for the vice-presidential campaign. "To be perfectly frank with you," McCarthy told his boss, "we have got to take the bit in our teeth here and go ahead and do something. You can't get a typewriter, a desk, or anything else unless you . . . go and get it yourself. That is just the situation here. The publicity bureau claims

17. When, during the 1944 campaign, FDR took a surprisingly slow train trip to the Northwest, reporters aboard the press car speculated that he might be ill and using the train ride to recuperate. According to Frances Perkins it was simply that he "wanted to go over that country [which he'd first seen during the 1920 race] and take a look at it after his administration" to see for himself how things had been improved. *Source:* Transcript of interview with Frances Perkins, Columbia Oral History Project, Columbia University.

18. They failed: On September 19, the Republicans took the governorship by more than three times that figure and captured all three congressional seats. A jubilant Harding repeated the old saying, "As Maine goes, so goes the nation."

Franklin's frustrating effort there in 1920 may account for some of his special joy sixteen years later when, running for reelection as President, he carried all but two of the forty-eight states. "As Maine goes," he liked to say then, "so goes Vermont."

that they cannot spend any money until further orders. . . . When all is said and done, you cannot win an election without money." And when William Church Osborn, the wealthy reformer who had been an early political ally of Franklin's, came into headquarters prepared to write out a check, he was kept standing in the foyer because no one recognized him.

Meanwhile, Tammany was "doing absolutely nothing" for the national ticket, concentrating all its resources on reelecting Al Smith as governor; they had even replaced Franklin's portrait with Smith's on Cox and Roosevelt posters all over the state. "It is a disgrace how they are acting," McCarthy said, "and enough to make one want to see the whole bunch of them out of the party."

The hard fact was that no one in the New York headquarters or anywhere else for that matter believed Cox stood much of a chance. It was not that people especially disliked the Democratic nominee. Neither he nor Harding had captured the public imagination; both were generally seen as pallid substitutes for the three colorful politicians whose domination of American public life had just come to an end: William Jennings Bryan, Theodore Roosevelt, and Woodrow Wilson.

"The conclusion is inevitable," wrote the editor of *Collier's* after Cox's nomination, "that each party went the worst way possible about the job of selecting its candidate for President." The *Nation* favored Eugene V. Debs, the radical labor leader whom the Socialists had nominated for President from his prison cell; it was a clear-cut choice, it said, between "Debs and dubs." "I had no use for Harding," the Kansas Progressive William Allen White recalled, "but I could not get excited about Cox . . . every time I considered voting for either of them I decided to vote for the other. I ended by thinking about Cox as I went into the election booth and so managed for a moment to justify a vote for Harding. I could have done it the other way quite as easily."

As the journalist Mark Sullivan remembered it, the insurmountable problem Cox and Roosevelt faced was their identification with the impaired President in the White House.

Wilson had presented the war to us as a fine spiritual adventure—and the four million Americans who participated had found it, most of them, disillusioning. Wilson had told us it was a "war to make the world safe for democracy"—and Americans had already begun to sense the decline of democracy that had begun with Communism in Russia in 1918, and was destined to put democracy on the defensive everywhere. Wilson had told us it was "war to end all wars"—and America had begun to feel that promise, too, would fail. Wilson had committed America to membership in a League of Nations—and America had become suspicious that meant commitment of America to send troops abroad on future occasions, repetitions of the experience that was already, and recently, dust and ashes in our mouths. Wilson, in short, was the symbol both of the war we had begun to think of with disillusion, and of the peace we had come to think of with cynicism. And Cox, by identifying himself with Wilson, took on Wilson's liabilities.

The Democratic cause was almost surely hopeless from the start, but Sullivan and other observers believed Cox did not help it by mounting such a shrill campaign—in a single month he travelled 22,000 miles through thirty-two states and delivered 394 scheduled speeches. In contrast to his chiseled, largely silent opponent, he looked "a little like a frontier 'bad man' shooting up the meeting," Sullivan observed. " 'Get off that front porch,' says Cox, 'and cut out that pink tea—I'm here with the rough stuff.' "

Harding would eventually be forced to leave his front porch, escorted to the Marion depot for his first campaign swing by brass bands and twenty-five hundred travelling salesmen who had rallied to the Republican candidate because Cox had once denounced drummers as "parasites and public nuisances." But he skillfully resisted Democratic demands to state just where he stood on the question of the League. Wilson "favors going into the Paris League and I favor staying out," he said, but he also declared himself in favor of an "Association of Nations," thus giving Republicans who favored the League at least some reason to stay within their party.

Now, still at Democratic Headquarters in New York on September 6, and hoping to galvanize the staff, Franklin dictated to Charles McCarthy a series of urgent memoranda to pass on to Senator Pat Harrison of Mississippi, chairman of the Democratic Speaker's Bureau, and George White of Ohio, chairman of the National Democratic Committee.

MEMORANDUM FOR SENATOR HARRISON

I spent some time with Mr. Roosevelt last night and one of the matters he wanted to take up here at Headquarters was this:—It seems that every time he or Governor Cox make reference in speeches to specific points which hit the other people rather hard, somebody comes back at them the very next day—for instance, when Mr. Roosevelt referred to the question of appropriations in his Chicago speech, Congressman [James] Good [of Iowa] came right back the next day, when young "Teddy" in Maine made the rash statement that the Republican Party won the war, and that no son or relative of anyone high in the administration had smelled powder, there was nobody to answer him.

Mr. Roosevelt thinks it very essential to have somebody here at Headquarters who can follow these things up, because he and Governor Cox are not in position to answer statements made by men like Mr. Good and young "Teddy," in other words, this should be left to lesser lights.

MEMORANDUM FOR MR. WHITE

I am frankly disappointed at the slowness in getting the business organization going. An executive committee ought to be running. There ought to be a conference of the leaders every morning. . . . We ought to get out one good statement every day in reply to the Republicans. . . .

I found in my Western trip and in Maine that the Federal office holders are not doing their share. Get more Congressmen and women on the stump. . . . We ought to have a dozen speakers in reserve to follow every speaker at five minutes' notice. . . . Make the Republican campaign ridiculous. Use TR, Jr's full statement about the Republican party winning the war. . . . Use, in the proper way, Republican whispering campaign in backwoods section of Maine that Cox is a Catholic and was born in Ireland. Use TR Jr's statement in Maine that the democrats have 60,000 *useless* clerks in the departments in Washington, and that on March 4th Harding if elected will *replace* them with 60,000 tried and true Republicans.

MEMORANDUM FOR MR. WHITE

As a suggestion I believe it would be a good idea to have somebody go into some country of New York State, and take a poll of all the ministers, clergymen, priests, etc. . . . on the question of the League. . . . If it seems to work out all right, before making anything public, try it in several other places . . . in other words, try to get a story that the churches of the country are behind the League of Nations

MEMORANDUM FOR MR. WHITE

I suggest that a telegram be sent to every State chairman asking him to make special efforts to get street banners strung up immediately. I have noticed Republicans very active and there is not one Democratic street banner that I have seen up to this time.

Senator Harrison thought a Democratic victory most unlikely. George White was so gloomy, according to the journalist Arthur Krock, that when a newspaperman asked him how he thought the Democrats would do in New Jersey, he answered, "We haven't got a Chinaman's chance," and Governor Cox asked Krock to serve as White's assistant just to keep him "from blurting out [further] embarrassing truths to the press about the dim prospects of the national ticket." The vice-presidential candidate's suggestions were received politely, dutifully read, and just as dutifully filed.

Charles McCarthy's burdens were eased somewhat in early September when Miss Marguerite A. Le Hand, an efficient young secretary who had worked for him at the Emergency Fleet Corporation in Washington, arrived to serve as his temporary assistant for the duration of the campaign at $40 a week.

Still, McCarthy told his boss, "The real work around Headquarters is being done by the revolving electric sign which has the pictures of Cox and Roosevelt on it."

Franklin would remain largely on his own.

In late September, he asked Eleanor to campaign with him. He genuinely wished her to be at his side—"I miss you so much," he wrote her early in the campaign. "It is very strange not to have you with me in all these doings"—but perhaps more important, it was the first national election in which women were to vote, and he thought the crowds would like a look at the candidate's wife.

Before boarding the *Westboro*, Eleanor travelled to Groton with James, the first of four sons she would escort to the school in which Franklin had seen that they were all enrolled at birth. "He seemed to me very young and very lonely when I left him," she remembered, "but it was a tradition in the family that boys must go to boarding school when they reached the age of twelve, and James would be thirteen the following December. . . . I never thought to rebel then, but now it seems to me too ludicrous to have been bound by so many conventions. I unpacked his trunk, saw that his cubicle was in order . . . said goodbye to Mr. and Mrs. Endicott Peabody," and hurried on to join her husband.

James was a thin, nervous, nearsighted child, unsettled by his mother's frequent unhappiness, unhappy himself at seeing so little of his father, sensitively attuned to the tensions that often gripped his home but fearful of leaving it. And he was poorly prepared academically. Eleanor especially despaired of his lack of interest in school-work. "His marks . . . have been disgraceful," she told Sara the previous winter when he was supposed to be preparing for Groton at St. Albans, the National Cathedral School in Washington; "I have told him this Spring was his last chance as if this continued we'd have to take him away from school & all its fun & have [him] taught at home. . . . He wept but he just doesn't try." She had been no happier with his performance in the spring: "James is worse. . . . I just told him I did not care to discuss it. . . . He wept as usual & it will have about as much effect as usual. . . ." In June, he had taken his entrance examinations, expecting to enter the second form, and was put back into the first. "Father," he wrote Franklin during the Democratic Convention, "I failed my groton exams for the second form. My marks were all low and they were all dew to careless and thoughtless work. I would like to take my Form exams again soon but not till you get back as I want to study up first."[19] He was miserably homesick during his first days at Groton, he remembered, too timid for a time even to ask his schoolmates for directions to the bathroom.

Eleanor joined her husband in Manhattan and would campaign alongside him for just over three weeks, as trains pulling the *Westboro* wound their way through the upper South, then west as far as Colorado and back again to New York.

"This is the most killing thing for a candidate I ever knew," she reported to Sara in her first letter from the train; it was also killing for a candidate's wife as unaccustomed as was Eleanor to the relentlessly public nature of national politics. "I never before had spent my days going on and off platforms," she remembered, "listening apparently with rapt attention to much the same speech, looking pleased at seeing people no matter how tired I was or greeting complete strangers with effusion."

Solid sleep was impossible. Speechmaking began early and ran late: "F. made 2 speeches & drove 26 miles over awful roads before we ever got any breakfast!" Eleanor reported from Kentucky. "There have

19. When his father did get back, James recalled, he "took it philosophically and did not rant or storm at me . . . he asked me why I had done so poorly and I came up with the ingenious alibi that I was still upset because of the excitement of the previous June when the anarchists tried to blow up Attorney General Palmer."

More than sixty years later, James Roosevelt still wondered why he'd "had so little" of his father during his youth; why "Father had no influence at all on me at Groton or at Harvard," had done "no working with me toward a future." *Sources:* James Roosevelt, *Affectionately, FDR*, pages 111–113; Interview with James Roosevelt.

been two town speeches since then and at least one platform speech every 15 minutes all day! We had coffee & sandwiches for lunch & a very hurried supper & now he still has to get off at Bowling Green for a speech in a hall! I will never be able to do without at least four large cups of black coffee *every* day!" There was no privacy—at St. Louis, Franklin's hair was cut in front of "an admiring audience of newspapermen"—no time even for laundry; arrangements had to be made to ship fresh clothing to stationmasters along the route. Eleanor asked Sara to please send to one stop "1 clean nightgown & shirt & 3 chemises & 3 drawers & any black stockings & handkerchiefs I may have. F. says he has enough."

Campaigning in Colorado, Eleanor received a telegram from Sara: James had collapsed at Groton with severe stomach pains; he was in the infirmary and Sara was already on her way to the school to care for him. Frightened, Eleanor planned to follow her as fast as she could, but Franklin urged her to stay aboard at least until she got further word. Eleanor agreed. "I'm going gaily on," she wrote nervously to her mother-in-law. Sara escorted her grandson to Boston to see a specialist who pronounced James's problem nervous indigestion, then took him home with her to Springwood, just as she had taken Franklin home whenever he fell ill at school a quarter of a century earlier. After several days of his grandmother's solicitous care in the big, serene house that was always the center of the Roosevelts' world, James returned, fortified, to Groton.

Eleanor stayed with the campaign. "This was the first time I ever remember not being on hand if one of the children was ill," she wrote later, "but it was probably a very good thing for the children to learn that they could not always be my first consideration." Unable to care for her distant son and uncertain always of her own worth unless she was fulfilling someone else's needs, she now found herself without a role aboard the *Westboro*. "I don't see that I'm of the least use on this trip," she wrote, and again, "my only use so far has been that people are curious to see his wife. . . ."

Franklin was the focus of everyone's attention. His "head should be turned," Eleanor reported to Sara,

> if it is ever going to be, for there is much praise and enthusiasm for him personally almost everywhere. We had a splendid meeting at Bowling Green last night, in the open at 10:30 p.m. must have been over a 100,000 people there. Franklin's voice is all right again & I should say he

came through yesterday finely & it certainly was a big day he must have talked to or tried to shake hands with at least 300,000 people, the newspapermen think. . . .

Of course, Franklin's looks bring all sorts of comments & then we get asked if he's "Teddy" frequently. I almost hope he does not get elected for so many people are coming to see us in Washington & I shan't remember their names or faces.

Franklin had already begun to urge those he met on the campaign trail to "Come and see me sometime!," an invitation which hundreds, perhaps thousands of near-strangers from all over the country would take literally over the coming years.

But despite the big, cheering crowds, Franklin was sure his campaign was being ignored: Republican newspapers refused to print his speeches, he charged; he was getting little support from headquarters. When he heard in Indiana in mid-October that Cox had challenged Harding to debate the League, he fired off a telegram to Senator Harrison at headquarters: WHY LEAVE ME OUT? I WOULD BE CHARMED TO DISCUSS THE LEAGUE AND LOTS OF OTHER THINGS WITH GOVERNOR COOLIDGE, ANY TIME, ANY PLACE. I AUTHORIZE YOU TO ACT AS MY SECOND AND TO ATTEND TO THE PRELIMINARIES.

The campaign grew harsher. The Republicans were "League liars,"[20] Franklin charged; their candidate was a "reactionary" indulging in "cheap trickery," and they were pandering to immigrant groups alienated by the League:

> . . . the Republican campaign managers are . . . making special appeals to the very small but dangerous element in our country which was not loyal or was of doubtful loyalty during the war. Republican leaders are making open solicitation of the Italian-American vote by suggesting to them a divided allegiance—by placing the interest of a foreign land above the interest of the United States, by doing deliberately the things which Theodore Roosevelt gave the last years of his life to stamp out.

The Democrats, he said, "want all-American votes only."

The Italian-American newspaper *Bolletino Della Sera* denounced this kind of attack as characteristic of "a rah-rah boy whose sole asset in politics consists in his name."

20. Conservative Republican senators who had been attacked by young Roosevelt should not lose heart, said the *New York Times*. "You who have been bludgeoned on the head by Theodore ought not to wince when tapped on the wrist by Franklin." *Source:* Frank Friedel, *Franklin D. Roosevelt: The Ordeal*, page 160.

"It is becoming almost impossible to stop F. now when he begins to speak," Eleanor wrote Sara from Cincinnati toward the end of the trip, "10 minutes is always 20, 30 is always 45 & the evening speeches are now about 2 hours! The men all get out & wave at him & when nothing succeeds I yank his coat tails! Everyone is getting tired but on the whole the car is still pretty good natured! They tell us Gov. Cox's is all on edge."[21]

In fact, the *Westboro* was considerably more good-natured than Eleanor liked. The days, filled with crowds and bad food and nonstop speechmaking, were dreary enough from her point of view—"I don't write every day," she told Sara, "because, except for different states and different crowds, the happenings are the same"—but the evenings were worse, given over to Bourbon, poker, cigars, and the kind of noisy, masculine horseplay that made her left out and uneasy.

She did not protest on her own behalf, of course, but she did tell Franklin that he should conserve his strength by getting to bed earlier and that he and his friends should in any case quiet down in the evenings—they were interfering with the sleep of Romeo Fields, the black porter who was studying for the ministry.

Help came from an unexpected quarter. Louis Howe was now aboard the train, having taken a month's leave from the Navy Department "to avoid the civil service rules," he told Eleanor. She had always shared her mother-in-law's distaste for her husband's closest aide. His manners, like his appearance, were rough; his air of jaded cynicism was distressing to a woman of unyielding principle; and, she would admit much later, she had felt excluded since their days in Albany by the extraordinary intimacy between this unkempt little man and her husband, jealous of the large role he played in a world which she had only rarely been allowed to penetrate. Above all, though she never publicly acknowledged it, she was resentful that Franklin had seen fit to consult his aide before telling her whether or not he wished to continue their marriage.

Now, suddenly, Howe began to court her favor. "In later years I

21. Things were not always peaceful aboard the *Westboro:* one day toward the end of the campaign, Louis Howe pulled off his jacket, cocked his small fists, and challenged Renah Camalier to fight. The big stenographer—who weighed some 250 pounds—restrained himself until Franklin could be summoned from his compartment to step in and calm him down. *Source:* Frank Freidel interview with Renah H. Camalier, Frank Freidel Papers, FDRL.

learned that he had always liked me," she wrote, "and thought I was worth educating, and for that reason he made an effort on this trip to get to know me."

But that was surely not the only reason. For all his gruffness, Louis Howe was discerning and shrewd. He sensed the claustrophobic effect life aboard the *Westboro* was having upon the wife Franklin so often ignored. Like her, he knew how hard one had to work, how high a price in self-esteem one often had to to pay, to remain at the center of Franklin's circle.[22]

If Franklin was finally to succeed in public life, Howe knew, he and Eleanor could no longer afford to be antagonists, must instead become partners, and the long train ride provided him with the opportunity he needed to win her over. He began by knocking on her compartment door from time to time to ask if he might discuss a speech with her. "I was flattered," she remembered, "and before long I found myself discussing a wide range of subjects."

They recited poetry to one another. Howe provided capsule histories of the towns through which they passed. With his help, Eleanor also "began to be able to understand some of our newspaper brethren and to look upon them as friends instead of enemies." She thought it funny when Howe got up a pool in Republican upstate New York to see who could predict the day's smallest track-side crowd (the loser had to walk up and down the platform wearing a huge and gaudy tie Howe

---

22. Howe knew from experience that Franklin's sense of humor even toward those most loyal to him could be callous, even cruel.

Both Democratic campaign trains happened to pull into Terra Haute, Indiana, at the same time one afternoon. The two candidates shook hands for the cameras and Cox made a speech—"his voice is much worse than F.'s," Eleanor reported to Sara—then, while she waited aboard the *Westboro*, Franklin rode along with Cox on the short run to Indianapolis. With him went Howe, McIntyre, Lynch, and Stanley Prenosil. There, after saying goodbye to the governor and with several hours to kill before they could catch a train back to Terra Haute, they rushed for a hotel suite and bath.

On the way, Howe stopped at a newsstand to buy an armful of evening papers, then settled into an armchair to read them while the others took turns at the tub. A bottle appeared and tumblers of whiskey were poured. Franklin told Howe to hurry up and take his bath; otherwise, they'd miss their train. Howe said "yes, yes," absently, but kept on reading, marking with a pencil stub stories he thought likely to yield material for speeches.

Finally, Franklin said, "Let's just give him a bath!" Prenosil filled the tub. All three laughing men lifted the little man off his feet, ripped off his trousers and his truss, then plunged him into the water and held him sputtering there while they scrubbed him with soap and towels.

Howe did his best to maintain his dignity: While his underwear dried on the radiator, he resumed marking his newspapers. *Source:* Lela Stiles, *The Man Behind Roosevelt,* page 71. (The Stiles account does not include the arrival of the whiskey, but it seems to me a safe detail to add; it was Franklin's first opportunity in weeks to have a drink out from under his wife's censorious eye.)

had ordered made up), and she gradually became relaxed enough to enjoy it when reporters made faces at her from the back of her husband's crowds, trying to force her to alter the earnest expression she felt she must adopt while pretending to listen to his all-too-familiar remarks. After a group of especially adoring women surrounded the candidate at a Jamestown, New York, luncheon—"worshippers at his shrine," Eleanor called them—the newspapermen got up a phony letter signed "the Burns Detective Agency," urging her to ask Franklin about his alleged infidelity, and slipped it under the door of her compartment. She managed to laugh and even kept the letter.

Howe continued to provide Eleanor with the interested sympathy she craved and so rarely got from her husband, and as the train rocked from town to town, she remembered, she slowly began to see that the little man whom she had once judged by "externals" had "rather extraordinary eyes and a fine mind."

He had still been "Mr. Howe" to Eleanor before the trip began, and she had hardly known his family. Before it ground to a halt at Buffalo the last week of October, he had become "Louis" and she had written ahead to Sara, asking her to invite his daughter, Mary, up from Vassar for tea at Springwood.

Toward the end of that month, hundreds of thousands of voters all across the country found in their mailboxes or slipped beneath the front door a circular addressed TO THE MEN AND WOMEN OF AMERICA—AN OPEN LETTER. It was signed by Dr. W. E. Chancellor, a negrophobic history professor who had devoted months to demonstrating to his own satisfaction that Harding was "not a White man . . . not a creole . . . not a mulatto, [but] a mestizo," whose election must be stopped in order to "save America from international shame and . . . domestic ruin." Rumors about Harding's alleged black ancestry had circulated in Ohio for years—"How do I know, Jim?" Harding once admitted to a friend. "One of my ancestors may have jumped the fence"—and the candidate himself had always carefully avoided dignifying them with public comment. But the story now seemed to be everywhere. A quarter of a million copies of the Chancellor flyer were seized at the San Francisco Post Office on orders from Woodrow Wilson himself. Two strangers in straw hats hurried through the corridors of a New York hotel passing out little pictures of the White House captioned "Uncle Tom's Cabin." A Republican committeeman expressed his panic to national party headquarters: "You have no conception of how the thing is flying over the state. . . . *It is affecting the woman vote. . . .*"

The Republicans were ready with a response. Harding's campaign manager, Harry M. Daugherty, issued a denial, complete with a reassuringly all-white Harding family tree. "No family in [Ohio] has a clearer or more honorable record than the Hardings," Daugherty said, "a blue-eyed stock from New England and Pennsylvania, the finest pioneer blood, Anglo-Saxon, German, Scotch-Irish, and Dutch."[23]

The Democrats denied having anything to do with distributing the circulars; both Wilson and Cox officially disassociated themselves from them.[24]

Republicans did not accept their denials. "In all of our political history," said the *New York Herald*, "there is nothing comparable to this foul eleventh-hour attack on a presidential candidate solely for the purpose of defrauding the Republican Party of its impending victory." Scott C. Bone, publicity director for the Harding campaign, lashed out at "conscienceless Democratic partisans."

Bone or his subordinates evidently then looked around for some-

23. In issuing this statement, Daugherty ignored the worldly counsel of Boss Penrose: "Don't say a thing about it. From what I hear we've been having a lot of trouble holding the nigger vote lately." *Source:* Andrew Sinclair, *The Available Man*, page 171.

24. According to Edith Wilson, her husband's secretary, Joseph Tumulty, had obtained a copy of one of Chancellor's flyers even before the campaign began and hurried to the South Portico of the White House where Wilson and his wife were having lunch, waving it like a flag. "Governor," he said, "we've got 'em beat! Here's a paper which has been searched out and is absolutely true, showing Harding has Negro blood in him. This country will never stand for them!"

Wilson said he would have nothing to do with such a charge "[e]ven if it is so: 'We cannot go into a man's genealogy; we must base our campaign on principles, not on back-stairs gossip.' "

In his book, *Wilson*, Tumulty indignantly denied ever having advocated disseminating the Chancellor material, and on October 8 he told the professor in writing that "under no consideration would the White House lend its influence" to the scheme. Tumulty's biographer, John Morton Blum, believed his subject and disbelieved Mrs. Wilson, but it seems at least possible that both accounts are true: Initially excited to have been handed something that might reverse the Republican tide, Tumulty later loyally disavowed it under orders from his chief.

In any case, Roosevelt's files contain at least one piece of evidence suggesting that some at Democratic Headquarters were, if not actively involved in distributing it, certainly eager to have it seen by the largest possible number of voters. Reporting to Franklin from New York on October 8, the same day that Tumulty officially turned away Dr. Chancellor, Charles McCarthy wrote: "I am going to say a few earnest prayers for what I hope will break between Saturday night and Monday morning. Of course, I am only hopeful of this, but if it does happen Cox and Roosevelt will be elected." The campaign treasury was still empty, he continued, but "if the good Lord has the way paved for what I hope he will be able to send you next week you and Cox are going to win the election alone."

I cannot imagine that the breaking of any other anti-Harding story could have held such promise of changing masses of votes. *Sources:* Edith Wilson, *My Memoir*, pages 305–306; Joseph Tumulty, *Wilson*, pages 278–280; Franklin D. Roosevelt Papers, Campaign of 1920, FDRL.

thing with which they could damage the reputation of one or the other of the Democratic nominees. Governor Cox was said to be have been a sharp businessman before he entered politics, and the sources of his considerable wealth were widely suspect in Ohio, but evidence of wrongdoing was hard to come by.[25]

Franklin presented an easier target. On the evening of Saturday, October 23, as he entered the Hotel Palatine at Newburgh, a man whom he vaguely recognized as a Washington reporter for the Providence *Journal* and whose name he thought was Fairbrother, stopped him halfway across the lobby and handed him a thick, sealed envelope. It was a letter from his employer, the newspaperman said, hurrying away; he hadn't read it, didn't know what it contained.

What it contained was a furious, intensely personal attack on Franklin's character, signed by his old nemesis, John R. Rathom. Roosevelt was "utterly lacking" in two characteristics, the editor charged, "the qualities of frankness and manliness."

Roosevelt had "aided and abetted" Josephus Daniels in appointing Thomas Mott Osborne as warden of the Portsmouth Naval Prison, Rathom continued, knowing that Osborne was a homosexual and therefore "unqualified to handle any body of men, large or small, in any station of life." And Osborne had then, with "Roosevelt's full knowledge and backing," routinely returned to active duty "men who had been convicted of crimes involving moral turpitude."

Much of Rathom's litany of charges was familiar to anyone who had read his anti-Roosevelt editorials of eight months before. Franklin's refusal to grant Captain Taussig the court of inquiry he had requested had been "cowardly"; his participation in the investigation of Portsmouth had ensured that it would be a "whitewash, the culmination of the political chicanery that has been in vogue ever since you and your late chief assumed office."

But the most serious-sounding attack was relatively new: A chief electrician named Clarence A. Parker had been court-martialed, convicted, and sentenced to ten years imprisonment for sodomy in February 1918. The next month, Daniels reduced his sentence to seven years. In June, Franklin signed an order placing Parker on probation and transferred him to a receiving ship at Boston whose unenthusiastic

25. Asked in 1960 by the writer Andrew Sinclair for whom he planned to vote in the presidential election of that year, an old Ohio farmer said he hadn't been much interested in politics since 1920: "*That* was an election," he said. "Of course, Cox was up to his elbows in filth. And Harding was a nigger." *Source:* Andrew Sinclair, *The Available Man*, page 169.

commanding officer twice urged that he be dishonorably discharged from the Navy "in view of the nature of his offenses." Daniels and Roosevelt refused, and when the Bureau of Navigation authorized Parker's discharge as "undesirable" anyway, Franklin wrote two testy memoranda to the chief of the Bureau of Navigation, ordering that Parker be permitted to re-enlist and asking, "Why is this not a case of insubordination on part of some officer in [the Bureau of Navigation]?"

Franklin seems in fact to have been less interested in the individual fate of the unfortunate Parker than angry that his and his chief's wishes had been ignored, but as Rathom described these events the inescapable implication was that Roosevelt was himself politically unprincipled, homosexual, or both:

> What interest you may have in this particular man must ever remain a mystery unless you care to explain. A charitable construction of your act might be that you wished to please the influential Mr. Osborne . . . as at that time you were contemplating a seat in the United States Senate from New York. . . . Yet even under the stress of campaign eagerness how decent men with the moral welfare of the Navy at heart could directly order the return to honorable service of a man convicted of unnatural offenses to mingle with and contaminate the good men of the service, and this at a time when the country was at war, is beyond all comprehension.

Still worse, according to Rathom, Franklin had so feared discovery in the midst of his controversy with Captain Taussig in January that he personally pulled Parker's file and destroyed incriminating evidence, "a cowardly and clumsy subterfuge."

The letter's closing paragraph was particularly vicious: "You, even more than Josephus Daniels, have been the evil genius of that department and you have earned the detestation and contempt of every patriotic and skilled naval officer with whom you came in contact."

Franklin was stunned by Rathom's letter because of the public doubts it raised about his masculinity, but also possibly because it stirred within him echoes of old private doubts about himself.

From his earliest days, Franklin's proximity to his mother, his unconscious adoption of many of her mannerisms and turns of phrase, even the physical resemblance to her that was already marked during his boyhood and grew steadily until her death—all had made some of those he met dismiss him as a "mama's boy."[26]

26. Among Rosy's first half-humorous thoughts at hearing the news of Franklin's nomination for Vice President was that he be sure to "[t]ell Ma when they ask for photographs of you at an early age . . . not to give out the one in a kilt and scotch bonnet!!!" *Source:* James Roosevelt Roosevelt Papers, FDRL.

The Oyster Bay Roosevelts, Alice Longworth remembered, privately called the youthful Franklin "Miss Nancy" "because he pranced around and fluttered." Corinne Robinson Alsop remembered his being dismissed as "handkerchief-boxy," after the painted figures of exquisite young men dancing the minuet that adorned the boxes in which satin handkerchiefs were then sold—"He had very, very narrow eyes, you know, very, very sloping shoulders." They had thought his tennis pathetic, his overeagerness to impress embarrassing, his table manners altogether too good, above all, his acquiescence in the wishes of his mother, that "domineering tartar," too demeaning. Franklin was said by some to be extremely attractive when he was young. "We never considered him so," Alice recalled. "But then we were a large, rough and boisterous family. Franklin used to sail a boat instead of sweatingly rowing it in the hottest weather as Father would insist on our doing. It was that kind of a difference."

That kind of a difference bothered Franklin, too. Acutely sensitive always to the impression he was making on others, he cannot have been unaware of how precious he seemed to some, and even as an adult, his overly enthusiastic efforts to overcome it—to seem just "one of the boys," as Mike Reilly, the Secret Service agent who knew him best, once put it—were sometimes embarrassing.

At Groton, he proved too light and too easily intimidated to be good at the contact sports the rector considered essential to the development of a Christian gentleman; he was a favorite with his schoolmasters but not his schoolmates, and was sufficiently slow to develop sexually to be bitterly disappointed when he failed to win the part of the female lead in his senior class play. He did no better at Harvard, leading cheers and exhorting the team to greater effort on the editorial page of the *Crimson* rather than struggling on the football field, and proving curiously reluctant to compete for the young women of his own age whom his classmates thought most desirable. (Alice Sohier, to whom he proposed marriage at twenty, was just seventeen; and Eleanor was, of course, his own retiring cousin.) His classmates routinely teased him about his good looks: A *Crimson* poster billed him as "Rosey Roosevelt, the Lillie of the Valley." Even as adults, he and Livy Davis, whose comparable looks ensured that he would suffer the same sort of kidding, sometimes ruefully addressed one another with cloying nicknames coined in college: "Sweetness," "Cunning Little Thing," "Dearest," "Old Lady," "Pretty Face."

At Albany, his Tammany opponents in the Senate had made much of their difficult colleague's dandified ways, and even at the Navy

Department there had been those amused by Franklin's fondness for capes and his predilection for designing overly elegant "costumes" for himself while travelling to the front.

Franklin Roosevelt may have been slight and laggard in his sexual maturing, but he was not homosexual, and most of those who knew him only as an older man, his neck thickened and his torso broadened by seven years of rugged, steady exercise, would have hardly recognized his slender, youthful self.[27]

But in the autumn of 1921, Franklin was still slim and boyish and almost too handsome, factors which among those who did not know

27. Still, some of Franklin's greatest admirers did occasionally speculate privately about what seemed to them to be the sizable feminine component in his makeup.

"You know," FDR's close adviser Thomas G. Corcoran once told the journalist Marquis Childs, "[Roosevelt] is the most androgynous human being I have ever encountered," and Childs himself agreed that "[T]here was in the man a kind of narcissism—I don't know whether to say a feminine narcissism, but it was the quality of the actor, the man who could be photographed . . . always with just the perfect camera angle."

The journalist John Gunther thought "he had some characteristics almost feminoid; I heard one lady say with asperity, 'If he lives long enough, he'll be like Queen Victoria.' "

While "It should be emphasized that, externally, Roosevelt's masculine qualities were pervasively dominant," wrote Louis Wehle, who had known Franklin since Harvard, he also had a "characteristically feminine quality." One need not share Wehle's archaic view of what constitutes "characteristically feminine" traits to find his memories of his old friend worthwhile; certainly many of the traits he lists were in fact characteristic of the way in which both Sara Delano Roosevelt and her son dealt with the world:

A psychologist might say, "Of course, sex determination swings biologically on a prenatal hairline of chance, anyway, and every individual has some traits of the other sex." However, some traits that we are all prone to regard as primarily feminine were more obvious in Roosevelt's mental makeup than in those of most men. To me, there was both a clue to this analysis and a partial confirmation of it in his almost literal resemblance to his mother, and in the extent to which he depended upon her even after he reached middle age.

He did not seem to arrive at conclusions in methodical ways, and was want to avoid discussion with members of his own Cabinet who developed and proved their points. To him a moment of boredom was a desperate ordeal. . . . His mind was sure to range ahead of any slow speaker's—perhaps even outside the topic being discussed—and he might interrupt with some suggestion of policy quite unrelated to the subject. By habit none too terse, I sometimes had to be on the alert to hold his interest, and watched with amused suspense how others lost it. . . .

He had other traits considered primarily feminine. Feeling, perhaps subconsciously, that orderly, logical analysis of a problem was especially difficult for him, he compensated by the habit of gambling, often successfully, on his eleventh-hour ability to handle it by inspiration. Despite his moral courage, he was, as I had occasions for observing, extremely sensitive to adverse criticism from friends, and was immediately depressed by it, although he would quickly recover his self-confidence or show of it. He shrank from private controversy. In listening to a proposal, he was inclined to avoid a plain negative answer, so that . . . many left his presence interpreting his response as Yes, even when he had not said it. . . .

Early in life he discovered his own personal charm and relied on it increasingly for persuading when he might fail to convince. . . .

Source: Transcript of interview with Marquis Childs, Columbia Oral History Project, Columbia University; John Gunther, *Roosevelt in Retrospect,* page 72; Louis B. Wehle, *Hidden Threads of History,* pages 115–117.

him might lend crude plausibility to Rathom's public suggestion that he was somehow personally implicated in a homosexual scandal at Portsmouth.

In any case, Franklin was greatly alarmed when he spoke with Thomas Osborne on the telephone that evening and learned that two Auburn, New York, newspapers had already received copies of the editor's attack: both papers planned to run it on Monday, the 25th. Each copy had arrived in an envelope whose return address in Manhattan was 18 West 44th Street, the office of the Republican National Committee. It seemed safe to assume that hundreds of other newspapers had received copies of the same defamatory letter.

There were just ten days left before Election Day. Not sure what to do at first, Franklin called Democratic Headquarters and asked Arthur Krock to come up to Hyde Park to help him plan a response in time for the morning papers. Krock and the Roosevelts spent Sunday evening together in the Springwood parlor. "I'll never forget how young and handsome he was," the newspaperman remembered, "and how young and charming his wife was. I was very much for him."

The next morning, Roosevelt filed a libel suit for $500,000 against Rathom—and against Scott C. Bone and Edward C. Clark of the Republican publicity department, whom he accused of knowingly spreading falsehoods about him all across the country in an effort to "blacken my character as a candidate. . . ."

Admiral Sims had sent Taussig to Rathom with details of the Portsmouth controversy and was highly pleased by the editor's letter. "You may be sure . . . the Providence *Journal* has all the goods," he told Admiral Fullam, and he assured Rathom he had nothing to worry about from Roosevelt: "I have seen [his] reply in the papers, and quite understand that it is only intended for use until after the election, as I have no idea that he would dare to bring a regular suit. There can be no doubt that the revealing of these facts has shown the people the kind of man he is, and it should have a very considerable effect on the election. It is to be hoped that the record he has made will eliminate him entirely from politics hereafter."

That was precisely what Franklin feared, and at least at first, he was deadly serious about his suit. His friend Thomas J. Spellacy, the U.S. District Attorney who had travelled to Europe with him as his legal adviser in 1919, granted Roosevelt's attorneys access to Rathom's file at the Department of Justice. While none of the material found there could be used as evidence in a civil suit, it provided plenty of damaging material for Franklin's attorney to use in cross-examining the man Franklin now called "that Rathom person."

The editor turned out to be a colossal liar. Nearly every alleged fact he had included in his colorful official autobiography turned out to be false: he had not been born or married where or when he said (although he had been divorced as an adulterer); he had never attended Harrow School, as he claimed; had not served four years in the Chinese Navy; did not cover either the Boer War or the war in the Sudan; and had been forced to flee to the United States from Canada, where, as a young newspaperman, he had been convicted of assaulting one woman and accused of blackmailing another. There even seemed to be some question as to whether he was entitled to the lordly middle name he sometimes used: "Revelstoke."

Best of all, from Franklin's point of view, on Thursday, October 28, three days after Rathom's "Open Letter" appeared in the newspapers, and two days after many of the same papers ran his own firm denial of every charge, the Attorney General authorized U.S. District Attorney Francis G. Caffey of the Southern District of New York to release to the press the full text of a "confession" Rathom had been forced to make to escape a federal indictment in 1918. In it, he had withdrawn a whole series of sensational claims he had made about his personal role in capturing alleged German agents. "In the interest of the public good," Caffey wrote, "and in fairness to Mr. Roosevelt, I think I ought now to say that I do not believe any attack by Mr. Rathom would be given credence by anyone who knows his record."[28]

28. Later, writing to his attorney, Judge Clarence Shearn, Franklin swore that no records had ever been destroyed and pointed out that dozens of offenses, serious as well as trivial, were loosely described under "scandalous conduct" and that in "exceptional cases" men in prison had been restored to duty since the earliest days of the American Navy: "The only difference in Mr. Daniels' policy as compared with the policies of his predecessors was that Mr. Daniels believed that in many cases where minor offenses had been committed by very young, newly enlisted boys, the old system did not give them sufficient chance to make good. . . ."

Daniels, he said, *had* restored "six or eight" men convicted of serious offenses to active service but only because he had become convinced that "the demands of justice" dictated an exception be made, and only at the recommendation of naval officers who had fully investigated the facts.

The surviving evidence suggests that Franklin was telling the truth. Louis Howe prepared for him a complete breakdown of the eighty-three cases to which Rathom had alluded. The overall category of "scandalous conduct leading to the destruction of good morals" under which most of these offenses were collected was broad indeed. Those men Franklin and Daniels had restored to service included one sailor who had stolen a horse; another who had "wilfully and maliciously raised the skirts of a woman unknown"; still others who had been imprisoned for "being intoxicated in church and leaving during sermon"; writing an indecent letter; receiving four dollars in stolen money; displaying "lewd and lacivious pictures"; and two men unlucky enough to have been "found on fire gratings of the ship lying together, each with his person indecently exposed and in contact with that of the other." The sentences initially meted out to

Franklin was evidently still anxious about the impact of Rathom's lurid charges, for that same day McCarthy felt the need to boost his spirits:

> I have heard some highly complimentary comments on your Brooklyn meetings. Also, Mr. Sinnott of the Newark *Evening News* who has just returned from the West and Middle West tells me that you made a very fine impression everywhere you went. He said that the comments on your plain talk and your willingness to more than meet the people half way reached the right spot. . . . Mr. McSwinney of the *Evening Post* tells me that he received the same reports from Mark Sullivan. I tell you these things because I believe what these people say, but I have not told you one half of the favorable comments I have heard from people because lots of them merely say them to be saying something, but I have real confidence in what the above men say.

As Election Day approached, Cox and Roosevelt assured one another that the opposition was weakening: WE ARE HAVING THE MOST REMARKABLE MEETINGS I HAVE EVER SEEN, Cox wired. THE FIGHT IS WON. Franklin assured Cox he would carry New York State. It is impossible to know now how much of this public confidence was bluff. Eleanor remembered later that Franklin had never really thought the ticket would win, and Marvin McIntyre recalled asking the candidate toward the end of the race if he had any illusions about actually being elected: "Nary an illusion," Roosevelt replied. Langdon Marvin, on the other hand, said Franklin told him he had been genuinely optimistic "because of all the applause," and Tom Lynch recalled a breakfast with

---

them also seemed capricious: a man who stole a five-dollar watch, and another found guilty of assaulting a five-year-old Haitian girl, received the same sentence: five years.

Charles McCarthy, now in private practice, eventually looked into all the cases and assured his former boss that "You have Rathom where the hair is short" in all but one. The names of offenders returned to duty had routinely been included among those of dozens of others in letters prepared for his signature by the Judge Advocate's Office; Franklin could have had no ulterior motive in any individual instance since he had never had the opportunity to know details of the cases against any of the men whose return to service he approved.

And the evidence on which Clarence Parker was originally convicted did seem shaky, the case for amelioration of his sentence therefore all the more plausible: he had been convicted of sodomy on the testimony of four men, at least two of whom may have had ulterior motives for charging that he propositioned them; there had been no corroborating witnesses; and twenty of Parker's fellow chief petty officers had attested that Parker had "always carried himself like a gentleman."

The only problem was that Parker's file was indeed missing, just as Rathom said it was, and weeks of searching failed to turn it up. It was eventually found in April 1921, locked in the desk of a lieutenant commander whose father had once been a reporter for the Providence *Journal*.

There, the trail was evidently allowed to end. The suit never got to court, perhaps because by then Franklin was braced for still more bad publicity growing out of the Senate investigation of the Newport scandal. *Source:* Franklin D. Roosevelt Papers, Business and Personal, FDRL.

Franklin aboard the *Westboro* during which Franklin expansively told him he would want him at his side in Washington after Inauguration Day on March 4.

"Listen, Frank, you're not going to Washington," Lynch said.

"Why not?"

"While you've been speaking, I've been getting around in the crowds. They'll vote for you, but they won't vote for Cox and the League."

Election Day was wet and cold at Hyde Park, and as Franklin, Eleanor, and Sara hurried into the little brick town hall to vote, rain dripped steadily from the eaves. Once inside, Sara and then Eleanor cast the first ballots of their lives for the smiling young son and husband who stood in line behind them, waiting to mark his own ballot for himself.

"In those earlier years," Steve Early told a mutual friend much later, Roosevelt "was just a playboy," he had not taken "life seriously enough . . . he couldn't be made to prepare his speeches in advance, preferring to play cards instead."[29]

But no amount of preparation could have stopped the Republicans that year. "This is not a landslide," Joseph Tumulty said after the votes were counted, "it is an earthquake." Harding and Coolidge won thirty-seven states, 61 percent of the popular vote, 404 of the 531 electoral votes. The Democrats took no state outside the old Confederacy. It was the worst electoral defeat since James Monroe swamped John Quincy Adams exactly a century earlier.

"We have torn up Wilsonism by the roots," said Henry Cabot Lodge. The Democratic President and his party had both been repudiated. "We had a chance to gain the leadership of the world," Wilson whispered to an aide. "We have lost it, and soon shall be witnessing the tragedy of it all."

And Franklin had suffered a more personal embarrassment: he had failed utterly in his mission to carry his own state. Every single Democratic candidate for state office had gone down with him to defeat; not one New York county had gone Democratic. (He may have taken some small personal comfort from the fact that his old rival, Al Smith,

---

29. FDR's own son would much later agree. "Up until 1921," Franklin D. Roosevelt, Jr., said, "Father was a rich playboy, living off his cousin's name and his mother's money." *Source:* Interview with Franklin D. Roosevelt, Jr.

whose reelection had so monopolized Tammany's attention during the campaign, had not made it back to Albany.)

"Franklin rather relieved not to be elected Vice President," Sara noted in her journal on Election Day. As always after a setback, Franklin was outwardly ebullient. The campaign had been "a darned fine sail!" he told one friend; he headed a letter to another, "Franklin D. Roosevelt, Ex. V.P., Canned. (Erroneously reported dead)," and declared to a third, "I do not feel in the least bit down-hearted. It seems to me that everything possible was done during the campaign, and no other course would have been honorable or successful. As long as the other people were going to win I am glad they have such a clear majority."

But this defeat, apparently so lightly brushed off at the time, evidently festered within him. In 1920, as at Groton almost three decades earlier, he believed that some injustice must underlie any loss he suffered. Sometimes he said it had been the hyphenated Americans who had done in the Democrats, people like his mother's inoffensive German-born gardener of twenty years, Sebastian Baumann. He had asked Baumann for whom he had voted, he told Josephus Daniels. "He said he voted for Harding. Why? Because of a letter from Germany telling him of lack of food and of clothes and it was because Wilson entered the war. Are you not an American citizen? 'Yes, but if America joins with England and France against Germany, I am a German.' "[30]

Twenty years later, Franklin had developed an even more eccentric theory to explain the Democratic disaster. In the midst of the presidential campaign of 1940, he took the time to tell an aide, Lowell Mellett, his version of just what it was that he was now sure had helped beat him and Cox twenty years earlier:

FDR: . . . There was a fellow once upon a time who was named Daugherty, and he helped run Harding's campaign against the Democrats. He was slick as hell. He went down through an agent to a Methodist minister in Marion, the town where Harding's mother and grand-mother came from. This friend of Daugherty's got hold of the Methodist minister and told him the story about Harding's mother having a Negro mother. In other words, Daugherty planted it on the Methodist minister, who was a Dem-

30. In fact, studies revealed that defections from the Democrats by "hyphenated Americans" were no greater than those among other groups. It was simply a Republican year. Source: Frank Freidel, *Franklin D. Roosevelt: The Ordeal*, page 88.

ocrat, and showed him certain papers . . . that proved the case. The Methodist minister, who was a Democrat, got all upset and he started the story all over the place. The press took it up, and it was the most terrific boomerang against *us*. . . .

Mellett: . . . I never heard of Daugherty planting that Negro story.

FDR: He planted it on *us*. [31]

At the end of November, Franklin and Hall hurried south to Lake Charles, Louisiana, to relax and hunt ducks and geese on a rich friend's rice plantation. The hunt turned out to be anything but restful. Rising before dawn on the morning of December 5, ready to shoot geese, Franklin and Hall were told that a fourteen-year-old boy named Elmer Olga had somehow become lost in the woods. An all-night search had failed to find him and a party of local people with dogs were setting off to try again. The Roosevelts joined the searchers as they fanned out and began crashing through the thickets. At about eleven o'clock the party heard six shots fired into the air up ahead. Franklin had bounded to the front of the pack and was signalling that he had found the boy unharmed.

Back at Hyde Park for Christmas, Franklin sent to all the men who had travelled the campaign trail with him a pair of gold cufflinks with their initials on one link and his on the other. The members of the Cuff Links Club would meet annually—and hilariously—to celebrate the candidate's birthday and reminisce about their first campaign together for the rest of Franklin's life. Thanking Roosevelt for his gift, Charles McCarthy wrote that he looked forward to the day when he could work again for the Democratic ticket, but with his boss's name at the top instead of the bottom.

Franklin looked forward to that day, too, and he brought with him

31. The rumors of Harding's black ancestry continued to fascinate Franklin. Even after he and Cox were defeated he eagerly shared the latest allegations with Josephus Daniels, who noted them in his journal on December 10, 1920: "FDR here. He said that in 1854 a man named Butler killed a man named Smith for calling his wife a negro. Later Gov. of Ohio at request of Harding's grandfather pardoned the murderer."

Although there evidently was a woman employee of the Republican National Committee named Virginia Phillips who was so horrified by the revelations about her party's nominee that she secretly urged the Democrats to distribute Dr. Chancellor's circulars, the tortured implausible, story that their dissemination was orchestrated by Harding's own campaign manager to arouse sympathy for his candidate is unique to FDR, so far as I know, the product, I believe, of his inability ever to accept defeat as in any way his own fault. *Sources:* E. David Cronon, ed., *The Cabinet Diaries of Josephus Daniels 1913–1921;* transcript of White House conversation that took place some time between August 22 and 27, 1940, quoted in "The FDR Tapes," *American Heritage* (February–March 1982).

out of the 1920 disaster a number of tangible assets which he hoped would help him get there. The campaign had made him for the first time something more than a Democratic echo of Theodore Roosevelt; for millions of voters he had become a vigorous, attractive personality in his own right. He had spoken and shaken hands with party leaders in almost every section of the country, amassing, along with a great deal of goodwill and thanks mostly to Louis Howe, thousands of file cards on which were noted the names, addresses, occupations, connections, special enthusiasms, and personal characteristics of more than two thousand influential Democrats, with many of whom he now began a genial correspondence as to how best to rebuild their battered party.

Franklin had no illusions about the immediate political future. The Democrats, he told Governor Cox, were not likely to return to the White House until an economic collapse drove the Republicans out. ("Thank the Lord we are both comparatively youthful!" he wrote Steve Early.) But when the time came, Franklin meant to be the man to whom his party turned.

"No one who heard your son . . . on Monday night," a friend of Sara's had written after hearing Franklin speak at Madison Square Garden on election eve, "need feel any concern for what the world would call his defeat. He is out of the reach of defeat. He is going his own way toward his own goal as steadily when voted down as when voted in. He is of a larger pattern than can be measured by any short sample of time. His *ideas* are as much beyond all power of defeat as he is himself. They are the *coming* ideas of the world. . . ."

Those ideas quickly proved malleable. As soon as he decently could, Franklin abandoned his support for U.S. entry into the League (Harding's election had ensured that America would not go in, in any case), and urged instead a separate peace with Germany, followed by negotiations with other countries aimed at reducing "the terrible burden of armaments from which all nations are suffering." By March of 1921, the man who had been the Wilson administration's loudest advocate of a Big Navy would declare himself "wholly out of sympathy with this talk about our having the greatest Navy in the world."

Among the letters of praise and commiseration Franklin received after the election was one filled with advice from his uncle, Fred Delano:

I am writing to express my sympathies but more than that to express my congratulations on the good, clean fight you have made. It would, of course, be too much to say that you made no mistakes; no fair person could expect it; but I think that your mistakes were trivial and unimportant when compared to your good and effective work.

You are young and if you learn to take care of your health will have many years of usefulness. You are endowed with a good and honorable name, with a pleasing personality, with many gifts denied to other men, and you have sufficient means so that you can afford to be a little independent—These are great gifts and they impose a heavy responsibility, but I look to see you make good in that undertaking. In the next two years you should seize the opportunity of looking after your personal affairs and of acquainting yourself with and getting in touch (as few public men do) with the way business is done and businessmen look at things. That is most desirable for you regardless of your future career and who shall say what that will be!

Franklin required little urging. With five children now attending fashionable and expensive schools, he needed to make a handsome living. He hoped, he said, soon to become one of the "younger capitalists."

Van-Lear Black made that possible. A yachtsman and Democratic fundraiser who owned the Baltimore *Sun* and had been an admirer of Franklin's since the party held its convention in his city a dozen years earlier, he offered Roosevelt a job on Wall Street as vice president in charge of New York, New Jersey, and New England for the Fidelity & Deposit Company of Maryland.

The Fidelity & Deposit Company—always "the F&D" to Franklin—was the fourth largest surety bonding concern in the nation. Its directors had been seeking "an executive with legal training, an alert mind and soundness of judgment which has not been warped by specialization." Franklin generally filled that bill, but it was his name, connections, and attractive personality that made them most eager to have him: The Fidelity & Deposit Company guaranteed contracts by both government and private industry; Franklin's contacts with politicians, labor leaders, and the New York banking community could be of enormous benefit to the business.

Black was a most understanding employer. Franklin's salary was fixed at $25,000 a year, five times what he had earned at the Navy Department, and he was required to spend just half of every weekday in the office. This would allow him to continue to practice law with

Grenville Emmet and Langdon Marvin and also leave him free to accept as many as he wished of the invitations to speak that arrived every week.

Much later, Franklin gave an aide a characteristically colorful version of how he got his job. "After we got licked that November," FDR said, he stopped off at Baltimore on the way south to shoot wildfowl. There, Van-Lear Black took him aside:

> "Look, we want to make you the head of New York, New Jersey and New England of the Fidelity and Deposit Company as vice-president" [he said].
>
> I said, "Van, there are two considerations. I don't want to give up my law practice entirely, want to keep my hand in. I will do this, if you wish, I'll make a contract to spend from one o'clock every day with the F&D. But up to one o'clock—noon—I'll be doing my law work. Your job with the F&D is partly giving out glad-hand stuff, so I'll spend my lunch hour for you," I said. "The other condition is that you let me look over your list of officers and vice-presidents. I've got to pick 'em. They may be all right, but *I've* got to pick 'em *myself.*"
>
> He said, "That's fair enough," and went out. And there on the list was [Harry] Daugherty, in charge of Ohio for the F&D.
>
> I said, "Mr. Black, I can't do that."
>
> "Well," he said, "he's been our agent there, he's handled all our legislative work in Ohio and I can't let him go. Well," he said, "I think he's going to the Cabinet."
>
> I said, "I think so, too, but I can't work for a company that Daugherty remains in."
>
> So, in order to get *me* for the F&D, the F&D fired Daugherty outright!

On January 7, 1921, Black toasted the arrival of his glamorous new employee with a lavish black-tie dinner at Delmonico's. Among the guests who welcomed Franklin Roosevelt to Wall Street were Adolph S. Ochs of the *New York Times*, Daniel Willard of the Pennsylvania Railroad, Owen D. Young of General Electric, Edward R. Stettinius of U.S. Steel, and Frank A. Munsey of *Munsey's* magazine. The main speaker of the evening, William P. G. Harding, governor of the Federal Reserve Board, talked glowingly of the new maturity now being evidenced by American business: Never again, he said, need American investors worry that the market might at any moment veer from

orgiastic extravagance to grim pessimism. Franklin applauded as
gravely as the rest.

His work for the F&D was largely "glad-hand stuff," just as he
remembered, pursuing business from celebrated acquaintances such as
Tex Rickard and Owen Young, chatting up old political allies, and,
with Louis Howe's help, exploiting the links to labor he had forged
during his years at the Navy Department. "I am going to take advantage of our old friendship," he wrote former Congressman James P.
Maher of Brooklyn, swept out of office in the same Republican tide
that had inundated Franklin, but now a real estate magnate in Brooklyn, "and ask if you can help me any in an effort to get . . . construction
bonds from the powers that be in Brooklyn. . . . As all of my friends
are your friends I feel . . . you can be of real help to me. I assure you
the favor will not soon be forgotten." J. C. Skemp of the Brotherhood
of Painters, Decorators and Paperhangers of America saw that all the
financial officers of his locals were bonded through Fidelity & Deposit.
"We have never forgotten," he told Howe, "that Mr. Roosevelt was
largely instrumental in securing recognition of painting as a basic
trade."

Black was pleased with the way things seemed to be going. Results
were "splendid," he told Roosevelt not long after he joined the firm.
"If you can hold expenses the results will actually be world-beating."
By 1923, the Fidelity & Deposit had moved from fourth to third place
among its competitors.

Franklin's mornings at his law office were no more demanding
than his afternoons at the F&D. Langdon Marvin recalled that he
"gave most of his time to cleaning up his political matters and writing
letters that had to do with it. I don't remember that he was active in
the practice of law."[32]

Now helping him handle his mail was twenty-three-year-old Marguerite Le Hand, nicknamed "Missy" because one of the smaller
Roosevelt children had trouble saying "Miss Le Hand." She had per-

---

32. He did later like to tell of a client who came to see him one morning not long after he
returned to the law. She was an elegant, elderly lady dressed in black and she told a tearful story:
the trustees of her late husband's estate, she said, had mismanaged it so badly that her income
had been halved and, not content with that, were now attempting to turn her own children
against her. Moved by her plight, Franklin suggested she return the next day, bringing with her
whatever documentary evidence she might have at home. In the meantime, she was not to worry;
he would be glad to defend her. A few minutes after she left, one of the wicked trustees called.
Had the lady been there? Yes, Franklin said. "Good God," said the caller. "She's escaped from
the asylum!" *Source:* Sara Delano Roosevelt, *My Boy Franklin*, pages 98–99.

formed ably at headquarters during the campaign, cheerfully keeping track of Franklin's constantly changing speaking schedule without complaint, and it was Eleanor who suggested that she be hired, temporarily at first, to help her husband clean up all the correspondence that had piled up while he was aboard the *Westboro,* and then permanently when he decided to divide his time between the law and the F&D. It had taken a bit of doing to get her to sign on; she initially worried that working for a lawyer would be "too dull." Franklin assured her that law was only a small part of what he had in mind. "Oh, that's all right," he said. "There'll be a lot besides legal briefs . . . a lot of interesting things."

His appointment diary was soon crowded with such things—speaking engagements, business dinners, and meetings of the growing number of civic groups that helped keep his name before the public and alive in influential circles: he continued to serve as a Harvard overseer; lobbied gently to be admitted to the Century Association (his father's favorite club, to which his half brother already belonged and to which he would be admitted in 1922); became president of the Boy Scout Foundation of Greater New York; member of the executive committee of the National Civic Foundation and the Near East Relief Committee; chairman of fund drives for Lighthouses for the Blind, the Woodrow Wilson Foundation, the Cathedral of St. John the Divine. And he talked expansively of writing several books.

Eleanor worried that he was signing up for too many outside activities even though, she told him, she understood his "remarkable faculty for getting through work when you get right down to it." And she confessed to a friend her irritation that Franklin, who had told her he would need to spend his evenings learning the bond business, was instead again accepting dinner invitations nearly every night of the week.

She was herself now often away from home. Franklin was at least momentarily out of public life, but his wife was more involved in it than ever before. The complex living conditions under which the Roosevelts resumed their New York existence in the months following the election had something do with her frequent absences. Thomas W. Lamont, the Morgan partner who had been the Roosevelts' tenant at 49 East 65th, had abandoned his lifelong Republican loyalties to vote for his landlord in the fall election—it was "an issue of idealism" he told the *New York Evening Post* in an interview which Sara proudly pinned into her personal scrapbook—but he was unwilling to give up his lease, which still had six months to run. And so the Roosevelts were forced to divide their family and their time: the smallest boys, John and Franklin Jr., stayed with their nurse in their grandmother's New York house; Anna and Elliott remained at Springwood with their British governess, Miss Sherwood. Eleanor spent Monday to Thursday in Manhattan and the weekends in Hyde Park, where Franklin joined her and the children whenever his crowded calendar allowed.

Even though she would be living until spring in one or another of her mother-in-law's homes, Eleanor resolved not to allow that fact to alter the independence she had begun to win for herself with such great effort. "I did not look forward to a winter of four days in New York with nothing but teas and luncheons and dinners to take up my time," she remembered. "The war had made that seem an impossible mode of living, so I mapped out a schedule for myself." She took daily lessons in typing and shorthand, and decided she also wanted to learn to cook. When it became clear that there was neither room nor time for her to practice her recipes in her mother-in-law's busy kitchen, she located a former cook, "now married, who had an apartment of her own, and . . . went twice a week and cooked an entire meal which I left with her for her family to criticize."

None of this pleased Sara. "My mother-in-law was distressed," Eleanor recalled, "and felt that I was not available, as I had been when I lived in New York before." To placate her, Eleanor joined the Monday Sewing Class and lunched regularly with her and the other members to provide them both with "a definite engagement together once a week."

But Eleanor also joined the board of the League of Women Voters, successors to the triumphant Woman Suffrage Association, and volunteered regularly to survey the *Congressional Record* and the Albany legislative calendar in search of bills likely to affect women. A tall, capable attorney named Elizabeth F. Read was assigned to help her understand the intricacies of legislation. Miss Read soon became a close friend; so did Esther Lape, the small, voluble companion with whom she lived on East 11th Street. Both women were impressed with Eleanor's practicality. "The rest of us were inclined to do a good deal of theorizing," Miss Lape remembered. "She would look puzzled and ask why we didn't do whatever we had in mind and get it out of the way." Eleanor found the two women good company, interested not only in the social and political issues that had come to concern her most, but also in poetry and French, enthusiasms Eleanor had only rarely indulged since leaving Allenswood and marrying Franklin.

"My husband was working hard," Eleanor later wrote tactfully of that winter and spring, "he went occasionally to men's dinners, and I remember many pleasant evenings with Elizabeth and Esther in their little apartment. Their standards and their interests played a great part in what might be called 'the intensive education of Eleanor Roosevelt. . . .'"

In April, Eleanor was a delegate to the national League convention at Cleveland and reported to Franklin from her hotel room:

Dearest Honey,
I've had a very interesting day and heard some really good women speakers. Mrs. [Carrie Chapman] Catt is clear, cold reason. Mrs. Larue Brown is amusing, apt, graceful, a Mrs. Cunningham from Texas is emotional and idealistic, but she made nearly everyone cry! I listened to Child Welfare all the morning and Direct Primaries all the afternoon, lunched with Margaret Norrie, drove out at five with Mrs. Wyllis Mitchell and called on Mrs. [Newton D.] Baker and heard some speeches on Child Welfare and attended a N.Y. delegate's meeting and am about to go to bed, quite weary. Meetings begin tomorrow at ten. . . .
                          Much, much love dear & I prefer
                          doing my politics with you!

In fact, though she may not have admitted it even to herself, she was learning to like doing her politics without her husband. She now "wrote fewer letters and asked fewer questions and gave fewer confidences," she remembered, "for I realized that in my development I was drifting far afield from the old influences. . . . I was thinking things out for myself and becoming an individual."

In May, attending a meeting of the Dutchess County League at Poughkeepsie, she introduced a resolution defending a Vassar professor against charges of disloyalty lodged by Vice President Coolidge. The Poughkeepsie *Eagle News* headlined its story: MRS. F. D. ROOSEVELT OFFERS RESOLUTION TAKING TO TASK HUSBAND'S VICTORIOUS RIVAL. The local press was "indignant," she noted in her journal. "Foolish of me to do anything of the kind."

This was the first recorded instance of a problem the Roosevelts never finally resolved, although they would face it again and again throughout the rest of their lives together; how far dared she go in public pursuit of goals that might damage her husband's political future.

There was something uncharacteristically feckless about Franklin's conduct in the spring of 1921. One Wednesday evening in May, and with Eleanor out of town, Franklin attended a reunion dinner at the Harvard Club. When Eleanor came home at midday on Thursday, the maid told her Mr. Roosevelt was still in bed. Frightened that he had fallen seriously ill, she hurried upstairs only to find that he was simply hung over "after a wild 1904 dinner & party." She was, she noted in her diary, "very indignant with him."

In early July, he and Eleanor travelled to Oldgate, the Connecticut home of Bamie Cowles, for the wedding of her son, Sheffield. At the groom's dinner, even some members of the normally boisterous Oyster Bay branch of the family found Franklin alarmingly noisy. Eleanor's Aunt Corinne charitably attributed Franklin's behavior to "the Roosevelt high spirits"; Eleanor herself was not amused.

One reason Franklin seemed to adjust so erratically to his new life out of government was simple boredom: the law had never interested him; neither did the surety bond business. Out of public office for the first time in a decade, he yearned again to wield power, missed being at the center of things.

Nor had his mood improved when the newspapers announced the name of the new Assistant Secretary of the Navy—Theodore Roosevelt, Jr.[33] The newspapers were filled with admiring stories about young Ted—THIRD ROOSEVELT AS ASSISTANT SECRETARY OF THE NAVY—in which Franklin had already become merely an amusing historical precedent. One Republican editorialist expressed confidence that for *this* young Roosevelt being Assistant Secretary of the Navy would prove a springboard to the White House, even though "for 'Fifth Cousin' it proved a political scaffold from which he suddenly dropped into oblivion." Another pointed out that when the Assistant Secretary attended the next Army-Navy Game and the massed sailors gave their cheer—

33. Admiral David W. Taylor was not cheered either. He had been in the Navy since before the Spanish-American War, and when the first rumors that the Harding administration planned to appoint TR, Jr. reached him on January 20, 1921, he came to see Josephus Daniels. "I have had to stand two Roosevelts," he said. "I cannot try another." *Source:* Josephus Daniels, *Cabinet Diaries.*

N-N-N-N!

A-A-A-A!

V-V-V-V!

Y-Y-Y-Y!

Roosevelt! Roosevelt! Roosevelt!—

it would be Ted, not Franklin, who would smile and bow and wave his thanks.[34]

34. Someone who had once worked very closely with Franklin in Washington—perhaps Louis Howe, Steve Early, or Livy Davis—sought to summarize his old boss's frustration in some lines Davis later sent to him:

> In that dear old navy office where I used to rule the sea
> There's another Roosevelt sitting—and I know he thinks of me;
> For my boss is back at Raleigh, and I hear the middies mourn
> "Come you back you gallant seaman, come you back to Washington
> Now the dirty work is done."

> And the gloomy days are gone and the joy has just begun
> Though I guessed that gang were yaller, yet it makes me feel right blue
> When I hear them praising Teddy for the jobs I used to do
> For I never would have braved the storm where Jimmy Cox was sunk
> If they hadn't made me stand for all that League of Nations bunk
> Blooming League of Nations stuff!

> For I didn't give a rap
> For a mandate over Yap
> I was there to blow the blasted German navy off the map.
> When the sun was on the golf links, and Josephus out to lunch
> I would call up Livy Davis, or some other of the bunch
> And the while we hacked the cover off the little bounding sphere
> I would whisper all my sorrows in his sympathetic ear,—
> In his sympathetic ear
> When he couldn't choose but hear
> All the inside dope and gossip of the naval atmosphere
> Yes, I once was happy, too—glad and carefree, just like you,—
> Chumming round with boys like Baker, Bryan or Bill McAdoo.

> But that's all shove[d] behind me, long ago and far away
> And there's no more admirals hanging round my office every day
> For I am learning back in Gotham what the Democrats all tells
> If you've heard the office calling you won't ever heed naught else
> No, you'll never heed naught else
> But those office-holding spells
> And the dinners and receptions with the diplomatic swells
> But they've clamped me in a vise
> And then shoved me on the ice
> And there's something sort of tells me they won't try the same thing twice.

> Boys, I'm tired of wasting lung power on this noisy New York mob
> For I'm pining every moment for that little navy job
> Though I dine with fifty aldermen from Albany to Queens
> And they fill me full of prophecies, I know just what it means
> Yes, I know just what it means
> For I've gone and spilled the beans
> And there's eight long years of waiting for the hope of other scenes.

But there was something else on Roosevelt's mind, as well. The Newport scandal would not go away. The Dunn Board, appointed by Daniels to look into the matter, had been slow to render its verdict. It had been in everyone's interest—Daniels' and Roosevelt's as well as that of the men of Section A—that the Navy wind up that work before the new Republican regime took over on March 4. "I am anxious," Daniels wrote Franklin, "to pass upon the findings of the Dunn board before my term of office expires. Is this not very important?"

Roosevelt was sure that it was. At the end of February, Daniels sent the board's "Findings, Opinions and Recommendations" to him for his comments before he gave his endorsement. "You know more about this than I do," Daniels said. Perhaps predictably, the board dealt gently with the Assistant Secretary: Roosevelt, it said, had merely been "unfortunate and ill-advised" when he "either directed or permitted the use of enlisted personnel to investigate perversion."

Franklin objected strenuously even to this mild criticism: such use of enlisted personnel had not been *his* idea, he said; the investigation had been going on for more than two months before he was told anything about it. "Frankly," he told Daniels, "I must decline to be made in any way the scapegoat for things which had their inception among the regular navy officers concerned."

As to the guilt of Lieutenant Erastus Hudson, the physician who had overseen the activities of Section A, of his subordinate, the former

---

Boys, I want to rule again
King of all the bounding main
Where the dreadnaughts ride the pillows and the braided seadogs reign.

Ship me somewhere south of Philly, where the worst is like the best
Where there ain't no Cox or Woodrow, and a man can throw a chest.
For I hear the navy calling, and it's there that I would be
Back among my mates and middies, looking lazy at the sea.
Back in dear old Washington
Where we helped to wreck the Hun
For I know the war is over and I'm missing half the fun
Take me back to Washington
Now the dirty work is done
And the gloomy days are gone and the joy has just begun.

Rosy sympathized with Franklin's annoyance at young Ted's takeover of the office his half brother would always in some sense consider his own, and loved to tell him stories of the usurper's supposed self-importance. After taking up his new duties at the Navy Department, young Ted had been unable to attend a family wedding, Rosy reported, and when his sister Helen Roosevelt Robinson asked his mother-in-law why he was not there, "Mrs. Alexander said 'he was very sorry not to come, but was detained by affairs of state.' Don't you love it? . . ."

(This last question, a standard phrase of FDR's in later years, was apparently a legacy of his exuberant half brother.)

detective Ervin Anold, and the men under their command, Daniels was faced with two divergent opinions: while the Dunn Board ruled that they had been misguided but had done nothing criminal, the Judge Advocate General ruled that men who had committed "acts of sexual perversion which are crimes *mala in se*" must face court-martial, a process that Franklin and Daniels knew could take months and yield still more embarrassing publicity.

To make matters worse, Hudson continued to call at Franklin's office, asking to be allowed to resign and hinting broadly that if permission were not granted he would have no choice but to testify further against Roosevelt and his former chief. "I hate to bother you again about this same matter," Franklin wrote Daniels, "but for each time that I write you our friend Dr. Hudson comes in to see me or telephones to me at least a score of times."

In a peremptory tone unusual even for him, Franklin urged his former chief to act fast to avert further trouble: "I want you to understand absolutely clearly, my dear Mr. Secretary, that if you approve [the Judge Advocate's view] you must inevitably find that the enlisted men . . . were guilty and recommend for immediate court-martial the names of such men who worked under Hudson as there is evidence against. . . ." The best way out was to submit the legal question to the Attorney General, who, Roosevelt was sure, would agree that the men had committed no crimes.

Daniels followed Franklin's advice, signing his final endorsement late on the night before Inauguration Day. "I have been sweating blood over the Newport case," he wrote to his former assistant the next morning, ". . . and I believe the conclusion reached is just to all concerned." In the end, the criticism of Franklin had been softened, and, just as Roosevelt had predicted, the Attorney General ruled in favor of leniency toward Lieutenant Hudson and his agents. "No sensitive man can criticize us for seeking to protect the enlisted men," Daniels assured Franklin. There would be no troublesome courts-martial: Hudson was censured for having failed to make sufficiently clear to Roosevelt the methods his men were employing at Newport, but permitted to resign honorably from the Navy.[35]

35. Dr. Hudson resumed private medical practice in New York, but continued to dabble in criminology and became a consultant to the city on fingerprinting. In 1933 he testified at the trial of Bruno Richard Hauptmann, the accused kidnapper of Charles A. Lindbergh's infant son, Charles Jr. He proved both overconfident and wrong on the witness stand, misremembering a key piece of evidence. Had the prosecutors not been able to demonstrate that his testimony was in error, Hauptmann might have gone free. *Source:* George Waller, *Kidnap*, paper 452-453.

The outgoing Secretary had done his best to blunt the Dunn Board's findings, but neither he nor Franklin could do anything about the Senate subcommittee also then investigating the Newport matter. It was in the hands of its two-man Republican majority, Chairman L. Heisler Ball of Delaware, and Henry W. Keyes of New Hampshire, whose fondness for Franklin Roosevelt had not been intensified by his recent run for the vice presidency.

Roosevelt had testified briefly before the senators shortly after the subcommittee was established in February 1920, and thought he had been promised then by Senator Ball an opportunity to be heard at greater length. Two months later, he had telephoned the chairman to ask when he might be expected to be called. "Not yet," Franklin remembered Ball saying, ". . . the Dunn Board is still investigating and as we may call other witnesses, I will let you know when we are ready for you."

Since the Dunn Board findings were delivered in March 1921, however, Franklin had heard nothing whatsoever from the subcommittee, and he knew that a parade of thirty other witnesses, some of them hostile to him, had been allowed to testify at length. As the weeks went by, and winter turned to spring and then to summer, the unbroken silence seemed increasingly ominous.

Franklin tried as best he could to put it from his mind. He hoped to spend most of the summer with his family at Campobello for the first time in eight years, and sent careful instructions to Captain Franklin Calder, the islander who saw to the Roosevelt boats and taught the children how to sail, to have the big, bark canoe newly pitched and the *Vireo* freshly varnished by the time Eleanor and the rest of the family arrived in early July.

Franklin joined them there on Sunday, July 10.

On the following Wednesday, a messenger from the nearby village of Welshpool bicycled through the cottage gate with a telegram:

> COMMITTEE READY TO REPORT MONDAY ON NEWPORT. LIBELLOUS RE-
> PORT OF MAJORITY. CAN YOU GO TO WASHINGTON AT ONCE ANSWER
> JOSEPHUS DANIELS

Franklin's worst fears had been confirmed: the subcommittee had gone back on its promise. The majority's findings, which Daniels warned were "libellous," were to be released to the press before Roosevelt had a chance to defend himself.

He wired the chairman immediately, demanding a hearing. Senator Ball wired right back, blandly denying ever having promised him a chance to testify; the transcript of his appearance before the Dunn Board had adequately covered all the necessary ground. If Roosevelt insisted on making an appearance, the subcommittee would hear him at ten o'clock on Monday morning, July 18.

Franklin left his cool island for heat-shrouded summer Washington, but when he reached the Capitol on Monday morning as instructed, Ball said again that the committee saw no need to hear him; his Dunn Board testimony had been sufficient. Franklin insisted he be allowed to speak, protesting that he had never even seen the testimony of the other witnesses, let alone been given a chance to respond to it. Ball agreed to allow him to look over the fifteen volumes of testimony, but they would need to have his statement by eight o'clock that evening.

Roosevelt had no choice but to agree to the chairman's conditions. On the way out of the hearing room, the Democratic member, Senator William H. King of Utah, assured him that the chairman had promised to delay releasing the majority report until Friday and had said that it could be amended if necessary before then.

Franklin was loaned an empty office in the Navy Department for the day. Steve Early and Missy Le Hand were called in to help. "Damn it, Steve," Franklin told Early as they began work, "this whole business is nothing but dirty politics. That's the point we've got to emphasize."

The majority report was about as damaging as it could possibly have been. Senators Ball and Keyes said they found Franklin's testimony before the Dunn Board "unbelievable" and "incredible."

He and Daniels, they charged, had permitted Lieutenant Hudson and other guilty parties to resign from the service and escape court-martial in order to cover up their own guilty acts.

Further, Roosevelt must have known and approved of the "most deplorable, disgraceful and unnatural" activities of Section A, and "If . . . he did not inquire and was not informed" about the methods its agents employed, he "was most derelict in the performance of his duty."

> The committee, however, cannot believe so. Franklin D. Roosevelt was a man of unusual intelligence and attainments, and . . . must have known the methods used and to be used to secure evidence. . . .
>
> The Committee is of the opinion that Secretary Daniels and Assistant Secretary Franklin D. Roosevelt showed an utter lack of moral per-

spective when they allowed men in the uniform of the United States Navy . . . to publicly testify to the beastly acts that had been performed upon them. . . . That Franklin D. Roosevelt, Assistant Secretary of the Navy, ever permitted or directed as he did, according to the opinion of both the Dunn court of inquiry and of this committee, the use of enlisted personnel for the purpose of investigating perversion, is thoroughly condemned as immoral and an abuse of the authority of his high office.

While a listless ceiling fan moved the humid air around the room, Franklin went to work in his shirtsleeves, teeth clenched on his pipe, angrily pencilling point after point on a lined yellow pad, then passing the pages on to be typed up by Missy. It was impossible in a single day to more than glance at the testimony—there were six thousand single-spaced pages of it—so he concentrated exclusively on preparing a refutation of the Republicans' most serious charges.

Late that afternoon, a friendly newspaperman stopped by with further alarming news: Senator Ball had again failed to keep his word. The majority report had already been released to the press.

Franklin continued to labor over his statement, finishing just in time to make it over to the Capitol and read it before the subcommittee while Early distributed the text to the newspapers. His tone was by turns angry and aggrieved. The Republicans had committed "a breach of faith," their report was meant for the "premeditated and unfair purpose of seeking what they mistakenly believe to be a partisan political advantage."

As soon as he had learned what was going on at Newport, he said, "IMMEDIATE ORDERS WENT OUT FROM ME . . . THAT DAY TO STOP IT." As for the committee's

insinuations that I must have known, that I supervised the operations, that I was morally responsible, that I committed all sorts of high crimes and misdemeanors. . . . THE SENATORS CANNOT CITE THE EVIDENCE IN THEIR SUPPORT. Throughout their report I accuse them of deliberate falsification of evidence, of perversion of facts, of misstatements of the record, and of a deliberate attempt to deceive. . . .

None of this worries me, nor does the report itself worry me personally. As an American one deplores bad faith and a conscious perversion of facts on the part of any Senator. As an American, irrespective of party, one hates to see the United States Navy, an organization of the nation, not of party, used as the vehicle for cheap ward politics. It rather amuses me to know that these Republican Senators consider me worthwhile attacking so maliciously and savagely. Perhaps they may later on learn what a boomerang is. . . . I only ask fair play.

Franklin was in fact deeply worried and not even remotely amused: if the majority report was generally believed, his political career, already in suspension, might actually be over. The story made headlines on the morning of July 20, just as he had feared it would, and his last-minute denials were mostly buried in the accompanying stories. Even the normally austere *New York Times* played it on the front page, and beneath a banner all the more potentially damaging for its genteel opacity:

LAY NAVY SCANDAL

TO F.D. ROOSEVELT

SENATE NAVAL SUB-COMMITTEE

ACCUSES HIM AND DANIELS

IN NEWPORT INQUIRY

DETAILS ARE UNPRINTABLE

But there was nothing more in the afternoon papers; public attention seemed focused on the new Harding administration rather than the alleged misdeeds of its predecessor. "I have talked to a good many people . . . and lots of them want to rush into print," Franklin assured Eleanor. "But in view of the fact that no [more] papers have taken it up it may seem best to drop the whole thing as far as letters to the paper are concerned and seek only for the present at least to file the complete brief and facts with the full Senate Committee, and watch what if anything they will do."

White with exhaustion, Franklin returned to New York by train and had a sound night's sleep at 47 East 65th Street for the first time in over a week.

But back in his Wall Street office the next day—where he was irritated to find enough unanswered mail and other matters to keep him from returning to Campobello for nearly two weeks—he continued to seethe at the treatment he had received from the Republican members of the subcommittee. Senator Ball had at least twice lied to him personally, yet his coldest anger was directed at Ball's colleague, Chairman Keyes. Perhaps Roosevelt expected no better of Ball, who was merely a graduate of public schools, of Delaware College and the University of Pennsylvania. Keyes, on the other hand, was a Harvard alumnus who had allowed partisanship to override the gentlemanly courtesy one Harvard man owed another no matter what their differences, and it was to him that he wrote a furious letter.

> Personal
> Senator Keyes
> Washington, D.C.   July 21, 1921
> Sir:
>   I have since seeing you on Monday had the opportunity of reading the report of the subcommittee signed by you.
>   As I believe in being frank, I am writing you in order that you may not labor under any misapprehension of my opinion:
>   I have had the privilege of knowing many thousands of Harvard graduates. Of the whole number I did not personally know one whom I believed to be personally and wilfully dishonorable. I regret that because of your recent despicable action I can no longer say that.
>   My only hope is that you will live long enough to appreciate that you have violated decency and truth, and that you will pray your maker for forgiveness.
>
>   Very truly yours,
>   Franklin D. Roosevelt

In the end, he thought better of mailing this letter, tucked it away in its envelope, and placed it in his files. Across the back of the envelope he scrawled in pencil: "Not sent—what was the use? FDR."

From Campobello that same day, Eleanor tried to reassure her husband: "It must be dreadfully disagreeable for you & I know it worried you though you wouldn't own it, but it has always seemed to me that the chance of just such attacks as this was a risk one had to take with our form of government & if one felt clean oneself, the rest did not really matter."

But for Franklin, it did really matter. A dozen years later, he was still fearful of the potential political damage his career might suffer if the opposition chose to rake up the old Newport scandal. Running for President in 1932, and working closely with Earle Looker, his extravagantly admiring campaign biographer, Roosevelt and Howe made sure that Franklin's lengthy press release written to refute the Ball subcommittee's charges was included in the text, word for word. Of the eighteen pages devoted to Franklin's almost eight years at the Navy

Department in Looker's *This Man Roosevelt,* nearly half are devoted to his version of what happened at Newport.

A week after his return from Washington to New York, on the morning of Thursday, July 28, Franklin and some fifty other prominent men associated with the New York Boy Scouts boarded Baron Collier's steam yacht at the Columbia Yacht Club and set sail for Bear Mountain, there to inspect the eighteen interconnected camps that served 2,100 city boys each summer.

It was a congenial gathering, and as the yacht moved slowly past the Palisades, "Big Bill" Edwards, a three-hundred-pound ex-football star who was now collector of Internal Revenue for the city, playfully placed Richard Enright, the city Police Commissioner, under citizen's arrest, charging that the innocent-looking cane he carried was in fact filled with illegal whiskey.

A mock court was set up and when the handle of the cane was unscrewed it turned out to be attached to a three-foot tube filled with golden brown liquid. Franklin volunteered to act as prosecutor. The phial was handed around so that everyone could sample it. Franklin was last. He smacked his lips, rolled his eyes. "May it please the court," he shouted to the watching crowd. "I find that the liquid in this container is nothing more than vanilla extract, and I move that the case be dismissed."

A good deal more vanilla extract may well have been consumed before the yacht finally docked at the Scout camp and the dignitaries in straw hats filed down the gangplank, because a little later—to the delight of the uniformed Scouts lined up along the bank—Big Bill Edwards fell spectacularly out of the canoe from which he was supposed to be inspecting them.

All in all, it was the sort of occasion Roosevelt always liked. There were parades and speeches and plenty of massed flags; earnest Scouts demonstrated sailor knots to Franklin, who kindly pretended not to know how to tie them; he posed for the newspapers surrounded by cheering boys; and he served as toastmaster at a campfire and fried-chicken dinner before sailing back to the city that evening.

With him went a mysterious virus, perhaps incubated somewhere among the Boy Scouts, inhaled or ingested at some point during the hot, hectic day, too small for any microscope to detect, but already moving through his bloodstream, multiplying as it moved.

CHAPTER

13

❧

FRANKLIN HAS BEEN QUITE ILL...

HE PATH that led up from the beach through a thick mat of wild
blueberry and raspberry bushes to the red clapboard hilltop cottage at Campobello was long, narrow, and steep, a daunting climb for
the smallest Roosevelts. But all five children raced one another up it
on arrival every summer, laughing as they ran. Despite the climb,
Franklin Jr. recalled, "it was a wonderful happy feeling when we
finally got there."

They had been especially eager to get there in the summer of 1921,
because for the first time in years their father was to be with them for
more than a few days at a time; and when he had been called away
almost as soon as he arrived in July to rush to Washington and defend
himself against the majority report of the Senate subcommittee investigating the Newport matter, they were understandably disappointed.

It was not that they lacked for things to do without him on the
island. Once morning lessons were over, the older children went to the
family tennis courts or ran down to the *Vireo*; Captain Calder taught
them the rudiments of sailing, but Franklin reserved the finer points
for himself and no child was allowed to go out alone until he had been
satisfied that he or she could play the eddies and make it back to the
mooring in a flat calm. For the younger children, an old dory had been
hauled part way up the hillside in front of the cottage so that they could
undertake their own imaginary voyages, raising and lowering the sail

and repelling boarders as they went. "We used to go all over the world in that dory right from that field," James remembered.

Closer to home, there was a good deal of cheerful bustle. A laundry wagon picked up dirty towels and bedding once a week, but the rest of the wash was done by the caretaker, Anna McGowan, and hung outside, on lines strung within a green lattice fence to keep it from being seen by intrusive passers-by.[1] There were twice-weekly visits by a butcher from Wilson's Beach. A dairyman brought milk and cream, butter and eggs. The children and their mother often took their seats in Captain Calder's open dory, powered by a noisy inboard motor which the smallest children called the "chug-chug," and crossed two choppy miles of sea to Eastport, where they shopped for fruit and vegetables and picked up newspapers and mail.

There were unauthorized and unscheduled diversions, as well. Unless the gate was kept tightly closed, half-wild cattle wandered into the garden to crop the nasturtiums and dahlias so carefully tended by the gardener, Nedley Wilson. The big resort hotel called the Tyn-y-Coed that had housed Franklin and his parents when they first came to Campobello while he was teething in 1883 had long since been abandoned, and Sara had declared its weatherbeaten silvery ruin off-limits to the children; it was full of nails and splinters, its floors sagged and seemed about to collapse, but Anna, James, and Elliott often slipped inside anyway to explore the dark, empty corridors. The boys also tried—with clothesline lariats and without much success—to lasso the sheep that helped keep the golf course clipped, and Chief, Anna's German Shepherd, once chased several terrified sheep into the sea, causing considerable concern within the family that the islanders who owned them might insist the dog be destroyed.[2]

1. For added modesty, Eleanor's underwear was dried inside a pillow case. *Source:* Interview with Linnea Calder, former Roosevelt employee.

2. When he returned briefly to the island as President in 1933, Franklin called the people of Campobello his "neighbors," but his actual closeness to them seems to have been somewhat exaggerated. There was always a considerable gulf between the fishermen and their families who occupied the island through the bitter winters, and the wealthy American visitors whom they found it profitable to serve in the summer, a gulf best symbolized perhaps by the seating in St. Anne's, the board-and-batten Episcopal church at Welshpool to which all the Roosevelts walked every Sunday morning; the pews in the center were reserved for the summer people; islanders sat along the walls.

When there was a rash of burglaries among the summer cottages in the winter of 1920–21, Franklin thought the "only practicable way" to ensure that it was not repeated "would be to have the owners of summer cottages combine in a statement to the islanders announcing definitely that they would not return to Campobello another year if further robberies occurred. I feel

James woke up in his first-floor room at five one morning to find a drunk sitting on the veranda, enjoying the view and cheerfully singing in a loud, cracked voice. Eleanor leaned out the living room window and ordered the intruder off the property. "Lady," he said, rising and starting down the stairs, "if you don't like my singing, I'll take it some place else."

The children's grandmother was not yet on the island that summer, did not plan to arrive until the beginning of September; a blessing for her daughter-in-law, perhaps, but another letdown for the children upon whom Sara doted, and who liked to bring her the baskets of wild raspberries for which, one grandchild remembered, she could be counted on to pay "exorbitant profits," provided there were "no stems, no leaves."

She had resumed her prewar custom of an annual trip to Europe where, at sixty-seven and unknown to Franklin and Eleanor, she and her niece Muriel Robbins Martineau had taken a twin-engine aeroplane across the English Channel. "It was five hours from London to Paris. I had been told about four hours, but I would not have missed it and if I do it again I shall take an open plane as one sees more and it is more like flying. Poor Muriel soon began to feel ill and had to lie on the floor all the way and had a horrid time."

DON'T DO IT AGAIN, Franklin cabled her when he got her letter describing her journey by air, and she wired back to say she would

---

morally certain that the inhabitants of Campobello Island could stop these robberies if they really wanted to.

The hardy islanders did their uncomplaining, courteous best to cater to the wealthy men and women who summered among them. But, as one member of an old island family said, the visitors "would have been surprised to know what we knew—and what we thought about them," and nearly a century later, stories of the summer people's more exacting demands were still being told privately among old Campobello families. Two concerned James Roosevelt, Franklin's father:

During one of his last summers on the island, Mr. James persuaded himself that there was something seriously wrong with his well; the water tasted bad. A crew was sent down the shaft to close it off, bail out all the water that remained, and scrub down the stone walls. Then it was refilled and allowed to settle before a ladle was ceremoniously dipped and handed up to Mr. James. He tasted it, grimaced, and ordered the men to repeat the whole process. They did, and the dipper was filled again. The old man insisted something still was wrong. The weary men climbed back down the well, but this time one carried a dead frog under his jacket so that when he climbed up again a little later, he could wave it in triumph and declare the problem solved. Gratified, Mr. James gravely tasted the water once more and pronounced it fine.

On another occasion, the elder Roosevelt asked an islander to post a letter for him in Welshpool, and gave him a nickel with which to buy a three-cent stamp. "Not wishing to embarrass Mr. Roosevelt," the man did not immediately walk the two miles back to his cottage to bring him his two cents change. Mr. James went into town personally to hunt him down and get his money back. *Sources:* Franklin D. Roosevelt Papers, FDRL; Confidential source, Campobello.

abandon plans to fly back to London before coming home, since he seemed so concerned.[3]

But there were plenty of interesting visitors to keep the children occupied, among them several members of the Fly Club, who arrived unannounced aboard a yacht looking for Franklin, and Prince Antoine Bibesco, a Rumanian diplomat, and his wife Elizabeth, the daughter of the leader of the British Liberal Party, Herbert Asquith. Mrs. Bibesco was accustomed to cocktails before dinner so Eleanor had to break open a drawer in Franklin's dresser to get at the whiskey hidden there; Jeff Newbold, Franklin's Hyde Park neighbor, who was also visiting the island, did the mixing.[4]

And there were other, steady guests occupying some of the cottage's eighteen bedrooms. James's tutor, Russell Lynt, had a room, his concentration on lessons temporarily undermined by his infatuation with Anna, now fifteen, coltish and high-spirited.[5] Jean Sherwood, tutor to the other children, was a boarder, too, and so was her mother, Mrs. Sidney Sherwood, whom Eleanor had invited to join the family for the summer. Mademoiselle Seline Thiel, the diminutive Swiss governess in charge of the smaller children, provided considerable excitement one afternoon when she fell off the *Vireo* and was so chilled after coming ashore that even Eleanor felt it necessary to lace her lemonade with illegal gin.[6]

3. Rosy, summering with Betty further north on the Upsalquitch River, was delighted: "So 'Mama' really did fly to Paris after all. We put her up to it long before leaving, and kept her up to the scratch until the very last moment, and told her she must on no account get talked out of it. I knew Franklin would have a fit!! I think it a splendid thing for her to have done and will make her feel years younger!!" *Source:* James Roosevelt Roosevelt Papers, FDRL.

4. This was a considerable concession for Eleanor to make to her guest; she was then an ardent believer in Prohibition. Sara took a more measured view. "I rather enjoy being where one had red and white wine on the table," she wrote from Paris, "very little said on the subject and no drinking of spirits, and I feel, as I always have, that we should have made our fight against *spirits* and the saloon, and encouraged the French habit of wine and water, but Americans really like their spirits now, just as the English do." *Source:* Joseph P. Lash, *Eleanor and Franklin,* page 266.

5. She would have a similar impact on James's next tutor.

6. This was Mlle Thiel's second icy plunge off Campobello. During his truncated island stay earlier that summer, Franklin took her out in a new sailing canoe; " . . . he wasn't too familiar with sailing canoes," James recalled, and "he did a maneuver which resulted in their tipping over and into the water they went. . . . Father was . . . very embarrassed, first . . . for having tipped over, but secondly because the young lady was a very good swimmer, a much better swimmer than Father was, and Father caught his foot . . . under the canoe and had a little difficulty freeing himself, and the young lady proceeded to free him and help him onto the little float that we had off the shore. . . . So I think he probably never told the story, but now it is a part of history." When Franklin learned of her second fall, he wrote to tell Eleanor that "As all good things come by three, tell Mlle to postpone her bath till she can fall off the rocks on our next cliff walk."

Louis and Grace Howe were also staying in the Roosevelt cottage, with their eleven-year-old son Hartley. Howe had finally left the Navy Department and, after toying with several job offers, had decided to remain at Franklin's side, ostensibly as his assistant at the Fidelity & Deposit, actually in order to continue with him to plan his political future, which both men now believed might begin again with a run for governor in 1922.

Howe stood in for Franklin at Campobello as best he could, patiently swatting fly balls to Hartley and to Elliott, still clumsy on his bowed legs, kindly assuring him that he had the makings of a ball player. He also helped the older children to carve model boats from balsa wood, a hobby he and their father shared, and he supervised the men trying to repair the gas engine that worked the windmill and without which on windless days no water could be pumped to the holding tank.[7]

Eleanor organized everything, seeing to the needs of her flood of guests; overseeing the staff of five and making sure that the Irish serving girls got to the Catholic church in Eastport on time for Sunday Mass; arranging for almost daily picnics, sending a servant on ahead to spread the blankets and distribute big wicker picnic baskets filled with sandwiches and Thermoses of drinks, hot and cold; and keeping her eye on the children from the porch, a huge megaphone suspended from its ceiling so that without having to lift it, she could project her high voice far enough to break up a quarrel on the beach far below or call the children in off the water for dinner.

In the evenings, she read aloud in the living room, where the combination of the day's activities, the flickering yellow light from the kerosene lamps, and the warmth of the fragrant driftwood fire soon made her listeners drowsy. "Grace and sometimes Louis snore before I get far," she told Sara, "and Russell goes to bed before I begin and Mlle won't go to bed but props her eyelids open with her fingers!"

Despite all that their mother did to keep them entertained, her children yearned for their father. "Campobello was his second home,"

Source: "Conversations Between the Four Roosevelt Brothers . . . ;" Elliott Roosevelt, ed., *FDR: His Personal Letters, 1905–1928,* page 516.

7. The children were in no hurry for this work to be completed: hot water was chronically in short supply at the cottage, and baths were limited to a depth of three inches for fear the small brass water heater in the kitchen would run out, but when the holding tank itself emptied, Franklin Jr. recalled, "*that* was a red letter day, a great, great occurrence, [because] we didn't have to take a bath." *Source:* "Conversations Between the Four Roosevelt Brothers. . . ."

James remembered; while on the island he "inundated us with fun. . . . Sometimes we felt we didn't have him at all, but when we did have him, life was as lively and as exciting as any kid could want it to be." Franklin was the center of things at Campobello, just as he was at Hyde Park, bursting with plans for picnics, always ready to sail or fish or camp, to lead the children and any friends who lived nearby in games of hare and hounds, bounding ahead of his pursuers along the rocky cliffs that edged the island.[8]

Back in New York, Franklin was nearly as eager to be back on the island as his children were to have him there, but he was still exhausted from his frustrating time in Washington and not looking forward to the long trip north, which involved three different trains and was wearying at the best of times. And so, when Van-Lear Black offered to carry him to Campobello aboard his 140-foot steam yacht *Sabalo*, he gratefully accepted.

They set sail on Friday, August 5. "I thought he looked tired when he left," Missy Le Hand wrote Eleanor, and both women hoped he would have a fine, lazy time aboard the *Sabalo*. The voyage was slower and less restful than they'd wished, however: off the coast of Maine the skies grew dark and the seas rough and the Maryland captain, to whom these waters were a mystery, finally turned over the wheel to Franklin. He held it for hours, shouting cheerful anecdotes into the fog and assuring his nervous passengers that he had guided huge destroyers through to Campobello safely in the past; they had nothing to worry about.

They arrived in Welshpool harbor late on Sunday the 7th to find the Roosevelt and Howe families assembled on the dock. As Franklin hugged the children one by one, they clamored to know what they would be doing the next day and the next. He promised to take all but the two youngest boys on a three-day fishing and camping trip up the St. Croix River, but they would have to wait just a little longer for his full attention. He led them all over the big yacht, then sent them home for the night, while he and Eleanor stayed aboard the *Sabalo* for an elegant dinner served on the broad fantail by stewards in uniform.

8. The children exulted in these ordeals, so reminiscent of the "point-to-point" marches his Cousin Theodore had led when he visited Oyster Bay as a small boy. Franklin's knowledge of the island's terrain and tides often allowed him to arrange for the "hounds" on his trail to be marooned on slippery rocks surrounded by a rising sea, and Eleanor, who found all such activities a trial, once said gently that "quite a number of persons really did not enjoy Father's games at all." *Source:* James Roosevelt (and Sidney Shallett), *Affectionately, FDR,* page 141.

Afterwards, they heard the sound of the horn that signalled that a school of fish had entered the weir just offshore, and the Roosevelts took Black and his party out to see the islanders sein herring. Crimson flares lit the dark water as fishermen hauled in nets seething with silver fish. It was an almost biblical scene, Eleanor thought; "you cannot help thinking of how the apostles drew in their nets and brought their boats in laden with fish."

Despite the rough trip and the tired feeling that he still seemed unable to shake, Franklin was up early the next morning to take Black and his friends fishing aboard the *Sabalo*'s tender; he was determined to return at least some of the hospitality his new boss had shown him following his defeat the previous November. "I baited hooks," he remembered, "alternating between the fore and aft cockpits . . . crossing beside the hot engine on a three-inch varnished plank." His foot slipped and he fell overboard into the Bay of Fundy. "I'd never felt anything as cold as that water!" he said. "I hardly went under, hardly wet my head, because I still had hold of the motor-tender, but the water was so cold it seemed paralyzing. This must have been the icy shock in comparison to the heat of the August sun and the tender's engine."

That evening he still felt tired and now his legs ached; a touch of lumbago, Franklin thought.

Tuesday afternoon, Black sailed south, perhaps exhausted by trying to match the pace set by his exuberant young employee, but pleading the press of business in New York.

Franklin was left alone with his family at last.

After lunch the next day, Wednesday, August 10, Franklin took Eleanor, James, and Elliott for a long sail. He held the tiller, as always, guiding the little boat smoothly but perilously close to jagged rocks; he was stern about safety whenever his children sailed alone, James remembered, but willing to take calculated risks when he was in command, supremely confident that his own encyclopedic knowledge of Campobello's currents and passages would get him out of any tight spots.[9]

To his eldest son, Franklin then seemed simply "the handsomest, strongest, most glamorous, vigorous, physical father in the world." James had always felt that way, and recalled sitting next to his father

9. Many years later, when Eleanor returned to the island with friends but without Franklin, she eagerly seized the tiller. "I never get a chance to sail the boat myself," she told a woman companion. "There are always men around. . . . One has always to let the men do the sailing." *Source:* Stephen O. Muskie, *Campobello,* page xix.

in the family Stutz back in Washington, marveling as his father effortlessly pushed the clutch pedal that his own small foot could not so
much as budge. On July 2, 1921, just before the family came up to
Campobello, his father had taken him to Jersey City to see the heavyweight champion, Jack Dempsey, fight the French challenger,
Georges Carpentier. The afternoon sun had been brutal and as soon
as the Frenchman was counted out in the fourth round, the onlookers
began pushing toward the exits and Franklin and his thirteen-year-old
son somehow got separated in the crush. James never forgot the feeling
of relief that flooded over him when he heard his father's familiar voice
calling his name and saw his tall figure pushing his way through the
crowd to find him.

Now, as the little boat darted in and out among the rocky islands
that guarded the entrance to the Cobscook River, the Roosevelts spotted tendrils of blue smoke rising above the dark pines on one of the
smaller islands: a forest fire. Franklin worked the *Vireo* as close as he
could—"almost on the beach," James recalled—and led Eleanor and
the children splashing toward shore. He tore evergreen boughs from
trees, armed each member of the party with one, and hurried them
inland, where they spent an hour or so battering at the flames that
squirmed and smoldered through the carpet of brown needles. When
the last ember was out, Franklin remembered, "Our eyes were bleary
with smoke, we were begrimed, smarting with spark-burns, exhausted."

They sailed back home across Cobscook Bay, past Friar's Head to
the long wooden slip that jutted out into Friar Bay in front of the
cottage.

It was about four o'clock and Franklin still felt curiously shaky. His
solution was more exercise: he challenged his children and Hartley
Howe to run with him to the family's favorite swimming place, a
shallow, landlocked freshwater pond called Lake Glen Severn, two
miles away on the other side of the island. They accepted, and he and
the children hurried inside to put on bathing suits, then pounded off
along the mossy path, past groves of stunted, lichen-covered trees and
clearings blanketed with purple fireweed. A horse and wagon driven
by a servant came along behind to bring them all home again.

When they reached the warm pond, Franklin and the children
splashed and whooped into the water and swam to the other side, then
they hurried up and over a low ridge, ran across several yards of sandy
beach, and hurled themselves into the frigid Bay of Fundy. Franklin

was disappointed that the shock of this plunge failed to yield "the glow I'd expected." He still felt strangely tired; his legs still ached.

Most of the children chose to jump into the wagon for the ride home, but when John and Elliott said they wanted to race, Franklin agreed to run with them.

He felt increasingly weary as he reached the cottage, and when he found that Captain Calder had brought the mail over from Eastport in his absence he sat down in his wet bathing suit to read it, "too tired even to dress. I'd never felt quite that way before."[10]

After about an hour he began to shiver, and when he could not seem to stop, told Eleanor he thought he'd best go upstairs to bed and have dinner on a tray; he did not want to risk infecting the children with whatever it was he was clearly coming down with. Eleanor sent up a tray of food at which he only picked. He was not hungry, had trouble sleeping, continued to tremble despite a heavy woolen blanket.

Early the next morning, when he swung his legs out of bed and started toward the bathroom just across the narrow hall, his left leg buckled beneath him. He steadied himself, made it into the bathroom and even managed to shave, although his head and back now throbbed with pain.

Something seemed very wrong, but he managed to get back into bed, and when Anna brought up his breakfast tray and anxiously asked her father how he was, he smiled and assured her he just had a little lumbago and a touch of fever. Eleanor took his temperature: the thermometer registered 102 degrees.

Clearly, Franklin was not going camping on the St. Croix and neither was she. Mrs. Sherwood and Grace Howe were put in charge of the expedition and the somewhat dispirited party set off that morning in Captain Calder's noisy motorboat, its deck piled with tents and supplies, two canoes lashed behind the stern. They were to be gone for three days, plenty of time, Eleanor thought, for Franklin to get better.[11]

The cottage was suddenly quiet and Eleanor could concentrate on caring for her husband, who seemed steadily to worsen. The pain in his back increased; he was having more and more trouble moving his

10. For the rest of her life, Sara believed against all medical argument that if her son had been *made* to change into nice dry clothes that afternoon, he would never have fallen ill. *Source:* Rita Halle Kleeman Papers, FDRL.

11. The youngest children, Franklin Jr. and John, stayed behind in the care of Mlle Thiel.

legs. "I tried to persuade myself that the trouble with my [left] leg was muscular, that it would disappear as I used it," Roosevelt remembered. "But presently it refused to work, and then the other. . . ."

Eleanor sent a local man in a motorboat sputtering across the Bay to Lubec to fetch Dr. E. H. Bennet, the local physician who saw to the children's ailments and had helped deliver Franklin Jr. He was a country doctor, perfectly well suited to set broken bones and soothe sore throats, but intimidated always when tending to the needs of the wealthy summer people on Campobello and frankly baffled by what now seemed to be wrong with Mr. Roosevelt. He looked Franklin over, and finally decided he must be suffering from a bad cold; he would be back in the morning to see how he was doing.

Roosevelt knew he did not have a cold. The next morning he could not stand without Eleanor and Howe holding him upright, and he had difficulty urinating. When Bennet and Eleanor conferred on Friday morning, they agreed they must have a second opinion. But how to find a qualified physician? There was only one telephone on the island, two miles away in the white clapboard Welshpool home of Mrs. Etta Mitchell, the telegraph and telephone operator, but she had to route all her calls through Eastport and connections were often bad.

Louis and Dr. Bennet chugged over to Lubec by boat, where Howe took over the doctor's telephone and began canvassing summer resorts up and down the Maine coast in search of a doctor willing to interrupt his holiday. At Bar Harbor, Howe finally located Dr. William Williams Keen, an eminent eighty-four-year-old Philadelphia surgeon who, when he learned who was ill, agreed to motor up to see the patient and to mention his mission to no one. But he would not be able to get there until Sunday morning.[12]

12. Dr. Keen's discretion had first been tested just a little more than twenty-eight years earlier, when he was called in upon the case of another important Democrat, President Grover Cleveland. In the summer of 1893, Cleveland was diagnosed as having a malignancy in the roof of his mouth. The United States was then undergoing a severe financial panic, and Cleveland's response to the bad news was a single word: "Secrecy." The country must not know. The President was slipped aboard a private yacht off Long Island, where a team of doctors, including Keen, successfully excised the cancer while a nervous steward stood by as an orderly.

One of the members of the surgical team later evidently leaked the story to a fellow physician who, in turn, confided in a reporter. But when the story appeared in the Philadelphia *Press* a month or so later, the White House indignantly denied that any such operation had ever taken place.

Dr. Keen himself confirmed the story in a 1917 magazine article nine years after Cleveland's death. *Source:* John Stuart Martin, "When the President Disappeared," *American Heritage* (October 1957).

Howe sat at the foot of the bed, helplessly rubbing Franklin's feet while they waited. "I don't know what's the matter with me, Louis," Roosevelt said again and again. "I just don't know."

Dr. Keen arrived about seven-thirty on Sunday morning, a slender, white-bearded old man with gold-rimmed spectacles.

After he had left again, Eleanor wrote Rosy:

> [Dr. Keen] made a most careful, thorough examination of [Franklin] this morning & he thinks a clot of blood from a sudden congestion has settled in the lower spinal cord temporarily removing the power to move though not to feel. I have wired to New York for a masseuse as he said that was vital & the nursing I could do & in the meantime Louis & I are rubbing him as well as we can. The doctor feels sure he will get well but it may take some months. I have only told Franklin he said he could surely go down [to New York] the 15th of Sept. He did say to leave then but not before on account of the heat . . . but it may have to be done on a wheelchair. The doctor thinks absorption [of the clot] has already begun as he can move his toes on one foot a little more which is very encouraging. . . .

The children, back now from their camping trip, were instructed to keep quiet and play out of earshot of the house, and not under any circumstances to enter their father's room. Hartley Howe remembered that his father ignored him entirely after he returned; he had moved into a closet-sized room with a door opening into Franklin's bedroom and all his attention now seemed focused on the well-being of the desperately ill man to whose career he had already devoted more than a decade. "From that time on," Eleanor wrote later, "[Louis] put his whole heart into working for my husband's future."

For two days, Eleanor and Louis took turns rubbing Franklin's legs, persevering despite the obvious pain it caused. Massage was agony, but it gave all three the sense that they were not entirely helpless, that there was something they could do about this terrifying malady. He did not improve: his toes froze again, he could no longer move at all below the waist. His bowels and bladder stopped functioning. Dr. Bennet had to show Eleanor how to administer an enema and, with Louis's help, lift her husband on and off the bedpan. He also taught her how to catheterize him, a delicate endeavor involving the insertion of a thin glass tube; if it were not done properly, infection would set in which was then virtually impossible to combat.

For Franklin—who had not been intimate with his wife for at least three years and perhaps for five—this unavoidable business must have been especially disagreeable; it would continue day and night for almost three weeks. For Eleanor it was a chance to perform what a friend would call "a service of love," and she was later uncharacteristically proud when one of her husband's physicians complimented her on her nursing skills.[13]

After the discovery of Franklin's romance with Lucy Mercer, he and Eleanor had agreed to stay together, but apart. He had dealt her self-esteem a brutal blow by his betrayal of her trust, and she had few remaining illusions about her husband: he had not proved serious or honorable enough for her (perhaps no one could have); she had found him too sinuous, too cautious, too willing to abandon principled positions and sacrifice old friends in the interest of personal advancement. She may no longer have been in love with her husband, as she once was, but she could again find solace now in being useful. Those who needed her invariably received intense devotion and concern; toward those who did not—including Franklin when he was well—she was merely unfailingly courteous.

Eleanor snatched what little sleep she could on the upholstered window seat in Franklin's room. Dr. Keen worried that round-the-clock nursing would weaken her own health. "You have been a rare wife and have borne your heavy burden most bravely," he told her later. "You will surely break down if you . . . do not have immediate relief. Even when the catheter has to be used your sleep must be broken at least once in the night. I hope that by having his urine drawn the last thing at night, [he will be able] to wait until the morning."

Franklin's fever soared. His hopes plummeted. Much later, he would confess to a friend that he lost his religious faith for a time, persuaded that the God who had always seemed to favor him had now inexplicably turned away.

By Monday night, August 15, Eleanor remembered, he "was out of his head."[14]

13. Eleanor evidently continued to perform these delicate tasks even after the arrival of Miss Edna Rockey, a trained nurse from New York, at the end of the month. *Source:* Eleanor Roosevelt, *This Is My Story,* page 332.

14. Fearing perhaps that such language could be construed to suggest that polio had permanently affected his mind, FDR asked her to delete this passage from the manuscript of her autobiography and she did. *Source:* Bernard Asbell, ed., *The FDR. Memoirs,* page 259.

Then, slowly, his temperature subsided; he was still in constant pain but his mind began to clear and some of his old optimism started to reappear. Perhaps God did not mean for him to die, after all.

On Thursday, Eleanor wrote Rosy that "I think he is getting back his grip and a better mental attitude, though he has of course times of great discouragement. We thought yesterday he moved his toes on one foot a little better which is encouraging."

That same day she got a letter from Dr. Keen. He had been ruminating on Mr. Roosevelt's case since returning to Bar Harbor, he said, and was now "inclined to believe" that a blood clot might not be the cause; it was more likely "a lesion of the spinal cord," a more serious affliction with a much slower rate of recovery. He also sent a bill for $600.

She could not bear to tell Franklin what Keen had said, as she wrote to his half brother, "it wrings my heart for it is all so much worse for a man than a woman."[15]

Rosy professed to be pleased by Keen's latest diagnosis:

> ... the last bulletins of the Drs seem to me reassuring. I like lesion better than clot, tho they seem to think that may take a little longer. I sent Dr. Murray a synopsis of your first letter and enclose his reply. He is very level-headed and I was awfully glad to hear approves of Dr. Keen. Usually he is very *difficile* about other Doctors. . . . I wrote him because I knew what he said would have great weight with Mama.[16]

But Louis Howe, who had himself once been misdiagnosed by doctors and had later been forced to stand by helplessly while his own infant son died of meningitis, was unwilling fully to trust any single physician's opinion. He wrote detailed letters to Franklin's Uncle Fred Delano in New York, asking that his nephew's symptoms be relayed

15. Rosy wrote directly to Franklin in the doggedly sunny tone all the Roosevelts seemed to adopt toward illness: "I am awfully distressed to hear about you. But I feel sure it is going to pass off very quickly. You are too young and hearty to play these old gentleman's tricks for any length of time. If you were my age, I should worry, but as it is, I don't. If it had happened on the yacht I might have guessed the reason, too much good food, *etc. etc. etc*!!!" *Source:* James Roosevelt Roosevelt Papers, FDRL.

16. Dr. Murray, evidently Rosy's own fashionable physician, agreed: Keen is "a clever man and his opinion is generally correct," he said. "If absorption of clot has really begun," as Keen said, then "motion in the feet & legs ought to begin soon. . . . The outlook is favorable. . . . These cases are not uncommon & often completely recover after weeks or months. At all events take the bright side as it is quite justifiable, and we all want to see this fine fellow restored to his former good health." *Source:* James Roosevelt Roosevelt Papers, FDRL.

to specialists there and in Boston for their opinions. They suspected infantile paralysis.[17]

"Dr. Keen, all doctors seem to know," Uncle Fred told Eleanor. "He is a fine old chap, but he is a Surgeon and not a connoisseur [of] this malady. I think it would be very unwise to trust to his diagnosis." Dr. Robert Williamson Lovett of Boston must be consulted immediately: "Pardon my being so insistent, but you & Mr. Howe ask for my best judgment and I give it to you." Lovett—"the great Dr. Lovett," Uncle Fred called him—was the leading American authority on infantile paralysis, Professor of Orthopedic Surgery at Harvard, chief surgeon at both Children's Hospital, Boston, and the New England Home for Crippled Children, chairman of the Harvard Infantile Paralysis Commission, developer of plans for treating patients of polio epidemics in three states, author of the standard work in the field.

"On Uncle Fred's urgent advice," Eleanor told Rosy, "which I feel I must follow on Mama's account, I have asked Dr. Keen to try to get Dr. Lovett here for a consultation to determine if it is I.P. or not. Dr. Keen thinks *not* but the treatment at this stage differs in one particular and no matter what it costs I feel and I am sure Mama would feel we must leave no stone unturned to accomplish the best results."[18] Dr. Keen tracked down his eminent colleague having dinner with friends near his summer home at Newport. Lovett agreed to come north.

On August 25, two weeks to the day since Franklin fell on the way to the bathroom, ten days after Louis and Eleanor had begun the agonizing massage, Dr. Lovett, Dr. Keen, and Dr. Bennet all arrived together at Campobello. Lovett was a tall, commanding man with a waxed gray mustache and dark, kindly eyes. He examined the patient gingerly—Franklin's muscles were too tender for him to go much beyond a superficial once-over. Roosevelt's face seemed partially paralyzed, Lovett noted. His arms were weak. The left thenar eminence—

17. One of them was young Dr. Samuel A. Levine, whom Delano saw in Boston on August 20. From the symptoms his visitor listed for him, Levine was certain Franklin had polio and urged that rather than wait for someone from Boston to make his way north to Campobello he contact a doctor in Bangor, Maine, and have a lumbar puncture done within twenty-four hours to relieve the pressure within the spine. This procedure reduced fever almost instantly, he said, and there was some reason to believe that it lessened the paralytic aftereffects as well. This was not done, with tragically crippling results—or so Dr. Levine, who later became an eminent cardiologist, always maintained. *Source:* Richard T. Goldberg, *The Making of Franklin D. Roosevelt*, page 30.

18. "I think you are right to have the second consultation," Rosy replied. "You have to damn the expense in such cases. All the same, I think $600 for his first outing was rather high. . . ." *Source:* James Roosevelt Roosevelt Papers, FDRL.

the fleshy part of the hand below the thumb—had lost its power. His bladder was still paralyzed but, thanks to Eleanor's care and patience with the catheter, there was no infection. No muscles in his immobilized legs seemed to have been totally destroyed as yet, but they were all very weak, most markedly so through the hips.

Lovett took his colleagues down the hall and into Anna's bedroom to discuss his findings before announcing them to the family.[19] When he emerged again, he was brisk and businesslike. The diagnosis was "perfectly clear," he said: it was poliomyelitis.

Eleanor reeled with the news. Were the children in danger, she first wanted to know. Lovett said no; if any of them were to fall ill they would have done so by now. But to be certain the disease did not spread to other families on the island she was to keep them isolated from other children.[20] And yes, James could safely go back to Groton when the term began, "on the proviso that the boy wears clothing which he did not wear at Campobello, that he puts on fresh underclothing, and that he takes a bath and washes his hair immediately before leaving."

As for Franklin, all massage must be stopped at once; it simply prolonged the already dreadful pain he was experiencing and might actually further damage his muscles. He was likely also to experience "mental depression and . . . irritability," and all those around him should therefore seek to bolster his spirits through steady encouragement. A registered nurse must be sent for to relieve Eleanor of some of the stress she had been under.

Otherwise, all they could do was wait. "[It] was a mild case within the range of possible complete recovery," Lovett remembered assuring Franklin, Eleanor, and Louis, but "I told them very frankly that no one could tell where they stood, that the case was evidently not of the severest type, that complete recovery or partial recovery to any point was possible. . . . [I]t looked to me as if some of the important muscles

19. Anna hid in the closet to listen and thereby learned what was wrong with her father before he himself did. *Source:* John W. Boettiger, *A Love in Shadow*, page 88.

20. This would keep them from attending church, the single bright spot, Franklin's sons remembered, in those otherwise dark weeks.

In later years, several of the children recalled that they had had the sniffles while their father was ill and wondered whether they, too, had not been struck with polio but in its most benign form. They may well have been. Grace Howe, too, later claimed to have noticed a curious stiffness in one leg the following winter, and modern studies suggest that for every person seriously afflicted by polio, some two hundred others exposed to the same virus suffered symptoms no more serious than those of a mild cold. *Source:* "Conversations Between the Four Roosevelt Brothers. . . ."

Franklin and Josephus Daniels gazing at the White House from the balcony of the old War and Navy Building, in May of 1918.

Three snapshots of the Vice-Presidential campaign from Anna Roosevelt's album: At the left, Franklin does his best to stir an upstate New York crowd; above, he stretches his legs between train rides with (left to right) Louis Howe, Tom Lynch, and Eleanor; below, he gratifies a group of the women whom Eleanor called "worshippers at his shrine" at Jamestown, New York, delighting himself and annoying his wife.

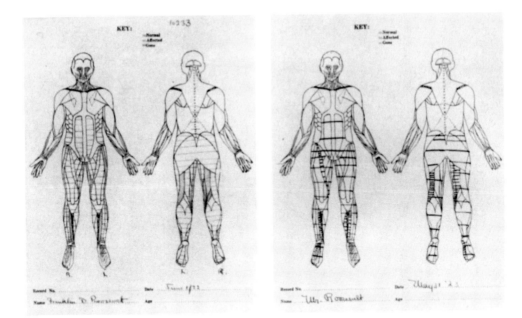

These previously unpublished muscle charts, drawn by Dr. Robert Lovett, show how little Franklin improved between June 1, 1922 and May 31, 1923. The horizontal lines—bright red in the originals—denote damaged muscles. Despite seven years of work, Roosevelt's charts would never show substantial progress toward recovery. (Photo credit: Boston Medical Library in the Francis A. Countway Library of Medicine)

Franklin's carefully nonchalant pose in this photograph, thought to have been made on the South porch at Springwood in the late spring of 1922, required that he lift his unbraced right leg into place with his hands.

Roosevelt at the Warm Springs pool in October, 1924, and on a Florida beach with (left to right) Missy Le Hand, Maunsell Crosby, and Frances de Rham during the second cruise of the houseboat *Larooco* in 1925.

When John W. Davis, the Democratic nominee for President, came to call at Springwood during the summer of 1924, Franklin still had to receive him unsteadily on crutches. The photograph at the right, taken a year later at Marion, Massachusetts, is sometimes said to show him standing on his unbraced legs, but most of his weight clearly rests on the shoulders of his long-time valet, LeRoy Jones, and Dr. William McDonald, and moments after the camera clicked, he sank back into the wheelchair that can just be made out behind him.

Marion Dickerman, Eleanor, and Nancy Cook on tour with an unidentified companion, mid-1920's. "I just hate to have Eleanor let herself look as she does," wrote her Auntie Bye. "Though never handsome she has always had a charming effect, but Alas and lackaday! Since politics have become her choicest interest all her charm has disappeared and the fact is emphasized by the companions she chooses to bring with her."

A possum hunt, staged for Roosevelt near Warm Springs. FDR is behind the wheel at the left, a suitably rustic corn cob pipe clenched in his teeth. The unhappy quarry is said to have been tied to the tree.

Roosevelt among friends at Warm Springs: At the left, he fishes for panfish while wearing his braces on the outside of his trousers in 1925. Above and below he practices walking with other polios: the skeletal man holding on to the railing behind him is Fred Botts, whom he made registrar of the Warm Springs Foundation; behind Botts is another fellow-patient, Miss Lois Foreman of Bellefont, Pennsylvania. An eyewitness recalled that "the three of them were roundly scolded for this line-up . . . walking was supposed to be very serious business."

The Roosevelt party returns to the Hyde Park railroad depot after Franklin's nomination for Governor in 1928. FDR grips the arm of his friend Henry Morgenthau, Jr. as he picks his careful way across the tracks to his waiting car, swinging each foot forward in a semi-circular arc. Later, photographs that so clearly showed his awkward gait were discouraged.

might be on the edge where they could be influenced either way—toward recovery, or turn into completely paralyzed muscles."[21]

Franklin was composed but silent for a time after Lovett and his colleagues left the cottage. He now seemed "really relieved that he knew the worst that could happen to him" Eleanor recalled. She would see the same expression on his face when she finally got in to see him on the afternoon of the day the Japanese attacked Pearl Harbor. He looked "very strained and tired" then, too, she remembered. "But he was completely calm. His reaction to any great event was always to be calm. If it was something that was bad, he just became almost like an iceberg, and there was never the slightest emotion that was allowed to show."[22]

But as the hours ticked by, his resolve this time began to melt. To do nothing, to be forbidden to do anything; to lie in bed hour upon hour, trying *not* to think of the fact that his aching legs were immovable, that they were weaker, flabbier, with every passing hour, unable even to urinate or move his bowels without having to call for help, would have been nightmarish for any man. But for Franklin Roosevelt—restless, exuberant, proud, energetic—it was very nearly insupportable. (It must have been nearly insupportable for Louis Howe and for Eleanor, too, who now knew that their tireless massaging of his legs may actually have furthered the crippling process which they were powerless to halt.)

On August 31, after six days of enforced immobility, he was at least momentarily unable to maintain his relentless cheer. When Dr. Bennet

21. What had really happened—though it was then still imperfectly understood by all physicians, including Dr. Lovett—was that some two weeks before, about the time Franklin attended the Boy Scout rally at Bear Mountain, he had somehow ingested the polio virus, usually transmitted in fecal matter or secretions of the nose. He was himself then still exhausted from his Washington struggle over the Newport scandal, and therefore an easy target for the ravenous virus which had travelled from the stomach to the bloodstream, overwhelming the body's natural antibodies as it multiplied, then entered the nerves and, finally, the spine, destroying nervous tissue, causing muscles to atrophy.

Dr. Keen had only reluctantly called in Dr. Lovett for his second opinion and was defensive about his own misdiagnosis, assuring Eleanor that Lovett had told him after examining the patient, "I do not recall any more puzzling or obscure case especially in its early manifestations than Mr. Roosevelt's." Then Keen added a footnote: "As to the financial side, will you kindly send me at your entire convenience a thousand dollars." *Source:* Elliott Roosevelt and James Brough, *Mother R.: Eleanor Roosevelt's Untold Story,* page 144.

22. Frances Perkins, who saw him earlier that same day, remembered that he was "very calm, very quiet, very pale." He seemed to make rather a point of reading dispatches and not looking up when members of his Cabinet entered the room, she thought. There was "a sort of studied quality about his calmness as though he was determined to have this outer aspect of calm. ... It's one way of controlling hysteria." *Source:* Transcript of interview with Frances Perkins, Columbia Oral History Project, Columbia University.

dropped in to see him that morning, he found his patient "unnerved," tearfully certain he was getting worse, not better. The muscles in his legs were more lifeless than they had been even during Lovett's visit; there had been a general "falling off." It seemed clear to him that stopping the massage had been a mistake: it had been painful, but at least he had felt he was *accomplishing* something by undergoing it. Doing nothing was intolerable.

Shaken, Dr. Bennet sent a night letter to Lovett:

ATROPHY INCREASING POWER LESSENING CAUSING PATIENT MUCH ANXIETY ATTRIBUTED BY HIM TO DISCONTINUANCE OF MASSAGE CAN YOU RECOMMEND ANYTHING TO KEEP UP HIS COURAGE AND MAKE HIM FEEL THE BEST IS BEING DONE OR TELL HIM THOSE CHANGES ARE UNAVOIDABLE HIS WIFE ANXIOUS TO AVOID WORRY ON HIS PART.

Franklin's mother was due to arrive in New York that same afternoon.

Still abroad when Franklin fell ill, Sara knew nothing of what had happened to her son, and her possible reaction was a source of concern to all the Roosevelts. Franklin had planned as always to be at the foot of the gangplank when she docked, and getting a stand-in who could gently break the news of his illness was one of the first things Eleanor tried to arrange from Campobello. Rosy seemed the obvious choice:

Do you think you can meet Mama when she lands? She has asked us to cable just before she sails & I have decided to say nothing. No letter can reach her now & it would simply mean worry all the way home & she will have enough once she gets here but at least then she can do things. I will write her a letter to quarantine, saying he is ill but leave explaining to you or if you can't meet her, to Uncle Fred or whoever does meet her.

Rosy agreed that Sara should be told nothing until she got back— "She would have forty thousand fits all the way over, and could do no good"—and he did go to meet her, arriving at the dock, a small, compact figure with a straw hat and white beard, armed with a pass from the collector of the Port of New York, which entitled him to board Sara's liner before anyone disembarked. But, as so often happened when Rosy ventured out into the workaday world, things didn't go perfectly. He struck "a perfect ass of a customs officer," he told Eleanor, "who notwithstanding the Collector's letter made himself very disagreeable and turned everything inside out. I never have run across any of that breed before. I think he was a left-over veteran of the Civil War! When the Assistant Appraiser came things were better." (He turned out to be a friend of Franklin's old friend and political ally, John K. Sague, the former Mayor of Poughkeepsie.) Rosy was waved through but when the gangplank was first lowered, the surging tide of newspaper reporters eager to seek out arriving celebrities carried him along with it, right past the room in which Sara and the other first-class passengers were waiting. "Found I could not get anywhere near where the passengers were," Rosy wrote, "and when I tried to get on shore I was slammed back again because I had no landing ticket!! It took an awful lot of bluff and brandishing of the (empty) envelope from the Collector's Office to get me ashore again in time to meet Ma at the gang plank when she came off!! Your Uncle Fred was there, too."

Rosy handed Sara the carefully worded letter from Eleanor:

Dearest Mama,

Franklin has been quite ill and so can't get down to meet you . . . to his great regret, but Uncle Fred and Aunt Kassie both write they will so it will not be a lonely homecoming. We are all so happy to have you home again dear, you don't know what it means to feel you near again.

The children are all very well and I wish you could have seen John's face shine when he heard us say you would be home soon.

. . . we are having such lovely weather, the island is really at its loveliest.

Franklin sends all his love and we are both so sorry we cannot meet you.

Ever devotedly
Eleanor

"It was a shock to hear the bad news," Sara wrote her sister Dora, " . . . but I am thankful I did not hear before I sailed." The long ride to Eastport—with its change of trains at Boston, and a second transfer at Ayers Junction, Massachusetts, for the final leg aboard a single car pulled by a tiny wood-burning engine—must this time have seemed interminable, but when she reached the cottage at last on the afternoon of September 1, she found her son apparently serene. His desperation of the day before carefully concealed, he put on the cheerful mask he had worn in his mother's presence since boyhood. She described their reunion in letters to her brother Fred and her sister Dora:

... I at once ... came up to a brave, smiling, and beautiful son, who said: "Well, I'm glad you are back, Mummy, and I got up this party for you!" He had shaved himself and seems very bright and *keen*. ...

... He made me tell him all about our four days in the devastated region [of France] and told me what he saw when there. ...

Below his waist he cannot move at all. His legs (that I have always been proud of) have to be moved often as they ache when long in one position. He and Eleanor decided at once to be cheerful and the atmosphere of the house is all happiness, so I have fallen in and follow their glorious example. ... Dr. [Bennet] just came and said, "This boy is going to get all right." They went into his room and I can hear them all laughing, Eleanor in the lead.

Even Eleanor was impressed with Sara's determination to seem hopeful: her husband's mother "was really very remarkable about this entire illness," she wrote, "and I am sure that, out of sight, she wept many hours but with all of us she was very cheerful."

It cannot have been easy for Sara to feign serenity in the face of her son's illness. Her girlhood had been filled with the deaths of relatives and siblings, her own life had very nearly been sacrificed in giving birth to her only child, and she always took even the most trivial illness suffered by Franklin or any of her grandchildren with deadly seriousness, rushing in to offer counsel, remedies, concern. And, for all his exuberance and vigor, Franklin had in fact often been ill, sometimes seriously, and Sara had tried always to be at his bedside during bouts of measles, kidney trouble, chronic sinusitis, sore throats, typhoid, tonsillitis, and influenza.

Her bottomless solicitude had been hugely comforting to him as a small child, but by the time he entered adolescence it had come to seem suffocating, a reminder of a dependence on his mother he no longer wished to acknowledge.

In any case, it now made Franklin uneasy and a week after his mother's return to the island, he insisted that she take Anna and travel south for a few days to attend the wedding of Uncle Fred's daughter, Louise. So far as possible, everyday life was to be resumed.

A cascade of mail arrived from solicitous friends and acquaintances who had heard that Franklin was ill but did not know how seriously. Eleanor and Louis—and for a week or so, Missy Le Hand, up from New York to help out—handled the correspondence for him, cheerfully accepting membership on his behalf on the Vassar board of trustees and the executive committee of the New York State Democratic Party even before Dr. Lovett offered his diagnosis. "Thanks to a severe ·chill which I lay to vagaries of the Bay of Fundy climate, which has more tide and more kinds of weather than any other place in the globe," Franklin said in a letter dictated to an old friend, "I am spending a considerably longer vacation than I intended under the stern eye of a doctor who refuses to allow me to more than look at my mail and sign a few letters each day."

In fact, Franklin was not signing any letters. Louis signed for him: both his boss's thumbs were now paralyzed and he could not hold a pen.

Howe and the Roosevelts continued to believe it essential that no hint of the true nature of Franklin's illness reach the press until his prognosis was clearer, and almost from the moment Franklin fell ill, Howe had done all he could to mislead outsiders as to its gravity, assuring the local Associated Press stringer who dropped over from Eastport every couple of days that while no certain diagnosis had yet been reached, the patient was improving daily and would soon be up and around again. The first newspaper story that he had been ill but was fast recovering did not appear until August 27, and it contained not a word about infantile paralysis.

"I am telling everybody who asks that you have a very severe rheumatic attack from 'excess bathing,'" Rosy told Franklin,

> which makes it very difficult for you to move!!! It is too silly for you to have an "infantile" disease. Anyway, I don't half believe it yet, and think still you will be well and over it long before the Drs think. Unless it develops into whooping cough or measles!! But seriously, the main thing is that they all (including Dr. Murray, who I have faith in) say there is no doubt of your getting completely over it. What a pity you are not running for something this Fall. Judging by the last time, when you were in bed, what a majority you would run up without legs!!!. . . .
>
> Poor Tom Lynch I told him today about you, and he burst out crying. He wanted to pack his grip and start right out for Campo but I dissuaded him from that as I thought it would complicate matters. I don't think anything should be said about infantile, until you are safely in NY and am warning all those who know, including Ma, to that effect.

Like Rosy, Louis Howe had been in New York on August 31, meeting an incoming liner: Mary Howe was returning from a summer in France, and while her father was warm and effusive in his greeting he did not even tell his own daughter what had really befallen Franklin.

While in the city, Louis dined twice with Uncle Fred, visited the F&D office in order to assure Roosevelt that "everything in connection with your affairs is in the best possible shape," and performed two other delicate missions for the family: "[Van-Lear] Black insisted on giving me ten quart bottles of rye," he told Franklin. "I positively and firmly declined to let you consume that quantity between the time of my arrival and the 14th, so I am leaving ten of them with Mrs. Ramsey, the Hibernian housekeeper at your mother's residence, trusting that there will be a half pint or so left by the time you return."

And before returning to Campobello he searched for a suitable watch with which Eleanor wished to reward Captain Calder for his help during her husband's illness.

> Dear Boss,
> . . . I love the way Eleanor telegraphed to go into Tiffany's to buy a watch for Calder without mentioning whether it was to be a $1200 Jorgenson or a Waterbury Radiolite; also to have it inscribed without mentioning what to inscribe on it. Lord knows, I have acted as your alter ego in many weird commissions, but I must positively and firmly refuse to risk my judgment on neckties, watches or pajamas.

He nonetheless bustled into the Fifth Avenue jewelers, took careful notes on a wide range of models with prices ranging from seventy-five to "130 plunks," and arranged for Eleanor to make her own final selection by telegram. "All [the watches] are of course, water-tight gold cases. You might gather from the prices that the works are 14 karat also, but they are not! Anything less than $75 is beneath the cognizance of Tiffany & Co. . . . They all have 'Tiffany & Co.' on the dial, so the captain can exhibit it to admiring neighbors."

The progressive atrophy about which Bennet had wired Lovett continued to alarm him and his patient: Franklin's legs were "more *flabby*" and his temperature was up again, the Lubec physician told Lovett in a follow-up letter. "When you stated that the improvements in 2 weeks would be considerable, did you mean *above* or *below* waist-line? If the *former*, it is working out correctly, if the *latter* not so. Will it be better to tell him frankly these changes must come and not to be discouraged?"

Lovett's answers were not reassuring. The ongoing atrophy, he believed, was most likely due to "over-exercising the muscles in the patient's efforts to see how they are." Complete rest remained the key to recovery; above all, the temptation to undertake "meddlesome therapeutic measures" must be resisted. In other words, Franklin must stop even attempting to move his lower limbs for fear that doing so might actually ensure that they never would.

Roosevelt might be gently lifted in and out of a bathtub filled with hot water once a day: "it is really helpful and will encourage the patient, as he can do so much more under water with his legs." Otherwise, "There is nothing that can be added to the treatments, and this is one of the hardest things to make the family understand. . . ."

Franklin's uncharacteristic outburst to Dr. Bennet had been predictable, too, Lovett said, evidence suggesting that he was nearing the end of the initial acute stage of the disease, when "a period of mental instability and nervous irritability is likely to occur in adolescents and older persons. . . ." When others were in the room, Franklin remained for the most part "wonderfully cheerful," Dr. Bennet noted, "a remarkable patient."

But he was now forbidden even to *try* to move, supported by pillows at the knees, the covers pinned to the top of the footboard because even their feather-light touch on his steadily shrivelling legs intensified his pain. Hour by hour, he watched the sea breeze stir the white curtains, traced the sun's slow course across the flowered wallpaper, tried not to hear the voices of his children running and playing without him and concentrate instead on those of Louis and Eleanor as they took turns reading aloud from the bundles of newspapers Captain Calder brought daily and from books borrowed from other cottages when the small family library was exhausted.

Franklin had always flourished on activity. His little red-covered appointment book for 1921 survives, its tiny pages peppered with appointments until shortly before he left for Campobello and utterly empty thereafter, except for a scattering of engagements—weekly F&D meetings, the State Democratic Convention in September, a gathering of trustees of the American Museum of Natural History— that he now knew he would be unable to keep.

For all their public bravado, neither he nor Eleanor nor Louis could be certain what sort of life might be possible for Franklin now. But they did know that none of their questions about it could be answered so long as they remained at Campobello.

He wanted desperately to get back to New York because, as Eleanor wrote, "if, as he hopes, he can carry on his various business activities, it can only be done there." For the moment at least, resumption of his business activities represented all to which Franklin dared aspire; his political career seemed at an end.

The logistics of getting Franklin back to New York proved formidable. To begin with, Dr. Bennet worried that local authorities anywhere between the island and the city might bar the progress of even so eminent a patient as Franklin Roosevelt out of fear that he would infect local citizens and prove "a menace to the public." To reassure him, Dr. Lovett armed the Roosevelts with a certificate attesting to Franklin's harmlessness more than a month after being stricken.

Howe first hoped to move Franklin by boat; provided the seas stayed calm, an ocean voyage would be far smoother than a rattling trip by train—and intrusive reporters could have no access to the patient.[23] In the end, Uncle Fred Delano overruled Howe, arranging to have a private railroad car dispatched to Eastport, there to be coupled to the regular train heading south.

But before Franklin could even begin the trip by rail, he would have to be carried out of the house, down the hillside and across two miles of choppy sea to Eastport, and there lifted aboard the train. Just lying in bed, Franklin was in almost constant pain; the unavoidable jouncing of that trip would be agony.

There was no choice. Captain Calder saw to it that a stretcher was fashioned from pine poles and sturdy sail canvas, and hired five islanders to help him.

On Tuesday morning, September 13, Franklin was gently wrapped in blankets for the journey. Despite his inability even to lift his head, much less sit up, Howe wanted him to appear as unaffected by his illness as possible, and so, since his left arm was still very weak and his left thumb remained incapable of gripping anything, his hat was placed over that hand.

Then he was lifted onto the makeshift stretcher. He did not complain as the six men, staggering a little under the clumsy weight of him, lifted the stretcher out of the bedroom, along the narrow hall, and down the stairs at an angle which must have been terrifying; had they

23. Rosy concurred: "What a pity he is not still in the Navy, and a destroyer handy to take [him] right through to Hyde Park!! Or that his Boss's yacht is not still hovering round somewhere!!" *Source:* James Roosevelt Roosevelt Papers, FDRL.

stumbled, his weakened arms and lifeless legs could not even have softened the impact of his fall.

They carried him through the living room and across the veranda with its sweeping view of the Bay.

The children stood watching. The door of Franklin's bedroom had been kept closed for more than a month, at first for fear the children would become infected themselves, then to keep them from tiring him. During all that time they had glimpsed their father only occasionally as one grown-up or another hurried in or out. Whenever Franklin saw one of them standing in the hall, James recalled, "He grinned at us, and he did his best to call out, or gasp out, some cheery response to our tremulous . . . greetings."

The children knew little about infantile paralysis except that it was "very serious," and that they were not to mention it to anyone outside the family for fear word of it would spread, but now they could see that whatever had befallen him, the father who had bounded off the *Sabalo* to take each of them into his arms was utterly changed.

Captain Calder and his men started slowly down the slope past the children's landbound dory toward the sea. They carried Franklin backward, his feet higher than his head, trying not to jostle him more than they could help. Looking back up at the cottage, he saw the worried faces of the smallest boys, Franklin Jr. and John, standing silently together on the porch.

He smiled as broadly as he could and lifted the hand on which his hat was balanced in a semblance of a wave.

"Don't worry, chicks, I will be all right," he said.

Then he was gone.

CHAPTER

14

TO THE END OF THE DRIVEWAY

I NFANTILE PARALYSIS was different from any other crisis Franklin had faced during his almost forty years. Charm had no effect upon it. He could not duck or dodge its impact. The kind of courage required to combat it was different in every way from the foolhardiness that had made him wish to see an enemy submarine on the way to Europe or risk German shelling on the Western Front. No play-acting, no bluster, no promises to be good if given just one more chance, could make this obstacle go away.

It had to be faced and fought, head-on, and that was something new for Franklin Roosevelt. To win that battle—which really meant simply not to lose it, not to allow his crippling to disable his career and destroy his future—would demand of him qualities not conspicuously displayed so far in his largely charmed life: patience, application, recognition of his own limitations, a willingness to fail in front of others and try again.

That struggle may be said to have begun on the way home from Campobello. From the slip below the cottage, Captain Calder and his crew carefully lowered Franklin's stretcher onto the deck of his dory. As the inboard motor muttered across the rough sea, Eleanor and Louis Howe sat beside him with Edna Rockey, the trained nurse who had come up from New York to help, and Duffy, the Roosevelts' sixteen-year-old Scottie. The impact of every wave hurt Franklin, but he did not complain. Howe had deliberately misdirected the handful of reporters at Eastport, assuring them Mr. Roosevelt would land at a wharf at one end of town, then directing Calder to head for the other: the less the press saw of this awkward transfer and his boss's condition the better.

The boat reached Eastport a little later than Louis had planned. The tide had begun to fall and as the islanders gingerly passed Franklin from the tossing boat to the steep steps that led up to dry land, the treads beneath their feet were green and slimy. "There was slipping and sliding," one witness recalled. Had they dropped him, Franklin would almost certainly have drowned.

A flatbed baggage truck was waiting at the top of the stairs. Franklin was loaded onto it and with Eleanor, Louis, Miss Rockey, Captain Calder, and his crew all walking beside it to shield him as much as possible from onlookers, he was hauled to the depot, trying not to cry out with pain as the tires stuttered over the cobblestones.

Things seemed to be going well: the reporters still had not reached the station from the distant wharf, but there was more delay when it was discovered that the steps of the private car were too steep and its door too narrow for Franklin to be carried directly onto the train. At the last minute the window frame of the sleeping compartment had to be knocked out so that he could be handed in and lifted off the stretcher and onto his berth. A cigarette was placed in his mouth and lit—his own hands could neither pick a cigarette from its pack nor place it in the new holder that was a gift from Louis nor light a match—and the Scottie was allowed to jump up and curl himself onto his master's chest.

Howe's timing turned out to have been perfect. The train started just as the reporters and townspeople reached the window, and they got only the briefest glimpse of Franklin, smiling and smoking in apparent comfort. "Mr. Roosevelt was enjoying his cigarette and said he had a good appetite," the *New York World* reported. "Although unable to sit up, he says he is feeling more comfortable."

Howe remembered that as the train finally pulled out of Eastport, sweat "rolled down my back . . . like old man river rolling to the sea."[1]

1. Franklin's passage was made more comfortable by the great care with which the engineer on the first leg of the journey took his train around the curves, and Franklin was careful to send a note of thanks to him through Captain Calder.

Later, when President, Franklin would insist that the trains that carried him all over the

The Roosevelts arrived at Grand Central Station the next day. Uncle Fred had arranged for their car to pull in at a siding well away from crowds and reporters. Dr. George Draper, a New York protégé of Dr. Lovett's known to Franklin and other old Groton friends as "Dan," stood waiting on the platform, along with an ambulance crew that was to take Roosevelt to the New York Presbyterian Hospital on Fifth Avenue and East 70th Street.[2] A handful of Franklin's friends waited with the doctor, among them Tom Lynch, whose conviction that Roosevelt would one day be President predated even Louis Howe's, and who had wept openly when word came of his illness. When he saw his usually animated friend being passed out the compartment window, pale and motionless, Lynch stepped forward to urge the porters to be especially careful. Franklin rolled his head toward the familiar voice. "Why hello, Tom," he said, smiling as though he were fully in charge of events, although in fact turning his head was nearly all he could do. "Why don't you come along in the ambulance? There are some things I want to talk to you about."

Lynch, afraid he would not be able to control his own emotions, mumbled something about having to get back to Poughkeepsie right away. "Tell him I'll be along later," he told Eleanor as the stretcher was being carried onto the freight elevator. Then he turned and fled from the station.

The news of Franklin's illness finally appeared on the front page of the *New York Times* the next morning, September 16:

F. D. ROOSEVELT ILL
OF POLIOMYELITIS
Brought on Special Car from Campobello,
Bay of Fundy, to Hospital Here
RECOVERING, DOCTOR SAYS
Patient Stricken by Infantile Paralysis
A Month Ago, and Use of Legs Affected

---

country not exceed 40 miles an hour: if they went much faster he faced the very real risk of being hurled from his seat. *Sources:* Joseph P. Lash, *Eleanor and Franklin*, page 272; Hugh Gallagher, *FDR's Splendid Deception*.

2. Dr. Draper had many links with the Roosevelts: his mother was Ruth Dana, the daughter of Charles A. Dana, editor of the *New York Sun* and an old friend of Sara and Mr. James; his sister was the monologist Ruth Draper, a girlhood friend of Eleanor and Isabella Ferguson.

The accompanying story reported Dr. Draper as having promised that while Mr. Roosevelt had lost the use of both legs below the knee "for more than a month . . . he definitely will not be crippled. No one need have any fear of any permanent injury from this attack."

Dr. Draper's public optimism about his new patient's prospects may have been based on Lovett's initial diagnosis of "a mild case." It may also have been intended to keep up Franklin's own morale.

In any case it seems to have had that effect, for that afternoon Franklin dictated a note to the *Times* publisher, Adolph S. Ochs:

> While the doctors were unanimous in telling me that the attack was very mild and that I was not going to suffer any permanent effects from it, I had, of course, the usual dark suspicion that they were just saying nice things to make me feel good, but now that I have seen the same statement officially made in the New York *Times* I feel immensely relieved because I know of course it must be so.
>
> I am feeling in the very best of spirits and have already been allowed to take up part of my somewhat varied interests.

Franklin's spirits may have been good but his physical condition was still so delicate and he was so exhausted from his painful journey that all visitors except Eleanor, Sara, and Louis were gently turned away when they tried to visit his hospital room. They left their calling cards, which Eleanor saved: Mrs. Theodore Roosevelt, Aunts Kassie and Corinne, Uncle Fred, Mrs. Frederick H. Vanderbilt, Lathrop Brown.

Others, further away, sent gifts and flowers and letters.

"Tough luck old scout. A few roses to cheer from Henry & Frances de Rahm."

"We cannot spare you. Frank Sague."

Eleanor's Aunt Maude dispatched a haunch of venison: "Tell Franklin that nothing short of a deer is good enough for him." Elliott Brown sent him two mallards; another old hunting companion sent along a brace of coots to be "drawn, split and broiled and served on toast."

Ted Roosevelt sent his terse condolences on the same stationery Franklin had used as Assistant Secretary of the Navy.

"So very sorry to hear that Franklin has been attacked by this horrid germ," wrote Endicott Peabody from Groton. "But I rejoice to know that he has now thrown it off and is on the road to recovery."

That road was never so smooth as the *New York Times* or Franklin's own consistently cheery notes implied. He continued to run an intermittent fever that sometimes rose as high as 102 degrees; his legs were still tender even to the touch of the sheets; and there were other alarming symptoms.

On September 24, nine days after Franklin was admitted, Dr. Draper reported to Lovett that his patient was not progressing as rapidly they had hoped.

> I am very much concerned at the very slow recovery both as regards the disappearance of pain, which is very generally present, and as to the recovery of even slight power to twitch the muscles. There is marked falling away of the muscle masses on either side of the spine in the lower lumbar region, likewise the buttocks. . . . There is marked weakness of the posterior part of the left deltoid [the thick, triangular shoulder muscle, used to raise the arm from the side]; very marked weakness of the right triceps; and an unusual amount of gross muscular twitching in the muscles of both forearms. He coordinates on the fine motions of his hands very well now so that he can sign his name and write a little better than before.
>
> The lower extremities present a most depressing picture. There is a little motion in the long extensors of the toes of each foot; a little in the perinei [pelvic girdle] of the right side; a little ability to twitch the bellies of the gastrocnemii, but not really extend the feet. There is a little similar power in the left vastus, and on both sides similar voluntary twitches of the ham-string masses can be accomplished.

There was still another problem that seemed to Draper nearly as serious as his patient's physical weakness: the ebullient optimism which Franklin seemed almost desperately to maintain despite his pain and weakness disturbed the doctor; his patient did not seem fully to grasp the seriousness of what had happened to him, was unable or unwilling to face the distressing facts of his condition.

He was "very cheerful and hopeful, and has made up his mind that he is going out of the hospital in the course of one two or three weeks on crutches," Draper told Lovett. "What I fear more than anything is that we shall find a much more extensive involvement of the great back muscles than we have suspected, and that when we attempt to sit him up he will be faced with the frightfully depressing knowledge that he could not hold himself erect."

To cushion this potential psychological blow, Draper suggested to

Lovett that he might devise a corset for Roosevelt to put on before he was lifted into a chair for the first time: "I thought we might explain the preparation of such a brace . . . as being merely a conservative method to prevent the inevitable strain on muscles set to work again for the first time."

Draper was so concerned about his patient's fragile psychological state that he had not yet even dared seriously to examine his arms and shoulders because he did not want to shake Franklin's own conviction that they were "untouched by the disease." Roosevelt's biceps still seemed to be in relatively good shape and he could haul himself up by a leather strap hung over his bed and so help himself be turned: "This of course gives him a great sense of satisfaction." So did the warm saline baths Dr. Lovett again prescribed to ease the stubbornly persistent tenderness in his legs.

> I feel so strongly after watching him now for over a week that the psychological factor in his management is paramount. He has such courage, such ambition, and yet at the same time such an extraordinarily sensitive emotional mechanism, that it will also take all the skill which we can muster to lead him successfully to a recognition of what he really faces without utterly crushing him.

After three weeks, Franklin was still confined to bed but feeling well enough for Missy Le Hand to be allowed into the sickroom for an hour or so each morning to take dictation. In addition to the customary flow of personal and political mail, Franklin had now begun to receive letters from other infantile paralysis patients and from anxious members of their families: an English father hoped he might have some advice to give about the care of his ten-year-old son; a man about Franklin's age sent him a photograph of himself smiling in his wheelchair and offered a blood transfusion, should his doctors deem it helpful; an elderly patient who signed herself a "young girl only 87½ years old" wrote a heartening note and included some inspirational verse, to which Franklin replied, "If I could feel assured that time could treat me so lightly as to leave me at eighty-seven and a half years with all my vigor, powers and only a cane required, I would consider that my future was very bright indeed. There are not many people who can equal that record, even though they have been fortunate enough not to have been fellow-sufferers, with you and me, of infantile paralysis."[3]

3. He would receive such letters from strangers and provide similarly encouraging answers for the rest of his life.

Correspondence helped keep him occupied but, as always, it was personal contact he craved most. When doctors warned that his three youngest children, who now visited him on the way home from the Buckley School every day, should not be allowed to jump up onto his hospital bed because it would tire him, he paid no attention, greeting them each afternoon with a wide grin and an invitation to "hop in!"[4]

Close friends were also allowed into the sickroom now, provided they didn't stay too long. Interviewed by the journalist Ernest K. Lindley eleven years later, many of them still recalled their visits to the hospital "eagerly and with tones of wonder. . . . Roosevelt gaily brushed aside every hint of condolence and sent them away more cheerful than they could make a pretense of being when they arrived. None of them has ever heard him utter a complaint or a regret or even acknowledge that he had had so much as a bit of hard luck."

Josephus Daniels was one of those granted permission to see him. Always emotional, he remembered Franklin as "young and debonair, striding and strong," and the sight of his former aide totally immobilized was deeply distressing to him. Franklin beckoned Daniels toward the bed, and when the older man came close, unable to mask his anguished sympathy, the patient landed a friendly but solid blow to his visitor's paunch that sent him reeling backwards. "You thought you were coming to see an invalid," he laughed. "But I can knock you out in any bout!"

From the first, Franklin seems to have seen it as his duty not only to appear always in the best of spirits himself but to bolster the spirits of all those who came to see him: no one entering his room was allowed a moment's lugubriousness; all commiseration was airily tossed aside.[5]

---

4. He continued this practice as President, welcoming any of his grandchildren who happened to be staying with him into his bed each morning at breakfast time.

5. His determination to make others comfortable about his condition began virtually with the onset of the disease. "He is clearly entitled to great credit for his remarkable courage and good cheer," Dr. Bennet told Eleanor, recalling how Franklin had acted even during the critical days at Campobello *"which has been such a comfort to all who tried to help . . . "* [author's italics].

And it extended to the end of his life. Admiral William Morr remembered that as a young officer during World War II he had been assigned to the White House map room from which the Allied effort against the Axis was being directed, a sanctum so secret that even Secret Service agents were barred from entering. One morning the door opened, a loud voice called out, "The President of the United States," and FDR rolled into the room in his wheelchair. It was Morr's duty to push the chair as the President surveyed the pins on the maps. Somehow, he recalled, "to my utter horror, I got the President stuck in a corner between a map of North Africa and a filing cabinet. Try as I did, I couldn't get the rear wheel of the wheelchair to come out, [and] as I pushed him into the file cabinet I thought of all the places they sent young naval officers

One admiring doctor told Franklin that if he had been the *son* of Theodore Roosevelt, he could not be more like him in the courage and zest he consistently displayed. Roosevelt was delighted with the compliment. "He was my distinguished cousin," he said, "and I married his niece!"

But the sources of Franklin's gallantry were more complex than his old wish to emulate his distinguished cousin. His curious childhood had been the proving ground for his determination to have no one ever be overly concerned about his condition, his consummate skill at pretending that his disability did not bother him and that it therefore need not bother anyone else.

Part of it was simple adherence to the standards of his time and class. "Children were brought up differently then," Franklin's cousin Laura Delano once told an interviewer. "You just never said you were sick. I've always thought this was very good training for Franklin because when he got infantile he never complained. You were somehow not conscious of his infantile."

That sort of well-mannered stoicism was especially encouraged among Delano children. Franklin had been trained from early boyhood to present a uniformly sunny surface to the world—to seem always "very nice . . . that is, always bright and happy," in his approving Grandfather Delano's words. "Not crying, worrying, infractious."

The fragile health of his father had further schooled him in the art of feigning good cheer. Franklin was nine when Mr. James suffered the first signs of the heart trouble that rendered him a semi-invalid for ten years before it killed him. During the difficult decade that followed, Franklin and his anxious mother had indulged together in a loving conspiracy to relieve the old man of all unnecessary worry, agreeing to work together to ensure that so far as possible nothing in or about their household should ever seem to be wrong. That effort sometimes demanded a startling degree of uncomplaining fortitude from Franklin. Travelling with his parents aboard their private railroad car shortly after the onset of his father's illness, the boy badly cut his head; rather than have his father worry he asked his mother to clean him up and keep the incident to herself, then put on a hat to hide the wound and spent the day on the observation platform waiting for a scab to form.

---

who got Presidents stuck in corners! Argentina, Adak, Iceland—and then the President turned and looked up with all the charm [of] which FDR was capable and said, "Young man, are you trying to *file* me?" *Source:* Unpublished memoir by William Morr, FDRL.

At fourteen, a Campobello friend accidentally knocked out one of Franklin's front teeth, leaving the pulsing nerve exposed; he told no one of it for hours, his proud mother remembered, and endured the extraction of the root that followed once it was discovered "without fuss."

His father's frailty and the ceaseless anxiety it inspired in his mother taught Franklin another hard-won lesson: unpleasant facts about which little could be done were best simply ignored. The three Roosevelts spent several summers at fashionable European spas so that Mr. James could undergo the water cures that they all fervently believed would prolong his life. It was in the interest of all three to pretend that they were merely on vacation, to enjoy the band concerts and handsome gardens and good food and avoid entirely the subject of the sick and dying who were all around them every day. Because all three knew that Mr. James could die at any time, they saw no need to speak of it, and even when alone together labored to maintain an air of almost perpetual cheer.[6]

There may have been something else behind the ebullient gaiety which Franklin constantly displayed but which he cannot always actually have felt. Although his wife would one day write that she had never heard him say he feared anything, his crippling had understandably frightened him. On Campobello, he had at first not known what was happening to him or even whether he would live, and had questioned God's apparent abandonment. He knew now that he would not die, believed that God had spared his life as inexplicably as He had paralyzed his legs, but he did not yet know the extent of the damage the disease had done to him or what sort of life it would allow him to lead.

The solicitous concern of those who gather around a patient's bedside, intended to calm, often merely alarms, for solicitude implies that there is something to be solicitous about, that there may be authentic justification for long faces and lowered voices. If the patient can will away the anxiety of his visitors, the fearful thing causing it, too, may at least momentarily be made to seem to disappear.

---

6. When Franklin was first told by his physicians in March of 1944 that he was suffering from high blood pressure and heart disease, he was sixty-two years old, precisely the same age as his own father had been when *he* was first diagnosed with the identical ailments. From then on, the President's doctors were astonished at how little interested he seemed in the progress of the disease, chatting away more or less merrily even while being examined, and failing to ask even the simplest questions about how he was doing.

When they finally managed to get the patient into a sitting position, Dr. Draper's worst fears about Franklin's upper body proved unfounded. "I was delighted to find that he had much more power in the back muscles than I had thought," Draper reported after examining him on October 11, "but I must say that the pelvic girdle and thighs, and, indeed, most of the leg muscles are in poor shape."

Dr. Lovett came down to New York to see Franklin on October 15. The patient was by then "just able to sit up [although] still tender in spots. He is cheerful and doing an hour or so of business each day. He has been in a chair once and I recommended pushing him around, and letting him go home when he wanted to."

Franklin did go home to East 65th Street almost two weeks later, on October 28. He had been in the hospital for six weeks by then, and immobilized for eleven. His chart read NOT IMPROVING.

He was carried up three flights of steps and put to bed in the quietest room in the house, thickly curtained and back from the street.

Because Franklin was for the moment out of public life—and would remain so, through no fault of his own, for the next seven years—it is virtually impossible to reconstruct his day-to-day activities during that time.[7] Everything he would do during those long years—his attempts to earn a living and keep his name alive in politics, his myriad hobbies and building projects and schemes to turn a fast profit, his efforts to work out a satisfactory relationship with his wife and mother and children—would all be subsumed by his single-minded struggle to regain his feet.

Three weeks after he left the hospital, he seems to have suffered a strange sort of relapse. His fever soared again, this time affecting his eyes; for several days he could not read, and his mother feared he would go blind. Then the fever fell as mysteriously as it had risen.

On November 25, Dr. Lovett came to the house to examine him again. During the course of his long career, Lovett had overseen the aftercare of more than fifteen hundred polio patients and had developed a course of treatment which he insisted his patients follow meticulously. The disease and its ravages developed in three stages, he

7. FDR himself foresaw this biographer's problem. In 1936, the second volume of Paul M. Angle's *Lincoln . . . Being the Day-by-Day Activities . . .* of the Civil War President, from birth to death, was published. Not long thereafter, speaking with potential members of the staff of his own Hyde Park Library, he suggested that one of their first tasks should be to compile a similar chronology of his own daily activities. It would have been a monumental task, but it is a pity no one made the attempt. *Source:* Interview with Margaret Suckley.

explained, and he assured Franklin that in his case the first, acute phase, which usually lasted from four weeks to three months and during which he insisted upon complete bed rest, was at last coming to an end.

The second stage just beginning should see "spontaneous improvement," which Franklin could expect to continue more or less steadily for the next two years. With the help of regular visits by a trained physiotherapist, Mrs. Kathleen Lake, Franklin could now start a carefully orchestrated regimen of exercise aimed at "trying to restore to their highest efficiency the affected muscles." Above all, it was imperative that Roosevelt follow orders and not try to do too much too fast: "The over-use of a muscle is . . . worse than its disuse," Lovett believed, and could actually lead to "permanent loss of returning power." The advice "often given to use affected limbs as much as possible," he said, "is . . . the worst advice that can be given. It is difficult to under-use such muscles but fatally easy to injure them by over-use."

At the end of two years, Franklin would enter the third and final, or "stationary" stage, in which no further improvement could be expected but Lovett might be able to employ surgery to correct any deformities that remained.

Franklin, who continued to assure his friends that he would be up and walking in a matter of weeks, asked: "When do we start?" and promised faithfully to do as he was told.

Mrs. Lake, brisk and businesslike, bustled up the stairs for the first time on the morning of December 1. New patients were often so discouraged that she had difficulty persuading them to do the arduous, painful, endlessly repetitive work of stretching the affected muscles. Franklin was a rare exception. He was almost too eager to begin, delighted to be doing something at last.

Mrs. Lake laid a horizontal board covered with oilcloth across Franklin's bed, then began gingerly to manipulate his limbs. Weeks of immobility had left every muscle stiff and weak. She lifted first one leg and then the other an inch or two off the board at first, slowly exercising each stiff, contracted muscle ten times while watching Franklin's drawn face for signs that he was experiencing so much pain that she should stop. Some paralytics found this initial stretching so ghastly that they could endure it just three days a week; Franklin insisted the physiotherapist come every morning and sought to make light of the slow, agonizing work, calling his exercise board "the Morgue," after the slabs on which corpses were laid out.

"Mrs. Lake works so long now every a.m.," Eleanor reported to

Sara, "that F. doesn't get up till after noon at least, except on Sundays when she doesn't come." "He is a wonderful patient," Mrs. Lake reported to Lovett not long after she began coming to the house, "very cheerful & works awfully hard." He professed to be content to move slowly, too: "He is perfectly satisfied . . . to remain as he is now & *not* get up on crutches, as he says he has plenty of occupation for his mind, everything is going well in the city, & he would rather strengthen his legs this way, than try to get up too soon."[8]

After the first seventeen days of therapy, he told Mrs. Lake he was encouraged, despite the pain: "he felt more power in his legs than he thought he had . . . & says that his feet feel warmer & do not get nearly so swollen sitting up."

Christmas was approaching, and James, then fourteen, was due home from Groton. He had not seen his father since he watched him being carried down the slope at Campobello, and he was frankly frightened at the prospect. "I went into his room," he remembered,

> striving manfully to assume an air of nonchalance, even gaiety, so as not to let him know how I really felt. . . .
>
> Pa read me like a book, and he worked a small miracle for me. He was propped up on pillows and those trapezes and rings over his bed on which he was already exercising his upper body upset me a bit. Pa instantly made me forget it. His chin still stuck out and he was grinning and he stretched out his arms to me. "Come here, old man," he said.
>
> I rushed over and received his embrace. . . . Then, even though I was a Roosevelt and a Grotonian, I cried a bit, but, with Pa squeezing me and slapping me on the back and carrying on enthusiastically about how "grand" I looked, I soon was chattering right along with him, telling him all about Old Peabody—only I didn't call him that—and the football team and prospects for spring baseball.

Franklin did his best to ease his children's terrors, pulling the covers back and displaying for them his withered legs, making a game out of naming the affected muscles and leading the sort of football-style cheers he had once led at Harvard when one or another seemed to show some slight improvement. "How we loved to talk about Pa's *gluteus maximus!*" James remembered.

He had his bed moved so that he and Elliott could wave to one

---

8. That was not what he was telling outsiders. "I . . . am getting along well and expect to be walking on crutches in a very few weeks," he wrote a friend after just seven days of exercises. "The doctors say that there is no question but that by the Spring I will be walking without any limp." *Source:* Frank Freidel, *Franklin D. Roosevelt: The Ordeal*, page 104.

another as the boy skated past the corner on his way to the Buckley School each morning, and sometimes had himself lowered to the floor so that he could challenge the boys to Indian wrestle with him. "You think you can take the old man!" he shouted to James. "Well, just get down here and try it!" No one could ever take him. "*God*, he was strong," Franklin Jr. remembered.

Franklin presided at Christmas as he always had, carving the turkey with as much flourish as he could muster sitting down, reading out Dickens's *Christmas Carol* in a firm, confident voice. But the trimming of the tree was very different from Christmases past. He had always placed and balanced every candle himself, clambering up and down a ladder until the whole tree was ablaze. "[H]e was still the impresario. . . . of course," James recalled, but his children now had to do the climbing, while he sat at the foot of the tree, fixing candles to the lowest limbs.[9]

For all the noisy good cheer Franklin paraded for the benefit of others, for all the energy and courage he poured daily into his struggle to regain the use of his legs, he was that winter the center of a second contest almost as bitter as his own, one whose harsh outlines have been softened and simplified somewhat by sentiment over the intervening decades.

Shortly after Christmas, Isabella Ferguson wrote Eleanor a letter praising her for the characteristic courage with which she was bearing up under the new burdens Franklin's illness had imposed upon her.

> Every inch of the last long & dreadful months stands amazingly vivid before me—as do you in your superb courage & determination. Dearest, it's an inspiration to see it all as I do constantly & let me say what I believe you'll understand. When great difficulties come to us in extreme youth we stagger along creditably because we are unable to see the whole truth & have abundant strength. When distress comes to us in older age we face up to it steadily & splendidly, partly thro resignation & a sense of finish[?]. When it comes to us at your & my ages, I believe it is the hardest of all tests because ours are the years when clear perception has come & with it the intense desire to live while we may. I wonder if you know what I mean. . . . It is above all hard to mark time at our ages, no matter what spiritual interpretation we try to attach to the cause.

9. "Even when I became a grown man with children on my own," James continued, "it sometimes hit me like a blow in the stomach to see Pa sitting there in his wheel chair, unable to reach the higher branches." *Source:* James Roosevelt (and Sidney Shalett), *Affectionately, FDR,* page 58.

Eleanor's reply to this letter has not survived, but we can be certain she did know what her best friend meant. Neither her own marriage nor Isabella's had turned out as they had hoped. Isabella, like Eleanor, was a sensitive, intelligent, able woman of extraordinary energy, for whom marriage and motherhood had failed to provide fulfillment. For a dozen years now, she had borne most of the responsibility for raising her children in a beautiful but harsh landscape, while steadily, faithfully seeing to the daily needs of her tubercular husband, who was far older than she and whose frustration at his own helplessness often took the form of dour silence. She had done all this without complaint, taking everything in stride with a cheerful spirit that Eleanor admired and envied but could herself only rarely summon. Now, with the children about to go off to school and her husband increasingly ill and distant, Isabella had begun to feel as if she were merely "marking time."[10]

10. Bob Ferguson would finally die of tuberculosis nine months later, on October 4, 1922. It took Isabella several weeks to bring herself to write to Eleanor about it:

> Oh my beloved Eleanor—
> ... The waters seem to have closed over my head—while you seem forever capable of striding ahead always in the pace that circumstances call for. My admiration knows no limit. May I someday profit by your example. Your dear friend Bob—has found rest. It is as tho my husband, brother, Father, & sick boy had left our house desolate. No words can describe the emptiness after all these years during which his spirit of progress—his desires & care for us—filled life's least nook & cranny & spelt the motive for our whole beings. Could there be a greater tribute to an invalid of thirteen years? ...
>   You'll be good enough to believe I helped Bob to longer years. It was inevitable that my abundant strength should be shared thus, but it seems as nothing in the balance with what he did & gave us. We'll talk of it some day, Eleanor. It can but live thro all time as all good does. ...
>   Eleanor, it would help so if I might compare your notes with mine. One doesn't stand still in the thirties, tho' I used to think one had one foot in the grave by then.
>   Your wholly devoted—
>   Isabella

When they did finally manage to compare notes, Eleanor learned that some time during her lonely years in the Southwest, Isabella had begun to find solace in the close friendship of one of her husband's oldest friends, General John Campbell Greenway, a vigorous former Rough Rider who had served with distinction on the Western Front and was now vice president of the Calumet & Arizona Mining Company. Now, she and Greenway planned to be married.

Some of Isabella's old friends had found unseemly the speed with which she agreed to marry again, but the Roosevelts, who now had more reasons than most to understand the extraordinary devotion she had shown to her husband during his long struggle against tuberculosis, stood by her, and Eleanor wrote immediately to her fiancé.

> My dear John,
>   I cannot call you anything else because, though I think I've only seen you once, I feel as though we have been friends a long time.
>   I have loved Isabella ever since I first met her & more & more as the years have gone by. No one else means to me what she does. ... Bless you both. ...

For her part, Isabella had been told of Franklin's infidelity and the terrible pain it had caused her old friend. Franklin had been "selfish, behaving *that* way," she told her daughter much later, and her youngest son remembered that Roosevelt's romance had been "the one thing that changed it for Mummy," making it impossible for her ever to think of him in quite the same way again. And Isabella was aware, too, of the wary arrangement the Roosevelts had made in order to maintain the outward form of their marriage while permitting each to develop a more detached life within its confines.

Now, Franklin's illness seemed to threaten even that arrangement, forcing Eleanor to refocus all her energies on her family, and especially on the care of her newly invalided husband, whose self-absorption had not been lessened by his illness, and the severity of whose crippling she may have believed was at least in part her fault, an unforeseeable by-product of the massage she and Louis had doggedly performed on Campobello under orders from Dr. Keen. Eleanor's hard-won and sharply critical "perception" of Franklin and of their marriage was clear enough and had not changed, but circumstances now seemed to dictate that she could no longer act upon it, that there was once again no way, in Isabella's words, for Eleanor to "live while we may." Eleanor felt trapped, was almost as confined psychologically as Franklin was physically.

Meanwhile, she did her best to reorganize her family's home to suit her husband's needs. Four of the five Roosevelts still lived in their tall but narrow brownstone that winter: even though James was away at Groton, the two youngest boys had to be moved to a fourth-floor room in Sara's adjoining house. A room had to be found in which Edna Rockey, the young nurse who had been in constant attendance since Dr. Keen urged Eleanor to hire someone to help her at Campobello, could rest between shifts.

And there was another permanent boarder. When Corinne Roosevelt Alsop was allowed in to see Franklin, she found him "as brave as a lion," she remembered, but what struck her most forcefully was not so much her cousin's courage as the fact that Louis Howe, to whom she had never even been previously introduced, was permitted to remain in the room during a visit by a member of the family and "completely controlled what we talked about and what we said."

Isabella and Greenway were married on November 4, 1923, precisely one year and one month after the death of Bob Ferguson. *Sources:* Eleanor Roosevelt Papers, FDRL; John S. Greenway Papers, Arizona Historical Society, Tucson.

Howe had come to stay, setting his family up in an apartment in Poughkeepsie (where Mary was attending Vassar) and visiting them there only on weekends. "It was," James Roosevelt recalled much later, "the closest thing to desertion I've ever seen."

Eleanor and Louis had cemented the friendship that began aboard the *Westboro* during Franklin's vice-presidential campaign throughout the long, frightening vigil at Franklin's bedside on Campobello. Now, faced with the triple tasks of caring for her crippled husband, looking after the rest of her family, and trying to hold onto whatever traces of independent life her altered circumstances permitted her, Eleanor clung fiercely to Howe. "She [had] called for help and Louis came," Frances Perkins remembered. " . . . I know that Mrs. Roosevelt loved Louis Howe. She loved him the way you love a person who has stood by you in the midst of the valley of the shadow and not been afraid of anything."

Their new intimacy irritated the children: Anna never forgot coming into the library one evening to find Howe sitting in a chair with her exhausted mother at his feet, her head back, eyes closed, while the little man slowly ran a brush through her long hair.[11]

Anna was sixteen that winter, already deeply affected by the old tensions between her parents, anxious over the incapacity of the father to whom she was devoted, and unhappy at Miss Chapin's fashionable school which her mother had mistakenly thought would accomplish for her daughter what Mlle Souvestre's Allenswood had done for her, when she was told that she must make a hard choice: she could hold onto her own large third-floor bedroom with its private bath, but only if she was willing to share it during the afternoons and early evenings with Miss Rockey; or she could give up her room to Howe and move into a much smaller room all to herself on the fourth floor. She resentfully chose to shift upstairs.

Howe was "an impossible guest," Franklin Jr. remembered. Because he had difficulty breathing, he was often unable to sleep and lit foul-smelling incense in his room, then coughed and paced until dawn. Despite the fits of coughing that racked his body, making it impossible for him to speak for minutes at a time, and leaving him gasping for air for still more minutes afterwards, he smoked incessantly, flicking ashes

11. Grace Howe, whose ancient resentment of her husband had not been lessened by his decision to move in with the Roosevelts, would one day accuse Louis of having an affair with Eleanor Roosevelt. He angrily denied it. He'd taken her to the movies once in a while, he said, but what of it? Franklin couldn't. *Source:* Confidential source.

wherever his mood suited. He was color-blind but determined that his ties, socks, and handkerchiefs all be of the same hue, so that Eleanor had to take the time to come to his room and make each morning's match-ups for him. He also relied upon her to tell him when the suit he had been wearing for several days was so soiled, wrinkled, and smeared with ashes that it had become "a disgrace" and had to go to the cleaners.

Howe collected Egyptian trinkets of all kinds and had a carved stone cat on his dresser, before which he set a tray of carefully arranged scarabs and semi-precious stones which Eleanor used to like to say were offerings to his personal god. If the maid moved the cat while dusting or one of the children dared tinker with the way the offerings were laid out, Louis would demand to know who had violated the sanctity of his room.

Like Anna, the younger children found Howe's constant gruff presence a trial, but the obvious respect which both their parents invariably showed him precluded their ever being openly rude. Instead, they worked out a more subtle revenge. Howe breakfasted with the family every morning at a table in whose center was a lazy susan against which he would prop his newspapers, one after the other—"He read more newspapers than any human being I've ever known," Eleanor said—absorbing the news while eating and smoking, oblivious to everything going on around him. Franklin Jr. and John learned that they could get a rise out of him by gently turning the lazy susan first one way and then the other until he had to stop reading and snap, "*Why* do you need so much butter?"

From the first, Louis and Eleanor were united in their view that so far as possible, Franklin must never be treated as an invalid. Dr. Draper agreed—"it was better for Franklin to make the effort to take an active part in life again and lead, as far as possible, a normal life," Eleanor remembered his saying. "Even if it tired him it was better for his condition."

Louis still maintained that Franklin's political future was bright. From the moment his chief was stricken, Howe had sought to play down in public the seriousness of Roosevelt's illness, seeing that reassuring stories were planted in the newspapers, writing cheery letters for Franklin when he had been too weak even to sign them, orchestrating his unwitnessed return to New York.

Was all this necessary, Eleanor had asked him then. "Do you really believe that Franklin still has a political future?"

"I believe," Howe said, "that someday Franklin will be President."

Eleanor, who later confessed that she always assumed the worst in any situation, privately thought any sort of return to political life, let alone a run for the presidency, "almost hopeless." She had come to terms with the fact that her husband would always be crippled, Frances Perkins remembered: "She had faced that. She . . . never fooled herself about his getting back the full use of his legs, which he did believe in. . . . [But] she thought he would die spiritually, die intellectually, and die in his personality, if he didn't have political hope."

To keep that hope alive, she supported Howe's every effort to keep him in contact with as many people as possible, ushering an almost unbroken stream of them up the stairs morning, afternoon, and evening.

She also joined her ally in exhorting Franklin to keep at his exercises. Habit may have had something to do with their shared impatience. Both his wife and his closest aide were long accustomed to having to cajole him into performing duties he disliked. Eleanor tried to accomplish it through earnest chiding, without notable success. Louis did better because he had a lighter touch, skillfully interspersing jokes and gossipy anecdotes among his promptings to get on with the job.

Franklin's exercises were difficult, boring, painful. Like all patients, he sometimes did not wish to perform them. Now, together, as they had separately in the past, Eleanor and Louis were determined that Franklin persevere.[12]

Lily Norton, an old family friend, visited Sara that autumn and wrote to a friend from Springwood:

It's a lovely region but tragedy rather overshadows this once so happy & prosperous family, for Mrs. R's only son, Franklin Roosevelt, was struck down in August with a terribly serious case of infantile paralysis. He is only 39—both too old & too young for such a fell germ to disable him.

---

12. Adding to Eleanor's impatience may have been her own frank lack of sympathy with illnesses in general and with those of her husband in particular. She believed him less hypochondriacal than his father had been or his brother was, but "over-conscious" of illness nonetheless, and, as her children had good cause to know, she thought giving in to almost any illness a sure sign of weakness.

During the course of their sixteen years together, she had also spent thankless weeks nursing Franklin through a good many maladies most adults experienced much earlier in their lives, while having patiently to assure his ever anxious mother that her boy would recover. Her decision never to treat her husband as an invalid may on some level have resulted in part from her wish that he remain under her care as briefly as possible. *Source:* Interview with Louis Eisner, FDRL.

He's had a brilliant career as assistant of the Navy under Wilson, & then a few brief weeks of crowded glory & excitement when nominated by the Democrats for the Vice Presidency. Now he is a cripple—will he ever be anything else? His mother is wonderfully courageous & plucky, but it's a bitter blow. . . .

For Sara, Franklin's future now seemed ordained: as soon as he could manage it, he must come home, to the shady lawns and river breezes of Hyde Park, where he could settle into a placid, comfortable invalid's life, and where she could herself tend to his needs precisely as she had tended to those of Mr. James, her first "beloved invalid" there, thirty years earlier.[13]

There was nothing extraordinary in her feeling that way. The future for the handicapped was then almost uniformly bleak. Public attitudes toward "cripples"—the stark word then in almost universal use to describe anyone who had suffered a physical handicap—had improved somewhat since the late nineteenth century, when they were often kept out of sight in locked rooms and even the names of the institutions newly created for their care hinted at their hopeless prospects: the Home for Incurables, the New York Society for the Ruptured and Crippled, the Home for Destitute Crippled Children.

But work to improve their lot was still largely undertaken not so much to benefit them as individuals as to ensure that they did not somehow injure society as a whole. "A failure in the moral training of a cripple," as one authority wrote not long before Franklin was felled, "means the evolution of an individual detestable in character, a menace and a burden to the community, who is only too apt to graduate into the mendicant and criminal classes."

Franklin Roosevelt had no fear that he would ever become a mendicant, but every precedent suggested that any sort of active and productive life outside his home was impossible, and Sara simply thought it

13. The novelist Thomas Wolfe, visiting on the Hudson, nicely caught what seems to have been the consensus about Franklin's future among Sara's Dutchess County neighbors in his novel *Of Time and the River:* "By the way, Ida," Mr. Joel growled. . . . "how is Frank? Have you been over to see them lately?"

"Yes Father," she answered, "we drove over last Tuesday and spent the evening with them. . . . He looks very well . . . but of course . . . he's never going to be any better—they all say as much . . . he'll never get back the use of his legs again—the man is a permanent cripple. . . ."

"Pity! Nice fellow, Frank! Always liked him! A little on the flashy order, maybe—like all his family . . . too easy-going, too agreeable . . . but great ability! . . . a little superficial, too . . . the whole lot is like that . . . go hell-for-leather at everything for three weeks at a time—and then forget . . . great opportunists, every one of them. . . ."

cruel for anyone to pretend otherwise. The painful exercises her son was enduring every day with such patience, the urging to do still more of them that came steadily from Eleanor and Howe, the daily visits from politicians and business associates, seemed woefully misguided to her. Her boy should be made as comfortable as possible and let alone.

A dozen years after Sara's death, her son's wartime friend, the British diplomat Nigel Law, wrote a warm assessment of Franklin that would have greatly pleased his mother:

> In my own mind I give him the highest praise an Englishman can give to a man, that he was a perfect example of the English Country Gentleman, and by that I mean (a type which is fast passing away) the landowner, whether large or small—with roots in his family estate who nevertheless disinterestedly devotes all his talents to his country, in local affairs, in Parliament, in the Army and, if need be, as a great Minister of State, Viceroy or Ambassador, and who, when the need of his services is past, returns once more to his fields and his library with relief.

That was precisely how Sara had always justified to herself Franklin's career in politics: he had been selflessly doing a gentleman's duty in the service of ordinary citizens less fortunate than he. Now, she felt, his illness had surely ended that obligation; no one could expect more of him than he had already given. And there was no need for him to worry about finances—she had plenty of money with which to make him comfortable. He deserved the rest he so obviously needed, and which she was more than happy to arrange for him.[14]

It pained her that Eleanor did not seem to grasp this as she did, even when she made her feelings on the subject clear. "My mother-in-law thought we were tiring my husband and that he should be kept com-

---

14. There was plenty of precedent for such an arrangement. When the son of Sara's friend and Dutchess County neighbor, Mrs. Robert R. Livingston, began to experience crushing migraines at an early age, for example, his solicitous mother successfully persuaded him to give up a promising career in law and settle for the pleasant, largely empty life of a Hudson River squire.

A century before Franklin was struck down at Campobello, a distant cousin, James Henry Roosevelt, was stricken at twenty-one with a crippling malady that may have been infantile paralysis. He was a bright and promising young man, a graduate of Columbia, planning to study law, and already engaged to Miss Julia Maria Boardman, a member of another old New York family. They intended to marry as soon as his practice was launched. But he fell ill just a month after being admitted to the New York Bar in 1821, leaving him unable to walk without crutches, and all concerned agreed that marriage for a cripple would be inadvisable. Young Roosevelt retired to his parent's estate. His fiancée never married, remaining his chaste friend for forty years. When he died in 1863, his large legacy helped New York establish the institution for "the reception and relief of sick and diseased persons" that became Roosevelt Hospital. *Sources:* Conversation with Clare Brandt, chronicler of the Livingstons; Nathan Miller, *The Roosevelt Chronicles*, pages 131–132.

pletely quiet," Eleanor wrote later, "which made my discussions as to his case somewhat acrimonious on occasion. She always thought she understood what was best, particularly where her child was concerned, regardless of what any doctor might say. I felt that if you placed a patient in a doctor's care, you must at least follow out his suggestions and treatment."[15]

When it seemed clear to Sara that Eleanor would not give in, she turned the full force of her frustration upon Eleanor's closest ally— Louis Howe.

Howe's constant presence in her son's home greatly displeased her. In fact, nothing about "that dirty, ugly little man" had ever pleased her. He symbolized for her everything that she always found most distressing about politics. He was soiled, rumpled, sardonic, not at all the sort of man with whom she wished her son to spend his time. She had always been polite to him, as she was to anyone who served Franklin, and had not openly complained when, shortly after Election Day in 1920, Eleanor had invited Howe and his family to stay at Springwood for a weekend—although her resentment could be read even in her resolutely tactful journal: "The Howes are here (4)."[16]

But now that her son's political career was clearly over, she saw no need to put up with Howe's presence a moment longer. She suspected that he had always been a sponger, interested chiefly in maintaining his hold on the glittering man who was his meal ticket, and she did not like his new closeness to her daughter-in-law, either. Anna may have told her of seeing Howe brush her mother's hair, and she now saw in her granddaughter's resentment at having to give up her bedroom to him a way to drive the interloper out.

"Granny, with a good deal of insight into my adolescent nature," Anna recalled, "started telling me that it was inexcusable that I, the only daughter of the family, should have a tiny bedroom in the back of the house, while Louis enjoyed a large, sunny front bedroom with

15. For the record, Sara herself explicitly denied ever having wished to "baby" her son, or to "make an invalid" of him. "All I did," she wrote him in 1934, "was say that if the doctors thought it best for you to have for some months a quiet life, I would keep Hyde Park open & live there for a time."

For a discussion of the extraordinary circumstances under which she felt she needed to defend herself in writing to her son, see Geoffrey C. Ward, *Before the Trumpet*, page 325.

16. Although the two families had spent several Christmases together in Washington, Roosevelt evidently did not know Howe's wife well then, either. "I have enjoyed Mrs. Howe," Eleanor assured Franklin, then on his way to Louisiana to hunt geese with Hall. "I don't think she would bore you and she's a plucky little thing."

his own private bath. Granny's needling finally took root. At her instigation, I went to Mother one evening and demanded a switch in rooms."

Eleanor—who was herself now forced to dress in her husband's bathroom and to snatch what little sleep she could on a cot set up each night in one of the boys' rooms—was not sympathetic. "[T]he situation grew in [Anna's] mind to a point where she felt that I did not care for her and was not giving her any consideration," she remembered. "It never occurred to her that I had far less than she had. . . . I realize now that my attitude toward her had been wrong. She was an adolescent girl and I still treated her like a child and thought of her as a child. It never occurred to me to take her into my confidence and consult with her about our difficulties or tell her just what her father was going through. . . . It never occurred to me that the time comes, particularly with a girl, when it is important to make her your confidante."

Anna slammed out of the room, filled with adolescent fury. Her mother would treat her with icy politeness for weeks.

Later, when Franklin no longer needed a nurse, Eleanor would shift Howe to a smaller room on the fourth floor, but that winter, she would afterwards write, was "the most trying . . . of my entire life."[17]

In late January, Mrs. Lake noticed that her patient seemed unusually "nervous & tired," although "nothing he is getting from me should cause this irritable condition." The stretching of his knees was now "really getting on his nerves . . . the fact that he sits every afternoon in his wheelchair with his knees bent rather counteracts the stretching in the morning." Every few days his calves seemed to become "congested [and] very painful to the touch," and his hamstrings again tightened.

Draper thought Mrs. Lake had simply been doing too much and cautioned her to ease up for a time. She thought there was more to it than that, "started a little private detective work," and through gentle but close questioning discovered that at Franklin's request, Miss

_____

17. Late in life, Eleanor attended the Broadway opening of *Sunrise at Campobello*, Dore Schary's sentimental account of Franklin's paralysis and his struggle to recover from it that later became a popular film. She admired the actors' performances, she said, especially Ralph Bellamy's bravura impersonation of her husband, but thought it had badly misrepresented her mother-in-law—for all her complexities, Sara was "never petty," Eleanor told friends. As for the play itself, she said it had as much to do with her and her family "as the man in the moon."

Rockey had been giving his legs unauthorized massages every evening. Was that true? she asked the patient.

"Oh, yes, every night before I go to sleep."

"How long?"

"Oh, just a little to rub the oil in to build up the muscles[.]"

"A further question settled the time to . . . two minutes hard rubbing (Swedish!) on each leg, & back massage, after he had been up & seeing people all the afternoon and evening."

"I persuaded him to cut that part out," she reported to Lovett, "& all this week the soreness has gradually disappeared & the last two days the knees are nearly straight, & in spite of a cold he hasn't been nearly so tired or nervous. . . . Also, as far as I can make out he has been having this same treatment right along, which probably accounts for the length of the sensitive period."

Franklin was contrite: "He keeps telling me over & over again that he does not wish to hurry, but wants to do what is absolutely the best thing for his ultimate recovery."

But if he was at least momentarily satisfied to maintain a slow but steady pace, Eleanor and Louis were not. Mrs. Lake reported her concern to Lovett: "The nurse seems to think that there is a good deal too much pushing ahead being done by the wife & Mr. H."

Franklin was pushing, too, in other ways, resolved to resume some semblance of his once frenetic life. He retained his offices on the boards of civic and charitable organizations, including the Cathedral of St. John the Divine, the Boy Scout Foundation of Greater New York, and the Woodrow Wilson Foundation,[18] and kept up a constant correspondence with Democratic leaders about the party's future, an effort which, he was pleased to see, kept his name sufficiently alive so that newspapers reported he was being talked up by Tammany leaders for the Senate in the fall.

The New York office of the F&D began holding strategy sessions in the Roosevelt library every Tuesday afternoon at four-fifteen but, although Howe managed to keep on top of his work, Roosevelt clearly

---

18. It took Franklin's illness to alter the ex-President's old rancor toward him. Even though Roosevelt had been one of the prime movers behind the creation of the foundation named in his honor, Wilson had remained chilly toward him, going so far as to have his secretary turn down his request for an autograph on one of two copies of Washington's Farewell Address which Franklin had had published in his honor.

But when news of Franklin's paralysis reached Wilson, himself confined to a wheelchair, he sent Eleanor his "heartfelt sympathy," and later reiterated to Roosevelt himself his gratitude for "your . . . friendship and unselfish devotion" to the objectives of the foundation. *Source:* Frank Freidel, *Franklin D. Roosevelt: The Ordeal*, pages 123–125.

worried that things would get away from him, that he would no longer be needed.[19] When the Newport News Shipbuilding Company purchased bonds through the F&D, Howe wrote an uncharacteristically plaintive letter to its president:

> . . . [I] am trying to let [Roosevelt] feel in every way that he is being of real service to his company in spite of the fact that he is confined to his house. You who know Mr. Roosevelt well can imagine how he chafes when feeling that he is not able to do all the things which his active mind suggests. . . . If by any chance the fact that this was Mr. Roosevelt's company influenced you in making this award, it would cheer Mr. Roosevelt tremendously if you would write him a little line to that effect.

Whatever the cause, Franklin again evidently overdid it. For shortly after his fortieth birthday on January 30, he suffered a severe setback: his hamstrings started to contract, again drawing his knees up toward his chest into an almost fetal position that if allowed to continue would make an upright stance impossible. Draper called in a colleague who agreed it was essential that "every effort . . . be concentrated on getting those legs out straight," and encased both of the bent, affected limbs in plaster from hip to ankle, leaving openings behind the knees into which wedges were to be hammered a little deeper each day to force them straight again.

Intermittent suffering now became unrelenting, and was compounded by a new anxiety: Franklin's totally immobilized left leg seemed to him to have lost what minute strength weeks of exercise had restored to it. Mrs. Lake had been home with a cold when he was placed in his cast, and when she returned, "found that they had put in four wedges only 22 hours after putting on a very straight cast, & that the patient became extremely worried at the complete loss of power in all the returning muscles. . . . He seemed extremely relieved to have me back & I was able to convince him that he could still set the muscles, and the power has slowly been returning again."

Roosevelt endured it all in silence for two ghastly weeks, hiding his agony from everyone who stopped in to see him.

"But Mother how does he stand the pain?" Franklin Jr. asked his mother one day.

"He does, dear. He does."

19. He had offered his resignation to the F&D as soon as his illness was diagnosed, but his employer had brushed it aside; Van-Lear Black was genuinely fond of Franklin and in any case, it was more Roosevelt's name and connections than his physical presence in the office that had made him seek him out in the first place.

Just two years earlier, the Providence *Journal* had publicly questioned both Franklin's candor and his manliness. His candor may still have been in question—indeed, infantile paralysis would eventually call upon all his highly developed skill at cavalier deception—but after the courage he displayed while facing this ordeal, no rational observer would ever again be able to challenge his "manliness."

The plaster came off in mid-February 1922. Mrs. Lake massaged Franklin's legs, saw that swelling in his left ankle caused by the cast came down, then began preparing him for his first attempt at standing up.

Virtually no measurable strength remained in Franklin's wasted lower limbs—with pitiless candor, one examining physician would later categorize them as "flail legs," and they were utterly incapable of supporting his weight. A specialist, Dr. Arthur Krida, measured him for a set of steel braces. When they arrived, they weighed fourteen pounds, ran all the way from his heels to above his waist, and were further strengthened at the hips by a leather pelvic band.

Once the braces were laboriously strapped on and the catches at his knees closed to ensure that his legs would not collapse beneath him, it took Mrs. Lake, Miss Rockey, Dr. Draper, and the Roosevelt butler just to get him on his feet. After seven months in bed, Roosevelt's ability to balance himself had vanished with the power to flex his feet and toes; the floor seemed infinitely far away; the strange steel supports atop which he swayed felt as alien, cumbersome, and treacherously unreliable as stilts. "Even with my back to a wall and braces locked at the knee," wrote one patient, recalling his own first attempt at standing with braces, "I [felt] brittle and vulnerable, and at least ten feet tall; thinking that if I fell I would shatter on the floor, like a tower of blocks."

Crutches were slid under his arms just to hold him upright at first, and then to help him begin to move about his room, surrounded always by hands ready to catch him if he started to fall. Since his hips were paralyzed, incapable of moving his legs individually, he was taught the rocking method of crutch-walking. Hanging heavily on his crutches, his arms and shoulders still weak, his legs straight out behind him, he was first instructed to think of himself as a tripod, his rigid, steel-encased limbs forming one point, his crutches the other two. To move, he had to use his neck muscles to thrust his head forward, tipping his body enough for his feet to be dragged along the floor toward the crutches. Then, he threw his head backward, thereby lifting his weight from the crutches long enough for him to slam them forward again so that the process could be repeated.

Despite the constant danger of falling and the awkwardness with which these initial attempts at walking were made, Franklin rejoiced at being on his feet at last and able, however haltingly, to move under his own power. His natural ebullience began to return by mid-March. So did his impatience. "He has all sorts of new ideas about developing his muscles & I have to discourage him periodically as tactfully as possible," Mrs. Lake reported, "otherwise he does considerably more harm than good & he does not in the least see why I'm so particular about the hip flexors, in spite of explanation.[20] Apart from that he is coming along quite well & seems satisfied. I am also giving him a few setting up exercises in the sitting position now, as his trunk muscles are still weak, & he welcomes any advance."[21]

To ease his restlessness and relieve his boredom, Mrs. Lake told Lovett, she tried to persuade her patient "to go for a drive at night, when he could be lifted into the car without people seeing him very much & he thought it a good idea, but as yet has not attempted it."

Roosevelt had willed himself to seem nonchalant about his condition in front of friends and family members. Privacy in the standard sense was no longer possible for a man incapable of dressing himself or getting to and from the bathroom on his own except by crawling. But he was wary of letting strangers observe his helplessness, and from the first he and Howe agreed that so far as humanly possible no outsider was ever to see him being carried. (The short trip home from the hospital had presumably been accomplished after dark.)

Franklin's frustration sometimes showed. To keep busy, he took it upon himself to catalogue all the books in his collection, filling out an index card for each one. Anna was helping him one day, clambering up and down a ladder to bring him armloads of books as he sat in his

20. Roosevelt's hip flexors—the muscles which permit the leg to straighten—were a source of considerable concern to his doctors; like his hamstrings, they showed signs of tightening which, if unchecked, would make it impossible for him ever to stand. The exercises aimed at loosening them were especially painful: Franklin lay on his stomach while Mrs. Lake rested one hand on his buttock, then gently bent his knee up behind him, and stretched the flexor by lifting his leg from the board. *Source:* Interview with Mary Hudson Veeder, one of Roosevelt's physiotherapists.

21. When Woodrow Wilson learned that Franklin had managed to stand upright, he sent his congratulations: "I am indeed delighted to hear you are getting well so fast and so confidently, and I shall try and be generous enough not to envy you." *Source:* Frank Freidel, *Franklin D. Roosevelt: The Ordeal,* page 125.

wheelchair, when she stumbled and her burden crashed to the floor. "I saw Father start," she remembered, and "an expression of pain passed swiftly over his face." She apologized, but he berated her for being "too careless for words," for being "no help at all," until she fled the room in tears, leaving him in his wheelchair surrounded by fallen books which he was unable to pick up.

After visiting Franklin at the end of March, Dr. Draper sent a progress report to Lovett. Roosevelt was a little better, he said, "walking quite successfully and seems to be gaining power in the hip muscles. The quadriceps are coming back a little, but they are nothing to brag of yet. Below the knee I must say it begins to look rather hopeless, but I know that even at this stage one cannot tell."[22]

And there was now a fresh worry:

> There has a situation arisen which may make it necessary for a little more of your expert diplomatic skill. Briefly, it is this. The patient has gotten the idea into his head that he must economise this Summer, and proposes, consequently, to rid himself of his nurses and have his wife take over the joint duties of Mrs. Lake and Miss Rockey. Obviously, this is an impossible plan. In the first place, Mrs. R. is pretty much at the end of her tether with the long hard strain she has been through, and I feel that if she had to take on this activity, that the whole situation would collapse.
>
> Another interesting thing in the complex tapestry is the fact that Mrs. Lake does not seem to fit perfectly smoothly into the picture. She is admirable as far as her technical work is concerned, and is accepted with the greatest satisfaction from this standpoint. As far as I can make out, the difficulty, if it amounts to a difficulty, is merely that she lacks the bubbling sense of humor which Miss Rockey possesses and which has been the mainstay of the whole outfit ever since the very beginning. On the other hand, I think Miss Rockey occasionally gets on the nerves of Mrs. R.

The tensions within the Roosevelt household were real enough that winter, but the accuracy of Dr. Draper's analysis of their cause seems faulty. It seems likely that while Franklin was conscientious about the exercises Mrs. Lake put him through, he did sometimes find her a stern and humorless taskmistress and resented her dismissal of his own ideas for improving his muscles—Franklin Roosevelt never enjoyed being told what to do by anyone.

22. It should be understood that whenever doctors and physiotherapists or Franklin himself reported favorably on his "walking," they meant simply his ability to be mobile while remaining upright on crutches or canes and wearing steel braces. Walking without such aids was never possible for him after he was stricken.

But it also seems most unlikely that concern about economizing alone would have prompted him to suggest that she and Miss Rockey be dismissed so that Eleanor could assume their duties. The more probable impetus behind Franklin's curious plan was Eleanor herself. Her earnest efforts to keep her husband at his exercises had earned only his resentment. She had met little but hostility from her daughter since she had forced Anna to vacate her room. Her mother-in-law's disapproval was unrelenting. The hard-won independent life that had once bolstered her always precarious spirits seemed to have been brought to a permanent halt.

And now Miss Rockey—young, attractive, high-spirited, and clearly dazzled by her husband's easy charm—had displaced her even in the sickroom, preventing her from performing for her husband the nursing duties in which she had taken such uncharacteristic pride on Campobello.

The sounds of delighted laughter she sometimes heard coming from behind her husband's door when his nurse was attending to him may have seemed to her evidence that he had charmed his admiring nurse into neglecting her duties—and may also have contained troubling echoes of the intimacy that had developed between Franklin and Lucy Mercer in her own home just a few years earlier.[23]

Whatever Draper understood of the real motivation for Franklin's odd plan, he was right that Eleanor was nearing the end of her tether. "[O]ne afternoon that spring, when I was trying to read to the youngest boys," she remembered,

> I suddenly found myself sobbing as I read. I could not think why I was sobbing, nor could I stop. Elliott came in from school, dashed in to look at me and fled. Mr. Howe came in and tried to find out what was the matter with me, but he gave it up as a bad job. The two little boys went off to bed and I sat on the sofa in the sitting room and sobbed and sobbed. I could not go to dinner in this condition. Finally, I found an empty room

23. Franklin evidently did not himself suggest dismissing his nurse and physiotherapist to Draper; "[I]t came to me indirectly," the doctor told Lovett, perhaps through Sara, who also may have worried about at least the appearance of her son's friendliness with Miss Rockey.

"I think jealousy between friends is stupid," Sara would tell a close friend many years later, "perhaps because I have so often been a victim of it." But jealousy between husbands and wives was unavoidable unless both parties were very careful. "Too much freedom often leads them into situations" that sparked it. An invalid, for example, was "completely dependent on a nurse or a secretary" who can devote herself entirely to his welfare, while the wife, who must divide her time among her husband, her children, and her household, inevitably comes to resent any intimacy that develops between him and any outsider.

Her own late husband, Sara thought, had been wise never to "keep a nurse longer than a few days if he were to be ill long." *Source:* Notepad of interviews with Sara Delano Roosevelt, Rita Halle Kleeman Papers, FDRL.

in my mother-in-law's house. . . . I locked the door and poured cold water on a towel and mopped my face. I eventually pulled myself together, for it requires an audience, as a rule, to keep on these emotional jags. That is the one and only time I ever remember in my entire life going to pieces in this particular manner.

In the end, and despite Eleanor's wish to play a more central role in her husband's struggle to recover, Draper told Lovett, "my feeling is that the best practical arrangement from the standpoint of peace in the family and general lubrication, would be to have Miss Rockey retained for the summer," and for Franklin to move out of his claustrophobic New York house to Springwood, "where he will have a much better opportunity to walk and be out of doors. . . ."

Lovett agreed, and the doctor's orders were followed to the letter. At the end of May, while Eleanor stayed in New York until the boys' school had ended, Franklin, Miss Rockey, and his valet went home to his mother at Hyde Park.[24]

Sara was pleased to have him where she believed he had always belonged. She had ramps installed in the upper and lower halls— "inclined planes," she called them—so that Franklin's wheelchair could proceed as smoothly as possible. The old trunk elevator which had once been used to move her invalid husband from floor to floor now moved her son; he even used his late father's old wicker-backed wheelchair for a time, before abandoning it for a smaller, more maneuverable model.[25]

Every hour of Franklin's day as a boy in this house had been carefully regulated by his mother, whose loving but autocratic presence had been constant even while he bathed until at least the age of eight and a half. "Mama left this morning," he wrote to his father then, "and I am to have my bath alone!"

Now, she again made certain that his daily routine was determinedly placid. She instructed the servants that her son must have absolute quiet. It was important that he rest, she told them, away from "all the bells" in New York. He was put to bed in the Blue Room, down the hall from his own, because it received more sun and stayed

24. Genuine regret as well as lingering resentment may be read in a postscript Eleanor added to a note to Franklin, written shortly after he left for Hyde Park: "The boys all said this morning, 'Oh! When will Father come? We want popsy!' " *Source:* Roosevelt Family Papers Donated by the Children, FDRL.

25. Later, he would have his own special chair made up—an armless wooden kitchen chair to which wheels and a holder for an ashtray were attached.

warm later at night. He remained in bed till ten or eleven o'clock in the morning, breakfasting on a tray and working out on a set of rings that hung over his bed, a routine that would first rebuild his upper body, then transform his slender back and shoulders and upper torso into those of a husky athlete.

Mrs. Lake came three days a week to oversee his exercises, after which he was dressed, wheeled into the elevator, taken downstairs, and pushed out onto the porch, where he read or whittled model boats or worked over his stamps, his fingers now sufficiently nimble to manipulate gummed hinges. Sometimes—Robert McGauhey, his mother's butler, remembered—he would ask to be wheeled around the library so that he could give directions as to how his books and leather-bound sets of magazines might be rearranged. When his half brother was at home next door, he often had himself pushed along the wooded path to the Red House for a chat in its dark living room, the walls hung with antlers and stuffed fish, Franklin in his wheelchair, Rosy with his gouty leg up on an elephant's-foot hassock.

Promptly at one, luncheon was served to Franklin and Sara in the Springwood dining room. A nap followed. Then, Franklin was wheeled back onto the porch for tea with his mother—unless it rained, in which case they took tea together in her snuggery, the cramped little chamber that was the real seat of power at Springwood. It cannot have been easy to thread a wheelchair to the tea table without knocking into the thicket of family photographs and ancestral portraits with which Sara had covered every shelf and tabletop in her favorite room.

Dinner was at seven. Afterwards, Franklin sat quietly in the library until it was eleven and time to be put to bed.

Even Sara soon sensed that her son was finding this life stultifying and began to import people to keep him company. His cousin Laura Delano and Margaret L. Suckley, a young and unmarried distant cousin of Eleanor's, both of whom became frequent and admiring companions, first got to know him well in his earliest days as an invalid, motoring down at Sara's request from their homes up the river. "Mrs. James would invite me and others to tea," Miss Suckley remembered, "because Franklin was lonely and needed to *see* people."[26]

---

26. Miss Suckley and Miss Delano would become two of his closest companions during the last White House years. "You're the only people I know," he told them once, "that I don't have to entertain." Both were with him at Warm Springs, Georgia, when he died. *Source:* Interview with Margaret L. Suckley.

He rarely referred to his paralysis, she recalled, but when he did, it was to say, "I'm not going to be defeated by a *childish* disease."

That theme ran through much of his correspondence about his crippling. "After many consultations among the medical fraternity," Franklin had written Langdon Marvin when he was first diagnosed, "my case has been diagnosed as one of poliomyelitis, otherwise infantile paralysis. Cheerful thing for one of my gray hairs to get!" The consistently jocular tone in which he wrote and spoke of it was misleading: it was in fact a source of shame and embarrassment to him that he had fallen victim to an illness ordinarily confined to children.

All his life, he had been thought immature for his age, too closely tied to his mother, not quite grown up. Now, polio threatened to make him literally a child again, restricted in what he could and could not do, increasingly dependent upon his mother and the kindness of others.

Some time that spring, Eleanor took a telephone call from Miss Nancy Cook, the executive secretary of the new Women's Division of the state Democratic Party. Would Mrs. Roosevelt have the time to attend a fund-raising luncheon and say a few words to the guests? Eleanor's initial impulse was to say no; she did not know Miss Cook, after all, and was still frankly terrified of speaking in public.

But Howe and Franklin insisted she accept, not so much because they thought it would do her good to resume a life of her own beyond the sickroom but because such appearances were a good way to keep the Roosevelt name before the public. She did so and turned up before the luncheon, outwardly serene but inwardly fearful, clutching a bouquet of posies for her hostess. Despite her apprehension, the luncheon speech went well and she forged a new friendship with Miss Cook and, soon thereafter, with Miss Cook's friend, Marion Dickerman.

Like her other close friends, Esther Lape and Elizabeth Read, the two women had been living together for some years. Miss Dickerman was tall and somewhat mournful-looking, with a voice and manner very like Eleanor's, an educator and social worker who had run for the New York legislature in 1919, the first woman ever to do so. Nancy Cook had been her campaign manager: she was short and sturdy, vigorous and capable, with close-cropped hair and big, excitable brown eyes. She "could do almost anything," Eleanor once wrote—jewelry making, gardening, pottery, cabinetry.

Increasingly, Eleanor now would move, alone, within a world made up largely of women, many of whom lived with other women in relationships that closely resembled conventional marriage. Just across the hall from Nancy Cook and Marion Dickerman, in their cooperative apartment building on 12th Street, lived still another couple with whom Eleanor would soon forge a close friendship: Molly Dewson, a former Red Cross worker in France and an executive with the National Consumer's League whom Eleanor would one day recruit for the Democratic Party, and her long-time partner Polly Porter, who divided her time between worker education and the breeding of Shetland sheep dogs.

To the members of Eleanor's family, her new companions were often targets of ridicule. "She had a number of women friends," Alice Longworth remembered, "whom we used to allude roughly to as her 'female impersonators.' My Cousin Helen [Roosevelt Robinson] had a horrible story—a delightful story—of being once in an adjoining room to one in which Eleanor and a couple of her female impersonators were having a pillow fight (apparently they used to leapfrog a lot as well). She had not had a very happy childhood, so of course it was nice for her to have some vigorous companions who adored her. Couldn't be better. More strength to all of them. Pillow fights were obviously as jolly a form of communication as any."

When speaking with political friends, Franklin sometimes seemed to share the family's scorn for his wife's new friends, calling them "she-males," and he laughed indulgently when Rosy denounced them as "Eleanor's parlor pinks." But, as so often with him, his attitudes shifted to suit the company he was keeping: he seems to have been genuinely fond of Cook and Dickerman, whom he called "our gang." They cheered Eleanor, he knew, and they kept her occupied with projects. And they liked him, in return, joining cheerfully in the mildly flirtatious conversation he enjoyed. "He seemed rather to like the solicitous feminine fussing," Molly Dewson remembered.

They all admired his courage. Miss Dewson never forgot how flattered she had been when, after dinner with the Roosevelts at the apartment of Nancy Cook and Marion Dickerman, Franklin accepted her unthinking invitation to have a look at her apartment, shuffling slowly across the hall on his crutches while she carried his straw hat. "You are too wonderful not to make a single complaint," she told him, and he only smiled back.

Franklin was pleased and grateful to be included in their activities, and, according to Miss Dickerman, was at least once wounded to be left out of them. When she and Eleanor thoughtlessly planned a women's picnic without him, he hinted broadly that he would like to come, and when they didn't issue an invitation swiftly enough, tears filled his eyes. They hurriedly asked him along, and saw that the car seat was taken out and dragged into the woods for him to sit on.[27]

Despite the differences that would always divide him from his wife, Franklin never stopped wanting to have and hold her approval. He now tried with almost pathetic eagerness to make her new friends think well of him, in the hope, perhaps, that they would help persuade Eleanor to think well of him, too. Marion Dickerman joined the family for dinner at Springwood one weekend late that spring, fresh from a visit to the coal mines of Pennsylvania and West Virginia, and filled with indignation at the conditions under which the miners there were forced to work and live. The Roosevelts listened with interested sympathy until she began to speak of the worst place she'd seen, the Vittondale Mine, where, not long before, hired thugs had savagely beaten union organizers. Sara, she noted, stiffened perceptibly as she spoke, and an awkward silence followed before someone changed the subject.

Later, in the library, Franklin asked Marion to stay up with him for a few minutes after the others had gone to bed, "if she was not too awfully tired." She stayed, and he asked her to tell him more about the Vittondale Mine.

"Did you know that that is a Delano mine?" he asked, when she had finished. She had not known and was deeply embarrassed. No wonder his mother "had been a little cool" toward her after dinner.

Franklin reassured her she'd done nothing wrong. Uncle Fred Delano saw to the Delano properties, he said, and he happened to be staying at Algonac. He would telephone him right away.

"You know, Uncle Fred," Miss Dickerman remembered Roosevelt telling his mother's younger brother, "as long as these conditions exist, my family does not want any income from that mine. And I'll appreciate your seeing to it."

Miss Dickerman's memory was not infallible: it is unlikely that Roosevelt would ever have taken quite so admonishing a tone with the

27. Told this story many years later, Franklin Roosevelt, Jr., found it impossible to believe that his father would ever have been so emotional about his handicap in public and suspected that Miss Dickerman had misinterpreted what she had seen; he had merely *pretended* to be sad to wangle an invitation. "The thing was to make *fun* of his predicament," his son remembered. "That got him what he wanted without allowing anyone to pity him." *Source:* Interview with Franklin D. Roosevelt, Jr.

dignified uncle whom he had been taught to revere. But the fact that he took the trouble to talk to him at all on a subject so delicate and in full view of a comparative stranger is clear evidence of how much Franklin wished to impress Eleanor's friends.

In June, Eleanor brought the children with her to Springwood for the summer and the fierce contest for Franklin's future resumed. Again exhorted to do still more by his wife, urged to rest by his mother, facing a life filled with just the sort of loneliness he had endured as an only child and that his early marriage and political career had once seemed permanently to have ended, Franklin was severely tried.

His doctors conferred by telephone and agreed that he must get away from his family for a time. The excuse Dr. Lovett used was that his patient needed to come to Boston to be fitted for new braces. The real reason, as Dr. Draper wrote, was to get him away from "the intense and devastating influence of the interplay of these high-voltage personalities. . . ."

Franklin travelled to Boston on the last day of June, moving into a three-room suite on the third floor of Phillips House, a residence maintained for wealthy patients adjacent to Massachusetts General Hospital. Miss Rockey occupied one bedroom, Franklin the other; a lounge allowed him to entertain friends.

Lovett made an exhaustive examination of his patient, meticulously grading each of the forty-four muscles he tested as "Normal," "Good," "Fair," "Poor," "Trace," or "Totally Paralyzed." Franklin's back muscles were now classified as "Good"; they had greatly strengthened since the initial onslaught of the disease. But not a single muscle below his ribcage was better than "Fair."

Franklin's muscles would not improve at Phillips House—though he assured his old friend Bertie Hamlin that they were "gaining very surely" and told Livy Davis that his recovery was "away ahead of schedule"—but the techniques by which he mimicked walking did. "Where [Miss Wilhemine Wright] has been of use to him," Dr. Lovett reported, "has been in teaching him new tricks about getting up and down out of a chair and attempting the stairs."

Wilhemine Wright, Lovett's assistant, was a pioneer in rehabilitation, a shrewd, no-nonsense therapist who believed that the "ability to use crutches properly is not innate, but must be learned, like dancing or skating." It was absurd to hand a pair of crutches to "the timid adult who has recently loss the use of his leg muscles" and expect him to walk, she wrote; "he doesn't know how to begin, and there are very few persons who know how to instruct him."

Franklin had daily sessions with Miss Wright in her clinic at the nearby Children's Hospital, a nearly helpless adult, six feet tall, making his slow, clumsy way among the children who formed the bulk of her patients.

The simple act of rising from a chair unaided had so far been beyond him. In order to stand, he had first to straighten each brace out before him, then lock the knees so that his legs would not bend, a posture that made it impossible for even the strongest patient to make it to his feet unaided.

"To rise from a chair [on his own]," Miss Wright explained, "the patient with two good arms and body, but two braced legs, must sit on the edge of his chair and with his hand place one foot across the other leg. He then turns toward the side of the leg and reaches behind him for the seat of the chair, turning himself completely over with his hands and then climbing up the back of the chair until his feet are on the floor. After that, it is an easy matter to push the hips back and straighten the body while balancing with the chair, and finally to place first one crutch and then the other under the arms."

It was a useful maneuver, a real breakthrough once Franklin had mastered it. But when performing it, he looked nothing like an able-bodied person rising from a chair, and so he would eventually have to abandon this technique in public, either remaining seated when others stood or allowing himself to be pulled to his feet behind a carefully positioned screen of aides.[28]

Climbing stairs was a still more serious challenge. If there was a

---

28. Even this was impossible without two trained assistants: while hauling him upright, his helpers had to wedge their feet in front of his so that his rigid legs would not simply slide out in front of him.

This problem yielded a rare flash of Rooseveltian anger at his condition. An onlooker at one of his first public appearances after being stricken, evidently unaware that he was handicapped, wrote to protest his having remained seated during a tribute to President Coolidge and received this blistering reply:

> As I wear steel braces on both legs and use crutches it is impossible for me to rise or sit down without the help of two people. After presiding at the opening of the meeting and turning it over to Bishop Manning I returned to my seat, sat down, and remained seated for the rest of the evening. It is, of course, not exactly pleasant for me to have to remain seated during the playing of the National Anthem and on other occasions when the audiences rise, but I am presented with the alternative of doing that or of not taking part in any community enterprises whatsoever.

Sources: Interviews with Hugh Gallagher, Mary Hudson Veeder, Alice Lou Plastridge-Converse; Frank Freidel, *Franklin D. Roosevelt: The Ordeal,* pages 186–187.

railing, Franklin was taught to hand one crutch to a companion (or place both crutches under his left arm), then reach forward along the railing with his right to haul himself up, step by step, until he neared the top. Since there was then no more railing on which to pull, he had to stop there, leaning on his crutches, then reach behind him to push himself the last step or two.

"To come downstairs," Miss Wright taught, "the patient who is supported between one crutch and the rail, must first push the foot nearest the wall over the edge of the step. He then jumps down onto the next step with his one crutch and, turning his face toward the rail, pulls his other foot off the upper step onto the one on which he is standing. He is left as far as possible from the rail and must jump himself back beside it before he can descend another step."

If there was no railing, things were even worse. The patient had to go up backwards, "holding his crutches as straight and near him as possible in order to get the maximum lift from them. As he raises his feet from the step and suspends himself on the crutches, he must endeavor to lift his hips up behind and fall forward . . . so that the weight of the head may balance the hips. It is the fear of leaning forward that prevents many patients from climbing stairs in this manner."[29]

It was a dangerous business, and learning it not the sort of thing that should be left to friends and family members, Miss Wright wrote, because the patient "must have absolute confidence in the strength and watchfulness of the instructor." She and an assistant clasped hands around Franklin as he struggled with his crutches, careful not to touch him unless absolutely necessary, but present if needed to break his fall.

Franklin eventually learned to pull himself up a few stairs, provided there was a handrail—Sara had a brass one installed right away on East 65th Street so that he could enter and leave his house without undue

---

29. Many years later, another patient vividly recalled the terrors he—and Franklin—first experienced trying to walk again:

> Lift yourself from the chair by your arms alone. Walk on your hands, clasped to the wooden poles. Force your arms to be legs, your hands to be feet. No cheating. The swing of your leg has to come from your shoulder. The move of foot has to originate from above the pelvis. You must lift yourself from the chair, out the door, and down the stairs with biceps, triceps and trapezius alone. No cheating. And know that if you make one mistep on the stairs, there are no gluteal muscles, no sartorius to rescue you. If one of your feet misses the step, you have nothing to catch you but your hands. And you must go down. Way down.

Source: Lorenzo Wilson Milam, *The Cripple: Liberation Front Marching Band Blues,* pages 56–57.

embarrassment and later added a ramp with railings to make access still easier, and Eleanor was pleased that he would now be able to "get in and out of a motor with ease." But despite Miss Wright's best efforts, Roosevelt could not "get up steps with only the crutches," he confessed to Lovett later that year, "and I doubt if this feat can be accomplished for a long time." (He evidently never did accomplish it.)

To the best of his ability, he continued to let no one know that any of these frustrations upset him. "He was the most charming man I've ever met," a house physician recalled. ". . . Whenever I saw him he was always smiling. A lot of people committed suicide with infantile. I think by the time he [came to Phillips House] he had made his adjustments. . . . I don't think it ever bothered him. He could walk with crutches and could lift himself up from the bathroom. I don't think it changed his style of life at all."

"I was anxious to get him on here, away from family and friends," Dr. Lovett wrote Sara,

> because I wanted to get hold of him alone and observe him as to whether I thought he had been persistently overdoing at home and what his resistance was. . . . He has been living very comfortably at Phillips House, has seen a few of his friends, gets out on the roof or the porch a good deal, takes an occasional automobile ride and looks very much better. Miss Wright has been able to teach him some new tricks about walking and managing himself which have increased his usefulness. . . .

Sara was delighted, so much "happier about my son now that he [is] under your care . . . I am so thankful that you have curtailed some of his work & that he is out of doors daily."

She reported family news to Franklin. Anna had the mumps but was "very good and happy." Eleanor had held a reception for forty mayors' wives under the Springwood trees; "she looks thin but I did not ask her how she felt." Mlle Thiel had told her that the children were "easier to manage here than . . . in town, but I fear they were not very good yesterday when poor Eleanor was here. They do stand a little in awe of me."

Sara had been especially pleased that by going to Boston, Franklin would be "near nice Livy"; Livingston Davis's good looks, Yankee background, and impeccable manners had always made her blind to his faults. In fact, Davis was then separated from his wife who was suing him for divorce and living what he and Franklin both liked to call "a spinster's life" in Boston.[30] He was delighted to see his friend, taking him for long drives, flirting with Miss Rockey, sitting up until the early hours of the morning with Franklin and other old Harvard friends, playing poker and drinking tumblers of Scotch from a bottle smuggled into Phillips House under his coat.

When Franklin returned to Hyde Park in July, he and the two youngest children had the Place largely to themselves. His mother had taken Anna, James, and Russell Sturgis, the son of old Campobello friends, with her to France for their first tour. Their two-month itinerary was exhaustive—Paris, Chartres, Soissons, Rheims, Verdun, Nancy, Strasbourg, Bourges, Vichy, Basle, Lucerne, Geneva, Interlaken, then back through France and on to London—but at sixty-seven, their grandmother was an indefatigable escort. "I think Eleanor's judgment about me is correct," Sara wrote, "so strong & tough that nothing tires me & I shall live for many, many years!"

She insisted that the children take turns sitting up front and speaking French with Albert, the chauffeur. At Versailles, she discovered they had just forty minutes before closing time, "so I took an excellent guide & wasted *no* time. The children had an intelligent visit. . . ."

No detail about her grandchildren was too small to escape her attention: "They eat well, & drink quarts of Evian water, but James

30. Alice Gardiner Davis had called upon Franklin and Eleanor in late February to explain that Livy's philandering and hard drinking and his inability to stay at one job for long had finally proved too much for her; she had no choice, she felt, but to leave him, taking their adopted son, Jamey, with her.

Not long afterwards, Livy's Boston attorney had written privately to Franklin. "[Davis] regards you as the fountain head of all wisdom, as well as his best friend," he told Roosevelt, and asked for his help in persuading Livy to "do the generous thing by Alice"; otherwise, he said, the prevailing feeling against him in and around Boston would only be intensified.

Franklin did his best: Alice was eminently fair-minded, he told the lawyer, deserved a generous settlement for all she had been through, and "seemed quite concerned . . . that Livvie is not really, seriously doing anything at the present time. . . . I know how much you have done to help poor old Livvie, and it is bully of you to have taken this interest when a lot of other people have turned a cold shoulder. . . ."

Livy was generous, in the end, though he balked briefly at the language of the summons served upon him: "cruel and abusive treatment *which seriously impaired health and endangered life.* . . . Really I must confess I was so blind that I had no idea it was as bad as that to live with me. . . . I would like to fight this charge. But I suppose I must continue to swallow my pride, hold my tongue, and swallow the medicine . . . I'm through with women. After the way [Alice] and her friends who had always cloaked themselves with smug holiness and righteousness have acted. [His lawyer] states that there is no form of cruelty equal to that of the righteous person who makes of the smallest detail a moral issue."

"Don't worry about legal language," Franklin urged him. "It is merely usual and customary. The main thing to do is get it over with!"

finds one egg *nothing* for breakfast with several rolls & two cups of chocolate! . . . *Private.* Anna has just become *indisposée.* . . . I shall have a chance to have her rest when not motoring, and if it seems best can stay two nights, instead of one at Verdun." She had her granddaughter's hair trimmed, as befit a young woman, and, she assured Eleanor, had been careful to have what was cut woven into a braid so that she could wear it while her hair grew out again in the fall.

But she kept her own trials to herself as long as she could and with the same cheerful stoicism she had instilled in her son. From London, weeks after it happened, she explained that she had suffered an accident at the start of the whirlwind visit to Versailles. Hurrying to catch the train in Paris, she fell down a long steep flight of stone steps.

> I happened to have on a pair of ready-made shoes with higher heels than I usually wear, and I caught my right heel and was thrown very hard, injuring or rather breaking a vein on the inside of my right leg. Of course I hopped up and swore it was nothing, but when we reached Versailles I bought lead wash and bandages and while the rest visited the Trianon, etc., I went to the Hotel de Reservoir and did up my leg. Then I wrote to you and told you of Versailles and then as a thank offering to the hotel, I had tea, after which Aunt Doe and the others called for me, and they all had tea and we returned to Paris, where I dined and lunched out, etc., etc. . . . I had a doctor.
>
> All of this is very uninteresting, but I suppose I have to tell you and I hope you will at once forget it. . . . I do not leave my room. Tomorrow the doctor will decide if the thing is going to absorb or not. I am really cross with myself, I have been so well, so nice and thin and active, never tired, and to do this was so unnecessary! I am saying to myself, it will be better tomorrow. I am sure it will not have to be opened, and [am] reading a good story by Balzac in a large, comfortable chair and my feet in another, and every 3 or 4 hours I get up and "do up" my game leg.[31]

Eleanor spent much of the summer with Franklin in Hyde Park, too, brushing up on her driving following a mishap in which she smashed the family Buick into one of the brownstone gateposts, and trying to learn to swim after having had to stand helplessly by one frightening afternoon while Depew fished Franklin Jr. out of the ice

---

31. In the end, surgery did not prove necessary. "The doctor here considers me a very remarkable tough old subject," she reported with pride, and then, concerned that she had made the physician seem to have been altogether too familiar, she added, "but he is very kind and polite in the way he expresses himself." *Source:* Roosevelt Family Papers Donated by the Children, FDRL.

pond when he lost his footing. Her swimming lessons, undertaken under direct orders from her husband who could not himself now serve as a reliable lifeguard for the children, took great dedication, for she had been terrified of water almost all her life. Traumatized at three, when the steamship on which she and her parents were travelling to Europe was rammed by another vessel and seemed sure to sink, she had been further terrified during a childhood visit to Oyster Bay when her Uncle Theodore ordered her to dive off the dock and she had dutifully done so, sinking like a stone, rather than confess to him that she could not swim. Now, she spent hours doggedly practicing the breast stroke, her head held well above the surface, legs kicking desperately, arms flailing.[32]

Franklin enjoyed teasing Eleanor about her fear of water, but his own terror of fire more than matched it. That fear, too, had its roots in childhood. Visiting his grandparents at Algonac at the age of two, he may have witnessed the hideous death of his lovely Aunt Laura whose robe, accidentally drenched with alcohol, burst into flame and sent her shrieking through the house and out onto the lawn; later, he helped put out a fire in the Springwood cellar beams and another in the Groton stables in which several horses were consumed. It was "a horrible scene," he had told his parents then, "the poor horses . . . lying under the debris with their hide entirely burned off and fearfully charred," all because *"there was no back door."* Far away from his family during the summers, he had often worried that there might be a fire in the Campobello cottage, issuing instructions for the filling of sand buckets, urging Eleanor to organize fire drills.

Now, his old terror was intensified by his new immobility, and Franklin Jr. remembered being allowed to scurry along beside his

---

32. She did not learn to dive until 1939, when she was fifty-six years old. Dorothy Dow, a junior member of the White House staff, taught her how. "She was anxious to perform for the President," Miss Dow noted in a letter home from Hyde Park,

> as he said he didn't believe she could do it. One day he drove over from the Big House [to Mrs. Roosevelt's nearby cottage] and sat at the edge of the pool. I sat down on the grass beside him, and he said, "I understand that you are the one who taught her all this." I acknowledged the fact. So, Mrs. R. walked out on the board, got all set in the proper form and went in as flat as could be. She could have been heard down at Poughkeepsie! I thought the President would explode with laughter. Mrs. R. came up red in the face, with a really grim expression, said nothing, walked out on the board again, and did a perfect dive. We all gave her a great big hand, and she was pretty proud of her accomplishment—which she certainly should have been.

Source: Dorothy Dow, *Eleanor Roosevelt: An Eager Spirit.* page 104.

father that summer as he crawled up and down the upstairs hall between his bedroom and the elevator, practicing his escape.[33]

At her husband's enthusiastic urging, Eleanor had plunged back into politics that summer: it was an election year and her active, public presence in party circles was the best way he and Howe could think of to keep the Roosevelt name in the newspapers. Eleanor was away from Springwood much of the time, organizing the Democratic women of Dutchess County, addressing luncheons, learning to suppress the unwelcome nervous giggle with which she had punctuated her first public appearances. "What are you laughing about?" Howe asked her after attending an early talk: "Have something to say, say it, and sit down."

She excused herself early from dinner with Rosy and Betty one evening, explaining that she had to speak in the village. "It's only the beginning," Rosy told Franklin after she had left. "Once they mount the soapbox, mark my words, they never get off."

One brief, bright spot that summer came when Franklin received a questionnaire asking for a short account of his contributions to the war effort from Benjamin Haviland, the Hyde Park town historian, then engaged in a history of the town during World War I. Franklin, still sensitive because he had not managed to get into uniform before the shooting stopped, was so pleased that someone had thought to include him among the veterans that he had Depew drive him over to the old man's home at East Park to convey his gratitude in person.

"He came to see me to thank me as the first one to recognize him as a boy of World War I from Hyde Park," Haviland remembered. "He informed me that it had been recommended to him by those who were doctoring him for his sickness that he was to have something to take up his attention . . . without being too weighty." He thought he might like to write a history of Hyde Park, Franklin explained, and wondered if Mr. Haviland would be willing to help him. Flattered by all the attention from the town's most celebrated citizen, Haviland said he would, and they became collaborators, delighting together in the minutiae of genealogy. Their relationship was cemented one day when Franklin boasted that he was a collateral descendant of Anne Hutchin-

---

33. Much later, the Secret Service would urge that the old hand-operated elevator be replaced by an electrically powered one. FDR refused, convinced that in a fire the power might go out and leave him trapped; he could do better, he was sure, by pulling himself down to safety before the thick rope burned through. *Source:* Interview with Franklin D. Roosevelt, Jr.

son, the dissenter banished from Massachusetts Bay Colony for her convictions and later killed by Indians on Long Island. "I told him I could beat him that one; that my great, great, great grandfather killed the Indian that killed Anne Hutchinson," Haviland remembered. The town historian had traced his family back to John Underhill, the hard-bitten soldier whom the Puritans also exiled and who later fought for the Dutch against the Long Island tribes. "When I told Mr. Roosevelt the reasons for this banishing of Underhill, that he was too intimate with Anne's sister . . . [a] shoemaker's wife, he said that made me his uncle. From that time on, he always called me 'Uncle Ben.' . . ."[34] (Haviland called Roosevelt "Franklin" even during the White House years, one of the very few Hyde Park citizens to dare do so.)

Roosevelt had always been interested in the history of the county in which his family had played a prominent part, and in 1914 he had joined Professor Helen Wilkinson Reynolds of Vassar in founding the Dutchess County Historical Society. Now, he devoted a good deal of time to it, driving out with Professor Reynolds to view overgrown cemeteries, seeing to the publication of historical documents, arranging to have the Holland Society of New York undertake a photographic survey of old Dutch houses, succeeding Uncle Ben Haviland as town historian. His interest was that of an enthusiastic antiquarian. It soothed him, he told Helen Reynolds, "to play with Dutchess County History."

"I am so pleased to get a clipping . . . ," Sara wrote Franklin while still abroad, "saying that Mr. Al Smith will accept the nomination for governor, [and] giving his letter to 'Frank.' It will save us from Hearst, who is a truly great danger, and I hope he will be nominated and elected. Eleanor's work among the women will, I trust, bear fruit."

It was Sara's loathing for William Randolph Hearst, not any special affection for Al Smith, that made her hope for a Smith victory. And it was Smith's loathing for Hearst that made him seek it.

Like Franklin, Smith had been forced out of active politics by the Republican landslide of 1920. For the first time in his life, he was earning a handsome income—$30,000 a year as chairman of the board

34. "I told Mr. Roosevelt that the story was true . . . but still there might be some discrepancies in some of the dates and things. . . . He said. 'Never mind the truth, it's a good story and the truth will take care of itself.' " In fact, Underhill was banished for religious dissidence. The adultery charge came later. *Sources:* George Palmer interview with Benjamin Haviland, National Park Service; *Dictionary of American Biography.*

of the United States Trucking Corporation, plus sizable additional fees as a director of other firms—and was able to spend time with his family.

He remained the most important Democrat in the state, and the gubernatorial nomination in 1922 was his for the asking. But he revelled in his new life as a prosperous "trucking boss." ("He was a man who was profoundly conscious of the fact that he had succeeded," Raymond Moley remembered. "He never entered that rarified atmosphere in which other notable men have questioned whether it is, after all, 'worthwhile.' ") And he might conceivably have sat out the race had his nearest rival not been Hearst, the flamboyant publisher who had been prowling the fringes of New York State politics since the century's turn, seeking some sure first foothold on his climb to the presidency. Now, Hearst had taken advantage of his great fortune and Smith's official absence to begin building support for his own candidacy for governor. The malleable mayor of New York, John F. Hylan, was under his control, other allies held important city offices, and he had started to build a skeleton machine upstate; some two hundred delegates to the upcoming convention in Syracuse were rumored to be leaning toward the publisher, provided Smith stayed in private life.

Al Smith was generally an amiable man, willing to forgive his opponents once the votes were counted. But he hated Hearst with a cold, steady hatred that startled even his own family and had only intensified with time. Its roots ran back at least to 1919, when, having beaten the publisher for the gubernatorial nomination and then trounced the Republican opposition, Governor Smith suddenly found himself the target of lurid, baseless assaults from Hearst's two powerful Manhattan dailies, the *American* and *Evening Journal.* The ostensible cause was New York City's milk supply. A prolonged producers' strike had reduced the flow of milk to the city and forced its price up to eighteen cents a quart, where it stayed even after the strike was over. The governor had no power to regulate prices, but he had tried nonetheless to bring relief by appointing a Fair Price Milk Committee and halting the sale of impure, unpasteurized milk to the poor.

Hearst did not allow these inconvenient facts to interfere with his campaign of villification. BABIES ARE DYING IN NEW YORK, said the *Evening Journal,* and it was Smith's fault: "Governor Smith! You have sold the babies to the Milk Trust as that other Judas, President Wilson, has sold the world to British tyranny." Hearst's cartoonists drew ragged, hollow-eyed children clutching at their desperate mothers while the governor, caricatured in spats and top hat, coldly ignored their pleas.

Already angry that anyone should accuse him, a son of the East Side streets and the proud father of five, of being insensitive to the plight of poor children, Smith travelled to Brooklyn to visit his sick mother. There, an attendant told him that Hearst's attacks were actually affecting her recovery from pneumonia: in her delirium she had been heard to murmur, "My son did not kill those babies. He was a poor boy. He loves children."

Doubly incensed, he challenged his tormentor to a debate at Carnegie Hall, and when Hearst backed off, claiming somewhat lamely that he had better things to do than answer the complaints of "faithless and unreliable public servants," the governor appeared on the stage alone. He declared that Hearst's newspapers were "like a cuttlefish that emits black ink," and denounced the publisher himself as a coward, a liar, "the pestilence that walks in darkness."

Now, Smith's own ambition nicely coincided with his sincere belief that his old enemy represented evil incarnate. Hearst was a philanderer, Smith believed (his liaison with the film star Marion Davies was already widely known), a phony Democrat (he had relentlessly attacked Woodrow Wilson before America entered the Great War and had supported Harding in 1920), and a heedless millionaire who feigned concern for New York's poor while building himself an ornate castle on a California hilltop.

Democratic leaders, fearful that Hearst might win the nomination only to lose the election, clamored for Smith to run; it was his duty, they said, to save the party. The ex-governor privately agreed, and asked Franklin, as the most prominent upstate Protestant in the party, to issue a public call for him to do so.

Glad to be asked to play even this symbolic role, Franklin wrote "Dear Al" an open letter on August 13:

> The Democratic party must put its best foot forward. Many candidates for office are strong by virtue of what they promise they will do. You are strong by virtue of what you have done. . . . I am taking it upon myself to appeal to you in the name of countless thousands of citizens of upstate New York. . . .
>
> . . . We realize that years of public service make it most desirable that you think now for a while of your family's needs. I am in the same boat myself—yet this call for further service must come first. Some day your

children will be even prouder of you for making this sacrifice than they are now.

In a reply addressed to "Dear Frank," Smith formally agreed to accept his party's draft.

Hearst swiftly shifted his tactics; with the governorship now denied him, he sought to run for the Senate instead, blandly dispatching emissaries to Smith, asking him to let bygones be bygones and promising heavy financial and newspaper support if he accepted his presence on the slate. Smith was adamant, telling every visitor that he would himself abandon the race rather than run alongside the man who had "nearly murdered" his mother, and Hearst finally withdrew rather than be humilated on the convention floor, his political career in ruins. Then, as a gesture toward those who had supported his defeated enemy, Smith agreed to the nomination of a Hearst ally, the Commissioner of Health of New York City, Dr. Royal S. Copeland.

AL NOMINATED WITH GREAT ENTHUSIASM, Howe wired Franklin from the convention at Syracuse. MORGENTHAU AND YOUR MISSUS LED THE DUTCHESS DELEGATION WITH THE BANNER THREE TIMES AROUND THE HALL.

"Everything went along first rate," Smith wrote Franklin. "I had quite a session with our lady politicians as Mrs. Roosevelt no doubt told you. I was delighted to see her taking an active part and I am really sorry that you could not be there, but take care of yourself—there is another day coming."[35]

To hasten that day, Franklin was working hard at Hyde Park. He only grudgingly performed the crutch-walking he had learned at Phillips House; it was slow and clumsy at best, the braces he had to wear while doing it were heavy and painful, and it did nothing to build up his legs.

What really interested him was full recovery of his muscles. He wanted to conquer his handicap, not merely adapt to it.

He labored with Mrs. Lake three mornings a week. Lovett had suggested that he try swimming in warm water, followed by light

35. Franklin lost little time in exaggerating his own role in Smith's nomination. "I had quite a tussle in New York to keep our friend Hearst off the ticket and to get Al Smith to run," he told Joseph E. Davies, "but the thing went through in fine shape."

In fact, Franklin had managed to avoid unnecessarily antagonizing Hearst, even accepting the purely honorary chairmanship of Copeland's Senate campaign, a gesture not lost on the publisher, who would prove to be instrumental in FDR's victory at the Democratic National Convention in 1932. *Source:* Frank Freidel, *Franklin D. Roosevelt: The Ordeal*, page 119.

massage and lying in the sun. He was helped to slide gently into the old ice pond behind the house in which he and his children had first learned to swim and was exhilarated by the relative ease with which his legs could be made to move beneath its surface. But its spring water was too frigid to allow him to remain submerged for long. His mother's chauffeur, Louis Depew, stood by whenever he swam, ready to haul him out when he got too cold. "One day he hollered to me—he was out there swimming," Depew remembered, "The water put me where I am, and the water has to bring me back." Later in the summer, his friend Vincent Astor offered Franklin the use of his heated pool at Rhinecliff and he had himself driven up there several times a week. "The legs work wonderfully in the water," he told Dr. Draper, "and I need nothing to keep myself afloat."

But his progress outside the pool was still painfully slow, and he began to cast about for other means of building up his strength, means of which Dr. Lovett did not necessarily approve.

At the suggestion of another polio,[36] he ordered built on the south lawn a set of parallel bars along which, resting his weight on his shoulders and arms, he dragged his legs back and forth each afternoon in hopes of building them up. He enjoyed having friends stop by during these workouts—Louis Howe or Missy Le Hand, the Morgenthaus, Margaret Suckley and Laura Delano, the Newbolds from next door. Franklin had always sought to remain the center of attention in any circle he entered, but non-stop talk now became a habit with him, his daughter remembered, "an unconscious habit formed when he realized he could not make an excuse and leave people because he was sedentary; and it was therefore, his responsibility to give them as good a time as possible while they were with him." His cheerful, almost ceaseless monologues on the Springwood lawn were calculated to hold his guests' attention and keep their minds as far as possible from pity as he struggled.

It did not always work. He missed his grip one afternoon while chattering away and fell, tearing several small ligaments in one leg that kept him off his feet for several days.

A Hyde Park neighbor wrote suggesting Franklin try both "intelligent massaging of the limbs for the diffusion of vitalizing magnetism" and something called the "Whiteley Exerciser," which required the

36. Here and in subsequent chapters I use this word—first widely used at Warm Springs—rather than "victim" or "sufferer" or "survivor" to denote someone who, like Franklin, contracted poliomyelitis and retained a residual paralysis.

patient to lean on crutches or over the back of a chair while rubber cables running from a motor to one of his ankles pulled and pushed the affected leg.

Whether he ever tried it is unknown, but he did devise apparatus of his own. Warned by Lovett that he was not yet ready to try a stationary rowing machine, he ordered built instead "an old-fashioned children's double-swing," he wrote a fellow patient. "I sit in one seat, put my feet in the other seat, and push down and pull up with my legs, thereby making the swing go forward and backward. It seems to develop the knee muscles in a splendid way."

He tried an oversized tricycle, too, brought home to him from Europe by Sara, the theory being that by having his feet strapped to the pedals and then asking McGauhey and Miss Rocky to push from behind, his legs would be exercised without having to expend any effort. He found it both clumsy and humiliating and asked that it be stored away in the barn.

In 1921, a French self-improvement advocate named Emile Coué had arrived in America, advocating the daily repetition of the slogan, "Day by day in every way I am getting better and better." Miraculous cures were said to have been produced, Coué institutes were formed in major cities, and several friends of Franklin's offered to write to the Frenchman on his behalf. Coué backed away, admitting he had had little luck with infantile paralysis patients; even his happy mantra couldn't revive dead nerves.

Franklin, who thought Coué "a really remarkable soul" who had done "perfectly splendid work," was not unduly discouraged. "In a way I have been following Coué's methods ever since I got this fool disease . . . ," he wrote one of the Frenchman's disciples. "I have been perfectly definite in my determination to throw away the crutches and every month that has gone by has found the nerve cells and muscles returning to better control."[37]

37. Coué's notions were second nature to the Delanos. Franklin's Uncle Fred reiterated the family code in a letter written shortly after his nephew was stricken:

My dear Franklin,

    I spent a restless night last night and thought a good deal about you, wondering how I could be of some service and as a result of that cogitation, I came to the conclusion that I ought to give you some "fatherly" advice. It won't do any harm and it may do some good!

    I do not remember the school book definition of philosophy, but since I passed 40, I have worked out ideas of my own on the subject. To my mind, philosophy means in substance, "making the best of the situation," or in other words taking things as they are, analyzing the facts, above all not *fooling* yourself, and by intelligent reasoning determining

Eleanor marvelled at Franklin's relentless optimism and did not wish to dampen it—he "never, ever admitted that he would not one day walk alone," she later told an interviewer. But she herself saw little sign that his legs were in fact improving. She was "not sanguine" about her husband's ever recovering the use of his limbs, she told Lovett privately, and was anxious now that Franklin begin to accept that fact and learn to adapt as best he could to his new circumstances. She accompanied him upriver to swim in the Astor pool because his doctor had encouraged him to exercise in warm water, but she worried aloud that he was failing to follow Lovett's other central directive for the summer: he was not working hard enough on his crutch-walking.[38]

When he reacted with anger to her prodding, she took her anxieties to Lovett himself, and the doctor wrote Franklin a chiding letter from his summer home at Newport.

I rather inferred from what she said that you had not been using your crutches and splints [braces] as much as I think you ought to. I probably misled you by telling you that the splints were not a treatment for your paralysis, which is perfectly true, but I think it is very important for you to do all the walking that you can within your limit of fatigue, with a view of your activities next winter. Walking on crutches is not a gift, but an art, acquired by constant practice just as any other game, and you will

---

the right course to pursue. I never worry, I accept things as they are, I "look forward and not back."

I realize that you are up against a hard problem, and hard cruel facts, and yet I feel the utmost confidence that you will emerge a better and a stronger man. It will give you time for reflection, and that alone is worth a good deal! In your rushing and busy life you have not had that. Now, as to your recovery, the doctors & nurses can do much. Experience can warn you what to avoid, but, after all, the constructive work of getting *well* depends largely on your own character, for though I have never been carried away with the preachments of the faith healers and the Christian Scientists, I think they have a kernel of truth in their dictum, a truth as old as time. . . . Of course, you mustn't rush things, because the Doctors tell me it is unwise to do active work for several weeks, but when you do begin, your attitude to yourself and to this recovery will mean everything. Marvelous "cures" have been effected by men I know, in consumption, paralysis, etc. by the will and determination of the Patient, and I feel so confident of your background of health and good habits and of your courage and good temper, that I refuse to be cast down. This does not mean that I am lacking in sympathy; that you have on every side and if prayers can save you, you do not have to lift your hand. My philosophy does not at all exclude the supernatural powers of our Heavenly Father, but I do think there is more truth than poetry in the saying, "God helps those who help themselves!"

38. That Eleanor's concern was justified seems to be borne out by the testimony of Mrs. William Plog, the wife of the Springwood manager, who was often on the grounds that summer: "I seen him walking with his crutches and his nurse *several times* [author's italics]."

Asked "Did he give up or keep on trying?" Mrs. Plog answered, "Well, I don't think he tried very often." *Source:* George Palmer interview with Mrs. William Plog, National Park Service.

have to put in quite a little time before you get about satisfactorily. In addition to this, you ought to practice getting up and down stairs, and helping yourself in every way with a view to your getting about acceptably next winter.

Franklin put in as much time as he could bear.[39] "It's a bit traumatic when you're fifteen years of age," wrote Anna, who returned to Hyde Park with James and her grandmother in time to witness Roosevelt's struggle late that summer, " . . . [to] see your father, whom you've regarded as a wonderful playmate, who took long walks with you, sailed with you, could out-jump you, and do a lot of things, suddenly, you look up and you see him walking on crutches—trying, struggling in heavy steel braces. And you see the sweat pouring down his face, and you hear him saying, 'I must get down the driveway today—all the way down the driveway.' "

The narrow drive that split the fields in front of Springwood and ran down to the Post Road between twin rows of elms was a quarter of a mile long at the most; it had been only a few moments' effortless exertion for a long-legged adolescent, dogs bounding at his heels.

Now, the drive seemed again an infinity for Franklin, longer even than when the feathery tops of the hay on either side of it marked out his small boy's world and he had toddled down it, holding his mother's hand. The old stone gateposts did not beckon anymore; they barred him, seemed even to recede, as he stumped slowly toward them in the summer heat.

39. Although he remained stubbornly sure that he and not Lovett had been right—refusing to wear his braces all summer "has been a good thing," he told Dr. Draper in August, "and has not done me one particle of harm." *Source:* Franklin D. Roosevelt Papers, Family, Business, and Personal, FDRL.

CHAPTER
15

❦

THE LIMITS OF HIS POSSIBILITIES

Franklin planned to return to Phillips House to have his braces refitted in late September 1922, and wrote Bamie Cowles to ask if he might stop for the night at Oldgate on the way. William Amory Gardner would be coming with him. Gardner, a wealthy and eccentric Groton schoolmaster whom almost four decades of boys fondly called "Uncle Billy Wag," had been Franklin's favorite teacher while at the school. Even as a young man, Gardner thought his own health so delicate that he played bridge standing up and clutching his heart for fear the excitement of the game would prove more than he could bear; now, he had been badly slowed by a genuine heart attack.

Bamie's husband, Admiral Cowles—"Mr. Bearo" to his wife, "a darling but not a ball of fire by any means," according to Corinne Alsop—had recently suffered a similar attack and also had to move with even greater caution than usual. Bamie herself was now almost wholly deaf, depending for what little she did hear on an elaborate and only intermittently effective amplifying device that sat on a table near her wheelchair.

Oldgate, she told her sister Corinne Robinson, had become "a home for incurables kept by an incurable. . . . It will be lovely to see [Franklin and Gardner] but I would much prefer having my invalids one by one. . . . Having an elevator that Hopkinson [the butler] has to run, everybody will have to get into it—all of which is a little painful."[1]

A visitor who dropped by during Franklin's visit never forgot the sight of Bamie and her guests sitting together in the Oldgate garden, with its velvet lawn rolling down to the Connecticut River. Gardner wheezed amiably in his chair next to the elderly and immobilized Admiral Cowles. Bamie, bent and gnarled and deaf, sat trapped in her wheelchair next to Franklin, trapped in his own, while he shouted into her listening device to make her laugh: "You felt such *gallantry* in all of them, you know, such humor, such complete elimination of any problem about bodies."

In front of strangers, things were very different for Franklin.

At around eleven o'clock on Monday morning, October 9, the Roosevelt Buick drew up in front of 120 Broadway, the building in which the Fidelity & Deposit office was located. Franklin Roosevelt was going back to the office for the first time in fifteen months, and every aspect of his return had been carefully mapped out by Missy Le Hand, who had seen to it that for his welcome-back luncheon at the upstairs Bankers Club he would have his own elevator "express and alone," to take him from his office to a private banquet room without ever having to wheel himself through the public dining room.

But first he had to reach his office. The uniformed chauffeur got out, came around the car, and opened the curbside back door. With his help, Franklin heaved himself onto the jump seat and held himself upright by holding onto the partition and the side of the open door. Then the chauffeur leaned down, tugged Roosevelt's braces out straight, and locked them.

A car pulled up behind him and began to honk impatiently. The chauffeur went back to speak to the driver, leaving his employer balanced precariously on the jump seat, his stiff legs protruding from the car in midair.

Passers-by stopped to watch. A few may have recognized the passenger. Most were just curious to see how the big cripple in the shiny car would manage getting out.

The chauffeur returned, pulled Roosevelt to his feet, leaned him up

---

1. When no elevator was nearby, Gardner climbed stairs backwards because, he said, it put less strain on his heart. Since this took a while, he read as he climbed to keep from becoming bored. *Source:* Interview with W. Sheffield Cowles, Jr.

against the car, and placed his hat on his head. Then he began gingerly to wedge first one crutch and then the other beneath his arms. As he did so, the hat tumbled off. A stranger picked it up, then wasn't sure what to do with it. The chauffeur, fearful of taking his hands off his employer until he was fully propped up on his crutches, asked the man if he would please put it back on Roosevelt's head. He did so, while Franklin laughed and thanked him. The crowd grew.

Franklin began to move. Hanging from his crutches, watching the ground before him carefully and trying not to see the people staring at him, he heaved himself across the sidewalk, his chauffeur at his side. Despite the chill October air, sweat ran off his face, drenched his shirt, patterned the shoulders of his jacket. He would always sweat heavily when attempting to walk in public, no matter what the weather—a sign both of the real exertion required to move and the added stress a proud man felt at having to display his helplessness before strangers.

Someone held the door open. Others stood aside to let him pass.

Franklin and the chauffeur started across the polished marble floor of the lobby toward the bank of elevators. Because Roosevelt's left leg was so much weaker than his right, the chauffeur had been instructed to wedge his foot against the rubber tip of the left crutch each time it slammed down to keep it from slipping too much on the ice-smooth floor. Somehow, halfway across the lobby, his foot failed to hold, and his employer's weight, all of it now concentrated on his left crutch, slowly, inexorably, shoved it aside. Franklin began to fall. The chauffeur tried to catch him by the shoulders but he was too heavy and Roosevelt went down, his crutches clattering loudly, his hat rolling across the floor.

Onlookers rushed to see what had happened, then stepped back unsure what to do, whether or not to look. Franklin wrestled himself to a sitting position, his rigid legs jutting out in front of him. His chauffeur struggled to pull him upright, but his weight, his braces, and the slippery floor combined to make it impossible. Roosevelt smiled and laughed. There was nothing to worry about, he assured the onlookers, as if this sort of thing happened all the time, and he personally found it hilarious. Finally, he called out to two husky young men to give him a hand.

Together, they and the chauffeur managed to haul him to his feet and hold him upright until the crutches were back in place and his hat was once more restored to his head. Then, still smiling and laughing, but with his knuckles white on the handles of his crutches and his legs alarmingly splayed for balance, he said, "Let's go!" and started for the elevators once more.

Describing the day to Livy Davis, he said only that he'd had a "Grand reception at 120 B'way, where I lunched and spent 4–5 hours," and he assured Van-Lear Black that it had been "a grand and glorious occasion." But he went back to Hyde Park the next day and did not return to the F&D for another two months. With his humiliating fall still fresh in his mind, he worked harder than ever at increasing his mobility, struggling day after chilly day down the long walk beneath the bare branches of the trees, toward his mother's front gate.

He evidently made it all the way down just once, in early November. "Several days ago," Edna Rockey reported to Dr. Lovett, "he was compelled to walk about one quarter of a mile which completely took him off his feet for about four days. Complained of pain on left side along the hip extending from the backbone around the side."

Franklin would never again attempt such a long journey.

The Roosevelts were at Hyde Park on Election Day, where Eleanor saw first-hand for the first time the hard-eyed brand of politics practiced by both sides in Dutchess County.

> . . .my husband had urged me to go out and drive the car and bring people in to vote, and I came home very irate because I had driven in two old ladies and one old gentleman who lived on a farm together . . . [who] had refused to come in until late in the afternoon. When I finally drove them in, the old man said to me, "Ain't no use to come to these polls early any more. When I was young you could get paid to by both parties several times during the day. Then you went in and voted as you chose, anyway. And nowadays they don't pay you the way they used to. The best you can hope for is a payment for each side before you go in. . . ."
>
> And I was horrified and I delivered a lecture on the vote being the one thing which rich and poor had alike, and that it was terrible to sell your vote. And he looked at me with great amusement . . . and said, "Oh, Ma'am, it's going out. Politics isn't what it used to be." And so when I got home . . . I was in a rage and before Judge Mack and my husband, I said, "Would you mind telling me why you people go on paying for votes? The Republicans do the same and they . . . vote just as they choose anyway. Why don't you just come to an agreement with the Republicans not to pay for votes?" and very benignly, they both looked at me and they said, almost in unison, "But how would we know that the Republicans kept their word?"

By early evening it was clear that Al Smith had easily defeated the incumbent Republican, Nathan Miller. Franklin was pleased that in his first tentative political sortie since his illness, he had managed to back a winner, but he knew that victory also meant that for the immediate future Smith would remain the most important Democrat in the state.[2]

In mid-November, the Roosevelts all moved back to New York for the winter and Franklin finally began to go down to the F&D office two or three mornings a week.

"I would go into the company office on business," remembered Francis R. Stoddard, a former Republican assemblyman who had known Roosevelt in Albany, "and [a friend] would sometimes say, 'stop in and say hello to Frank Roosevelt.' I would say, 'I'm sorry, I'm busy. Next time, I'll drop in to see him.'" And when the next time came, as like as not, Roosevelt was not present, his model ships and naval prints the only sign that he ever had been. A hard rain, snow on the ground, or just the threat of frigid weather was enough to keep him home.

Franklin's absences may not have bothered Van-Lear Black, but Roosevelt's insistence that he be made to feel still in charge of things from afar was often hard on Vincent Cullen, the manager who did the unglamorous work of keeping things going while he was away. The two men had never got on well together. Cullen had come to resent taking orders from a glamorous politician who, even before his illness, rarely spent much time on company business, and Franklin, for his part, grew mistrustful of this humorless, hardworking subordinate who sometimes dared question his directives and seemed to threaten his position.

Roosevelt had big plans for the F&D that called for the opening of two new branch offices, one in Brooklyn, the other in Albany to handle upstate affairs, keep an eye on the legislature, and drum up state business. Both were to report to him. Cullen objected that his small staff would be unable to handle the added work and when he proved unable to persuade his chief of that, quietly lobbied the head office so

---

2. In his letter of congratulations, Franklin was careful to remember Smith's beloved mother: "The splendid personal tribute to you . . . must have been the utmost satisfaction to your mother, and though I have never had the honor of meeting her, I hope you will tell her from me that she has every right to be proud of her boy."

"My mother was opposed to me running any more for public office from the standpoint of my own health," Smith answered, "but when she saw the returns on election night she forgot all about everything else." *Source:* Franklin D. Roosevelt Papers, Family, Business, and Personal, FDRL.

that when the two new offices did finally open in January 1922, Albany was instructed to bypass the New York office and report directly to Baltimore.

Franklin had not been consulted and was furious. "I had of course understood that I am in charge of the New York office, with *responsibility* for the New York office," he told Colonel Edgar A. Hamilton, the vice-chairman of the F&D. "I have seen no letter conferring upon Mr. Cullen powers other than that of manager of the New York office, and subject to me."

Hamilton sought to mollify him: "You realize, of course, that when the home office officials are in New York it is not always possible to get up to see you and confer on what would seem to be relatively unimportant matters, and we have always assumed that in expressing his wishes, Mr. Cullen was speaking after conferring . . . with you. . . . [W]e need you and depend on you now more than perhaps we ever did before."

Roosevelt was not persuaded, and when the new Albany office failed to foresee two pending bills in the New York State legislature that seemed likely to hamper F&D business, he rubbed it in in letters to the home office:

> I knew of course that this sort of thing was bound to happen. Just as long as you attempt to run upstate New York from Baltimore you may be able to crawl along, but you cannot make the progress in that section, nor can you protect the company half as well, as if it were under my jurisdiction.
>
> Please don't for a moment think that this is either a threat or a boast, but I happen to know more about upstate New York than anybody in Baltimore. Think this over.

Later, a caller at the Roosevelt home casually mentioned to Franklin that he was looking forward to the annual F&D brokers' party. Roosevelt had not heard of it and felt left out. He wrote an angry memorandum to Cullen, to which the manager replied instantly:

> I do not quite understand your note. You have probably been misinformed or misunderstand about the party. It is the regular brokers' party, the same as we have given heretofore, and has been the custom. I have selected the brokers to attend, because I am personally acquainted with nearly all of them, and naturally I signed the invitations.

Again, Franklin was not mollified:

> As it turned out I was neither misinformed or misunderstood about the party. Has it ever occurred to you that as a General Vice President &

Director of the F&D, occupying an office in the New York office, it might be embarrassing and somewhat disconcerting to be asked by an outsider about the broker's party and to be compelled to show utter ignorance?

My objection is not to the party nor to your sending out the invitations for this party, if it is confined to regular brokers.

Please do make a definite effort to keep me more informed. A one-sided cooperation is an impossible thing. You will, I am sure, be the first to admit that I have never interfered with your end of the work, nor have blocked your plans, but on the other side I must ask that I be kept informed from now on far more than I have been heretofore.

Franklin D. Roosevelt[3]

Franklin continued to receive business callers at home. One of them was Lowell Mellett, then the editor of the Washington *Daily News* (and much later administrative assistant to FDR), who had never met him and who for some reason had never known he had been ill. The butler pointed him upstairs where Roosevelt stood, leaning on the bannister, to greet him. With a smiling toss of his head, Franklin indicated that Mellett was to walk on ahead into the library, then followed along behind, chatting amiably. "I realized then that Roosevelt was propelling himself forward by clasping the railing, hand over hand," Mellett remembered. "I never got over the hurt of seeing him in his crippled state, either then or afterward."

That was precisely the impact Franklin was afraid his condition would have on strangers, and in the struggle to appear himself unaf-

---

3. In 1924, Colonel Hamilton wrote Franklin to ask if, since he was to be away from the office so much, he would mind if Cullen were made a vice president "to act in your absence" in signing important documents. A vice president's signature was often legally required, he explained, and it was risky to have someone else signing his name for him; there was "always the danger of serious consequences, particularly when it is known generally that you are at such a distance."

Franklin wrote back from aboard a houseboat off Florida. He was "very glad to get [Cullen] elected," he said. "I like Cullen and think he has done very well with the details of the work of the New York office," but "I do not mind saying to you, confidentially, however that I do not think he has cooperated sufficiently with me. There are many leads . . . in which I could be of assistance but he practically never calls on me for any. In fact, during the whole of the past year I do not think he has consulted me in any way on more than one or two perfectly unimportant subjects." Cullen was also reluctant to get to know "more of the big men of New York city" to whom Franklin said he had offered to introduce him, and "I am quite frank in saying that a good many papers have had my name signed to them when I could have signed them perfectly well myself. . . ." Then he added, "What I have written is not in a spirit of criticism."

Cullen got his vice presidency, but by early 1928, he had had enough of Franklin Roosevelt and left the F&D to work for the rival National Surety Company, at what Roosevelt described as "fabulous salaries and commissions," taking with him for good measure the main agent in the Brooklyn office. Their sudden departure momentarily alarmed Franklin, who told the press he planned to abandon some of his less important activities to concentrate more fully on the F&D. There is little evidence that this actually happened, but the F&D continued to do well. *Sources:* Franklin D. Roosevelt Papers, Family, Business, and Personal, FDRL; Frank Freidel, *Franklin D. Roosevelt: The Ordeal*, page 141.

fected by it, no achievement, no matter how minute it might seem to others, went unheralded. One morning a secretary brought him checks to sign on behalf of the Woodrow Wilson Foundation.

"Wait a moment," he said. "I want to show you something."

Then, while she watched, he leaned forward, pinched the crease of one trouser leg between thumb and forefinger, lifted that leg, and crossed it over the other one. The result looked almost normal.

"Now," he said, beaming with pride, "what do you think of that!"

Franklin never did return to his law office at 52 Wall Street. There were several steps in front of that building when he first fell ill and no railing, he reminded his partner, Grenville Emmet, and although it had recently been remodelled, two high steps remained and "the question of even two steps is a very difficult one as I have to be actually lifted up and down them." Besides, he said, his interests increasingly ran to "practical things along the lines of business administration" rather than the law, and so he felt he should end their partnership.

He and his former partners remained friends, although Langdon Marvin was at least initially upset. "I don't want to protest," he wrote Roosevelt, "but I should like to know what you really have in mind. You and I have been associated together for fourteen years—in name at least—and I had hoped for closer association in the future so that it is a very real sorrow for me to have the association end. And I can't help but ask why."

Privately, Marvin's colleagues were relieved. Franklin had done little useful work for the firm before his illness and virtually none afterwards, though no one had wanted further to discourage him by telling him so while he was fighting so hard to recover. "He's a nice fellow," Albert de Roode, a member of the firm, told Frances Perkins before the break-up. "I feel sorry for him. But we can never make a lawyer of him. . . . He comes to conclusions. He hasn't got the patience to work things out." Marvin later put it more tactfully: "I had always thought him a great business getter, but he was too busy with other things to bother much about clients. So we got very little business out of him, but we had a deep affection and friendship for him."

Franklin placed the blame elsewhere. "The other partners are dear, delightful people," he told Van-Lear Black, "but their type of law business . . . is mostly estates, wills, etc. all of which bore me to death. . . . Also, I get not one red cent out of my connection with them, whereas if I were with some live people, working along other lines, I could be of material assistance [to the F&D] on reorganizations, receiverships, etc., pulling my own weight in the boat and incidentally making some money out of it."

What he really had in mind was a new firm "with my name at the head instead of at the tail," and he soon had his wish, for there had been at least one positive result of his humiliating October fall in the lobby at 120 Broadway. One of the men who had helped pull Franklin to his feet and dust him off was Basil O'Connor, a stubby red-haired attorney, ten years his junior, with an office right next door to the F&D.

O'Connor more than filled Franklin's desire for a "live" partner. He was a fast-talking tinsmith's son from Taunton, Massachusetts, who had entered Dartmouth at sixteen and earned the title Most Likely to Succeed after putting himself through school by playing the violin in a dance band he'd organized himself; he had even launched his own fraternity after the established ones turned him down. When too much study at the Harvard Law School rendered him temporarily blind, he kept up with his classes by persuading fellow students to read to him.

By the time he and Roosevelt rode up in the elevator together, O'Connor had managed to build a successful one-man practice, arranging lucrative contracts between oilmen and refiners all over the world.

The two men instantly liked each other: Franklin admired the young lawyer's aggressiveness and attention to detail; O'Connor admired Roosevelt's courage and good humor and saw the great advantages that could come from identifying himself with so celebrated a name. They decided to form a new partnership. Franklin was to offer "general legal advice" at a salary of $10,000 a year; O'Connor would do the day-to-day work. The firm would be called Roosevelt & O'Connor.[4]

The Great Depression, FDR told his fellow countrymen in his first Fireside Chat of 1934, was "the after-effect of that unfortunate decade [the twenties] characterized by a mad chase for unearned riches, and an unwillingness of leaders in almost every walk of life to look beyond their own schemes and speculations."

During that decade, Franklin pursued his own schemes and specu-

4. Although Franklin and O'Connor began working together in 1923, they did not officially announce their new partnership until New Year's Day, 1925.

To soften the blow to his old friend and partner Langdon Marvin, Franklin assured him his new partnership was "only . . . a tentative arrangement" dictated by "my physical infirmities." In fact, it lasted until the day Roosevelt died. *Source:* Franklin D. Roosevelt Papers, Family, Business, and Personal, FDRL.

lations as blindly as did any other leader. In business, Eleanor once admitted, her husband "was not experienced and not always wise." Money itself never interested him greatly. He had been raised to think any discussion of it vulgar, a tenet adhered to so strongly within the Roosevelt family that he had no idea of the size of his mother's income, and his wife had no idea of his.

He had once had both a restless body and a restless mind. Now, only his mind could roam. It was the excitement of speculation that drew him—business was always a "game" to him, a game of chance as much as skill—and he was usually careful not to risk too much money on any single gamble.

During the twenties, Roosevelt saw money to be made in everything from selling advertising space in taxicabs to harnessing the tidal power of Passamaquoddy Bay. A partial list of the schemes for which Roosevelt had high hopes included a South American substitute for coffee called *Yerba Maté* that went nowhere; an oil-drilling firm that found then-worthless gas, instead of oil; a resort chain that was to have stretched from Lake Placid to southern Georgia for which he could never find sufficient backing; an equally underfinanced plan to merge several small intercoastal shipping lines; a fleet of dirigibles meant to ply the skies between Chicago and New York that was quickly supplanted by aeroplanes; and a plan to corner the live lobster market by holding the catch in pounds until the price of lobsters rose. (Prices fell instead, and this scheme, promoted by his indefatigable friend Pat Homer, cost Roosevelt $26,000 before he could get out.)

Roosevelt was also director of three different companies formed to take advantage of the collapse of the German mark—only one, United European Investors, Inc., made any money—and he was on the board of the Sanitary Postage Service Corporation which peddled pre-moistened stamps from slot machines. To Roosevelt's subsequent regret, this last firm eventually merged with the Consolidated Automatic Merchandising Corporation, or CAMCO, which ran three entirely automated stores in Manhattan—meant to be pilot projects for a national chain—and sold everything from Baby Ruth Candy Bars to Watkins Emulsified Cocoanut Shampoo from special slot machines that said "thank you" after each transaction. A fellow CAMCO director, Dr. Glenn Frank of the University of Wisconsin, saw the elimination of ordinary clerks as liberating, converting the salesman "from a mere bundle wrapper into a counselor in consumption," but labor understandably took a very different view. Schemes that displaced workers were not popular after the crash and the Republicans eagerly seized upon Roosevelt's connection with the firm during his first contest for the presidency. FDR had been a director but claimed to have been only nominally involved.[5]

By 1923, Franklin had already lent his name to so many questionable schemes that the general secretary of the Society for Promoting Financial Knowledge wrote him a sorrowful letter:

> I have noted with a great deal of concern the use of your name to further the sale of stocks of new promotions, that, while undoubtedly sincere in conception, are business risks of the more hazardous type and I am wondering if your attention has been called to the fact that these securities are being offered for public subscriptions as "safe investments." . . . It seems such a pity that a distinguished and honored name should be commercialized in such a manner, when there are so many opportunities for employing the prestige that it carries in activities designed to promote some common good.

Those responsible for the promotion that had prompted this chastisement, Roosevelt assured the general secretary, had used his name without permission: "You know how difficult it is for a man more or less in public life to keep his name from being used without authorization for all kinds of enterprises, but I try to be vigilant in this matter."

His vigilance was always relative—or rather, his congenital enthusiasm for novel projects often rendered it irrelevant.[6]

Franklin's misadventures on the stock market were not forgotten by his fellow plungers, and when, as President, he seemed to blame the influence of speculators for the Depression, and vowed to drive the money changers from the temple, many of his former colleagues were embittered. "He must have known that the men who were concerned [in the '29 crash]," his old Harvard rival Walter Sachs said later, "his . . . classmates, like [Eugene] Thayer, who was later president of the Chase bank . . . men like myself . . . we may have been subject to poor

5. CAMCO went under when the voluble machines proved easy to jam, unable to tell a genuine coin from a slug, and sometimes recalcitrant about yielding up the products for which they had so politely accepted payment. Guards finally had to be hired to protect the machines from irate customers.

6. Talking with Rexford Tugwell many years later, FDR's Secretary of Agriculture and second Vice President, Henry A. Wallace, recalled his initial impression that FDR was a "daring adventurer . . . I reached the conclusion . . . that I would under no circumstances, ever have any business dealings with him." Then, almost in the same breath, he added that Roosevelt had been "a Godsend to the country at the time he came"; a less daring and adventurous man with "a more plodding type of mind" would have been unable to launch the New Deal or conduct World War II. *Source:* Interview with Henry A. Wallace, Rexford G. Tugwell Papers.

judgment or been carried away . . . but . . . we meant to do the right thing. Those are the things I couldn't quite forgive him."

In February 1923, Franklin received from an old friend in England an elixir which she was sure would help him regain his feet. "It may be monkey glands or perhaps it is made out of the dried eyes of the extinct three-toed rhinoceros," he wrote Dr. Draper. "You doctors have sure got imaginations. Have any of your people thought of distilling the remains of King Tut-Ankh-Amen? The serum might put new life into some of our mutual friends. In the meantime, I am going to Florida to let nature take its course—nothing like Old Mother Nature, anyway."

He had rented a sixty-foot houseboat, the *Weona II,* for $1,500 and planned to spend several weeks aboard her, cruising among the Florida Keys. It had taken a good deal of careful planning: measured drawings of the two flights of steps aboard were made so that a way could be devised of getting him from one deck to another.

Then there was the delicate question of LeRoy Jones, the black valet whom Franklin called "Roy" and without whose care he could not get through the day: Could a place be found for him aboard? J. Fred Tam, the Manhattan yacht broker through whom the rental arrangements were made, thought he might fit in with the four-man crew so long as, "for the purpose of discipline," he was willing to take his orders from the master and that he "had not been impregnated with the present so-called 'rights,' and is of the willing kind, as most well brought-up darkies are. . . ."

Eleanor accompanied Franklin for the first few days aboard the *Weona II* but did not enjoy herself. There was nothing much for her to do aboard, and she was rarely happy unless immersed in work. "I had never considered holidays in winter or escape from cold weather an essential part of living," she remembered, "and I looked upon it now as a necessity and not a pleasure. I tried fishing but had no skill and no luck. When we anchored at night and the wind blew, it all seemed eerie and menacing to me."

It all seemed marvellous to Franklin. He was once again in charge of things, cultivated long, nautical sideburns, and called himself "the Admiral" in the jaunty ship's log he began keeping the day Eleanor left.

Old friends came down to sail and fish—Livy Davis, Lewis Cass Ledyard, Jr., and his wife, Ruth, Henry and Frances de Rahm, John

R. Lawrence, another old Harvard friend, now a New England wool manufacturer, and his wife Lucy. Life aboard was distinctly informal. "Bring the following," he told Livy before coming. "Oldest known outfit—flannel or khaki trousers, tennis shirts and perhaps a couple of flannel shirts; soft slippers for on deck; one sweater. No glad rags—not even a razor is necessary, but I insist on a tooth brush—I will have a comb on board! If you and Johnnie [Lawrence] want to leave your tuxedoes and rah rah flannels at Miami do so, but don't for the love of Pete, clutter up my boat with that gear!"

All the male passengers except Franklin started the day with a swim *"au naturel."* During the day they fished, raced model boats when the sea was flat, took turns trying to shoot birds on the wing. Ledyard hooked and landed a 42-pound Jewfish. ". . . I thought we left New York to get *away* from the Jews," his wife said, and Franklin thought the remark so good he included it in his log. "The tip end of Florida is where Jonah had his trying experience," he told Livy, "he was a Hebrew and hence cast up."

Louis Howe spent a few days on board. He brought with him F&D paperwork which demanded Franklin's attention, went fishing with very little luck, scribbled some doggerel in the log:

> Colder, colder grew the night, we really suffered pain
> We'd sat and sat with rod and reel and fished and fished in vain
> And that, we thought, was reason fair to take to rum again.

They took often to rum, spending each evening on deck feeling "very comfortable" as they played records on a wind-up gramophone, watched the moonlight on the water, and listened to Franklin reminisce about his days at the Navy Department until he signalled that it was time for bed by calling out to his valet, "Oh, Roy!"

"I'm sure this warmth and exercise is doing lots of good," Franklin wrote his mother. ". . . I am sunburned and in fine shape. [My friends] have been dear and look after me all the time. They are great fun to have on board in this somewhat negligée existence. All wander round in pyjamas, nighties and bathing suits!"

Franklin paid tribute to that negligée existence in verse:

COMMUNITY LIFE

> You can slack off peak halyards—and eat with your knife,
> You can dine in your shirtsleeves, and so can your wife—
> These are some of the joys of community life!

*   *   *   *

When they first come on board they think it's so nice—
  With staterooms and comforts sans price—
  Till they suddenly realize that every partition
  Sounds intimate echoes of each guest's condition
Of mind and of body—For whispers of details
The wall in its wisdom with great gusto retails.

*   *   *   *

  When Henry turns over in bed with a groan,
Then Ruth thinks it's Cass who has uttered a moan—
  When Ledyard hits out with his elbow at night
  Then Franklin thinks Henry has got in a fight—
  If Rosy gets coughing he lies without curses
For well he knows soon will appear his trained nurses
  To tuck him up comfy and give him a drink—
Those angels of mercy in soft mauve and pink—

No secrets of thought between husband and wife
  Can safely be had in Community Life . . .

  Just to show you how quickly this al fresco mood
  Got ahold of our guests—got right into their blood—
  On the second day morn at breakfast quite early
Ruth appeared in her nighty—and slippers—yes, really!
And Cass wore a bathrobe that looked like a monk's
While Henry was happy in nothing but trunks—
  And as for Frances . . . [7]

  F.D.R.

At Miami, James M. Cox came aboard for a visit. "Jim's eyes filled
with tears when he saw me," Franklin told a friend much later, "and
I gathered from his conversation that he was dead certain that I had
had a stroke and that another one would soon completely remove me.
. . . Jim from that day on always shook his head when my name was
mentioned and said in sorrow that in effect I was a hopeless invalid and
could never resume any active participation in business or political
affairs."

---

7. According to a bit of her own doggerel, read aloud at dinner one evening, Frances de
Rham had evidently gone for a swim without her bathing suit and been spotted by her companions.

  A female went swimming—she was far from a peach
  She was as the Lord made her, so what could she do
  But call herself, gaily, a true 32."

Source: Weona II log, Franklin D. Roosevelt Papers, Family, Business, and Personal, FDRL.

In fact, Franklin had met and mastered a host of logistical problems during his cruise and proudly reported on all of them to Dr. Lovett. He had learned to move easily between decks, he said, by sitting on the stairs and lifting himself up and down, one step at a time, and he managed to fight fish weighing up to forty pounds without being strapped to the swivel chair. When the passageways proved too narrow for crutches, he got around below decks by hanging from the beams and using his shoulder muscles to swing his legs forward. He had exercised his quadriceps religiously on deck by rocking in a small rocking chair: "The tendency at first was to cheat by rocking with the body, but within a few days I could rock back and forth by using only the knee and the lower leg and foot muscles." And he made his way down the tall side of the boat from the top deck to the surface of the sea—a distance of ten feet—by an ingenious arrangement of his own devising: a section of the side rail was cut out at the base of the forward davit from which a board was suspended like the seat of a child's swing. "I then sat on the deck, put my feet through the swing, pulled it under me, the davit was . . . swung out and I was lowered into the motor boat or . . . into the water. It was perfectly easy once in the water to slide out of the swing and to get back into it."

From the time of this first voyage and even after his return to politics forever reshaped his life, Franklin seems to have been happiest when in command of his own ship, out of sight of staring strangers and out of earshot of his turbulent family. At sea, he could set the rules and handle the logistics, and there was never the slightest need for the self-consciousness that inevitably attends atrophied limbs—the embarrassment that when ashore made him hastily drape a towel over his diminished legs or hide them behind a newspaper if even a close friend's camera was present.[8]

When he returned to Hyde Park, tanned and vigorous, his mother burst into tears. With the sideburns grown on the cruise, flecked now with gray, he so resembled his late father that she said she could not bear to look at him again until he shaved them off.

---

8. Even after he was back in politics full time and vacationing on land, he enjoyed pretending to be at sea. Over the front door of the "Little White House" which he built for himself at Warm Springs, Georgia, a ship's lantern burned whenever he was home, and the semicircular sundeck in the back, which commanded a handsome prospect of woods and rolling hills that stretched for some twenty miles before the forest grew up to block it, was built to resemble a ship's fantail. Later, at "Shangri-La," the Maryland presidential retreat which became Camp David, he called his visits "cruises" in the Navy blue-and-gold guest book he titled his log.

Kathleen Lake examined Franklin shortly after he got back and found him "immensely improved . . . in all ways, looking at least ten years younger, able to set the right knee, a thing I have been working for all winter & with slight assistance able to sit up from lying position, feet much improved, etc."

But the improvement was short-lived, she noted: "Feeling much better, he plunged headlong into work & people in to dinner every night, & in two weeks he came down with a bad cold, looked a perfect wreck & practically lost everything he had gained, including the setting of the right quadriceps.

"After a week of that I persuaded him to go up to Hyde Park & try a complete rest . . . for ten days, which he did, with excellent results. Nobody went with him except his servant."

The real obstacle to more consistent progress remained his family, Mrs. Lake believed. "If only his wife could be persuaded that he does not need urging on all day & entertaining all evening, I think he would not be so tired and would do better physically. You would not believe that two weeks could make such a difference. He himself begins to understand how the city affects him & his knee going back like that was a real surprise. But he is so surrounded by the family, all giving him advice & ordering him round that he gets quite desperate & it was that that made me suggest Hyde Park quite alone . . . he, & they, now realize that it was a good move."

Even on his own in the country, his overall condition remained fragile. He spent another weekend at Hyde Park, sat outside too long in the damp river breeze, and "got cold in his right leg . . . & the quadriceps which was coming back has once more disappeared." Sometimes, Anna or a servant led him around the garden on a horse, while he did his best to grip his mount's sides with his knees. "He manages a good deal better than I thought possible," Mrs. Lake reported, but after a few minutes the withered muscles of his thighs became so exhausted they would begin to tremble uncontrollably and he would have to be lifted down.

In late April, Franklin wrote to Dr. Lovett himself. A year had now gone by since he had last been examined and he assumed the doctor would wish to have a look at him. Would Lovett's office therefore reserve him a room at Phillips House on May 26?

Miss Rockey had left him to take another job the previous autumn, but "I have a colored boy who helps me get about. I suppose that I can perfectly well . . . have the colored boy come in every morning and get me up and help me about. He would, of course, sleep at a hotel."

Lovett saw Franklin on May 31, precisely one year and one day after his first examination at Phillips House. His skill at walking on crutches had increased. "I am very well satisfied with Mr. Roosevelt's condition," the doctor reported to Eleanor. "He handles himself definitely better than he ever has. . . ."

But his legs remained stubbornly unchanged. Of the same forty-four muscles whose strength Lovett had carefully gauged a year earlier, seven now showed very slight improvement and seven had actually deteriorated.

Twelve months of hard, lonely work had yielded no measurable overall improvement whatsoever.

That news must have been at least momentarily crushing for Franklin, but he skillfully masked the fact from Livy Davis and the other old friends who came to see him during his ten days in Boston and to whom he later pronounced his visit "a bully stay."[9]

Throughout his treatment, he had chafed under Lovett's strictures. Now, he refused to accept his judgment as final. The rules his doctor laid down were drawn from the experiences of ordinary patients, after all, and rules written for others had never applied to Franklin Roosevelt. Dr. Lovett's other patients routinely stopped improving after two years; Franklin vowed he would not.

For his part, Lovett found his patient's dogged independence merely irritating, his indiscriminate interest in unorthodox treatments of all kinds evidence only of his unwillingness to keep to an admittedly tedious course of exercises.[10]

9. While in Boston, Franklin tried to find his old friend a new job that would take his mind of his troubles. Perhaps Davis would like to head a delicacy importing firm, he had suggested before coming. He was sure there would be money in it and "there is no reason why a gentleman should not go into this any more than into the manufacture of ladies' underclothes like our friend, John Lawrence."

Livy was not keen on "the specialty biz." "If you had ever kept house as I have," he told Roosevelt, "you would realize that the catalogues of Park & Tilford & S. S. Pierce carry a line of imported delicacies which are ordinarily overlooked by housewives. In other words, such companies are already equipped & functioning along this line and yet have difficulty indoctrinating people to buy."

10. Many years later, Lovett's widow would recall her husband having said that whatever progress Roosevelt made toward recovery was due more to Eleanor's exhortations than to his own efforts. She and Louis Howe were "the taskmasters" and he would have greatly increased his mobility had he listened to them more often. *Source:* Herman Hagedorn interview with Corinne Alsop, Theodore Roosevelt Association.

"You had to do what Lovett said or he would have nothing to do with you," a physician on his staff remembered. "That visit in . . . May and early June was the end of it. We never saw [Roosevelt] after that."[11]

Over the coming months and years, Franklin's avid, hopeless search for novel remedies would intensify, not diminish.

He eagerly exchanged advice with other polios. Reginald W. Bulkley, a paralyzed New Jersey attorney whom Franklin had come to know at Phillips House, enclosed a leaflet for a compact folding wheelchair; Roosevelt thought he might order one for use aboard ship and, in exchange, urged Bulkley to "try swimming, even if you have to lie on your back with some bamboo poles as a support under you to help float you."

Margaret H. Staton of New York City, victim of an accident in infancy that had paralyzed one side of her body, championed the work of a local shoemaker "who will make a balance for the body, whether the trouble is in ankle, knee or hip, through an inner mold which he takes in plaster and builds an ingenious shoe around. . . . It is a beautiful shoe, too! . . . My whole being is changed with the lifting of the mental strain. . . . I used to be so sensitive about myself that I would cry if people stared, but now I stop others like a traffic cop and tell them my message of 'saving soles.' "

Franklin thanked her for her letter but said he was afraid he had "no use for such a shoe as yet . . . my knees will not bear my weight."

A friend in the insurance business in Kansas offered to send him "a wonderful belt" called the "I-on-a-co," which, he said, must be effective since the Kansas City *Star* had accepted advertisements for it and "this paper will not under any circumstances take on unethical products."

> The I-on-a-co is simple in operation. Merely plug it into an electric light socket and put it over your body for ten minutes or so, once or twice a day. . . . Your Doctor may "poo poo" the idea, as most learned physicians do when any new medical theory is advanced. My personal view is that . . . the old quinine capsule is about the only thing we have in this modern world that hasn't been improved through electricity in the past twenty-five years. I hope that you will enjoy the exhilarating effect, and that it will stimulate circulation way beyond your expectations.

11. Dr. Lovett died in England the following summer.

"Great stuff!" Franklin wrote back. "I shall be delighted to try the I-on-a-co. It sounds like a substitute for a cocktail."

He looked into all manner of mechanical appliances. The orthopedic corsets built by Dr. Gabriel Bidou of Paris, for example, promised to transform the life of all "paralytics [who were] burdens not only to their families and friends, but to the charities of the state" by entirely encasing affected limbs in housings of leather, rubber, and steel, and employing springs to replace missing muscles. Bidou's corsets may have helped some grievously crippled patients, but they made their wearers resemble giant, armored insects and Franklin did not sign up for one.

He did have dealings with the Roth Orthopedic Institute of New York, however, whose pamphlet "Facts Concerning the Crippled and Deformed" was filled with grotesque photographs of the afflicted interspersed among bright promises and dire warnings:

> There should be no delay in securing our treatment after a "moderate recovery" is partially accomplished (a symptom which we have pointed out as most deceptive, in that it has given you hope that you are actually recovering from the difficulty when in fact you are getting worse, and need immediate treatment), as it may develop all the different after-effects which required long and tedious treatment, or it may even make an operation necessary. Taken in time, the Roth apparatus will arrest the cause for an operation and the operation will not be necessary.

When he later complained that a brace the Institute had built for him was too heavy, Adolph Roth himself wrote offering to replace it with "a new snap-joint apparatus with lighter weight steel, without any obligation," and when he got no immediate response to his letter, telephoned Eleanor. Afterwards, she wrote a note to her husband on the corner of Roth's original letter: "This man talked to me for *hours* on the phone & feels that you have not written him. Please do. I don't want to talk to him again."

At the urging of a mutual friend, Arthur M. Van Rensselaer of Woodmere, New York, the manufacturer of a vehicle especially built for the handicapped and called the Moto-Chair sent him several brochures. It was electrically powered and hand-driven, capable of going 40 miles an hour yet light enough for two men to carry, guaranteed to "go through crowded city traffic as easily as water passes through a sieve," and built "about level with the curb, so that the car may be entered without taking an upward step." "Many cripples," Van Rensselaer promised, "will find in the Moto-Chair the first and only practicable means for keeping in contact with the world outside of their own homes."

Franklin thought the Moto-Chair "most interesting":

> My chief difficulty in regard to it is that when I am in the country I like to spend a lot of time in the woods and our wood roads are extremely rough. Some of them are practicable for a Ford car, but I fear that the Moto-Chair would not give enough clearance or enough power to get over some of the rough places. This autumn I have been able to sit on a horse and be led around the place. Of course I would fall off if the horse tripped and what I need, even more than a motor-chair, is a horse which is constitutionally unable to trot, and which is also guaranteed against sidewise motions.

The Moto-Chair may not have suited Franklin's needs, but mobility remained a central issue with him. Like the other paralyzed patients for whom the device had been intended, he was eager to find "a practicable means for keeping in contact with the outside world," some means of locomotion that would allow him to explore all by himself the woods and fields he had loved since boyhood, out from under the bottomless solicitude of his mother and the incessant prodding of his wife.

Sara bought him a big motorized tricycle, but like the Moto-Chair, it was not up to the Springwood forest roads. "Mr. Roosevelt didn't like it," Depew recalled. "He never used it."[12]

He still had to rely upon others simply to leave his mother's house.

Franklin received a letter from a twenty-seven-year-old polio named Paul Hasbrouck, who had served in World War I, been a secretary to a Maryland senator before he was stricken, and now lived with his parents in Poughkeepsie. He, too, had been a patient of Dr. Lovett's, had reached an apparent plateau in his recovery, and wondered what new regimens Roosevelt might have discovered.

Franklin answered that

> I have . . . found for myself one interesting fact which I believe to be a real discovery, and that is that my muscles have improved with greater rapidity when I could give them sunlight. Last winter I went to Florida and was much in the open air under the direct rays of the sun with very

---

12. Sara did, however. When as an old lady she injured her leg, she rode on it to and from her farm to see that the tenant was faithfully carrying out her orders. *Source:* George Palmer interview with Chauncey Depew, National Park Service.

few clothes on, and there is no doubt that the leg muscles responded more quickly at that time than when I am at home when I am, of necessity, more in the house. This summer also I have made a real effort to sit in the sun for several hours every day, and the improvement has undoubtedly been much more rapid. I am about to try a new artificial light for use this winter. This light is said to give 4 times the strength of the sun's rays with the red or burning rays of the sun extracted. It is like a lamp on a high stand which can be attached to any electrical fixture. If it seems to me good I will let you know more about it. My theory is that by exercise we can only develop the muscles up to a certain point, i.e., that it is necessary to build up the nerve centers of the lower spine in order to make more exercise possible. I suppose you have found, as I have, that too much exercise stops or slows up the improvement.

His theory—and the light with which he hoped to test it—had in fact been given him by two Kansas City osteopaths whom he swore to secrecy. "I have told [them]," he assured Mrs. Lake, "that I do so only as a supplementary experiment and that I have not given up on Lovett, do not intend to, and want to be able to discuss the case with Lovett at any time." But "it is absolutely a fact that the mornings I am able to sit in the sun for an hour or two my legs do not get cold in the evening; whereas, if the day is cloudy and I do not get my sunbaths, the legs freeze up from about 5 p.m. on. Don't you (in your purely private and non-professional capacity) agree with me that it can do no harm to try it out at least for a month or two?"[13]

Mrs. Lake's reply has not survived, but Franklin's faith in his own ability to revivify lifeless nerves was unshakable. "An outside doctor," he told Paul Hasbrouck, "said to me the other day that 'There is one thing about this infantile paralysis which you may be sure of—you will get progressively better year after year until you die.' That is mighty encouraging!"

It was also entirely false.

"Polio was a storm," one of Roosevelt's physiotherapists would remember teaching her patients. "You were what remained when it had passed." It would take Franklin Roosevelt five more years finally to accept the fact that he could never again be what he had been before the storm hit.

13. Franklin's belief in the healing power of sunlight persisted for years and became an important part of the aftercare offered at Warm Springs, Georgia. "There was nothing to it," a physiotherapist who worked there in its earliest days recalls, "but we believed there was." *Source:* Interview with Mary Hudson Veeder.

The Roosevelts' friend the economist Adolph Miller, visiting Springwood that summer, came upon Franklin all alone one morning, carving the hull of a model boat, his knife moving expertly over a chunk of balsa wood.

Most of Roosevelt's hobbies had initially been undertaken when he was still a small boy and had provided him then with ways of escaping for a time his mother's loving but adamant efforts to direct his every moment. Now, unable once again to evade his mother or his wife at will, he turned to his old hobbies with renewed enthusiasm. Hunting, the diversion he had followed most avidly as a boy, was clearly no longer possible.[14] But he spent hours at his more sedentary pursuits, poring over his stamps, arranging and rearranging his books, and crafting small shelves for them with carpenter's tools given him long before he went to Groton. He could no longer go himself in search of bargains in printshops, but he dispatched Louis Howe to auction houses and art galleries to ferret out new naval prints to add to those that already blanketed the Springwood walls.

Toy boats had always been an enthusiasm, but since his illness they had become something of an obsession, shared with Louis Howe and his own eldest boys who raced their trim little vessels across the Hudson against his, competing for a Roosevelt cup in the spring and a Hyde Park cup in autumn.

Franklin had initially been most interested in authentic rigging for his miniature craft and had built what he described as two "fairly accurate models of the *Resolute* and the *Reliance*," but after he was himself immobilized, he developed a new passion: seeing how fast a small boat could be made to sail. He began using balsa for the hulls, oiled silk instead of wood for decks, and aluminum for the spars, and by the time of Miller's visit had managed to make his best model so sleek and light and beautifully balanced that she could skim across the

14. He still dreamed of returning to the field, however, writing to Richard E. Byrd in November of 1922—when he was still unable even to make his way into his office building—that "By next Autumn I will be ready to chase the nimble moose with you."

He was somewhat more realistic two years later when George K. Shuler, the New York State Treasurer, asked him to become a governor of a new hunting club being formed in Virginia by veterans of the Great War. "Some day," he replied, "I hope to go down there with you and prove that I can kill more ducks than you have killed Huns. However . . . it would be ridiculous for me to be a Governor in view of the fact that everybody knows I am on crutches and could not get within . . . 100 miles of the place. You had better get someone with 2 legs instead of four!"

He was never able to hunt waterbirds again, but one day in Georgia he did manage to shoot some quail from his wheelchair as beaters drove the birds over his head. *Sources:* Kenneth S. Davis, *FDR: The Beckoning of Destiny*, page 682; Franklin D. Roosevelt Papers, FDRL; Interview with Robert Copeland.

broad river in just over ten minutes, while her proud builder followed in a rowboat, his mother's chauffeur at the oars.

As Franklin chatted with Adolph Miller, his knife slipped suddenly, taking with it a sizable chunk of the toy hull. He looked petulant for a moment, Miller noted, like a child about to cry. Then he brightened. "That's all right," he said. "I have a new idea. I always wanted to try a new experiment and I can do it on this hull."

Miller marvelled at his friend's new-found patience, his willingness to build upon apparent disaster and move on.

But for Franklin, no toy boat, however swift, could make up for the old joy of sailing his own yacht. He longed to be back at the helm and was frankly envious that Livy Davis was then conducting full-scale experiments he could only hope to match in miniature. Still unattached and without a serious job, Livy had joined several professors at the Massachusetts Institute of Technology who were spending their summer on the Charles River aboard his yacht the *Papoose,* trying to discover scientifically "what makes a boat go," their experiments underwritten by "a small group of yachting enthusiasts."

"Johnnie Lawrence and I went down on the 'Squaw' to Glen Cove for three days' racing," he told Franklin in mid-July, "and struck the most magnificent weather imaginable, for there was a broiling hot sun the whole time, and each day we had the whole gamut of wind from a dead calm . . . to lee-rails under, with boiling foam at bow. We spoke of you continuously and only wished that you were with us, for it would have been absolutely feasible, and would have been the greatest thing in the world for you, for most of the time we wore no clothes at all, and consequently got burned to a crisp."

Franklin answered that he'd love nothing more than a sail, had in fact been planning a three-week excursion from New York to Buzzard's Bay and back, but had been unable to locate a boat large enough to accommodate both him and "the faithful Roy."

"It is a shame about the boat, . . ." Livy replied, ". . . but from any . . . that I know, I should think that Roy would present a very difficult problem for he can hardly sleep in the forecastle [with the others], and the only place I can think of to stow him is on a mattress on top of a pile of rope in the lazarette. The only solution I see is to have a boat with a stateroom and take along [Miss] Rockey. Eh, what?"

On second thought, Livy suggested, why didn't Franklin come aboard the forty-foot *Squaw,* belonging to their mutual friend John L. Lawrence, a veteran of the *Weona II* cruise, whose own legs had been weakened by illness. Livy would come, too, and Roy could stay ashore; " . . . both of us and the whole crew . . . ought to be able to substitute for him."

Franklin accepted the invitation, then came down with a cold and had to delay his sail, and finally grew almost plaintively concerned that he might be imposing himself upon his able-bodied friends: "I want you to find out frankly from Johnny whether it is really convenient for me to go . . . in view of the postponement of everything by one week," he wrote Livy. "Also find out when he wants to race her again as of course I would have to be off her by that time and if it is the least bit upsetting to his plans to have me come on the postponed date do not hesitate to let me know."

Lawrence assured Livy that he looked forward to Franklin's visit. "It will be grand. . . ," Franklin told Livy, his teasing tone restored, "and so nice to think that you will brush my teeth and wash my face and hands for me every night and morning."

The sail went well. The sun and sea air and easy company did wonders for Roosevelt's morale. Lawrence anchored off Bertie Hamlin's summer home at Matapoisett, and she rode out to the yacht in a gas launch with a basket of fresh vegetables to find Franklin "brown as a berry and in his usual fine spirits. He had been lowered into the bay for a swim . . . was very broad shouldered and heavy—I suppose this must be expected now."

Franklin was convinced that "pulling myself about the decks" had strengthened his legs, and shortly after returning to shore, he and Lawrence agreed to go in together and purchase for $3,750 a secondhand houseboat called the *Roamer*. They renamed her the *Larooco* (for "Lawrence, Roosevelt and Company" and pronounced to rhyme with "cocoa") and planned to sail her off Florida each winter, enjoying the fishing while building up their limbs.

Eleanor's apparent inability to see beneath her husband's sunny exterior to the authentic anguish his paralysis inevitably produced was sometimes startling. He cannot, for example, have enjoyed this peremptory and tactless note, written that autumn: "Couldn't you have LeRoy send me *at once* 2 prs of your golf stockings for [James]? . . . as you don't use them now they are really better used and you can get new [ones] later."

Now, already concerned that Franklin was straining the limits of Van-Lear Black's generosity by spending so little time at the New York office, she worried aloud that the purchase of a used houseboat sight unseen was both a risky proposition and a strain on family finances. Her husband gave in to an outburst of despair and self-pity so uncharacteristic as to have remained in his wife's mind for the rest of her life. "Well," he said, "I suppose I'd better do all I can to learn to move about as much as possible. I don't want to be a useless burden to the rest of my family."

"His bitterness was a shock," Eleanor remembered. She hastily withdrew her objection "and . . . never forgot again that much of his gallant joking was merely a way of forcing himself to accept cheerfully what he could not help."

That joking quickly resumed. "The new partnership has decided to have a dark-haired Swede by the name of Davis to slack off the peak halyards," he wrote Livy, "[to] shake up the drinks and act as trained nurse for any invalids who may be on board. In other words, you are invited for the whole trip, rent free, provided you do the usual chores in which you are so expert."

Livy was delighted. He seems to have wanted nothing more in life than to serve his friend in any capacity asked of him. In a gesture which must have been genuinely moving for both of them, he surprised Franklin by presenting him with his old ensign as Assistant Secretary of the Navy. "A million thanks for the old astnav flag," Roosevelt wrote him. "I . . . will take it south with me and some day when we get up around the corner in the lonely reaches of the Shark River, we will 'hist' the old rag to the mast-head and salute it with 17 rum swizzles."[15]

15. Livy's life that autumn was especially empty, as can be read between the lines of a resolutely hearty October letter to Franklin: The brokerage firm with which he was at least nominally involved seemed on the edge of going under, he had sold the big house in which he and Alice had lived and taken a room at the Myopia Hunt Club at Hamilton, Massachusetts:

My life has been so crammed full lately that 24 hours provide only a moitié of what I am endeavoring to accomplish. In the first place I have sold the place in Milton. . . . The new owner has taken over Michael [the butler] and bought the hens, coal and wood and a lot of furniture. He is a delightful fellow named Ralph S. Richmond, and I left a bottle of champagne in the cellar, asking him and his charming wife to drink it the first night they are in residence. To Michael I gave a lot of furniture and deposited 1,000 bucks in a Savings Bank to his credit in recognition of fifteen years of faithful and devoted service.

I never realized that there was so much furniture in the world as an enormous storeroom covering the whole of the stable contained all the left over furniture of father's houses in Boston & Worcester. This I am trying to dispose of by gift, sale, etc. But what in Hell can I do with 21 specimens of stuffed birds? I have offered them to the Natural History Museum, the Museum in Harvard, some schools, etc. without success and finally to the Perkins [Institute] for the Blind thinking that at least they couldn't see them but they also refused them. . . .

My old hunter "King George" developed an incurable kidney trouble so that I had to dispose of him so he is now running with the hounds he followed so many years, as it is the

Isabella Ferguson came east with her children that autumn, and had her first glimpse of Franklin since his illness. She no longer admired him as she once had; he was too much of an opportunist, she now thought, and had caused her friend Eleanor too much pain for her to overlook. But his valor astonished her in spite of herself, and afterwards, on her way home, she wrote him a personal tribute:

> Dear Franklin,
>
> It is only on second thought that your victory comes over me—because, on first thought, we cannot realize that your life has in any way become handicapped. You have so entirely created a normal attitude. Eleanor had prepared me for your great courage, but even so, I didn't realize to what an extent you had mastered the discouragement of it all. . . . Please accept the admiration of an old friend & the faith that the quality of your life is only strengthened—*for us all,* you are doing something that it is not given many to do.

The annual dinner of the Cuff Links Club, made up of the small band of men who had ridden aboard the *Westboro* with Franklin or worked in his headquarters in 1920, was to be held at the Roosevelts' New York home on January 26, 1924, four days before his forty-second birthday. As always, Louis Howe was in charge, and full of elaborate plans with which to entertain his chief.

This time the dining room was to be fitted out as if it were the wardroom of a battleship, he explained to Charles McCarthy, and the

---

custom here to feed them to the hounds instead of burying them. I have therefore been looking for a male hunter for the last three weeks . . . [and have] fallen in love with a green Irish roan only four years old. . . . I am living here and get up three mornings a week when it's all dark and frosty and ride him for three hours, schooling him over jumps the afternoons of the other days. It is marvelous trying to outwit him without using reins . . . merely moral suasion. . . .

The crowd here are marvelously hospitable and cordial and we have many wonderful dinners. Game, champagne, etc. Last night 12 girls & 12 men all in pink except one with songs & stories until after midnight.

Eager to help find his troubled friend something to do, Franklin eventually arranged that he become a commission agent for the F&D in Boston. "Davis has the right connections," he assured Van-Lear Black. "Somerset Club, etc., etc., is generally liked and can make the work pay if he gets out and hustles. . . . The experiment [will] cost us nothing."

"I really believe you could make a good thing out of it," Roosevelt assured Livy. "It means lots of work and the use of a good deal of imagination in landing new prospects. Nevertheless, ready-made jobs in more interesting things are not lying around, and with your acquaintance in the whole of New England I am certain you could make it profitable."

Livy tried it but hustling and hard work were beyond him, and he did not represent the F&D for long.

guests were to impersonate workers at the Brooklyn Navy Yard host-
ing a dinner in the candidate's honor,

> still maintaining the fiction that we [are] on our campaign trip. We might
> start out with an amusing dialogue between Admiral [William V.] Pratt
> and the Master Mechanic in which Pratt insists that all the boys come
> aboard whether they have washed their hands or not . . . get [Marvin]
> McIntyre to get sailor suits from the Department for our four sweetest
> singers. They can dress in my room before dinner, and appear as the
> Colorado Star Quartette. Also, some other goat must represent the Ma-
> rines. Apropos of Haiti, he should present Franklin with a couple of skulls
> of Haytians which he dug up from the local graveyard for amusement.
> You will probably remember the unfortunate incident.
>
> The more I think of it the more possibility this seems to give, and I
> am getting quite keen for it as I write. A special radio from "Little Ted"
> has infinite possibilities in it.
>
> Get the gang together and let me know the date for the big drunk.

The big drunk was a highlight of every Roosevelt winter, filled
always with teasing and laughter and good times remembered. But
beneath the hilarious surface of these nostalgic evenings in the 1920s
was always the troubling fear that because of Franklin's paralysis there
might be no more good times to look forward to.

That grim prospect would seem even more likely the following
month, when what Isabella had called Franklin's mastery of the discouragement of it all underwent perhaps its severest test.

Before boarding the train for Florida and his cruise aboard the
Larooco in February, Franklin was examined by Dan Draper. ". . . I
am very much disheartened about his ultimate recovery," Draper
wrote Lovett after Roosevelt had left his office. "I cannot help feeling
that he has almost reached the limit of his possibilities. I only hope I
may be wrong in this."

It had been two full years since Franklin had entered the second
phase of treatment. He now seemed to be moving into the "stationary"
stage during which, Lovett and Draper had both warned him, no
further improvement could be expected. His doctors could do nothing
more for him.

Franklin was on his own.

Whatever Franklin's private thoughts as he lay in his berth on the
long trip to Florida, by the time the train pulled into Jacksonville with

Roy and Missy Le Hand on February 2, he seemed only eager to get out on the water and was full of plans for his new boat.

As he was carried aboard, it was clear she needed a good deal of work. The *Larooco* was seventy-one feet long and looked like "a floating tenement," John Lawrence remembered, boxlike, peeling, stained. There were no sails; power was provided by two ancient thirty-five-horsepower engines. Franklin's stateroom with an attached bath was on the port side of the bow; he quickly had its brass double bed dismantled and replaced with twin bunks; the big, stained mattress was carried on deck for sunbathing. Across the narrow passageway were two smaller cabins for guests, each with two beds. Above them, reached by a short staircase, was a big room that doubled as wheelhouse and stateroom where he unpacked his fishing gear and placed on the shelves his "Library of the World's Worst Literature." Above that was a broad deck, shaded by a tattered canvas canopy.

Sailing master Robert S. Morris was in charge; his wife Dora did the cooking. The elderly couple from Connecticut were paid a combined salary of $125 a month. A young mechanic saw to the recalcitrant engines.

Before his boss went south, Louis Howe had equipped him with an elaborate new "Log of the Houseboat *Larooco,* Being a More or Less Truthful Account of What Happened (expurgated for the Very Young)"; it was bound in black leather stamped in gold, dedicated to Saints Ananias and Sapphira, "the patron saints of liars and fishermen," and illuminated with watercolors: Franklin and Lawrence on their knees on a desert island importuning mermaids; a Jewfish with a prominent nose and a sort of crest from which hung the triple balls of a pawnbroker's sign.

There is no hint of discouragement anywhere in the log's uniformly blithe pages. The boat's interior badly needed painting; the walls of Franklin's stateroom leaked whenever it rained. Nothing seemed to bother him: when the steering cable slipped three days out, blowing the boat sideways and lodging her "gracefully" on a sandbar, he took the opportunity to go fishing in a twenty-three-foot sea-skiff bought from a local sportsman.

But the impact on Franklin of Dr. Draper's devastating verdict was evident to the person aboard who knew him best. Many years later, Missy Le Hand told Frances Perkins, "there were days on the *Larooco* when it was noon before he could pull himself out of depression and greet his guests wearing his lighthearted façade." When she remembered those days, a friend recalled, her eyes filled with tears.

Missy Le Hand's presence aboard the houseboat—and Eleanor's absence from it—was further evidence of the delicate arrangement under which the Roosevelts were now living their lives.

If it had initially been thought that Roosevelt, forced by his condition to stay put and remain out of politics, would be brought closer to the wife and children he had seen so little of before he fell ill, that illusion was quickly dissipated. "Those were the lonely years," James recalled. "For a long while during this time of illness and recovery we had no tangible father, no father-in-being, whom we could touch and talk to at will—only an abstract symbol, a cheery letter writer, off somewhere on a houseboat . . . fighting by himself to do what had to be done. . . . Looking back on this period, I must say in all honesty that neither Anna, nor my brothers, nor I had the guidance and training that I think Father would have given us had he not been involved in his own struggle to re-establish a useful life for himself."[16]

That struggle, Franklin had come to believe, could not be waged effectively at home for more than a few weeks at a time. "I miss you very much . . . ," Eleanor wrote Franklin aboard the *Larooco*, "but I imagine it is as well you are far away from all entanglements." The tensions caused by those entanglements remained too great. "Franklin Roosevelt," Frances Perkins remembered, "more than the average person, had to be let alone and had to have an opportunity to see what he could do without help. If help were to be given to him, it must be in such a subtle and imperceptible way that it didn't appear to *be* help. I . . . put it on the grounds of the way people feel towards their mother who likes to give them good advice. At a certain age they have to throw it off or they never learn to do it themselves."

Eleanor would later blame her mother-in-law for her husband's frequent absences, and certainly no one was more ready to help him than Sara. "She always complained that she never saw Franklin alone," Eleanor wrote, "but if they were left alone together . . . they often disagreed. Those two were too much alike in certain ways to be left long alone. Franklin was as determined as she was, and as the years

16. In February 1925, John Roosevelt, then just nine, sent his far-off father a caricature of himself: It had a huge head, an oversized toothy grin, a powerful torso with long outspread arms—and miniscule legs. *Source:* James Roosevelt (and Sidney Shallett), *Affectionately, FDR,* page 171.

passed he went ahead and did everything he wanted to do, in spite of the fact that he had a great respect and love for his mother. But . . . she continued to the last to try to guide his life."[17]

But if his mother was too much like Franklin to remain alone with him for very long without conflict, his wife was too little like him for him to savor her company: too humorless, too admonitory, too easily aggrieved, too unwilling to relax. Her own attempts at guiding his life were as deeply resented as his mother's. "One of the great quarrels she had with her lot," Frances Perkins once said of Eleanor, "is that Franklin didn't listen to her. . . . That's her gripe. I shouldn't say that, but it's true. He never did rely on her. He liked her as a reporter . . . [but] when most men would have asked their wives what they thought, he didn't."

Increasingly over the past two difficult years he had turned to Missy for the easy companionship his wife was never able to provide. That he now allowed his secretary to witness aboard the *Larooco* the private despair that he hid so completely even from his wife and mother is evidence of the extraordinary degree of trust he had come to place in her.

Missy was twenty-five in the winter of 1924, attractive but not beautiful, with intense dark blue eyes, a strong jaw, black hair already threaded with silver, and a remarkably low, throaty voice. She was a Roman Catholic, the third child of an Irish gardener from Somerville, Massachusetts, who drank too much and deserted his family early on. During her many years with the Roosevelts she was acutely conscious of the disparity between his family and her own—Margaret Suckley once marvelled that such a pleasant and well-mannered young woman had had "no background at all"—and, perhaps in an attempt to exaggerate the gentility of her upbringing, she would one day tell the author of a magazine profile that her parent had been "in real estate." But she remained fond of her errant father (much as Eleanor was of hers), and his early abandonment of her may have made her especially susceptible to the appeal of a man like Roosevelt, who was nearly twice her age and often signed his notes to her "Father."

She was hugely capable and disciplined, handling all of Franklin's correspondence, keeping track of his scattered interests, screening his visitors and managing through patient, unfailing courtesy to placate

17. Anna thought this passage greatly overdrawn, evidence of her mother's "own stress over Granny," rather than genuine tension between mother and son. *Source:* Interview with Anna Roosevelt Halsted by Bernard A. Asbell, Anna Roosevelt Halsted Papers, FDRL.

even those she turned away. But it seems clear that in the four years since she had agreed—at Eleanor's suggestion—to leave the Democratic National Committee and work for Franklin full time, clearing up his correspondence after the vice-presidential contest, her devotion to him had grown well beyond what might have been expected of even the most dedicated employee. In New York, she slept on a relative's sofa on the East Side so that she could reach the Roosevelt home at any hour, had become a fixture there, and at the F&D office was almost as omnipresent as Louis Howe—and was at first as deeply resented by the children, to whom she represented yet another barrier between them and their father.[18]

She often accompanied Roosevelt to Hyde Park for working weekends, called him "FD"—"Effdee" in her letters—a name no one else dared use, and had allowed her life to be absorbed by his, taking on as if by osmosis his likes and dislikes, his favorite drinks and games and books, even his turns of phrase: "Your speech was *too* lovely," she wrote him once; her own rest had been "perfectly grand."

Now, aboard the *Larooco,* she threw herself wholeheartedly into the good times upon which he insisted. She helped him paint the battered wicker furniture a "booful blue," spent evening after evening at the game he insisted on calling "Ma and Pa Cheezey," fished alongside him patiently for hours even though she sunburned easily. When the boat put in here and there to allow guests to come aboard—William H. Kelly, the Democratic boss of Syracuse, J. C. Penney, the department store magnate, James Cox and his wife—Missy acted as Franklin's hostess, encouraging him to tell his favorite stories, seeing that everyone's glass was filled with illicit rum brought aboard by the mechanic.

Theodore Roosevelt had filled his own infrequent moments of rest with writing, managing in the course of his career to write a four-volume history of the winning of the West, a chronicle of the naval war of 1812, biographies of Thomas Hart Benton, Gouverneur Morris,

18. Franklin Jr. once told a friend that it was the constant presence of Missy Le Hand, not Louis Howe, that he had most resented in his youth. She had so much of his father, he remembered, and he had so little; and she seemed invariably to agree with whatever his father said. "Are you always agreeable?" he asked her once. "Don't you ever get mad and flare up? Do you always smile?"

"Missy looked as if she would burst into tears," he remembered. *Sources:* Interview with Franklin D. Roosevelt, Jr.; Joseph P. Lash, *Eleanor Roosevelt: A Friend's Memoir,* page 210.

and Oliver Cromwell, and twenty-nine other volumes, along with countless articles and some 150,000 letters.

During his years at the Navy Department, Franklin, too, had often talked of writing when he had the time. "In regard to my own actual pen-to-paper possibilities," he once told his old friend George Marvin, "I am always in the delightful frame of mind of wanting to say 'Yes' to anything in the way of writing, be it a magazine article or a 12-volume history of the Navy—always provided the work is to be done next week, or the week after."

Time was clearly no longer a problem; he had little else, in fact, as several friends gently pointed out the moment they heard of his illness. On September 15, 1921, for example—the day he arrived from Campobello on a stretcher and entered New York Presbyterian Hospital—Livy Davis had written him a characteristically jaunty letter:

Dear old Rosy,
        . . . I wish to Gosh there was something I could do for you now. As soon as you are ready let me know and I'll beat it to N. Y. and we'll have an old time talk fest. Seems as if your convalescence will afford you an opportunity to do a little of the writing of which you have spoken so often. The chief difficulty, I should judge, would be in choosing where to begin.
        . . . setting aside your authority to dissertate with monographs upon . . . Flora, Fauna and Ornithology from Pisinrinco Harbor to Poughquog, N.Y., the following subjects with examples leap into my mind:

1. Highmuckamucks; or Lunching and Dining in Europe.
2. Efficiency: The Indecisions of a Secretary: JD [Josephus Daniels].
3. Pep, or the Heroism of an Admiral in War Time: [Admiral Parks.]
4. Wind: or How to Run a Gov. Bureau: S. McG. & "Sure to be Sammy." [Samuel McGowan, Paymaster General]
5. The Effect of Loquacity on Achievement: Sims
6. The Ladies of Washington: or Thirty Days & Evenings as a Bachelor.
7. Frivolities of a Capital: Or Picnicking as an Art.
8. My own attempt is entitled: "On the Trail of a Roosevelt; or 29 Concussive Nights in a different place and bed."[19]

19. By omitting several of these titles and mixing up the rest in his *FDR*, Ted Morgan has tried to make them prove his thesis that "Franklin had repeatedly been involved in sexual escapades and that Lucy Mercer was not his only mistress." That may be true, but Livy's suggested topics offer little evidence of it. Only number six suggests Roosevelt's flirtations. (The proposed subject of Livy's "own attempt" is clearly not sexual adventuring but an account of

Franklin did make several attempts at serious writing during his years of treatment. He managed to publish an article, "Shall We Trust Japan?" in *Asia* magazine, although before the manuscript was ready for the printer its editor had to do a good deal of additional research and writing of his own. (The article argued that while economic competition was inevitable between the United States and Japan, war was not, a considerable change of heart for Franklin since his days as an eager anti-Japanese belligerent in 1913, and evidence of the influence of Woodrow Wilson's anti-imperialism upon him.)

He wrote an overwrought and wholly admiring sketch of Alexander Hamilton, whom he credited with having "ordered the finances of the country and . . . removed for all time the risk of disturbance of the state." Then, he excitedly reviewed his friend Claude G. Bowers's book *Jefferson and Hamilton* for the *New York World*. From this volume he learned, apparently for the very first time, that the struggle between the ideas of government put forth by its two great protagonists had continued throughout the nation's history. The book was "thrilling," he said, it made him "breathless" and feel "like saying 'At last.' " Thereafter, he would scorn Hamilton as "a fundamental believer in an aristocracy of wealth and power," and identify himself instead with Jefferson, who "brought the government back to the average voter. . . ."

A life of John Paul Jones had long interested him and with Louis Howe's help he had amassed a considerable collection of original material. But he never made much headway, even when someone suggested he try a scene-by-scene scenario for a movie.

He attempted a little volume of lives of neglected early American seafarers, and abandoned that, too.

And aboard the *Larooco* in early 1924, when Missy was called suddenly away by the death of her father—she would be gone for nearly two weeks—he wrote out the first fourteen pages of a history of the United States. He began it in the "highly primitive" Europe of A.D. 1000 and, with roughly a thousand years to go, may have simply

---

his exhausting trip to the front with his friend in 1918.) In reading Livy Davis's journals and letters, valuable as they are, his own chronically tumid state must always be kept in mind.

Isabella Ferguson had a suggestion for Franklin, too. She was writing a play, she told Eleanor, and wondered if he would like to be her long-distance collaborator: "I can handle the first two acts which are in the West, [but] I can't do anything with the Third in London & would he mind just taking the London Act off my hands? I don't mind a bit what he does with the characters, in fact their future is a terrible responsibility to me now." Franklin did not take this on. *Sources:* Ted Morgan, *FDR*, page 203; Eleanor Roosevelt Papers, FDRL.

felt the remaining task too daunting. In any case, he gave it up, returning to it from time to time to make tiny emendations in pen and pencil but never adding anything to the story.

It had just been "something to do," he told an adviser who asked him about it during his presidency. "I thought all our histories lacked movement and a sense of direction. The nation was clearly going somewhere right from the first. I thought I could do better with that idea than had been done before." He could not. He had little of his cousin's literary talent or industry, would always be less skilled as playwright than actor, acutely sensitive to how words made him sound and wonderfully adept at altering the words of others to make himself sound better, but pedestrian at putting them together himself.[20]

At around two-thirty in the afternoon of Monday, February 4, the *Larooco* anchored off St. Augustine and those on board saw that flags ashore were flying at half-mast. Woodrow Wilson had died at last in his dark house on S Street in Washington. "Our own ensign," Franklin noted in his log, "will remain at half mast for 30 days."

Wilson's death had been expected for some time—Franklin had written out a statement for the press as soon as he heard the former President's recovery was unlikely—"Woodrow Wilson in his life gave mankind a new vision of pure democracy." But the newspapers describing Wilson's death and funeral that Franklin sent Missy ashore to pick up every day or two also brought political news that brightened Franklin's spirits.

20. He did not like to dwell on this frailty. When Harry Hopkins first went to London on his behalf he asked his emissary to find out from Winston Churchill "who writes his stuff." On his return, Hopkins told friends how much he dreaded having to tell the Boss that the British Prime Minister wrote it himself.

FDR never entirely abandoned his dream of publishing a best-seller. In late 1926, Houghton Mifflin published in book form a commencement address he had given at Milton Academy. It sold fewer than 350 copies. As President a decade later, he contracted with Bennett Cerf, the head of Random House, to publish his public papers and addresses in five volumes. Samuel Rosenman was to handle the editing. Cerf was delighted but unsure of how the books would do, and sought to lower the President's sights a little by reminding him that a collection of Herbert Hoover's papers had sold just 2,000 sets.

It didn't work. "Hoover sold 2,000!" Roosevelt laughed. "We'll sell a million!"

In fact, the books appeared at the height of the Court-packing fight in 1937, and sold just 7,000 sets. (Subsequent volumes were published by Harper.) "We discovered," Cerf recalled, "that anybody who had $15 to spend on books at one time hated Franklin Roosevelt." To prove it, he cited the order he received from a Boston bookseller: "We'll buy as many sets as you can deliver, bound in [Roosevelt's] own skin." *Source:* Transcript of interview with Bennett Cerf, Columbia Oral History Project, Columbia University.

The entirely unexpected death of President Harding six months earlier had at first seemed to offer the Democrats a realistic chance to regain the presidency in 1924. But the succession of Calvin Coolidge had dashed those hopes. "I cannot help feeling," Franklin had written then, "that Harding's unfortunate taking off has helped rather than hurt the Democratic Party. Coolidge . . . is not a world beater," but it "looks to me now as if he would be nominated next year. He will be considered, of course, a Conservative, and that means that we must nominate a Progressive without fail."

Al Smith was the party's leading progressive, but far out in front of all other candidates was William G. McAdoo, Wilson's son-in-law and wartime Secretary of the Treasury, a Georgia-born New York corporation lawyer who had moved to California and enjoyed wide support among both Southern and Western delegates. He enjoyed enthusiastic support from rural Drys and labor unions as well as from the powerful but clandestine Ku Klux Klan, whose special ferocity was reserved that year for Roman Catholics.

But now the Florida newspapers headlined the discovery of a dangerous, potentially fatal flaw in McAdoo's candidacy that threatened to scuttle his hopes for the presidency. An ongoing Senate investigation that winter had revealed that in exchange for massive bribes, Albert Fall, the Secretary of the Interior, had secretly leased federal oil reserves, meant to provide the Navy with petroleum, to two private corporations—Wyoming's Teapot Dome had been tapped by the Mammoth Oil Company, headed by Harry F. Sinclair, and the California Elk Hills Reserve had been laid open to Edward L. Doheny's Pan-American Petroleum and Transport Company.

Secretary Fall had been forced to resign (and later went to prison), and now, just a few days before Wilson's death, the committee learned that, over the years, Doheny had paid McAdoo some $250,000 for his "influence."[21]

It suddenly seemed at least possible that Smith, the champion of the Eastern cities with whom Franklin had identified himself since 1920, might mount a convincing challenge to the badly tarnished McAdoo. If he did, Franklin hoped a role might be found for him to play.

And there was still more good news: the oil scandal also seemed

21. On behalf of the F&D, Franklin himself had once tried to get to Doheny through McAdoo. Arranging for a salesman to call upon McAdoo in the spring of 1922, he added that Doheny is "a good friend of mine and I feel sure will be very glad to have you place the business our way." *Source:* Kenneth S. Davis, *FDR: The Beckoning of Destiny,* page 697.

to have permanently sidelined Franklin's only serious rival within the Roosevelt family. Edward Denby, the Secretary of the Navy and Ted Roosevelt's superior, had also been forced to leave his post because he had approved turning over the oil fields to the Interior Department (although no evidence was ever offered that he had done so for personal gain), and Ted and Archie Roosevelt were suspected of complicity: Ted because his wife owned shares in Sinclair's firm; Archie because he had been on its payroll overseas.

"I am sending you clippings from which you will see that little Ted appears to be down and out as candidate for governor," Louis Howe wrote Franklin when the story first broke. "This will amuse you." And a week later he passed along still more gossip. "I hear *sub rosa* that Mrs. Ted has a fine bunch of Sinclair stock, and that the knowledge [led] to the extreme haste in putting brother Archy on the stand. The general position of the newspaper boys is politically he is as dead as King Tut, for the moment at least."[22]

Meanwhile, he and Missy continued their cruise. Also aboard for much of the time was Maunsell Schieffelin Crosby, a friend and Dutchess County neighbor of Franklin's whom Sara had encouraged her son to ask along because he shared many of the interests of which she approved: stamp collecting, forestry, fishing, and ornithology. During Crosby's several weeks aboard the *Larooco* he and Franklin spotted ninety-nine species of birds and caught barracuda and mackerel on the offshore reefs, and silvery tarpon closer to shore, careful to keep their quarry well away from the twisting mangrove thickets in which they tried to hide themselves when hooked.

They went ashore from time to time to buy provisions and pick up the mail, and sometimes Crosby drove Franklin around among the fast-growing resort communities. In Miami they drew up in front of William Jennings Bryan's home, and the old man of whom Franklin

---

22. Ted, too, thought his political career had come to an end until his wife showed him the receipt proving she had sold the shares in 1921, well before any illicit leases were granted, and at his brother's urging Archie not only resigned from the Sinclair firm but volunteered to testify before the Senate committee investigating the matter and even attempted to persuade a fellow employee to offer further evidence against Secretary Fall.

Rosy shared his half-brother's pleasure in the embarrassment Teapot Dome caused Oyster Bay. "What an oily business all round in Washington!" he wrote Franklin. "The only good things is that . . . Ted [is] apparently eliminated. I don't think that Archie R. covered himself with glory. It is hardly what the British call 'cricket' to rush in as an involuntary informer against his Employer!! I rather think Ted thought it a good way to help save his own bacon!!!" *Source:* James Roosevelt Roosevelt Papers, FDRL.

had often been so scornful came out to the car for "a nice chat." Roosevelt was unimpressed by Palm Beach: "not having been here since 1904," he noted, "I found the growth of mushroom millionaires' houses luxuriant. The women we saw went well with the place—and we desired to meet them no more than we wished to remain in the harbor even an hour more than necessary."

Franklin read with interest the reports he received about the doings of his far-off children. Sara was to attend James's confirmation at Groton in March. "Little Franklin," Louis Howe wrote, "came home from dancing class all puffed up with pride at having won a gold medal and the prize for being the best tango dancer. Johnny's nose is out of joint and he professes a great contempt for the terpsichorean art generally." And Franklin reported back the good times he was having. "Today Maunsell and I took the motor boat to an inlet, fished, got out on the sandy beach, picnicked and swam and lay in the sun for hours," he told his mother. "I know it is doing the legs good, and though I have worn the braces hardly at all, I get lots of exercise crawling around, and I know the muscles are better than ever before." (Just once during the whole ten-week cruise, on April 6, did Franklin record having exercised "with canes and crutches" as instructed by Dr. Lovett.)

Unmentioned in his letters home were the almost endless problems the ancient houseboat encountered simply remaining afloat. Her motors routinely ceased to function and had to undergo laborious repairs; wind and rain kept Franklin and Missy below decks for days on end; the boat ran aground six times in a single day, and often got lost in the maze of inlets and mangrove swamps. Disasters and delays like these would have enraged the haughty and hyperkinetic Franklin Roosevelt who had toured the Western Front just a few years earlier. Paralysis was teaching him a degree of patience he had never shown before.

As promised, Livy Davis came down for a few days, curiously subdued and suffering from a series of ailments which seem to have been at least in part psychosomatic. He arrived, Franklin said, looking "like a sick child . . . from shingles, boils, bunions and cold in the head," and he somehow managed while fishing around the pilings of a railroad bridge in choppy water to lose his pants. He came back to the *Larooco*, Franklin teased, "minus trousers—to the disgust of the two ladies [Missy and Mrs. Morris]. Earlier he had exercised on the top deck a la nature. Why do people who *must* take off their clothes go anywhere

where the other sex is present? Capt. Morris remarked that some men get shot for less."[23]

Franklin's complaint about Livy's lack of modesty was a longstanding joke between them, but he did find his friend alarmingly changed: openly resentful of the presence of others, morose, unable to function for long without a drink. The hold-ups that Franklin now took in stride agitated him. "[P]oor old Livy was with me for over two weeks," Franklin reported to John Lawrence after their mutual friend had left. "I think there is something seriously wrong with him. He was upset the whole time—magnified everything, got in wrong with everybody and got everyone in wrong with everybody else."[24]

This turned out to be the last trip Livy and Franklin ever took together: Davis did not come along the following winter, though he longed to do so. "I can picture you," he wrote Franklin then, "divanating in local garb consisting of a j-strap beneath a cotton plant with a mint julep in one hand the latest utterance of [William Jennings Bryan] in the other with Missie clad—God knows how—langorously fanning you with a punkah. O Boy make the most of it for you will soon be way up yonder where the *days* are six months long!"

In the summer of 1927, Davis would become engaged to a second wealthy woman from Maine, Georgia Appleton, and invited "dear old Rosy" to be his best man at the August 31 wedding at Bar Harbor: "O Rosy at the dawn of our real lives we do so want you to be present that while possibly we should not ask it, we do hope you will make a superhuman effort." In the end, Franklin did not go, lunching instead with the newlyweds when they came to New York the following week, and over the coming years he heard less and less from the man who had once called himself "your jolly boy."

23. Several Roosevelt biographers have taken this passage seriously, as evidence of Roosevelt's censoriousness. I think they are wrong. Like adolescent schoolboys, Franklin and Livy had enjoyed teasing one another about their alleged modesty at least since their Haitian trip together. Livy had been a passenger aboard the *Weona II* when the men swam naked every morning and had himself joked before coming about bringing along only a single pair of shorts "as I suspect you have gotten Missy thoroughly indoctrinated by this time to the clothing we wear."
Had Franklin really been upset by his friend's behavior he would never have mentioned the incident in the pages of his log, from which all substantive or unpleasant topics were ruthlessly banished. Nor would he have made another joke about Davis's disrobing a few days later, or added, still later in the log, that Mrs. Morris had spotted Livy aboard the train that took him north again and cheerily shaken a towel at him in farewell.

24. Precisely what happened will probably never be known. The pages from the *Larooco* log that covered activities aboard from March 23 to April 5 were evidently removed by someone before it was deposited at the Franklin D. Roosevelt Library.

Livy and his new wife attended Franklin's first inauguration as governor in 1928, but stayed away from his second one two years later, explaining that, "having seen your life under these conditions . . . I would greatly prefer to come up sometime . . . when you are leading a normal existence."

In January of 1931, Livy wrote Franklin to say that a friend of his had "been seized by an irresistible desire to write a book on your life—Oh Boy! Just think what I could tell him"—and asking for an appointment on the would-be author's behalf.

Franklin was jocular but firm in turning him away.

Your friend who wants to write a bibli-ous-ography of me can't be kept from doing so if he insists. No law covers a situation like that. However, there are some six or seven other scribes in the field at the present moment and from present appearances it looks as if sometime this summer there will appear simultaneously in all book shops a whole library of authentic, imaginative or apocryphal stories concerning my daily habits over the past forty-nine years.

Of course if this friend of yours insists, he may see me for fourteen and a half minutes and I will tell him the story of my life in that period. I doubt if I could give him the other half minute.

Seriously, do call off the dogs. Why anybody should be interested, I do not know, but I prophesy that these proposed volumes will bust his publisher.

There was at least one more letter. In May, Livy reported that he had recently seen William Phillips, and that "Bill is all excited about your [presidential] candidacy next year and the universal opinion here-abouts is that you will not only receive the nomination but will be overwhelmingly elected."

Early in the morning on January 11, 1932, ten days before his celebrated classmate entered his name in the North Dakota Democratic primary, formally announcing his candidacy for President of the United States, Livy slipped out of his house in Brookline, hurried across the neatly clipped lawn, entered the woodshed, and closed the door. A few moments later, passers-by heard a shot. Livingston Davis had shot himself through the head.

"Livy's death certainly was a great shock," Franklin wrote to a mutual friend, "and I shall miss him dreadfully. I cannot understand it. He seemed to me the last person in the world who would brood, because he always talked things over with his friends."

On Inauguration Day, Roosevelt made a point of seeing that his old companion's widow had a good seat for the ceremonies.[25]

Franklin's ten weeks aboard the *Larooco* provided Eleanor with still more uninterrupted time for her own work with the Women's Division of the Democratic Party. "You need not be proud of me, dear," she wrote her husband. "I'm only being active again till you can be again—it isn't such a great desire on my part to serve the world and I'll fall back into habits of sloth quite easily! Hurry up, for as you know my ever present sense of the uselessness of all things will overwhelm me sooner of later!"

In fact, she was less easily overwhelmed now, more certain of her ability to function on her own. An unsuspected, steely toughness was increasingly apparent beneath her uniformly ladylike exterior. She had failed to persuade Al Smith to put two women on the ticket with him before the convention, but she did exact his promise to name women to high office in his administration. Frances Perkins visited headquarters one day and overheard Eleanor laying down the law to a Democratic committeewoman by long-distance telephone: It was not enough to print up handbills and hold Democratic meetings; she said firmly. "Don't waste your breath, don't waste your gasoline. . . ." There was no point in preaching to the converted. Ways had to be found to spread the word among potentially sympathetic Republicans, and she, Nancy Cook, and Marion Dickerman made expeditions by automobile into the countryside where they gently overcame the objections of old-line leaders uneasy about organizing women. When she and a fellow volunteer stopped at the home of the chairman of one rural county and his wife claimed he was out, Eleanor (who had seen him scuttle inside at her car's approach), answered, "All right, we will just sit here on the steps until he comes." After an hour or so, the chairman's wife came onto the porch again to say that she really had no idea when her husband would be home. "It doesn't matter," Mrs. Roosevelt said. "We have nothing else to do. We'll wait." After another hour or so, the sheepish chairman emerged to talk business with his visitors.

25. "He was a grand companion," FDR wrote from the White House for the 1934 report of his Harvard class, ". . . the kind of comrade who conversed at the right time, and was always full of fun and good nature." He liked to think, he said, that the years he and Livy had worked together at the Navy Department "were the happiest and most fruitful of his life. He always continued to talk about them and to rejoice in the interesting and delightful adventures of those days. As one of his classmates who knew him and cared for him greatly, I shall always be grateful for his affection and his companionship during these many years."

By April, women in all but five counties had been organized, and the Women's Division had proved itself a force to be reckoned with. But Eleanor had no illusions as to how far women still had to go to become equal partners in politics. Men were happy to call upon women's organizational skills, she told a woman reporter, but they were unwilling to share power. She summarized the patronizing view even the most modern-minded men still held toward their activist wives: "You are wonderful. I love and honor you. . . . Lead your own life, attend to your charities, cultivate yourself, travel when you wish, bring up the children, run your house, I'll give you all the freedom you wish and all the money I can but—leave me my business and politics." If women wanted to help control events, she continued, they must master the mechanics of politics, be willing to confront male politicians on their own terms.

At the state convention in Albany in early April, she did just that. Her antagonist was Charles F. Murphy, "the Quiet Boss" of Tammany whom her husband had first battled thirteen years earlier, and the issue was selection of delegates-at-large for the national convention in July. She explained the struggle in a letter to Franklin, still aboard the *Larooco:*

> I have wanted you home the last few days to advise me on the fight I'm putting up on two delegates and two alternates at large. Mr. Murphy and I disagree as to whether the men leaders shall name them or whether we shall, backed by the written endorsement of 49 Associate County chairmen. I imagine it is just a question of what he dislikes most, giving me my way or having me give the papers a grand chance for a story by telling the whole story at the women's dinner Monday night and by insisting on recognition on the floor . . . and putting the names in nomination. There's one thing I'm thankful for. I haven't a thing to lose and for the moment you haven't either.

Murphy was not inclined to let her have her way, and so, at the Women's Dinner at the Ten Eyck Hotel, in whose corridors Franklin had once lobbied against Murphy's Senate candidate Billy Sheehan, she warned the Quiet Boss of what was coming.

> It is always disagreeable to take stands. It is always easier to compromise, always easier to let things go. To many women and I am one of them, it is extraordinarily difficult to care about anything enough to cause disagreement or unpleasant feelings, but I have come to the conclusion

this must be done for a time until we can prove our strength and demand respect for our wishes.

The next day, April 14, she led a delegation that called upon Governor Smith to ask that he back them in their struggle. Smith agreed and Murphy surrendered: the women, not he, would pick their own delegates-at-large.

Eleven days after his defeat by Eleanor, on April 25, 1924, Boss Murphy died suddenly of a heart attack. Franklin, just back from Florida, issued a statement mourning the loss of New York's "most powerful and wisest leader."

A few days later, two of Al Smith's closest aides, Belle Moskowitz and State Supreme Court Justice Joseph Proskauer, came to call at 47 East 65th Street. Citizens for Smith needed a chairman, they said. A Protestant. Someone who could appeal to the broadest possible spectrum of potential voters. Someone neither tainted by Tammany nor identified with either the dry or the wet faction of the party. Someone like Franklin Roosevelt.

Would he be willing to take the job?

Franklin explained that his disability would keep him from rushing around the state attending meetings.

That would not present a problem, his visitors assured him as they took their leave; if he would lend his name, they would do the work.

Roosevelt agreed. The Republican *New York Herald-Tribune* wrote that while Murphy's death had robbed the Democrats of a crafty political leader, Roosevelt's "prestige and principles" more than made up for the loss.[26]

Franklin Roosevelt was at least nominally back in active politics. Neither he nor Howe thought Smith could win the Democratic nomination: the governor was too Catholic, too citified, too defiantly wet

26. Accompanying its story about Franklin's new job, the *New York Post* printed a photograph of Eleanor, prompting Josephus Daniels to write his former assistant to say how glad he was to learn he was "not the only 'squaw' man in the country. . . . I have had that experience on similar occasions and have always wondered how the newspapermen knew so well who was at the head of the family."

Franklin responded in the same vein:

You are right about the squaws! Like you I have fought for years to keep my name on the front page and to relegate the wife's to the advertising section. My new plan, however, seems admirable—hereafter for three years my name will not appear at all, but each fourth year (Presidential ones) I am to have all the limelight. Why don't you adopt this too? It will make it much easier to put that Democratic national ticket of Daniels and Roosevelt across in 1928 or 1932.

Source: Joseph P. Lash, *Eleanor and Franklin,* page 287.

to appeal to Protestant delegates much outside the Eastern cities. When Franklin tried to persuade Smith to declare the Prohibition issue a "red herring," and assert that "A temperate people are a happy and contented people, and to that all my acts and words will bend," Smith refused, calling instead for immediate repeal of the Eighteenth Amendment and, if that proved impossible, for weakening the Volstead Act to permit the manufacture and sale of beer and wine.

One afternoon at Smith headquarters in the Biltmore Hotel, a mutual friend remembered, Franklin was chatting with some prairie Democrats who had asked to see the candidate, when the governor entered,

> like a breeze, in swallowtail coat, a silk hat at a rakish angle and with the usual cigar in his mouth. "Hello, hello, my boy, and how's things?" he said, addressing Roosevelt. The latter introduced his callers as delegates from Kansas. "Hello, boys," said Smith, shaking hands. "Glad to see you. Y'know, the other day some boys were in from Wisconsin and I learned somethin'. I always thought Wisconsin was on this side of the lake. It's on the other side. Glad to know it. Glad to know more about the place where the good beer comes from."

But even if Smith had been a more broadly appealing presidential aspirant—Roosevelt and Howe agreed—it was now again unlikely that any Democrat could win the White House in November. No one blamed Coolidge for the scandals that had taken place under his predecessor. The economy seemed still to be in good shape. The Democrats themselves were badly split between Wets and Drys, Catholics and Protestants, city and country.

Still, by leading the struggle for Smith, Franklin would maintain his position as an important New York leader and help cleanse himself of the taint of anti-Catholicism which had clung to him ever since his fight against Blue Eyed Billy Sheehan.

Boss Murphy's death had given Franklin the chairmanship. Now, the death of a second prominent Tammany Democrat again indirectly benefited Roosevelt. Smith had originally counted upon Bourke Cockran, the Irish-American attorney and orator who had nominated him at San Francisco four years earlier, to do the job again. But Cockran had died the year before, and Smith had been slow to name a replacement.

He was still puzzling over the problem a few days before the convention opened. "Who ought to put me in nomination?" Smith asked his aide, Judge Joseph Proskauer.

Proskauer thought for a moment, then said, "Frank Roosevelt."
"For God's sake, why?"

Franklin had been a steady supporter since 1920, and the governor
sympathized with his battle to regain his feet, but the old social and
cultural gulf between the two men had never closed and Smith had
never overcome his initial impression of Roosevelt as a state senator:
priggish, devious, showy, impractical, overly refined. "Franklin," he
once told a friend, "just isn't the kind of man you can take into the
pissroom and talk intimately with."

Proskauer thought no more of Franklin than Smith did. His reasons for suggesting his name were purely pragmatic. Smith needed
Roosevelt, the judge told him, "because you're a Bowery mick and he's
a Protestant patrician and he'd take some of the curse off you."[27]

Smith grudgingly agreed, and took Proskauer with him to see
Roosevelt in the tiny office he occupied at Democratic Headquarters.
Franklin was cordial but coy. "Oh, Al," he said, "I'd love to do it, but
I'm so busy here working with delegates I have no time to write a
speech." (Much later, FDR would claim that Smith had asked him at
this meeting to "audition" and that he had refused; this seems to have
been pure fantasy.)

Then he turned to Proskauer: "Joe, will you write a speech for
me?"

Proskauer said he would—indeed, he had already written it and
had included a phrase drawn from a poem by William Wordsworth.
Al Smith, it said, was the " 'Happy Warrior' of the political battlefield."[28]

Roosevelt read Proskauer's draft, was not happy with it, and spent
the weekend at Hyde Park enthusiastically writing an address of his
own. When his mother's tenant, Moses Smith, happened by him that
weekend as he sat on a blanket in the sun dictating to Missy Le Hand,

27. In retrospect, Eleanor agreed that the governor's feelings for her husband were never
more than politically motivated: "With Al Smith, I always felt that he never really did anything
more than look with a kindly but very condescending eye upon this younger man and they really,
fundamentally had very little in common. . . ."

Writing in 1927, the journalist Henry F. Pringle offered the reasons reporters were privately
told Roosevelt had been picked to nominate Smith: "Franklin D. Roosevelt . . . lives near
Poughkeepsie and does not bear the Tammany brand. . . ." *Sources:* Interview with Eleanor
Roosevelt, Robert D. Graff Papers, FDRL; Henry F. Pringle, *Alfred E. Smith, A Critical Portrait*,
page 305.

28. Wordsworth's original lines:
　　This is the Happy Warrior; this is he
　　Whom every man in arms should wish to be.

he sang out: "Mose, what do you think I'm doing? I am writing a speech to nominate Al Smith for President!"

Back in New York on Monday he told Proskauer that he could not possibly deliver the address the judge had composed. "It's too poetic. You can't get across Wordsworth's poem to a gang of delegates." Proskauer was no happier with Roosevelt's. The two men argued for a time before Proskauer suggested that they put the question before "somebody who has good publicity sense . . . someone like Herbert [Bayard] Swope," managing editor of the *New York World*.

Roosevelt agreed; Swope was a friend of his. But "Swope made a faux pas," Proskauer remembered. "We hadn't told him who had written them and he read Frank's speech first, threw it on the floor and said, 'Joe, this is the goddamnedest, rottennest speech I've ever read!' Then he read mine and he said, 'This is the greatest speech since Bragg nominated Cleveland.' "[29]

Roosevelt was not pleased and continued to argue. It was nearing midnight. Finally, Proskauer said, "Frank . . . I have enough authority from the Governor to tell you that you're either going to make that speech, or you're not going to make any."[30]

"All right," Roosevelt said. "I'll make the goddamned speech and it'll be a flop."

Franklin's uncharacteristic flash of anger was likely sparked in part by simple if unacknowledged fear. The Smith nomination would mark his first public appearance in nearly three years, and it would be made in front of the very men and women whom he must impress if he were to look forward to a full-time return to politics. Somehow, he must be able first to reach the platform, then to make his way to the lectern in

29. General Edward S. Bragg's seconding speech for Grover Cleveland at the Democratic Convention of 1884 had included the resonant line: "They love him for the enemies he has made." As he went on speaking in praise of his candidate, the galleries cheered on the old soldier who had commanded all that was left of the Union Iron Brigade at Petersburg, chanting, "A little more grape, General! A little more grape!"

30. "[F]rom that night [until] the day he died, [Roosevelt] never mentioned that speech to me," Proskauer recalled. "I got indirectly a version of his theory; he had a genius for self-deception. He'd write these statements and come to believe them."

At an Albany dinner, according to Proskauer, Judge Irving Lehman asked FDR, "How did you ever get onto that wonderful idea of the happy warrior?"

"I'll tell you how it was, Irving," Roosevelt answered. "I wrote a speech. I gave it to Joe Proskauer to read, and he said it was fine, and I said, 'No, it ought to have a phrase in it to give it punch.' He thought a minute, and said, 'Why don't you call Al the happy warrior?' and I said 'fine,' and I stuck it in." *Source:* Transcript of interview with Joseph Proskauer, Columbia Oral History Project, Columbia University.

plain view of thousands of delegates whose pleasure at seeing him again could be turned instantly to fatal pity if he stumbled.

He remained unable to stand without braces or move without crutches, but he was determined not to be seen in a wheelchair on the convention floor and began to practice a new maneuver: James, tall and strapping now at sixteen, was called upon to stand to his left so that his father could grip his arm; most of his weight rested heavily on the crutch under his right arm. Slow forward movement was made possible by pivoting his body with his shoulders. To relieve the anxiety of onlookers—so as not to "scare everybody half to death," as Franklin said—he and James engaged in loud banter as they made their painful way along, laughing together as if no real exertion were involved, nodding and smiling and locking eyes with onlookers to take their attention from their slow, hitching progress. ("I began to be close to him then," James recalled, "when I helped him get ready for that speech. I began to know what he needed, how I could help him.")

Franklin was in his seat when the opening gavel fell for the first session on June 24, and he attended every session thereafter. His arrival each morning was carefully orchestrated. He was driven to a side entrance of the Garden, lifted out of his automobile and into his wheelchair, then wheeled inside by his son. When they reached the entrance to the hall closest to the New York Delegation, James would lock his father's braces and pull him to a standing position so that he could enter the hall upright.

To make passage up the aisle as easy as possible, the Roosevelts arrived early and left late. Franklin's only other concession to his condition was to ask for an especially sturdy aisle seat with arms to help ensure that he did not topple sideways and so that he could help to raise and lower himself, and he made sure that James stood nearby during demonstrations to protect him from injury in case over-exuberant delegates jostled past too closely.

Just four years earlier in San Francisco he had made an unforgettably vigorous impression, carrying the New York State standard in the demonstration for Woodrow Wilson, vaulting chairs on his way to the platform, rushing from delegation to delegation shaking hands and greeting friends.

The contrast he now presented was almost unbearable. Looking down from the galleries and watching his slow, ungainly arrivals and departures each day, visitors took to applauding his courage, a gesture at once kindly meant and deeply humiliating.[31]

If he were to resume active political life, he knew he had to prove himself capable of evoking more than mere sympathy. "Nobody knows how that man worked," Marion Dickerman remembered. "They measured off in the library of the Sixty-Fifth Street house . . . the distance to the podium, and he practiced getting across that distance. Oh, he struggled."

Roosevelt was scheduled to speak at twelve noon on Thursday, June 26, and as the hands on the big clock behind the platform edged toward twelve, Eleanor and the rest of the children, along with Sara, Marion, and Nancy, looked on silently together from the gallery.

Franklin and James left their seats on the floor and made their slow, steady, determinedly smiling way up the aisle. Marion mumbled a prayer. Eleanor knitted fiercely.

Finally, they reached the rear of the dais. Franklin leaned stiffly on one crutch, gripping James's arm while he was introduced. "Outwardly [Father] was beaming, seemingly confident and unconcerned," James recalled, "but. . . . his fingers dug into my arm like pincers—I doubt that he knew how hard he was gripping me. His face was covered with perspiration."

Joseph Guffey, the national committeeman from Pennsylvania, stood nearby. Franklin whispered loudly to him: "Go and shake the pulpit!" Guffey evidently didn't understand at first, and Roosevelt "almost fiercely" repeated his request: he wanted to be certain that the Speaker's stand would not suddenly collapse under his weight as he leaned on it. Guffey shook it and reported back that it was sturdy.

Then it was time. "Let's go," Franklin said.

James handed him his second crutch and he began moving slowly toward the podium alone, sweat beading his brow, jaw grimly set, eyes on the floor—left crutch forward and weight shifted to it, right leg hitched forward, right crutch forward, left leg hitched forward, again and again—following in full view of twelve thousand delegates, alternates, and spectators the lurching fifteen-foot path he had laboriously

---

31. The 1924 Democratic Convention was the first to be covered by radio. Listening at home, Franklin's old Dutchess County ally, Morgan Hoyt, heard faint applause, followed by the announcer's explanation: "I don't know what it is, but I rather imagine that Franklin D. Roosevelt is coming in. He always gets a hand . . . for the gallant fight he is making. . . . Yes, it is. There he comes slowly down the aisle on his crutches. . . ." *Source:* George Palmer interview with Morgan Hoyt, National Park Service.

traced in his library. Frances Perkins, sitting near the rostrum, remembered that no one in the Garden seemed to breathe. Roosevelt looked "so pale, so thin, so delicate," she was afraid that if he did make it to the microphone he would be unable to summon the strength to make himself heard.

It seemed to take an age, but when he finally stood at the podium, unable even to wave for fear of falling, but grinning broadly, head thrown back and shoulders high, in the exaggerated gesture that would now become a trademark, the delegates rose to their feet and cheered for three minutes, and as they did so the sun broke through the clouds above the Garden skylight and poured down upon him.

Elated at being back in the center of events from which his paralysis had threatened forever to bar him, Franklin allowed his rich tenor to ring through the Garden with a new and telling passion:

> You equally who come from the great cities of the East and the plains and hills of the West, from the slopes of the Pacific and the homes and fields of the Southland, I ask you in all sincerity, in the balloting on that platform tomorrow, to keep first in your hearts and minds the words of Abraham Lincoln—"With malice toward none, with charity to all."

When he reached the speech's final words he very nearly sang them:

> . . . He has a power to strike at error and wrongdoing that makes his adversaries quail before him. He has a personality that carries to every hearer not only the sincerity but the righteousness of what he says. He is the "Happy Warrior" of the political battlefield. . . . Alfred E. Smith.

" . . . [T]he crowd just went crazy," Marion Dickerman remembered. "Oh it was stupendous, really stupendous!"

Frances Perkins saw that while Franklin continued to smile, his hands were now trembling and white-knuckled as they gripped the podium. He had been on his feet for well over thirty minutes and no provision seemed to have been made to shield his departure from the stage. "I saw around him all those fat slob politicians—men," she remembered, "and I knew they wouldn't think of it." She whispered to the woman beside her to follow her and rushed onstage to stand in front of Franklin as he turned to leave.[32]

---

32. This would become a standard ending to FDR's public appearances. While the audience continued to applaud, supporters would hurry up ostensibly to congratulate him, actually to shield his exit. Women, Miss Perkins remembered, were ideal for the purpose because their skirts masked the most. *Source:* George Martin, *Madame Secretary*, pages 184–185.

While the band swung into "The Sidewalks of New York" and the Smith delegates flooded into the aisles, Franklin at last permitted James to bring his wheelchair to the rear of the platform, to unlock his braces so that he could ease himself into it, and wheel him offstage. Behind him, the demonstration he set off lasted well over an hour.

That evening, the New York Delegation was to attend a reception at the Roosevelts'. Marion Dickerman arrived early to see if she could help Eleanor with the preparations and the butler asked her to come upstairs at once. Mr. Roosevelt wished to see her.

She found him sitting up in bed, pale and clearly exhausted, but smiling and holding wide his arms.

"Marion," he said, as they embraced, "I *did* it!"[33]

Despite the convention's universally warm feelings for Franklin, his plea for tolerance and compromise went unheeded by the deeply divided delegates. Most members of the platform committee wanted a plank deploring the practices of the powerful Ku Klux Klan, without denouncing it by name. A minority demanded a stronger and more specific condemnation of the hooded legion. McAdoo, not wishing to alienate any of the rural delegates who had helped give him his sizable but not decisive lead, refused to take sides. Smith, well behind McAdoo but with enough votes to deny his rival victory, refused to equivocate. The Klan was un-American, he told the press: "I had infinitely rather lose the nomination on an issue of principle, than be successful through resorting to subterfuge."

The two Klan planks reached the convention floor on the evening of June 29. The debate was savage and prolonged. William Jennings Bryan led the battle for McAdoo and the tepid plank, bent and shaky now but with the same thunderous voice that had three times made him the Democratic standard-bearer. Tammany had packed the Garden's galleries with Smith supporters whose fervor for their candidate

---

33. That Franklin was acutely sensitive to the delicate line between admiration for his pluck and pity for his condition is further evidenced in a letter he wrote to his half brother in January of 1922, after making another appearance at Madison Square Garden, this time as chairman of the building fund drive for Rosy's pet charity, the Cathedral of St. John the Divine.

I was scared to death when I stumped forward to call the meeting to order, as everybody had long faces and Pritchard's prayer only made the atmosphere more church-like. I had to do something as my own short address was exceedingly solemn, so I started off by grinning at the audience and remarking that it seemed natural to be back in Madison Square Garden again. That broke the ice and from then on all was smooth sailing.

Source: James Roosevelt Roosevelt Papers, FDRL.

was exceeded only by their raucous impatience with parliamentary procedure. As the old orator struggled to be heard, they jeered and cursed and chanted, "Oil, Oil, Oil."

"All the bums of New York" were there, Frances Perkins recalled, and their obscene catcalls "sort of sickened the [out-of-town] delegates because they screamed so much. . . . They thought that the meeting in Madison Square Garden was to make Al Smith President. . . . Why bother with all this other stuff?" Their behavior served only to confirm the country delegates' already dark suspicion of the big cities and their candidate.

A riot was prevented only by the presence of a beefed-up force of disciplined police officers—mostly Irish, but ecumenically willing to crack Catholic as well as Protestant heads if the job required it.

Roosevelt did what he could as a gentleman to soothe the wounded feelings of delegates appalled by Smith's supporters. Later, according to the Atlanta *Journal,* Georgians who attended the convention would prove "especially cordial" to him "because they appreciate the interest Mr. Roosevelt showed in them, and his courtesy in apologizing, as an Al Smith leader, for unfortunate and embarrassing incidents in connection with the convention."[34]

But nothing Franklin or anyone else could do could eliminate the bitterness that made the 1924 convention the most exhausting in history. It took thirteen hot days and 103 ballots before the delegates finally abandoned their first choices and nominated the conservative attorney and former Ambassador to London, John W. Davis of West Virginia. "The two factions lost everything that they had fought over," H. L. Mencken remembered. "It was as if Germany and France had fought over Alsace-Lorraine for centuries, then handed it over to England."[35]

As the *New York Herald-Tribune* wrote while the balloting was still

34. One such incident was entirely accidental. When a Georgian was recognized to second McAdoo's nomination, the band struck up "Marching Through Georgia" under the impression that it was the state song.

35. Davis would later find nearly every element of the New Deal distasteful, and at a wedding in early 1936 vowed that if the Democrats were returned to power and taxes rose, he would be forced to move to England. Sara Delano Roosevelt was also a wedding guest and suggested mildly that Mr. Davis might look into the British tax system before doing anything so rash.

About a year later, her son having been reelected by an unprecedented margin, she happened upon Davis again at another dinner and expressed elaborate astonishment at seeing him; she had assumed, she said, that he had long since settled in England. Davis covered his face with his hands and said, "Wasn't it wicked of me?" *Source:* Rita Halle Kleeman notepad, Kleeman Papers, FDRL.

going on, it was the riveting presence of Franklin Roosevelt the delegates would remember most enthusiastically.

> From the time Roosevelt made his speech in nomination of Smith . . . he has easily been the foremost figure on floor or platform. That is not because of his name. There are many Roosevelts. [How especially pleased Franklin must have been to read those words at last.] It is because without the slightest intention or desire to do anything of the sort, he has done for himself what he could not do for his candidate.
>
> Believing Roosevelt to be out of reach, the delegates cast a lingering look at him over their shoulders and renewed the search for somebody who could be nominated. . . . But always back to Roosevelt their gaze would go, and more than once it was found expedient to hush a little delegation which was talking about sending up his name, lest unforeseen results might happen. . . .

On his return home from the convention, Tom Pendergast, the distinctly unsentimental boss of Kansas City, spoke for many: ". . . you know I am seldom carried away," he told a friend, ". . . but I want to tell you that had Mr. Roosevelt . . . been physically able to withstand the campaign, he would have been named by acclamation. . . . He has the most magnetic personality of any individual I have ever met. . . ."

It is some measure of the emotional distance Eleanor Roosevelt now carefully kept from her husband that when she came to write about these events in her autobiography she remembered that "The brightest spot in the whole convention for me was the fact that Isabella Ferguson, who had now remarried, had come on for the convention. She was now Mrs. John C. Greenway, and he was [an alternate] delegate from Arizona."[36]

Eleanor was still not convinced that her husband's return to public life was permanent, that he could ever actually attain the presidency. "At that time," Frances Perkins remembered, ". . . Mrs. Roosevelt

---

36. Both Isabella and her new husband had always been Theodore Roosevelt Republicans, but Greenway had decided to join the Democrats in 1924, "after supporting the Col.," as Isabella wrote, "for 22 years," and his wife followed him into the party. The following year, Isabella gave birth to a son, Jack. Her second husband died of complications following gallbladder surgery in 1926.

Isabella then launched into her own career in politics: elected Democratic National Committeewoman from Arizona in 1928 and again in 1932, she seconded Franklin's nomination at Chicago, then served two terms in Congress. In 1940 she publicly opposed FDR's bid for a third term, an act which Franklin never forgave but which Eleanor did her best to overlook.

didn't have his comeback in mind. He was still pretty sick and pretty weak." But "I do hope that he'll keep in political life," Eleanor told Miss Perkins that summer. "I want him to keep himself interested in politics. This is what he cares for more than anything else. I don't want him forgotten. I want him to have a voice. . . . It's good for him."

Franklin played no further active part in the 1924 campaign, but Eleanor did. Her political convictions had much to do with that decision: when the all-male National Platform Committee failed to adopt the progressive planks she and her women's subcommittee had drawn up for the national platform, including calls for an end to child labor, a minimum wage, and an eight-hour day, she helped lead the successful fight to include them in the state party platform.

But her personal feelings—and those of Louis Howe—added impetus to her activity. Relations between the two branches of the Roosevelt family had not improved since 1920. Nicholas Longworth had especially infuriated Sara earlier in the year by pronouncing Franklin "a denatured Roosevelt," and no one in the Hyde Park circle—but especially not Howe—had forgotten Ted Jr.'s 1920 denunciations of his Democratic cousin as a "maverick." Now, they saw a way to get even.

By the time the Republicans of New York State met that summer, the oil scandal that had lightly touched Ted and Archie Roosevelt had so largely died away that they felt they could safely nominate Ted to challenge Al Smith for governor.

Smith ignored Teapot Dome during the campaign, warning his followers not to mention it for fear of creating sympathy for his attractive young opponent. Democratic newspapers ignored it, too.

But Howe could not. The campaign now provided him with what he saw as an irresistible opportunity to ensure that the earlier reports of Ted's political death had not been exaggerated. "He's been waiting to get even for he says a long time!" Eleanor said of Howe, and she proved his willing instrument. "From all we heard," Mrs. Theodore Roosevelt, Jr., wrote much later, "no one [among the Democrats] even mentioned oil, except Ted's cousin, Mrs. Franklin D. Roosevelt. . . ."

One afternoon that autumn, a bizarre vehicle turned into the driveway at Oldgate, Bamie Cowles's house in Farmington, Connecticut—an automobile over which was fitted a giant *papier-mâché* teapot whose spigot somehow poured forth authentic clouds of steam. Out of it stepped Eleanor, Marion, and Nancy, all wearing brown riding pants.

("If you think [Eleanor] looked bad in skirts," Bamie's son remembered, "you should have seen her in those pants!")[37]

At Howe's eager urging, they had spent several days following Ted Jr. around the state, speaking to the large, curious crowds the teapot drew: the Republican candidate for governor, Eleanor told one roadside gathering, was "a personally nice young man whose public service record shows him willing to do the bidding of his friends." Now, she and her friends had driven across the Connecticut border in hopes of finding beds for the night and, because Eleanor's Auntie Bye was so fond of her niece, she provided them. "Mother liked Eleanor," W. Sheffield Cowles, Jr., remembered, "so she just swallowed it."[38]

It had been "a rough stunt," Eleanor admitted in later years, and it had repercussions within the family. Ted Roosevelt—who was badly beaten by Smith despite Calvin Coolidge's easy victory in the state— never forgave her. Neither did his wife. Sixteen years later, complimenting Corinne Alsop in 1936 for being "a grand political enemy" because she never let political differences damage family feeling, Eleanor said she was "a little distressed" to hear that Ted's wife had refused even to be introduced by her son Elliott at a non-partisan meeting in Fort Worth, Texas. "It seems to me unfortunate," she said, "to harbor that kind of political feeling."[39]

37. Bamie evidently agreed, writing to her niece Corinne Alsop:

I just hate to have Eleanor let herself look as she does. Though never handsome, she always had to me a charming effect, but Alas and lackaday! Since politics have become her choicest interest all her charm has disappeared, and the fact is emphasized by the companions she chooses to bring with her. I am so sorry, and feel a good deal as I used to about Kate Marquand when she was in one of her very virtuous moods and spent her entire time taking charge of the Girls' Clubs: I told her that while doing that kind of work it was more than ever important that her front hair should be becomingly arranged; that she would have far more influence over the girls than if she assumed an uncompromisingly plain aspect.

Years later, Corinne, who was fond of Eleanor but sometimes found her "tediously noble," suggested that her curious clothing was evidence of a certain lack of humor: "Otherwise how could one who knew little about children and seemed to care less . . . have edited *Babies, Just Babies* [the child-care magazine Eleanor agreed to edit for a time while First Lady]; nor could one order two similar brown tweed suits for herself and Nancy Cook with plus-fours. They were a sight . . . no artist could paint."

Source: Alsop Family Papers, Houghton Library, Harvard University.

38. Campaigning for his own party in 1916, Franklin, too, had sought refuge with Bamie, wiring her: ARE YOU WILLING TO TAKE IN A DEMOCRAT FOR THE NIGHT? She always was, provided the name was Roosevelt.

39. Sara, too, was grateful for the dignified way in which Corinne Alsop kept her personal and political feelings carefully segregated. "For this you are *kind*," she wrote on November 10, 1936. "You must be disappointed [by the colossal Democratic victory]. I have not minded enemies or *anyone's* standing for their principles, but I do mind the lies and *inventions* of jealous people. I have always been my son's severest critic, but I really do not see how people can say *bad* things

Back in June, as the roll calls droned on at the Democratic Convention, Franklin had spent time talking to an old friend, George Foster Peabody, a Wall Street banker and frequent campaign contributor, whose winter home at Columbus, Georgia, was not far from the tiny, threadbare town of Bullochville. There, he had recently bought a half-interest in the Meriwether Inn, a rundown resort hotel on a pine-covered hillside from which flowed thermal waters, known as Warm Springs since the Civil War for their supposed ability to cure an eclectic variety of diseases. The place was in terrible shape and ten miles from the nearest paved road, Peabody admitted, but he believed it could be made into a going proposition again. Franklin might like to try its waters sometime.

Roosevelt expressed only mild, polite interest.

But later in the summer, Peabody wrote him a letter and enclosed in it a testimonial from a young Georgia polio in whom the warm, mineralized waters seemed to have brought about miraculous improvement. Louis Joseph had been confined to a wheelchair since childhood, he said. Visiting Warm Springs with relatives three years before, he had begged to be allowed to swim in the big outdoor pool and when immersed in the buoyant water had felt instantly able to move his legs as never before. Three seasons of steady swimming, combined with hours of walking back and forth across the bottom of the pool, had enabled him to walk on dry land with the aid of two canes.

---

about him. Still, I do not forget how furious I used to be with the horrid things said about Theodore, and how I always defended him. . . ."

Characteristic of the more unforgivingly Republican Roosevelts was a letter sent to FDR during the 1932 campaign against Herbert Hoover and written by Mary Willis Roosevelt, the second wife and widow of Theodore Roosevelt's uncle, James Alfred Roosevelt.

Dear Franklyn,

I shall not sail under false colors, but tell you, that, because of your running mate [Congressman John Nance Garner] of Texas, and your silly attitude about that "forgotten man" and all the rest that you have said about the President in your very bad political strategy, in attacking him, a thing that has always been considered bad form in politics I am unreservedly against you—

James who saw hundreds of men a week in his work, said there were no "forgotten men" but plenty who thought they were owed something for *nothing*, was dead against such ideas of socialistic patting them on the back, as you are handing out. You have only belittled yourself by talking like this, and I know many people who, because of it, have decided they will *not* vote for you. . . .

In replying, FDR could not resist addressing this very distant cousin as "Dear Marye," then added: "Thank you very much for writing to me. It is good to hear from you. I am sorry that you feel as you do, but I must tell you quite frankly that it really never occurred to me that you would vote for me." *Sources:* Alsop Family Papers, Houghton Library, Harvard University; James Roosevelt (and Sidney Shallet), *Affectionately, FDR,* pages 233–234.

Franklin's interest was now piqued and Peabody's partner in the Bullochville venture hurried north to see him. Tom Loyless was a Georgia newspaper columnist, a gaunt, gray-haired Democrat who had waged a fight against the Ku Klux Klan that had lost him his own newspaper and nearly got him killed, and who had since channeled his improving zeal into transforming the old resort he remembered fondly from his boyhood into an up-to-date health spa.

Franklin Roosevelt was celebrated and wealthy and a polio, just the sort of man whose backing Loyless needed to help him make that transformation. He described the Louis Joseph case in greater detail and promised that Joseph himself would be available to talk to Mr. Roosevelt about it whenever he chose to come down.

Franklin agreed to stop by in early October and have a look at the place.[40]

40. Had William A. Milliken of Washington written Franklin a couple of weeks earlier, history might have been quite different. "If you feel strong enough to stand the trip," he told Franklin, "there is a water in Tenn., near Knoxville, known as 'Tate Springs.' I know of some most remarkable cures by it. Some sound like a miracle. Secretary [of the Treasury Andrew] Mellon's father was cured there after trying everything in Europe and all the Doctors. I believe . . . a week or two there will do you a world of good. I fully believe it saved my life in 1884 when I had worn myself down by over-work. . . . Pardon my taking this liberty but we need just now all the brainy, honest men in existence."

Franklin wrote back on September 5 to thank him for the tip, "especially as I had only ten days ago about decided to go down to some Springs in Georgia this autumn which seem to me very similar to Tate Springs."

CHAPTER

16

OLD DOCTOR ROOSEVELT

I N THE AUTUMN of 1924, more than three years after infantile paralysis had done its damage to him, Franklin Roosevelt was still waging
a two-front war against the disease. Despite uniformly discouraging
counsel from his doctors and in the face of his wife's impatience with
what she considered his unwillingness to face reality, he remained
determined that he would somehow find a way to restore his wasted
muscles to something like their old strength, would one day stride
forward as he once had, without braces or crutches or canes, to reenter
political life and resume his interrupted climb to the presidency. The
laws governing ordinary polios, he remained convinced, did not apply
to him. He could not be President unless he could walk; therefore, he
would walk.

But if he could not finally manage that—and no one claims ever
to have heard him even suggest that he would not succeed—he knew
that he would have to discover a better way to *seem* to walk than on
crutches, to relieve the anxiety of his old supporters and reassure new
ones that he was up to the job. He had demonstrated dramatically at
the New York convention in June that he was no longer entirely
immobilized, but he knew better than any of those who had cheered
him then how precarious his balance was, what a physical toll the
simple act of standing took.

His years now fell into a regular pattern: as few weeks in New
York as he could get away with and still keep his job with the F&D;

the rest spent wherever he seemed most likely to make progress toward recovery.

A physiotherapist once asked him just what it was he hoped to achieve by continuing to exercise, year after arduous year. He wanted to stand easily in front of people, he said, so that they would forget he was crippled.

If he could not do that, he knew, he had no future.

That effort now took him to Georgia.

Some fifty people were gathered around the Southern Railway station at Bullochville shortly after dark on Friday, October 3, 1924. It was a big crowd for a little town, home then to just 470 citizens. A famous man was said to be coming in on the evening train from Atlanta, and famous men rarely came to Bullochville anymore. Among those who had turned out to see him were all the town's most prominent citizens, including E. B. Doyle, the farmer who served as part-time mayor, the town's lone physician, Dr. Neal Kitchens, and the two newcomers who were trying to revive the old Warm Springs resort just up the road, George Foster Peabody and Tom Loyless.

The train pulled in slowly, all the cars but the last battered sleeper hissing past the short platform. A porter opened the rear door and jumped down to put the steps in place. Two women got off first. One was tall and gaunt, the other younger but with dark hair streaked with gray; she smiled widely as she shook hands with Peabody and Loyless and their companions.

Then the famous man himself appeared, grinning broadly and shouting greetings, but leaning heavily on crutches. His broad shoulders filled the door, a young woman in the crowd remembered, but his legs seemed to dangle "like strings." A black man stood behind him, apparently his servant. Another black man, recruited by Loyless, stepped up to help. Together, they lifted him gingerly down to the platform. "How nice of you all to welcome us!" he said, once he was again safely leaning on his crutches.

Franklin Roosevelt had come to see Warm Springs for himself. There did not seem to be much to see at first: the tiny depot with its twin entrances marked WHITE and COLORED; the three-storied Tuscawilla Hotel, right next door, the largest building in town with a big rusty Coca-Cola sign hanging over the unpaved street; and, as the car pulled away from the station and started up the red clay road, a scattering of shacks lit by kerosene lamps and half-hidden among the pines.

Then, even those lights disappeared as they turned off the main road and rattled through deep woods for half a mile or so, before pulling up in front of a small whitewashed cottage whose owners, Mr. and Mrs. William Hart of nearby Columbus, had agreed to let the Roosevelts occupy it for as long as they liked. It was not prepossessing, either; the scuttling of squirrels chasing one another back and forth across the roof kept Franklin from sleeping late the next morning, and when Eleanor woke up, she remembered, sunlight streamed in through cracks in the walls.

The pines that surrounded the cottage were fragrant and the weather was pleasant, but there were no spectacular views as there were at Campobello, and the Meriwether Inn, the huge, turreted resort hotel that loomed in the distance, was clearly a firetrap, despite the fresh coats of yellow, green, and white paint that George Peabody had hastily authorized when he learned his wealthy visitor really was coming south. The cluster of fourteen derelict cottages and a separate dancing pavilion that went with it—"one of the most perfect dancing floors to be found at any Southern Summer resort," according to Peabody's latest brave brochure—were in still worse shape.

But it was the mineralized waters, not the hotel, that had drawn Franklin to Warm Springs, and Peabody and Loyless made sure that shortly after he had downed his breakfast, Louis Joseph came knocking on the cottage door. Joseph, who entered the living room on his own feet, as advertised, using one cane but wearing no braces, was living testimony to the springs' restorative powers, and Franklin eagerly interrogated him about his case. Joseph's recovery was not perhaps as complete or startling as Peabody had initially made it out to be. He had discarded his braces almost as soon as he arrived in Warm Springs in 1922, so it seemed unlikely that his time in the pool had actually had much to do with that initial breakthrough; he still had to use a cane except when inside his house—otherwise "I might fall down," he told a later interviewer—and he was not at all sure that it was the warm water itself that had helped him so much as the daily exercising he had done while his legs were submerged in it. All he knew was that he had been able to walk in steadily shallower water until he could do so on land.

Joseph had come a long way back from infantile paralysis, much further than Roosevelt had. Were Franklin to progress anywhere near so far, he would be exultant.

Roosevelt wanted to try the pool that same afternoon. His first sight of it was not especially reassuring. The season had ended. The bright blue surface of the water in the big T-shaped pool was undisturbed by any other swimmers, and the cement that surrounded it was cracked and stained. He would have to be undressed and then helped on with his bathing suit in the public dressing room, his helplessness and his wasted limbs exposed to the curious gaze of anyone who happened in. Roy did his best to limit his employer's humiliation, fashioning a private cubicle in the dressing room by hanging canvas over ropes, then got him ready, wheeled him to the pool's edge, and gently helped him down into the water.

It felt wonderful—astonishingly buoyant, according to another first-time bather, with "a perceptible soft, sulphurous . . . odor," and blessedly warm. Poor circulation was a chronic problem with polios. Cold water quickly made withered muscles ache. Able-bodied bathers often found the 90-degree water at Warm Springs too warm to stay in for long without feeling enervated, but paralytics could comfortably remain for up to two hours.

Lying back in it for the first time, one polio later marvelled, "all friction and weight of limbs disappears. . . ." Immersed until only his head and neck were above the surface, Franklin found that his unbraced legs would hold him upright. By thrashing his powerful arms and shoulders he could move himself back and forth across the pool, his largely useless limbs suspended below and behind him, and when Louis Joseph suggested that he grip the edge of the pool as he faced the water, and see if he couldn't raise his stronger leg—the right— toward the surface, he thought he could feel it begin to respond, lifted in part by the astonishingly supportive water.

As he swam and splashed, Tom Loyless arrived at poolside, bringing with him Dr. James Johnson, a young physician from Manchester, four miles away. Johnson was a general practitioner and no expert on infantile paralysis, but he had monitored Louis Joseph's progress with interest, and suggested to Roosevelt that if the Joseph case was any guide, he could expect to feel positive effects in three weeks or so.

Franklin was predisposed to believe him: he had adamantly refused to accept Dr. Lovett's grim forecast as to his further recovery, clinging instead, to the one hint of hope that Lovett had ever given him, the fact that a handful of his patients who had exercised regularly in warm water had shown unexpected gains in strength. Besides, the whole Roosevelt family believed in the efficacy of mineralized waters for every sort of ailment. Franklin and his mother were both convinced that the summers they had spent with Mr. James at Bad Nauheim and other European spas had greatly prolonged his life, and Sara now took the waters annually as a preventive; Rosy took them, too, believing them salutary for all his afflictions, genuine and imaginary.

After Franklin's swim, Loyless drove the Roosevelts and Missy through the Georgia countryside. Franklin loudly admired the pines and peach orchards and mountain views. Eleanor privately deplored the untidiness, the poverty, the tumbled-down shanties of the blacks; she was put off by the expansive friendliness of their new neighbors and horrified when she saw that there was no butcher shop in town, that live, trussed-up chickens had to be bought at a nearby farm, brought home squawking, and dispatched on the premises.

She started back to New York the next day. "It is too bad that Eleanor had to leave so soon," Franklin told his mother, "but she and I both feel it is important for her not to be away at the end of the [Al Smith] campaign as long as I have to be myself."

The fact that Missy Le Hand was to stay on with him in his cottage after Eleanor left was carefully not mentioned. Sara was already troubled at how little time her peripatetic daughter-in-law spent with Franklin—to the end of her days she would end her letters to him, "I hope dear Eleanor is with you"—and she now found Missy's new proximity to her son frankly worrisome. She was not fooled when he tried to divert her attention the same way he had while seeing young women whose names he did not wish her to know during his years at Groton and Harvard—by simply failing to mention her presence in his otherwise chatty letters home—nor was she mollified when he later told her Missy's presence was required to help him keep up a "huge and constant local correspondence."

Eleanor knew better, and Franklin was more candid with her:

> [Life is] just the same day after day and there is no variety to give landmarks. The mornings as you know are wholly taken up with the pool and four of the afternoons we have sat out on the lawn, or as Roy calls it, the "yard," and I have worked at stamps or cheques or accounts or have played rummy with Missy. The other three afternoons we have gone motoring with Mr. and Mrs. Loyless and we have seen the country pretty thoroughly. I like him ever so much and she is nice but not broad in her interests, but she chatters away to Missy in the back seat and I hear an occasional yes or no from Missy to prove she is not sleeping.

One evening, Franklin wheeled himself out onto the cottage porch and called out to Tom Loyless and his sister and a few friends to

"Come on over" and have a cocktail. Missy did the mixing, and as she emerged from the kitchen in her apron, the tray of drinks rattling cheerfully, a knock was heard at the door. Roosevelt called out, "Come in, come in."

It was the local Baptist preacher, come to talk over his community's future with the distinguished visitor. Without missing a step, Missy put the tray down on a side table, draped a tablecloth over the glasses, and slipped back into the kitchen. Roosevelt remained suitably grave during the pastor's visit, but when he had left the cottage at last, Loyless remembered, Missy and Franklin were "agonized with laughter."[1]

Between 1925 and 1928, Franklin would spend more than half his time—116 of 208 weeks—away from home, struggling to find a way to regain his feet. Eleanor was with him just four of those 116 weeks, and his mother was with him for two.

Missy Le Hand was with him for 110 of them. Despite her own delicate health—she tired easily and had a weak heart, the aftereffect of childhood rheumatic fever—it was she, not Eleanor, who remained at his side during all those months of discouragement, frustration, and enforced idleness, she who would stay with him day after day through all the Albany and White House years until a stroke felled her in 1941.

It seems clear that she was in love with him. Her few surviving notes to Franklin are loving, tolerant, wifely: "*Please* have the dentist come down if the tooth is not *all* well"; "Thank you for your nice letters—you are sweet to write. I know how many things you *want* to do"; "Gosh, it will be good to get my eyes on you again", "This place is horrible when you are away." She took enthusiastic interest in all his hobbies—"I am sending you the envelopes of the foreign correspondence [for the stamps], but am keeping the letters for Mr. Howe, OK?"; "Have a swell time. I'm glad you got your tarpon—get a lot more"—and was perfectly content to take part in them simply for the pleasure of being in his company. When she took a rare vacation away from him in 1926, she sent him a pressed flower she had found

---

1. Eleanor's presence during Prohibition days had the same inhibiting effect as the pastor's. In 1932, a Southern editor, arriving at the Roosevelt cottage with something in a paper bag, asked before entering, "Is Mrs. Roosevelt here?" Told she was not, he said, "Then it's all right. I just brought a jug of corn for the Governor."

Meriwether County remained dry long after Prohibition ended—it is still hard to buy a drink there—and, according to Henry A. Wallace, it later fell to Henry Morgenthau, Jr., to see that the Little White House was well stocked with decent liquor before the President arrived. *Sources:* Frank Freidel, *FDR and the South*, page 20; Interview with Henry A. Wallace, Rexford G. Tugwell Papers.

imbedded beneath the gleaming surface of a Norwegian glacier, along with a pledge that "I'm going to be so good when I get back and never get cross or anything. Isn't that wonderful?"

She was attractive if not beautiful, intelligent and amusing, and over the years she would draw a number of suitors, including the patrician diplomat William C. Bullitt, and Earl Miller, the strapping New York State policeman, whose apparent closeness to Eleanor would itself spawn gossip during the 1930s. Missy deflected them all. Wondering why, one close friend finally concluded that "she was just too devoted and interested in FDR. She never met anybody that would come up to Roosevelt."

The precise nature of his feelings for her are harder to fathom. Many years later, at a Delano dinner party in Manhattan during which the subject of Franklin's early romance with Lucy Mercer came up, his outspoken cousin Laura Delano would declare that "Missy was the only woman Franklin ever loved, *everybody* knows that."

He may well have loved her. Clearly he relished her company and relied on her for the amusement and emotional support and affectionate praise his mother had raised him to expect from the women closest to him, but which his wife was rarely able to summon. The contrast between the two women could not have been more clear: Missy shielded him from importunate visitors; Eleanor encouraged them to call upon him if they shared her views. Eleanor upbraided him for things he'd left undone; Missy praised him for all that he managed to accomplish and showed for his daily health the solicitude Eleanor thought unnecessary.[2]

Missy relaxed and amused him, made herself available around the clock, offered sound advice when asked—and almost always remembered to maintain a discreet silence until then. "She was [also] the frankest of the President's associates," the speechwriter Samuel Rosenman recalled, "never hesitating to tell him unpleasant truths or to express an unfavorable opinion about his work," but, unlike his wife, she rarely opposed him in public and was invariably careful to make him see the advantage to *him* of an alternative course of action.[3]

2. Sitting just outside his White House office, Missy was ever alert to the slightest sign of illness. "Catching a sound as the door swings open to admit a caller," a journalist noted, "she will march in. 'Why are you sneezing?' Or 'Did you cough?' " *Source:* Doris Fleeson, "Missy— To Do This," *The Saturday Evening Post*, January 8, 1938.

3. The speechwriter Samuel Rosenman recalled the way she sometimes made her opinions felt. During the 1936 campaign, Henry Morgenthau, Jr., suggested that the President might consider delivering as a campaign address at Forbes Field in Pittsburgh a speech that had been prepared for him on the topic of fiscal policy. FDR listened quietly as his old friend began to

And she shared in Franklin's extravagant love of nonsense. He once received at Warm Springs a barely literate letter from a maker of arch supports and foot appliances named Charles Ritz, asking questions Roosevelt considered intrusive. It is impossible to imagine Eleanor working with him to fill out the gag responses he and Missy got up to amuse themselves (but did not send):

Can you walk without a cain or some assistants?
I cannot walk without a *CAIN* because I am not *ABEL*. (This is very subtle but perhaps you can get "Punch" to print it.)

Does both your shoes fit you even?
They fit me EVEN unless by accident I put on an ODD shoe—Ha Ha

Are you inclined to have a weakness also in the ankle?
I have my little weaknesses like anybody else. (Rotten)

Are you sure of your step?
We all have to watch our steps with so many Prohibition agents around. (Not so good.)

Have you any pain below the hips? If so, tell me where.
My principal pain is in the neck when I get letters like this.

"Missy's sense of humor is very much like Roosevelt's," a perceptive journalist wrote:

She has a trilling laugh and finds something humorous in almost every situation. She watches her man so closely that she can see the slightest changes in his emotional attitude before they have become apparent to anyone else. She knows when Roosevelt's thick layer of Dutch stubbornness is coming to the surface before he knows it himself. She knows when he is really listening to the person who is talking to him and when he is merely being polite.

She was protective of her special relationship with her boss. A close friend once marvelled at the way, through the sheer infectious power of his laughter, FDR seemed able to make all his listeners laugh, no matter how bad the joke. "That's his political laugh," Missy explained, but later, when the friend used the phrase herself, "she got madder than hell. *I* wasn't supposed to say that."

---

read it aloud. "The President realized right away," Rosenman recalled, "that it would never do [but] was apparently steeled to hear it to the end. Missy was not quite so polite. At the end of the second page she stood and with great firmness announced: 'By this time all of the bleachers are empty, and the folks are beginning to walk out of the grandstand.' As she sauntered out of the room, we all burst into laughter, including the Secretary of the Treasury himself." *Source:* Samuel I. Rosenman, *Working with Roosevelt*, page 113.

But for all her intimacy with Franklin—and perhaps to ensure that it would not be intruded upon too often—she was careful always to maintain the warmest possible relations with Eleanor. "I have had such a happy year," she wrote her one Christmas in the White House:

> I hope you know how very much I appreciate being with you—*not* because of the [White House]—but because I'm *with you!*
>
> I hope you have as Merry a Christmas as you should have for all you have done for others. I know the "doing" has been fun for you, too. I love you so much. I never can tell you how very much.
>
> As ever
> Missy

For her part, Eleanor was privately scornful of Missy's largely unqualified admiration for her husband, but she was also grateful to her for performing the daily services for him that she was disinclined to do herself, and often troubled by the way her husband accepted the younger woman's strenuous devotion as somehow his due.[4]

Whether Franklin expressed his affection for Missy physically is unknown and unknowable. He could have: infantile paralysis had not rendered him impotent—examining physicians specifically noted that it had not. And some visitors, startled by Missy's constant presence aboard the *Larooco,* or at Warm Springs (where she often occupied her own bedroom in Franklin's cottage), or, later, elsewhere, including the Governor's Mansion and at the White House (she had her own quarters in both residences), thought there was enough circumstantial evidence to suggest that Missy was Franklin's mistress as well as his

---

4. In this last, her daughter Anna once suggested, she was being hypocritical:

I think this applied with Mother as well as with Father. The people who worked with them had to be just as if they had no lives of their own. I think both of them unwittingly and unknowingly even to themselves—it never occurred to them that these people lived their lives through them, and had nothing of their own. The same is true of Mother's [long-time secretary] Miss [Malvina] Thompson. She never—for years and years—had a life of her own. They [Missy and Miss Thompson] were "attachments."

. . . I used to just cringe sometimes when I'd hear Mother at 11:30 at night say to Tommy, "I've still got a number of columns to do. Come on, you've got to take a column." And this weary, weary, woman who'd just been working . . . and didn't have Mother's stamina would sit down at a typewriter. . . . I remember one time when Tommy with asperity said, "You'll have to speak louder, I can't hear you." And [Mother's] reply was, "If you will listen, you can hear *perfectly* well!"

Source: Bernard Asbell, *The FDR Memoirs,* page 246; Bernard Asbell, interview with Anna Roosevelt Halsted, Anna Roosevelt Halsted Papers, FDRL.

faithful secretary and companion—and to relish spreading stories about their relationship during the presidential years.[5]

Grace Tully, Missy's colleague and successor, later denied them all. "Missy let none of this bother her . . . ," she wrote, "and knew because of the high esteem in which she was held by her associates that nothing these people could say could in any way harm her or her reputation, which was beyond reproach."

Long after both Franklin and Missy were dead, troubled friends and family members continued to do their best to paper over the undeniable fact of her constant presence at his side, not because they disapproved of it—no one, in Roosevelt's circle or out of it, seems ever actively to have disliked Missy; one of Franklin's intimates thought her "a saint"—but because they feared it might damage the posthumous reputation of her employer.[6]

Even the Roosevelt children divided over the exact nature of their father's relationship with his secretary. Elliott would one day put his name to a book alleging that they had been lovers, but his sole evidence seems to be that once, aboard the *Larooco,* he saw Missy playfully sit on his father's lap while wearing her bathrobe, and that her bedroom had been next to his in the Governor's Mansion. "I think Missy became utterly and completely devoted to this man. . . . ," Anna once said. "She *was* the office wife, quote, unquote." But she joined her brothers James and Franklin Jr. in doubting that their association went beyond that. Elliott's alleged evidence proved little, they argued: their father was paralyzed, after all, and frequently received visitors in his bedroom, where he read and dictated much of his mail.[7]

5. Once, when FDR urged Joseph P. Kennedy to be a bit more circumspect about his long-time liaison with the movie star Gloria Swanson, Kennedy is supposed to have shot back, "Not until you get rid of Missy Le Hand!" It seems unlikely that even Joe Kennedy would have been so crudely defiant of the touchy man whose favor he needed, but that the story was widely believed in Washington is evidence of the ubiquity of the rumors about the President and his secretary. *Source:* Michael P. Beschloss, *Kennedy and Roosevelt,* page 113.

6. Years later, John Lawrence would loyally allege, for example, that "I spent about a month each year with [Roosevelt] on *Larooco.* When neither [of us] had guests, Louis Howe and Missy LeHand were aboard." In fact, Lawrence spent just a few days aboard the houseboat of which he was co-owner, on its third cruise in 1926, and Louis Howe visited the boat just once that same year. Guests came and went; Franklin and Missy were the *Larooco*'s permanent passengers.

7. Something besides propriety may have been at work to keep the closeness between Franklin and his secretary platonic. Infantile paralysis invariably has psychological as well as physical aftereffects, and among some polios—especially those, like Roosevelt, who had always been skittish of emotional commitment and genuine intimacy and proud of their good looks and athletic physiques—the possibility of further failure and humiliation posed by sex ultimately proves too great a risk to run.

Raymond Moley believed that the relationship between the President and his secretary was

The fact that Eleanor remained obliged to Missy at least suggests that while relations between her husband and his secretary may sometimes have seemed flirtatious (Roosevelt flirted constantly and harmlessly with almost all the women in his circle, except his wife), they were not physical—or at least that Eleanor assumed they were not.

Marion Dickerman thought that Eleanor avoided "the belittling emotion of jealousy" when it came to Missy, largely because she could not believe that anyone could ever replace Lucy Mercer in her husband's affections, and certainly not a mere secretary. For all her emotional estrangement from Franklin, Eleanor never fell entirely out of love with him, and in later years did prove acutely jealous of several women whom she felt monopolized his attention: Betsy Cushing, James's vivacious first wife; Princess Martha of Norway, who was a frequent guest at Hyde Park and in the White House during the war; Harry Hopkins's second wife, Louise, who lived in the White House; even her own daughter, Anna, to whom FDR turned for cheerful companionship during the last, lonely year of his life. ("She was apprehensive of anyone whom she felt got too close," Anna remembered.) All of these women belonged to the same class to which she and her husband belonged and therefore could legitimately be seen by her as rivals. For all her intimacy with her husband, Missy Le Hand seems to have remained, at least in Eleanor's eyes, an employee.

Sara was not so complacent. She had disapproved so strongly of Franklin's having lived aboard the *Larooco* with his secretary the year before, in fact, that when Missy returned to the boat after her father's funeral, Eleanor thought it best not to mention it to her mother-in-law. "I haven't yet told Mama that Missy is back," she assured Franklin then. "I think she has more peace of mind when she doesn't know things!"

Franklin's mother eventually came to accept the presence of the sunny, unassuming young woman whose devotion to her son was matched only by her own: "Much love [to] . . . nice little 'Missy,'" she would write Franklin later. "She knows what I think of her." But at

---

free of sexual intimacy, but for still another reason: "Everyone assumed [Roosevelt] was indifferent to sex. I always attributed this to religion, his class upbringing and that sort of thing. But he was interested in a different kind of relationship with a woman, friendly and close without being sexually intimate. We're so obsessed today with sex that we can't understand a relationship that doesn't include it. But there's no doubt that Missy was as close to being a wife as he ever had—or could have." *Sources:* Raymond Moley, *The First New Deal,* pages 273–275. For a fuller discussion of the special problems sex sometimes poses for polios, see Hugh Gallagher, *FDR's Splendid Deception,* pages 130–141.

least while Sara was in residence at Springwood and her son came home to stay, arrangements were always made for his secretary to sleep elsewhere.

Franklin swam and sunbathed at the pool every morning, and nearly everyone in town managed to drop by to shake his hand. He enjoyed the attention, was cordial to everybody. Many years later an old man who had been a small boy then remembered timidly asking Mr. Roosevelt why he used such a long cigarette holder. "Because," Franklin laughed, "my doctor told me to stay as far away from cigarettes as possible."

Peabody and Loyless persuaded the town to change its name from Bullochville to Warm Springs, and Roosevelt was invited to officiate at the town hall ceremony.

"On Wednesday," Franklin told his mother toward the end of his two-week stay in Georgia, "the people of Warm Springs are giving me a supper and reception in the Town Hall and on Friday evening, our last day, I am to go to Manchester . . . for another supper and speech. I think every organization and town in Georgia has asked me to some kind of party. . . .

"When I get back [to New York] I am going to have a long talk with Mr. George Foster Peabody. I feel that a great 'cure' for infantile paralysis and kindred diseases could well be established here."

Franklin wanted to buy Warm Springs. He had persuaded himself that the shabby old resort could become fashionable and profitable again while simultaneously providing aftercare for polios.

Almost no one except Tom Loyless agreed. Eleanor doubted her husband had the patience to make a go of such an ambitious undertaking. Basil O'Connor, who took the train down from New York at Franklin's request so that he could discuss the plans with Loyless in person, advised his partner against full involvement: a hard choice would have to be made right away between vacation spot and medical facility, O'Connor argued, or both would surely fail. George Peabody's asking price was appallingly high—$200,000, roughly twice what he had paid for it just a few years earlier—and the attorney was privately concerned that if Roosevelt committed himself to the Georgia resort, he would have still less time for the law practice that was already suffering from his prolonged absences.

Franklin was unperturbed. Warm Springs offered him an opportunity to be in complete, personal charge of a big project and, for all his prominence and fame, Franklin Roosevelt had never run anything on his own. Despite his many broad hints about who was *really* in charge of the Navy Department, during his showy time there he had always finally had to answer to Josephus Daniels; his running mate had set the agenda when he ran for Vice President in 1920; at the F&D, he was merely one of several vice presidents answerable to a committee of Baltimore businessmen. Even at home, he was not really in charge: his mother owned his Manhattan and Hyde Park houses; it was she, not he, who gave the orders at Springwood.

Warm Springs would be his alone, and it would become a haven for him from both the women who had been dominant in his life, a place free from the formality that prevailed at Hyde Park and that left him at liberty to do as much or as little exercising as he wished, to indulge in the sort of undergraduate good times that he liked, that made Eleanor uneasy, and with which Missy saw no need ever to interfere.

In Roosevelt's mind, then, the resort's risks were easily outweighed by its promise. About the same time, Cleburne Gregory, a reporter for the Atlanta *Journal,* was sent down to see Franklin by his publisher, Major Jack Cohen, an influential Democrat who may have been doing Peabody and Loyless a favor by providing a little free publicity for their struggling facility. In any case, Gregory swam and chatted with Roosevelt for three days, then returned to Atlanta to write his story, which appeared as the lead article in the *Journal*'s Sunday supplement on October 26, beneath the headline FRANKLIN ROOSEVELT WILL SWIM TO HEALTH. Alongside it ran a carefully posed photograph of a grinning Roosevelt at the edge of the pool, a newspaper spread across his legs so that while they were clearly seen to be reduced in strength it was impossible to assess the full extent of the damage infantile paralysis had done to them.

Franklin left Warm Springs for New York the day the story first ran, but the article was soon syndicated all over the country:

> Franklin D. Roosevelt, New York lawyer and banker, Assistant Secretary of the Navy during the World War, and Democratic nominee for Vice President is literally swimming his way back to health and strength at Warm Springs, Georgia. . . .
>
> Mr. Roosevelt and Mr. Loyless, in adjoining cottages, are the only residents of the dozen or so small cottages surrounding the [Meriwether Inn] at the present time. The hotel has closed for the winter season. . . . The distinguished visitor has the large swimming pool to himself two hours or more each day. . . .

He swims, dives, uses the swinging rings and horizontal bars over the water and finally crawls out on the concrete pier for a sun bath that lasts another hour. Then he dresses, has lunch, rests a bit on the delightfully shady porch, and spends the afternoon [being driven] over the countryside, in which he is intensely interested. . . .

"I am deriving wonderful benefit from my stay here," Mr. Roosevelt said. "This place is great. See that right leg? It is the first time I have been able to move it at all in three years."[8] Mr. Roosevelt does not attribute any medicinal effects to the Warm Springs water, but he gives the water credit for his ability to remain in it for two hours or more without tiring in the least, and the rest of the credit for his improvement is given to Georgia's sunshine.

Not only are the swims and sun baths delightful innovations to Mr. Roosevelt, but his method of living is enchanting. . . . Living a full half mile from the town of . . . Bullochville, he is protected from the intrusion of the curious. . . .

"The best infantile paralysis specialist in New York told me that the only way to overcome the effects of the disease was to swim as much as possible, and bask in the sunlight," [he said]. "Conditions here are ideal for both prescriptions. The water in some way relaxes muscles drawn taut by the disease, and gives the limbs much greater action. The sunshine has curative effects, I understand."

So marked have been the benefits in his case, Mr. Roosevelt plans to return to Warm Springs in March or April and remain for two or three months. At that time he will build a cottage on a hilltop.

"Say! Let's get one of the hot dogs this man makes just outside the swimming pool. They're great," Mr. Roosevelt challenged With him everything in Warm Springs is "Great" or "Fine" or "Wonderful." That is the spirit that has carried him to remarkable heights for a man just past his fortieth year, and it is the spirit that is going to restore him to his pristine health and vigor, for political and financial battles and successes in the years to come.

"Anna," eleven-year-old Franklin Jr. wrote to his sister in early February, 1925, "Chief is very well but seems to grow more and more lonesome, like me and Johnny. The house seems just like an emty waistbasket. Now that Father has left, Mother seems always to be on the go."
Franklin had spent three chilly months in New York and Hyde Park after leaving Warm Springs, then left his family again for Florida. He was carried back aboard the *Larooco* on February 2, 1925. The

8. The reporter evidently heard this wrong: Roosevelt had long been able at least to twitch his right leg; it was his left that remained almost totally lifeless.

houseboat's second cruise began badly: the New York train was twenty-four hours late reaching Miami; someone had stolen much of the furniture over the winter and all of it had to be replaced before they could get under way; the entire executive council of the American Federation of Labor and their wives—thirty in all—had to be entertained on deck.

Even the fishing seemed slow at first. But on the 11th, off Conch Reef, Franklin's luck seemed to turn. Fishing from their launch, he, Missy, and a boy from a friend's yacht caught more than a dozen barracuda. Franklin's was the largest by far, thirty-five pounds, played and landed on light tackle.

A heavy rain squall came up as they headed home with their catch and they raced down a shallow, twisting creek to reach the *Larooco* before dark. They found her at the mouth of the creek, pounding furiously at anchor in the rising wind. The launch reached the houseboat's side, and Missy managed to scramble up onto the deck, but when Franklin started to swing himself aboard, his hand slipped on the wet rail and he was hurled back to the floor of the launch, landing with all his weight on the limp left leg bent beneath him.

The knee exploded in pain. Roy and the rest of the crew got to him right away, but rather than try to pass him up to the houseboat deck in the spattering rain, they opened the galley window and handed him through it.

Franklin was in agony, convinced that he had not only torn but shattered his knee, and fearful that his withered leg's chronically poor circulation might now cause gangrene. The nearest physician was at Miami, more than a full day's run away. Missy sat with Franklin the whole way as the little houseboat moaned and shuddered through the choppy sea.

At Miami, she hurried ashore to find a doctor. When he came aboard, he said that ligaments in the knee had been badly torn but nothing was broken. The physician strapped up the leg, and warned that it would take weeks to heal.

Old friends arrived—Maunsell Crosby, Frances De Rham, Tom Lynch—but Franklin stayed in bed for a solid week before he dared have his brace strapped on or allowed himself to be carried on deck, and he would be forced to watch from the sidelines for much of the voyage as his guests fished, swam, and explored the tangled woods along the shore. For a full month he even left to others the keeping of his jaunty log.

He was still fully in charge in the evenings, however. One day,

Tom Lynch caught a huge grouper from which an excellent chowder was made—"so excellent," Frances De Rahm noted in the log, that with the rum cocktails that accompanied it, the chowder "inspired our dear Admiral to give a most graphic and amusing account of his political career from the beginning" that did not end until three the following morning, when he shouted, "Oh, Roy!" his signal that he wished his valet to come and put him to bed.

He did his best always to seem cheerful, working over his stamps while others splashed around the boat, pretending not to mind when Missy and Frances were unable to rush back fast enough from a shopping expedition to bring him ice cream before it melted.

The *Larooco* docked at Key West on May 10, and when the newspapers were brought aboard everyone was pleased to "find the Admiral occupying most of the front pages . . . with project for rejuvenating [the] Democratic Party. Much excitement. *Many* pictures of the Admiral. . . ."

Ever since the Democratic disaster of 1920, Franklin and Louis Howe had sought to revivify their battered, sundered party, calling again and again for regular conferences to ensure that the warring factions were heard from, and the creation of a full-time national machine financed by the largest possible numbers of ordinary citizens rather than the traditional handful of rich contributors. Their goal, Roosevelt said, was to make the Democrats "unequivocally the party of progressive and liberal thought."

Their efforts had redoubled in 1924, when they sent a circular letter to every delegate and alternate who attended the tumultuous New York convention, asking for his or her proposals for doing better next time. The response had been both massive and dispiriting: the fissures within the party ran deeper than even Franklin and Howe had feared. Southerners thought northerners ignored them. Westerners charged the party was run by an unholy coalition between North and South. The party's dismal fortunes were variously said to be the fault of Bryan, Smith, McAdoo, Socialists, Wets, Drys, immigrants, farmers.

Undaunted, Franklin and Howe issued an open letter to Senator Thomas J. Walsh of Montana, permanent chairman of the 1924 convention, calling for a national conference to develop common themes and refocus Democratic fire where it rightfully belonged—on the Republicans. (The headlines that so pleased Franklin and his party at Key West accompanied publication of this letter.)

In the end, Franklin's new effort at party unity would yield little more than headlines. Any proposal that came from Roosevelt was suspect to Al Smith's enemies because of the public alliance the two New Yorkers had forged. Some thought Franklin's scheme simply a not-so-subtle attempt at swinging the spotlight of leadership to himself—and his desire to be made "temporary chairman" of the proposed conference lent credence to that suspicion. Still others thought publicizing the party's problems would just make them more intractable.

Back in New York, Louis Howe was struggling to handle all the delicate correspondence this controversy inspired. "I find it hard to put complicated situations clearly on paper," he wrote Franklin, "and, to be brutally frank, even harder to get a reply from you in time to count much." He arrived in Florida five days later, with a briefcase full of letters for his boss to sign—Franklin had urged him to "prepare as many letters for my signature as possible [before coming down]. You know perfectly well that I will answer none of them in longhand"— and was immediately thrown overboard at Roosevelt's orders, still wearing his dingy suit. "L.H. is finally bathed in the ocean," Franklin noted. "Under protest."

Howe was there, along with Eleanor and others, for the Roosevelts' twentieth wedding anniversary on March 17. The dinner table was covered with a green paper tablecloth—Franklin and Eleanor had been married on St. Patrick's Day—and there were amusing place cards drawn by Howe, gag gifts (including "a pair of *linnen* panties" for Franklin), several rounds of toasts, and a speech by Henry Morgenthau.

Franklin spent the night of his anniversary in his cabin. His wife slept on deck, trying to ignore the snoring of Louis Howe.

The next day, she and Missy left for New York together by train. "Missy weeps because last A.M. on boat!" Eleanor wrote Marion Dickerman in disbelief. She herself could hardly wait to get away.

Franklin was soon to move on to Warm Springs.

Tom Loyless had been working there all winter, trying to ready the old resort for what he hoped would be a flood of new summer visitors. "A bit tired," he wrote Franklin aboard the *Larooco* in March, "but I enjoy it, all except my experience for the past week or more, with a booze-fighting house-mover. Have been having five or six of the hotel cottages moved around a bit—and the man I gave the contract to has been drunk [since] soon after I got started. I must say I can't much blame him, but it is hard on me, as I never know where he is going to take the next one—and I don't think he does. I have tried some stunts myself, in days past, with more or less liquor in me, but I never tried to move houses."

"Your visit certainly put Warm Springs on the map," Loyless told Franklin. He had received hundreds of letters from polios or members of their families asking for information about the miracle pool in which Franklin Roosevelt was said in the newspapers to be swimming his way back to health. They wanted to swim there, too. A few polios simply turned up at the depot, some helped off the train by anxious relatives, others on their own, all asking the way to the healing waters.

Loyless had turned the first few away, explaining that there were as yet no facilities for them. But by the time Franklin moved back into the Hart cottage on April 2, 1925, several had managed to find rooms in the village and were clamoring to be allowed into the pool. Still another was carried off the train the day Roosevelt arrived, in fact, a painfully thin young Pennsylvanian named Fred Botts who had wanted to be an opera singer until polio confined him to his bedroom eight years earlier; the railroad had refused to permit him and his wheelchair to ride in a Pullman, so he had come all the way to Warm Springs in the mail car, seated inside a sort of wooden cage banged together by the brother who escorted him so that he would not be hurled about too badly by the jarring train.

At first, Franklin was annoyed that other polios had come to Warm Springs. He had deliberately arrived almost a month before the regular season opened on May 1, just so that he could work on his own legs in peace. But he also felt at least partially responsible for so many having been drawn to the place simply because he had once been there and, for better or worse, he now felt obligated to see what he could do to help the newcomers who continued to arrive.[9]

He remembered those earliest days in a talk given at Warm Springs several years later:

9. He would later publicly confess his embarrassment at the winter's spate of misleading newspaper stories about his first stay in Georgia.

There I was, large as life, living proof that Warm Springs . . . had cured me of 57 different varieties of ailments. Most of the diseases from which I had suffered were apparently fatal, but Warm Springs evidently had got each just in time, giving me a chance to go out and catch another incurable malady and dash back here to get rid of it. That enterprising youngster who syndicated the article must have made several fortunes out of it but he never even sent me a five per cent commission. . . . Every human being, male or female, between Florida and Alaska who has a stomach ache, a cold in the nose or a gouty toe, it would seem writes to old Dr. Roosevelt, with the firm belief that I can point out to them, from personal experience, how to get cured.

Source: Donald Scott Carmichael, *FDR Columnist.*

> One day Mr. Loyless and some of the neighbors—the Harts, Miss [Georgia] Wilkins, and Josephs and some of us—were sitting around when a messenger came up the hill to Mr. Loyless and said, "Two people have been carried off the train down at the station. What shall we do with them? Neither of them can walk."
>
> Well, we held a consultation. . . . We decided that we would take care of them in the village overnight, and then, in a couple of days, we could fix up what is now "The Wreck," and put them in it. Well, before we could put that cottage in order, eight others had arrived. . . . We did not know what to do with them. . . .

At poolside, Franklin found himself in the company of eight to ten eager but largely helpless men and women who looked to him for guidance. He had had no special training in physiotherapy, and, despite four years of work with the leading American experts in rehabilitation, had experienced little measurable success in rebuilding his own muscles. Everything would have to be improvised.

None of this seems to have discouraged him for a moment.

He asked Dr. Johnson of Manchester to examine each of the newcomers. "He came and looked them over," Roosevelt remembered, "and guaranteed that they did not have heart trouble or something from which they would suddenly die. . . ." Then Franklin administered as best he could the muscle tests Dr. Lovett had performed upon him with such uniformly discouraging results. It was important, he knew, for every polio to understand how much or how little muscle he or she actually had to work with, and to set an individual standard against which progress or the lack of it could be measured regularly.

He had a railing installed around the inside of the pool so that he and the others could hold on safely, ordered a platform built twelve inches beneath the surface of the water to use as an exercise table, and hired two local youths to help polios slide in and out of the pool. (Their duties soon included pushing wheelchairs around the grounds, and they and their legion of successors became known as "push boys.")

> . . . I undertook to be doctor and physiotherapist, all rolled into one. . . . I taught them all at least to play around in the water. I remember there were two quite large ladies; and when I was trying to teach them an exercise I had really invented, which was the elevating exercise in the medium of water, one of these ladies found great difficulty in getting both feet down to the bottom of the pool. Well, I would take one large knee and I would force this large knee and leg down until the foot rested firmly on the bottom. And then I would say, "Have you got it?" and she would say, "Yes," and I would say, "Hold it, hold it." Then I would reach up

and get hold of the other knee very quickly and start to put it down and then number one knee would pop up. This used to go on for half an hour at a time; but before I left . . . I could get both knees down at the same time. . . . So you see, these girls who think they are physiotherapists don't know anything about it. I invented it first.

Roosevelt did not invent physiotherapy, of course, but he was an authentic pioneer in its application, and his eager, infectious enthusiasm galvanized polios who until they met him had been utterly without hope.

Polios often seemed "addled" when they got to Warm Springs, one of the first physiotherapists remembered. The impact of the disease was so devastating, both for them and for their families, that "they no longer knew who they were or what they were. At Warm Springs they found out."

Rehabilitative care was still primitive in 1924. It had not been long since a leading American "authority" on infantile paralysis, Dr. R. C. Elmslie, suggested that "when a leg is completely useless—i.e., when it cannot be swung forward and backward—it is better to amputate it through the thigh." Once the acute symptoms had receded, most polios were simply sent home from the hospital. The lucky ones got professional nursing care; the rest were dependent upon the custodial care of solicitous but untrained family members. A good many were simply locked away in their bedrooms.[10]

Massive feelings of guilt and alienation enveloped many of them— they came to believe that by falling ill they had failed to live up to the expectations of others to whom they had then become a burden. Often shut away without ever having even talked with another polio, sometimes further damaged by inadequate or incompetent aftercare, and persuaded that they were an embarrassment to their families, they felt themselves permanently set apart from the rest of the world. Some succumbed to what one polio called "the secret pleasure of the invalid, that complete dependence upon others which releases one . . . from the obligations of life." Others became embittered, ashamed to leave their rooms, to be seen by outsiders.

Almost all had felt powerless to improve until they arrived at the Warm Springs pool and suddenly found themselves surrounded by

10. In the coming years it would become the unofficial duty of the Warm Springs staff and its supporters to "dig polios out of the countryside" and see that they came south for treatment. Eleanor Roosevelt stumbled upon one man who had been deserted by his wife and forced to live in his wheelchair in the kitchen of his upstate home for three years. She saw to it that he was sent to Georgia. *Source:* Interview with Mary Hudson Veeder.

other polios, some of whom at least were worse off than they, and being asked to *do* something about it at last.

A later polio remembered both the sudden shock of being hit by infantile paralysis and the no less startling sense he got at Warm Springs that its ravages really did not mean the end of everything:

> To see your body changed irrevocably; to find yourself helpless, set apart from others, and yet to know that within you are unchanged; to realize, with a shock, that although others may never look at you or think of you in quite the same way again, you are still the same person; that is to begin to know what your body is. It is not you at all. The real you . . . is something quite apart, unchanging . . . a constant.

That process of realization began during the spring of 1925, and Roosevelt was its catalyst, seeming to know by instinct and example how to infuse others with his own unconquerable spirit.

It is unlikely that Franklin Roosevelt ever thought himself merely one more member of any crowd, but he came as close to it as he ever did in those early days in Georgia. He was in charge of the exercises at the pool, but he also toiled alongside the others in the warm water, then sprawled on a cot in the sun, chatting happily with anyone who passed by.

He was having a wonderful time. "You would howl with glee," he told an old friend,

> if you could see the clinic in operation at the side of the pool, and the patients doing various exercises in the water under my leadership—they are male and female of all ages and weights. In addition to all this I am consulting architect and landscape engineer for the Warm Springs Co.— am giving free advice on the moving of buildings, the building of roads, setting out of trees and remodelling the hotel. We, i.e., the Company plus F.D.R., are working out a new water system, new sewage plant, fishing pond, and tomorrow we hold an organization meeting to start the Pine Mountain Club which will run the dance hall, tea room, picnic grounds, golf courses and other forms of indoor and outdoor sports. I sometimes wish I could find some spot on the globe where it was not essential and necessary for me to start something new—a sand bar in the ocean might answer, but I would probably start building a sea wall around it and digging for pirate treasure in the middle.

Roosevelt also appointed himself "Vice President in Charge of Picnics," organizing expeditions into the countryside by automobile. His favorite site was Dowdell's Knob, a rocky overhang 1,395 feet above sea level, reached by a dirt track that threaded its precarious way along the crest of nearby Pine Mountain. Roosevelt and his friends dressed informally for these excursions, but the black men who waited on them wore white jackets, just as the Roosevelt servants had for family picnics at Campobello. A car seat was dragged out for him to sit on—he was so at ease among his friends and fellow polios that he sometimes wore his hated braces on the outside of his trousers so that he could adjust the knee catches or take them off without help—and he spent hours watching the slowly shifting shadows of the clouds moving over the forests and fields of the valley far below.

Whenever a polio seemed about to give in to despair, Roosevelt once told a friend, he or she should be brought up to Dowdell's Knob right away: one look at the glorious view would provide them with the will to go on.[11]

Franklin volunteered for still another task at Warm Springs, taking over Tom Loyless's weekly column in the Macon *Daily Telegraph* when Loyless seemed too exhausted and too preoccupied with Warm Springs to continue it. (He was in fact dying of cancer, although no one yet knew it.)

"Roosevelt Says" ran for eight weeks. Franklin was glad, he wrote, to have "returned to my former profession—I used to edit the college paper in the old days." He professed to like everything about Georgia, but especially its Democratic newspapers—"one reason why my digestion is perfect down here. Back home my digestion starts the day all right, but after reading the morning papers at the breakfast table, things go wrong. By the time I have finished reading the evening papers, I am a hopeless dyspeptic."

He offered predictable opinions on safe issues—civil service reform, a streamlined tax system, government run on a solid "business basis"—and artfully balanced views on controversial ones: while he wanted America to "act like a man" abroad, he wrote, "No American, of course, wants any entangling alliance." "We lack a sense of humor and of proportion if we forget that not so very long ago we were immigrants outselves. . . . ," but, "I agree that for a good many years to come European immigration should remain greatly restricted. We have, unfortunately, a great many thousand foreigners who got in here and must be digested. For fifty years the United States ate a meal altogether too large—much of the food was digestible, but some of it

11. Frail and ashen, FDR himself would spend several hours at Dowdell's Knob, staring out at the view, on the afternoon of the day before he died in 1945.

was almost poisonous. The United States must, for a short time, stop eating, and when it resumes should confine itself to the most readily assimilable foodstuffs."

Those foodstuffs did not include the Japanese, according to Roosevelt, who were "not capable of assimilation into the American population."

> . . . Anyone who has traveled in the Far East knows that the mingling of Asiatic blood with European or American blood produces, in nine cases out of ten, the most unfortunate results. . . . The argument works both ways. I know a great many cultivated, highly educated and delightful Japanese. They have all told me that they would feel the same repugnance and objection to have thousands of Americans settle in Japan and intermarry with the Japanese as I would feel in having large numbers of Japanese coming over here and intermarrying with the American population.
>
> In this question, then, of Japanese exclusion from the United States it is necessary only to advance the true reason—the undesirability of mixing the blood of the two peoples. . . . The Japanese people and the American people are both opposed to intermarriage of the two races—there can be no quarrel there.[12]

The Warm Springs resort season officially began on May 1. Vacationers checking into the Meriwether Inn were startled to find a new sort of visitors already in place: men and women on crutches stumped loudly through the lobby; others wheeled themselves up and down the corridors; wheelchairs crowded the space between the tables in the dining room; polios exercised their atrophied limbs in the swimming pool.

The sight of so many afflicted people was distressing to the summer visitors—who knew whether their condition was contagious? Their presence in the pool dining room might actually be dangerous. Finally, a delegation of guests waited upon Loyless. Their vacations were being

---

12. Roosevelt himself had never "traveled in the Far East," of course, and the names of the "great many . . . delightful Japanese" whom he claimed to know have been lost to history.
His columns were offered for syndication but found no takers. In the White House, twelve years later, FDR had copies of the columns bound in pigskin and stamped in gold:

> Roosevelt Says
> Being an Exegesis of the New Deal,
> April–May, 1925

On the flyleaf he added:

> My first effort as a columnist—
> proving that no one can write a column on public affairs once a day, or twice a week.
> Franklin D. Roosevelt, 1937

Source: Donald Scott Carmichael, *FDR Columnist.*

ruined, they said; they had not bargained for spending their holidays in a hospital; the unfortunates would have to go, or they themselves would be forced to leave Warm Springs.

To placate them, Loyless and Franklin opened a second dining room in the basement, redoubled their efforts to fix up the colony of old cottages so that all the polios could be moved out of the inn and housed there, and began to dig a second, smaller pool for their exclusive use, connected by a channel with the old one but concealed within a shed.

Some guests left anyway. Their ignorant squeamishness seemed only to deepen Franklin's faith in the future of Warm Springs, and he wrote John Lawrence, tactfully suggesting that they now consider selling the *Larooco* so that he could devote more time to it.

> The two months in Florida this year and last did me an undoubted amount of good, yet I realize that on a houseboat it is very difficult to get the kind of exercise I need, i.e., swimming in warm water. The sharks make it impossible to play around in deep water for any length of time, and the sand beaches are few and far between, and even on them I get sunlight chiefly but very little swimming. There is now no question that this Warm Springs pool does my legs more good than anything else. ... Therefore, from the sole consideration of getting my legs better I must contemplate next winter giving up the Florida trip and coming here instead. This would have been impossible up to now as there were no heating facilities for the cottages or bathhouses, and these are needed in February and March. Now, however, they are putting in heat and next winter I will be able to come here instead of going to Florida.

Lawrence, who had yet to find the time to spend so much as a day on the houseboat he and Franklin had purchased together, may privately have been relieved. Certainly, he was agreeable. Selling the boat was fine with him, he wrote. "I am delighted to hear you are getting better, and also that you are trying to save the Democratic Party from wine, women and Hollering. ... Go to it. We shall need a sound party to keep the Republicans in line, and don't forget that I am looking forward to being one of the 10,000 Secretaries of the Navy that you have pledged 8 years from now, when you have the honor of calling the White House your own and swimming in the fountain."[13]

Despite the trouble Loyless was having just holding onto his handful of regular customers, and the dearth of medical personnel trained

13. "Eight years from now" was 1933, the year FDR did come to call the White House his own.

to deal with his new ones, Franklin continued to believe that once the resort was properly restored it could simultaneously turn a profit and serve as a rehabilitation center.

For the first time in his life, Franklin had become fully engaged in something that promised to benefit others as well as himself. He was already calling himself "Old Doctor Roosevelt," and his genuine interest in the rehabilitation of those who exercised under his care is evident in every line of the progress report on his first seven patients which he banged out on his typewriter at the end of his visit and sent to Dr. Frank Ober, Dr. Lovett's successor in Boston.

1. Miss [Elizabeth] Retan from Newton, Mass., a patient of Dr. Osgood—one leg and both arms practically normal—uses brace on other leg but can walk short distance without it. Has improved remarkably I think since coming here.

2. Mr. Philpot, 19, from Alabama, one leg about 60% of normal, the other leg about 40%, abductors and adductors weak, does not wear braces but walks with crutches. Has improved much in 3 weeks, but is inclined to overdo and required constant supervision.

3. [Lambert] Hersheimer . . . [Dr. Ober's own patient] is. . . . thoroughly unsatisfactory, . . . largely because of his mental attitude. His mother has no control over him and he hates this place because it is dull, and against the wish of his mother is leaving soon. He has undoubtedly improved, but has not given himself a fair chance, because he wants to get away and will not admit any gain here. He is too fat, has not exercised regularly and I am particularly sorry that your case should be the one which has been most difficult to deal with. Please, therefore, discount what he tells you about 50%!

4. Mr. Botts from Pennsylvania—a case of 8 years' standing—has practically nothing below the hips—came here very emaciated and looking like a T.B. case. Dr. Johnson and I have been trying to build him up physically and he shows general physical improvement and states his general physical condition is far better than at any time since the illness. Five or six important muscles of which there was no trace can now be felt, glutei greatly improved, quadriceps in one knee returning, abductors strengthened and adductors have reappeared. He uses braces. When he came here could walk only a few steps, yesterday he walked half a mile in them. It is, of course, doubtful if he gets rid of the braces, but his improvement has really been extraordinary and he is tremendously keen ˄nd a willing patient.

5. Mrs. [Thelma] Steiger of Missouri has had polio 3 ½ years—a very

bad case from the waist down. On first examination showed nothing below the hips—there are now distinct traces of quadriceps, ham strings and foot muscles. This also is a very difficult case as there is very little to start on.

6. Mr. [Paul] Rogers of Wisconsin—about 35 years old—the worst case of all. The history shows that he probably killed his muscles by returning to work 3 weeks after getting polyo. . . . Has practically nothing below the waist except slight glutei, adductors and abductors. Has bad foot drop and stiffening. A hard case to work on as he had made up his mind that nothing could ever be done. He has, however, improved with the exercise and shows traces in toes and ham strings and one quadriceps.

7. My own case—the gain I made here last autumn did not continue during the winter. During the past 6 weeks, however, it has started in again, *all* muscles have undoubtedly strengthened. Here is a rough and ready measurement—when I came here last autumn I could only stand up in water without support at level of top of shoulders. When I left I could stand up with shoulders 2 inches out of water. Today, I can stand up with shoulders 4 inches out of water. That represents a gain, I think, of about 20 pounds on my knees.

All in all, I consider this pool the best after-care treatment for polyo. The temperature is about 85 [degrees] and the water does not debilitate. We, the patients, go into the pool at about 10 a.m., stay in half an hour, swimming and exercising at a raised platform with bars, then we lie in the sun for half an hour, then go in again for half an hour and come out and lie in the sun for a final half hour.

It is absolutely essential that the place have a doctor and "exercise lady," especially as over 600 polyo patients have written Mr. Loyless or me, asking about coming here.

The physical progress made by Roosevelt and his fellow polios that first spring may have been slight, but the psychological strides they made were unmistakable. That same autumn, a South Carolina physician wrote to ask Franklin about his own treatment and Roosevelt responded with a five-part program for recovery based on "my own experience and that of hundreds of other cases I have studied." It called for gentle exercise and massage, "swimming in warm water—lots of it," "Sunlight—all the patient can get," and *"Belief on the patient's part that the muscles are coming back and will eventually regain recovery of the affected parts"* (author's italics). Roosevelt infused his fellow polios with that belief.

Assessing those same weeks, Fred Botts would later write of all the patients who *"nearly"* put aside their wheelchairs with the encouragement of "The Honorable Franklin D. Roosevelt from New York City, dearest of friends and noblest of mentors. . . ."

Franklin was encouraged by his own progress and by that of the other polios at Warm Springs, but he was not content to rely on any one place alone in his relentless search for something, *anything,* that would restore strength to his legs. On August 4, 1925, after just two months back in New York, he was off again in search of further help, headed this time for Louis Howe's cottage at Horseneck Beach, Massachusetts, on the shore of Buzzard's Bay in whose warm waters some of Dr. Lovett's patients were said to have made unexpected progress.

"The car . . . will be crowded," Franklin told Sara, "Louis and I on the back seat with various packages tucked around and under us, one colored treasure on a little seat, the other in front with [the chauffeur, Montford] Snyder and several score suitcases, braces, crutches, canes, sandwiches thrown in for good measure. However, it saves $11 for each person to travel thus to the beach."

Bachelor life at Horseneck Beach was spartan. Franklin lived in the barn just behind the Howe cottage, Mary Howe remembered,

> all cozied up and compact just for one person. He had a servant . . . come to dress and undress him, and there were two planks of wood from his door leading right down to the beach, and somebody could push him or he would move his own wheelchair and then get off and hump his way into the water backwards, dragging his legs. The two of them [Franklin and her father] would work on their boats, talk politics, look at stamps, read detective stories by lamplight, and Dad worked out some sliding clothesline to send messages. FDR was working on a movie script about John Paul Jones. And once he said, "Look Louis, I can wiggle my toe. . . ."

At nearby Marion, Massachusetts, lived Dr. William McDonald, a neurologist who had persuaded himself that even severely paralyzed patients could be helped through rigorous exercise in the Bay combined with a no less challenging onshore regimen of massage, exercise, and round-upon-plodding-round of a specially designed "walking board"—a wooden oblong, fitted out with rails.

McDonald was a voluble, eccentric, little man—he typed his own hectic letters, peppered with "Hells" and "Damns" in red and green, spent his winters chronicling his travels in Africa and Asia with a movie camera, and insisted on being called "Billie" by the four well-to-do patients he worked with at one time—but Franklin's Uncle Fred Delano had heard good things about him while visiting the old Delano homestead at Fairhaven, and it was apparently at his urging that the physician examined Franklin at Howe's cottage.

"Net result," Franklin wrote Dr. Draper,

> he told me he would get me on my feet without braces. I accepted the offer and came here [to Marion, where Bertie Hamlin's brother-in-law rented him a cottage on] August 25th. . . .
>
> Of course I have seen the methods of practically all the others doctors in the country—the Lovett Method, Golthwaite Method, Hibbs Methods, St. Louis Method, Chicago Method, etc., etc. They are all good in their way, but McDonald uses what they use and goes one step further. The principle of the others is the exercise of individual muscles, primarily in the line of straight pull. McDonald's exercises give all this, but in addition exercises the muscles in coordination with each other, i.e., the pull outside of the direct plane. . . . In other words, McDonald seeks functioning as the primary objective and he has certainly succeeded in dozens of cases. It seems so worthwhile that I shall keep on with this until November, and I thought you would be really interested because I know that you had no hard and fast opinions about the restoring of function in polyo cases. In addition to all this, McDonald himself is a peach—talks your language and mine!

Sara shared her son's high hopes for McDonald—who, after all, came recommended by the brother she revered.

> I was very glad to get your letter of Tuesday, and all my thoughts are in Marion, and tomorrow, I can think of you there and beginning the treatment. I feel so hopeful and confident! Once able to move about with crutches and without braces, strength will come and now for the first time in more than a year I feel that *work* is to be done for *you*, my dearest. . . .

McDonald's regimen was "very strenuous for the patient," Franklin reported to his mother. "Yesterday I swam for 1 ½ hours in the morning, had the exercises with the Dr. at 4 and then tried the walking board for ½ hour. He seems pleased with the general line up and I feel with him that things have now got to the point with the muscles in general where there is something to work on and I can go right at it. Braces are of course laid aside, he is hot against them, and confirms what I have told you for two years and you would not believe."

Part of McDonald's appeal for Roosevelt was that he shared his belief that braces were to be avoided as much as possible as symbols of weakness, a tacit admission that the legs locked within them could never be restored.

On August 31, just six days after his arrival, Franklin wrote Van-Lear Black, "This time I think I have hit it. Dr. McDonald has gone one step further than the others and his exercises are doing such wonders that I expect in the course of another 10 days to be able to stand up without braces. What I did before in the way of swimming at Warm Springs was all to the good, but now I begin to see actual daylight ahead. . . ."

About that same time, Franklin evidently managed to stand for a moment—with Dr. McDonald and Roy supporting him under the shoulders—while wearing only his left brace, and was so pleased that he wired Black the news of this EXTRAORDINARY achievement.[14]

Roosevelt's initial appointment had not been universally popular among the F&D's regular employees, many of whom felt he was being paid a lot to do little, and while everyone now sympathized with his physical affliction, there continued to be those in both the New York and Maryland offices who felt it might be best for the smooth running of the firm if Roosevelt would retire or at least relinquish some of his responsibilities rather than to continue as such a highly paid part-time employee.

Franklin did his best from Marion to persuade Black that he was on top of things, even though away. "Things in the office are going exceedingly well," he reported, "and we are really getting a lot of new business through my political connections. Last night I spoke over the radio and already this morning a brand new bond has come in as a result!"

He needn't have worried: his employer remained steadfast, scrawling his congratulations in pencil:

Dear F.D.R.

You don't know how delighted we are here at the good news your telegram of yesterday contained. Certainly your improvement must be great when you use the word "extraordinary"—for from my knowledge of your expressions you are not given to the use of superlatives. Am writing this long-hand for I want to repeat what I told you personally some months ago and that is your job is to centre on getting well and

14. A photograph showing Franklin supported by his valet, Roy, and McDonald may have been taken at this dramatic moment. As Hugh Gallagher first noted, Roosevelt's wheelchair waits just behind him. Clearly he was not expected to stand for long. *Source:* Hugh Gallagher, *FDR's Splendid Deception,* picture portfolio between pages 142 and 143.

nothing else. This so far as I am personally concerned and my business interests. So as your stay at Marion is doing you so much good for heaven's sake stride around there as long as you are being benefited. . . .

Please don't [fidget] or change your mind as to going down to the Georgia Springs after you leave Marion. While the going is good, let's keep on going, and cinch getting entirely well.

The children were disappointed that their father planned to stay on at Marion into the fall. "So glad to know that you are trying out a new Dr.," Franklin Jr. wrote bravely, but the new model boat his father had sent him was "an awful job to put together. I wish you were here to help me. We all miss you a lot."

Franklin worked every day all fall with McDonald and his three other patients, all of them women much younger than he. They exercised together all morning, had lunch, then crawled together up the long flight of steps to the exercise room at the top of McDonald's beachfront house for several more hours of work.

In the evenings, McDonald, Franklin, and Missy—who joined him as soon as he moved to Marion—played cards, worked over stamps (the doctor collected them too), or watched mile upon mile of McDonald's home movies.[15]

One day in early December, Franklin managed to walk almost a block—from the house to the wharf's edge—still leaning on crutches but wearing only his left brace. McDonald walked on his left side, Roy on his right. When he reached the dock, his knees shaking, his torso trembling, he stopped and said, "I can walk! I can walk!" Then they helped him back down into his wheelchair.[16] He went home to Hyde

15. Roosevelt also did his best to stay in touch with the political world, and the political emissaries who came and went at his cottage greatly enlivened the normally tranquil seaside colony. Bertie Hamlin remembered one especially exotic visitor, encountered one November afternoon when she stopped by for tea.

After he had gone—Franklin told me [the stranger] was an East Side Jew—a tailor—from New York. He had come over on the boat the previous night and had been over once before to spend the day. Franklin said he had a chance in this way to learn a great deal about conditions in [the young man's life]—his clubs and other organizations—at first hand. He felt he got to the bottom of situations that could and should be remedied—the scandalous housing conditions—labour—schools—churches and the family life. He [admired] the patience of people [under] unbearable tenement living—the lack of decent provisions for sanitary purposes—sometimes one water faucet for a whole house—and that in some cases the properties were owned by wealthy people who left the care to agents who had no interest but to exact the rent.

Source: Frank Freidel. Franklin D. Roosevelt: The Ordeal, page 206.

16. Several biographies allege that Roosevelt managed to make this walk with a cane, not crutches. They are in error, as Franklin's own report to his mother written November 17, 1925, makes clear. Source: Elliott Roosevelt, ed., FDR: His Personal Letters, 1905–1928, page 591.

Park in December, convinced that he was at last on the road to real recovery.

It was almost all illusion. A new physiotherapist was hired to help him for a month, Miss Alice Lou Plastridge, a Vermonter who had worked with Dr. Lovett and Wilhemine Wright at Boston. She never forgot her introduction to Springwood:

> Mr. Roosevelt's mother met me at the front door. . . . At the foot of the winding stairway she called, "Eleanor, Eleanor, come down. Miss Plastridge is here." You would have thought I was the Queen of Spain.
>
> Eleanor was also very cordial. She then called, "Anna, Anna come down, Miss Plastridge is here." We . . . walked down a long hall to the library. It was a beautifully appointed room with rows and rows of books. We talked at the doorway when I heard a deep voice from the far end of the room.
>
> "Aren't you *ever* going to come and speak to me?" It was Mr. Roosevelt.

Miss Plastridge began working with Franklin in his bedroom the next morning, putting him through his exercises on a slab stretched across wooden horses. She found him an amiable, voluble patient—she especially enjoyed listening to his big plans for Warm Springs—but she also found their daily sessions disheartening. "We worked for a couple of weeks and I knew we weren't getting anywhere . . . ," she remembered. "Since his polio onset was in 1921, there wasn't any particular motion in his legs. He didn't have much to use and he didn't know the right way to use what he had."

His braces were far too heavy, she noted, and his crutch-walking was clumsy and impatient: "His arms were enormously strong, though his hands always shook, and he used everything with great *force*. He would pound down on the floor and you would think the floor would break under him, his effort was so great. [But he] would just drag his legs along."

Then, trying to ease himself down into a chair one evening, Franklin badly sprained his back. The doctor called Miss Plastridge the next morning, asking her to go out and buy a "baker," a portable device that would surround Roosevelt's throbbing back with heat. She did as she was told, made her patient as comfortable as she could—there was angry swelling "the size of your fist" all along his spine, she remembered—and went home.

When she opened his bedroom door the next morning, he all but shouted at her.

"What are *you* here for? Have you forgotten about my back?"

"I thought we might do just a little work."

"I can't do *anything* without hurting."

"Will it hurt your back to move your toes?"

"Yes," glaring now, "it will."

"Then you're not doing it right."

Roosevelt was furious. "All right. Put up the table and prove it!"

Miss Plastridge did, pushing and pulling his muscles an inch at a time, and stopping at the slightest sign of pain. As she did so, she began to explain where each muscle was, and urged him to concentrate on that particular spot as she worked it.

Gradually, she taught him how to "localize" some of his stronger muscles so that when walking on crutches he began to be able to hitch one leg forward, then the other, rather than merely drag them along together.

"He [learned] not to use his whole body when just trying to move his foot," Miss Plastridge recalled. It was a major improvement, the most important since he was first pulled upright onto his braced legs four years earlier. At the Springwood dinner table a few days before Christmas, Franklin placed a small box in front of Miss Plastridge.

"Open it," he said.

Inside was a token of his gratitude, a gold ring with a lapis stone. She would wear it every day for the rest of her life.[17]

Frances Perkins was a frequent visitor to Hyde Park, and left a vivid memory of life there as millions of Americans believed it to be during the Roosevelt presidency:

> Many times in summer when I would be told that "the family [is] on the lawn," I approached through the library and saw through the open door an unforgettable picture: Mrs. Sara Roosevelt in a . . . light summery dress with ruffles . . . sitting in a wicker chair and reading; Mrs. [Eleanor] Roosevelt in a white dress and white tennis shoes with a velvet band around her head to keep the hair from blowing, sitting with her long-legged, graceful posture in a low chair and knitting, always knitting; Roosevelt looking off down the river at the view he admired, with a book, often unopened, in one hand, and a walking stick in the other; dogs playing nearby, and children romping a little farther down the lawn. The scene was like a Currier and Ives print of Life along the Hudson.

17. In 1929, Roosevelt would appoint Miss Plastridge director of physical therapy at the Warm Springs Foundation. When I spoke to her in 1988, Alice Lou Plastridge-Converse was, at ninety-nine, the oldest member of the American Physical Therapy Association.

In fact, after the mid-1920s, the Roosevelt family was rarely so united and life at Springwood rarely so tranquil as that, and Eleanor spent as little time as she decently could at her mother-in-law's home. Since 1918, the relationship between the Roosevelts had become more merger than marriage, an affectionate and effective partnership based on a shared past and mutual interests, but without passion or intimacy.

Some time toward the end of the busy summer of 1924, Franklin and Eleanor, Nancy Cook and Marion Dickerman had taken the time to spread a picnic on the grassy shore of the Fall Kill, a cold, clear stream that gurgled prettily through land Franklin had bought for himself a little less than two miles east of Springwood.

It was a lovely place and a beautiful day, and Eleanor lamented that this would be one of the last picnics of the year; her mother-in-law was soon to close the big house for the winter. Franklin then suggested that the three women build a cottage on the bank of the stream. Cook and Dickerman could live there year-round if they liked, and Eleanor could join them whenever she had the time. He would give them a life interest in the land and supervise the construction himself. It was a generous gesture, but it also gave him another interesting project to oversee. "My missus and some of her female political friends want to build a shack on a stream in the back woods," he wrote to his friend the contractor Elliott Brown in the affectionately patronizing tone in which he often discussed his wife's activities; the stream could be dammed to form a pond, and its water diverted to fill a pool in which he might exercise. He signed on Henry Toombs, a Georgia-born New York architect already at work on Warm Springs, and told his wife, "If you three girls will just go away and leave us alone, Henry and I will build the cottage."[18]

They built the cottage, dug the pool and, just a few yards further back·from the stream, added a big gray stucco factory in which Eleanor and her friends hoped to oversee the manufacture of handcrafted re-production furniture. It was officially inaugurated on New Year's Day, 1926, with a luncheon to which Franklin, Sara, Nancy, Marion, Eleanor, Mlle Thiel, and Alice Plastridge were all invited. Everyone, including Sara, sat on kegs of nails for a (non-alcoholic) cocktail—except

18. A physiotherapist at Warm Springs who knew both Roosevelt and Toombs well said that Toombs was Franklin's favorite architect in part because when FDR claimed to have designed buildings for which the professional was actually responsible, "Henry knew enough to keep quiet." *Source:* Interview with Mary Hudson Veeder.

Franklin, for whom a straight-backed chair had been brought over from Springwood.

When luncheon was announced, the women suddenly realized that there was no man available to carry Roosevelt to the table. "Being hale and hearty," Miss Plastridge remembered, "I said to one of the ladies, equally hale and hearty, 'Let's make a chair of arms and carry him in.' He heard me suggest this, . . . [l]ooked at me with the greatest disdain, slid off his chair . . . and crept into the dining room, with all of us hovering over him, trying to help. He turned his head from side to side, making funny remarks at all of us, all the way in."

Eleanor, Marion, and Nancy all slept in the same big, dormitory-like bedroom in the stone cottage for a time, in a proximity so close that some visitors were startled; even the towels were embroidered with their three intertwined initials.

Some have speculated that such clues and the blizzard of effusive letters Eleanor wrote to Cook and Dickerman—and, later, to the journalist Lorena Hickok—implied a physical as well as an emotional attachment to them, that she turned to women for solace after her sexual relationship with Franklin had ceased.

This may, of course, be true. No living witness knows, and the written evidence is inconclusive. It is true that several of the women of whom Eleanor was most fond were homosexual. But she wrote letters no less passionate, no less suggestive of a physical relationship, to women who were not—Isabella Greenway during her early years, and later, to the dancer Mayris Chaney—and to at least three men as well: the good-looking state policeman Earl Miller; her friend and biographer Joseph P. Lash; and Dr. David Gurewitsch, her physician during her last years.[19]

19. Her letters to Hickok were undeniably the most ardent of all, especially during 1933 and 1934, and Hickok's feelings seem clearly to have been those of a smitten lover. But in at least one letter to her friend, written in 1935, Eleanor suggests strongly that while she was aware of Hickok's sexual longing for her, she did not reciprocate it: had Hickok ever had a husband, she told her friend, that "would have satisfied certain cravings."

I suspect something else accounts for the special fervor of Eleanor's letters during this time. She was in fact more desperate during the early New Deal years than at any time since her discovery of her husband's romance with Lucy Mercer in 1918. Her husband's election to the presidency seemed to her to signal an end to the independent life she had so painstakingly and precariously constructed for herself. She was to be an appendage again, as she had been during the early years in Albany and Washington and during the winter following Franklin's being stricken with polio, to have no life of her own—a feeling driven home with brutal force when she asked Franklin to give her a specific job and was refused on the grounds that Missy Le Hand would not like it.

Her epistolary output was staggering, both in its emotional fervor and in its volume. There are so many thousands of her letters in so many collections at the Hyde Park Library that no one has ever made a count, and thousands more never made it into the archives. It was as if she feared that if she didn't weave this great net of letters, her friends, acquaintances, even her children would somehow drop away. She lavished gifts on scores of people, kept track of their birthdays and their offspring, flew to their bedsides when they were ill, and offered hours of counsel and consolation when they were in trouble. Many of Eleanor's letters were remarkably ardent; her warmth and the intensity of her attachment must sometimes have seemed overwhelming even to those who welcomed it most.

Her powerful feelings for Cook and Dickerman were not unique, then, but her love for the new home she shared with them and the life they led together there was unprecedented. The stone cottage at Val-Kill was the first home Eleanor Roosevelt ever felt was truly her own. Even before she was orphaned at ten she had been rootless, parcelled out to relatives in a succession of exiles and abandoments that had helped persuade her she was somehow odd, unattractive, unable to count on anyone's unconditional love. At three, she asked her aunt, "Where is Baby's home now?" and received no satisfactory answer; there was none to give. At eighteen she told another aunt, "I have no real home," and could not stop her weeping. Even Franklin had failed to provide her with such a home. Springwood was unequivocally his mother's house, and it was Sara who had rented, staffed, and furnished their first dwelling, built their second one to adjoin her own (and kept the deeds to both), and gave them their third—the cottage at Campobello, right next door to her own—as a gift.

The closest thing to contentment Eleanor had felt during her young life came at Allenswood, the English boarding school where she spent what she called the three "happiest years of my life." She had

---

Hickok, whose interest was primarily in Mrs. Roosevelt, not the President, and who seems to have sensed intuitively the painful fragility of the First Lady's self-esteem, eagerly provided the unqualified admiration and support for which she yearned no less than did her husband.

Eleanor's eggshell-thin sense of her own worth is hauntingly reflected in a letter she wrote to Hickok just three days after FDR's inaugural. Her friend had given her a ring, and she had worn it during the ceremonies. "Oh! I want to put my arms around you," she wrote. "I ache to hold you close. Your ring is a great comfort. I look at it & think she does love me, or I wouldn't be wearing it!"

Her fears of being trapped in the White House proved groundless, of course. She became a world figure, peripatetic and hugely admired, and as she did so her need for Hickok diminished. She wrote more than two hundred letters to her in 1933, only forty-two in 1942. *Sources:* Joseph P. Lash, *Love, Eleanor* and *A World of Love*. See also Geoffrey C. Ward, "First Among First Ladies," *New York Times Book Review*, June 13, 1982.

felt safe and relatively serene at Allenswood. No longer responsible for
the turbulent younger brother whom she believed her special charge,
blessedly beyond the reach of her unhappy Hall relatives, she had been
sought out instead by worshipful younger girls to whom she could be
terribly kind, and by her teachers, especially the elderly but imposing
headmistress, Mademoiselle Marie Souvestre, whose every word she
sought to remember. It had been at Allenswood, her cousin Corinne
Alsop wrote, that "Eleanor for the first time was deeply loved, and
loved in return."

The life she now led with her friends at Hyde Park was as close
as a married woman in her forties and with five children could come
to recreating the one she had known at boarding school. Although the
Val-Kill pool was always open to Franklin and his friends, and a stone
barbecue was built near his accustomed seat on the sloping lawn so that
whenever they had a picnic he could grill his own hamburgers and
steaks as blood-rare as he liked, Val-Kill was a woman's world, into
which men intruded only when invited, a place where intense and
introspective friendship and shared confidences of a kind impossible to
imagine from Franklin or his mother were actively encouraged, where
Eleanor's earnest views were not laughed away, as they often were
even by her own children,[20] and where allowances could be made for
her sometimes unsteady disposition. "I hate to think you've been unhappy, dear," she wrote Miss Dickerman after some minor misunderstanding between her and her housemates, "it is new for me to have
anyone know when I have 'moods' much less have it make any real
difference & if you'll try not to take them too seriously I'll try not to
let myself have them!"

Marion and Nancy helped Eleanor with the children, motored
with her to Campobello in the summers, planned with her to buy the
Todhunter School for Girls in New York. There, beginning in September of 1927 when she dropped off her youngest son, John, at
Groton, she would get a chance to be to other girls what Mlle Souvestre had been to her, "a stimulating vivid personality." Eleanor taught
history, drama, English, and current affairs at Todhunter three days
a week, but she especially enjoyed leading field trips, shepherding her
wealthy, uniformed girls through courtrooms and settlement houses

20. She once told Marion Dickerman about a luncheon at which she and the labor leader Rose
Schneiderman had tried to discuss labor affairs with her own sons: "R was left as I always am
with the boys, feeling quite impotent to make a dent, because they regard me as a woman to be
dutifully and affectionately thought of because I am their mother but even tho' I hold queer
opinions they can't be considered seriously as against those of their usual male environment!"
Source: Kenneth S. Davis, *Invincible Summer*, page 55.

and Ellis Island, and past the same sort of squalid tenements that had made such a lasting impression on her just before her marriage and that she had then insisted on having her young fiancé see as well.

One evening not long after they moved into their cottage, sitting together by the fireplace, Eleanor told her two closest friends the story of her discovery of Franklin's romance with Lucy Mercer and of the grim bargain she and he had made in its aftermath in the interest of the children and her husband's career. The curious coolness the two women had often noticed between the Roosevelts was now explained, but Eleanor extracted a promise in exchange for telling them the secret that still gnawed at her: Marion and Nancy were not to choose sides between her and her husband; they, too, were to help keep up amiable appearances.

Sara professed at first to be pleased by the cottage her son had built for his wife—"Eleanor is so happy over there that she looks well and plump, don't tell her so," she wrote him not long after Val-Kill opened, "it is very becoming"—but she was never really reconciled to Eleanor's having her own Hyde Park home.

"Can you tell me *why* Eleanor wants to go over to the Val Kill cottage to sleep every night?" she once asked one of her daughter-in-law's closest friends. "Why doesn't she sleep here? This is her home."

"Perhaps it's quieter there," the friend responded carefully, "and she can swim?"

"Well, I think she belongs *here.*"

Eleanor did not think so. "The peace of it is divine," she told Franklin the first summer she spent at Val-Kill, and for the rest of her life she would consider it her real home, the center of her hard-won autonomous life.[21]

---

21. Eleanor still stayed overnight at Springwood whenever her husband or her children were there, sleeping in her sparsely furnished bedroom between her husband's and her mother-in-law's much larger ones. But sometimes the strain became too great, and one summer day, Marion Dickerman recalled, she turned up at the cottage in tears. For three days, she refused even to take a telephone call from Springwood. Finally, Dickerman, who felt it her duty whenever possible to "build bridges back to Franklin" for her friend, called Roosevelt and told him to come and talk to his wife.

"But will she talk to *me?*" he asked.

She thought Eleanor would, and so he came over alone, driving the hand-controlled Ford he had mastered, his arrival announced by the rattling of the wooden bridge across the creek. He parked as close as he could to the cottage and waited.

Eleanor went out and reluctantly joined him in the front seat of the open car. The two talked in low tones for nearly two hours, or so Dickerman remembered, before Franklin started up his car again and took his wife back with him temporarily to his mother-in-law's house.

In 1938, FDR began to build his own small fieldstone retreat still further from Springwood, on a hilltop above Val-Kill that offered a spectacular view of the Hudson and the wooded mountains beyond it. The house was designed to fit his special needs: everything was on one

Eleanor accompanied Franklin south on February 1, 1926, for the first few days of the third and final cruise of the *Larooco*. (Roosevelt and Lawrence had tried to sell the houseboat over the winter, but had found no buyer and Franklin thought it would be wasteful not to go aboard one last time so long as she was still his.) It was a tense train trip. Eleanor had not wished to go—"Dear Marion, I love you and miss you sadly . . . ," she had written from the train. "I'm so tired of doing just what I'm doing now!"—and things were not made easier for her when William Hart, the owner of the first cottage the Roosevelts had occupied in Georgia, boarded their Pullman at Savannah and he "& F. . . . talked 'Warm Springs' every minute & will till we reach Jacksonville. . . ."

Eleanor liked life aboard the *Larooco* no better than she ever had:

> We are having a killing time with our engines & now are on our way to Miami but tied up to the mango bushes in one of the passages while they find out why our clutch is slipping. My face is covered with mosquito bites in spite of citronella & my only fear is that when we reach Miami they'll think I have small pox!
>
> Florida is queerer each year & the people make me long to know why they are here. We have a mechanic on the boat today who brought his wife because they're living in a tent & I suspect she wouldn't be left alone. Well, she's a little German dressmaker and the most unhappy, out of place person, now what is she doing here?
>
> We're off again! I wish you were here, it would do you good. . . . Franklin is trying to walk on deck & it seems to go quite well so I hope he'll do it every day.
>
> Much love to Nan and you, life is quite empty without your dear presence.

Maunsell Crosby and another guest were also aboard, and still more were on the way, Eleanor told Marion, "so we are going to be quite

---

floor, the doors had no sills to interfere with his wheelchair; the stove was built especially low so that he could reach the burners while seated. "A great hobby of his," a man who helped landscape the place recalled, "was to go up there and scramble himself eggs. He would go up there and go in the kitchen and scramble himself eggs. . . . He loved that."

He called it "Top Cottage," and was most annoyed when the press began to call it his "Dream House." His mother was upset that he built it at all—she felt that both her children were deserting her—and made him promise that he would never spend the night in it so long as she was alive. He evidently kept that pledge even after she died: "Whenever he came [to Hyde Park] he always wanted to go his Hill Cottage, and sit up there and rest," the landscaper recalled, "but I have never seen him up there after dark. He always left there before dark."

The little house still stands on its summit, concealed among tall trees and in private hands. *Sources:* Kenneth S. Davis, *Invincible Summer;* George Palmer interview with Russell W. Linaka, National Park Service.

crowded on board & I may try to leave Thursday night, the day Missy arrives, as I don't know where she will sleep if I don't! I'm sleeping on deck."

She left on Friday, the 12th, grateful for the excuse that the imminent arrival of Oswald and Lady Cynthia Mosley afforded her. Mosley was then a Socialist member of parliament, tall and striking, with a carefully barbered mustache. His wife was the daughter of Lord Curzon. They were officially studying American industry but unofficially enjoying a social whirl that saw them enthusiastically entertained by those whom Mosley called "fabulous American millionaires"; one of their hosts managed to have Cole Porter serenade them at dinner.

Among those who had sought them out in New York were the Franklin Roosevelts. Years later, Mosley recalled the first of several visits to East 65th Street:

> The meeting was both impressive and strange. [Roosevelt] was alone in the room with his wife, seated on a chair from which he could not rise to greet us. He was completely paralyzed below the waist. . . . What a contrast between this magnificent man with his fine head and massive torso, handsome as a classic Greek and radiating charm, though completely immobile, and the exceptionally ugly woman, all movement and vivacity with an aura of gentle kindness, but without even a reflection of his attraction. How did they come together?

The two politicians got on so well that Franklin had asked the Mosleys to join him in Florida. They came aboard at Tavernier on February 15, and spent four days fishing and sunning and swimming. Mosley caught twelve barracuda—"a fish about the size of a salmon," he told a friend in England, "but much more powerful and the fiercest animal in the water—Legend has it that they go for the balls and a nasty mess results . . . really a most amusing trip."

"F.D.R. reminded me of one of the great hostesses of Europe," Mosley remembered, "so solicitous of his guests, so active and imaginative in devising fresh amusements. . . . We . . . set bait for shark at night when the boat was at rest. Much commotion would then ensue during dinner and I . . . [climbed] down the ladder on the side of the boat to finish the shark with F.D.R.'s revolver, under the lights flashed by the coloured crew. Next day it was impossible to swim near the boat, for many sharks would be attracted by the blood."

They swam together, too, staying in the shallow "milk-warm water" just off the beach so that Roosevelt could exercise his legs "while we without much difficulty would beat off with wooden oars the relatively harmless little sand sharks who would come wriggling in to have a look. . . ."

But "[t]he best fun," Mosley continued, "was going fast in a motor-boat over the shallow lagoons [Franklin at the helm] to get the sting-ray. It would lie flat on the bottom, easily visible, and the business was to get the harpoon into it and to pass on at speed before the sting tail came lashing over to retaliate."

And in the evenings, sitting on deck in blue wicker chairs sipping the sweet rum drinks Missy handed around but which Franklin insisted on mixing himself, they talked politics. "Drank heavily all day." Cynthia Mosley wrote in the log, "resulting in a coalition between the progressive Democrats and Socialists of England. Red flag nailed to mast and so to bed."[22]

Roosevelt and Lawrence again put the *Larooco* up for sale in March. The asking price was $14,000; for an additional $500 the buyer could have all the bed linen, china, kitchenware, and furniture, plus the motorized dory. "She has just finished a very successful 2 months' cruise," Franklin told the man he hoped would handle the sale; she was "the most comfortable of all the smaller houseboats I have seen in Florida. Am only offering her because I cannot be in Florida the next 2 winters."[23]

He planned to spend those winters in Warm Springs.

Anna visited her father there in early April. She was almost twenty now, and had come to share her mother's suspicion that her father was fooling himself, both about his own prospects and those of Warm Springs.

Ma, it's awfully hard to tell whether Father is walking better or not. He doesn't walk very much, & doesn't exercise over much. However he does

22. Oswald Mosley left the Socialists and founded the British Union of Fascists in October 1932, an action which at least at first failed to alter Franklin's fondness for him. When Cynthia Mosley wrote to congratulate him on his election as President in November, Franklin thanked her, then added his greetings to "to that fine husband of yours." In March 1933, responding to congratulations from the Mosleys on his inauguration, he wrote, "there will be still occasional chances for fishing and I hope we may have a repetition of that jolly trip sometime soon." *Source:* Oswald Mosley, *My Life.*

23. In the end, the partners were not able to sell their boat. The *Larooco* was laid up at the Pilington Yacht Basin, about two miles up the Fort Lauderdale River. In September, a savage hurricane smashed into the Florida coast and drove the houseboat four miles inland, where it lodged in a pine forest. Franklin tried to sell it as a hunting lodge without success before it was finally cut up for salvage. "So ended a good old craft with a personality," Roosevelt wrote on the last page of the log. "On the whole it was an end to be preferred to that of gasoline barge or lumber lighter." *Source:* Elliott Roosevelt, ed., *FDR: His Personal Letters, 1905–1928,* page 609.

handle himself better & can go up 2 steps. He is entirely "off" Dr. McDonald now—Says he was ruining his legs—might get him to walk but would deform his legs. Dr. [LeRoy C.] Abbott was here & started him off on this tack, as far as I can gather. Dr. A. told him he must wear 2 braces. He now wants to spend the summer between Warm Spr., Hyde Park & N.Y.! I don't know whether you know all this, but anyhow, it sounds interesting.

The one & only topic of conversation is *Warm Springs!*

Roosevelt's single-mindedness was understandable. Tom Loyless had died of cancer in March, and, with the opening of the season just a few weeks away, Franklin now found himself in charge of every detail. He hired Egbert T. Curtis, the young fiancé of one of Missy Le Hand's closest friends, to serve as manager of the Meriwether Inn. There were twenty-three polios at the pool, more than double the number with whom he had exercised the previous spring, and he persuaded Dr. Leroy W. Hubbard, a tall, white-mustached veteran of Northern epidemics now in charge of rehabilitation for the New York State Department of Public Health, to come down to oversee their treatment and gauge their progress. Hubbard's hand-picked "exercise lady," a stout, red-faced physiotherapist named Helena T. Mahoney, drove down from New York and began working with them in the pool.

Meanwhile, the final papers were being drawn up for Franklin's purchase of the old resort—the battered old inn, its cottages and pools, and twelve hundred undeveloped acres of land.

Eleanor herself arrived in Georgia a few days later. She still found the place repellent. The poverty was unrelieved. The hilarity that accompanied evening cocktails excluded her. There was nothing useful for her to do, and she thought Franklin was not doing enough, either about his own exercising or on behalf of the F&D. She also felt she was intruding upon Missy's territory. ("Missy," she wrote Marion Dickerman, ". . . is keen about everything here, of course!")

On the afternoon of April 24, she quarreled openly with Franklin about his plans. Warm Springs would cost him $195,000, almost two thirds of his fortune, at a time when all five of his children were attending private schools and only a few months after he had been forced to sell some of his beloved naval prints at auction just to bring in enough extra income to help pay for his recuperative trips to the South.

Sara could always be counted upon to make up the difference, Franklin assured Eleanor; she would never let her grandchildren go unschooled.

Eleanor was not persuaded. It seemed to her that she had heard it all before. Franklin "never went anywhere in the world that he didn't want to buy something and stay there," she told an interviewer many years later. He had once looked into buying his own island off Nova Scotia; had come back from Haiti in 1917 full of plans for purchasing the island of La Gonave; and, while sailing off Florida during his third cruise aboard the *Larooco,* had got so excited by the idea of developing part of one of the Keys that he brought Henry Morgenthau, Jr., down to see if he'd like to join him in investing. (He was still rueful a year later when he discovered that the land they had passed up at $450 an acre was going for $2,000.)[24]

Warm Springs seemed to Eleanor like just one more expensive enthusiasm with which he could be counted upon quickly to grow bored.

But this time even she realized that she was wrong. Franklin was genuinely committed to this new scheme, she told Marion after she had heard him out, and he was resentful of the criticism he had received about it from friends and family members: "he feels . . . that he's trying to do a big thing which may be a financial success & a medical and philanthropic opportunity for infantile & that all of us have raised our eyebrows & thrown cold water on it. There is nothing to do but make him feel one is interested & to try to keep his points before him 1st that he must use it in winter himself 2nd that he cannot honorably neglect the F&D because of Mr. Black's kindness to him. . . ."[25]

24. He continued to hatch similar schemes to the end of his life. In the spring of 1945, just before starting out on his final trip to Warm Springs, he told Eleanor that at the end of his fourth term he planned to take a freighter around the world and hoped she would come along. If she did not think she could stand a long freighter journey because it would make her seasick, she could follow by plane, he said, meeting him at important stops. "I said that was all right with me," she remembered.

A few days later he had an entirely new notion. The Near East now interested him, she recalled, " 'certainly some of those countries, with reforestation and proper farming and conservation, you could bring back some of their deserts. And I think it would be fun to go and live there for two or three years and see what we could do about it.' And I gave him one look, and I said, 'My heavens, haven't we met enough crisis. Aren't you tired of crisis?' "

Roosevelt agreed they'd been working hard, "but it could be interesting you know, really would be fun." *Source:* Interview with Eleanor Roosevelt, Rexford G. Tugwell Papers, FDRL.

25. Eleanor may have been chastened by her husband's anger, but her feelings about Warm Springs remained unchanged: "Franklin is expecting to leave here on May 5th," she told Marion in the same letter. "He will return here for a week in August, either with Elliott or me & won't *that* be a hot little jaunt." *Source:* Kenneth S. Davis, *Invincible Summer,* pages 61–62.

The next day, April 27, Franklin and Eleanor drove to Atlanta to attend uninvited the annual convention of the American Orthopedic Association. Twice, Franklin had asked to be permitted to address the meeting about the work he and Dr. Johnson were doing at Warm Springs; twice he had been summarily refused: Roosevelt was not a physician, Dr. Johnson was a mere general practitioner; neither was qualified to become a member of the organization and only members would be given the floor. Roosevelt would be wasting his time.

Franklin paid no attention, drew up in front of the convention hotel, and began working the lobby and corridors in his wheelchair, shaking doctors' hands and talking up Warm Springs with the same relentless charm with which he had canvassed delegates at the San Francisco Democratic Convention six years before. Before he left he managed to obtain unofficial approval for continuing the Warm Springs experiment and the promise of a physicians' committee to evaluate the next batch of patients to be treated in the pool.

Two days later, Franklin signed the deed. Warm Springs, with all its problems and its bright potential, now belonged to him.

Eleanor left for New York, and wrote Franklin a conciliatory letter from Val-Kill:

> . . . I know you love creative work, my only feeling is that Georgia is somewhat distant for you to keep in touch with what is really a big undertaking. One cannot, it seems to me, have *vital* interests in widely divided places, but that may be because I'm old and rather overwhelmed by what there is to do in one place, and it wearies me to think of even undertaking to make new ties. Don't be discouraged by me; I have great confidence in your extraordinary interest and enthusiasm.

Anna, the oldest of the Roosevelt children, was twenty on May 3, 1926, tall and slender, tomboyish and high-spirited. Hers had not been an easy adolescence. The continuing strain between her parents puzzled and worried her. She greatly missed her father who, since 1921, seemed always to be elsewhere, struggling to recover his strength, and she remained resentful of the persistent presence of Louis Howe, who now often seemed to monopolize her mother's attention as he once had her father's.

She rebelled against the social conventions to which her mother had meekly submitted and now insisted that she follow. After completing Miss Chapin's finishing school at eighteen, Anna was told she must endure a formal coming out during Tennis Week at Newport in the summer of 1924. "I wasn't going to come out," she remembered announcing. "And Granny said, 'You are.' And I went to Mother and she said, 'Yes, you must!' . . . She *made* me. I couldn't go to Father . . . because he'd just say, 'That's up to Granny and Mother. You settle all this with them'. . . . He would never give me the time of day." She could never reconcile the contradiction between the nineteenth-century customs her mother and grandmother insisted she observe—she still could not go to the movies without a chaperone—and the liberated, progressive talk she had been hearing from guests at the family table since childhood.

The trauma of Tennis Week was further intensified for her when her elderly cousin, Susie Parish, with whom she was staying, blurted out the fact of her father's unfaithfulness and the consternation it had caused within the family and without. Anna was horrified—although she now at least partly understood the chill that so often seemed to hang between her parents—but she lived silently with the secret for a full year until her mother, for reasons no one now knows, independently confirmed the story to her. "I felt very strongly on Mother's side . . . ," Anna remembered. "I think that was . . . a woman thing. . . . I think I was probably putting myself a little fearfully into mother's shoes."[26]

Her anger at her unfaithful father was quickly replaced by irritation with the vigilant grandmother who took her to Europe that summer. "Granny and I have been bickering all day," Anna confided to her diary not long after they boarded ship. "And it's been my fault all the time. . . . Oh! Damn!"

Sara was attended during the voyage by her pretty young French ladies' maid, Fabienne Pellerin. She soon attracted the attention of a bold ship's officer, who quickly found a friend for Anna, too.

> Fabienne and I for the second night went up on the top deck and talked with 2 officers [out of sight of the other first-class passengers]. It's piles of fun but gee! You have to be careful, because they're so free with their arms and hands and some of the things they say about women, etc. would shock most American young men to death. It wouldn't be exactly safe for a girl to go up alone with these officers, that's all I can say!! Wouldn't Granny be het up if she knew!!

Sara evidently was het up, or quickly became so, because as soon as they reached Italy, where Anna's blue eyes and yellow hair drew what seemed to her grandmother an alarming amount of flattering

---

26. Anna never mentioned the story to her brothers, who learned of their father's romance with Lucy Mercer only after his death.

attention, she engaged an English governess named Miss Bates to act as her granddaughter's chaperone for the rest of the trip.

Anna had completed finishing school, survived her formal debut, toured Europe; now, her parents thought she ought to go to college. She did not wish to do so. (In this, at least, she had her grandmother's backing. College made young women "bookworms," Sara said, and drove away the right sort of suitors.) Franklin wanted his daughter to try at least one year at Cornell. Anna refused even to consider it. He insisted. She reluctantly allowed that since she had always loved dogs and horses and life on the Place, she might be willing to study agriculture so that she could someday help her father with his farming experiments around Springwood. She finally spent a summer semester at the Agricultural Experimental Station at Geneva—so angry at being forced to attend that she refused to speak to her mother during the drive there, and would not answer any of her letters—then made a desultory try at a four-month course in agriculture at Cornell.

Studies did not interest her. Suitors did. Long letters from at least three ardent young men had followed her around Italy; a fellow student at Geneva proposed to her; others pursued her at Cornell.

Most persistent was Curtis Dall, a tall, balding broker with Lehman Brothers, ten years older than Anna. He was educated at Princeton, served in World War I as a naval aviator, was pleasant, bland, and utterly conventional: his greatest pleasures, he once wrote, were football weekends at Princeton, house parties in the country, and carriage rides through Central Park.

In March of 1926, Dall and Anna became engaged.

A special train brought guests up from New York for the June wedding. There were 480 wedding gifts. Endicott Peabody officiated at St. James, and Franklin came north from Georgia to give the bride away.

But not even Anna's wedding was without its underlying strains. Sara had been so delighted that her unconventional granddaughter had found such a suitable husband that she presented the young couple with a richly furnished cooperative apartment in Manhattan, instructing her granddaughter not to tell her mother of the gift if she thought she might disapprove. Eleanor was furious. "I am so angry at her for offering something to a child of mine without speaking to me . . . & for telling her not to tell me that it is all I can do to be decent. . . .," she told Franklin. "Sometimes I think constant irritation is worse for one than real tragedy. . . ."

The tensions that had riven her family had proved too much for

Anna. "I got married when I did," she remembered later, "because I wanted to get out."

Franklin had been "entirely 'off' " Dr. McDonald in April, according to his daughter, persuaded then that the eccentric neurologist's regimen was actually harmful, that he must accept the fact that he needed to wear both of his braces in order to get around. But in August he was back at Marion, struggling again to walk under McDonald's direction with only his left brace strapped on. Such seemingly erratic veering from one kind of treatment to another resulted not so much from Roosevelt's impatience, his unwillingness to stick to any one remedy for long, as Eleanor suspected, as from his adamant refusal to concede the basic, brutal fact of his condition even to himself: Nothing was working, nothing *could* work, because there were no nerves left to power the muscles he still hoped to rebuild.

Eleanor and the two youngest boys were with Franklin this time, living in a handsome ivy-grown cottage near McDonald's home. Even so, one of McDonald's colleagues remembered, "[f]undamentally, he was a loner. His marriage was a failure but I doubt this bothered him to any extent."

Roosevelt was "hypomanic" in his buoyancy most of the time, the doctor recalled, and "had to be reminded, at times, not to hog all the conversation." His old tendency to fill every second of silence with talk had in fact grown more marked since his crippling, in part because uninterrupted talk offered him an outlet for energy otherwise pent up, but also because of the need, common among handicapped persons but exaggerated in Roosevelt's case, to entertain as well as converse. Unable to move on his own, dependent on others for the performance of the simplest tasks, and uneasy always that his listeners might remain with him only out of kindness, it became important for him to be able simultaneously to talk people into doing his bidding and to relieve himself of the burden of asking for their help by putting on a nonstop show—"walking on your tongue," one polio has called it.[27]

But there were also days, the Marion physician added, when Roosevelt was reluctant to undergo the full regimen of exercises, and "Eleanor would be called to straighten him out. I can see her now, taking over like an old master sergeant: 'Franklin, there are certain

27. Edward Hermann, the fine actor who played Roosevelt in the television version of Joseph P. Lash's *Eleanor and Franklin,* made a careful study of his character before beginning the filming. He believes that Roosevelt's broad, expansive gestures were also carefully crafted to draw people to him and keep them at his side. *Source:* Interview with Edward Hermann.

things that we have to do to get you better' . . . Franklin's invariable answer was, 'Oh———!' "

Bertie Hamlin, whose summer home was nearby, sometimes stopped by to see Franklin in the afternoons. For two or three hours a day, she remembered, he made his way around and around an oblong wooden railing, pulling himself along, hand-over-hand, "talking and laughing and dragging his legs after him. Almost always someone or several people were sitting around. . . . never a word of regret or complaint from him."

Old friends like the Hamlins who remembered Franklin in his active youth and now saw him unable even to stand unaided were invariably impressed by his steadfast good cheer; what had once seemed to some of them a heedless adolescent attitude toward life now seemed a conscious act of courage; the inbred grandiosity that had once put people off had been transformed into a sign of his unconquerable spirit. Roosevelt's refusal to indulge in self-pity or to seek sympathy for his crippling was as practical as it was courageous, of course. No nation in history had ever chosen a crippled man to lead it; pity was poison to his political future.

One evening, Franklin was carried into dinner at the Hamlins by Roy and his driver, who were then sent away, not to return until nine-thirty.

"We wondered how we would spend the evening—probably staying in the dining room," Mrs. Hamlin remembered. "But when dinner was over—Franklin pushed back his chair and said, 'See me get into the next room.' He dropped down on the floor and went in on his hands and knees and got up into another chair himself. My husband was so overcome at such courage and seeing the superb young fellow so pleased at being able to do this—that on the plea of hearing the telephone, he went into the den for awhile."[28]

"Polio," Roosevelt's son Franklin Jr. said, "taught Father to concentrate on the things he was physically able to do and not waste time thinking about the things he could not." He was in fact able to do that to an extraordinary degree, to appear so unruffled by his handicap that even many ordinarily shrewd people close to him were

28. In fact, crawling on "his hands and knees" would have been difficult for Franklin; his shrunken thighs were barely strong enough to support the weight of his body. The actor Ralph Bellamy, preparing for his role as FDR in the play *Sunrise at Campobello*, once asked Eleanor whether, when her husband had crawled from one room to another, he had done so face-down. "*Never* face down," she said. "Always face-up, in a sitting position, drawing his body after him. He deliberately did something to distract you, so that you were never conscious of seeing anything but that wonderful head."

persuaded that his crippling really did not affect him—and therefore need not alarm them. Even Rexford G. Tugwell, among the least sentimental of his aides, once said that Roosevelt was "never bothered by polio."

President and Mrs. Roosevelt once attended a big picnic at the Dutchess County home of Henry and Eleanor Morgenthau. After the steamed clams and broiled chicken and sweet corn picked fresh from the Morgenthaus' own garden, Dorothy Dow, a young member of the White House staff, reported to her mother, "we all went inside . . . for dancing. . . . Mrs. Roosevelt organized a Virginia Reel, and the President sat there and called it and laughed so one could have heard him back at Hyde Park. . . . There were eleven couples in the set and we kept going and kept going until we were all breathless—except Mrs. R, of course—and the President finally just sat back in his chair, with his tongue hanging out, and called quits."

FDR, Miss Dow was sure, "was having the time of his life."

He was not. Even if, as caller, he had technically been in charge of the dancers' movements, it is inconceivable that any man so fond of dancing as he had been in his youth could have felt unmixed pleasure at watching twenty-two people—his own wife prominent among them—furiously dancing around and around the wheelchair from which he could not move. That anyone could ever have believed he was is testimony to the consummate skill with which he was able to persuade almost everyone who saw him that he was utterly oblivious to his paralysis.[29]

There was talk early that summer at Marion of nominating Roosevelt for senator. Franklin enjoyed the attention, and the steady stream of callers it produced, but he had no interest whatsoever in serving in the Senate, where he would inevitably have been forced to take sides on many of the issues that were tearing his party apart, would no longer be able to appear above the factionalism that scarred so many other prominent Democrats and from which his struggle against his crippling now safely shielded him.

"There are two good reasons why I can't run for the Senate . . . ," he told a friend. "The first is that my legs are coming back in such fine

29. Very occasionally, Franklin did let his irritation show. While governor, he held a late-night meeting with Louis Howe and Lieutenant Governor Herbert Lehman in his Albany office. The meeting began with both Howe and Lehman seated in chairs, but as the three men discussed a difficult decision, Lehman got up and began to pace back and forth across the office. Franklin watched from his chair as long as he could stand it, then turned to the motionless Howe and said, "Louis, for heaven's sake, stop *fidgeting!*"

shape that if I devote another two years to them I shall be on my feet again without my braces. The 2nd is that I am temperamentally unfitted to be a member of the uninteresting body known as the United States Senate. I like administrative or executive work, [and] do not want to have my hands and feet tied and my wings clipped for 6 long years."[30]

Party leaders picked Robert F. Wagner for the Senate nomination weeks before the New York State Convention that would make it official, but when Franklin agreed to deliver the keynote address, Louis Howe worried that his presence might somehow be misinterpreted as a sign of his availability:

> I have been warned of a plan to get you up to make a speech and then demand you to accept a stampeded convention with everybody yelling "We want Franklin!" This is, of course, a possibility, but I hope your spine is sufficiently strong to assure them that you are still nigh to death's door for the next two years. Please try and look pallid and worn and weary when you address the convention so it will not be too exceedingly difficult to get by with the statement that your health will not permit you to run for anything for 2 years more.

No such chanting was heard during Roosevelt's speech, but he had a fine time talking up Al Smith and ridiculing Coolidge prosperity. The President was in the thrall of grasping millionaires ("Calvin Coolidge would like to have God on his side," he said, "but he *must* have Andrew Mellon"), and he had done nothing to help farmers or end a national coal strike: "The people of the East have well learned through months of struggle to get coal for their furnaces and stoves, the hard meaning of the slogan 'Keep cool with Coolidge.'

" . . . [A] nation which is unwilling by government action to tackle new problems caused by the immense increase of population and the astounding strides of science, is headed for decline and ultimate death."[31]

Shortly after Franklin's appearance at the convention, his old friend Louis Wehle, who had been among the first to promote him for

30. With memories of his frustrating career in the state Senate in mind, he was still more candid with George Foster Peabody: "My explosions would come at too frequent intervals to be effective." *Source:* Frank Freidel, *Franklin D. Roosevelt: The Ordeal*, page 216.

31. His address was broadcast nationally, and he asked Josephus Daniels whether, in his zeal to defend Al Smith's governorship, he had seemed to ally himself too closely with the Wets. ". . . [Y]ou took only a light bath and came out in fine shape . . . ," his old chief assured him. "Nobody could call you an [immersionist] like Al Smith; they would rather think you took yours by sprinkling . . . or pouring." *Source:* Alfred B. Rollins, Jr., *Roosevelt and Howe*, page 225.

Vice President in 1920, wrote to see whether, if Smith won the Democratic presidential nomination in 1928, Roosevelt might be persuaded to run for governor. Franklin demurred, asking for a moratorium on all further political offers while he continued to concentrate on his recovery:

> I must give principal consideration for at least 2 years more to getting back the use of my legs. Up to now I have been able to walk only with great diff. with steel braces and crutches, having to be carried up steps, in and out of cars, etc. etc. Such a situation is, of course, impossible in a candidate. I am, however, gaining greatly and hope, within a year, to be walking without the braces, with the further hope of then discarding the crutches in favor of canes and eventually possibly getting rid of the latter also. The above are necessarily only hopes, as no human being can tell whether the steady improvement will keep up.

It had not kept up that summer at Marion. Despite all his valor and hard work, Roosevelt walked no better in September when he left than he had on his arrival in July. He resolved not to return the following year and concentrate instead on Warm Springs—a decision he evidently failed to convey clearly to Dr. McDonald.

Sara was never entirely reconciled to this decision—Marion was close to the old Delano homestead at Fairhaven, McDonald had been recommended by Uncle Fred, Warm Springs was altogether too far from Hyde Park to suit her—and when the first brochures advertising the Georgia resort appeared, she wrote to tell her son that "Dr. McDonald was much hurt that all letters and circulars speak of Warm Springs as being the only place that had helped you," while "I consider that the first *real* improvement you made was with Dr. McDonald."

Franklin answered with unusual asperity: "Of course, I can't be responsible for *all* the silly and untrue stories which gossip spreads. *No* circular about Warm Springs. . . . has spoken of Warm Springs as being the only place which has helped me. . . . If Dr. McDonald is hurt I am sorry, but he has no cause to be. I am not giving to the public any history of my own case—if I did I should include Dr. Lovett, Mrs. Lake, etc., etc."

Whether or not he had cause for it, McDonald's sense of grievance evidently grew, and in 1932, when FDR was running for President, he may have begun to think of taking a cruel revenge. Charles Hamlin took the problem to Uncle Fred and his son-in-law, James L. Houghteling, who, in turn, wrote to Roosevelt's campaign manager, Jim

Farley, on August 31 to warn him of it. "Since FDR stopped going to Marion," Houghteling told Farley,

> McDonald has, as I understand developed an incurable disease and begun to lose his eyesight and is consequently in a very sensitive and irritable frame of mind. When the Governor on his sailing vacation put in at Marion . . . for the night he did not go ashore, as he planned for an early start the following day. Doctor McDonald, however, seems to have believed that FDR came ashore, and was bitterly hurt at not having a visit from him. This led him to make some very critical remarks about FDR— which seem to have come to the ears of Julian Mason of the New York *Evening Post.* Julian is bitterly against the Governor, and is yellow through and through and will stop at nothing; I have known him all my life and am qualified to speak. He went down and interviewed Doctor McDonald and came away saying that he had enough stuff to blow Franklin Roosevelt out of the water. Whether this McDonald material has to do with the Governor's health, or some imaginable factor of a scandalous nature, I do not know [but] Mason's . . . remarks about blowing out of water sounds like something explosive.

Since the issue of Roosevelt's health had been at least muted in 1932 by having him examined by three distinguished physicians and pronounced fit to run, it seems most likely that McDonald's "explosive" material dealt with Franklin's private life—probably the frequent presence at Marion of Missy Le Hand.

In any case, Franklin was concerned enough to seek to head him off with a hearty note. "Dear Billy," he wrote, "I have been meaning for weeks to write to you." Nothing would have pleased him more than to have dropped in on his old friend, he said, but he had struck a bargain with the press, promising that he would not land anywhere if they would let him cruise along the coast without being pestered. He had sent Jimmy ashore to buy provisions armed with a personal message to the doctor but he had become distracted and failed to deliver it. "I do hope," he concluded, "that one of these days we can meet and have a good chat about old times. I hear from many people of your fine courage. That is like you! Keep it up."

Dr. McDonald subsided.

CHAPTER

17

~~~

IT WAS TIME

Have you been good boys and girls while Papa was away?" Franklin sang out to his fellow polios as he was wheeled to the pool on his first morning back in Warm Springs, September 21, 1926. He would spend nearly half of the next two years—349 days—with them in Georgia, a much higher proportion of his time than he would ever be able to spend there again.

He ordered a cottage built for himself, all on one level with a driveway that could bring him right up to the edge of a shady terrace, and with Dr. Hubbard and Miss Mahoney now overseeing the medical side of things, he began to focus his attention on trying to make good on his promise to the press that, once renovated, "the Springs will rank with the most frequented resorts in the country" and "rival Pinehurst in the North Carolina Mountains."

Roosevelt had a three-step program, he assured the *New York Times:* first, he intended to get the pools in operation, then to build a health resort for those whom the waters aided, and, "Third, the building of a cottage colony around the magnificent country club as a community center which will be available to people who are willing to maintain their part of the colony on a scale in keeping with their resources and their positions in life." To lure such wealthy colonists, Roosevelt promised a quail-shooting preserve, riding stables and bridle paths, a lake for bass fishing, a "magnificent" clubhouse, and two eighteen-hole golf courses.

No detail was too small to engage his energy. He pencilled the costs of refurbishing the old hotel on a legal pad:

Beds 26 @ $30
Dressers 26 @ $28
Writing tables 50 @ $3
Bedroom Chairs 26 @ $6
Dining Room Dishes, Silver, Glass $2,000. . . .

" . . . [Y]ou needn't worry about my losing a fortune," he assured his mother that autumn, "for every step is being planned either to pay for itself or to make a profit on." But in the end, while a few wealthy individuals did build cottages among the pines—providing Franklin with congenial company in the evenings and plenty of friends to take on picnics—all but a handful of them were either polios themselves or, like Henry Pope of Chicago and James T. Whitehead of Detroit, the parents of polios hoping to take advantage of the pool and the program of physiotherapy conducted there.[1]

Warm Springs never became remotely fashionable: the promised lake was never dug and the two eighteen-hole golf courses dwindled to one, with just nine holes.

It is further evidence of Eleanor's increasing distance from her husband that once, when asked to recall the psychological impact of his illness upon him, she replied that the only thing she had noticed was that she had never heard him speak of golf after he was stricken, although it had once been his favorite game. In fact, he spoke of it often at Warm Springs, where he helped design and supervise the laying out of the course with a network of roads and specially reinforced bridges so that those polios, like himself, who could not play but liked to watch as well as those who could play but could not walk long distances, could drive from hole to hole. After the course was completed, he liked to drive with Missy or the pretty young wife of a Warm Springs physician at his side, shouting bawdy advice to the players and carry-

---

1. The strict standards Franklin set for those who wished to build cottages on his land actually worked against luring the very wealthy: no structure was to be more than a single story high, to contain more than two bedrooms, or to be painted any other color but white. Trees were to be left uncut, roads unpaved.

Franklin may not have been too deeply disappointed that they stayed away. Urging his Cousin Bamie to come down for a visit in 1927, he assured her that she would love "the informality and truly languid southern atmosphere of the place! My one fear is that this gentle charm will appeal to some of our rich friends who are suffering from nervous prosperity and that they will come down . . . and ruin our atmosphere." *Sources:* Interview with Mary Hudson Veeder; Elliott Roosevelt, ed., *FDR: His Personal Letters, 1905–1928*, page 624.

ing with him a silver pitcher of martinis with which to toast good shots—and bad.

"It looked like an old-time hostelry in any quiet mountain resort of the Eastern states," a 1926 Warm Springs visitor recalled. "Porch chairs, a great dining room, with Negro waiters, parked automobiles with state licenses from far and near, big trees of oak and pine. . . . Only after a first look did you see the fleet of wheelchairs, filled for the most part with youth, and the crutches, canes and braces." But that second look continued to drive away paying guests. The public misconception that polio was somehow perpetually contagious died hard. Even Sara, who made a brief visit that fall and gamely agreed to build herself a cottage she never planned to occupy just to encourage her son, was alarmed at the proximity of so many polios, and when, two years later, she learned that her two youngest grandchildren were to visit, she sent her son and daughter-in-law an admonitory letter:

> You no doubt think me very fussy not to want the boys to go into the patients' pool, but quite aside from any danger to them, if they or anyone were to develop the disease after being at Warm Springs, it would give a "black eye" to the place, and especially if the pool is used by well people. I know you will not like my interference but after all, sometimes one has a right to interfere. This is only for you two and is to be destroyed at once.

Some time in 1926, Franklin sketched out an ingenious set of hand controls for an automobile: slender steel rods were to be welded to the foot pedals, then brought within the driver's reach through holes bored in the dashboard and tipped with wooden "spools." A local mechanic and blacksmith named Ponder thought he could bang out what Mr. Roosevelt had in mind. Franklin bought a battered Model T Ford with a high body and wooden spoked wheels for $50, and Ponder went to work.

About a week later, the blacksmith drove up to the cottage in which Roosevelt was staying while a crew of carpenters worked to finish his own. Franklin wheeled himself out to see his new car, and insisted on going for a drive right away, watching carefully as the mechanic pushed and pulled the spools to start and stop. Just outside of town, Roosevelt took over, the car shuddering jerkily at first as he accustomed himself to the controls, then proceeding smoothly. He was exultant, driving back through Warm Springs at 25 miles an hour, then roaring over to Manchester, then back to Warm Springs again, where he pulled up in front of the drug store, honking his horn and shouting, "Let's have a Coke!"

When the soda jerk emerged from the store with the cold drinks, Franklin was still gleeful. "How do you like my new car? It's the latest model!"

After almost five years of unbroken dependence on others, Franklin was free at last to move about on his own. He couldn't get enough of it, becoming almost as familiar to the people along the dusty roads of Meriwether County as the rural mail carrier—except, one resident remembered, "the mail carrier did take Sunday off."

"Roosevelt drove well," one frequent passenger wrote; "his useless feet and legs did not prevent him from controlling the car with the negligent ease of a practiced and confident driver; and we went along steadily enough with frequent stops for short lectures about the countryside."

"He just dearly loved to leave the road," Vice President Henry A. Wallace remembered of his three visits to Warm Springs, "and weave that car in and out among the long leaf pines. . . . Really, very reckless driving. I had seen him do the same thing in a motor boat when he would get off his yacht. He wanted to show that he could go faster than anybody, when he had the right kind of motor behind him."

Thereafter, leisurely drives became a central feature of every visit to Hyde Park, too, and the sight of FDR waving and smiling at the wheel of his blue car became a common one up and down the Hudson.

He also eventually had roads built over the old Springwood forest paths he'd known as a boy, so that he could "look over the woods and renew the scenes of his childhood . . . ," according to Frank Draiss, the laborer who helped build them for him. "When it came to laying out the roads, . . . [h]e would tell me just what he wanted to do—just where he wanted to go. And he would drive up and say, 'Well, now, Frank, I want to go this way.' So I would clear a path out so he could drive his car up and make a place for him to turn around and from that point on he would point out some place else he wanted to [go] . . . where he used to roam around on horseback."[2]

---

2. Sometimes, driving along the twisting forest roads at Hyde Park, it would delight the President to see if he could elude the Secret Service escort Congress required to remain with him at all times. "[T]hey had a terrible time . . . ," Eleanor recalled, "and on one occasion when he'd led them through his tree plantations in the lower woods, they appeared at the house and said, 'Where is the President?' I said, 'I don't know, he has not come back,' and the look on the men's faces was perfectly desperate, and they said, 'Our big car got stuck in the mud and we couldn't follow him, now where is he?' . . . at that moment [FDR] drove up looking triumphant and said, 'Oh, were you looking for me?'"

He did the same thing from time to time at Warm Springs. Very early one cold morning,

To the end of his days, Franklin Roosevelt liked to portray himself as "a tree farmer" from Hyde Park, and enjoyed telling stories whose point was the special, genial rapport he enjoyed with the villagers near whom he had lived since boyhood. But his actual relationship with the people of Hyde Park was always considerably more rarefied than he liked to admit.

During World War II, for example, it amused FDR and his special emissary Harry Hopkins to devise a clandestine code with which to correspond with one another across the Atlantic by secret cable. Important Allied leaders were given secret names, drawn from those Hyde Park men and women Roosevelt knew best:

Plog (William A. Plog, estate superintendent at Springwood) was General George C. Marshall, Chief of Staff of the U.S. Army.

Keuren (one of Plog's workers) was General Dwight D. Eisenhower, Supreme Commander of the Allied Expeditionary Force in Western Europe.

Moses Smith (the Roosevelt's outspoken tenant farmer since 1920) was the British Prime Minister, Winston S. Churchill.

Mr. Bee (Christian Bie, the caretaker at Top Cottage, the private Hyde Park retreat the President began building for himself in 1938) was Sir Alan Brooke, Chief of the Imperial General Staff.

Mrs. Johannsen (Mrs. Nellie Johannsen, who ran a gas station and tea shop not far from Val-Kill) was Sir Stafford Cripps, British Minister of Aircraft Production.

Depew (Louis Depew, Sara's chauffeur for many years) was General Carl Spaatz, commander of the U.S. 8th Air Force.

Robert (Robert McGaughey, Springwood's British butler) was General Mark Clark, commander of the Fifth Army.

The President may have intended this code to reflect the democratic spirit in which the war was being fought; may really have thought it somehow symbolic of an ordinary American neighborhood,

---

a Secret Service agent left his post for a moment to fetch himself and his Marine companion a cup of hot coffee. This was the Marine's first morning on guard duty and when, moments after his companion left, FDR himself drove past, smiling and lifting one big hand from the wheel in greeting, the dazzled young man merely saluted smartly.

"Anything happen?" the agent asked when he got back.

"Naw," said the Marine. "But the President's gone."

The agent paled and sounded the alarm. Secret Service agents and Marines fanned out through the countryside but did not find Roosevelt for nearly an hour. When they did, he was parked by the side of the road at his farm, talking with his black tenant, Mack Copeland. *Sources:* Transcript of interview with Eleanor Roosevelt, Robert D. Graff Papers, FDRL; Interviews with Charles Doggett and Robert Copeland.

mobilized to resist totalitarianism. (That is clearly what the playwright and speechwriter Robert E. Sherwood intended when he first reported it in his biography of Hopkins.)

Yet the names FDR chose to represent the leaders of the Allied cause were not those of neighbors so much as retainers. It cannot have been an accident that every one of them belonged to a person whose first duty it was to serve Franklin Roosevelt and his family.

No matter with whom he came into contact, Franklin always set the rules. He made up Runyonesque names for his close associates— "Sammy the Rose" for Samuel Rosenman; "Harry the Hop" for Harry Hopkins; "Henry the Morgue" for Henry Morgenthau, Jr.—to which they all answered cheerfully enough. Whenever possible, first-time visitors to his office were called by their first names, an aide sometimes whispering the name into the smiling President's ear even as he extended his big hand.

He made a special point of addressing royalty by their first names— England's king and queen were George and Elizabeth; Norway's crown princess was Martha. This especially delighted FDR's secretary, Bill Hassett, who noted in his journal that it taught "royalty . . . a lesson in the variations of democracy which could not be learned out of [Lord] Bryce or de Tocqueville."[3]

Not everyone agreed. Dean Acheson, who, like Franklin, had attended Groton and was himself accustomed to a certain deference, many years later described the impact of the President's instant familiarity upon him in a letter to Hassett, written after reading the published version of Hassett's wartime diary, *Off the Record with FDR*.

> You would call it, indeed you have called it, his democracy—his calling sovereigns and commoners by their first name. But it was not, I think, democracy. It was the Hudson Valley equivalent of the attitude of continental royalty. Not English royalty, which is a royalty conceived in a kind of middle class respectability, by Wesleyanism, out of Queen Victoria. His was the royalty of the Tudors and Stuarts and Bourbons and Hapsburgs—and even the pushy Hohenzollerns—to whom all other royalty were equals, and no one else mattered at all, so far as their opinion of oneself was concerned. They might be used, flattered, found interesting, treated with camaraderie in the army, on the playing field, [in the] shooting butt, etc. But basically nothing they thought of the sovereign affected

3. Hassett was particularly pleased one day at Springwood when he slipped into the library with a message for another of FDR's royal guests, Crown Princess Juliana of the Netherlands. "I whispered the fact to the President. Said he, 'Juliana, Bill has a message for you,' which I then delivered and that was all there was to it." *Source:* William D. Hassett, *Off the Record with FDR*, page 50.

his thought of himself. So when he called me "Dean" on our first meeting and thereafter, I did not like it.[4]

It should be remembered, too, that while FDR called everyone else by their first names, he was to all of them—kings, queens, senators, secretaries, servants—"Mr. President."[5]

Certainly he took the community stewardship he had learned from his father with great earnestness. He was an active and assertive senior vestryman of his father's old church, and took an interest in everything from what to name new public schools to what should be included in the historical murals his friend Olin Dows was painting for the town post office. No detail of local life seemed too small to capture his attention. In February of 1940, clearly prompted by a stern talk from his mother, he wrote the following memorandum to the Postmaster General: "At the Poughkeepsie Post Office there are approximately twenty-five steps leading up from the street to the front door. I hear considerable complaints from elderly people, especially in the Winter, who are forced to use these steps without a hand-rail. What can you do?"

A hand rail was installed.

He also gently saw to it that the overdue library books Sara borrowed from the James Roosevelt Memorial Library were returned. (Since his mother had endowed the library in her husband's memory in 1927, she herself saw no reason to take back any book she especially liked.) And after her death, he would bring all of his political skills to bear—without success—on ameliorating a longstanding dispute between the two women left in charge, the librarian and custodian.

Franklin was still more concerned with the details of Springwood

4. To be fair, it should be added that there were other reasons for the chilly tone that suffused Acheson's memories of FDR. The President had demanded his resignation as Undersecretary of the Treasury in an angry dispute over the buying of gold in 1933. Acheson left office quietly, then, and, to the President's astonishment attended the swearing in of his successor. FDR called him over after the oath taking and spoke to him as one Grotonian to another. "I'm mad as hell at you," he said, "but for you to come here today is the best act of sportsmanship I've ever seen!" When another Undersecretary later left office noisily, FDR suggested that he look up Acheson's actions to see how a gentleman should act under such circumstances. In 1941, FDR appointed Acheson Assistant Secretary of State.

"I always had the greatest respect for him," Acheson told Hassett. "He packed a tremendous wallop, and I am one of the . . . individuals who . . . found himself on the receiving end of it. But I did not like him, even though I experienced his magnanimity, too. . . ." *Sources:* Arthur M. Schlesinger, Jr., *The Coming of the New Deal,* pages 242–244; William D. Hassett Papers, FDRL.

5. Robert Sherwood remembered how startled he was when a Roosevelt cousin entered the room in which he and the President were working over a speech and addressed him as "Franklin." *Source:* John Gunther, *Roosevelt in Retrospect,* page 40.

itself, and after his mother's death, Plog reported directly to him in numbing detail every expenditure on the Place—"4 saws sharpened—$2.00; Shoe horse with Never-Slips—$4.00; 1 sink plunger—$2.00 . . . 6 rat and mouse traps—$6.00." The President himself decided how and when coal was to be delivered; agreed that a worker named John De Grof "should be raised to $3.00 a day, but I do not think we can give him milk or coal"; was pleased to see that Springwood hens had laid 923 eggs in October 1942, a jump of 113 from September.

He was a sympathetic but not notably open-handed employer. Moses Smith, his tenant farmer, lived with his wife and four sons in a battered old farmhouse with four chimneys that was somewhat grandly called "Woodlawns" and stood on the first parcel of land Franklin had bought for himself in 1911. Parts of the house, at least, dated from the late eighteenth century. There was no indoor plumbing; no electricity until 1926. And the roof leaked.

One day in the mid-twenties, Franklin visited the house, with Eleanor, Nancy Cook, and Marion Dickerman. All were appalled by conditions, inside and out, and improvements were evidently promised. When, at least a full decade later, nothing had been done, Mrs. Smith, normally a reticent woman, took it upon herself to write to "Hon. Pres. F. D. Roosevelt":

Dear Sir:—

I am sorry to trouble you but . . . I would like to recall to your mind the period before you were elected Governor, when you and Mrs. Roosevelt, Miss [Marion] Dickerman and Miss [Nancy] Cook were here for a while one afternoon, and upon leaving you noticed the dining room and the kitchen floors, and told me you would give me new flooring. Of course, they are worse now, and when the heater was put in the house, Mose had to go under the kitchen floor and brace it up, because the weight of the hot water tank made it sag. I wanted him to tell you, but he said that you were too busy; now I feel that it is my duty to tell you the condition of the house, as it is an old one and well worth saving.

When it rains I have to put pails under the leaks in the kitchen and bathroom, and on the north side of the house it beats in and ruins the wall paper. I did the dining room over this spring, and it is a mess—so I am asking you to please roof the house and fix the north side, and to give me the new floorings which you promised so long ago, also the new back porch. I certainly would appreciate the heating system, for we nearly freeze every winter as it is impossible to heat the front part of the house with the small fireplaces there. . . .

The President wrote back, not to her but to her husband, wishing, he said, "that you and your family should be comfortable and well-housed"; he agreed to fix the leaky roof, brace the floor, and put in new flooring, and make other necessary repairs, all for no more than $343— "That, I think, is all I can really afford at this time." There would be no heat.[6]

FDR himself continued, publicly at least, to consider the people of Hyde Park his neighbors, and their continuing reluctance to support him for office both baffled and wounded him. (In nine political contests—two for state senator in 1910 and 1912, one for Vice President in 1920, two for governor, and four for President, he managed to carry his home town just three times—twice for state senator and once again, for reelection as governor, in 1930.)

In 1940, he decided to make a special effort to win over the village, and ordered that a personal letter be delivered to every doorstep. ("Bless his heart," said Marion Dickerman, who remembered his laboring over the letter in hopes of striking just the right note, "he did *so* want to carry his own town.") Its tone was uncharacteristically wistful:

> Dear Friend:
> The greatest happiness that election day can bring me will be the news that you, my neighbors, supported me with your vote. No matter how great the pressure of national and international affairs which we have shared together, I have constant inspiration from the friendship back home.
>
> FDR, your neighbor

It did not work, though he won just under half the vote against Wendell Willkie, and came closer to winning Hyde Park that presidential year than he had before or would again.[7]

6. FDR's largesse was always limited. He often went about without any cash, borrowing a dollar from his valet, Irvin McDuffie, for the collection plate at church, and he thought that a five-dollar tip was sufficient for the porter who served him aboard the presidential car *Magellan* that took him to and from Hyde Park for weekends during the war. One veteran of these trips, Sam C. Mitchell, finally used his seniority with the Brotherhood of Sleeping Car porters to be reassigned to the press car, where every reporter could be expected to ante up two dollars, for a total of $40 to $50. *Sources:* Typescript of an interview with Irvin McDuffie, Little White House Archives, Warm Springs; David Brinkley, *Washington Goes to War,* page 168.

7. The rewards for Roosevelt's most loyal Hyde Park supporters, the members of the Roosevelt Home Club, founded in 1929, included quadrennial opportunities to bask—at a suitable distance—in reflected glory. Evaretta Killmer, the wife of one member, never forgot attending FDR's first inauguration:

Roosevelt carried Warm Springs and Meriwether County all four times he ran for President, by victory margins that ranged from 12 to 1 to 1 to 50 to 1, and his relationship with their people would be subtly different from his relationship with the people of Hyde Park and Dutchess County. It would be false to history—and to Roosevelt's character and upbringing—to suggest that he ever truly felt himself one of them; and after Roosevelt's death, some of those who had known him best in Georgia were amused by the number of townspeople who claimed to have been his close friends: "Of *course*, he waved at everybody and remembered their names," a physiotherapist remembered. "He was a *politician.*" But at least some citizens of Warm Springs did become individuals to him in ways that the people of his own town rarely did, beginning with old Mr. Watts, the gray-bearded mailman, who wove his inebriated way up the path to whatever cottage Franklin happened to be staying in every morning. Watts read all postcards entrusted to his care and reported whatever news they contained to the addressee before handing them over; he also did his cheerful best to read letters in envelopes, too, holding them up to the sun as he walked, to see if he could make out enough to get at least the gist.

Franklin talked politics with local leaders, including Judge Henry Revill, who stood just over five feet and weighed well over three hundred pounds, and Uncle Jake Jarrell, the county sheriff, who made moonshine whiskey when he was not upholding the law. He spoke to the combined Sunday Schools on "Woodrow Wilson, the Peerless Statesman," and gave a talk called "My Three Trips to the White House" before a luncheon meeting of the Warm Springs Chamber of Commerce at the Tuscawilla Hotel. The roomful of bankers and shop-

President Roosevelt showed us every courtesy. He even sent one of the nicest Drum Corps in Washington, to meet us at the train. And when we passed by, in the march . . . why he sat in a little enclosed glass case like. . . . And he had a cape around him and a stove-pipe hat, and he took it off and waved it at us when we passed by . . . and Tom Mix, with his big black horse, rode out of the side street and rode ahead of us, so as to make us rather conspicuous. And his horse was all decorated with red, white and blue ribbons. It was beautiful.

They did not get to greet the President himself at the White House reception that followed the inaugural procession, but Eleanor shook each member's hand, and when it was learned that Mrs. Killmer had been one of the instructors at Sara's sewing school and had also sewed all the napkins and tablecloths for Franklin's wedding, Sara asked that she and three other Hyde Park friends be brought in to see her in a separate room, "which was very pleasing to me." *Source:* Interview with Evaretta Killmer, George Palmer interviews, National Park Service.

keepers, farmers and small-town politicians was riveted by his genial memories of his first boyhood visit in 1893, when his father's friend Grover Cleveland had expressed his hope that ten-year-old Franklin would *never* grow up to be President; the job was already too big for any man.

Then he recalled for his audience the 1905 inauguration of his Cousin Theodore, and finished up with a few moving remarks about his various interviews with Woodrow Wilson, so courageous in the face of his own crippling illness.

When he had finished, the audience, genuinely fond of the big friendly man who was working so hard to transform their town, and unaccustomed to hearing first-hand such stories of great men, stood and cheered.

Georgians were open and friendly, Franklin liked to say, especially when contrasted with his neighbors at Marion who had gone for days at a time without so much as a wave. People flocked to the door of Franklin's new cottage—"*too* sweet," he assured his mother when it was finished—often bringing gifts: vases of flowers and armsful of firewood, country hams and pigs' feet and freshly shot quail and possum, homemade pies and jars of fruit.

And he ventured out alone along the slithery red clay roads, pulling into farmyards to talk crops and livestock, parking in front of the drug store for a soda, nosing into "the Cove," a deep hollow on the Flint River, to buy corn whiskey and listen to country fiddling. "He was a man that could talk to you," a farmer remembered. "He had sense enough to talk to a man who didn't have any education, and he had sense enough to talk to the best educated man in the world; and he was easy to talk to. He could talk about *anything.*"

He could also listen, and the stories he heard from the poor people of Meriwether County stayed with him into the presidency, stories about the lack of electricity in the countryside and the exorbitant rates paid for it in town; about bad schools and low farm prices, failed banks and lost savings.

The widow of a local storekeeper remembered Roosevelt's occasional telephone calls to her husband:

"Mrs. Killian. Is Sam there?"

"Yes, sir."

"May I speak to him? What are you doing, Sam? You real busy? How about coming over for a little confab?"

"You see," Mrs. Killian told an interviewer. "You see, he wanted to learn every figure in this town by their first name. And he'd call 'em. He wanted to know *every* white person. He really, truly was a neighbor."

Eleanor Roosevelt was appalled by the conditions under which the blacks of Meriwether County lived, and is said to have begun inquiring into their welfare as she and her husband rode from the railroad depot to the Hart cottage on their very first visit to Warm Springs. (Fifty years later, an interviewer asked one elderly white resident of nearby Manchester what she and her friends had thought of *Mrs.* Roosevelt. "We didn't like her a bit," she said. "She ruined every maid we ever had.")

Her husband was not inclined to intrude upon Southern folkways, although he was sometimes amused by them. Once, driving down a Georgia road, FDR began to tease his corpulent Alabama-born military aide, General Edwin "Pa" Watson. If Southern gentlemen were sincere believers in white supremacy, he asked, why was there so much obvious evidence of miscegenation in the South? As they drove, a small, light-skinned boy was seen walking along the road. FDR stopped the car and asked Watson to find out his father's name. He didn't know, the boy said. Did he know his own name? Yes, sir, he finally said, "Franklin D. Roosevelt." Watson never tired of telling that story on his Boss, and Roosevelt never tired of laughing at it.[8]

8. With race as with so many things, Franklin's real private views proved maddeningly elusive, as apparently changeable and variegated as the visitors who streamed through his office.

His courtesy and good manners in the presence even of black servants was unfailing, the badge of a gentleman: Lizzie McDuffie, the Roosevelt's maid and wife of Irvin McDuffie, the former Atlanta barber who succeeded Roy as his valet in 1927, wrote that she "always found Mr. Roosevelt courteous. He was Democratic without posing, and a true friend of the Negro race without paternalism." And his solicitude for individual blacks was genuine; when Dr. G. David Houston, a black Harvard classmate who had been graduated cum laude and gone on to head several high schools and teach English at Howard University, died in 1940, the President extended his condolences to his widow and generously added, "He and I were real friends in college," though that was hardly true.

And when, in the spring of 1943, President-elect Edwin Barclay of Liberia spent the night at the White House, FDR made a point of reminding Bill Hassett, born in Vermont, that this marked the first time a black man had ever been an overnight guest in the executive mansion; Booker T. Washington had been merely a luncheon guest in TR's time. The implication clearly was that he shared the New Englander's pleasure in this sign of racial progress.

But a month or so earlier, planning Barclay's visit with Elmer Davis, director of the Office of War Information, and Jonathan Daniels, the Southern-born son of his old Navy Department chief, FDR had joked about the supposed incidence of venereal disease among black U.S. troops stationed in Liberia. He said an officer had told him that venereal disease had affected 100 percent of the Liberians.

"I suppose they all get it before they are grown," FDR added, "as I understand there is no such thing as chastity in Liberia after the age of five or six."

Davis then suggested to Roosevelt that in light of President Barclay's upcoming visit, they should "wash off the toilet seat with Lysol."

FDR roared.

Roosevelt believed local prejudice against blacks ran too deep to be altered by any action of his—when it was suggested that a cottage for black polios be opened at Warm Springs, he would quietly help see to it that separate but hardly equal facilities were begun for them at the nearby Tuskegee Institute. But he did do what he could to allay local fears of Al Smith's Catholicism. "One morning . . . around daylight," Roosevelt liked to say he remembered,

> somebody banged on the shutters. . . . So I got into a little wheelchair and went over and opened up the shutters and there was an old gentleman from over in Shiloh Valley.
>
> He said, "Mr. Roosevelt . . . we are all upset about you. . . . We people over in Shiloh Valley, we are sort of old-fashioned and we believe the written word."
>
> And I said, "Yes, what happened?"
>
> "Well the preacher on Sunday, after church, he gave us a lot of handbills . . . and if what those handbills say is true, we don't see how you can be supporting this fellow, Smith."
>
> I said, "Why not?"

His visitor then passed a handbill through the window. Since Rome recognized only Catholic rites, it declared, Smith's election as President would invalidate all Protestant marriages and render all Protestant children illegitimate.

Roosevelt laughed. "I think I am legally married to my wife even if Smith has been governor of New York . . . [and] I have got five pretty husky kids and I have every reason to believe they are legitimate."

This dawn visitor, like so many of the everyday citizens whose opinions Roosevelt routinely mustered to bolster his own opinions, was almost surely a phantom, but the anti-Catholicism that prevailed in the Georgia hills was real enough—Warm Springs employees had

---

Even Daniels was a little abashed by this exchange, noting in his diary, "Such is the conversation in the presidential office on occasion."

Evidently still amused by the prospect of Barclay's visit a month later, the President sent a gag memorandum to Steve Early, whose animosity toward blacks had, at the height of the 1940 presidential campaign, caused him to knee in the groin a black New York policeman who had dared delay his boarding the President's train at Pennsylvania Station.

May 21, 1943
Memorandum to Early

In view of the fact that Pa [Edwin Martin Watson, FDR's military aide] . . . will . . . be away on the 26th, and in view of the condition of Mac's health [Marvin McIntyre, the President's secretary, was ill with emphysema], I hope you will be agreeable to acting as civilian aide to President Barclay during his visit.

FDR

Sources: Jonathan Daniels, *White House Witness*, pages 165–166.

been astonished to find that Miss Mahoney, though a Catholic, was an entirely admirable physiotherapist—and Roosevelt worked hard to overcome it, making speech after reassuring speech about the governor whenever and wherever he was invited.

Not long after his return to Warm Springs in the fall of 1926, Franklin began to buy up tracts of land on which he hoped to experiment with agriculture, just as he had in Hyde Park. He would eventually own some 1,750 acres, most of them located on the crest of Pine Mountain and bought from the part-time mayor of Warm Springs, Ed Doyle, who served as his farm manager for monthly wages higher than anything he'd ever made when the land he worked was his.

"I want to farm just like the local farmers do," Franklin told the county agent. "The only difference is, I want to make a profit."

Meriwether County had once been corn and cotton country, but prices had fallen, the boll weevil descended annually, and neither traditional crop yielded a reliable profit any longer. Most local farmers lost money during the twenties—and would face disaster during the thirties. Roosevelt would not allow Doyle to plant cotton on his land, hoping to demonstrate that by modern farming methods and a shrewder choice of crops, the Georgia hills could be made profitable.[9]

He planted long-leaf pine, only to find it too slow-growing to be profitable and too resinous for the local sawmills to handle. He tried beef cattle, apples, peaches, Concord grapes. Nothing worked.

Nor was Roosevelt's agricultural expertise always all that he believed it was: Mack Copeland, his black tenant during the 1930s, was once told to have all Mr. Roosevelt's cattle lined up along the road one afternoon so that the President could drive up and inspect them from his car. Two animals were "right thin," Copeland's son Robert remembered many years later, so he and his brother were instructed to build a little enclosure among the trees and well back from the road and to keep them penned there until the President drove off again. FDR never noticed their absence.

The Roosevelt farm never once made money, remembered Rexford Tugwell, who visited it several times with the president during the 1930s; it "seemed always to require expenditure for wages, for upkeep, for improvements and for extensions; but it was a delight [to

9. Old habits died hard. At one Meriwether County meeting, called to discuss raising poultry for profit, an old farmer was outraged when the discussion turned to the relative merits of various feeds: "Feed 'em? Feed 'em? Hell, if I have to feed 'em, I don't want 'em!" *Source:* Theo Lippman, Jr., *The Squire of Warm Springs,* page 106.

FDR] nevertheless. . . . It pleased him so much because it offered a challenge. He always tended to believe that something could be done with apparently hopeless enterprises. The more difficult the problem it often seemed the more satisfaction in maneuvering for improvement. There can hardly ever have been a more dismal prospect than was offered by farming that ridge of Pine Mountain. All his efforts would come to very little in the end; but he had not yet . . . accepted the inevitable. He was still hopeful."

He did not accept the inevitable about polio, either, and in January of 1927 he at last got some news that seemed to encourage his perennial hope of recovery: the American Orthopedic Association had officially declared that all twenty-three patients with whom Dr. Hubbard and Miss Mahoney had worked over the past months had clearly benefited from their time in Georgia, and it recommended "the establishment of a permanent hydrotherapeutic center at Warm Springs."

A new, nonprofit Georgia Warm Springs Foundation was created, and Franklin set about finding likely donors, with Louis Howe's enthusiastic help. Howe believed there was now real reason to think that all the time his boss spent in Warm Springs was finally going to pay off, and he threw himself into fund raising with all the ingenuity and zeal he customarily poured into politics. Franklin himself would be the best money-getter, he assured his boss—"a little concentrated work when we can lead our victims up to your desk for lunch is a far safer way of handling the important people" than leaving the job to others—but he also suggested hiring a photographer to take pictures for the Sunday supplements, "particularly if any part of the golf links can be dressed up to look like golf links."

> I am also wondering if it will be possible to get some before-and-after photographs of some of these youngsters. . . . I am not at all certain whether a still photograph would show the improvement after some months' treatment, but you are an ingenious cuss and might think of some way in which this could be done. Perhaps just one photograph showing them doing a hundred yard dash or shoveling coal or something [or] another after treatment, together with the statement that when they arrived it required two stretchers and an ambulance to get them down to the pool, might do the trick.
>
> As every patent medicine faker has discovered, nothing lures the "come on" like a before-and-after photograph. Why, God only knows.

My idea would be to use these in your conversations with malefactors of great wealth. . . .

Sara tried to raise money among her sister Kassie's rich neighbors at Tuxedo Park. Eleanor helped, too. But in the end, while most of the Roosevelts' friends wished Franklin well, they sent no money.[10]

He went right on with the work.

Paul Hasbrouck, the young polio from Poughkeepsie with whom Franklin had corresponded off and on about aftercare for two years, arrived that April for treatment. The "tremendous scale of the operations in preparation of opening here this summer has amazed me," Hasbrouck wrote home. "Workmen remodeling the cottages, the hotel—building a . . . third swimming pool and laying out a nine-hole golf course to be enlarged later to 18 holes."

Roosevelt and his Ford seemed to be everywhere at once, directing the work, stopping to chat with townspeople, greeting new patients as they arrived: there would be eighty of them in 1927, and there was a scramble to find places for them all to stay. He personally answered letters from would-be patients, too, writing a mother anxious to bring her child to Georgia:

> The Foundation takes patients in the cottages at cost, $42 a week, which includes board, lodging, medical treatment, physiotherapy, pool charges, etc.
>
> If you prefer to be together in the Hotel, the rates there are from $4.50 to $8 a day; if you would care to rent a cottage and keep house I feel sure I could get one of the privately owned cottages & the owners usually rent them for about $125 a month. It is just possible that one of the hotel cottages will be vacant, but this I cannot be certain of for a week or two. . . . I will do everything possible.

And he saw to it that the bills for indigent patients were paid out of a Patients' Aid Fund. When that was depleted, he asked that the bills be sent to him personally at Hyde Park. No one was to be turned out.

Franklin made the rules. He wanted no uniformed attendants, no hospital atmosphere, and so there were none; the dozen lithe, tanned young graduates of Peabody College at Nashville whom Miss Mahoney hired as physiotherapists, or "physios," wore one-piece bathing

10. Warm Springs would not be free of financial worries until Roosevelt was President and the national "March of Dimes" was organized, first to raise funds for the foundation, then to aid polio research nationally. The announcement that Dr. Jonas Salk had at last succeeded in developing a vaccine against infantile paralysis was made by Basil O'Connor in 1955, on the tenth anniversary of Roosevelt's death.

suits, then still considered daring, while working with polios in the pool.

Paul Hasbrouck described his room in one of the refurbished hotel cottages—"really a section of a long barrack-like bungalow. My room is completely lined with new-smelling and new-looking boards—floor, walls and ceiling. There is a congoleum rug on the floor." Furnishings were plain but serviceable: a bed, chiffonier, washstand with pitcher of water. But a modern bathroom was just off the shady porch that ran along the back of the building, and a push boy occupied his own room nearby to help the polios do what they could not do themselves.

"There *were* no back bedrooms for polios at Warm Springs," a physiotherapist remembered. "That was Roosevelt's doing. He meant it to be *their* world, no one else's."

It was "just a wonderful place to be," a polio recalled, and at its core was Franklin's invincible zest. "He was the kind of man who would come into a room and make it his. When he came in, the *dynamo* was there."

From the time he first reluctantly left Springwood to enter Groton at fourteen, Franklin Roosevelt had sought both to excel at everything he did—to be always in charge of things—and to fit in, to get on "very well with the fellows," as he had wistfully written his parents then. During his whole boyhood, it had been the natural order of things that Franklin be liked and admired by everyone—parents, servants, governesses, tutors—but his efforts to replicate that world had not worked at school or in college, in Albany or in Washington.

They worked at Warm Springs. It was his creation: polios and physios alike looked to him for leadership; but he also was its most eagerly sought-after resident, the laughing, vigorous center of things. His arrivals at the battered depot were always triumphant, his departures accompanied by heartfelt shouts of "Come back soon!" "His greatest contribution was himself," one polio remembered, "the apparent ease with which he handled himself. His example proved to us that 'A polio could do *anything*—even be President of the United States.'"

He was a privileged member of his community, living in his own cottage, only infrequently dining with the other polios, but he exercised alongside them, offered them hearty encouragement as he drove past in his open automobile, and shared their distinctive, biting humor, sometimes shocking to outsiders but enormously satisfying to people for whom laughter had rarely been a large part of life before getting off the train in Georgia.

The polios dismissed all able-bodied persons as "A.B.'s." Those among them only lightly affected were "fakes." Favorite stories were repeated through the years. When a car slowed so that its occupants could gawk at a group of polios sitting on the lawn, one boy in a wheelchair sang out, "If you come back at five, you can watch us being fed!" A hugely fat man named Doyle, so immobilized that his cigars had to be stuck one after another into his face by a push boy, was asked by a solicitous visitor if he'd had infantile paralysis. "No," he said. "Just testing wheelchairs." Another polio who had been helped onto the toilet by a push boy and then forgotten for much of the day was crowned "King Arthur" at a dinner ceremony for all the time he'd put in on the throne.

Around Thanksgiving time each year, Franklin presided at a banquet celebrating "Founder's Day." Children drew straws to see who sat next to him while he carved a huge turkey with all the theatrical flourish he displayed on Christmas Day at Hyde Park. There were songs by Fred Botts, a menu that promised such delicacies as "quadriceps on toast," "Potato Crips," and "Tibia Turnovers," and skits and musical numbers especially recast for the occasion. One woman recalled appearing as part of a quartet of primping "Powder-puff" girls in wheelchairs who sang "I won't dance, don't ask me." FDR and the rest of the polios shouted with laughter, she remembered, and when some of the veteran reporters who had accompanied the President down from Washington were seen to be wet-eyed at the sight of such lovely girls unable even to stand the polios laughed all the harder and FDR hardest of all.

". . . [W]e who sat with him in our wheelchairs, opposite his wheelchair," a polio who attended Founder's Day remembered, "learned, possibly with surprise . . . that the President was, like ourselves, a polio first, and man and President after that. Only we could sense the endless tedium of his days, the being lifted in and out of chairs, of bed, bathtub, pool. And know that war and politics and the glory of his fame were outside of all this, strung like beads on the thread of the waiting days. . . ."

Roosevelt's example sustained and inspired the polios at Warm Springs. But they sustained him, too, and he would return as often as he could to be among the men, women, and children who shared with him that painful secret.[11]

11. He managed to get back to Georgia for what would be his last Founder's Day in 1944. A patient who saw him helped from the train noted that he was so thin and white that he looked like Woodrow Wilson in his final days. But he took his traditional place behind the wheel of his

The atmosphere at the pool had changed somewhat since Franklin's first spring as "Old Doctor Roosevelt." The morning routine on the submerged exercise tables was slow, serious business now. Each muscle, beginning with the toes, was put through its arc of motion ten times, in total silence, imposed by the big sign that hung overhead:

ABSOLUTE QUIET
IS ESSENTIAL FOR THIS WORK
PLEASE DO NOT
TALK OR MOVE AROUND UNNECESSARILY

This rule applied even to Roosevelt, and from the sidelines Miss Mahoney made sure it was obeyed. "She was hard on you, but fair," a physio remembered, and if the rule of silence were broken or she sensed that one of her girls had somehow been less than attentive to her work, she would call out, "Please come to my sitting room after you are finished."

But once exercises were over, those patients who were up to it could move to the adjacent play pool, where Franklin often led them in wild, shouting games of water polo against the physios, his thin hair plastered flat, cheeks puffed with effort as he hurled the ball like a bullet and ducked anyone who came too close. (Despite Roosevelt's enthusiasm, the physios usually won at water polo, but they lost at baseball, which the polios played from wheelchairs while their able-bodied opponents had to do the best they could with their feet tied together.)

"Part of the daily program is walking, which takes place from 3:00 to 4:00 . . . under the superintendence of Miss Mahoney and Dr. Hubbard," Paul Hasbrouck reported to his family in April 1927. "This walking is for *quality* more than *quantity,* that is, patients are corrected in the way they walk. [The rails on the ramp] are for those, like Mr. Roosevelt, who need something to take hold of on both sides; but the aim is to become independent of the rails. On yesterday afternoon— Miss Mahoney's birthday—Mr. Roosevelt . . . presented her with an

open car with his Scottie, Fala, at his side. As happened whenever he came back to Warm Springs, the polios had been arranged to greet him in a semicircle in front of the handsome, white-columned center called Georgia Hall that he had ordered built for them not far from the site of the old Meriwether Inn. "As he turned into the circular drive he slowed," one of them recalled, "and when he reached us he stopped. Then, sitting in silence, he smiled. He raised his arms above his head, clasping his hands like a victor, and in our chairs we smiled back at him, and wept." Source: Bentz Plagemann; *My Place to Stand,* page 202.

old-fashioned buggy whip (tagged with a sentiment appropriate to the occasion), for use in training her performers."

Franklin had reason to be especially grateful to Miss Mahoney that April: she had begun to work out with him a new way of walking.

He had learned to make reasonably steady and relatively safe progress with a cane in his right hand and a crutch under his left arm. (That was how he had reached and left the microphones at the 1926 New York State Convention, and Miss Mahoney had recently reported to Eleanor that "it is good to see him walk around the house with a crutch and cane and stand up to the table and do and get what he wants. His balance improves & I am sure you will find him doing more and more on his feet.")

But the difference in height between cane and crutch made that gait distressingly ungainly. He had also worked hard to master walking with two canes—managing on one occasion to take seventeen uninterrupted steps that way—but the side-to-side lurch that cane-walking entailed also struck uninitiated onlookers as alarming, and the slightest nudge could knock him to the ground.

Neither method remotely resembled normal walking, neither would allow him to "pass" in the greater, able-bodied world beyond Warm Springs.

To help him do that, Miss Mahoney had recently worked out a variant better calculated to ease his audience's anxiety. Three years earlier, he had made his way up the aisle of the Democratic Convention leaning on one crutch while gripping James's rigid right arm. Now, she began to teach him to do the same thing with a single cane.

Miss Mahoney wrote to Eleanor asking that he be allowed to defer his return to New York in order to make further progress:

> Dear Mrs. Roosevelt,
>
> Mr. Roosevelt is doing so very well I want you to know it. He is walking with two canes at exercise and also with my arm and a cane. His muscles are greatly improved—his knees especially much stronger. He has shown such interest and attention to this work. . . . I do dread having it interrupted and do hope he will stay just as long as possible for we always have to go back some each week he goes away. Even two weeks or so longer will help to establish what we have. We hope you will persuade Mr. Roosevelt to stay a bit longer. . . .

Eleanor consulted Louis Howe, who wrote to reassure Franklin.

> Your Missus has shown me a letter from Miss Mahoney, urging her to urge you to stay at W.S. for at least two weeks longer and giving as her

reason that your improvement has been so real and remarkable that to leave just now would be to set everything back just as you were going over the top—The letter apparently was approved by Dr. Hubbard although his name was not used. I can't tell you how pleased I am, old man, at the details she gives of the way you have come back. I have always felt you would.

"Now I am not going to advise one way or the other because I concluded long ago that you knew more about your case and what to do for it than the doctors did," Howe went on, but so far as the F&D was concerned, Roosevelt needn't hurry north since Van-Lear Black was vacationing in Paris and not expected back until midsummer, the professional fund raiser they had been forced to hire for Warm Springs couldn't start until June 1, and "About politics the only better place for you to be just now and for the next month . . . than Georgia would be Alaska or China. The minute you get in range the newspapers are going to put all kinds of questions up to you [about Smith's presidential candidacy] some of which will be awkward either to ignore or answer.

"So to sum up I think you can rest your decision on whether staying on is going to do you the good at a critical stage in your recovery that Miss Mahoney thinks it is or not. There is no pressing need of coming back before the first of June that I can see."

Roosevelt stayed as long as he could.[12]

That same April, Missy Le Hand, so outwardly cheerful and self-contained, fell ill, first with what seems to have been a mild heart attack, and then with frightening bouts of delirium and depression—"a little crack-up," Grace Tully would gently call it later; "a nervous breakdown," a close friend admitted—whose symptoms were so severe that Dr. Hubbard removed even her fountain pen from her room for fear she would harm herself. What brought on her collapse no one now knows, but it took months for her fully to recover and she would be driven to despondency several more times over the coming years.[13]

12. His skill at walking did steadily improve, but the growing power that both Franklin and Miss Mahoney thought they had detected proved illusory: "My . . . legs continue to improve," Franklin reported to Dr. McDonald, "especially the waist muscles, and I get about quite comfortably with canes, [but] I cannot get rid of that brace on the left leg yet. It is still a mystery why that left knee declines to lock. It is very strong, and I suppose some day I shall discover why I cannot put my full weight on it."

13. In June of 1941, Missy was felled by a stroke that paralyzed her left arm and leg and made it all but impossible for her to speak. She would live on for three years, prone to uncontrollable fits of weeping, worried constantly about the man to whom she had devoted her life but whom she could no longer help.

Roosevelt dutifully visited her bedside in the White House each evening for a while—

That same month, Franklin received at Warm Springs a letter postmarked Aiken, North Carolina, from Lucy Mercer Rutherfurd. Its occasion was the birth of Anna's daughter, Anna Eleanor, on March 25.

> I hear that you are a grandfather and though I do not know exactly just what one's feelings are on that question—still I am sure—in your case—it

---

wheeling his chair up to her bed, recounting with too-desperate cheer the day's happenings, trying not to notice her painful, futile efforts to get out a word or two.

Then she was sent to Warm Springs. When Franklin visited her there in November she was able only to say the single word "yes." Moments after he left her, Secretary of State Cordell Hull called him back to Washington. There, consumed by the war that had burst upon him and made uneasy always by any evidence that the world was not so sunny as he pretended it was, he seems to have put her from his mind, unable to summon the energy just to hold the telephone while she tried to force herself to form comprehensible words at the other end. When he failed to place a call to her even on Christmas Eve, Eleanor was appalled. So, evidently, were the relatives who now cared for her in their home in Somerville, Massachusetts, and one of them wrote the President:

> She started crying New Year's Eve about 11:30 and we couldn't stop her, and then she had a heart spell and kept calling "F.D. come please come, Oh, F.D."—it really was the saddest thing I ever hope to see. We were all crying. She was very depressed all through the holidays and that was the climax. She was especially expecting you to call on Christmas Day and when we sat down to dinner, her eyes filled with tears and she said, "A Toast to the President's health," and then again during dinner another toast to you.
>
> She loves her gift and kept saying "Sweet, lovely, beautiful, I love it," but was very much disappointed at not getting your picture so will you please send her one. She asked me to have you do this.
>
> She received a beautiful, lengthy letter from Secretary [Harold] Ickes and was delighted. Also from Mr. Baruch. Mrs. Roosevelt's gifts were lovely and she was pleased to think she wrapped them herself. That meant so much to her.
>
> She watches for the Postman every trip . . . she is waiting now for your message to Congress and will watch the clock from the minute she awakens.
>
> She worries so about you all the time. . . .

On the evening of July 30, 1944, Missy was taken to the movies. A newsreel showed Roosevelt looking gaunt and shrunken, dark lines below his eyes, cheeks drawn, collar too large for his thin neck. She became agitated and had to be taken home, where she suffered a cerebral hemorrhage while poring over old photographs of him. She died the next morning. FDR was aboard a destroyer off Hawaii when he got the news.

"You and I lost a very dear friend," Grace Tully told him when he got back to Washington. "And he was about to cry," she remembered, "and so was I, and he said, 'Yes, poor Missy.' But he never liked to talk about those things . . . he didn't want to show any emotion." In his will, written after her stroke but before she died and never altered afterwards, he provided that up to half the annual income from his estate be used to pay her medical bills; the remainder was to go to Eleanor. ("If it embarrasses Mother," he told James. "I'm sorry. It shouldn't, but it may.")

Missy left her most precious possession—a small bookcase Franklin had once made for her with his own hands—to her favorite niece.

On March 27, 1945, just before leaving on his final trip to Warm Springs, Roosevelt sent a night letter to the shipyard that was to launch a cargo vessel named in her honor:

> MRS. ROOSEVELT AND I SEND WARM GREETINGS TO ALL WHO ATTEND THE LAUNCHING OF THE S.S. MARGUERITE A. LE HAND IN THE HOPE THAT A CRAFT WHICH BEARS SO HONORED A NAME WILL MAKE A SAFE JOURNEY AND ALWAYS FIND A PEACEFUL HARBOR.
>
> FRANKLIN D. ROOSEVELT

is a subject of congratulation—for all concerned. . . . I was interested to hear a little about your project from Livy Davis who was here. . . . I hope that you and Eleanor and the children are all very well and that Warm Springs is booming. . . .

> V sincerely yours,
> Lucy Rutherfurd.

Franklin evidently answered, for Lucy soon wrote again, this time from aboard the SS *Belgenland,* which was taking her and her large family to Europe:

I should think you and Eleanor should try it sometime—of course the worst is yet to come and the score in trunks is difficult to keep. . . . Bessie Kittredge's sister who cannot walk went abroad last year—they had a special chair made that would fit easily in the French trains—I am not sure it was collapsible—it simplified things a good deal—I could find out about it more definitely if you ever wanted to know. I hope you have a happy summer and that I shan't go home to find you President—Nor Secretary of State—nor yet a physical wreck from too much work for Al Smith or any other potentates!

> Ever yrs sincerely
> Lucy R.[14]

In early May, other old memories were sadly stirred. Rosy Roosevelt, seventy-three now and just back in Hyde Park after his customary warm winter in Bermuda, caught a cold that developed almost overnight into pneumonia. On May 7, suddenly, he died.

14. Lucy's cheerful, decorous letters continued to find Franklin wherever he was, and they were never again to be entirely out of touch, although Eleanor seems to have been totally unaware of it.

FDR quietly arranged for Lucy to watch each of his four inaugurations from a White House limousine, and about 1940 began calling her once or twice a week, sometimes murmuring in his overconfident French to avoid being overheard. She called him, too, and Missy and Grace Tully left standing instructions with the switchboard that she should always be put directly through to the Boss.

Sometime after Missy's stroke in 1941, Franklin and Lucy began to see as well as speak to one another again, driving through Rock Creek Park together in the afternoons and sometimes dining at the White House when Eleanor was away. Winthrop Rutherfurd died in 1944, after a long illness. Thereafter, Roosevelt sometimes stopped his train en route to Hyde Park from Washington to visit the Rutherfurd estate at Allamuchy, New Jersey, and Lucy spent time with him at Hobcaw Barony, Bernard Baruch's South Carolina estate.

During the last, increasingly lonely months of the President's life, she joined the little band of other women—including Anna, Margaret Suckley, and Laura Delano—who devoted much of their time to trying to ease his burdens and see to his failing health. Once, home on leave from the Navy, Franklin Jr. bounded into his father's office unannounced to find him having his wasted legs massaged by a strange woman who was introduced to him only as "my old friend, Mrs. Winthrop Rutherfurd."

She was with him in Warm Springs on April 12, 1945. Hers was the last face he saw before he died. *Source:* Interview with Franklin D. Roosevelt, Jr.

Franklin had always shared a little of his mother's scorn for his half brother (who was, after all, not her son but that of Mr. James's first wife): both felt that too much had been given Rosy for him to have done so little with his life. But Franklin had also relished his high good humor, shared his sense that life was meant to be enjoyed, not endured, and been especially grateful for the cheerful, bantering attitude Rosy had taken toward his paralysis.

"It is very hard to realize . . . that he is no longer there," Franklin wrote his Cousin Bamie, who had once hoped to marry Rosy and had remained his friend all their lives, "and in so many more ways than I had realized, I depended on his companionship and on his judgment."

Roosevelt hurried north for the funeral and interment at St. James.

When his half brother's will was finally read, it provided Franklin with a sizable legacy that eased the burden of his Warm Springs debt. But Rosy had also bequeathed to him all of his beloved guns and angling gear, posthumous symbols of the Roosevelt faith shared by both half brothers that in the face of all the odds, Franklin would one day hunt and fish again.

Nineteen twenty-eight looked even less like a Democratic year than had 1924. Calvin Coolidge had announced the previous summer that he did not choose to run again for President, but the country still seemed too prosperous to turn to the Democrats, and the most likely Republican nominee, Secretary of Commerce Herbert Hoover, was hugely popular because of the work he had done in Europe during and after World War I.

Opposition to Al Smith's presidential candidacy within his party had greatly lessened, in large part because of the widespread belief among his enemies that no Democrat could win in November, that denying him the nomination was not worth the effort it would require.

Franklin had been publicly aligned with Smith since 1924, and both he and Eleanor had come repeatedly to Smith's defense when his religion came under attack. Privately, however, Franklin still shared at least some of Louis Howe's scorn for the governor. "I am becoming more and more convinced that Al will be nominated and will not be elected," Louis told Franklin that spring.

> Hell is being raised in R.I., Conn. & Mass. because the Pope has excommunicated several people because they dared to bring a civil suit against the Bishop for misusing a charity. . . . This is pretty direct interference

and all the R.I. & Mass. Protestants are stirred up over it. [George R.] Van Namee [Smith's former secretary, now a member of the state public service commission] is weeping because Al's youngest daughter is to be married on June 10 at Albany and *insists* on having the Cardinal himself with his full Cardinal's court perform the ceremony. Won't the News Reels look nice in the happy Southland on this . . . not one item of papal pomp in the ceremony will be cut from the film. I hope the young couple won't have to kiss the Cardinal's toe as part of the ceremony.

And Franklin and Howe had fresh cause for resenting the presidential candidate for whose nomination they had been working for so long. For several years now, Roosevelt had been at loggerheads with Smith's abrasive friend Robert Moses, chairman of the New York State Council of Parks. The trouble began in 1924, when Smith appointed Franklin chairman of the Taconic State Park Commission with what he thought was a clear mandate to see that a splendid new 125-mile highway linked the Bronx River Parkway with Albany, thereby opening up his beloved Hudson Valley. Roosevelt then sought to have Louis made the commission secretary at a salary of $5,000 a year. Moses, whose jealousy of his own prerogatives more than matched Roosevelt's, and who had both the governor's ear and a visceral contempt for Franklin, had indignantly refused to appoint anyone so devoted to the career of another man to a body which he believed should owe its allegiance to him alone, and he had done so in a manner calculated to enrage. If Roosevelt wanted a "secretary and valet" on the commission, he said, he would have to foot the bill himself.

In January 1928, allocations for all the regions had been approved—except for the Taconic. "I wasn't born yesterday!" Franklin wrote Smith. "You and I have been in this game so long that I now realize the mistake I made . . . was in not playing the kind of politics that our friend Bob Moses used. . . . You know just as well as I that Bob has skinned us alive this year."

Roosevelt saw no option, he said, but to resign.

Not only did the governor remain unmoved by Franklin's arguments, but he wrote him a five-page letter remarkable both for its length—rare for Al Smith, who was embarrassed by his lack of grammar—and for its tone of irritated condescension:

I know of no man I have met in my whole public career who I have stronger affection for than for yourself. Therefore, you can find as much fault with me as you like. I will not get into a fight with you for anything or for anybody. But that does not stop me from giving you a little tip and the tip is don't be so sure about things that you have not the personal handling of yourself. I have lived, ate, and slept with this park question for three and one-half years. I know all about it. . . . When I told you at the Hotel Biltmore that the legislative leaders would not stand for these appropriations, I was telling you what I knew to be a fact and you were guessing at it. . . .

Roosevelt did not resign his chairmanship. Each man still coveted the other's support, and when Smith asked him again to deliver the nominating speech for him at the Houston convention in June, he happily agreed. It would give him another moment in the spotlight and permit him to demonstrate again to the delegates how far he had come since 1924.

A slight, pretty, young Warm Springs physio named Mary Hudson, with whom Franklin had often practiced his new walk, remembered the sudden extraordinary interest he began to show in perfecting it that spring. "He came every day," she remembered, "and always on time. You knew he was getting ready for something."

He was wheeled to the end of the walking ramp in front of the cottages each afternoon, had his braces locked, and then was helped to stand. He gripped Miss Hudson's right arm with his left, took the cane in his right hand, and started haltingly along the ramp, struggling to master what the physiotherapists called a two-point walk": "One, two, one, two," Mary Hudson recalled. "Right cane thrown forward and left foot forward together. Lift right leg and left arm comes down with pressure."

"He was such a big man, his braces were so long, and when they locked them at the knees, it was hard to teach him to hold his balance and walk." Inside those braces, his legs were in little better shape than they had been the year before or the year before that, the physio remembered more than half a century later. "If you don't get [muscle development] back the first year or so, you don't get it back. He had [Poor to Very Poor muscles] and could hope only to maintain that. . . . He didn't really have any muscles at all."[15]

15. When I showed the physiotherapist Roosevelt's muscle charts, she amended this memory slightly: "He had a *few* Fair muscles, but in the wrong places to help him walk." He had virtually no glutei, for example, and so could not lock his hips to stand without braces, but he possessed relatively strong perineals (graded as "Fair" on the chart), the muscles below the knee which, without equally strong ones to oppose them, simply splayed his feet. *Source:* Interview with Mary Hudson Veeder.

How then did he do it? "It's all up here," she answered, tapping her forehead. "He just *decided* to do it. He walked on sheer determination. He was ready. It was time."

At some point that spring the Warm Springs photographer is thought to have made movies of Roosevelt learning his new walk. Such films—and still photographs as well—were often made at Warm Springs to record a patient's progress. Some time during the intervening years, perhaps at Roosevelt's own request or that of one of his aides, the film seems to have been destroyed as part of the overall effort he and his supporters made to reveal as little as possible about his paralysis.[16]

From the moment he was carried down the hill at Campobello with his immobilized hand hidden beneath his hat to the very last day of his life, Roosevelt and his intimates worked together to ensure that as few people as possible knew the full extent of his disability. His polished skill at duplicity, his positive delight in secrecy, in knowing things that others didn't—qualities that had once helped alienate his wife and disappoint his mother, had put off prospective political allies, and might well have destroyed his career at the Navy Department had he worked for a less forgiving man than Josephus Daniels—now superbly served his purposes.

Franklin Roosevelt was the most photographed and filmed American of his time. He happily had himself pictured astride horses at Warm Springs (although he had largely given up riding as too dangerous long before he went there), gripping the helm of sailboats, tanned

16. It is evidence of the extraordinary hold that Roosevelt retains on those who knew him that the former Warm Springs employee who told me of this film made me promise not to divulge her name. "Don't say it came from me," she said, almost half a century after secrecy about the President's condition had ceased to matter.

Curiously, it may have been Louis Howe who persuaded Franklin that Warm Springs should invest in a movie camera. In the spring of 1927, he wrote his boss that such a purchase would both provide good publicity and aid treatment.

My next idea of a "stunt" for the press is to get a little amateur moving picture outfit and tell of your being the first to think of using movie pictures both to keep [a] . . . record of the improvement made in walking etc. by the patients [and] to encourage their morale by taking pictures of them from time to time so that they can see for themselves how much better their muscles function. I think it's a darn good idea. Wouldn't you like to have a film of how you walked, say, two years ago? And wouldn't it help you to correct wrong carriage & etc. if you could see for yourself just what you did wrong? Think it over. *I'm not talking about movies for public exhibition but for the patients' own use.* [Author's italics] It would also be a darned good story properly worked up as something new in diagnosis and treatment and the camera with projection machine and all only costs about $150.

Source: Louis Howe papers, FDRL.

and grinning in the stern chairs of deep-sea fishing boats, splashing in the Warm Springs pool, and appearing to stand unaided when actually leaning against a wall or automobile or holding tightly to the arm of one or another of his sons. In all of the pictures he looked vigorous, healthy, strong. Precisely three photographs of him in his wheelchair are known to have survived (two were snapped in private by Margaret Suckley and never seen publicly during his lifetime; the third, published in *Life* magazine, was made at Hyde Park but at a great distance and conveys little of his crippling).

Whenever possible, the public's natural curiosity about Roosevelt's condition was firmly deflected. He himself disliked speaking of it: he wanted no "sob stuff" written about him, he said, and Steve Early had standing orders to tell any new reporter requesting information about his paralysis that it was "an old story," not worth writing up again.[17]

Millions of Americans assumed FDR was merely "lame."

We owe to an amateur movie maker the single motion-picture glimpse we have of the walk Mary Hudson helped Franklin Roosevelt master in the summer of 1928—less than a minute of silent black-and-white footage.

It was made five years later, on the afternoon of August 26, 1933. It was warm and sunny in Poughkeepsie, and a large crowd had gathered on the Vassar College campus for a Dutchess County reception in honor of the region's most illustrious citizen. Roosevelt had motored over from Hyde Park, and his open Packard had brought him to within a few steps of the outdoor platform from which he would speak. As he finished his remarks, a local physician named Harold Rosenthal stationed himself next to the car. He had his 16-mm movie camera with him and was eager to get some close-up film of FDR to show his family and friends.

Rosenthal began filming as Roosevelt and his aides left the specially built ramp that led down from the platform, perhaps thirty feet away. FDR wears a dark sports jacket and white summer pants. His left hand grips the right arm of his stocky bodyguard, Gus Gen-

17. Even the President's mother was monitored for indiscretions. Visiting London in the summer of 1934, Sara was pleased to report to her son, she was invited "quite alone" for tea at Buckingham Palace: "I gave the King your message & he was pleased. . . . The Queen . . . was very nice & asked much about you as he did & how you could get about. I even got up & stood behind a chair & put one hand lightly on the back as you do."

Sara later evidently described this scene to her biographer, Rita Halle Kleeman, who included it in the first draft of her manuscript. Anna got wind of it, asked to see the offending paragraph, and insisted on her father's behalf that even this gentle story about his handicap be deleted. *Source:* Anna Roosevelt Halsted Papers, FDRL.

nerich; his right hand grips a cane on which he leans heavily, his index finger pointing straight down the shaft to keep its tip from slipping. As he starts to move forward along the dappled path, a member of his party steps out from behind him and hurries toward the camera. His expression is pleasant but purposeful; he is a Secret Serviceman and he silently orders Rosenthal to stop filming. The doctor complies, but not before we have clearly seen FDR take three unsteady steps, his head and torso rocking alarmingly from side to side, as he heaves himself forward from the hips. It is suddenly, shockingly clear that nothing works below those hips: his legs, encased in hidden braces, are utterly stiff and so wasted there seems nothing of substance within his billowing trousers.

The camera stops, then starts again—Dr. Rosenthal was not easily discouraged. Roosevelt is now so close that his broad shoulders and big profile fill the screen. Only the ghost of his customary smile is present; his jaw is set, his eyes downcast; he looks uneasy, even irritated, as his awkwardness is captured by the loudly whirring camera just inches away. (FDR is waiting while, out of the frame, an aide opens the car door so that he can be helped to turn around and fall back onto the seat; the aide will then unsnap his braces, allowing his knees to bend while he swings himself into a normal sitting posture.) Again, the film is interrupted, and when it resumes, FDR is safely in his seat—and transformed: his head cocked companiably, the famous grin in place, he shouts greetings to old friends in the crowd. He is himself again.[18]

18. Even with all the work they did with Roosevelt, one of his physiotherapists remembered, "when he was going to make a big public appearance somewhere we always held our breath for fear he'd fall."

He did fall—or almost fall—several times as President, most memorably at Franklin Field in Philadelphia on the last night of the 1936 Democratic National Convention. Spotlights followed him as he made his halting way toward the microphones through cheering party leaders to accept his renomination for the presidency. He gripped James's arm with his left hand and held his cane in his right, but when he spotted the poet Edwin Markham, an elderly man with a white mane and flowing beard, in the crowd, he stopped, shifting his cane to his left hand, and extending his right in greeting. Somehow, his delicate balance proved faulty: his body began to twist, and the knee-lock on his left braces snapped open under the sudden pressure. His leg collapsed beneath him, and he would have gone down, had not Gus Gennerich, following along on his right, stepped forward, caught him beneath the arm, and held him up. In the confusion, the pages of his speech fell from James's hand and splashed across the stage beneath the feet of the startled dignitaries.

Roosevelt subsequently gave his own off-the-record account of this incident to several reporters, including Walter Trohan of the Chicago *Tribune*, who made careful notes:

There I was hanging in the air, like a goose about to be plucked, but I kept on waving and smiling, and smiling and waving. I called to Jimmy out of the corner of my mouth to fix the pin.

"Dad," Jimmy called up, "I'm trying to pick up the speech."

"I'm telling everyone you are going to Houston without crutches," Eleanor wrote Franklin at Warm Springs, "so mind you stick at it!"

This time, Roosevelt needed no urging, and he took an extra ten days getting to Houston, travelling by train through the Midwest, shaking hands with F&D clients, and speaking on Smith's behalf, largely so that he and eighteen-year-old Elliott, who was to provide his support this time, could perfect their walking before smaller audiences. It was especially important, Franklin impressed upon his son again and again, that both of them seem always to be having a grand time, no matter what sort of strain their mutual effort actually demanded.

On the evening of June 27, 1928, the fifteen thousand spectators who cheered Franklin's slow, smiling progress to the podium at Houston without the crutches that had been so conspicuous in New York four years before included Marion Dickerman and Nancy Cook, but not Eleanor. "I had no desire to take part in the hurly-burly of a convention," she explained later; "the 1924 convention had given me all I wanted of that type of experience." But she heard her husband anyway, at Springwood, just one of the fifteen million Americans who that evening listened to the radio as Franklin Roosevelt described the qualities he believed essential in a great President, qualities which he was ascribing to Smith but which many had already come to see as abundantly present in him.

"To hell with the speech," I said . . . "Fix the God-damned brace. If it can't be fixed there won't be any speech." But I didn't lose a smile or a wave.

By this time I was mad clear through. First, I was mad because Jack Garner [the Vice President, who had introduced him] had mangled my name . . . calling me "Delaney." . . . Then I was mad because Ed Halsey, the Senate Secretary, got in front of me when I was waving to the crowd, and I must confide to you that Ed has the broadest beam in a body renowned for its posterior spread.

I was mad at the mayor of Philadelphia, who kept leaning over to confide how many police they had on duty in the park, at the station and along the route. I have to tell you that the mayor has one of the worst cases of halitosis ever blown in my face. I was mad at the lights which were so bright I couldn't see a soul in the blackness beyond.

I was mad at the speech which scattered on the floor. Finally, and above all, I was mad at the damned brace which had picked that moment of all moments to break down.

I could feel Jimmy fumbling and then I heard the pin snap back into place. My balance was restored and the weight was lifted from poor Gus. Jimmy shuffled the pages into proper order, but with some difficulty because he was flustered.

Roosevelt continued to grin, and before resuming his shuffling progress toward the podium, extended his hand toward the horrified Markham again, greeting the old poet as if nothing whatsoever had happened.

"I was still mad when I began [the speech] . . . ," Franklin continued. "It wasn't until I reached the line about 'economic royalists' . . . and heard the mighty roar from the crowd that I knew I had them, so I gave them the business." It was one of the most memorable addresses of his life, in which he pledged not only to meet but to master his enemies. *Source:* Walter Trohan, *Political Animals*, pages 82–83.

... [The] quality of soul which makes a man loved by little children, by dumb animals, that quality of soul which makes him a strong help to those in sorrow or trouble, that quality which makes him not merely admired, but loved by all the people—the quality of sympathetic understanding of the human heart, of real interest in one's fellow man. Instinctively, he senses the popular need because he himself has lived through the hardship, the labor and the sacrifice which must be endured by every man of heroic mould who struggles up to eminence. . . . Between him and the people is that subtle bond which makes him their champion and makes them enthusiastically trust him with their loyalty and their love.

America needs . . . a pathfinder, a blazer of the trail to the high road that will avoid the bottomless morass of crass materialism that has engulfed so many great civilizations of the past . . . one who has the will to win—who not only deserves success but commands it. Victory is his habit—the happy warrior, Alfred E. Smith!

The impact of his speech, and of the dramatic manner in which he delivered it—head held high this time, braced legs spread wide apart to provide balance, one arm free now to wave and gesture—was extraordinary.[19] Even the resolutely Republican Chicago *Tribune*, published by Robert R. McCormick, Franklin's fellow Grotonian and ardent critic, was momentarily dazzled: Roosevelt, it said, "is the only Republican in the Democratic Party." The *New York Times* thought the speech "a model of its kind—limpid and unaffected . . . without a single trace of fustian."[20]

Will Durant, writing for the *New York World*, was adulatory:

Here on the stage is Franklin Roosevelt, beyond comparison the finest man that has appeared at either convention. . . . A figure tall and proud even in suffering; a face of classic profile; pale with years of struggle against paralysis; a frame nervous and yet self-controlled with that tense, taut unity of spirit which lifts the complex soul above those whose calmness is only a stolidity; most obviously a gentleman and a scholar. A man softened and cleansed and illumined with pain. What in the name of Croker and Tweed is he doing here?

Nothing better could be said for the Governor of New York than that Franklin Roosevelt loves him. . . . This is a civilized man; he could look

19. In part to hide his tremulous hands—a family trait inherited from his father and passed on to his sons, but exacerbated in his case by polio—Roosevelt developed broad, expansive gestures, invariably waving with his whole arm instead of just his hand as he once had, and signing documents with a bold flourish.

20. Smith himself thought this so apt that he sent a copy of it to Roosevelt, with a scrawled note in the margin: "Dear Frank, This must be right because it brought tears in the Mansion when you spoke it. Al."

[British Prime Minister David] Balfour and [French Premier Raymond] Poincaré in the face. For the moment we are lifted up.[21]

Roosevelt also acted as Smith's floor manager (Smith's first choice had been Frank Hague, the New Jersey boss whose noisome reputation for corruption had already begun to spread, and whose distinctly urban style would only have added further to the fears Smith inspired in rural delegates; "Thank God," Howe said, when he heard that Hague had been bypassed.) All went well, and Smith was nominated on the first ballot.[22]

Franklin privately professed to be unhappy about the tepid party platform, which managed to waffle on both foreign policy and the League, writing to the old Wilsonian Newton D. Baker, "If you or I had been the candidate, we would have ordered it otherwise." But in fact his own positions on both those issues were at least as equivocal as was the platform he had actually helped to write, and he was privately appalled when in his acceptance speech Smith seemed again to go out of his way to alienate dry sentiment.

He also argued strenuously against Smith's appointment of John J. Raskob as chairman of the Democratic Committee. Raskob was a confirmed Wet, a self-made and conservative millionaire (whose entry in *Who's Who* still listed him as a Republican), and a devout Catholic. Franklin, who claimed to Sara that he had himself disdained to take the job—although there seems to be no evidence to indicate that it was ever actually offered to him—was privately indignant that Raskob got it. "I had especially hoped that the publicity end of things would have been

21. Sara was taking the waters at Vosges that summer. Bernard Baruch stopped at her table in the hotel dining room one evening. He had been at Houston, he told her, and had greatly admired her son's speech, then added that "Elliott was perfect, helping you and taking the sheets as they fell from your hand. How lovely to have had James 4 years ago and Elliott now!" *Source:* Roosevelt Family Papers Donated by the Children, FDRL.

22. In the end, the stickiest problem Franklin faced came on the final day, when Herbert Lehman pointed out to him that no one had thought to ask a Jewish clergyman to deliver an invocation. He told the story to Henry Morgenthau, Jr.

"Yes, we have no rabbi today!" . . . when I got to the platform, I found that four policemen and several firemen were searching Houston to try to find either of the rabbis. No report had been received from these sleuths and they had dashed out and acquired a willing baptist to meet the emergency. There was the baptist brother on the stand, and just as I was about to introduce him to the assembled mob your good rabbi was led in in handcuffs, delivered over to me and the day was saved.

Apparently, the rabbis in Houston, like the Catholic priests, were backward about coming forward. The other sky pilots were so anxious to pray for our souls (or rather make political speeches to us) that the authorities had to draw lots!

Source: Frank Freidel, *Franklin D. Roosevelt: The Ordeal,* page 242.

put under some really big men with imagination and organizing ability," he told Van-Lear Black, "but . . . it is a situation in which I can find little room for active work." He did not wish to be one of Smith's "yes-men," he continued, and there was little appeal for him in working in a campaign actually being run by Belle Moskowitz "with the aid of the General Motors publicity and advertising section."

Eleanor actively headed the women's division, her unhappiness with Smith's opposition to Prohibition outweighed by her enthusiasm for his progressive program as governor and her anger at the Protestant bigotry now being focused upon him. But Franklin, who had expected to be a close Smith adviser, found himself shunted aside instead, to an office at National Committee Headquarters in the General Motors Building where he was asked to busy himself with organizing the Division of Commerce, Industry and Professional Activities set up to raise campaign contributions from businessmen through a torrent of letters sent out over his signature. "I rarely get to see the Governor himself," he confessed to a friend, "and can communicate only by way of other people."

Smith's gruff condescension always annoyed Roosevelt. "Do you remember," he later asked a veteran of the 1928 campaign, "when at headquarters . . . I was treated by Raskob and Mrs. Moskowitz all the time I was there in July, August and the first part of September as though I was one of those pieces of window dressing that had to be borne with because of a certain political value in non-New York City areas?"

In fact, Franklin stopped coming regularly to his office in mid-July, retreating instead to Springwood (now his alone because his mother was away in Europe and his wife was working on the campaign), and leaving Louis Howe behind to represent his interests as best he could. Even the task of signing fund-raising letters was turned over to two secretaries whom Howe called "the forgers" for their skill at imitating Roosevelt's confident signature.[23]

23. Shortly after his retreat up the Hudson, Ferdinand Hoyt, his old political ally from the 1910 campaign, came to see him with a proposition. He and his brother Morgan had bought an old and struggling local newspaper, the *Standard,* and thought that if Franklin could be talked into writing a weekly column for them, circulation would soar. Roosevelt was initially reluctant, Morgan Hoyt remembered; "at first he was too tired . . . he wanted to take a rest . . . he didn't feel able. . . . But upon Ferd's rather insist[ing] in saying that it would be a great help to Smith. . . . He says, 'I will do anything to help Al.' " (An added incentive was that the Hoyts hoped to syndicate the column, thereby spreading Roosevelt's name to breakfast tables all across the country.)

He dictated the columns—called "Between Neighbors"—to Missy at Hyde Park and had

But if Roosevelt was rarely at headquarters, he was rarely far from the minds of those who ran it. The party chieftains agreed that he was the right man to run for governor that fall. His great name and Hudson River origins would appeal to upstate Republicans. So would his ancient reputation as an enemy of Tammany, though he was now in fact the machine's cooperative ally. He was a Protestant, which would help offset Smith's Catholicism, and he was a master of ambiguity on the issue of Prohibition. Perhaps most important, no other potential nominee had so few enemies. Without him, Smith's anxious advisers argued, the presidential nominee might not win New York's forty-five electoral votes—and without New York, he could not possibly reach the White House. With the 200,000 upstate votes they thought Roosevelt carried with him, Smith would at least have a chance.

Smith agreed, although his enthusiasm for Roosevelt was, as always, purely political; he still thought Franklin a lightweight Mama's boy saddled with a meddlesome wife, his sole assets his name and smile and crooning voice—"not quite bright," in his friend Robert Moses' estimation. It was actually fortunate for Franklin that Smith felt that way toward him, of course, for if he had truly respected Roosevelt, had he thought him ever capable of mounting an effective challenge to his own supremacy in his home state, he might never have undertaken to talk him into running for governor. When a political ally, Daniel E. Finn, asked Smith whether he was afraid that in trying to persuade Roosevelt to run, "you are raising up a rival who will some day cause you trouble?" Smith answered, "No, Dan, he won't live a year."[24]

The pressure on Roosevelt to accept the nomination built steadily all summer. He did his best to resist it. He shared with Howe the continuing fear that 1928 would be yet another good year for the

---

them ready to be picked up at Springwood every Monday morning. In writing them, he adopted a lofty, nonpartisan tone: You could no longer "fool people into believing that the nation . . . is going to the dogs," he wrote, "just because one political party happens to be in power." He deplored religious bigotry and the fact that rumors were spreading about the personal lives of Smith and Hoover: "As I happen to be a personal friend of both of these gentlemen it makes me a little hot under the collar. . . ." And he deplored single-issue voters with "merry-go-round minds [that] start at a given point, move with great rapidity and keep on coming back time after time to the same point . . . who see in a national campaign only one conceivable issue."

Franklin kept it up for ten weeks, until his own unforeseen nomination for governor made his pose of nonpartisanship impossible to sustain any longer. *Sources:* Donald Scott Carmichael, *FDR Columnist;* George Palmer interview with Morgan Hoyt, National Park Service.

24. "That remark of Al Smith's was sincere," FDR said when Finn told him of it ten years later. "There were a good many people at that time . . . who believed—some honestly and some because they wanted to—that I was headed for a tombstone." *Source:* Elliott Roosevelt, ed., *FDR: His Personal Letters, 1928–1945,* pages 771–772.

Republicans. But he was also deeply involved in making a go of Warm Springs, into which he had sunk most of his personal fortune, and did not wish to interrupt the steady exercise he was still persuaded would somehow return him to his feet.

But his own smiling, vigorous appearance on his son's arm at Houston had badly undercut his old claim that he physically could not yet mount an effective campaign. (His father's paralysis, Franklin Roosevelt, Jr., believed, had been a perverse sort of political blessing, for had he not been paralyzed he might have won his party's nomination long before the country was ready for a Democratic President—and before he was himself really prepared to run. Had he been nominated too early, "he would have been over-eager and likely have made a fool of himself, the way he did in 1920.")

Old friends who had not seen Franklin for some time now spoke of a physical transformation in him. Still slim and boyish before his illness—James Cox remembered him as having been "almost gawky" eight years earlier—he had become beefy, with broad shoulders, a deep chest, and big arms whose biceps, he liked to tell visitors, were bigger than Jack Dempsey's. "Frank, you look like a gorilla!" Louis Wehle told him when he saw him that year. His condition was "a marvel" in view of "the low state of his health only three years before"; he had gained "much in weight and color, and his vigor seemed greater than it had been before."

Several Smith aides came up to Hyde Park that summer, to swim in the pool at Val-Kill and to urge Franklin to think again about the governorship. He enjoyed the attention and one afternoon, sitting on the edge of the pool, his thin calves beneath the green water, he told some of them that he thought so much of Al that "I'll run for anything to help him." Then, with a wink and in a stage whisper intended to be heard by Sara, sitting beneath an umbrella on the sloping lawn and soon to embark upon her annual voyage to Europe, he added: *"But don't let my mother know about this!"*

Sara was not amused by Franklin's teasing. "If this costs me my son," she took one visitor aside to say, "I shall never forgive you. It's asinine."

For once, she and Louis Howe were in agreement. Howe was not worried about his boss's health—he knew how rugged Roosevelt really was in spite of his useless legs—but he was terribly concerned that a run for the governorship would bring a premature end to his political life. Smith was going to lose to Hoover, Howe was certain of it, and he would likely drag down any candidate for governor. But because no man so severely handicapped as Franklin had ever even *run* for an important political office, much less won it, Roosevelt's own physical condition, not the weakness of the national candidate, might well be blamed for his defeat. Then, too, Howe thought it most likely that Hoover would go on to win a second term as President, in 1932. The prudent thing for Franklin to do was wait to run for governor until that year, and then be ready for the White House four years after that.

MY CONVICTION THAT YOU SHOULD NOT RUN IS STRONGER THAN EVER AND ELEANOR AGREES WITH ME, Louis wired Franklin in Warm Springs where he went in late September, in part to put still more distance between himself and the clamoring party leaders. IF THEY ARE LOOKING FOR A GOAT WHY DONT WAGNER SACRIFICE HIMSELF?

Smith called Franklin from the campaign trail in Milwaukee to ask him to reconsider. Roosevelt again turned him down; he did not want to abandon his efforts to walk. (In this he was following Howe's advice: THERE IS NO ANSWER TO THE HEALTH PLEA, he had warned his boss, ANY OTHER REASON WILL BE OVERRULED BY THE GOVERNOR HIMSELF.) "Well, you're the doctor," Smith finally said.

To make his decision still clearer, Roosevelt dictated to Missy a lengthy public telegram, explaining again that AS I AM . . . ONLY FORTY-SIX . . . I OWE IT TO MY FAMILY AND MYSELF TO GIVE THE PRESENT CONSTANT IMPROVEMENT A CHANCE TO CONTINUE, and sent it to the governor in Rochester, where the state convention was about to convene to choose its nominee on October 1.[25]

Smith took Roosevelt at his word, but when he reached Rochester he found both his own Tammany allies and the upstate delegates among whom Franklin had always been a favorite in open revolt. The Republicans had now nominated for governor Albert Ottinger, the able state attorney general, whose Jewish faith and strong record as a crime fighter could be expected to make deep inroads into normally Democratic precincts in New York City. Only Roosevelt, the leaders

25. While the "constant improvement" was invisible to others, Roosevelt's hope remained bright. Filling out a medical questionnaire for a life insurance firm in 1930, two years after his steely decision to return to active politics had foreclosed further improvement at Warm Springs, he tersely—and inaccurately—described his case and his prospects for a complete comeback: "Ant[erior] poliomyelitis, Aug. 1921. Acute symptoms 2 mos. Starting 1922, started walking with braces. Definite, steady muscle gain . . . past 2 years. . . . Can contract muscles of quad. extensors & in calves of legs. *Prospect of . . . walking without braces good—perhaps in year or two.*" [Author's italics] *Source:* The Robert Forbes Collection, *Forbes* Magazine.

now felt still more strongly, could offset Ottinger's appeal by winning upstate votes.

Smith agreed to try once more to change Roosevelt's mind. Howe, worried that Franklin's inbred dislike of ever directly displeasing anyone would make him cave in to Smith's entreaties, did his best to stir old resentments at the governor's slights. He wired that a friendly newspaperman had told him REAL PRESSURE COMES FROM LEADERS AND JOBHOLDERS WHO FEEL YOU WILL BE ELECTED GOVERNOR AND PATRONAGE MADE SECURE AND THAT GOVERNOR DOES NOT REALLY CONSIDER YOUR NOMINATION VITAL TO HIS PERSONAL SUCCESS THERE IS CERTAIN GRIM HUMOR IN THIS DEMAND ON ONE WHO COULD NOT GET A PARK APPROPRIATION THREE MONTHS AGO. . . . IF YOU CHANGE YOUR MIND AND RUN PLEASE WIRE ME.

Smith tried to get through to Franklin at Warm Springs the next morning. There was only one telephone at the foundation, in a booth in the lobby of the old inn, and Roosevelt was exercising in the pool a quarter of a mile away when the governor's call came. He told the bell boy who found him at poolside to tell Smith, "I've gone on a picnic—you don't know where—and I won't be back all day. Say after that I am going to a meeting somewhere—a long way off—and that you don't know which direction." Then he had himself dressed and hurriedly took off with Missy and a picnic hamper for Dowdell's Knob until late afternoon so that no one could reach him.

At Rochester that evening, Smith called Eleanor to his suite on the fifth floor of the Seneca Hotel and pleaded with her to help him persuade her husband to accept the nomination. Franklin's Warm Springs debts could be taken care of, the governor promised, and Herbert Lehman, an efficient and vigorous administrator whom Roosevelt liked and admired, would run for lieutenant governor and help lighten his burdens, leaving him plenty of time for further recuperation.

Eleanor gently refused. "I feel that this is Mr. Roosevelt's problem," she said. "I am not trying to influence him either way."

Would she at least get him on the telephone?

She agreed to try.

That evening, Franklin was to give a speech on Smith's behalf at Manchester, and he was there, seated on the platform of the school auditorium, having been carried up three flights of stairs, when word reached him that his wife was calling him on a public telephone at the

City Drug Store, four blocks away. She was told to stay on the line. He finished his brief talk, shook hands with well-wishers, and then, laughing and smiling to ease the discomfort of the crowd, endured being carried back down the stairs. With Missy and Egbert Curtis, the hotel manager who had driven his car, he was driven down to the drug store and helped into the phone booth, his braced legs jutting through the door so that it could not be closed.

Eleanor was annoyed at having had to wait so long for him—she had a train to catch back to Manhattan where she was to teach at Todhunter the next morning—and was not amused by the obvious glee with which he started to tell her of how hard he had been making it for Smith to track him down. She told him quickly that she was only calling because Raskob and Smith had asked her to, handed over the receiver, and rushed out of the room to catch her train.

She could hear the governor shouting, "Hello Frank!" as she hurried down the corridor.

But in the Georgia telephone booth, surrounded by onlookers and with Missy watching anxiously, Franklin claimed the connection had suddenly gone bad. "It's no use . . . ," he shouted into the receiver. "I can't hear you."

An operator came on with an urgent message from the governor: As soon as Mr. Roosevelt got back to Warm Springs would he please go to the Meriwether Inn? Smith would call him there again.

The five-mile drive from Manchester through the Georgia night took less than fifteen minutes, barely time for Franklin to steel himself against what he knew would be a very hard sell. Missy was steadfastly opposed to his running—"Don't you *dare*," she told him as they drove. Her concern for his further recovery was one factor in her opposition, and she shared Louis Howe's conviction that 1928 was the wrong year, but she also knew that a return to public life would inevitably curtail their time together.[26]

A few minutes later, Mary Hudson, the physio who had helped Franklin master his new walk in the weeks leading up to the Houston convention, bustled into the big lobby of the Meriwether Inn, back from a movie date. She was startled to see Missy in the lobby so late.

"What are you doing here?" she asked.

---

26. Anna, now living on an estate near Tarrytown with her husband and infant daughter, was fully in favor of his running: GO AHEAD AND TAKE IT, she had wired her father—and he had wired her back YOU OUGHT TO BE SPANKED.

"He's over on the telephone," Missy answered.

There was no need to ask who "he" was, Mary Hudson remembered. Roosevelt was sitting in his wheelchair just outside the telephone booth, holding the receiver to his ear and shouting his responses so that he could be heard over the mouthpiece inside.

John J. Raskob was on the other end of the telephone. Roosevelt owed it to the party to run, he said.

Franklin countered that he had his health to think about. Besides, he could not leave the Warm Springs Foundation at this delicate stage; he had too much money invested in it, for one thing, some $250,000.

"Damn the Foundation," Raskob said. "We'll take care of it." He would personally make up Roosevelt's losses.[27]

Before Franklin could respond, the financier handed the telephone to the governor. In his familiar gritty voice, Smith bore down: Roosevelt *must* take the nomination. All he would have to do was make a couple of radio speeches, get elected, then go right back to Warm Springs to continue his treatments. He'd have to come back to Albany for his inauguration, of course, and to send his annual message to the legislature, and he would sometimes have to sign bills. But he could spend all the rest of of his time—nine months of every year—in Georgia.

"Don't hand me that baloney," Franklin said.

Herbert Lehman took the phone. If Franklin agreed to run, he said, he would accept the nomination for lieutenant governor and fill in whenever he was needed. They would make a great team.

Smith came back on.

"Frank," he shouted. "I told you I wasn't going to put this on a personal basis, but I've got to." As a favor to him, he was asking Roosevelt to accept the nomination; without him, he might lose the presidency. Unstated but unmistakably present beneath the governor's genial rasp was the threat that if Franklin refused this final appeal, he could expect no help from Smith or his allies whenever his turn at the great prize came.

---

27. In fact, he sent Franklin a check for that sum right away. Roosevelt returned it to him, explaining that it was enough for him to know that the financier was willing to underwrite him.

He remained personally hostile to Raskob, however, and in 1936, to counter a rumor that the millionaire had paid him to run for governor, he dictated a memorandum for use by his aides in which he claimed (falsely) that Raskob had pledged to pay $50,000 to the foundation "but has never made good. . . ." In fact, he had personally contributed more than twice as much as that to Warm Springs. *Sources:* Frank Freidel, *Franklin D. Roosevelt: The Ordeal,* page 255; Theo Lippman, Jr., *The Squire of Warm Springs,* page 52.

Franklin tried to laugh it off. Smith's prospects were not so desperate as all that, he said.

Smith stopped him: "I just want to ask you one more question. If those fellows nominate you tomorrow and adjourn, will you refuse to run?"

For a long moment Franklin did not speak.

Missy anxiously watched his face. "Don't you dare," she said. "Don't you *dare.*"

He was sure his friends could understand why he did not wish to run, Roosevelt finally said. And he could not consent to having his name placed in nomination. But if the delegates acted on their own, he really wasn't sure what he would do.

"All right," Smith said with delight. "I won't ask you any more questions!"

"I'll call you tomorrow," Franklin shouted. He handed the receiver to Missy to hang up.

Waiting outside by the car, Curtis was impatient to know what was happening. "He was in there for quite a while," Curtis remembered.

When the door of the inn finally opened and Missy emerged at Franklin's side, she looked grim. So did Roosevelt, and although the night was cool, Curtis noted that his brow was beaded with perspiration and sweat had soaked through his shirt. No one spoke as Franklin was wheeled down the hotel ramp and helped back into his car.

Curtis got behind the wheel and they started back toward the hillside cottage where Franklin and Missy were to spend another night together. No one said anything.

Finally, Curtis could bear the silence and the suspense no longer.

Was Mr. Roosevelt going to run? he asked.

"Curt," Franklin said, "when you're in politics, you've got to play the game."

Shortly after eleven o'clock in the morning on Election Day, November 6, 1928, Franklin and his mother were driven to Hyde Park to cast their votes. A band of photographers and newsreel cameramen was waiting as their automobile pulled up in front of the brick town hall. Franklin greeted them with a wave and a broad smile. As the chauffeur came around to help him out of the car, he called out: "No movies of me getting out of the machine, boys," and they dutifully lowered their cameras.

That evening, Roosevelt's family, friends, and closest supporters gathered in his suite at the Biltmore Hotel for what they hoped would be a celebratory buffet dinner.[28]

But by nine o'clock, it was clear that the Democrats were going down to disastrous defeat. Even the South, unshakably Democratic since the Civil War, had split, and early returns indicated that Al Smith had failed even to carry his own state, and that Franklin, though running slightly ahead of the national ticket, was likely to go down with him.

Eleanor had been frankly ambivalent about her husband's candidacy. REGRET THAT YOU HAD TO ACCEPT BUT KNOW THAT YOU FELT IT OBLIGATORY, she had wired him when she learned he had agreed to be nominated. During the campaign she had worked almost entirely for Smith, rarely appearing with her husband. "Governor Smith's election mean[s] something," she told a friend, "but whether Franklin spends 2 years in Albany or not matters . . . comparatively little. It will have pleasant and unpleasant sides for him and the good to the State is problematical."

The good to Eleanor was problematical, too. Once again, she feared, her life independent of her husband was to be curtailed; if he won, she would be reduced to pouring tea and seeing to seating arrangements, unable to be her own woman.[29]

Frances Perkins was at the dinner, too. She had not much liked Franklin Roosevelt when she first met him, and had only slowly warmed to him over the intervening years. But she had been greatly impressed by the courage and patience he had displayed during the campaign. "He was really kind of scared" when he first began to tour, she had been shrewd enough to see, but he had disguised that fear magnificently, and at campaign stops she had found herself eagerly

28. Missy Le Hand was missing, lying in bed at home listening anxiously to the returns over the radio: she had fallen ill with what may have been a second nervous collapse within days of Roosevelt's decision to run and had played no part in the campaign.

29. "If the rest of the ticket didn't get in, what does it matter," she told a reporter when all the returns were finally in. "No, I am not excited about my husband's election. I don't care. What difference can it make to me?"

"I sometimes wonder," she wrote much later, "whether I really wanted Franklin to run. I imagine I accepted his nomination and later his election as I had accepted most of the things that had happened in my life thus far; one did whatever seemed necessary and adjusted one's personal life to the developments in other people's lives."

Chastised by a close friend for failing to care enough about FDR's reelection to the presidency in 1936, she would answer, "One can be personally indifferent & yet do one's duty." It was not Franklin himself but the things he stood for—or that she wanted him to stand for—to which she would devote the balance of her life after his death. *Sources:* Joseph P. Lash, *Eleanor and Franklin*, page 320; Eleanor Roosevelt, *This I Remember*, page 46.

helping him maintain the illusion of mobility. "You could sort of lift your hand to fix your hat and that would make [your] coat hang like a large screen," she remembered, while behind it, he snapped his legs straight so that he could emerge from his automobile.

She had been impressed by his gallantry at the 1924 convention, but now it seemed to her to be accompanied by a new equanimity. "He didn't waste himself over trifles," she recalled. "He was good natured about it. He didn't fuss. . . . If the car didn't stop at Oriskany Falls because the road was out—making his speech about the battle monument there irrelevant—he'd draw up by the common in the center of Skaneateles and greet all comers pleasantly. . . . He'd learned to take what they bring him. If you can't use your legs and they bring you milk when you wanted orange juice, you learn to say, 'That's all right, I'll drink it.' "[30]

At first, Roosevelt was defiant in the face of the bad news. "We'll stay around until it is over," he assured his aides as the discouraging returns came in: he was still running ahead of Smith, but barely. "I have an idea that some of the boys upstate are up to their old tricks of delaying the vote and stealing as many as they can from us."

"His jaw was set," the speechwriter Samuel Rosenman remembered, "quite the way I saw it, years later, the day after Pearl Harbor."

He asked to be put through by telephone to the sheriffs of several counties.

"This is Franklin Roosevelt," he told them. "I am watching the returns here at the Biltmore Hotel in New York City. The returns from your county are coming in mightly slowly and I don't like it. I shall look to you, if they are unduly delayed, and I want you personally

---

30. For all the pain and suffering it had caused him, she later concluded, his illness taught him more than patience and forbearance.

I would like to think that he would have done the things he did even without his paralysis, but knowing the streak of vanity and insincerity in him, I don't think he would have unless somebody had dealt him a blow between the eyes. It's a dreadful thing to say. . . . [but] a person without humility cannot make out in this sorry world. . . . An old priest . . . once said to me, "Well, you know, humility is the first and greatest of the virtues. If we don't learn it of our own accord, the Lord will surely teach it to us by humiliation, because there's no other way to live." It is true so often that people who just continue to be proud and arrogant do get some frightful lesson by humility, which is an awful thing to accept, but . . . very educative.

It is impossible now to gauge the degree of humility Franklin may have felt before and after infantile paralysis, but it seems safe to add that with Franklin Roosevelt, humility was always relative. *Source:* Transcript of interview with Frances Perkins, Columbia Oral History Collection, Columbia University.

to see that the ballots are not tampered with. If you need assistance to keep order or to see that the vote is counted right, call me here at this hotel and I shall ask Governor Smith to authorize the State Troopers to assist you."

This was a largely empty threat. Unless he were elected, Roosevelt had no power over state troopers and had no assurance from Smith that he would actually take such drastic action.

Around midnight, the governor and his wife visited Roosevelt headquarters. Smith's defeat had been overwhelming.

"Well, the time hasn't come yet when a man can say his beads in the White House," the bitter candidate had told friends at his headquarters in the Sixty-Ninth Regiment Armory, but in front of the Roosevelts he struggled to maintain his cheerful composure. It was not easy. "I'll never forget how very strange he looked," Frances Perkins recalled. "So unlike himself. He had that kind of glassy eye that I never saw on him before. . . . The eye of a man who's steeling himself."

Katie Smith could not hide her tears. She had borne up well during the past months despite vicious (and entirely unfounded) rumors that she drank too much—even some campaign workers were said privately to have called her "pretty cheap stuff"—but she now found the humiliation of the unprecedented beating her husband had suffered difficult to bear.

After a few long, awkward minutes, the Smiths left for their private suite. It was Katie's birthday, the governor explained, and they wanted to be with the children for the cutting of the cake.

The morning papers arrived, with front-page stories that detailed the defeat of both Smith and Roosevelt.

Even Franklin's stubbornly maintained good cheer began to wear down, and not long after the Smiths left his suite and the newspapers had been scanned, he thanked everyone and said he was going home to East 65th Street to get some sleep. With Eleanor and Anna walking slowly beside his chair, he allowed himself to be wheeled down the corridor and into the elevator.

The newspapermen put on their hats and coats and left. The story seemed over. Campaign workers locked their offices and straggled out behind them. Someone turned off the lights in the ballroom.

Louis Howe stayed behind. Uncharacteristically quiet and still more ashen than usual, he paced the corridor, hands clasped behind his back, in the agitated attitude that members of the Roosevelt staff had come to call his "Felix the Cat routine." He had been appalled when Franklin accepted the nomination: BY WAY OF CONGRATULATIONS DIG UP TELEGRAM I SENT YOU WHEN YOU RAN IN SENATORIAL PRIMARIES, he had wired when he got the bad news. MESS IS NO NAME FOR IT . . . FOR ONCE I HAVE NO ADVICE TO GIVE.

His worst fears now seemed realized. They should have waited. Everything for which he and Franklin had worked so hard had been in vain. Party leaders had long memories and little room for sentimentality: they would not quickly forget that Roosevelt had failed to help Smith carry his own state, would likely be wary of ever again nominating a man so severely crippled to run for any important office, let alone the presidency.

One big room stayed open. Inside, a team of operators worked a bank of telephones, making one long-distance connection after another so that Jim Farley, secretary of the Democratic State Committee, and Edward J. Flynn, Democratic chairman from the Bronx, could continue to badger upstate officials about the slow pace with which the ballots from their precincts were coming in. Several tally men sat around a table, pencilling in the latest returns.

"I made up my mind to sit out the night," Frances Perkins recalled, "on the ridiculous theory that if I didn't give up, somehow the result would be changed. Only one other person seemed to have that idea," she noted, "Sara Delano Roosevelt. . . . She wasn't going to desert her boy."

Sara's feelings about her son's candidacy had been as ambivalent as Eleanor's at first, though for entirely different reasons. She had still not reconciled herself to his returning to politics after his illness, but once he had determined to do so, she had not wished to have him disappointed. "Eleanor telephoned me before I got my papers that you have to 'run' for the governorship," she had written him when she got the news: "Well, I am sorry if you do not feel you can do it without too much *self* sacrifice, & yet if you run I do not want you to be defeated! . . . However, all will be well whatever happens. Now what follows is *really private*. In case of your election I know your salary is smaller than the one you get now. I am prepared to make the difference up to you."

Now, she refused to concede. "I'll stay with you," Sara told Miss Perkins. "I don't think it's over by a long shot." The two women sat quietly, side by side on a sofa in the corridor, trying to make sense of snatches of overheard telephone conversations and keep track of the vote count, watching Howe pace, blue smoke surrounding his pallid, anxious face.

Some time after one o'clock, Ed Flynn asked to be put through to Franklin.

A butler answered and explained that Mr. Roosevelt had gone to bed. Flynn persisted.

There was a long pause, and then he heard the candidate's voice, blurred with fatigue. The Bronx boss told him he was now running far enough ahead of Smith so that it seemed at least possible that he would carry the state, after all. Franklin didn't believe it. Flynn was wrong, he said, and "crazy to wake him up." He hung up.

Nonetheless, at 2:00 a.m., Flynn issued a statement to the press, threatening to dispatch an army of "1,000 lawyers" upstate to probe fraud at the polls. The threat evidently had the effect he wanted, for the upstate returns now began to be reported more rapidly. Sara and Miss Perkins listened as the votes tumbled in—"forty votes here, one hundred votes there . . . seventy-five votes somewhere else. They mounted up."

By four o'clock, everything had changed: a narrow Roosevelt victory seemed certain.

There was no champagne with which to drink a toast—Prohibition was still in effect—and so Miss Perkins called room service and she and Sara solemnly saluted Franklin with tumblers of milk.

Then the doorman found the two women a taxi. Miss Perkins insisted on dropping Mrs. Roosevelt before heading home herself. As they drove through the dark, empty streets, she remembered, her elderly companion was "ecstatic."

The taxi drew up before the twin Roosevelt houses and the old lady got out. As Miss Perkins drove off again, she could see Sara start up the steps, eager to get inside, to see her son and share his triumph.

ACKNOWLEDGMENTS

I have now devoted the better part of eight years of my life to chronicling the first forty-six of Franklin Roosevelt's, and a great many people were kind enough to help me along the way. Most of them are thanked in the Source Notes that follow, but several need to be acknowledged here as well, and in greater detail.

I want to thank the descendants of Isabella Ferguson Greenway King, who provided me with good company, vivid memories, and a wonderful place to stay in their forebear's lovely creation, the Arizona Inn at Tucson, while examining her papers: her children, John S. Greenway and Martha Ferguson Breasted; her daughter-in-law, Mrs. Robert Munro Ferguson; and her granddaughter, Patty Doar. I am also grateful to Johanne Stevens, who has spent years organizing the family collections and without whose help I could never have found all that I did find at the Arizona Historical Society. A biography of Isabella is being prepared by A. Blake Brophy of Tucson, and I am grateful to him for letting me read his early chapters in manuscript.

I have written elsewhere of the rare generosity of the scholars who have studied FDR before me, but I want here especially to thank two men—Alfred B. Rollins, Jr., who shared with me more than a quarter century's worth of insights into the oddly symbiotic relationship between Roosevelt and Louis Howe; and Frank Freidel, whose pioneering footprints are everywhere among the archives and who opened to me transcripts of conversations with nine crucial, long-dead witnesses, with most of whom he alone had taken the trouble to speak.

I worked with original documents and published materials at Columbia University, the New-York Historical Society Library, the New York Society Library, the New York Public Library, the Francis A. Countway Library of Medicine and the Houghton Library at Harvard, and am grateful to the staffs of all of them. But the bulk of my work inevitably was done at the Franklin D. Roosevelt Library, and I want to thank by name all of those whose patience, good humor, and willingness to look further on my behalf made working in its daunting collections such an unalloyed pleasure: the director, Dr. William R. Emerson, Supervisory Archivists Frances Seeber and Raymond Teichman, as well as Elizabeth Denier, Susan Elter, John Ferris, Sheryl Griffith, Marguerite Hubbard, Paul McLaughlin, Robert Parks, Irene Prentiss, and Mark Renovitch. I shall miss them all.

I am also especially grateful to four present and former members of the National Park Service staff—Diane Boyce, Susan J. Brown, Donald McTernan, and Emily Wright—who answered my questions and allowed me to prowl behind the barriers at Springwood and Val-Kill in search of clues, and to Charles Barnes and his staff at the Little White House at Warm Springs, Georgia, who invited me down to meet a number of local people who remembered Roosevelt. And I want to thank Sheila Rothman, whom I've never even met, but who heard of my work from a mutual friend and generously sent me important materials on the care of invalids in the early part of the century, and Dr. John A. Gable of the Theodore Roosevelt Association, whose omniscience about the "other" Roosevelts proved invaluable.

Forty-five people—their names are listed in the Bibliography—put up with my questions, sometimes several times, during the course of my work. But I want to make special mention of three interviewees without whose vivid memories this book could not have been written: Linnea Calder, who brought life on Campobello alive for me; Mary Hudson Veeder, who did the same for Warm Springs and the struggle against polio FDR waged there; and Margaret Suckley, whose understanding of the Roosevelts is both sensitive and authoritative.

Several members of the Roosevelt family were helpful, but two proved especially important: Curtis Roosevelt, many of whose shrewd judgments about the role class played in the way his grandparents faced the world I have cheerfully adopted as my own; and the late Franklin D. Roosevelt, Jr., who offered me access to the journals of Helen Roosevelt Robinson and frank insights into his parents' lives, and whose enthusiasm for *Before the Trumpet* meant more to its author than he ever knew.

I want to thank my friend and agent Carl Brandt, and my editors at Harper & Row, M. S. Wyeth and Terry Karten, for their sympathy and patience when the plans for this book began to shift. I'm also grateful to my amazingly alert copyeditor, Ann Adelman, and production editor, Pamela Montgomery.

Several friends took the time to read and comment upon all or part of the manuscript: Professor Michael Simpson of the University of Wales, whose knowledge of World War I naval affairs on both sides of the Atlantic is virtually encyclopedic, kindly waded through the story of Franklin's sometimes stormy years at the Navy Department and saved a hopelessly landlocked author from disaster; my friend and fellow polio Hugh Gallagher, who patiently took my telephone calls, and then was good enough to read through the chapters having to do with infantile paralysis that grew out of them; Professor Charles B. Strozier, who made sure that I did not push the psychological evidence farther than it would go; and Richard F. Snow, the managing editor of *American Heritage* magazine, for whose friendship, steady encouragement, and unrivalled eye for literary excess I am again grateful.

And, as always, I am most grateful to my wife Diane, who not only read every word but lived through every page.

SOURCE NOTES

PREFACE

Three witnesses to FDR's birthday visit to Justice Holmes recorded their memories of the event: Donald Hiss, in Kathie Loucheim, ed., *The Making of the New Deal: The Insiders Speak;* James Roosevelt, in his own book, *Affectionately, FDR: A Son's Story of a Lonely Man* (written with Sidney Shalett); and Felix Frankfurter in *Felix Frankfurter Reminisces* (ed. Harlan B. Phillips). I have drawn details from all three versions.

PROLOGUE: THE END OF ALGONAC

Rita Halle Kleeman was Sara Delano Roosevelt's friend and biographer. After Mrs. Roosevelt's death, she also became her champion. Her book, *Gracious Lady: The Life of Sara Delano Roosevelt,* appeared in 1935, six years before its subject died, and Mrs. Kleeman had always intended one day to publish a revised edition, with a final chapter devoted to Sara's years as the President's mother. Toward that end, she conducted a number of additional interviews with her, both at Hyde Park and in her home in Manhattan, taking discreet notes in pencil on a tiny spiral pad.

In the event, however, her publisher proved unwilling to cooperate, and no other publisher could be found. Meanwhile, Mrs. Kleeman grew increasingly resentful of how her late friend was being portrayed in the growing library of books and articles by and about the Roosevelts. When James Roosevelt published *Affectionately, FDR: A Son's Story of a Lonely Man,* in 1959, she wrote to say how pleased she was to find that it gave "a balanced picture of your grandmother," rather than depicting her as "the dreadful ogre of the legend which has been a source of deep grief to her many friends and which—as you children would be the last to know—is almost universally believed."

The author of that "legend," or so Mrs. Kleeman believed, was Eleanor Roosevelt, whose resentment of her late mother-in-law grew more and more evident in her autobiographical books and writings. It seems clear that Mrs. Kleeman did not much like Eleanor Roosevelt; she deplored her political views, thought her "grudging," believed that Eleanor's portrait of Sara as "selfish, domineering, jealous" was her own "subconscious revenge on her mother-in-law for having had the charm and beauty that she herself lacked, and because *she,* and not her mother-in-law, as she said . . . was jealous of Franklin's love." (The feeling seems to have been mutual. Eleanor never acknowledged the copy of *Gracious Lady* Mrs. Kleeman sent to her and later told her she thought it had been a mistake to publish such a book during its subject's lifetime; it had been impossible to be "objective.") According to Mrs. Kleeman, "Mrs. James Roosevelt's sister [Kassie Collier] and brother [Frederic A. Delano] realized this and sorrowed over it. Often they asked if I, as a writer, could do nothing about it."

She did what she could. In 1954, the centennial of Sara's birth, Mrs. Kleeman wrote at least two magazine articles defending her old friend, filled with anecdotes drawn from notes made during her last talks with Sara. She was unable to find a publisher for these, either. After her death, her papers—including both unpublished articles; an after-dinner speech; correspondence with friends, editors, and members of the Roosevelt and Delano families; and her stenographer's pad filled with notes—were deposited at the FDRL. "I want to leave this record," she wrote in a note accompanying them, "before, I too, like so many of those who loved [Sara, am] gone—to present her as her friends saw her—for future delvers for the truth."

I have drawn heavily upon Mrs. Kleeman's notes and unpublished manuscripts in writing the Prologue and subsequent portions of this book; one need not share all of her conclusions about either of the two most important women in Franklin Roosevelt's life to find the first-hand evidence she uncovered about them and their relationship invaluable.

The story of Sara Delano Roosevelt's last days and death is touched upon in many of the biographies of her son, and I have gleaned what I could from all of them, as well as from newspapers and magazines. I believe my account to be the fullest ever given.

The President's carefully worded cable, suggesting that his mother accept the unobtrusive aid of a nurse, her no less careful reply, and his wishful pencilled note are all among the Sara Delano Roosevelt Papers, Roosevelt Family Papers, FDRL.

James Roosevelt recounted his grandmother's brave final exit from Campobello in *Affectionately, FDR*, pp. 317–318. Sara's brother, Frederick A. Delano, told FDR of his last visit with his sister in a letter written September 27, 1941, FDRL. Franklin D. Roosevelt, Jr., told me of his grandmother's feelings toward Mrs. Collier.

My description of Sara's bedroom as it must have been when her son last visited her there is based primarily upon two sources: the Kleeman Papers, and a photograph of the room made by a photographer working for the Historic American Building Survey in July of 1941 (kindly located for me by Diane Boyce of the National Park Service). The small bedside photographs which Mrs. Kleeman saw and I describe are not visible in the photograph, presumably because Sara had taken them with her to Campobello for the summer. The Kleeman Papers also record Sara's delight in her room and the memories it stirred, her pleasure in her son's successes and his smile, and her interest in his radio broadcasts.

Sara's early assertion that she could always visualize just what Franklin was doing no matter where he was is found in a letter written to him at Groton, Roosevelt Family Papers Donated by the Children, FDRL; her later reaffirmation of that power in the face of a possible visit from him was expressed in one of her last letters, written to Munro Robinson, August 6, 1941, Roosevelt Family Papers, FDRL. (Robinson's first name is misspelled "Monroe" in the letter, which Sara evidently dictated to a companion.)

James Roosevelt's tribute to country life is from a letter he wrote in 1878 to Anna Roosevelt, Theodore Roosevelt Collection, Houghton Library, Harvard University.

Sara told Frances Perkins of a mother's duty toward her children's friends, *The Roosevelt I Knew*, p. 67.

Eleanor described to her daughter, Anna, how "bright" Sara had seemed after FDR arrived to sit with her, and recalled details of the funeral in the library, Bernard Asbell, ed., *Mother and Daughter: The Letters of Eleanor and Anna Roosevelt*, pp. 136–137.

It was Helen Roosevelt Robinson who recorded in her diary Eleanor's taking charge of things and Franklin's courage in the hours after his mother's death; Franklin D. Roosevelt, Jr., graciously allowed me to examine her voluminous journals.

Eleanor's confidence that FDR would remember only pleasant things about his mother was expressed in a letter to her aunt, Maude Gray; her more private views were given in a letter to Joseph P. Lash; both appear in Lash, *Eleanor and Franklin*, pp. 642–643.

Mike Reilly, the chief of the President's Secret Service detail, left the fullest account of the falling tree and the President's arrival at the cemetery, *Reilly of the White House*, pp. 83–85.

Robert E. Sherwood's assessment of the hidden impact on FDR of his mother's death is from his *Roosevelt and Hopkins*, p. 385.

The story of FDR's sudden sorrow at discovering the relics of his childhood was told by Grace Tully in her *FDR, My Boss*, p. 105. Mrs. Kleeman had helped Sara pack the box, and it was she who told Eleanor's secretary, Malvina Thompson, of its existence; her September 28, 1941, memorandum to Miss Thompson, enumerating the carton's contents, is among the Kleeman Papers, FDRL.

1: THE WONDERFUL HUSBAND

The thirty-seven letters and postcards the newlywed Roosevelts faithfully wrote home to Sara during their ten weeks overseas form the heart of this honeymoon chapter; they fill eighty-five pages of *FDR: His Personal Letters, 1905–1928*, edited by Elliott Roosevelt. But I have also drawn upon Sara's few surviving letters to her "dear children," written from Hyde Park and Campobello (Roosevelt Family Papers Donated by the Children); her scrapbook and her sporadic and skeletal journal for that summer (Roosevelt Family Papers); and a miscellaneous collection of bills, receipts, and other documents known as the "Honeymoon Papers" (Franklin D. Roosevelt Papers); all at the FDRL.

The social delicacy required of the commander of a transatlantic liner is nicely set forth in John Malcolm Brinnin, *The Sway of the Grand Saloon*, pp. 341–342.

Eleanor's memory of her nervousness upon arrival at Springwood on her wedding night is recalled in Alfred Steinberg, *Mrs. R.*, p. 54. She recounted the story of the torn first edition and the lesson it taught her in her last book, *You Learn by Living*, p. 29, and she told an interviewer, Louis Eisner, of Franklin's surprise at her insecurity, FDRL. Her domestic ineptitude is described in *This Is My Story*, pp. 126–127.

Sara's need for the solace only Franklin could provide was expressed in a letter written to him at Harvard in 1901, and confirmed by Nelly Blodgett in her letter of January 9 of that same year; both are among the Roosevelt Family Papers Donated by the Children, FDRL. Her tiny prayer book, with its poignant portrait and inscription, was only recently discovered among the books in her Springwood bedroom, and was shown to me by Diane Boyce of the National Park Service.

Franklin's pledge to his mother that his marriage would never alter things between them may be found in *FDR: His Personal Letters, Early Years*, p. 518.

Corinne Robinson Alsop recalled her own early ignorance about sex in her unpublished memoir, Alsop Family Papers, Harvard, quoted here by courtesy of her son, John Alsop. Alice Roosevelt Longworth's memories of her own relative sophistication and Eleanor's reaction to it are from *Mrs. L.*, by Michael Teague, p. 57. Eleanor's questioning of her grandmother is described in *You Learn by Living*, p. 28.

Anna Roosevelt remembered her mother's dispiriting warning about what to expect from sex in an interview with Bernard Asbell, *The FDR Memoirs*, p. 222. Sara's brisk dismissal of her grandson's query is quoted in Lash, *Eleanor and Franklin*, p. 146, and was confirmed for me by Franklin Roosevelt, Jr.

Eleanor confided her own inability to be spontaneous and her need to deny natural desires in a 1934 letter to her close friend, Lorena Hickok quoted on p. 1 of Lash, *Love, Eleanor*. Her love letters to Franklin are among the Franklin D. Roosevelt Papers, FDRL.

Franklin's over-eager courting of Alice Sohier is described in my book, *Before the Trumpet: Young Franklin Roosevelt, 1882–1905*, pp. 252–255, 315–316.

Warren Delano II's description of his amiable grandson was given in letters to his son, Warren III, and to his brother, Franklin Hughes Delano, for whom the boy was named, Delano Family Papers, FDRL.

Eleanor described Franklin's nightmares and sleepwalking in *This Is My Story*, pp. 135–136.

The poetic vow of perpetual fidelity Eleanor elicited from Franklin is recorded in Lash, *Eleanor and Franklin*, p. 108.

Franklin's earlier flirtation with Aline Cholmley is recorded in his Line-A-Day Diary, kept while a student at Harvard, Franklin D. Roosevelt Papers, FDRL.

Eleanor's stories of her miserable time at Cortina and with the Foljambes, and of Franklin's failed plot to shock his Aunt Dora, are to be found in *This Is My Story*, pp. 130–134. The grim lesson she learned from her childhood experience with disappointment is described in *You Learn by Living*, p. 26.

Louis Auchincloss kindly told me of the reaction of one member of his family to Eleanor's primness when in the presence of married women dining with men not their husbands.

Eleanor's account of the Roosevelt's mostly blissful stay in Florence is given in *This Is My Story*, pp. 128–130.

I was fortunate enough to have been the first Roosevelt biographer to examine the voluminous papers recently deposited at the Arizona Historical Society in Tucson by the descendants of Isabella Selmes Ferguson Greenway King, Eleanor's great and lifelong friend. Letters pertaining to that crucial friendship, as well as to the Roosevelts and other important members of their circle, may be found in five separate but interrelated collections: the Dinsmore, Flandrau, Greenway, Munro Ferguson, and Selmes Papers.

Letters from Isabella Ferguson Greenway are also to be found scattered through the Eleanor Roosevelt Papers, FDRL; the relationship between these two complicated and sensitive women deserves an independent study of its own.

My brief sketch of Robert Ferguson is drawn from conversations with his daughter, Martha Ferguson Breasted, as well as from Joseph P. Lash, *Eleanor and Franklin* and *Love, Eleanor;* Edmund Morris, *The Rise of Theodore Roosevelt,* Sylvia Jukes Morris, *Edith Kermit Roosevelt;* and Eleanor Roosevelt, *This Is My Story,* pp. 134–137.

Eleanor twice told of her embarrassing political ignorance and of her terror at the prospect of making a public speech; first in *This Is My Story,* pp. 136–137, and again in *You Learn by Living,* pp. 15–16.

The pencilled draft of Franklin's earliest speech is among the Franklin D. Roosevelt Papers, FDRL; it appears here for the first time in its entirety. The Scottish newspaper account of its delivery, only slightly garbled, is still in Sara's scrapbook, Roosevelt Family Papers, FDRL.

Theodore Roosevelt's discussion with a reporter about the Portsmouth Treaty negotiations, the reminiscences of New York Congressman Herbert Parsons, the visitor to Sagamore Hill to whom TR told his news with such ebullience, and the praise from the *New York World,* are all from Herman Hagedorn, *The Roosevelt Family of Sagamore Hill,* pp. 229–231.

Franklin's last-minute purchase of a portrait of TR and its high price are both confirmed by the detailed receipt filed with the "Honeymoon Papers," Franklin D. Roosevelt Papers, FDRL. The silver-point drawing was one of three made by the artist at a White House banquet, and its present whereabouts are unknown; the other two are at the Theodore Roosevelt Birthplace in New York City, according to the files of the Theodore Roosevelt Collection, Beinecke Library, Harvard University. I am grateful to the curator of that collection, Walter F. Dailey, for doing what he could to track them down on my behalf.

2: MR. FRANKLIN

Franklin's trotting triumph and the Roosevelt's homecoming from Europe are both noted in Sara's journal, supplemented here by a study of photographs made that afternoon at the Poughkeepsie Fair Grounds, FDRL. The memories of young Franklin and his resemblance to his father may be found in the interviews with local people conducted by Fred Rath and George Palmer in 1945; FDRL. Henry Noble MacCracken's idiosyncratic books, *Blithe Dutchess!* and *Old Dutchess, Forever!,* contain some useful information about the extraordinary enthusiasm for trotting and fine horses that once gripped the county. The visitor who recalled Mr. James's determination to drive during his final days was Margaret Chanler Alrdich, who told the story in her *Family Vista,* p. 190.

Price Collier's thoughts on the importance of horses to a genuine gentleman were found in Sara's scrapbook, FDRL. The child's drawing of a man driving a high-stepping horse is among the Kleeman Papers, FDRL. Sara's letter to Franklin explaining the importance of riding while attending classes at Columbia is among the Roosevelt Family Papers Donated by the Children, FDRL. The Roosevelts' Hudson River neighbor, Olin Dows, lovingly recalled the care that went into grooming horses for public appearances in his *Franklin Roosevelt at Hyde Park,* p. 74.

Sara's description of her lifelong ambition for her son was given to a *New York Times* reporter, S. J. Woolf, and appeared in an article called "His Mother Tells About the President," February 18, 1934.

Franklin's amusement at the small size of his rented New York home is expressed in a letter written during his honeymoon, *FDR: His Personal Letters, 1905–1928*, p. 72.

Sara's birthday letter to her pregnant daughter-in-law is among her papers, Roosevelt Family Papers Donated by the Children, FDRL. Franklin's wish to have many children was recalled for me by Alice Sohier's granddaughter, Emily Shaw; see my *Before the Trumpet* for further details. Eleanor remembered her fears about childbirth, the comfort she got from her pregnant friend, and the lesson she drew from having come through the ordeal unscathed in *You Learn by Living*, pp. 33–34. Sara's efforts to help Eleanor ready herself for motherhood and her admiration for her daughter-in-law's stoicism are given in her journal, FDRL.

The Roosevelt-Longworth wedding was exhaustively covered by the newspapers. I have drawn heavily upon accounts that appeared in the *New York Times, Herald*, and *Tribune*, especially for the details of what those, like Franklin, who were kept out of the Porcellian meeting could hear through the dining room door; a present-day club member, who prefers to remain anonymous, kindly explained to me the tradition of the "Brothers' Room." I have taken additional wedding details from Sylvia Jukes Morris, *Edith Kermit Roosevelt*, pp. 304–307, and from Alice Longworth's own memories as given in Michael Teague, *Mrs. L.*, pp. 123–129, Howard Teichman, *Alice*, and Carol Felsenthal, *Alice Roosevelt Longworth*.

Anna's arrival is sketchily described in Sara's journal, FDRL; Helen Roosevelt Robinson's description of the baby and of Franklin's obvious pleasure in her comes from her diary, kindly shown to me by Franklin D. Roosevelt, Jr. Eleanor's memories of her wan early efforts at caring for her baby are all from *This Is My Story*, pp. 142–146.

Dr. L. Emmett Holt's dicta on the proper way to raise children are all from his book, *The Care and Feeding of Children: A Catechism for the Use of Mothers and Children's Nurses*, a copy of which my friend Marjorie Iseman lent to me. Eleanor herself described her attempt to give Anna more fresh air and the trouble it caused with the neighbors in *This Is My Story*, p. 151.

James Roosevelt described his father's reluctance to involve himself in household matters in his *Affectionately, FDR*, p. 39. Anna's memories of her own early and lasting devotion to her father are quoted in *Mother and Daughter: The Letters of Eleanor and Anna Roosevelt*, edited by Bernard Asbell, p. 19. Eleanor's description of Anna longing after her father is quoted in John R. Boettiger, *A Love in Shadow*, p. 50; her chiding letters to Franklin at Cambridge and from Oldgate are among the Roosevelt Family Papers Donated by the Children, FDRL. Her own memory of her high standards and her disapproval of her husband for missing church are in *This Is My Story*, pp. 149–150. The beginnings of Franklin's two aborted works of fiction were found among the Roosevelt Family Papers Donated by the Children, FDRL. Aunt Ella Bulloch's memories of Elliott Roosevelt's love of domesticity are from a 1905 letter, Eleanor Roosevelt Papers, FDRL. Eleanor's dutiful participation in her mother-in-law's genteel charities is noted in Sara's journals, FDRL. Her emphasis on the importance of being useful is from *This Is My Story*, p. 13; her icy memory of having been just one of many who served her husband's purposes is from the second volume of her autobiography, *This I Remember*, p. 349. She told interviewer Louis Eisner of the success FDR had in arranging his life to suit himself, FDRL.

Corinne Alsop's memories of her New Year's visit to Springwood and of Franklin's irritation at his mother is from her unpublished essay about her cousin, Alsop Family Papers, Harvard University, and appear here by courtesy of her son, John Alsop. Olin Dows includes a sketch and description of the New Year's dances at Crumwold in his *Franklin D. Roosevelt at Hyde Park*, pp. 65–66. Eleanor's illness and operation and her reactions to them are noted in Sara's journal and more fully described in *This Is My Story*, p. 146.

My portrait of Columbia and its School of Law as Franklin knew them is drawn from a number of sources, but I was greatly helped in my research by Paul R. Palmer, curator of the "Columbiana" Collection which is now housed in the Low Memorial Library, and benefited, as well, from the wise counsel of Professor Arthur W. Murphy of the current faculty. Among the books and articles I consulted: Columbia University (Staff of the Foundation for Research in Legal History), *A History of the School of Law, Columbia University;* Columbia University, *Bulletin of Information, 1905–1906* and *1906–1907;* Horace Coon, *Colossus on the Hudson;* Frederick Paul Keppel (Dean of Columbia College), *Columbia;* John A. Kouwenhoven, *The Columbia Historical Portrait of New York;* Brander Matthews, et al., eds., *A History of Columbia University 1754–1904;* Robert A. M. Stern, Gregory Gilmartin, and John Massengale, *New York 1900: Metropolitan Architecture and Urbanism, 1890–1915;* Judith Green, "FDR and Columbia: Bringing the Best to the New Deal," *Columbia Law Alumni Observer* (February–March 1982).

Sara's strong views on where her son should attend law school were expressed in a 1901 letter, Roosevelt Family Papers Donated by the Children, FDRL. Beverley R. Robinson recalled the long hours and hard work he endured at Columbia, Columbia Oral History Project, Columbia University. Eleanor's inquiry about Franklin's fellow students is quoted in Joseph P. Lash, *Eleanor and Franklin*, p. 135; the rough ethnic tally of his law school class was also made by Lash. The law school graduate who was so anxious to assure posterity that his classmates were graduates of Ivy League schools was H. Alexander Smith, Columbia Oral History Project, Columbia University.

The name of the law student who so disliked Franklin is not known, but a long interview with him appears in *This Man Roosevelt*, by Earle Looker, pp. 49–52. Franklin's own pencilled notes for several Columbia classes are among his papers, FDRL. His verses about Professor William S. Redfield appear on the flyleaf of his textbook, recently acquired by the Franklin and Eleanor Roosevelt Institute, FDRL. Jackson E. Reynolds' stern critique of his former student, and his description of the help Franklin may have received in obtaining his job with Carter, Ledyard & Milburn, can be found in his interview by the Columbia Oral History Project, Columbia University. Edmund L. Baylies's letter offering Franklin a position as a clerk is on display at the FDRL.

The overheard conversation between FDR and Nicholas Murray Butler is from Horace Coon, *Colossus on the Hudson*, p. 99.

The letters to Sara upon which I based my account of the Roosevelts' summer at Campobello in 1907 all appear in *FDR: His Personal Letters, 1905–1928*, pp. 86–139. (I have restored the names of those summer residents Franklin and Eleanor found so trying, deleted when the letters were first published.) Sara's responses are among the Roosevelt Family Papers Donated by the Children, FDRL. Eleanor also left an account of those weeks in *This Is My Story*, pp. 143, 147–149.

Franklin's three years with Carter, Ledyard & Milburn resist detailed reconstruction. Louis M. Stanton (a former partner and now a judge) kindly provided me with access to what little record of Roosevelt's tenure remains with the firm. Confidentiality still demands that clients' files remain closed, and court transcripts of the civil cases Franklin handled between 1907 and 1910 no longer survive. My account is therefore largely based upon Franklin's own pencilled notes and briefs and his skeletal correspondence with clients, filed as Law School and Law Practice Correspondence and Papers, Franklin D. Roosevelt Papers, FDRL. His mock self-advertisement is on display at the FDRL. His own memory of what it was like to start work without practical training was given at a 1941 press conference, and appears in Samuel I. Rosenman, ed., *The Public Papers and Addresses of Franklin D. Roosevelt*, pp. 457–458. Eleanor offered her assessment of her husband's liking for the law and the lessons he learned from it to Louis Eisner, FDRL. His opponent's account of Franklin's kindness is from Earle Looker, *This Man Roosevelt*, pp. 49–52.

Franklin's letter to Eleanor about his gift to the Minturn Hospital is among her papers, FDRL. The former clerk who recalled both Mr. Ledyard's ability and his temper was Grenville Clark; that assessment and his account of the unwise trip he and Franklin took to the Polo Grounds are both from Gerald T. Dunne, *Grenville Clark: Public Citizen*, p. 21. Other details of office life come from another former clerk, Edward De T. Bechtel, an interview with whom appeared in the "Talk of the Town" section of *The New Yorker*, April 21, 1945. Jackson E. Reynolds recalled the commodore's brutal verdict on Franklin's potential as a lawyer, Columbia Oral History Project, Columbia University.

I found Herman Bassman's indictment and Franklin's sketchy notes for Bassman's defense among his Law School and Law Practice Correspondence and Papers, Franklin D. Roosevelt Papers, FDRL.

Eleanor's memories of the birth of James and the harrowing summer she spent with her two babies at Seabright are in *This Is My Story*, pp. 157–159. Sara's account of the birth of her first grandson and Franklin's delight in it is from her journal; her letter on the subject of Seabright along with the note she sent with the hat for Franklin's trip are among the Roosevelt Family Papers Donated by the Children, FDRL. My accounts of the Kentucky and Newfoundland trips are based on Franklin's letters to Eleanor, *FDR: His Personal Letters, 1905–1928*, pp. 140–150.

James' christening is described in Sara's journal, FDRL; the croquet that followed was noted in Helen Roosevelt Robinson's diary, courtesy of Franklin D. Roosevelt, Jr.

3: ALMOST THERE

FDR's pleasure in Helen Robinson's gift of her grandmother's journals and his feelings about the life they describe are found in his letters to her in PPF 498, FDRL. Eleanor's letter to Bamie is quoted in Joseph P. Lash, *Eleanor and Franklin*, p. 166. Franklin's letter to Edmund Baylies is among his Papers as a State Senator, FDRL.

The clipping that included Judge Howland's enthusiasm for the law is still pinned in Sara's personal scrapbook, FDRL. Grenville Clark recalled Franklin's heady vision of his own future in the *Harvard Alumni Bulletin*, April 28, 1945.

Eleanor told the interviewer Louis Eisner of the importance of Theodore Roosevelt to her husband's decision to enter politics, FDRL. Mr. James's memory of his own genteel skittishness about actually taking part in politics is from his brief penciled autobiography, Roosevelt Family Papers, FDRL. The effusive 1896 account of Rosy in London is in Sara's scrapbook, FDRL. Sara drew her somewhat wistful distinction between political participation and becoming a politician in a 1911 letter to Franklin, Roosevelt Family Papers Donated by the Children, FDRL.

The story of Theodore Roosevelt's determined entry into politics and the ambivalence of his family toward that course is told in David McCullough, *Mornings on Horseback*, pp. 189–190, 251–255; Edmund Morris, *The Rise of Theodore Roosevelt*, pp. 142–145; and in TR's own *An Autobiography*, pp. 55–58. Mittie Roosevelt described Mr. James' reading of the newspaper story about her oldest son in a letter to TR's brother, Elliott, Eleanor Roosevelt Papers, FDRL. TR's exhortation to the Groton boys is from the summer 1900 number of *The Grotonian*, FDRL. The Reverend Billings' sermon is among Sara's papers; his hopes for Franklin and Eleanor were expressed in a letter congratulating them on their wedding in 1905, Eleanor Roosevelt Papers, both at the FDRL. Mike Reilly remembered FDR's difficulties at being one of the boys in his *Reilly of the White House*, p. 57.

Ella Bulloch's letter wondering at the political ambitions of the younger Roosevelt generation is quoted in Joseph P. Lash, *Eleanor and Franklin*, p. 168. Eleanor's memory of her family's traditional political loyalty is from *This Is My Story*. Sara's assertion that her late husband's hatred of Tammany and vice took precedence over party loyalty is from a letter she wrote to Franklin in 1901, Roosevelt Family Papers Donated by the Children, FDRL. Franklin expressed his distaste for being identified with New York City in a 1915 letter to F. F. Moon, Franklin D. Roosevelt, Papers as Assistant Secretary of the Navy, FDRL.

Sara's sketch of her 1905 Christmas gift is on display at the FDRL; her memories of her decision to build twin houses is from Rita Halle Kleeman, *Gracious Lady*, and from Mrs. Kleeman's notes, Kleeman Papers, FDRL. Eleanor's own memories of her misery at being smothered in the new house and of Franklin's genuine puzzlement at it are from *This Is My Story*, pp. 152–153, 162–163. Her diary, with its terse, unhappy entries, is among her papers at the FDRL. Hall's letter reporting that he had registered the new baby at Groton is in the Roosevelt Family Papers Donated by the Children, FDRL.

Eleanor told the story of her terrifying ride at least twice, in *This Is My Story*, pp. 162–163, and in a recorded tour of Springwood and its stables, of which the National Park Service was good enough to offer me a transcript.

My accounts of the troubled Campobello summer of 1909 and of the illness and death of the first Franklin Jr. are based upon Eleanor's letters to Franklin and on Sara's journal, all at the FDRL. Eleanor's account of her own deep depression following the baby's death is from *This Is My Story*, pp. 164–165, 168; her account of Franklin's reaction to the same event is from her interview with Louis Eisner, FDRL.

Relatively little is known of Franklin's connection with the Milk Committee. I have sketched its work from articles scattered through various New York dailies between 1909 and 1911, including the *Sun, Herald, Tribune,* and *Times*.

Sara's account of the sad 1909 Christmas and her explanation for Franklin's absences are both from her journal, FDRL.

The story of Franklin's First Hurrah is described in all the standard biographies. In preparing my version I consulted all of them and found particularly helpful Kenneth S. Davis, *FDR: The Beckoning of Destiny*, pp. 225–242; Frank Freidel, *Franklin D. Roosevelt: The Apprenticeship*, pp. 76–96; Ernest K. Lindley, *The Democratic Roosevelt*, pp. 66–76; Henry Noble MacCracken, *Blithe Dutchess*, pp. 74–94; Alfred B. Rollins, *Roosevelt and Howe*, pp. 16–32; and Elliott Roosevelt, ed., *FDR: His Personal Letters, 1905–1928*, pp. 151–160. Thomas Mott Osborne's first, favorable impression of Franklin is described in Rudolph W. Chamberlain, *There Is No Truce: A Life of Thomas Mott Osborne*, p. 169. The precise sequence of events that summer and autumn is difficult to trace, but I have done my best to provide the one that seems most plausible.

Eleanor's recollection of her own distracted reaction to Franklin's political plans is from *This Is My Story*, p. 166. Sara's memory of her response is from Rita Halle Kleeman, *Gracious Lady*, p. 253.

The presence of the young Roosevelts at TR's triumphant homecoming is confirmed by news photographs and by invitations, reviewing stand tickets, and the like in the Franklin D. Roosevelt Papers, Family, Business, and Personal, FDRL. TR's fondness for FDR was recalled by Sara to Rita Halle Kleeman, *Gracious Lady*, p. 204.

Several of the men who first met Franklin during the 1910 campaign offered their memories of it, and I have drawn heavily upon those, including interviews with Morgan Hoyt, Thomas Leonard, and John Mack conducted by Fred Rath and George Palmer of the National Park Service; an interview with Harry Hawkey; and an article, "Roosevelt Enters Politics," by Morgan H. Hoyt, first published in *The Franklin D. Roosevelt Collector* (November 1951); all at the FDRL. FDR offered his own version of his entrance into politics before a Vassar audience on August 26, 1933, Samuel I. Rosenman, ed., *The Public Papers and Addresses of Franklin D. Roosevelt*, Vol. 2: *The Year of Crisis, 1933*, pp. 338–345. Excerpts from his 1910 stump speeches were compiled from a number of Dutchess County newspapers by a member of the FDRL staff in 1948, and may be found among his Papers as State Senator. I also consulted Franklin's bills and check stubs, FDRL.

My brief account of TR's return to politics is based upon Mark Sullivan, *Our Times*, Vol. 4: *The War Begins, 1909–1914*, pp. 440–461; Joseph L. Gardner, *Departing Glory: Theodore Roosevelt as Ex-President*, pp. 169–195; and William Manners, *TR and Will: A Friendship That Split the Republican Party*, pp. 163–186.

Eleanor's letters to Franklin from Hyde Park and Campobello are among her papers, FDRL; her third-person memory of her sense of betrayal was written for a magazine article in 1931 and is quoted here from Joseph P. Lash, *Eleanor and Franklin*, p. 157. Anna's memory of being tied up is from a memorandum she wrote to herself, and is quoted here from Bernard Asbell, ed., *Mother & Daughter: The Letters of Eleanor and Anna Roosevelt*, pp. 20–21. Eleanor's recollection of how youthful her husband looked as he set out on his political career is from *This Is My Story*, p. 167. The friend who recalled his high spirits is quoted but not named in John Gunther, *Roosevelt in Retrospect*, p. 201; his victory in the Campobello bareback race was recalled by an eyewitness, Stephen Chalmers, speaking to the author of "The Enigma," an anonymous profile of FDR that first appeared in *Fortune* Magazine (December 1933); it is quoted here from Don Wharton, ed., *The Roosevelt Omnibus*, pp. 96–97.

Eleanor's wan birthday note and Hall's letter to Eleanor cheering the arrival of Elliott are both among the Roosevelt Family Papers Donated by the Children, FDRL. The song Franklin and Connell sang to keep warm is given in Joseph P. Lash, *Eleanor and Franklin*, p. 169.

Eleanor's memory of Franklin's early speaking style is from *This Is My Story*, p. 167. FDR's own memory of his embarrassment is from William D. Hassett, *Off the Record with FDR*, p. 159. Sara's proud election night tally is among her son's Papers as State Senator, FDRL.

4: THE AWFULLY MEAN CUSS

Franklin's turbulent time in the state Senate is described in all of his biographies. I have drawn especially heavily on four of them: Ernest K. Lindley, *Franklin D. Roosevelt: A Career in Progressive Democracy*, pp. 77–111; Frank Freidel, *Franklin D. Roosevelt: The Apprenticeship*, pp. 97–133; Kenneth S. Davis, *FDR: The Beckoning of Destiny, 1882–1928*, pp. 239–269; and Alfred B. Rollins, Jr., *Roosevelt and Howe*, pp. 16–45. In most cases below, when quoted material comes from one or more of these accounts, it has seemed redundant to cite specific pages.

But I have also worked extensively with Roosevelt's own Papers as State Senator at the FDRL, and have listed these and all other sources in detail.

My portrait of Albany, both when Franklin first knew it as a child and as it was when he moved there as a freshman legislator, owes much to William Kennedy's vivid, fragmentary, idiosyncratic book *Albany!;* Huybertie Pruyn's lively memories of the comfortable world in which she was brought up on Elk Street are quoted in it on pp. 106–113.

The signature of the writer of the letter meant to reassure Franklin and Eleanor about Albany society is indecipherable (at least by me), but he then worked for the Wall Street firm of Potter, Choate & Prentice, and his letter is filed among papers having to do with the Roosevelts' Albany homes, Papers as State Senator, FDRL. Eleanor's failure to remember whether or not she helped pick out the State Street house is noted in *This Is My Story*, p. 168. Franklin's brief 1911 journal is among his Papers as State Senator, FDRL; he only kept it for a week.

My account of Al Smith's first experience of Albany is from Richard O'Connor, *The First Hurrah: A Biography of Alfred E. Smith*, pp. 50–51. Smith's own story of his first visit to the Roosevelt home in Albany was retold by his daughter, Emily Smith Warner, in her interview by the Columbia Oral History Project, Columbia University; Francis R. Stoddard's memories of his early interest in Senator Roosevelt's career come from his interview in the same collection.

Eleanor's obsessive tidiness is described in *This Is My Story*, pp. 170–171; her memories of her wet nurse, James' illness, and her own "dual existence" are all found between pp. 168 and 173 of that same book. Franklin's recollections of the governor's inauguration, his own first constituents' reception, the festivities that followed, and his early views on Tammany and the Senate fight are all from his journal, FDRL. Sara's brief comments upon some of the same topics appear in her diary. Her proud letter to Eleanor and Franklin is among the Roosevelt Family Papers Donated by the Children, FDRL.

Theodore Roosevelt's memories of his own debut in politics are from *An Autobiography*, pp. 57–58. The extraordinary initial impact he made on his fellow legislators is described in Edmund Morris, *The Rise of Theodore Roosevelt*, pp. 159–202, and David McCullough, *Mornings on Horseback*, pp. 251–275.

Franklin's less flamboyant arrival and Thomas Grady's baleful view of it were described by W. Axel Warn in the *New York Times*, January 22, 1911.

My brief portrait of Charles F. Murphy is drawn largely from Alfred Connable and Edward Silberfarb, *Tigers of Tammany Hall: Nine Men Who Ran New York*, pp. 231–268, and M. R. Werner, *Tammany Hall*, pp. 482–566. Eleanor's account of the Sheehan fight, the insurgents' conclaves in her home, her growing interest in politics, and her outrage over Tammany tactics are all from *This Is My Story*, pp. 173–176. Anna's memory of eavesdropping on the insurgents in the library is from her son John Boettiger's book, *A Love in Shadow*, p. 59. The fulsome praise of Franklin's alleged philanthropy is from a clipping found among his Papers as State Senator, FDRL.

Mr. James' scorn for the Irish is documented on p. 47 of my *Before The Trumpet: Young Franklin Roosevelt, 1882–1905*. James Farley's early denial of FDR's snobbery is from his *Behind the Ballots*, p. 349; his later bitterness at not having been treated as an equal by FDR is on p. 68 of *Jim Farley's Story: The Roosevelt Years*. Eleanor's recollection of the strained lunch with the Sheehans is in *This Is My Story*, p. 174.

Langdon Marvin's letters to Franklin congratulating him, trying to set up a new law partnership, and pleading for more business are among the Papers as State Senator, FDRL. His memories of how the partnership worked out and Franklin's minor role in it are from the transcript of his interview by the Columbia Oral History Collection, Columbia University.

Franklin's dismissal of his Tammany opponents as ignorant is from a clipping found among his Papers as State Senator, FDRL. Sara's account of her interview with TR and the cautious counsel he offered in the Sheehan fight are from a letter in the Roosevelt Family Papers Donated by the Children, FDRL.

My account of Frederic A. Delano's career is based upon a brief autobiographical sketch meant only for his descendants and kindly lent to me by his great-grandson, Frederic D. Grant, Jr. FDR's reference to his Uncle Fred's influence upon him as a planner is from an article he wrote for *Survey* magazine in 1932, and is quoted here from Frank Freidel, *Franklin D. Roosevelt: Launching the New Deal*, p. 78.

Langdon Marvin's invitation to speak at the Harvard dinner and Franklin's fretful acceptance of it are among FDR's Papers as State Senator, FDRL. The lyrics of all the songs sung at the Legislative Correspondents' Association dinner are printed on the program, Papers as State Senator, FDRL.

Judge Joseph Proskauer's harsh memory of Franklin's lingering reputation as an inept spoiler comes from his reminiscence in the Columbia Oral History Collection, Columbia University.

It was Frank Freidel who first took note of FDR's imaginative 1928 account of the end of the Sheehan struggle—see his *Franklin D. Roosevelt: The Apprenticeship*, p. 116—and the "author's italics" are really his.

Franklin's bad luck with early newspaper photographs is recounted in a newspaper clipping found among his Papers as State Senator, FDRL.

His encounters with Senator Frawley are described in newspaper clippings in the scrapbooks filed with his Papers as State Senator, FDRL. I told of young Franklin's short boxing career on p. 135 of *Before the Trumpet*, but did not then know of his opponent's size or age or the bout's actual outcome; the winner's son, Jeffrey Potter, kindly filled me in.

The story of Franklin's 1911 illness, his final days in Albany that summer, and his vacillations about closing the New York house are all to be found in his letters to Eleanor and Sara, Elliott Roosevelt, ed., *FDR: His Personal Letters, 1905–1928*, pp. 163–174. Eleanor's angry letter to Franklin is quoted here from Joseph P. Lash, *Eleanor and Franklin*, pp. 174–175. Sara's mention of "our" children and her birthday gift are both from her journal, FDRL.

Eleanor's memories of her reluctance to join the "gayer and younger group" at Albany are from *This Is My Story*, p. 180.

Frances Perkins' memories of the young Roosevelt's patrician arrogance are from her *The Roosevelt I Knew*, pp. 9–14, and from her interview by the Columbia Oral History Project, Columbia University.

Corinne Robinson's account of a point-to-point hike with TR is from her worshipful little book, *My Brother Theodore Roosevelt*.

The story of the trick played on Franklin and his friend Senator Wainwright is described in Lela Stiles, *The Man Behind Roosevelt*, pp. 29–30. Franklin's views on woman suffrage, the Gaynor Charter, Sunday baseball, conservation, and other issues are scattered through his Papers as State Senator, FDRL. Richard Connell's admiring letter to Franklin was also found there.

Robert S. Binkerd's disappointing dinner with Franklin was described by him in his interview by the Columbia Oral History Project, Columbia University. The Good Government man who remembered Franklin mostly for his unreliability was Laurence Arnold Tanzer; the former page was Reuben A. Lazarus; the recollections of both men are found in the same collection.

Again, Frances Perkins' memories of the fight for the fifty-four-hour bill are from her book *The Roosevelt I Knew*, pp. 13–14, and from her interview by the Columbia Oral History Project. The most thorough and persuasive version of the last-minute vote and Franklin's dubious role in it appears in George Martin's excellent biography, *Madame Secretary: Frances Perkins*, pp. 91–100, 495–496. The author of the richly detailed *Saturday Evening Post* article called "The Winner" that claimed Franklin had played a pivotal part in winning passage of the bill was Louis Howe.

My discussion of Franklin's attitudes toward agricultural and moral legislation owes much to two articles by Alfred B. Rollins, Jr., "Young F.D.R. and the Moral Crusaders," and "Young Franklin D. Roosevelt as the Farmer's Friend," in the January 1956 and April 1962 issues of *New York History: Quarterly Journal of New York State Historical Association*.

Franklin's remarks on the importance of "cooperation" as a solution to American ills were given in full in the Troy *Record*, March 4, 1912, Papers as State Senator, FDRL.

5: THE SPLENDID TRIUMPH

Franklin's exuberant account of his trip to Panama with Hall and J. Mayhew Wainwright is drawn from his letters to Sara and Eleanor, published in Elliott Roosevelt, ed., *FDR: His Personal Letters, 1905–1928*, pp. 180–190, as well as from an additional letter, intended for Eleanor but perhaps never sent, entitled "An Account of an Unsentimental Journey of Two Politicians and an Undergraduate," and found among the Eleanor Roosevelt Papers, FDRL. (Since this letter was clearly addressed to Eleanor, I have assumed that the second one— "A Further Account of an Unsentimental Journey," etc—with its use of the word "nigger," was meant for her, too.) I have drawn upon David McCullough's monumental history of the Panama Canal, *The Path Between the Seas*, for details of what Franklin and his companions saw and the numbers of tourists aboard the everyday trains.

My account of the Roosevelts' visit to Bob and Isabella Ferguson and the life the Fergusons led in New Mexico draws upon Isabella and Bob's letters to Eleanor, Eleanor Roosevelt Papers, FDRL; Eleanor's *This Is My Story*, pp. 182–185; Eleanor's letters to Isabella, the Munro Ferguson Family Correspondence, Arizona Historical Society, Tucson; and my interview with Martha Ferguson Breasted. Sara's chagrin at not being allowed to come even so far as Philadelphia is from a letter she wrote to Franklin, Roosevelt Family Papers Donated by the Children.

The grim medical advice then doled out to tuberculosis patients by helpless physicians is drawn from "The White Plague," a memoir by Elizabeth C. Mooney, *American Heritage* (February–March 1979).

Franklin's activities on behalf of Woodrow Wilson—and himself—in the spring, summer, and fall of 1912 are detailed in all of his biographies. I have found most useful: Frank Freidel, *Franklin D. Roosevelt: The Apprenticeship*, pp. 134–156; Ernest K. Lindley, *Franklin D. Roosevelt: A Study in Progressive Democracy*, pp. 102–111; Kenneth S. Davis, *FDR: The Beckoning of Destiny, 1882–1928*, pp. 270–305; and Alfred B. Rollins, Jr., *Roosevelt and Howe*, pp. 46–56. In the notes that follow I have again cited only those items that do not appear in these overlapping accounts.

My account of Hall's flirtations and his resentment of Sara's interference in them comes from his letters to his sister, Eleanor Roosevelt Papers, FDRL. I have also used Eleanor's memories of the wedding and her ambivalence about it in *This Is My Story*, pp. 186–187, as well as the account by Joseph P. Lash in *Eleanor and Franklin*, p. 181.

Eleanor's bafflement at the Baltimore convention is nicely conveyed in *This Is My Story*, pp. 187–189. Franklin's private opinion of Josephus Daniels after their first meeting was many years later conveyed to his secretary, William D. Hassett, who in turn told Daniels' son, Jonathan, about it; it is quoted here from Jonathan Daniels, *The End of Innocence*, p. 54.

Franklin's letter to Eleanor about his hectic lobbying for renomination is in Elliott Roosevelt, ed., *FDR: His Personal Letters, 1905–1928*, pp. 193–194. Sara's response to her son's renomination is among the Roosevelt Family Papers Donated by the Children; as is her *sotto voce* warning about Theodore Douglas Robinson, Jr. Isabella's letters about "Uncle Theodore" are among the Eleanor Roosevelt Papers, FDRL.

The account of the Roosevelts' sudden, violent illness is drawn primarily from Sara's journal, FDRL, and Eleanor's *This Is My Story*, pp. 190–192.

Louis Howe's impatience at the pace with which Harry Hawkey drove was attested to in notes written by Hawkey himself, PSF Hyde Park, FDRL.

My portrait of Howe and his early career draws heavily upon the first eight chapters of *Roosevelt and Howe*, the shrewd, elegant study by Alfred B. Rollins, Jr., and, to a far lesser extent, upon Lela Stiles, *"The Man Behind Roosevelt": The Story of Louis McHenry Howe*. It has benefited greatly too from a long, useful conversation with Dr. Rollins and from careful scrutiny of the notes for his book, on deposit at the FDRL. I have also consulted the Louis Howe Papers and the Franklin D. Roosevelt Papers as State Senator and Assistant Secretary of the Navy, FDRL.

My source for most of the material about Thomas Mott Osborne is drawn from Rudolph W. Chamberlain, *There Is No Truce*. It is a fascinating but inadequate study (for the reasons cited in the footnote on page 474); much more needs to be done with this important, quixotic reformer.

Sara's terse notice of Howe's presence is from her journal; Eleanor's more open hostility toward him is recalled in *This Is My Story*, pp. 192–194.

Franklin's determinedly cheery note about his prospects for the 1913–14 legislative session is among the Eleanor Roosevelt Papers, FDRL.

Robert Wagner's private satisfaction at seeing young Franklin pass from the Albany scene was described by his son, Robert F. Wagner, Jr., in the ABC Television documentary series, *FDR & His Times*.

6: THE ENDLESS ADDICTION

Franklin's years as Secretary of the Navy are touched upon in all his biographies, and in writing this chapter as well as chapters 8 and 9, I have drawn heavily upon all of them. Most helpful have been Frank Freidel, *Franklin D. Roosevelt: The Apprenticeship*, chapters 9 through 21, and Kenneth S. Davis, *FDR: The Beckoning of Destiny, 1882–1928*, chapters 11 through 19. I also owe a good deal to Joseph P. Lash, *Eleanor and Franklin*, and to Alfred B. Rollins, *Roosevelt and Howe*.

In addition, I have consulted the voluminous scrapbooks Franklin's office kept for him during his first Washington years, as well as his own Papers as Assistant Secretary of the Navy and those of Louis Howe, FDRL.

Franklin's letter to his mother about his new job and her obvious pleasure in his holding it are in Elliott Roosevelt, ed., *FDR: His Personal Letters, 1905–1928*, pp. 199–200. His terse anniversary note to Eleanor is among her papers, FDRL. Endicott Peabody's congratulatory letter is among the Papers as Assistant Secretary of the Navy, FDRL. Bamie's letter to Robert Ferguson is in the Robert Ferguson Papers, Arizona Historical Society in Tucson.

The preinaugural taunting prompted by Franklin's youth is recounted in Frank Freidel, *Franklin D. Roosevelt: The Apprenticeship*, p. 157n. Roosevelt's own indiscreet ebullience about what his cousin had done in the Assistant Secretary's job and what he himself might do is from the *New York Sun*, March 19, 1913. Eleanor's shocked reaction to it is quoted in Joseph P. Lash, *Eleanor and Franklin*. The familiar story of Theodore Roosevelt and the Asiatic Squadron is perhaps best told in Edmund Morris, *The Rise of Theodore Roosevelt*, pp. 600–603.

Eleanor often reported on events at Campobello and in Washington to her friends Isabella and Robert Ferguson, and I have here quoted letters from both the Eleanor Roosevelt Papers at the FDRL and the Ferguson and Greenway Papers at the Arizona Historical Society in Tucson. The letters between Eleanor and Franklin that do not appear in Elliott Roosevelt, ed., *FDR: His Personal Letters, 1905–1928*, may be found among the Eleanor Roosevelt Papers and the Roosevelt Family Papers Donated by the Children, FDRL.

Woodrow Wilson's views on Mexico are from Ray Stannard Baker, *Woodrow Wilson: Life and Letters President 1913–1914*, pp. 236–351.

My account of Elliott's accident at Campobello has benefited from the unpublished "Conversations Between the Four Roosevelt Brothers Recorded at the Roosevelt Cottage on Campobello Island on June 22, 24, and 25, 1979," kindly lent to me by the superintendent of the Roosevelt Campobello International Park Commission.

Eleanor recalled the agonies of settling into Washington in *This Is My Story*, pp. 208–209. James Roosevelt remembered his stint as his mother's reluctant footman in an interview with me: the late Laura Chanler White told me of her carriage rides with her distracted friend.

Alice Longworth's memories of her exile at Rookwood are from Michael Teague, *Mrs. L.*, p. 137; her recollections of dinner at the Roosevelts are on pp. 156–157. The Washington social circles in which the young Roosevelts moved most easily are elegantly described in Jonathan Daniels, *The End of Innocence*. I have also drawn upon the unpublished reminiscences of Huybertie [Mrs. Charles] Hamlin, FDRL, as well as transcripts of interviews with William Phillips and Adolph Miller, Columbia Oral History Project, Columbia University.

The often turbulent relationship between the young Roosevelt and Josephus Daniels is detailed in his son Jonathan's *The End of Innocence*, and further examined in *The Time Between the Wars* and *Washington Quadrille*, by the same author. I have drawn heavily upon these volumes in this chapter, as well as in chapters 7, 8, 9, and 10, and have supplemented these with the *Cabinet Diaries of Josephus Daniels*; his own genial and discursive autobiography, *Tar Heel Editor; Editor in Politics; The Wilson Era: Years of Peace 1910–1917; The Wilson Era: Years of War and After 1917–1923*; the autobiography of Mrs. Josephus Daniels, *Recollections of a Cabinet Minister's Wife* and Joseph L. Morrison, *Josephus Daniels: The Small-d Democrat*. I have also consulted an unpublished interview with Daniels conducted by Frank Freidel in 1947, Frank Freidel Papers, FDRL.

Eleanor's memories of her husband's early brashness when dealing with Secretary Daniels are from her interview with Louis Eisner, FDRL. The story of Joseph Kennedy's frustrating confrontation with FDR is told in Michael R. Beschloss, *Kennedy and Roosevelt*, pp. 44–47. (It should be noted that this tale was evidently based on newspaper interviews with Kennedy during the 1930s; Beschloss could find no contemporary evidence for the standoff at the Navy Yard.)

My portrait of Louis Howe at the Navy Department is drawn very largely from the Papers as Assistant Secretary of the Navy, and his own files, FDRL. George Marvin's harsh memory of him at work in Franklin's office is from his unpublished "Notes on Franklin D. Roosevelt as Assistant Secretary of the Navy 1913–1920," Frank Freidel Papers, FDRL. James Roosevelt recalled to me the startling *lèse-majesté* his father tolerated from Howe and no one else.

My account of Franklin's murky role as political power broker in New York State is based upon his voluminous patronage correspondence with political leaders all over the state, forty-three boxes of it, filed among the Papers as Assistant Secretary of the Navy, FDRL.

Franklin's feverish tour of Western installations during the Mexican crisis was well covered by the newspapers, and a large collection of clippings can be found in his scrapbooks, Papers as Assistant Secretary of the Navy, FDRL.

The events that led up to his abortive Senate race are also well documented in his scrapbooks. Eleanor's criticism of his slap at William Church Osborn is from a letter in the Roosevelt Family Papers Donated by the Children, FDRL.

Mrs. Charles Hamlin left an account of the Cape Cod Canal ceremonies in her unpublished memoir, FDRL. Eleanor's admiring reaction to her husband's hard work at the department is from the Roosevelt Family Papers Donated by the Children, FDRL.

The late W. Sheffield Cowles, Jr., told me of his mother's alarming call from Rosy and its anticlimactic outcome. Marion Dickerman was the friend of Eleanor who paid tribute to Rosy's masculine charm, Oral History Project, Columbia University. Eleanor's amusement at her mother-in-law's discomfiture was expressed in letters to Isabella Ferguson, Arizona Historical Society, Tucson. The curious role Betty Riley Roosevelt subsequently played within the family was separately described to me by James and Franklin Roosevelt, Jr., and by Margaret Suckley.

Isabella described the Campobello atmosphere to her husband, Robert, Arizona Historical Society, Tucson, where Franklin's letter telling of the birth of Franklin Jr. was also found.

Rosy's fervent anti-Semitism is amply documented in his papers, FDRL, where Franklin's amused wire is also filed. Eleanor's early hostility toward Jews—and Catholics—appears in letters written to her mother-in-law, Roosevelt Family Papers Donated by the Children.

My account of Franklin's friendship with Henry Morgenthau, Jr., is drawn from John Morton Blum, *Roosevelt and Morgenthau,* and from the four published volumes of *The Morgenthau Diaries,* edited by Blum. The interpretation of it as a severely limited relationship is my own. The statistics on Jews in the New Deal, Jewish voting patterns, and wartime American attitudes toward Jews all come from Otis L. Graham, Jr., and Meghan Robinson Wander, eds., *Franklin D. Roosevelt: His Life and Times. An Encyclopedic View.* A former Roosevelt neighbor who wishes to remain anonymous recalled to me his father's bewilderment at FDR's willingness to work with Jews.

Isabella Ferguson Greenway's daughter, Martha Ferguson Breasted, kindly recalled for me her "Uncle Franklin's" showy visit to York Harbor.

Franklin's complicated relationship with his Harvard class is documented among his Papers as Assistant Secretary of the Navy and among his own papers, Harvard College Class of 1904: General Correspondence, FDRL.

7: THE PLACE

Two of the Roosevelt children published accounts of their bringing up. *Affectionately, FDR: A Son's Story of a Lonely Man,* James Roosevelt's first book (written with Sidney Shalett), is the best of them, at once loving and honest in its portrayal of his complex parents and his grandmother.

Elliott Roosevelt's three books—*An Untold Story: The Roosevelts of Hyde Park, A Rendezvous with Destiny: The Roosevelts of the White House,* and *Mother R: Eleanor Roosevelt's Untold Story* (all written with James Brough)—are considerably less useful; much that is included in them has appeared in other published works, and one must dig hard for reliable new material.

A second book by James Roosevelt (with Bill Libby), *My Parents: A Differing View,* written in part to soften the harsh portrait presented by his younger brother, suffers somewhat from the same problem.

Anna Roosevelt died in 1975, never having written the memoir she had finally decided to attempt. But she did grant a long interview to Bernard Asbell, who later used it in two of his own fine books about the Roosevelts, *The FDR Memoirs* and *Mother & Daughter: The Letters of Eleanor and Anna Roosevelt.* And *A Love in Shadow,* her son, John R. Boettiger's, sensitive account of his parents' marriage, includes many insights about his mother's early years at Springwood.

I have drawn upon all these books, along with Joseph P. Lash's *Eleanor and Franklin,* especially pp. 192–199. But I have also benefited greatly from conversations with James Roosevelt and Franklin D. Roosevelt, Jr., and with John R. Boettiger and Curtis Roosevelt, and have examined carefully all the letters that the adult Roosevelts wrote to one another during the children's early years in various collections, FDRL.

The story of Franklin's exuberant Raleigh speech is given in Jonathan Daniels, *The End of Innocence,* pp. 68–69. His hopeful letter from England, outlining his plans for renovating Springwood, is found in Elliott Roosevelt, ed., *FDR: His Personal Letters, 1905-1928,* p. 84. Sara's reveries about Mr. James' hovering presence in his old house are from a 1901 letter to her sister Dora Forbes, Roosevelt Family Papers Donated by the Children, FDRL, and an undated letter to Bamie, Anna Roosevelt Cowles Papers, Houghton Library, Harvard University. Rosy's rueful letter about the costly Hyde Park road and Sara's suggestion that she and her son take better care of their woods are from the same collection. The farm journal which Franklin kept faithfully from 1911 to 1914 is at the FDRL, with William Plog's notes still tucked inside its cover.

My account of Franklin's youthful interest in forestry, his purchasing of land, and his planting of trees is based on three main sources: Nelson C. Brown, "Personal Reminiscences of F.D.R.": F. Kennon Moody, *FDR and His Neighbors: A Study of the Relationship Between Franklin D. Roosevelt and the Residents of Dutchess County,* pp.

91–112; and Charles W. Snell, "Franklin D. Roosevelt and Forestry at Hyde Park." Copies of all three unpublished manuscripts are available at the FDRL.

William Plog's memory of Sara's close attention to farm matters is from an interview with him by George Palmer, National Park Service. James Roosevelt remembered his father's mock-horror at the cost of eggs and the size of the dairy herd in *Affectionately, FDR*, p. 50. FDR's tribute to his mother's strawberries was paid in remarks inaugurating his library in 1941. The guest who remembered Springwood cream so fondly was Marion Dickerman, Columbia Oral History Project, Columbia University. James Roosevelt remembered the shipments he received in Cambridge and his parents' very different reactions to them, and speculated as to his father's seriousness about trying to modernize Springwood in conversation with the author.

The story of the Crum Elbow controversy is based on Moody, *FDR and His Neighbors*, pp. 164–166, FDRL. Sara's reaction to Franklin's effort to rename her estate is from Doris Faber, *The Mothers of American Presidents*, p. 64.

The account of the renovation of Springwood is based upon a number of sources, including Olin Dows, *Franklin D. Roosevelt at Hyde Park*, pp. 80–81; Clare and Hardy Steeholm, *The House at Hyde Park*, pp. 122–128; F. L. Rath, Jr., *Home of Franklin D. Roosevelt National Historic Site, Hyde Park New York: Preliminary Guard Manual* (unpublished; National Park Service); and George Y. Wilkins, *A Report on the Birthplace and Home of Franklin Delano Roosevelt* (unpublished, National Park Service).

Sara's enthusiasm for Franklin's sketches, her plans for the library, and her pleasure in the finished house are all from letters among the Roosevelt Family Papers Donated by the Children, FDRL. Her delight in the scale model he built is quoted in Olin Dows, *Franklin D. Roosevelt in Hyde Park*, p. 80.

Sara is quoted as calling the new Springwood a "hotel" in a 1915 letter from Eleanor to Isabella Ferguson, Ferguson Family Correspondence, Arizona Historical Society, Tucson.

Anna Roosevelt told Bernard Asbell of her special affection for Hyde Park and of her memories of her father there; a copy of her complete interview is among her papers, FDRL. She also wrote "The Place," an eloquent essay about Springwood's special meaning for her, which appears in its entirety as chapter 6 of John R. Boettiger's *A Love in Shadow*. James Roosevelt's memories of the special meaning Springwood held for him and the good times he had with his father and grandmother there are given an entire chapter in his *Affectionately, FDR*, pp. 44–58. Eleanor Roosevelt offered her own memories of life there in a recorded tour of the house, of which the National Park Service was kind enough to give me a transcript, as well as in a pamphlet, *Franklin D. Roosevelt and Hyde Park: Personal Recollections*, National Park Service.

Unless indicated otherwise, all the quotations in this and the following sections come from one or another of these sources.

Eleanor's letter to Isabella about Franklin's impending visit and her children's excitement about it is from an undated letter, Ferguson Family Correspondence, Arizona Historical Society, Tucson.

Eleanor's initial enthusiasm for the new Springwood is from a 1916 letter to Isabella Ferguson, Ferguson Family Correspondence, Arizona Historical Society, Tucson.

Her subsequent bitterness was most openly expressed in her posthumously published article, "I Remember Hyde Park: A Final Remembrance," *McCall's* (February 1963).

The little household account book in which Franklin tallied the linens is among Sara's papers, FDRL.

The member of the family who recalled Sara's public grooming advice for her daughter-in-law and Eleanor's response to it was W. Sheffield Cowles, Jr., in conversation with the author.

The unnamed visitor who worried about the state of the Roosevelt children's noses is quoted in Jonathan Daniels, *The End of Innocence*.

Eleanor's somewhat austere view of motherhood is from *This Is My Story*, p. 300.

Anna recalled her mother's curious reaction to James' poison ivy, her own feelings about kissing her parents and grandparents, the hierarchy of nurses and governesses, and her mother's failures and successes as a parent in interviews and private memoranda quoted in both Asbell and Boettiger.

Sara's intense interest in her grandchildren is documented in her letters and journals, and in Rita Halle Kleeman's *Gracious Lady*, pp. 252–255. Eleanor's harsh assessment of Sara's motives is from the *McCall's* article cited above. The story of "Old Battle Axe" was first told in James Roosevelt, *Affectionately, FDR*, pp. 40–42. Eleanor's memory of how she felt after she had fired this sadist is from Joseph P. Lash, *Eleanor and Franklin*, pp. 198–199. Eleanor's memory of finding James weeping in his father's arms is from her pamphlet, *Franklin D. Roosevelt and Hyde Park*, p. 7.

James Roosevelt's continuing bafflement that he had so little of his father during his boyhood was conveyed to the author in conversation.

Eleanor remembered her anxiety at coming home to her children in *This Is My Story*, pp. 212–213. Sara's tributes to her grandchildren are from letters among her papers, Roosevelt Family Papers Donated by the Children. James Roosevelt tells of Elspeth Connochie and his curtailed visits in *Affectionately, FDR*, pp. 41–42.

The story of the Hyde Park burglaries is told in *Affectionately, FDR*, pp. 56–57, and Elliott Roosevelt, ed., *FDR: His Personal Letters, 1905–1928*, pp. 315–316, and in Franklin's correspondence with Colonel Archibald Rogers, Papers as Assistant Secretary of the Navy, FDRL.

8: TOO DAMNED SLOW FOR WORDS

My account of the Roosevelts' trip to the Panama-Pacific Exposition is drawn from a wide variety of sources. Most useful were the scrapbooks found among the Papers as Assistant Secretary of the Navy, FDRL. For additional details about the exposition itself, I consulted Ben MaComber's guidebook, *The Jewel City*, and the anonymously written souvenir booklet, *State of New York at the Panama-Pacific Exposition*.

Eleanor's memories of the trip are from *This Is My Story*, pp. 219–226.

My sketch of Vice President Thomas Marshall is drawn mainly from Gene Smith, *When the Cheering Stopped*, and Marshall's own amusing book, *Recollections of Thos R. Marshall, Vice President and Hoosier Philosopher—A Hoosier Salad*. FDR's memories of Marshall were dictated in the White House on July 28, 1941, and are filed in PSF 151 (Anecdotes).

William Phillips' account of the breakfast table confrontation between the Roosevelts is from the transcript of his Oral History interview at Columbia University; a somewhat gentler version of it is given on p. 70 of Phillips's privately printed memoir, *Ventures in Diplomacy*.

Theodore Roosevelt's journey up the Amazon, his return to politics, and the story of the Barnes libel trial are most memorably described in Joseph L. Gardner, *Departing Glory*, pp. 228–350, and in Henry F. Pringle, *Theodore Roosevelt: A Biography*, pp. 572–577, and I have relied heavily upon these works throughout this chapter.

The struggle between TR and Woodrow Wilson is described in the standard biographies of both men, but is most thoroughly discussed in John Milton Cooper's *The Warrior and the Priest. Woodrow Wilson and Theodore Roosevelt*.

Secretary Daniels' struggle with Augustus Gardner is recounted in Jonathan Daniels' two books, *The End of Innocence* and *Washington Quadrille*, and is made plain in his own diaries and autobiography, as well. Wilson's fury at Daniels' anonymous traducers is quoted from Ray Stannard Baker, ed., *Woodrow Wilson: Life & Letters*, Vol. 7, p. 15. William Phillips' memory of young Franklin's habit of seeming to agree with everyone with whom he spoke is from his *Ventures in Diplomacy*. Admiral Fiske's recollection of the same thing was given in testimony before a Senate investigating committee and is quoted here from Tracy Barrett Kittredge, *Naval Lessons of the Great War*, p. 221.

The aide who recalled Franklin's being rattled at the thought of an office visit by his Cousin Theodore was Vice Admiral Wilson Brown; the story appeared in an excerpt from his memoir, *Four Presidents as I Saw Them*, in *American Heritage* (February 1955), p. 80.

The story of FDR's appendicitis and Louis Howe's role in misdiagnosing it is told in Lela Stiles, *"The Man Behind Roosevelt."*

Frances Parkinson Keyes recalled the visit of the two Washington ladies to Eleanor shortly after the birth of John Aspinwall Roosevelt in her memoir, *Capital Kaleidoscope: The Story of a Washington Hostess*.

Franklin's correspondence with Admiral W. Sheffield Cowles is found among the Roosevelt Family Papers Donated by the Children. The admiring newspaper story about his good looks is from one of his scrapbooks. The first woman who thought him so good-looking was Margot Oxford; the name of the second is not known. Both are quoted in John Gunther, *Roosevelt in Retrospect*, p. 214. Eleanor's acerbic portrait of the "typical Metropolitan Club young man" her husband almost became is from her interview with Louis Eisner, FDRL.

Nigel Law described his high times with Franklin in a letter to Jonathan Daniels, quoted in his *Washington Quadrille*.

My account of the polio epidemic of 1916 is based on New York newspapers of the time, plus Richard Carter, *Breakthrough: The Saga of Jonas Salk*, and John Rowan Wilson, *Margin of Safety*. Admiral William D. Leahy recalled his trip with the Roosevelt children to Frank Freidel, Frank Freidel Papers, FDRL.

Franklin's chastening correspondence with TR about the readiness of the Great White Fleet is among his Papers as Assistant Secretary of the Navy, FDRL.

My account of Franklin's tour of Haiti is based upon separate accounts written by Livingston Davis, George Marvin, and FDR himself, all at the FDRL. I have also consulted two books by Hans Schmidt, *The United States Occupation of Haiti: 1915–1934*, and *Maverick Marine: General Smedley D. Butler and the Contradictions of American History*, as well as Butler's own autobiography (written with Lowell Thomas), *Old Gimlet Eye*. That overeager Marines did offer Franklin two *caco* skulls as souvenirs is based upon jokes made about the incident by Louis Howe, found among his papers, FDRL.

    Eleanor Roosevelt recalled her serenity in the face of Franklin's heady plan to purchase La Gonave in an interview with Rexford G. Tugwell, Rexford G. Tugwell Papers, FDRL.

9: HONNEUR OBLIGE

Franklin's brief, telegraphic diary, with its notes on Woodrow Wilson's second inaugural and hints of his own dissatisfaction with the President, is at the FDRL. Wilson is quoted on the insidious *"Junkertburm"* in Josephus Daniels, *The Wilson Era, Years of Peace.* . . . p. 285.

    The Harvard friend to whom Franklin wrote the lofty letter about the importance of personal loyalty was Edwyn Johnstone. George Creel recalled his suspicions about Howe's loyalty to Daniels in his Oral History interview, Columbia University Oral History Collection, Columbia University.

Daniels recalled his own melancholy at the outbreak of war in his diary and autobiography. My sketch of Admiral William S. Sims is based largely on Elting Morison, *Admiral Sims and the Modern Navy*. Franklin's self-serving version of Sims' appointment appeared in newspaper clippings in his scrapbooks.

Eleanor Roosevelt recalled Wilson's declaration of war in *This Is My Story*, p. 245. Huybertie Hamlin's unpublished memoir at the FDRL includes the story of Franklin's preoccupation with scuttling sounds heard overhead during the President's address.

James Roosevelt and Franklin D. Roosevelt, Jr., each recalled for me the volcanic impact of their great-uncle's visit to their home. The encounter between TR and Wilson, which Franklin helped arrange, is described in the standard biographies of both men. Eleanor's memories of TR's anger and frustration at being kept from the battlefront and his urging that Franklin enter the armed services are from separate interviews with Louis Eisner, Frank Freidel, and the producers of *FDR*, the ABC television series; all are at the FDRL.

    The story of Franklin's attempt to force his chief to hasten mobilization is found in a clipping in one of his scrapbooks. Admiral Benson's anti-British sentiments and the exchanges between Admiral Sims and Admiral Jellicoe are all from Morison's *Admiral Sims and the Modern American Navy*.

    James Roosevelt recalled with some embarrassment his childhood visit to Marshal Joffre in *Affectionately, FDR*, pp. 79–80.

Franklin's scheme to undermine his chief with the help of the novelist Winston Churchill is fully documented in his correspondence as Assistant Secretary of the Navy, FDRL.

The story of Franklin's longstanding relationship with Lucy Mercer Rutherfurd remains shadowy, despite the best efforts of a host of biographers. FDR's secretary, Grace Tully, inadvertently revealed in her 1949 book *FDR, My Boss*, that Mrs. Rutherfurd had been present (along with two other persons) at the moment the President suffered his fatal hemorrhage at Warm Springs. Jonathan Daniels was the first to attempt a full account of it, in his *The End of Innocence*, published in 1954, and then, in considerably expanded form, in *Washington Quadrille*, published in 1968. Since then, Joseph Alsop, Bernard Asbell, Kenneth S. Davis, Joseph P. Lash, and Ted Morgan have all had their say about it; and so, in one way or another, have three of the Roosevelt children—Anna, James, and Elliott—and one grandchild, John R. Boettiger.

In attempting to piece together what happened for this book, I have been grateful to the authors of all these earlier accounts and have done my best to follow the faint documentary trail that winds through various collections at the FDRL. The interpretation of it that I offer—and the altered chronology of events it suggests—are my own, of course.

The story of Eleanor's first timid emergence into public life as a Red Cross worker during World War I is best described in *This Is My Story*, pp. 250–263, and in Joseph P. Lash, *Eleanor and Franklin*, pp. 208–219.

Eleanor's clash with her Grandmother Hall is quoted from *This Is My Story*, pp. 251–252. The precise nature of the quarrel that yielded Sara's extraordinary letter to her "Dearest Franklin & Dearest Eleanor" has been the subject of some controversy among Roosevelt biographers: Jonathan Daniels, for one, believed it had been sparked directly by the Lucy Mercer affair. When Eleanor was asked about it by her son, James, she said she believed the issue had been her husband's refusal to pledge unequivocally that Springwood would remain in the family "forever." Given the emotional impact the recent Algonac fire had had on all the Delanos, including Sara, and the anxiety she always felt about holding onto Springwood and keeping it unchanged, that explanation seems entirely plausible to me.

10: A BREATHLESS, HUNTED FEELING

Livingston Davis' journals are the source of much of this chapter; he kept daily notes on his activities with and without Franklin from the time he joined the Navy Department until the spring of 1919. Other central sources are Franklin's letters from Europe, Papers as Assistant Secretary of the Navy, FDRL; Frank Freidel's *Franklin D. Roosevelt: The Apprenticeship*, pp. 336–372, and *The Ordeal*, pp. 3–16; and Joseph P. Lash, *Eleanor and Franklin*, pp. 208–236. Eleanor's letters to Isabella are all from the Isabella Ferguson Greenway Papers, Arizona Historical Society, Tucson.

I have also had the benefit of two conversations with Professor Michael Simpson of the University College of Swansea, who gave me access to his unpublished article, "The Moral Equivalent of San Juan Hill: Franklin D. Roosevelt Goes to War, July to September, 1918," upon which I have drawn heavily. In addition, he shared with me discoveries among the Sims Papers at the Library of Congress which I have used both in this and the following chapter. I am most grateful to him.

The story of the visit to Franklin of Harry Hooker and Cathleen Nesbitt is from her autobiography, *A Little Love & Good Company.*

Eleanor's letters to Sara, written in the uneasy spring of 1918, are among the Roosevelt Family Papers Donated by the Children, FDRL.

Both Josephus Daniels and his wife recalled their wait with Franklin for the first air-mail delivery in their autobiographies. Woodrow Wilson's lecture on religious tolerance is given in Ray Stannard Baker, *Woodrow Wilson: Life and Letters:* Vol. 8, *Armistice,* p. 260. Daniels' growing irritation at Franklin is amply set forth in his published diaries.

Franklin's speech in which he declared his hatred of war is quoted here from Samuel I. Rosenman, ed., *The Public Papers and Addresses of Franklin D. Roosevelt,* Vol. 5, p. 289. My account of his 1918 trip to Europe is drawn from his own letters home, both as they are found among the Roosevelt Family Papers at the FDRL, and as they appear in edited form in Elliott Roosevelt, ed., *FDR: His Personal Letters, 1905–1928,* pp. 374–441, as well as the Davis diary and memoirs subsequently written by Davis and Edward McCauley, Jr., and from interviews conducted by Frank Freidel with R. H. Camalier, John Hancock, and John S. Hancock, Frank Freidel Collection, FDRL. Details of his party's terror when the big army gun opened up are from Franklin's story as told to K. M. Maas, the widow of Lieutenant Commander Charles O. Maas, who accompanied him to the front, PSF 151, FDRL.

My account of Quentin Roosevelt's death is based largely upon "The Search for Quentin Roosevelt," an unpublished article by William Jeanes, editor of *Car and Driver,* who kindly agreed to share his conclusions with me. The impact of that death on Theodore and Edith Roosevelt is described most memorably in Sylvia Jukes Morris, *Edith Kermit Roosevelt,* pp. 412–427, but some additional details are here taken from Joseph C. Gardner, *Departing Glory,* pp. 389–395. TR's sorrowful letter to Bob Ferguson is among the Robert Ferguson Papers, Arizona Historical Society, Tucson. Eleanor's letter to Franklin is from the Roosevelt Family Papers Donated by the Children, FDRL.

FDR's remarks about Churchill, made to Joseph P. Kennedy, are from Kennedy's unpublished memoir, and are quoted here from Michael Beschloss, *Kennedy and Roosevelt,* pp. 200 and 230.

Eleanor's thoughts about her grandmother's dependency and the toll it took on her and on her children are from *This Is My Story,* pp. 299–301. Her correspondence with Louis Howe is filed with Howe's papers, Franklin D. Roosevelt, Papers as Assistant Secretary of the Navy, FDRL.

The children's letters to their father are among the Roosevelt Family Papers, FDRL; the one from his mother is from the Roosevelt Family Papers Donated by the Children, FDRL.

My account of the near-collapse of the Roosevelt marriage is inevitably based very largely on the works of Joseph P. Lash, in whom Eleanor confided her side of the story, supplemented by Joseph Alsop, *FDR: A Centenary Remembrance*, pp. 67–74. Edith Roosevelt's memory of Eleanor's early doubts about her ability to hold onto Franklin is from Michael Teague, *Mrs. L.*, p. 158.

Eleanor's memories of hardships overcome in the fall of 1918 are from *This Is My Story*, pp. 267–272. Corinne Alsop's assessment of the crisis and its impact are from her unpublished memoir, Alsop Papers, Houghton Library, Harvard University.

Eleanor published a lengthy account of the Roosevelts' trip to Europe in 1919 in *This Is My Story*, pp. 273–293, here supplemented by her travel diary, FDRL, and by letters she and Franklin wrote home to Sara, published in Elliott Roosevelt, ed., *FDR: His Personal Letters, 1905–1928*, pp. 442–471. Joseph P. Lash was the first to notice the grim story told by the photograph of the haggard Roosevelts aboard the *Aztec*, in his *Eleanor and Franklin*.

The death of Theodore Roosevelt and its impact are memorably recounted in Sylvia Jukes Morris, *Edith Kermit Roosevelt;* Joseph C. Gardiner, *Departing Glory;* and Henry F. Pringle, *Theodore Roosevelt*.

The late W. Sheffield Cowles, Jr., told me of Franklin's difficulties at speechmaking aboard the *George Washington* and of his on-deck talks with him about roads not taken.

Josephus Daniels recalled his conversation with Newton D. Baker in his autobiography.

11: THE SIMON-PURE POLITICIAN

Sara Delano Roosevelt's presence at Algonac when she learned of Franklin's nomination is attested to by a letter from Annie Hitch, found among the Eleanor Roosevelt Papers, FDRL. SDR's diary for the early part of 1920 is sporadic and does not become daily until the end of July, when her son's campaign was about to begin; there is no entry for July 5. My description of Algonac as it was rebuilt is from Frederic A. Delano's privately printed pamphlet, *Algonac*, and from a visit to the site. Sara's letters to Franklin are among the Roosevelt Family Papers Donated by the Children, FDRL.

Eleanor's letter to her Auntie Bye about the Roosevelts' future plans is among the Anna Roosevelt Cowles Papers, Houghton Library, Harvard University. Josephus Daniels' admonitions to Franklin, Franklin's reassuring replies, and Roosevelt's boastful letter to Livingston Davis are all from Frank Freidel, *Franklin D. Roosevelt: The Ordeal*, pp. 21–22.

My account of the effort to clean up Newport is based largely upon documents found in the "Newport Case" files in two collections: Franklin D. Roosevelt, Papers as Secretary of the Navy, and Franklin D. Roosevelt Papers, Family, Business, and Personal, FDRL. Included among them is Josephus Daniels's own account of the case, written on March 3, 1921. I have also drawn upon Ted Morgan, *FDR*, pp. 234–245, though my conclusions about the case are somewhat different from his, and upon

Lawrence R. Murphy, *Perverts by Official Order*, the first full-scale study of the investigation and its aftermath.

Documents pertaining to the Portsmouth case may be found among the Franklin D. Roosevelt Papers, Family, Business, and Personal, FDRL, in a file called "Rathom Case." I have also consulted two books on Thomas Mott Osborne, *There Is No Truce*, by Rudolph Chamberlain, and Frank Tannebaum's *Osborne of Sing Sing*. Admiral William Sims's resentments are spelled out in Elting Morison's biography, *Admiral Sims*, which is also the source of his letter to Admiral Fullam.

Eleanor's letters to Isabella Ferguson describing her new domestic tranquility and the reasons for it, her concerns about "Revolution," and her lobbying efforts at the Navy Department, are among the Greenway Papers at the Arizona Historical Society, Tucson. Her letters to Sara are in the Roosevelt Family Papers Donated by the Children; her journal is with her own papers; both at the FDRL. Her explanation of her decision to hire an all-black domestic staff is from *This Is My Story*, pp. 295–296.

Eleanor described her visit to St. Elizabeth's Hospital at least twice in print, in *This Is My Story*, pp. 257–258, and *You Learn by Living*, pp. 29–30; my account combines details from both versions. Her letters to Franklin are among the Roosevelt Family Papers Donated by the Children; his responses are among the Roosevelt Family Papers. The story of Eleanor's weeping appears in Arthur M. Schlesinger, Jr., *The Crisis of the Old Order*, p. 369, and Elliott Roosevelt and James Brough, *An Untold Story*, pp. 84–85.

My account of Eleanor's elaborate martyrdom after leaving her husband to dance on at the Chevy Chase Club is drawn from two different sources: Joseph Alsop, *FDR: A Centenary Remembrance*, pp. 67–68; and Joseph P. Lash, *Eleanor and Franklin*, pp. 243–244. Her struggles with her mother-in-law are tersely noted in her journal and her letter to Sara, Roosevelt Family Papers Donated by the Children.

Eleanor's fascination with the Saint-Gaudens statue is documented in Joseph P. Lash, *Eleanor and Franklin*, p. 237, and in Doris Faber, *The Life of Lorena Hickok*, p. 115. The interpretation of what it may have meant to her is mine.

My account of Woodrow Wilson's fight for the League and physical collapse is based upon Gene Smith, *When the Cheering Stopped*, Arthur Walworth, *Woodrow Wilson*, Robert H. Ferrell, *Woodrow Wilson & World War I 1917–1921*, Tom Schachtman, *Edith & Woodrow*, Edith Wilson, *My Memoir*, John Morton Blum, *Joseph Tumulty*, Josephus Daniels, *The Wilson Era: Years of War and After*, Mark Sullivan, *The Twenties*, and Jonathan Daniels, *The Time Between the Wars, The End of Innocence*, and *Washington Quadrille*.

Eleanor's memories of Wilson's Boston reception are from *This Is My Story*, pp. 292–293.

Franklin's fighting liberal speech and its impact are most fully described in Frank Freidel, *Franklin D. Roosevelt: The Ordeal*, pp. 52–55.

The bombing of A. Mitchell Palmer's home is described in Alice Roosevelt Longworth's *Crowded Hours*, pp. 282–283, James Roosevelt's *Affectionately, FDR*, pp. 60–61, Geoffrey Perrett's *America in the Twenties*, and in Eleanor's letter to Sara, Roosevelt Family Papers Donated by the Children, FDRL. I also consulted the *New York Times* and *Washington Post* accounts. Palmer's fervid response to it is quoted from

Arthur M. Schlesinger, Jr., *The Crisis of the Old Order,* pp. 42–43. Franklin's thoughts on free love are in Frank Friedel, *Franklin D. Roosevelt: The Ordeal,* p. 18.

Alice Longworth's explanation of her loathing for Wilson is from Michael Teague, *Mrs. L.,* p. 167. Her activities at the depot and outside the White House are from her *Crowded Hours,* pp. 285–286.

Details about the Washington race riots are from Herbert Shapiro, *White Violence and Black Response,* pp. 153–154. Franklin's letters about it are in Elliott Roosevelt, ed., *FDR: His Personal Letters, 1905–1928,* pp. 479–480, and Frank Freidel, *Franklin D. Roosevelt: The Ordeal,* p. 30.

Sources for my continuing account of Wilson's ordeal are given above, but most of this section is based upon Gene Smith's *When the Cheering Stopped.* The story of Franklin's cheerful identification with royalty is from the transcript of the interview with William Phillips, Columbia Oral History Project, Columbia University. Josephus Daniels' terse account of Franklin's unhappiness at not being allowed to receive the king of Belgium is from *The Cabinet Diaries of Josephus Daniels.*

Alice Longworth's memory of her reaction to news of Wilson's illness is from Michael Teague, *Mrs. L.,* p. 169; her letter to her Auntie Bye is from the Alice Roosevelt Cowles Papers, Houghton Library, Harvard University. Eleanor's reaction to the defeat of the League is from a letter in the Greenway Papers, Arizona Historical Society, Tucson.

Admiral Sims' criticisms of the medal awards are spelled out in detail in Elting Morison's *Admiral Sims,* pp. 433–439, and Tracy Barrett Kittredge, *Naval Lessons of the Great War,* pp. 41–73; Daniels' own very different account of the medals controversy is given in his *The Wilson Era-The War Years and After,* pp. 492–499. Admiral Fullam's letters describing Franklin's clandestine support for Sims are among the Sims Papers at the Library of Congress and were brought to my attention by Professor Michael Simpson.

Mrs. Sims' letter to Eleanor and Franklin's anxious reply are among his Papers as Assistant Secretary of the Navy, FDRL.

Bertie Hamlin's encounter with Franklin is from her unpublished article, "Some Memories of Franklin Delano Roosevelt," FDRL. Franklin's discouraged letter is from Frank Freidel, *Franklin D. Roosevelt: The Ordeal,* p. 56.

Eleanor's inquiry about Herbert Hoover's popularity in the Southwest is from the Greenway Papers, Arizona Historical Society, Tucson. My account of the abortive Hoover presidential boom is drawn from Richard Norton Smith, *The Shattered Dream;* David Burner, *Herbert Hoover: A Public Life;* and Hoover's own *The Memoirs of Herbert Hoover.* Louis Wehle described his efforts on Franklin's behalf in his *Hidden Threads of History.* Franklin's own enthusiastic letter about the Great Engineer is quoted from Frank Freidel, *Franklin D. Roosevelt: The Ordeal,* p. 57.

My documentary sources for the continuing Portsmouth controversy are cited above but they have been here supplemented by Frank Freidel's notes on his interview with Captain J. K. Taussig, Frank Freidel Papers, FDRL.

Josephus Daniels noted his own shock at Franklin's Brooklyn speech in his diary. His son, Jonathan, offers further details in his *The End of Innocence,* pp. 306–308. Livy

Davis' disbelieving letter is among Franklin's Papers as Assistant Secretary of the Navy, FDRL.

My account of the death and burial of Eleanor's Aunt Edith is drawn from *This Is My Story*, pp. 307–309. The story of how the Roosevelts learned of Lucy Mercer's marriage is from Joseph Alsop, *FDR: A Centenary Remembrance*, pp. 71–72. Eleanor's letter announcing that news to Sara is among the Roosevelt Family Papers Donated by the Children, FDRL.

My account of the Lord Grey affair is drawn from Jonathan Daniels, *The End of Innocence*, pp. 296–299, and *Washington Quadrille*, pp. 136–143, 179–183, 191–192; Gene Smith, *When the Cheering Stopped*; and Arthur Walworth, *Woodrow Wilson*. Eleanor described the fateful Christmas dinner in *This Is My Story*, pp. 305–306.

The struggle between Sims and Daniels is detailed in Elting Morison, *Admiral Sims*, and Tracy Barrett Kittredge, *Naval Lessons of the Great War*, both of which are heavily weighted toward the admiral's view. Daniels offers his own no less partisan version of events in *The Wilson Era-The War Years and After*, pp. 499–507. Jonathan Daniels also describes the conflict in *The End of Innocence*, pp. 313–314. Frank Freidel, *Franklin D. Roosevelt: The Ordeal*, details Franklin's reactions to the contest, pp. 39–40, 48–50. The exchange between Sims and Fullam is from the Sims Papers at the Library of Congress.

Sources for my account of the continuing Newport scandal are given above.

Woodrow Wilson's sad spring drive is described in *Starling of the White House*, by Colonel Edmund W. Starling, pp. 156–157. The President's dismissive remarks about the leading candidates for the presidential nomination were made to Senator Carter Glass and are given in Gene Smith, *When the Cheering Stopped*, pp. 160–161.

The account of the Republican Convention is based primarily upon Mark Sullivan, *The Twenties*, Francis Russell, *The Shadow of Blooming Grove*, and Andrew Sinclair, *The Available Man*. Corinne Alsop's remarks before the convention are from the Alsop Papers, Houghton Library, Harvard University.

Two longhand chapters of an unpublished memoir by Vice Admiral John L. McRea, then Admiral Rodman's aide, FDRL, provided the details of Franklin's and Daniels' accommodations at the San Francisco convention. The convention itself is memorably described in H. L. Mencken, *A Choice of Days*. Frank Freidel gives the most detailed attention to Franklin's role at the convention in *Franklin D. Roosevelt: The Ordeal*, pp. 61–69. A scrapbook among the Franklin D. Roosevelt Papers, Vice-Presidential Campaign of 1920, FDRL, yielded varying newspaper accounts of the struggle for the New York standard.

My sketch of Al Smith and his rise to prominence is drawn from Frank Graham, *Al Smith American*, Oscar Handlin, *Al Smith and His America*, Matthew and Hannah Josephson, *Al Smith: Hero of the Cities*, Richard O'Connor, *The First Hurrah*, Henry F. Pringle, *Alfred E. Smith: A Critical Study*, Emily Smith Warner (with Hawthorne Daniel), *The Happy Warrior*, and from the transcript of an interview with Frances Perkins, Columbia Oral History Project, Columbia University.

Frances Perkins recalled her impressions of Franklin at the convention in *The Roosevelt I Knew*, p. 27, and in the transcript of her interview, Columbia Oral History Project, Columbia University.

There are various accounts of Boss Murphy's reaction to the notion of nominating Roosevelt for Vice President; I have used Edward Moore's own recollection left among his papers at his death and reprinted in Arthur Krock, *Memoirs*, pp. 152–153.

Al Smith's tempered enthusiasm for Roosevelt is quoted from Matthew and Hannah Josephson, *Al Smith: Hero of the Cities.*

12: THE BRILLIANT CAMPAIGN

Franklin's homecoming to Hyde Park is described in clippings in Scrapbooks, Franklin D. Roosevelt Papers, Campaign of 1920, FDRL. Sara's proud letter to her son is among the Roosevelt Family Papers Donated by the Children, FDRL.

The warm congratulatory letters from Herbert Hoover and the comparatively chilly wire from Woodrow Wilson are both from Frank Freidel, *Franklin D. Roosevelt: The Ordeal*, pp. 68–69. The Democratic candidates' visit to Wilson is described in James M. Cox, *A Journey Through My Years*, and in all the standard biographies of FDR; Mrs. Wilson's memory of Franklin's expression is from Alden Hatch, *Edith Bolling Wilson.*

Criticism of Franklin's destroyer journey to Campobello is from clippings in a scrapbook found among the Franklin D. Roosevelt Papers, Campaign of 1920, FDRL.

The most complete account of Eleanor's reactions to the 1920 campaign are given in Joseph P. Lash, *Eleanor and Franklin*, pp. 249–258, and my account in this chapter and the next relies heavily upon it. Eleanor's initial agony at intrusions by the press is recalled in *This Is My Story*, p. 314. I viewed the silent film footage of the Roosevelts at Campobello at the FDRL.

Ted Morgan includes Franklin's letter to Ellery Sedgwick in his *FDR: A Biography*, p. 228.

Franklin's farewell letter to Josephus Daniels and Daniels' grateful response are both given in Carroll Kilpatrick, *Roosevelt and Daniels*, pp. 67–68.

The standard biographies give detailed accounts of Franklin's official notification at Springwood. Josephus Daniels noted the interruption by the airplane in his *The Wilson Era, The War Years and After*, p. 270. Eleanor expressed her sympathy for her mother-in-law in *This Is My Story*. Sara's encounter with the ordinary citizens of Poughkeepsie is in Rita Halle Kleeman, *Gracious Lady.*

My sketch of Warren Delano III is based upon the memorial pamphlet *Warren Delano* written by his brother, Frederick A. Delano, and an interview with Laura Franklin Delano Adams Eastman. My account of his death is based on the *New York Times* for September 10, 1920.

For a more detailed account of the origins and extent of Delano Republicanism, see Geoffrey C. Ward, *Before the Trumpet*. Mrs. Hitch's reaction to her decorated automobile is from an interview with two granddaughters of her chauffeur, Mrs. Catherine F. Connell and Mrs. Gabrielle O'Neill, Eleanor Roosevelt Oral History

Project, FDRL. James Roosevelt and Laura Eastman both recalled the awe their Great-Aunt Kassie inspired in all who met her in interviews with the author; Eleanor confessed her envy of her looks in a letter to Franklin, Roosevelt Family Papers Donated by the Children.

My account of life at Tuxedo owes a good deal to Frank Kintrea, "Tuxedo Park," *American Heritage* (August–September 1978). Herbert C. Pell's memories of life there are from the transcript of an interview with him, Columbia Oral History Project, Columbia University. The colloquy between Franklin and Sara is from Grace Tully, *FDR, My Boss.*

Bronson Chanler himself kindly drove me through the grounds of Steen Valetje while he told me of his schoolboy encounter there with FDR.

Franklin K. Lane's fond, knowing letter to Franklin is from *The Letters of Franklin K. Lane,* pp. 351–352.

Roosevelt's first national campaign is most thoroughly detailed in Frank Freidel, *Franklin D. Roosevelt: The Ordeal,* pp. 70–91, and I owe much to it.

Renah Camalier's nickname is given in a reminiscent letter he wrote to Louis Howe in 1924, Louis Howe Papers, FDRL.

The journalist who offered Franklin advice on how to identify with Theodore Roosevelt was J.W. Holcombe, and he is quoted here from Ted Morgan, *FDR,* p. 229. Franklin's explanation of his being picked to run for Vice President is from Emil Ludwig, *Roosevelt: A Study in Fortune and Power.* The newspaper headlines attesting to Franklin's closeness to TR are all from scrapbook clippings, Franklin D. Roosevelt Papers, Campaign of 1920, FDRL, and Corinne Robinson's warm letter is from the same collection. The late W. Sheffield Cowles, Jr., told me of Theodore Roosevelt, Jr.'s, envy of his distant cousin.

Eleanor confessed her doubts about the campaign in a letter to Charles McCarthy. Her letters to Franklin and to Sara are among the Roosevelt Family Papers Donated by the Children. Franklin's letter to her is reproduced in Elliott Roosevelt, ed., *FDR: His Personal Letters,* 1905–1928, pp. 508–509. His telegram is in the Franklin D. Roosevelt Papers, Campaign of 1920, FDRL.

Steve Early's candid letters from the field are in the Franklin D. Roosevelt Papers, Campaign of 1920, FDRL, as are the clippings about Franklin's winning smile. Eleanor's reassuring letter about the Republican newspapers being merely patronizing is with the Roosevelt Family Papers Donated by the Children. Franklin's instructions to headquarters not to release material until Stanley Prenosil had wired his story appear on the bottom of a telegram in which he suggested a debate with Calvin Coolidge, Franklin D. Roosevelt Papers, Campaign of 1920, FDRL. My account of the Centralia lynching is based upon John McClelland, Jr., *Wobbly War: The Centralia Story.*

Charles McCarthy's complaints about how things were going at headquarters and Franklin's energetic memoranda are among the Franklin D. Roosevelt Papers, Campaign of 1920, FDRL. Arthur Krock's memories of George White's gloomy forecasts are from the transcript of an interview with him, Columbia Oral History Project, Columbia University, and Krock's *Memoirs.*

My examination of public sentiment toward the candidates and toward Wilson is based upon Frank Sullivan, *The Twenties*, Francis Russell, *The Shadow of Blooming Grove*, Andrew Sinclair, *The Available Man*, and William Allen White, *The Autobiography of William Allen White*.

Eleanor recalled her ambivalent feelings upon leaving James at Groton in *This Is My Story*; her subsequent feeling that boarding schools were not necessarily a good idea are from *This I Remember*, the second volume of her autobiography, published after her husband's death. My account of James' first difficult days at school are from his book, *Affectionately, FDR*, pp. 110–117. Franklin's telegram is with the Franklin D. Roosevelt Papers, Campaign of 1920, FDRL; his quarrel with the hyphenated Americans and the response of the *Bolletino Della Serra* are both from scrapbook clippings in the same collection.

The account of Eleanor's time aboard the *Westboro* is based largely upon *This Is My Story*, pp. 313–321, Joseph P. Lash, *Eleanor and Franklin*, pp. 249–258, and Lela Stiles, *"The Man Behind Roosevelt,"* pp. 67–74. The phony letter from the Burns Agency is among the Franklin D. Roosevelt Papers, Campaign of 1920, FDRL.

The story of the attempts to smear Harding is drawn from Francis Russell, *The Shadow of Blooming Grove*, Mark Sullivan, *The Twenties*, Andrew Sinclair, *The Available Man*, and John Morton Blum, *Joseph Tumulty*.

My account of Franklin's public battle with John R. Rathom is drawn from documents contained in the "Rathom Case" file in the Roosevelt Family Papers, (Business and Personal), FDRL. These include photostats of government documents proving Rathom's dubious background, Franklin's own account of how he received the open letter, and brief histories of each of the eighty-three cases upon which Rathom based his attack. Arthur Krock twice recalled his working up a reply with Franklin: in his Columbia Oral History Project transcript, Columbia University, and in his *Memoirs*, p. 152. Admiral Sims' satisfaction with Rathom's attack and his reassurances to the editor are among his papers at the Library of Congress. Charles McCarthy's uncharacteristically cheery letter is among the Franklin D. Roosevelt Papers, Campaign of 1920, FDRL.

Eleanor recalled FDR's pessimism in *This Is My Story*, p. 320. Tom Lynch told Ernest K. Lindley of FDR's optimism, and he included the story in his *Franklin D. Roosevelt*, p. 198.

Steve Early compared Franklin to a playboy in conversation with Harold Ickes, as recalled in Ickes' *Diary*.

Franklin's remark that the campaign had been a fine sail is from Alfred Steinberg, *Mrs. R.*, p. 121; his supposed interview with his mother's gardener was recorded in *The Cabinet Diaries of Josephus Daniels;* and his bizarre version of how the rumors of Harding's black ancestry were spread is from the transcript of a White House conversation with Lowell Mellett that took place between August 22 and 27, 1940, and is quoted from "The FDR Tapes," *American Heritage* (February–March 1982).

The story of the rescue of Elmer Olga is from a scrapbook clipping, Franklin D. Roosevelt Papers, Campaign of 1920, FDRL. The friend who wrote so glowingly to Sara of her son's ideals was Elizabeth Chapman, the same woman who shielded

Warren Delano's body from the eyes of gawkers in September 1920; her letter is among the Eleanor Roosevelt Papers, FDRL.

Fred Delano's counsel is with the Franklin D. Roosevelt Papers, Campaign of 1920, FDRL. Franklin's colorful story of how he got his job is from a conversation with Lowell Mellett, "The FDR Tapes," *American Heritage* (February–March 1982). Langdon Marvin's memories of Franklin at the law office are from the transcript of his Columbia Oral History Project interview, Columbia University.

My sketch of Marguerite Le Hand is based largely upon Bernard Asbell, ed., *The FDR Memoirs*, John Franklin Carter, *The New Dealers*, and an article by Doris Fleeson that appeared in *The Saturday Evening Post*.

Eleanor's account of her new New York life is drawn from Joseph P. Lash, *Eleanor and Franklin*, and from *This Is My Story*, pp. 322–327.

Franklin's unusually heavy drinking is hinted at in Eleanor's diary, FDRL. The late W. Sheffield Cowles, Jr., described Franklin's boisterous behavior at his wedding to me. Scrapbook clippings about TR Jr. are found in the Franklin D. Roosevelt Papers, Campaign of 1920, FDRL.

My account of the Section A scandal is based on documents found together in the "Newport Matter" file, Roosevelt Family Papers (Business and Personal), FDRL.

Clippings describing the Boy Scout outing are in the Franklin D. Roosevelt Papers, 1920–1928, FDRL.

13: FRANKLIN HAS BEEN QUITE ILL...

My account of Campobello and the good times the Roosevelts customarily had there is based upon my own stay on the island, as well as interviews with Linnea Calder, the daughter of the cottage caretaker, and another old Campobello hand who prefers to remain anonymous, and with James and Franklin D. Roosevelt, Jr. I have also benefited greatly from the unpublished transcript, "Conversations Between the Four Roosevelt Brothers recorded at the Roosevelt Cottage on Campobello Island on June 22, 24, and 25, 1979," which was kindly lent to me by Harry W. Stevens, superintendent of the Roosevelt Campobello International Park and Natural Area. I have also drawn upon *Campobello: Roosevelt's "Beloved Island,"* by Stephen O. Muskie, *Campobello The Outer Island,* by Alden Nowlan, James Roosevelt (with Sidney Shallett), *Affectionately, FDR* (pp. 131–145), and Elliott Roosevelt, *An Untold Story* (pp. 133–134).

The onset of infantile paralysis was obviously the central event of Franklin's adult life. Yet, except for a brief outline of the events of the week of August 8, 1921, written to a physician interested in his case, Franklin left no detailed account of what happened to him, and Eleanor's account of the same events, written in 1935 when it was in the family's interest not to dwell on the seriousness of Franklin's condition, is curiously distant and lacking in detail.

Every Roosevelt biographer has had to tell this central story, of course, and I have benefited from the work of all of them, but found especially moving the account in Kenneth S. Davis, *FDR: The Beckoning of Destiny*, pp. 646–661. Three books on the subject of Roosevelt's polio alone also proved useful: Richard T. Goldberg, *The Making of Franklin D. Roosevelt*, Jean Gould, *A Good Fight*, and, especially, *FDR's Splendid Deception* by Hugh Gallagher, whose understanding of the true meaning of Roosevelt's incapacity is fuller than that of any other writer.

I should perhaps add here that I contracted infantile paralysis myself in 1950 and bring a certain hard-won expertise to this and the following chapters.

But in piecing together this central story, I have so far as possible gone back to original sources: Franklin's own letters from Campobello display only the serene and cheerful face he presented to the world, revealing almost nothing of what he must have felt inside; Eleanor's letters to Rosy, Fred Delano, Louis Howe, and Missy Le Hand, and their responses, sketch at least the outlines of what happened on the island; correspondence with his first physicians, W. W. Keen and Edward H. Bennet, offers fragmentary clues. All are at the FDRL.

The most valuable evidence of what life was like for Roosevelt during the first weeks and months of his convalescence—much of which must still be read between the lines—is to be found among the papers of Franklin's Boston physician, Dr. Robert W. Lovett, now at the Francis A. Countway Library of Medicine, Boston. I am most grateful to that library's curator, Richard Wolfe, for helping to make the collection accessible to me. Included among Lovett's papers are notes on his own examinations of the patient, muscle charts starkly detailing the extent of his crippling, and correspondence with the first doctors to see Roosevelt at Campobello, as well as with Franklin's New York physician, Dr. George W. Draper, Franklin's physiotherapist, Mrs. Kathleen Lake, and his nurse, Edna T. Rockey. I have drawn very heavily upon the Lovett Papers in this and the three chapters that follow.

Since the context in which it appears makes clear the source of most of the material in this chapter, I will account here only for items that might otherwise prove puzzling to the reader.

Details of Eleanor's crowded life in the weeks before her husband's arrival at Campobello, Sara's exultant letter about her cross-Channel flight, and her startled son's reply are all from Joseph P. Lash, *Eleanor and Franklin*, pp. 264–267.

The friend to whom Eleanor said she had performed a "service of love" for Franklin was Joseph P. Lash. Eleanor's comparison between her husband's reaction to the news that he had infantile paralysis and that the Japanese had attacked Pearl Harbor is from an interview, Robert D. Graff Papers, FDRL.

Linnea Calder provided details of how the islanders carried Roosevelt from his cottage, and James and Franklin Jr. both recalled for me watching their father disappear down the hill. The latter recalled the artifice with which Howe disguised Roosevelt's useless left hand beneath his hat.

14: TO THE END OF THE DRIVEWAY

Again, my account of Roosevelt's attempts to recover his strength is based on the sources listed for Chapter 13, with special emphasis on the Lovett Papers and some of my own memories of trying to get back on my feet after infantile paralysis.

The Roosevelt sons remembered the frightening trip by sea to Eastport in "Conversations Between the Four Roosevelt Brothers. . . ." Elliott, who followed along in a separate boat with James, recalled the slippery footing. Louis Howe told Lela Stiles of his great relief when the train pulled out for New York, and she reported it in *"The Man Behind Roosevelt."*

The condolences and calling cards of Franklin's visitors are among the Eleanor Roosevelt Papers, FDRL.

Franklin's correspondence with polios and their parents is scattered throughout his papers at the FDRL. Josephus Daniels recalled his first interview with Roosevelt after infantile paralysis in his autobiography. The story of the admiring doctor comes from a handwritten note by the editor of the newspaper in which it evidently appeared. My *Before the Trumpet* includes considerable discussion of Roosevelt's family training in withholding complaints and appearing always to be cheerful.

Dr. Lovett's grim prognosis is here based both on his papers and on his voluminous writings about polio and its progress, listed under Articles in the Bibliography. James Roosevelt remembered his Christmas visit in *Affectionately, FDR,* and in an interview with me, Franklin Jr. recalled his father's prodigious strength.

My account of Isabella's relationship with Eleanor is based on their correspondence in Arizona and Hyde Park. Eleanor left her own account of the tense winter and spring of 1922 in *This I Remember.* James Roosevelt told me of Louis Howe's virtual abandonment of his family. Frances Perkins reflected on the relationship between Eleanor and Louis Howe in her reminiscence, Columbia Oral History Collection, Columbia University. Franklin Jr. told me of Howe's odd behavior and the subtle revenge he and John took.

My discussion of public attitudes toward polio owes much to Hugh Gallagher's *FDR's Splendid Deception.* Nigel Law's encomium to his great friend is from Jonathan Daniels, *The End of Innocence,* p. 159. Anna Roosevelt Halsted recalled her grandmother's plot to oust Louis Howe from her house in her reminiscence in the Columbia Oral History Collection, Columbia University.

Louis Howe's letters to F&D clients are among the Franklin D. Roosevelt Papers, Family, Business, and Personal. Franklin Jr. recalled for me his query about how his father stood the pain of his casts.

The physician who recalled Roosevelt's "flail legs" was Dr. Raymond H. Baxter, and he is quoted in Richard T. Goldberg, *The Making of FDR,* p. 88. The polio who recalled his first use of braces was Bentz Plagemann, *My Place to Stand,* p. 237. Anna's recollection of her father's momentary anger is quoted here from John Boettiger, *A Love in Shadow,* p. 94.

Robert McGauhey recalled the details of Franklin's first days back at Springwood in an interview with George Palmer of the National Park Service, FDRL. Margaret Suckley told me of her first afternoons with Roosevelt.

My account of Eleanor's first tentative moves beyond the household owe much to Joseph P. Lash, *Eleanor and Franklin.* Alice Longworth's scorn for her new friends is from *Mrs. L.* by Michael Teague. Molly Dewson is quoted in Susan Ware, *Partner and I.* The Marion Dickerman stories are from Kenneth Davis, *Invincible Summer,* and the Dickerman reminiscence in the Columbia Oral History Collection, Columbia University.

Franklin's charts—the weakened muscles noted in angry red—are among the Lovett Papers.

The lessons taught by Wilhemine Wright are clearly set forth in her articles.

Sara's letters from Europe are among the Roosevelt Family Papers Donated by the Children. My *Before the Trumpet* includes a discussion of Roosevelt's fear of fire.

Benjamin Haviland told George Palmer of his friendship with FDR, National Park Service, FDRL. Roosevelt's interest in Dutchess County history is recounted in F. Kennon Moody, *FDR and His Neighbors.* . . .

The account of Al Smith's war with William Randolph Hearst and his willingness to return to politics in 1922 is based on the sources given for my portrait of Smith in Chapter 11 and Frank Freidel, *Franklin D. Roosevelt: The Ordeal.*

Louis Depew recalled Franklin's enthusiasm for swimming to George Palmer, National Park Service, FDRL. His correspondence with other polios is scattered through his papers, FDRL. Anna's memories of his struggle to reach the Albany Post Road comes from her reminiscence, Columbia Oral History Collection, Columbia University.

15: THE LIMITS OF HIS POSSIBILITIES

Again, all correspondence with Drs. Lovett and Draper and Mrs. Lake is to be found among the Lovett Papers, Francis A. Countway Library of Medicine, Boston.

Bamie's concerns about Franklin's upcoming visit to Oldgate were expressed to her niece, Corinne Alsop, and are among her papers at the Houghton Library, Harvard University. W. Sheffield Cowles, Jr., described the visit both to me and to David McCullough.

My account of Franklin's fall while returning to the F&D is based upon Turnley Walker, *Roosevelt and the Warms Springs Story.* Walker, himself a polio, learned the details from talks with Basil O'Connor. I base my supposition that Roosevelt fell on his very first visit to Wall Street since the onset of paralysis on a letter from Mrs. Lake among the Lovett Papers that suggests he left for Hyde Park immediately after making this lone appearance.

Eleanor Roosevelt described the Election Day encounter that so appalled her to an interviewer, Robert Graff Papers, FDRL.

Francis Stoddard recalled his swift visits to the F&D in his reminiscence, Columbia Oral History Collection, Columbia University. Franklin's sparring with Vincent Cullen may be seen in their letters and memoranda to one another, Franklin D. Roosevelt Papers, Family, Business, and Personal, FDRL. Lowell Mellett described his visit to the Roosevelt townhouse, Reminiscences by Contemporaries, FDRL. The secretary's memory is from John Gunther, *Roosevelt in Retrospect*, p. 232.

Roosevelt's correspondence with Langdon Marvin about the ending of their partnership, Franklin D. Roosevelt Papers, Family, Business, and Personal, FDRL. Albert de Roode's patronizing view of Roosevelt's aptitude as a lawyer is recalled by Frances Perkins in her reminiscence, Columbia Oral History Collection, Columbia University.

Eleanor told Rexford G. Tugwell of her husband's unsteady business career, Rexford G. Tugwell Papers. My survey of his investments owes much to Frank Freidel, *Franklin D. Roosevelt: The Ordeal*, and Kenneth S. Davis, *FDR: The Beckoning of Destiny*. Walter Sach's bitter remarks are from his reminiscence, Columbia Oral History Collection, Columbia University.

The *Weona II* log is among the Franklin D. Roosevelt Papers, Family, Business, and Personal, FDRL. Eleanor recalled her distaste for life aboard in *This Is My Story*.

Dr. Lovett's young colleague was Dr. Albert Brewster, quoted in Richard T. Goldberg, *The Making of FDR*, p. 52.

Franklin's correspondence with various polios is scattered through his papers for the period and in the Paul Hasbrouck Papers, FDRL. Mary Hudson Veeder compared polio to a passing storm in an interview with me.

Adolph Miller's visit to Hyde Park is described in his reminiscence, Columbia Oral History Collection, Columbia University. Franklin's account of his boat carving is quoted from Frank Freidel, *Franklin D. Roosevelt: The Ordeal*, pp. 114–115. His correspondence with Livy Davis is in Franklin D. Roosevelt Papers, Family, Business, and Personal, FDRL. Eleanor recalled Franklin's uncharacteristic bitterness and her own shock at it in *This I Remember*, pp. 25–26.

Louis Howe's plans for an elaborate Cuff Links Club skit are from the Howe Papers, FDRL.

The *Larooco* logs are among the Franklin D. Roosevelt Papers, Family, Business, and Personal, FDRL. Franklin's feeling that he had to be in control of things was remembered by Frances Perkins in her reminiscence, Columbia Oral History Collection, Columbia University. Eleanor's memories of tensions between her husband and her mother-in-law are from *This I Remember*. My account of the relationship between FDR and Missy Le Hand owes much to Bernard Asbell, *The FDR Memoirs*.

All of Roosevelt's writings are at the FDRL.

The details of Eleanor's life apart from Franklin are from Joseph P. Lash, *Eleanor and Franklin*. Claude Bowers described Al Smith's breezy visit with the Wisconsin delegates in his *My Life*. Various details about the convention and the Roosevelt speech are drawn from newspaper accounts, the reminiscences of Joseph Proskauer, Frances Perkins, and Marion Dickerman in the Columbia Oral History Collection, Columbia University, and from the biographies of Al Smith listed among the sources for Chapter 11.

Eleanor's surprisingly vague memory of the convention is from *This Is My Story*. Her thoughts about Franklin's future are from the Frances Perkins reminiscence, Columbia

Oral History Collection, Columbia University. W. Sheffield Cowles, Jr., recalled for me Eleanor's campaign visit to Oldgate and his mother's reaction to it.

16: OLD DOCTOR ROOSEVELT

There are several books which deal seriously with Roosevelt and Warm Springs and I have drawn upon all of them: Turnley Walker, *Roosevelt and the Warm Springs Story*, Theo Lippman, Jr., *The Squire of Warm Springs*, Jean Gould, *A Good Fight*, Ruth Stevens, *Hiya Neighbor!*, Hugh Gallagher, *FDR's Splendid Deception*, Frank Freidel, *FDR and the South*, Richard T. Goldberg, *The Making of FDR*, Donald Scott Carmichael, *FDR Columnist*, and Chapter 1 of Rexford G. Tugwell, *In Search of Roosevelt*.

I have consulted all the files touching upon Warm Springs at the FDRL, and have examined what records remain of the Roosevelt era at Warm Springs itself. In addition, I spoke at length with two of the physiotherapists who worked with Roosevelt, Mary Hudson Veeder and Alice Lou Plastridge-Converse, and talked as well with several polios and former push boys. I also benefited greatly from watching the home movies made by his Warm Springs neighbor, Lynn Pierson, FDRL.

I will offer sources here only for those items which, so far as I know, appear in none of the standard published works on FDR.

Louis Joseph described his case to Rexford G. Tugwell, Rexford G. Tugwell Papers, FDRL.

Bernard Asbell did the arithmetic about the amount of time Roosevelt and Missy Le Hand spent together for his *FDR Memoirs*, and also conducted important interviews with Anna Roosevelt Halsted and Mr. and Mrs. Egbert Curtis that touched upon that relationship, FDRL. Missy Le Hand's letters to FDR are among the Franklin D. Roosevelt Papers, Family, Business, and Personal, FDRL. Grace Tully paid tribute to her old colleague in a memorandum she wrote criticizing John Gunther's *Roosevelt in Retrospect*, FDRL. Marion Dickerman's views on Eleanor and jealousy are from Kenneth Davis, *Invincible Summer*. Sara's letters to Franklin are all from the Roosevelt Family Papers Donated by the Children, FDRL.

Franklin Jr.'s sad letter to Anna is from the Roosevelt Family Papers Donated by the Children, FDRL. The *Larooco* logs are among the Franklin D. Roosevelt Family Papers, Family, Business, and Personal, FDRL. Louis Howe's exasperated letter to Franklin is among the Howe Papers.

Mary Hudson Veeder told me of the many "addled" polios whom she and her colleagues helped to recover their senses. Bentz Plagemann recalled what Warm Springs did for him in *My Place to Stand*, p. 183.

Franklin's correspondence with John Lawrence and Livy Davis is all in the Franklin D. Roosevelt Papers, Family, Business, and Personal, FDRL. His letter to Dr. Ober is among the Lovett Papers at the Francis A. Countway Library of Medicine, Boston.

Mary Howe's memories of the cottage her father and Franklin shared is from Lela Stiles, *"The Man Behind Roosevelt."* My portrait of Dr. William McDonald is based on his letters to FDR, Franklin D. Roosevelt Papers, Family, Business, and Personal, FDRL.

Alice Lou Plastridge-Converse told me of what she had been able to do for Roosevelt over the telephone. She also told that story to Dr. Jay Schleichkorn and it appears in his article, "Physical Therapist, 98, Recalls Rehabilitating Franklin Roosevelt," *PT Bulletin*, March 15, 1988.

Frances Perkins recalled an idyllic afternoon at Springwood in her *The Roosevelt I Knew*. My account of Val-Kill's creation and the life Eleanor led there is based on Kenneth Davis, *Invincible Summer*, Joseph P. Lash, *Eleanor and Franklin*, and on my own article, "Eleanor Roosevelt Drew Her Strength from a Sanctuary Called Val-Kill," *Smithsonian Magazine* (October 1984). Alice Lou Plastridge-Converse told me of the inaugural luncheon. Corinne Alsop's memory of Allenswood and its impact upon Eleanor is from a letter she wrote to Archibald MacLeish and is among her papers at the Houghton Library, Harvard University.

My account of the Mosleys' stay aboard the *Larooco* is based on three books: Oswald Mosley, *My Life;* Nicholas Mosley, *Rules of the Game;* and Richard Sidelsky, *Oswald Mosley*.

Roosevelt's notes on the sale of the *Larooco* are from the Robert Forbes Collection, *Forbes* Magazine. Anna's report on her father is from *Mother and Daughter*, edited by Bernard Asbell. The story of her trip abroad and decision to marry is drawn largely from her son's book, *A Love in Shadow*, pp. 93–116, supplemented by Curtis Dall's eccentric memoir, *My Exploited Father-in-Law*.

Franklin Roosevelt, Jr., reflected on what polio had meant to his father's career in conversation with the author.

Dorothy Dow reported on FDR and the square-dancers in her memoir, *Eleanor Roosevelt: An Eager Spirit*.

Louis Howe's letter expressing concern about a convention stampede is among his papers, FDRL. Roosevelt's letter to Louis Wehle is in his book, *Hidden Threads of History*. John Houghteling's letter to James Farley and Roosevelt's to William McDonald are among the Franklin D. Roosevelt Papers, Family, Business, and Personal, FDRL.

17: IT WAS TIME

Franklin's list of suggested changes for the Meriwether Inn is from the collection of the Franklin and Eleanor Institute, FDRL. Ann Irwin Bray told me of her mother's cheerful drives around the Warm Springs golf course with FDR. Henry A. Wallace remembered Franklin's exultant driving in an interview with Rexford G. Tugwell, FDRL. Frank Draiss recalled his road building to George Palmer, National Park Service Interviews, FDRL.

My account of Roosevelt's relationship with Hyde Park residents owes much to L. Kennon Moody, *FDR and His Neighbors*, but also to a careful examination of Roosevelt's correspondence with William Plog, FDRL. Dean Acheson's letter about Roosevelt's special sense of himself is among the William D. Hassett Papers, FDRL. Marion Dickerman recalled Roosevelt's last-ditch effort to win Hyde Park in her reminiscence, Columbia Oral History Collection, Columbia University.

James Roosevelt told the story of his father, Pa Watson, and the little boy to Rexford G. Tugwell, Rexford G. Tugwell Papers, FDRL.

Mary Hudson Veeder wanted me to know that Roosevelt was a politician before he was a citizen of Warm Springs.

Paul Hasbrouck's letters home offer a vivid picture of Warm Springs in 1927, FDRL. Hugh Gallagher loaned me a copy of Franklin's letter to the polio's anxious mother.
      Mary Hudson Veeder explained about the lack of back bedrooms, showed me the Founder's Day programs from which I got the grisly-sounding menu items, and paid tribute to Miss Mahoney's even-handed but stern justice.
      Virginia Shipp recalled being a Powder-puff girl. Bentz Plagemann's *My Place to Stand* contains a choice sampling of Warm Springs humor.
      The correspondence about letting Franklin stay a little longer in Georgia is from the Franklin D. Roosevelt Papers, Family, Business, and Personal, and Louis Howe Papers, both at the FDRL.

There are a number of letters from Miss Mahoney to Franklin and Eleanor concerning Missy Le Hand's collapse in the Franklin D. Roosevelt Papers, Family, Business, and Personal, FDRL. Lucy Mercer Rutherfurd's letters are in the same collection. Rosy's will is at the FDRL.

Mary Hudson Veeder told me of working with FDR to perfect his walk in the spring of 1928.
      Dr. Harold Rosenthal's home movies are at the FDRL.
      Elliott Roosevelt told me of the preparations he and his father made for the Houston appearance. Roosevelt's letters to Van-Lear Black are in the Franklin D. Roosevelt Papers, Family, Business, and Personal, FDRL.
      Eddie Dowling recalled his visit to Franklin to persuade him to run for governor, transcript of his interview, Columbia Oral History Collection, Columbia University. He said it took place in Georgia, which cannot be true since Sara was not there that summer, and so I have assumed that the scene he describes took place at Val-Kill.

Mary Hudson Veeder told me of the evening Smith talked Roosevelt into accepting his party's nomination. Other details come from Bernard Asbell's interview with Egbert Curtis.
      My account of election night, 1928, is drawn from the biographies of Al Smith given in the source notes for Chapter 11, supplemented by newspaper accounts, the memoirs of James Farley, Samuel Rosenman, and Ed Flynn, and the reminiscence of Frances Perkins, Columbia Oral History Collection, Columbia University.

BIBLIOGRAPHY

UNPUBLISHED MATERIAL

MANUSCRIPT COLLECTIONS CONSULTED AT THE FRANKLIN D. ROOSEVELT
LIBRARY

Bye, George
Delano Family Papers
Delano, Frederic A.
Olin Dows
Early, Stephen T.
Forbush, Gabrielle
Franklin D. Roosevelt Library, Inc.
Franklin D. Roosevelt Memorial Foundation
Freidel, Frank
Hackett, Henry T. and John
Hall Family
Halsted, Anna Roosevelt
Harper and Brothers
Hasbrouck, Paul
Hassett, William D.
Hickok, Lorena
Howe, Louis M.
Joseph, Nannine
Kleeman, Rita Halle
Lape, Esther
Livingston Family
McIntyre, Ross T.
Marvin, Langdon P.
Mellett, Lowell
Morgenthau, Henry, Jr.
O'Connor, Basil
Perkins, Frances
Rollins, Alfred B.
Roosevelt, Anna Eleanor
Roosevelt, Anna Eleanor and Franklin D. (Reminiscences by Contemporaries)
Roosevelt, Franklin D.: Papers Pertaining to Family, Business, and Personal
    Affairs
Roosevelt, Franklin D.: Papers as New York State Senator, 1910–1913

Roosevelt, Franklin D.: Papers as Assistant Secretary of the Navy, 1913–1920
Roosevelt, Franklin D.: Papers as Vice-Presidential Candidate, 1920
Roosevelt, Franklin D.: Papers, 1920–1928
Roosevelt, Franklin D.: Papers as President, Alphabetical File
Roosevelt, Franklin D.: Papers as President, Official File
Roosevelt, Franklin D.: Papers as President, President's Official File
Roosevelt, Franklin D.: Papers as President, Secretary's File
Roosevelt, James (son of the President)
Roosevelt Family
Roosevelt Family: Papers Donated by the Children of Franklin D.
and Eleanor
Rosenman, Samuel I.
Schary, Dore
Secret Service
Suckley, Margaret L.
Tugwell, Rexford G.

Note: I have also drawn heavily upon the audiovisual section of the FDRL. Its thousands of photographs and miles of film seem to me to be indispensable to anyone who wants to understand the Roosevelts or the different worlds in which they moved.

OTHER MANUSCRIPT COLLECTIONS CONSULTED

Alsop Family Papers, Houghton Library, Harvard University
Cowles, Anna Roosevelt, Papers, Houghton Library, Harvard University
Howe, Mark Anthony de Wolfe Papers, Houghton Library, Harvard University
Peabody, Endicott Papers, Groton School
Robinson, Corinne Roosevelt Papers, Houghton Library, Harvard University
Roosevelt, Theodore, Collection, Houghton Library, Harvard University
Roosevelt, Theodore, Collection, Theodore Roosevelt Birthplace, New York City
Sherwood, Robert E., Papers, Houghton Library, Harvard University

AUTHOR'S INTERVIEWS

Anderson, Benjamin
Boettiger, John R.
Bray, Ann Irwin
Breasted, Martha Ferguson
Calder, Linnea
Caldwell, Mary
Childs, Marquis
Cone, Marell
Copeland, Robert
Corr, Maureen
Cowles, W. Sheffield, Jr.
Doar, Patty

Doggett, Charles
Eastman, John, Jr.
Eastman, Laura Franklin Delano Adams
Fetters, James
Fish, Hamilton
Freidel, Frank
Ferguson, Mrs. Robert Munro
Greenway, John S.
Gurewitsch, Edna
Hermann, Edward
Keyserling, Mary D.
Lash, Joseph P.
Loftin, Vernon
Loftin, Elmer
Morgan, Gerald
Morgan, Thomas
Pike, Suzanne
Plastridge-Converse, Alice Lou
Roosevelt, Curtis
Roosevelt, Elliott
Roosevelt, Franklin D., Jr.
Roosevelt, James
Rush, Tom
Shaw, Bramwell
Shaw, Emily
Shipp, Virginia
Suckley, Margaret L.
Trotter, William
Veeder, Mary Hudson
White, Laura
White, Peter
Whitehead, Dr. Mark
Woodall, Sue

ORAL HISTORY TRANSCRIPTS

Oral Histories, FDRL

Dickerman, Marion
Forbush, Gabrielle
Roosevelt, Anna Eleanor
Rosenman, Samuel I.

Robert D. Graff Papers, FDRL

Arnold, Thurman
Ashurst, Harry

Barrett, Daniel M.
Batchelder, Antoinette (Toi)
Biddle, Francis
Budenz, Louis
Calder, Franklin
Celler, Emmanuel
Cohen, Benjamin
Corcoran, Thomas
Cornell, Douglas
Craig, May
Delano, Laura
Dows, Mrs. Tracy
Fish, Hamilton
Flanagan, Hallie
Fortas, Abe
Frankfurter, Felix
Golden, Paulina
Hickok, Lorena
Hopkins, William
Howe, Hartley E.
Ickes, Jane
Johnson, Felton
Kannee, Henry
Krock, Arthur
Kunze, Fred
Lucas, Scott
Masten, Harvey
McCormack, John
McGauhey, Isabel
Mitchell, Samuel
Morgan, Mrs. Gerald
Mott, William
Nathan, Robert
Parks, Lillian Rogers
Patman, Wright
Porter, Paul
Queseda, Pete
Robinson, Helen Roosevelt (Mrs. Theodore Douglas)
Romagna, Jack
Roosevelt, Anna Eleanor
Roosevelt, James
Smith, Arthur
Smith, A. Merriman
Stiles, Lela
Suckley, Margaret L.
Theis, William

Tully, Grace
Wheeler, Burton K.

Eleanor Roosevelt Oral History Transcripts, FDRL

Bell, Minnewa
Berge, Otto
Boettiger, John R.
Calhoun, Gilbert
Connell, Catherine, and O'Neill, Gabrielle
Corr, Maureen
Curnan, Archie H. ("Tubby")
Daniels, Jonathan
Dows, Olin
Drewry, Elizabeth B.
Entrup, Marguerite
Farley, Harold
Gellhorn, Martha
Gurewitsch, Edna P.
Gurievitch, Grania
Halsted, Diana Hopkins
Halsted, James A.
Harriman, W. Averell
Hoffman, Anna Rosenberg
Kidd, Gordon
Lash, Trude
McVitty, Honoria Livingston
Nixon, Edgar; Deyo, Jerome; and Stickle, William
Redmond, Roland
Roosevelt, Elliott
Roosevelt, James
Seagraves, Eleanor
Tugwell, Rexford G.

National Park Service Val-Kill Transcripts, FDRL

Berge, Otto
Boettiger, John R.
Corr, Maureen
Curnan, Archie ("Tubby")
Entrup, Marguerite
Gellhorn, Martha
Levy, William Turner
Redmond, Roland
Roosevelt, Elliott
Wotkyns, Eleanor

*National Park Service, Transcripts of Interviews by George Palmer
and Fred Rath*

Campbell, Mary
Clay, John
Curan, Charles Van
Depew, Louis
Dickinson, Mr. and Mrs. Grant
Draiss, Frank
Farley, Theresa P.
Hackmeister, Louise
Haviland, Benjamin
Hoyt, Morgan
Killmer, Evaretta
Killmer, Thomas
Leonard, Thomas F.
Linaka, Russell W.
Mack, John
Martin, Alfred
McGauhey, Robert
McGirr, Newman
Morgan, Mary Newbold
Plog, Mrs. William
Plog, William A.
Robinson, Helen Roosevelt (Mrs. Theodore Douglas)
Simon, Louis
Smith, Moses
Thompson, Mildred L.
Traudt, James; and Knauss, Alex
Tully, Grace L.

Columbia University Oral History Collection Transcripts

Albright, Horace
Arnold, Henry H.
Baldwin, Raymond Earl
Battle, Samuel J.
Binkerd, Robert S.
Bowers, Claude G.
Bowles, Chester
Braden, Spruille
Canfield, Cass
Cerf, Bennett
Chamberlain, Thomas Gassner
Childs, Marquis
Clark, Grenville
Clay, Lucius
Creel George

Daniels, Jonathan Worth
Davis, John W.
Davison, Frederick
Davison, Fredrick Trubee
Delano, William Adáms
Dewey, Thomas E.
Dickerman, Marion
Dowling, Eddie
Farley, James A.
Flynn, Edward J.
Francis, Clarence
Gerard, James W.
Halsted, Anna Roosevelt
Hamilton, Carl
Henshaw, Frederick
Isaacs, Stanley M.
Jackson, Robert H.
Johnson, Alvin
Kerr, Florence
Keyserling, Leon H.
Krock, Arthur
Land, Emory
Lazarus, Reuben A.
Lehman, Herbert
Lippmann, Walter
Mahoney, Jeremiah
Marvin, Langdon P.
Marvin, Mary
Miller, Adolph
Moley, Raymond
Moscow, Warren
O'Brian, John Lord
Pell, Herbert C.
Perkins, Frances
Phillips, William
Poletti, Charles
Proskauer, Joseph M.
Reed, Stanley
Reynolds, Jackson E.
Robinson, Beverley R.
Roosevelt, Anna Eleanor
Rosenman, Dorothy
Rosenman, Samuel I.
Sachs, Walter E.
Schaick, George S. van
Schiefflin, William Jay
Schlesinger, Arthur M.

Smith, Alexander H.
Smith, H. Alexander
Stoddard, Francis Russell
Straus, Nathan
Tanzer, Laurence Arnold
Theodore Roosevelt Association (Interviews with Corinne Roosevelt Alsop, Mr.
      and Mrs. W. Sheffield Cowles, Jr.)
Tugwell, Rexford G.
Wadsworth, James Wolcott
Wagner, Robert F., Jr.
Wallace, Henry Agard
Warburg, James Paul
Warner, Emily Smith
Wheeler, Burton K.
Wickard, Claude A.
Williams, James Thomas, Jr.

THESES AND REPORTS

Note: This list does not include the considerable number of unpublished
      manuscripts and drafts by FDR, Eleanor Roosevelt, members of their
      families and their friends upon which I drew, almost all of which are to be
      found scattered among the various manuscript collections at the FDRL.
      The titles and locations of these are given in the source notes for the
      individual chapters.

Coady, Joseph William. *Franklin D. Roosevelt's Early Washington Years
      (1913–1920).* Ph.D. dissertation, St. John's University, 1968.
Ferdon, Nona S. *Franklin D. Roosevelt: A Psychological Interpretation of His
      Childhood and Youth.* Ph.D. dissertation, University of Hawaii, 1971.
Fogel, Nancy. *Change in Hyde Park: Interviews with 24 People.* Senior thesis,
      Vassar College, 1979.
Moody, F. Kennon. *FDR and His Neighbors: A Study of the Relationship Between
      Franklin D. Roosevelt and the Residents of Dutchess County.* Ph.D.
      dissertation, SUNY, Albany, 1981.
Rath, Fred L. *Home of Franklin D. Roosevelt National Historic Site, Hyde Park,
      New York: Preliminary Guard Manual.* Prepared for the National Park
      Service, 1948.
Roosevelt International Park Commission. *Conversations Between the Four Roosevelt
      Brothers Recorded at the Roosevelt Cottage on Campobello Island on June 22,
      24, and 25, 1979.*
Snell, Charles W. *Historic Site and Grounds Report Bellefield Mansion and Estate,
      Home of Franklin D. Roosevelt.* Prepared for the National Park Service,
      1950.
Wilkins, George Y. *A Report on the Birthplace and Home of Franklin D. Roosevelt.*
      Prepared for the National Park Service, 1950.

PUBLISHED MATERIALS

BOOKS BEARING DIRECTLY UPON THE ROOSEVELTS AND DELANOS

Adamic, Louis. *Dinner at the White House.* New York, 1946.

Alsop, Joseph. *FDR: A Centenary Remembrance.* New York, 1982.

Asbell, Bernard. *When FDR Died.* New York, 1961.

——. *The FDR Memoirs.* New York, 1973.

——. ed., *Mother and Daughter: The Letters of Eleanor and Anna Roosevelt.* New York, 1982.

Bellush, Benjamin. *Franklin D. Roosevelt as Governor of New York.* New York, 1956.

Beschloss, Michael P. *Kennedy and Roosevelt: The Uneasy Alliance.* New York, 1980.

Bishop, Jim. *FDR's Last Year.* New York, 1974.

Blum, John Morton, ed. *From the Morgenthau Diaries:*
    Vol. 1: *Years of Crisis.* Boston, 1959.
    Vol. 2: *Years of Urgency.* Boston, 1965.
    Vol. 3: *Years of War.* Boston, 1967.

——. *Roosevelt and Morgenthau.* Boston, 1970.

——. *The Progressive Presidents.* New York, 1980.

Boettiger, John R. *A Love in Shadow.* Boston, 1968; New York, 1978.

Brough, James. *Princess Alice.* Boston, 1975.

Burns, James MacGregor. *Roosevelt: The Lion and the Fox.* New York, 1956.

——. *Roosevelt: The Soldier of Freedom.* New York, 1970.

Busch, Noel. *What Manner of Man.* New York, 1944; Chicago, 1977.

Carmichael, Donald Scott. *FDR Columnist.* Chicago, 1947.

Churchill, Allen. *The Roosevelts: American Aristocrats.* New York, 1956.

Dall, Curtis B. *FDR: My Exploited Father-in-Law.* Washington, D.C., 1970.

Dallek, Robert. *Franklin D. Roosevelt and American Foreign Policy, 1932–1945.* Oxford, 1979.

Daniels, Jonathan. *White House Witness 1942–1945.* Garden City, N.Y., 1975.

Davis, Kenneth S.
    Vol. 1: *FDR: The Beckoning of Destiny, 1882–1928* New York, 1971.
    Vol. 2: *FDR: The New York Years, 1928–1933.* New York, 1985.
    Vol. 3: *FDR: The New Deal Years, 1933–1937.* New York, 1986.

——. *Invincible Summer: An Intimate Portrait of the Roosevelts.* New York, 1974.

Day, Donald, ed. *Franklin D. Roosevelt's Own Story.* Boston, 1951.

Delano, Daniel W., Jr. *Franklin Roosevelt and the Delano Influence.* Pittsburgh, 1946.

Dow, Dorothy. *Eleanor Roosevelt: An Eager Spirit.* New York, 1984.

Dows, Olin. *Franklin Roosevelt at Hyde Park.* New York, 1949.

Faber, Doris. *The Mothers of American Presidents.* New York, 1968.

Farley, James A. *Behind the Ballots: The Personal History of a Politician.* New York, 1938.

——. *Jim Farley's Story: The Roosevelt Years.* New York, 1948

Farr, Finnis. *FDR.* New Rochelle, N.Y., 1972.

Felsenthal, Carol. *Alice Roosevelt Longworth.* New York, 1988.

Fish, Hamilton. *FDR: The Other Side of the Coin.* New York, 1976.

Flynn, John T. *Country Squire in the White House.* New York, 1940.

———. *The Roosevelt Myth.* Garden City, N.Y., 1948.

Franklin D. Roosevelt Library. *The Press Conferences of Franklin D. Roosevelt* (22 vols.).

Freedman, Max, ed. *Roosevelt and Frankfurter: Their Correspondence, 1928–1945.* Boston, 1967.

Freidel, Frank.

    Vol. 1: *Franklin D. Roosevelt: The Apprenticeship.* Boston, 1952.

    Vol. 2: *Franklin D. Roosevelt: The Ordeal.* Boston, 1954.

    Vol. 3: *Franklin D. Roosevelt: The Triumph.* Boston, 1956.

    Vol. 4: *Franklin D. Roosevelt: Launching the New Deal.* Boston, 1973.

———. *FDR and the South.* Baton Rouge, La., 1967.

Gallagher, Hugh Gregory. *FDR's Splendid Deception.* New York, 1985.

Gardner, Joseph. *Departing Glory: Theodore Roosevelt as ex-President.* New York, 1973.

Geddes, Donald Potter, ed. *Franklin Delano Roosevelt: A Memorial.* New York, 1945.

Goldberg, Richard Thayer. *The Making of Franklin D. Roosevelt: Triumph Over Disability.* Cambridge, 1981.

Gosnell, Harold. *Champion Campaigner.* New York, 1952.

Gould, Jean. *A Good Fight: The Story of FDR's Conquest of Polio.* New York, 1960.

Graff, Robert D., Ginna, Robert Emmett, and Butterfield, Roger. *FDR.* New York, 1963.

Graham, Otis L., Jr., and Wander, Meghan Robinson, eds. *Franklin D. Roosevelt: His Life and Times: An Encyclopedic View.* Boston, 1985.

Greer, Thomas H. *What Roosevelt Thought: The Social and Political Ideas of Franklin D. Roosevelt.* East Lansing, Mich., 1958.

Gunther, John. *Roosevelt in Retrospect.* New York, 1950.

Gurewitsch, A. David. *Eleanor Roosevelt: Her Day.* New York, 1973.

Hagedorn, Herman. *The Roosevelt Family of Sagamore Hill.* New York, 1954.

Hallgren, Mauritz A. *The Gay Reformer: Profits Before Plenty Under Franklin D. Roosevelt.* New York, 1935.

Hareven, Tamara. *Eleanor Roosevelt: An American Conscience.* Chicago, 1968.

Harrity, Richard, and Martin, Ralph G. *Eleanor Roosevelt: Her Life in Pictures.* New York, 1958.

Hart, Albert Bushnell, ed. *Theodore Roosevelt Encyclopedia.* New York, 1941.

Hassett, William D. *Off the Record with FDR.* New Brunswick, N.J., 1958.

Hershan, Stella K. *A Woman of Quality.* New York, 1970.

Hickok, Lorena. *The Road to the White House: FDR: The Pre-Presidential Years.* New York, 1962.

Hoff-Wilson, Joan, and Lightman, Marjorie, eds. *Without Precedent: The Life and Times of Eleanor Roosevelt.* Bloomington, Ind., 1984.

Hough, Richard. *The Greatest Crusade: Roosevelt, Churchill and the Naval Wars.* New York, 1986.

Johnson, Gerald W. *Roosevelt: An American Study.* New York, 1942.

Kearney, James R. *Anna Eleanor Roosevelt: The Evolution of a Reformer.*

Kemp, Barbara H., and Cherasky, Shirley. *Eleanor Roosevelt's Washington* (pamphlet). Washington, D.C., 1984.

Kinnaird, Clark, ed. *The Real FDR.* New York, 1945.

Kleeman, Rita Halle. *Gracious Lady: The Life of Sara Delano Roosevelt.* New York, 1935.

Larabee, Eric. *Commander in Chief: Franklin Delano Roosevelt, His Lieutenants & Their War.* New York, 1987.

Lash, Joseph P. *Eleanor Roosevelt: A Friend's Memoir.* Garden City, N.Y., 1964.

———. *Eleanor and Franklin.* New York, 1971.

———. *Eleanor: The Years Alone.* New York, 1972.

———. *Roosevelt and Churchill 1939–1941.* New York, 1976.

———. *FDR: An Intimate History.* Garden City, N.Y., 1983.

———. *Love, Eleanor: Eleanor Roosevelt and Her Friends,* Vol. I. Garden City, N.Y., 1982.

———. *A World of Love: Eleanor Roosevelt and Her Friends,* Vol. II. Garden City, N.Y., 1984.

———. *Life Was Meant to Be Lived: A Centenary Tribute.* New York, 1984.

Leuchtenberg, William E. *Franklin D. Roosevelt and the New Deal, 1932–1940. In the Shadow of FDR: From Harry Truman to Ronald Reagan.* Ithaca, N.Y., 1983.

Lindley, Ernest K. *Franklin D. Roosevelt: A Career in Progressive Democracy.* New York, 1932.

———. *The Roosevelt Revolution.* New York, 1933.

———. *Halfway with Roosevelt.* New York, 1936.

Lippman, Theo, Jr. *The Squire of Warm Springs: FDR in Georgia, 1924–1945.*

Longworth, Alice Roosevelt. *Crowded Hours.* New York, 1933.

Looker, Earle. *This Man Roosevelt.* New York, 1932.

Lorant, Stefan. *FDR: A Pictorial Biography.* New York, 1950.

———. *The Life and Times of Theodore Roosevelt.* Garden City, N.Y., 1959.

Loucheim, Katie, ed. *The Making of the New Deal: The Insiders Speak.* Cambridge, 1983.

Ludwig, Emil. *Roosevelt: A Study in Fortune and Power.* New York, 1938.

Mackenzie, Compton. *Mr. Roosevelt,* New York, 1944.

Maclcish, Archibald. *The Eleanor Roosevelt Story.* Boston, 1965.

Marks, Frederick W., III. *Wind Over Sand: The Diplomacy of Franklin Roosevelt.* Athens, Ga., 1988.

McCullough, David. *Mornings on Horseback.* New York, 1981.

McIntyre, Ross T. *White House Physician.* New York, 1946.

Manners, William. *TR and Will: A Friendship That Split the Republican Party.* New York, 1969.

Miller, Nathan. *The Roosevelt Chronicles.* Garden City, N.Y., 1979.

———. *FDR: An Intimate History.* Garden City, 1983.

Moley, Raymond. *After Seven Years.* New York, 1939.

————. *The First New Deal.* New York, 1966.

Morgan, Ted. *FDR: A Biography.* New York, 1985.

Morison, Elting E., ed. *The Letters of Theodore Roosevelt,* 8 vols., Cambridge, 1951, 1952, 1954.

Morris, Edmund. *The Rise of Theodore Roosevelt.* New York, 1979.

Morris, Sylvia Jukes. *Edith Kermit Roosevelt.* New York, 1980.

Nesbitt, Henrietta. *White House Diary.*

Partridge, Bellamy. *The Roosevelt Family in America.* New York, 1936.

Perkins, Dexter. *The New Age of Franklin Roosevelt 1932–1945.* Chicago, 1957.

Perkins, Frances, *The Roosevelt I Knew.* New York, 1946.

Pringle, Henry F., *Theodore Roosevelt: A Biography.* New York, 1931.

Rigdon, William McKinley, and Derieux, James. *White House Sailor.* Garden City, N.Y., 1962.

Rixey, Lillian. *Bamie.* New York, 1963.

Rollins, Alfred B., Jr. *Roosevelt and Howe.* New York, 1962.

————, ed. *Franklin D. Roosevelt and the Age of Action.* New York, 1962.

Robinson, Corinne (Roosevelt). *My Brother Theodore Roosevelt.* New York,

Robinson, Edgar E. *The Roosevelt Leadership 1933–1945.* Philadelphia, 1955.

Roosevelt, Eleanor, ed., *Hunting Big Game in the Eighties.* New York, 1933.

Roosevelt, Eleanor. *This is My Story.* New York, 1937.

————. *My Day.* New York, 1938.

————. *This I Remember.* New York, 1949.

————. *Franklin D. Roosevelt and Hyde Park* (pamphlet). Washington, D.C., 1949.

————. *On My Own.* New York, 1958.

————. *The Autobiography of Eleanor Roosevelt.* New York, 1961.

————. *You Learn by Living.* New York, 1960.

————. *The Wisdom of Eleanor Roosevelt.*

Roosevelt, Elliott, ed. *FDR: His Personal Letters: Early Years* (Vol. I). New York, 1947.

————. *FDR: His Personal Letters, 1905–1928* (Vol. II). New York, 1948.

————. *FDR: His Personal Letters, 1928–1945* (2 vols.). New York, 1950.

————. *As He Saw It.* New York, 1946.

————, and James Brough, *An Untold Story: The Roosevelts of Hyde Park.* New York, 1973.

————, and James Brough. *A Rendezvous with Destiny: The Roosevelts of the White House.* New York, 1975.

————, and James Brough. *Mother R.: Eleanor Roosevelt's Untold Story.* New York, 1978.

Roosevelt,. Franklin Delano. *How I Am Going to Conduct My Responsibilities.* East Aurora, N.Y., 1982.

Roosevelt, James, with Sidney Shalett. *Affectionately, FDR: A Son's Story of a Lonely Man.* New York, 1956.

————, with Bill Libby. *My Parents: A Differing View.* Chicago, 1976.

Roosevelt, Nicholas. *A Front Row Seat,* Oklahoma City.

Roosevelt, Sara Delano (as told to Isabel Leighton and Gabrielle Forbush). *My Boy Franklin.* New York, 1933.

Roosevelt, Theodore. *Theodore Roosevelt: An Autobiography.* New York, 1925.

——. *Letters to Anna Roosevelt Cowles.* New York, 1924.

Roosevelt, Mrs. Theodore, Jr. *Day Before Yesterday.* Garden City, N.Y., 1959.

Rosenman, Samuel I. *Working with Roosevelt.* New York, 1952.

——, ed. *The Public Papers and Addresses of Franklin D. Roosevelt.* 13 vols., New York, 1938–50.

Sandifer, Irine Reiterman. *Mrs. Roosevelt As We Knew Her.* New York.

Schlesinger, Arthur M., Jr. *The Age of Roosevelt: The Crisis of the Old Order, 1919–1933.* Boston, 1957.

——. *The Age of Roosevelt: The Coming of the New Deal.* Boston, 1958.

——. *The Age of Roosevelt: The Politics of Upheaval.* Boston, 1960.

Schriftgiesser, Karl. *The Amazing Roosevelt Family, 1603–1942.* New York, 1942.

Sherwood, Robert E. *Roosevelt and Hopkins.* New York, 1948.

Steelholm, Clara and Hardy. *The House at Hyde Park.* New York, 1950.

Steinberg, Alfred. *Mrs. R: The Life of Eleanor Roosevelt.* New York, 1958.

Stiles, Lela. *"The Man Behind Roosevelt." The Story of Louis McHenry Howe.* Cleveland, 1954.

Sutton, Anthony C. *Wall Street and FDR.* New Rochelle, N.Y., 1975.

Teague, Michael. *Mrs. L.: Conversations with Alice Roosevelt. Longworth.* Garden City, N.Y., 1981.

Teichman, Howard. *Alice: The Life and Times of Alice Roosevelt Longworth.* Englewood Cliffs, N.J., 1979.

Tittle, Walter. *Roosevelt as an Artist Saw Him.* New York, 1948.

Tugwell, Rexford G. *The Democratic Roosevelt.* New York, 1957.

——. *The Art of Politics as Practiced by Three Great Americans: Franklin Delano Roosevelt, Luis Munoz Marin and Fiorello H. LaGuardia.* Garden City, N.Y., 1958.

——. *In Search of Roosevelt.* Cambridge, 1972.

——. *Roosevelt's Revolution.* New York, 1977.

Tully, Grace. *FDR, My Boss.* New York, 1949.

"Unofficial Observer" (pseudonym for John Carter Vincent). *The New Dealers.* New York, 1934.

Venkataramani, M.S., ed. *The Sunny Side of FDR.* Columbus, Ohio, 1973.

Wagenknecht, Edward. *The Seven Worlds of Theodore Roosevelt.* New York, 1958.

Walker, Turnley. *Roosevelt and the Warm Springs Story.* New York, 1953.

Ward, Geoffrey C. *Before the Trumpet: Young Franklin Roosevelt, 1882–1905.* New York, 1985.

Wharton, Don, ed. *The Roosevelt Omnibus.* New York, 1934.

White, William S. *Majesty and Mischief: A Mixed Tribute to FDR.* New York, 1961.

Wolfskill, George, and John A. Hudson. *All But the People: Franklin D. Roosevelt and His Critics, 1933–1939.* London, 1969.

Young, James C. *Roosevelt Revealed.* New York, 1936.

Youngs, J. William. *Eleanor Roosevelt: A Personal and Public Life.* Boston, 1985.

Zevin, Ben D., ed. *Franklin D. Roosevelt: Nothing to Fear.* New York, 1946.

BOOKS ON ASPECTS OF THE ROOSEVELTS' WORLD

Adams, Henry H. *Harry Hopkins: A Biography.* New York, 1977.

Albion, Robert G. *Makers of Naval Policy.* Annapolis, Md., 1980.

Aldrich, Margaret Chanler. *Family Vistas: The Memoirs of Margaret Chanler Aldrich.* New York, 1958.

Allen, Frederick Lewis. *Only Yesterday.* New York, 1931.

———. *Since Yesterday.* New York, 1940.

Ashburn, Frank D. *Peabody of Groton.* New York, 1944.

Auchincloss, Louis. *Life, Law and Letters: Essays and Sketches.* Boston, 1979.

Baker, Ray Stannard. *Woodrow Wilson: Life and Letters.* 8 vols., New York, 1939.

Beach, Edward L. *The United States Navy: 200 Years.* New York, 1986.

Berg, Roland H. *The Challenge of Polio: The Crusade Against Infantile Paralysis.* New York, 1943.

Berle, Beatrice Bishop. *A Life in Two Worlds.* New York, 1983.

Blum, John Morton. *Joe Tumulty and the Wilson Era.* Boston, 1951.

Brandt, Clare. *An American Aristocracy: The Livingstons.* Garden City, N.Y., 1985.

Brinkley, David. *Washington Goes to War.* New York, 1988.

Brinnin, John Malcolm. *The Sway of the Grand Saloon: A Social History of the North Atlantic.* New York, 1972.

Brownell, Will, and Billings, Richard N. *So Close to Greatness: A Biography of William C. Bullitt.* New York, 1988.

Burner, David. *Herbert Hoover: A Public Life.* New York, 1979.

Burns, James MacGregor. *The American Experiment: The Workshop of Democracy.* New York, 1985.

Butler, Smedley D. (as told to Lowell Thomas), *Old Gimlet Eye: The Adventures of Smedley D. Butler.* New York, 1933.

Caro, Robert A. *The Power Broker: Robert Moses and the Fall of New York.* New York, 1975.

———. *The Path to Power: The Years of Lyndon Johnson.* New York, 1982.

Carter, John Franklin ("The Unofficial Observer"). *The New Dealers.* New York, 1934.

Carter, Richard. *Breakthrough: The Saga of Jonas Salk.* New York, 1966.

Cebula, James E. *James M. Cox: Journalist and Politician.* New York, 1985.

Chamberlain, Rudolph W. *There Is No Truce: A Life of Thomas Motto Osborne.* New York, 1935.

Clark, James C. *Faded Glory: Presidents out of Power.* New York, 1985.

Columbia University (Staff of the Foundation for Research in Legal History), *A History of the School of Law, Columbia University.* New York.

———. *Bulletin of Information, 1905–1906.* New York, 1905

———. *Bulletin of Information, 1906–1907.* New York, 1906.

Connable, Alfred, and Edward Silberfarb. *Tigers of Tammany Hall: Nine Men Who Ran New York.* New York.

Coon, Horace. *Colossus on the Hudson.* New York.

Cooper, John Milton, Jr. *The Warrior and the Priest: Woodrow Wilson and Theodore Roosevelt.* Cambridge, 1983.

Cowles, Virginia. *The Astors.* New York, 1979.

Cox, James M. *Journey Through My Years: An Autobiography.* New York, 1946.

Cronon, E. David (ed.). *The Cabinet Diaries of Josephus Daniels, 1913–1921* Lincoln, Nebr., 1963.

Daniels, Jonathan. *The End of Innocence.* New York, 1954.

——. *Washington Quadrille: The Dance Beside the Documents.* Garden City, N.Y., 1968.

——. *The Time Between the Wars.* Garden City, N.Y., 1966.

Daniels, Josephus.

——. *Our Navy at War.* New York, 1922.

——. *Editor in Politics.*

——. *Tar-Heel Editor.* Chapel Hill, N.C., 1940.

——. *The Wilson Era: Years of Peace 1910–1917.* Chapel Hill, N.C., 1944.

——. *The Wilson Era: Years of War and After 1917–1923.* Chapel Hill, N.C., 1946.

Daniels, Mrs. Josephus (Adelaide Worth Bagley Daniels). *Recollections of a Cabinet Minister's Wife 1913–1921.* Raleigh, N.C., 1945.

Davis, Fred. *Passage Through Crises: Polio Victims and Their Families.* San Francisco, 1963.

Draper, George. *Acute Poliomyeltis.* Philadelphia, 1917.

——. *The Patient and the Physician.* New York, 1927.

——. *Infantile Paralysis.* New York, 1935.

Dunn, Robert. *World Alive: A Personal Story.* New York, 1956.

Dunne, Gerald T. *Grenville Clark: Public Citizen.* New York, 1986.

Faber, Doris. *The Life of Lorena Hickok: E.R.'s Friend.* New York, 1980.

Ferrell, Robert H. *Woodrow Wilson and World War I 1917–1921.* New York, 1986.

Flynn, Edward J. *You're the Boss.* New York, 1947.

Furman, Bess. *Washington By-Line.* New York, 1949.

Gekle, William F. *The Hacketts and the Roosevelts and Other River Families.* Poughkeepsie, N.Y., 1984.

Gerard, James W. *My First Eighty-Three Years in America.*

Gerber, Morris. *Old Albany.* Albany, N.Y., 1965.

Graham, Frank. *Al Smith: American.* New York, 1945.

Grant, James. *Bernard Baruch: The Adventures of a Wall Street Legend.* New York, 1983

Hacker, Louis M., and Hirsch, Mark D. *Proskauer: His Life and Times.* Montgomery, Ala., 1978.

Handlin, Oscar. *Al Smith and His America.* Boston, 1958

Harbaugh, William H. *Lawyer's Lawyer: The Life of John W. Davis.* Oxford, 1973.

Hatch, Alden. *Edith Bolling Wilson: First Lady Extraordinary.* New York, 1961.

Hoftstadter, Richard. *The American Political Tradition and the Men Who Made It.* New York, 1949.

Holbrook, Stewart H. *The Age of the Moghuls.* New York, 1949.

Holt, Dr. L. Emmett. *The Care and Feeding of Children: A Catechism for the Use of Mothers and Children's Nurses.* 1916.

Hoover, Herbert. *The Memoirs of Herbert Hoover* (3 volumes). New York,

1951–1952.

Hoover, I.H. ("Ike"), *Forty-Two Years in the White House.* Boston, 1934.

Hunter, Lieutenant Francis T. *Beatty, Jellicoe, Sims and Rodman.* Garden City, N.Y., 1919.

Ickes, Harold L. *The Secret Diary of Harold L. Ickes.* 3 vols., New York, 1953–54.

Johnson, Walter. *William Allen White's America.* New York, 1947.

Josephson, Matthew. *The Money Lords.* New York.

———, and Josephson, Hannah. *Al Smith: Hero of the Cities.* Boston, 1969.

Kavaler, Lucy. *The Astors: An American Legend.* New York, 1972.

Keyes, Frances Parkinson. *Capital Kaleidoscope: The Story of a Washington Hostess.* New York, 1972.

Kilpatrick, Carroll. *Roosevelt and Daniels.* Chapel Hill, N.C., 1952.

Kittredge, Tracy Barett. *Naval Lessons of the Great War.* Garden City, N.Y., 1921.

Knox, John C. *A Judge Comes of Age.* New York, 1940.

Kouwenhoven, John A. *The Columbia Historical Portrait of New York.* New York, 1953.

Krock, Arthur. *Memoirs: Sixty Years on the Firing Line.* New York, 1967.

Lamont, Thomas W. *Across World Frontiers.* New York, 1951.

Lane, Franklin K. *The Letters of Franklin K. Lane.* Boston, 1922.

Lash, Joseph P. *Dealers and Dreamers.* Garden City, N.Y., 1988.

Lawrence, Bill. *Six Presidents, Too Many Wars.* New York, 1972.

Littell, Norman M. (edited by Jonathan Dembo), *My Roosevelt Years.* Seattle, 1987.

Lord, Walter. *The Good Years: From 1900 to the First World War.* 1960.

Lovett, Robert W. *The Treatment of Infantile Paralysis.* New York, 1916.

MacCracken, Henry Noble. *Blithe Dutchess.* New York, 1950.

———. *Old Dutchess, Forever/*New York, 1958.

McEneny, John J. *Albany: Capital City on the Hudson.* Albany, N.Y., 1981.

McClelland, John Jr. *Wobbly War: The Centralia Story.* Tacoma, Wash., 1987.

McCullough, David. *The Path Between the Seas.* New York, 1977.

McCullough, Edo. *World's Fair Midways.* New York, 1977.

McJimsey, George. *Harry Hopkins: Ally of the Poor and Defender of Democracy.* Cambridge, 1987.

Martin, George. *Madame Secretary: Frances Perkins.* Boston, 1976.

Marx, Rudolph. *The Health of the Presidents.* New York, 1960.

Matthews, Brander, et al., eds. *A History of Columbia University 1754–1904.*

Mee, Charles L., Jr. *A Visit to Haldeman and Other States of Mind.* New York, 1977.

Mencken, H. L. *A Choice of Days.* New York, 1980.

Milam, Lorenzo Wilson. *The Cripple: Liberation Front Marching Band Blues.* San Diego, 1984.

Miller, Nathan. *The US Navy: An Illustrated History.* New York, 1977.

Moley, Raymond. *27 Masters of Politics in a Personal Perspective.* New York, 1949.

Morison, Elting E. *Admiral Sims and the Modern American Navy.* Boston, 1942.

Morrison, Joseph L. *Josephus Daniels Says . . . An Editor's Political Odyssey:*

———. *From Bryan to Wilson, to FDR, 1894–1913.* Chapel Hill, N.C., 1962.

———. *Josephus Daniels: The Small-d Democrat.* Chapel Hill, N.C., 1968.

Morse, Arthur D. *While Six Million Died.* New York, 1968.

Moscow, Warren. *Politics in the Empire State.* New York, 1984.

Mosley, Nicholas. *Rules of the Game. Sir Oswald and Cynthia Mosley 1896–1933.* London, 1982.

Mosley, Sir Oswald. *My Life.* New Rochelle, N.Y., 1968.

Murphy, Lawrence R. *Perverts by Official Order.* New York, 1988.

Muskie, Stephen O. *Campobello: Roosevelt's "Beloved Island."* Camden, Maine, 1982.

Nesbitt, Cathleen. *A Little Love & Good Company.* New York, 1983.

O'Connor, Richard. *The First Hurrah: A Biography of Alfred E. Smith.* New York, 1965.

Paul, John. *A History of Poliomyletis.* New York, 1971.

Peabody, Francis W., Draper, George, and Dolchez, Alphonse R. *A Clinical Study of Poliomyelitis.* New York, 1912.

Perrett, Geoffrey. *America in the Twenties: A History.* New York, 1982.

Phillips, Harlan B., ed. *Felix Frankfurter Reminisces.* New York, 1960.

Phillips, William. *Ventures in Diplomacy.* Boston, 1952.

Pink, Louis H. *Gaynor, The Tammany Mayor Who Swallowed the Tiger.* New York, 1967.

Plagemann, Bentz. *My Place to Stand.* New York, 1949.

Pringle, Henry F. *Alfred E. Smith: A Critical Portrait.* New York, 1927.

Reilly, Michael F. *Reilly of the White House.* New York, 1947.

———. *The President Makers.* Boston, 1976.

Savell, Isabella. *The Executive Mansion in Albany: An Informal History, 1856–1960.* Albany, N.Y., 1960.

Schmidt, Hans. *The United States Occupation of Haiti, 1915–1934.* New Brunswick, N.J., 1971.

———. *Maverick Marine: General Smedley D. Butler and the Contradictions of American Military History.* Lexington, Ky., 1987.

Schwarz, Jordan A., *Liberal: Adolf A. Berle and the Vision of an American Era.* New York, 1987.

Shapiro, Herbert. *White Violence and Black Response.* Amherst, Mass., 1988.

Shoumatoff, Alex. *Russian Blood.* New York, 1982.

Sinclair, Andrew. *The Available Man: The Life Behind the Mask of Warren Gamaliel Harding.* New York, 1965.

Skidelsky, Robert. *Oswald Mosley.* New York, 1975.

Smith, Arthur D. Howden. *Mr. House of Texas.* New York, 1940.

Smith, A. Merriman. *Thank You, Mr. President.* New York, 1946.

———. *Merriman Smith's Book of Presidents: A White House Memoir.* New York, 1972.

Smith, Gene. *When the Cheering Stopped.* New York, 1964.

———. *The Shattered Dream.* New York, 1970.

Smith, Richard Norton. *An Uncommon Man: The Triumph of Herbert Hoover.* New York, 1984.

———. *The Harvard Century: The Making of a University to a Nation.* New York, 1986.

Starling, Edmund W. *Starling of the White House.* New York, 1946.

Steel, Ronald. *Walter Lippmann and the American Century.* Boston, 1980.

Stern, Robert A.M., Gilmartin, Gregory, and Massengale, John. *New York 1900: Metropolitan Architecture and Urbanism 1890–1915.* New York, 1984.

Stevens, Ruth. *Hi-Ya Neighbor!* Atlanta, 1947.

Strauss, Elaine. *In My Heart I'm Still Dancing.* New Rochelle, N.Y., 1979.

Sullivan, Mark. *Our Times: The United States 1900–1925.*

    Vol. 1: *The Turn of the Century.* New York, 1931.

    Vol. 2: *America Finding Herself.* New York, 1932.

    Vol. 3: *Pre-War America.* New York, 1930.

    Vol. 4: *The War Begins 1909–1914.* New York, 1932.

    Vol. 5: *Over Here 1914–1918.* New York, 1933.

    Vol. 6: *The Twenties.* New York, 1935.

Tannebaum, Frank. *Osborne of Sing Sing.* Chapel Hill, N.C., 1933.

Thomas, Lately. *A Pride of Lions: The Chanler Chronicle.* New York, 1971.

Trohan, Walter. *Political Animals.* Garden City, N.Y., 1975.

Waller, George. *Kidnap.* New York, 1970.

Ware, Susan. *Partner and I: Molly Dewson, Feminism, and New Deal Politics.* New Haven, 1987.

Warner, Emily Smith (with Hawthorne Daniel). *The Happy Warrior.* Garden City, N.Y., 1956.

Wecter, Dixon. *The Saga of American Society: A Record of Social Aspiration, 1607–1937.* New York, 1937.

Wehle, Louis B. *Hidden Threads of History: Wilson Through Roosevelt.* New York, 1953.

Weiss, Nancy J. *Farewell to the Party of Lincoln: Black Politics in the Age of FDR.* Princeton, 1983.

Werner, M.R. *Tammany Hall.* New York, 1928.

Whalen, Richard J. *The Founding Father.* New York, 1963.

White, William Allen. *The Autobiography of William Allen White.* New York, 1946.

William, Kennedy. *Albany!* New York, 1985.

Williams, T. Harry. *Huey Long.* New York.

Wilson, Edith. *My Memoir.* Indianapolis, 1939.

Wilson, John Rowan. *Margin of Safety.* Garden City, N.Y., 1963.

Wyman, David S. *The Abandonment of the Jews: America and the Holocaust 1941–1945.* New York, 1984.

Zukowsky, John, and Stimson, Robbe Pierce. *Hudson River Villas.* New York, 1985.

JOURNALS AND NEWSPAPERS

I consulted the *New York Times* most frequently, but often supplemented it with other New York newspapers, especially the *Graphic, Herald, Journal, Sun, Tribune, Herald-Tribune,* and *World.*

Any biographer is fortunate in that from the first Franklin Roosevelt made sure that his files included a nearly exhaustive trove of clippings about himself, gleaned from hundreds of newspapers both foreign and domestic, all of them conveniently available in folders and scrapbooks among his papers at the FDRL.

ARTICLES

Basso, Hamilton. "The Roosevelt Legend." *Life*, November 3, 1947.

Boyle, Robert H. "Step in and Enjoy the Turmoil." *Sports Illustrated*, June 13, 1977.

Chauncey, George, Jr. "Christian Brotherhood or Sexual Perversion? Homosexual Identities and the Construction of Sexual Boundaries in the World War One Era." *Journal of Social History* (Winter, 1985).

Davis, Kenneth S. "FDR As a Biographer's Problem." *The American Scholar* (Winter 1983–84).

Duffy, John. "Franklin Roosevelt: Ambiguous Symbol for Disabled Americans." *Midwest Quarterly* (Autumn 1987).

Erickson, Joan. "Nothing to Fear." *Daedalus* (Spring 1964).

Fabricant, Noah D. "FDR's Nose and Throat Ailments." *Eye, Ear, Nose and Throat Monthly* (February 1957).

———. "FDR's Tonsillectomy and Poliomyletis." *Eye, Ear, Nose and Throat Monthly* (June 1957).

———. "FDR, the Common Cold and American History." *Eye, Ear, Nose and Throat Monthly* (March 1958).

Fleeson, Doris. "Missy—To Do This." *Saturday Evening Post*, January 8, 1938.

Iseman, Marjorie F. "My Father and Mrs. Roosevelt's Dogs." *American Heritage* (August 1974).

Looker, Earle. "Is FDR Physically Fit to Be President?" *Liberty*, July 25, 1931.

Lovett, Robert W. "A Plan of Treatment in Infantile Paralysis." *Journal of the American Medical Association*, August 5, 1916.

———. "The After-Care of Paralytics as a Public Problem." *Journal of the American Medical Association*, February 10, 1917.

———. "The After-Care of Infantile Paralysis." *Journal of the American Medical Association*, April 7, 1917.

———. "Fatigue and Exercise in the Treatment of Infantile Paralysis. . . ." *Journal of the American Medical Association*, July 21, 1917.

———. "The Diagnosis, Prognosis and Early Treatment of Infantile Paralysis." *Journal of the American Medical Association*, May 27, 1922.

Martin, John Stuart. "When the President Disappeared." *American Heritage* (October–November 1957).

Morris, Edmund. "Theodore Roosevelt, President." *American Heritage* (June–July 1981).

Pollard, Charyll C. "FDR—Collector." *Prologue* (Winter 1969).

Potter, David M. "Sketches for the Roosevelt Portrait." *Yale Review* (Autumn 1949).

Rollins, Alfred B., Jr. "Young FDR and the Moral Crusaders." *New York History* (January 1956).

——. "Young Franklin D. Roosevelt as the Farmer's Friend." *New York History* (April 1962).

——. "Was There Really a Man Named Roosevelt?" in George Athan Billias and Gerald Grob, eds., *American History: Retrospect and Prospect*, New York, 1971.

——. "The View from the State House: FDR," in Martin L. Fausold, ed., *The Hoover Presidency: A Reappraisal*. Albany, N.Y., 1974.

Roosevelt, Anna. "How Polio Helped Father." *Woman* (July 1949).

Schleichkorn, Jay. "Physical Therapist, 98, Recalls Rehabilitating Franklin Roosevelt." *PT Bulletin*, March 15, 1988.

Sill, Leonora. "Bird Lover of Hyde Park." *Audubon* (June 1955).

Tugwell, Rexford G. "The Two Great Roosevelts." *The Western Political Quarterly* (March 1952).

Ward, Geoffrey C. "Matters of Fact: Mrs. Roosevelt Faces Fear." *American Heritage* (October–November 1984).

——. "Eleanor Roosevelt Drew Her Strength from a Sanctuary Called Val-Kill." *Smithsonian Magazine* (October 1984).

——. "How Teddy Roosevelt Took Charge!" *Success!* (April 1985).

——. "Matters of Fact: FDR's Twenty-Four-Year War." *American Heritage* (June–July 1985).

——. "The House at Hyde Park." *American Heritage* (April–May 1987).

——. "Matters of Fact: Ollie and Old Gimlet Eye." *American Heritage* (November 1987).

Whitehead, James L. "A President Goes Birding." *Conservationist* (May–June 1977).

Wilson, Theodore A., and McKinzie, Richard D. "The Masks of Power: FDR and the Conduct of American Diplomacy," in Frank J. Merli and Theodore A. Wilson, eds., *Makers of American Diplomacy*, New York, 1974.

Wright, Wilhemine G., "Crutch-Walking as an Art." *American Journal of Surgery* (December 1926).

INDEX